THE BICENTENNIAL EDITION

OF THE

WORKS OF JOHN WESLEY

General Editor RICHARD P. HEITZENRATER

Textual Editor FRANK BAKER

THE WORKS OF
JOHN WESLEY

VOLUME 23

═══

JOURNAL AND DIARIES

VI

(1776–86)

EDITED BY

W. REGINALD WARD

(JOURNAL)

AND

RICHARD P. HEITZENRATER

(DIARIES)

ABINGDON PRESS

NASHVILLE

1995

The Works of John Wesley, Volume 23
JOURNAL AND DIARIES, VI, 1776-86

Copyright © 1995 by Abingdon Press

All rights reserved.
No part of this book may be reproduced in any manner whatsoever without written permission of the publisher except brief quotations embodied in critical articles or reviews. For information address Abingdon Press, Nashville, Tennessee.

Library of Congress Cataloging in Publication Data
(Revised for vol. 23)

Wesley, John, 1703–1791.
The works of John Wesley.

(The Bicentennial edition of the works of John
Wesley)
Some vols. are reprinted from the Oxford ed.
Includes bibliographical references and indexes.
Contents: v. 1. Sermons I, 1-33— [etc.] —
v. 22. Journal and diaries V, (1765–75) —
v. 23. Journal and diaries VI, 1776–86).
1. Methodist Church. 2. Theology—18th century.
3. Wesley, John, 1703–1791—Diaries. I. Outler,
Albert Cook. 1908-1989. II. Wesley, John, 1703–1791.
Works. 1984 (Bicentennial ed.) III. Title.

IV. Series.
BX8217.W5   1984   230'.7   83-22434
ISBN 0-687-46210-X (v. 1)

ISBN 0-687-46227-4 (vol. 23)
ISBN 0-687-46226-6 (vol. 22)
ISBN 0-687-46225-8 (vol. 21)
ISBN 0-687-46223-1 (vol. 20)
ISBN 0-687-46222-3 (vol. 19)
ISBN 0-687-46214-2 (vol. 9)
ISBN 0-687-46221-5 (vol. 18)
ISBN 0-687-46213-4 (vol. 4)
ISBN 0-687-46212-6 (vol. 3)
ISBN 0-687-46211-8 (vol. 2)
ISBN 0-687-46210-X (vol. 1)

THE MONOGRAM USED ON THE CASE AND HALF-TITLE IS
ADAPTED BY RICHARD P. HEITZENRATER FROM ONE OF
JOHN WESLEY'S PERSONAL SEALS

MANUFACTURED IN THE UNITED STATES
OF AMERICA

THE BICENTENNIAL EDITION OF
THE WORKS OF JOHN WESLEY

THIS edition of the works of John Wesley reflects the quickened interest in the heritage of Christian thought that has become evident during the last half-century. A fully critical presentation of Wesley's writings had long been a desideratum in order to furnish documentary sources illustrating his contribution to both catholic and evangelical Christianity.

Several scholars, notably Professor Albert C. Outler, Professor Franz Hildebrandt, Dean Merrimon Cuninggim, and Dean Robert E. Cushman, discussed the possibility of such an edition. Under the leadership of Dean Cushman, a Board of Directors was formed in 1960 comprising the deans of four sponsoring theological schools of Methodist-related universities in the United States: Drew, Duke, Emory, and Southern Methodist. They appointed an Editorial Committee to formulate plans, and enlisted an international and interdenominational team of scholars for the Wesley Works Editorial Project.

The works were divided into units of cognate material, with a separate editor (or joint editors) responsible for each unit. Dr. Frank Baker was appointed textual editor for the whole project, with responsibility for supplying each unit editor with a critically developed, accurate Wesley text. The text seeks to represent Wesley's thought in its fullest and most deliberate expression, in so far as this can be determined from the available evidence. Substantive variant readings in any British edition published during Wesley's lifetime are shown in appendices to the units, preceded by a summary of the problems faced and the solutions reached in the complex task of securing and presenting Wesley's text. The aim throughout is to enable Wesley to be read with maximum ease and understanding, and with minimal intrusion by the editors.

This edition includes all Wesley's original or mainly original prose works, together with one volume devoted to his *Collection of Hymns* (1780) and another to his extensive work as editor and publisher of extracts from the writings of others. An essential feature of the project is a Bibliography outlining the historical settings of the works published by Wesley and his brother Charles, sometimes jointly, sometimes separately. The Bibliography also offers full analytical data for identifying each of the two thousand editions of these 450 items that were published during the lifetime of John Wesley, and notes the location of copies. An index is supplied for each unit, and a General Index for the whole edition.

The Delegates of the Oxford University Press agreed to undertake publication, but announced in June 1982 that because of severe economic problems they would regretfully be compelled to withdraw from the enterprise with the completion in 1983 of vol. 7, the *Collection of Hymns*. Abingdon Press offered its services, beginning with the publication of the first volume of the *Sermons* in 1984, the bicentennial year of the formation of American Methodism as an autonomous church. The new title now assumed, however, refers in general to the bicentennial of Wesley's total activities as author, editor, and publisher, from 1733 to 1791, especially as summarized in the first edition of his collected works in thirty-two volumes, 1771-74.

Dean Robert E. Cushman of Duke University undertook general administration and promotion of the project until 1971, when he was succeeded as President by Dean Joseph D. Quillian, Jr., of Southern Methodist University, these two universities having furnished the major support and guidance for the enterprise. During the decade 1961-70, the Editorial Committee supervised the task of setting editorial principles and procedures, and general editorship was shared by Dr. Eric W. Baker, Dean William R. Cannon, and Dean Cushman. In 1969 the Directors appointed Dr. Frank Baker, early attached to the project as bibliographer and textual editor for Wesley's text, as Editor-in-Chief also. Upon Dean Quillian's retirement in 1981, he was succeeded as President of the project by Dean James E. Kirby, Jr., also of Southern Methodist University. In 1986, the Directors appointed Richard P. Heitzenrater as General Editor to begin the chief editorship of the project with the *Journal and Diaries* unit. Dean Dennis M. Campbell of Duke University was elected President of the project in 1990.

Other sponsoring bodies have been successively added to the original four: Boston University School of Theology, the Conference of the Methodist Church of Great Britain, The General Commission on Archives and History of The United Methodist Church, The United Methodist Board of Higher Education and Ministry, and the World Methodist Council. For the continuing support of the sponsoring institutions the Directors express their profound thanks. They gratefully acknowledge also the encouragement and financial support that have come from the Historical Societies and Commissions on Archives and History of many Annual Conferences, as well as the donations of private individuals and foundations.

On June 9, 1976, The Wesley Works Editorial Project was incorporated in the State of North Carolina as a nonprofit corporation. In 1977, by-laws were approved governing the appointment and duties of the Directors, their Officers, and their Executive Committee.

The Board of Directors

President: Dennis M. Campbell, Dean of The Divinity School, Duke University, Durham, North Carolina

Vice-President: Joe Hale, General Secretary of The World Methodist Council, Lake Junaluska, North Carolina

Secretary: John Harnish, Associate General Secretary of the Division of the Ordained Ministry, The United Methodist Board of Higher Education and Ministry, Nashville, Tennessee

Treasurer: Thomas A. Langford, The Divinity School, Duke University, Durham, North Carolina

General Editor: Richard P. Heitzenrater, The Divinity School, Duke University, Durham, North Carolina

Textual Editor: Frank Baker, The Divinity School, Duke University, Durham, North Carolina

Neil Alexander, Book Editor of The United Methodist Church, Nashville, Tennessee

Kenneth L. Carder, Bishop of The United Methodist Church, Nashville Area

Judith Craig, Bishop of The United Methodist Church, Ohio West Area

Janet Fishburn, Acting Dean of The Theological School of Drew University, Madison, New Jersey

R. Kevin LaGree, Dean of Candler School of Theology, Emory University, Atlanta, Georgia

Robin Lovin, Dean of Perkins School of Theology, Southern Methodist University, Dallas, Texas

Robert C. Neville, Dean of Boston University School of Theology, Boston, Massachusetts

Jean Miller Schmidt, Iliff School of Theology, Denver, Colorado
Charles Yrigoyen, Jr., Executive Secretary of The Commission
    on Archives and History of The United Methodist Church,
    Drew University, Madison, New Jersey

CONTENTS

SIGNS, SPECIAL USAGES,
ABBREVIATIONS

[ ]   Indicate editorial insertions or substitutions in the original text, or (with a query) doubtful readings.

< >   Indicate conjectural readings in manuscripts where the original text is defective.

. . .   Indicate a passage omitted by the writer from the original and so noted by Wesley, usually by a dash.

[. . .]   Indicate a passage omitted silently by Wesley from a text he was quoting, to which the present editor is drawing attention; the brackets are not used in editorial annotations and introductions.

(( ))   Enclose passages within a manuscript struck through for erasure.

[[ ]]   Enclose passages supplied by the present editors from cipher or shorthand, from an abstract or similar document in the third person, or reconstructed from secondary evidence.

a,b,c   Small superscript letters indicate footnotes supplied by Wesley.

1,2,3   Small superscript figures indicate footnotes supplied by the editor.

Cf.   Before a scriptural or other citation by Wesley, indicates that he was quoting with more than minimal inexactness, yet nevertheless displaying the passage as a quotation.

See   Before a scriptural citation indicates an undoubted allusion, or a quotation which was not displayed as such by Wesley, and which is more than minimally inexact.

Wesley's publications. Where a work by Wesley was first published separately, its title is italicized; where it first appeared within a different work such as a collected volume, the title appears within quotation marks. References such as *'Bibliography*, No. 3' are to the forthcoming Bibliography in this edition (Vols. 33–34), which has a different numbering system from Richard Green's *Wesley Bibliography*.

Book-titles in Wesley's text are italicized if accurate, and given in roman type with capitals if inaccurate. If a title consists of only one generic word which forms a major part of the original title, it is italicized; but if it is inaccurate (such as 'Sermons' for a volume entitled *Discourses*), it is printed in lower case roman.

Abbreviations. Works and institutions frequently cited are abbreviated thus:

BCP   The Book of Common Prayer, London, 1662.

Bibliography   Frank Baker, *A Descriptive and Analytical Bibliography of the Publications of John and Charles Wesley* (in preparation), Vols. 33–34 in this edn.

Curnock	Nehemiah Curnock, ed., *The Journal of the Rev. John Wesley, A.M.*, 8 vols., London, Epworth Press, 1938.
CWJ	Thomas Jackson, ed., *The Journal of the Rev. Charles Wesley, M.A.*, 2 vols., London, Wesleyan Methodist Bookroom, 1849.
Jackson	Thomas Jackson, ed., *The Works of the Rev. John Wesley*, 4th edn., 14 vols., London, Mason, 1840-42.
JW	John Wesley (1703-91).
JWJ	John Wesley's *Journal*.
OED	Sir James A. H. Murray, et al., *A New English Dictionary on Historical Principles*, 11 vols., Oxford, Clarendon Press, 1884-1933.
SPCK	Society for Promoting Christian Knowledge
SPG	Society for the Propagation of the Gospel
Telford	John Telford, ed., *The Letters of the Rev. John Wesley*, 8 vols., London, Sharp, 1931.
Works (1771-74)	John Wesley, *The Works of the Rev. John Wesley, M.A.*, 32 vols., Bristol, Pine, 1771-74.
WHS	*The Proceedings of the Wesley Historical Society*, 1898– .

A N

EXTRACT

FROM THE

Rev. Mr. *JOHN WESLEY*'s

JOURNAL,

FROM

January 1, 1776, to Auguſt 8, 1779.

XVIII.

L O N D O N:

Printed by J. PARAMORE, at the Foundry, Moorfields:
And ſold at the New Chapel, City-Road; and at the Rev. Mr.
Weſley's Preaching-Houſes, in Town and Country. 1783.

Journal

From January 1, 1776, to August 8, 1779

January 1, 1776, about eighteen hundred of us met together, in London, in order to renew our covenant with God.[1] And it was, as usual, a very solemn opportunity.

Tuesday 2, I set out for Bristol. Between London and Bristol, I read over that elegant trifle, *The Correspondence between Theodosius and Constantia.*[2] I observed only one sentiment which I could not receive, that 'Youth is the only possible time for friendship, because everyone has at first a *natural* store of sincerity and benevolence; but as in process of time men find everyone to be false and self-interested, they conform to them more and more, till in riper years they have neither truth nor benevolence left.' Perhaps it may be so with all that know not God, but they that do, escape 'the corruption that is in the world'[3] and increase both in sincerity and in benevolence as they grow in the knowledge of Christ.

Sat. 6. I returned to London. And I returned just in time. For on Sunday 7, the severe frost set in, accompanied with so deep a snow as made even the high road impassable.[4] For some days before the frost broke up, it was observed, by means of the thermometer, that the cold was several degrees more intense than that in the year 1741. But God then removed the cup from us, by a gentle, gradual thaw.

Sun. 14. As I was going to West Street Chapel, one of the chaise springs suddenly snapped asunder. But the horses instantly stopping, I stepped out, without the least inconvenience.

At all my vacant hours in this and the following week I endeav-

[1] On the origins of this service, see Aug. 6, 1755 (21:23 in this edn.).
[2] John Langhorne, *The Letters that Passed between Theodosius and Constantia, after she had taken the veil* (London, 1763; 2nd edn., 1764). This volume was succeeded by *The Correspondence between Theodosius and Constantia from their first acquaintance to the departure of Theodosius* (London, 1764). These were reprinted in two volumes. in 1782.
[3] 2 Pet. 1:4.
[4] The *Gentleman's Magazine* 46 (1776):44, noted of this day that 'the greatest fall of snow that has been known in England in the memory of man began. It was attended with a high easterly wind which drifted it in many places to an incredible depth.' By the end of the month, temperatures of zero Fahrenheit were being recorded at Chatham, and the salt waters of the Medway had frozen over (ibid., p. 117). The agricultural outcome, as in 1741, was excellent: 'a warm spring and a hot dry summer produced an early and good harvest.' E. L. Jones, *Seasons and Prices; The Role of the Weather in English Agricultural History* (London, 1964), pp. 139, 146.

2

oured to finish the 'Concise History of England'.[5] I am sensible it must give offence, as in many parts I am quite singular—particularly with regard to those greatly injured characters, Richard the Third and Mary Queen of Scots. But I must speak as I think; although still waiting for and willing to receive better information.   5
Sun. 28. I was desired to preach a Charity Sermon in All Hallows Church, Lombard Street. In the year 1735, above forty years ago, I preached in this church, at the earnest request of the church wardens, to a numerous congregation, who came, like me, with an intent to hear Dr. Heylyn. This was the first time that,   10
having no notes about me, I preached extempore.[6]
Wednesday, Feb. 14. I preached at Shoreham. How is the last become first! No society in the county grows so fast as this, either in grace or number. The chief instrument of this glorious work is Miss Perronet, a burning and a shining light.[7]   15

[5] *A Concise History of England*, 4 vols. (London, 1776); see *Bibliography*, No. 357). JW dated the preface Aug. 10, 1775, and admitted that the work was 'extracted chiefly from Dr. Goldsmith, Rapin and Smollett' with 'ten thousand dull passages . . . omitted', and with corrections and reference to the activity of God in history inserted. JW's strong views on Richard III and Mary Queen of Scots have already been made clear; see June 17, Nov. 10, 1769 (22:188-89, 210 in this edn.).

[6] No contemporary record is extant of Wesley's preaching in All Hallows in 1735. His diary indicates his having preached 'extempore' on the Beatitudes on Nov. 10, 1734, at the Castle in Oxford. But in his journal of the Georgia voyage (18:137, cf. 313), he says he 'first preached extempore' on the quarter-deck of the Simmonds off Gravesend on Sunday, Oct. 19, 1735. The qualification about having no notes may be important in this present entry, or perhaps Wesley meant that his first preaching extempore in a church was at All Hallows.

The force of this sudden recollection, nevertheless, arose from the fact that John Heylyn (see 18:241, n. 15 in this edn.) was not merely a writer much used by JW in his youth, but a favourite preacher with the religious societies in the early days of the English awakening; and it was doubtless in their company that JW had been called on to preach extempore. William Myles paraphrases this entry and adds that extempore preaching 'is now universally practised by all the Methodist Preachers and also by many Ministers of the Established Church, especially those who are considered as *Gospel Ministers*: but at that time as for several years after it was looked upon as a very uncommon and wonderful thing in these kingdoms.' *A Chronological History of the People Called Methodists* (Liverpool, 1800), p. 3.

All Hallows (where JW preached again on Oct. 22, 1786, and Dec. 28, 1788) was one of the last of the city churches to be rebuilt after the Great Fire, being completed only in 1694. With lavish gifts from the bankers, the furnishings were of the finest; and when, just before the Second World War, the building, already completely hemmed in by other structures, was found to be endangered by soil subsidence, the campanile, porch, and furnishings were moved to a new church at Twickenham. The rector of All Hallows, 1755 to his death in December 1776, was Thomas Broughton, M.A., formerly an Oxford Methodist.

[7] John 5:35. Damaris Perronet (1727-82), who died unmarried, was a pillar of the Methodist society at Shoreham. Luke Tyerman's description of her as 'bold, mascu-

Fri. 23. I looked over Mr. Bolt's *Considerations on the Affairs of India*.[8] Was there ever so melancholy a picture! How are the mighty fallen![9] The Great Mogul, Emperor of Hindustan,[10] one of the mightiest potentates on earth, is become a poor, little, impotent slave to a company of merchants! His large, flourishing empire is broken in pieces and covered with fraud, oppression, and misery! And we may call the myriads that have been murdered happy in comparison of those that still groan under the iron yoke! Wilt not thou visit for these things, O Lord?[11] Shall the fool still say in his heart, There is no God![12]

Sun. 25. I buried the remains of William Evans,[13] one of the first members of our society. He was an Israelite indeed, open (if it could be) to a fault, always speaking the truth from his heart.

Wed. 28. I looked over a volume of Lord Lyttleton's *Works*.[14]

line-minded', which passed into the *DNB* (*sub* Vincent Perronet), began as a description of her handwriting as 'careless, bold and masculine'. *The Life and Times of John Wesley*, 3 vols. (London, 1870-71), 3:54; and Tyerman MSS, 2, fol. 138, in Methodist Archives, Manchester. There is nothing particularly masculine about the content of her letters (ibid., fols. 137-48). For a letter of JW to her, see John Telford, ed., *The Letters of the Rev. John Wesley*, 8 vols. (London, 1931), 5:233; hereafter cited as Telford. Cf. *The Proceedings of the Wesley Historical Society* 14 (1923):95; 16 (1927):44; hereafter cited as *WHS*.

[8] William Bolts, *Considerations on India Affairs, particularly respecting the present state of Bengal, and its dependencies. With a map of those countries, chiefly from actual survey*, 3 vols. (London, 1772-75). Bolts was a free merchant who, after defying for years the efforts of the Bengal government to suppress him, had been deported in 1769 and brought American merchants back with him with a view to taking Verelst, Governor of Bengal, to court. The book is a copiously documented attack on Verelst and Clive. L. S. Sutherland, *The East India Company and Eighteenth-Century Politics* (Oxford, 1952), pp. 220-21; N. L. Hallwood, *William Bolts; A Dutch Adventurer under John Company* (Cambridge, 1920), pp. 123-31. Horace Walpole thought Bolts, who bankrupted himself in his campaign, unfair; *The Last Journals of Horace Walpole*, ed. J. Doran and A. F. Steuart, 2 vols. (London, 1890-1910), 1:72. But he seems to have influenced a moralizing passage in JW's sermon, No. 69, on 'The Imperfection of Human Knowledge', II.4 (2:579 and n. 50 in this edn.).

[9] 2 Sam. 1:19, etc.

[10] Orig., 'Indostan'.

[11] See Jer. 5:9 etc.

[12] See Ps. 14:1; 53:1.

[13] William Evans, jeweller, of Woodsclose, Clerkenwell, had been a member of one of the bands at City Road in 1745; Thomas Jackson, ed., *The Journal of the Rev. Charles Wesley, M.A.*, 2 vols. (London, 1849), 2:245, hereafter cited as *CWJ*; see also George J. Stevenson, *City Road Chapel, London, and its Associations, Historical, Biographical, and Memorial* (London, 1872), p. 34. Although Evans had once been the object of serious accusations in the society, he had long been much admired by JW; Telford, 5:15, 16, 118.

[14] *The Works of George, Lord Lyttelton, now first collected together; with some other pieces never before printed*, ed. G. E. Ayscough (London, 1774; frequently reprinted). For Lyttelton and JW's view of him, see Aug. 31, 1770 (22:245, n. 48 in this edn.).

He is really a fine writer, both in verse and prose—though he believed the Bible, yea, and feared God! In my scraps of time I likewise read over Miss Talbot's *Essays*, equal to anything of the kind I ever saw.[15] She was a woman of admirable sense and piety, and a far better poet than the celebrated Mrs. Rowe.[16] But here too,

Heaven its choicest gold by torture tried![17]

After suffering much, she died of a cancer in her breast.

Friday, March 1. As we cannot depend on having the Foundery[18] long, we met to consult about building a new chapel. Our petition to the city for a piece of ground lies before their committee. But when we shall get any farther, I know not. So I determined to begin my circuit as usual, but promised to return whenever I should receive notice that our petition was granted.

On Sunday evening, I set out, and on Tuesday reached Bristol. In the way I read over Mr. Boehme's *Sermons*,[19] Chaplain to Prince George of Denmark, husband of Queen Anne. He was a

---

[15] Catherine Talbot, *Essays on Various Subjects*, 2 vols. (London, 1772). Catherine Talbot (1721-70) was something of a celebrity in her day, though her works on religious and moral themes were published after her death. The posthumous child of Edward Talbot, archdeacon of Berkshire and brother of the later Lord Chancellor, she was taken with her mother into the household of Thomas Secker, acted as his almoner, and mixed with the great as he rose to be Primate. Her work was frequently reprinted. JW recommended her *Essays* to Ann Bolton and printed her appreciative remarks in the *Arminian Magazine* 14 (1791):590.

[16] On Elizabeth Rowe and JW's estimate of her, see July 2, 1769 (22:193 in this edn.).

[17] Altered from Pope's *Epitaph on Mrs. Corbet* who, like Mrs. Rowe and Miss Talbot, died of cancer; *The Works of Alexander Pope*, ed. Whitwell Elwin and William John Courthope, 10 vols. (rev. edn., London, 1871-89), 4:386. JW also quoted from this *Epitaph* on May 5, 1757 (21:101, n. 74 in this edn.).

[18] Orig., "Foundry". JW's usual spelling was 'Foundery'.

[19] Anton Wilhelm Boehme (1673-1722), an alumnus of Halle (see Dec. 1, 1764; 21:495, n. 61 in this edn.), was expelled from Waldeck in an anti-pietist drive in 1698, and raised from an impoverished private tutorship in London to a court chaplaincy by Prince George of Denmark. Boehme, who was very prominent in the SPCK, became such a public figure in English religious society as well as among the Germans resident in London, that George I reappointed him after Anne's death. Boehme was a prolific author in both German and English, one of the notable intermediaries between the Protestant crisis in the Holy Roman Empire and Britain, and as none of his works were volumes of sermons, it is impossible to determine what title JW had in his hands. It may have been his *Sämtliche Erbauliche Schriften*, edited by the Pietist theologian J. J. Rambach at the Danish port of Altona (3 vols., 1731-33), vol. 1 of which included his *Discourses and Tracts for Promoting the Common Interest of True Christianity* (1717). Boehme's work is discussed in Arno Sames, *Anton Wilhelm Böhme (1673-1722): Stu-*

person of very strong sense and, in general, sound in his judgment. I remember hearing a very remarkable circumstance concerning him, from Mr. Fraser, then chaplain to St. George's Hospital. 'One day', said he, 'I asked Mr. Boehme, with whom I was
5 intimately acquainted, "Sir, when you are surrounded by various
persons, listening to one and dictating to another, does not that
vast hurry of business hinder your communion with God?" He
replied, "I bless God, I have just then as full communion with
him as if I was kneeling alone at the altar." '
10 　　Wed. 6. I went down to Taunton and at three in the afternoon
opened the new preaching-house.[20] The people showed great eager-
ness to hear. Will they at length know the day of their visitation?[21]
　　Thur. 7. I returned to Bristol, which I left on Monday 11, and
having visited Stroud, Painswick, and Tewkesbury, on Wednesday
15 20, came to Worcester. Thursday 21, I was much refreshed
among this loving people, especially by the select society, the far
greater part of whom could still witness that God had saved them
from inward as well as outward sin.
　　Sat. 23. About noon, I preached in the town hall at Evesham, to
20 a congregation of a very different kind. Few of them, I doubt,
came from any other motive than to gratify their curiosity. However, they were deeply attentive, so that some of them, I trust,
went away a little wiser than they came.
　　I had been informed that Mr. Weston, the minister of [Chip-
25 ping] Campden,[22] was willing I should preach in his church. But
before I came he had changed his mind. However, the vicar of
Pebworth was no weathercock. So I preached in his church Sunday 24, morning and evening.[23] And I believe not in vain.

dien zum ökumenischen Denken und Handeln eines Halleschen Pietisten (Göttingen, 1989).
Cf. D. L. Brunner, *Halle Pietists in England* (Göttingen, 1993).
　[20] This was an octagon chapel; another Taunton chapel was purchased from J. Lack-
ington in 1811, and when, after a long period in low water, this chapel was completely
refurbished in 1832, the original octagon was sold as a contribution towards the cost.
Wesleyan Methodist Magazine 56 (1833):219.
　[21] See Luke 19:44.
　[22] William Weston (1711-91) matriculated from St. John's College, Cambridge, in
1728, graduated B.A., 1731/2; M.A., 1735; B.D., 1742. He was a fellow of St. John's,
1735-67, and succeeded his father as vicar of Empingham, 1735-43. He was vicar of
Camden, 1744-91; rector of Meppershall, Beds., 1765-91; and prebendary of Lincoln,
1771-91. JW read his ingenious *Dissertations on Some of the Most Remarkable Wonders of
Antiquity* (1748) in 1788 (see Apr. 2, 1788).
　[23] An invitation to preach in Pebworth in 1768 had been foiled by the squire; see Mar.
18, 1768 (22:121, n. 23 in this edn.).

Mon. 25. I went on to Birmingham. I was surprised to hear that a good deal of platina was used there. But upon inquiry I found, it was not the true platina, an original metal between gold and silver (being in weight nearest to gold, even as 18 to 19), but a mere compound of brass and spelter.[24]

Wed. 27. I preached at Dudley in the midst of antinomians and backsliders, on 'We beseech you not to receive the grace of God in vain.'[25] In the evening, I preached to our old flock at Wednesbury, and the old spirit was among them. Friday 29, about eight, I preached to a very large congregation, even at Wolverhampton; and at six in the evening, to a mixed multitude in the marketplace at Newcastle-under-Lyme. All were quiet now, the gentleman who made a disturbance when I was here last[26] having been soon after called to his account.

Sun. 31. I preached at Congleton. The minister here having much disobliged his parishioners,[27] most of the gentry in the town came to the preaching, both at two in the afternoon and in the evening. And it was an acceptable time. I believe very few, rich or poor, came in vain.

Monday, April 1. I went on to Macclesfield. That evening, I preached in the house; but it being far too small, on Tuesday 2, I preached on the Green, near Mr. Ryle's door.[28] There are no mockers here, and scarce an inattentive hearer. So mightily has the word of God prevailed!

Wed. 3. Having climbed over the mountains, I preached at the New Mills in Derbyshire.[29] The people here are quite earnest and

---

[24] 'Platina' was an old name for platinum, but if JW's recollection of its specific gravity was correct, it must have been a mixture of some kind. 'Spelter' was zinc or zinc alloy.

[25] Cf. 2 Cor. 6:1 (*Notes*).

[26] See March 17, 1775 (22:444 in this edn.).

[27] There was a long-standing contest for the patronage of the 'higher chapel' in Congleton between the corporation who built it, and the rectors of Astbury to whose parish it was a chapel of ease. The corporation succeeded in carrying the appointment of Richard Sandbach in 1768, but speedily fell out with him, he claiming the freehold of the chapel and charging the representatives of a deceased alderman half a guinea for burying him. Immediately after JW's visit, the mayor and justices prosecuted Sandbach in the ecclesiastical courts for 'having refused to visit sick people, and privately to baptize weak sickly infants', and they got rid of him in 1785; S. Yates, *History of the Ancient Town and Borough of Congleton* (Congleton, 1820), pp. 75-81. Sandbach then moved to London, and 'becoming a changed character, acted more in harmony with the sacredness of his profession'. J. B. Dyson, *The History of Wesleyan Methodism in the Congleton Circuit* (London, 1856), p. 76.

[28] On John Ryle see Apr. 3, 1774 (22:402, n.59 in this edn.).

[29] His host here was James Beard, a pillar of the New Mills society who did much to build a new chapel there. *Methodist Magazine* 35 (1812):533.

artless, there being no public worship in the town but at our chapel; so that they go straight forward, knowing nothing of various opinions and minding nothing but to be Bible Christians.

Thur. 4. I began an answer to that dangerous tract, Dr. Price's
5 *Observations upon Liberty*;[30] which if practised would overturn all government and bring in universal anarchy. On Easter Day the preaching-house at Manchester contained the congregation pretty well at seven in the morning. But in the afternoon, I was obliged to be abroad, thousands upon thousands flocking
10 together. I stood in a convenient place, almost over against the Infirmary, and exhorted a listening multitude[31] to 'live unto him who died for them and rose again'.[32]

Tuesday 9, I came to Chester and had the satisfaction to find an earnest, loving, well-established people. Wednesday 10, in the
15 evening the house at Liverpool was well filled, with people of all ranks. Friday 12, I visited one, formerly a captain, now a dying sinner. His eyes spoke the agony of his soul, his tongue having well-nigh forgot its office. With great efforts he could but just say, 'I want — Jesus Christ!' The next day he could not utter a word.
20 But if he could not speak, God could hear.

Mon. 15. About noon, I preached in the new house at Wigan,[33]

[30] Richard Price, *Observations on the Nature of Civil Liberty, Principles of Government, and the Justice and Policy of the War with America* (London, 1776; frequently reprinted). Richard Price (1723-91), a liberal nonconformist of advanced Arian views, became the best-known Dissenter in the country in consequence of the success of this pamphlet, and drew upon himself formidable opposition, including JW's *Some Observations on Liberty* (1776) and *Calm Address to the Inhabitants of England* (1777). Price's unblushing premise that 'all civil government, so far as it can be denominated *free*, is the vesture of the people. It originates with them. It is conducted under their direction; and has in view nothing but their happiness. All its different forms are no more than so many different modes in which they choose to direct their affairs. . . . And all *magistrates* are trustees or deputies for carrying regulations into execution' (Price, *Observations*, pp. 6-7), might well seem anarchy to JW.

[31] One of whom, Thomas Marsland (1756-1841), who became a pillar of Stockport Methodism, was taken halfway to conversion. 'The word came with great power to his heart: he cried earnestly to God for mercy. Mr. Wesley endeavoured to encourage him; but he did not at that time obtain what his soul so much desired. However, on August 12, 1778, Mr. Wesley again visited Stockport, and while he was preaching divine light broke upon Mr. Marsland's mind; and he at once beheld, by the eye of faith, the Saviour as dying for him. Immediately his soul was filled with joy and peace . . . and from that time to the day of his death, [he] continued in connexion with the Wesleyan society.' *Wesleyan Methodist Magazine* 66 (1843):792-93.

[32] Cf. 2 Cor. 5:15.

[33] The money for which had been largely raised in one of his earliest appointments by Samuel Bradburn, 'the Methodist Demosthenes'. B. Gregory, *From Cobbler's Bench to President's Chair* (London, 1895), pp. 31-32.

to a very quiet and very dull congregation. But considering what the town was some years ago, wicked even to a proverb, we may well say, 'God hath done great things already.'[34] And we hope to see greater things than these.[35] In the evening, I was obliged to preach abroad at Bolton, though the air was cold and the ground 5 wet. Tuesday 16, I preached about noon at Chowbent,[36] once the roughest place in all the neighbourhood. But there is not the least trace of it remaining. Such is the fruit of the genuine gospel.

As we were considering in the afternoon what we should do, the rain not suffering us to be abroad, one asked the vicar for the 10 use of the church, to which he readily consented. I began reading prayers at half-hour past five. The church was so crowded—pews, alleys, and galleries—as I believe it had not been these hundred years, and God bore witness to his word.

Wed. 17. After preaching at Bury about noon, I went on to 15 Rochdale and preached in the evening to a numerous and deeply serious congregation. Thursday 18, I clambered over the horrid mountains to Todmorden, and thence to Heptonstall, on the brow of another mountain. Such a congregation scarce ever met in the church before. In the evening, I preached in the Croft[37] 20 adjoining to the new house at Halifax.

Fri. 19. I preached at Smith House, for the sake of that lovely woman, Mrs. Holmes.[38] It does me good to see her, such is her patience, or rather thankfulness, under almost continual pain.

Sun. 21. After strongly insisting at Dawgreen on family religion, 25 which is still much wanting among us, I hastened to Birstall Church,[39] where we had a sound, practical sermon. At one, I preached to many thousands at the foot of the hill, and to almost as many at Leeds in the evening.

Mon. 22. I had an agreeable conversation with that good man, 30

---

[34] Cf. Ps. 126:4 (BCP).
[35] See John 1:50.
[36] Orig., 'Chaw-bent'.
[37] J. U. Walker, *A History of Wesleyan Methodism in Halifax and its Vicinity* (Halifax, 1836), pp. 142-43, prints 'the croft' in lower case; it was evidently a field beside the new chapel, then building, and completed the following year.
[38] On Elizabeth Holmes, see 19:270, n. 82 in this edn.
[39] The vicar of Birstall, 1774-1800, was Henry Watkins M.A. (*c.* 1743-1829). He was also vicar of Conisborough 1770-1829, canon of York 1773-1829, canon of Southwell, 1774-1829, rector of Barnborough, 1815-29, and chaplain to the Bishop of Exeter in 1800. He is said probably to have been 'chaplain to the Archbishop or one of the bishops during most of his career', but evidence for this is not forthcoming. H. C. Cradock, *A History of the Parish of Birstall, Yorkshire* (London, 1933), pp. 266-67.

Mr. O———.[40] O that he may be an instrument of removing the
prejudices which have so long separated chief friends!

Tue. 23. I preached in the press-yard[41] at Rothwell, and have
seldom seen a congregation so moved. I then spoke severally to
5 the class of children and found every one of them rejoicing in the
love of God. It is particularly remarkable that this work of God
among them is broke out all at once: they have all been justified
and one clearly sanctified within these last six weeks.

Wed. 24. I went on to Otley,[42] where the word of God has free
10 course and brings forth much fruit. This is chiefly owing to the
spirit and behaviour of those whom God has *perfected in love*.[43]
Their zeal stirs up many, and their steady and uniform conversation has a language almost irresistible. Friday 26, I preached in the
new chapel at Eccleshall, to a people just sprung out of the dust,
15 exceeding artless and exceeding earnest, many of whom seem to
be already *saved from sin*. O why do we not encourage all to expect
this blessing every hour, from the moment they are justified! In
the evening, I preached at Bradford on 'The wise man that builds
his house upon a rock',[44] that is, who builds his hope of heaven on
20 no other foundation than *doing these sayings* contained in the Sermon on the Mount—although in another sense, we build not
upon his *sayings*, but his *sufferings*.

Sat. 27. I preached in the church at Bingley,[45] perhaps not so
filled before for these hundred years. Sun. 28. The congregation at
25 Haworth was far greater than the church could contain. For the
sake of the poor parishioners, few of whom are even awakened to

---

[40] Perhaps Francis Okeley, the Moravian minister at Bedford, on whom see Mar. 9,
1758 (21:136, n. 45 in this edn.).

[41] The word 'press-yard' was already obsolete in JW's day; it was derived from the
name of a yard in the old Newgate prison in which tortures were carried out, and from
which, later, prisoners started for the place of execution.

[42] To the house of Elizabeth Ritchie (see 22:406, n. 88 in this edn.) who wrote about
this time: 'I have been with Mr. Wesley to the various places he has visited in this country, and have had, while travelling, many valuable opportunities for conversation. . . . I
have enjoyed uninterrupted sunshine.' Agnes Bulmer, *Memoirs of Mrs Elizabeth Mortimer* (London, 1836), p. 61.

[43] See 1 John 4:12, 18.   [44] Cf. Matt. 7:24.

[45] Thomas Taylor described how 'at 10 1/2, to the surprise of many, [JW] preached
in Bingley Church, from Acts xxiv.25. I never saw him weep while preaching before
now. He spoke awfully and the congregation heard attentively'; Tyerman, *John Wesley*,
3:225-26. The vicar of Bingley from 1741 till his death in 1797 was Richard Hartley
(1717-97), who entertained JW in 1784 (see below, Diary, July 18, 1784). He had
entered Trinity College, Cambridge, as a sizar in 1734, and graduated B.A. in 1738. He
was usher of Wakefield School, 1738-39.

this day, I spoke as strongly as I possibly could upon these words, 'The harvest is past, the summer is ended, and we are not saved.'[46]

The church at Colne is, I think, at least twice as large as that at Haworth. But it would not in any wise contain the congregation. I preached on 'I saw a great white throne coming down from heaven'.[47] Deep attention sat on every face. And I trust, God gave us his blessing.[48]

Mon. 29. About two, I preached at Padiham in a broad street to a huge congregation. I think the only inattentive persons were the minister and a kind of gentleman. I saw none inattentive at Clough in the evening. What has God wrought since Mr. Grimshaw and I were seized near this place by a furious mob and kept prisoners for some hours! The sons of him who headed that mob now gladly receive our saying.

Tue. 30. In the evening, I preached in a kind of square at Colne to a multitude of people, all drinking in the word. I scarce ever saw a congregation wherein men, women, and children stood in such a posture! And this in the town wherein thirty years ago no Methodist could show his head! The first that preached here was John Jane, who was innocently riding through the town when the zealous mob pulled him off his horse and put him in the stocks! He seized the opportunity and vehemently exhorted them 'to flee from the wrath to come'.[49]

Wednesday, May 1. I set out early and, the next afternoon, reached Whitehaven—and my chaise-horses were no worse for travelling near a hundred and ten miles in two days.

In travelling through Berkshire, Oxfordshire, Bristol, Gloucestershire, Worcestershire, Warwckshire, Staffordshire, Cheshire, Lancashire, Yorkshire, Westmorland, and Cumberland, I dili-

---

[46] Jer. 8:20.

[47] A conflation of Rev. 20:11 and 21:2.

[48] Thomas Taylor's diary amplifies this entry: 'The next day (Sunday) I heard him [JW] at Keighley in the morning, and then at Haworth Church. Afterwards the sacrament was administered, but in too great a hurry. Several hundreds communicated in less than an hour. We then dined in haste and confusion and drove off to Colne. I rode fast and got thither before Mr. Wesley. The street was filled with people waiting to welcome him, but, when about two miles from Colne, his chaise broke down, which somewhat delayed his coming. He mounted a horse, however, and so arrived in safety. The crowd was so great that it was with difficulty we got into the church. The sexton led us to the reading desk and thereby I got a seat. Mr. Wesley's text was Revelation 20:12 [cf. however, n. 47 above]. At the beginning he was rather flat, but, at the end, he spoke many awful things.' See Tyerman, *John Wesley*, 3:226.

[49] Matt. 3:7. On John Jane, see 20:324, n. 49 in this edn.

gently made two inquiries. The first was concerning the increase or decrease of *the people*; the second, concerning the increase or decrease of *trade*. As to the latter, it is, within these two last years, amazingly increased in several branches in such a manner as has not been known in the memory of man—such is the fruit of the entire civil and religious liberty which all England now enjoys! And as to the former, not only in every city and large town, but in every village and hamlet, there is no decrease, but a very large and swift increase. One sign of this is the swarms of little children which we see in every place. Which then shall we most admire, the ignorance or confidence of those that affirm population decreases in England? I doubt not but it increases full as fast here as in any province of North America.[50] ·

Mon. 6. After preaching at Cockermouth and Wigton, I went on to Carlisle and preached to a very serious congregation. Here I saw a very extraordinary genius, a man blind from four years of age, who could wind worsted, weave flowered plush, on an engine and loom of his own making; who wove his own name in plush, and made his own clothes and his own tools of every sort. Some years ago, being shut up in the organ-loft at church, he felt every part of it and afterwards made an organ for himself, which judges say is an exceeding good one. He then taught himself to play upon it, psalm-tunes, anthems, voluntaries, or anything which he heard. I heard him play several tunes with great accuracy, and a complex voluntary; I suppose all Europe can hardly produce such another instance. His name is Joseph Strong.[51] But

[50] JW's economic observations were more to the point than the anti-American inferences he wished to draw from them. The mid-1770s were indeed years of upswing in the trade cycle, marked by cheap food, low bankruptcy rates, a strong pound, and a good price for Consols (Consolidated Annuities, the government securities of Great Britain). And, as those who founded Sunday schools did not need JW to tell them, the increase in the population had become very noticeable in the younger age-groups. In the American colonies, however, the effects of rates of births and deaths, which were both more favourable than those in England, were compounded by heavy immigration to give gross rates of population growth higher than in any European country.

[51] The following paragraph appeared in a copy of the *Newcastle Chronicle*, the date of which has not been traced. 'Joseph Strong, a native of Carlisle, who was blind from birth, displayed an extraordinary genius for mechanics. The following affords a striking instance of his ingenuity and perseverance: At the age of 15 he one afternoon secreted himself in Carlisle Cathedral during Divine Service. When the service was over and the gates were shut, he proceeded to the organ loft and examined every part of the instrument. This took him till midnight; and having satisfied himself respecting the construction, he began to try the tone of the different stops and the proportion they bore to each other. Eventually his nocturnal music was discovered, and the Dean, after reprimand-

what is he the better for all this, if he is still 'without God in the world'?[52]

Tue. 7. I went on to Selkirk. The family came to prayer in the evening; after which the mistress of it said, 'Sir, my daughter Jenny would be very fond of having a little talk with you. She is a strange lass. She will not come down on the Lord's Day but to public worship, and spends all the rest of the day in her own chamber.' I desired she would come up, and found one that earnestly longed to be altogether a Christian. I satisfied her mother that she was not mad, and spent a little time in advice, exhortation, and prayer.

Wed. 8. We set out early, but found the air so keen that before noon our hands bled as if cut with a knife. In the evening, I preached at Edinburgh and, the next evening, near the riverside in Glasgow. Friday 10, I went to Greenock.[53] It being their fast-day before the Sacrament (ridiculously so called; for they do not fast at all, but take their three meals just as on other days), the congregation was larger than when I was here before, and remarkably attentive. The next day I returned to Glasgow and, on Sunday 12, went in the morning to the High Kirk (to show I was no bigot), and in the afternoon to the Church of England chapel. The decency of behaviour here surprises me more and more. I know nothing like it in these kingdoms, except among the Methodists. In the evening the congregation by the riverside was

ing him for the method he had taken to gratify his curiosity, gave him permission to play whenever he pleased. He then set to work and made himself a chamber-organ, upon which he used to play both for amusement and devotion. At the age of 20, he could make himself almost every article of wearing apparel, and his household furniture (save few exceptions) was of his own manufacture. Besides he constructed various pieces of machinery, and among them was a model of a loom with a figure representing a working man upon it. Though he indulged his fancy in the manner above stated, he also followed with great assiduity the business of a diaper weaver, at which he was accounted a good workman.' *WHS* 4 (1904):179.

[52] Eph. 2:12.

[53] JW was accompanied by James Rogers and Thomas Rutherford. The latter describes how between six and seven he set out on horseback for Greenock. 'That was the only time I ever travelled with him when he rode on horse back and it was one of the highest treats of that kind I ever enjoyed. As he could not read or write, as he did when travelling in his carriage, he gave himself up to conversation, which was at once replete with information and entertainment. We had got but a very little way out of town, when we passed a gentleman's seat. Mr. Wesley asked me what the name of it was, but alas, tho' I had passed it repeatedly, I could not tell! He said, "When I can learn nothing else, I like to learn the names of houses and villages as I pass them". His words carried reproof to my heart, and covered me with shame.' *Methodist Magazine* 31 (1808):489-90.

exceeding numerous, to whom I declared 'the whole counsel of God'.[54] Monday 13, I returned to Edinburgh and, the next day, went to Perth, where (it being supposed no house would contain the congregation) I preached at six on the South Inch,[55] though 5 the wind was cold and boisterous. Many are the stumbling-blocks which have been laid in the way of this poor people. They are removed, but the effects of them still continue.

Wed. 15. I preached at Dundee to nearly as large a congregation as that at Port Glasgow. Thursday 16, I attended an ordina- 10 tion at Arbroath. The service lasted about four hours. But it did not strike me. It was doubtless very grave. But I thought it was very dull.

Fri. 17. I reached Aberdeen in good time. Saturday 18, I read over Dr. Johnson's *Tour to the Western Isles*.[56] It is a very curious 15 book, wrote with admirable sense and, I think, great fidelity—although in some respects he is thought to bear hard on the nation, which I am satisfied he never intended. Sun. 19. I attended the morning service at the kirk, full as formal as any in England—and no way calculated either to awaken sinners or to 20 stir up the gift of God in believers. In the afternoon, I heard a useful sermon at the English chapel and was again delighted with the exquisite decency, both of the minister and the whole congregation. The Methodist congregations come the nearest to this. But even these do not come up to it. Our house was sufficiently 25 crowded in the evening. But some of the hearers did not behave like those at the chapel.

---

[54] Cf. Acts 20:27.

[55] The South Inch, a 'beautiful green . . . through which by an avenue of trees, we enter Perth [from Moncrieff hill]. . . . It was the scene of the athletic sports and games of our ancestors. Here the quoit was thrown, the arrow shot, and the ball struck with an energy and power compared to which the senseless efforts of modern arms appear ridiculous and contemptible. Within these few years [1800], that monster *improvement* has levelled a little eminence which stood at one end of this green and bore the name of the Scholars Knoll'—doubtless a good natural pulpit; *Memorabilia of the City of Perth* (Perth, 1806), p. 6. The Inches were also used for common grazing. James Scott, *Statistical Account of the Town and Parish of Perth* (Perth, 1796), p. 14.

[56] Samuel Johnson, *A Journey to the Western Islands of Scotland* (London, 1775). JW's generous judgment is illuminated by Johnson's latest editor, Mary Lascelles: 'Johnson's sympathies, and antipathies were clearly engaged by what he learned in the Highlands, and (even more notably) in the Isles. He exposes his full powers of apprehension to the impact of what had happened, was happening, and was likely to follow. . . . So delicate is the equipoise that readers, from that day to this, have drawn opposite inferences from them.' See Mary Lascelles, ed., in *Works*, 16 vols. (Yale edn., New Haven, 1958-93), 9:xv, n. 7.

Mon. 20. I preached about eleven at Oldmeldrum,[57] but could not reach Banff[58] till near seven in the evening. I went directly to the parade and proclaimed to a listening multitude, 'The grace of our Lord Jesus Christ'.[59] All behaved well but a few gentry, whom I rebuked openly. And they stood corrected. 5

After preaching, Mrs. Gordon, the Admiral's widow,[60] invited me to supper. There I found five or six as agreeable women as I have seen in the kingdom—and I know not when I have spent two or three hours with greater satisfaction. In the morning, I was going to preach in the assembly-room, when the Episcopal minis- 10 ter sent and offered me the use of his chapel.[61] It was quickly filled. After reading prayers, I preached on those words in the Second Lesson, 'What lack I yet?'[62] and strongly applied them to those in particular who supposed themselves to be 'rich' and 'increased in goods and lacked nothing'.[63] I then set out for Keith. 15

Banff is one of the neatest and most elegant towns that I have seen in Scotland. It is pleasantly situated on the side of a hill, sloping from the sea, though close to it, so that it is sufficiently sheltered from the sharpest winds. The streets are straight and broad. I believe it may be esteemed the fifth, if not the fourth, 20 town in the kingdom. The county, quite from Banff to Keith, is the best peopled of any I have seen in Scotland. This is chiefly if not entirely owing to the late Earl of Findlater.[64] He was indefati-

---

[57] For a previous visit to John Likly, minister of Oldmeldrum, see June 8, 1764 (21:469, n. 37 in this edn.).

[58] Orig., 'Bamff'.

[59] 2 Cor. 8:9, the text Wesley usually cites in his diary and Sermon Register, and verified in this instance by a first-hand account given in n. 63 below.

[60] William Gordon was promoted Admiral in 1762, having been gazetted Captain in 1744; he died in 1768. His widow died at the house in Banff after a long illness in April 1794. *Gentleman's Magazine* 64 (1794):384; *Scots Magazine* 56 (1794):179.

[61] The Episcopal chapel in Banff had been burnt down by Cumberland in 1746 during the rebellion; Samuel Lewis, *A Topographical Dictionary of Scotland*, 2 vols. (London, 1846), 1:102. But there was now a qualified chapel (i.e., one which took the oaths to the Hanoverians), the minister of which was Charles Cordiner. Cf. below, May 14, 1784. *Ex inf.* Dr. Gavin White.

[62] Matt. 19:20.

[63] Cf. Rev. 3:17. This visit elicited a slightly querulous comment from two members of the Methodist society at Banff, William and Isabel McPherson: 'Mr. Wesley was here on the 20th of May last and preached on the Parade from 2 Corinthians viii. 9. He supped at Lord Banff's, and next night at Admiral Gordon's Lady's house, with a great number of great ones; and at their request he preached in the English chapel to an elegant and crowded congregation.' Tyerman, *John Wesley*, 3:225, n. 1.

[64] James Ogilvy, sixth Earl of Findlater and third Earl of Leafield (*c.* 1714-70), was one of the celebrated improving landlords among the Scottish aristocracy, doing much for

gable in doing good, took pains to procure industrious men from
all parts and to provide such little settlements for them as enabled
them to live with comfort.

5   About noon, I preached at the New Mills,[65] nine miles from
Banff, to a large congregation of plain, simple people. As we rode
in the afternoon the heat overcame me, so that I was weary and
faint before we came to Keith. But I no sooner stood up in the
market-place than I forgot my weariness—such were the seriousness and attention of the whole congregation, though as numerous
10   as that at Banff. Mr. Gordon, the minister of the parish,[66] invited
me to supper, and told me, his kirk was at my service. A little society is formed here already and is in a fair way of increasing. But
they were just now in danger of losing their preaching-house, the
owner being determined to sell it. I saw but one way to secure it
15   for them, which was to buy it myself. So (who would have thought
it!) I bought an estate, consisting of two houses, a yard, a garden,
with three acres of good land. But he told me flat, 'Sir, I will take
no less for it than sixteen pounds ten shillings, to be paid, part
now, part at Michaelmas, and the residue next May.'[67]
20   Here Mr. Gordon showed me a great curiosity. Near the top of
the opposite hill a new town is built, containing, I suppose, a hundred houses, which is *a town of beggars*.[68] This, he informed me,
was the professed, regular occupation of *all the inhabitants*. Early

bleaching and the manufacture of linen and damask, as well as for agriculture and
forestry. His New Keith (Lewis, *Scotland*, 2:3) was one of the famous planned villages of
Scotland, which self-consciously imitated the model villages of southern England, but
paid rather more heed than they to function rather than ornament. T. Christopher
Smout, *A History of the Scottish People, 1560–1830* (rev. edn., London, 1972), pp. 275-76.
    [65] Probably Newmills of Boyne, a village 1 mile north-west of Cornhill and about
halfway between Banff and Keith; cf. below n. 68.
    [66] George William Algernon Gordon, A.M. (*c.* 1733-94), minister of Keith, 1771-94.
    [67] The precise nature of the transaction highly abbreviated here is still not clear. The
owner of the property bought by JW was George Smout, mason of Cairnie, who had
acquired it from the Earl of Findlater. The 'three acres' (actually 4 acres 2 roods 32
perches) was a tenancy, part of the 500 acres laid out in allotments by the earl. The tenancy seems, however, to have been attached to the two houses JW bought. Unstated
complications arose about this which led JW in 1789 to appoint trustees (Telford,
8:110) headed by William McPherson, weaver, Banff (on whom see May 20, n. 63,
above). Regular worship in the chapel ceased in 1827, and it was sold in 1835. After use
in turn as a school and drill hall, a free church chapel and an Episcopal manse, the property reverted to its original form of two dwelling-houses. *WHS* 9 (1914):155-56.
    [68] This was the new town of Newmill, a village of about one hundred small holdings,
founded in the middle of the eighteenth century by Lord Fife. Boasting a market, it is
also described as 'a colony from various districts of the Highlands, who, being indigent,
and supported by begging, or their own alertness, are allured there by the abundance of
moss . . . during the summer months they range this and the neighbouring parishes, and

in spring they all go out and spread themselves over the kingdom. And in autumn they return and do what is requisite for their wives and children.

Wed. 22. The wind turning north, we stepped at once from June to January. About one, I preached at Inverurie,[69] to a plain, earnest, loving people, and before five came to Aberdeen. Thursday 23, I read over Mr. Pennant's journey through Scotland[70]—a lively as well as judicious writer. Judicious, I mean, in most respects; but I cannot give up to all the deists in Great Britain the existence of witchcraft, till I give up the credit of all history, sacred and profane. And at the present time I have not only as strong, but stronger, proofs of this from eye and ear witnesses than I have of murder, so that I cannot rationally doubt of one any more than the other.

Fri. 24. I returned to Arbroath and lodged at Provost Grey's.[71] So, for a time, we are in honour! I have hardly seen such another place in the three kingdoms as this is at present. Hitherto there is no opposer at all, but everyone seems to bid us God-speed! Saturday 25, I preached at Westhaven (a town of fishermen) about noon, and at Dundee in the evening. Sun. 26. I went to the new church, cheerful, lightsome, and admirably well finished.[72] A young gentleman preached such a sermon, both for sense and language, as I never heard in North Britain before. And I was informed his life is as his preaching. At five we had an exceeding large congregation, and the people of Dundee in general behave better at public worship than any in the kingdom, except the Methodists and those at the episcopal chapels. In all other kirks, the bulk of the people are bustling to and fro before the minister has ended his prayer. In Dundee all are quiet, and none stir at all till he has pronounced the blessing.

are a great encroachment upon what is truly the property of the native poor.' Sir John Sinclair, *The Statistical Account of Scotland*, 12 vols. (Edinburgh, 1791-99), 5:423-24; see also *WHS* 4 (1904):214; 9 (1914):155.

[69] Orig., 'Inverary'.

[70] Thomas Pennant, *A Tour in Scotland, 1769* (Chester, 1771). He also published supplements to this tour and a *Voyage to the Hebrides, MDCCLXXII* (Chester, 1776), which were frequently reprinted, and appeared as vols. 12-14 of his *Collected Works*. In *Works* 12:169 he speaks of 'the imaginary crime of witchcraft'.

[71] There was no eighteenth-century Provost Grey at Arbroath. The entry is doubtless an error for David Greig, Provost 1775-77, and for three subsequent periods. George Hay, *History of Arbroath to the Present Time* (Arbroath, 1876), pp. 341, 389.

[72] Dundee became the head of a circuit in 1765, while services in Dundee itself were being held 'in a large hall above the vaults of an old Franciscan nunnery'; W. F. Swift, *Methodism in Scotland* (London, 1947), p. 48. In 1773, the society moved into a disused chapel in Tully Street, where they remained for almost a century.

Mon. 27. I paid a visit to St. Andrews, once the largest city in the kingdom.[73] It was eight times as large as it is now, and a place of very great trade. But the sea rushing from the north-east gradually destroyed the harbour and trade together; in consequence of which, whole streets (that were) are now meadows and gardens. Three broad, straight, handsome streets remain, all pointing at the old cathedral, which by the ruins appears to have been above three hundred feet long and proportionably broad and high; so that it seems to have exceeded York Minster and to have at least equalled any cathedral in England.[74] Another church, afterwards used in its stead, bears date 1124. A steeple standing[75] near the cathedral is thought to have stood thirteen hundred years.

What is left of St. Leonard's College[76] is only a heap of ruins. Two colleges remain. One of them has a tolerable square,[77] but all the windows are broke, like those of a brothel. We were informed, 'The students do this, before they leave the college.' Where are their blessed governors in the meantime? Are they all fast asleep? The other college[78] is a mean building, but has a handsome library newly erected. In the two colleges, we learned, were about seventy

[73] St. Andrews had been the principal episcopal burgh at a time when the episcopate mattered much to the Scottish kingdoms, and with Aberdeen, Perth, and Dundee, attained a pre-eminence in foreign trade, and declined after abolition of episcopacy. It is, however, hazardous to estimate social decline from the size of ecclesiastical ruins, and at the time JW was writing, St. Andrews was still to be reckoned among the dozen or so largest Scottish towns. Smout, *Scottish People*, p. 243n.

[74] The cathedral was 350 feet long (as compared with York's 375 feet), 65 feet broad, and crossed from north to south by a transept 180 feet long. J. Grierson, *Delineations of St. Andrews* (3rd edn., Cupar, 1838), p. 93.

[75] 'A square prism of one hundred and eight feet in height', part of the chapel of St. Regulus. Grierson (*Delineations*, pp. 89, 91) reported that all the oldest Scottish writers reckoned this building to 'the end of the fourth or beginning of the fifth century', though there was no literary account of it earlier than the thirteenth century.

[76] St. Leonard's College was founded in 1512. In 1747, the revenues of St. Salvator's and St. Leonard's colleges were found to be insufficient, and the buildings of St. Leonard's ruinous beyond repair, so the two colleges were united.

[77] St. Salvator's College, founded in 1458. 'The buildings of this college formed an extensive square, inclosing a quadrangular court about 230 feet long and 180 wide, decorated with piazzas on the north side' (Grierson, *Delineations*, p. 156). In 1827 these buildings were found by a royal commission to be ruinous beyond repair. A Treasury minute to replace them was followed by the Reform Act, and the scheme was never completed.

[78] St. Mary's College, founded 1552. Like both Samuel Johnson and James Boswell, JW seems to have mistaken the upper rooms of the University Library, built in 1764, for the library of St. Mary's College. Johnson, *Western Islands* (Yale edn., 1971), p. 7; Boswell, *Tour to the Hebrides* in *Boswell's Life of Johnson*, ed. G. B. Hill and L. F. Powell, 6 vols. (Oxford, 1934–60), 5:480; see also Grierson, *Delineations*, p. 205.

students, near the same number as at Old Aberdeen. Those at
New Aberdeen are not more numerous, neither those at Glasgow.
In Edinburgh, I suppose, there are a hundred. So four universities contain three hundred and ten students![79] These all come to
their several colleges in November and return home in May! So   5
they *may* study five months in the year and lounge all the rest! O
where was the common sense of those who instituted such colleges! In the English colleges everyone *may* reside all the year, as
all my pupils did. And I should have thought myself little better
than a highwayman if I had not lectured them every day in the   10
year but Sundays.

We were so long detained at the passage[80] that I only reached
Edinburgh time enough to give notice of my preaching the next
day. After preaching at Dunbar, Alnwick, and Morpeth, on Saturday, June 1, I reached Newcastle.   15

Mon. 3. I visited Sunderland, where the society then contained
three hundred and seventy-two members. Thursday 6, I
preached at Darlington and Barnard Castle; on Friday, in Teesdale and Weardale. Here many rejoiced with joy unspeakable[81] and
seemed determined never to rest till they had recovered that great 20
salvation which they enjoyed some years ago. Saturday 8, as we
rode to Sheep Hill, we saw and heard at a distance much thunder
and rain and lightning. The rain was before and behind and on
each side—but none fell upon *us*. About six, I preached at Sheep
Hill. It rained hard very near us; but not a drop came upon *us*.   25
After eight I reached Newcastle, thoroughly tired. But a night's
rest set me up again. On Monday and Tuesday I met the classes. I
left three hundred and seventy-four in the society, and I found
about four hundred. And I trust they are more established in the
'faith that worketh by love'.[82]   30

While I was here, I talked largely with a pious woman whom I
could not well understand. I could not doubt of her being quite

---

[79] The average attendance at St. Andrews was indeed about 70 (Grierson,
Delineations, p. 174). But the comparison with Oxford is misplaced as well as odious. All
over Europe (including Oxford and Cambridge) student enrollments fell in the eighteenth century, and many German universities had well under a hundred students at
this time. Edinburgh, however, was now entering upon its period as the 'Athens of the
North'; and, as for 'the blessed governors' in the previous century, much of the best in
Scottish universities was often to be found in Aberdeen, where there was less clerical
control than elsewhere.
[80] Queensferry.
[81] See 1 Pet. 1:8.
[82] Cf. Gal. 5:6.

sincere, nay, and much devoted to God. But she had fallen among some well-meaning enthusiasts, who taught her so to 'attend to the *inward voice*' as to quit the society, the preaching, the Lord's Supper, and almost all *outward means*. I find no persons harder to
5   deal with than these. One knows not how to advise them. They must not act contrary to their conscience, though it be an erroneous one. And who can convince them that it is erroneous? None but the Almighty.

Mon. 17. After preaching at Durham, I went on to Darlington.
10   The society here, lately consisting of nine members, is now increased to above seventy, many of whom are warm in their first love. At the love-feast many of these spoke their experience with all simplicity. Here will surely be a plentiful harvest, if tares do not grow up with the wheat.[83]
15   Wed. 19. I preached to my old, loving congregation at Osmotherley and visited once more poor Mr. Watson,[84] just quivering over the grave.

Part of this week I read, as I travelled, a famous book, which I had not looked into for these fifty years. It was Lucian's
20   *Dialogues*.[85] He has a good deal of humour, but wonderful little judgment. His great hero is Diogenes, the cynic, just such another brute as himself. Socrates (as one might expect), he reviles and ridicules with all his might. I think there is more sense in his Timon than in all his other dialogues put together. And yet
25   even that ends poorly, in the dull jest of his breaking the heads of all that came near him. How amazing is it that such a book as this should be put into the hands of schoolboys!

Mon. 24. I went on to Scarborough. I think the preaching-house here is the most elegant of any square room which we have
30   in England.[86] And we had as elegant a congregation. But they were as attentive as if they had been Kingswood colliers.

Tue. 25. I visited a poor backslider, who has given great occasion to the enemy to blaspheme. Sometime since, he felt a pain in

---

[83] See Matt. 13:26.

[84] On Thomas (or John) Adams (*alias* Watson) see Mar. 28, 1745 (20:58, n. 34 in this edn.).

[85] Lucian of Samosata, *Dialogi; graece* (1st edn., Florence, 1496, constantly reprinted). Nineteenth-century writers found Lucian's assaults on popular religion 'admirable'. *Dictionary of Classical Antiquities*, ed. H. Nettleship and J.E. Sandys (London, 1891), p. 363.

[86] On the Scarborough preaching-house in Church Stairs Street, see June 21, 1772 (22:338, n. 86 in this edn.).

the soles of his feet, then in his legs, his knees, his thighs. Now it has reached his stomach and begins to affect his head. No medicines have availed at all. I fear he has sinned a sin unto death[87]—a sin which God has determined to punish by death.

Fri. 28. I am seventy-three years old and far abler to preach than I was at three-and-twenty. What natural means has God used to produce so wonderful an effect? (1) Continual exercise and change of air, by travelling above four thousand miles in a year. (2) Constant rising at four. (3) The ability, if ever I want, to sleep immediately. (4) The never losing a night's sleep in my life. (5) Two violent fevers and two deep consumptions. These, it is true, were rough medicines, but they were of admirable service, causing my flesh to come again as the flesh of a little child. May I add, lastly, evenness of temper? I *feel* and *grieve*; but, by the grace of God, I *fret* at nothing. But still 'the help that is done upon earth', he 'doth it himself.'[88] And this he doth in answer to many prayers.[89]

Monday, July 1. I preached about eleven to a numerous and serious congregation at Pocklington. In my way from hence to Malton, Mr. C—— (a man of sense and veracity) gave me the following account. 'His grandfather, Mr. H——, he said, about twenty years ago, ploughing up a field two or three miles from Pocklington, turned up a large stone, under which he perceived there was a hollow. Digging on, he found at a small distance a large, magnificent house. He cleared away the earth and, going into it, found many spacious rooms. The floors of the lower story were of mosaic work, exquisitely wrought. Mr. C—— himself counted sixteen stones within an inch square. Many flocked to see it from various parts, as long as it stood open. But after some days, Mr. P—— (he knew not why) ordered it to be covered again. And he would never after suffer any to open it, but ploughed the field all over.[']'[90] This is far more difficult to account for than the subterraneous buildings at Herculaneum.[91]

---

[87] See 1 John 5:16.

[88] Ps. 74:13 (BCP).

[89] Compare this self-assessment with the one made on his 71st birthday, June 28, 1774 (22:418 in this edn.).

[90] The neighbourhood of Pocklington abounds in such remains. *Notes and Queries* (1883), 2:477.

[91] A city some 5 miles south-west of Naples at the western foot of Vesuvius, badly damaged by the earthquake of 63 A.D. and overwhelmed by the eruption of Vesuvius in 69. There were rich discoveries of its architectural heritage in the 18th century. A. F. Pauly, ed., *Paulys Real-Encyclopaedie*, 33 vols. (Stuttgart, 1893-1972), 8:532-48.

History gives us an account of the time when, and the manner how, these were swallowed up. The burning mountain is still assured, and the successive lavas that flowed from it still distinguishable. But history gives no account of this, nor of any burning
5 mountains in our island. Neither do we read of any such earthquake in England as was capable of working that effect.

Tue. 2. I went to York.[92] The house was full enough in the evening, while I pointed the true and the false way of expounding those important words, 'Ye are saved through faith.'[93]
10 Wednesday 3, I preached about noon at Tadcaster, with an uncommon degree of freedom, which was attended with a remarkable blessing. A glorious work is dawning here, against which nothing can prevail, unless the ball of contention[94] be thrown in among the plain people by one or two that have lately
15 embraced new opinions. In the evening, I preached at York on the fashionable religion vulgarly called *morality*. And showed at large from the accounts given of it by its ablest patrons, that it is neither better nor worse than *atheism*.

Thur. 4. I met the select society and was a little surprised to
20 find that instead of growing in grace, scarce two of them retained the grace they had two years ago. All of them seemed to be sincere, and yet a faintness of spirit ran through them all.

In the evening, I showed to a still more crowded audience the nature and necessity of Christian love—ἀγάπη, vilely rendered
25 *charity* to confound poor English readers. The word was sharper than a two-edged sword,[95] as many of the hearers felt. God grant the wound may not be healed till he himself binds it up.

Fri. 5. About eleven, I preached at Foggathorpe,[96] a lone house a few miles from Howden. Abundance of people were gathered
30 together, notwithstanding heavy rain. And they received the truth in the love thereof. I came to Howden a little before three, when a large congregation was soon gathered. All were serious, the more so because of a few claps of thunder that rolled over our heads.

---

[92] Miss Mortimer and Elizabeth Ritchie shared in the class meeting and other spiritual exercises which were held on this occasion. J. Lyth, *Glimpses of Early Methodism in York and the Surrounding District* (York, 1885), pp. 126–30.

[93] Eph. 2:8 (*Notes*).

[94] Wesley seems here to be thinking of the proverbial 'bone of contention', but in his sermon No. 104, 'On Attending the Church Service' (1787), §33, he refers to those who 'have no better business than to toss the ball of controversy to and fro' (3:478 in this edn.).

[95] See Heb. 4:12.

[96] Orig., 'Fogguthorp'. Foggathorpe is a village 8 miles west of Market Weighton.

I preached at Swinefleet in the evening. These are the most sensible and gentlemen-like farmers that I have seen anywhere. And many of them are 'rooted and grounded in love',[97] and have adorned the gospel many years.

Sat. 6. I went on to Epworth and found my old friend Mr. Hutton in the deepest melancholy. I judged it to be partly natural, partly diabolical; but I doubt not he will be saved, though as by fire.[98]

Tue. 9. I preached at Brigg in the morning. All behaved well but a few gentlemen (so called) who seemed to understand no more of the matter than if I had been talking Greek.

I went thence to Horncastle and to Spilsby with Mr. Br[ackenbury].[99] While he was at Cambridge he was convinced of sin, though not by any outward means, and soon after justified. Coming to Hull, he met with one of our preachers. By long and close conversation with him, he was clearly convinced, it was his duty to join with the people called Methodists. At first, indeed, he staggered at lay preachers; but after weighing the matter more deeply, he began preaching himself and found a very remarkable blessing both on his own soul and on his labours.

After visiting a few more places in these parts, on Saturday 13, I returned to Epworth. Sunday 14, I preached in the morning at Gringley,[1] about one at Owston, and at four in Epworth market-

[97] Eph. 3:17.
[98] See 1 Cor. 3:15. 'William Hutton, mercer and grocer, a man in good repute in the town, with whom JW stayed when at Epworth.' George J. Stevenson, *Memorials of the Wesley Family* (London, 1876), 348; Telford, 3:220; 6:35, 169.
[99] Robert Carr Brackenbury (1752-1818) was described in his obituary as 'of Raithby Hall, Co. Lincoln, formerly a celebrated character on the turf. Though possessed of an ample fortune, he was for many years a zealous preacher among the Methodists, and he is stated to have bequeathed £1600 for the spreading of the gospel'; *Gentleman's Magazine* 88 (1818, pt. 2):376. Brackenbury, a magistrate, was indeed the owner of several country houses and thousands of acres, but he was admitted to St. Catherine's College, Cambridge, in 1769, with a view to the ministry of the Church. JW's high opinion of him, despite a somewhat petulant reception in 1780 of the news that he was married (Telford, 7:34), persisted; the following month he gave him an open invitation to preach in Methodist preaching-houses (*WHS* 28 [1951]:55) and frequently had him as a travelling companion. In 1782, his wife died in consequence of a trivial accident, and from 1784-90 JW appointed him as assistant in the Channel Islands without the formality of admitting him by Conference; he made him a member of the Legal Hundred, and was attended by him on his death bed. From 1790, Brackenbury was stationed as a supernumerary in circuits within reach of Raithby Hall, at which he built a chapel for Methodist use; *WHS* 20 (1936):170-74. He died 'having solemnly expressed the wish that his fame might not be made the subject of human panegyric'; *Methodist Magazine* 42 (1819):696; Mrs. Richard Smith, *Raithby Hall; or, Memorial Sketches of R. C. Brackenbury* (London, 1859).
[1] Orig., 'Gringly'.

place, where God 'struck with the hammer of his word and broke the hearts of stone'.[2] We had afterwards a love-feast, at which a flame was soon kindled; which was greatly increased while Mr. Cundy[3] related the manner how God perfected him in love—a testimony which is always attended with a peculiar blessing.

Mon. 15. I preached at Doncaster, in one of the most elegant houses in England[4] and to one of the most elegant congregations. They seemed greatly astonished. And well they might, for I scarce ever spoke so strongly on 'Strait is the gate, and narrow is the way, that leadeth unto life.'[5] Tuesday 16, at Sheffield I talked at large with one whose case is very peculiar. She never loses a sense of the love of God, and yet is continually harassed by the devil and constrained to utter words which her soul abhors, while her body feels as if it was in a burning flame. For this her father turned her out of doors, and she had no money, nor any friend to take her in. To cut her off from every human comfort, our wise Assistant turned her out of [the] society. Yet in all this she murmured not, 'neither charged God foolishly'![6]

Wed. 17. Having been desired by one of Chesterfield[7] to give them a sermon in the way, I called there—but he did not come to

---

[2] Cf. CW, *Hymns and Sacred Poems* (1749), 1:319; see *Collection of Hymns* (1780), No. 82:

> Come, O thou all-victorious Lord
> Thy power to us make known;
> Strike with the hammer of thy word,
> And break these hearts of stone.

The hymn was 'Written before preaching at Portland' (Dorset, June 1746), and the lines are reminiscent of seeing the quarrymen at work (see 7:181 in this edn.).

[3] Richard Condy (or Cundy), who died in 1800, appeared in the stationing minutes for the first time at the following Conference, and was appointed to Epworth where JW now encountered him. JW found him 'a valuable man. I seldom converse with him but he does me good' (Telford, 6:252). In 1780 ill-health compelled him to desist from travelling, but in 1784 he was appointed as the first master at a school in the Whitefriar Street Chapel in Dublin; C. H. Crookshank, *History of Methodism in Ireland*, 3 vols. (Belfast, 1885), 1:390. From 1785-92, he travelled in Ireland; he then returned to English circuits, becoming a supernumerary in 1799.

[4] What JW meant here by 'elegant' is indicated by his description of the chapel on a previous visit (July 7, 1770) as 'one of the neatest in England'. This use of the word 'elegant' common in his day, survives in connection with scientific formulae, processes, and solutions to problems. *OED*.

[5] Matt. 7:14.

[6] Cf. Job 1:22.

[7] This change of heart may have owed something to the rough play which greeted the first Methodist arrival in Chesterfield three years before. Tyerman, *John Wesley*, 3:226, summarising Tyerman MSS, 3, fol. 12 (Methodist Archives, Manchester).

own me. So after resting awhile at another house, I stood at a small distance from the main street and proclaimed salvation by faith to a serious congregation. After preaching at a few other places, on Thursday the 18th, I preached at Nottingham, and having no time to lose, took chaise at noon and, the next evening, Friday 19, met the committee at the Foundery.[8]

Wed. 24. I read Mr. Jenyns's admired tract on *The Internal Evidence of the Christian Religion*.[9] He is undoubtedly a fine writer; but whether he is a Christian, deist, or atheist, I cannot tell. If he is a Christian, he betrays his own cause by averring that 'All *Scripture is* not *given by inspiration of God*;[10] but the writers of it were *sometimes* left to themselves and consequently made *some mistakes*.' Nay, if there be *any* mistakes in the Bible, there may as well be a thousand. If there be one falsehood in that book, it did not come from the God of truth.

Sun. 28. Perceiving the immense hurt which it had done, I spoke more strongly than ever I had done before on the sin and danger of indulging 'itching ears'.[11] I trust, here at least that plague will be stayed.

Friday, August 2,[12] we made our first subscription toward build-

[8] According to Curnock (6:117, n. 1), the Foundery Chapel, though held on a lease which had still some time to run, was believed by JW to be threatened by wider schemes for the redevelopment of Finsbury and Moorfields. Negotiations with the Committee for letting City lands were begun, and by March 1776 it was resolved to open a subscription for a new Foundery Chapel. Eventually, the City granted a lease of 59 years on the site in City Road on which Wesley's Chapel still stands. Telford, 6:179, 189, 206; Stevenson, *City Road*, pp. 64–65.

[9] Soame Jenyns, *A View of the Internal Evidence of the Christian Religion* (London, 1776). Soame Jenyns (1704–87), M.P. for Cambridgeshire 1742–54, for Dunwich 1754–58, and Cambridge 1758–80, became a commissioner for trade and plantations in 1775, and wrote a good deal of poetry as well as tracts of a philosophical, economic and political kind. His *View of the Internal Evidence*, which created controversy, rapidly went through ten editions and was much translated, marked his personal transition from scepticism to some kind of belief, but was thought by *cognoscenti* to lack seriousness. Lewis Namier and John Brooke, *The House of Commons 1754-90*, 3 vols. (London, 1964), 1:681-82. JW spells his name 'Jenyng'.

[10] Cf. 2 Tim. 3:16.

[11] 2 Tim. 4:3.

[12] JW's activities during this week are amplified in a letter from Hannah Ball to Patty Chapman (*The Methodist Recorder* [London, 1897], p. 1026): 'The first night I was in London [Aug. 3] I went to a prayer meeting at West Street Chapel. The next morning at 6 met Molly Rockull's band, where I found one precious soul entirely given up to God. . . . I had a coach and went to the Foundery. Mr. Wesley preached from these words: "Wherefore let him that thinketh he standeth take heed lest he fall". The discourse was very excellent and encouraging to me. After the sermon the sacrament was given to a great number of communicants. Then I went to Mr. Parkinson's to dine. After that to the Foundery again, and had an opportunity of being present when Mr.

ing a new chapel.[13] And at this and the two following meetings above a thousand pounds were cheerfully subscribed.

Sun. 4. Many of the preachers being come to town, I enforced that solemn caution in the Epistle for the day, 'Let him that standeth take heed lest he fall.'[14] And God applied it to many hearts. In the afternoon, I preached in Moorfields to thousands, on Acts 2:32, 'Him hath God raised up, whereof ye are all witnesses.'[15]

Tue. 6. Our Conference began,[16] and ended on Friday the 9th, which we observed with fasting and prayer, as well for our own nation as for our brethren in America.[17] In several conferences we

Wesley met the leaders of the bands and classes. He also baptized a woman. I was glad to be present. . . . I heard him preach in Moorfields to a very great multitude. The sun was very hot, and I was much fatigued. After that we returned to the Foundery, where was a general love-feast. It was very full and hot, but a refreshing season. . . . [Tuesday] Was not able to rise in the morning without doing myself hurt, so rested till afternoon, and then went to the Foundery and heard Mr. Wesley preach again, and found it good to be there. . . . On Thursday heard Mr. Wesley again at the Foundery. Afterwards met in the bands and spoke my experience. . . . Sunday morning [11th] at 6 I met Molly Rockull's band again. . . . Spent a little time with Mr Wells in conversation. I did not see him any more, but firmly believe I shall meet him at God's right hand. Mr. Wesley read prayers and preached and gave the Sacrament. After it was over [he] prayed extempory and Mr. Charles Wesley after him. He (Mr. Charles) was very excellent in prayer. I was much pleased to see him. He looks a very gracious man. In the afternoon I had the privilege through a friend, to be a few moments with Mr. John Wesley alone. He asked how you did, but did not say anything about your not writing to him. I also had the opportunity to meet with the leaders of bands and classes. His brother read prayers, and he preached again. He met the Society, and then took his leave, giving the hymn-book to Mr. Mather to sing a few verses for him. Here I could but drop a tear, being much affected'.

[13] See above, July 19, 1776, n. 8 in this edn.

[14] 1 Cor 10:12.   [15] Orig. cited as, 'Acts ii.31'.

[16] The minutes of this Conference already reveal the impact of the American war; no preachers were stationed in America, and the number of members there was simply repeated from the previous year. There were also complaints that Ireland made practically no contribution to the yearly expenses, a defect ascribed to the leaders meeting independently of the assistant. The implication of one resolution is that JW helped support Miss Owen's school at Publow, and entered two girls in it. The 'grand hindrance of the work of God' was perceived to be Calvinism, which preachers were to oppose without returning 'railing for railing'.

[17] There was much reason for concern at a Methodist as well as at a national level. The Virginia Methodists joined with the Baptists to overthrow the Anglican establishment in the colony, and their rapid expansion created a case for Methodist ordination so that the people might receive the sacraments no longer available from the clergy. Ordinations indeed began at the Fluvanna Conference in 1779, and Francis Asbury, JW's one English preacher remaining, in virtual confinement at Delaware, had called a preparatory conference of preachers who were prepared to allow sacraments to be received from Anglican clergy only. How Asbury managed to get his way with the southern preachers at the next Conference in Virginia is not known.

have had great love and unity. But in this there was over and above, such a general seriousness and solemnity of spirit as we scarcely have had before. Sun. 11. About half an hour after four I set out, and at half an hour after eleven on Monday came to Bristol. I found Mr. Fletcher a little better,[18] and proposed his taking a journey with me to Cornwall, nothing being so likely to restore his health as a journey of four or five hundred miles. But his physician would in no wise consent. So I gave up the point. Tue. 13. I preached at Taunton and afterwards went with Mr. Brown[19] to Kingston. The large old parsonage-house is pleasantly situated, close to the churchyard, just fit for a contemplative man. Here I found a clergyman, Dr. Coke, late Gentleman Commoner of Jesus College in Oxford, who came twenty miles on purpose. I had much conversation with him, and an union then began which I trust shall never end.[20]

---

[18] On John Fletcher, see Mar. 13, 1757 (21:88 in this edn.). Fletcher's health had not been good for some years, and it had been thought that effects of excessive study and austerity of living might be repaired by 'exercise in the open air'; Joseph Benson, *The Life of John William de la Fléchère* (3rd edn., London, 1812), pp. 172-73 (hereafter, *Fletcher*). To these disabilities were now added 'a violent cough, accompanied with spitting of blood', for which JW prescribed, with perfect confidence, 'a constant exercise, together with a change of air'; John Wesley, *A Short Account of the Life and Death of the Rev. John Fletcher* (1786), vol. 14 in this edn.; Jackson 11:304. Fletcher nevertheless accompanied JW in November 'through Oxfordshire, Northamptonshire and Norfolk; [reporting] I hope I am rather better than worse' (Benson, p. 189). See below, Nov. 13, 20, and 23, 1776.

[19] On James Brown, see Apr. 19, 1764 (21:454, n. 69). It has often been believed that Thomas Coke acted briefly as his curate on his expulsion from South Petherton in 1771. Certainly Brown introduced Coke to Methodist theology.

[20] Thomas Coke (1747-1814) was to become one of the leading figures in international Methodism for the rest of his days. The son of a prosperous apothecary at Brecon, he matriculated at Jesus College, Oxford, in 1764, and after briefly flirting with scepticism, he was confirmed in the faith by reading Thomas Sherlock. He was ordained deacon in 1770 and priest in 1772, and was now curate of South Petherton. With many good qualities Coke combined a strong vein of pomposity and instability, and, according to Moore, exemplified them at his first meeting with JW. 'Mr. Wesley, with marked sobriety, gave him an account of the way in which he and his brother proceeded in Oxford, and advised [Coke] to go on in the same path, doing all the good he could, visiting from house to house, omitting no part of the clerical duty; and counselled him to avoid every reasonable ground of offence. [Coke] was exceedingly surprised, and indeed, mortified. "I thought" said he when he related the account to me, "he would have said, 'Come with me, and I will give you employment according to all that is in your heart.' " However, he proceeded to turn his parish 'into a kind of Methodist circuit', and was dismissed amidst celebrations led by bell-ringing and hogsheads of cider. He attended the Bristol Conference in 1777, and was first stationed as a preacher in 1778. Coke's views were characterised by breadth rather than practicality, and he was much used by JW in the extension of the work beyond England. President of the Irish Conference from the beginning of that office in 1782, he published a plan for a missionary society in 1784,

Wed. 14. I preached at Tiverton, and on Thursday went on to
Launceston. Here I found the plain reason why the work of God
had gained no ground in this circuit all the year. The preachers
had given up the Methodist testimony.[21] Either they did not speak
5   of perfection at all (the peculiar doctrine committed to our trust),
or they spoke of it only in general terms, without urging the
believers to 'go on to perfection',[22] and to expect it every moment.
And wherever this is not earnestly done the work of God does not
prosper.
10   Fri. 16. I was going to preach in the market-place at Camelford,
where a few are still alive to God, when a violent storm drove us
into the house—that is, as many as could squeeze in. The fire
quickly kindled among them and seemed to touch every heart.
My text was, 'What dost thou here, Elijah?'[23] And God himself
15   made the application. A flame was once more raised in this town.
May it nevermore be put out!

In the evening, I preached in Mr. Wood's yard[24] at Port Isaac to
most of the inhabitants of the town. The same spirit was here as at
Camelford and seemed to move upon every heart. And we had all
20   a good hope that the days of faintness and weariness are over and
that the work of God will revive and flourish.

Sat 17. We found Mr. Hosken at Cubert,[25] alive, but just tottering over the grave. I preached in the evening on 2 Cor. 5:1-4,
probably the last sermon he will hear from me. I was afterwards
25   inquiring if 'that scandal of Cornwall, the plundering of wrecked

assisted JW in his ordinations in the same year, and went off to America as superintendent, later getting the title changed to 'bishop'. Hastiness characterised his attempts to
secure a union between the Methodists and the Protestant Episcopal Church in America, as later, in England, his effort to succeed JW as leader of the Methodist community;
this was frustrated by the preachers. His management of home and foreign missions was
financially disastrous, and he was, in effect, sacked by the American Methodist Conference in 1808. Coke, however, remained in the front rank of the English Methodist
preachers, serving as secretary of Conference from 1791 till his death, with the exception of five years, in two of which he was president, and he inspired a good deal of personal loyalty among the missionaries. A good modern account of him is given in John
Vickers, *Thomas Coke, Apostle of Methodism* (London, 1969).
  [21] The erring preachers for East Cornwall in 1775 (who had allowed a membership
loss of 8) were Richard Rodda, William Whitaker, Richard Wright, and John Roberts. It
is not quite clear why they were singled out for rebuke, for in 1775 West Cornwall
reported a heavy loss of membership, which the preachers then appointed had done
almost nothing to repair.
  [22] Heb. 6:1 (*Notes*).   [23] 1 Kgs. 19:9, 13.
  [24] On Richard Wood, merchant, see Aug. 27, 1768 (22:154 and n. 58 in this edn.).
  [25] Orig., 'Hoskins, at St. Cuthbert's'. On Joseph Hosken see Sept. 7, 1765 (22:18, n.
79 in this edn.). He died in 1780.

vessels', still subsisted. He said, 'As much as ever, only the Methodists will have nothing to do with it. But three months since, a vessel was wrecked on the south coast, and the tinners presently seized on all the goods—and even broke in pieces a new coach which was on board and carried every scrap of it 5 away.' But is there no way to prevent this shameful breach of all the laws, both of religion and humanity? Indeed there is. The gentry of Cornwall may totally prevent it whenever they please. Let them only see that the laws be strictly executed upon the next plunderers, and, after an example is made of ten of these, 10 the next wreck will be unmolested. Nay, there is a milder way. Let them only agree together to discharge any tinner or labourer that is concerned in the plundering of a wreck, and advertise his name, that no Cornish gentleman may employ him any more, and neither tinner nor labourer will any more be concerned in 15 that bad work.

Sun. 18. The passage through the sands being bad for a chaise, I rode on horseback to St. Agnes, where the rain constrained me to preach in the house. As we rode back to Redruth, it poured down amain and found its way through all our clothes. I was tired 20 when I came in, but after sleeping a quarter of an hour all my weariness was gone.

Mon. 19. I joined together once more the select society, who are continually flying asunder, though they all acknowledge the loss they have sustained thereby. At eleven I met fifty or sixty 25 children. How much depends upon these? All the hope of the rising generation. Tuesday 20 in the evening, I preached at Helston, where prejudice is at an end, and all the town, except a few gentry, willingly hear the word of salvation.

Wed. 21. I preached at Penzance, in a gentleman's balcony, 30 which commanded the market-place,[26] to a huge congregation, on 'Without holiness no man shall see the Lord.'[27] The word fell heavy, upon high and low, rich and poor. Such an opportunity I never had at Penzance before.

Thur. 22. I preached at six in the market-place at St. Just's. Two 35 or three well-dressed people walked by, stopped a little, and then went on. So they did two or three times. Had it not been for shame, they might have heard that which is able to save their souls.

---

[26] Said to be the balcony of the Star Inn, later the venue of Quarterly Meetings. John Pearce, ed., *The Wesleys in Cornwall* (Truro, 1964), p. 159, n. 155.
[27] Cf. Heb. 12:14.

Fri. 23. The congregation both morning and evening was large, and great was our rejoicing in the Lord. Saturday 24, in the evening, I preached in a meadow at St. Ives to one of the largest congregations I had seen in the county. Sunday 25, I met the chil-
5 dren—the most difficult part of our office. About five in the evening, I began preaching at Gwennap[28] to full twenty thousand persons. And they were so commodiously placed in the calm, still evening that everyone heard distinctly.

Tue. 27. About noon, I preached in the Piazza adjoining to the
10 Coinage Hall in Truro.[29] I was enabled to speak exceeding plain on 'Ye are saved through faith.'[30] I doubt the antinomians gnashed on me with their teeth; but I *must* declare 'the whole counsel of God'.[31] In the evening, I preached in an open space at Mevagis-sey[32] to most of the inhabitants of the town; where I saw a very
15 rare thing—men swiftly increasing in substance, and yet not decreasing in holiness.

Wed. 28. The rain drove us into the house at St. Austell, where I think some of the stout-hearted trembled. The next evening, I preached at Methrose[33] and was pleased to see an old friend with
20 his wife, his two sons and two daughters.[34] I believe God sent a message to their hearts, as they could not help showing by their tears.

Sunday, September 1. I got to Plymouth Church a little after the service began. I admired the seriousness and decency of the
25 congregation—none bowed or curtsied or looked about them. And at the Lord's Supper, although both the ministers[35] spoke so low in delivering the elements[36] that none who were not very near could hear a word they said, yet was the congregation as still as if no one had been in the church. I was likewise agreeably surprised

---

[28] On Gwennap Pit, see Sept. 5, 1762 (21:388 and n. 75 in this edn.).
[29] On this building see Aug. 16, 1773 (22:386, n. 78 in this edn.). The upper storey was supported by arches, from beneath which JW spoke to the people in the square.
[30] Eph. 2:8 (*Notes*).
[31] Cf. Acts 20:27.
[32] Orig., 'Mevegissey'.
[33] Orig., 'Medros'.
[34] Perhaps the Meager family; see Aug. 25, 1755 (21:24, n. 91 in this edn.).
[35] The vicar of St. Andrew's, Plymouth, 1769-1824, was John Gandy (1742-1824). He matriculated from Sidney Sussex College, Cambridge, 1756, and graduated B.A. in 1762. He was vicar of Whitchurch, Devon, 1767-69, and Prebendary of Exeter, 1777. J. B. Rowe, *The Ecclesiastical History of Old Plymouth* (Plymouth, 1873), p. 55.
[36] This word is capitalized in both 1783 and 1788 editions, apparently reflecting JW's preference at this period—though the word is one he seldom used.

at their number—when I was at the church in Hull, I think we had six communicants beside those that came with me. Here I suppose were full three hundred.

Immediately after service, I went to the quay and preached on those words in the Epistle for the day, 'The Scripture hath concluded all under sin, that the promise by faith of Jesus Christ might be given to them that believe.'[37] I wondered at the exquisite stupidity of the hearers, particularly the soldiers, who seemed to understand no more of the matter than so many oxen. So I told them in very plain terms. And some of them were ashamed.

Mon. 2. In my way to Exeter I read over an ingenious tract[38] containing some observations which I never saw before. In particular, that if *corn* sells for twice as much now as it did at the time of the Revolution, it is in effect *no dearer* than it was then, because we have now twice as much money; that if other things sell now for twice as much as they did then, corn ought to do so too; that though the price of all things increases as money increases, yet they are really *no dearer* than they were before; and, lastly, that to petition Parliament to alter these things is to put them upon impossibilities and can answer no end but that of enflaming the people against their governors.

Wed. 4. I was desired to call at Ottery, a large town eleven miles from Exeter. I preached in the market-house to abundance of people, who behaved with great decency. At five, I preached in the market-place at Axminster to a still larger congregation. I have seldom heard people speak with more honesty and simplicity than many did at the love-feast which followed. I have not seen a more unpolished people than these—but love supplies all defects. It supplies all the essentials of good breeding, without the help of a dancing-master.

Thur. 5. I went on to Corfe Castle in the Isle of Purbeck. At six, I preached in the yard adjoining to the preaching-house. It was a season both of conviction and consolation. Friday [6], I preached at the new house in Melcombe[39] to as many as it would

---

[37] Gal. 3:22. This was the Thirteenth Sunday after Trinity.

[38] [Charles Smith], *A Short Essay on the Corn Trade, and the Corn Laws. Containing a General Relation of the Present Method of Carrying on the Corn Trade, and the Purport of the Laws Relating Thereto in this Kingdom* (London, 1758). JW's seeming free-trade sympathies in this comment are the more odd as corn prices were in a declining phase which lasted till 1780.

[39] Orig., 'Malcomb'. Melcombe Bingham is 5 miles north of Puddletown; Higher Melcombe and Melcombe Horsey are nearby hamlets.

well contain.[40] About noon, I stood upon the cross at Bruton,[41] and proclaimed 'the grace of our Lord Jesus Christ'.[42] Many seemed to be astonished; all were quiet, and a few deeply affected.

5　In the evening, I preached at Shepton Mallet, where the people in general appeared to be more serious ever since the late, terrible riot in which two of them were killed.[43] On Saturday, I went on to Bristol.

Mon. 9. I began what I had long intended, visiting the society from house to house, setting apart at least two hours in a day for 10 that purpose. I was surprised to find the simplicity with which one and all spoke, both of their temporal and spiritual state. Nor could I easily have known by any other means how great a work God has wrought among them. I found exceeding little to reprove, but much to praise God for. And I observed one thing 15 which I did not expect: in visiting all the families without Lawford's Gate[44]—by far the poorest about the city—I did not find so much as one person who was out of work.

Another circumstance I critically inquired into: what is the real number of the people? Dr. Price says (doubtless to encourage our 20 good friends the French and Spaniards): 'The people of England are between four and five millions, supposing them to be four or four and a half on an average in one house.'[45] I found in the fami-

---

[40] Edn. C omits this sentence. A–B read 'Friday 5'. All three follow here with 'Friday 6. About noon . . .'. Corfe Castle to Bruton was nearly forty miles as the crow flies, but perhaps possible in a chaise; cf below Apr. 17, 1777.

[41] 'In the market place there is a curious hexagonal market cross, supported by six pillars at the angles, and a larger one in the centre. The roof consists wholly of the ribs of arches, which, springing from the centre, diverge from pillar to pillar, and are finely ornamented with sculpture. This edifice is eighteen feet high, the top flat, and encompassed with a stone balustrade; it was built, as Leland informs us, by John Ely, the last abbot of Brewton.' J. Collinson, *History and Antiquities of the County of Somerset*, 3 vols. (Bath, 1791), 1:211.

[42] 2 Cor. 8:9.

[43] JW writes as if the riots were far more recent than those mentioned on Feb. 12, 1748, or even the corn riots of 1766; J. Latimer, *The Annals of Bristol in the Eighteenth Century* (Bristol, 1893; reprint 1970), p. 378. Shepton Mallet was a town busily employed in the manufacture of woollen cloth and knitted stockings (Collinson, *History of Somerset*, 3:459), and its history of riot really began twenty years after JW's death when those industries were destroyed by machine competition elsewhere; J. E. Fairbrother, *Shepton Mallet: Notes on its History* (Shepton Mallet, 1859), pp. 25–26. It may be that war circumstances had caused a recent dislocation.

[44] On the settlement outside Lawford's Gate, see July 29, 1750 (20:354 in this edn.).

[45] Richard Price's *Essay on the Population of England and Wales* was not published till 1780, but he had introduced material of this kind into the appendix of the second edition of his *Appeal to the Public on the Subject of the National Debt* (London, 1772). JW's reference seems not to be a quotation, but accurately reported that Price accepted (from

lies which I visited about six in a house. But one who has lately made a more general inquiry informs me, there are without Lawford's Gate seven in a house. The same information I received from one who has lately made the inquiry concerning the inhabitants of Redcliff. Now, if at four in a house we are four millions, must we not at seven in a house be seven millions?

But even this is far short of the truth, for a plain reason—the houses are miscomputed. To give one instance. The houses without Lawford's Gate are computed to be a thousand. Now at the sitting of the Justices, some years since, there were two hundred public houses. Was then one house in five a public house? No, surely—one in ten at the utmost. If so, there were two thousand houses and, consequently, fourteen thousand persons. I believe there are now full twenty thousand. And these are nothing near a quarter of the present inhabitants of Bristol.[46]

Wed. 11. I preached about one at Bath, and about six, in a meadow near the preaching-house in Frome, besought a listening multitude 'not to receive the grace of God in vain'.[47]

Thur. 12. I spent about two hours in Mr. Hoare's gardens at Stourton.[48] I have seen the most celebrated gardens in England, but these far exceed them all: (1) in the situation, being laid out on the sloping sides of a semi-circular mountain; (2) in the vast basin[49] of water enclosed between them, covering, I suppose, sixty acres of ground; (3) in the delightful interchange of shady groves and sunny glades, curiously mixed together. Above all, in the

other statisticians) a multiplier of 4 to 4 1/2 for converting households to heads of population, and thought that there had been a marked depopulation during the century. Of course the real issue between him and JW was whether an independent America was a good thing or a bad. It is now reckoned that the population of England and Wales at this time was about seven millions.

[46] An estimate of the population of Bristol (including Clifton and Bedminster) in 1775, which used a household multiplier little less than that favoured by JW, yielded a figure of only 35,440. Latimer, *Annals of Bristol*, p. 422.

[47] Cf. 2 Cor. 6:1. The Frome circuit stewards' book records: 'Sept. 1776. Mr. Wesley's turnpikes, 4/-'. S. Tuck, *Wesleyan Methodism in Frome* (Frome, 1837), p. 46n.

[48] Henry Hoare, banker, bought Stourhead in 1720. Sir Richard Colt Hoare engagingly found it 'a difficult and nice task . . . to perform . . . to describe my own works and my own plans in the direction of the fine property which my worthy grandfather had ceded to me during his lifetime', and did not shrink from the claim that in the Italianate Stourhead, 'cheerfulness and variety of outline predominate throughout the whole demesne; and the hand of Taste has most happily seized the opportunity of improving on the outline of Nature', particularly in the creation of a large lake in place of formal fishponds and improved planting. R. C. Hoare, *The History of Modern Wiltshire*, 6 vols. (London, 1822-44), 1:63-88,

[49] Orig., 'bason'.

lovely grottoes, two of which excel everything of the kind which I
ever saw: the fountain-grotto, made entirely of rock-work,
admirably well imitating nature; and the castle-grotto, into which
you enter unawares, beneath a heap of ruins. This is within totally
5 built of roots of trees, wonderfully interwoven. On one side of it is
a little hermitage, with a lamp, a chair, a table, and bones upon it.
Others were delighted with the temples, but I was not: (1)
because several of the statues about them were mean; (2) because
I cannot admire the images of devils, and we know the gods of the
10 heathens are but devils; (3) because I defy all mankind to reconcile statues with nudities either to common sense or common
decency.
Returning from thence through Maiden Bradley, we saw the
clumsy house of the Duke of Somerset,[50] and afterwards the
15 grand and elegant one of Lord Weymouth,[51] beautifully situated
in a lovely park.
Friday 13. I went on to Midsomer Norton,[52] where the rector,

[50] Much of this house had been pulled down in 1717, though its condition then is
illustrated in Colen Campbell, *Vitruvius Britannicus*, 5 vols. (London, 1717-71), 2:56.
It then 'consisted of three ranges round a forecourt facing E[ast], and wings extending
N[orth] and S[outh] from the E[ast] ends and the W[est] ends of this main composition and two extending W[est]'. N. Pevsner, *Wiltshire* (Harmondsworth, 1963), p. 320.
[51] Longleat is enthusiastically characterized by N. Pevsner (*Wiltshire*, pp. 35, 308-13)
as 'a milestone in English 16th century architecture. It is the first compleatly Eliza-
bethan house, large, self-assured, all of a piece, built round two courtyards with unified
fronts to all sides, displaying most prominently its grid of large mullioned and tran-
somed windows and confining to a secondary role the (originally French) orders of
pilasters and the medallions for busts.' In 1783 Mrs. Boscawen 'did not tell Lady Weymouth all I thought of Longleat, lest it shou'd sound like flattery, but to me it appear'd
the *very finest* place I ever saw in my life . . . . Mr. Hoare's [Stourhead] I have since
seen; it has many pretty *opera* scenes in it, but it is not in the style of Longleat—far
from it'. *The Autobiography and Correspondence of Mary Granville, Mrs. Delany*, ed.
Lady Llanover, 6 vols. (London, 1861-62), 3:140-41.
[52] Two generations later an anecdote of this visit was related by Richard Treffry; *Wesleyan Methodist Magazine* 65 (1842):136. JW 'was entertained at the house of Mr. [Eli-
jah] Bush, who was a Local Preacher, and kept a large boarding-school in that place.
While Mr. Wesley was there two of the boys had a quarrel, and fought and kicked each
other most fiercely. While thus engaged, Mrs. Bush went into the schoolroom, and
parted them, and brought them into the parlour, where Mr. Wesley was about to take
tea with Mr. Bush and the family. In a most kind and affectionate manner, Mr. Wesley
talked to them, and concluded his advice by repeating those lines of Dr. Watts:

> Birds in their little nests agree;
> And 'tis a shameful sight,
> When children of one family
> Fall out, and chide, and fight.

He then said, "You must be reconciled. Go and shake hands with each other", which
they did. "Now", said he, "put your arms round each other's neck and kiss each other".

being applied to, cheerfully granted me the use of his church, and himself made one of the congregation. I preached on those words in the Second Lesson, 'O thou of little faith, wherefore didst thou doubt?'[53] About two, I preached in the new house at Paulton, to a plain, simple, loving people; and spent the evening, in Kingswood, endeavouring to remove some little offences which had arisen in the family.[54]

Wed. 18. About one, I preached at Bath, as usual to a crowded audience; in the afternoon, at Keynsham, where at length we see some fruit of our labours. Thursday 19, finding few would come to the room at Pill, I preached in the market-place. Many attended, and I am persuaded God cut some of them to the heart. About six, I preached at Pensford and spent the evening with the lovely family at Publow.[55] Saturday 21, I preached in the Paddock at Bedminster. It is plain (notwithstanding what some affirm) that the time of field-preaching is not past, while the people flock to it from every quarter.

Sun. 22. After reading prayers, preaching, and administering the Sacrament at Bristol, I hastened away to Kingswood and preached under the trees to such a multitude as had not been lately seen there. I began in King Square a little before five, where the word of God was quick and powerful.[56] And I was no more tired at night than when I rose in the morning. Such is the power of God!

After settling all things at Bristol and Kingswood, and visiting the rest of the societies in Somersetshire, Wiltshire, and Hants., I returned in October to London with Mr. Fletcher.[57]

When this was done Mr. Wesley said, "Come to me"; and, taking two pieces of bread and butter, he folded them together, and desired each to take a part. "Now", said he, "you have broken bread together". He then gave them a cup of tea, and told them, they had both drunk of the same cup. And after putting his hands upon their heads, he blessed them; when they went into their schoolroom and forgot their animosities. The next morning when the scholars came into prayers, Mr Wesley singled out these two boys, took them in his arms, and sent them away with his blessing. This anecdote was related to the writer by a magistrate of Berkshire, who was one of the boys thus kindly reprehended and instructed.'

[53] Matt. 14:31.

[54] Though Kingswood was never without its troubles, it was enjoying a share of peace and prosperity at this time.

[55] Orig., 'Peblow'. JW had used 'Peblow' before. On Hannah Owen's school at Publow, see Sept. 6, 1772 (22:348, n. 41 in this edn.).

[56] See Heb. 4:12.

[57] JW arrived in London about mid-October. His letters help fill in this seven-week gap in the Journal.

Sunday, November 10. I was desired to preach at St. Vedast's Church, Foster Lane,[58] which contained the congregation tolerably well. I preached on those words in the Gospel for the day (how little regarded even by men that fear God!), 'Render to Caesar the things that are Caesar's, and unto God the things that are God's.'[59]

Wed. 13. I set out with Mr. Fletcher to Norwich. I took coach at twelve, slept till six, and then spent the time very agreeably in conversation, singing, and reading. I read Mr. Bolt's account of the *Affairs in the East Indies*[60]—I suppose much the best that is extant. But what a scene is here opened. What consummate villains! What devils incarnate were the managers there! What utter strangers to justice, mercy, and truth![61] To every sentiment of humanity! I believe no heathen history contains a parallel: I remember none in all the annals of antiquity. Not even the divine Cato, or the virtuous Brutus, plundered the provinces committed to their charge with such merciless cruelty as the English have plundered the desolated provinces of Hindustan.

When we came to Norwich, finding many of our friends had been shaken by the assertors of the *horrible decree*,[62] I employed the three following mornings in sifting the question to the bottom. Many were confirmed thereby, and I trust will not again be removed from the genuine gospel.

Thur. 14. I showed in the evening what 'the gospel' is, and what it is to 'preach the gospel'. The next evening, I explained at large the wrong and the right sense of 'Ye are saved by faith.'[63] And many saw how miserably they had been abused by those vulgarly called 'Gospel Preachers'.[64]

---

[58] The rector of St. Vedast's, 1744-79, was Theophilus Lewis Barbault (or Barbauld; 1709-79), who had been a scholar of Trinity College, Cambridge, in 1725 and graduated M.A. in 1731. St. Vedast's was a church built by Wren (1695-1700) with a steeple added, 1709-12. It was burned out in the Second World War, and has since acquired furnishings from many sources. Pevsner, *London* (2nd edn., London, 1962), 1:166-67, 689.

[59] Cf. Matt. 22:21. This was the Twenty-third Sunday after Trinity.

[60] For this book see above, Feb. 23, 1776.

[61] See Ps. 89:14.

[62] I.e., the decree of reprobation; cf. Calvin, *Institutes* III.xxxiii.7, and see *Letters*, Apr. 30, 1739 (25:640 in this edn.).

[63] Cf. Eph. 2:8 (*Notes*).

[64] The covert reference here is to James Wheatley, whose interest in his Norwich Tabernacle was sold to the Countess of Huntingdon just before his death in 1775, and to the student preachers introduced (along with others) by the Countess. A. C. H. Seymour, *The Life and Times of Selina, Countess of Huntingdon*, 2 vols. (London, Painter, 1840), 2:343-46.

Sun. 17. In the morning, we had about a hundred and fifty communicants and a remarkable blessing. In the afternoon and in the evening, we were crowded enough. Monday 18, we set out for Yarmouth. Here I knew not where to preach, the mayor refusing me the use of the town hall. But the chamberlain gave me the use of a larger building, formerly a church.[65] In this a numerous congregation soon assembled, to whom I described the 'sect which is everywhere spoken against'.[66] I believe, all that were attentive will be a little more candid for the time to come.

Tue. 19. I opened the new preaching-house at Lowestoft,[67] a new and lightsome building. It was thoroughly filled with deeply attentive hearers. Surely some of them will bear fruit unto perfection.[68] Wednesday 20, Mr. Fletcher preached in the morning, and I at two in the afternoon. It then blew a thorough storm, so that it was hard to walk or stand, the wind being ready to take us off our feet. It drove one of the boats which were on the strand from its moorings out to sea. Three men were in it, who looked for nothing every moment but to be swallowed up. But presently, five stout men put off in another open boat and, rowing for life, overtook them and brought them safe to land.

Thur. 21. I preached at Beccles. A duller place I have seldom seen. The people of the town were neither pleased nor vexed, as 'caring for none of these things'.[69] Yet fifty or sixty came into the house either to hear or see. The people of Loddon seemed in the evening of another spirit, resolved to 'enter in at the strait gate'.[70] Friday 21, we had a solemn parting with our friends at Norwich, and on Saturday evening, I brought Mr. Fletcher back to London considerably better than when he set out.

Fri. 29. We considered the several plans which were offered for the New Chapel.[71] Having agreed upon one, we desired a surveyor to draw out the particulars with an estimate of the expense.

---

[65] 'The Dutch church, . . . now [1825] used for the public library'. A. Watmough, *History of Methodism in the Town and Neighbourhood of Great Yarmouth* (London, 1826), p. 62.

[66] Cf. Acts 28:22.

[67] Orig., 'Lestoffe'. This chapel, subsequently greatly enlarged, was demolished in 1907 to make room for new schools. *Wesleyan Methodist Magazine* 48 (1825):365; *Methodist Recorder* (Sept. 5, 1907).

[68] See Luke 8:14.

[69] Cf. Acts 18:17 (*Notes*).

[70] Matt. 7:13; Luke 13:24.

[71] In City Road, London.

We then ordered proposals to be drawn up for those who were willing to undertake any part of the building.

Monday, Dec. 2. I set out for Bedford in the Diligence,[72] and came thither at four in the afternoon. I found great freedom of speech in the evening and perceived God was reviving his work in this people.

Tue. 3. I crossed over to St. Neots and had an hour's friendly conversation with Mr. V[enn].[73] O that all men would sit as loose to opinions as I do! That they would *think and let think*! I preached in the evening to a numerous congregation with much enlargement of spirit. Wednesday 4, I preached at Godmanchester, and on Thursday returned to London.

In the way I read over Mr. Gray's works,[74] and his life wrote by Mr. Mason.[75] He is an admirable poet, not much inferior to either Prior or Pope. But he does not appear, upon the whole, to have been an amiable man. His picture, I apprehend, expresses his character—sharp, sensible, ingenious, but at the same time proud, morose, envious, passionate, and resentful. I was quite shocked at the contempt with which he more than once speaks of Mr. Mason. One full as ingenious as himself, yea, full as good a poet (as even *Elfrida*[76] shows, as much as Mr. Gray despises or affects

[72] JW uses several of the generic terms for public coaches, of which a great variety served England at varying speeds and varying costs. We follow him in capitalizing Diligence, as in using lower case for coach and most other generic terms (except in the instance where he uses 'diligence' on May 16, 1777). The Diligence, referred to in Smollett's *Roderick Random*, seems to have been re-introduced from continental Europe about this time as one of the specially named rapid services. See *OED*; Charles G. Harper, *The Manchester and Glasgow Road: London to Manchester*, 2 vols. (London, 1924), p. 20; and cf. below, Feb. 3, May 16, 1777; Oct. 26, 1778; Oct. 19, 1783; Feb. 25, Aug. 8, 1785; Oct. 10, 13, 1786.

[73] On Henry Venn see Feb. 27, 1759 and July 20, 1761 (21:178, 336 in this edn.). His health having collapsed, Venn had accepted the small rectory of Yelling, Hunts., some 12 miles from Cambridge and 6 from St. Neots, in 1771.

[74] Thomas Gray, *Poems, with Memoirs of his Life and Writings* by W. Mason (York, 1775). Thomas Gray (1716-71; spelled 'Grey' by JW) formed a bridge between the Augustan poets with whom JW compares him, and later romantic tastes. Appointed Professor of Modern History at Cambridge in 1768, he lived in seclusion and did not dine in college, ill-health and shyness making him a poor mixer in unfamiliar society.

[75] William Mason (1725-97), educated at St. John's College, Cambridge, graduating M.A. in 1749, became the friend, admirer, imitator, and protege of Thomas Gray, through whose influence he was elected fellow of Pembroke College in 1749. He wrote a good deal of poetry on the government side, became a royal chaplain in 1757, and canon of York in 1762. In 1775 he published a memoir of Thomas Gray, supported the reform movement of 1780, and was later a follower of Pitt.

[76] William Mason, *Elfrida, a Dramatic Poem written on the Model of the Antient Greek Tragedy* (London, 1752).

to despise it), and over and above possessed of that modesty and humanity wherein Mr. Gray was so greatly deficient.

Friday the 13th was the National Fast.[77] It was observed not only throughout the city, but (I was afterwards informed) throughout the nation, with the utmost solemnity. I shall not wonder if God should now interpose and send us prosperity, since at length we are not too proud to acknowledge, 'there is a God that judgeth the earth.'[78]

Monday 16, I preached at Canterbury, on Tuesday at Dover, Wednesday about eleven, at poor, dry, dead Sandwich. But I now found more hope for the poor people than I had done for many years. In the evening, I preached at Margate to a very genteel and yet very serious congregation. And I believe (although it blew a storm) near a hundred were present in the morning.

Thur. 19. I had another truly comfortable opportunity at Canterbury. God lifted up the hands that hung down[79] and gave many a strong hope that they should yet see good days after all the days of darkness and heaviness. Friday 20, I returned to London and, on Sunday 22, buried the remains of Elizabeth Duchesne,[80] a person eminently upright of heart, yet for many years a child of labour and sorrow. For near forty years she was zealous of good works and at length shortened her days by labouring for the poor beyond her strength. But her end was peace. She now rests from her labours, and her works follow her.[81]

Tue. 31. We concluded the year with solemn praise to God for continuing his great work in our land. It has never been intermitted one year or one month since the year 1738, in which my brother and I began to preach that strange doctrine of *Salvation by Faith*.

Wednesday, January the first [1777], we met, as usual, to renew

---

[77] This day, 'the day appointed for the observance of a solemn fast and humiliation', was oddly reported by the *Annual Register* (1776), p. 199: 'The same, it may be said, was kept with uncommon marks of devotion, by people of all ranks and religions, not only throughout the cities of London and Westminster, but England in general; at least, it does not appear, that ministers and churchwardens of any but two adjoining parishes near Portsdown Hill, Hants., [i.e., immediately behind the Portsmouth naval base], have been called to account for not attending their duty on the occasion'.

[78] Ps. 58:11 (BCP).   [79] See Heb. 12:12.

[80] In the 1750s, Elizabeth Duchesne had been one of the London friends and coadjutors of both John and Charles Wesley. She was recalled by the former during the Protestant excitement of 1780, as having been told by a Catholic priest, 'You are not heretic! You have the experience of a real Christian!' 'And would you', she asked, 'burn me alive?' He said, 'God forbid! unless it were for the good of the Church!' Telford, 3:199; 4:36; 6:372-73; *CWJ*, 2:209.

[81] See Rev. 14:13.

our covenant with God.[82] It was a solemn season, wherein many found his power present to heal, and were enabled to urge their way with strength renewed.

Thur. 2. I began expounding in order the Book of Ecclesiastes. I never before had so clear a sight either of the meaning or the beauties of it. Neither did I imagine that the several parts of it were in so exquisite a manner connected together, all tending to prove that grand truth, that there is no happiness out of God.

Wed. 8. I looked over the manuscripts of that great and good man, Charles Perronet.[83] I did not think he had so deep communion with God; I know exceeding few that equal him. And had he had an university education, there would have been few finer writers in England.

Mon. 13. I took the opportunity of spending an hour every morning with the preachers, as I did with my pupils at Oxford. And we endeavoured not only to increase each other's knowledge, but to 'provoke one another to love and good works'.[84]

Wed. 15. I began visiting those of our society who lived in Bethnal Green hamlet.[85] Many of them I found in such poverty as few can conceive without seeing it. O why do not all the rich that fear God constantly visit the poor! Can they spend part of their spare time better? Certainly not. So they will find in that day when 'every man shall receive his own reward, according to his own labour.'[86]

Such another scene I saw the next day in visiting another part of the society. I have not found any such distress, no, not in the prison of Newgate. One poor man was just creeping out of his sick-bed to his ragged wife and three little children—who were more than half naked and the very picture of famine—when one bringing in a loaf of bread, they all ran, seized upon it, and tore it in pieces in an instant. Who would not rejoice that there is another world?

---

[82] On the Covenant Service, see Aug. 6, 1755 (21:23, n. 82 in this edn.).

[83] On Charles Perronet, see May 20, 1748 (20:227, n. 56 in this edn.). A number of these MSS appeared in *Arminian Magazine* 4 (1781):213-17, 275-78, 329-33, 386-87, 436-39, 494-96, 604-6.

[84] Cf. Heb. 10:24.

[85] Bethnal Green was notorious in the eighteenth century for the poverty of its population of weavers, its licensing abuses, the noisomeness of its sewers and its liability to typhus, its rack-renting and sub-letting, and the skill of its landlords in avoiding contributing to the poor rate. M. Dorothy George, *London Life in the Eighteenth Century* (2nd edn., London, 1925), pp. 67, 71, 80, 85, 98, 177, 305.

[86] 1 Cor. 3:8.

Mon. 20. Mrs. T[erry] gave us a remarkable account. On Saturday the 11th instant, her little boy, a child of eminent piety between five and six years old, gave up his spirit to God. She was saying to one in the house, 'My son is gone to glory.' A youth standing by cried out, 'But I am going to hell.' He continued praying all Sunday and Monday, but in utter despair. On Tuesday he found a hope of mercy, which gradually increased. The next morning he rejoiced with joy unspeakable, knowing his sins were blotted out. And soon after, Henry Terry (the son of many tears to his poor mother) slept in peace.

Tue. 21. I dined at Mr. A——'s. A month or two ago he had a trial worthy of a Christian. He saw his little son (between four and five years old) crushed to death in a moment. But he did not murmur: he could say, 'The Lord gave, and the Lord hath taken away'![87]

Sun. 26. I preached again at All Hallows Church, morning and afternoon. I found great liberty of spirit, and the congregation seemed to be much affected. How is this? Do I 'yet please men'?[88] Is the offence of the cross ceased?[89] It seems, after being scandalous near fifty years, I am at length growing into an honourable man!

Thur. 30. I had a visit from Mr. B——,[90] grown an old, feeble, decrepit man! Hardly able to face a puff of wind or to creep up and down stairs! Such is the fruit of cooping one's self in a house! Of sitting still day after day.

Monday, February 3. Hearing there was some disturbance at Bristol,[91] occasioned by men whose tongues were set on fire

---

[87] Job 1:21.
[88] Cf. Gal. 1:10.
[89] Gal. 5:11.
[90] Probably Thomas Broughton, Lecturer of All Hallows, on whom see 18:234, n. 89 in this edn. Broughton, secretary of the SPCK from 1743, was to be found for five hours in every working day 'in the Society's house, first in Bartlett's Buildings, Holborn, and afterwards in Hatton Garden. . . . On Sunday morning, December 21, 1777, in Hatton Garden, Broughton put on his ministerial robes, and according to his wont, retired into his room till church-time. The bells were ringing and he continued in his closet. They ceased but he made no appearance. His friends entered and found him on his knees—dead.' Luke Tyerman, *The Oxford Methodists* (London, 1873), pp. 349, 359.
[91] On Jan. 16, 1777, attempts were made by an arsonist to fire three ships in Bristol docks at low tide. These fires were quickly put out but were followed by a series of attempts to burn down warehouses. Both in Bristol and London there were efforts to make political capital out of the fires, 'Tories forgetting that some of the principal merchants were Americans, and that an American was the chief sufferer by the fire, [taunt-

against the government, I went down in the Diligence and, on Tuesday evening, strongly enforced those solemn words, 'Put them in mind to be subject to principalities and powers, to speak evil of no man.'[92] I believe God applied his word and convinced
5 many that they had been out of their way.

Finding the repeated attempts to set fire to the city had occasioned a general consternation, on Wednesday 5, I opened and applied those words to a crowded audience, 'Is there any evil in the city, and the Lord hath not done it?'[93] On Thursday, I wrote *A*
10 *Calm Address to the Inhabitants of England*.[94] May God bless this, as he did the former,[95] to the quenching of that evil fire which is still among us! On Saturday, I returned to London.

Saturday, February 15. At the third message, I took up my cross and went to see Dr. Dodd[96] in the Compter.[97] I was greatly
15 surprised. He seemed, though deeply affected, yet thoroughly

ing] the Whigs with having instigated the outrages; while the latter as foolishly retorted that the whole affair was a factious manoeuvre of the Ministerialists'. Some weeks later (at the expense of the Corporation and Merchants' Society) a Scotsman who had briefly resided in Bristol was arrested in Lancashire and brought to confess that he was James Aitken, *alias* Jack the Painter, who had fired the rope-house at Portsmouth dockyard in 1770. He was subsequently hanged at Portsmouth on a gallows 67 feet high. See Oct. 12, 1770 (22:256 in this edn.); Latimer, *Annals of Bristol*, pp. 426-28.

[92] Cf. Titus 3:1-2.
[93] Cf. Amos 3:6.
[94] See *Bibliography*, No. 365. In this pamphlet, JW ascribed the outbreak of war in America to an entirely unreasonable desire for independence in the colonies, dating back to the 1730s and inflamed by opposition politicians at home looking for a cause.
[95] *A Calm Address to our American Colonies* (1775). JW now described the fate of this pamphlet: 'The ports being just then shut up by the Americans, I could not send it abroad as I designed. However, it was not lost; within a few months, fifty, or perhaps an hundred thousand copies in newspapers and otherwise, were dispersed throughout Great Britain and Ireland. The effect exceeded my most sanguine hopes. The eyes of many people were opened.' *Calm Address to . . . England* (1777), pp. 3-4.
[96] On William Dodd, 'macaroni parson' and forger, see Mar. 5, 1767 (22:71 in this edn.). JW's surprise at the summons was due to the fact that Dodd had often spoken against him in the days of his prosperity. JW was accompanied on this visit by Charles, who had a longstanding interest in victims of the law. Among these he considered Dodd to be, and wrote an eloquent 'Prayer for Dr. Dodd under Condemnation' in verse. Mary Bosanquet also corresponded with Dodd about his personal salvation, and the Wesley brothers detected signs of genuine penitence; Thomas Jackson, *The Life of the Rev. Charles Wesley, M.A.*, 2 vols. (London, 1841), 2:309-13. Or as Horace Walpole coarsely put it: 'Those gentry the Methodists will grow very troublesome, or worse; they were exceedingly unwilling to part with that impudent hypocrite, Dr. Dodd, and not less to have forgery criminal. . . . I cannot bear a militant arch-inquisitor, or an impostor in a tabernacle'; *Horace Walpole's Correspondence*, ed. W. S. Lewis, 48 vols. (New Haven, Yale University Press, 1937-83), 28:319. JW believed Dodd's end was edifying. 'Some Account of the late Dr. Dodd', *Arminian Magazine* 6 (1783):358-60.
[97] The Compter (Counter) was the name of several urban prisons for debtors, one of which was in London.

resigned to the will of God. Mrs. Dodd[98] likewise behaved with the utmost propriety. I doubt not, God will bring good out of this evil. Tuesday 18. I visited him again and found him still in a desirable state of mind, calmly giving himself up to whatsoever God should determine concerning him.

Wed. 19.[99] I was desired to see one that after she had been filled with peace and joy in believing[1] was utterly distracted. I soon found, it was a merely natural case—a temporary disorder, common to women at that period of life.

Tue. 25. I spent an agreeable hour with Dr. C[onyer]s,[2] a deeply serious man, who would fain reconcile the Arminians and Calvinists. Nay, but he must first change *their hearts*.

Sunday, March 2, being a warm sunshiny day, I preached in Moorfields in the evening. There were thousands upon thousands, and all were still as night. Not only violence and rioting, but even scoffing at field-preachers, is now over.

Today I received from an eye-witness a particular account of a late remarkable occurrence. Capt. Bell, a most amiable man, beloved of all that knew him and just engaged to one which he tenderly loved, sailed from England last autumn. On September 20, he was hailed by the *Hawke*, a small sloop, Capt. Arthur Crawford, commander, who told him, he came from Halifax in His Majesty's service, cruising for American privateers. Capt. Bell invited him to breakfast, entertained him with all kindness, and made him some little presents; but on his cursing and swearing at the Americans, mildly reproved him, and he desisted. Mr. M'Aness, the supercargo,[3] seeing him walk round the ship and diligently observe everything in it, told Capt. Bell, 'Be upon your

---

[98] The fate of Mrs. Dodd (who died on July 14, 1784) was immortalized in Thomas Jackson's most eloquent periods (*Charles Wesley*, 2:312-13): 'The loss of Dr. Dodd's character, his imprisonment, his trial, his condemnation, the suspense connected with the unsuccessful attempts to obtain a commutation of punishment, and, above all, the terrible execution, were too much for the affectionate and sensitive mind of Mrs. Dodd to sustain. Reason fled; and the unfortunate lady died a maniac, at Ilford, in Essex. Such were the bitter fruits of unsanctified pulpit popularity!'

[99] Orig., Wed. 23.

[1] See Rom. 15:13.

[2] On Richard Conyers, see Apr. 17, 1764 (21:452-53, n. 62 in this edn.). He had moved south from Helmsley after the death of his wife, and was now and for the remainder of his life, vicar of St. Paul's, Deptford. Despite JW's cool comment, John Fletcher continued to look to him to carry through the work of reconciliation. *Arminian Magazine* 6 (1783):386-88.

[3] Supercargo: 'An officer on board a merchant ship whose business it is to superintend the cargo and commercial transactions of the voyage.' *OED*.

guard, this is certainly an enemy!' But the Captain answered, 'It cannot be, no man can act so base a part.'

Capt. Crawford returned to his own ship and, sailing under the stern of the other while Capt. Bell and some others were standing on the quarterdeck, ordered his men to fire at him. They did so, and shot him in the belly, so that his bowels came out. But he did not fall. He ordered them to fire again. He fell and, while his men were carrying him away, Crawford took the vessel.

Capt. Bell being conveyed into the cabin, sent and desired to speak with Capt. Crawford. But he would not come. He then desired to speak with his own sailors, one by one. One of them saying, 'Sir, you have been basely murdered,' he replied, 'Love your enemies; pray for them that despitefully use you. What are our sufferings to those which our Lord endured for us?' He then desired the account which St. John gives of our Lord's sufferings to be read to him. He desired his love to all that loved the Lord Jesus; particularly to her he was about to marry. Then bidding them all farewell, he died in peace, about two hours after receiving the second shot.

But what did Capt. Crawford do amiss? Have not the English also taken American ships by surprise? Yes, but not with such circumstances. For, first, he hoisted no colours nor ever summoned the ship to yield; second, he fired on men who thought nothing of the matter, and pointed the men to Capt. Bell in particular! So it was deliberate murder. Such is the mercy, such the gratitude, of American rebels![4]

Mon. 10. In the evening, I preached at Reading. How many years were we beating the air[5] at this town! Stretching out our hands to a people as stupid as oxen! But it is not so at present. That generation is passed away, and their children are of a more excellent spirit.[6] After preaching at Newbury and Ramsbury[7] in the way, on Wednesday 12, I went on to Bristol.

Sun. 16. I preached at St. Werburgh's,[8] the first church I ever

---

[4] This sentence is omitted from edn. C (1791), almost certainly on the initiative of James Creighton (see *Bibliography*, No. 36).

[5] See 1 Cor. 9:26.

[6] See Prov. 12:26; 17:27.

[7] Orig., 'Romsbery'.

[8] Orig., 'St. Warburgh's'. JW's diary for Apr. 1, 1739, carries no mention of St. Werburgh's. While he possibly could have preached here prior to this date (he had preached in Gloucester on May 14, 1732), the probability is faint. The 2 o'clock entry for Apr. 1, 1739 (19:383 in this edn.) reads: 'At St. Peter's, read Prayers, Sermon' (and virtually the

preached in at Bristol. I had desired my friends not to come thither, but to leave room for strangers. By this means the church was well filled, but not overmuch crowded—which gives occasion to them that seek occasion, as it is a real inconvenience to the parishioners.   5

Fri. 21. I preached at Bath. I often wonder at this: our chapel[9] stands in the midst of all the sinners, and yet going or coming to it I never heard an immodest word, but prayers and blessings in abundance.

Sun. 23. I preached at St. Ewen's Church,[10] but not upon justi- 10 fication by faith. I do not find this to be a profitable subject to an unawakened congregation. I explained here, and strongly applied, that awful word, 'It is appointed unto men once to die.'[11]

Mon. 24. I left Bristol and, preaching at Ramsbury, Witney, Oxford, and High Wycombe in my way, on Thursday came to 15 London, whence I cannot be long absent while the New Chapel is building.[12] Friday 28, I received an affectionate message from a great man—but I shall not wonder if the wind changes.[13]

Sunday 30. Easter Day was a solemn and comfortable day, wherein God was remarkably present with his people. During the 20 Octave[14] I administered the Lord's Supper every morning, after

same entry is repeated on the following Sunday). Whether JW himself actually preached on these two occasions is not certain. In any case, St. Werburgh's does not appear in these early records and one wonders if this statement embodied a *lapsus memoriae*. The vicar of St. Werburgh's was Richard Symes, on whom see Apr. 19, 1764 (21:454, n. 69 in this edn.).

[9] At this time the Methodist society 'met in an obscure room in Avon-street'; *Wesleyan Methodist Magazine* 48 (1825):286. The street was described by John Wood as 'thirty feet broad and [containing] fifty-one houses, which from a regular and tolerable bigness have fallen into an irregularity and meanness not worth describing'. *WHS* 6 (1907):56.

[10] Orig., 'St. Ewin's'. This ancient (*c.* 1130) but tiny church was originally dedicated to St. Auden (Audoenus, Audoin, *c.* 610-84), later corrupted to Oven, Owen, or Ewen. In 1787-88 it was consolidated with the parish of Christ Church, and was pulled down for the rebuilding of Christ Church; William Barrett, *History and Antiquities of the City of Bristol* (Bristol, Pine, 1785), p. 475-79. The vicar from 1762 was Romney Penrose, (*c.* 1733-86), son of an earlier vicar of the same name. He matriculated from Wadham College, Oxford, took a B.C.L. degree from St. John's College, and became a fellow in 1756.

[11] Heb. 9:27.

[12] On this see above, July 19, 1776.

[13] Curnock surmised that this was either Lord North or Lord Dartmouth, but it was a couple of years since JW had written to them about public affairs. JW's letter to Mrs. Johnston, Mar. 28, 1777 (Telford, 6:260-61), opens the possibility that the missive he received may have been from the Archbishop of Canterbury or the King.

[14] Octave: 'The eighth day after a feast counting inclusively and so the same day a week after, or the same day and the whole intervening week inclusively. The number of

the example of the Primitive Church. Sunday, April 6, I began a journey through some of our societies to desire their assistance towards the expense of the New Chapel. I preached at Birmingham on Monday 7, in Congleton on Tuesday, and on Wednesday,

5 went on to Macclesfield. The new church here is far the most elegant that I have seen in the kingdom. Mr. Simpson[15] read prayers, and I preached on the first verse of the Second Lesson, Hebrews 11. And I believe many felt their want of the faith there spoken of. The next evening, I preached on Hebrews 12:14, 'without holi-

10 ness, no man can see the Lord.' I was enabled to make a close application, chiefly to those that expected to be saved by faith—I hope none of them will hereafter dream of going to heaven by any faith which does not produce holiness.

Fri. 11. I preached at Stockport about ten, and at Manchester

15 in the evening. Monday 14, I preached about noon at Warrington, and in the evening at Liverpool, where many large ships are now laid up in the docks which had been employed for many years in buying, or stealing, poor Africans and selling them in America for slaves.[16] The *men-butchers* have now nothing to do at this laudable

20 occupation. Since the American war broke out there is no demand for *human cattle*. So the men of Africa[17], as well as Europe, may enjoy their native liberty.[18]

Wed. 16. About noon, I preached at Wigan; in the evening at the new house in Bolton,[19] crowded within and without, on 'the

25 wise man, who built his house upon a rock'.[20] Many here are following his example and continually increasing both in the knowledge and love of God.[21]

Thur. 17. I called upon Mr. Barker[22] at Little Leigh, just totter-

feasts with octaves was greatly increased during the Middle Ages, but in 1955 the Roman Church suppressed all octaves except those of Christmas, Easter, and Whitsuntide. The BCP contains special proper prefaces for feasts with octave'; J. S. Purvis, *Dictionary of Ecclesiastical Terms* (London, 1962), p. 129.

[15] On David Simpson and Christ Church, Macclesfield, see Apr. 3, 1774 (22:402, n. 59 in this edn.).

[16] The slave trade was not declared illegal in Great Britain until 1807.

[17] Orig., 'Afric'.

[18] JW had published his (very hostile) *Thoughts upon Slavery* in 1774 (vol. 15 in this edn.).

[19] This chapel, opened in 1776, is believed to have been built on the meadow outside the town which produced the hay for the preachers' horses. A house for the preachers was built on one side and Christopher Hopper built himself a house on the other.

[20] Cf. Matt. 7:24.

[21] See Col. 1:10.

[22] On Daniel Barker, see Mar. 21, 1775 (22:445, n. 57 in this edn.).

ing over the great gulf. Being straitened for time, I rode from
thence to Chester. I had not for some years rode so far on horseback, but it did me no hurt. After preaching, I took chaise and
came to Middlewich a little before the Liverpool coach in which I
went on to London.   5
    I have now finished Dr. Gell's *Essay toward an Amendment of the
Last Translation of the Bible.*[23] This part only takes in the Penta-
teuch, but many other texts are occasionally explained. Surely he
was a man mighty in the Scriptures[24] and well acquainted with the
work of God in the soul. And he plainly shows that the antinomi-   10
ans and anti-perfectionists were just the same then as they are now.
    Monday [21] was the day appointed for laying the foundation
of the New Chapel.[25] The rain befriended us much by keeping
away thousands who purposed to be there. But there were still
such multitudes that it was with great difficulty I got through   15
them to lay the first stone. Upon this was a plate of brass (covered
with another stone) on which was engraved, 'This was laid by Mr.
John Wesley, on April [21], 1777.' Probably this will be seen no
more by any human eye, but will remain there till the earth and
the works thereof are burned up.[26]   20
    Sun. 27. The sun breaking out, I snatched the opportunity of
preaching to many thousands in Moorfields. All were still as night
while I showed how 'The Son of God was manifested to destroy
the works of the devil.'[27]
    Mon. 28. At one, I took coach and, on Wednesday evening,   25
preached at Newcastle upon Tyne. I love our brethren in the
southern counties, but still I find few among them that have the
spirit of our northern societies. Saturday, May 3, I went to Sunderland and strongly enforced, 'Render unto Caesar the things
that are Caesar's.'[28] Monday 5, having finished my business in   30

[23] Robert Gell, *An Essay towards the Amendment of the English Translation of the Bible*
(London, 1659). JW had read Gell while he was at Oxford, and again early in 1741
(19:452, 468, in this edn.). At the same time CW encountered him, declaring, 'Never
man, uninspired, spoke as this man speaks. I wonder where the devil has had him so
long.' *CWJ*, 1:285–86.
    [24] Acts 18:24.
    [25] On this scheme see above, Mar. 27, 1777, and July 19, 1776; see also Wesley's ser-
mon on this occasion, on Num. 23:23 (3:577–92 in this edn.). A curious pair of typo-
graphical errors appears in this account. The date of the entry originally stood as 'Monday, 2', and of the inscription in brass as 'April 1', a different digit in each date being
omitted. *WHS* 2 (1900):122.
    [26] See 2 Pet. 3:10.
    [27] Cf. 1 John 3:8.   [28] Cf. Matt. 22:21, etc.

these parts, I set my face southward again and, after preaching at
Durham about eleven, went on to Darlington. I have not lately
found so lively a work in any part of England as here. The society
is constantly increasing and seems to be all on fire for God. There
5 is nothing among them but humble, simple love—no dispute, no
jar of any kind. They exactly answer the description that David
Brainerd gives of his Indian congregation.[29] I particularly desired
both the preachers and leaders to have an especial care over them
and if possible to prevent either the devil or his agents from poi-
10 soning their simplicity. Many of them already know that 'the
blood of Jesus Christ' hath 'cleansed them from all sin.'[30]

Wed. 7. I went to Yarm. There I found a lovely young woman
in the last stage of a consumption, but such a one as I never read
of, nor heard any physician speak of but Dr. Wilson.[31] The seat of
15 the ulcers is not the lungs but the windpipe. I never yet knew it
cured. My housekeeper died of it last year. This young woman
died in a few weeks.

Thur. 8. About eleven, I preached at Osmotherley. I found my

[29] On David Brainerd and his *Life* (published by Jonathan Edwards, abridged by JW)
see Dec. 9, 1749 (20:315, n. 98 in this edn.). In his diary, Brainerd frequently contrasts
the carelessness of white hearers with the attention and responsiveness of Native Americans, as in the following passage: 'August 5 [1745, Crossweeksung, NJ]. In the morning
I discoursed to the Indians at the house where we lodged: Many of them were then
much affected and appeared surprizingly tender, so that a few words about their soul's
concerns would cause the tears to flow freely, and produce many sobs and groans. In the
afternoon, they being returned to the place where I have usually preached amongst
them, I again discoursed to them there. There were about 55 persons in all, about 46
that were capable of attending divine service with understanding: I insisted upon 1 John
4:10, "Herein is love", etc. They seemed eager of hearing; but there appeared nothing
very remarkable, except their attention, till near the close of my discourse, and then
divine truths were attended with a surprizing influence, and produced a great concern
among them. There was scarce three in 40 that could refrain from tears and bitter cries.
They all, as one, seemed in an agony of soul to obtain an interest in Christ, and the
more I discoursed of the love and compassion of God in sending his Son to suffer for
the sins of men; and the more I invited them to come and partake of his love, the more
their distress was aggravated, because they felt themselves unable to come. It was surprizing to see how their hearts seemed to be pierced with the tender and melting invitations of the Gospel, when there was not a word of terror spoken to them.' Jonathan
Edwards, *An Account of the Life of David Brainerd (1749)*, ed. Norman Pettit, in vol. 7
(1985) of *Works*, 10 vols. (Yale edn., New Haven, 1957-92), 7:306-7.

[30] Cf. 1 John 1:7.

[31] Andrew Wilson (1718-92) was the son of a Scots minister, and graduated M.D. at
Edinburgh in 1749. He practised in Newcastle and later in London. By this time he was
physician to the medical asylum, and a decided Hutchinsonian in his views; he wrote
extensively on philosophical and medical subjects. JW had read his *An Enquiry into the
Moving Powers Employed in the Circulation of the Blood* when it appeared in 1774 (see
June 24, 1774; 22:418, n. 25 in this edn.), and was to refer to his skill again on Feb. 24,
1779, below.

old friend, Mr. Watson,[32] who first brought me into this country, was just dead, after living a recluse life near fifty years. From one that attended him I learned that the sting of death was gone,[33] and he calmly delivered up his soul to God.

Fri. 9. I went to Malton, hoping to meet Miss R[itchie][34] there; but instead of her I found a letter which informed me that she was on the brink of the grave, but added, 'Surely my Lord will permit me to see you once more in the body.' I would not disappoint the congregation, but as soon as I had done preaching set out, and about four in the morning came to Otley. I minutely inquired into the circumstances of her illness. She is dropped suddenly into the third stage of a consumption, having one or more ulcers in her lungs, spitting blood, having a continual pain in her breast and a constant hectic fever, which disables her from either riding on horseback or bearing the motion of a carriage. Meantime she breathes nothing but praise and love. Short-lived flower! And ripe for a better soil.

Sat. 10. After travelling between ninety and a hundred miles, I came back to Malton and, having rested an hour, went on to Scarborough and preached in the evening. But the flux which I had had for a few days so increased that at first I found it difficult to speak. Yet the longer I spoke the stronger I grew. Is not God a present help?

Sun. 11. I experienced a second time what one calls *febris ex insolatione*.[35] The day was cold, but the sun shone warm on my back as I sat in the window. In less than half an hour, I began to shiver and soon after had a strong fit of an ague. I directly lay down between blankets and drank largely of warm lemonade. In ten minutes the hot fit came on, and quickly after I fell asleep. Having slept half an hour, I rose up and preached. Afterwards I met the society. And I found no want of strength, but was just as well at the end as at the beginning.

---

[32] On Thomas Adams, *alias* Watson, see Mar. 28, 1745 (20:58, n. 34 in this edn.).

[33] 1 Cor 15:55-56.

[34] Orig., 'R——y'. On Elizabeth Ritchie of Otley see May 2, 1774 (22:406, n. 88 in this edn.), and below, May 27, 1777. She in fact recovered from this ailment, and survived to nurse JW in his last illness and, in 1801, to marry Harvey Walklate Mortimer, a widower with six children, whom she had refused many years before.

[35] This name for sunstroke is thought to come from a medical textbook of the time. The *OED* gives an example of the English equivalent, 'insolation', from 1758, but it had disappeared from J. M. Good's *History of Medicine* (London, 1795) and his *Study of Medicine*, 4 vols. (London, 1822).

Monday 12, I preached at Bridlington; Tuesday 13 in the morning, at Beverley, and in the evening, at Hull, on 'Narrow is the way that leadeth unto life.'[36] And yet, blessed be God, there are thousands walking in it now who, a few years since, thought
5 nothing about it.

Wed. 14. At eleven, I preached at Pocklington, with an eye to the death of that lovely woman, Mrs. Cross. A gay young gentleman with a young lady, stepped in, stayed five minutes, and went out again with as easy an unconcern as if they had been listening
10 to a ballad-singer. I mentioned to the congregation the deep folly and ignorance implied in such behaviour. These pretty fools never thought that for this very opportunity they are to give an account before men and angels!

In the evening, I preached at York. I would gladly have rested
15 the next day, feeling my breast much out of order. But notice having been given of my preaching at Tadcaster, I set out at nine in the morning. About ten the chaise broke down. I borrowed a horse; but as he was none of the easiest, in riding three miles I was so thoroughly electrified that the pain in my breast was quite
20 cured.[37] I preached in the evening at York, on Friday took the Diligence, and on Saturday afternoon came to London.

Whit Sunday the 18th, our service at the Foundery began as usual at four. I preached in West Street Chapel in the forenoon, and at the Foundery in the evening. In the afternoon, I buried the
25 body of Joseph Guilford, a holy man and a useful preacher.[38] Surely never before did a man of so weak talents do so much good! He died as he lived, in the full triumph of faith, vehemently rejoicing and praising God!

Tue. 20. I met the committee for building, which indeed was
30 my chief business at London. We consulted together on several articles and were confidently persuaded that He who had incited us to begin would enable us to finish.

Sat. 24. My brother and I paid another visit to Dr. Dodd and spent a melancholy and useful hour. He appears, so far as man
35 can judge, to be a true, evangelical penitent.

To ease my journey, I went to Stevenage on Sunday evening. Monday 26, I went on to Witham Common, and on Tuesday

---

[36] Matt. 7:14 (*Notes*).
[37] Cf. July 26, 1775 (22:459, n. 19).
[38] On Joseph Guilford, see Feb. 5, 1763 (21:405, n. 52 in this edn.). JW himself wrote a graceful account of Guilford's last days in *Arminian Magazine* 6 (1783):23-24.

reached Sheffield. The next day I went to Leeds and, after preaching in the evening, pushed on to Otley. Here I found E[lizabeth] R[itchie] weaker and happier than ever. Her life seemed spun out to the last thread. I spent half an hour with her, to

> Teach her, at once, and learn of her, to die.[39]   5

I then rested two or three hours and took chaise at two on Thursday 29, hoping to reach Whitehaven in the evening, but I could only get to Cockermouth. Friday 30, I went on to Whitehaven, where I found a little vessel waiting for me. After preaching in the evening, I went on board about eight o'clock, and   10 before eight in the morning landed at Douglas in the Isle of Man.[40]

Douglas exceedingly resembles Newlyn in Cornwall, both in its situation, form, and buildings; only it is much larger and has a few houses equal to most in Penzance. As soon as we landed I was   15 challenged by Mr. Booth, who had seen me in Ireland and whose brother has been for many years a member of the society in Coolalough—a chaise was provided to carry me to Castletown. I was greatly surprised at the country. All the way from Douglas to Castletown it is as pleasant and as well cultivated as most parts of   20 England, with many gentlemen's seats. Castletown a good deal resembles Galway, only it is not so large. At six, I preached near the castle, I believe, to all the inhabitants of the town. Two or three gay young women showed they knew nothing about religion; all the rest were deeply serious. Afterwards I spent an hour   25 very agreeably at Mrs. Wood's,[41] the widow of the late Governor. I

---

[39] Cf. Alexander Pope, *Eloise to Abelard, ll.* 326-27:

> Present the cross before my lifted eye,
> Teach me, at once, and learn of me, to die.

There are many allusions to this poem in the hymns of the Wesley brothers.

[40] A mission in the Isle of Man had been begun in 1775 by John Crook at the behest of the Liverpool society. This work not merely introduced Methodism to the island, but led to Crook's entering the Methodist itinerancy; *Arminian Magazine* 4 (1781):537; *Methodist Magazine* 31 (1808):3-10, 49-57, 97-105, 145-51, 193-202. See J. I. West, 'John Wesley in the Isle of Man', *Proceedings of the Isle of Man Natural History and Antiquarian Society* 6 (1958): 15-27, and below, June 6, 1781.

[41] John Wood of Dumfries, an army captain and protégé of the Duke of Atholl, had been appointed governor in 1761. The island was sold to the Crown in 1765. He died in March 1777. His kindness to Methodists was doubtless the reason why JW called on his widow. J. I. West, 'Wesley in the Isle of Man', pp. 62-63.

was much pressed to stay a little longer at Castletown, but my time was fixed.

Sunday, June 1. At six, I preached in our own room and, to my surprise, saw all the gentlewomen there. Young as well as old were now deeply affected and would fain have had me stayed, were it but an hour or two. But I was forced to hasten away, in order to be at Peel Town[42] before the service began.

Mr. Corlett[43] said he would gladly have asked me to preach, but that the bishop[44] had forbidden him, who had also forbidden all his clergy to admit any Methodist preacher to the Lord's Supper. But is any clergyman obliged, either in law or conscience, to obey such a prohibition? By no means. The *will* even of the king does not bind any English subject, unless it be seconded by an express law.[45] How much less the will of a bishop! 'But did not you take an oath to obey him?' No, nor any clergyman in the three kingdoms. This is a mere *vulgar error*. Shame that it should prevail almost universally.

As it rained, I retired after service into a large malt-house. Most of the congregation followed and devoured the word. It being fair in the afternoon, the whole congregation stopped in the churchyard; and the word of God was with power. It was a happy opportunity.

Mon. 2. The greater part of them were present at five in the morning. A more loving, simple-hearted people than this I never saw. And no wonder, for they have but six Papists and no Dissenters in the island. It is supposed to contain near thirty thousand people, remarkably courteous and humane. Ever since smuggling was suppressed, they diligently cultivate their land; and they have a large herring fishery, so that the country improves daily.[46]

---

[42] Orig., 'Peele-town'.

[43] Orig., 'Corbett'. Henry Corlett was vicar of St. Germain, Peel, from 1761 till his death in 1801. He was one of the clergy trained at Bishop's Court, Kirkmichael, by Thomas Wilson, Bishop of Sodor and Man, 1697-1755, and translated the book of Exodus for the Manx Bible. *WHS* 5 (1905):81.

[44] Richard Richmond (1727-80), matriculated from St. John's College, Cambridge, 1747; graduated LL.B., 1752; LL.D., 1758. He was rector of Walton on the Hill, Lancs., 1757-80, chaplain to the Duke of Atholl, and consecrated bishop 1773. The bishop's pastoral letter warned his flock in very strong terms against the ministries of 'unordained, unauthorised and unqualified persons from other countries', and required his ministers to 'repel' any of them who presented himself at Holy Communion. Tyerman, *John Wesley*, 3:229.

[45] For another expression of JW's views on the relationship of English law and monarchial will, see Sermon 96, 'On Obedience to Parents', I.6 (3:365 in this edn.).

[46] This character was borne out by John Murlin, who paid a successful preaching visit to the island in 1758: 'After I left them, some of them sent to Whitehaven, desiring to

The old castle at Peel[47] (as well as the cathedral built within it) is only a heap of ruins. It was very large and exceeding strong, with many brass guns, but they are now removed to England. I set out for Douglas in the one-horse chaise, Mrs. Smyth[48] riding with me. In about an hour, in spite of all I could do, the head-   5
strong horse ran the wheel against a large stone. The chaise overset in a moment, but we fell so gently on smooth grass that neither of us was hurt at all. In the evening, I preached at Douglas to near as large a congregation as that at Peel, but not near so serious. Before ten we went on board and, about twelve on Tuesday 3,   10
landed at Whitehaven. I preached at five in the afternoon, and hastening to Cockermouth found a large congregation waiting in the castle-yard. Between nine and ten, I took chaise and, about ten on Wednesday 4, reached Settle. In the evening, I preached near the market-place, and all (but two or three *gentlefolks*) were seriously   15
attentive. Thursday 5, about noon, I came to Otley,[49] and found

have another preacher. But it was some years before another preacher went, there being so little probability of doing any considerable good while the whole island was a nest of smugglers. The Duke of Atholl was then king of the isle; but the case is now widely altered. Since it was purchased of the Duke and united to the Crown of England, that detestable trade is rooted out. A considerable part of the island is cultivated. At one part of it, a herring-fishery is established; at another a large linen-manufactory.' Thomas Jackson, ed., *Lives of Early Methodist Preachers*, 6 vols. (4th edn., London, 1871), 3:298.

[47] Three of the four churches on the island were in a worse state than the castle, which down to fairly recent times had been used as prison to the island. Romantic writers of JW's time were apt to stress the grandeur of the castle; George Waldron, *A Description of the Isle of Man* (1744; Manx Society edn., Douglas, 1865), pp. 9, 13, 89. But after the Crown repossessed the island in 1765, it was used as a sheepwalk; John Feltham, *Tour through the Isle of Man in 1797 and 1798* (Douglas, 1861) p. 185. By 1822 its remains could be flattered only as 'venerable ruins'; Samuel Haining, *A Historical Sketch and Descriptive View of the Isle of Man* (Douglas, 1822), p. 164.

[48] This was the first wife of the Rev. Edward Smyth, whose sister-in-law had entertained JW in Ireland (see Apr. 2, 1775; 22:445, n. 59 in this edn.). Edward Smyth married twice: (1) Agnes Higginson (Seymour, *Huntingdon*, 2:189), 1756–83; and (2) a Miss Dawson, sister-in-law to Dr. Murray, Dean of Ardagh (ibid., 2:193n.). Mrs. Smyth's account of the episode reflected somewhat severely on JW's capabilities as a driver: 'He told me when we got into the carriage that he could drive a chaise forty years ago; but, poor dear man! his hand seemed out of practice, as I thought we should be overturned several times. At last, one of the wheels being mounted on one side of a ditch, we were both pitched out in a great plain as the Lord in mercy ordered it; for had we been overset in some parts of the road, it is more than probable we should have been killed on the spot. I found no bad effects from the fall at the time; but the next morning I was scarce able to stir, and felt so sore and bruised that I thought it likely I should lay my bones in the churchyard at Douglas.' *The Christian's Triumph over Sin, the Devil and the Grave, Exemplified in the Life, Death, and Spiritual Experience of that Chosen Vessel, Mrs. Agnes Smyth* (London, 1783), pp. 42–43.

[49] JW preached at various places in this district, energetically begging funds for the City Road Chapel. Tyerman, *John Wesley*, 3:243.

E[lizabeth] R[itchie] just alive, but all alive to God. In the evening, it seemed as if the departing saint had dropped her mantle upon the congregation. Such an awe was upon them while I explained and applied, 'They were all filled with the Holy Ghost.'[50]

5   Fri. 6. I preached at Bradford,[51] where a blessed work has increased ever since William Brammah was here. 'Hath not God chosen the foolish things of the world to confound the wise?'[52] Sun. 8. About one I took my stand at Birstall; thousands upon thousands filled the vale and the side of the hill. And all, I found,
10 could hear. Such another multitude assembled near Huddersfield in the evening. Many of these had never heard a Methodist preacher before, yet they all behaved well.

Mon. 9. I spent one hour more at Otley. *Spectaculum Deo dignum!*[53] I have not before seen so triumphant an instance of the
15 power of faith. Though in constant pain, she has no complaint: so does the glory of God overshadow her and swallow up her will in his! she is indeed

All praise, all meekness, and all love.[54]

Wed. 11. I had appointed to preach in the new preaching-house
20 at Colne.[55] Supposing it would be sufficiently crowded, I went a

---

[50] Acts 2:4; 4:31.

[51] Orig., 'Bradforth'. William Brammah, a native of Sheffield, was an itinerant from 1762 till his death in 1780. The writer of his obituary described him as 'a plain, honest man, of deep piety and great zeal for the cause and interest of the Redeemer's kingdom.' His talents for the ministry were remarkably small, so that it was almost proverbial, 'Hear Mr. Brammah *once*, and you will hear all he has to say, let his text be what it will.' Charles Atmore, *The Methodist Memorial; being an Impartial Sketch of the Lives and Characters of the Preachers* (Bristol, 1801), p. 64. He was clearly a source of affectionate anxiety to JW who kept advising him to 'sleep early and rise early, and [deny] himself with regard to tobacco and eating flesh suppers', to stop 'screaming and the use of spirituous liquors'; he had less patience with his wife Alice, who was given to fits of religious excitement. Telford, 5:28, 116, 347; 6:17-18, 226; A. Steele, *A History of Methodism in Barnard Castle and the Principal Places in the Dales Circuit* (London, 1857), pp. 82-83; J. W. Laycock, *Methodist Heroes in the Great Haworth Round* (Keighley, 1909), p. 333.

[52] Cf. 1 Cor. 1:27.

[53] Cf. Seneca, *De Providentia* ('On Providence'), ii. 9. See also JW's quotation of the same phrase in Sermon 59, 'God's Love to Fallen Man' (1782), I.7 (2:429 and n. 48 in this edn.), where he enlarges the quotation in keeping with Seneca's context: 'See a sight worthy of God—a good man struggling with adversity and superior to it'.

[54] CW, *Short Hymns on Select Passages of Holy Scriptures* (1762), II.49; *Poetical Works*, 10:57; cf. the *Collection of Hymns* (1780), 332:16 (7:489 in this edn.). See also below, May 21, 1783.

[55] JW here clearly makes the best of what had been a bad business. The building scheme had been in difficulties throughout, and the western gable had been blown

little before the time, so that the galleries were but half full when I came into the pulpit. Two minutes after, the whole left-hand gallery fell at once with a hundred and fifty or two hundred persons. Considering the height and the weight of people, one would have supposed many lives would have been lost. But I did not 5 hear of one. Does not God give his angels charge over them that fear him?[56] When the hurry was a little over, I went into the adjoining meadow and quietly declared the whole counsel of God.

On Thursday and Friday, I preached at Halifax, Dawgreen, Horbury, and Wakefield. On Saturday I wrote *Thoughts upon* 10 *God's Sovereignty.*[57] To a cool man I think the whole matter will appear to rest on a single point: as *Creator* he could not but act according to his own sovereign will, but as *Governor* he acts, not as a mere Sovereign, but according to justice and mercy.

Mon. 16. I met the class of children at Rothwell.[58] This con- 15 sisted last year of eleven young maidens. They are increased to twenty. I think, seventeen or eighteen of them are now rejoicing in the love of God. And their whole behaviour is suitable thereto, adorning the doctrine of God our Saviour.[59]

Afterwards I went on to Rotherham and was glad to find that 20 the society is not discouraged by the death of that good man William Green, who had been as a father to them from the beginning.[60] He never started either at labour or suffering, but went on calm and steady, trusting God with himself and his eight chil-

down before the roof could be put on. At another point the money to pay wages ran out, and, though the crisis is said to have been surmounted with the aid of a special providence, it is probably significant that the collapse here reported was due to 'the malevolence of a carpenter who had purposely cut the timber too short' (Tyerman, *John Wesley*, 3:243). Though there were no fatalities, the injury toll was clearly extensive, and Alexander Mather found himself 'obliged . . . to travel through many societies, in order to defray these large expenses of taking care of those that were hurt, and rebuilding the gallery.' Jackson, *Early Methodist Preachers*, 2:185-86; 5:47.

[56] See Ps. 91:11; Matt. 4:6.

[57] See *Bibliography*, No. 367, and vol. 12 of this edn. (Jackson, 10:361-63.)

[58] This work among children at Rothwell had attracted JW's attention on his previous visit, above, Apr. 23, 1776; it proved somewhat disappointing in the end, see below, Apr. 12, 1780.

[59] See Titus 2:10.

[60] William Green, who died in 1777, was teaching at a school in Thorpe at the time of his conversion, *c.* 1741, and became a class-leader and local preacher. His second wife was Jane Holmes; see June 16, 1742 (19:278, n. 29 in this edn.). He subsequently had a school at Rotherham where he introduced Methodism after great persecution. His school was the preaching-house till 1761, when he took the lead in getting the chapel built. He provided hospitality for the preachers, a horse for taking them over a wide area, and was an active distributor of JW's publications.

dren, even while all the waves and storms went over him.[61] He died as he lived, in the full assurance of faith,[62] praising God with his latest breath.

Tue. 17. I preached in the market-place at Chesterfield on 'It is appointed unto men once to die.'[63] Although the congregation was numerous, yet I did not observe any either trifling or inattentive hearers. In the evening, I preached at Derby. It was supposed the people would be afraid to come, as part of the roof had lately fallen in.[64] (Indeed it fell an hour before the congregation met; otherwise many must have been hurt.) But they were not afraid: the house was well filled, and even the rich attended with seriousness.

Wed. 18. I preached at Nottingham to a serious, loving congregation. There is something in the people of this town which I cannot but much approve of: although most of our society are of the lower class, chiefly employed in the stocking-manufacture, yet there is generally an uncommon gentleness and sweetness in their temper and something of elegance in their behaviour, which, when added to solid, vital religion, make them an ornament to their profession.

Thursday 19, I did not reach Leicester till the congregation had waited some time; so I began immediately to enforce, 'Believe on the Lord Jesus Christ, and thou shalt be saved.'[65] I had designed not to call here at all, supposing it would be lost labour. But the behaviour of the whole congregation convinced me that I had judged wrong. They filled the house at five in the morning and seemed determined to 'stir up the gift of God which was in them'.[66] Saturday 21, I returned to London.

Wednesday 25, I saw Dr. Dodd[67] for the last time. He was in exactly such a temper as I wished. He never at any time expressed the least murmuring or resentment at any one; but entirely and calmly gave himself up to the will of God. Such a prisoner I scarce ever saw before, much less such a condemned malefactor. I should think, none could converse with him without acknowledging that God is with him.

Thur. 26. I read the truly wonderful performance of Mr. Row-

---

[61] See Ps. 42:9 (BCP).
[62] Heb. 10:22.　　　　　　　　　　　　　　　　　　　　　　　　[63] Heb. 9:27.
[64] The Derby historians kindly pass over this incident in silence.
[65] Acts 16:31.
[66] See 2 Tim. 1:6.
[67] On William Dodd, see above, Feb. 15, 1777.

land Hill.[68] I stood amazed! Compared to him Mr. Toplady[69] himself is a very civil, fair-spoken gentleman! Friday 27, I wrote an
answer to it:[70] 'Not rendering railing for railing'[71] (I have not so
learned Christ[72]) but speaking the truth in love![73]

Sat. 28. I have now completed my seventy-fourth year; and by
the peculiar favour of God I find my health and strength, and all
my faculties of body and mind, just the same as they were at four
and twenty.

Mon. 30. I set out for Northamptonshire and preached in the
evening at Stony Stratford. Mr. Canham had prepared a large and
commodious place, but it would not contain the congregation.
However, all without, as well as within, except one fine lady, were
serious and attentive.

Tuesday, July 1. I preached in the evening at [Maids'] Moreton,[74] near Buckingham; the thunder, attended with heavy rain,
was likely to rob us of our whole congregation. We cried to God.
The thunder and rain ceased, and we had a fair sunshiny evening.
A large number of people flocked together, some of whom came
twelve or fourteen miles. And they did not lose their labour, for
God accompanied his word with the demonstration of his Spirit.[75]

Wed. 2. The house was more than filled at five, and chiefly with

---

[68] This was Hill's pamphlet, *Imposture Detected and the Dead Vindicated* (London,
1777), succinctly described by Richard Green as 'a miserable piece of writing, marked
by the lowest degree of rude abuse, fitter for Billingsgate than for the pen of a Christian
minister'; *Anti-Methodist Publications issued during the Eighteenth Century* (London,
1902; repr. New York, 1973), pp. 129-30. To this JW replied (see n. 70 below), as did
Thomas Olivers with *A Rod for the Reviler* (London, 1777). Rowland Hill (1744-1833)
of Hawkstone Park, Shropshire, was the sixth son of Sir Rowland, and a younger
brother of Sir Richard Hill (on whom see July 11, 1772; 22:341, n. 3 in this edn.). Educated at St. John's College, Cambridge, where he graduated B.A. in 1769, he encountered much opposition to his earnest pursuit of 'curious' religion. He was refused ordination by six bishops in succession owing to his refusal to give up irregular preaching,
and was never able to proceed beyond deacon's orders. As a result a chapel was built for
him at Wotton, Glos., which he served for part of every year, and in 1783, the Surrey
Chapel in London, which he filled with great congregations. In the next generation Hill
was one of the leading exponents of 'catholic christianity', but he was now strongly on
the Calvinist side in the predestination controversy, and he replied to JW's *Answer* with
A Full Answer to the Rev. J. Wesley's Remarks upon a late Pamphlet (Bristol, 1777).
[69] On A. M. Toplady, see Nov. 29, 1775 (22:474, n. 86 in this edn.).
[70] *An Answer to Mr. Rowland Hill's Tract, entitled 'Imposture Detected'* (1777); see *Bibliography*, No. 368 (9:402-15 in this edn.).
[71] 1 Pet. 3:9.
[72] See Eph. 4:20.
[73] Eph. 4:15.
[74] Orig., 'Marton'. Maids' Moreton was a parish 1 mile north-east of Buckingham.
[75] See 1 Cor. 2:4.

genteel young women, of whom (I learned) there is a large number in this village, remarkable both for sense and seriousness.
After dinner we went on to Oxford, where also we had a very serious congregation. So all the seed sown here has not fallen either
5   on stony or thorny ground.[76]
In the afternoon, I went to Witney and, the evening being fair
and mild, preached on Wood Green to a far larger congregation
than the house could have contained. I spent the rest of the
evening profitably and agreeably with a few of the excellent ones
10 of the earth.[77] I was ready to say, 'It is good for me to be here.'[78]
No! Go thou and preach the gospel!
Thur. 3. I was much comforted at Stroud among an earnest,
serious, loving people. Friday 4, I preached in dull Gloucester at
ten, and at six in the new house at Tewkesbury. Saturday 5, I sent
15 my chaise straight to Worcester, and myself took horse for Bengeworth. The church was tolerably filled. Afterwards I went down
with Mr. Beale[79] to his house—the same in which Mr. Benjamin
Seward lived[80] three or four and forty years ago. In the evening, I
preached in the little chapel at Broad Marston.
20   Sun. 6. I preached in Pebworth Church morning and afternoon, and at Bengeworth in the evening. The church, large as it
is, was well filled, and many for the present were much affected. I
preached there once more at eight in the morning, and then rode
on to Worcester. On Tuesday evening, the rector of the parish was
25 at the preaching, a candid, sensible man.[81] He seemed much surprised, having never dreamed before that there was such a thing

---

[76] See Mark 4:5, etc..
[77] The Bolton family, on whom see July 15, 1773, and Oct. 14, 1775 (22:383-84 and n.
67; and 469 in this edn.).
[78] Cf. Matt.17:4, etc.
[79] Mr. Beale (d. 1805) was rector of Bengeworth. He was a man of universal charity,
said to support all the principal charitable institutions in the locality. He was a witness
in the case of George Lukins of Yatton, a man who believed himself possessed of seven
devils. *Arminian Magazine* 12 (1789):375.
[80] Benjamin Seward (born *c.* 1705) appeared frequently in the early history of the
Wesley brothers (see 19:31, n. 44; 172, n. 75 in this edn.). A native of Badsey near Evesham, he matriculated from St. John's College, Cambridge, 1721, was converted in
1739, and wrote hymns. In 1739 he fell seriously ill; his brother Henry ascribed his
madness to CW, and threatened to beat the latter on Bengeworth Common. Luke
Tyerman, *The Life of the Rev. George Whitefield*, 2 vols. (2nd edn., London, 1890),
1:163.
[81] It is not clear who this was. Valentine Green, *The History and Antiquities of the City
and Suburbs of Worcester* (London, 1896), 2:43-67, describes a dozen parishes in
Worcester together with their incumbents.

as common sense among the Methodists! The society here, by patient continuance in well-doing, has quite overcome evil with good:[82] even the beasts of the people[83] are now tame and open not their mouths against them. They profited much when the waves and storms went over them. May they profit as much by the calm! 5

Wed. 9. I went through a delightful vale to Malvern Wells, lying on the side of a high mountain and commanding one of the finest prospects in the world—the whole vale of Evesham.[84] Hitherto the roads were remarkably good, but they grew worse and worse till we came to Monmouth. Much disturbance was 10 expected here,[85] but we had none; all were deeply attentive.

About six in the evening on Thursday 10, I preached on the Bulwark at Brecon.[86] Friday 11, I called upon Mr. Gwynne, just recovering from a dangerous illness.[87] But he is not recovered from the seriousness which it occasioned. May this be a lasting 15 blessing!

Saturday 12. We dined at Llandilo. After dinner we walked in Mr. Rice's[88] park, one of the pleasantest I ever saw, it is so finely watered by the winding river running through and round the

---

[82] Rom. 12:21.

[83] Ps. 68:30 (BCP).

[84] JW's penchant for a highly developed countryside has here led him into error; he beheld the Severn valley, beyond which, just to the east, was the Vale of Evesham.

[85] In 1770, Alexander Mather had attempted to open a licensed preaching-house in Monmouth, but was repelled by the opposition of a churchwarden and a show of mob force (Jackson, *Early Methodist Preachers*, 2:184). It may have been on the occasion of this visit by JW that the young Thomas Wilks (1759-1830), later a Methodist convert, 'was strongly inclined to disturb that venerable man, but was restrained by an invisible power'; *Wesleyan Methodist Magazine* 53 (1830):573. The Monmouth Methodists experienced more bitter and prolonged persecution than any others in Wales. A. H. Williams, ed., *John Wesley in Wales, 1739-90* (Cardiff, 1971), p. 93, n. 1.

[86] The Bulwark was an open area of ground in front St. Mary's Chapel and behind the old Walton Gate in Brecon. See Meredith Jones's town plan (1744) prefixed to vol. 2, pt. 1, of Theophilus Jones, *A History of the County of Brecknock* (Brecknock, 1805-9).

[87] Marmaduke Gwynne, CW's father-in-law, had died in 1769. His son and heir, Howell, moved to Llanelwedd Hall near Builth, leaving Garth to *his* heir, a second Marmaduke. JW might have called on either of these Gwynnes; the health of each was precarious, Howell dying in 1789, and Marmaduke in 1784. Williams, *Wesley in Wales*, p. 93, n. 2.

[88] Orig., 'Rees's'. George Rice (1724-79), one of Newcastle's political managers in Wales, was one of the Carmarthenshire Whigs who, 1738-64, struggled violently with the West Wales Tories, led by Sir John Philipps of Picton Castle, Jacobite son of the early benefactor of the Holy Club, to control the borough of Carmarthen, and was himself M.P. for the county, 1754-79. Successfully working his passage at the accession of George III, Rice became a commissioner of trade and plantations in 1761. The castle admired by JW, though of ancient origin, was built and enlarged in the thirteenth century.

gently rising hills. Near one side of it, on the top of a high eminence, is the old castle, a venerable pile, at least as old as William
the Conqueror and 'majestic, though in ruins'.[89]

In the evening, I preached to a large congregation in the market-place at Carmarthen. I was afterwards informed, the mayor
had sent two constables to forbid my preaching there. But if he
did, their hearts failed them, for they said not one word.

Sun. 13. We had a plain, useful sermon from the vicar,[90] though
some said, he 'did not preach the gospel'! He preached what these
men have great need to hear, lest they seek death in the error of
their life.[91]

In the evening, I explained to a huge congregation who it is
'that builds his house upon a rock'.[92] I believe many had ears to
hear, even of the young and gay, to whom I made a particular
application.

Mon. 14. I reached Llwyn-gwair[93] about noon. In the evening
Mr. Pugh[94] read prayers, and I preached at Newport. This is the
only town in Wales which I had then observed to increase.

In riding along on the side of Newport Bay, I observed on the
ground a large quantity of turfs. These are found by removing the
sand above the high-water mark, under which there is a continued
bed of turf, with the roots of trees, leaves, nuts, and various kinds
of vegetables. So that it is plain, the sea is an intruder here and
now covers what was once dry land. Such probably was the whole
bay a few centuries ago.[95] Nay, it is not at all improbable that formerly it was dry land from Aberystwyth[96] to St. David's Point.

Tue. 15. Mr. Bowen carried me in his chaise to Cardigan. This
is the second town I have seen in Wales which is continually
increasing both in buildings and in number of inhabitants. I
preached at noon, five or six clergymen being present with a
numerous congregation. And a more attentive one I have not seen;

---

[89] Milton, *Paradise Lost*, ii.305.

[90] John Rogers (1708–96), matriculated from Jesus College, Oxford, 1724; took B.A. from Christ Church, 1730; vicar of St. Peter's, Carmarthen, 1752–96.

[91] See Wisd. 1:12.

[92] Cf. Matt. 7:24.

[93] Orig., 'Llwynguair'. The home of the Bowen family, on whom see Aug. 20, 1772 (22:346–47 and n. 32 in this edn.).

[94] David Pugh, on whom see Aug. 20, 1772 (22:347 and n. 33 in this edn.).

[95] Changes in coastlines have been indicated by changes in the course of rivers at Aberystwyth, and there are legends of a buried city beneath the sea. Williams, *Wesley in Wales*, p. 94, n. 1.

[96] Orig., 'Aberystwith'.

many likewise appeared deeply affected. If our preachers constantly attended here, I cannot think their labour would be in vain.
Wed. 16. About nine, I preached again in Newport Church and
found much liberty among that poor, simple people. We dined
with Admiral Vaughan[97] at Trecwn, one of the most delightful   5
spots that can be imagined. Thence we rode to Haverfordwest,
but the heat and dust were as much as I could bear. I was faint for
a while, but it was all gone as soon as I came into the congregation. And after preaching and meeting the society, I was as fresh
as at six in the morning.   10
  Thur. 17. I preached at Roch[98] and took a view of the old castle
built on a steep rock. A gentleman wisely asked Mr. S[tokes],[99]
'Pray is this *natural* or *artificial?*' He gravely replied, 'Artificial, to
be sure; I imported it from the north of Ireland.'
  Fri. 18. The more I converse with the society at Haverford   15
[west],[1] the more I am united to them. Saturday 19, about eleven, I
preached at Houghton, two miles short of the ferry. There was an
uncommon blessing among the simple-hearted people. At Pembroke in the evening, we had the most elegant congregation I have
seen since we came into Wales. Some of them came in dancing and   20
laughing as into a theatre. But their mood was quickly changed, and
in a few minutes they were as serious as my subject, Death. I believe,
if they do not take great care, they will remember it—for a week!

---

[97] John Vaughan, post captain 1746, admiral of the blue 1787, died unmarried, 1789;
WHS 11 (1917):23; Williams, *Wesley in Wales*, p. 94, n. 2. JW visited this house five
times, and the Admiral and his sisters were much attracted to him. The topographer
Richard Fenton was both enthusiastic and back-handed about Trecwn. He held that 'in
point of situation, [it] yields to very few spots in the county, as possessing every ingredi-
ent of fine scenery'; on the other hand the valley ought to be turned into a trout-lake,
and 'of this place it may be said, what is not applicable to many places in the county,
that the possessor, to improve it, has nothing to do but to cut down trees judiciously,
the growth at present being too crowded.' Richard Fenton, *A Historical Tour through
Pembrokeshire* (London, 1811), pp. 343-44.
[98] Orig., 'Roach'. Roch 'derives its name from a rocky mountain ridge rising abruptly
from the plain, and the summit whereof is occupied by an ancient castle. . . . It was gar-
risoned for the king during the [civil] war, and in 1644 was besieged by the parliamen-
tarians, under the command of Captain Edwards to whom, after a defence of two days,
it was surrendered,' and by whom it was largely dismantled. Samuel Lewis, *A Topographical Dictionary of Wales*, 2 vols. (London, 1844), 2:361.
[99] John Rees Stokes of Cuffern near Roch. Williams, *Wesley in Wales*, p. 95, n. 1.
[1] This society had delighted JW on a previous visit (see Aug. 16, 1769; 22:199 in this
edn.). The particular remark about his pleasure here may owe something to the fact that
a pillar of the work was Catherine Warren, sister to the wife of J. R. Stokes; *WHS* 30
(1956):132-33. But also, the unmentioned fact was that the Haverfordwest society had
thrived in competition with the Moravians there.

Sun. 20. The congregation at St. Daniel's was more than the church could contain. After reading prayers, I preached an hour (an uncommon thing with *me*) on 'Not every one that saith unto me, Lord, Lord!'[2] Many were cut to the heart, and at the Lord's Supper, many were wounded and many healed. Surely now at least, if they do not harden their hearts, all these will know the day of their visitation.[3]

Mon. 21. Having been much pressed to preach at Jeffreyston,[4] a colliery six or seven miles from Pembroke, I began soon after seven. The house was presently filled and all the space about the doors and windows, and the poor people drank in every word. I had finished my sermon when a gentleman, violently pressing in, bade the people get home and mind their business. As he used some bad words, my driver spake to him. He fiercely said, 'Do you think I need to be taught by a chaise-boy?' the lad replying, 'Really, sir, I do think so,' the conversation ended.

In the evening, I preached in the market-place at Carmarthen to such another congregation as I had there before. And my heart was so enlarged towards them that I continued preaching a full hour. Tuesday 22, I preached at Llanelli[5] about one, and at Swansea in the evening.

Wed. 23. I preached in Swansea at five, in Neath between eight and nine, and about one at Margam. In the road between this and Bridgend we had the heaviest rain I ever remember to have seen in Europe. And it saved John Prickard's life.[6] For presently man and beast were covered with a sheet of lightning; but as he was thoroughly wet it did him no harm. In the evening, I preached in Oldcastle Church near Bridgend.

---

[2] Matt. 7:21.

[3] See Luke 19:44.

[4] Orig., 'Jetterson'. Jeffreyston was a parish 7 miles south of Narberth. The special nature of its coal made it popular with London malters, 'it being free from all bituminous qualities'. Lewis, *Wales*, 1:436.

[5] Orig., 'Llanelly'.

[6] John Prickard (1744–84), a native of New Moat, Pem., had a religious upbringing from his parents, and as a young man was a follower of Whitefield and Howell Davies. His conversion experience in 1768, however, involved a turning away from his Calvinistic antecedents to Arminian Methodism, and he quickly became a successful class-leader, exhorter, and local preacher. He was loathe to offer for the English itinerancy and thought of volunteering for the West Indies or even Africa, but was admitted by the English Conference in 1774. He travelled in Wales, England, and Ireland, but died after a debilitating illness at an early age and was characterized in the Conference minutes as 'a man thoroughly devoted to God, and an eminent pattern of holiness'. Jackson, *Early Methodist Preachers*, 4:170-97; Atmore, *Memorial*, pp. 336-42.

Thur. 24. I preached to a large and serious congregation in the town hall at Cowbridge. Friday 25 about eleven, I read prayers and preached at Llantwit [Major] Church[7] to a very numerous congregation. I have not seen either so large or so handsome a church since I left England. It *was* sixty yards long, but one end of it is now in ruins. I suppose it has been abundantly the most beautiful, as well as the most spacious, church in Wales.

In the evening, I preached at Mrs. Jones's house in Font-y-gary.[8] For the present, even the genteel hearers seemed affected—and God is able to continue the impression.

Sat. 26. I breakfasted at Fonmon Castle and found a melancholy pleasure in the remembrance of past times. About noon, I preached at Penmark,[9] and in the evening, in that memorable old castle at Cardiff.

Sunday 27. I preached in the town hall, and again in the afternoon to a crowded audience, after preaching in a little church at Caerphilly.[10] In the evening, I preached in Mr. M[atthews]'s hall at Llandaff,[11] and God applied his word (I think) to every heart.

Monday 28, I preached at Newport, and in the evening reached Bristol.

---

[7] This complicated structure was later described by Lewis (*Wales*, 1:460-61): 'The present *church*, dedicated to St. Illtyd, and a spacious and venerable pile of building, erected, according to an old manuscript, by R. Neville, Earl of Warwick and Lord of Glamorgan, in the reign of Henry VI, and comprising in addition to that portion of it in which divine service is performed, a more ancient structure, separated only from the former by the tower, to the west of which it is situated. From this latter a door opened into a dilapidated building, in a line with it, called the Lady Chapel, the walls of which were ornamented with busts and figures of saints, now destroyed; this chapel which is almost a ruin, was forty feet and a half in length. The old church which was sixty-four feet and a half long is said to have been deserted on account of the dampness of its situation, but this would have equally operated against the erection of a contiguous structure of larger dimensions'. The modern church is 98 feet long. It contained monuments to members of the 'Westley' family, said to be a branch of JW's own; *WHS* 3 (1902):131-32. The incumbent was Joshua Powell (born *c.* 1720), who matriculated from Jesus College, Oxford, in 1739.

[8] Orig., 'Fontegary'. Mary, née Forrest, widow of Robert Jones of Fonmon (see 19:282, and 227, n. 9 in this edn.) moved to Font-y-gary when her son attained his majority and took possession of Fonmon on July 7, 1742. JW had made a special visit to Fonmon to comfort her after the death of her husband.

[9] The Joneses of Fonmon were buried in the church here, though the text does not say explicitly that it was in the church that JW preached. On Sept. 1, 1745, CW had been refused Communion in this church. *CWJ*, 1:404.

[10] Orig., 'Carp Lylly'. The 'little church' was St. Martin's, a chapel of ease to Eglwysilan, rebuilt in the early nineteenth century.

[11] Thomas Matthews of Llandaff Court, on whom see Aug. 27, 1763 (21:426, n. 36 in this edn.).

Wed. 30. I spent an hour or two with Mr. Fletcher,[12] restored to
life in answer to many prayers. How many providential ends have
been answered by his illness! And perhaps still greater will be
answered by his recovery.

5   Friday, August 1. I desired as many as could to join together in
fasting and prayer that God would restore the spirit of love and of
a sound mind[13] to the poor deluded rebels in America.[14] In the
evening, we had a watch-night at Kingswood, and I was agreeably
surprised to observe that hardly anyone went away till the whole
10   service was concluded.

Tue. 5. Our yearly Conference began.[15] I now particularly
inquired (as that report had been spread far and wide) of every
Assistant, 'Have you reason to believe from your own observation
that the Methodists are a fallen people?[16] Is there a decay or an
15   increase in the work of God where you have been? Are the societies in general more dead or more alive to God, than they were
some years ago?' The almost universal answer was, 'If we "must
know them by their fruits", there is no decay in the work of God
among the people in general. The societies are not dead to God—
20   they are as much alive as they have been for many years. And we

[12] Fletcher of Madeley had been nursed through a serious illness by his friends, Mary
and Charles Greenwood, at Stoke Newington, and in April 1777 was taken to James Ireland's at Brislington, just outside Bristol, where he took the Hotwells waters. By
December it was feared that nothing could save him but the air of his native Switzer-
land, and he set off for France and that country with Ireland's two daughters, not
returning till April 1781; Benson, *Fletcher*, pp. 206, 212, 222-23. The sensation made by
Fletcher's attendance at the following Conference was described by an eye-witness. S.
Dunn, *Life of Adam Clarke* (London, 1863), pp. 126-27; Luke Tyerman, *Wesley's Designated Successor* (London, 1882), pp. 396-97; J. S. Simon, *John Wesley; The Last Phase*
(London, 1934), pp. 115-16.
[13] See 2 Tim. 1:7
[14] This sentence was omitted from edn. C (?1791).
[15] At this Conference the question was asked for the first time, 'What preachers have
died this year?' and a sentence of appreciation was added about each of the four names
reported, the beginning of the roll of honour of preachers who have died in the work
which has continued ever since. The most substantial items of business consisted of
objections to preachers and the methods by which they were selected. This corporate
self-examination also became a permanent feature of the Methodist system.
[16] This discussion (not minuted in the record) appears to have arisen from charges
made by John Helton, who had been appointed assistant for the Bristol circuit in 1776,
but now resigned from the itinerancy, announcing his conversion to Quakerism. On his
evolution, see Apr. 29, 1770 (22:227, n. 64 in this edn.). George Smith, the Wesleyan
historian, believed that this episode precipitated JW's decision to launch, the following
New Year's Day, the *Arminian Magazine* to disseminate (among other things) reliable
material about the principles of his movement. *History of Wesleyan Methodism*, 3 vols.
(5th edn., London, 1866), 1:411-12.

look on this report as a mere device of Satan to make our hands
hang down.'

'But how can this question be decided?' *You*, and *you* can judge
no farther than you see. You cannot judge of one part by another,
of the people of London, suppose, by those of Bristol. And none 5
but myself has an opportunity of seeing them throughout the
three kingdoms.[17]

But to come to a short issue. In most places, the Methodists are
still a poor, despised people, labouring under reproach and many
inconveniences. Therefore, wherever the power of God is not, 10
they decrease. By this then you may form a sure judgment. Do
the Methodists in general decrease in number? Then they
decrease in grace; they are a fallen, or at least, a falling people.
But they do not decrease in number. They continually increase,
therefore they are not a fallen people. 15

The Conference concluded on Friday as it began, in much love.
But there was one jarring string: John Helton[18] told us, he must
withdraw from our connexion. Because he saw the Methodists
were a fallen people. Some would have *reasoned* with him, but it
was lost labour, so we let him go in peace. 20

Mon. 11. I returned to London. Thursday 14, I drew up proposals for the *Arminian Magazine*.[19] Friday 15, the committee for
the building met; which is now ready for the roof. Hitherto God
has helped us![20]

Sun. 17. In the calm, fair evening, I took the opportunity to 25
preach in Moorfields.[21] The congregation was (at least) as large as

[17] Edn. C omits this paragraph.

[18] Orig., 'Hilton', as in *Minutes* for 1768, 1775, 1776. Otherwise he is listed as Helton,
and it was with that name that in 1778 (as a Quaker) he published *Reasons for Quitting
the Methodist Society*.

[19] See *Bibliography*, Nos. 371-84. The proposals were for a monthly magazine to 'contain no news, no politics, no personal invectives, nothing offensive either to religion,
decency, good nature, or good manners', and, on the positive side, to 'maintain that
God *willeth all men to be saved*, by *speaking the truth in love*; by arguments and illustrations drawn partly from Scripture, partly from reason; proposed in as inoffensive a
manner as the nature of the thing will permit. Not that we expect those on the other
side of the question will use *us* as we use *them*.' Tyerman, *John Wesley*, 3:281.

[20] See 1 Sam. 7:12.

[21] This is the last record in the *Journals* of JW's preaching in Moorfields. Within a
decade the fields had been half covered with brokers' houses, and even the southern
part of the area, the quadrangles planted with elms before the Bethlehem Hospital,
which was fashionably favoured as the 'City Mall', became 'very much neglected'.
S. W. Fores, *New Guide for Foreigners to the Cities of London and Westminster* (London,
1787), street map; B. Lambert, *History and Survey of London and its Environs* (London,
1806).

I ever saw there. As yet I do not see any sign of the decay of the work of God in England.

Mon. 18. I went down to Bristol again and read in the way Dr. M'Bride's *Practice of Physic*.[22] Undoubtedly it is an ingenious book, yet it did not answer my expectation. Several things I could contradict from my own experience. E.g., he says, 'All fevers are attended with thirst and vigilia.' Nay, in two violent fevers I had no thirst at all and slept rather more than when I was in health.

Tue. 19. I went forward to Taunton with Dr. Coke,[23] who, being dismissed from his curacy, has bid adieu to his honourable name and determined to cast in his lot with us. In the evening, I endeavoured to guard all who love or fear God against that miserable *bigotry*[24] which many of our mistaken brethren are advancing with all their might.

Wednesday 20, I preached at Tiverton; Thursday 21, at Launceston; Friday 22 about ten, in Bodmin. Thence I went unto Cubert[25] and found that venerable old man, Mr. Hosken,[26] calmly waiting for his discharge from the body. Saturday 23 at noon, I preached in Redruth, and in the evening, on the cliff of St. Ives. In the following week, I visited most of the western societies, and on Saturday 30, had the Quarterly Meeting. I now inquired particularly whether the societies were increasing or decreasing. I could not hear of a decrease in any, but several were swiftly increasing, particularly those of St. Just, Penzance, and Helston.

Sun. 31. I preached in the morning at St. Agnes, in the evening to the huge congregation in Gwennap[27]—larger (it was supposed) by fifteen hundred or two thousand than ever it had been before.

Saturday, September 27.[28] Having abundance of letters from Dublin, informing me that the society there was in the utmost

---

[22] David McBride, *A Methodical Introduction to the Theory and Practice of Physic* (London, 1772). On the author, see Apr. 19, 1774 (22:405, n. 79 in this edn.).

[23] On Thomas Coke, see above, Aug. 13, 1776.

[24] I.e., the Calvinist version of the doctrines of election and predestination, which as recently as the 14th (see above) JW had promised to controvert in an 'inoffensive . . . manner'.

[25] Orig., 'St. Cuthbert's'.

[26] Orig., 'Hoskins'; see Sept. 7, 1765 (22:18, n. 79 in this edn.).

[27] On Gwennap Pit, see Sept. 5, 1762 (21:388, n. 75 in this edn.).

[28] This gap of almost a month in the *Journal* is entirely unexplained, and is in no way made good by JW's letters. It began, however, with a letter from Gwennap to his wife on September 1. In this letter JW reiterated his former terms for a reconciliation, that she should restore his papers and promise to take no more, and added a third that she should withdraw her slanders against his good name. These terms were not, however, accepted. Telford, 6:273-74.

confusion[29] by reason of some of the chief members whom the preachers had thought it needful to exclude from the society, and finding all I could *write* was not sufficient to stop the growing evil, I saw but one way remaining—to go myself, and that as soon as possible. So the next day, I took chaise with Mr. Goodwin[30] and made straight for Mr. Bowen's at Llwyn-gwair[31] in Pembrokeshire, hoping to borrow his sloop and so cross over to Dublin without delay. I came to Llwyn-gwair on Tuesday 30. The next day, October 1, the captain of a sloop at Fishguard,[32] a small seaport town ten or twelve miles from Llwyn-gwair, sent me word he would sail for Dublin in the evening; but he did not stir till about eight the next evening. We had a small, fair wind. From Fishguard to Dublin is about forty leagues. We had run ten or twelve, till at about eight in the morning, Friday 3, it fell dead calm. The swell was then such as I never felt before, except in the Bay of Biscay. Our little sloop, between twenty and thirty tons, rolled to and fro with a wonderful motion. About nine, the captain finding he could not get forward, would have returned, but he could make no way. About eleven I desired we might go to prayer. Quickly after, the wind sprung up fair; but it increased, till about eight at night it blew a storm. And it was pitch dark, so that having only the captain and a boy on board, we had much ado to work the vessel. However, about ten, though we scarce know how, we got safe into Dublin Bay.

Sat. 4. Between seven and eight, I landed at Ringsend. Mr.

---

[29] There were many signs of prosperity in the Dublin Society. Great numbers were attracted by the preaching of the Rev. Edward Smyth and Samuel Bradburn, and there were important conversions, including Henry Moore, later JW's literary executor and biographer. But Bradburn was charged with teaching false doctrine, i.e., opposing Calvinism, by Solomon Walker, 'a gentleman of considerable influence and wealth in connection with the society', and when John Hampson, the superintendent, called a meeting of the trustees of the Widows' Alms House to elect a successor to a deceased trustee, accusations of dishonesty were made against the Treasurer. These charges proved unfounded, and the superintendent proceeded to enforce discipline on a considerable scale. It was this confusion which bought JW across. Crookshank, *Ireland*, 1:301-14; Telford, 6:275-76.

[30] John Goodwin (*c.* 1739-1808), a native of Cheshire, began to preach soon after a youthful conversion and became an itinerant in 1768. 'His character was unblemished during the whole of his ministry, and his affection for his colleagues was generally acknowledged'; *Methodist Magazine* 31 (1808):421. JW moreover trusted his judgment in Irish matters (*WHS* 20 [1935]:51) and had stationed him in Dublin, 1770-72.

[31] Orig., 'Llyngwair'. On George Bowen, see Aug. 20, 1772 (22:346-47 and n. 32 in this edn.).

[32] Orig., 'Fishgard'.

McKenny[33] met me and carried me to his house. Our friends presently flocked from all quarters and seemed equally surprised and pleased at seeing me. I moved no dispute, but desired a few of each side to meet me together at ten on Monday morning. In the evening, although on so short a warning, we had an exceeding large congregation, on whom (waiving all matter of contention) I strongly enforced those solemn words, 'I must work the work of him that sent me, while it is day; the night cometh when no man can work.'[34]

Sun. 5. I was much comforted at St. Patrick's, where an uncommon awe seemed to rest on the whole assembly. In the evening, I preached on Eph. 4:30, etc., being the conclusion of the Epistle for the Day. Nothing could be more seasonable, and I read it as a presage of good.

Mon. 6. At ten, I met the contending parties: the preachers on one hand and the excluded members on the other. I heard them at large, and they pleaded their several causes with earnestness and calmness too. But four hours were too short to hear the whole cause, so we adjourned to the next day. Meantime, in order to judge in what state the society really was, I examined them myself, meeting part of them today and the rest on Tuesday and Wednesday. Four and thirty persons, I found, had been put out of or left the society; but notwithstanding, as there were last quarter four hundred and fifty-eight members, so there are just four hundred and fifty-eight still. At the desire of the members lately excluded, I now drew up the short state of the case, but I could in no wise pacify them. They were all civil, nay it seemed affectionate to *me*, but they could never forgive the preachers that had expelled them—so that I could not desire them to return into the society; they could only remain friends at a distance.

Thur. 9. I was desired by some of our friends to clear up the point of *imputed righteousness*;[35] I did so by preaching on, 'Abraham believed God, and it was imputed to him for righteousness.'[36] In opening these words I showed what *that faith* was which was imputed to *him* for righteousness, *viz.*, faith in God's promise to

---

[33] Orig., 'M'Kenny'; James McKenny, hosier and haberdasher, 68 Stephen Street, Dublin. *WHS* 5 (1905):77.

[34] John 9:4.

[35] JW had published a leaflet, *Thoughts on the Imputed Righteousness of Christ* on this very subject at Dublin in 1762.

[36] Jas. 2:23 (*Notes*); Rom. 4:3 (*Notes*).

'give him the land of Canaan',[37] faith in the promise that 'Sarah should conceive a son',[38] and the faith whereby 'he offered up Isaac on the altar.'[39] But Christ is not in any of these instances the direct or immediate object of Abraham's faith, whereas he is the direct, immediate object of that faith which is *imputed to us* for   5 righteousness.

Sat. 11. I visited many, sick and well, and endeavoured to confirm them in their love towards each other. I was more and more convinced that God had sent me at this time, to heal the breach of his people.   10

Sun. 12. We had a lovely congregation in the morning to whom I closely applied St. Peter's words, 'I exhort you as strangers and pilgrims, abstain from fleshly desires which war against the soul.'[40] To the mixed multitude in the evening, I applied our Lord's words, 'All things are ready; come unto the marriage.'[41] I   15 then took a solemn and affectionate leave of the society and cheerfully commended them to the Great Shepherd, more in number and, I am persuaded, more established in grace than they had been for twenty years.

Mon. 13. In the morning we went on board, but the wind being   20 right a–head and blowing hard, we made but little way till night, and the sea was so rough that I could not sleep till midnight. Tuesday 14. After beating up and down several hours more, the captain thought best to run under the Caernarvonshire shore. About noon, we put out to sea again, but the storm increased and,   25 about four, carried away our bowsprit and tore one of the sails to tatters. But the damage was soon repaired, and before six, by the good providence of God, we landed at Holyhead.

Wanting to be in London as soon as possible, I took chaise at seven and hastened to Bangor Ferry.[42] But here we were at a full   30 stop; they could not, or would not, carry us over till one the next day, and they then gave us only two miserable horses, although I had paid *beforehand* (fool as I was)[43] for four. At Conway Ferry we were stopped again, so that with all the speed we could possibly

[37] Cf. Gen. 17:8. etc.
[38] Cf. Gen. 21:2.
[39] Cf. Gen. 22:2, 9.
[40] Cf. 1 Pet. 2:11 (*Notes*).
[41] Matt. 22:4.
[42] From here on October 15, JW wrote back to Mrs. Wm. Smyth in Dublin, giving a full account of the adventurous voyage. Telford, 6:282–83.
[43] A reminiscence of *stultus ego* in Virgil *Eclogues*, I.20, 21.

make, even with a chaise and four, we travelled eight and twenty miles yesterday, and seventeen today! Thursday in the afternoon, we reached Chester; Friday morning, Lichfield; and on Saturday morning, London.

5   Mon. 20. I went to High Wycombe; but good Mr. James,[44] having procured a drummer to beat his drum at the window of the preaching-house, I only prayed and sung by turns from six to seven—and many of the people were much comforted. In the rest of the week I visited the societies at Oxford, Witney, Finstock,
10   and Wallingford, and had reason to believe that many received the seed in honest and good hearts.

Mon. 27. I preached at Stony Stratford; the congregation was large and attentive. So it always is, yet I fear they receive little good for they 'need no repentance'.[45] Tuesday, I preached at Tow-
15   cester; on Wednesday, at Whittlebury; and on Thursday, at Northampton. And some of even that heavy congregation seemed to feel 'The night cometh, when no man can work.'[46]

Monday, November 3. I began visiting the classes in London, in which I was fully employed for seven or eight days. Afterwards,
20   I visited those in the neighbouring towns and found reason to rejoice over them.

Sun. 16. I was desired to preach a charity sermon in St. Margaret's Church, Rood Lane.[47] In the morning, I desired my friends not to come; in the afternoon it was crowded sufficiently,
25   and I believe many of them felt the word of God 'sharper than any two-edged sword'.[48]

Mon. 17. I went to Norwich and preached there in the evening; the house was far too small, the congregation being lately

---

[44] Perhaps James Price, B. A., vicar of Wycombe, 1763–88, and four times mayor of the town. Henry Kingston, *The History of Wycombe* (Wycombe, 1848), p. 81; Thomas Langley, *History and Antiquities of the Hundred of Desborough* (London, 1797), pp. 84–85.

[45] Luke 15:7.   [46] John 9:4.

[47] St. Margaret Pattens, built by Wren (1684–89), was crowned by one of his most remarkable towers (1698–1702), and with a west front on Rood Lane. This church which possesses some of the earliest post-Reformation plate, is now a clergy centre for the sees of London, Southwark and Chelmsford. The incumbent at this time was Peter Whalley M.A., D.D. (1723–76), who matriculated from St. John's College, Oxford, in 1740, graduating B.A. in 1744, and B.C.L. in 1768. He was Master of Christ's Hospital in 1768 and subsequently of St. Olave's school, Southwark, and from 1766 rector of St. Margaret Pattens, and St. Gabriel Fenchurch, and vicar of Horley, Surrey. He edited Thomas Bridge's *History and Antiquities of Northamptonshire* (2 vols., 1762–91) and the works of Johnson. Eliza Wesley, daughter of Samuel Wesley and sister of Samuel Sebastian Wesley, was organist at this church, 1846–86.

[48] Heb. 4:12.

increased very considerably. But I place no dependence in this people, they wave to and fro like the waves of the sea.

Wed. 19. I went over to Loddon and preached at one to a much more settled congregation. In the evening, I preached at Norwich and afterwards administered the Lord's Supper to the society. And I was almost persuaded that they will no longer be tossed to and fro with every wind of doctrine.[49]

Thur. 20. Abundance of people were present at five, and we had a solemn parting. I went to [King's] Lynn the same day and, Saturday 22, taking chaise soon after twelve, reached London in the afternoon.

Sun. 23. I preached in Lewisham Church[50] for the benefit of the Humane Society, instituted for the sake of those who *seem* to be drowned, strangled, or killed by any sudden stroke. It is a glorious design, in consequence of which many have been recovered that must otherwise have inevitably perished.

Mon. 24. I spent the afternoon at Mr. Blackwell's[51] with the B[ishop] of [London].[52] His whole behaviour was worthy of a Christian bishop: easy, affable, courteous. And yet all his conversation spoke the dignity which was suitable to his character.

Having been many times desired, for near forty years, to publish a magazine, I at length complied, and now began to collect materials for it.[53] If it once begin, I incline to think it will not end but with my life.[54]

---

[49] See Eph. 4:14.

[50] This sermon was written on Friday, Nov. 21, and published as a pamphlet. In his 1809 edition of Wesley's *Works,* Joseph Benson gave it the title, 'The Reward of Righteousness', by which it is still known; see No. 99 (3:399-414 in this edn.).

[51] On Ebenezer Blackwell, see Aug. 20-21 and Feb.10, 1751 (20:398, and 379, n. 54 in this edn.).

[52] The occasion of JW's meeting the bishop, Robert Lowth, here, was that Blackwell's second wife, Mary Eden, was a niece of Mrs. Lowth. Robert Lowth (1718-87) was educated at New College, Oxford, graduating B.A. in 1733. In 1741 he was appointed professor of poetry in Oxford, and delivered learned lectures on Hebrew poetry, which were published in 1753 and frequently reprinted. In 1748, he accompanied Henry Bilson-Legge on his Berlin embassy, and in 1749 he went abroad again as tutor to two sons of the Duke of Devonshire. His preferment was then rapid. Archdeacon of Winchester in 1750, he was offered the See of Limerick in 1755, but exchanged it for the English preferments of James Leslie, which included a Durham Prebend. In 1766 he became Bishop of Oxford, being translated to London in 1777, and declined the primacy on grounds of health in 1783. For his controversy with Warburton, see Jan. 5, 1766 (22:28, n. 18 in this edn.).

[53] Cf. above, Aug. 14, 1777.

[54] In one form or another, and under various titles, the journal which JW began in 1778 as the *Arminian Magazine* lasted until 1969.

Monday, December 1. I spent some hours both morning and afternoon in visiting the sick at the west end of the town, but I could not see them all. Wednesday 3, I visited as many as I could on the north-east part of the town. I spent the evening at [Stoke] Newington with Mr. Fletcher, almost miraculously recovering from his consumption;[55] and on Thursday 4, he set out with Mr. Ireland[56] for the south of France.

Tue. 9. I visited the chief societies in Bedfordshire and Huntingdonshire, and returned by Hertford, where (for once) I saw a quiet and serious congregation. We had a larger congregation at Barnet in the evening than ever, and a greater number of communicants. Will this poor, barren wilderness at length blossom and bud as the rose?

Sat. 13. Being strongly urged to lay the first stone of the house which was going to be built at Bath, on Sunday 14, after preaching at West Street Chapel in the morning and at St. Paul's, Shadwell[57] in the afternoon, I went to Brentford. I preached at six, and taking chaise at twelve on Monday 15, easily reached Bath in the afternoon. Tuesday 16, I paid a short visit to Bristol; preached in the evening and morning following, Wednesday 17, and at one laid the foundation of the new chapel at Bath.[58] The wind was piercing cold, yet scarce any of the congregation went away before the end of the sermon. After preaching at the room in the evening, I took chaise and, the next afternoon, reached London.

Just at this time there was a combination among many of the post-chaise drivers on the Bath road, especially those that drove in the night, to deliver their passengers into each other's hands. One driver stopped at the spot they had appointed, when another waited to attack the chaise. In consequence of this many were robbed. But I had a good Protector still; I have travelled all roads

[55] On Fletcher's convalescence with the Greenwoods of Stoke Newington, see above, July 30, 1777.

[56] On James Ireland of Brislington, Bristol, see above, July 30, 1777.

[57] The incumbent, 1741–98, was Joseph Butler M.A. (1716–98).

[58] The trustees of the chapel in King Street were known as proprietors, each having a £100 share in it, a share which had to be transferred to a new trustee on the death of the original proprietor, but which might be disposed of by sale before that event. The proprietors had an annual dinner at the Christopher Inn (the cost of which was charged to the trust accounts) to settle accounts and declare a dividend. JW was a proprietor and drew his dividend, but never appeared at the dinner. *WHS* 1 (1898):127. Mary Bosanquet was present on this occasion and gives Wesley's text as Num. 23:23. She also confirmed that 'the people were very attentive, though the cold was severe'; Henry Moore, *The Life of Mrs. Mary Fletcher* (London, 1818), p. 125.

by day and by night for these forty years, and never was interrupted yet.

Thur. 25. I buried the remains of Mr. Bespham, many years master of a man-of-war. From the time he received the truth in love, he was a pattern to all that believe. His faith was full of mercy and good fruits;[59] his works shall praise him in the gates.[60]

Sat. 27. A few days since, my assistant, Mr. Baynes,[61] by far the strongest person in our family, was taken ill of a fever. He was immediately attended, both by an apothecary and a physician, but their labour was in vain: this morning God called him into the world of spirits. I had no desire to part with him, but God knew what was best both for him and me!

Wed. 31. We concluded the old year and began the new with prayer and thanksgiving. Four or five of the local preachers assisted me. I was agreeably surprised, their manner of praying being so artless and unlaboured, and yet rational and scriptural both as to sense and expression.

Thursday, January 1, 1778. We had a very solemn opportunity of renewing our covenant with God.[62] Tuesday 6, I spent an agreeable and a profitable hour with three German gentlemen, two of them Lutheran ministers, and the third, Professor of Divinity at Leipzig. I admired both their good sense, seriousness, and good breeding.[63] How few of our clergy exceed or equal them!

Mon. 19. I went over to Tunbridge Wells and preached in the large Dissenting Meeting[64] to a numerous congregation, and deep attention sat on every face. Tuesday 20, I went on through miserable roads to Robertsbridge, where an unusually large congregation was waiting. Thence, we went on to Rye, where the house

---

[59] Jas. 3:17.

[60] See Prov. 31:31.

[61] On William Baynes, see Oct. 25, 1757 (21:129, n. 6 in this edn.).

[62] On the Covenant Service see above, Aug. 6, 1755 (21:23, n. 82 in this edn.).

[63] For similar appreciative comments, so unlike the nineteenth-century stereotype of the eighteenth-century rationalist pastor, see Jan. 28, 1757 (21:84 in this edn.), and below, Jan. 12, 1779.

[64] This was the Presbyterian Meeting-House on Little Mount Sion, opened in 1720. During the pastorates of William Johnstone and Mr. Skinner (1752-84), it flourished very greatly, and was made available to the preachers of the Countess of Huntingdon (Seymour, *Huntingdon,* 2:125) as well as to JW; Methodists enjoyed its hospitality till their own chapel was built in 1812. Presbyterianism then decayed in Tunbridge Wells, and the chapel was taken over by a congregation of Independents, 1830-48. The evangelical links of this chapel continued: Primitive Methodists occupied it, 1854-57. *WHS* 10 (1915):197-99; E. F. Ellen, 'Early Presbyterianism at Tunbridge Wells', *Journal of the Presbyterian Historical Society of England* 2 (1920-21):222-24.

was sufficiently crowded as usual. How large a society would be here, could *we* but spare them in *one* thing![65] Nay, but then all our labour would be in vain. One sin allowed would intercept the whole blessing.

5　　Mr. Holman's widow being extremely desirous I should lodge at Cadborough[66] two miles from Rye, I ordered my chaise to take me up at the preaching-house immediately after the service. She had sent a servant to show me the way, which was a road dirty and slippery enough cast up between two impassable marshes; the

10　man waited awhile and then went home, leaving us to guide ourselves. Many rough journeys I have had, but such a one as this I never had before; it was one of the darkest nights I ever saw; it blew a storm, and yet poured down with rain. The descent in going out of the town was near as steep as the ridge of a house; as soon as we

15　had passed it, the driver being a stranger, knew not which way to turn. Joseph Bradford,[67] whom I had taken into the chaise, perceiving how things were, immediately got out and walked at the head of the horses (who could not possibly keep their eyes open, the rain so violently beating in their faces) through rain, wind, mud, and water,

20　till in less than an hour he brought us safe to Cadborough.

Wednesday 21. I went back to Shoreham. Mr. P[erronet],[68] though in his eighty-fifth year, is still able to go through the whole Sunday service. How merciful is God to the poor people of Shoreham! And many of them are not insensible of it.

25　　Monday, February 2. I had the satisfaction of spending an hour with that real patriot, Lord [Dartmouth].[69] What an unheard of

---

[65] See Nov. 22, 1773 (22:393 in this edn.): 'They will not part with the accursed thing, smuggling.'

[66] Orig., 'Carborough'. The hospitable widow was Priscilla, widow of John Holman, June 1, who died in 1777, and who herself died in 1780. See Dec. 11, 1769.

[67] On Joseph Bradford, see June 17, 1775 (22:457, n. 4 in this edn.).

[68] On Vincent Perronet, see Aug. 14, 1744 (20:35, n. 74 in this edn.).

[69] William Legge, second Earl of Dartmouth (1731-1801), president of the Board of Trade, 1765-66; Secretary State for the Colonies 1772-75; Lord Privy Seal, 1775-82; Lord Steward of the Household, April-December 1783. Dartmouth was the leading evangelical aristocrat of day, was thought of to take charge of the work of the Countess of Huntingdon, had she not come through her serious illness in 1767, and by his kindness and church patronage was of great service to evangelical clergy in the establishment. JW's encomium of him as a 'real patriot', however, was based on the fact that after first taking office with the Rockingham Whigs, he stayed on in the government of Lord North, with whom he had travelled abroad as a young man, and after wavering a good deal on the American issue came (like JW) finally to the view that there was no avoiding the use of force. JW wrote him letters on the state of the nation in 1775, knowing that religion formed a bond between him and the King, George III.

thing it is, that even in a court he should retain all his sincerity! He is indeed (what I doubt Secretary Craggs[70] never was):

Statesman, yet friend to truth.[71]

Perhaps no prince in Europe, besides King George, is served by two of the honestest and two of the most sensible men[72] in his kingdom!   5
This week I visited the society and found a surprising difference in their worldly circumstances. Five or six years ago, one in three among the lower ranks of people was out of employment, and the case was supposed to be nearly the same through all London and Westminster. I did not now, after all the tragical outcries   10
of want of trade that fill the nation, find one in ten out of business—nay, scarce one in twenty, even in Spitalfields.
Sun. 15. I buried the remains of Richard Bourke,[73] a faithful labourer in our Lord's vineyard; a more unblameable character I have hardly known. In all the years that he has laboured with us, I   15
do not remember that he ever gave me occasion to find fault with

[70] James Craggs the younger (1686–1721), after a brief diplomatic career, rose rapidly through the confidence of Marlborough and Sunderland to become Secretary of State for the Southern Department at the time of the split in the Whig Party in 1718, becoming an inveterate enemy of Hanoverian influence in the British government. An effective man of business and a debater, he was believed by the opposition to be (like his father) deeply implicated in the South Sea scandal. Before there could be revelations, however, Craggs died in March 1721, perhaps by suicide, having already outlived by a month his son, who had fallen victim to smallpox.
[71] This quotation is part of Pope's epitaph 'On James Craggs, Esq.', in Westminster Abbey, and also forms the close of 'To Mr. Addison', Epistle VII in *Epistles to Several Persons (Moral Essays,* 1781). On the monument see Pevsner, *London,* 1:418.
[72] The Earl of Dartmouth and Lord North. Frederick North, Lord North (1732–93), after taking over the government in 1780, successfully reconstituted a court party which restored stability to English politics until its reputation was damaged by failures in the American War of Independence, and it was weakened by some losses in the election of 1780. North finally resigned in 1782, the King regarding this as an act of desertion. North for his part entered on a course of opposition, which was broken only by the brief and bitter interlude in office of the Fox-North coalition in 1783. That JW could in one paragraph sing the 'patriot' virtues and applaud Lord North, illustrates both how greatly his judgment had been affected by the outbreak of the American War, and why he could be regarded as angling for preferment. In terms of propaganda, 1778 was indeed a bad year for him; in addition to the continuing Calvinist controversy, and a clash of arms with Thomas Maxfield, JW had to bear a good deal of popular ridicule. Green, *Anti-Methodist Publications,* Nos. 505-20.
[73] Orig., 'Burke'. This preacher was stationed in 1765 variously as Burk, Burke, and Bourke, but his own signature of 1771 used the last spelling. Atmore (*Memorial,* p. 71) adds little to the splendidly succinct tribute to 'Bourke' in the Conference minutes of 1778: 'a man of faith and patience, made perfect through sufferings, one who joined the wisdom and calmness of age with the simplicity of childhood'.

him in anything. He was a man of unwearied diligence and patience, and 'his works do follow him.'[74]

Tue. 17. I wrote *A Serious Address to the Inhabitants of England*[75] with regard to the present state of the nation, so strangely misrep-
5 resented both by ignorant and designing men; to remove, if possible, the apprehensions which have been so diligently spread, as if it were on the brink of ruin.

Thur. 26. I committed to the earth the remains of George Parsons. He has left very few like him, so zealously, so humbly, so
10 unreservedly devoted to God. For some time his profiting has appeared to all men;[76] he ripened apace for eternity.[77] He was as a flame of fire wherever he went, losing no occasion of speaking or working for God; so he finished his course in the midst of his years and was quickly removed into the garner.

15 Friday 27 was the day appointed for the National Fast, and it was observed with due solemnity: all shops were shut up, all was quiet in the streets, all places of public worship were crowded, no food was served up in the King's house till five o'clock in the evening. Thus far at least we acknowledge God may direct our paths![78]

20 Sunday, March 1, I preached at Brentford in the evening; Monday 2, at Newbury; and the next evening, at Bath. Wednesday 4, I went on to Bristol. I found the panic had spread hither also, as if the nation were on the brink of ruin.[79] Strange that those who love God should be so frightened at shadows! I can compare
25 this only to the alarm which spread through the nation in King William's time, that on that very night the Irish Papists were to cut the throats of all the Protestants in England.[80]

---

[74] Cf. Rev. 14:13.

[75] See *Bibliography*, No. 386. Wesley's eventual title used 'People' for 'Inhabitants'. In this pamphlet JW made extensive use of the arguments of Josiah Tucker, dean of Gloucester (on whom see 19:86, n. 72 in this edn.), an anti-Methodist writer a generation earlier, to argue that the American War was not proving ruinous to Britain. What might prove disastrous was the 'ignorance, yea, contempt of God [which] is the present characteristic of the English nation'.

[76] See 1 Tim. 4:15.

[77] See John Flavel: 'ripening apace for heaven'; *Husbandry Spiritualized*, in *Works* (4th edn., London, 1740), 2:272.

[78] See Prov. 3:6.

[79] 'The nation has leaped from outrageous war to a most humiliating supplication for peace, with as little emotion as one passes in an ague from a shivering fit to a burning one.' Horace Walpole to Sir Horace Mann, Mar. 5, 1778, *Horace Walpole's Correspondence* (Yale edn.), 24:359.

[80] In December 1688 London, especially, was in the grip of one of the recurrent Catholic panics that were a feature of British history, especially in the period when the

Mon. 9. On this and the following days, I visited the society and found a good increase. This year I myself (which I have seldom done) chose the preachers for Bristol; and these were plain men and likely to do more good than has been done in one year for these twenty years.[81]

Fri. 13. I spent an hour with the children at Kingswood, many of whom are truly desirous to save their souls.[82]

Mon. 16. I took a cheerful leave of our friends at Bristol and set out once more for Ireland. After visiting Stroud, Gloucester, and Tewkesbury, on Wednesday 18, I went over to Bewdley and preached about noon at the upper end of the town to most of the inhabitants of it.

Thur. 19. I preached to a large congregation in the church at Bengeworth and spent a little time very agreeably with the rector, a pious, candid, sensible man.[83] In the evening, I preached at Peb-

Puritan menace began to fade. At this moment 'a bold man ventured to . . . publish another declaration in the prince [of Orange]'s name. . . . It set forth the desperate designs of the papists, and the extreme danger the nation was in by their means, and required all persons immediately to fall on such papists as were in any employments, and to turn them out, and to secure all strong places, and to do everything else that was in their power in order to execute the laws, and to bring all things again into their proper channels. . . . It was never known who was the author of so bold a thing. . . . The King was under such a consternation that he neither knew what to resolve on, nor whom to trust. The pretended declaration put the city in such a flame, that it was carried to the Lord Mayor, and he was required to execute it. The apprentices got together, and were falling upon all mass-houses, and committing many irregular things. Yet their fury was so well governed, and so little resisted that no other mischief was done; no blood was shed. . . . The prospect from Ireland was more dreadful. Tyrconnel gave out new commissions for levying thirty thousand men. And reports were spread about that island, that a general massacre of the Protestants was fixed to be November.' Gilbert Burnet, *History of his Own Time* (London, 1875), pp. 503-10; T. B. Macaulay, *History of England from the Accession of James II*, 3 vols. (Everyman edn., London, 1906), 2:112-13.

[81] In this sentence, clearly penned long after the event (this journal extract concludes in 1779 and was not published till 1783), JW leaps ahead to the summer Conference and the events which followed it. The three preachers he appointed were John Goodwin (the existing superintendent), James Wood, and John Valton. The latter describes the sequel. He did not want to come 'being awed at the idea of standing before so many wise and holy persons as there were in Bristol and Bath. . . . But [JW] still kept to his appointment in spite of all remonstrances. . . . I have cause to rejoice that I had in Mr. John Goodwin and Mr. James Wood the kindest of colleagues. In Paulton the work broke out wonderfully; and about eighty souls were added to the society and a preaching-house was soon afterwards erected. The effect of the word upon the poor colliers was such as I had never witnessed before. At Fishponds, also, we had a blessed revival of religion. This was indeed, a year of consolation' (Jackson, *Early Methodist Preachers*, 6:97-98).

[82] On revivals among the children at Kingswood, see May 5, 1768, and Sept. 16-29, 1770 (22:129-31, 251-54).

[83] On Beale, rector of Bengeworth, see above, July 5, 1777.

worth Church, but I seemed out of my element. A long anthem was sung, but I suppose none beside the singers could understand one word of it. Is not that 'praying in an unknown tongue'?[84] I could no more bear it in any church of mine than Latin prayers.

5   Fri. 20. I preached at Birmingham. Saturday 21, calling at Wolverhampton, I was informed that 'some time since, a large, old house was taken, three or four miles from the town, which receives all the children that come, sometimes above four hundred at once. They are taught *gratis*, reading, writing, and popery 10 and, when at age, bound out apprentices.'[85]

In the evening, I preached in the shell of the new house at Newcastle-under-Lyme; and thence hastened forward, through Burslem, Congleton, Macclesfield, and Stockport, to Manchester. I found it needful here also to guard honest Englishmen 15 against the vast terror which had spread far and wide. I had designed going from hence to Chester in order to embark at Parkgate, but a letter from Mr. Wagner informing me that a pacquet was ready to sail from Liverpool, I sent my horses forward and followed them in the morning. But before I came thither the wind 20 turned west. So I was content.

Sun. 22. I was much refreshed by two plain, useful sermons, at St. Thomas's Church,[86] as well as by the serious and decent behaviour of the whole congregation. In the evening, I exhorted all of our society who had been bred up in the church to continue 25 therein.

Tue. 31. We went on board the *Duke of Leinster*,[87] and fell down the river with a small side wind. But in the morning, after a dead calm, a contrary wind arose and blew exceeding hard. Wednesday, April 1. The sea was rough enough. However, I went to sleep

---

[84] See 1 Cor. 14:13, 14.

[85] This school, designed to cater for boys 'whose parents were in more confined circumstances than those of Standon Lordship' (later St. Edmund's College), was created by Bishop Challoner (on whom see 19:319, n. 69 in this edn.) at Betley near Newcastle-under-Lyme in 1762 against much Catholic lay opposition. On Lady Day 1763, the boys were moved in a covered waggon to Sedgley Park, a property rented from Lord Ward, who had to face some lively exchanges in Parliament for his action. Over the years the greater part of the Catholic clergy of the Midlands and many prominent laymen were educated here, but JW exaggerates the numbers attending by a factor of four. E. H. Burton, *The Life and Times of Bishop Challoner*, 2 vols. (London, 1909), 2:35-38; F. C. Husenbeth, *History of Sedgley Park School, Staffs.* (London, 1856), pp. 8-15.

[86] On which, see Apr. 24, 1757 (21:94, n. 64 in this edn.).

[87] Captain Pearson; *WHS* 5 (1905):77. Two months later, leaving Dublin 'with 200 haymakers and other passengers', this packet sprung a leak and foundered, though without loss of life.

about my usual time, and in the morning found myself in Dublin Bay, and about seven we landed at the Quay.

I was soon informed that one of our friends, a strong, lively, healthy man, Mr. Ham, had died the day before. From the time he was taken ill he was a mere self-condemned sinner, deeply con- 5 vinced of his unfaithfulness to God, and declaring:

> I give up every plea beside,
> Lord, I am damned; but thou hast died.[88]

'When my wife dies', said he, 'let her be carried to the Room; she has been an honour to her profession. But I will not, I am not 10 worthy; I have been no credit to you.' He continued full of self-condemnation, till after a week's illness his spirit returned to God.[89]

I daily conversed with many of the society and had the satisfaction to find them both more united together and more alive to 15 God than they had been for some years. Saturday, I began meeting the classes and was agreeably surprised. I had heard that near a hundred persons had left the society; on strict inquiry I found about forty were wanting—the present number being about four hundred and sixty—and therefore were more loving and unani- 20 mous than I ever knew them before.

Sun. 5. Meeting the society in the evening, I largely explained the reasons of the late separation[90] and strongly exhorted all our brethren 'not to *render railing for railing*'.[91]

Tue. 7. I set out for the country and reached Tyrrellspass. It 25 being a mild evening, I preached to a numerous congregation. The next evening it was larger still, and the power of the Lord was present to heal.[92]

Thur. 9. Between eight and nine, I preached in the court-house at Mullingar to a more serious congregation than I ever saw there 30 before. In the evening, I preached in the court-house at Longford to a far more numerous and equally serious congregation.

Fri. 10. About eleven, I preached at Abbeyderg,[93] and before one

---

[88] John and Charles Wesley, *Hymns and Sacred Poems* (1739), p. 94; cf. *Collection of Hymns* (1780), no. 128, st. 6 (7:239 in this edn.).
[89] See Eccles. 12:7.
[90] See above, Oct. 6, 1777.
[91] Cf. 1 Pet. 3:9.
[92] Luke 5:17.
[93] Orig., 'Abbydarrig'.

set out for Athlone. The sun shone as hot as it uses to do at mid-summer. We had a comfortable time, both this evening and the next day, all being peace and harmony. Sunday 12, God spoke in his word, both to wound and to heal.[94] One young woman came to
5   me just after service, who then first rejoiced in God her Saviour.[95]

    Mon. 13. About noon, I preached at Ballinasloe to a large con-gregation, some of whom seemed to be much affected; so did many at Aughrim in the evening. Tuesday 14, I went on to Eyre-court.[96] The wind was now piercing cold, so that I could not
10 preach abroad. And there was no need, for the minister not only lent me his church but offered me a bed at his house; but I was obliged to go forward. At six in the evening, I preached at Birr to a congregation of deeply-attentive hearers.

    Wed. 15. I met many of my old friends at Coolalough and had a
15 numerous congregation in the evening. Thursday 16, I preached in the riding-house in Tullamore. The commanding officer ordered all the soldiers to be present, and attended himself with the rest of the officers, while I explained, 'Render unto Caesar the things that are Caesar's, and unto God the things that are
20 God's.'[97]

    Friday 17 (Good Friday), I preached at Tullamore in the morn-ing, and Mountmellick in the evening. Saturday 18, I preached at Portarlington in the evening, and about eight in the morning to a very genteel, yet attentive audience on 'Acquaint thyself now with
25 him, and be at peace.'[98] I returned to Mountmellick before the church began, at which I would always be present, if possible. I would fain have preached abroad in the afternoon, but the weather would not permit, so we made all the room we could in the house and had a solemn and comfortable meeting.

30   Mon. 20. Mr. Jenkins, the vicar of Maryborough,[99] read prayers, and I preached on 'Repent and believe the gospel.'[1] The congregation was far larger than when I was here before, and abundantly more attentive. Several clergymen were present and several gentlemen, but they were as serious as the poor.

---

[94] See Deut. 32:39.
[95] See Luke 1:47.
[96] On JW's friends here, see July 2, 1760 (21:266–67, n. 49 in this edn.).
[97] Cf. Matt. 22:21.
[98] Job 22:21.
[99] Thomas Jenkins had invited JW to preach in his church on Apr. 24, 1775 (22:448 in this edn.).
[1] Cf. Mark 1:15.

Tue. 21. We found the election for Parliament men had put all Kilkenny in an uproar. In consequence of this, we had a small, dead congregation. But another cause of this was the bitter and perpetual quarrels between the chief members of the society. I talked largely with the contending parties, and they promised bet- 5
ter behaviour for the time to come.

Wed. 22. I went on to Clonmel where, our room being small and the weather unfavourable for preaching abroad, we procured the largest room in the town, which was in the Quaker's work-house.[2] I had scarce sat down when a young man came and said, 10
'My father and mother send their kind respects and would be glad of thy company this evening.' His mother (now Mrs. Dudley) was my old acquaintance, Molly Stokes.[3] I went at four and spent an hour very agreeably. But much company coming in, Mr. Dudley desired I would call again in the morning. I then told him 15
what his wife was reported to say of me. He answered me, it was an utter mistake, that she had never spoke a disrespectful word concerning me.

Thur. 23. Several of our brethren from Cork met at Rathcor-mack.[4] I was glad to find Mr. Rankin with them, just arrived from 20
America.[5] When we came to Cork, the congregation was waiting, so I began without delay.

Sun. 26. I earnestly exhorted a numerous congregation at eight to 'Abstain from fleshly desires'[6]—a necessary lesson in every place, and nowhere more so than in Cork. At St. Peter's Church I 25
saw a pleasing sight, the Independent Companies, raised by pri-

[2] This may be a reference to the fact that there had been artificial attempts to stimulate the manufacture of textiles in Clonmel, which fell foul of English protectionist legislation. Samuel Lewis, *A Topographical Dictionary of Ireland*, 2 vols. (2nd edn., London, 1846), 1:356.

[3] Mary Stokes (1750–1823) was born in Bristol, the daughter of Joseph and Mary Stokes. JW much esteemed her spiritual gifts, in the early 1770s corresponding with her about their cultivation (Telford, 5:230–44, *passim*); he rebuked her harshly when she proposed to become a Quaker (ibid., 5:334–35). Undeterred, she took this step, and in 1777 married Robert Dudley of Clonmel, where JW now met her. *The Life of Mary Dudley*, ed. Hannah Dudley (London, 1825), pp. 27–31.

[4] Orig., 'Rathcormick'.

[5] On Thomas Rankin, see Sept. 8, 1765 (22:19–20, n. 82 in this edn.). After he and George Shadford left America in 1778, only Francis Asbury of the ten American appointments made by JW was left. At the Conference of 1782, Asbury was given charge of the American work on the double ground of election by the preachers and JW's 'original appointment', a curious foreshadowing of the Christmas Conference of 1784.

[6] 1 Pet. 2:11 (*Notes*).

vate persons associating together without any expense to the government.[7] They exercised every day and, if they answer no other
end, at least keep the Papists in order, who were exceedingly alert
ever since the army was removed to America.

5   Mon. 27. In going to Bandon, I read Abbé Raynal's[8] *History of
the Settlements and Trade of the Europeans in the Indies*.[9] I would be
glad to propose a few queries. I ask, (1) Is not this *Philosophical
History* (so called) in many parts profoundly dull—exactly fitted to
spread a pleasing slumber over the eyes of the gentle reader? (2)
10 Are there not several passages quite obscure? Is this the fault of the
author, or the translator? (3) Are there not several assertions which
are false in fact? Such as that of the healthiness of Batavia? —one
of the unhealthiest places in the known world. (4) Do not many of
his assertions so border upon the marvellous that none but a disci-
15 ple of Voltaire[10] could swallow them? As the account of milk-white
men, with no hair, red eyes, and the understanding of a monkey?
(5) Is not Raynal one of the bitterest enemies of the Christian revelation that ever set pen to paper? Far more determined and less
decent than Voltaire himself? As where he so keenly inveighs
20 against that horrid *superstition*, the depriving men of their *natural
liberty* of whoredom! Does he not take every opportunity of
wounding Christianity, through the sides of *superstition* or *enthusi-*

---

[7] When armed conflict began in America in 1775, Irish and Scots-Irish were prominent in it, and the whole British opposition saw the conflict as an extension of their own
struggle. There was therefore bound to be a vivid Irish response, the more so as the
American war encouraged the government to recruit Catholic troops (the Catholics
being among the government's few friends) and to forbid the export of Irish provisions.
The demands of the American war and the need to concentrate what units there were in
the south led to the formation of volunteer corps in West Cork as early as 1774, and by
1778 there were said to be thirty-eight corps in Cork and Tipperary alone; in due course
a few Catholics were here accepted into the volunteers. Not surprisingly Dr. Johnson
'called it rebellion', and the movement created serious problems for the government,
which found it hard to profit in Ireland from the fact that a high proportion of American loyalists were also Irish, and that two Irish units were formed for American service.
R. B. McDowell, *Ireland in the Age of Imperialism* (Oxford, 1979), pp. 238-74.

[8] Orig., 'Resnal'—as again in sections (5) and (6).

[9] Abbé G. T. F. Raynal, *A Philosophical History of the Settlements and Trade of the
Europeans in the East and West Indies*, J. Justamond, tr. (London, 1776). Some of JW's
criticisms are a matter of taste, but the conclusion of the work (4:392-93) gives grounds
for his more vitriolic attacks. Religion (it is alleged) is the simple creation of men's fears
and misfortunes, and Christianity only gained a grip on men because of the troubles
entailed on them by the overthrow of the Roman republic and the evils of the empire.
'But a religion that arose in the midst of public calamity must necessarily give its
preachers a considerable influence over the unfortunate persons who took refuge in it.'
The evil of sacerdotalism was there from the beginning.

[10] On whom, see Feb. 3, 1770 (22:215, n. 25 in this edn.).

asm? Is not the whole laboured panegyric on the Chinese and the Peruvians a blow at the root of Christianity? Insinuating all along that there are no Christians in the world so virtuous as these heathens? Prove this fact, and it undeniably follows that Christianity is not of God. But who can prove it? Not all the baptized or unbaptized infidels in the world. From what authentic history of China is that account taken? From none that is extant; it is pure romance flowing from the Abbé's fruitful brain. And from what authentic history of Peru is the account of the Peruvians taken? I suppose from that pretty novel of Marmontel,[11] probably wrote with the same design. (6) Is not Raynal one of the most bitter enemies of *monarchy* that ever set pen to paper? With what acrimony does he personally inveigh against it as absolutely, necessarily, essentially subversive, not only of liberty, but of all national industry, all virtue, all happiness? And who can deny it? Who? The Abbé himself? He totally confutes his own favourite hypothesis. For was not Atahualpe[12] a monarch? Yea, a far more absolute one than the King of France? And yet was not Peru industrious, virtuous, and happy under this very monarch? So the Abbé peremptorily affirms, as it were on purpose to confute himself. And is not the Emperor of China, at this day, as absolute a monarch as any in Europe? And yet who so industrious, according to Raynal, who so virtuous, so happy as his subjects?—so that he must totally give up either his argument against Christianity, or that against monarchy. If the Peruvians were, and the Chinese are, the most industrious, virtuous and happy men, then monarchy is no way inconsistent with the industry, virtue, and happiness of a people. But if the Peruvians were, in these respects, and the Chinese are, no better than other men (which is the very truth), then the argument against Christianity falls to the ground.

From the largeness and seriousness of the congregation here I should have imagined the work of God was much increased, but upon inquiry I found just the contrary; near one-third of those

[11] Orig., 'Marmontell'. Jean François Marmontel, *Les Incas, ou la Description de L'empire de Perou* (Paris, 1777; Eng. tr. Dublin, 1777). Marmontel, an Encyclopaedist, attacked the brutality of the Spaniards on grounds that could hardly be palatable to JW: 'Les partisans du fanatisme s'efforcent de le confondre avec la religion: c'est là leur sophisme éternel. Les vrais amis de la religion la séparent du fanatisme, et tachent de la délivrer de ce serpent caché et nourri dans son sein. Tel est le dessein qui m'anime'(1:xxv).

[12] Orig. 'Atabalipe'. Atahualpa, or Atahuallpa (1500?-1533), the last Inca king of Peru. See William Prescott, *History of the Conquest of Peru* (1847).

were wanting whom I left in the society three years ago, yet those who remained seemed much in earnest. In the evening, God clothed his word with power; few appeared to be unaffected. And I was sorry I could not spend a little more time where 'the fields' were so 'white to the harvest'.[13]

Wed. 29. I returned to Cork and met the classes. O when will even the Methodists learn not to exaggerate! After all the pompous accounts I had had of the vast increase of the society, it is not increased at all; nay, it is a little smaller than it was three years ago. And yet many of the members are alive to God. But the smiling world hangs heavy upon them.

Sunday, May 3. I was a little surprised at a message from the gentlemen of the Aughrim society (a company of volunteers[14] so called), that if I had 'no objection', they 'would attend at the New Room in the evening'. They did so, with another independent company, who were just raised, The True Blues. A body of so personable men I never saw together before: the gentlemen in scarlet filled the side gallery, those in blue, the front gallery; but both galleries would not contain them all; some were constrained to stand below. All behaved admirably well, though I spoke exceeding plain on, 'We preach Christ crucified.'[15] No laughing, no talking; all seemed to hear as for life. Surely this is a token for good.[16]

Mon. 4. I went to Kilfinnane,[17] in the neighborhood of which there is a considerable revival of the work of God. The rain continuing, I preached in a large, empty house, and again at five in the morning. Probably I shall see that no more in the present world.[18] We then went on, through abundance of rain, to Limerick.

I felt in the evening the spirit of the congregation the same as many years ago, but in one circumstance I observed a considerable change. I used to have large congregations at my first coming to Limerick, but from the first day they gradually decreased. It was not so now, but poor and rich, Protestants and Papists, flocked together from the beginning to the end. Had they a presage that they should see my face no more?[19]

---

[13] Cf. John 4:35.
[14] On the volunteers, see above, Apr. 26, 1778.
[15] 1 Cor. 1:23.
[16] See Ps. 86:17.
[17] Orig., 'Killfinnan'.
[18] Edn. C (?1791) omits this sentence. In fact, JW preached at Kilfinnane again three times on May 13, 1778, May 14, 1787, and May 11, 1789. See below.
[19] Edn. C (?1791) omits this sentence.

Thur. 7. I preached once more to the loving, earnest, simple-hearted people of Newmarket. Two months ago, good Philip Guier[20] fell asleep, one of the Palatines that came over and settled in Ireland between sixty and seventy years ago. He was a father both to this and the other German societies, loving and cherishing them as his own children. He retained all his faculties to the last and, after two days illness, went to God.

Fri. 8. Finding the poor people at Ballingarrane,[21] whom I had not seen these five years, were very desirous to see me once more, I went over in the morning. Although the notice was exceeding short, yet a large number attended.

Sat. 9. I wrote *A Compassionate Address to the Inhabitants of Ireland*[22]—through which, as well as through England, the mock-patriots had laboured to spread the alarm, as though we were all on the very brink of destruction.

Sun. 10. I examined the society and have not known them for many years so much alive to God! And I do not remember to have ever found them so loving before—indeed the whole city seemed to breathe the same spirit. At three in the afternoon, I preached my farewell sermon on 1 Cor. 13:13, and setting out immediately, reached Snugborough[23] before eight o'clock.

Tue. 12. Setting out early, I intended to lodge at Claregalway, but we found there was no lodging to be had. However, they told us there was a good inn at Shrule,[24] not many miles farther; and

[20] Orig., 'Geier'. When the Palatine community (see May 12, 1749; 20:272, n. 75 in this edn.) began to go morally downhill, Philip Guier was among those who sought to reclaim them. Master of the German school at Ballingarrane, he was made JW's first local preacher in 1752. Among his scholars, educationally and spiritually, were Philip Embury (see June 23, 1758; 21:155, n. 6 in this edn.) and Thomas Walsh (see Sept. 2, 1752; 20:438-39, n. 47 in this edn.). An active preacher out of school, he was supported by gifts in kind from his flock. Among the more charming legends attaching to Irish Methodism is the story that even a century after his death 'Romanists as well as Protestants were accustomed to salute the Methodist minister as he jogged along on his horse [to Ballingarrane], and to say "There goes Philip Guier who drove the devil out of Ballingarrane." ' Tyerman, *John Wesley*, 2:146; Crookshank, *Ireland*, 1:57.

[21] Orig., 'Ballingrane'.

[22] See *Bibliography*, No. 387 (Jackson, 11: 148-54). This pamphlet, published in June as part of JW's anti-radical and anti-American crusade, is a sort of jeremiad in reverse. JW held that though the international and the domestic situations were threatening, they were not as bad as they were made out; and, more importantly, that if God would spare Sodom should ten righteous men be found in it, he would certainly spare a Britain in which 'religion, true scriptural religion . . . [was] continually increasing in every part of the kingdom'.

[23] Orig., 'Snegborough'.

[24] Orig., 'Shreuil'.

there we found a house, but it afforded no food either for man or beast. So we were obliged to push on for Ballinrobe, which we reached about eleven o'clock. We came this day sixty-eight (English) miles—a good day's work for a pair of horses.

5   Wed. 13. I preached in the evening to a large congregation, but most of them dead as stones. The next morning, I crossed over to Hollymount and preached to more than the house would contain. In the afternoon, we came to Castlebar and had a lively congregation in the evening. Here we found the same spirit as at Limerick
10   and solemnly rejoiced in God our Saviour.[25]

Sun. 17. Although the weather was rough and boisterous, the people flocked at nine from all quarters, Papists and Protestants, and God sent down a gracious rain, especially upon the backsliders. In the evening, the court-house was exceedingly crowded,
15   and the fire of love ran from heart to heart. One eminent backslider,[26] who had drank in iniquity like water, was utterly broken in pieces and resolved to cut off the right hand at once and to be altogether a Christian.

When we came into the house I told them, 'God has more work
20   to do in this family.' Two of John Carr's[27] sons and four of his daughters were present. I prayed for them in faith; they were all soon in tears, their hearts were broken, and I left them mere sinners.

Mon. 18. There were two roads to Sligo, one of which was several miles shorter, but had some sloughs in it. However, having a
25   good guide, we chose this. Two sloughs we got over well; on our approaching the third, seven or eight countrymen presently ran to help us: one of them carried me over on his shoulders, others got the horses through, and some carried the chaise. We then thought the difficulty was past, but in half an hour we came to another
30   slough. Being helped over it, I walked on, leaving Mr. Delap,[28]

[25] See Luke 1:47.
[26] This episode doubtless led JW to write his sermon, *A Call to Backsliders*, which was dated 'Sligo, May 20, 1778', and published at Dublin the following June (see Sermon 86, 3:211-26 in this edn.). This pamphlet, like the *Compassionate Address*, offered a message of hope; many indeed perished through presumption, but many more perished from despair, 'thinking it impossible they should escape destruction'. Against this JW insists that 'there can be no analogy or proportion between the mercy of any of the children of men and that of the most high God.' Even some who had fallen from sanctifying grace had been restored.
[27] John Carr was an Irish local preacher. Crookshank, *Ireland*, 1:180.
[28] Andrew Delap, Irish itinerant 1774-78. He was the orphaned son of a naval officer, brought up by his uncle Samuel, the county treasurer of Donegal. Of good education and pleasing personality, his professional prospects were much injured by a severe

John Carr, Jos[eph] Bradford,[29] and Jesse Bugden,[30] with the chaise, which was stuck fast in the slough. As none of them thought of unharnessing the horses, the traces were soon broke. At length they fastened ropes to the chaise and to the stronger horse; and the horse pulling and the men thrusting at once, they thrust it through the slough to the firm land. In an hour or two after, we all met at Ballynacarrow.[31]

While I was walking, a poor man overtook me, who appeared to be in deep distress. He said he owed his landlord twenty shillings rent, for which he had turned him and his family out of doors, and that he had been down with his relations to beg their help, but they would do nothing. Upon my giving him a guinea, he would needs kneel down in the road to pray for me, and then cried out, 'Oh! I shall have a house, I shall have a house over my head!' So perhaps God answered that poor man's prayer by the sticking fast of the chaise in the slough!

Tue. 19. In the evening, I preached at Sligo in the old courthouse, an exceeding spacious building. I know not that ever I saw so large a congregation here before, nor (considering their number) so well-behaved. Will God revive his work even in this sink of wickedness? And after so many deadly stumbling-blocks!

Upon inquiry, I found, there had been for some time a real revival of religion here.[32] The congregation have considerably increased, and the society is nearly doubled. We had in the evening a larger congregation than before, among whom were

speech impediment, and he proposed to join an army corps about to embark for foreign service. Attending the preaching of John Smith with some irreverent fellows, he was disconcerted by Smith's prophecy that he would become a preacher, and his conversion soon afterwards was completed by the preaching of a lady Quaker. Against family opposition, he joined the Methodists and began to accompany John Smith on his rounds. Convinced that he should become a preacher, Delap prayed to be released from his speech impediment; his prayer was answered, and he entered the itinerancy in 1774. He disappears from the stationing minutes in 1779.

[29] On Joseph Bradford's personal relation to JW, see June 17, 1775 (22:457 and n. 9 in this edn.).

[30] Jesse Bugden was an Irish local preacher. Crookshank, *Ireland*, 1:318.

[31] Orig., 'Ballinacurrah'.

[32] After a division in the Sligo circuit, the Methodists turned from controversy to evangelism, and evoked a good deal of confessional violence. Charles Graham, 'the apostle of Kerry', however, called down divine wrath upon one of his assailants, whose death within a week put an end to assaults on the preachers. In the four years 1778-82 the membership at Sligo virtually trebled, and the circuit was again divided. 'Numbers were led to seek and obtain the pearl of perfect love'; Crookshank, *Ireland*, 1:319; W. Graham Campbell, *The Apostle of Kerry; or, The Life of Charles Graham* (Dublin, 1868), pp. 28-29.

most of the gentry of the town. And all but one or two young gentlemen (so called) were remarkably serious and attentive.

I now received an intelligible account of the famous massacre at
Sligo.[33] A little before the Revolution, one Mr. Morris, a popish
gentleman, invited all the chief Protestants to an entertainment.
At the close of which, on a signal given, the men he had prepared
fell upon them and left not one of them alive. As soon as King
William prevailed, he quitted Sligo. But venturing thither about
twenty years after, supposing no one then knew him, he was discovered and used according to his deserts.

Thur. 21. I went on to Peter Taylor's near Swanlinbar.[34] At six,
I preached in a large room in the town, designed for an assembly,
where rich as well as poor behaved with the utmost decency.

Fri. 22. We went through a lovely country to Belturbet,[35] once
populous, now greatly decayed. At eleven, I preached in the
Armoury, a noble room, to a very large and very serious congregation. At six, I preached in the court-house at Cavan to a larger
congregation than that at Belturbet.

Sat. 23. I was desired to preach once more at Cootehill, which I
had not seen for many years. The use of the Presbyterian meeting-house being procured, I had a very extraordinary congregation. To many church-people were added Seceders, Arians,
Moravians, and what not; however, I went straight forward, insisting that 'Without holiness no man shall see the Lord.'[36]

After dinner we went on to Clones, finely situated on the top of

---

[33] A castle was built in Sligo in the thirteenth century, and the town suffered a long
history of violence at the hands of contending parties, which reached a peak during the
civil wars of the mid- and late-seventeenth century. The legend JW here relates
with such confident relish is related, *mutatis mutandis*, of the year 1641, and also of
much earlier periods when the enemies were rival septs.

[34] Peter Taylor is described by Crookshank as 'of Gortnaleg' (*Ireland*, 1:278), now
spelled Gortnahey. A good part of the Swanlinbar known to JW was destroyed by fire
in 1786, but the town remained fashionable as a spa, being 'distinguished for its mineral
waters which are strongly impregnated with sulphur, earth, sea-salt, and fossil alkali,
and in their medicinal effect are both alterative and diaphoretick: they are esteemed
highly efficacious as a restorative from debility.' Lewis, *Ireland*. 2:539.

[35] Belturbet, 12 miles from Cavan, was incorporated into a borough early in the seventeenth century, to further the plantation of Ulster. In 1618, by an indenture to the charter, Sir Stephen Butler granted endowments and privileges to the corporation, and the
corporation covenanted that the inhabitants should be ready at all times to be mustered
and trained to arms whenever required by Sir Stephen, his heirs, or assigns, or by the
Muster-master General of Ulster, or any of the king's officers duly authorised.' It
remained a barrack-town in the nineteenth century, but its commercial prosperity was
impeded by the shoals in the river Erne in dry weather.

[36] Cf. Heb. 12:14.

a hill in the midst of a fruitful and well-cultivated country, and the people seemed as sprightly as the place. I preached in the Green Fort,[37] near the town, to abundance of people, but no tri-flers. Sunday 24, I preached there again at nine to a still larger congregation, but the far largest of all was in the evening, the people coming in from all parts of the country.

There is something very peculiar in this people; they are more plain, open, and earnest, than most I have seen in the kingdom. Indeed some of our Irish societies, those in Athlone, Limerick, Castlebar, and Clones, have much of the spirit of our old York-shire societies.[38]

Mon. 25. I went through a pleasant country to Aghalun.[39] A very large congregation was soon assembled, and the rich seemed to be as attentive as the poor. So they were also in the evening at Sidaire.[40]

Tue. 26. We went on to Lisleen.[41] Wednesday 27. I received a very remarkable account from Mrs. Brown,[42] a gentlewoman in the neighbourhood. She said, 'Six years ago my daughter Jane, then seventeen years old, was struck raving mad: she would strike anyone she could, particularly her father; she cursed and swore horribly; she never slept, and let her hands be bound ever so fast over night, they were loose in the morning. The best physicians were consulted, and all means used, but to no purpose. On Thursday, December 28 last, she violently struck her father on the breast; the next day, Friday 29, she was perfectly well, without using any means at all; and she has continued ever since, not only in her senses, but full of faith and love.'

[37] 'An extensive, artificial mound of earth, very steep and rather difficult of access, being on the summit of a considerable hill'. Lewis, *Ireland*, 1:348.
[38] Crookshank notes of Clones (*Ireland*, 1:328) that 'early morning meetings were reg-ularly and numerously attended in this town, there was much life in the society, and the zeal and consistency of the members had a good influence on the community at large,' in particular in killing the subscriptions to silver plate on which the local horse-racing depended.
[39] Orig., 'Aughalan', later known as Brookeborough; see May 25, 1773 (22:371 in this edn.); see also, Crookshank, *Ireland*, 1:252 and note.
[40] Orig., 'Sidare'.
[41] Orig., 'Loghean'.
[42] Mrs. Brown, 'a respectable widow who lived at Creevy' with her son George, who became a preacher, had been impressed by Wesley's preaching at Magheralough; see June 10, 1771 (22:279, n. 10 in this edn.). She also brought a subsequently 'godly and zealous woman, Mrs. Margaret Johnstone [d. 1781]—a member of the noble family of Annadale—to religious decision'; see May 26, 1773 (22:373, n. 29 in this edn.), and Mar. 28, 1777.

Thur. 28. Between nine and ten, I preached at a village called Magheracolton[43] to a large and serious congregation, and in the evening at Londonderry. Considering the largeness and serious-ness of the congregations, I wonder no more good is done here.

5 Monday, June 1. I went over to the New Buildings and took my honourable post in the Mill-Deep;[44] attention sat on every face. So it usually does when *the poor* have the gospel preached.[45] I preached at Londonderry in the evening on 'I am not ashamed of the gospel of Christ.'[46] How happy would many of those be, if 10 they had but thoroughly learned this lesson!

Wed. 3. I took an account of the present society, a little smaller than it was three years ago. Thursday 4, I took my leave of this affectionate people, and about eleven, preached at Limavady.[47] In the afternoon, I went on to Kilrea and was cordially received by 15 Mr. Haughton, once a travelling preacher, now a magistrate and rector of a parish;[48] but the church wherein it was at first proposed I should preach is, as I found, a mere heap of ruins, so I preached in the new meeting-house,[49] a very large and commodious build-ing. Abundance of people flocked together; some of them seemed 20 not a little affected, and all were seriously attentive; surely some will bring forth good fruit.[50]

Fri. 5. We went on to Coleraine. As the barracks here are empty,[51] we hired one wing, which by laying several rooms into one, supplied us with a spacious preaching-house; but it would 25 not contain a third of the congregation; but standing at the door, I had them all before me in the barrack-square.

Sat. 6. I was desired to take a ride to the celebrated Giant's

---

[43] Orig. 'Magharacolton'.

[44] Wesley's editors, Jackson and Curnock, treated this as an error, reading '. . . in the Mill. Deep attention sat . . .'.

[45] See Matt. 11:5, etc.

[46] Rom. 1:16.

[47] Orig. 'New Town, Limaviddy'. 'This place [about 13 miles east from London-derry] has reverted to its old name of Limavady, derived from the castle of the O'Cahans on the brow of a romantic glen . . . called *Lima-vaddy* or "the Dog's Leap".' Lewis, *Ireland*, 2:401.

[48] On John Haughton, see May 21, 1750, and Aug. 10, 1756 (20:338, n. 92; and 21:73, n. 76 in this edn.). An elaborate rectory had been built by the previous incumbent in 1774, but the church was rebuilt by the Miners' Company only in the eighteenth cen-tury. Lewis, *Ireland*, 2:165.

[49] Lewis (*Ireland*, 2:165) says this was 'for Presbyterians in connexion with the Gen-eral Assembly'.

[50] See Matt. 7:17.

[51] Presumably because of the military demands of the American War.

Causeway.[52] It lies eleven English miles from Coleraine. When we came to the edge of the precipice, three or four poor boys were ready to hold our horses and show us the way down. It being dead low water, we could go anywhere and see everything to the best advantage. It is doubtless the effect of subterraneous fire. This manifestly appears from many of the stones which composed the pillars that are now fallen down; these evidently bear the mark of fire, being burned black on one or the other surface. It appears likewise from the numerous pumice stones, scattered among the pillars; just such pillars and pumices are found in every country which is or ever was subject to volcanoes.

In the evening, I saw a pleasing sight. A few days ago a young gentlewoman,[53] without the knowledge of her relations, entered into the society; she was informed this evening that her sister was speaking to me upon the same account. As soon as we came into the room she ran to her sister, fell upon her neck, wept over her, and could just say, 'O sister, sister!' before she sunk down upon her knees to praise God. Her sister could hardly bear it; she was in tears too, and so were all in the room. Such are the first-fruits at Coleraine. May there be a suitable harvest!

Sun. 7. I breakfasted with Mr. Boyd,[54] the twin soul for humility and love with Mr. Ch[apman][55] of Staplehurst, I read prayers for

[52] JW was here upon a tourist track already popularised by Mrs. Delany and the Earl-Bishop of Derry, who built a footpath for visitors. There are reckoned to be about 37,000 basalt columns in the Causeway, the southern end of a line of volcanic intrusions extending to Skye.

[53] Henry Moore, later JW's literary executor and biographer, recalls this event in a memorial to his wife (1756-1818): 'This young gentlewoman . . . was Miss Anne Young, at that time twenty-two years of age—and afterwards my beloved partner. And her sister on whose account she was so affected was Miss Isabella Young, the present Mrs. Rutherford. This affecting scene took place in one of the apartments immediately under the preaching room. The preacher who was present [presumably John Prickard, on whom see above, July 23, 1777] informed me that it was too much for Mr. Wesley. After looking on for some moments he ran into an adjoining apartment and shut the door'; *Methodist Magazine* 36 (1813):443-53. Coleraine was a Protestant town, and perhaps for that reason it had been possible to form a strong society 'of manufacturing people' without attracting any of the Presbyterian upper classes, until the Young sisters joined. Isabella Young married the preacher Thomas Rutherford (stationed at Derry in 1779) in 1780 and died in 1819; *Methodist Magazine* 31 (1808):531; 42 (1819):762-64.

[54] Charles Boyd (1708-81), educated at Trinity College, Dublin, B.A. 1731, was rector of Rothlin 1747-66, and of Killowen 1772-81. Killowen was on the other side of the River Bann from Coleraine with which it was connected by a bridge, and of which it became a suburb. Lewis, *Ireland*, 2:118.

[55] Orig., 'Sh——', apparently a misprint. The reference is to the Rev. Jacob Chapman, Presbyterian minister of Staplehurst, on whom see Nov. 2, 1763 (21:437, n. 84 in this edn.).

him and administered the Sacrament to such a number of communicants as I suppose never met there before.[56] A little before the time
of preaching, the rain ceased, and we had a wonderful congregation
in the barrack-yard in the evening. Many of them were present at
5 five in the morning, when I left them full of love and good desires.
About nine, I preached in the town hall at Ballymoney,[57] about
twelve at another little town, and in the evening at Ballymena.

Tue. 9. We rode through a small village wherein was a little
society. One desiring me to step into a house there, it was filled
10 presently; and the poor people were all ear while I gave a short
exhortation and spent a few minutes in prayer. In the evening, as
the town hall at Carrickfergus[58] could not contain the congregation, I preached in the market-house on 'Fear God and keep his
commandments, for this is the whole of man.'[59] The people in
15 general appeared to be more serious and the society more earnest
than they had been for many years.

Thence we went to Belfast,[60] the largest town in Ulster, said to
contain thirty thousand souls. The streets are well laid out, are
broad, straight, and well-built. The poorhouse stands on an emi-
20 nence, fronting the main street and having a beautiful prospect on
every side over the whole country. The old men, the old women,
the male and the female children, are all employed according to
their strength, and all their apartments are airy, sweet, and clean,
equal to anything of the kind I have seen in England.

25   I preached in the evening on one side of the new church[61] to far

---

[56] Crookshank notes (*Ireland*, 1:321) that 'the late Hon. Richard Jackson M.P. and his
excellent lady, who were present, seemed to rejoice in showing [JW] every mark of respect.'

[57] Orig., 'Ballymannely'.

[58] Here JW was met by the preacher Jonathan Kern and the stocking-weaver William
Black who accompanied him round the circuit. Crookshank, *Ireland*, 1:321.

[59] Eccles. 12:13.

[60] At this time Belfast, with about 12,000 inhabitants, was one of a group of towns
vying for the third place among Irish cities. Its great importance was as the commercial
centre of the linen industry, and it was the advantage of a port with an industrial hinter-
land, which Belfast shared (on a much more modest scale) with Glasgow and Liverpool,
that provided the basis for its meteoric growth after this time. It was the new building
which caught JW's eye. The poorhouse (1774) already bore the marks of Belfast's
industrial progress, for in 1777 two Belfast entrepreneurs set the children in it to work
on cotton-spinning, and later filled vacant rooms in the house with their machinery.
Belfast was also a dissenting capital, not unlike some of those in America. A single
parish church was outstripped by four Presbyterian churches, and the dominant Presbyterian ethos is reflected in JW's description of the place.

[61] The new church beside which JW preached was St. Anne's, built in 1777 at the
expense of the Marquess of Donegal who managed the Belfast corporation (the countess's name was Anne). It consisted 'of a nave and a chancel, with a lofty Ionic tower sur-

the largest congregation I have seen in Ireland—but I doubt the bulk of them were nearly concerned in my text, 'And Gallio cared for none of these things.'[62]

Thur. 11. About nine, I preached to five or six hundred people in the old church at Newtownards.[63] The sight of these vast buildings and large gardens running to decay through the extinction of the family that lately owned them (so successful was the scheme of those wretches who purposely educated poor Mr. C——, the last of the family, in such a manner as to ensure his not living long and his dying without issue) always makes me pensive. But still our comfort is, there is a God that judgeth the earth.[64]

About twelve, I preached at Kircubbin.[65] Thence we went to Portaferry[66] and found a ready passage to Strangford. I stood on

mounted by a Corinthian cupola covered with copper, forming one interesting and conspicuous object for many miles around' (Lewis, *Ireland*, 1:190). But the porticos had to be replaced as inferior to the rest of the building, and in the twentieth century the whole was demolished to make way for the present St. Anne's Cathedral. McDowell, *Ireland*, pp. 16, 35-37, 160; George Benn, *A History of the Town of Belfast from the Earliest Times to the Close of the Eighteenth Century*, 2 vols. (London, 1877), pp. 565-668; George Benn, *History of Belfast* (London, 1880), p. 83.

[62] Acts 18:17 (*Notes*).

[63] Orig., 'Newtown, Clannibois'. Now Newtownards, 8 miles east of Belfast. The changing name of the town reflects the history of the property. The Dominican monastery in the place passed at the Dissolution to Lord Clandeboy, by whom it was assigned to Viscount Montgomery of the Ardes. The church in which JW preached was subsequently converted into a courthouse, and replaced by a cruciform building in 1817. 'Mr. C——' was Robert Colvill (d. 1749), who sold the manors of Newtown and Mount Alexander to the Stewart family, later Marquesses of Londonderry. 'Colvill was still a minor when his mother married [Baron] Bessborough, and Bessborough managed all his affairs for him. Even after he came of age he continued to be of a suicidal disposition, "wild and indecent" in his conversation and "disordered in his understanding". In 1721 he made a will by which he left his Co. Down property to Bessborough's second son, John Ponsonby; from 1731-44 Bessborough held the manor of Newtown on which the borough stood in trust for him [and Ponsonbys frequently represented the borough in Parliament]. In 1744 the link between the Ponsonbys and Co. Down was severed. By that time Colvill had fallen entirely under the influence of his mistress, one Martha Launders, who turned him against Bessborough, and prevailed on him to sell [to Stewart] the whole of the estate which John Ponsonby was due to inherit.' A. P. W. Malcolmson, 'The Newtown Act of 1748; Revision and Reconstruction', *Irish Historical Studies* 18 (1973):317. See also *Ulster Journal of Archaeology* 5 (1899):144-45; 6 (1900):14-15.

[64] Ps. 58:11 (BCP).

[65] Orig., 'Kirkhubly'. If Lewis is right, the area was sparsely populated at this time: 'This town, which is situated on the shore of Strangford Lough, is of very recent origin, having been built since the year 1790, previously to which time there were not more than five houses in the place' (Lewis, *Ireland*, 2:197). JW was the guest of Joseph Napier of St. Andrews, who fitted up a barn for him to preach in and accompanied him on some of his rounds. *Wesleyan Methodist Magazine* 87 (1864):553.

[66] Portaferry was a substantial town on the east side of the entrance to Strangford Lough, opposite Strangford itself, with which it was linked by a ferry.

the point of a rock which projected into a large circular cavity that contained, in the hollow and round the edge of it, all the multitude who flocked together. I spoke longer than I used to do and was no more weary when I had done than I was at six in the morning. After service we went to Downpatrick, where I slept in peace.[67]

Fri. 12. I walked through the town, I suppose one of the most ancient in Ulster. I was informed, it was once abundantly larger than it is now, consisting of the Irish town, then inhabited by none but Roman Catholics, and the English town, encompassed with a wall and a deep ditch filled with water.[68] At the head of the English town stands the Abbey on a hill which commands all the country. It is a noble ruin and is far the largest building that I have seen in the kingdom. Adjoining to it is one of the most beautiful groves which I ever beheld with my eyes: it covers the sloping side of the hill and has vistas cut through it every way. In the middle of it is a circular space twenty or thirty yards in diameter. I would have preached there, but the rain drove into the house[69] as many as could crowd together.

Sat. 13. I took my stand in the middle of the Grove, the people standing before me on the gradually rising ground, which formed a beautiful theatre; the sun just glimmered through the trees, but did not hinder me at all. It was a glorious opportunity. The whole congregation seemed to drink into one spirit.

Sun. 14. I preached at Dunsfort[70] in the morning. In the evening, the congregation in the Grove exceeded even that at Belfast, and I verily believe all of them were 'almost persuaded to be Christians'.[71]

---

[67] JW was here the guest of a Mr. Richardson who, with his wife, mother, and two daughters became Methodist. Crookshank, *Ireland,* 1:322.

[68] Downpatrick, built on a group of small hills on the south shore of the western branch of Strangford Lough, was 'divided according to ancient usage into three districts called respectively the English, Irish and Scottish quarters' (Lewis, *Ireland,* 1:478). The town's claim to ancient lineage was based on its having been the chosen residence of St. Patrick who founded two abbeys there. One of these appears to have been the first cathedral of the diocese, and it suffered heavily in military operations by Danes, Scots, and again at the Reformation. As a result, in 1663 Charles II erected the church at Lisburn as a cathedral for the Diocese of Down and Connor. But in 1790, part of the ruins were restored by government grant and public subscription, the cathedral thus built being 'a stately embattled edifice chiefly of unhewn stone'.

[69] A preaching-house erected in 1777 by the Rev. Edward Smyth (on whom see above, June 2, 1777).

[70] Orig., 'Dunsford'; a parish 3 1/2 miles east from Downpatrick.

[71] Cf. Acts 26:28.

Mon. 15. I left Downpatrick with much satisfaction, and in the evening, preached in the Linen Hall at Lisburn to near as large a congregation as that in the Grove, but not near so much affected. Afterwards I went to my old lodging at Derryaghy,[72] one of the pleasantest spots in the kingdom; and I could relish it *now*! How does God bring us down to the gates of death and bring us up again!

Tue. 16. I preached at eight to a lively congregation under the venerable old yew,[73] supposed to have flourished in the reign of King James, if not of Queen Elizabeth.

Wed. 17. At eleven, our brethren flocked to Lisburn from all parts, whom I strongly exhorted, in the Apostle's words, to 'walk worthy of the Lord'.[74] At the love-feast which followed we were greatly comforted, many of the country people declaring with all simplicity, and yet with great propriety both of sentiment and expression, what God had done for their souls.

Thur. 18. I preached at Ballinderry[75] (in my way to Lurgan)[76] where many flocked together, though at a very short warning. We had four or five times as many in the evening at Lurgan—but some of them wild as colts untamed.[77] However, they all listened to that great truth, 'Narrow is the way that leadeth to life.'[78]

Fri. 19. I preached about noon to a serious company at Derryanvil, and then went on to Cockhill. I preached here at the bottom of the garden; the table was placed under a tree, and most of the people sat on the grass before it. And everything seemed to concur with the exhortation, 'Acquaint thyself now with him, and be at peace.'[79]

Sat. 20. I travelled through a delightful country to Charlemont,

---

[72] I.e., the house of Mrs. Edward Gayer, where JW had been dangerously ill in 1775. See June 17, 1775 (22:456 and n. 6 in this edn.).

[73] Curnock (6:199, n. 2) notes that this yew was still standing in the early years of this century, 'though looking very small'.

[74] Col. 1:10.

[75] In this village there was a Moravian interest.

[76] On the following morning, JW opened a chapel here. The society here, which may even have predated Whitefield's visit in 1751, had hitherto met in the house of Isaac Bullock, the first Methodist convert in the place; he had entered the breach at Havana in 1762 and was one of the few to survive; *Wesleyan Methodist Magazine* 50 (1827):800-801. On the painting presented to the chapel by the local inventor of the speaking statue, see Apr. 26, 1762 (21:362, n. 89 in this edn.). Cf. Raymond Gillespie, *Wild as Colts Untamed: Methodism and Society in Lurgan, 1750-1975* (Lurgan, 1977), pp. 6-7.

[77] Cf. Apr. 24, 1759 (21:188, n. 38 in this edn.).

[78] Matt. 7:14 (*Notes*).

[79] Job 22:21.

where Captain Tottenham[80] was the commanding officer. We lodged with him in the castle, which stands on an eminence and commands the country on all sides. A tent was set up in the castle-yard, where all the soldiers were drawn up at eleven, with abundance of people from many miles round, who were all attention. In the evening their number was considerably enlarged, but still all heard as for life.

Sun. 21. I preached at nine in the Avenue at Armagh,[81] to a large and serious congregation. It was increased fourfold at six in the evening, but many were there who behaved as if they had been in a beargarden.

Mon. 22. I took a walk to the primate's,[82] and went through the house and all the improvements. The house is neat and handsome but not magnificent, and is elegantly but not splendidly furnished. The domain is beautifully laid out in meadow-ground, sprinkled with trees, on one side of which is a long hill covered with a shrubbery, cut into serpentine walks. On each side of the shrubbery is a straight walk, commanding a beautiful prospect. Since this Primate came, the town wears another face: he has repaired, and beautifully, the cathedral, built a row of neat houses for the choral vicars, erected a public library and an infirmary, procured the free school to be rebuilt of the size of a little college, and a new-built horse-barrack, together with a considerable number of convenient and handsome houses; so that Armagh is at length rising out of its ruins into a large and populous city. So much good may any man of a large fortune do, if he lays it out to the best advantage!

Tue. 23. I went on to Tandragee,[83] one of the pleasantest towns

---

[80] On the origins of Charlemont, see Apr. 19, 1769 (22:179-80, n. 63 in this edn.). It continued into the nineteenth century 'a place of great strength, fortified with bastions, a dry ditch, and escarp and counterscarp . . . two ravelins, one in front, the other in the rear of the works, surrounded by a glacis which runs along side of the Blackwater', the ordnance depot for the north of Ireland, the headquarters of the artillery for Ulster, and down to 1835 the seat of a military governor (Lewis, *Ireland*, 1:311). Charles Tottenham (1738-1806) became Captain of the 50th Foot in 1770, M.P. for Clonmires 1761-76, and Tetford 1776-83, and was raised to the Irish peerage as Viscount Ely in 1789. In 16 years he received five separate peerage creations, in 1801 becoming Marquess of Ely in the Irish peerage, and Baron Loftus in that of the United Kingdom.

[81] M'Geough's avenue, on which see Apr. 17, 1769 (22:178-79, n. 58 in this edn.).

[82] On Archbishop Richard Robinson and his improvements, see June 5, 1773 (22:374, n. 35 in this edn.).

[83] Orig., 'Tandrogar'. This judgment on Tandragee, a town built and filled with English colonists by Oliver St. John in the early seventeenth century, was echoed by nineteenth-century observers. 'Its general appearance is prepossessing; and, as seen from a

in Ireland. As it was a fair, calm evening, I had designed to preach in the avenue to the castle, but being desired to preach in the courtyard, I took my place under a tall, spreading tree in the midst of a numerous congregation, who were still as night. There could not be devised a more pleasing scene: the clear sky, the setting sun, the surrounding woods, the plain unaffected people, were just suitable to the subject, 'My yoke is easy, and my burden is light.'[84]

Wed. 24. For exactly two months we have had only two days without rain. In the evening, I preached in the same lovely place. I dined, supped, and lodged at Dr. Leslie's,[85] the rector, a well-bred, sensible, and, I believe, a pious man. We had family prayers before supper, which he read with admirable propriety and devotion; and I know not that I have spent a more agreeable evening since I came into the kingdom.

Thur. 25. I walked round Dr. Leslie's domain. A pleasanter spot I never saw: it lies on the top of a fruitful hill at a small distance from the town, and commands the whole view of a lovely country, east, west, north, and south; and it is laid out with the finest taste imaginable. The ground I took for a park I found was an orchard, tufted with fruit-trees and flowering shrubs and surrounded with a close, shady walk. I spent another hour with the amiable family this morning, and it was an hour I shall not soon forget; but it will never return! For one, if not more, of that lovely company are since removed to Abraham's bosom! In the evening, I preached to a large congregation at Newry and, on Saturday morning,[86] returned to Dublin.

I had now just finished Xenophon's Κυροπαιδεία,[87] some parts of which I think are exceeding dull, particularly his numerous speeches and, above all, the tedious dialogue between Cyrus

distance, ascending from a beautiful vale, through which the river Cusher winds between lofty banks richly wooded at one extremity, the demesne of Tandragee crowning the other, the town forms a strikingly picturesque feature in the landscape' (Lewis, *Ireland,* 2:549). The castle founded by the O'Hanlons, was also rebuilt by St. John, and completely destroyed by the O'Hanlons in 1641. Reconstructed in 1684 and now owned by the dukes of Manchester, it was again in decay, and was taken down and lavishly rebuilt in 1812. Close to it was 'the elegant residence of the rector', where JW stayed.

[84] Matt. 11:30.

[85] Orig., 'Lesley's'. On Henry Leslie, see June 13, 1773 (22:375-76, n. 39 in this edn.).

[86] On June 26, Samuel Bradburn noted: 'Went to the Man-o'-war [50 miles from Newry] to meet Mr. Wesley. Slept there'. *Memoirs of the late Rev. Samuel Bradburn,* ed. Eliza Weaver Bradburn (London, 1816), p. 62.

[87] The *Cyropaedia* (or *Education of Cyrus*) was popular among the Romans and has found favour with recent editors. 'It is historical but not history; it has much Socratic dialogue, but it is not philosophy; it has discussions of many questions of education,

and Cambyses. But what a beautiful picture does he draw of Cyrus! What an understanding! And what tempers! Did ever a heathen come up to this? Not since the world began. Few, exceeding few, even of the best instructed Christians have attained so
5 unblameable a character.

Sun. 28. I am this day seventy-five years old, and I do not find myself, blessed be God, any weaker than I was at five-and-twenty. This also hath God wrought![88]

All this week, I visited as many as I could and endeavoured to
10 confirm their love to each other, and I have not known the society for many years so united as it is now.

Saturday, July 4. A remarkable piece was put into my hands, the *Life of Mr. Marsay*,[89] and I saw no reason to alter the judgment which I had formed of him forty years ago. He was a man of
15 uncommon understanding and greatly devoted to God. But he was a consummate enthusiast. Not the word of God, but his own imaginations, which he took for divine inspirations, were the sole rule both of his words and actions. Hence arose his marvellous instability, taking such huge strides backwards and forwards; hence his fre-
20 quent darkness of soul—for when he departed from God's word, God departed from him. Upon the whole, I do not know that ever I read a more dangerous writer, one who so wonderfully blends together truth and falsehood, solid piety, and wild enthusiasm.

Tue. 7. Our little Conference began, at which about twenty
25 preachers were present.[90] On Wednesday we heard one of our friends at large upon the 'Duty of *leaving the Church*'; but after a full discussion of the point, we all remained firm in our judgment that it is our duty *not to leave the Church*, wherein God has blessed us and does bless us still.[91]

ethics, politics, tactics, etc., but it is not an essay. It is biographical but it is not biography; it contains also, in the episode of Panthea and Abrodatas, one of the most charming love stories in literature. We may best call it an historical romance—the western pioneer in that field of literature.' Xenophon, *Cyropaedia*, Loeb edn., ed. W. Miller (London, 1925), 1:viii, xii.

[88] See Num. 23:23, used as his text, Apr. 21, 1777, on laying the foundation of City Road Chapel, London (see Sermon 112, 3:577-92 in this edn.). JW was not the only one to note the day with gratitude. Samuel Bradburn records: 'At 9 o'clock this morning Mr. Wesley married me to my lovely Betsy.' Bradburn, *Memoirs*, p. 62; Thomas W. Blanshard, *The Life of Samuel Bradburn, the Methodist Demosthenes* (London, 1870), p. 71.

[89] Orig., 'Morsay'. On this work, see July 10, 1775 (22:458, n. 13 in this edn.).

[90] Twenty-seven preachers received Irish stations at this Conference.

[91] This was the first Irish Conference of which the minutes were separately printed (see vol. 10 in this edn.), though William Myles's statement that its resolutions were

Sun. 12. After I had several times explained the nature of it, we solemnly renewed our covenant with God. It was a time never to be forgotten; God poured down upon the assembly the Spirit of grace and supplication, especially in singing that verse of the concluding hymn:

> To us the covenant-blood apply,
>   Which takes our sins away;
> And register our names on high,
>   And keep us to that day.[92]

This afternoon Mr. Delap,[93] one of our preachers, walking through the city, met a crowd of people running from a mad dog who had bit several persons; he walked on, took up a large stone, struck the dog on the head, and knocked him down; he then leaped upon him and dispatched him, while the people crowded round and gave him abundance of thanks.

On Monday, Tuesday, and Wednesday, I visited many of those who had left the society; but I found them so deeply prejudiced that till their hearts are changed I could not advise them to return to it.

Thur. 16. I went with a few friends to Lord Charlemont's[94] two

---

adopted by the English Conference and published in the minutes is incorrect. He describes, clearly with accuracy, how Edward Smyth 'revived the controversy respecting the Church of England, and laboured with all his might and with manifest uprightness of mind, to persuade Mr. Wesley and the brethren to separate from it'; *Chronological History*, p. 141. The outcome of the discussion is thus formally recorded in the Irish Minutes (Tyerman, *John Wesley*, 3:270):

'Q. 23. Is it not our duty to separate from the Church, considering the wickedness both of the clergy and of the people?
A. We conceive not. (1) Because both the priests and the people were full as wicked in the Jewish Church, yet God never commanded the Holy Israelites to separate from them. (2) Neither did our Lord command his disciples to separate from them; if He did not command just the contrary. (3) Because from hence it is clear, that this would not be the meaning of those words asked by St. Paul, come out from among them, and be ye separate'.

[92] CW, *Short Hymns on Scriptures* (1762), 2:37; see *Collection of Hymns* (1780), No. 518 (7:711 in this edn.).
[93] On Andrew Delap, see above, May 18, 1778.
[94] James Caulfield (1728-99), fourth Viscount, created first Earl of Charlemont in the Irish peerage in 1763. Charlemont delighted to play the independent politician. Raised to the earldom for pacifying without bloodshed the threat of serious disorder in northern Ireland, he at once opposed the address of thanks for the Peace of Paris, and was cut off from further court favour. It was this which led him in 1773, despite moving in the most prestigious literary circles in London, to dispose of his town house and concen-

or three miles from Dublin. It is one of the pleasantest places I have ever seen. The water, trees, and lawns, are so elegantly intermixed with each other, having a serpentine walk running through a thick wood on one side and an open prospect both of land and sea on the other. In the thickest part of the wood is the Hermitage, a small room, dark and gloomy enough. The Gothic Temple, at the head of a fine piece of water which is encompassed with stately trees, is delightful indeed; but the most elegant of all the buildings is not finished; the shell of it is surprisingly beautiful, and the rooms well contrived both for use and ornament. But what is all this, unless God is here? Unless he is known, loved, and enjoyed? Not only 'vanity', unable to give happiness, but 'vexation of spirit'.[95]

Sun. 19. In the evening, I went on board the *Prince of Orange*;[96] but the wind failing, we soon stuck upon a sand-bank; we got clear of it about five in the morning and set sail. All the day before there had been a strong north-east wind. This had raised the sea to an uncommon degree, which affected me full as much as a storm. However, lying down at four in the afternoon, I fell asleep and slept most of the time till four in the morning. About six, we landed on Liverpool quay, and all my sickness was over.

Tue. 21. We had, as usual, a very numerous and very serious congregation. Wednesday 22, I went on to Bolton. The new house here is the most beautiful in the country; it was well filled in the evening, and I believe many of the audience tasted largely of the powers of the world to come, while I enlarged upon our Lord's words, 'Neither can they die any more: for they are equal to angels, and are the children of God, being the children of the resurrection.'[97]

Fri. 24. I preached at Bury and Rochdale and, the next evening,

---

trate his efforts in Ireland. The outward signs of this change of interest were to build a house in Rutland Square, Dublin, and reconstruct the residence at Merino, now visited by JW. A friend and patron of Grattan, he backed the movement for the repeal of the legislative restraints on the Irish parliament. JW visited Merino again with great delight in 1787 (see below, July 3, 1787); his opprobrious remarks on this occasion may owe something to the fact that Charlemont had been an admirer, though not a disciple, of David Hume. Francis Hardy, *Memoirs of the Political and Private Life of James Caulfield, Earl of Charlemont* (London, 1810); Thomas Rodd, ed., *Original Letters principally from Lord Charlemont [and others] to Henry Flood* (London, 1820); Henry Grattan, *Memoirs of the Life and Times of the Rt. Hon. Henry Grattan*, 5 vols. (London, 1839-46), 1:252, 281.

[95] Eccles. 1:14. etc.
[96] Captain Pattison. *WHS* 5 (1905):77.
[97] Luke 20:36 (*Notes*).

at Halifax. Sunday 26, the house was tolerably well filled at eight. Understanding there was great need of it, I preached on 'Render unto Caesar the things that are Caesar's, and unto God the things that are God's.'[98] I spoke with all plainness and yet did not hear that anyone was offended.[99]

At one, I preached on those words in the Gospel for the Day, 'Reckon ye yourselves to be dead unto sin, but alive unto God, through Jesus Christ our Lord.'[1] Such a time I have not known for some years; the house was extremely crowded, but I believe there was not only no inattentive, but no unaffected hearer. In the evening, I preached at Bradford to such a congregation as I have not seen since I left London.

Saturday, August 1. I was desired to take a view of Busfield's[2] improvements near Bingley. His house stands on the top of a hill clothed with wood, opposite to another which is covered with tall oaks. Between the hills runs the river; on the top, at the bottom, through the midst, and along the side of his woods, he has made partly straight, partly serpentine walks, some of which command a lovely prospect. He is continually making new improvements, but will not that thought frequently intrude:

> Must I then leave thee, paradise? Then leave
> These happy shades and mansions fit for gods?[3]

Sunday 2. At one, I preached at the foot of Birstall hill to the

---

[98] Cf. Matt. 22:21, etc.

[99] The point of this reference is that in the Turvin Valley near Mytholmroyd there had been a notorious trade in clipping the legal currency and coining the clippings, highly organized by David Hartley of Turvin. This abuse went on almost unchecked, despite the execution of Hartley in 1770, until one of his sons saved his own life by informing on the others, who were hanged at York in 1774 and 1775, and gibbeted in Halifax. One of the counterfeiters had been a founder member of a local independent church, and he too was denounced from the pulpit by his pastor. This episode is studied by J. Styles, '"Our Traitrous Money Makers": The Yorkshire Coiners and the Law', in J. Brewer and J. Styles, *An Ungovernable People* (London, 1983), pp. 172-249.

[1] Cf. Rom. 6:11. This was the Sixth Sunday after Trinity; Wesley's text was part of the Epistle for the Day (not the Gospel, which was Matt. 5:20).

[2] Orig., 'Bushfield'. Johnson Atkinson Busfield (1738-1817) was the elder son of Christopher Atkinson, the Oxford Methodist (see below, May 2, 1779), and the elder brother of Miles Atkinson, whom JW encountered in Leeds. He was turning a large farmhouse known as Spring Head into the improved residence called Myrtle Grove. He married (1) Elizabeth, daughter of William Busfield of Ryshworth Hall, Bingley, in 1775, and (2) Susannah, relict of John Deardon of The Hollens. He took the surname and arms of Busfield in 1772. Busfield is thought to have heard JW preach at Bingley in 1776; he gave frequent assistance to the Methodist cause. Laycock, *Haworth Round*, pp. 336-37.

[3] Cf. Milton, *Paradise Lost*, xi.269-71. See also JW's use of the same abridgement, Aug. 13, 1759 (21:225 in this edn.).

largest congregation that ever was seen there. It was supposed there were twelve or fourteen thousand; but there were some thousands more at Leeds—I think it was the largest congregation I have seen for many years, except that at Gwennap in Cornwall.

5 Tue. 4. Our Conference began;[4] so large a number of preachers never met at a Conference before. I preached morning and evening till Thursday night; then my voice began to fail, so I desired two of our preachers to supply my place the next day. On Saturday, the Conference ended.

10 Sun. 9. I preached at eight in the market-place at Dewsbury to some thousands of serious people, as Mr. Powley[5] would not permit me to preach in the church 'because it would give offence'!

After visiting Bradford and Halifax, I struck across to Manchester and Stockport, and went on by moderate journeys to 15 London. Having soon finished my business there, on Monday 17, Dr. Coke, my brother,[6] and I, took coach for Bristol; and early on

---

[4] There were more than a large number of preachers present, as Thomas Taylor recalls in his diary:

> Aug. 5. Today we permitted all sorts to come into the Conference, so that we had a large company. The forenoon was occupied in speaking upon preaching-houses. In the afternoon, the sending of missionaries to Africa was considered. The call seems doubtful. Afterwards the committee met, and we were an hour and a half in speaking what might have been done in five minutes. We are vastly tedious, and have many long speeches to little purpose.
> Aug. 6. This day has been employed chiefly in stationing the preachers.
> Aug. 7. We were engaged in conference till after one o'clock; and then the sacrament began, at which, I think, two thousand were present.

JW declined to take action to prevent the abuse of power by trustees after his death, and with characteristic confidence pronounced that the reason 'why . . . so many of our preachers fall into nervous disorders' was that they had 'not sufficiently observed Dr. Cadogan's rules—to avoid indolence and intemperance'. In particular they must 'every day use as much exercise as [they] can bear; or murder [themselves] by inches'. *Minutes* (1778).

[5] Orig., 'Pawley'. Matthew Powley (1740-1806) matriculated from Queen's College, Oxford in 1760, graduating B.A. 1764; M.A. 1768. He became perpetual curate of Slaithwaite in 1767 and vicar of Dewsbury, a living to which he was presented by the King at the behest of Lord Dartmouth, 1777-1806. At Oxford, Powley was associated with Thomas Haweis and was almost expelled from the college in 1761. He remained attached to the Olney circle and was recommended to Lady Huntingdon by Venn and Berridge, 'both of whom esteemed him very highly for his indefatigable diligence and zeal in the service of the Church of Christ', and he preached at her chapel in Bath (Seymour, *Huntingdon*, 2:21). He preached and wrote against Fletcher of Madeley. William Cowper, *The Letters and Prose Writings of William Cowper*, J. King & C. Ryskamp, eds., 5 vols. (Oxford, 1979-86), 1:565-66; 2:59-61; see also 1:349, 427, 432; 2:xxvi, 507, 542.

[6] CW wrote to his wife this day: 'Soon after five this morning, my brother and Dr. Coke took me up. . . . On Wednesday my youthful brother sets out for Cornwall. He seems as active and zealous as ever'. *CWJ*, 2:269.

Thursday 20, I set out for Cornwall. I preached at Taunton that evening; Friday 21, at Exeter;[7] and on Saturday, reached the Dock.

Sun. 23. At seven, I preached in our room, and at one, on the quay at Plymouth. The common people behaved well, but I was shocked at the stupidity and ill-breeding of several officers, who kept walking and talking together all the time with the most perfect unconcern. We had no such Gallios[8] in the evening at the Dock, though the congregation was four times as large. Surely this is an understanding people; may their love be equal to their knowledge.

Mon. 24. In the way to Methrose,[9] Mr. Furz[10] gave me a strange relation, which was afterwards confirmed by eye- and ear-witnesses:

> In July 1748, Martin Hoskins, of Sithney, being in a violent passion, was struck raving mad and obliged to be chained down to the floor. Charles Sk——[11] went to see him. He cried out, 'Who art thou? Hast thou faith? No! Thou art afraid.' Charles felt an inexpressible shock and was raving mad himself. He continued so for several days, till some agreed to keep a day of fasting and prayer. His lunacy then ended as suddenly as it began; but what was peculiarly remarkable was, while he was ill, Martin was quite well, as soon as he was well, Martin was as ill as ever.

Thence I went on to Redruth, Helston,[12] and Penzance. On Thursday 27 in the evening, I preached in the market-place at St. Just. Very few of our old society are now left; the far greater part of them are in Abraham's bosom, but the new generation are of the same spirit, serious, earnest, devoted to God, and particularly remarkable for simplicity and Christian sincerity.

Fri. 28. The stewards of the societies met at St. Ives, a company of pious, sensible men. I rejoiced to find that peace and love prevailed through the whole circuit: those who styled themselves 'my Lady's Preachers',[13] who screamed and railed and threatened to

---

[7] Orig., 'Exon'.

[8] In Acts 18:12-17, Gallio, deputy of Achaia, declining to protect Paul against Jewish charges, or to interfere in matters of Jewish law, is reported to have 'cared for none of these things'.

[9] Orig., 'Medras'.

[10] On John Furz, see Aug. 3, 1762 (21:383, n. 58 in this edn.).

[11] Probably Charles Skelton, on whom see May 30, 1749 (20:278, n. 96 in this edn.).

[12] Orig., 'Halston'.   [13] I.e., preachers of the Countess of Huntingdon.

swallow us up, are vanished away. I cannot learn that they have made one convert—a plain proof that God did not send them.

One was mentioning today a wonderful oration which Mr. Rowland H[ill][14] had lately made. I thought Mr. Toplady 'had not left behind him his fellow',[15] but see!—

> . . . *uno avulso, non deficit alter*
> *Aureus, et simili frondescit virga metallo!*[16]

Sat. 29. I found the venerable old man at Cubert[17] pale, thin, and scarce half alive; however, he made shift to go in a chaise to the preaching and, deaf as he was, to hear almost every word. He had such a night's rest as he had not had for many months, and in the morning seemed hardly the same person. It may be God will give him a little longer life for the good of many.

Sun. 30. About five, I preached in the amphitheatre at Gwennap,[18] it was believed, to four-and-twenty thousand. Afterwards, I spent a solemn hour with the society, and slept in peace.[19]

Mon. 31. About eleven, I preached to a large and serious congregation near the town hall in Bodmin, and about six in the evening, at Launceston—a town as little troubled with religion as most in Cornwall.

Tuesday, September 1. I went to Tiverton. I was musing here on what I heard a good man say long since: 'Once in seven years I burn all my sermons, for it is a shame if I cannot write better sermons now than I could seven years ago.' Whatever others can do, I really cannot. I cannot write a better sermon on *The Good Steward* than I did seven years ago;[20] I cannot write a better on *The Great Assize* than I did twenty years ago;[21] I cannot write a better

---

[14] On whom see above, June 26, 1777.

[15] Cf. Shakespeare, *Julius Caesar*, V.iii.100-1: 'It is impossible that ever Rome should breed thy fellow.' For Augustus Montague Toplady, see Nov. 29, 1775 (22:474, n. 86 in this edn.).

[16] Cf. Virgil, *Aeneid*, vi.143-44 (with '*uno*' for '*primo*'): 'When the first is torn away, a second fails not, golden too, and the spray bears leaf of the selfsame ore' (Loeb).

[17] Orig., 'St. Cuthbert's'; for the 'venerable old man', Joseph Hosken of Cubert, now nearing the end of his days, see Sept. 7, 1765 (22:18-19, n. 78 in this edn.). Wanting 'a worn-out preacher to live with him, to take care of his family, and to pray with them morning and evening', Hosken had offered a home to John Haime (on whom see Feb. 1, 1744; 20:8-9, n. 39 in this edn.) in 1766. Jackson, *Early Methodist Preachers*, 1:306.

[18] For which see Sept. 5, 1762 (21:388, n. 75 in this edn.).

[19] Probably as a guest of the Skinner family at Little Carharrack. *WHS* 4 (1904):194.

[20] See Sermon 51 (2:281-98 in this edn.).

[21] See Sermon 15 (1:354-75 in this edn.).

on *The Use of Money* than I did near thirty years ago;[22] nay, I know not that I can write a better on *The Circumcision of the Heart* than I did five and forty years ago.[23] Perhaps, indeed, I may have read five or six hundred books more than I had then and may know a little more history or natural philosophy than I did. But I am not sensible that this has made any essential addition to my knowledge in divinity. Forty years ago I knew and preached every Christian doctrine which I preach now.

Thur. 3. About noon, I preached at Cathanger[24] about eight miles from Taunton. It was an exceeding large house, built (as the inscription over the gate testifies) in the year 1555 by Sergeant Walsh, who had then eight thousand pounds a year, perhaps more than equal to twenty thousand now. But the once famous family is now forgotten, the estate is mouldered almost into nothing, and three-quarters of the magnificent buildings lie level with the dust. I preached in the great hall, like that of Lincoln College, to a very serious congregation. In the evening, I preached at South Petherton, once a place of renown and the capital of a Saxon kingdom— as is vouched by a palace of King Ina[25] still remaining, and a very large and ancient church. I suppose the last blow given to it was by Judge Jeffreys,[26] who after Monmouth's rebellion hanged so

[22] See Sermon 50 (2:263–80 in this edn.).

[23] See Sermon 17 (1:398–414 in this edn.).

[24] 'The manor house, a venerable old edifice in the form of an L is still standing, inhabited by a farmer. . . . The great hall is lofty, and has a ceiling of good masonry divided into lozenges. . . . Over the entrance of the porch is cut in stone, JOHN WALSHE, ANNO DNI 1559, SERJEANT AT LAWE'; Collinson, *Somerset*, 1:42. According to Collinson, Walsh was made a Justice of the King's Bench in 1563.

[25] 'Ina had a palace here. The inhabitants show an old house near the church which still bears that prince's name, but which in reality was the erection of more modern times, as the old palace must long ago have been level with the ground'; Collinson, *Somerset*, 3:107. Ine, Ini, or Ina (d. 726) was king of the West Saxons, 688–725 or 726, and the strongest king in southern England in that time. He did much to create an organized church out of isolated monasteries and mission stations in Wessex, and gave evidence of broad views in his code of West Saxon law; F. M. Stenton, *Anglo-Saxon England* (Oxford, 1943), pp. 70-73. Three Roman villas have been found in and about the town. The oldest parts of the church, the chancel and lower tower, date from the late thirteenth century. Pevsner, *South and West Somerset* (Harmondsworth, 1958), p. 292.

[26] Orig., 'Jeffries'. George Jeffreys, first Baron Jeffreys of Wem (1648-89), ap-pointed Lord Chief Justice of England in 1683 despite his notoriously overbearing conduct, was president of a commission of five judges sent to the West of England two days after the defeat of Monmouth's rebellion at the battle of Sedgmoor in 1685. There has been dispute as to the number of executions and transportations which followed his 'Bloody Assize'. A modern estimate has put the figure at 150 and 800 respectively; G. H. Clark, *Later Stuarts* (Oxford, 1940), p. 115. But Jeffreys's brutal behaviour and the granting of

many of the inhabitants and drove so many away, that it is never likely to lift up its head again.

Fri. 4. I spent some time in the evening, and an hour in the morning, with the lovely children at Publow.[27] Such another company of them I never saw, since Miss Bosanquet[28] removed from Leytonstone.

Sat. 5. I returned to Bristol. Sunday 6 at eight, I preached[29] near the Drawbridge;[30] at two, near Kingswood School under the tree which I planted for the use of the next generation; and at five, near King Square[31] to a very numerous and exceeding serious congregation.

Mon. 7. In my way to Bath I read a pamphlet which surprised me exceedingly. For many years I had heard the King severely blamed for 'giving all places of trust and profit to Scotchmen'. And this was so positively and continually affirmed that I had no doubt of it. To put the matter beyond all possible dispute the writer appeals to the Court Calendar[32] of the present year, which contains the names of all those that hold places under the King. And hereby it appears that of four hundred and fifty odd places, just *eight* are possessed by Scotchmen; and of the hundred and fifty-one places in the Royal Household, *four* are possessed by Scots, and no more.

Ought not this to be echoed through the three kingdoms to show the regard to truth these wretches have, who are constantly endeavouring to inflame the nation against their Sovereign, as well as their fellow-subjects!

Tue. 8. In the evening, I stood on one side of the market-place of Frome and declared to a very numerous congregation, 'His commandments are not grievous.'[33] They stood as quiet as those

---

rebels to courtiers as slaves for the plantations were enough to perpetuate bitter resentment among populations already suffering from industrial depression. The assize sat at Winchester, Salisbury, Dorchester, Exeter, Taunton, and Bristol, and it is not clear why JW thought South Petherton was especially badly afflicted.

[27] On Hannah Owen's school at Publow, see Sept. 6, 1772 (22:348, n. 41 in this edn.).

[28] On Mary Bosanquet, later Mrs. Fletcher, see Dec. 1, 1764 (21:495, n. 60 in this edn.).

[29] CW: 'Sunday, September 6th, I rode with my brother in his chaise to Kingswood, and had a feast indeed with our beloved colliers.' *CWJ*, 2:271.

[30] The old Drawbridge was removed in 1897, the river Frome covered over, and a fixed bridge (St. Augustine's) constructed. Curnock, 6:210, n. 4.

[31] Orig., 'Kings-Square'.

[32] Orig., 'Kalender'.

[33] 1 John 5:3.

at Bristol, a very few excepted, most of whom were, by the courtesy of England, called *gentlemen*. How much inferior to the keelmen and colliers!

On Wednesday and Thursday I made a little excursion into Dorsetshire, and on Saturday returned to Bristol. Sunday 13, we had a comfortable opportunity at the Room in the morning, as well as at the Square in the afternoon, where the congregation was considerably larger than the Sunday before. But on Sunday 20, it was larger still. Now let the winter come; we have made our full use of the Michaelmas summer.[34]

On Monday, Tuesday, and Wednesday, on meeting the classes, I carefully examined whether there was any truth in the assertion that above a hundred in our society were concerned in unlawful distilling. The result was that I found two persons, and no more, that were concerned therein.

I now procured a copy of part of Mr. Fl[etcher]'s late letter to Mr. [Ireland], which I think it my duty to publish as a full answer to the lying accounts which have been published concerning that bad man:

> Mr. Voltaire finding himself ill, sent for Dr. Fronchin, first physician to the Duke of Orleans, one of his converts to infidelity, and said to him, 'Sir, I desire you will save my life. I will give you half my fortune if you will lengthen out my days only six months. If not, I shall go to the devil, and carry you with me.'[35]

Thur. 24. I read prayers and preached in Midsomer Norton Church. Thence, I went to Bradford on a sultry hot day, such as were several days this month, and preached on the 'seed that fell among thorns.'[36] God strongly applied his word.

Tue. 29. I preached at Almondsbury[37] to a large number of

[34] Michaelmas is September 29. Although *OED* notes 'Michaelmas spring', i.e., an autumnal spring, 'Michaelmas summer' is not recorded. The first record in the *OED* of the American counterpart, 'Indian summer', is for 1794.

[35] The quotation is from a letter of John Fletcher to James Ireland of July 15, 1778. Ireland had accompanied him on a journey of convalescence abroad and then returned, fulfilling a promise to send him 'some anecdotes concerning our two great philosophers, Voltaire and Rousseau', the former being JW's 'bad man'; Benson, *Fletcher*, p. 236. According to C. J. Abbey and J. H. Overton, however, 'it is said that Voltaire, when challenged to produce a character as perfect as that of Jesus Christ, at once mentioned Fletcher of Madeley.' *The English Church in the Eighteenth Century*, 2 vols. (London, 1878), 2:113. On James Ireland, see above, July 30, 1777.

[36] Cf. Matt. 13:7, 22.

[37] Orig., 'Almsbury'. Almondsbury was a village 7 miles north of Bristol, which JW was to visit frequently in later years. The connection is explained by John Valton who,

plain people, who seemed just ripe for the gospel. We observed
Friday, October 2, as a day of fasting and prayer for our King and
nation.[38] We met as usual at five, at nine, at one, and in the
evening. At each time, I believe, some found that God was with
5   us—but more especially in the concluding service.

Sat. 3. Visiting one at the poorhouse, I was much moved to see
such a company of poor, maimed, halt, and blind,[39] who seemed to
have no one caring for their souls. So I appointed to be there the
next day, and at two o'clock had all that could get out of bed,
10 young and old, in the great hall. My heart was greatly enlarged
towards them, and many blessed God for the consolation.

Monday I went with my brother to the Devizes[40] and preached
in a large commodious room. This and the following evening we
preached at Salisbury.[41] Wednesday 7, we went on to Winchester.
15 I had thoughts of preaching abroad, if haply anything might
awaken a careless, self-conceited people. But the rain would not
permit, and it made the road so heavy that we could not reach
Portsmouth Common till near six.

Thur. 8. One of our friends whom I have known several years,
20 Mrs. Sarah M[aitlan]d,[42] and on whose veracity I could depend,
was mentioning some uncommon circumstances. I desired her to
relate them at large, which she readily did as follows:

Six or seven years ago a servant of my husband's died of the
smallpox. A few days after, as I was walking into the town, I met
25 him in his common, everyday clothes, running towards me. In
about a minute he disappeared.

during a spell in Bristol, had made the friendship of two substantial Methodists, Mr.
and Mrs. Purnel. 'They also had a country house at Almondsbury. . . . Mr. Purnel was
now dead, and the family had, in consequence of considerable losses in mercantile life,
laid aside their carriage. The widow now lived entirely at Almondsbury, with a view to
foster the infant [Methodist] cause in that parish. She, and Miss [Elizabeth] Johnson
and Mrs. Wait of Belton [on whom see Oct. 22, 1760; 21:284–85, n. 19 in this edn.]
were reckoned three of the most pious women among the Methodists in the west of
England.' Valton married Judith Purnel on Dec. 1, 1786. Jackson, *Early Methodist
Preachers*, 6:120–23.

[38] The editors of neither the *Annual Register* nor the *Gentleman's Magazine* thought
the solemnities of this day worth recording.

[39] See Luke 14:21.

[40] CW wrote to his wife on October 1 (*CWJ*, 2:280–81): 'Probably I have taken my last
leave of Bristol. Certainly I shall never more be separated eight weeks from my family. .
. . I am nourishing myself up for a journey with my philosophical brother.'

[41] Orig., 'Sarum'.

[42] This Sarah Maitland is probably to be identified with Penny Maitland, wife of
General Maitland and sister of Martin Madan, who corresponded with JW on perfection in 1763. Jackson, 12:257; *WHS* 5 (1906):144–46.

Mr. Heth, a surgeon and apothecary, died in March 1756. On the 14th of April following, I was walking with two other women in the High Street about day-break, and we all three saw him, dressed as he usually was, in a scarlet surtout, a bushy wig, and a very small hat. He was standing and leaning against a post, with his chin resting on his hands. As we came towards him (for we were not frighted at all), he walked towards us and went by us. We looked steadily after him and saw him till he turned into the markethouse.

Not long after this, Mr. Sm— died. Ten or twelve days after, as I was walking near his house about eleven o'clock, in a bright, sun-shiny day, I saw him standing at his chamber window and looking full upon me; but it was with the most horrid countenance that I ever saw. As I walked on, I could not keep my eyes off of him, till he withdrew from the window, though I was so terrified with his ghastly look that I was ready to drop down.

Fri. 9, I returned to London and, Sunday 11, buried the remains of Eleanor Lee. I believe she received the great promise of God, entire sanctification, fifteen or sixteen years ago and that she never lost it for an hour. I conversed intimately with her ever since, and never saw her do any action, little or great, nor heard her speak any word, which I could reprove. Thou wast indeed 'a mother in Israel'![43]

Tue. 13. I took a little tour into Oxfordshire and preached in the evening at Wallingford.[44] Wednesday 14, I went on to Oxford and, having an hour to spare, walked to Christ Church, for which I cannot but still retain a peculiar affection. What lovely mansions are these! What is wanting to make the inhabitants of them happy? What without which no rational creature can be happy—the experimental knowledge of God. In the evening, I preached at Finstock to a congregation gathered from many miles round. How gladly could I spend a few weeks in this delightful solitude! But I must not rest yet. As long as God gives me strength to labour, I am to use it. Thursday 15, I preached at Witney. Since Nancy B[olton] has been detained here, the work of God has greatly revived. Mysterious providence! That one

---

[43] Judg. 5:7.

[44] JW's efforts here led to the formation of a society which before the end of the century had grown to about fifty members and had a chapel. The latter, however, was private property, and when the owner died, it was sold and converted into tenements, and the society dwindled to nothing. For this and subsequent efforts to introduce Methodism into Wallingford, see *Wesleyan Methodist Magazine* 58 (1835):215-16.

capable of being so extremely useful should be thus shut up in a corner![45]

Fri. 16. I was desired to preach at Thame[46] on my return to London. I came thither a little after ten. The mob had been so troublesome there that it was a doubt with the preachers whether the place should not be given up. However, I thought it might not be amiss, before this was done, to make one trial myself. But I found it impracticable to preach abroad, the wind being so exceeding sharp. I went therefore into a large building, formerly used by the Presbyterians. It was quickly filled, and more than filled, many being obliged to stand without. Yet there was no breath of noise; the whole congregation seemed to be 'all but their attention dead'.[47] We had prayed before that God would give us a quiet time, and he granted us our request.

Immediately after, a strange scene occurred. I was desired to visit one who had been eminently pious, but had now been confined to her bed for several months and was utterly unable to raise herself up. She desired us to pray that the chain might be broken. A few of us prayed in faith. Presently she rose up, dressed herself, came downstairs, and I believe had not any farther complaint. In the evening, I preached at High Wycombe, and on Saturday returned to London.

Mon. 19. About noon, I reached Mr. Fary's near Little Brickhill.[48] I designed to preach in the house, but the number of people obliged me to preach abroad in spite of the keen east winds. Tuesday 20, I preached about noon at Hanslope,[49] and in the evening at [Maids'] Moreton near Buckingham. Wednesday 21, I preached about noon at Silston (properly Silverstone),[50] and then walked with a company of our friends to Whittlebury.[51] This is the flower

[45] This tribute to Nancy Bolton (on whom see July 15, 1773; 22:383-84, n. 67 in this edn.), from 'Mysterious' to the end, is omitted from edn. C (?1791).

[46] Thame was a market town 13 miles east of Oxford. JW returned on Oct. 17, 1782.

[47] Cf. William Congreve, *On Mrs. Arabella Hunt singing*, 'Let me be all, but my attention, dead', ver. 1, *l*. 12, *Poems on Several Occasions*, in *Works*, 3 vols. (London, 1710), 3:875. See also, below, June 15, 1783, and Mar. 2, 1787.

[48] Orig., 'Little Brickhil'.

[49] Orig., 'Hanslip'.

[50] Silverstone was the name already in use in the early nineteenth century. The village is 3 miles south-west of Towcester.

[51] On the origins of the chapel here, see June 23, 1763 (21:419, n. 11 in this edn.). The connection between Maids' Moreton and Whittlebury is explained in the memoir of Mrs. Anna Cordeux (1759-1824), who as a young unmarried woman joined the Methodists at Whittlebury; *Wesleyan Methodist Magazine* 48 (1825):297-98. 'Two pious ladies at Maids Moreton, near Buckingham, in the year 1778, invited her to live with

of all our societies in the circuit, both for zeal and simplicity. Thursday 22, I preached at Towcester, on Friday at Northampton, and on Saturday returned to London.

Mon. 26. I set out in the Diligence to Godmanchester, hoping to be there by six in the evening. But we did not come till past eight; so most of the people being gone, I only gave a short exhortation. At five in the morning we had a large congregation, but a much larger in the evening. Wednesday 28 about noon, I preached at St. Neots,[52] and afterwards visited a lovely young woman, who appeared to be in the last stage of a consumption and was feebly gasping after God. She seemed to be just ripe for the gospel, which she drank in with all her soul. God speedily brought her to the blood of sprinkling,[53] and a few days after, she died in peace.

I preached in the evening at Bedford, and the next day, Thursday 29, at Luton. We had a miserable preaching-house here,[54] but Mr. Cole[55] has now fitted up a very neat and commodious room, which was thoroughly filled with well-behaved and deeply attentive hearers. How long did we seem to be ploughing upon the sand here! But it seems there will be some fruit at last.

Fri. 30. I preached at noon to fifty or sixty dull creatures at poor, desolate Hertford, and they heard with something like seriousness. In the afternoon, I went on to London.

Sunday, November 1, was the day appointed for opening the New Chapel in the City Road.[56] It is perfectly neat, but not fine, and con-

them. As there were no Methodists there, she could not consent to go, except in the condition that the Methodist preachers should be allowed to come to the village and preach in a licensed place once a fortnight, and be entertained at their house.' After a short visit to London, she returned to Whittlebury and notes of this occasion, 'Mr. Wesley coming to visit, put some of us into band. I was appointed with four more to meet on Wednesday evening.' She was later prominent in London Methodism.

[52] Orig., 'St. Neot's'. Another young female convert at this service was Sarah Rutter whose story is related in *Arminian Magazine* 15 (1792):238–40.

[53] Heb. 12:24.

[54] An upper room in the market-place; *Wesleyan Methodist Magazine* 124 (1901): 922. The first chapel, given by William Cole, was not opened till 1780. Frederick Davis, *The History of Luton with its Hamlets, etc.* (Luton, 1855), pp. 118–19.

[55] On William Cole and his wife, see Apr. 30, 1754 (20:486, n. 64 in this edn.).

[56] On the origins of this project, see above, July 19, 1776. This was the first chapel built, as distinct from acquired, by JW in London. A newspaper report of this occasion, preserved by JW himself (Richmond College Interleaved Journal, quoted by Curnock, 6:216n), records that 'the first quarter of an hour of his sermon was addressed to his female auditory on the absurdity of the enormous dressing of their heads; and his religious labours have so much converted the women who attended at this place of worship that widows, wives and young ladies appeared on Sunday without curls, without flying

tains far more people than the Foundery. I believe, together with the Morning Chapel, as many as the Tabernacle.[57] Many were afraid that the multitudes crowding from all parts would have occasioned much disturbance. But they were happily disappointed—there was none
5   at all; all was quietness, decency, and order. I preached on part of Solomon's prayer at the dedication of the temple, and both in the morning and afternoon (when I preached on the 'hundred forty and four thousand standing with the Lamb on Mount Zion'),[58] God was eminently present in the midst of the congregation.

10 Mon 2. I went to Chatham and preached in the evening to a lively, loving congregation.[59] Tuesday 3, I went by water to Sheerness. Our room being far too small for the people that attended, I sent to the Governor to desire (what had been allowed me before)[60] the use of the chapel. He refused me (uncivilly enough),
15 affecting to doubt whether I was in orders! So I preached to as many as it would contain in our own room.

Wed. 4. I took a view of the old church at Minster,[61] once a spacious and elegant building. It stands pleasantly on the top of a hill and commands all the country round. We went from thence to
20 Queensborough,[62] which contains above fifty houses and sends two members to Parliament. Surely the whole Isle of Sheppey[63] is now but a shadow of what it was once.

caps, and without feathers: and our correspondent further says that the female sex never made a more pleasing appearance.'

[57] Whitefield's nearby Tabernacle in Tottenham Court Road (see 22:259 in this edn.).

[58] 1 Kgs. 8:22; 2 Chron. 6:12, etc.; cf. Rev. 14:1.

[59] Another newspaper cutting in the Richmond College Interleaved Journal reports: 'Mr. Wesley in his discourse on Monday advised his congregation not to drink smuggled liquors, telling them they might as well rob the King on the highway as deprive him of his lawful duties. His text was "Render unto Caesar the things which are Caesar's, and unto God the things which are God's".'

[60] See Dec. 16, 1767 (22:116, n. 97 in this edn.).

[61] Minster was the principal parish in Sheppey. 'The church which is dedicated to St. Mary and St. Sexburg (as was the monastery) is supposed by some to have been the very church of it, but by others, that it only adjoined to it; at present it consists of two aisles and two chancels. The steeple is at the west end, being a large square tower, with a turret at the top, in which there is a clock and a ring of five bells. It was formerly higher than it is at present, as appears by the remains. There was formerly a building adjoining to the east end of the north chancel, as appears by the door-case and some ornaments on the outside of it'; E. Hasted, *History and Topographical Survey of the County of Kent*, 12 vols. (2nd edn., Canterbury, 1797–1803), 6:217, 226-27.

[62] Writing in 1798, Hasted took a more optimistic view of Queensborough: 'Formerly, whilst the castle was standing, a place of much more consequence than it is at present, yet as to its size and number of its inhabitants, it was much less so,' the number of houses having increased since Elizabeth's reign from 23 to 120 or more (ibid., 6:237-38).

[63] Orig., 'Sheepy'.

Thur. 5. I returned to Chatham and, on the following morning, set out in the stage-coach for London. At the end of Strood,[64] I chose to walk up the hill, leaving the coach to follow me. But it was in no great haste; it did not overtake me till I had walked above five miles. I cared not if it had been ten; the more I walk, the sounder I sleep.

Sun. 15. Having promised to preach in the evening at St. Antholin's Church,[65] I had desired one to have a coach ready at the door when the service at the New Chapel was ended. But he had forgot; so that after preaching and meeting the society, I was obliged to walk as fast as I could to the church. The people was so wedged together that it was with difficulty I got in. The church was extremely hot; but this I soon forgot, for it pleased God to send a gracious rain upon his inheritance.[66]

Thur. 26. I fulfilled the dying request of Ann Thwayte by burying her remains and preaching her funeral sermon. In all the changes of those about her she stood steadfast, doing and suffering the will of God. She was a woman of faith and prayer, in life and death adorning the doctrine of God her Saviour.[67]

Sun. 29. I was desired to preach a charity sermon in St. Luke's

---

[64] A district north-west of Rochester, on JW's route.

[65] JW had preached at this church (which was united with St. John Baptist, Walbrook) in 1738; see May 19, 1738, and *Diary* Apr. 21, 1738 (18:241, 576 in this edn.). The rector, 1774–1810, was the Hon. Jerome de Salis (1751–1810). He had matriculated from Queen's College, Oxford, in 1757, graduating B.A. in 1761, and M.A. in 1765. He was also vicar of Wing, Bucks., from 1757, a royal chaplain and count of the Holy Roman Empire.

[66] See Ps. 68:9 (BCP).

[67] See Titus 2:10. Anne Thwayte was the wife of James Thwayte (1733–1803) and was described *c.* 1803 as 'a very religious young woman who was a blessing to him while she lived'; *WHS* 22 (1940):141. The 'changes of those about her' relate to the vicissitudes of her husband, a moralizing account of which found its way into the papers of Thomas Jackson. Born of Yorkshire Quaker stock, Thwayte joined the Methodist society at the age of 21, and soon afterward came to London and married. Prayer-meetings after preaching services held in their house were of notable evangelistic effect. In 1758 he began to preach, frequently travelling with JW, though he never received a circuit appointment. In 1764 he was among the dozen Methodist preachers who purchased ordination from Erasmus, the Greek bishop, and was among the last half dozen whom a gathering of preachers hastily assembled by JW decided should not be 'owned as clergymen', 'received as preachers', or even remain 'members of society'. He thereupon built a chapel for himself, called 'Chappel Court in the Borough, Southwark', which for a time was as successful as his business as a jeweller and silversmith, and to the reproaches of his wife he fell into the sin of vanity. Finally his plate was stolen while he conducted public worship, his business failed, his congregation diminished to two, and, a broken man, he rejoined the Methodists in 1797. Cf. Walter Wilson, *The History and Antiquities of the Dissenting Churches and Meeting-houses in London*, 4 vols. (London, 1808–14), 4:319.

Church, Old Street.[68] I doubt whether it was ever so crowded before. And the fear of God seemed to possess the whole audience. In the afternoon, I preached at the New Chapel and, at seven, in St. Margaret's, Rood Lane,[69] full as much crowded as St. Luke's. Is then 'the scandal of the cross ceased'![70]

Tuesday December 1, I went to Rye. Here, as in many other places, those who begin to flee from the wrath to come are continually 'received to doubtful disputations'[71]—puzzled and perplexed with intricate questions concerning absolute and unconditional decrees![72] Lord, how long wilt thou suffer this? How long shall these well-meaning zealots destroy the dawning work of grace and strangle the children in the birth?

Wed. 2. In the evening, I preached at Robertsbridge and spoke with all possible plainness, both for the sake of threescore children and of a large congregation of serious, attentive people. Thursday 3, many at Sevenoaks seemed deeply affected while I was applying those words, 'Do you now believe?' Especially while I was reminding them of the deep work which God wrought among them twelve or fourteen years ago.[73] Friday, going on to Shoreham, I found Mr. P[erronet] once more brought back from the gates of death;[74] undoubtedly for the sake of his little flock— who avail themselves of his being spared too, and continually increase not only in number but in the knowledge and love of God.[75]

Sun. 6. I buried the remains of Merchant West, snatched away in the midst of his years. From a child he had the fear of God and was serious and unblameable in his behaviour. When he was a journeyman he was reverenced by all that wrought in the shop with him; he was a pattern of diligence in all things, spiritual and

---

[68] This church was well known to the young JW; see Aug. 3, 1740 (19:163, n. 40, and 429 in this edn.). The rector from 1775 till his death in 1795 was Henry Waring.

[69] St. Margaret Pattens, built in the 1530s when an older building was taken down, and a rood or cross set up in the churchyard (hence Rood Lane) to collect money for the new church. For the church as JW knew it, and for its first rector, Peter Whalley, see above, Nov. 16, 1777.

[70] Cf. Gal. 5:11.

[71] Cf. Rom. 14:1.

[72] JW's worry on recent visits to Rye had been not predestination but smuggling. See Nov. 22, 1773 (22:393 in this edn.), and Jan. 20, 1778, above.

[73] See Nov. 17, 1762 (21:398 in this edn.).

[74] Cf. John 16:31. Vincent Perronet, vicar of Shoreham (on whom see Aug. 14, 1744; 20:35, n. 74 in this edn.), survived till 1785.

[75] BCP, Communion, Humble Access.

temporal. During a long and severe illness, his patience was unshaken, till he joyfully resigned his spirit to God.

Mon. 7. I took a little journey to Canterbury[76] and Dover, and was much comforted among a loving, earnest people. Friday 11, I preached at Lambeth in the chapel newly prepared by Mr. Edwards,[77] whose wife has seventy-five boarders. Miss Owen[78] at Publow takes only twenty, thinking she cannot do her duty to any more.

Fri. 18. I called upon Colonel Gallatin.[79] But what a change is here! The fine gentleman, the soldier, is clean gone, sunk into a feeble, decrepit old man, not able to rise off his seat and hardly able to speak.

Sun. 20. I buried what was mortal of honest Silas Told.[80] For many years he attended the malefactors in Newgate without fee or reward; and I suppose no man for this hundred years has been so successful in that melancholy office. God had given him peculiar talents for it, and he had amazing success therein. The greatest part of those whom he attended died in peace, and many of them in the triumph of faith.

Friday (Christmas Day), our service began at four as usual in the New Chapel. I expected Mr. Richardson[81] to read prayers at West Street Chapel, but he did not come; so I read prayers myself and preached and administered the Sacrament to several hundred people. In the afternoon, I preached at the New Chapel, thor-

---

[76] The occasion for JW's visit to Canterbury is revealed in a letter from Damaris Perronet to JW, July 6, 1778: 'I saw Mr. F[enwick] at Canterbury, and hope he sees now where this false meteor has led him. I am far from thinking his uneasiness is only disappointment. . . . I told him it was the envy of Satan, who was imposing on his understanding in order to hinder his usefulness: and that Methodism was not intended to turn people from one outward thing to another, but to bring spirituality among all. . . . I think his gifts are improved, and that he is fervent in prayer. There is a *good* prospect at Canterbury, and before this fell out, there was a *great* one.' Michael Fenwick, preacher at Canterbury, 1778, seems to have received no further circuit appointment till 1789. For his eccentric character, see July 25, 1757 (21:117, n. 57 in this edn.).

[77] Mr. Edwards had begun Methodist services in his dining-room (*Methodist Recorder*, Dec. 4, 1913) and had shortly to enlarge the chapel (which was also used by the school). On a later visit (see Nov. 29, 1787) JW spoke highly of Mrs. Edwards's school. A water colour of the chapel is reproduced in Curnock 6:219 and *WHS* 5 (1905):65. He was probably the class-leader who introduced Fletcher (later of Madeley) to Methodist ways. Patrick P. Streiff, *Jean Guillaume de la Fléchère* (Frankfurt, 1984), p. 66.

[78] On whom see Sept. 6, 1772 (22:348, n. 41 in this edn.).

[79] On Bartholomew Gallatin, see Apr. 24, 1751 (20:386, n. 89 in this edn.).

[80] On whom see Nov. 13, 1748 (20:253, n. 89 in this edn.).

[81] On John Richardson, former curate of Ewhurst, see Apr. 19, 1764 (21:455, n. 69 in this edn.).

oughly filled in every corner; and in the evening, at St. Sepulchre's,[82] one of the largest parish churches in London. It was
warm enough, being sufficiently filled; yet I felt no weakness or
weariness, but was stronger after I had preached my fourth sermon than I was after the first.

Thur. 31. We concluded the old year with a solemn watch-
night and began the new with praise and thanksgiving. We had a
violent storm at night—the roaring of the wind was like loud
thunder. It kept me awake half an hour. I then slept in peace.

Friday, January 1, 1779. At length we have a house capable of
containing the whole society. We met there this evening to renew
our covenant with God. And we never met on that solemn occasion without a peculiar blessing.

Tue. 12. I dined and drank tea with four German ministers.[83] I
could not but admire the wisdom of those that appointed them.
They seem to consider not only the essential points, their sense
and piety, but even those smaller things, the good breeding, the
address, yea, the persons of those they send into foreign countries.

Sun. 24. I visited a young woman in such terrible fits as I scarce
ever saw before. And she was hardly out of one when she fell into
another, so that it seemed she must soon lose her reason, if not
her life. But Dr. Wilson[84] in one or two days' time restored her to
perfect health.

Monday, February 8. Finding many serious persons were much

[82] St. Sepulchre's, on Snow Hill, Holborn, was a gothic church rebuilt in the fifteenth
century, much damaged in the Great Fire, and (it is believed) restored by Wren on a
roomier scale than any of his other parish churches (Pevsner, *London*, 1:163). The vicar
from 1767 was Thomas Weales (1722-84). He matriculated from St. John's College,
Oxford, graduating B.A. 1742, M.A. 1747, B.D. 1755, D.D. 1756; and was an under-
master at Merchant Taylors' School, 1745-48.

[83] These were almost certainly the ministers of the four German congregations in
London, which (besides the German court chapel at St. James's, mostly attended by
officials of the Hanoverian embassy and chancellery) were the Lutheran and Reformed
congregations in the Savoy, the Hamburg, or Trinity Church in Trinity Lane (formerly
Swedish), and the George congregation in Goodmansfields. Their names in the order of
congregations were Adam Lampert, Carl Gottfried Woide, Johann Christoph Beuthin
and Wachsel. Distinguished court chaplains had from the beginning in Queen Anne's
reign been appointed through the Halle foundations; but despite JW's good impression
of the others, they complained bitterly of congregational election of ministers by arti-
sans who had got rich quickly, and found that opulent merchants subscribed but did not
attend, lesser men conformed to the Church of England, or also ceased church attendance, while 'travelling Germans are more interested in Ranelagh or Vauxhall than the
German churches.' J. G. Burckhardt, *Kirchengeschichte der deutschen Gemeinden in London* (Tübingen, 1798).

[84] On Andrew Wilson, see above, May 7, 1777.

discouraged by 'prophets of evil',[85] confidently foretelling very heavy calamities which were coming upon our nation, I endeavoured to lift up their hands by opening and applying those comfortable words, 'Why art thou so heavy, O my soul? Why art thou so disquieted within me? O put thy trust in God; for I will yet give him thanks, who is the help of my countenance and my God.'[86]

Wednesday 10 was the National Fast.[87] So solemn a one I never saw before. From one end of the city to the other there was scarce anyone seen in the streets. All places of public worship were crowded in an uncommon degree, and an unusual awe sat on most faces. I preached on the words of God to Abraham, interceding for Sodom, 'I will not destroy the city for his sake.'[88]

Mon. 15. I went to Norwich in the stage-coach with two very disagreeable companions, called a gentleman and gentlewoman, but equally ignorant, insolent, lewd, and profane. Wednesday 17, I went to Yarmouth and preached to a large and serious congregation. Thursday 18, I preached at Lowestoft,[89] where is a great awakening, especially among youth and children, several of whom, between twelve and sixteen years of age, are a pattern to all about them. Friday 19, I preached at Loddon,[90] and afterwards talked with a girl sixteen years of age. She was justified two months since, and has not yet lost the sight of God's countenance for a moment, but has been enabled to rejoice evermore and to pray without ceasing.[91] But being surrounded with relations who neither loved nor feared God, they were pressing upon her con-

---

[85] Cf. Jer. 28:8.

[86] Ps. 43:5-6 (BCP).

[87] The mood changed rapidly, for on the following day Horace Walpole was fearing violence as well as merriment on the 12th 'with the full triumph of Admiral Keppel . . . from Portsmouth', i.e., his acquittal by court martial. He added: 'The good people of Edinburgh have set but an ugly example. There has been a serious insurrection against the papists, and two Mass-houses were burned; and the Provost quieted the tumult only by promising that the toleration of Popery would not be extended to Scotland. This will be agreeable news to the Americans who did not expect to see the administration reproved by Scots.' Horace Walpole to Sir Horace Mann, Feb. 11, 1779. *Horace Walpole's Correspondence*, 24:438-39.

[88] Cf. Gen. 18:32. This is the first of four occasions that JW records using this text; in the other cases he uses the correct biblical phrase 'for ten's sake'. See June 6, 1780; Dec. 11, 1781; Mar. 26, 1782.

[89] Orig., 'Loestoffe'.

[90] A market town 10 miles south-east of Norwich, where in 1786 there was a class of 37 members. *WHS* 3 (1901):74.

[91] 1 Thess. 5:16-17.

tinually, till by little and little she sunk back into the world and
had neither the power nor form of religion left.

Sun. 21. I returned to Norwich and took an exact account of
the society. I wish all our preachers would be accurate in their
accounts and rather speak under than above the truth. I had heard
again and again of the increase of the society. And what is the
naked truth? Why, I left in it two hundred and two members—
and I find one hundred and seventy-nine![92] Sunday 21 at twelve, I
took coach and in the morning reached London.

Sun. 28. Immediately after preaching at Spitalfields, I hasted
away to St. Peter's, Cornhill,[93] and declared to a crowded congregation, 'God hath given us his Holy Spirit.'[94] At four, I preached
in the New Chapel for the benefit of the Reformation Society.
This also I trust will be a means of uniting together the hearts of
the children of God of various denominations.[95]

Monday, March 1. I went to Bristol. Thur 4. I went over to
Paulton[96] and preached at noon to the liveliest people in all the
circuit. This people are now just of the same spirit as those of
Bristol were forty years ago.

Thur. 11. I opened the New Chapel at Bath.[97] It is about half as

---

[92] Edn. C (?1791) omits the foregoing five sentences.

[93] As the Diary shows, JW was often at St. Peter's in 1740, and he was to preach there twice again, on Nov. 25, 1779, and Feb. 4, 1780 (see below). The rector, 1744–97, was John Thomas (1709–97), who matriculated from Queen's College, Oxford, in 1725 and graduated B.A. in 1730. On him see *Gentleman's Magazine* 67 (1797, pt. 1):166. The church was rebuilt by Wren, 1677–82, and is much commended by Pevsner, *London*, 1:162-63. It is now the church of the Royal Tank Regiment and other regiments.

[94] 1 Thess. 4:8.

[95] Wesley had preached a sermon before this Society for the Reformation of Manners on Jan. 30, 1763 (see Sermon 52; 2:300–323 in this edn.). JW's concern here for unity among Protestants anticipates his attitude with regard to the Gordon Riots the follow-ing year, which led to controversy not only at that time, but for fifty years or more after his death.

[96] Orig., 'Poulton'. Paulton was a parish 9 1/2 miles south-west of Bath. Seven weeks later John Valton wrote to JW that 'the work of God is still in a prosperous state at Poulton [*sic*]. We have now got a hundred members in that society, and the prospect of more. We have had but three or four justified since you were here; but most of the new members are currently and conscientiously walking in all the ordinances and command-ments of God. Many of them are painfully athirst for God, and are constrained, under the means, to cry aloud to him who is able to save. The fig-tree has put forth a few branches, by which I gather that the summer is near, and I daily expect that they will be brought to God in great abundance.' *Arminian Magazine* 12 (1789):388–89. A chapel was built at Paulton by Josiah Gregory, of whom there is an uninformative panegyric in *Methodist Magazine* 36 (1813):834. He died in 1811. *Wesleyan Methodist Magazine* 50 (1827):832.

[97] On which see above, Dec. 17, 1777.

large as that at London and built nearly upon the same model. After reading prayers, I preached on 'We preach Christ crucified, to the Jews a stumbling block, and to the Greeks foolishness.'[98] I believe God sent his word home to many hearts. We concluded the service with the Lord's Supper. 5

Mon. 15. I began my tour through England and Scotland, the lovely weather continuing such as the oldest man alive has not seen before, for January, February, and half of March. In the evening, I preached at Stroud, the next morning at Gloucester, designing to preach in Stanley at two, and at Tewkesbury in the 10 evening. But the minister of Gretton[99] (near Stanley) sending me word, I was 'welcome to the use of his church', I ordered notice to be given that the service would begin there at six o'clock. Stanley Chapel was thoroughly filled at two. It is eighteen years since I was there before,[1] so that many of those whom I saw here then, 15 were now grey-headed—and many more gone to Abraham's bosom. May we follow *them* as they did Christ!

I was preparing to go to Gretton when one brought me word from Mr. Roberts that he had changed his mind; so I preached in Mr. Stephen's orchard to far more than his church would have 20 contained. And it was no inconvenience either to me or them, as it was a mild, still evening.

Wed. 17. I preached at Tewkesbury about noon, and at Worcester in the evening. Thursday 18, upon inquiry, I found there had been no morning preaching since the Conference! So the people 25 were of course weak and faint. At noon, I preached in Bewdley in an open space at the head of the town to a very numerous and quiet congregation. Here Mrs. C[lark] informed me, 'This day twelvemonth I found peace with God; and the same day my son, till then utterly thoughtless, was convinced of sin. Some time 30 after, he died, rejoicing in God and praising him with his latest breath.'[2]

Fri. 19. I preached in Bengeworth Church about noon and,

---

[98] 1 Cor. 1:23.

[99] Orig., 'Gratton'. Gretton was a chapelry in the parish of Winchcombe which in turn was close to Stanley Pontlarge. The vicar of Winchcombe and Gretton, 1778-93, was Richard Roberts.

[1] On JW's last visit to Stanley Pontlarge, see Mar. 10, 1761 (21:310, n. 80 in this edn.).

[2] This testimony is complemented by one by JW himself on a visit to Bewdley on Mar. 16, 1786: 'Prejudice is here now vanished away. The life of Mr. Clark turned the tide; and much more his glorious death.'

about six, in Pebworth Church. Saturday 20, I went on to Birmingham. Sunday 21, just at the time of preaching at [West] Bromwich Heath, began such a storm as that which ushered in the year. Yet as no house could contain the people, I was constrained
5 to stand in the courtyard.[3] For a moment I was afraid of the [roof] tiles falling on the people, but they regarded nothing but the word. As I concluded, we had a furious shower of hail: hitherto could the prince of the power of the air go,[4] but no farther.

After preaching at Wednesbury, Darlaston, Dudley, and
10 Wolverhampton, on Wednesday 24, I went on to Madeley. In the way I finished a celebrated *Essay on Taste*.[5] And is this the treatise that gained the premium? It is lively and pretty, but neither deep nor strong. Scarce any of the terms are accurately defined, indeed *defining* is not this author's talent. He has not by any means a clear
15 apprehension, and it is through this capital defect that he jumbles together true and false propositions in every chapter and in every page.

To this *Essay* three extracts are subjoined. The first is much to the purpose. The second is a superficial, empty thing. Is this a
20 specimen of 'the great Mr. Alembert'?[6] But I was most surprised at the third. What, is this extracted from 'the famous Montesquieu'?[7] It has neither strength nor clearness nor justness of

---

[3] The courtyard of Mr. Whyley's house, on which see Mar. 19, 1774 (22:400, n. 40 in this edn.).
[4] Eph. 2:2.
[5] Alexander Gerard, *An Essay on Taste*, first published at London, 1759. The edition referred to is that of Edinburgh, 1764, which contained *Three Dissertations on the Same Subject by Voltaire, d'Alembert and Montesquieu*. Alexander Gerard, on whom see May 3, 1761 (21:317, n. 19 in this edn.), won the prize offered in 1756 by the Philosophical Society of Edinburgh for the best essay on taste. He treated the subject more broadly than had been common, holding that taste consists chiefly 'in the improvement of those principles which are commonly called the powers of the imagination'. JW enlarged on his present criticism in 'Thoughts upon Taste', conceding, however, that defective as the book was, it was the best on the subject available. *Arminian Magazine* 3 (1780):662-67; Jackson, 13:465-70.
[6] Jean Le Rond, known as D'Alembert (1717-83), French mathematician, philosopher, and man of letters. He was called Jean Le Rond from having been abandoned at birth at the church of Saint-Jean le Rond. Early known for his contributions to mathematics, he was appointed by Diderot to assist him with the preparation of the *Encyclopaedia*, and wrote the preliminary discourse, which contained a philosophic history of the origin of ideas and a family tree of all the sciences and arts, and won him the congratulations of Montesquieu. The *Encyclopaedia* was also a vehicle for one of his chief interests, aesthetics or the principles of taste, which he held to be based on incontestable principles.
[7] Charles de Secondot, Baron de la Brede et de Montesquieu (1689-1755), French man of letters and political theorist, President of the Parlement of Bordeaux, 1716-26,

thought! And is this the writer so admired all over Europe? He is no more to be compared to Lord Forbes[8] or Dr. Beattie,[9] than a mouse to an elephant.

Thur. 25. I preached in the new house which Mr. Fletcher has built in Madeley Wood.[10] The people here exactly resemble those at Kingswood, only they are more simple and teachable. But for want of discipline, the immense pains which he has taken with them has not done the good which might have been expected.

I preached at Shrewsbury in the evening, and on Friday 26, about noon, in the assembly-room at Broseley.[11] It was well we were in the shade, for the sun shone as hot as it usually does at midsummer. We walked from thence to Coalbrookdale and took a view of the bridge[12] which is shortly to be thrown over the

and European traveller. Known in JW's lifetime as the expositor of the theory of the division of powers and as a philosophical novelist, he obtained a great posthumous reputation as a moralist with the publication of excerpts from his diary.

[8] Alexander Forbes, 4th and last Baron Forbes of Pitsligo (1678-1762), a Jacobite who fought in the risings of 1715 and 1745 (after which he remained in hiding for many years), and correspondent of the Quietists. His *Essays Moral and Philosophical* were published in 1734, but his *Thoughts concerning Man's Condition*, written in 1732, appeared only posthumously in 1763.

[9] James Beattie (1735-1803), Scottish poet, schoolmaster, and professor of moral philosophy and logic at Marischal College, 1760. A friend of Dr. Johnson, he appended to his *Essay on Truth* (1770) an essay 'On poetry and music as they affect the mind'.

[10] Madeley Wood was a constant thorn in the flesh of John Fletcher, whether from the violence of the colliers there, or the opposition of a clergyman who publicly charged him 'with rebellion, schism and being a disturber of the public peace' and threatened to enforce the Conventicle Act against him; Benson, *Fletcher*, pp. 65, 69, 296, 299. In 1777 he began, largely at his own expense, to build a house at Madeley Wood where his classes could meet, wanting somewhere 'about the centre of my parish, where I should be glad the children might be taught to read and write in the day, and the grown-up people might hear the Word of God in the evening when they can get an evangelist to preach it to them: and where the serious people might assemble for social worship when they have not a teacher'. J. Randall, *Short but Comprehensive Sketch of the Lives . . . of Rev. John and Mrs. Mary Fletcher* (1879), p. 17, quoted in R. F. Skinner, *Nonconformity in Shropshire, 1662-1816* (Shrewsbury, 1964), p. 74.

[11] This was part of a town-hall of extraordinary versatility built in 1777: 'a handsome brick building, in the centre of the town, supported on pillars and arches, the basement forming a spacious market place: on the first storey is a room wherein the courts and public meetings are held (used also as an assembly-room) and two smaller apartments appropriated to the use of the Sunday school, there is a small prison attached to it for the confinement of debtors, and for criminals previous to their committal by the borough magistrates.' Lewis, *England*, 1:353; cf. Charles Hulbert, *History and Description of the County of Salop* (Shrewsbury, 1837), p. 342. Fletcher had a society in Broseley for many years, though it was outside his parish. Skinner, *Nonconformity in Shropshire*, p. 72.

[12] This bridge, designed and executed in iron by Abraham Darby III of Coalbrookdale (1750-91), was the first of its kind. It was begun in 1769, opened in 1779, and earned Darby the gold medal of the Society of Arts in 1787. JW returned to see it in service on April 20, 1781 (see below), making the Delphic comment that 'it will not soon be imitated.'

Severn. It is one arch, a hundred feet broad, fifty-two high, and eighteen wide—all of cast iron, weighing many hundred tons. I doubt whether the Colossus of Rhodes weighed much more.

Saturday 27, I preached at Newcastle-under-Lyme; Sunday 28, at Burslem, morning and afternoon. Monday 29, I went on to our loving brethren at Congleton and preached on the nature of Christian *zeal*.[13] A measure of this they have already, but they want much more. Tuesday 30 and the next day, I preached at Macclesfield.[14] The hearts of many were enlarged. And the society, I found, was increasing both in number and strength.

Thursday, April 1. About one, I preached at New Mills in Derbyshire. A commodious preaching-house, lately built,[15] has proved a blessing to the whole country. They flock together from every quarter and are thankful both to God and man. In the evening, I preached at Stockport, where I received a strange account of poor William Hamilton, who left us to join the Quakers and is as miserable as he can live, afraid to see any man lest he should kill him. O what a poor exchange has this unhappy man made!

April 2. About one, I opened the new chapel at Davyhulme.[16] April 4, Easter Day, was a solemn festival. In the afternoon, I preached at Oldham to such a congregation as I have not seen since I was at the Cornish amphitheatre.[17] And all, beside a few giddy children, were seriously attentive.

Mon. 5. I preached at Northwich.[18] I used to go from hence to Little Leigh. But since Mr. Barker[19] is gone hence, that place knows us no more. I cannot but wonder at the infatuation of men that really love and fear God, and yet leave great part of, if not all, their substance to men that neither love nor fear him! Surely if I did little good with my money while I lived, I would at least do good with it when I could live no longer.

---

[13] Cf. JW's Sermon 92, 'On Zeal', from Gal. 4:18 (3:308-21 in this edn.).

[14] A meeting was held at the house of John Ryle (on whom see Apr. 3, 1774; 22:402, n. 59 in this edn.), the former mayor of the town, at which JW met preachers from the neighbourhood. Benjamin Smith, *Methodism in Macclesfield* (London, 1875), p. 136.

[15] On the origins of the New Mills chapel, see above, Apr. 3, 1776.

[16] Orig., 'Davyholme'.

[17] I.e., Gwennap Pit, on which see Sept. 5, 1762 (21:388, n. 75 in this edn.).

[18] Joseph Benson, in his MS diary, relates: 'On April 5, Mr. Wesley preached on the different degrees of glory to be dispensed to the righteous at the day of judgment; but I could not quite agree with everything he said'. Methodist Archives, Manchester.

[19] On Daniel Barker of Little Leigh, see Mar. 21, 1775 (22:445, n. 57 in this edn.).

Tue. 6. I went to Mr. S[almon]'s[20] at Nantwich, a nephew of Mr. Matthew S[almon][21] who was, fifty years ago, one of our little company at Oxford and was then both in person, in natural temper, and in piety, one of the loveliest young men I knew. Mr. Joseph S[almon] was then unborn and was for many years with- 5 out God in the world. But he is now as zealous in the works of God as he was once in the works of the devil. While I preached, it was a season of strong consolation—but one young gentlewoman refused to be comforted. She followed me into Mr. S[almon]'s all in tears; but would neither touch meat nor drink. After I had 10 spent a little time in prayer, she broke out into prayer herself. And she did not cease till God turned her sorrow into joy unspeakable.

After preaching at Alpraham and Chester, on Wednesday I went on to Warrington. The proprietor of the new chapel[22] had sent me word that I was welcome to preach in it. But he had now 15 altered his mind; so I preached in our own, and I saw not one inattentive hearer.

[20] Joseph Whittingham Salmon. JW printed a letter of his of 1777 telling of his call to preach with the comment: 'What a lovely simplicity! What pity that such a spirit as his should fall among thieves!' *Arminian Magazine* 11 (1788):217-18. His reservation seems to have been about the mysticism apparent in a rambling funeral sermon he preached for his wife in 1785, *The Robes of the Saints Washed in the Blood of the Lamb* (Leeds, 1785); Tyerman, *Oxford Methodists*, p. 62n. He also published a volume of verse, *Moral Reflections in Verse, begun in Hawkestone Park, etc.* (Nantwich, 1796). Miss Salmon was also a Methodist and an intimate friend of Elizabeth Ritchie (later Mrs. Mortimer) and Hester Ann Rogers.

[21] Matthew Salmon, b. 1714, matriculated from Brasenose College, Oxford, 1730, and graduated B.A. 1733. He was an Oxford Methodist and highly esteemed (Tyerman, *Oxford Methodists*, p. 61); he proposed to accompany JW to Georgia, but was prevented by extreme pressure from his parents (ibid., pp. 64, 65, 335). Like John Clayton, whose advice he sought, he became alienated from the Methodists. He wrote *A Foreigner's Companion through the Universities of Oxford and Cambridge* (1748), in which he alleges (p. 25) that 'when I happened to be at Oxford, in 1742, Mr. [Charles] Wesley, the Methodist of Christ Church, entertained his audience two hours and, having insulted and abused all degrees, from the highest to the lowest, was in a manner hissed out of the pulpit by the lads' (see Sermon 3, *Awake, Thou That Sleepest*, 1:142-158 in this edn.). CW, citing the comment in his journal and accepting the barb, replied, 'And high time for [the lads] to do so, if the historian said true; but, unfortunately for him, I measured the time by my watch, and it was within the hour; I abused neither high nor low, as my sermon, in print, will prove; neither was I hissed out of the pulpit, or treated with the least incivility, either by young or old. What, then, shall I say to my old high-Church friend, whom I once so admired? I must rank him among the apocryphal writers . . .'. *CWJ*, 2:70-71.

[22] The 'proprietor of the new chapel' erected in 1778 in Bank Street is unknown; 'our own' chapel in Back Dallom Lane was erected in 1755 by William Gandy, a local Presbyterian, and held by a trust 'for Protestant Dissenters to use their religious exercise therein'. It was, however, mapped in 1772 as a 'Methodists' Meeting'. It subsequently became the booking-office of Warrington's first railway-station, and still later was converted into cottages. *WHS* 8 (1911):60-61; 9 (1913):90-92.

I preached at Liverpool in the evening and the next day; at Wigan on Friday; on Saturday and Sunday at Bolton. Monday 12, I preached at Bury about one, and in the evening at Rochdale. Now was the day of visitation for this town. The people were all on fire. Never was such a flame kindled here before, chiefly by the prayer-meetings scattered through the town. Tuesday 13, I preached at nine to a crowded audience in the new house at Bacup;[23] at one in the shell of the house at Padiham,[24] where there is at length a prospect of peace, after abundance of disturbance caused by one who neither fears God nor reverences man. In the evening, I preached at Colne, but the people were still in such a panic that few durst go into the left-hand gallery.[25] Wednesday 14, after a delightful ride through the mountains, I preached first in Todmorden,[26] and then in Heptonstall Church.[27] I afterwards lodged at the Ewood, which I still love for good Mr. Grimshaw's sake.[28]

Thur. 15. I went to Halifax, where a little thing had lately occasioned great disturbance. An angel blowing a trumpet was placed on the sounding-board over the pulpit. Many were vehemently against this; others as vehemently for it. But a total end was soon put to the contest, for the angel vanished away.[29] The congrega-

[23] The chapel here was erected for a society of 14 members chiefly by John Maden (1724-1809), one of William Darney's converts, with a capital, after the purchase of the site, of sixpence. *Methodist Magazine* 34 (1811):525.

[24] The building here was imperilled by a claimant to the site who repeatedly pulled down at night what was built in the day, and when, with the aid of Methodist nightwatchmen, the chapel was almost complete, sent toughs with pick-axes to break down the doors. Alexander Mather, the Lancashire superintendent, clearly believed that he had managed a difficult situation with great skill, when he got the claimant to accept half the site and pay £5 for the damage he had caused. JW, however, complained that his graphic account of his triumph 'omitted one considerable branch of his experience, teaching what is properly termed "the great salvation",' and this Mather had to supply separately (Jackson, *Early Methodist Preachers*, 2:186-89). The chapel preserved its own memorial, viz., a sun-dial inscribed 'They thrust sore at me that I might fall; but the Lord hath helped me, and taken part against them that hated me.' Tyerman, *John Wesley*, 3:291.

[25] On the recent disaster here, see above June 11, 1777.

[26] Orig. 'Todmarden'.

[27] For Tobit Sutcliffe, the friendly incumbent, see Apr. 18, 1774 (22:404, n. 72 in this edn.).

[28] On Ewood and the Grimshaw family, see July 4, 1772 (22:339, n. 94 in this edn.).

[29] This episode evoked vintage Tyerman: 'Several of the Halifax Methodists, thinking that the sounding board would be improved by some kind of ornament, opened a subscription for that purpose, and, a fortnight before Wesley's visit, procured the celestial trumpeter which Wesley mentions. John Murlin, one of the preachers, determined not to preach under the angel's expanded wings. Discussion sprang up in the midst of

tions, morning and evening, were very large, and the work of God seems to increase in depth as well as extent.

Sun. 18. In the morning, I preached in Haworth Church, but in the afternoon I could not: thousands upon thousands were gathered together, so that I was obliged to stand in the church-yard. And, I believe, all that stood still were able to hear distinctly.

Mon. 19. I preached in Bingley Church[30] to a numerous con-gregation. I dined with Mr. Busfield in his little paradise,[31] but it can give no happiness unless God is there. Thence, I went to Otley. Here also the work of God increases, particularly with regard to sanctification. And I think everyone who has experi-enced it retains a clear witness of what God has wrought.

Thur. 22. I was a little surprised at a passage in Dr. Smollett's *History of England*, Vol. 15, pp. 121-22:[32]

> *Imposture* and *fanaticism* still hang upon the skirts of religion. Weak minds were seduced by the *delusions* of a *superstition*, styled *Methodism*, raised upon the affectation of superior sanctity and *pretensions* to divine illumination. Many thousands were infected with this *enthusiasm* by the endeavours of a few, obscure preach-ers, such as Whitefield and the two Wesleys, who found means to lay the whole kingdom under contribution.

Poor Dr. Smollett! Thus to transmit to all succeeding genera-tions a whole heap of notorious falsehoods!

'*Imposture* and *fanaticism*!' Neither one nor the other had any share in the late revival of scriptural religion, which is no other than the love of God and man, gratitude to our Creator, and goodwill to our fellow-creatures. Is this *delusion* and *superstition*?

which Wesley came. The leaders were summoned; a heated discussion followed; and the votes, for and against the angel were equal. Just at this juncture, John Hatton of Lightcliffe entered, and gave a vote for the angel's removal. Immediately the carved image was taken down; John Murlin hewed it in pieces; and before midnight it was burned in the chapel yard. Great was the consternation of these simple Methodists, when, at the five o'clock preaching, next morning, they found their pet angel had van-ished. Quarrelling ensued; and several influential members, in angelic indignation, left the society'; *John Wesley*, 3:292; Walker, *Halifax Methodism*, p. 150.

[30] For a previous visit and the incumbent, see above, Apr. 27, 1776.

[31] For the improvements at Myrtle Grove, see above, Aug. 1, 1778.

[32] Tobias George Smollett's *Compleat History of England* reached a second edition in 11 vols. (London, 1758-60), was supplemented by a *Continuation of the Complete [sic] History of England*, 5 vols. (London, 1755), which was modified and re-entitled *The His-tory of England from the Revolution to the Death of George II (designed as a continuation of Mr. Hume's History)* (London, 1790). The passage quoted is slightly abbreviated from the original, but accurately conveys its sense.

No, it is real wisdom, it is solid virtue. Does this fanaticism 'hang upon the skirts of religion'? Nay, it is the very essence of it. Does the Doctor call this 'enthusiasm'? Why? Because he knows nothing about it. Who told him that these 'obscure preachers made
5   *pretensions* to divine illumination'? How often has that silly calumny been refuted to the satisfaction of all candid men! However, they 'found means to lay the whole kingdom under contribution'. So does this frontless[33] man, blind and bold, stumble on without the least shadow of truth!

10   Meantime what faith can be given to his *History*? What credit can any man of reason give to any fact upon *his* authority?[34]

In travelling this week I looked over Baron Swedenborg's account of heaven and hell.[35] He was a man of piety, of a strong understanding, and most lively imagination. But he had a violent
15   fever when he was five-and-fifty years old, which quite overturned his understanding. Nor did he ever recover it; but it continued 'majestic, though in ruins'.[36] From that time he was exactly in the state of that gentleman at Argos:

20   *Qui se credebat miros audire tragoedos,*
        In vacuo laetus sessor, plausorque theatro.[37]

        Who wond'rous tragedies was wont to hear
        Sitting alone in the empty theatre.

His words, therefore, from that time were *agri somnia*,[38] the dreams of a disordered imagination—just as authentic as
25   Quevedo's *Visions of Hell*.[39] Of this work in particular I must

[33] 'Having no front; 1. *fig.* unblushing, shameless, audacious . . . (now rare)'. *OED*.

[34] Nevertheless JW had drawn upon Smollett's *History* for his own *Concise History of England*, 4 vols. (1776–77), for which see *Bibliography*, No. 357.

[35] Emanuel Swedenborg, *De Coelu et ejus mirabilibus et de inferno* (London, 1750). Eng. tr. *Treatise concerning Heaven and Hell, containing a relation of many wonderful things therein, as heard and seen by the author, translated from the Latin* (London, 1778). On the author, to whom JW had been temporarily attracted, see Feb. 28, 1770 (22:216, n. 32 in this edn.).

[36] Milton, *Paradise Lost*, ii.305.

[37] Horace, *Epistles*, II.ii.129–30. The translation may well be JW's own. Cf. H. R. Fairclough in Loeb edn. (1926): 'Once at Argos there was a man of some rank, who used to fancy that he was listening to wonderful tragic actors, while he sat happy and applauded to the empty theatre—a man who would correctly perform all other duties of life. . .'.

[38] Horace, *Art of Poetry*, 7: 'a sick man's dreams'.

[39] *The Visions of Dom Francisco [Gomez] de Quevedo Villegas . . . made English by R. L.* [Sir Roger l'Estrange] (London, 1667; frequently reprinted). It is not surprising that

observe that the doctrine contained therein is not only quite unproved, quite precarious from beginning to end, as depending entirely on the assertion of a single, brainsick man; but that in many instances it is contradictory to Scripture, to reason, and to itself. But over and above this, it contains many sentiments that are essentially and dangerously wrong. Such is that concerning the Trinity; for he roundly affirms God to be only one Person, who was crucified. So that he revives and openly asserts the long-exploded heresy of the Sabellians and Patripassians—yea, and that of the Anthropomorphites, affirming that God constantly appears in heaven in the form of a man.[40] And the worst is, he flatly affirms, 'None can go to heaven who believes three Persons in the Godhead,' which is more than the most violent Arian or Socinian ever affirmed before.

Add to this that his ideas of heaven are low, grovelling, just suiting a Mahometan paradise, and his account of it has a natural tendency to sink our conceptions both of the glory of heaven and of the inhabitants of it, whom he describes as far inferior both in holiness and happiness to Gregory Lopez[41] or Monsieur de Renty.[42] And his account of hell leaves nothing terrible in it. For, first, he quenches the unquenchable fire.[43] He assures us there is no fire there. Only he allows that the governor of it, the devil, sometimes orders the spirits that behave ill to be 'laid on a bed of hot ashes'. And, secondly, he informs you that all the damned enjoy their favourite pleasures. He that delights in filth is to have his filth—yea, and his harlot too! Now how dreadful a tendency must this have in such an age and nation as this! I wish those pious men, Mr. Clowes[44] and

---

JW took exception to the catalogue of follies contained in the *Visions*, but it is not clear on what he based his conviction that they were anti-Trinitarian.

[40] Sabellianism, a modalist form of monarchianism, was named for a now obscure theologian, Sabellius. The modalist monarchians, seeking to safeguard the unity of the Godhead, held that the only differentiation in it was a mere succession of modes or operations. They were also called Patripassians, as it was a corollary of their doctrine that the Father suffered as the Son. Anthropomorphites attributed human characteristics to God to a degree unacceptable to the orthodox.

[41] On whom see Aug. 31, 1742 (19:294, n. 73 in this edn.).

[42] On whom see Jan. 6, 1738 (18:208, n. 74 in this edn.).

[43] See Matt. 3:12.

[44] John Clowes (1743-1831), educated by John Clayton (on whom see 18:131, n. 45 in this edn.), matriculated from Trinity College, Cambridge, 1761; graduated B.A. 1766; and was elected fellow of Trinity 1769. In the same year he became the first vicar of St. John's, Manchester, recently built by his kinsman, Edward Byrom, and held the living till his death. A reading of William Law led him to the study of English, French, and

Cookworthy,[45] would calmly consider these things before they usher into the world any more of this madman's dreams.

Mon. 26. I preached at Huddersfield, where there is a great revival of the work of God. Many have found peace with God. Sometimes sixteen, eighteen, yea, twenty in one day. So that the deadly wound they suffered when their predestinarian brethren left them is now fully healed—and they are not only more lively, but more in number than ever they were before.[46]

Tue. 27. I saw a melancholy sight indeed! One that ten years ago was clearly perfected in love, but was worried by Mr.—— day and night, threaping[47] him down he 'was in a delusion', that at length it drove him stark mad. And so he continues to this day. Observe! It was not perfection drove this man mad, but the incessant teasing[48] him with doubtful disputations.[49]

German mystics. In 1773, he was introduced to the work of Emanuel Swedenborg and to his first English translator, Thomas Hartley, and this was the beginning of a lifelong devotion to Swedenborg's works and their translation. On his contribution to the Swedenborgian movement, see W. R. Ward, 'Swedenborgianism: Heresy, Schism, or Religious Protest?' in *Schism, Heresy, and Religious Protest*, Studies in Church History 9 (Cambridge, 1972), pp.303-9; *A Memoir of the late Rev. John Clowes, written by himself* (Manchester, 1834); Theodore Compton, *Life and Correspondence of the Reverend John Clowes* (3rd edn., London, 1898).

[45] Orig., 'Clotworthy', an error for William Cookworthy (1705-80), a Devonshire Quaker. His father died and almost all the family property was lost during the South Sea Bubble, but he and his brother restored the family fortunes by creating a successful wholesale drug business. Cookworthy evinced strong religious feelings only at the age of 31, when he retired from business and, after probation, was accepted as a minister in the Society of Friends. He laboured energetically and with acceptance among them for the rest of his life, even though he adopted Swedenborgian views. He admired Swedenborg and was portrayed in his *Relics* reading him (John Prideaux, ed., *Relics of W. Cookworthy* [London, 1853]), and like him had strong scientific interests which made him welcome among men of science and knowledge (such as Captain Cook). He is indeed principally remembered for discovering deposits of Cornish china clay and its possibilities for manufacturing porcelain comparable with that of Meissen and Sèvres. Though his efforts in this direction were unprofitable, he contributed enormously to the development of pottery manufacture. He was on good terms with the Methodist excise-man and preacher at Port Isaac (Prideaux, *Relics*, pp. 19-20, and below, Aug. 31, 1779), and preferred the teachings of JW to those of Whitefield. See also J. Harrison, *Memoir of William Cookworthy* (London, 1854); A. Douglas Selleck, *Cookworthy 1705-80 and his Circle* (Plymouth, 1978).

[46] 'Prayer-meetings, early and late, frequent preaching services, judicious button-holing, and holy living told mightily for good. Aged and grey-haired men and women, young men and maidens . . . sought and found salvation . . . well-nigh lost souls became trophies of saving mercy.' Joel Mallinson, *History of Methodism in Huddersfield, Holmfirth, and Denby Dale* (London, 1898), p. 38.

[47] This word which survives only in Scots and northern dialect, means, in its transitive form, to rebuke or reprove, or (as here) 'to persist in asserting . . . , to maintain obstinately or aggressively'. *OED*.

[48] Orig., 'teizing'.

[49] Rom. 14:1.

Wed. 28. I had promised to preach at six in the morning to the poor prisoners at Whitley.[50] Though the ground was covered with snow, so many people flocked together that I was constrained to preach in the court of the prison. The snow continued to fall, and the north wind to whistle round us—but I trust God warmed many hearts.

I preached at Wakefield in the evening; Thursday 29, at Rothwell and Leeds, and on Friday noon, at Harewood. In the afternoon, we walked to Mr. Lascelles's house.[51] It is finely situated on a little eminence, commanding a most delightful prospect of hill and dale, and wood and water. It is built of a fine white stone with two grand and beautiful fronts. I was not much struck with anything within. There is too much sameness in all the great houses I have seen in England: two rows of large, square rooms with costly beds, glasses, chairs, and tables. But here is a profusion of wealth: every pane of glass, we were informed, cost six and twenty shillings. One looking-glass cost five hundred pounds, and one bed, six hundred. The whole floor was just on the plan of Montague House, now the British Museum.[52] The grounds round the house are pleasant indeed, particularly the walks on the riverside and through the woods. But what has the owner thereof save the beholding them with his eyes?

Saturday, May 1. I looked over the first volume of Mr. Bryant's *Ancient Mythology.*[53] He seems to be a person of immense reading

---

[50] Orig., 'Whiteley'. Whitley was 3 miles south-west of Dewsbury.

[51] Edward Lascelles (1740-1820), M.P. for Northallerton 1761-74 and 1790-96, created Baron Harewood of Harewood in 1796 and Viscount Lascelles and Earl of Harewood in 1812. Harewood House was begun in 1759 to designs by John Carr, though the exteriors admired by JW owed much to the younger Robert Adam. The south façade was entirely remodelled by Sir Charles Barry in the mid-nineteenth century. The lavish interior furnishing was made possible by the fortune accumulated by Edward's father Henry (who bought the estate) in the rubber trade and as a customs collector in the West Indies. Pevsner, *West Riding*, pp. 245-46.

[52] 'Since their establishment in 1753, the various collections which formed the basis of the British Museum had been housed in Montague House, designed in a French style by Robert Hooke, reconstructed after a fire in 1686 and purchased by the Trustees for £10,250 in 1754. 'By the early nineteenth century this "disgraceful place" as John Wilson Croker called it, "known by the name of the British Museum," appeared increasingly unsuitable', and a programme of rebuilding begun by Saunders and implemented by Smirke led to the creation of the present building after the Napoleonic Wars. *History of the King's Works*, ed. H. M. Colvin (London, 1963-73), 6:403-4.

[53] Jacob Bryant, *A New System; or, An Analysis of Ancient Mythology: Wherein an attempt is made to divest tradition of fable, and reduce the truth to its original purity*, 3 vols. (London, 1774-76). JW abridged the first two volumes of the original edition in *Arminian Magazine* 6 (1783) and 7 (1784).

and indefatigable industry. But I have two objections to the whole
work: (1) that his discoveries, being built chiefly on etymologies,
carry no certainty in them; (2) that were they ever so certain, they
are of no consequence. For instance, whether Chiron was a man
or a mountain, and whether the Cyclops were giants or watch-
towers, are points of no manner of importance either to me or any
man living.

Sun. 2. Dr. Kershaw,[54] the vicar of Leeds, desired me to assist
him at the Sacrament. It was a solemn season. We were ten clergymen and seven or eight hundred communicants. Mr. Atkinson[55] desired me to preach in the afternoon. Such a congregation
had been seldom seen there. But I preached to a much larger in
our own house at five, and I found no want of strength.

Fri. 7. After having visited the intermediate societies,[56] I came to
Darlington and found some of the liveliest people in the north of
England. All but one or two of the society are justified, great part
of them partakers of the great salvation; and all of them seem to
retain their first simplicity and to be as teachable as little children.

Sun. 9. I preached in the market-place, and all the congregation behaved well but a party of the Queen's Dragoons.[57] Monday
10, I preached at Barnard Castle and saw a quite different behaviour in the Durham militia, the handsomest body of soldiers I
ever saw except in Ireland. The next evening they all came, both
officers and soldiers, and were a pattern to the whole congregation. In my journey to Brough (where I preached at noon) I read
over a volume of Dr. Blair's *Sermons*.[58] He is an elegant,[59] but not a

[54] Samuel Kirshaw (d. 1786), vicar of Leeds from 1751. He matriculated from St.
Catherine's College, Cambridge, in 1724, and graduated B.A. 1728, M.A. 1731, and
D.D. 1760. He was rector of Ripley in 1759.

[55] Miles Atkinson (1741-1811) was the second son of Christopher Atkinson, one of the
original Oxford Methodists, vicar of Thorp Arch and Walton; Tyerman, *Oxford
Methodists*, pp. 371-73. He matriculated from Peterhouse, Cambridge, in 1759, and was
6th Wrangler in 1763. He was vicar of Kippax 1783-1811, lecturer of the parish church
in Leeds 1769-70, and founded St. Paul's, Leeds, largely at his own expense. He was
rector of Walton on the Hill, Lancs., 1780-88; vicar of Leek, Staffs., 1785-1803. He was
the brother of Johnson Atkinson Busfield (on whom see above, Aug. 1, 1778). Two volumes of his *Practical Sermons* (London, 1812) were published posthumously.

[56] On the 5th, JW preached three times in York.

[57] JW put the troops down by speaking of the tolerance required by the King,
George III. G. Jackson, *Wesleyan Methodism in the Darlington Circuit* (Darlington,
1850), p. 23.

[58] Hugh Blair, *Sermons*, 5 vols. (London, 1777-1801). Johnson helped to secure publication of these sermons. Boswell, *Johnson*, 3:97.

[59] In 1762 Blair became the first Regius Professor of Rhetoric and Belles Lettres at
Edinburgh.

deep writer, much resembling, but not equalling, Mr. Seed.[60] I do not remember that any day in January, February, or March, was near so cold as this.

Wed. 12. After preaching at Cotherstone[61] and in Teesdale, I went a little out of my way to see one of the wonders of nature.[62] The river Tees rushes down between two rocks and falls sixty feet perpendicular into a basin of water sixty feet deep. In the evening, I preached to the lovely congregation in Weardale, and the next day went on to Newcastle.

Sun. 16. I preached at Gateshead Fell in the morning, and in the new house near Sheep Hill at noon. Here the work of God greatly revives: many are lately convinced of sin, and many enabled from day to day to rejoice in God their Saviour.[63]

Mon. 17. About noon, I preached at [North] Shields, and in the evening, at Sunderland. Tuesday 18, I read prayers and preached in Monkwearmouth Church and, Thursday 20, returned to Newcastle. Sunday 23 in the morning, I preached at Ballast Hills; about two, at the Fell; about five, at the Garth Heads.[64] The congregation was double to that at the Fell. And I trust God gave us a double blessing.

Mon. 24. I preached at five in the Orphan House; about nine, at Plessey; at noon, in the market-house at Morpeth.[65] Many soldiers who were marching through the town came in, and the power of the Lord was present to heal. In the evening, I preached in the court-house at Alnwick;[66] and at night was no more tired than in the morning.

Tue. 25. We walked through the castle.[67] Two of the rooms are

[60] On Jeremiah Seed, see May 23, 1765 (21:512, n. 49 in this edn.).

[61] Orig., 'Cuthburton'. Cotherstone was a small township in the parish of Romaldkirk, 3 miles north-west from Barnard Castle.

[62] High Force, 5 miles north-west of Middleton in Teesdale.

[63] See Luke 1:47.

[64] On the Ballast Hills, see June 26, 1774 (22:418, n. 36 in this edn.); on Garth Heads, see June 14, 1761 (21:328, n. 60 in this edn.).

[65] 'The town-hall is a plain structure of hewn-stone with a piazza and turrets, erected in 1714 by Sir John Vanbrugh at the expense of the family of Howard; it is generally appropriated to meetings for public business, and the lower part is occasionally used as a theatre' (Lewis, *England*, 3:304). It was renewed after fire damage in 1869-70. Pevsner, *Northumberland*, p. 215.

[66] The new town-hall built in 1771.

[67] The following favourable comments reveal JW in harmony with the taste of the day. The first Duke of Northumberland inherited a ruined castle in 1750, and proceeded in the 1760s greatly to improve it with the aid of masons like Matthew and Thomas Mills, and artists like James Paine and Robert Adam, who 'gave Alnwick the

more elegant than even those at Harewood House. But it is not a
profusion of ornaments (they are exceeding plain and simple), it
is not an abundance of gold and silver, but a *je ne sais quoi*[68] that
strikes every person of taste.

5   In the evening, I preached in the town hall at Berwick. Many
officers as well as soldiers were there, and the whole congregation
seemed much affected. Shall we see fruit at Berwick also?

   Wed. 26. We had such a congregation at Dunbar as I have not
seen there for many years. Thursday 27, I went on to Edin-
10 burgh.[69] I was agreeably surprised at the singing in the evening. I
have not heard such female voices, so strong and clear, anywhere
in England!

   Fri. 28. I went to Glasgow and preached in the house, but the
next evening by the riverside. Sunday 30 at seven, I spoke exceed-
15 ing strong words in applying the parable of the sower. In the
afternoon, I went to the English chapel.[70] But how was I surprised! Such decency have I seldom seen even at West Street or
the New Room in Bristol. (1) All, both men and women, were
dressed plain—I did not see one high-head.[71] (2) No one took
20 notice of anyone at coming in but, after a short ejaculation, sat
quite still. (3) None spoke to anyone during the service, nor
looked either on one side or the other. (4) All stood, every man,
woman, and child, while the Psalms were sung. (5) Instead of an
unmeaning voluntary was an anthem, and one of the simplest and
25 sweetest I ever heard. (6) The prayers, preceding a sound, useful
sermon, were seriously and devoutly read. (7) After service, none
bowed or curtsied or spoke, but went quietly and silently away.

most complete and fanciful decorations he ever designed' (Pevsner, *Northumberland*,
p. 69). All these were, however, swept away in massive reconstructions by the fourth
Duke in the 1850s.
  [68] See Apr. 29, 1766 (22:39, n. 73 in this edn.).
  [69] It was on this visit that Johnson provided Boswell with an introduction to JW to
discuss Elizabeth Hobson's ghost story; see May 27, 1768 (22:137-46 in this edn.).
  [70] 'The English episcopal chapel stands on the east side of the lane leading from St.
Andrew's Square to the Green. It was erected in 1751, and is a neat building, but by its
low situation is exposed to the inundations of the river. It contains a handsome well-
tuned organ . . . and is in every respect handsomely laid out. . . . In winter this chapel is
heated by stoves. . . . The members of the Scottish Episcopal Church attend divine
worship in an apartment of the Grammar School.' *A Picture of Glasgow* (Glasgow,
1812), p. 94.
  [71] A high head-dress. In his 'Large' Minutes for 1780 (p. 13), JW introduced the following rule for members of the bands: 'Give no ticket to any that wear calashes, high-
heads, or enormous bonnets.' *Minutes of the Methodist Conferences* (London, 1862),
1:481; cf. above, Nov. 1, 1778, n. 56.

After church, I preached again by the riverside to a huge multi-tude of serious people; I believe, full as many more as we had the Sunday before at Newcastle. Surely we shall not lose all our labour here!

Monday 31, I returned to Edinburgh and, June 1, set out on my northern journey. In the evening, I preached at Dundee. The congregation was, as usual, very large and deeply *attentive*. But that was all. I did not perceive that anyone was *affected* at all. I admire[72] this people! So decent! So serious! And so perfectly unconcerned!

Wed. 2. We went on to Arbroath, where was near as large a congregation as at Dundee, but nothing so serious; the poor Glas-sites[73] here, pleading for a merely notional faith, greatly hinder either the beginning or the progress of any real work of God. Thursday 3, I preached at Aberdeen, to a people that can *feel* as well as *hear*. Friday 4, I set out for Inverness and, about eight, preached at Inverurie[74] to a considerable number of plain, country people, just like those we see in Yorkshire. My spirit was much refreshed among them, observing several of them in tears. Before we came to Strathbogie (now new-named Huntly),[75] Mr. Bracken-bury[76] was much fatigued. So I desired him to go into the chaise and rode forward to Keith.

Mr. Gordon, the minister,[77] invited us to drink tea at his house. In the evening, I went to the market-place. Four children, after they had stood awhile to consider, ventured to come near me; then a few men and women crept forward till we had upwards of a hundred. At nine on Sunday 6, I suppose they were doubled, and some of them seemed a little affected. I dined at Mr. Gordon's, who behaved in the most courteous, yea, and affectionate manner. At three, I preached in the kirk, one of the largest I have seen in the kingdom, but very ruinous. It was thoroughly filled, and God was there in an uncommon manner. He sent forth his voice, yea, and that a mighty voice, so that I believe many of the stout-

---

[72] Used in its early sense of 'to view with wonder or surprise', without necessarily approving. *OED.*

[73] On the Glassites (or Sandemanians), see Oct. 29, 1745 (20:97, n. 74 in this edn.).

[74] Orig., 'Inverary'. Inverurie is a royal burgh 16 miles north-west of Aberdeen.

[75] Huntly was in the district of Strathbogie and the site of the ruins both of Strathbogie Castle and of Huntly Castle, which superseded it. The town took its name from the Gordon family, earls of Huntly, whose seat it was till they moved to Fochabers.

[76] On Robert Carr Brackenbury, see above, July 9, 1776.

[77] On whom see above, May 20, 1776.

hearted trembled. In the evening, I preached once more in the market-place, on those awful words, 'Where the worm dieth not, and the fire is not quenched'.[78]

Mon. 7. I came to Grangegreen near Forres,[79] about twelve
5   o'clock. But I found the house had changed its master since I was here before, nine years ago.[80] Mr. Grant (who then lived here in his brother's house) was now Sir Lodowick Grant, having succeeded to the title and estate of Sir Alexander,[81] dying without issue. But his mind was not changed with his fortune; he received
10 me with cordial affection and insisted on my sending for Mrs. Smith and her little girl,[82] whom I had left at Forres. We were all here as at home, in one of the most healthy and most pleasant situations in the kingdom. And I had the satisfaction to observe my daughter sensibly recovering her strength, almost every hour.[83] In
15 the evening all the family were called in to prayers, to whom I first expounded a portion of Scripture. Thus ended this comfortable day. So has God provided for us in a strange land.

Tue. 8. I found another hearty welcome from Mr. Dunbar, the minister of Nairn.[84] A little after ten, I preached in his kirk, which
20 was full from end to end. I have seldom seen a Scotch congregation so sensibly affected. Indeed, it seemed that God smote the rocks and brake the hearts of stone in pieces.[85]

In the afternoon, I reached Inverness, but found a new face of things there. Good Mr. M'Kenzie[86] had been for some years
25 removed to Abraham's bosom. Mr. Fraser,[87] his colleague, a pious man of the old stamp, was likewise gone to rest. The three present ministers are of another kind,[88] so that I have no more place in the kirk—and the wind and rain would not permit me to preach on

---

[78] Mark 9:44, 46, 48.

[79] Orig., 'Fores'. Grangegreen is about 2 miles west of Forres.

[80] See June 7, 11, 1764 (21:469-71 in this edn.).

[81] See June 11, 1764 (21:469, n. 34 in this edn.).

[82] Née Jane Vazeille, JW's stepdaughter. For her and her 'little girl', see June 20, 1774 (22:416 and n. 31 in this edn.).

[83] Edn. C (?1791) omits the sentence, 'And . . . hour.'

[84] On Patrick Dunbar, see Apr. 30, 1770 (22:228, n. 65 in this edn.).

[85] See 1 Kgs. 19:11.

[86] Orig., 'Mackenzie'. On Murdach M'Kenzie, who had died in 1774, see Apr. 27, 1770 (22:226, n. 61 in this edn.).

[87] On Alexander Fraser, who had died in 1778, see June 10, 1764 (21:470, n. 41 in this edn.).

[88] The three charges in Inverness were at this date held by Robert Rose (1st charge, 1774-99), George Watson (2nd charge, 1778-98), and another Alexander Fraser (3rd charge 1778-98); cf. n. 87 above.

the Green. However, our house was large, though gloomy enough. Being now informed (which I did not suspect before) that the town was uncommonly given to drunkenness, I used the utmost plainness of speech, and I believe not without effect. I then spent some time with the society, increased from twelve to between fifty and sixty; many of these knew in whom they had believed, and many were 'going on to perfection';[89] so that all the pains which have been taken to stop the work of God here have hitherto been in vain.

Wed. 9. We had another rainy day, so that I was again driven into the house. And again I delivered my own soul to a larger congregation than before. In the morning, we had an affectionate parting, perhaps to meet no more. I am glad, however, that I have made three journeys to Inverness. It has not been lost labour.

Between ten and eleven, I began preaching at Nairn. The house was pretty well filled again. And many more of the gentry were there than were present on Tuesday. It pleased God to give me again liberty of speech in opening and applying those words, 'God is a spirit, and they that worship him must worship him in spirit and in truth.'[90]

About two, we reached Sir Lodowick Grant's. In the evening, we had a very serious congregation. Afterwards, I spent an hour very agreeably with the family and two or three neighbouring gentlemen.

Fri. 11. We did not stop at Keith, but went on to Strathbogie. Here we were in a clean, convenient house and had everything we wanted. All the family very willingly joined us in prayer. We then slept in peace.

Sat. 12. About one, I preached at Inverurie to a larger congregation than before and was again refreshed with the simplicity and earnestness of the plain country people. In the evening, I preached at Aberdeen. Sunday 13, I spoke as closely as I could, both morning and evening, and made a pointed application to the hearts of all that were present. I am convinced, this is the only way whereby we can do any good in Scotland. This very day I heard many excellent truths delivered in the kirk. But as there was no application, it was likely to do as much good as the singing of a lark. I wonder the pious ministers in Scotland are not sensible of

[89] Cf. Heb. 6:1 (*Notes*).
[90] John 4:24.

this. They cannot but see that no sinners are convinced of sin, none converted to God, by this way of preaching. How strange it is, then, that neither reason nor experience teaches them to take a better way!

Monday 14, I preached again at Arbroath; Tuesday 15, at Dundee; and Wednesday 16, at Edinburgh. Thursday 17, I examined the society. In five years I found five members had been gained! Ninety-nine being increased to a hundred and four. What then have our preachers been doing all this time? (1) They have preached four evenings in the week and on Sunday morning—the other mornings they have fairly given up. (2) They have taken great care not to speak too plain, lest they should give offence. (3) When Mr. Brackenbury preached the old Methodist doctrine, one of them said, 'You must not preach such doctrine here. The doctrine of perfection is not calculated for the meridian of Edinburgh.' Waiving, then, all other hindrances, is it any wonder that the work of God has not prospered here?

On Friday and Saturday, I preached with all possible plainness. And some appeared to be much stirred up. On Sunday 20, I preached at eight and at half an hour past twelve, and God gave us a parting blessing.

I was in hopes of preaching abroad at Dunbar in the evening, but the rain would not permit. Monday 21, I preached in the court-house at Alnwick and, finding the people were greatly alarmed with the news of the French and Spanish fleets,[91] I opened and applied, 'Say ye to the righteous, it shall be well with him.'[92] I believe many laid hold of the promise and were not a little comforted.

Tue. 22. Finding the panic had spread to Newcastle, I strongly enforced those words, 'The Lord sitteth above the water-floods;

---

[91] The panic here reported by JW was felt also in the heart of the government. The Royal Navy was overstretched with the demands of supplying America and Gibraltar, fighting the French in the West Indies, keeping the French fleet in port at home, and guarding the Channel; and it was not assisted by the courts-martial of Keppel and Palliser. Spain entered the war, and her fleet met up with the French; they planned a landing at Gosport or the Isle of Wight. For two months from late June, the government was preparing for an actual invasion, with an inefficiency intensified by its own inner divisions and poor morale. For two and a half months the combined enemy fleet was only a few hours' sail from an ill-defended Plymouth. The event proved that morale and disorganisation were even worse in the Franco-Spanish fleet, and they returned in September to Brest without an engagement. Herbert Butterfield, *George III, Lord North, and the People, 1779–80* (London, 1949), pp. 41–70.

[92] Isa. 3:10.

the Lord remaineth a King for ever.'[93] Wednesday 23, I rested here. Lovely place! And lovely company! But, I believe, there is another world. Therefore I must 'arise and go hence'![94]

Thursday 24, I preached at Stockton-on-Tees at noon, and at Yarm in the evening. Friday 25 at two in the afternoon, I preached to a lovely congregation at Potto,[95] and to such another at Hutton Rudby. I was afterwards agreeably surprised in examining the select society. Many of them have been members thereof for near twenty years. And not one of them has lost the pure love of God ever since they first received it.

Sat. 26. After preaching at Stokesley and Guisborough I went on to our loving, earnest brethren at Whitby—just of the same spirit with those at Darlington in the opposite point of the circuit.

Sun. 27. I preached at eight in the room, and at five, in the market-place to a huge congregation. They were deeply attentive, but no more affected than the stones they stood upon.

Mon. 28. I preached in the new preaching-house at Robin Hood's Bay, and then went on to Scarborough. Tuesday 29, I spent agreeably and profitably with my old friends and, in my way to Bridlington,[96] Wednesday 30, took a view of Flamborough Head.[97] It is an huge rock, rising perpendicular from the sea to an immense height, which gives shelter to an innumerable multitude of sea-fowl of various kinds. I preached in the evening at Bridlington and afterwards heard a very uncommon instance of paternal affection. A gentleman of the town had a favourite daughter, whom he set up in a milliner's shop. Some time after, she had a concern for her soul and believed it her duty to enter into the society. Upon this her good father forbade her his house, demanding all the money he had laid out, and required her instantly to sell all her goods in order to make the payment!

In this journey I looked over the *History of Whitby*,[98] in which are many curious things. Among others there is an account of St.

[93] Cf. Ps. 29:9 (BCP).

[94] Cf. John 14:31.

[95] A small township 5 miles south-west of Stokesley.

[96] Orig., 'Burlington'.

[97] 'Flamborough Head is . . . one of the greatest natural curiosities in the kingdom. The cliffs which are of white limestone rock, extend in a range from five to six miles, and rise in many places to an elevation of 300 feet perpendicularly from the sea; at the base are several extensive caverns' (Lewis, *England*, 2:214). Curnock raised this estimate to 450 feet.

[98] L. Charlton, *History of Whitby and Whitby Abbey* (York, 1779). The passage about the Percy family's origins in Normandy is on p. 50.

Ninian, a monk of Whitby Abbey, long before the Conquest.
Here is also an account of the father of the Percy family: he came
over with William the Conqueror and took his name from a town
in Normandy. So the pretty tale of *piercing the eye* of the Scottish
5 King proves to be mere invention!

Thursday, July 1. This is the first of eighteen or twenty days
full as hot as any I remember in Georgia. And yet the season is
remarkably healthy. I preached in Beverley at noon, and at Hull in
the evening. Saturday 3, I reached Grimsby and found a little
10 trial. In this and many other parts of the kingdom, those striplings
who call themselves Lady Huntingdon's Preachers have greatly
hindered the work of God. They have neither sense, courage, nor
grace to go and beat up the devil's quarters in any place where
Christ has not been named; but wherever we have entered as by
15 storm and gathered a few souls, often at the peril of our lives, they
creep in and by doubtful disputations[99] set everyone's sword
against his brother.[1] One of these has just crept into Grimsby and
is striving to divide the poor little flock. But I hope his labour will
be in vain, and they will still hold the unity of the Spirit in the
20 bond of peace.[2]

Sun. 4. I had designed to preach abroad at Louth, but the rain
drove us into the house. In the evening, I expounded and strongly
applied the story of Dives and Lazarus.[3] The whole congregation,
except a few *poor gentlemen*, behaved with decency.

25 Mon. 5. I preached about eleven at Langham Row[4] to a congregation gathered from many miles round on 'How amiable are thy
tabernacles, O Lord of Hosts!'[5] As a great part of them were
athirst for *perfect love*, they drank in every word. In the afternoon
we went to Raithby.[6] It is a small village on the top of a hill. The

---

[99] Rom. 14:1.
[1] See Ezek. 38:21.　　　　　　　　　　　　　　　[2] See Eph. 4:3.
[3] Luke 16:19-31.
[4] Orig., 'Longham-Row'. A tiny hamlet, some 7 or 8 miles from Alford, but important to JW as the home of George Robinson, for many years one of the stewards of the
Grimsby circuit (see below, June 18, 1780; cf. *WHS* 6 [1908]:79, 91), near which was an
octagon chapel erected about 1770. He gave an account of the origins of Methodism
here in a letter to JW, July 6, 1775; *Arminian Magazine* 10 (1787):496-98. For an example of George Robinson's services to the preachers, see *Methodist Magazine* 21
(1798):231.
[5] Ps. 84:1.
[6] Raithby is a village 2 miles west from Spilsby. Brackenbury (on whom see above,
July 9, 1776) built himself Raithby Hall in place of Penton House where he was born
(Pevsner, *Lincolnshire*, p. 337). Pevsner describes the chapel as a 'plain' creation in the
'offices'.

shell of Mr. Brackenbury's house was just finished, near which he has built a little chapel. It was quickly filled with deeply serious hearers. I was much comforted among them and could not but observe, while the landlord and his tenants were standing together, how

5

Love, like death, makes all distinctions void.[7]

Tue. 6. After an absence of near twenty years,[8] I once more visited poor Coningsby and preached at eleven in their new preaching-house to a plain, simple people. In the evening, I took my usual stand in the market-place at Horncastle. The wild men were 10 more quiet than usual; I suppose because they saw Mr. Brackenbury standing by me, whom they knew to be in commission for the peace for this part of the county.

Wednesday 7, I preached at Sturton and Gainsborough; and Thursday 8, at Scotter, where the poor people walk 'in the fear of 15 God, and in the comforts of the Holy Ghost'.[9] In the evening, I preached at Owston and, on Friday 9, went on to Epworth. How true is this trite remark:

Nescio qua natale solum dulcedine cunctos
Ducit, et immemores non sinet esse sua![10]

20

The natal soil to all how strangely sweet!
The place where first he breathed who can forget?

In the evening, I took my usual stand in the market-place, but had far more than the usual congregation. Saturday 10, taking a solitary walk in the churchyard, I felt the truth of 'One generation 25 goeth, and another cometh.'[11] See how the earth drops its inhabitants as the tree drops its leaves.[12]

---

[7] Matthew Prior, *Solomon*, II.242; in *Literary Works of Matthew Prior*, ed. H. B. Wright and M. R. Spears, 2 vols. (Oxford, 1959), 1:340. Prior may here have been imitating Edmund Waller's 'Love, strong as death, and like it levels all' (*Divine Love*, Canto VI.39), and was in his turn utilized by CW in his hymn on the Communion of Saints; *Hymns and Sacred Poems* (1740), p. 195; *Collection of Hymns* (1780), No. 504 (7:694 in this edn.).

[8] See Apr. 4, 1759 (21:182 in this edn.). Coningsby is a mile from Tattershall in the soke of Horncastle.

[9] Cf. Acts 9:31 (*Notes*).

[10] Ovid, *Epistulae ex Ponto* ('Epistles from the Black Sea') I.iii.35-36. The translation is probably Wesley's own; cf. *WHS* 5 (1905):88.

[11] Cf. Eccles. 1:4, and the following note.

[12] Cf. Oct. 13, 1786, where this is treated as a quotation. See also Sermon 29, Sermon on the Mount, IX', § 28: 'The generations . . . shook off the earth, as leaves off of their

Sun. 11. About eight, I preached at Misterton,[13] and about one, at Upperthorpe.[14] But good Alice Shadford[15] was not there. She was long 'a mother in Israel',[16] a burning and shining light,[17] an unexceptionable instance of perfect love. After spending near a hundred years on earth, she was, some months since, transplanted to paradise.

So general an outpouring of God's Spirit we had seldom known as we had at Epworth in the afternoon:

> Like mighty wind, or torrent fierce
> It did opposers all o'errun.[18]

O that they may no more harden their hearts, lest God should swear, 'They shall not enter into my rest!'[19]

Mon. 12. I preached at Crowle, and afterwards searched the churchyard to find the tomb of Mr. Ashbourn.[20] We could find nothing of it there. At length we found a large flat stone in the church. But the inscription was utterly illegible, the letters being filled up with dust. However, we made a shift to pick it out and then read as follows:

> Here lieth the body of Mr. Solomon Ashbourn. He died in 1711, and solemnly bequeathed the following verses to his parishioners.
>
> 'Ye stiff-necked and uncircumcised in heart and ears, ye do always resist the Holy Ghost. As your fathers did, so do ye.' Acts vii.54.
>
> 'I have laboured in vain. I have spent my strength for nought, and in vain. Yet surely my judgment is with the Lord; and my work with my God.' Isai. xlix.4.

---

trees' (1:648, n. 102 in this edn.), and Sermon 70, 'The Case of Reason Impartially Considered', II.2 (2:594, n. 29 in this edn.), where JW quotes in Greek Homer's *Iliad* vi.146, which compares the generations of men to the generations of leaves.

[13] Misterton is 5 miles north-west of Gainsborough. JW addressed a great crowd on John 7:37, 39. *Wesleyan Methodist Magazine* 79 (1856):301.

[14] Orig., 'Overthorpe'.

[15] For whom see Sept. 8, 1750 (20:361, n. 78 in this edn.).

[16] Judg. 5:7.

[17] John 5:35.

[18] John and Charles Wesley, *Hymns and Sacred Poems* (1739), p. 187; cf. *A Collection of Hymns* (1780), No. 445:5-6 (7:624 in this edn.). See also Henry More, *Divine Dialogues* (London, 1668), 2:506.

[19] Heb. 3:11.

[20] On Solomon Ashbourn, vicar of Crowle 1669-1711, see July 18, 1770 (22:241, n. 24 in this edn.).

But that generation which was abandoned to all wickedness is gone; so are most of their children. And there is reason to hope that the curse entailed on them and their children is gone also. For there is now a more lively work of God here than in any of the neighbouring places.

Tue. 13. About noon, I preached at Swinefleet[21] under the shade of some tall elms. At six in the evening, I preached on the Green at Thorne to a multitude of people. The work of God goes on swiftly here; many are awakened, many converted to God. Wednesday 14, I preached to an elegant congregation at Doncaster; in the evening, to a numerous one at Rotherham. Thursday 15, I preached in Paradise Square in Sheffield to the largest congregation I ever saw on a week-day. Friday 16, I preached in the evening at Derby to many genteel and many plain people. Saturday 17, I preached at noon in Castle Donington, but in the open air, for there was no enduring the house.[22] Yet they persuaded me to preach within at Nottingham in the evening, but the house was as hot as an oven. Sunday 18, I made shift to preach in the Room at eight, but at five I went to the cross. We had a London congregation—and all as well behaved as if they had been in Moorfields.

One who had left us to join the Quakers desired to be present at the love-feast; in the close of which, being able to contain himself no longer, he broke out and declared, he must join us again. I went home with him and, after spending some time in prayer, left him full of love and thankfulness.

Mon. 19. At five, our house was quite filled with people and with the presence of God. Farewell, ye loving lovely followers of the Lamb.[23] May ye still adorn the doctrine of God your Saviour![24]

About nine, I preached in the market-place at Loughborough; about noon, at Griffydam;[25] and in the evening, at Ashby[-de-la-Zouch]. Tuesday 20, I preached in Markfield Church about noon, and in the evening at Leicester, where we had an exceeding solemn time while I described the Son of Man coming in his glory.[26]

Wed. 21. The house was filled at five, and we had another

---

[21] Swinefleet was a chapelry in the parish of Whitgift, 5 miles south from Howden.
[22] When this chapel had been built in 1771 or 1772, it was reckoned to be the best in the neighbourhood. *Wesleyan Methodist Magazine* 46 (1823):753.
[23] See Rev. 14:4.
[24] See Titus 2:10.
[25] Griffydam is a locality 3 miles north of Coalville. This was JW's only recorded visit.
[26] Matt. 25:31. See below, July 16, 1783 (and Diary).

solemn opportunity. About eight, calling at Hinckley, I was desired to preach, as also at Foleshill,[27] ten or twelve miles farther. When I came to Coventry, I found notice had been given for my preaching in the park,[28] but the heavy rain prevented. I sent to the
5 mayor, desiring the use of the town hall. He refused, but the same day gave the use of it to a dancing-master. I then went to the women's market. Many soon gathered together and listened with all seriousness. I preached there again the next morning, Thursday 22, and again in the evening. Then I took coach for London. I
10 was nobly attended: behind the coach were ten convicted felons, loudly blaspheming and rattling their chains,[29] by my side sat a man with a loaded blunderbuss, and another upon the coach.

Sun. 25. Both the chapels were full enough. On Monday, I retired to Lewisham to write. Tuesday, August 3, our Conference
15 began,[30] which continued and ended in peace and love.[31] Sunday 8, I was at West Street in the morning, and at the New Chapel in the evening, when I took a solemn leave of the affectionate congregation. This was the last night which I spent at the Foundery. What hath God wrought[32] there in one and forty years!

---

[27] Orig., 'Forcell'.

[28] The park, outside the old city walls, was part of the estate of the Duke of Cornwall, leased to the city and used as a recreation ground and for horse racing. Whitefield preached there in 1751. The town hall was St. Mary's Hall, originally a guildhall and one of the notable pieces of Coventry architecture. W. Reader, *New Coventry Guide* (Coventry, n.d.), pp. 181-200. The Women's Market was a building open at the sides on the market square.

[29] The rattling and the blasphemy are equally explained by the fact that the men were jammed into a 'basket' without seats or springs, the basket being 'the overhanging back compartment on the outside of a stage-coach'; *OED*. Cf. Oliver Goldsmith: 'It has shook me worse than the basket of a stage-coach'; *Collected Works*, ed. A. Friedmore (Oxford, 1966), 5:202.

[30] The principal item at this short Conference was a decrease in membership of some 2300. Since America, which at the last Conference had been reckoned at nearly 7000 members, was now omitted from the total, this decline might seem immaterial; but it afflicted twenty circuits including some of the strongest. It was ascribed to worldly-mindedness and political radicalism. Preachers were absolutely forbidden to 'speak evil of those in authority, or . . . prophesy evil to the nation', and were required to work a good deal harder in Scotland.

[31] In one respect it did not. JW's stepson-in-law, William Smith of Newcastle, attended the Conference, partly with a view to negotiating a reconciliation between JW and his wife, Smith's mother-in-law. He reports: 'I talked very freely with both parties upon the subject and did all in my power to lay a foundation for future union, but alas! all my attempts proved unsuccessful. I had to leave matters no better than I found them. It is indeed a melancholy affair, and I am affraid [sic] productive of bad consequences.' William Smith to Joseph Benson, Newcastle, Sept. 21, 1779, MS letter, Methodist Archives, Manchester.

[32] Num. 23:23.

A N

E X T R A C T

FROM THE

Rev. Mr. *JOHN WESLEY's*

J O U R N A L,

FROM

AUGUST 9, 1779, to AUGUST 26, 1782.

XIX.

───────────────────

L O N D O N:

Printed by *J. Paramore*, at the Foundry, Upper Moorfields.
And sold at the New Chapel, City-Road, and at the Rev. Mr.
Wesley's Preaching Houses in Town and Country. 1786.

Journal

From August 9, 1779, to September 3, 1782

Monday, August 9, 1779, I set out for Wales with my brother and his family. In the evening, I preached at Oxford; the next at Witney. Wednesday, we went on to Gloucester, where I preached with much satisfaction to a crowded audience. Thursday 12, we went on to Monmouth, where the late storm is blown over.[1] I preached at six in the evening, but did not observe one inattentive person then, any more than at five in the morning.

Friday 13, as I was going down a steep pair of stairs, my foot slipped, and I fell down several steps. Falling on the edge of one of them, it broke the case of an almanac which was in my pocket all to pieces. The edge of another stair met my right buckle and snapped the steel chape[2] of it in two. But I was not hurt. So doth our good Master give his angels charge over us! In the evening, I preached at Brecon[3] and, leaving my brother there, on Saturday 14, went forward to Carmarthen.

This evening and in the morning, Sunday 15, the new preaching-house[4] contained the congregation. But in the afternoon, we had, I think, the largest congregation I ever saw in Wales. I preached on the Gospel for the Day, the story of the Pharisee and the Publican, and I believe many were constrained to cry out for the present, 'God be merciful to me a sinner!'[5]

Mon. 16. In the evening, I preached in the market-place again to a very serious congregation, many of whom were in tears, and felt the word of God to be sharper than a two-edged sword.[6]

Tue. 17. Having some steep mountains to climb, I took a pair of post-horses. About four miles from the town one of them began to kick and flounce without any visible cause, till he got one of his

---

[1] The Methodists in Monmouth had recently (notably during Alexander Mather's visit in 1771) had much trouble from the mob; Jackson, *Early Methodist Preachers*, 2:184; *Arminian Magazine* 16 (1793):399.

[2] 'Chape . . . 4. The part of a buckle by which it fastened to a strap'. *OED*.

[3] Orig., 'Brecknock'.

[4] The first Wesleyan preaching-house in Carmarthen, in the yard of the Red Lion. *Bathafarn; The Journal of the Historical Society of the Methodist Church in Wales* 25 (1971):40–41, 45.

[5] Luke 18:13. This was the Eleventh Sunday after Trinity; the BCP gives the Gospel for the day as Luke 18:9.

[6] Heb. 4:12.

legs over the pole. Mr. Broadbent[7] and I then came out of the chaise and walked forward. While the drivers were setting the chaise right, the horses ran back almost to the town, so that we did not reach Llwyn-gwair[8] till between two and three o'clock. Mr. Bowen[9] was not returned from a journey to Glasgow. However, I spend a very comfortable evening with Mrs. Bowen and the rest of the family.

Wed. 18. I preached about ten in Newport Church, and then we went on to Haverfordwest. Here we had a very different congregation, both as to number and spirit. And we found the society striving together for the hope of the gospel. Thursday 19, we went over to Trecwn,[10] one of the loveliest places in Great Britain. The house stands in a deep valley, surrounded with tall woods, and them with lofty mountains. But as Admiral Vaughan[11] was never married, this ancient family will soon come to an end. At two, I preached in Newcastle Church,[12] and in the evening, at Haverford[west].[13]

Fri. 20. Many of us met at noon and spent a solemn hour in intercession for our King and country.[14] In the evening, the house was thoroughly filled with people of all denominations. I believe they all felt that God was there, and that he was no respecter of persons.

Sat. 21. I went to Pembroke. Understanding that a large number of American prisoners were here, in the evening, I took my

[7] John Broadbent (1751-94), born at Leeds and converted young, was admitted on trial to the itinerancy at the Conference of 1772, and taken into full connexion the following year. 'He was fervent, lively, and zealous in the pulpit; and, having naturally a weak constitution, he frequently so exhausted himself in preaching, that he was ready to drop down when he concluded his sermon. He continued to travel as long as he was able, but was constrained to yield at last, a short time before his death'; Atmore, *Memorial*, pp. 68-69. He was just completing a year's appointment to the Glamorgan circuit. He was named in the Deed of Declaration and was present at JW's deathbed.

[8] Orig. 'Llynguare'.

[9] On George Bowen, see Aug. 20, 1772 (22:346, n. 32 in this edn.).

[10] Orig., 'Fracoon', a misprint for 'Tracoon'.

[11] On John Vaughan, see above, July 16, 1777. The house is now demolished, though an ornamental stone marks the spot where JW is said to have preached. Williams, *Wesley in Wales*, p. 101, n. 1.

[12] St. Peter's Church, Little Newcastle, 7 1/2 miles north of Haverfordwest. Cf. below, Aug. 22, 1779.

[13] Orig., 'Ha'rford', here and on the 22nd.

[14] The invasion scare was still at its peak, and the Irish situation very serious. Worse was to come in the autumn in the shape of the radical movements in Middlesex and Yorkshire. It was not merely a palsied government which seemed to be disintegrating under the pressure of military failure; control of Ireland and the domestic political system seemed to be failing also.

stand over against the place where they were confined, so that they all could hear distinctly. Many of them seemed much affected. O that God may set their souls at liberty!

Sun. 22. Mr. Rees,[15] a neighbouring clergyman, assisting me, I began at St. Daniel's between nine and ten. The congregation came from many miles round, and many of them were greatly refreshed. While we rode to Haverford[west] after dinner, I think it was full as hot as it uses to be in Georgia, till about five o'clock a violent shower exceedingly cooled the air. But it ceased in half an hour, and we had then such a congregation as was scarce ever seen here before. And though many of the gentry were there, yet a solemn awe spread over the whole assembly.

Mon. 23. I came once more to Carmarthen. Finding the people here (as indeed in every place) under a deep consternation, through the terrible reports which flew on every side, I cried aloud in the market-place, 'Say ye unto the righteous, it shall be well with him.'[16] God made it a word in season to them, and many were no longer afraid.

Tue. 24. Setting out immediately after preaching, about eight I preached at Kidwelly, about nine miles from Carmarthen, to a very civil and unaffected congregation. At eleven, though the sun was intensely hot, I stood at the end of the churchyard in Llanelli and took occasion from a passing-bell strongly to enforce those words, 'It is appointed unto men once to die.'[17] About six, I preached at Swansea to a large congregation, without feeling any weariness.

Wed. 25. I preached at five and about eight in the town hall at Neath. In the afternoon, I preached in the church near Bridgend[18] to a larger congregation than I ever saw there before. And at six in the town hall at Cowbridge, much crowded and hot enough. The heat made it a little more difficult to speak, but by the mercy of God I was no more tired when I had done than when I rose in the morning.

Thur. 26. I preached at five and again at eleven. I think this was the happiest time of all. The poor and the rich seemed to be equally affected. O! how are the times changed at Cowbridge

---

[15] William Rees, perpetual curate of Little Newcastle, 1770–82. Williams, *Wesley in Wales*, p. 101, n. 5.
[16] Isa. 3:10.
[17] Heb. 9:27.
[18] St. Mary's, Nolton. Williams, *Wesley in Wales*, p. 102, n. 1.

since the people compassed the house where I was and poured in stones from every quarter;[19] but my strength was then according to my day.[20] And (blessed be God!) so it is still.

In the evening, I preached in the large hall at Mr. Mathews's[21] in Llandaff. And will the rich also hear the words of eternal life! 'With God all things are possible.'[22]

Fri. 27. I preached at Cardiff about noon and at six in the evening. We then went on to Newport and, setting out early in the morning, reached Bristol in the afternoon. Sunday 29, I had a very large number of communicants. It was one of the hottest days I have known in England. The thermometer rose to eighty degrees—as high as it usually rises in Jamaica.

Being desired to visit a dying man on Kingsdown, I had no time but at two o'clock. The sun shone without a cloud, so that I had a warm journey. But I was well repaid, for the poor sinner found peace. At five, I preached to an immense multitude in the Square. And God comforted many drooping souls.

Mon. 30. I set out for the west, and in the evening, preached at Taunton on 'Walk worthy of the Lord.'[23] Tuesday 31, after preaching at Cullompton about noon, in the evening, I preached at Exeter in a convenient room, lately a school—I suppose formerly a chapel.[24] It is both neat and solemn, and is believed to contain four or five hundred people. Many were present again at five in the morning (Sept. 1) and found it a comfortable opportunity. Here a gentleman, just come from Plymouth, gave us a very remarkable account: 'For two days the combined fleets of France and Spain lay at the mouth of the harbour. They might have entered it with perfect ease. The wind was fair; there was no fleet to oppose them; and the island, which is the grand security of the

---

[19] See May 7, 1743 (19:325 in this edn.).
[20] See Deut. 33:25.
[21] On Thomas Matthews, see Aug. 27, 1763 (21:426, n. 36 in this edn.).
[22] Matt 19:26, etc.
[23] Col. 1:10.
[24] This building was not a chapel but the old high school, founded by the Dean of Exeter in 1343 and rebuilt in 1445 and 1561. It was the fourth home of the Exeter Methodists, the first being (in the mid-1740s) in Theatre Lane, behind the Guildhall, the second a room over Northgate (demolished in 1769); the third in Rank Lane. In 1776, JW had encouraged George Gidley, an excise officer, then of Port Isaac, to assist the small Exeter society in any way he could, and it was he who had secured the use of the Dean and Chapter property here referred to. *WHS* 4 (1904):149-50; 12 (1920):141-42; Telford 6:201; *Wesleyan Methodist Magazine* 94 (1871):324; Elijah Chick, *History of Methodism in Exeter and the Neighbourhood* (Exeter, 1907), p. 32.

place, being incapable of giving them an hindrance. For there was scarce any garrison, and the few men that were there had no wadding at all and but two rounds of powder.' But had they not cannon? Yes, in abundance—but only two of them were mounted! 'Why then did they not go in, destroy the dock, and burn, or at least plunder, the town?' I believe, they could hardly tell themselves. The plain reason was, the bridle of God was in their teeth;[25] and he had said, 'Hitherto shall ye come, and no farther.'[26]

After preaching at Tiverton, Halberton, Taunton, and South Brent[27] in the way, on Saturday [September] 4, I returned to Bristol.

Sunday 5, being willing to make the best of the fine weather, I preached at eight on the quay on 'The Lord sitteth on the water-floods: the Lord remaineth a King for ever.'[28] At ten I began the service at Kingswood and, in the afternoon, preached in the Avenue to a multitude of people; but we had five or six times as many at King's Square. And great was our rejoicing in the Lord.

Mon. 6. I preached on David's prayer, 'Lord, turn the counsel of Ahithophel into foolishness.'[29] And how remarkably has he heard this prayer with regard to the French Ahithophels!

Wed. 8. I preached at Paulton,[30] where the people are still all alive. And the society is still as one family; consequently it increases both in grace and number. At six, I preached at Pensford and spent a pleasant evening with the lovely family at Publow.[31] Where is there such another? I cannot tell; I doubt, not in Great Britain or Ireland.

Sun. 12. I found it work enough to read prayers and preach and administer the Sacrament to several hundred people. But it was comfortable work, and I was no more tired at the end than at the beginning.

Mon. 13. I preached at Bath and Bradford; on Tuesday, at the end of the new house in Frome. Wednesday 15, I preached at Motcombe[32] and Shaftesbury; Thursday 16, at Shepton Mallet.

---

[25] See Isa 30:28.

[26] Cf. Job 38:11. On these events see above, June 21, 1779, and note.

[27] South Brent was a parish and former small market town 6 miles south-west of Axbridge, in the area of present-day East Brent.

[28] Cf. Ps. 29:9 (BCP).

[29] Cf. 2 Sam. 15:31.

[30] On Methodism here, see above, Mar. 4, 1779.

[31] Hannah Owen's school; see Sept. 6, 1772 (22:348, n. 41 in this edn.).

[32] Orig., 'Malcom'. Motcombe was a parish 2 miles north-west of Shaftesbury.

Here also, as well as at Paulton (the two most unlikely places in the circuit), a spreading flame is kindled. I preached at Coleford in the evening. Among this plain, simple people, the power of God is always present.

Sun. 19. The rain would not suffer me to preach abroad. On Monday, Tuesday, and Wednesday, I examined the society and found a large number had been called home this year. A few are still tottering over the grave, but death hath lost its sting.[33]

Thur. 23. I preached in the afternoon near the Fishponds. The people here had been remarkably dead for many years. But since that saint of God, Bathsheba Hall,[34] with her husband, came among them, a flame is broke out. The people flock together in troops and are athirst for all the promises of God.

In the evening, one sat behind me in the pulpit at Bristol who was one of our first masters at Kingswood.[35] A little after he left the school, he likewise left the society. Riches then flowed in upon him, with which, having no relations, Mr. Spencer[36] designed to do much good—after his death. 'But God said unto him, Thou fool!'[37] Two hours after, he died intestate and left all his money to—be scrambled for!

Reader! If you have not done it already, make your will before you sleep!

Fri. 24. James Gerrish,[38] Junior, of Rode[39] near Frome, was for several years zealous for God. But he too grew rich and grew lukewarm, till he was seized with a consumption. At the approach of death, he was 'horribly afraid';[40] he was 'in the lowest darkness

---

[33] See 1 Cor. 15:55.

[34] JW preached the funeral sermon for Bathsheba Hall (1745-80) on Oct. 1, 1780, and published seven extracts of her diary in the *Arminian Magazine* 4 (1781):35ff. She was converted, after a serious childhood, at the age of eighteen, while resident in the household at the Foundery. After returning to Bristol, she suffered recurrent illness, but about 1779 'began to be useful to others, both by her prayers and private exhortations', a usefulness which increased after her marriage to John Hall. Marriage, however, did not mend her health, and she died in 1780. JW describes the journal, which closed in 1775, as 'exceedingly artless and simple; [it] affords little variety; but [it] is the genuine picture of a soul renewed in love, and wholly devoted to God'; it is indeed an example of the religious vocabulary which a contemporary Methodist might use to reveal, or (as in this case) to veil her transactions with God.

[35] William Spencer; see June 22, 1751 (20:392, n. 5 in this edn.).

[36] Orig., 'Spenser'—for his own spelling see *Letters*, 26:320-21 in this edn.

[37] Luke 12:20.

[38] He appears in Tuck's *Methodism in Frome* as 'James Girrish, married baker, Road'.

[39] Orig., 'Road'. Rode was a parish 4 miles north-east of Frome. There had been many Quaker Gerrishes here. *Victoria County History; Wiltshire*, 3:116.

[40] Jer. 2:12.

and in the deep'.[41] But he 'cried unto God in his trouble' and was 'delivered out of his distress'.[42] He was filled with peace and joy unspeakable,[43] and so continued till he went to God. His father desired I would preach his funeral sermon, which I accordingly
5 did this day at Rode. I concluded the busy day with a comfortable watch-night at Kingswood.

Mon. 27. I preached at Pill. On Wednesday, I opened the New Chapel in Guinea Street. Thursday 30, I preached at Almonds-bury[44] on communion with God, while deep awe sat on the face of
10 all the people. Friday, October 1, I took a solemn leave of the children at Kingswood. Several of them have been convinced of sin again and again, but they soon trifled their convictions away.

Sun. 3. I preached once more in the square to a multitude of people, and afterward spent a solemn hour with the society in
15 renewing our covenant with God.

Mon. 4. I left Bristol, preached at the Devizes at eleven, and in the evening at Salisbury.[45] Tuesday 5, I preached at Whitchurch,[46] where many, even of the rich, attended and behaved with much seriousness. Wednesday 6, at eleven, I preached in Winchester,
20 where there are four thousand five hundred French prisoners. I was glad to find they have plenty of wholesome food and are treated in all respects with great humanity.

In the evening, I preached at Portsmouth Common. Thursday 7, I took a view of the camp adjoining to the town and wondered
25 to find it as clean and neat as a gentleman's garden. But there was no chaplain! The English soldiers of this age have nothing to do with God!

Fri. 8. We took chaise as usual at two, and about eleven came to Cobham.[47] Having a little leisure, I thought I could not employ it
30 better than in taking a walk through the gardens. They are said to take up four hundred acres and are admirably well laid out. They far exceed the celebrated gardens at Stowe,[48] and that in several respects: (1) in situation, lying on a much higher hill and having a finer prospect from the house; (2) in having a natural river, clear

---

[41] Cf. Ps. 88:5 (BCP).
[42] Cf. Ps. 107:6, etc. (BCP).
[43] 1 Pet. 1:8.
[44] Orig., 'Amesbury'. On the Almondsbury connection, see above, Sept. 29, 1778.
[45] Orig., 'Sarum'.
[46] Whitchurch was a small market town 12 miles north of Winchester.
[47] On these gardens, see Oct. 5, 1771 (22:291, n. 69 in this edn.).
[48] Orig., here and below, 'Stow'; see n. 51.

as crystal, running beneath and through them; (3) in the buildings therein, which are fewer indeed, but far more elegant—yea, and far better kept, being nicely clean, which is sadly wanting at Stowe; and lastly, in the rock-work, to which nothing of the kind at Stowe is to be compared.   5

This night I lodged in the new house at London.[49] How many more nights have I to spend there?

Mon. 11. I began my little tour into Northamptonshire. In the evening, I preached at Stony Stratford, the next day, at Hanslope[50] and at [Maids'] Moreton a little mile from Buckingham. Wednes-   10 day 13, having so lately seen Stourhead and Cobham gardens, I was now desired to take a view of the much more celebrated gardens at Stowe. The first thing I observed was the beautiful water which runs through the gardens to the front of the house. The tufts of trees, placed on each side of this, are wonderfully pleas-   15 ant. And so are many of the walks and glades through the woods, which are disposed with a fine variety. The large pieces of water interspersed give a fresh beauty to the whole. Yet there are several things which must give disgust to any person of common sense: (1) the buildings called temples are most miserable, many of them   20 both within and without. Sir John Vanbrugh's[51] is an ugly, clumsy lump, hardly fit for a gentleman's stable; (2) the temples of Venus and Bacchus, though large, have nothing elegant in the structure. And the paintings in the former, representing a lewd story, are neither well designed nor executed; those in the latter are quite   25 faded, and most of the inscriptions vanished away; (3) the statues are full as coarse as the paintings; particularly those of Apollo and the Muses—whom a person not otherwise informed might take to be nine cook-maids; (4) most of the water in the ponds is dirty and thick as puddle; (5) it is childish affectation to call things here   30 by Greek or Latin names, as Styx and the Elysian Fields; (6) it was ominous for my lord to entertain himself and his noble com-

[49] I.e., 'Wesley's House' on the south side of the City Road Chapel.

[50] Orig., 'Honslip'.

[51] Sir John Vanbrugh (1664–1726), dramatist, architect, and herald. After his first success at Castle Howard, Vanbrugh was employed on a number of prestigious mansions, notably Blenheim and Floors Castle (cf. below, May 27, 1784), where the final effect was one of magnificence rather than comfort, and weight rather than elegance. His share in the landscape planning at Stowe is uncertain, and was not perhaps dominant. The profusion of buildings in the grounds which so disgusted JW (and others) delighted Horace Walpole with its 'inexpressible richness', and is unique to this estate. Not all that were built or are mentioned by JW survive. Pevsner, *Buckinghamshire*, pp. 251-52.

pany in a grotto built on the bank of Styx, that is, on the brink of
hell; (7) the river on which it stands is a black, filthy puddle,
exactly resembling a common sewer; (8) one of the stateliest monuments is taken down, the Egyptian Pyramid. And no wonder,
considering the two inscriptions which are still legible: the one,

> *Linquenda tellus, et domus, et placens*
> *Uxor: neque harum, quas colis, arborum*
> *Te praeter invisas cupressos,*
> *Ulla brevem dominum sequetur!*[52]

the other,

> *Lusisti satis, edisti satis, atque bibisti:*
> *Tempus abire tibi est: ne potum largius aequo*
> *Rideat, et pulset lasciva decentius aetas.*[53]

Upon the whole, I cannot but prefer Cobham gardens to those
at Stowe, for (1) the river at Cobham shames all the ponds at
Stowe; (2) there is nothing at Stowe comparable to the walk near
the wheel, which runs up the side of a steep hill, quite grotesque
and wild; (3) nothing in Stowe gardens is to be compared to the
large temple, the pavilion, the antique temple, the grotto, or the
building at the head of the garden, nor to the neatness which runs
through the whole.

But there is nothing even at Cobham to be compared (1) to the
beautiful cross at the entrance of Stourhead gardens, (2) to the vast
body of water, (3) the rock-work grotto, (4) the temple of the sun,
(5) the Hermitage. Here too everything is nicely clean, as well as in
full preservation. Add to this that all the gardens hang on the sides
of a semicircular mountain. And there is nothing, either at Cobham or Stowe, which can balance the advantage of such a situation.

On this and the two following evenings, I preached at Whittlebury, Towcester, and Northampton. On Saturday, I returned to
London.

[52] Horace, *Odes*, II.xiv.21–24: 'Earth we must leave, and home and darling wife; nor of
the trees thou tendest now will any follow thee, its short-lived master, except the hated
cypress' (Loeb); quoted and translated above, July 5, 1756 (21:64, n. 36 in this edn.);
quoted also in Sermon 28, 'Sermon on the Mount, VIII', § 19 (1:624 in this edn.).
[53] Horace, *Epistles*, II.ii.214–16: 'You have played enough, have eaten and drunk
enough. 'Tis time to quit the feast, lest, when you have drunk too freely, youth mock
and jostle you, playing the wanton with better grace' (Loeb).

Mon. 18. I set out for Sussex and, after visiting the societies there, returned to London on Saturday the 23rd. I was in hopes, by bringing her with me, to save the life of Miss A. of Ewhurst, far gone in a consumption. But she was too far gone; so that though that journey helped her for awhile, yet she quickly 5 relapsed and, soon after, died in peace.[54]

Sun. 24. I preached a charity sermon in Shadwell Church.[55] I spoke with all possible plainness. And surely some out of an immense multitude will receive the truth and bring forth fruit with patience.[56]   10

Mon. 25. I set out for Norwich. Tuesday 26, I went on to Yarmouth, on Wednesday to Lowestoft,[57] on Friday to Loddon. Saturday 30, I came to Norwich again.

Monday, November 1, I crossed over to [King's] Lynn and settled the little affairs there; on Wednesday 4, went on to Colch- 15 ester and, on Friday, to London. Saturday 5, I began examining the society, which usually employs me eleven or twelve days.

Sat. 13. I had the pleasure of an hour's conversation with Mr. G[alloway],[58] one of the members of the first Congress in America. He unfolded a strange tale indeed! How has poor K[ing] 20 G[eorge] been betrayed on every side! But this is our comfort: there is One higher than they. And He will command all things to work together for good.[59]

The following week I examined the rest of our society but did

---

[54] Query, Ann Holman. See *WHS* 19 (1934):112-14.
[55] See above, Dec. 14, 1777.
[56] See Luke 8:15.
[57] Orig., 'Loestoffe'.
[58] Joseph Galloway (1730-1803) was born in Maryland and early attained eminence as a lawyer and politician at Philadelphia, becoming speaker in the General Assembly of Pennsylvania. In this capacity he tried to maintain harmony with England, believing that the differences in the empire were basically constitutional and could be overcome by a written constitution, his final scheme for which he published after becoming a member of the first Continental Congress in 1774. In December 1776, he joined the British army under Sir William Howe under an indemnity, and enjoyed well-paid offices in Philadelphia till that town was evacuated in 1778; he returned to England. In 1779, he published attacks on Howe for his misconduct of the war, and subsequently two pamphlets on the general significance of the rebellion. JW, who here met him for the first time, defended him both privately and publicly against the attacks he encountered (Telford, 7:21, 48), and reprinted and distributed his *Reflections on the Rise and Progress of the American Rebellion* (1780); ibid., 7:121; *WHS* 9 (1913):7-9. JW's hope that Galloway would write a 'true account of the American revolution' (Telford, 8:234) was unfulfilled (Galloway turned to the study of prophecy), but JW took his niece Sarah to meet the American and his daughter in 1791. Curnock, 8:134; cf. Telford, 8:238.
[59] See Rom. 8:28.

not find such an increase as I expected. Nay, there was a considerable decrease, plainly owing to a senseless jealousy that had crept
in between our preachers, which had grieved the Holy Spirit of
God[60] and greatly hindered his work.[61]

5   Mon. 22. My brother and I set out for Bath, on a very extraordinary occasion. Some time since, Mr. Smyth, a clergyman whose
labours God had greatly blessed in the north of Ireland, brought
his wife over to Bath, who had been for some time in a declining
state of health. I desired him to preach every Sunday evening in
10 our chapel while he remained there. But as soon as I was gone
Mr. McNab,[62] one of our preachers, vehemently opposed that;

---

[60] See Eph. 4:30.

[61] The nature of this dispute was at root the same as that which immediately followed
at Bath, the relations between JW's unordained preachers, and his few ordained assistants, such as his brother, and, in the following entry, the Rev. Edward Smyth. Trouble
had been brewing at City Road since the new chapel was opened, for part of the original
intention had been that on Sundays the chapel should be served only by ordained men,
and the liturgy used, morning and evening. Although CW did not seem the best suited
for the congregations, he nevertheless claimed the right to preach there 'twice every
Sunday . . . : (1) Because after you [JW], I have the best right. (2) Because I have so
short a time to preach anywhere. (3) Because I am fully persuaded I can do more good
there than in any other place'; letter of June 16, 1779, *Arminian Magazine* 12
(1789):441. The issue at Bath was similar. McNab, whom JW described in 1771 as 'a
sound and good preacher; but too warm and impatient of contradiction' (Telford,
5:219), an estimate confirmed by Christopher Hopper (Curnock, 6:270, n. 1), had been
appointed superintendent of the Bristol circuit (which included the Bath chapel) at the
Conference of 1779, and he resisted the intrusion of Edward Smyth. JW's brutal summary of the twelfth of the 'Rules of a Helper' hardly touched the point that McNab was
labouring where JW appointed, in a superintendent's office, which he believed controlled access to the pulpits of the circuit. McNab's expulsion was clearly regarded as
unjust by many of the preachers, and at the next Conference JW received him back.
The very prospect of this had caused CW to resist John's pressing invitation to attend
the Conference on the grounds '(1) I can do no good; (2) I can prevent no evil; (3) I am
afraid of being a partaker of other men's sins . . . ; (4) I am afraid of myself; you know I
cannot command my temper, and you have not the courage to stand by me.' The weakness of CW's position, and of the lengths JW went to defend it, was that in the City
Road Chapel deed of Aug. 6, 1779, JW had retained the right personally to appoint the
preachers there during his lifetime, and envisaged handing it over thereafter to a committee of trustees named in his will. The will (dated Feb. 20, 1784) appointed the
trustees (four clergy and eight preachers) and conveyed to them also the right to appoint
preachers to the chapel at Bath. Shortly after this episode, CW was relieved of his reading duties at City Road at the request of the trustees. Tyerman, *John Wesley*, 3:305-13;
Simon, *John Wesley; The Last Phase*, pp. 147-49.

[62] Alexander McNab (1745-97) was born at Killin near Perth and after school went to
sea. Returning to Edinburgh for maritime professional studies, he became attracted by
Methodist preaching and was eventually converted. After serving as a class-leader, he
began to preach in June 1766, and the following Conference was received into the itinerancy. Appointed to Edinburgh in 1777, he found the chapel in a ruinous condition,
and became responsible for a debt of £500 incurred for repairs. Atmore's judgment on
the Bath affair (*Memorial*, p. 294) was 'Mr. Charles Wesley entered seriously into the

affirming it was the common cause of all the lay preachers; that they were appointed by the Conference, not by *me*, and would not suffer the clergy to ride over their heads—Mr. Smyth in particular,[63] of whom he said all manner of evil.[64] Others warmly defended him. Hence the society was torn in pieces and thrown into the utmost confusion.

Tue. 23. I read to the society a paper which I wrote near twenty years ago on a like occasion.[65] Herein I observed that 'the rules of our preachers were fixed by *me*, before any Conference existed,' particularly the twelfth: 'Above all, you are to preach *when* and *where* I appoint.' By obstinately opposing which rule Mr. McNab has made all this uproar. In the morning at a meeting of the preachers, I informed Mr. McNab that as he did not agree to our fundamental rule, I could not receive him as one of our preachers till he was of another mind.[66]

Wed. 24. I read the same paper to the society at Bristol, as I found the flame had spread thither also. A few at Bath separated from us on this account, but the rest were thoroughly satisfied. So on Friday 26, I took coach again and, on Saturday, reached London.

In this journey I read Dr. Warner's *History of Ireland* from its

business, and in the opinion of many, prevailed upon Mr. [John] Wesley, contrary to his judgment to dismiss Mr. McNab from the connection. At the next Conference . . . through the honesty and influence of the preachers, he was restored again, and travelled a few years longer, but the wound he had received not being healed, he desisted and settled at Sheffield', becoming the esteemed pastor of a small congregation till his death.

[63] The tradition continued in Methodist historiography. Tyerman relates that 'Mr. McNab's subsequent appointments were honourable both to Wesley and himself. . . . Mr. Smyth went back to Ireland; but, in 1782, became one of Wesley's London curates, with a salary of sixty guineas yearly. In 1786, he was appointed minister of Bethesda Chapel, Dublin, where he rent the Methodist society, and took with him above a hundred persons, among whom were the richer members of the Dublin Methodists. He then removed to Manchester, where he officiated as curate of St. Clement's and St. Luke's churches'; *John Wesley*, 3:313.

[64] Matt. 5:11.

[65] Quite likely, a paper written for the benefit of the Norwich preachers in 1760; the second quotation that follows is from JW's 1766 manifesto (see *Minutes*, 1:60-62). Frank Baker, *John Wesley and the Church of England* (London, 1970), p. 383.

[66] CW made it a matter of bitter reproach after the Conference of 1780 that his brother did not stick to this resolution: 'Your *will*, I perceived, was to receive Mr. McNab, unhumbled, unconvinced, into your confidence and into your bosom. He came uninvited, and openly accused your *curate* for obeying your orders: you suffered it; and did not give Mr. McNab the gentlest reproof for disobeying them and drawing others into his rebellion; and endeavouring to engage all the preachers in it; making an actual separation at Bath, and still keeping up his separate society. My judgment was, never to receive Mr. McNab as a preacher *till he acknowledged his fault.*' John Whitehead, *The Life of the Rev. John Wesley, M.A.*, 2 vols. (London, Couchman, 1793-96), 2:380.

first settlement to the English conquest.[67] And after calm deliber-
ation, I make no scruple to pronounce it a mere senseless
romance. I do not believe one leaf of it is true from the beginning
to the end. I totally reject the authorities on which he builds: I
5 will not take Flagherty's or Keating's[68] word for a farthing. I
doubt not, Ireland was, before the Christian era,[69] full as bar-
barous as Scotland or England. Indeed, it appears from their own
accounts that the Irish in general were continually plundering and
murdering each other from the earliest ages to that period. And so
10 they were ever since, by the account of Dr. Warner himself, till
they were restrained by the English. How then were they converted by St. Patrick (cousin-german[70] to St. George!)? To what
religion? Not to Christianity. Neither in his age nor the following
had they the least savour of Christianity, either in their lives or
15 their tempers.

Sun. 28. I preached a charity sermon at St. Peter's, Cornhill.[71]
Monday 29, I visited the societies in Kent and returned on Saturday.

Sunday, December 5. In applying those words, 'What could I
20 have done for my vineyard which I have not done?'[72] I found such
an uncommon pouring out of the convincing Spirit as we have
not known for many years. In the evening, the same Spirit enabled
me strongly to exhort a numerous congregation to 'Come boldly
to the throne of grace'[73] and to 'make all their requests known
25 unto God with thanksgiving.'[74]

---

[67] Ferdinando Warner, *The History of Ireland* (London, 1763). Warner, who wrote
widely on theological and literary topics, had the idea of this work while collecting
material in Dublin for his *Ecclesiastical History of England to the Eighteenth Century*
(London, 1756–57), but, when he failed to obtain financial support from the Irish House
of Commons, gave it up after one volume. John Nichols, *Literary Anecdotes of the Eighteenth Century*, 9 vols. (London, 1812), 2:415.

[68] JW is harsh on Warner here. Warner prized O'Flaherty (R. O'Flaherty, *Ogygia*
[London, 1685]) for rejecting many romantic tales and greatly improving the chronol-
ogy of ancient Irish history. But he included G. Keating among the mass of native Irish
writers who 'all betray so much vanity, and deal so much in the fabulous, as, gives an air
of romance to the whole, or to speak it in the most favourable and candid terms, as
makes it appear to be mythological rather than a real history.' See G. Keating, *The General History of Ireland*, trans. D. O'Connor (Dublin, 1723); Warner, *History of Ireland*,
1:i–ii.

[69] Orig., 'aera'.

[70] I.e., first cousin.

[71] On St. Peter's, Cornhill, see above, Feb. 28, 1779.

[72] Cf. Isa. 5:4.

[73] Heb. 4:16 (*Notes*).

[74] Cf. Phil. 4:6.

Tue. 7. I preached in Rotherhithe[75] Chapel, a cold, uncomfortable place, to an handful of people who appeared to be just as much affected as the benches they sat upon.

Thur. 9. In speaking on those words, 'Set thy house in order; for thou shalt die and not live,'[76] I took occasion to exhort all who had not done it already, to settle their temporal affairs without delay. Let not any man who reads these words put it off a day longer!

Mon. 13. I retired to Lewisham and settled the society book. Fifty-seven members of the society have died this year, and none of them 'as a fool dieth'.[77] An hundred and seventy have left the society. Such are the fruits of senseless prejudice.[78]

Sat. 25. We began the service at the New Chapel as usual at four in the morning. Afterwards, I read prayers and preached and administered the Lord's Supper at West Street; in the afternoon, I preached at the New Chapel again, then met the society, and afterwards the married men and women; but after this I was no more tired than when I rose in the morning.

Wed. 29. Mr. Hatton, lately come from America, gave us an account of his strange deliverance. He was Collector of the Customs for the eastern ports of Maryland and zealous for King George. Therefore the rebels resolved to dispatch him, and a party was sent for that purpose under one Simpson, who owed him five hundred pounds. But first he sent him the following note:

> Sir,
>   We are resolved to have you dead or alive. So we advise you to give yourself up, that you may give us no more trouble.
>   I am, sir,
>   Your obedient servant.

Mr. Hatton not complying with this civil advice, a party of riflemen was sent to take him. He was just going out, when a child told him they were at hand and had only time to run and get into a hollow which was under the house. The maid clapped to the trap-door and covered it over with flax. They searched the

---

[75] Orig., 'Redriff'. This colloquial or, according to Samuel Lewis (*England*, 3:622), corrupt version of Rotherhithe appears also at Feb. 23, 1768; and in the Diary, June 6, 1740 (22:119 and 19:422 in this edn.).

[76] Isa. 38:1.

[77] 2 Sam. 3:33.

[78] I.e., the disputes surrounding CW.

house from top to bottom, opened all the closets, turned up the beds, and finding nothing, went away. He was scarce come out, when another party beset the house and came so quick that he had but just time to get in again. And the maid, not having flax enough at hand, covered the door with foul linen. When these also had wearied themselves with searching and went away, he put on his boots and great-coat, took a gun and a rug (it being a sharp frost), and crept into a little marsh near the house. A third party came quickly, swearing he must be about the house, and they would have him if he was alive. Hearing this, he stole away with full speed and lay down near the sea-shore between two hillocks, covering himself with seaweeds. They came so near that he heard one of them swear, 'If I find him, I will hang him on the next tree.' Another answered, 'I will not stay for that, I will shoot him the moment I see him.'

After some time, finding they were gone, he lifted up his head and heard a shrill whistle from a man fifty or sixty yards off. He soon knew him to be a deserter from the rebel army. He asked Mr. H[atton] what he designed to do, who answered, 'Go in my boat to the English ships, which are four or five and twenty mile off.' But the rebels had found and burned the boat. So knowing their life was gone if they stayed till the morning, they got into a small canoe (though liable to overset with a puff of wind) and set off from shore. Having rowed two or three miles, they stopped at a little island and made a fire, being almost perished with cold. But they were quickly alarmed by a boat rowing toward the shore. Mr. Hatton standing up said, 'We have a musket and a fusee. If you load one as fast as I discharge the other, I will give a good account of them all.' He then stepped to the shore and bade the rowers stop and tell him who they were, declaring he would fire among them if any man struck another stroke. Upon their answering, he found they were friends, being six more deserters from the rebel army. So they gladly came on shore and brought provisions with them to those who before had neither meat nor drink. After refreshing themselves, they all went into the boat and cheerfully rowed to the English ships.

Fri. 31. We concluded the year at West Street with a solemn watch-night.[79] Most of the congregation stayed till the beginning of the year and cheerfully sang together:

[79] On watch-night services, see Apr. 9, 1742 (19:258, n. 50 in this edn.).

Glory to God, and thanks, and praise,
Who kindly lengthens out our days, etc.[80]

Sunday, January 2, 1780. We had the largest congregation at the renewal of our covenant[81] with God which ever met upon the occasion. And we were thoroughly convinced that God was not   5
departed from us. He never will, unless we first depart from him.

Tue. 18. Receiving more and more accounts of the increase of popery, I believed it my duty to write a letter concerning it, which was afterwards inserted in the public papers.[82] Many were grievously offended. But I cannot help it. I must follow my own con-   10
science.

Sat. 22. I spent an hour or two very agreeably in Sir Ashton

---

[80] Cf. CW, *Hymns for New Year's Day* (1750 onwards), the first lines of the first hymn:

> Wisdom ascribe, and might, and praise
> To God, who lengthens out our days.

George Osborn, ed., *The Poetical Works of John and Charles Wesley,* 13 vols. (London, Wesleyan Conference Office, 1868-72), 6:9. The second line in the text duplicates line 3 of hymn VII in that collection,

> Sing to the great Jehovah's praise!
> All praise to him belongs:
> Who kindly lengthens out our days
> Demands our choicest songs.

[81] On the origins of the Covenant Service, see Aug. 6, 1755 (21:23, n. 82 in this edn.).

[82] This letter (dated Jan. 12, 1785) defending the Protestant Association from its critics, was published in *The Public Advertiser* and was subsequently enlarged as a broadsheet (Telford, 6:370-73); disdaining all persecution, it argued that 'no Roman Catholic does or can give security for allegiance or public behaviour,' since it was 'a Roman Catholic maxim established not by private men but by a public council, that "no faith is to be kept with heretics." ' JW's letter evoked a substantial counterblast by Arthur O'Leary (1729-1802), a Capuchin friar of Cork, to which JW replied in *Arminian Magazine* 4 (1781):296-300, 352-60. On May 12, 1787 (see below), JW notes that he was invited 'to breakfast with my old antagonist, Father O'Leary. I was not at all displeased at being disappointed. He is not the stiff, queer man that I expected, but of an easy genteel carriage, and seems not to be wanting either in sense or learning.' O'Leary was the more sensitive to JW's charges as, while he was in the Capuchin monastery at St. Malo in the Seven Years' War, he had ministered to British prisoners of war there, many of them Irish and Catholic, and had resisted pressure from Choiseul, the French foreign minister to get them to transfer their allegiance to France; he had recently defended Catholic oaths of loyalty and urged on the Irish their undivided loyalty to the Crown in the event of French invasion. O'Leary was an apostle of Enlightenment who thought that the progress of knowledge would speedily terminate differences of confessional opinion, and his loyalist utterances were encouraged by secret service pensions. His equivocal position in Ireland led him to leave in 1789 and take employment in the Spanish embassy in London.

Lever's Museum.[83] It does not equal the British Museum in size, nor is it constructed on so large a plan, as it contains no manuscripts, no books, no antiquities, nor any remarkable works of art. But I believe, for natural curiosities, it is not excelled by any museum in Europe. And all the beasts, birds, reptiles, and insects, are admirably well ranged and preserved. So that if you saw many of them elsewhere, you would imagine, they were alive! The hippopotamus, in particular, looks as fierce as if he was just coming out of the river, and the old lion appears as formidable now as when he was stalking in the Tower.

Sun. 28. In the evening, I retired to Lewisham to prepare matter (who would believe it?) for a monthly magazine.[84] Friday, February the 4th, being the National Fast,[85] I preached first at the New Chapel and then at St. Peter's, Cornhill.[86] What a difference in the congregation! Yet out of these stones God can raise up children to Abraham.[87]

Thur. 17. I preached at Dorking and could not but reflect, in this room I lodged the first time I saw *poor* Mr. Ireland[88]—

[83] Sir Ashton Lever (1729-88) of Alkrington Hall near Oldham, was from an early age a devotee of outdoor sports and collecting in the field of natural history, to which he later added savage costumes and weapons. This collection attracted much attention, and in 1774 he took Leicester House in Leicester Square to display it in sixteen rooms, at a charge of 5s. 3d. per person. He grew eccentric and impaired his fortune by expenditure on the museum. In 1783 he offered the collection, then valued by a parliamentary committee at £53,000, for a moderate sum to the British Museum, but the trustees declined to buy. In 1788, he obtained an act to dispose of the collection by a lottery of 36,000 guinea tickets, of which only 8000 were sold. The winner displayed the collection for some years on the South Bank before disposing of it in 7829 lots in a monster auction in 1806.

[84] Believe it or not, JW had been editing and writing the *Arminian Magazine* for over two years. JW often retired to Lewisham for high pressure literary work, and it is a question whether this note has not been displaced from Nov. 24, 1777, where (also at Lewisham) he describes the origin of the *Arminian Magazine*.

[85] On this occasion Richard Watson preached a Whiggish sermon at Cambridge, declaring that the King's best friends were those who detested 'alike despotism and republicanism'. *Gentleman's Magazine* 50 (1780):169.

[86] On this church, see above, Feb. 28, 1779.

[87] See Matt. 3:9.

[88] Richard Ireland (1700-80) of Reigate Place. On Dec. 19, 1770, JW had preached at Dorking and then at Reigate, by which is probably meant Reigate Place. On the next visit, Dec. 17, 1771, the visit to Reigate Place is made explicit, and the house is described by JW. The entry of Nov. 15, 1775, implies that there was regular preaching at Reigate Place, but there is no further mention of the house in the *Journal* (see 22:260, 302, 471 in this edn.). The implication seems to be that a society in that house was given up owing to some estrangement between JW and Richard Ireland; *WHS* 28 (1952):85-88. 'Emphatically poor' is a reference to the passage from Abraham Cowley's essay, 'Of Avarice', *Essays, Plays, and Sundry Verses*, ed. A. R. Waller (Cambridge, 1906), p. 437, frequently quoted by JW:

emphatically poor! Poor beyond expression—though he left four-score thousand pounds behind him!

Thur. 24. I met the building committee, according to whose representation our income at last nearly answers our expenses. If so it will clear itself in a few years.

Mon. 28. Taking the post-coach, I reached Newbury time enough to preach to a crowded audience. Tuesday 29 and Wednesday, I preached at Bath, where brotherly love is now restored. Thursday, March 2, I went into Bristol and enjoyed much peace among a quiet, loving people. On Monday, Tuesday, and Wednesday, I examined the society and had reason to rejoice over them.

Mon. 13. I set out for the north and, in the evening, preached at Stroud, where is a considerable increase of the work of God. Tuesday 14, I preached in the church at Pitcombe,[89] but it would by no means contain the congregation. In the evening, I preached at Tewkesbury, and on Wednesday the 15th, at Worcester to a very serious congregation. Thursday 16 about noon, I began preaching at Bewdley, in an open space at the head of the town. The wind was high and exceeding sharp, but no one seemed to regard it. In the middle of the sermon came a man beating a drum, but a gentleman of the town soon silenced him. Friday 17 about noon, I preached at Bengeworth[90] Church to the largest congregation I ever saw there; and in Pebworth Church about six, to a larger congregation than I had seen there before. I found uncommon liberty in applying those words (perhaps a last warning to the great man of the parish, Mr. Martin[91]), 'Whatever thy hand findeth to do, do it with thy might.'[92]

Sat. 18. I went on to Birmingham and, Sunday 19, preached at eight in the morning and at half past one in the afternoon; in the evening, at Wednesbury. Monday 20, I reached Congleton and

---

The Beggars but a common fate deplore,
The Rich poor Man's Emphatically poor.

Cf. July 21, 1760, and Sermon 131, 'The Danger of Increasing Riches', I.1 (21:269 and 4:179 in this edn.).

[89] Orig., 'Pitchcombe.' Pitcombe, Glos., was a village 2 miles north of Stroud.
[90] On Beale, the rector of Bengeworth, see above, July 5, 1777.
[91] Probably Capt. Robert Martin; see Ralph Bigland, *Historical, Monumental, and Genealogical Collections relative to the County of Gloucester*, 2 vols. (London, 1791-92), 2:318.
[92] Eccles. 9:10.
[93] John 11:43.

preached to a lively congregation on our Lord's words, 'Lazarus,
come forth!'[93] Tuesday 21, I preached in the New Chapel at Macclesfield;[94] Thursday 23, at Stockport and Manchester.

On Good Friday, I preached at seven in Manchester, about one
5   in Oldham, and in Manchester at six. Saturday 25, I went on to
Bolton, where the work of God is continually increasing. On
Easter Day, I set out for Warrington. Mr. Harmer[95] read prayers
both morning and afternoon. We had a large congregation in the
morning, as many as the church could well contain in the after-
10   noon, and more than it could contain in the evening. At last there
is reason to hope that God will have a steady people even in this
wilderness.

The next evening, when a few of the society were met together,
the power of God came mightily upon them. Some fell to the
15   ground, some cried aloud for mercy, some rejoiced with joy
unspeakable.[96] Two or three found a clear sense of the love of
God, one gay young woman in particular, who was lately much
prejudiced against this way but is now filled with joy unspeakable.

Monday, Tuesday, and Wednesday, I spent at Liverpool, being
20   undetermined whether to proceed or not. At length I yielded to
the advice of my friends and deferred my journey to Ireland.[97] So

[94] The Sunderland Street Chapel began as the private property of John Ryle, and was
not put on a properly executed trust-deed for some months; Smith, *Methodism in Macclesfield*, pp. 49-50. Benson records: 'March 22. Mr. Mayer and I rode to Macclesfield
to meet our old father in the gospel, Mr. Wesley, and were glad to find him, though at
the age of seventy-eight [actually 76] look as well, and able to preach as much and
strongly, as though he had been no more than forty.' Curnock, 6:269, n. 1.

[95] John Harmer, one of the Anglican clergymen whom JW attempted to rally in 1764
(see Apr. 19, 1764; 21:455, n. 69 in this edn.), seems to have acted in 1766 as a preacher
in Lady Huntingdon's connection, but speedily withdrew without an explanation; Seymour, *Huntingdon*, 1:487-88. He is then said to have joined JW, 1766-72; William
Myles, *Chronological History* (3rd edn., London, 1803), p. 301. There is, however, no
trace of him in the stationing minutes. He was vicar of Butlers Marston, near Kington
in Warwickshire, 1779-84, and minister of Kineton. He appears to have come to Warrington as assistant to the evangelical vicar of St. James's, James Glazebrook, in 1777,
and there in 1788 baptized Peter Phillips, one of the later pioneers of the Quaker
Methodists. *WHS* 6 (1908):121-24; 8 (1911):83.

[96] See 1 Pet. 1:8.

[97] The nature of this advice (and of the man to whom it was given) is indicated in a
letter from Christopher Hopper to Joseph Cownley, Colne, Apr. 6, 1780: 'I have seen
and heard the old gentleman [JW] at Bolton and Manchester. He is still the same man,
full of spirits, and full of business, and perhaps too full of himself. But he is in the
Lord's hands. I hope his latter end will be peace and glory. You have doubtless seen
Mr. Wesley's letter to the printer of the *The Public Advertiser* in vindication of an
Appeal from the Protestant Association to the people of Great Britain. A Romish priest
[Arthur O'Leary, on whom see above, Jan. 18, 1780] has answered it. The Papists in
Ireland are ready to take up arms against us. They are all in a flame. Mr. Wesley

I preached at Northwich about noon, and in the evening at Alpraham[98] in the midst of all the old Methodists. We had a very different congregation at Nantwich in the evening. But as many as could get into the house or near the door behaved very seriously.

Saturday, April 1, I returned to Chester and found many alive 5 to God, but scarce one that retained his pure love. Sunday 2, I reached Warrington about ten. The chapel was well filled with serious hearers, and I believe God confirmed the word of his grace. Hastening back to Chester, I found a numerous congregation waiting, and immediately began, 'This is the victory that 10 overcometh the world, even our faith.'[99]

Monday 3, I returned to Manchester and, Tuesday 4, strongly applied, 'What could I have done for my vineyard, which I have not done?'[1] At present there are many here that 'bring forth good grapes',[2] but many swiftly increase in goods. And I fear very few 15 sufficiently watch and pray that they 'may not set their hearts upon them.'[3]

Wednesday 5, I preached at Bolton; Thursday 6 about noon, at Bury; and at Rochdale in the evening. Friday 7, I went to Delph,[4] a little village upon the mountains, where a remarkable work of 20 God is just broke out.[5] I was just set down when the minister sent

received several letters from the preachers and others, who seem of an opinion that it would not be safe for the little man to appear in Paddy's land this year. He has therefore thought it prudent to stay in his own country. I think it is but a little bravado, but I cannot tell; those creatures are not to be trusted; perhaps they would cut our throats if they could. They shall dethrone the Pope before I will give them the right hand.' Curnock, 6:270-71n.

[98] JW had been visiting Alpraham since 1749, staying with the Cawleys at Moat Hall; see Oct. 19, 1749 (20:309, n. 75 in this edn.). His arrival now was the occasion of a general holiday in the neighbourhood. *Wesleyan Methodist Magazine* 80 (1857):220.

[99] 1 John 5:4.

[1] Cf. Isa. 5:4.

[2] Cf. ibid.

[3] Cf. Deut. 32:46.

[4] Orig. 'Delf'.

[5] Delph was a chapelry in the parish of Rochdale. Around this optimistic entry a picturesque legend grew up. Heginbottom, the incumbent of Saddleworth, was blind, and engaged a curate called Stones, whose principal interests were his dogs and gun. This enthusiasm occasioned a blunt rebuke from one of the mountain men of Saddleworth, which led to Stones's conversion, and, in turn, to a revival in the district based on powerful cottage prayer-meetings. The revival in turn led to Stones's loss of his job, and to the people at Delph taking counsel about their spiritual future. They took advice from Joseph Benson, then superintendent of the Manchester circuit, who had preached the first Methodist sermon in the district as recently as October 1779. A room was hired for worship in Delph, and following JW's visit, Conference gave permission for the erection of a preaching-house at Saddleworth. *Wesleyan Methodist Magazine* 76 (1853):786.

me word, I was welcome to preach in his church. On hearing this, many people walked thither immediately, near a mile from the town. But in ten minutes he sent word, his mind was changed. We knew not then what to do, till the trustees of the Independent Meeting offered us the use of their house. It was quickly filled, and truly God bore witness to his word. In the evening, I preached at Huddersfield. Saturday 8 about noon, I opened the new house at Mirfield[6] and, in the evening, preached at Dawgreen. Sunday 9, I went on to Birstall and took my stand at the front of the house, though the north-east wind whistled round about. I preached again between four and five, pointing them to the great Bishop and Shepherd of their souls.[7]

Monday 10, I preached in the prison at Whitley,[8] in the evening at Morley, and on Tuesday morning at Cross Hall.[9] The family here are much grown in grace since I saw them last. Most of them now enjoy the great salvation and walk worthy of their vocation. And all around them 'see their good works, and glorify their Father which is in heaven.'[10]

In the evening, I preached to a very genteel congregation at Wakefield. Wednesday 12, after preaching at Rothwell, I inquired what was become of that lovely class of little girls, most of them believers, whom I met here a few years since.[11] I found, those of them that had pious parents remain to this day. But all of them whose parents did not fear God are gone back into the world.

In the evening, I preached in the new house at Leeds.[12] Thursday 13, I opened the new house at Hunslet. On Friday, I preached at Woodhouse. Sunday 16, our house at Leeds was full at eight, yet everyone heard distinctly. In the afternoon, I preached at the old church, but a considerable part of the people could not hear. Indeed the church is remarkably ill constructed. Had it been built with common sense, all that were in it, and even more, might have heard every word.

Mon. 17. I left Leeds in one of the roughest mornings I have

---

[6] 'A good chapel' was built in Mirfield, a very early centre of Methodist activity in the West Riding, in 1779. *Wesleyan Methodist Magazine* 61 (1838):537.

[7] See 1 Pet. 2:25.

[8] Orig., 'Whitelee'.

[9] The Yorkshire home of Miss Bosanquet, on whom see Dec. 1, 1764 (21:495, n. 60 in this edn.). For a previous visit, see July 7, 1770 (22:239 and n. 12).

[10] Cf. Matt. 5:16.

[11] See Apr. 23, 1776.

[12] On the site of the Old Boggard House.

ever seen. We had rain, hail, snow, and wind in abundance. About nine, I preached at Bramley; between one and two, at Pudsey. Afterwards, I walked to Fulneck, the German settlement.[13] Mr. Moore[14] showed us the house, chapel, hall, lodging-rooms, the apartments of the widows, the single men, and single women. He showed us likewise the workshops of various kinds, with the shops for grocery, drapery, mercery, hardware, etc., with which, as well as with bread from their bakehouse, they furnish the adjacent country. I see not what but the mighty power of God can hinder them from acquiring millions:[15] as they (1) buy all materials with ready money at the best hand; (2) have above an hundred young men, above fifty young women, many widows, and above an hundred married persons, all of whom are employed from morning to night without any intermission in various kinds of manufactures, not for journeymen's wages, but for no wages at all, save a little very plain food and raiment; as they have (3) a quick sale for all their goods and sell them all for ready money. But can they lay up treasure on earth and at the same time lay up treasure in heaven?[16]

In the evening, I preached at Bradford, where I was well pleased to find many, both men and women, who had never suffered any decay since they were *perfected in love*. Wednesday 19, I went to Otley; but Mr. Ritchie[17] was dead before I came. But he

[13] I.e., the Moravian settlement. JW had visited the settlement at an early stage; see Apr. 28, 1747 (20:169-70, and n. 5 in this edn.).

[14] John Moore (1745-90) is mentioned as a 'labourer's child' in the first list of the Fulneck congregation, 1746; Daniel Benham, *Memoirs of James Hutton* (London, 1856), p. 232. He became Congregation's Warden there in 1776 (and in this capacity acted as JW's guide), moved to Bath in 1780, and to Bristol, where he eventually died, in 1782.

[15] JW is here naive. The Moravians were still labouring to pay off Zinzendorf's debts. In any case, the complexity of the relation between the Moravian settlements and their economic milieu comes out in the fact that the settlement at Herrnhut long retained its original economic character. The economic functions of that at Fulneck were killed in the following century by the competitive power of Yorkshire capitalism. It was only at Bethlehem, Pennsylvania, where the settlement developed into the headquarters of the Bethlehem Steel Corporation, that an enterprise begun by the Moravians developed into something which 'acquired millions' and competed in the capitalist world on capitalist terms. This theme is adumbrated in Gillian Lindt Gollin, *Moravians in Two Worlds* (New York, 1967). In 1770, James Hutton had complained to CW of JW's strictures in this vein, and had then received a conciliatory reply. *Moravian Messenger*, n.s., 12 (1875):423-24.

[16] See Matt. 6:19-20.

[17] John Ritchie (d. 1780) was born in Edinburgh, becoming a naval surgeon. Abandoning this profession, he moved into Wharfedale, married Beatrice Robinson (1728-1808; *Methodist Magazine* 32 [1809]:174-75), and settled at Otley. In 1754 she was converted, and her second child, Elizabeth, JW's intimate, later Mrs. Mortimer, was born; see May 2, 1774 (22:406, n. 88 in this edn.). From this time on the Ritchies were generally JW's hosts when he was in the area.

had first witnessed a good confession. One telling him, 'You will be better soon', he replied, 'I cannot be better. For I have God in my heart. I am happy, happy, happy in his love.'

Mr. Wilson,[18] the vicar, after a little hesitation, consented that I should preach his funeral sermon. This I did today. The text he had chosen was, "To you that believe he is precious."[19] Perhaps such a congregation had hardly been in Otley Church before! Surely the right hand of the Lord bringeth mighty things to pass![20]

Sun. 23. Mr. Richardson[21] being unwilling that I should preach any more in Haworth Church, Providence opened another—I preached[22] in Bingley Church,[23] both morning and afternoon. This is considerably larger than the other. It rained hard in the morning. This hindered many, so that those who did come got in pretty well in the forenoon; but in the afternoon, very many were obliged to go away.

After preaching at several other places on Monday[24] and Tuesday, Wednesday 26, I preached in Heptonstall Church,[25] well filled with serious hearers. In the evening, I preached near Todmorden in the heart of the mountains. One would wonder where all the people came from. Thursday 27, I preached in Todmorden Church with great enlargement of heart. In the afternoon, we went on to Blackburn. It seemed the whole town was moved. But the question was, Where to put the congregation? We could not stand abroad because of the sun. So as many as could squeezed into the preaching-house.[26] All the chief men of the town were there. It seems as if the last will be first.

---

[18] Henry Wilson was instituted vicar of Otley on July 23, 1760, and was dead before May 18, 1782. Borthwick Institute, York, MS Inst. A.B., 14:117; 15:309.

[19] Cf. 1 Pet. 2:7.

[20] Ps. 118:16 (BCP).

[21] On John Richardson, see Apr. 19, 1764, and Aug. 3, 1766 (21:454, n. 69, and 22:55, n. 40 in this edn.).

[22] Mr. D. C. Dews of Leeds draws my attention to a recently identified item in Keighley Public Library, the MS Commonplace Book of Allen Edmundson, 1779-83. This shows that JW preached at Keighley on Saturday, April 22, on Isaiah 59:1, 2, and on the 23rd at Bingley on Acts 20:27 in the morning and Matt. 7:24-28 in the afternoon and that night at Keighley on John 14:23. Joseph Bradford was with him and preached at Keighley in the morning and at Bingley at 1 p.m.

[23] The vicar of Bingley was Richard Hartley, on whom see above, Apr. 27, 1776.

[24] JW preached at Keighley at 5 a.m. on 2 Pet. 2:9. Edmundson, MS Commonplace Book.

[25] On the incumbent, Tobit Sutcliffe, see Apr. 18, 1774 (22:404 and n. 72 in this edn.).

[26] In 1780, not long before JW's visit, the Old Calendar House, in what was later called Chapel Street, was obtained for Methodist use. W. Jessop, *An Account of Methodism in Rossendale and the Neighbourhood* (Manchester, 1880), p. 140.

Sun. 30. We had a lovely congregation at Colne, but a much larger at one and at five. Many of them came ten or twelve miles. But I believe not in vain. God gave them a good reward for their labour.

Monday, May 1. We reached Grassington about ten. The multitude of people constrained me to preach abroad. It was fair all the time I was preaching, but afterwards rained much. At Pateley Bridge the vicar offered me the use of his church. Though it was more than twice as large as our preaching-house, it was not near large enough to contain the congregation. How vast is the increase of the work of God! Particularly in the most rugged and uncultivated places! How does he 'send the springs' of grace also 'into the valleys, that run among the hills'![27]

Tuesday 2, we came to Ripon and observed a remarkable turn of providence. The great hindrance of the work of God in this place has suddenly disappeared.[28] And the poor people, being delivered from their fear, gladly flock together to hear his word. The new preaching-house was quickly more than filled. Surely some of them will not be forgetful hearers!

In the afternoon, we travelled through a delightful country, the more so when contrasted with the horrid mountains. The immense ruins of Jervaulx Abbey[29] show what a stately pile it was once. Though we were at a lone house, a numerous congregation assembled in the evening, on whom I enforced, 'This is life eternal, to know thee, the only true God, and Jesus Christ whom thou hast sent.'[30]

Wed. 3. Judging it impracticable to pass the mountains in a carriage, I sent my chaise round and took horse. At twelve, I preached at Swaledale to a loving people, increasing both in grace and number. Thence we crossed over another range of dreary mountains and, in the evening, reached Barnard Castle. Not being yet inured to riding, I now felt something like weariness.

[27] Cf. Ps. 104:10.
[28] The reference is probably to a letter (Telford, 5:22) which JW had addressed in 1766 to Francis Wanley (1709-91), dean of Ripon , rector of Stokesley and prebendary of York (all 1750-91), a magistrate who had refused justice to Methodists, who had suffered rough handling at the hands of the mob. *The History of Ripon, Comprehending a Civil and Ecclesiastical Account of that Ancient Borough* (Ripon, 1801), p. 110; Jackson, *Early Methodist Preachers*, 4:160.
[29] Orig., 'Garvaix'. Jervaulx was one of the Cistercian houses in which the North Riding was rich; the order moved in in 1156. The church was 264 feet long. Pevsner, *North Riding*, pp. 203-4.
[30] John 17:3 (*Notes*).

But I forgot it in the lively congregation, and in the morning it was gone.

Thur. 4. About eight, I preached to a serious congregation at Cotherstone,[31] and about one at Newbiggin in Teesdale. We doubted how we should get over the next mountain, the famous Pikelaw,[32] after so long and heavy rains. But I scarce ever remember us getting over it so well. We found the people in Weardale,[33] as usual, some of the liveliest in the kingdom, knowing nothing and desiring to know nothing save Jesus Christ and him crucified.[34]

Fri. 5. Notice having been given without my knowledge of my preaching at Nenthead,[35] all the lead-miners that could got together, and I declared to them, 'All things are ready.'[36] After riding over another enormous mountain, I preached at Gamblesby[37] (as I did about thirty years ago) to a large congregation of rich and poor. The chief man of the town was formerly a local preacher, but now keeps his carriage. Has he increased in holiness as well as in wealth? If not, he has made a poor exchange.

In the evening a large upper room, designed for an assembly, was procured for me at Penrith. But several of the poor people were struck with a panic for fear the room should fall. Finding there was no remedy, I went down into the court below and preached in great peace to a multitude of well-behaved people. The rain was suspended while I preached, but afterwards returned and continued most of the night. Saturday 6, I went on to Whitehaven and, in the evening, exhorted all who knew in whom they had believed to 'walk worthy of God in all well-pleasing; being fruitful in every good work and increasing in the knowledge of God'.[38]

Sun. 8. I preached at eight, at two, and at five, but could not preach abroad because of the rain. We were in hopes of sailing for the Isle of Man the next morning, as a little vessel was waiting for us. But the wind then turned full against us. By this means I had

[31] Orig., 'Cuthbedson'.
[32] The route from Newbiggin to Weardale over Pikelaw (or Pike Low) reaches almost 2000 feet in height.
[33] Orig., 'Weredale'.
[34] 1 Cor. 2:2.
[35] Orig. 'Ninthead'.
[36] Matt. 22:4.
[37] Gamblesby was small township in the parish of Addingham, 10 miles north-east of Penrith.
[38] Cf. Col. 1:10 (*Notes*).

an opportunity given me of meeting the select society. I was
pleased to find that none of them have lost the pure love of God
since they received it first. I was particularly pleased with a poor
Negro. She seemed to be fuller of love than any of the rest. And
not only her voice had an unusual sweetness, but her words were
chosen and uttered with a peculiar propriety. I never heard either
in England or America such a Negro speaker (man or woman)
before.

Tue. 9. Finding no hopes of sailing, after preaching morning
and evening, I went to Cockermouth. Wednesday 10, at eight, I
preached in the town hall:[39] but to the poor only—the rich could
not rise so soon. In the evening, I preached in the town hall at
Carlisle.[40] And from the number and seriousness of the hearers, I
conceived a little hope that even here some good will be done.

Thur. 11.[41] I reached Newcastle and, on Friday 12, went to
Sunderland. Many of our friends prosper in the world. I wish
their souls may prosper also. Sunday 14, I preached at Gateshead
Fell at two o'clock and hoped to preach at the Garth Heads[42] at
five. But the rain drove us into the house. But all was well. For
many found God was there.

Mon. 15. I set out for Scotland and, Tuesday 16, came to
Berwick-upon-Tweed. Such a congregation I have not seen there
for many years. Perhaps the seed which has so long seemed to be
sown in vain may at length produce a good harvest.

Wed. 17. I went on to Dunbar. I have seldom seen such a congregation here before. Indeed, some of them seemed at first dis-

[39] Lewis says of Cockermouth: 'The Moot-hall, formerly an old dilapidated structure,
inconvenently situated in the market-place, has been rebuilt in a much more commodious manner, and on a more eligible site.' *England*, 1:585.

[40] 'The town-hall and council chamber are conspicuously situated in the centre of the
city; and to which you ascend by a flight of steps from the promenade. In these most of
the public business is done, and the corporation records kept.' John Housman, *A Topographical Description of Cumberland, Westmorland, Lancashire, and a Part of the West Riding of Yorkshire* (Carlisle, 1800), p. 410.

[41] JW's route is said to have taken in Wolsingham, Co. Durham, where he stayed in
the old house at the top of the causeway, as a guest of Titus and Hannah Angus.
Methodist Recorder (Winter No., 1904), p. 38.

[42] 'Adjoining [Keelmen's Hospital] is a small field, called the Garth-heads, where
hundreds of children and youths, from the unwholesome lanes in Sandgate, may be
almost constantly seen amusing themselves. It was formerly much more extensive';
Eneas Mackenzie, *A Descriptive and Historical Account of the Town and Country of New-
castle-upon-Tyne*, 2 vols. (Newcastle, 1827), 1:185. A Presbyterian meeting-house at
Garth Heads, opened in 1722, had to be converted into a house to give some support to
its minister before the end of the eighteenth century; ibid., 1:384n.

posed to mirth, but they were soon serious as death. And truly
the power of the Lord was present to heal[43] those that were willing
to come to the throne of grace.[44] Thursday 18, I read with great
expectation Dr. Watt's *Essay* on liberty.[45] But I was much disap-
5 pointed. It is abstruse and metaphysical. Surely he wrote it either
when he was very young or very old. In the evening, I endeavoured to preach to the hearts of a large congregation at Edinburgh. We have cast much 'bread upon the waters' here. Shall we
not 'find it' again, at least, 'after many days'?[46]

10 Fri. 19. I preached at Joppa,[47] a settlement of colliers, three
miles from Edinburgh. Some months ago, as some of them were
cursing and swearing, one of our local preachers going by,
reproved them. One of them followed after him and begged he
would give them a sermon. He did so several times. Afterwards
15 the travelling preachers went, and a few quickly agreed to meet
together. Some of these now know in whom they have believed
and walk worthy of their profession.

Sat. 20. I took one more walk through Holyrood House,[48] the
mansion of ancient kings. But how melancholy an appearance
20 does it make now! The stately rooms are dirty as stables; the
colours of the tapestry are quite faded; several of the pictures
are cut and defaced. The roof of the royal chapel is fallen in; and
the bones of James the Fifth[49] and the once beautiful Lord

---

[43] Luke 5:17.

[44] Heb. 4:16 (*Notes*).

[45] Isaac Watts, *An Essay on the Freedom of the Will in God and in Creatures, and on Various Subjects Connected Therewith* (1732), in *The Works of Isaac Watts*, ed. G. Burder, 6 vols. (London, 1810-11), 6:241-80. Watts published this work at the age of 58 when he was neither very old nor very young. The work cannot be justly described as abstruse or metaphysical, and on the subject of the divine decree declines 'to be too positive and presumptuous upon either side of such sublime and abstruse reasonings'; but it did try to reconcile the liberty of men with the electing liberty of God, and therein lay its offence.

[46] Eccles. 11:1.

[47] In 1846, Lewis gave a quite different account of this place: 'A modern and neat village, situated on the sea-side, and on the great road between Edinburgh and Musselburgh. It may be said to form a suburb of the large and fashionable village of Portobello, which is visited on account of its excellent beach, and its proximity to Edinburgh, as a bathing place in the summer season. In the vicinity are some handsome villas.' *Scotland*, 1:591.

[48] For previous visits, see May 11, 1761, and May 14, 1768 (21:320 and 22:133, n. 1 in this edn.).

[49] James V (1512-42), King of Scotland from 1513 and proclaimed competent to rule from 1524. James's youth gave an opening for the endemic faction-warfare of Scotland; his maturity did much to precipitate the Reformation for he obtained papal sanction for the legitimation of two of his natural children, the regent Moray, and the father of the

Darnley[50] are scattered about like those of sheep or oxen. Such is human greatness! Is not a 'living dog better than a dead lion'![51]

Sun. 21. The rain hindered me from preaching at noon upon the Castle Hill. In the evening the house was well filled, and I was enabled to speak strong words. But I am not a preacher for the people of Edinburgh. Hugh Saunderson[52] and Michael Fenwick[53] are more to their taste.

Tue. 23. A gentleman took me to see Roslin Castle,[54] eight miles from Edinburgh. It is now all in ruins, only a small dwelling-house is built on one part of it. The situation of it is exceeding fine, on the side of a steep mountain, hanging over a river from which another mountain rises, equally steep and clothed with wood. At a little distance is the chapel, which is in perfect preservation both within and without. I should never have thought that it had belonged to anyone less than a sovereign prince! The inside being far more elegantly wrought with variety of scripture histories in stonework than I believe can be found again in Scotland, perhaps not in all England.

---

fifth Earl of Bothwell, and of five others, still babies, to be abbots of Kelso and Melrose, priors of St. Andrews and Pittonweem, abbot of Holyrood, prior of Coldingham, and abbot of Charterhouse.

[50] Henry Stuart, Lord Darnley (1545-67), son of the Earl of Lennox, was sent by his mother to France in 1560 with a view to marriage with Mary Stuart. After being confined in London by Queen Elizabeth, he was released and received into royal favour in 1562, and in 1565 allowed to go to Scotland at Mary's request. He was refused the crown matrimonial and conspired with Protestants to obtain it. He attempted to leave the country but fell ill; and before he could rejoin the Queen he was murdered.

[51] Eccles. 9:4.

[52] On Hugh Saunderson, who had been stationed in Edinburgh 1771-73, see June 4, 1774 (22:412, n. 19 in this edn.).

[53] On Michael Fenwick, see July 25, 1757 (21:117, n. 57 in this edn.), and Dec. 7, 1778. The comparison is unkind, for Fenwick (who seems never to have been stationed in Edinburgh) 'was not permitted to travel in a circuit, nor was he acknowledged as a preacher, for several years before his death . . . but his preaching occasionally was connived at, and a small pittance was allowed him annually by the Conference, to preserve him from want and distress.' Atmore, *Memorial*, pp. 123-24.

[54] Roslin, to the south of Edinburgh, was the principal residence of the St. Clairs, earls of Orkney, from the early twelfth century. It suffered damage both by accident and by English raids, and was besieged and taken for the last time by General Monk in 1650. The chapel, a collegiate foundation, was created by William de St. Clair in 1446 and dedicated to St. Matthew the Apostle. Stripped of its ornaments at the time of the Reformation, the chapel was sacked by a mob in 1688 who went on to plunder the castle. It was restored, however, by General St. Clair and maintained by the earls of Rosslyn, whose burial place was in the vault. It is claimed to be 'one of the richest specimens of the decorated English style of architecture'. Lewis, *Scotland*, 2:429; *An Account of the Chapel of Roslin* (Edinburgh, 1790); William Mac Dowall, *New Guide to Roslyn* (3rd edn., Edinburgh, 1840).

Hence we went to Dunbar. Wednesday 24 in the afternoon, I went through the lovely garden of a gentleman in the town who has laid out walks hanging over the sea and winding among the rocks: one of them leads to the castle wherein that poor injured
5 woman, Mary Queen of Scots, was confined.[55] But time has well-nigh devoured it; only a few ruinous walls are now standing.

Thursday 25, we went on to Berwick. Friday 26, in returning to Alnwick, we spent an hour at H[ulne], an ancient monastery.[56] Part of it the Duke of Northumberland has repaired, furnished it
10 in a plain manner, and surrounded it with a little garden. An old inscription bears date 1404, when part of it was built by the fourth Earl of Northumberland. How many generations have had their day since that time and then passed away like a dream![57] We had a happy season at Alnwick with a large and deeply attentive
15 congregation.

Sat. 27. At noon, I preached in the town hall at Morpeth, and God applied his word to many hearts. In the afternoon, I preached to the loving colliers at Plessey, and then went on to Newcastle.

20 Sun. 28. Between eight and nine in the morning, I preached at Gateshead Fell on fellowship with God, a subject which not a few of them understand by heartfelt experience. The congregation at Sheep Hill about noon was far too large for any house to contain. Such was the power of God that I almost wondered, any could
25 help believing. At five, I preached at the Garth Heads to a still more numerous congregation. But there were few among them

[55] Mary, Queen of Scots, took refuge in Dunbar Castle after the murder of David Rizzio in 1565, and subsequently appointed the Earl of Bothwell its governor. She also passed six days here, together with her court, in a tour along the coast in the following year; and upon the murder of Darnley in 1567, Bothwell, attended by a thousand horsemen, arrested the Queen on her progress to Stirling and carried her and her retinue by force to Dunbar, where he detained her prisoner for twelve days. Soon after her marriage with Bothwell, she remained here for some time, while levying forces from Lothian and the Merse against the people who had taken arms to oppose the Earl; and, marching with these to Carberry Hill, she there joined the hostile party, abandoning Bothwell. The castle was given up to the Earl of Murray, who had been appointed Regent of Scotland, and was soon demolished.
[56] Hulne Priory, one of the earliest English foundations of the Carmelites founded about 1240. The ruins lie picturesquely in the park of Alnwick Castle, and prominent among them is a tower added by the Percys in 1488. JW's reference is to a Gothic summer-house, built by the first Duke shortly after 1776, during the 'Adam' phase of the rebuilding at Alnwick, with pretty stucco-work inside. Pevsner, *Northumberland*, pp. 195-96.
[57] See Job 20:8.

who remembered my first preaching near that place in the Keel-
man's Hospital. For what reason the wise managers of that place
forbade my preaching there any more, I am yet still to learn.[58]

Wed. 31. Taking my leave of this affectionate people, I went to
Mr. Parker's at Shincliffe[59] near Durham. The congregation being   5
far too large to get into the house, I stood near his door. It seemed
as if the whole village were ready to receive the truth in the love
thereof. Perhaps their earnestness may provoke the people of
Durham to jealousy.

In the afternoon, we took a view of the castle at Durham,[60] the   10
residence of the bishop. The situation is wonderfully fine, surrounded by the river and commanding all the country. And many
of the apartments are large and stately, but the furniture is mean
beyond imagination! I know not where I have seen such in a gentleman's house, or a man of five hundred a year, except that of the   15
Lord-lieutenant in Dublin. In the largest chambers the tapestry is
quite faded, beside that it is coarse and ill-judged. Take but one
instance. In Jacob's vision you see, on the one side, a little paltry

---

[58] On this first visit, see Nov. 14, 28, 1742 (19:301-2, n. 92 in this edn.). The present
visit delighted JW's stepson-in-law, William Smith. 'Mr. W. left us last week, after a
short but very pleasing and profitable visit. I never was better pleased with him in my
life, nor do I remember ever to have been more profited by his preaching. As the doctrine is the same, so I found it was attended with the same peace and joy and power now
as it was 25 years ago. . . . His congregations at N[ew] C[astle] were very large, and he
preached some admirable sermons indeed.' MS letter, William Smith to Joseph Benson, Newcastle, June 6, 1780, in Methodist Archives, Manchester.

[59] Shincliffe is a village 2 miles south-east of Durham. Thomas Parker (d. 1829)
resided near Durham for five years. Educated for business, he turned from this career,
qualified as a barrister, and had recently settled in Durham, where he developed a good
practice in the field of commercial law. Two or three years before, he had become a
Methodist and was a remarkably zealous and successful preacher. 'The amenity of his
look, the melody of his voice, and plainness and correctness of his language, and, above
all, the pure and consolatory Gospel doctrines that he preached gave him a mastery over
the feelings of his congregation that was often irresistible.' It was to his labours that the
sudden expansion of the small Durham society was due. After four or five years, he followed his professional fortune to Hull, becoming counsel to the Hull Dock Company
and settling at Beverley, where he signed Coke's plan for a missionary society in 1784.
In 1790 he came to London, still a local preacher, but became a Swedenborgian owing,
it was believed, to 'the solicitations of his lady, who was the sister of the most influential
follower of the Baron, and had embraced his sentiments'. After a short time, he moved
to Glasgow where he failed to make a success of an invention he had patented. *Circa*
1780 he published an attack on the East India Company, and *c*. 1784 a two-volume
scripture commentary. *Wesleyan Methodist Magazine* 53 (1830):577-80n.

[60] Durham Castle was begun a few years after the Norman Conquest and was public
evidence of the palatine power exercised by the bishop. It now forms part of the buildings of University College, Durham, and the tapestries, to be seen in the Senate rooms,
appear in better condition than JW found them.

ladder and an angel climbing it in the attitude of a chimney-sweeper; on the other side, Jacob staring at him from under a large silver-laced hat!

Thursday, June 1. About ten, I preached at Aycliffe, a large village twelve miles from Durham, all the inhabitants whereof seem now as full of goodwill as they were once of prejudice.

I preached at Darlington in the evening.[61] It is good to be here: the liveliness of the people animates all that come near them. On Friday evening, we had a love-feast at which many were greatly comforted by hearing such artless, simple accounts [of][62] the mighty works of God.

Sat. 3. At noon, I preached to a large congregation at Northallerton.[63] The sun shone full in my face when I began, but it was soon overcast. And I believe, this day, if never before, God gave a general call to this careless people. In the evening, I preached at Thirsk. When I was here last, a few young women behaved foolishly. But all were deeply serious now and seemed to feel that God was there.

Sunday 4. The service began about ten at Staveley[64] near Boroughbridge. Mr. Hartley, the rector, read prayers. But the church would scarce contain half the congregation, so that I was obliged to stand upon a tombstone both morning and afternoon. In the evening, I preached at Boroughbridge to a numerous congregation, and all were attentive except a few soldiers, who seemed to understand nothing of the matter.

Mon. 5. About noon, I preached at Tockwith,[65] and then went on to York. I was surprised to find a general faintness here, one fruit of which was that the morning preaching was given up.

Tuesday 6 was the Quarterly Meeting, the most numerous I ever saw. At two, was the love-feast, at which several instances of the mighty power of God were repeated, by which it appears that his work is still increasing in several parts of the circuit.

An arch news-writer published a paragraph today, probably designed for wit, concerning 'the large pension which the famous

[61] On this visit JW preached on the steps of the market cross; one enthusiastic lady described 'his countenance as truly angelic'. Jackson, *Methodism in Darlington*, p. 28.

[62] Orig., 'it'.

[63] In the yard of Jacky Wren, a weaver. J. Ward, *Methodism in the Thirsk Circuit* (Thirsk, 1860), p. 36.

[64] Staveley was a parish 3 miles south-west of Boroughbridge. The Hartleys seem to have been patrons as well as rectors (Lewis, *England*, 3:178).

[65] Tockwith was a township 5 miles north-east of Wetherby.

Wesley received for defending the King'.[66] This so increased the congregation in the evening that scores were obliged to go away. And God applied that word to many hearts, 'I will not destroy the city for ten's sake!'[67]

Wed. 7. I preached at Pocklington and Swinefleet. Thursday 8, I preached on the Green at Thorne to a listening multitude. Only two or three were much *diverted* at the thought of 'seeing the dead, small and great standing before God'![68]

Fri. 9. About noon, I preached at Crowle and, in the evening, at Epworth on 'I will not let thee go, except thou bless me.'[69] Saturday 10 in the evening, I preached at Owston and, passing the Trent early in the morning, on Sunday 11, preached at Kirton,[70] about eight, to a very large and very serious congregation. Only before me stood one, something like a gentleman, with his hat on, even at prayer. I could scarce help telling him a story. In Jamaica, a Negro passing by the Governor, pulled off his hat. So did the Governor. At which, one expressing his surprise, he said, 'Sir, I should be ashamed if a Negro had more good manners than the Governor of Jamaica.'

About two, I preached at Gainsborough, and again at five, to a very numerous congregation. We had then a love-feast,[71] and one

---

[66] The paragraph originally appeared in the *London Courant*. It read: 'The famous preacher Wesley may now be ranked among the pensioned hirelings of the Court; and has been busily employed in some parts of Yorkshire very lately putting forth his pious political tenets. The established churches in many places have been laid open to him, particularly at Halifax and Bingley, where in his sermons he has repeatedly exhorted his disciples to purchase a 4d. book which he calls *A True Statement or Account of the War in America*', the work he published for Joseph Galloway (see Nov. 13, 1779). Lyth, *Methodism in York*, pp. 137–38.

[67] Cf. Gen. 18:32.   [68] Rev. 20:12.
[69] Gen. 32:26.

[70] Kirton in Lindsey, 18 miles north from Lincoln. Methodist preaching had begun here in 1774 at the invitation of Mrs. Elizabeth Turner (1734–1812) and five or six friends. Her religious sensibilities had been greatly stimulated under Baptist preaching, but the invitation to the Methodist preachers proved a thorny path to spiritual progress. Her husband was willing to accompany her to church and to the Baptist meeting, but opposed her joining the Methodist class; and there was village violence against other Methodist converts. JW is here adding his impetus to a new society formed under difficulties; *Methodist Magazine* 36 (1813):529–30. Early difficulties created in Kirton by social climbing are referred to in *Methodist Magazine* 28 (1805): 555-56.

[71] This was the love-feast, held at Gainsborough Old Hall, at which Robert Moss (1771–1849) 'solemnly covenanted, in the presence of God, angels, and the Rev. John Wesley and the church there assembled, that I would be a Methodist as soon as I was old enough'. This vow was so well fulfilled that he is said almost to the end to have beamed 'with the glow of an almost youthful health, and with the tempered cheerfulness of sanctified intelligence and benignity'. *Wesleyan Methodist Magazine* 79 (1856):301.

of the most lively which I have known for many years. Many
spoke, and with great fervour as well as simplicity, so that most
who heard blessed God for the consolation.

   Mon. 12. About eleven, I preached at Newton on Trent to a
5 large and very genteel congregation. Thence, we went to Newark,
but our friends were divided as to the place where I should
preach. At length they found a convenient place, covered on three
sides and on the fourth open to the street.[72] It contained two or
three thousand people well, who appeared to hear as for life. Only
10 one big man, exceeding drunk, was very noisy and turbulent, till
his wife (*fortissima Tyndaridarum!*)[73] seized him by the collar, gave
him two or three hearty boxes on the ear, and dragged him away
like a calf. But at length he got out of her hands, crept in among
the people, and stood as quiet as a lamb.

15   Tue. 13. I accepted of an invitation from a gentleman at Lincoln, in which I had not set my foot for upwards of fifty years.[74] At
six in the evening, I preached in the Castleyard to a large and
attentive congregation. They were all as quiet as if I had been at
Bristol. Will God have a people here also?

20   Wednesday 14, I preached again at ten in the morning. In the
middle of the sermon a violent storm began; on which Mr.
Wood,[75] the keeper, opened the door of the court-house, which
contained the whole of the congregation. I have great hope some
of these will have their fruit unto holiness and, in the end, ever-
25 lasting life.[76]

   Heavy rain drove us into the house at Horncastle in the evening.
Thursday 15, I preached at Raithby. Two of Mr. Brackenbury's

---

[72] This is said to have been a covered shambles or meat-market, one end opening on
Market Place, the other abutting on Middlegate. A town hall was later built on the site.
WHS 4 (1904):239.

[73] Horace, *Satires*, I.i.100, 'of right virago strain' (Fawkes). 'Yet a freedwoman cleft
him twain with an axe, bravest of the Tyndarid breed' (Loeb). Clytemnestra, daughter
of Tyndareus, slew her husband Agamemnon with an axe. Possibly the freedwoman's
name was Tyndaris.

[74] JW had in fact ridden through Lincoln on July 13, 1770, and had stayed a few hours
on Aug. 29, 1749 (22:240 and 20:296 in this edn.). The present entry indicates clearly
enough, however, his conviction that the gospel would not flourish in that cathedral
town. Tyerman reports (*John Wesley*, 3:327) that 'for seven years after this there was
not a Methodist in Lincoln'; when Methodism obtained a foothold there it was by an
act of policy from a woman of independent means from the outside, Mrs. Fisher. *Wesleyan Methodist Magazine* 48 (1825):290; William Leary, *Methodism and the City of Lincoln* (Lincoln, 1969), pp. 9–10.

[75] JW preached where the magistrates usually sat. A. Watmough, *A History of
Methodism in the Neighbourhood and City of Lincoln* (London, 1829), p. 20.

[76] See Rom. 6:22.

brothers[77] spent the evening with us. Friday 16, we went on to Boston, the largest town in the county, except Lincoln. From the top of the steeple[78] (which I suppose is by far the highest tower in the kingdom), we had a view not only of all the town, but of all the adjacent country. Formerly this town was in the Fens. But the Fens are vanished away. Great part of them is turned into pasture and part into arable land. At six, the house contained the congregation, all of whom behaved in the most decent manner. How different from those wild beasts with whom Mr. Mitchell and Mr. Mather had to do![79] Saturday 17, the house was pretty well filled in the morning, and many were much affected. A gentleman who was there invited me to dinner and offered me the use of his paddock. But the wind was so exceeding high that I could not preach abroad—as I did when I was here before just six and twenty years ago.[80] And Mr. Thompson,[81] a friendly Anabaptist, offering me the use of his large meeting-house, I willingly accepted the offer. I preached to most of the chief persons in the town on 1 Cor. 13:1-3. And many of them seemed utterly amazed. 'Open their eyes, O Lord, that they sleep not in death!'[82]

Sun. 18. I gave them a parting discourse at seven, and, after adding a few members to the little society and exhorting them to cleave close to each other, I left them with a comfortable hope that they would not be scattered any more.

---

[77] On Robert Carr Brackenbury, see above July 9, 1776.

[78] Boston Stump. St. Botolph's Church, Boston, 'is a giant among English parish churches. [It] is 282 feet long, and the Stump, the most prodigious of English parochial steeples, is 272 feet high.' The steeple seems to have been raised in stages in order to outdo the steeple at Louth, and it is possible that it obtained the name of the Stump from an unfulfilled intention further to raise even the present tower by a spire. Pevsner, *Lincolnshire*, pp. 463-64; see also, Sept. 13, 1761 (21:341, n. 21 in this edn.).

[79] Alexander Mather's bad experience at Boston had been in the autumn of 1757 (Jackson, *Early Methodist Preachers*, 2:172-75); on Mather, see Mar. 10, 1761 (21:309, n. 78 in this edn.). Thomas Mitchell's affray had been with the 'lions of Wrangle', nine miles away, in 1751 (Jackson, *Early Methodist Preachers*, 1:248-50); on Mitchell, see Apr. 3, 1752 (20:414 and n. 35 in this edn.), and on Wrangle see July 8, 1751 (20:396-97 in this edn.).

[80] JW had preached in the paddock at Boston on Apr. 3, 1759 (21:182 in this edn.).

[81] William Thompson, minister of the Boston Baptist Church (1762-95), was a friend of Dan Taylor and a founding father of the New Connexion of General Baptists, the Baptist equivalent of JW's movement; A. C. Underwood, *A History of the English Baptists* (London, 1947), pp. 151, 153. His church is said to be the only one of the ancient Baptist churches to be regularly united with the Baptist New Connexion from its formation in 1770. Pishey Thompson, *History and Antiquities of Boston* (Boston, 1856), p. 262.

[82] Cf. Ps. 13:3 (BCP).

About noon, I preached in the market-place at Wainfleet,[83] once
a large seaport town till the harbour was blocked up by sand. The
congregation behaved exceeding well. We now passed into
Marshland, a fruitful and pleasant part of the county. Such is
Langham Row in particular, the abode of honest George Robinson[84] and his fourteen children. Although it was a lone house, yet
such a multitude of people flocked together that I was obliged to
preach abroad. It blew a storm, and we had several showers of
rain; but no one went away. I do not wonder that this society is the
largest as well as the liveliest in these parts of Lincolnshire.

Mon. 19. I preached at Louth, where the people used to be
rough enough, but now were serious and calmly attentive. Such a
change in a whole town I have seldom known in the compass of
one year.

Tue. 20. After preaching at Tealby, I went on to Grimsby,
where I am still more at home than in any place in the east of Lincolnshire, though scarce any of our first members remain—they
are all safe lodged in Abraham's bosom. But here is still a loving
people, though a little disturbed by the Calvinists, who seize on
every halting soul as their own lawful prey.[85]

Wed. 21. I preached at Scotter to a lovely, simple-hearted people, and at Epworth in the evening.

Thur. 22.[86] I preached once more at Crowle to a numerous and
deeply serious congregation. Everyone thought, 'Can any good
come out of Crowle?'[87] But God's thoughts were not as our
thoughts![88] There is now such a work of God in this as is in few of
the places round about it.

---

[83] Wainfleet is 39 1/2 miles east from Lincoln. The waters of the creek on which it
stood were much reduced by the drainage of the East Fen. JW, accompanied by Joseph
Bradford and John Peacock, was here entertained by Mrs. Elizabeth Webster (1745-
1835) who had been converted at the age of 20, and whose home was a base for the
preachers for 50 years. *Wesleyan Methodist Magazine* 58 (1835):806.

[84] On Langham Row and George Robinson, see above, July 5, 1779.

[85] CW had written of the 'wolf' or devil that

> He seizes every straggling soul,
> As his own lawful prey.

Poetical Works, 5:34. The reference is to the activities of the preachers of Lady Huntingdon's connexion.

[86] JW's first visit to Crowle on July 8, 1748, had a rowdy reception (see 20:232 in this
edn.); on his last visit on June 27, 1788, he was still hopeful of good results.

[87] Cf. John 1:46.

[88] See Isa. 55:8.

Sat. 24. I preached about noon at Belton;[89] there was the dawn of a blessed work here. But 'My Lady's Preachers', so called, breaking in, set everyone's sword against his brother. Some of them revive a little, but I doubt whether they will ever recover their first love.

Sun. 25. Sir William Anderson,[90] the rector, having sent an express order to his curate, he did not dare to gainsay. So at ten, I began reading prayers to such a congregation as I apprehend hardly ever assembled in this church before. I preached on Luke 8:18, part of the Second Lesson. Not a breath was heard; all was still 'as summer's noontide air'.[91] And I believe our Lord then sowed seed in many hearts which will bring forth fruit to perfection.[92]

After dinner, I preached at Westwoodside.[93] The high wind was a little troublesome. But the people regarded it not. We concluded the day with one of the most solemn love-feasts I have known for many years.

Mon. 26. Finningley Church was well filled in the evening, and many seemed much affected. Tuesday 27, I preached at Doncaster about noon, and to a larger congregation at Rotherham in the evening. Wednesday 28, I went to Sheffield. But the house[94] was not ready, so I preached in the square.

I can hardly think I am entered this day into the seventy-eighth year of my age. By the blessing of God I am just the same as when I entered the twenty-eighth. This hath God wrought,[95] chiefly by

---

[89] A village 2 miles north of Epworth. Here the patronage of the living was in the hands of the Huntingdon family, and James Glazebrook, the first student at Trevecca and now vicar of St. James's, Warrington, was shortly to be presented by the Countess's daughter, the Countess of Moira. The peculiarity of Belton near Epworth was that there was a settlement of Dutch and French Protestants, brought over by Cornelius Vermuyden to assist in fen-draining during the reign of Charles II. They had had their own church, and Calvinist traditions for the Countess to exploit, but 'the females of the hamlet who intermarried with these strangers retained their maiden names after marriage, not choosing to adopt those of their foreign husbands'. Lewis, *England,* 1:176.

[90] Sir William Anderson (1722-85), rector of Epworth, 1757-84. He was rector of Lea, Lincs., 1743-85, and succeeded as baronet in 1765. He was succeeded in the rectory and the baronetcy by his son, Charles (1768-1846). Joshua Gibson (1742-1808) was curate of Epworth from 1762. The ill feeling between him and JW became open (see below, July 6, 1788), though the latter's final reference to him is a kindly one (see July 4, 1790).

[91] Milton, *Paradise Lost,* ii.308-9.

[92] See Luke 8:14.

[93] Westwoodside is a village 1 mile west of Haxey and some 3 miles south-west of Epworth.

[94] Norfolk Street Chapel, which was opened on June 29, 1780 (see below). JW preached in Paradise Square; see above, July 15, 1779.

[95] See Num. 23:23.

my constant exercise, my rising early, and preaching morning and evening.

Thur. 29. I was desired to preach at Worksop, but when I came they had not fixed on any place. At length they chose a lamentable one, full of dirt and dust, but without the least shelter from the scorching sun. This few could bear. So we had only a small company of as stupid people as ever I saw. In the evening, I preached in the old house[96] at Sheffield, but the heat was scarce supportable. I took my leave of it at five in the morning and, in the evening, preached in the new house, thoroughly filled with rich and poor to whom I declared, 'We preach Christ crucified.'[97] And he bore witness to his word in a very uncommon manner. Saturday, July 1, I preached once more at Rotherham. Sunday 2 at eight, I preached at Sheffield. There was afterward such a number of communicants as was never seen at the old church before. I preached again at five, but very many were constrained to go away. We concluded our work by visiting some that were weak in body but strong in faith, desiring nothing but to do and suffer the will of God.

Monday 3 and Tuesday 4, I preached at Derby. Wednesday 5, at a church eight miles from it.[98] In the afternoon, as I was going through Stapleford in my way to Nottingham, I was stopped by some who begged me to look into their new preaching-house. Many following me, the house was soon filled, and we spent half an hour together to our mutual comfort. In the evening, I preached at Nottingham. Wednesday 5, I preached in Loughborough about eleven, and in the evening at Leicester. I know not how it is that I constantly find such liberty of spirit in this place!

Thur. 6. The room at five, according to custom, was filled from end to end. I have not spent a whole day in Leicester for these fifty-two years. Surely I shall before I die. This night we spent in Northampton, then went on to London.

Sun. 9. We had a full congregation at the New Chapel and found God had not forgotten to be gracious.[99] In the following days, I read over with a few of our preachers the large *Minutes* of

[96] This was a house purchased in Mulberry Street in 1759 and converted into a preaching-house. *Wesleyan Methodist Magazine* 58 (1835):607.

[97] 1 Cor. 1:23.

[98] Perhaps Risley, a chapelry 7 1/2 miles east from Derby and 2 miles north-west of Long Eaton.

[99] See Ps. 77:9.

the Conference and considered all the articles, one by one, to see whether any should be omitted or altered.[1]

Sunday 16 was a day of much refreshment and strong consolation to many who are persuaded that God will revive his work and bind up the waste places.[2] Monday 17, my brother and I set out for Bath. I preached at Reading in the evening. On Tuesday evening, I preached at Ramsbury Park.[3] On Wednesday, we reached Bath.

A year ago there was such an awakening here as never had been from the beginning. And in consequence of it, a swift and large increase of the society. Just then Mr. McNab,[4] quarrelling with Mr. Smyth, threw wildfire among the people and occasioned anger, jealousies, judging each other, back-biting, and tale-bearing without end. And in spite of all the pains which have been taken, the wound is not healed to this day.

Both my brother and I now talked to as many as we could and endeavoured to calm and soften their spirits. And on Friday and Saturday, I spoke severally to all the members of the society that could attend. On Friday evening, both in the preaching and at the meeting of the society, the power of God was again present to heal, as also on Saturday, both morning and evening; and a few are added to the society.

Sun. 23. I preached (after reading prayers) at ten, at half hour past two, and in the evening. Very many heard; I hope some *felt* what was spoken. We have sown; O may God give the increase![5]

Monday 24, I went on to Bristol. While I was at Bath, I narrowly observed and considered the celebrated cartoons,[6] the three first in particular. What a poor *designer* was one of the finest painters in the world! (1). Here are two men in a boat, each of them more than half as long as the boat itself! (2). Our Lord saying to Peter, 'Feed my sheep,' points to three or four sheep standing by him. (3). While Peter and John heal the lame man, two

---

[1] The outcome of this conversation was the fourth edition of the 'Large' *Minutes* published in November 1780 (vol. 10 in this edn.), originally derived from the first edition of 1753 and from the doctrinal and disciplinary minutes of 1749. The fifth edition, garnering the work of JW's lifetime in shaping a formal connexional discipline was published in 1789. Jackson, 8:299-338.

[2] See Isa. 51:3.

[3] See Mar. 3, 1775 (22:444, n. 55 in this edn.).

[4] On this episode, see above, Nov. 22, 1779.

[5] See 1 Cor. 3:6.

[6] Apparently replicas of Raphael's cartoons, the originals of which were at Hampton Court. Cf. Dec. 22, 1774 (22:441, n. 37 in this edn.).

naked boys stand by them! For what? O pity that so fine a painter should be utterly without common sense!

In the evening, I saw one of the greatest curiosities in the vegetable creation, *the nightly Cereus*.[7] About four in the afternoon, the dry stem began to swell. About six it gradually opened, and about eight it was in its full glory. I think the inner part of this flower, which was snow white, was about five inches diameter; the yellow rays which surrounded it, I judged, were in diameter nine or ten inches. About twelve it began to droop, being covered with a cold sweat; at four it died away.

The people at Bath were still upon my mind. So on Thursday 27, I went over again, and God was with us of a truth whenever we assembled together. Surely God is healing the breaches of this poor, shattered people.

Sun. 30. Forty or fifty of our preachers being come, we had a solemn opportunity in the morning. We had the most numerous congregation in the afternoon which has been seen here for many years. And will not the Lord be glorified in our reformation rather than our destruction?[8]

Tuesday, August 1, our Conference began. We have been always hitherto straitened for time. It was now resolved, for the future we allow nine or ten days for each Conference,[9] that everything relative to the carrying on of the work of God may be maturely considered.

[7] *Cereus grandiflorus* which behaves as JW describes, the flowers dying at sunrise and not opening again. It is a native of the West Indies, and was introduced in 1700 to the Royal Gardens at Hampton Court.

[8] This gloomy comment and the entry which preceeds it, refer to the contest of authority with McNab. See above, Nov. 22, 1779.

[9] For a gathering specially extended in length, the minutes of the 1780 Conference are extraordinarily uninformative. It is probable, however, that the insistence of the 'Large' *Minutes* that Methodism was a movement within the Church occasioned some demur (Simon, *Wesley, Last Phase*, p. 162), for CW detected 'the working of principles unfavourable to that strict Churchmanship which he believed to be essential', and left Conference (he said for the last time) writing verses which commenced:

> Why should I longer, Lord, contend,
> My last important moments spend,
> In buffeting the air?
> In warning those who will not see,
> But rest in blind security,
> And rush into the snare.

On Aug. 5 JW wrote to Miss Bosanquet (Telford, 7:29) that 'the case of the church we shall fully consider by-and-by; and I believe we shall agree that none who leave the Church shall remain with us.'

Fri. 4. I preached on a convenient piece of ground at one end of Redcliff[10] Parade. Great part of the immense congregation had never heard this kind of preaching before. Yet they were deeply attentive while I opened and applied those awful words, 'I saw the dead, small and great, stand before God.'[11]

Sun. 6. We had the largest numbers of communicants that had ever met at the New Room, and the largest congregation at five that had ever met near King Square. Wednesday 9, we concluded the Conference in much peace and love.

Friday 11. The sultry heat continuing, I would not coop myself up in the chapel but preached again near Redcliff Parade with much comfort and peace.

Mon. 14. For fear of the violent heat, we set out for Cornwall very early in the morning. But we feared where no fear was. For that very day the heat was at an end, and a mild rain began, which at intervals followed us almost to the Land's End.

After preaching at South Brent, Taunton, and Cullompton, on [Wednesday] 16, we came to Exeter. It is still a day of small things here for want of a convenient preaching-house.[12] Thursday 17, I went on to Plymouth. Here I expected little comfort. A large preaching-house was built. But who was to pay for it? I preached in it at six, at five in the morning, and on Friday evening. And from the number and spirit of the hearers, could not but hope that good will be done here also.

Sat. 19. I snatched the opportunity of a fair evening to preach in the square at Plymouth Dock. Sunday 20 at seven in the morning and at five in the evening, I preached at the Dock; in the afternoon in Plymouth House. It was crowded sufficiently. After preaching I made a collection for the house, which amounted to above five and twenty pounds. When I had done, Mr. Jane said:[13] 'This is not all. We must have a weekly collection both here and at the Dock. Let as many as can subscribe sixpence a week for one year. I will subscribe five shillings a week. And let this be reserved

---

[10] Orig., 'Radcliff'.

[11] Rev. 20:12.

[12] This seems a derogatory comment after the efforts so recently made in Exeter (see above, Aug. 31, 1779), but in addition to the usual troubles of Methodism in cathedral towns, the Exeter society suffered separations (see below, Aug. 15-18, 1782) and did not become the head of an independent circuit till 1808. Note the comment in the next entry condemning the Plymouth society for building too convenient a meeting-house.

[13] Nehemiah Jane, a quarterman in the dockyard. R. N. Worth, *History of Plymouth* (Plymouth, 1870), p. 258.

for the payment of the debt.' It was done, and by this simple method the most pressing debts were soon paid.

Mon. 21. I preached to a large and quiet congregation in the main street at St. Austell. Tuesday 22, I preached at Mevagissey, in the evening at Helston. Wednesday 23, I went on to Penzance. it is now a pleasure to be here, the little flock being united together in love. I preached at a little distance from the preaching-house. A company of soldiers were in town, whom, toward the close of the sermon, the good officer ordered to march through the congregation. But as they readily opened and closed again, it made very little disturbance.

Thur. 24. I preached near the preaching-house at St. Just. God applied his word with power, more especially at the meeting of the society, when all our hearts were as melting wax.[14] Friday 25, I preached in the market-place at St. Ives to most of the inhabitants of the town. Here is no opposer now. Rich and poor *see*, and very many *feel* the truth.

I now looked over a volume of Mr. K[nox]'s *Essays*.[15] He is a lively writer of middling understanding. It is prim, affected, and highly frenchified. I object to the beginning so many sentences with participles. This does well in French, but not in English. I cannot admire his judgment in many particulars. To instance in one or two. He depresses Cowley beyond all reason, who was far from being a mean poet. Full as unreasonably does he depress modern eloquence. I believe I have heard *speakers* at Oxford, to say nothing of Westminster, who were not inferior to either Demosthenes or Cicero.

Sat. 26. We had our Quarterly Meeting at Redruth, where all was love and harmony. Sunday 27, it was supposed, twenty thousand people were assembled at the amphitheatre in Gwennap.[16] And yet all, I was informed, could hear distinctly in the fair, calm evening.

---

[14] See Ps. 22:14.

[15] Vicesimus Knox, *Essays, Moral and Literary* (London, 1778), Vol. 2, Essay 7, 'On the Merits of Cowley as a Poet'. In this sprightly piece Knox begins by arguing that Cowley's editor, Dr. Sprat, 'by placing [him] in the first rank of poets, in effect degraded him from the subaltern station which he had else preserved unmolested', and ended by claiming that Cowley as a prose writer, 'as well as they whom he imitated, Donne and Jonson, were unquestionably possessed of great learning and ingenuity; but they all neglected the graces of composition, and will, therefore, soon be numbered among those once celebrated writers, whose utility now consists in filling a vacant place on the upper shelf of a deserted library' (pp. 76, 83-84). See also Essay 160, 'Cursory Remarks on the Eloquence of the Pulpit'.

[16] On Gwennap Pit, see Sept. 5, 1762 (21:388, n. 75 in this edn.).

Mon. 28. I preached at Wadebridge[17] and Port Isaac. Tuesday 29, at Camelford and Launceston. Hence we hastened toward Bristol by way of Wells, where (the weather being intensely hot, so that we could not well bear the room) I preached on the shady side of the market-place on 'By grace ye are saved through faith.'[18] As I was concluding a sergeant of the militia brought a drum. But he was a little too late. I pronounced the blessing and quietly walked away. I know not that ever I felt it hotter in Georgia than it was here this afternoon.

Sunday, September 3. I preached three times at Bath and, I believe, not without a blessing.[19] Wednesday 6, I preached at Paulton. The flame kindled last year still continues to burn here. And (what is strange) though so many have set their hand to the plough, there are none that look back.[20] In all the number, I do not find so much as one backslider.

Thursday 7, I spent an hour with the children, the most difficult part of our work. About noon, I preached to a large and serious congregation at Chew Magna;[21] in the evening, to a still more serious company at Stoke,[22] where Mr. Griffin[23] is calmly waiting for the call that summons him to Abraham's bosom.

Mon. 11. As I drew near Bath, I wondered what had drawn

---

[17] Orig., 'Wedebridge'. Wadebridge, 6 miles north-west of Bodmin, was a place where Methodism had to be reintroduced after being driven out by persecution. *Methodist Recorder* (Winter No., 1902), p. 96.

[18] Eph. 2:8 (*Notes*).

[19] Events on September 4 are supplied in the diary of Robert Roe: 'I went to hear Mr. Wesley. His sermon seemed as if for me alone. He observed, "It is a blessing to have preventing, enlightening or convicting grace; but this is not the salvation I am treating of. Unless we have the love of God shed abroad in our hearts we cannot be saved. It is well to make a beginning; but we must go forward, or perish everlastingly. We are both justified and sanctified by faith, and have a direct witness of the Spirit without which neither can exist. Others progress by our fruits: a calm, gentle, resigned, patient mind in all states and situations". I went with him to Mr. Castleman's and had a good time. At night he said, "It is a shame this poor weak thing should go home tonight: let him have my bed"; but I declined it.' *Arminian Magazine* 7 (1784):524.

[20] See Luke 9:62.

[21] A substantial Somerset parish 3 miles west of Pensford.

[22] Chew Stoke, a small parish 4 miles west of Pensford.

[23] John Griffin, who was survived by a wife, still living in 1790, and by a son of the same name who died, a lifelong Methodist and benefactor, on Nov. 17, 1832; *Wesleyan Methodist Magazine* 55 (1832):906. His wife, a connection of the Somerset Bourchier family, was a mainstay of Methodism in the village; and through their son and the marriages of their grand-daughters into the Harper and Hellier families, they became the ancestors of a group of families long active in the Anglican and Methodist ministry and in West-country Methodism. *WHS* 7 (1910):142; *Methodist Recorder* (Winter No., 1896), p. 79.

such a multitude of people together, till I learned that one of the Members for the City had given an ox to be roasted whole.[24] But their sport was sadly interrupted by heavy rain, which sent them home faster than they came; many of whom dropped in at our chapel, where I suppose they never had been before.

Tue. 12. At the invitation of that excellent woman, Mrs. Turner,[25] I preached about noon in her chapel in Trowbridge. As most of the hearers were Dissenters, I did not expect to do much good. However, I have done my duty; God will look to the event.

Thur. 14. I read prayers and preached in Clutton Church;[26] but it was with great difficulty because of my hoarseness, which so increased that in four and twenty hours I could scarce speak at all. At night I used my never-failing remedy, bruised garlic applied to the soles of the feet. This cured my hoarseness in six hours; in one hour it cured my lumbago, the pain in the small of my back which I had had ever since I came from Cornwall.

Wed. 20. I preached in the market-place at Pill to the most stupid congregation I have lately seen. Thursday 21, I married Mr. Horton[27]

[24] The rejoicing at Bath, a corporation borough with 30 voters, was in the camp of Lord Camden, recorder of the borough, who at a late stage had put up his son, John Jeffreys Pratt, as a candidate. A week before the election one of the sitting members, Sir John Sebright, died, and, the government failing to find another candidate in time, Pratt and the other sitting member, Abel Moysey, son of an eminent Bath physician, were returned unopposed. Namier and Brooke, *House of Commons*, 3:366.

[25] Joanna Turner, née Cook, (1732-84), was the daughter of John Cook, a West of England clothier, and claimed to have been a 'ring-leader in all the vain amusements of the town' as a young woman. On a visit to London, she heard the leading evangelical preachers and was introduced to the societies of Whitefield and JW, where she met her cousin Elizabeth Johnson (see above, Sept. 29, 1778), a devout Bristol class-leader. Joanna Cook joined Whitefield's movement and formed a society in Trowbridge. Four years after her marriage to Mr. Turner in 1766, she built the Tabernacle at Trowbridge—the opening sermon was by James Rouquet, the old master at Kingswood (*WHS* 9 [1914]:131)—where JW now preached. In 1772, she wrote JW a letter declaring her sympathy with his work, though she did not share his views; *Methodist Magazine* 21 (1798):46-47. JW prepared (though he did not publish) an abridgment of a memorial of her life, given him by her husband; *WHS* 4 (1903):57-59. But the *Arminian Magazine* 13 (1790):223-24 did carry an elegy on her death, praising her works of charity as well as her piety. Her family links with Methodism continued; one of her nieces married Adam Clarke, and another married Joseph Butterworth. Mary Wells, *The Triumph of Faith over the World, the Flesh, and the Devil, Exemplified in the Life, Death, and Spiritual Experience of . . . Mrs. Joanna Turner* (Bristol, 1787); T. Mann, *A Brief History of the Tabernacle Church, Trowbridge* (Trowbridge, 1884), pp. 1-20.

[26] Clutton was a mining parish 3 miles south of Pensford.

[27] The wedding was at Bedminster Church; *WHS* 7 (1909):17. John Horton, drysalter (1740-1802), was a member of the Common Council of London, and one of the executors of JW's will. After JW's death he left the connexion. He was, however, a model of the catholic Christianity of that generation, and when in 1799 he returned to Bristol (after what the obituary writers imply were serious financial difficulties), his relations

and Miss Durbin;[28] may they be patterns to all around them! Sunday 24, I preached in Temple Church, the most beautiful and the most ancient[29] in Bristol.

Sunday, October 1. I preached as usual, morning and evening, at the room. About two, I preached a funeral sermon at Kingswood for that blessed saint, Bathsheba Hall,[30] a pattern for many years of zealously doing and patiently suffering the will of God. In the evening, about seven hundred of us joined in solemnly renewing our covenant with God.

Mon. 2. After preaching at the Devizes, I went on to Salisbury. Tuesday 3, I walked over to Wilton and preached to a very serious congregation in the new preaching-house. I found at Salisbury the fruit of Captain Webb's preaching:[31] some were awakened, and one perfected in love.[32] Yet I was a little surprised at the remark of some of our eldest brethren, that they had never heard perfection preached before.

Wed. 4. The preaching-house at Whitchurch,[33] though much enlarged, could not contain the congregation in the evening. Some genteel people were inclined to smile at first, but their mirth was quickly over. The awe of God fell upon the whole congregation, and many 'rejoiced unto him with reverence'.[34] Saturday 7, I returned from Portsmouth to London.

Mon. 16. I went to Tunbridge Wells and preached to a serious

with the preachers were cordial, and he is said to have told his son he would rather 'see him a Methodist Preacher than Archbishop of Canterbury'. 'He was a lover of good men of every denomination; very sensible, well-read, serious without gloom, cheerful without levity, and polite without ceremony'; *Methodist Magazine* 26 (1803):211-15. His Islington house at Highbury Place was one of JW's London retreats for rest and writing. *WHS* 10 (1915):85.

[28] Mary Durbin (1752-86) was the daughter of Henry Durbin (see Mar. 27, 1762), a chemist and a member of the Baldwin Street religious society even before JW's first arrival in Bristol; Bulmer, *Mrs. Mortimer*, pp. 169-70. Durbin (1711-99) was one of the trustees of the Portland Chapel who tried unsuccessfully to exclude Henry Moore from its pulpit in 1794; *Wesleyan Methodist Magazine* 68 (1845):319-20n. Another of his daughters became 'deranged in her faculties'. *WHS* 8 (1912):117.

[29] Temple Church was founded in 1145, but St. James's was older, having been founded in 1130. George Heath, *The History and Antiquities of Bristol* (Bristol 1797), pp. 110-18, 123, 129-30.

[30] On whom, see above, Sept. 23, 1779.

[31] On Thomas Webb, see Feb. 2, 1773 (22:359, n. 73 in this edn.). The implication of the reference to Elizabeth Bushell, in the next note, is that Webb did preach perfection.

[32] Elizabeth Bushell (born *c.* 1757), who married James Trimen (for whose obituary see *Wesleyan Methodist Magazine* 53 [1830]:718) *c.* 1783. John B. Dyson, *Methodism in the Isle of Wight* (Ventnor, 1865), pp. 96-98.

[33] Whitchurch, a market town 12 miles north from Winchester.

[34] Cf. Heb. 12:28.

congregation on Rev. 20:12. Tuesday 17, I came back to
Sevenoaks, and in the afternoon walked over to the Duke of
Dorset's seat.[35] The park is the pleasantest I ever saw, the trees are
so elegantly disposed. The house, which is at least two hundred
years old, is immensely large. It consists of two squares, considerably bigger than the two quadrangles in Lincoln College. I believe
we were shown above thirty rooms, beside the hall, the chapels,
and three galleries. The pictures are innumerable—I think four
times as many as in the castle at Blenheim. Into one of the galleries
opens the king's bedchamber, ornamented above all the rest. The
bed curtains are cloth of gold and so richly wrought that it
requires some strength to draw them. The tables, the chairs, the
frames of the looking-glasses, are all plated over with silver. The
tapestry, representing the whole history of Nebuchadnezzar, is as
fresh as if newly woven. But the bed curtains are exceeding dirty
and look more like copper than gold. The silver on the tables,
chairs, and glass, look as dull as lead. And to complete all, King
Nebuchadnezzar among the beasts, together with his eagle's claws,
has a large crown upon his head and is clothed in scarlet and gold.

Monday 23, I visited for a few days the societies in Northamptonshire. Monday 30, I went to High Wycombe, where the new
preaching-house was well filled in the evening. Tuesday 31,[36] we
had such a congregation at noon in Oxford as I never saw there
before. And what I regarded more than their number was their
seriousness; even the young gentlemen behaved well, nor could I
observe one smiling countenance, although I closely applied these
words; 'I am not ashamed of the gospel of Christ.'[37]

Sunday, November 5, I preached at the New Chapel on Luke
9:55, 'Ye know not what manner of spirit ye are of,'[38] and showed
that, supposing the Papists to be heretics, schismatics, wicked

---

[35] The descent of the manor of Knole since the Sackville family (earls and later dukes
of Dorset), first obtained an interest in it early in the seventeenth century, had been of
exceptional complexity; but lately, exchanges of property covered by an Act of Parliament had led to their obtaining the fee simple; the family now resided all the time and
could improve the estate. Hasted, *Kent*, 3:70-73. Vita Sackville-West (1892-1962), who
would have inherited Knole (her birthplace) in the 1920s had she been male, wrote an
account of *Knole and the Sackvilles* (London, W. Heinemann, 1923), which describes
her growing up among the treasures mentioned in JW's account. Knole is now in the
National Trust.

[36] This entry indicates that the effort to prevent members of the university attending
evangelical conventicles made in the expulsions of 1768 was already nugatory.

[37] Rom. 1:16.

[38] Luke 9:55.

men, enemies to us and to our church and nation, yet we ought not to persecute, to kill, hurt, or grieve them, but barely to prevent their doing hurt.[39]

In the ensuing week, I finished visiting the classes and had the satisfaction to find that the society is considerably increased, both in number and strength, since the Conference.

Mon. 20. I went on the Chatham and, finding the society groaning under a large debt, advised them to open a weekly subscription. The same advice I gave to the society at Sheerness. This advice they all cheerfully followed, and with good effect. On Friday 24, we agreed to follow the same example at London, and in one year we paid off £1400.[40]

Mon. 27. I went to Bedford and preached in the evening. Tuesday 28, I preached at St. Neots. Wednesday 29 at ten, I preached in Godmanchester, and about six, in the new house at Huntington. I have seldom seen a new congregation behave with such seriousness. Thursday 30, I came to Luton and found that child of sorrow and pain, Mrs. Cole,[41] was gone to rest. For many years she had not known an hour's ease; but she died in full, joyous peace. And how little does she regret all that is past, now the days of her mourning are ended!

Monday, December 4. I visited the eastern societies in Kent and, on Friday, returned to London. Sunday 10, I began reading and explaining to the society the large *Minutes* of the Conference.[42] I desire to do all things openly and above board. I would have all the world, and especially all of our society, see not only all the steps we take, but the reasons why we take them.

Sat. 16. Having a second message from Lord George Gordon[43]

[39] Whether or not (as Curnock supposed) this sermon was prompted by the first of Lord George Gordon's requests to JW to visit him in the Tower (see below, Dec. 19, 1780), it undoubtedly betrays uneasiness at the contribution which his preaching and publishing had made to the Gordon riots.

[40] Each of these debt redemption schemes bore the marks of that established at Plymouth by Mr. Jane. See above, Aug. 20, 1780.

[41] On Mrs. Cole, née Clayton, see Apr. 30, 1754 (20:486, n. 64 in this edn.).

[42] JW had read the draft of the 'Large' *Minutes* to a group of the preachers on July 9, 1780.

[43] Lord George Gordon (1751-93), a younger son of the third Duke of Gordon, served in the navy, and rose to the rank of lieutenant. He contested Inverness-shire against General Fraser so effectively that the latter purchased the seat of Ludgershall for him in 1774. In 1779 he became president of the Protestant Association formed to secure the repeal of the Act of 1778 reducing Catholic disabilities. The mass procession to present the association's petition ended in rioting on a great scale early in June 1780, a feature of which was (entirely unconfessional) attacks on prisons and the houses of those prominent in the administration

earnestly desiring to see me, I wrote a line to Lord Stormont,[44] who on Monday the 18th sent me a warrant to see him. On Tuesday 19, I spent an hour with him at his apartment in the Tower. Our conversation turned upon popery and religion. He seemed to
5 be well acquainted with the Bible and had abundance of other books, enough to furnish a study. I was agreeably surprised to find he did not complain of any person or thing, and cannot but hope his confinement will take a right turn and prove a lasting blessing to him.

10 Fri. 22. At the desire of some of my friends, I accompanied them to the British Museum. What an immense field is here for curiosity to range in! One large room is filled from top to bottom with things brought from Tahiti;[45] two or three more with things dug out of the ruins of Herculaneum! Seven huge apartments are
15 filled with curious books, five with manuscripts, two with fossils of all sorts, and the rest with various animals! But what account will a man give to the Judge of quick and dead[46] for a life spent in collecting all these?[47]

Sun. 25. Desiring to make the most of this solemn day, I
20 preached early in the morning at the New Chapel; at ten and four, I preached at West Street and, in the evening, met the society at each end of the town.

Fri. 29. I saw the indictment of the Grand Jury against Lord George Gordon. I stood aghast! What a shocking insult upon truth
25 and common sense! But it is the usual *form*. The more is the shame. Why will not the Parliament remove this scandal from our nation?[48]

of the law, such as Lord Mansfield and Sir John Fielding. Gordon was confined for eight months in the Tower (where JW encountered him) but was acquitted of a charge of high treason in February 1781. In November 1784, he again appeared as a Protestant hero, championing the Dutch against Joseph II, and claiming to be able to recruit hundreds of sailors who threatened to pull down Pitt's house. He became a Jew, partly, it is said, to persuade Jews to withhold loans for the conduct of wars; and was imprisoned for libels on the British government and Marie Antoinette from 1788 till his death.

[44] David Murray (1727-96), eighth Viscount Stormont in the Scottish peerage, who succeeded under special remainder as second Earl of Mansfield in 1793. He was secretary of state in the government of Lord North, 1779-82, and it was in this capacity that JW approached him.

[45] Orig., 'Otaheite'.

[46] Acts 10:42.

[47] JW's almost automatic recurrence to the theme of the transience of this world's goods, is singularly inappropriate both to the permanent intellectual significance of the collections, and to the instinctive engagement with them of his own intellectual curiosity.

[48] Horace Walpole's account is more laconic: 'Lord George Gordon carried before the King's Bench, He made a very long speech; against the opinion of his counsel, Kenyon

Saturday 30. Waking between one and two in the morning, I observed a bright light shine upon the Chapel. I easily concluded, there was a fire near, probably in the adjoining timber-yard.[49] If so, I knew it would soon lay us in ashes. I first called all the family to prayer. Then going out, we found the fire about an hundred yards off, and had broke out while the wind was south. But a sailor cried out, 'Avast! Avast! The wind is turned in a moment!' So it did, to the west, while we were at prayer, and so drove the flame from us. We then thankfully returned, and I rested well the residue of the night.

Sun. 31. We renewed our covenant with God.[50] We had the largest company that I ever remember; perhaps two hundred more than we had last year. And we had the greatest blessing. Several received either a sense of the pardoning love of God or power to love him with all their heart.

Monday, January the first, 1781. We began as usual, the service at four, praising Him who maugre[51] all our enemies had brought us safe to the beginning of another year.

Sunday 7. Much of the power of God rested on the congregation while I was declaring how 'the Son of God was manifested, to destroy the works of the devil.'[52]

Sunday 14. I preached at St. John's, Wapping.[53] Although the church was extremely crowded, yet there was not the least noise or disorder while I besought them all, 'by the mercies of God to present themselves a living sacrifice, holy, acceptable to God'.[54]

Thur. 18. Hearing Mr. Holmes[55] was extremely weak, I went

and Erskine, pleaded not guilty; ordered for trial on the Monday sen'night.' Walpole, *Last Journals*, 2:345.

[49] Mr. Tooth's in Worship Street. Stevenson, *City Road*, p. 78.

[50] On the Covenant Service, see Aug. 6, 1755 (21:23, n. 82 in this edn.).

[51] 'Maugre . . . B. *adv.* and *prep.* In spite of, notwithstanding'. *OED*.

[52] 1 John 3:8 (*Notes*). This was Wesley's sermon, 'The End of Christ's Coming' (2:471-84 in this edn.). Although he had been preaching from this text since at least 1742, he did not put the sermon on paper until now, finishing the transcription on January 20. It first appeared in the *Arminian Magazine* 4 (1781):360-66, 408-14.

[53] JW had preached here on Feb. 26, Apr. 23 and May 19, 1738. The rector of St. John's Wapping, Dec. 31, 1748-1800, was Francis Willis (1729-1807). Willis matriculated from Lincoln College, Oxford, in JW's time there, graduated B.A. from St. Alban Hall, and M.A. in 1741 from Brasenose College, the patrons of this living. He was also physician to George III, and established a private lunatic asylum at Greatford, Lincs. The church was replaced by another in 1790, which was itself destroyed, all but the tower, in World War II.

[54] Cf. Rom. 12:1.

[55] Rev. Edward Holme, from 1757 vicar of Birling, 7 miles north-west from Maidstone. He matriculated from Queen's College, Oxford, in 1732, aged 21, graduating

down to Birling[56] and found him very near worn out, just tottering over the grave. However he *would* creep with me to the church, which was well filled, though the night was exceeding dark. I preached on 'Repent and believe the gospel.'[57] The congregation appeared to be quite stunned. In the morning, I returned to London.

Tue. 23. I went to Dorking and buried the remains of Mrs. Attersal,[58] a lovely woman snatched away in the bloom of youth. I trust it will be a blessing to many, and to her husband in particular.

Thur. 25. I spent an agreeable hour at a concert of my nephews.[59] But I was a little out of my element among lords and ladies. I love plain music and plain company best.

Monday, February 12. I went to Norwich. The house was extremely crowded in the evening, and the whole congregation appeared to be wounded. Consequently many attended in the morning. Tuesday 13, I was desired to preached that evening on 'Work out your own salvation with fear and trembling; for it is God that worketh in you both to will and to do his good pleasure.'[60] Even the Calvinists were satisfied for the present and readily acknowledged that we did not ascribe our salvation to our own works, but to the grace of God.

Wed. 14. To awaken if possible the careless ones at Loddon, at

---

B.A. in 1737, and M.A. in 1741. He conveyed land at Leybourne and an endowment for a free school for poor children of neighbouring parishes, managed by trustees who included friends of JW. One of these, Joseph Beardmore, who married Miss Mary Owen of Publow, was also a trustee for JW's new chapel. Hasted, *Kent*, 2:202, 210.

[56] Orig., 'Burling'.

[57] Mark 1:15.

[58] According to Curnock (6:303, n. 3), the Dorking parish register records under Oct. 28, 1777, 'Joseph Attersole to Sarah Polding, by licence, by Samuel Goodinge, vicar', but there is no record of the burial in the registers of the church or chapel. For a Miss Attersol at Dorking, see Nov. 23, 1772 (22:354, n. 54 in this edn.).

[59] CW's two surviving sons, Charles (1757-1834) and Samuel (1766-1837), were musically talented and, as soon as they could publicly perform together, they began in 1779 to give an annual series of subscription concerts at their father's house, 1 Chesterfield Street, Marylebone. JW's discomfort at the present visit may be illuminated by the recollection of one lady present that 'Mr. John Wesley went in full canonicals, and she in rich silk and ruffles' (Stevenson, *City Road*, 460). Among the others present was General Oglethorpe, come to hear the sons of his old secretary. 'Meeting with Mr. John Wesley, [he] kissed his hand, and showed him every mark of profound respect'; Thomas Jackson, *Life of Charles Wesley*, 2 vols. (London, 1841), 2:347. CW gives a full account of his two boys in *CWJ*, 2:140-66. See also Adam Clarke, *Memoirs of the Wesley Family*, 2 vols. (London, 1836), 2:371-75.

[60] Cf. Phil. 2:12-13.

two in the afternoon, I opened and enforced those awful words, 'Where their worm dieth not, and the fire is not quenched.'[61] In the evening, I applied those gracious words, 'All things are ready; come unto the marriage.'[62]

After spending Thursday and Friday with the affectionate people at Lowestoft, on Saturday I returned to Norwich. Here I found about fifty missing out of the two hundred and sixteen whom I left in the society a year ago. Such fickleness I have not found anywhere else in the kingdom; no, [not][63] even in Ireland.

Sun. 18. The Chapel was full enough, both in the afternoon and the evening. I declared to them the whole counsel of God, and on Monday, returned to London.

Wed. 21. Being the National Fast, I preached at the New Chapel in the morning, and at West Street in the afternoon. At this, as well as the two last public fasts, all places of public worship were crowded. All shops were shut up, all was quiet in the streets, and seriousness seemed to spread through the whole city. And one may hope even this outward acknowledgment of God is in a measure acceptable to him.

Sunday 25. My brother, Mr. Richardson,[64] and Mr. Buckingham[65] being ill, I went through the service at Spitalfields alone. The congregation was much larger than usual; but my strength was as my day, both here, the New Chapel, and afterwards at St. Antholin's Church.[66] The service lasted till near nine, but I was no more tired than at nine in the morning.

Friday, March 2. We had our General Quarterly Meeting and found the money subscribed this year for the payment of the public debt was between fourteen and fifteen hundred pounds.

Sun. 4. At eight in the evening, I took coach for Bristol with Mr. Rankin[67] and two other friends. We drove with two horses as far as Reading. Two more were then added with a postillion, who knowing little of his business, instead of going forward turned quite round on a sloping ground, so that we expected the coach to overturn every moment. So it must have done, but that the coach-

---

[61] Mark 9:44, 46, 48.

[62] Matt. 22:4.

[63] Orig., 'nor'.

[64] John Richardson, former curate of Ewhurst, and now JW's helper, on whom see Apr. 19, 1764 (21:455 in this edn.).

[65] William Buckingham, on whom see Sept. 7, 1760 (21:274, n. 81 in this edn.).

[66] On this church, see above, Nov. 15, 1778.

[67] On Thomas Rankin, see Sept. 8, 1765 (22:19, n. 82 in this edn.).

man instantly leaped off and, with some other men, held it up till we got out at the opposite door. The coach was then soon set right, and we went on without let or hindrance.

After spending two or three days at Bath, on Thursday 8, I
5 went forward to Bristol. On Monday the 12th and the following days, I visited the society, but was surprised to find no greater increase, considering what preachers they had had.[68]

Sun. 18. I preached morning and evening at the Room, in the afternoon at Temple Church. The congregation here is remark-
10 ably well behaved; indeed so are the parishioners in general. And no wonder, since they have had such a succession of rectors as few parishes in England have had.[69] The present incumbent truly fears God. So did his predecessor, Mr. Catcott[70] who was indeed as eminent for piety as most clergymen in England. He succeeded
15 his father, a man of the same spirit, who I suppose succeeded Mr. Arthur Bedford, a person greatly esteemed fifty or sixty years ago for piety as well as learning.

---

[68] John Pawson (on whom see, June 21, 1767; 22:86, n. 4 in this edn.), Thomas Rankin, and Thomas Tennant (1741-93), a Londoner who never completely freed himself from depression, deep feelings of guilt, and of fear of death, who was admitted to the itinerancy on trial in 1770 after travelling in the spring with JW himself. Ill health and pain compelled him to desist from travelling in 1792. Atmore, *Memorial*, pp. 414-16.

[69] JW's recollection here is confused. The living was a vicarage; the elder Catcott was rector of St. Stephen's, not vicar of Temple; and at least one of his predecessors, Henry Becher, had been among his opponents. The succession was as follows (*WHS* 3 [1902]:157-58):

> Apr. 4, 1693, Arthur Bedford (on whom see Oct. 6, 1738; 19:15, n. 46 in this edn.).
> Apr. 25, 1713, William Cary.
> Nov. 16, 1723, Samuel Curtis.
> Feb. 10, 1738/39, Henry Becher.
> Jan. 11, 1743/44, Thomas Jones.
> May 17, 1755, John Price.
> Aug. 21, 1779, Joseph Easterbrook.

Joseph Easterbrook (1751-91), in the words of his memorial, was 'a faithful and laborious minister of the gospel, whose life corresponded with his profession'; *WHS* 9 (1913):96. The son of the city bellman, Easterbrook was educated at Kingswood School, taught at Trevecca College, and, obtaining episcopal ordination, was presented to the living of Temple Church by the corporation. He succeeded James Rouquet as chaplain of Newgate jail, and it was his 'invariable rule to send those who were awakened under his ministry, and who came to him for advice, to meet in class, and . . . to unite themselves to the [Methodist] Society'; Atmore, *Memorial*, pp. 110-16; *WHS* 19 (1934):101-3. His funeral sermon was preached by Henry Moore.

[70] Alexander Catcott (1725-79), son of the master of Bristol Grammar School, is remembered principally as a student of the Creation and the Flood, which he thought occurred when the internal waters broke out and dissolved the earth, an hypothesis which appeared to him confirmed by his geological and druidical studies.

Mon. 19. For several years the severe weather has begun the very day I set out from Bristol. But the mild weather now continued seven or eight days longer. This evening, I preached at Stroud; Tuesday 20, at Stroud, Gloucester, Tewkesbury, and Worcester. Wednesday 21 at noon, I preached in Bewdley, and at Worcester in the evening. Thursday 23, I preached in Bengeworth Church and had some conversation with that amiable man, Mr. B[eale].[71] I preached in the evening at Pebworth Church on those words in the Lesson, 'Godliness with contentment is great gain.'[72]

Sat. 24. I was invited to preach at Quinton[73] five miles from Birmingham. I preached there at noon in the open air to a serious and attentive congregation. Some of them appeared to be very deeply affected. Who knows but it may continue? In the evening, I had another comfortable opportunity with our friends at Birmingham.

Sun. 25. I preached at Birmingham, Dudley, and Wednesbury. Monday 26, I preached at noon in Mr. Barker's large parlour at Congreve near Penkridge.[74] Many stood in the next room, and many in the garden near the windows. And I believe all could hear. I brought strange things to the ears of those that had been used to softer doctrines. And I believe not in vain. They seemed to receive the truth in the love thereof.

In the evening, I preached at Newcastle-under-Lyme. Mr. Scott[75] and two or three of his preachers were present. They have

---

[71] Rector of Bengeworth, on whom see above, July 5, 1777.

[72] 1 Tim. 6:6.

[73] Not Quinton, Warwicks., near Chipping Camden, which JW had visited on Oct. 19, 1743, and Mar. 15, 1772 (see 19:343 and 22:310 in this edn.), but Quinton, a locality 5 miles west of Birmingham. This visit was doubtless in response to a letter from Ambrose Foley of Mar. 18, 1778, declaring that he had been engaged for some years 'in reading your sermons to a considerable company, who wish well to your labours of love; and as they are some of them but babes in Christ, an instructive lesson might (with the Divine blessing) greatly establish their faith, and much good be done to others. If you have an hour or two to spare, my house which is a good one, and my heart, which is a bad one, are both open for you'; *WHS* 5 (1905):92-93. JW was frequently in touch with the Foleys over the next couple of years. Telford, 7:69, 87, 109, 167.

[74] Penkridge is an ancient settlement and substantial parish 6 miles south of Stafford. Congreve, 2 miles south-west of Penkridge, had a working forge for much of the eighteenth century. The ironmaster's name was Thomas Barker. *Victoria County History; Staffordshire*, 5:106, n. 10.

[75] Jonathan Scott (1735-1807), son of Richard Scott of Scott's Hall, Kent and Belton, Shrops., and formerly captain in the 7th Dragoons. He was converted by the preaching of William Romaine in 1766, left the army, and working from Staffordshire outwards, became the most successful evangelist among the Independents in the north-west. He

lately begun to preach both here and at Burslem.[76] If they would go and break up fresh ground we should rejoice. But we cannot commend them for breaking in upon our labours after we have borne the burden and heat of the day.

Tuesday 27. I went a little out of my way in order to open the new preaching-house at Shrewsbury.[77] I did not so much wonder at the largeness as at the seriousness of the congregation. So still and deeply attentive a congregation I did not expect to see here. How apt are we to forget that important truth, that 'all things are possible with God.'[78]

Wed. 28. I returned to Burslem. How is the whole face of this country changed in about twenty years![79] Since the potteries were introduced, inhabitants have continually flowed in from every side. Hence the wilderness is literally become a fruitful field. Houses, villages, towns have sprung up. And the country is not more improved than the people. The word of God has had free course among them. Sinners are daily awakened and converted to God, and believers grow in the knowledge of Christ. In the evening, the house was filled with people and with the presence of God. This constrained me to extend the service a good deal longer than I am accustomed to do. Likewise at the meeting of the society, many were filled with strong consolation.

After preaching at Congleton, Macclesfield, and Stockport in my way, on Friday the 30th, I opened the new chapel at Manchester,[80]

helped to found churches in Newcastle-under-Lyme, Hanley, Stone, Uttoxeter, Stoke-on-Trent, Whitchurch, Nantwich, and many other places. In 1776, a group of Congregational ministers at Lancaster ordained him to the unique office of 'presbyter or teacher at large'. He was much patronized by Lady Glenorchy, and he had some distinguished preaching assistants, including George Burder and John Wilson. It was a group of these assistants who now accompanied him. Seymour, *Huntingdon*, 1:317-19; R. Tudur Jones, *Congregationalism in England, 1662-1962* (London, 1962), pp. 155-56; Dugald Macfadyen, 'The Apostolic Labours of Captain Jonathan Scott', *Transactions of the Congregational Historical Society* 3 (1907-8):48-66.

[76] Orig., 'Borslem'.

[77] Built at the expense of John Appleton, currier, and situated in Hills Lane; *WHS* 4 (1904):222; *Arminian Magazine* 13 (1790):636-40. JW's next visit to Shrewsbury (see below, Aug. 5, 1784) was to preach Appleton's memorial sermon.

[78] Cf. Matt. 19:26, etc.

[79] On JW's first visit, he had commented on the number of potters; see Mar. 8, 1760 (21:245-46 in this edn.). Josiah Wedgwood (1739-95) had then only recently become a master potter. In 1760, however, Wedgwood had opened new works at Etruria, and the whole area had rapidly developed. In particular an enormous export market was tapped; in 1781 Wedgwood claimed that five-sixths of the manufactures of North Staffordshire were exported.

[80] The Oldham Street Chapel, then on the outskirts of the town.

about the size of that in London. The whole congregation behaved with the utmost seriousness. I trust much good will be done in this place.

Sunday, April 1. I began reading prayers at ten o'clock. Our country friends flocked in from all sides. At the Communion was such a sight as I am persuaded was never seen at Manchester before: eleven or twelve hundred communicants at once, and all of them fearing God.

Tue. 3. I took a solemn leave of our affectionate friends here and went on to Bolton. The society here are true, original Methodists. They are not conformed to the world, either in its maxims, its spirit, or its fashions, but are simple followers of the Lamb. Consequently they increase both in grace and number.

Wed. 4. I went over to Wigan and preached a funeral sermon for Betty Brown, one of the first members of this society, one of whom, John Layland, gave me the following artless account of her:

> She met with us in a class about twenty years, even to the Sunday before her death, which was on Friday, March 2. Going to market that day in good health, she returned (as she often did) without her husband, ate her supper and went to bed. About midnight he came and found her body, but the spirit was fled! Her love for God, for his cause, and for her brethren and sisters, was truly remarkable. So was her pity for backsliders. At home and abroad she was continually intent on one thing. We cannot forget her tears and prayers, which we doubt not the Lord hath heard.
>
> A little before her death, sitting with my sisters, she seemed in deep thought and broke out, 'I will go to God!' One of them being surprised, said, 'Pray, Betty, what do you mean?' She only replied, 'I will go to God.' So that, if I think right, she was the beloved of God, the delight of his children, a dread to wicked men, and a torment to devils.

Thur. 5. I went to Chester. The house was well filled with deeply attentive hearers. I perceived God had exceedingly blessed the labours of Jonathan Hern[81] and William Boothby.[82] The con-

---

[81] Jonathan Hern had been admitted to the itinerancy in 1769 and till the Conference of 1780 served in Ireland; from this time he served in English circuits till he desisted from travelling at the Conference of 1791.

[82] William Boothby travelled 1776–90 and was a supernumerary at Wakefield 1790–1801. He was the victim (legendary style) of mob violence stirred up by a clergyman at Colchester in 1784; the latter is said to have been 'smitten with paralysis shortly afterwards and never preached again'. *WHS* 18 (1931):16.

gregations were much larger than they used to be. The society
was increased, and they were not only agreed among themselves
but in peace with all round about them.

Fri. 6. I went to Alpraham and preached the funeral sermon of
good old sister Cawley.[83] She has been indeed a mother in Israel, a
pattern of all good works.[84] Saturday 7 at noon, I preached at Preston on the Hill,[85] and in the evening, at Warrington. Sunday 8,
the service was at the usual hours. I came just in time to put a stop
to a bad custom which was creeping in here. A few men who had
fine voices sang a psalm which no one knew, in a tune fit for an
opera, wherein three, four, or five persons, sung different words at
the same time! What an insult upon common sense! What a bur-
lesque upon public worship! No *custom* can excuse such a mixture
of profaneness and absurdity.

Mon. 9. Desiring to be in Ireland as soon as possible, I hastened
to Liverpool and found a ship ready to sail; but the wind was contrary, till on Thursday morning the captain came in haste and told
us the wind was come quite fair. So Mr. Floyde,[86] Snowden,[87]
Joseph Bradford,[88] and I, with two of our sisters,[89] went on board.
But scarce were we out at sea, when the wind turned quite foul
and rose higher and higher. In an hour I was so affected as I had
not been for forty years before. For two days I could not swallow
the quantity of a pea of anything solid, and very little of any liquid.

---

[83] The wife of Richard Cawley, on whom see Oct. 19, 1749 (20:309-10, n. 75 in this edn.). Cf. *Wesleyan Methodist Magazine* 135 (1912):746-48. On Richard Cawley's conversion and early career, see James Everett, *Wesleyan Methodism in Manchester and its Vicinity* (Manchester, 1827), pp. 139-75.

[84] Titus 2:7.

[85] A small township then in the parish of Runcorn, 4 miles north-east of Frodsham.

[86] John Floyde (1749-98), an itinerant 1770-82. 'A sensible, pious man' and acceptable preacher, he desisted from travelling after a severe illness from which he was cured by prayer (see below, Apr. 24, 1782) and developed a successful profession as surgeon and apothecary, first at Halifax, then at Leeds, ministering meanwhile at the Stainland Chapel. This was originally built as a chapel of ease to Halifax parish, but its stated pastors were Wesleyan, Independent, and Methodist New Connexion, until in the early nineteenth century it came into the hands of an Episcopal minister who frequently exchanged pulpits with Methodist preachers; Walker, *Wesleyan Methodism in Halifax*, pp. 102-4. His serving again as a Methodist local preacher seemed to some of his brother itinerants symptomatic of increasing worldliness, and the sickness and financial embarrassment of his last years seemed to them an appropriate visitation. Atmore, *Memorial*, pp. 142-44.

[87] On George Snowden, an itinerant who had commenced in the Irish work, see May 3, 1775 (22:449, n. 75 in this edn.).

[88] On Joseph Bradford, who for the years 1774-79 had been regularly appointed JW's travelling companion, see June 17, 1775 (22:457, n. 9 in this edn.).

[89] One of whom, as appears below, was Mrs. Snowden.

I was bruised and sore from head to foot and ill able to turn me on the bed. All Friday, the storm increasing, the sea of consequence was rougher and rougher. Early on Saturday morning the hatches were closed, which, together with the violent motion, made our horses so turbulent that I was afraid we must have killed them lest they should damage the ship. Mrs. S[nowden] now crept to me, threw her arms over me, and said, 'O Sir, we will die together!' We had by this time three feet [of] water in the hold, though it was an exceeding light vessel. Meantime we were furiously driving on a lee shore, and when the captain cried, 'Helm alee,' she would not obey the helm. I called our brethren to prayers, and we found free access to the throne of grace. Soon after, we got, I know not how, into Holyhead harbour after being sufficiently buffeted by the winds and waves for two days and two nights.

The more I considered the more I was convinced, it was not the will of God I should go to Ireland at this time. So we went into the stage-coach without delay and, the next evening, came to Chester.

I now considered in what place I could spend a few days to the greatest advantage. I soon thought of the Isle of Man and those parts of Wales which I could not well see in my ordinary course. I judged it would be best to begin with the latter. So after a day or two's rest, on Wednesday 18, I set out for Brecon, purposing to take Whitchurch (where I had not been for many years)[90] and Shrewsbury in my way. At noon, I preached in Whitchurch to a numerous and very serious audience; in the evening, at Shrewsbury, where, seeing the earnestness of the people, I agreed to stay another day.

Here I read over Sir Richard Hill's letter to Mr. Madan[91] on his defence of polygamy.[92] I think it is home to the point, and wish always to write (if I must write controversy) in just such a spirit.

[90] Whitchurch, Shrops.; for JW's last recorded visit see Mar. 27, 1772 (22:313 in this edn.), a disastrous expedition in which JW's coach stuck fast and had to be abandoned.

[91] Sir Richard Hill, *The Blessings of Polygamy Displayed, in an Affectionate Address to Rev. Martin Madan, Occasioned by his Late Work 'Thelyphthora'* (London, 1781). Hill being a Shropshire baronet, JW might well feel the need to be *au fait* with the controversy at this moment.

[92] Martin Madan, *Thelyphthora: or, A Treatise on Female Ruin* (2nd edn., London, 1780; 2nd enl. edn., 3 vols., 1781). In this work Madan defended polygamy on the basis of the Mosaic law which he held to be in accordance with Christianity properly understood. Since these doctrines had been held by JW's brother-in-law Westley Hall (on whom see May 13, 1738; 18:238, n. 9 in this edn.), it is not surprising that the Methodist reply was left to Joseph Benson, in numerous instalments in *Arminian Magazine* 6 (1783) and 7 (1784).

Not knowing the best way from hence to Brecon, I thought well to go round by Worcester. I took Broseley in my way and thereby had a view of the iron bridge over the Severn[93]—I suppose the first and the only one in Europe. It will not soon be imi-
5 tated.

In the evening, I preached at Broseley and, on Saturday 21, went on to Worcester. I found one of our preachers, Joseph Cole,[94] there, but unable to preach through his ague. So that I could not have come more opportunely. Sunday 22, I preached at seven in
10 our own room. At three, the service began at St. Andrew's.[95] As no notice had been given of my preaching there, only as we walked along the street, it was supposed the congregation would be small. But it was far otherwise. High and low, rich and poor, flocked together from all parts of the city. And truly God spoke in
15 his word, so that I believe most of them were 'almost persuaded to be Christians'.[96] Were it only for this hour alone, the pains of coming to Worcester would have been well bestowed.

Monday 23. Being informed it was fifty miles to Brecon,[97] we set out early, but on trial we found they were computed miles.[98]
20 However, taking fresh horses at the Hay[-on-Wye], I just reached it in time, finding a large company waiting. Wednesday 25, I set out for Carmarthen. But Joseph Bradford was so ill that, after going six miles, I left him at a friend's house and went only myself.[99] I came in good time to Carmarthen and enforced those

---

[93] On this see above, Mar. 26, 1779.

[94] Joseph Cole (1749-1826) was admitted to the itinerancy on trial in 1780, and travelled 'with an unblemished reputation and considerable success' till compelled by advancing years to retire in 1815. He then settled in Carmarthen. 'He was blessed with a peculiar talent for reproving sin with effect. . . . Persons occupying respectable stations in society have [in numerous instances] acknowledged the propriety of his remarks and thanked him for his admonitions.' *Wesleyan Methodist Magazine* 49 (1826):642-43.

[95] St. Andrew's, Worcester. The vicar in 1784 was W. Wormington (1745-1828), who moved on to become vicar of Norton with Lenchworth, Co. Worcs., in 1785. John Noake, *Worcester Sects; or, A History of the Roman Catholics and Dissenters of Worcester* (London, 1861).

[96] Cf. Acts 26:28.

[97] Orig., 'Brecknock'.

[98] 'Computed miles', often estimated and quite inaccurate, were the basis of postal charges; the computed distances frequently differed from 'measured' or real miles. The measured distance is said to be about 60 miles; see Curnock, 6:314, n. 1.

[99] Williams, *Wesley in Wales*, p. 104, n. 1: 'Wesley left Joseph Bradford . . . at Beilie, a farm some 1 1/2 miles from Defynnog; he remained there for three months. His hosts were Walter Williams and his wife, both of whom were members of the Brecon society. The husband died on 12 Mar. 1797 aged 54, and his wife (formerly the widow of the Methodist John Watkins of Glanusk) on 12 Feb. 1825, aged 88. When Wesley called there

solemn words on a serious congregation, 'Now he commandeth all men everywhere to repent.'[1]

Thursday 26. I went on to Pembroke and, in the evening, preached in the town hall. Friday 27, I preached at Jeffreyston,[2] seven miles from Pembroke, to a large congregation of honest colliers. In the evening, I preached in Pembroke town hall again to an elegant congregation and afterwards met the society, reduced to a fourth part of its ancient number. But as they are now all in peace and love with each other, I trust they will increase again. Sunday 18, we had in the evening the most solemn opportunity which I have had since we came into Wales, and the society seemed all alive and resolved to be altogether Christians.[3]

Sun. 29. At seven, I preached in the room, on 'Lazarus, come forth!'[4] And about ten, began at St. Daniel's.[5] The church was filled as usual, and the Second Lesson gave me a suitable text, 'Almost thou persuadest me to be a Christian!'[6] I applied the words as closely as possible. And I doubt not, some were more than 'almost persuaded'. In the evening, I preached at Haverfordwest to the liveliest congregation I have seen in Wales.

Mon. 30. I met about fifty children, such a company as I have not seen for many years. Miss Warren[7] loves them, and they love her. She has taken true pains with them, and her labour has not been in vain. Several of them are much awakened, and the behav-

on his last journey in 1790 [Aug. 9] at 6 a.m. [at 5, according to the Diary] he blessed one of their grandchildren who later became the Rev. W. R. M. Williams M.A., a chaplain in the service of the East India Company. *Eurgrawm*, 1861, 372-75; 1862, 17-18.'

[1] Acts 17:30.

[2] Orig., 'Jefferson'.

[3] See Acts 26:28-29, and below.

[4] John 11:43.

[5] This visit is recorded in the diary of James Chubb (1749-1826), a Methodist excise man, who rode from Pembroke to hear JW ('about 1500 attended the sacrament') and afterwards dined with him 'at Mr. Llewellin's'. JW started out first on a pony, and though Chubb 'rode at the rate of seven miles an hour', he did not catch up till JW was detained at a ferry. 'It is about 9 miles and Mr. W. 76 [77]', he adds. A few days later JW exhorted the society 'not to indulge themselves with too much sleep. . . . He allowed six hours for a man and seven for a woman in health.' *WHS* 29 (1953):24.

[6] Cf. Wesley's Sermon No. 2, from this text (1:131-41 in this edn.).

[7] Catherine Warren ('my dear Kitty' to JW) was a member of a county family of Longridge, Pem., and sister to Lady Kensington. JW had been in correspondence with her since at least 1778, and a phrase in the first surviving letter, 'you have now a sufficient sphere of action wherein you may employ whatever talents you have received' (Telford, 6:308), suggests that he had already committed to her a number of boys to teach, a number which had here increased to fifty. In 1784 she had given up the work (Telford, 7:229), but had resumed it by the following year; *WHS* 30 (1956):132. See also above, July 18, 1777.

iour of all is so composed that they are a pattern to the whole congregation.

Tuesday, May 1. I rode to St. David's, seventeen measured miles from Haverfordwest.[8] I was surprised to find all the land for the last nine or ten miles so fruitful and well cultivated. What a difference is there between the westermost[9] parts of England and the westermost parts of Wales! The former (the west of Cornwall) so barren and wild! The latter, so fruitful and well improved! But the town itself is a melancholy spectacle. I saw but one tolerable good house in it. The rest were miserable huts indeed. I do not remember so mean a town even in Ireland. The cathedral has been a large and stately fabric, far superior to any other in Wales. But a great part of it is fallen down already, and the rest is hastening into ruin—one blessed fruit (among many) of bishops residing at a distance from their see. Here are the tombs and effigies of many ancient worthies, Owen Tudor[10] in particular. But the zealous Cromwellians broke off their noses, hands, and feet, and defaced them as much as possible. But what had the Tudors done to them? Why, they were progenitors of *kings*.

Thur. 3. About ten, I preached at Spittal,[11] a large village about six miles from Haverfordwest. Thence we went to Trecwn[12] and spent a few hours in that lovely retirement, buried from all the world in the depth of woods and mountains. Friday 4 about eleven, I preached in Newport Church, and again at four in the evening. Saturday 5, I returned to Haverfordwest.

Sat. 6. I preached in St. Thomas's Church,[13] on 'We preach Christ crucified.'[14] It was a stumbling-block to some of the hearers. So the Scripture is fulfilled. But I had amends when I met the society in the evening.

[8] Orig., 'Ha'rford'. According to Lewis (*Wales*, 1:274), 16 miles. JW's demonstration of prickly royalism was perhaps more appropriate to the state of the American War than of St. David's Cathedral; this had suffered violence throughout its history, but in the civil war suffered more in property than in fabric; W. B. Jones and E. A. Freeman, *History & Antiquities of St. David's* (London, 1856), p. 337 ff. Some of the ruin which distressed JW was rectified in 1798 when John Hash (who may have been born at Cardigan) rebuilt the west front and chapter house.

[9] During Wesley's lifetime this was slowly displaced by 'westernmost', of which *OED* notes the first use in 1705, and the last use of 'westermost' in 1821.

[10] In fact the tomb of his son Edmund, the father of Henry VII.

[11] A small parish 5 miles north from Haverfordwest.

[12] Orig., 'Tracoon'. The home of Admiral Vaughan, on whom see above, July 16, 1777.

[13] The rector of St. Thomas's, Haverfordwest, 1777-99, was William Cleaveland.

[14] 1 Cor. 1:23.

Mon. 7. About ten, I preached near the market-place in Narberth,[15] a large town ten miles east from Haverfordwest. Abundance of people flocked together. And they were all still as night. In the evening, I preached to an equally attentive congregation at Carmarthen.

Tue. 8. I had a large congregation at Llanelli and at Swansea. Some months since, there were abundance of hearers at Neath, but on a sudden one lying tongue set the society on fire till almost half of them were scattered away. But as all, offended or not offended, were at the town hall, I took the opportunity of strongly enforcing the Apostle's words, 'Let all bitterness, and wrath, and anger, and clamour, and evil-speaking, be put away from you, with all malice.'[16] I believe God sealed his word on many hearts, and we shall have better days at Neath.

About three, I preached in the church near Bridgend and, at six, in the town hall at Cowbridge. Thursday 10, I preached in our room[17] about ten, on 'I am not ashamed of the Gospel of Christ.'[18] May God deliver us from this evil disease which eats out all the heart of religion! In the evening, I preached in the town hall at Cardiff, but the congregation was almost wholly new. The far greater part of the old society, Ann Jenkins, Thomas Glascott, Arthur Price, Jane Haswell, Nancy Newell,[19] and a long train, are gone hence and are no more seen![20] And how few are followers of them, as they were of Christ!

Mon. 14. Before I reached Monmouth, one met and informed me that Mr. C.,[21] a Justice of the Peace, one of the greatest men in

[15] Orig. 'Nerbeth'. Methodism was introduced into Narberth by James Chubb, the exciseman (on whom see above, Apr. 29, 1781), who during a year's residence there arranged for Methodist preachers to call fortnightly, got them a room to preach in, and kept on good terms with the Calvinistic Methodists. *WHS* 29 (1953):28.

[16] Eph. 4:31.

[17] The Cowbridge society, led by Isaac Skinner, had been given permission by the previous Conference to build a preaching-house. *Minutes*, 1:147.

[18] Rom. 1:16.

[19] Anne Jenkins, the widowed mother of James Jenkins (1745; Curnock, 6:316, n. 21), Thomas Glascott, and Arthur Price remained permanently in JW's recollection as pillars of Cardiff sanctity; see Aug. 30, 1771 (22:289, n. 56 in this edn.). On Glascott see also Sept. 1, 1758 (21:164, n. 48 in this edn.). Janes Haswell and Nancy Newell are otherwise unknown, but are remembered in distinguished company.

[20] See Ps. 39:15 (BCP).

[21] Probably the same as 'Mr. G.' of Aug. 15, 1788; William Catchmay[d] (1747-93), who assumed the name of Gwinnett on Aug. 17, 1782, on inheriting Shurdington, near Chippenham, from Mary, widow of George Gwinnett. J. A. Bradney, *A History of Monmouthshire*, 4 vols. (London, 1904-32), 2 (pt. 2):215-17. On the disorders in Monmouth, see above, Aug. 12, 1779.

the town, desired I would take a bed at his house. Of consequence, all the rabble of the town were as quiet as lambs. And we had a comfortable opportunity both night and morning. Surely this is the Lord's doing!

5   Tue. 15. We went through miserable roads to Worcester. Wednesday 16 about ten, I preached in the large meeting at Kidderminster,[22] to a numerous congregation. With much difficulty, we reached Shrewsbury[23] in the evening and found the people waiting. There has been no tumult since the new house was built.

10 So far God has helped us.

    Thur. 17. I preached at Whitchurch and Nantwich. Friday 18 at eleven, in the chapel near Northwich and, in the evening, at Manchester. Sunday 20, I found much enlargement in applying to a numerous congregation the lovely account given by St. James

15 of 'pure religion and undefiled'.[24] In the afternoon, I preached a funeral sermon for Mary Charlton,[25] an Israelite indeed. From the hour that she first knew the pardoning love of God, she never lost sight of it for a moment. Eleven years ago she believed that God had cleansed her from all sin.[26] And she showed that she had not

20 believed in vain by her holy and unblameable conversation.

    Mon. 21. I went over to Warrington and preached in the evening. Fearing many of the congregation rested in a false peace, I endeavoured to undeceive them by closely applying those words, 'Ye shall know them by their fruits.'[27] Tuesday 22 about eleven, I preached at

25 Chowbent,[28] and in the evening, at Bolton where the people seemed to be on the wing, just ready to take their flight to heaven.

    Wed. 23. Having appointed to preach at Blackburn, I was desired to take Kabb[29] in my way. But such a road sure no carriage

---

[22] This meeting had until lately been led by Benjamin Fawcett (on whom see Mar. 13, 1771; 22:265, n. 58 in this edn.), a man who did not shrink from unconventional methods. On his death in 1780 the meeting divided, the Independents retaining the meeting-house and the Arians building a new chapel.

[23] Orig., 'Salop', the ancient name.

[24] Jas. 1:27.

[25] Tyerman *(John Wesley,* 3:333) possessed MS correspondence and the diaries of Samuel Bardsley, the itinerant, which showed that Molly Charlton was the one and only sweetheart Bardsley ever had, and that the pair wished to marry. The difficulty of providing for married preachers was, however, so great that JW and John Pawson intervened to break off their engagement.

[26] See 1 John 1:7.

[27] Matt. 7:16.

[28] A village in the chapelry of Atherton, which is 2 miles north-east from Leigh.

[29] Much discussion of this name early in the present century yielded no certain result, even the suggestion that JW was endeavouring to use the word 'cab' forty years ahead of

ever went before! I was glad to quit it and use my own feet. About twelve I found a large number of plain, artless people just fit for the gospel. So I applied our Lord's words, 'If any man thirst, let him come unto me and drink.'[30] In the evening, I preached in the new house at Blackburn.[31]

Thur. 24. I went on to Preston, where the old prejudice seems to be quite forgotten. The little society has fitted up a large and convenient house,[32] where I preached to a candid audience. Everyone seemed to be considerably affected; I hope in some the impression will continue.

Fri. 25. We went on to Ambleside and, on Saturday, to White-haven. Sunday 27, I preached in the morning and evening in the house; in the afternoon in the market-place. But abundance of people went away, not being able to bear the intense heat of the sun.

Wed. 30. I embarked on board the packet-boat for the Isle of Man. We had a dead calm for many hours. However, we landed at Douglas[33] on Friday morning. Both the preachers[34] met me here and gave me a comfortable account of the still increasing work of God.

Before dinner we took a walk in a garden[35] near the town, wherein any of the inhabitants of it may walk. It is wonderfully

anyone else. The likeliest possibility is that Nab Farm, Turton, is meant, and that Kabb represents a lapse of memory or an uncorrected printer's error. *WHS* 4 (1904):247-48; 6 (1907):14-16.

[30] John 7:37.   [31] See above, Apr. 27, 1780.

[32] JW seems to have been premature both in his comment on prejudice and on the ability of the Preston society to fit itself out with convenient premises. With the travelling preachers visiting Preston only once a fortnight, leadership was provided by an ex-Presbyterian local preacher, Roger Crane (1758-1836), who became a Methodist only in 1777. 'Being greatly inconvenienced by the want of a suitable place of worship, he and two other young men determined, if possible, to accomplish the erection of a commodious chapel; which considering the spirit of hostility then prevailing in the town towards Methodism, was a work of no small hazard and enterprise. The number in the society was about fifty; these were chiefly poor and unable to render much assistance; but they did what they could, Mr. Crane taking the general oversight of the building . . . and the chapel was opened in the year 1787.' *Wesleyan Methodist Magazine* 62 (1839):532.

[33] On the origins of Methodism in the Isle of Man, see above, May 30, 1777.

[34] John Crook and Thomas Readshaw. The latter, who is listed in none of the standard works of reference, was stationed in the *Minutes* on more than one occasion at this time, but seems to have been regarded as 'one of our old local preachers', particularly popular in the north-east, who became a Methodist in 1750, and died suddenly in 1788, 'truly happy in the Lord'. *Methodist Magazine* 32 (1809):305-6; James Rosser, *History of Wesleyan Methodism in the Isle of Man* (Douglas, 1849), p. 96.

[35] Hill's garden, a promenade near the sea, closed to the public in 1790. The Nunnery Gardens still existed in Curnock's time (6:318), but were then private.

pleasant, yet not so pleasant as the gardens of the Nunnery (so it is still called) which are not far from it. These are delightfully laid out and yield to few places of the size in England.

At six, I preached in the market-place to a large congregation, all of whom except a few children and two or three giddy young women were seriously attentive.

Saturday [June 2]. I rode to Castleton through a pleasant and (now) well cultivated country. At six, I preached in the market-place to most of the inhabitants of the town on 'One thing is needful.'[36] I believe the word carried conviction into the hearts of nearly all that heard it. Afterwards, I walked to the house of one of our English friends, about two miles from the town. All the day I observed, wherever I was, one circumstance that surprised me. In England we generally hear the birds singing morning and evening, but here the thrushes and various other kinds of birds were singing all day long. They did not intermit, even during the noonday heat, where they had a few trees to shade them.

Sun. 3 (Whitsunday). I preached in the market-place again about nine, to a still larger congregation than before, on 'I am not ashamed of the Gospel of Christ.'[37] How few of the genteel hearers could say so? About four in the afternoon, I preached at Barrule[38] on the mountains to a larger congregation than that in the morning. The rain began soon after I began preaching, but ceased in a few minutes. I preached on 'They were all filled with the Holy Ghost,'[39] and showed in what sense this belongs to us and to our children.

Between six and seven, I preached on the seashore at Peel[40] to the largest congregation I have seen in the island. Even the society nearly filled the house. I soon found what spirit they were of. Hardly in England (unless perhaps at Bolton) have I found so plain, so earnest, so simple a people.

Mon. 4. We had such a congregation at five as might have been expected on a Sunday evening. We then rode through and over the mountains to Barregarrow,[41] where I enforced on an artless,

---

[36] Luke 10:42.   [37] Rom. 1:16.

[38] Orig., 'Barewle'. Barrule village stands on the present main road from Castletown to Peel at a height of 679 feet. Nearby is South Barrule, a hill of 1586 feet, commanding an extensive view, where an annual service was long held to commemorate JW's visit.

[39] Acts 2:4, etc.

[40] Orig., 'Peele'.

[41] Orig., 'Beergarrow'. Barregarrow is a locality on the western side of the Isle about 5 1/2 miles north-east of Peel.

loving congregation, 'If any man thirst, let him come unto me and drink.'[42] A few miles from thence we came to Bishop's Court, where good Bishop Wilson[43] resided near threescore years. There is something venerable, though not magnificent, in the ancient palace. And it is undoubtedly situated in one of the pleasantest spots of the whole island.

At six in the evening, I preached at Ballaugh,[44] but the preaching-house would not contain one half of the congregation, of which the vicar, Mr. Gelling,[45] with his wife, sister, and daughter, were a part. He invited me to take a breakfast with him in the morning (Tuesday 5th), which I willingly did. He read family prayers before breakfast in a very serious manner. After spending a little time very agreeably, I went on to Kirk Andreas.[46]

Here also I was obliged to preach in the open air, the rain being suspended till I had done. In the afternoon, we rode through a pleasant and fruitful country to Ramsey,[47] about as large as Peel and more regularly built. The rain was again suspended while I preached to wellnigh all the town, but I saw no inattentive hearers.

Wed. 6. We had many of them again at five, and they were all attention. This was the place where the preachers had little hope of doing good. I trust they will be happily disappointed.

This morning we rode through the most woody, and far the pleasantest part of the island, a range of fruitful land lying at the foot of the mountains, from Ramsey, through Sulby, to Kirk Michael. Here we stopped to look at the plain tombstones of

---

[42] John 7:37.

[43] Thomas Wilson (1663-1755), Bishop of Sodor and Man from 1697 till his death. He entered Trinity College, Dublin, as a sizar in 1685, and graduated B.A. in 1686. After curacies in South Lancashire, he was pressed into the bishopric of Sodor and Man by Lord Derby. Finding Bishop's Court ruinous, he rebuilt it extensively from his own pocket, and became an energetic planter, farmer, miller, and physician. He built churches and took up Thomas Bray's scheme for establishing parochial libraries; see Feb. 26, 1737 (18:175, n. 53 in this edn.). He also prepared a catechism and a translation of the First Gospel and other religious literature into Manx. His attempts to enforce ecclesiastical discipline involved him in conflict with the civil authority. He was a friend of Oglethorpe and the Georgia Trustees (see 18:136, n. 4 in this edn.), and in 1749 was appointed by Zinzendorf to be 'antistes' of the reformed tropus of the Moravian church. In the nineteenth century his *Works* were edited by John Keble and reprinted in the 'Library of Anglo-Catholic Theology', 7 vols. in 8 (Oxford, Parker, 1847-63).

[44] Orig., 'Balleugh'. Ballaugh is a village 7 miles west of Ramsey.

[45] Orig., 'Gilling'; Daniel Gelling, rector of Ballaugh from 1778 till his death in 1801, was formerly rector of Mallow. *WHS* 5 (1905):83.

[46] Orig., 'Andrews'. Andreas was 4 miles north-west of Ramsey.

[47] Orig., 'Ramsay'. Ramsey is a resort on the east coast of the Isle, 7 miles south of Point of Ayr.

those two good men, Bishop Wilson and Bishop Hildesley,[48] whose remains are deposited side by side at the east end of the church. We had scarce reached Peel before the rain increased, but here the preaching-house contained all that could come. After-
5   wards Mr. Crook[49] desired me to meet the singers. I was agreeably surprised. I have not heard better singing either at Bristol or London. Many, both men and women, have admirable voices. And they sing with good judgment. Who would have expected this in the Isle of Man!
10   Thur. 7. I met our little body of preachers.[50] They were two and twenty in all. I never saw in England so many stout, well-looking preachers together. If their spirit be answerable to their look, I know not what can stand before them. In the afternoon, I rode over to Dalby[51] and preached to a very large and very serious congregation.

[48] Mark Hildesley (1698–1772), Bishop of Sodor and Man from 1755. He was a fellow of Trinity College, Cambridge, 1723; rector of Holwell, Beds., 1735–67; prebendary of Lincoln, 1754; and chaplain to Lord Bolingbroke and Viscount St. John. His energies as bishop were largely consumed by completing the provision of the Bible in Manx for his flock.

[49] John Crook (1742–1805), the son of a South Lancashire physician of some property who wasted his substance in extravagance, fell out with his wife, went to sea, and died. Crook had so far received a classical education, but his mother soon marrying a second dissipated husband, he was apprenticed to a manual trade, and, being badly treated, enlisted as a private soldier. His conversion began under a sermon preached in the Methodist preaching-house at Limerick in 1770, and was assisted by his marrying a woman of piety and good sense from Cork. Bought out of the army by an uncle, he became a class-leader and local preacher in Liverpool, and his usefulness encouraged the Liverpool society, at the instigation of a member formerly resident in the Isle of Man, to send him there as a missionary in 1775 (see above, May 30, 1777). He quickly won a response, and, though he suffered mob violence encouraged by the clergy, was protected by the governor John Wood (on whom see above, May 30, 1777). The bishop (Richard Richmond; see above, June 1, 1777), however, excommunicated the Methodist preachers as 'unordained, unauthorized, and unqualified persons from other countries', and attacked their 'crude and pragmatical and inconsistent, if not profane and blasphemous ex tempore effusions'; Tyerman, *John Wesley*, 3:229–31). Crook was admitted to the itinerancy on trial in 1775, and taken into full connexion the following year. A second tour of service in the Isle of Man, 1778–81, saw the Methodist membership increase some two and a half times to 1597, and he was appointed there a third time, 1786–88. Most of his other service was in Ireland, and in 1791, the year of JW's death, he was President of the Irish Conference. In 1798, he returned again to the Isle of Man, but contracted a 'severe scorbutic complaint in his legs', which compelled him to spend some of his remaining years as a supernumerary and which ultimately killed him. A man of wide reading, humility, and power in prayer, Crook clearly occupied a place of special esteem in the itinerancy of his day, notwithstanding that glamourous appointments never came his way. He took a special interest in the singing and musical side of his services. A memoir which quotes extensively from his diary was published in *Methodist Magazine* 31 (1808):3–10, 49–57, 97–105, 145–51, 193–202.

[50] I.e., the local preachers.

[51] Orig., 'Dawby'. Dalby is a hamlet near the west coast 4 miles south of Peel.

Fri. 8. Having now visited the island round, east, south, north, and west, I was thoroughly convinced that we have no such circuit as this, either in England, Scotland, or Ireland. It is shut up from the world and, having little trade, is visited by scarce any strangers. Here are no Papists, no Dissenters of any kind, no Calvinists, no disputers. Here is no opposition, either from the Governor[52] (a mild, humane man), from the Bishop[53] (a good man), or from the bulk of the clergy. One or two of them did oppose for a time, but they seem now to understand better. So that we have now rather too little than too much reproach, the scandal of the cross being for the present ceased. The natives are a plain, artless, simple people, unpolished—that is, unpolluted. Few of them are rich or genteel; the far greater part, moderately poor. And most of the strangers that settle among them are men that have seen affliction. The local preachers are men of faith and love, knit together in one mind and one judgment. They speak either Manx or English and follow a regular plan, which the Assistant gives them monthly.

The isle is supposed to have thirty thousand inhabitants. Allowing half of them to be adults, and our societies to contain one or two and twenty hundred members, what a fair proportion is this! What has been seen like this in any part either of Great Britain or Ireland?

Sat. 9. We would willingly have set sail, but the strong northeast wind prevented us. Monday 11, it being moderate, we put to sea; but it soon died away into a calm. So I had time to read over and consider Dr. Johnson's tour through Scotland.[54] I had heard that he was severe upon the whole nation, but I could find nothing of it. He simply mentions (but without any bitterness), what he approved or disapproved. And many of the reflections are extremely judicious, some of them very affecting.

Tue. 12. The calm continuing, I read over Mr. Pennant's *Tour through Scotland*.[55] How amazingly different from Dr. Johnson's! He is doubtless a man both of sense and learning. Why has he then *bad English* in almost every page? No man should be above writing correctly.

[52] The Governor of the Isle of Man, 1777-91, was Edward Smith.
[53] George Mason (1731-83), Bishop of Man from 1780. Mason graduated M.A. from Cambridge in 1763, and B.D. and D.D. from New College, Oxford in 1770.
[54] See above, May 18, 1776.
[55] See above, May 23, 1776.

Having several passengers on board, I offered to give them a sermon, which they willingly accepted. And all behaved with the utmost decency while I showed, 'His commandments are not grievous.'[56] Soon after, a little breeze sprung up which, early in the morning, brought us to Whitehaven.

Thur. 14. I had a design to preach at noon in the town hall at Cockermouth.[57] But Mr. Lowthian[58] offering me his meeting-house, which was far more convenient, I willingly accepted his offer. By this means I had a much more numerous audience, most of whom behaved well.

At seven, I preached at Mr. Whyte's in Tallentire,[59] a little village four miles from Cockermouth. Many assembled here who had hardly seen or heard a Methodist before. I believe some of them did not hear in vain. After this I saw Mr. Whyte no more. God soon called him into a better world. Friday 15 in the evening, I preached in the town hall at Carlisle,[60] and on Saturday 16, reached Newcastle.

Sun. 17. In the morning, I preached at the Ballast Hills,[61] in the afternoon at Gateshead, and at five at the Garth Heads. Today I heard a remark at All Saints' Church[62] which I never read or heard before, in confirmation of that assertion of Abraham, 'If they hear not Moses and the prophets.'[63] 'The thing has been tried. One did rise from the dead, in the sight of a multitude of people. The namesake of this Lazarus rose from the dead. The very Pharisees

---

[56] 1 John 5:3.

[57] On this building, see above, May 10, 1780.

[58] Orig., 'Lothian'. T. Lowthian, Independent minister of Cockermouth, 1764–83. William Whellan, *History and Topography of the Counties of Cumberland and Westmorland* (Pontefract, 1860), p. 306.

[59] Orig., 'Ballantyn'. Tallentire was a township in the parish of Bridekirk 3 miles north from Cockermouth; there was and remained no place of worship there.

[60] On this building, see above May 10, 1780.

[61] The Ballast Hills was an area near the mouth of the Tyne where the ships that carried Tyne coal to London, and returned laden with ballast, deposited the ballast before taking on a fresh cargo.

[62] A perpetual curacy within the original town parish of St. Nicholas (patron, the vicar) and one of the four ecclesiastical districts into which Newcastle was divided. The remark reported was doubtless that of the perpetual curate, George Stephenson (who died in 1791). Stephenson came to All Saints as second curate in 1755, and was first curate from 1774 till his death. He was also curate of St. Nicholas, South Gosforth, 1762–91; curate of Cramlington, 1763–66; rector of Longbenton 1769–91; and chaplain to Trinity House, Newcastle. Mackenzie, *Account of Newcastle*, 1:321; *A History of Northumberland*, 15 vols. (Newcastle, 1893-1940), 13:338, 402; Durham Diocesan Records, Bishop's transcript.

[63] Luke 16:31.

could not deny it. Yet who of them that believed not Moses and the prophets was thereby "persuaded to repent"?[64]

Wed. 20. I went over to Sunderland and preached evening and morning to a lovely congregation. Thursday 21, I read prayers and preached in Monkwearmouth Church and, Friday 22, returned to Newcastle.

Sat. 23. I went over to Hexham and preached in the marketplace to a numerous congregation on 'I saw the dead small and great, stand before God.'[65] None were rude or uncivil in any respect, and very few were inattentive. Sunday 24, I preached in the morning at Gateshead Fell, about noon at a village called Greenside,[66] ten miles west of Newcastle, to the largest congregation I have seen in the north—many of whom were Roman Catholics. In the evening, I preached once more at the Garth Heads (some thought, to the largest congregation that had ever been there) on those words in the service, 'Comfort ye, comfort ye my people, saith your God.'[67]

After preaching at many places in the way, on Wednesday 27, I preached at York. Many of our friends met me here, so that in the evening the house would ill contain the congregation. And I know not when I have found such a spirit among them; they seemed to be all hungering and thirsting after righteousness.[68]

Thur. 28. I preached at eleven in the main street at Selby to a large and quiet congregation, and in the evening at Thorne. This day I entered my seventy-ninth year. And by the grace of God, I feel no more of the infirmities of old age than I did at twenty-nine. Friday 29, I preached at Crowle and at Epworth. I have now preached thrice a day for seven days following—but it is just the same as if it had been but once.

Sat. 30. I went over to Owston and found the whole town was moved. One of the chief men of the town had been just buried,

---

[64] Cf. Luke 16:30-31.

[65] Rev. 20:12.

[66] Greenside is a village 2 miles south-west of Ryton, and was then a straggling line of pitmen's cottages. It is not clear why Catholicism should persist so strongly in a manor held by the bishop, though Greenside had been among the lands forfeited in 1570 by John Swinburne for his support of the revolt of the northern earls. A large house was converted into a Methodist preaching-house in this year, 1781. William Fordyce, *A History of the County Palatine of Durham*, 2 vols. (Newcastle, n.d.), 2:670-71; William Hutchinson, *The History and Antiquities of the County Palatine of Durham*, 3 vols. (Newcastle, 1785-94), 2:438-39.

[67] Isa. 40:1.

[68] See Matt. 5:6.

and his wife a few days before. In a course of nature they might
have lived many years, being only middle aged. He had known the
love of God, but had choked the good seed by hastening to be
rich. But Providence disappointed all his schemes, and it was
thought he died of a broken heart. I took that opportunity of
enforcing, 'Whatsoever thy hand findeth to do, do it with thy
might; for there is no work, nor device, nor knowledge, nor wisdom in the grave whither thou goest.'[69]

Sunday, July 1. I preached as usual at Misterton, at
Upperthorpe,[70] and at Epworth. Monday 2, I preached at Scotter
about eight, at Brigg at noon, and in the evening in the old
churchyard at Grimsby to almost all the people of the town on
'Blessed are the dead which die in the Lord.'[71] The late proof of it
is in the glorious death of Robert Wilkinson,[72] and the behaviour
of his widow,

So firm, yet so soft; so strong, yet so resigned,[73]

I believe will hardly be forgotten, by any that were witnesses of it.

[69] Eccles. 9:10.
[70] Orig., 'Overthorpe'.
[71] Rev. 14:13.
[72] Robert Wilkinson, who died on Dec. 8, 1780, had first heard evangelical preaching as a young man at Rookhope, a lead-mining village in Co. Durham. His conversion took place in Lent 1767, after he had heard a good deal of Methodist preaching in Weardale, and his account of it gives a vivid impression of the release from inner tension which signified salvation to so many Methodists. 'At night . . . I could not help roaring for the disquietness of my soul. . . . I then felt I must perish eternally, unless some way to escape were found which I knew not of. . . . My neighbours said I was beside myself, for I could not rest in my bed. I often rose and wandered into the fields, weeping and bewailing my desperate state.' Release came during prayer and spiritual reading with a Methodist friend, and the following year he began to exhort around Carlisle, being admitted a preacher on trial in 1769 (Jackson, *Early Methodist Preachers*, 6:212-14). George Shadford describes how, in the last days of Wilkinson's life, his prayer at a love-feast 'pierced the heaven, the power of God came down on people like a torrent of rain; and they were so affected that they wept and rejoiced abundantly.' A similar occasion of powerful and mixed emotions was produced by his wife at his funeral at Grimsby. Even at the end 'he had a severe conflict with Satan, and he was as in an agony,' but emerged with confessions of triumph. 'When the minister repeated the following words in the Burial Service, "Not to be sorry as men without hope", Mrs. Willkinson was so over-whelmed with the power of God, that she could not refrain from exclaiming, "Sorry! No! Glory be to God! . . . Glory and praise and blessing, be ascribed unto God for ever and ever." All who heard her were very deeply affected, and most of the people were melted into tears, some for sorrow and others for joy.' (Atmore, *Memorial*, pp. 502-7). It is this episode to which JW refers.
[73] Cf. Pope's 'Epitaph on Mrs Corbet', line 8, quoted by JW on May 5, 1757 (21:101, n. 74 in this edn.), and Feb. 28, 1776.

Tue. 3. I preached at Cleethorpes[74] three miles from Grimsby; here likewise there has been an outpouring of the Spirit. I was reminded here of what I saw at Cardiff almost forty years ago. I could not go into any of the little houses, but presently it was filled with people, and I was constrained to pray with them in every house, or they would not be satisfied. Several of these are clearly renewed in love and give a plain, scriptural account of their experience. And there is scarce a house in the village wherein there is not one or more earnestly athirst for salvation.

Wed. 4. I called upon an honest man and, I hope, took him out of the hands of an egregious quack, who was pouring in medicines upon him for what he called 'wind in the nerves'! In the evening, I preached at Louth, now as quiet as Grimsby. When shall we learn 'to despair of none'?[75]

Thur. 5. I had the pleasure of meeting Mr. Brackenbury[76] again, though still exceeding weak. His chapel was thoroughly filled in the evening—I trust, with sincere hearers.

Fri. 6. I crossed over to Langham Row, where the high wind would not suffer me to preach abroad. But the house tolerably contained the congregation, most of whom attended again at five in the morning.

Today I finished the second volume of Dr. Robertson's *History of America*.[77] His language is always clear and strong, and frequently elegant. And I suppose his history is preferable to any history of America which has appeared in the English tongue. But I cannot admire, first, his intolerable prolixity in this history, as well as his history of Charles the Fifth. He promises eight books of the history of America and fills four of them with critical dissertations. True, the dissertations are sensible, but they have lost their way—they are not history. And they are swelled beyond all proportion, doubtless for the benefit of the author and the bookseller, rather than the reader. I cannot admire, secondly, a Christian divine writing a history with so very little of Christianity in it. Nay, he seems studiously to avoid saying anything which might

[74] Orig., 'Claythorp'. This is indeed Cleethorpes 3 miles east of Grimsby, not the much more distant Claythorpe near Alford.

[75] Wesley may well have been thinking of Horace's counsel: '*Nil desperandum*'— 'never despair' (*Odes*, I.vii.27).

[76] On Robert Carr Brackenbury, see above, July 9, 1776.

[77] William Robertson, *History of America*, 2 vols. (London, 1777). Compare JW's views of Robertson's other works on Nov. 10, 1769, and Apr. 28, 1772 (22:210, n. 6; 319-20, n. 6 in this edn.).

imply that he believes the Bible. I can still less admire, thirdly, his speaking so honourably of a professed infidel;[78] yea, and referring to his masterpiece of infidelity, *The Sketch of the History of Man*, as artful, as unfair, as disingenuous a book, as even Toland's

5 *Nazarenus*.[79] Least of all can I admire, fourthly, his copying after Dr. Hawkesworth[80] (who once professed better things) in totally excluding the Creator from governing the world! Was it not enough never to mention the Providence of God where there was the fairest occasion? without saying expressly, 'the *fortune* of

10 Cortez'[81] or *chance* did thus or thus? So far as *fortune* or *chance* governs the world, God has no place in it.

The poor American, though not pretending to be a Christian, knew better than this.[82] When the Indian was asked, 'Why do you think "the beloved ones" take care of *you*?' he answered, 'When I

15 was in the battle, the bullet went on this side and on that side; and this man died, and that man died. And I am alive! So I know, the beloved ones take care of *me*.'

It is true, the doctrine of a particular providence (and any but a particular providence is no providence at all) is absolutely out of

20 fashion in England. And a *prudent* author might write this to gain the favour of his gentle readers. Yet I will not say, this is real prudence, because he may lose hereby more than he gains—as the majority even of Britons, to this day, retain some sort of respect for the Bible.

25 If it was worth-while to mention a little thing after things of so much greater importance, I would add, I was surprised that so sensible a writer, in enumerating so many reasons why it is so much colder in the southern hemisphere than it is in the northern—why it is colder, for instance, at forty degrees south than at

---

[78] Henry Home, Lord Kames (1696-1782), on whom and his book, see May 25, 1774 (22:410, n. 11 in this edn.).

[79] John Toland, *Nazarenus: or Jewish, Gentile and Mahometan Christianity* (London, 1718).

[80] John Hawkesworth (1715?-73), a professional scribbler of humble origins, who cooperated with Johnson and others on the *Adventurer*, edited Swift, and has already appeared in JW's journal as editor of Captain Cook's voyages; see Dec. 17, 1773 (22:394, n. 20 in this edn.). It was this latter work which gave the offence, for in the introduction he refused to attribute any of the critical escapes from danger 'to the particular interposition of Providence'; since chance had no role in the government of the world, he 'must necessarily refer every event to one cause . . . as well the sufferings as the enjoyments of life'. John Hawkesworth, *An Account of the Voyages undertaken . . . for Making Discoveries in the Southern Hemisphere*, 3 vols. (London, 1773), 1:xix-xxi.

[81] Orig. 'Certiz'.

[82] This conversation is more fully reported, July 20, 1736 (18:166-67 in this edn.).

fifty north latitude—should forget the main, the primary reason, namely, the greater distance of the sun. For is it not well known that the sun (to speak with the vulgar) is longer on the north side the line than the south? That he is longer in the six northern signs than the southern, so that there is a difference (says Gravesande[83]) of nine days? Now if the northern hemisphere be obverted to the sun longer than the southern, does not this necessarily imply that the northern hemisphere will be warmer than the southern? And is not this the primary reason of its being so?

Sat. 7. I designed to go from hence to Boston, but a message from Mr. Pugh[84] desiring me to preach in his church on Sunday, made me alter my design. So procuring a guide, I set out for Rauceby. We rode through Tattershall, where there are large remains of a stately castle.[85] And there was in the chancel of the

---

[83] Guillaume Jacques Gravesande, *Philosophiae Newtonianae Institutiones, in usus academicos* (Lugduni Batavorum, 1723). The author notes (p. 298), 'diutius in percurrendis sex signis primis haeret Sol, quam in sex posterioribus, daturque differentia novem dierum.'

[84] John Pugh (1744–99), matriculated from Hertford College, Oxford, 1767, graduating B.A. in 1771. He was vicar of Rauceby 1771–99. Pugh was one of the Oxford evangelicals whose career was not impeded by the expulsion of the six from St. Edmund Hall in 1768, and he also formed a link between the evangelicals of Joseph Jane's day and the evangelical machine of the Wilberforce era, for he presided over a meeting in Rauceby vicarage in 1795 which accepted his suggestion, as Jane's executor, that a legacy from the latter be applied to the support of missionaries; this was one of the influences in the creation of the Church Missionary Society a few years later; J. S. Reynolds, *The Evangelicals at Oxford, 1735–1871* (Oxford, 1953), pp. 36, 42, 69, n. 2. His obituary recorded that 'possessed of considerable property and of that liberal spirit which "deviseth liberal things", his employment and pleasure were to help forward the interests of Religion, and to administer both to the temporal and spiritual necessities of his fellow creatures. In his parish he was as laborious as a feeble constitution would allow; but the exertions of his bounty were by no means confined to those of his own charge. He was a firm friend to the Church of England and the existing form of government.' *Gentleman's Magazine* 69, pt. 1 (1799):440.

[85] The castle and collegiate church at Tattershall, a market town about 20 miles southeast of Lincoln, were founded in the middle of the fifteenth century by Sir Ralph Cromwell, Lord Treasurer under Henry VI, and incorporated special provisions for almshouses and teaching, the school to be in close connection with the college, on the pattern of Henry VI's contemporaneous foundation at Eton; A. Hamilton Thompson, *The English Clergy and their Organization in the Later Middle Ages* (Oxford, 1947), p. 155. Much of the castle was demolished during the Interregnum. At the dissolution of the monasteries, all the collegiate buildings except the church were taken down. The church, as well as its painted glass windows, was a thing of beauty, but when in 1754 the Earl of Exeter removed them to install in the chapel at Burleigh (T. Allen says Stamford Baron) on the condition that they were replaced with plain glass, no action was taken, and the church remained exposed to the weather with unglazed windows for fifty years; Lewis, *England*, 4:280. J. D. Le Couteur says that the ancient glass was *given* in 1757 by the patron Lord Fortescue to the Earl of Exeter, who removed it to his own church of St. Martin's, Stamford Baron, where it exists for the most part in a very jumbled condi-

old church the finest painted glass (so it was esteemed) in England, but the prudent owner, considering it brought him in nothing by staying there, lately sold it for a round sum of money.

Here I met with such a ferry as I never saw before. The boat was managed by an honest countryman who knew just nothing of the matter, and a young woman equally skilful. However, though the river was fifty yards broad, we got over it in an hour and an half. We then went on through the Fens in a marvellous road, sometimes tracked and sometimes not, till about six, we came to Rauceby[86] and found the people gathered from all parts. I preached on those words in the Second Lesson, 'There is neither Jew nor Gentile, Barbarian, Scythian, bond nor free; but Christ is all and in all.'[87]

Sun. 8. The congregation was still larger. Hence I rode over to Welby and preached in Mr. Dodwell's Church[88] in the afternoon and in the evening to a numerous and serious congregation. Monday 9, I preached at Grantham in the open air (for no house would contain the congregation), and none made the least disturbance, any more than at Newark (where I preached in the evening) or in the Castle yard at Lincoln on Tuesday 10. Wednesday 11, I preached at Newton on Trent and Gainsborough.

After visiting many other societies, I crossed over into the West Riding of Yorkshire.[89] Monday 23, I preached at Yeadon to a large

tion; *English Medieval Painted Glass* (2nd edn., London, 1978), p. 163. The Tattershall parishioners 'very justifiably raised a riot in an endeavour to prevent this scandalous spoliation'; W. F. Rawnsley, *Highways and Byways in Lincolnshire* (London, 1914), pp. 387–88. Under the Act 33 George III, *c.*150 (1793), the unsound ferry was replaced by a three-arched bridge and the road to Sleaford turnpiked. Thomas Allen, *The History of the County of Lincoln*, 2 vols. (London, 1834), 2:76, 78; William Albert, *The Turnpike Road System in England, 1663–1840* (Cambridge, 1972), p. 217.

[86] The joint parish of North and South Rauceby, 4 miles west of Sleaford.

[87] Cf. Col. 3:11.

[88] Welby was a small parish 4 miles north-east of Grantham. William Dodwell (1751–1824), rector of North and South Stoke and of Welby 1775–1824, was a generous benefactor by will of the Wesleyan Missionary Society and the Bible Society, as well as the village school; Tyerman, *John Wesley*, 3:356; Lewis, *England*, 4:444. Some Wesleyan preachers preached in his kitchen, where prayer-meetings were also held in the Methodist manner. He and Pugh of Rauceby once attended the Methodist Conference at JW's invitation. Though a fervent preacher of renewal, Dodwell irked his parishioners with the nervous irritability, which cost him all his housekeepers and which worsened with age. But the Methodists did not attempt to form a society and establish regular preaching at Welby till 1803. T. Cocking, *History of Wesleyan Methodism in Grantham and its Vicinity* (London, 1836), pp. 291–303.

[89] On July 21, JW preached at Keighley in the morning on Josh. 24:15; on the 22nd, twice at Bingley Church, on Matt. 5:20 and Mark 16:16. At 5 a.m. the following morning, July 23, he preached again at Keighley on Hab. 2:14. Edmundson MS Commonplace Book.

congregation. I had heard the people there were remarkably dead; if so, they were now remarkably quickened—for I know not when I have seen a whole congregation so moved.[90] Tuesday 24, we had fifty or sixty children at five, and as many or more in the evening, and more affectionate ones I never saw. For the present, at least, God has touched their hearts. On Wednesday and Thursday, I preached at Bradford and Halifax. On Friday, at Greetland[91] Chapel and Huddersfield. After preaching, I retired to Longwood House,[92] one of the pleasantest spots in the county. Saturday 28, I preached at Longwood House, at Mirfield, and at Dawgreen. Sunday 29, I preached at eight before the house. I expected to preach at one as usual under the hill at Birstall. But after the church service was ended, the clerk exclaimed with a loud voice, 'The Rev. Mr. Wesley is to preach here in the afternoon.'[93] So I desired Mr. Pawson[94] to preach at one. The church began at half hour past two, and I spoke exceeding plain to such a congregation as never met there before. In the evening, I preached at Bradford[95] to thousands upon thousands on 'The wages of sin is death; but the gift of God is eternal life through Jesus Christ our Lord.'[96]

Mon. 30. I crossed over to Tadcaster at noon, and in the evening to York. Hence I took a little circuit through Malton, Scarborough, Beverley, Hull, and Pocklington, and came to York again.

Sunday, August 5. At the old church in Leeds[97] we had eighteen clergymen and about eleven hundred communicants. I preached there at three; the church was thoroughly filled, and I believe most could hear while I explained the New Covenant which God has now made with the Israel of God.

[90] Yeadon retained this character for a couple of generations; in the first half of the nineteenth century it enjoyed a revival every seven years. W. R. Ward, *Religion and Society in England, 1790-1850* (London, 1972), p. 264.

[91] Orig., 'Greatland'.

[92] 'Longwood House is situated about two miles from Huddersfield, and at that time was the dwelling place of Mr. Whitaker, a gentleman of considerable property; here Mr. Wesley was invariably entertained when in the neighbourhood.' Walker, *Halifax Methodism*, p. 158.

[93] The vicar of Birstal was Jonas Eastwood.

[94] On John Pawson, see June 21, 1767 (22:87, n. 6 in this edn.).

[95] In the New Market. Edmundson, MS Commonplace Book.

[96] Rom. 6:23.

[97] The vicar of Leeds, after a long and disputed election, was Samuel Kershaw. Educated at Catherine Hall, Cambridge, he proceeded B.A. 1727, M.A. 1731, and D.D. 1740. He also succeeded his father as rector of Ripley. R. V. Taylor, *Biographia Leodensis* (London, 1865), pp. 183-85.

Mon. 6. I desired Mr. Fletcher, Dr. Coke,[98] and four more of
our brethren, to meet every evening that we might consult
together on any difficulty that occurred.[99] On Tuesday our Conference began, at which were present about seventy preachers
whom I had severally invited to come and assist me with their
advice in carrying on the great work of God. Wednesday 8, I
desired Mr. Fletcher to preach. I do not wonder he should be so
popular, not only because he preaches with all his might, but
because the power of God attends both his preaching and prayer.
On Monday[1] and Tuesday, we finished the remaining business
of the Conference and ended it with solemn prayer and thanksgiving.

Wed. 15. I went to Sheffield. In the afternoon, I took a view of
the chapel lately built by the Duke of Norfolk. One may safely say,
there is none like it in the three kingdoms—nor, I suppose, in the
world. It is a stone building, an octagon, about eighty feet diameter. A cupola which is at a great height gives some, but not much,
light. A little more is given by four small windows which are
under the galleries. The pulpit is moveable. It rolls upon wheels

---

[98] On John Fletcher, see Mar. 13, 1757 (21:88-89, n. 33 in this edn.); on Thomas
Coke, Aug. 13, 1776.

[99] The minutes of this Conference give no hint of the difficulties in which JW thus
sought the assistance of this informal inner cabinet. But Thomas Taylor in his MS
diary complained that 'many things are exceedingly wrong; but whom to trust to
attempt amendment I know not. I sometimes think the whole head is sick, and the
whole heart faint'; Tyerman, *John Wesley*, 3:361. In particular the cost of providing hospitality was falling too heavily on the Leeds society, though JW had taken it upon himself to limit the attendance by personal invitation. As it was, the preachers had to maintain their own horses during Conference, and JW must bear the odium of his act of
authority. The cost of maintaining preachers' wives was also becoming insupportable;
they must 'admit no more married preachers, unless in defect of single preachers', but
at the same time require societies that had no manse to hire lodgings for the preacher's
wife. The Baildon society complained that they were exhorted to attend the parish
church, but the parson preached anti-Methodist doctrine; with the utmost hesitation
JW conceded that if the minister began to preach absolute decrees or ridicule Christian
perfection, Methodists 'should quietly go out of the church; yet attend it again at the
next opportunity'; *Arminian Magazine* 5 (1782):182-83. William Hey (1736-1819), a
distinguished surgeon and (later) twice mayor of Leeds, presented a paper complaining
that Methodists were moving into practical dissent from the Church; JW cut him short,
and he left the society; John Pearson, *Life of William Hey, Esq., F.R.S.*, 2 vols. (London,
1822), 2:93-103. Coke brought doctrinal charges against Bradburn and Benson which
were dismissed; John W. Etheridge, *The Life of the Rev. Thomas Coke* (London, 1860),
pp. 64-67. Preachers were required not to publish anything till it had been corrected by
JW, and then the profits were to go into a common stock. Small wonder that JW
appealed to the unction of John Fletcher to keep Conference on keel.

[1] JW preached at Leeds at 5 a.m. on 1 Cor. 10:13. Edmundson, MS Commonplace
Book.

and is shifted once a quarter, that all the pews may face it in their turns—I presume the first contrivance of the kind in Europe.[2]

After preaching in the evening to a crowded audience and exhorting the society to brotherly love, I took chaise with Dr. Coke[3] and, travelling day and night, the next evening came to 5 London. We observed Friday the 17th as a fast day and concluded it with a solemn watch-night. Having finished my business in town for the present, on Sunday 19 at eight in the evening, I took coach, with my new fellow-traveller, George Whitfield,[4] and on Monday evening preached at Bath. Tuesday 21, I went on to Bris- 10 tol and, after resting a day, on Thursday 23, set out for Cornwall.

Finding after breakfast that I was within a mile of my old friend, G. S[tonehouse],[5] I walked over and spent an hour with him. He is all-original still, like no man in the world either in sentiments or anything about him. But perhaps if I had his immense 15 fortune, I might be as great an oddity as he.

About six in the evening, I preached at Taunton to a numerous congregation. I found the letters concerning popery[6] had much abated prejudice here. Friday 24, I preached at Cullompton[7] about noon, and at Exeter in the evening. Saturday 25, I preached 20 in the square at Plymouth Dock to a quieter congregation than

[2] This was a chapel connected with Shrewsbury Hospital 'for perpetuall maintenaunce of twentie poor persons', created by Henry Howard in 1666 in accordance with the will of Gilbert, Earl of Shrewsbury, who died in 1616, and was first occupied in 1673. The Howard family, later dukes of Norfolk, retained an interest in this benefaction, and in 1770 Edward, the fifteenth Duke, endowed the hospital with £1000 which was applied by the trustees to the repair of flood damage and the creation of the chapel here referred to; Joseph Hunter, *Hallamshire. The History and Topography of the Parish of Sheffield* (London, 1819), pp. 179–81. The buildings were demolished in the nineteenth century.

[3] On Thomas Coke, see above, Aug. 13, 1776.

[4] George Whitfield (1753–1832), was born near Hexham, and had a conventional Anglican upbringing. Converted as a young man, he was frequently appointed as JW's travelling companion from this time on, accompanying him to Holland in 1783 and Scotland in 1784. He first appears in the stationing minutes in 1785. At JW's request, he acted as Book Steward from 1789 till Robert Lomas was brought in to reorganize the Book Room in 1805; Ward, *Religion and Society*, p. 101. 'He was a man of liberal opinions, and aimiable disposition,' who served in the itinerancy for over 50 years; but, as his derisory obituaries show, he shared the common fate of many of JW's inner circle who survived into the age of Bunting, of being forgotten; *Wesleyan Methodist Magazine* 56 (1833):156; 61 (1838):161–66.

[5] George Stonehouse, on whom see May 10, 1738 (18:237–38, n. 7 in this edn.). He sold his Islington living to join the Moravians, and within a short time left them.

[6] Doubtless *Popery Calmly Considered* (1779; vol. 13 in this edn.; Jackson, 10:140–58), and *The Protestant Association* (1781; vol. 16 in this edn.).

[7] A market town 12 miles north–east of Exeter.

usual. Sunday 26 between one and two, I began in the new house in Plymouth.[8] The large congregation was all attention, and there seemed reason to hope that even here we shall find some fruit of our labour. In the evening, I preached again in the square, on the
5   story of the Pharisee and Publican, to such a congregation for number and seriousness together as I never saw there before.

Mon. 27. I was desired to preach at Trenuth[9] at noon, *a little way* (they said) out of the road. The 'little way' proved six or seven miles, through a road ready to break our wheels in pieces.
10 However, I just reached St. Austell[10] time enough to preach. And God greatly comforted the hearts of his people.

Tue. 28. Between nine and ten, we had such a storm of rain as I do not remember to have seen in Europe before. It seemed ready to beat in the windows of the chaise and in three minutes
15 drenched our horsemen from head to foot. We reached Truro, however, at the appointed time. I have not for many years seen a congregation so universally affected. One would have imagined, everyone that was present had a desire to save his soul.

In the evening, I preached in the High Street at Helston. I
20 scarce know a town in the whole county which is so totally changed. Not a spark of that bitter enmity to the Methodists in which the people here for many years gloried above their fellows.[11]

Going through Marazion I was told that a large congregation was waiting. So I stepped out of my chaise and began immedi-
25 ately. And we had a gracious shower.[12] Some were cut to the heart, but more rejoiced with joy unspeakable.[13]

In the evening, I preached in the market-place at Penzance. I designed afterwards to meet the society. But the people were so eager to hear all they could that they quickly filled the house from
30 end to end. This is another of the towns wherein the whole stream of the people is turned, as it were, from east to west.

---

[8] The first Methodist preaching-house in the three towns was erected in 1779 in Lower Street, Plymouth, chiefly by the exertions of Redstone, a carpenter, and Nehemiah Jane, on whom see above, Aug. 20, 1780. Richard Nicholls Worth, *History of the Town and Borough of Devonport* (Plymouth, 1870), p. 66; Worth, *Plymouth*, p. 258.

[9] No satisfactory identification of this place has been made; it may have been Trenouth, a mile east of St. Cleer, not far from Liskeard, which was about halfway between Plymouth and St. Austell.

[10] Orig., 'St. Austle's'.

[11] The Journal is silent about this, though even on his second visit on Sept, 3, 1755, JW described the town as 'once turbulent enough' (see 21:26 in this edn.).

[12] I.e., an outpouring of grace.

[13] See 1 Pet. 1:8.

We had a happy season, both at St. Just on Thursday evening, and in the market-place at St. Ives on Friday. Saturday September 1, I made an end of that curious book, Dr. Parsons's *Remains of Japhet*.[14] The very ingenious author has struck much light into some of the darkest parts of ancient history. And although I can- 5 not entirely subscribe to every proposition which he advances, yet I apprehend he has sufficiently proved the main of his hypothesis, namely: (1) that after the flood, Shem and his descendants peopled the greatest parts of Asia; (2) that Ham and his children peopled Africa;[15] (3) that Europe was peopled by the two sons of 10 Japhet[h], Gomer and Magog—the southern and south-western by Gomer and his children, and the north and the north-western by the children of Magog; (4) that the former were called Gomerians, Cimmerians, Cimbrians, and afterwards Celtiae, Galatae, and Gauls; the latter were called by the general name of Scythi- 15 ans, Scuiti, Scots; (5) that the Gomerians spread swiftly through the north of Europe as far as the Cimbrian Chersonesus (including Sweden, Denmark, Norway, and divers other countries), and then into Ireland, where they multiplied very early into a considerable nation; (6) that some ages after, another part of them who 20 had first settled in Spain, sailed to Ireland under Milea, or Milesius, and, conquering the first inhabitants, took possession of the land; (7) that about the same time the Gomerians came to Ireland, the Magogians or Scythians came to Britain, so early that both still spoke the same language and well understood each other; (8) 25 that the Irish spoke by the Gomerians and the Welsh spoke by the Magogians are one and the same language, expressed by the same seventeen letters, which were long after brought by a Gomerian prince into Greece; (9) that all the languages of Europe, Greek and Latin in particular, are derived from this; (10) that the ante- 30 diluvian language, spoken by all till after the flood and then continued in the family of Shem, was Hebrew, and from this (the Hebrew) tongue many of the eastern languages are derived. The foregoing particulars this fine writer has made highly probable. And these may be admitted though we do not agree to his vehe- 35 ment panegyric on the Irish language—much less receive all the

---

[14] James Parsons, *Remains of Japhet; being Historical Inquiries into the Affinity and Origin of the European Languages* (London, 1767). This was the last work of James Parsons (1705-70), a Barnstaple physician and antiquary, who wrote largely on these themes, and for *Japhet* acquired a knowledge of ancient Irish and Welsh.
[15] Orig. 'Africk'.

stories told by the Irish poets or chroniclers as genuine, authentic history.

At eleven, I preached in Camborne[16] church-town, and I believe the hearts of all the people were bowed down before the Lord. After the Quarterly Meeting in Redruth, I preached in the market-place on the first principle, 'Ye are saved through faith.'[17] It is also the last point. And it connects the first point of religion with the last.

Sun. 5. About five in the evening, I preached at Gwennap.[18] I believe two or three and twenty thousand were present. And I believe God enabled me so to speak that even those who stood farthest off could hear distinctly. I think this is my *ne plus ultra*.[19] I shall scarce see a larger congregation till we meet in the air.

After preaching at Bodmin, Launceston, Tiverton, and Halberton, on Wednesday 5 about noon, I preached at Taunton. I believe it my duty to relate here what some will esteem a most notable instance of enthusiasm.[20] Be it so or not, I aver the plain fact. In an hour after we left Taunton, one of the chaise horses was on a sudden so lame that he could hardly set his foot to the ground. It being impossible to procure any human help, I knew of no remedy but prayer. Immediately the lameness was gone, and he went just as he did before. In the evening, I preached at South Brent, and the next day, went on to Bristol.

Fri. 8. I went over to Kingswood and made a particular inquiry into the management of the school. I found some of the rules had not been observed at all—particularly that of rising in the morning. Surely Satan has a peculiar spite at this school! What trouble has it cost me for above these thirty years! I can *plan*, but who will *execute*! I know not, God, help me![21]

Sun. 9. In the calm, sunshiny evening, I preached near King

[16] Orig., 'Cambourn'.
[17] Eph. 2:8 (*Notes*).
[18] On Gwennap Pit, see Sept. 5, 1762 (21:388, n. 75 in this edn.).
[19] 'The point of highest achievement.' *OED*.
[20] I.e., a supposed supernatural manifestation.
[21] This dispirited comment is the more striking since JW had just sent off to the press his *Plain Account of Kingswood School* (1781; Jackson, 13:289-301), for the most part written long before and recently serialized in *Arminian Magazine* 4 (1781), in which he extolled the education in the school as superior to that which was offered by the universities. The unsatisfactory side of the school was immortalized in the following year by Adam Clarke, who never got over his ill-reception by the headmaster, Thomas Simpson; Joseph Butterworth Bulmer Clarke, ed., *An Account of the . . . Life of Adam Clarke*, 3 vols. (London, 1833), 1:153-69. In the following year JW in effect got rid of Simpson for not maintaining discipline. Simpson set up his own school at Keynsham, of which

Square. I know nothing more solemn than such a congregation praising God with one heart and one voice. Surely they who talk of the *indecency* of field-preaching never saw such a sight as this.

Mon. 10. I preached at Paulton and Shepton Mallet to a lively, increasing people in each place. Tuesday 11, I found the same cause of rejoicing at Coleford, and the next evening at Frome. Thursday 13, I preached at Rode and at Bradford[-on-Avon]. Friday 14, after an interval of thirty years, I preached again in Trowbridge.[22] About two, I preached near the church in Freshford, and then spent a day or two at Bath.

On Monday 17, I preached at Chew Magna and [Chew] Stoke; on Tuesday, at Clutton and Pensford. But Pensford is now a dull, dreary place, the flower of the congregation being gone.[23]

Thur. 20. I went over the Mangotsfield,[24] a place famous for all manner of wickedness and the only one in the neighbourhood of Kingswood which we had totally neglected. But on a sudden light is sprung up even in this thick darkness. Many inquire what they must do to be saved. Many of these have broke off outward sin and are earnestly calling for an inward Saviour. I preached in the main street to almost all the inhabitants of the town on 'Believe in the Lord Jesus Christ, and thou shalt be saved.'[25]

Fri. 21. I preached at Thornbury,[26] where I had not been before for near forty years. It seems as if good might at length be done here also,[27] as an entire new generation is now come up in the room of the dry, stupid stocks that were there before.

On Monday 24 and the following days, I met the classes at Bristol and was not a little surprised to find that the society is still decreasing. Certainly we have all need to stir up the gift of God that is in us[28] and with all possible care to 'strengthen the things that remain'.[29]

his son became vicar. A. G. Ives, *Kingswood School in Wesley's Day and Since* (London, 1970), pp. 96–97; Jackson, 13:301–2.

[22] JW's memory is failing; he had visited Trowbridge on Sept. 12, 1780, when he preached in Mrs. Turner's chapel. His first visit had been twenty-seven years earlier, Sept. 17, 1754 (20:492 in this edn.).

[23] That is, Hannah Owen was there no longer. Mrs. Owen had taken her two younger daughters to London about 1780. Elizabeth Owen, the eldest, who remained, married W. Pine and set up a school at Pensford. Mary, the third daughter, married Joseph Beardmore, on whom see above, Jan. 18, 1781.

[24] A large parish 5 miles north-east of Bristol, 2 miles north of Kingswood, noted for its output of coal and paving-stone; Methodism did not take root here.

[25] Acts 16:31.

[26] JW's previous visit to this substantial market town 24 miles south-west of Gloucester had been on Feb. 17, 1746; see 20:113 in this edn.

[27] See below, Sept. 10, 1789.   [28] See 2 Tim. 1:6.   [29] Rev. 3:2.

Thur. 27. I preached at Bath and Bradford[-on-Avon] and, on Friday, at Trowbridge. How long did we toil here and take nothing![30] At length it seems the answer of many prayers is come. Friday 28 about noon, I preached at Keynsham, and not without hopes of doing good even here. Since Miss Owen[31] has removed from Publow, Miss Bishop[32] has set up a school here. And it is worthy to be called a *Christian school*. It *is* what the school at Publow *was*!

Sat. 29. I spent an hour with Mr. Henderson[33] at Hanham and particularly inquired into his whole method. And I am persuaded there is not such another house for lunatics in the three kingdoms: he has a peculiar art of governing his patients, not by fear but by love. The consequence is, many of them speedily recover and love him ever after.

Thursday, October 4. I was importuned to preach the condemned sermon at Bristol. I did so, though with little hope of doing good, the criminals being eminently impenitent.[34] Yet they

[30] For early Methodism at Trowbridge, see Sept. 17, 1754 (20:492 in this edn.). In 1781, John Mason managed a class in Trowbridge and made a convert of John Knapp. Knapp's house became a home for preachers (Adam Clarke was received in it when he left Kingswood), and he also rented a scribbling- (or carding-) shop which was fitted up as a place of worship and which later afforded the site for the first chapel. *Methodist Recorder* (Mar. 6, 1902):13–14; (May 11, 1905):10; *WHS* 6 (1908):115.

[31] On Hannah Owen's school, see Sept. 6, 1772 (22:348, n. 41 in this edn.); Sept. 18, 1781.

[32] Mary Bishop had been the partner in one of JW's most active spiritual correspondences for a dozen years. She had a school in Bath, but in 1777 she was taken ill at Miss March's house 'with a spitting of blood & apparent consumption', and was thought unlikely to teach again. However, 'her school [was] her daily bread' and, after treatment at Wells, she now set up again here (see Tyerman MSS, 2, fol. 158, Methodist Archives, Manchester). Much of JW's correspondence with her turned on the dangers of Calvinism, but he did not spare advice on the education in the school. JW published a conflated version of many of his letters to Miss Bishop as 'profitable' devotional reading; *WHS* 7 (1909):84. Later she married Mr. Mills, a Quaker. For JW's letters to her see Telford, vols. 5–8, *passim*.

[33] Richard Henderson, an Irishman who came to England in 1762, was certainly an itinerant preacher by the following year (Jackson, *Early Methodist Preachers*, 4:26), and travelled till the Conference of 1771. He had an excellent name as an aimiable man and a preacher, but 'was naturally of a timid, diffident, reasoning spirit; of a melancholy habit which frequently led him to view himself in an unfavourable light. And being inclined to *deep thinking*, he began to criticize and philosophise upon the scriptures, which greatly impeded his usefulness, and bewildered his mind. Hence he gave up the work of the ministry, and buried his most excellent talent in the earth. He settled at Hanham near Bristol, where he kept a private asylum for lunatics for some years' (Atmore, *Memorial*, p. 183), which JW visited five times; *WHS* 3 (1902):158–61. Impeccable Methodist sources assessed his death as 'not the rejoicing of a babe but the adoration of a father'; Atmore, *Memorial*, p. 184. His son, who had a considerable reputation in Oxford, predeceased him. See Mar. 13, 1789.

[34] The criminals executed on October 12 were Benjamin Loveday and John Bourke.

were for the present melted into tears, and they were not out of God's reach.

Sun. 7. I took my leave of the congregation in the New Square in a calm, delightful evening. Monday 8, I preached at the Devizes about eleven, at Salisbury in the evening.

Tue. 9. I preached at Winchester, where I went, with great expectation, to see that celebrated painting in the cathedral, 'The Raising of Lazarus'.[35] But I was disappointed. I observed, (1) there was such a huddle of figures that had I not been told I should not ever have guessed what they meant; (2) the colours in general were far too glaring, such as neither Christ nor his followers ever wore. When will painters have common sense!

Wed. 10. I opened the new preaching-house just finished at Newport[36] in the Isle of Wight. After preaching, I explained the nature of a Methodist Society, of which few had before the least conception.[37] Friday 11, I came to London and was informed that my wife died on Monday. This evening she was buried, though I was not informed of it till a day or two after.[38]

Mon. 15. I set out for Oxfordshire and spent five days with much satisfaction among the societies. I found no offences among them at all, but they appeared to walk in love. On Friday 19, I returned to London.

Sun. 21. About ten at night, we set out for Norwich and came thither about noon on Monday. Finding the people loving and peaceable, I spent a day or two with much satisfaction, and on Wednesday went on to Yarmouth. There is a prospect of good here also, the two grand hinderers having taken themselves away.[39]

[35] This picture has been considered the best work of Benjamin West (1738-1820), an historical painter of American Quaker origin, who settled in England in 1763. According to Curnock, the picture was first placed above the altar, then moved to the south transept, then sold to America.

[36] An account of the financing of this building scheme, which cost £572. 13s. 4 1/2d, is given in Dyson, *Methodism in the Isle of Wight,* pp. 108-10.

[37] In a letter of July 24, 1781, to Jasper Winscom, JW reports having written 'a few lines to Fanny Bewis, which I believe will check the Independency of our friends at Newport'. *WHS* 19 (1933):68.

[38] Mrs. Wesley was buried in Camberwell churchyard. In death, her name was inevitably publicly and painfully linked with that of her husband. 'Died Mrs. M. Wesley, aged 71, wife of Mr. John Wesley, the celebrated Methodist, Oct. 8, 1781'. *Gentleman's Magazine* 51 (1781):491.

[39] On Benjamin Worship and John Simpson, see Jan. 20, 1761 (21:300, n. 54 in this edn.). Their story is recapitulated below, Oct. 22, 1783. A new start had in fact been made in Yarmouth in 1780, when James Wood, Superintendent at Norwich, corresponded with Samuel King, a brazier, who was later a local preacher at Yarmouth

At Lowestoft I found much life and much love. On Friday, I preached at Loddon and, on Saturday, returned to Norwich.

Sunday 28. I preached at Ber Street to a large congregation, most of whom had never seen my face before. At half an hour after two and at five, I preached to our usual congregation and, the next morning, commended them to the grace of God.

Mon. 29. I went to Fakenham and, in the evening, preached in the room built by Miss Franklin, now Mrs. Parker.[40] I believe most of the town were present. Tuesday 30, I went to Wells,[41] a considerable seaport twelve miles from Fakenham, where also Miss Franklin had opened a door by preaching abroad, though at the peril of her life. She was followed by a young woman of the town, with whom I talked largely, and found her very sensible and much devoted to God. From her I learned 'that till the Methodists came they had none but female teachers in this country,[42] and that there were six of these within ten or twelve miles, all of whom were members of the Church of England'. I preached about ten in a small, neat preaching-house, and all but two or three were very attentive. Here are a few who appear to be in great earnest. And if so, they will surely increase.

At two in the afternoon, I preached at Walsingham, a place famous for many generations. Afterwards I walked over what is left of the famous abbey, the east end of which is still standing. We then went to the friary, the cloisters and chapel whereof are

(*WHS* 3 [1901]:74), and was given permission to preach in the General Baptist Chapel which had been first built for the Methodists. Requests were received to re-form the Methodist society, and, when Wood left the circuit in 1782, there were about sixty members, for whom JW opened a substantial preaching-house in the following year. Seeds of future dissidence were already present in Yarmouth, however; among the new society members was the mother of Dr. Warren, later the leader of the Wesleyan Methodist Association. Watmough, *Methodism in Great Yarmouth*, pp. 71-75.

[40] 'Molly Franklin and Sister Proudfoot are good women,' wrote JW in 1782 of the leaders of a somewhat disorderly society at Fakenham; Telford, 7:117. John Prickard (on whom see above, July 23, 1777), who was stationed in the Lynn circuit at the Conference of 1781 and was taken severely ill, related that 'Mr. and Mrs. Parker spared no pains or expense in providing everything convenient for me'; Jackson, *Early Methodist Preachers*, 4:193. Prickard also suffered the same violence as Miss Franklin (as is reported in the next entry). Atmore, *Memorial*, p. 340.

[41] Wells-next-the-Sea, a commercial port situated on an inlet about a mile from the sea.

[42] This is a curious sidelight on the propagation of religious awakening, and one which, despite exceptions such as Molly Franklin and Mary Sewell (*WHS* 3 [1901]:74), seems to have been inadequately exploited by the Methodists of this locality in JW's day. In the mid-1780s there were two female local preachers only on the Norwich circuit.

almost entire.[43] Had there been a grain of virtue or public spirit in Henry the Eighth, these noble buildings need not have run to ruin.

Wed. 31. I went to [King's] Lynn and preached in the evening to a very genteel congregation. I spoke more strongly than I am accustomed to do and hope they were not all *sermon-proof.* Friday, November 2, I returned to London.

Mon. 5. I began visiting the classes and found a considerable increase in the society. This I impute chiefly to a small company of young persons who have kept a prayer-meeting at five every morning. In the following week, I visited most of the country societies and found them increasing rather than decreasing. Sunday 18, I preached at St. John's, Wapping,[44] and God was present both to wound and heal. Monday 19, travelling all night, I breakfasted at Towcester and preached there in the evening and the following morning. Tuesday 20, we had a pleasant walk to Whittlebury. This is still the loveliest congregation as well as the liveliest society in the circuit.[45] Thursday 22, we had a large congregation at Northampton. On Friday, I returned to London.

Mon. 26. I took a little tour through Sussex, and, Wednesday 28, I preached at Tunbridge Wells in the large Presbyterian meeting-house[46] to a well-dressed audience, and yet deeply serious. On Thursday, I preached at Sevenoaks. Friday 30, I went on to Shoreham to see the venerable old man.[47] He is in his eighty-ninth year and has nearly lost his sight, but he has not lost his understanding, nor even his memory, and is full of faith and love. On Saturday, I returned to London.

---

[43] This description does not make quite clear what JW saw. To the priory, which became one of the most famous pilgrimage places in medieval England, belong the remains of the church, and into the east range of its buildings was built the abbey house in the late eighteenth century. The remains of the friary, 200 yards away, now consist principally of the guest-house and kitchen. N. Pevsner, *North-east Norfolk and Norwich* (repr. London, 1970), pp. 187-89.

[44] On this church, see above, Jan. 14, 1781.

[45] JW had always enjoyed meeting the society at Whittlebury (see June 23, 1763; 21:419 in this edn.), a parish 3 miles south of Towcester, where bone-lace was manufactured by the women. But owing to the opposition of the rector, Henry Beauclerc (1746-1817), the chapel beside which he preached in 1763 was not completed for another twenty years, and JW had to seek protection for the Methodist cause there in the Court of King's Bench. Telford, 7:193.

[46] On this meeting-house, see the note at Jan. 19, 1778.

[47] Vincent Perronet, on whom see Aug. 14, 1744 (20:35, n. 74 in this edn.). He lived until 1785.

Sunday, December 2, I preached at St. Swithin's Church[48] in the evening. About eight, I took coach and reached St. Neots in the morning. I preached in the evening to a larger congregation than I ever saw there before. Tuesday 4, about nine, I preached for the first time at Buckden,[49] and in the evening at Huntingdon. Wednesday 5, I was at Bedford. On Thursday 6th, our house at Luton was thoroughly filled, and I believe the people *felt* as well as heard those words, 'Where their worm dieth not, and the fire is not quenched.'[50] On Saturday I was in London.

Monday 10, I went to Canterbury and preached in the evening on 'Casting all your care on God'.[51] It was a word in season. Tuesday 14, finding abundance of people troubled as though England were on the brink of destruction, I applied those comfortable words, 'I will not destroy the city for ten's sake.'[52] Wednesday 12, I preached at Chatham and, the next day, returned to London.

Friday 21, we observed all over England as a day of fasting and prayer, and surely God will be entreated for a sinful nation. Friday 28, by reading in Thurloe's Memoirs[53] the original papers of the treaty at Uxbridge,[54] *agnovi fatum Carthaginis*,[55] I saw it was then

---

[48] JW had last preached in this church, 'for the last time', on Dec, 17, 1738 (19:28, and n. 19 in this edn.). The rector of St. Swithin's, 1776–1805, was Richard Palmer (1714–1805), who matriculated from Jesus College, Cambridge, in 1732; graduated B.A., 1736; M.A., 1766; and received a Lambeth D.D. He became rector of Scott Willoughby in 1740, chaplain to the Commons and prebendary of Canterbury, 1769–81. St. Swithin's Church was destroyed during World War II and not rebuilt.

[49] Orig., 'Bugden'.

[50] Mark 9:44, 46, 48.

[51] Cf. 1 Pet. 5:7.

[52] Cf. Gen. 18:32.

[53] John Thurloe, *Collection of State Papers; Containing Authentic Memorials of the English Affairs from 1638 to the Restoration of King Charles II; published from the originals; with a life of Thurloe* (London, 1742).

[54] 'The propositions of the Houses [of Parliament] presented to the King at Oxford, and subsequently discussed at the Treaty of Uxbridge' were presented to the King on Nov. 24, 1644, and answered by him two months later. They represented terms for peace between the two parties, stiffened by the parliamentary victory at Marston Moor and the need to preserve a united front between Parliament and the Scots. They required among other things, not only the 'three kingdoms', but the King, to take the Solemn League and Covenant, the abolition of episcopacy, and the reformation of religion, measures against Papists. They also included long lists of named persons for whom there should be no pardon or access to court. The papers are conveniently reprinted in *The Constitutional Documents of the Puritan Revolution, 1625–60*, ed. S. R. Gardiner (3rd edn., Oxford, 1906), pp. 275–87. Though severe, the terms not unfairly represented the real situations of the parties to the negotiations, and Charles I did not help himself by confirming his character as a man impossible to negotiate with.

[55] 'I recognize the fate of Carthage.' Cf. Livy, xxvii.51: 'C. Claudius consul, quum in castra redisset, caput Hasdrubalis . . . projici ante hostium stationes . . . jussit. Hannibal,

flatly impossible for the King to escape destruction. For the Parliament were resolved to accept no terms unless he would (1) give up all his friends to beggary or death, and (2) *require* all the three kingdoms to swear to the solemn league and covenant. He had no other choice! Who then can blame him for breaking off that treaty? 5

Tuesday, January 1, 1782, I began the service at four in West Street Chapel, and again at ten. In the evening, many of us at the New Chapel rejoiced in God our Saviour.[56]

Sunday 6. A larger company than ever before met together to 10 renew their covenant with God.[57] And the dread of God, in an eminent degree, fell upon the whole congregation.

Mon. 14. Being informed that through the ill conduct of the preachers things were in much disorder at Colchester,[58] I went down, hoping to 'strengthen the things which remained, that 15 were ready to die'.[59] I found that part of the class-leaders were dead and the rest had left the society; the bands were totally dissolved. Morning preaching was given up, and hardly any, except on Sunday, attended the evening preaching. This evening, however, we had a very large congregation, to whom I proclaimed 'the 20 terrors of the Lord'.[60] I then told them, I would immediately restore the morning preaching. And the next morning, I suppose an hundred attended. In the day-time, I visited as many as I possibly could in all quarters of the town. I then inquired who were proper and willing to meet in band. And who were fittest for leaders, either of bands or classes. The congregation this evening was 25 larger than the last, and many again set their hands to the plough. O may the Lord confirm the fresh desires he has given, that they may no more look back!

Friday, March 1.[61] We had a very solemn and comfortable 30

tanto simul publico familiarique ictus luctu, angoscere se fortunam Carthaginis dixisse fertur.'—'C. Claudius the consul, on returning to the camp, ordered Hasdrubal's head to be flung down in front of the enemy's outposts. Hannibal, smitten at once by so great public and private grief, is reported to have said that he recognized the fortune of Carthage.'

[56] See Luke 1:47.

[57] On the Covenant Service, see Aug. 6, 1755 (21:23, n. 82 in this edn.).

[58] Among the remedial measures still to come was a complete change of circuit staff at the next Conference.

[59] Cf. Rev. 3:2.

[60] Cf. 2 Cor. 5:11.

[61] The gap, virtually three months in the journal at this point, merely takes to its logical conclusion JW's recent habit of giving a very perfunctory account of his residence in London for the first two months of the year.

watch-night at West Street.[62] Sunday 3, I took coach and the next evening had a watch-night at Bath. Tuesday and Wednesday, after meeting the classes, I visited as many as I could, chiefly of the sick and poor. Thursday 7, I preached about eleven at Keynsham, and in the evening at Bristol. Friday 8 and most of the following days, I visited Mr. C[astlema]n,[63] just hovering between life and death. What a blessing may this illness be! On Monday, Tuesday, and Wednesday, I visited the classes and found a little increase. Friday 15, I opened the new house at Freshford.[64] In the afternoon, I called at Mr. Henderson's at Hanham[65] and spent some time with poor, disconsolate Louisa.[66] Such a sight, in the space of fourteen

[62] On watch-night services, see Apr. 9, 1742 (19:258, n. 50 in this edn.).

[63] John Castleman, a Bristol surgeon of 6 Dighton Street, an address just off King Square, where JW often preached, and where his printer, William Pine, and another Bristol friend he often visited, Nathaniel Gifford, also lived. JW was taken to Castleman's house when in a fever in 1783 (see below, Aug. 8, 1783), and in the following year he performed the ordinations for America in his room there; Henry Moore, *The Life of the Rev. John Wesley*, 2 vols. (London, 1824-25), 2:330-32. Mrs. Castleman, née Letitia Fisher (1738-1822), 'genteel, yet a Christian', was a pupil of Molly Maddern at Kingswood. Telford, 7:63; *WHS* 2 (1900):103-9.

[64] Orig., 'Freatford', apparently a misprint. Freshford was a parish 4 miles south-east from Bath which JW passed through as early as 1739, and at which he preached as early as 1749. The chapel here owed much to Paul Hart (1727-1809), who was converted under Methodist preaching *c.* 1750 and became a member of the society then formed in the village. 'Sometime Mr. Hart, with others of his friends, would on a Sabbath morning, walk as far as Kingswood to hear the Word of God preached, and converse with the pious colliers, and from thence proceed to Bristol, to hear another sermon, and afterwards return in the evening, a journey of not less than thirty-six miles. . . . Twice a week he visited Coomb [i.e., Combe Hay] and Dunkerton, two villages but three or four miles distant, and gave an exhortation to such as assembled to receive it. He and three others . . . purchased a dwelling house, and fitted it up for a place of worship. . . . And in the year 1782, finding the place too small for the congregation, they agreed with a builder to erect a new chapel,' the four making up a shortfall of £80 in the subscriptions, and handed the chapel over to trustees for the use of preachers appointed by Conference. *Methodist Magazine* 33 (1810):83.

[65] Orig., 'Hannam', Richard Henderson's asylum; see above, Sept. 29, 1781.

[66] Much of the following entry about 'poor disconsolate Louisa' had already appeared in the *Arminian Magazine* 5 (1782):324-25, as JW's personal commentary upon a full story he reprinted from the *St. James's Chronicle* under the heading 'A Tale of Real Woe', which included an attempt to solicit information about the mysterious young woman. The story, which had much press coverage, is usefully summarized in John Latimer, *The Annals of Bristol in the Eighteenth Century* (Frome, 1893), pp. 425-26:

In the year 1776, a woman, described as extremely young, of prepossessing appearance and graceful manners, but obviously of disordered intellect, entered a house at Flax Bourton [near Bristol] and asked for a little milk. After obtaining refreshment she wandered about the fields, and finally took shelter under a haystack, where she remained three or four days. Some ladies in the vicinity, having become acquainted with her condition, she was supplied with food, but neither solicitations nor threats induced her to sleep in a house ['she said *men*

years, I never saw before! Pale and wan, worne with sorrow, beaten
with wind and rain, having been so long exposed to all weathers,
with her hair rough and frizzled, and only a blanket wrapped
round her, native beauty gleamed through all. Her features were
small and finely turned, her eyes had a peculiar sweetness, her   5
arms and fingers were delicately shaped, and her voice soft and
agreeable. But her understanding was in ruins. She appeared
partly insane, partly silly and childish. She would answer no question concerning herself, only that her name was Louisa. She

lived there', William Roberts, *Memoirs of the Life and Correspondence of Mrs.
Hannah More*, 4 vols. (3rd edn., London, 1835), 1:122], and as her mental
derangement increased she was removed to St. Peter's Hospital in Bristol. How
long she was detained there is unknown, but she regained her liberty in 1777 or
1778, and immediately returned to the stackyard at Bourton, where, strange to
say, she remained nearly four years, receiving food from the neighbouring gentry, but obstinately refusing the protection of a roof, even in winter. Throughout
this period 'Louisa' or 'Maid of the Haystack' as she was called, declined to give
any account of her birthplace, parentage, or past life, though from casual
remarks it was inferred that her family was of high distinction. A peculiar accent
led observers to suppose that she was a foreigner. . . . In 1781 the condition of
the poor woman excited the interest of Miss Hannah More who with the assistance of friends [especially Lord and Lady Bathurst] had her removed to a private lunatic asylum at Hanham [where JW now encountered her]; while the
mystery of her antecedents was sought to be cleared up by the publication of 'A
Tale of Real Woe' in a London newspaper. Although no pains were spared to
elicit information by publishing translations of this story in the chief towns of
France and Germany (Roberts, *Memoirs*, 1:240; cf. p. 272), the results for some
years were wholly negative. But in 1785 an anonymous pamphlet, written in
French but probably printed in Belgium, made its appearance under the title of
'The Unknown; A True Story'. According to the writer, 'a young lady, who,
from the attentions paid to her by the Duke of York and other high personages,
was believed to be a natural daughter of the Emperor Francis I, had lived in
magnificent style at Bordeaux from 1765 to 1769; she had then been arrested at
the instance of the Empress, carried off to Belgium, and eventually conducted to
the coast near Ostend, where £50 'was put into her hands, and she was abandoned to her wretched destiny'. The purpose of the pamphleteer, who did not
produce a vestige of evidence in support of his story, was to identify the Bristol
'Maid of the Haystack' with the alleged half-sister of the Queen of France. And
in spite of the improbabilities surrounding his assumptions . . . Miss More and
others appear to have firmly believed in the bare assertions of a masked libeller
of the house of Austria, whose work was translated into English and went
through three editions. In the meantime the alienation of Louisa degenerated
into helpless idiocy, and she was removed to a lunatic house connected with
Guy's Hospital, London, where she died in December, 1800. Miss More continued to the last to contribute towards her maintenance, and paid the expenses of
her funeral.

Reprinted in *WHS* 3 (1902):161-62. The appeal for information abroad was due to the
fact that when addressed in French she appeared uneasy; and when addressed in German she burst into emotional tears. See also below, Mar. 6, 1784, and Sept. 15, 1785.
Delany, *Autobiography*, 2nd ser., 3:145.

seemed to take no notice of any person or thing, and seldom spoke above a word or two at a time. Mr. Henderson has restored her health, and she loves him much. She is in a small room by herself and wants [i.e., lacks] nothing that is proper for her.

5   Some time since, a gentleman called, who said he came two hundred miles on purpose to inquire after her. When he saw her face, he trembled exceedingly, but all he said was, 'She was born in Germany and is not now four and twenty years old!'

In the evening, I preached at Kingswood School and afterwards
10 met the bands. The colliers spoke without any reserve; I was greatly surprised. Not only the matter of what they spoke was rational and scriptural, but the language, yea, and the manner, were exactly proper. 'Who teacheth like Him?'[67]

Mon. 18. I left our friends at Bristol with satisfaction, having
15 been much refreshed among them. In the evening and the next day, I preached at Stroud; Wednesday 20, at Gloucester, Tewkesbury, and Worcester.

Fri. 22. About two in the morning, we had such a storm as I never remember. Before it began, our chamber-door clattered to
20 and fro exceedingly. So it sounded to us; although, in fact, it did not move at all. I then distinctly heard the door open and, having a light, rose and went to it. But it was fast shut. Meantime the window was wide open. I shut it and went to sleep again. So deep a snow fell in the night that we were afraid the roads would be
25 impassable. However, we set out in the afternoon and made shift to get to Kidderminster. We had a large congregation in the evening, though it was intensely cold; and another at seven in the morning, Saturday 23, and all of them were deeply serious. It was with a good deal of difficulty we got to Bridgnorth,[68] much of the
30 road being blocked up with snow. In the afternoon, we had another kind of difficulty: the roads were so rough and so deep that we were in danger every now and then of leaving our wheels behind us. But by adding two horses to my own, at length we got safe to Madeley.

35   Both Mr. and Mrs. Fletcher[69] complained that, after all the pains they had taken, they could not prevail on the people to join

---

[67] Job 36:22.

[68] Orig., 'Bridgenorth'. Bridgnorth, Shrops., is a town on the cliff above the river Severn, about 13 miles west of Wolverhampton.

[69] On John Fletcher, see Mar. 13, 1757 (21:88, n. 33 in this edn.), and on his wife, née Mary Bosanquet, Dec. 1, 1764 (21:495, n. 60 in this edn.). Their marriage (described in Benson, *Fletcher*, pp. 314–30) had taken place on Nov. 12, 1781.

in society, no, nor even to meet in a class. Resolving to try, I preached to a crowded audience on 'I am not ashamed of the gospel of Christ.'[70] I followed the blow in the afternoon, by strongly applying those words, 'Awake, thou that sleepest,'[71] and then enforcing the necessity of Christian fellowship on all who desired either to awake or keep awake. I then desired those that were willing to join together for this purpose to call upon Mr. Fletcher and me after service. Ninety-four or ninety-five persons did so; about as many men as women. We explained to them the nature of a Christian society, and they willingly joined therein.

Mon. 25. I spent an agreeable hour at the boarding-school in Sheriffhales.[72] I believe the Miss Yeomans are well qualified for their office. Several of the children are under strong drawings. We then went on to Newcastle-under-Lyme. (This is the name of a little river which runs near the town.) Tuesday 26, I found many at Burslem, too, under sad apprehensions of the public danger. So I applied to these also those comfortable words, 'I will not destroy it for ten's sake.'[73]

Thur. 28. Coming to Congleton, I found the Calvinists were just breaking in and striving to make havoc of the flock.[74] Is this brotherly love? Is this doing as we would be done to? No more than robbing on the highway. But if it is *decreed*, they cannot help it. So we cannot blame them.

Good Friday, March 29. I came to Macclesfield just time enough to assist Mr. Simpson[75] in the laborious service of the day. I preached for him morning and afternoon, and we administered the Sacrament to about thirteen hundred persons. While we were administering, I heard a low, soft, solemn sound, just like that of an Aeolian harp. It continued five or six minutes, and so affected

---

[70] Rom. 1:16. [71] Eph. 5:14.

[72] Orig., 'Sheriffe-Halen'. Sheriffhales was a substantial parish 3 miles north from Shifnal. There seem no adequate grounds for Telford's identification of the Misses Yeoman with the Mary and Rebecca Yeoman of the *Letters*.

[73] Gen. 18:32.

[74] The reference here is to the evangelistic activity of Captain Jonathan Scott (on whom see above, Mar. 26, 1781). His application to preach in the Methodist preaching-house having been refused, he held repeated open-air services in front of it, and gave notice that Sir Richard Hill (on whom see July 11, 1772; 22:341, n. 2 in this edn.), the violence of whose polemic against JW was notorious, would also come. The refusal to allow Scott the use of the preaching-house gave offence to a number of families, and, when a Calvinist cause was formed, they joined it and helped build the Mill Street Chapel; Dyson, *Congleton*, pp. 84–85. Similar difficulties were experienced with Scott at Macclesfield. Smith, *Macclesfield*, p. 192.

[75] On David Simpson, see Apr. 3, 1774 (22:402, n. 59 in this edn.).

many that they could not refrain from tears. It then gradually died away. Strange that no other organist[76] (that I know) should think of this! In the evening, I preached at our room. Here was that *harmony* which art cannot imitate.

5   Saturday 30. As our friends at Leek, thirteen miles from Macclesfield, would take no denial, I went over and preached about noon to a lovely congregation. God bore witness to his word in an uncommon manner, so that I could not think much of my labour.

Easter Day, March 31. I preached in the church[77] morning and
10   evening, where we had about eight hundred communicants. In the evening we had a love-feast, and such an one as I had not seen for many years. Sixteen or eighteen persons gave a clear, scriptural testimony of being renewed in love. And many others told what God had done for their souls, with inimitable simplicity.

15   Monday, April 1. We set out in the morning for Chapel-en-le-Frith.[78] But such a journey I have seldom had, unless in the middle of January. Wind, snow, and rain we had in abundance, and roads almost impassable. However, at last we got to the town and had a good walk from thence to the chapel through the driving
20   snow, about half a mile. But I soon forgot my labour, finding a large congregation that were all athirst for God.

Tue. 2. About ten, I preached at New Mills to as simple a people as those at Chapel[-en-le-Frith]. Perceiving they had suffered much by not having the doctrine of perfection clearly explained
25   and strongly pressed upon them, I preached expressly on the head and spoke to the same effect in meeting the society. The spirits of many greatly revived, and they are now 'going on to perfection'.[79] I found it needful to press the same thing at Stockport in the evening. Thursday 4, I preached at noon in the new
30   preaching-house at Ashton[-under-Lyne][80] to as many as the

[76] The organist was Aeneas Maclardie, father of Sarah, the first wife of Jabez Bunting. Thomas Percival Bunting, *Life of Jabez Bunting*, 2 vols. (London, 1859-87), 1:130n.

[77] The vicar of Leek, 1758-85, was Simon Mills, also rector of Norbury. John Sleigh, *History of the Ancient Parish of Leek* (Leek, 1862), p. 77.

[78] Wesley's first visit to Chapel-en-le-Frith was Apr. 28, 1745 (see 20:64, and n. 63 in this edn.).

[79] Cf. Heb. 6:1 (*Notes*).

[80] After a revival in 1775, three societies had formed in the neighbourhood, and that in Ashton, despite a sudden drop in membership to 15, was the first to build a preaching-house. This was made possible by the gift of a site in Harrod's Yard, a generous loan from a sympathizer, George Wilson, and collecting through the town and district. It was completed late in 1781. Edward Alan Rose, *Methodism in Ashton-under-Lyne*, 2 pts. (Ashton, 1967-68), 1:21-23.

house would hold. The inscription over the door is, 'Can any good come out of Nazareth? Come and see.'[81] In the evening, I preached at Manchester.

Fri. 5. About one, I preached at Oldham and was surprised to see all the street lined with little children—and such children as I never saw till now. Before preaching they only ran round me and before me; but after it, a whole troop, boys and girls, closed me in and would not be content till I shook each of them by the hand. Being then asked to visit a dying woman, I no sooner entered the room than both she and her companions were in such an emotion as I have seldom seen. Some laughed, some cried, all were so transported that they could hardly speak. O how much better is it to go to the poor than to the rich. And to the house of mourning, than to the house of feasting![82]

About this time I had a remarkable letter; part of it was as follows:

The work of God prospers among us here; I never saw anything equal to it. The last time I was at St. Just the leaders gave me an account of seventy persons who had found either pardon or perfect love within the last fortnight. And the night and morning I was there, twenty more were delivered. One and twenty likewise were then added to the society, most of whom have found peace with God.

Christopher Watkins[83]

Sat. 13. I preached at St. Helen's, a small but populous town ten or twelve miles from Liverpool, in Joseph Harris's house,[84] who is removed hither from Kingswood to take care of the copper-works. Surely God has brought him hither for good. The people seem to be quite ripe for the gospel.

---

[81] John 1:46.

[82] See Eccles. 7:2.

[83] Christopher Watkins (1750-1805), itinerant, at this time Superintendent of the West Cornwall circuit. 'A man of God, zealous to promote his glory, and the salvation of immortal souls', his ministry was eventually cut short by severe illness. *Methodist Magazine* 28 (1805):522.

[84] Joseph Harris lived next to the Navigation Tavern, on a site subsequently absorbed by Pilkington's glass works. Two of the largest concerns of the eighteenth century, The British Cast Plate Glass Company and the copper smelting works of the Parys Mine Company of Anglesey, had recently been attracted to Ravenhead by John Mackay's development of the high-grade Rushy Park coal seam; Harris was manager of the copper works from 1779 to about 1789. T. C. Barker and J. R. Harris, *A Merseyside Town in the Industrial Revolution: St. Helen's, 1750-1900* (Liverpool, 1954), pp. 36, 83; *Methodist Recorder* (Aug. 14, 1902), p. 11.

I was waked at half past two this morning, as was Mr. Broadbent[85] also, by a very loud noise, like a vast crack of thunder accompanied with a bright flash of light. It made the whole room shake, and all the tables and chairs therein jar. But (what is strange) none in the house or in the town heard it beside us.

Mon. 15. I saw an uncommon sight—the preaching-house at Wigan filled, yea, crowded! Perhaps God will cause fruit to spring up, even in this desolate place.

I had now leisure to transcribe a letter wrote last May from Amherst in Nova Scotia by a young man[86] whose father, some years since, went thither with his whole family:

> In the year 1779, I saw if I would go to heaven I must lead a new life. But I did not know I wanted an inward change, or see the deplorable state I was in by nature, till I was at a prayer-meeting held at Mr. Oxley's. While they were praying, my heart began to throb within me, my eyes gushed out with tears, and I cried aloud for mercy, as did most that were in the room, about fourteen in number. One indeed could not hold from laughing when we began to cry out, but it was not long before he cried as loud as any. In a few moments, it pleased God to fill Mrs. Oxley with joy unspeakable. After this, we went almost every night to Mr. Oxley's to sing and pray. Going thence one night and seeing the northern lights, I thought, 'What if the day of judgment be coming?' I threw myself down on the ground and cried to the Lord for mercy. On Sunday, Mr. Wells, an old Methodist, came to Amherst and gave us an exhortation, in which he said, 'Sin and repent, sin and repent, till you repent in the bottomless pit.' The words went like a dagger to my heart, and I continued mourning

---

[85] On John Broadbent, itinerant, JW's travelling companion, see above, Aug. 17, 1779.

[86] William Black (1760-1834), born at Huddersfield, was taken to Nova Scotia by his mother in 1775, following his father who had left in 1774. His mother's instruction and the good conduct of the captain made a religious impression on him, but, as related here, it was not till 1779 that he was converted under Methodist influence. He began to exhort in the neighbourhood, making a great emotional impact, and gradually preached over a wide area. After devoting himself entirely to evangelism, he was taken into full connexion in 1786. To this work 'he brought a constitution of more than ordinary strength; a sound, strong, and discriminating judgment; the very desirable possession of great Christian prudence; an ardent thirst for the attainment of knowledge'; and a reputation as 'the Apostle of Methodism in Nova Scotia'. He was esteemed both by Coke and JW, with whom he corresponded frequently, and in 1789 was appointed 'presiding elder, or general superintendent, of the missions in Nova Scotia, New Brunswick, and Newfoundland'. He visited the West Indies in 1793 with Coke, but the Nova Scotia district would not release him for that mission. He became a supernumerary in 1812, but continued active. An account of his experience was published in Jackson, *Early Methodist Preachers*, 5:242-95.

after God for five weeks and four days, till our monthly meeting. I was then strongly tempted to put an end to my life, but God enabled me to resist the temptation. Two days after, an old Methodist, after praying with me, said, 'I think you will get the blessing before morning.' About two hours after, while we were singing a hymn, it pleased God to reveal his Son in my heart. Since that time I have had many blessed days and many happy nights.

One Sunday night, after my brother Dicky and I were gone to bed, I asked him, 'Can you believe?' He answered, 'No.' I exhorted him to wrestle hard with God, and got up to pray with him. But he was unbelieving still, so I went to sleep again. Yet not being satisfied, after talking largely to him, I got up again and began praying for him, being fully persuaded that God would set his soul at liberty. And so he did. He pardoned all his sins and bade him 'Go in peace.'

It being now between twelve and one, I waked my brothers, John and Thomas, and told them the glad tidings. They got up. We went to prayer, and when we rose from our knees, Tommy declared, 'God has blotted out all my sins.' I then went to my father and mother (who were both seeking salvation) and told them the joyful news. My father said, 'Willy, pray for *us*.' I did, and earnestly exhorted him to wrestle with God for himself. So he did, and it was not long before God set his soul also at liberty. The next morning, it pleased him to show my sister Sally his pardoning love. Blessed be his name for all his benefits!

Not long after, Mr. Oxley's son came to our house and lay with me, and complained of his hardness of heart. After I had talked with him a little while, the Lord laid his hand upon him in a wonderful manner, so that he rolled up and down and roared as in the agonies of death. But between one and two in the morning, he likewise could rejoice in God his Saviour. These are a few of the wonderful works of God among us. But he is also working on the hearts of the inhabitants in general.

William Black, Junior

Mon. 22.[87] I preached about eleven in Todmorden Church, thoroughly filled with attentive hearers, in the afternoon in Heptonstall Church, and at the Ewood[88] in the evening. Wednesday 24, the flood caused by the violent rains shut me up at Longwood

---

[87] On the previous day, Apr. 21, JW had preached at Colne in the morning on Matt. 7:24–25; at noon on Acts 18:17; and at 4 p.m. on 1 Pet. 5:8. Edmundson, MS Commonplace Book.

[88] On the Grimshaw family farm, see July 4, 1772 (22:339–40, n. 94 in this edn.).

House.[89] But on Thursday the rain turned to snow, so on Friday I got to Halifax, where Mr. Floyde[90] lay in a high fever, almost dead for want of sleep. This was prevented by the violent pain in one of his feet, which was much swelled and so sore it could not be
5   touched. We joined in prayer that God would fulfil his word and 'give his beloved sleep'.[91] Presently the swelling, the soreness, and the pain were gone. And he had a good night's rest.

Sat. 27. As we rode to Keighley,[92] the north-east wind was scarce supportable, the frost being exceeding sharp and all the
10 mountains covered with snow. Sunday 28, Bingley Church[93] was hot, but the heat was very supportable both in the morning and afternoon. Monday 29, I preached at Skipton-in-Craven, at Grassington, and at Pateley Bridge. Tuesday 30, I found Miss Ritchie[94] at Otley, still hovering between life and death. Thursday,
15 May 2, I met the select society,[95] all but two retaining the pure love of God, which some of them received near thirty years ago. On Saturday evening, I preached to an earnest congregation at Yeadon. The same congregation was present in the morning, together with an army of little children—full as numerous, and
20 almost as loving, as those that surrounded us at Oldham.

Sun. 5. One of my horses having been so thoroughly lamed at Otley that he died in three or four days, I purchased another. But as it was his way to stand still when he pleased, I set out as soon as possible. When we had gone three miles the chaise stuck fast. I walked
25 for about a mile and then borrowed a horse, which brought me to Birstall before the prayers were ended. I preached on those words in the Gospel, 'Do you now believe?'[96] which gave me an opportunity of speaking strong words both to believers and unbelievers. In the evening, I preached at Leeds on St. James's beautiful description of
30 pure religion and undefiled, 'To visit the fatherless and widows in their affliction, and to keep himself unspotted from the world.'[97]

---

[89] On Longwood House, see above, July 28, 1781.

[90] On John Floyde, still an itinerant, see above, Apr. 9, 1781.

[91] Cf. Ps. 127:2.

[92] JW preached on Gen. 18:32. Edmundson, MS Commonplace Book.

[93] On Bingley Church and vicar, see above, Apr. 27, 1776. JW preached in the morning on Matt. 7:24–25. Edmundson, MS Commonplace Book.

[94] Elizabeth Ritchie (on whom see May 2, 1774; 22:406, n. 88 in this edn.) had been much worn down by the illness of both her parents and the death of her father, but she lived to nurse JW on his deathbed.

[95] On the select society, see Oct. 13, 1749 (20:307, n. 66 in this edn.).

[96] John 16:31. This was the Fifth Sunday after Easter.

[97] Jas. 1:27.

Thur. 9. I preached at Wakefield in the evening. Such attention sat on every face that it seemed as if everyone in the congregation was on the brink of believing. Friday 10, I preached at Sheffield. Saturday 11, about noon at Doncaster, and in the evening at Epworth. I found the accounts I had received of the work of God here were not at all exaggerated. Here is a little country town containing a little more than eight or nine hundred grown people, and there has been such a work among them as we have not seen in so short a time either at Leeds, Bristol, or London.

Sun. 12. About eight, I preached at Misterton, about one at Upperthorpe.[98] Many of the Epworth children were there, and their spirit spread to all around them. But the huge congregation was in the market-place at Epworth, and the Lord in the midst of them. The love-feast which followed exceeded all. I never knew such an one here before. As soon as one had done speaking, another began. Several of them were children; but they spoke with the wisdom of the aged, though with the fire of youth. So out of the mouth of babes and sucklings did God perfect praise.[99]

Mon. 13. I preached at Thorne. Never did I see such a congregation here before. The flame of Epworth hath spread hither also: in seven weeks fifty persons have found peace with God.[1]

Tue. 14. Some years ago four factories for spinning and weaving were set up at Epworth. In these a large number of young women and boys and girls were employed. The whole conversation of these was profane and loose to the last degree. But some of these, stumbling in at the prayer-meeting, were suddenly cut to the heart. These never rested till they had gained their companions. The whole scene was changed. In three of the factories no more lewdness or profaneness were found; for God had put a new song in their mouth, and blasphemies were turned to praise. Those three I visited today and found religion had taken deep root in them. No trifling word was heard among them, and they watch over each other in love. I found it exceeding good to be there, and we rejoiced together in the God of our salvation.[2]

---

[98] Orig., 'Overthorpe'.

[99] See Matt. 21:16.

[1] This is a circumstantial description of revival by contagion, reminiscent of Jonathan Edwards's *Faithful Narrative*, on which see Oct. 9, 1738 (19:16, n. 50 in this edn.).

[2] A fuller account of the revival in Epworth, including that among the factory girls, had been recently received by JW, and was later published in *Arminian Magazine* 7 (1784):45-50, 103-6. Among the converts received into the Epworth society at this time were the brothers of Alexander Kilham, later the first Methodist reformer. Alexander

Wed. 15. I set out for the other side of Lincolnshire. Thursday 16, I preached in the new house at Barrow [upon Humber].[3] I was well pleased to meet with my old fellow-traveller, Charles Delam-otte,[4] here. He gave me an invitation to lodge at his house, which I
5 willingly accepted of. He seemed to be just the same as when we lodged together five and forty years ago. Only he complained of the infirmities of old age, which through the mercy of God, I know nothing of.

Hence I went by Hull, Beverley, Bridlington,[5] and then has-
10 tened to Newcastle upon Tyne,[6] where I preached on Sunday the 26th. Monday 27, I set out for Scotland, and Wednesday 29, reached Dunbar. The weather was exceeding rough and stormy. Yet we had a large and serious congregation. Thursday 30, find-ing the grounds were so flooded that the common roads were not
15 passable, we provided a guide to lead us a few miles round, by which means we came safe to Edinburgh.

Fri. 31. As I lodged with Lady Maxwell[7] at Saughton Hall (a good old mansion-house three miles from Edinburgh), she desired me to give a short discourse to a few of her poor neigh-
20 bours. I did so, at four in the afternoon, on the story of Dives and Lazarus. About seven, I preached in our house at Edinburgh and

was working away from home at Ouston, but was much influenced at second-hand by these events. Alexander Kilham, *The Life of . . . Alexander Kilham, Methodist Preacher* (Nottingham, 1799), pp. 8–14.

[3] Barrow upon Humber, a parish 3 miles east of Barton-upon-Humber. The preach-ing-house at Barrow was built in 1780. *WHS* 8 (1912):130.

[4] Orig., 'Delamot'. On Charles Delamotte, one of the original party to Georgia, see Oct. 14, 1735 (18:136, n. 2 in this edn.).

[5] Orig., 'Burlington'.

[6] Via Sunderland on May 25; Telford, 7:123.

[7] Darcy Brisbane (*c.* 1742–1810), who in 1759 married Sir Walter Maxwell, Bart., of Pollock. He died two years later. Six weeks later her son, the only child of the marriage, also died. These bereavements were the first step in her conversion, which was gradu-ally carried through with the assistance of Whitefield and JW, whose correspondent she became. She mostly resided in or near Edinburgh and was often present at the 5 a.m. preaching. She established her school in Edinburgh for the Christian education of poor children in 1770, and by the time of her death had educated 800 children in it. She moved to Saughton Hall for a time on grounds of health, opened her house to the vil-lagers, and 'engaged different ministers to preach unto them the unsearchable riches of Christ'. She was a close friend and coadjutor of Lady Glenorchy, but did not go with her in her breach with JW. In 1780 she took under her wing Lady Henrietta Hope (on whom see May 12, 1772; 22:323, n. 26 in this edn.), third daughter of John, Earl of Hopetoun, and superintended her conversion. She also became a correspondent of Eliz-abeth Ritchie. She opened a number of chapels, including the Hope Chapel at Bristol. Her letters and diary form the substance of John Lancaster, *The Life of Darcy, Lady Maxwell* (2nd edn., London, 1826). See also A. J. Hayes, *Edinburgh Methodism, 1761–1975* (Edinburgh, 1976), pp. 31–33.

fully delivered my own soul. Saturday, June 1, I spent a little time with forty poor children whom Lady Maxwell keeps at school. They are swiftly brought forward in reading and writing, and learn the principles of religion. But I observe in them all the *ambitiosa paupertas*.[8] Be they ever so poor, they must have a scrap of *finery*. Many of them have not a shoe to their foot—but the girl in rags is not without her ruffles.

Sun. 2. Mr. Collins[9] intended to have preached on the Castle Hill at twelve o'clock, but the dull minister kept us in the kirk till past one. At six the house was well filled, and I did not shun to declare the whole counsel of God. I almost wonder at myself. I seldom speak anywhere so roughly as in Scotland. And yet most of the people hear and hear, and are just what they were before.

Mon. 3. I went on to Dundee. The congregation was large and attentive as usual. But I found no increase either of the society or of the work of God. Tuesday 4, the house at Arbroath[10] was well filled with serious and attentive hearers. Only one or two pretty flutterers seemed inclined to laugh, if any would have encouraged them. Wednesday 5, we set out early, but did not reach Aberdeen till between five and six in the evening.

---

[8] Cf. Juvenal, *Satires* III.182-83:

> *Hic vivimus ambitiosa / Paupertas omnes—*
> Here [at Rome] we all live in ambitious poverty.

Love of finery among the poor would be seen by some as ambitious or pretentious poverty.

[9] Brian Bury Collins, who later assumed the name of Collinsbury, 1754-1807, matriculated from St. John's College, Cambridge, in 1771, and graduated M.A. in 1780. He was ordained after great hesitation by the Bishop of Chester at the request of Lady Townshend, and after being curate to Pugh (on whom, see above July 7, 1781) at Rauceby, became an assistant to David Simpson at Macclesfield. He regarded himself as having 'an unlimited preaching commission', and as an apostle of evangelical unity; but Charles Atmore found him painfully divisive in the Newcastle society in 1789 (*Wesleyan Methodist Magazine* 68 [1845]:117; W. W. Stamp, *The Orphan House of John Wesley* [London, 1863], p. 147). There was a strong desire for the sacraments which, as an ordained man, he could administer; and there was talk of building a chapel for him and inviting Methodist preachers to settle there too (John Pawson to Charles Atmore, May 4, 1789; Tyerman MSS, 3, fol. 164, Methodist Archives, Manchester). JW took him to Bath in the McNab case (see above, Nov. 22-23, 1779), but later found him 'not very adviseable' (Telford, 7:247). He is said to have 'made rather too free with liquor towards the close of his days. A son of his lies interred in the City Road burying ground' (Tyerman MSS, 1, fol. 55 [margin], Methodist Archives, Manchester, the first item of an interesting correspondence between Collins and George Merryweather, fols. 55-61). A selection of his correspondence is printed in *WHS* 9 (1913):25-35.

[10] Orig., 'Arbroth'.

The congregations were large both morning and evening, and
many of them much alive to God. Friday 7, we received a pleasing
account of the work of God in the north. The flame begins to
kindle even at poor, dull Keith,[11] but much more at a little town
5 near Fraserburgh,[12] and most of all at Newburgh, a small fishing
town fifteen miles from Aberdeen, where the society swiftly
increases, and not only men and women, but a considerable number of children are either rejoicing in God or panting after him.
   Sat. 8. I walked with a friend to Mr. Leslie's[13] seat, less than a
10 mile from the city. It is one of the pleasantest places of the kind I
ever saw, either in Britain or Ireland. He has laid his gardens out
on the side of a hill, which gives a fine prospect both of sea and
land, and the variety is beyond what could be expected within so
small a compass. But still

15   *Valeat possessor oportet*
           Si comportatis rebus bene cogitat uti?[14]

Unless a man have peace within, he can enjoy none of the things
that are round about him.
   Sun. 9. We had a lovely congregation in the morning, many of
20 whom were athirst for full salvation. In the evening, God sent forth
his voice, yea, and that a mighty voice. I think few of the congregation were unmoved, and we never had a more solemn parting.
   Monday 10, we went to Arbroath; Tuesday 11, to Dundee; and
Wednesday 12, to Edinburgh. We had such congregations both
25 that evening and the next as had not been on a weekday for many
years; some fruit of our labours here we have had already. Perhaps
this is a token that we shall have more.
   Fri. 14. We travelled through a pleasant country to Kelso,[15]

---

[11] On Keith, see above, May 20, 1776; June 4, 1779.
[12] Orig., 'Fraserburg'.
[13] Orig., 'Lesley's'.
[14] Cf. Horace, *Epistles* I.ii.49-50, 'The possessor must be sound in health if he thinks
of enjoying the stores he has gathered' (Loeb). Wesley's original has 'oportat', 'compar-
tatis bene relas', and 'uta'—probably misprints caused by Wesley's hand-writing.
[15] JW's visit to Kelso was at the invitation of Mrs. Planche (1744-89), the Highland
widow of a Swiss Protestant, and he lodged with her brother. She had heard the itinerant, William Hunter, preach in Scotland, and, making the journey down to Alnwick to
hear him again, she was converted and admitted to the society. Finding herself isolated
in Kelso, she wrote to JW to send Hunter over to that town; he came on several occasions, preaching with success, and the result of his efforts, together with JW's visit, was
that a society was formed; *Arminian Magazine* 14 (1791):416-23. The Kelso society
never built a chapel.

where we were cordially received by Dr. Douglas.[16] I spoke strong words in the evening concerning judgment to come, and some seemed to awake out of sleep. But how shall they keep awake, unless they 'that fear the Lord, speak often together'?[17]

Sat. 15. As I was coming downstairs, the carpet slipped from under my feet, which, I know not how, turned me round and pitched me back, with my head foremost, for six or seven stairs. It was impossible to recover myself till I came to the bottom. My head rebounded once or twice from the edge of the stone stairs. But it felt to me exactly as if I had fallen on a cushion or a pillow. Dr. Douglas ran out, sufficiently affrighted. But he needed not. For I rose as well as ever, having received no damage but the loss of a little skin from one or two of my fingers. Doth not God 'give his angels charge over us, to keep us in all our ways'?[18]

In the evening and on Saturday 16, I preached at Alnwick. Monday 17, I preached at Rothbury in the Forest, formerly a nest of banditti,[19] now as quiet a place an any in the county. About one,

[16] Not as Curnock (6:358, n. 1) supposed, minister of Kelso. The only Douglas serving in the area at this moment was Robert (1747–1820), minister of Galashiels from 1770, who did not take his D.D. from Aberdeen till 1797. He provided the security for the capital which made Galashiels a manufacturing town, and sold Sir Walter Scott the estate on which Abbotsford was built; Hew Scott, *Fasti Ecclesiae Scoticanae*, 7 vols. (Edinburgh, 1915–28), 2:178. JW's friend was doubtless the benevolent Dr. Douglas who, when a school of arts was commenced by voluntary subscription in Kelso in 1824, took over a mathematical class. James Haig, *Topographical and Historical Account of the Town of Kelso* (Edinburgh, 1825), p. 127.

[17] Cf. Mal. 3:16.

[18] Cf. Ps. 91:11.

[19] Rothbury was a small town 11 miles south-west of Alnwick; the surrounding hills are known as Rothbury Forest—which Curnock said 'was a spot so fierce and uncivilized that no man would pass through it if he could avoid doing so' (6:358, n. 2). JW's picturesque description derives from a biography of Bernard Gilpin (1517–83), the Protestant 'apostle of the North', which JW serialized in *Arminian Magazine* 1 (1778):407–8. It contains a story of Gilpin's dealing with armed factions in the parish of Rothbury. 'During the two or three first days of his preaching, the contending parties observed some decorum and never appeared at church together. At length, however, they met. One party had been early at church, and just as Mr. Gilpin began his sermon the other entered. They stood not long silent. Inflamed at the sight of each other, they began to clash their weapons, for they were all armed with javelins and swords. When the tumult in some degree ceased, Mr. Gilpin proceeded, but again the combatants began to brandish their weapons and draw towards each other. Mr. Gilpin stepped from the pulpit, went between them, and addressing the leaders, put an end to the quarrel for the present. They promised him, however, that till the sermon was over, they would again make no more disturbance. He then went again into the pulpit and spent the rest of the time in endeavouring to make them ashamed of what they had done. His discourse affected them so much that they promised to forbear all acts of hostility while he continued in the county.' This is not so much a story of *banditti* as a description of the way Gilpin continued in a Protestant context the traditional role of the parish priest in

I preached at Saugh house,[20] a lone house, twelve miles from Rothbury. Though it was sultry hot, the people flocked from all sides, and it was a season of refreshment to many. In the evening, I went to Hexham and preached near the old priory[21] to an immense multitude. Very many were present again in the morning and seemed to drink in every word that was spoken.

Tue. 18. After preaching about one at Prudhoe, I went to Newcastle. Wednesday 19 and the following days, I examined the society. I found them increased in grace, though not in number. I think four in five, at least, were alive to God. To quicken them more, I divided all the classes anew, according to their places of abode. Another thing I observed, the congregations were larger, morning and evening, than any I have seen these twenty years.

Sun. 23. I preached about eight at Gateshead Fell, about noon at Burnopfield, and at the Garth Heads in the evening. My strength was as my day. I was no more tired at night than when I rose in the morning.

Mon. 24. I came to Darlington just in time, for a great stumbling-block had lately occurred. But my coming gave the people a *newer thing* to talk of. So I trust the *new thing* will soon be forgotten.[22]

Wednesday 26, I preached at Thirsk; Thursday 27, at York. Friday 28, I entered into my eightieth year, but, blessed be God, my time is not 'labour and sorrow':[23] I find no more pain or bodily infirmities than at five and twenty. This I still impute (1) to the power of God, fitting me for what he calls me to; (2) to my still

containing factional friction in the parish. Neither the Protestant nor the Catholic attempts to drive the parish as a focus of unity had much hope of success, and the Catholic evolution from avuncular social advice to individualized auricular confession with its own special furniture was an evasion of the problem. On this theme, see J. Bossy, 'Blood and Baptism; Kinship, Community and Christianity in Western Europe from the Fourteenth to the Seventeenth Centuries', in *Sanctity and Secularity; the Church and the World*, Studies in Church History 10 (Oxford, Blackwells, 1973), pp. 129-43. This was JW's only visit to Rothbury.

[20] A mile east of Cambo, where there was a plaque recording that JW preached there on his 79th birthday, June 17, 1782, O.S., and where annual services were once held; Curnock, 6:358, n. 3.

[21] The first church here was built by Wilfrid, *c.* 675-80; most of what JW could see dated from the period 1180-1250; this in turn has been substantially modified (especially the east front) by further building, 1850-1910. Pevsner, *Northumberland*, pp. 171-79.

[22] This may have been the purchase of a preacher's house, and the division of expenses, the preacher's to the circuit, JW's to the Darlington society. Jackson, *Methodism in Darlington*, p. 28.

[23] Ps. 90:10.

travelling four or five thousand miles a year; (3) to my sleeping, night or day, whenever I want it; (4) to my rising at a set hour; and (5) to my constant preaching, particularly in the morning. Saturday 29, I went on to Leeds and, after preaching, met the select society,[24] consisting of about sixty members, most of whom can 5 testify that 'the blood of Jesus Christ cleanseth from all sin.'[25]

Monday, July 1. Coming to Sheffield just at the time of the Quarterly Meeting,[26] I preached on Acts 9:31, 'Then had the churches peace, and were edified; and walking in the fear of the Lord, and in the comfort of the Holy Ghost, were multiplied.'[27] This is eminently 10 fulfilled in all these parts—at Sheffield, in particular.

Tue. 2. I found a serious as well as a numerous congregation at Nottingham.[28] Thursday 4, I preached at Derby. I trust the work of God will now prosper here also. All the jars of our brethren are now at an end, and they strive together for the hope of the gospel. 15

Saturday 6, I came to Birmingham and preached once more in the old, dreary preaching-house.[29] Sunday 7, I opened the new house[30] at eight, and it contained the people well; but not in the evening—many were then constrained to go away. In the middle of the sermon a huge noise was heard, caused by the breaking of a 20 bench on which some people stood. None of them was hurt, yet it occasioned a general panic at first, but in a few minutes all was quiet.

Wed. 11. I read prayers and preached in the church at Darlaston,[31]

---

[24] On the select society, see Oct. 13, 1749 (20:307, n. 66 in this edn.).

[25] Cf. 1 John 1:7.

[26] On the Quarterly Meeting, see June 23, 1760 (21:264, n. 34 in this edn.).

[27] Cf. Acts 9:31.

[28] G. H. Harwood believed that JW lengthened his stay here to arrange to secure the new chapel to the connexion. *History of Wesleyan Methodism in Nottingham* (Nottingham, 1872), pp. 51-52.

[29] Thomas Taylor added the silver lining: 'I have reason to think that our preaching out of doors in Birmingham was a happy means of increasing the blessed work: for before that time we were cased up in an old shabby building, in an obscure, dirty back street; but soon after our going out of doors, a large new chapel was built; and since that two more.' Jackson, *Early Methodist Preachers*, 5:49.

[30] The Cherry Street Chapel. The alarm arose from the collapse of a carpenter's bench on which too many people stood. But after the disaster in Yorkshire, the local *Gazette* was authoritatively primed to report that the chapel was 'one of the firmest buildings of the kind in the Kingdom'. W. C. Sheldon, *Early Methodism in Birmingham* (Birmingham, 1903), pp. 29-31.

[31] Orig., 'Darleston'. The rector was, according to Curnock, Titus Neve (*c.* 1720-*c.* 1789), who matriculated from Balliol College, Oxford, in 1738, graduating B.A. in 1742, and becoming sacrist of the Collegiate Church of Wolverhampton. His son-in-law, John Read, was the first steward (1835) of the Walsall circuit. *Methodist Recorder* (June 13, 1901), pp. 13-15.

and in the evening returned to Birmingham. Friday 12, I walked through Mr. Boulton's curious works.[32] He has carried everything which he takes in hand to a high degree of perfection and employs in the house about five hundred men, women, and children. His gardens, running along the side of a hill, are delightful indeed, having a large piece of water at the bottom, in which are two well-wooded islands. If faith and love dwell here, then there may be happiness too. Otherwise all these beautiful things are as unsatisfactory as straws and feathers.

Sat. 13. I spent an hour in Hagley Park,[33] I suppose inferior to few if any in England. But we were straitened for time. To take a proper view of it would require five or six hours. Afterwards I went to the Leasowes[34]—a farm so called—four or five miles from Hagley. I never was so surprised. I have seen nothing in all England to be compared with it. It is beautiful and elegant all over. There is nothing grand, nothing costly; no temples, so called; no statues (except two or three which had better have been spared). But such walks, such shades, such hills and dales, such lawns, such artless cascades, such waving woods, with waters intermixed, as exceed all imagination! On the upper side, from the openings of a shady walk, is a most beautiful and extensive prospect. And all this is comprised in the compass of three miles! I doubt if it be exceeded by anything in Europe.

[32] On Matthew Boulton's 'curious works', see Mar. 22, 1774 (22:400, n. 47 in this edn.).

[33] Hagley Hall was built for the first Lord Lyttelton, Viscount Cobham, 1754-60, by Sanderson Miller in the Palladian tradition. The grounds (to which JW doubtless refers) had already been begun before that date and were rich in ornaments including a (deliberately) ruined castle. Pevsner, *Worcestershire*, pp. 177-78; Delany, *Autobiography*, 2nd ser., 3:134.

[34] Orig., 'Leeasows'. The home of William Shenstone the poet (1714-63), Leasowes was a property near Halesowen, and not far from Hagley, acquired by the grandfather of the poet. On the death of his guardian in 1745, William Shenstone took the property into his own hands, and made it his main life's work to beautify the place, acquiring a significant niche in the history of landscape gardening. Shenstone's income, however, was less than that of JW, and was often so depressingly short of his ambitions, as to lead the spiteful to declare that he only enjoyed Leasowes when the eminent came to see it. At the end of his life Shenstone was hoping to receive a pension from Lord Bute, and it was on a visit in connection with this application that he caught the chill from which he died, a death said by Johnson to have been 'hastened by his anxieties' (*Lives of the Poets*, Everyman edn., 2:323), but hardly the romantic fatality imagined by JW. Little remains of Shenstone's garden furnishings, and in its present state the house seems to date from the nineteenth century. Pevsner, *Worcestershire*, p. 182; Marjorie Williams, *William Shenstone; A Chapter in the Eighteenth-Century Taste* (Birmingham, 1935); Richard Graves, *Recollections of some Particulars in the Life of the Late William Shenstone* (London, 1788).

The father of Mr. Shenstone[35] was a gentleman farmer, who bred him at the university and left him a small estate. This he wholly laid out in improving the Leasowes, living in hopes of great preferment, grounded on the promises of many rich and great friends. But nothing was performed till he died at forty-eight—probably of a broken heart!

Sunday 14. I heard a sermon in the old church at Birmingham,[36] which the preacher uttered with great vehemence, against these 'hare-brained,[37] itinerant enthusiasts'. But he totally missed his mark, having not the least conception of the persons whom he undertook to describe.

Mon. 15. Leaving Birmingham early in the morning, I preached at nine in a large schoolroom at Coventry. About noon, I preached to a multitude of people in the brick-yard at Bedworth.[38] A few of them seemed to be much affected. In the evening, I preached at Hinckley, one of the civilest towns I have seen.

Wednesday 17, I went on to Leicester; Thursday 18, to Northampton; and Friday 19, to Hinxworth[39] in Hertfordshire. Adjoining to Miss Harvey's[40] house is a pleasant garden. And she has made a shady walk round the neighbouring meadows. How gladly could I repose awhile here! But repose is not for *me* in this world. In the evening many of the villagers flocked together, so that her great hall was well filled. I would fain hope, some of them received the seed in good ground and will bring forth fruit with patience.[41]

---

[35] Orig., 'Shenston'.

[36] The rector of St. Martin's, Birmingham, 1781-1829, was Charles Curtis (1757-1820), who was also rector of Solihull, 1781-1829. He had been admitted at St. John's College, Cambridge, in 1775, graduated B.A. 1779, M.A. 1782.

[37] Orig. 'hair-brained', a common alternate spelling, perhaps suggesting a different connotation of the term.

[38] Bedworth was a ribbon-weaving parish 5 miles north of Coventry, on the main Coventry-Leicester road.

[39] Hinxworth was a small parish 4 miles north of Baldock.

[40] The unfruitfulness of the early Methodist preaching at Baldock was ascribed to 'there being no one to receive the preachers, and many to load them with reproach'. Miss Harvey's hospitality helped to meet the need, and in addition 'she built at her own expense, a good chapel at Stevenage, one at Baldock, and one at Biggleswade, and also an excellent house for the residence of the preachers; all of which she settled on the Methodist plan; besides leaving a handsome legacy [of £3000] to support the infant cause so dear to her heart. Her private charities to her poor neighbours were great, her life exemplary, her faith in the great Redeemer unswerving, and her end peace'; *Wesleyan Methodist Magazine* 52 (1829):291. Many members of her family, which was connected with the Harveys of Finningley (on whom see above, Nov. 11, 1779), were buried in Hinxworth churchyard. Robert Clutterbuck, *The History and Antiquities of the County of Hertford*, 3 vols. (London, 1815-27), 3:531.

[41] Luke 8:15.

Sat. 20. We reached London. All the following week the congregations were uncommonly large. Wednesday 24, my brother and I paid our last visit to Lewisham and spent a few pensive hours with the relict of our good friend, Mr. Blackwell.[42] We took one more walk round the garden and meadow, which he took so much pains to improve. Upwards of forty years this has been my place of retirement when I could spare two or three days from London. In that time, first Mrs. Sparrow[43] went to rest, then Mrs. Dewal,[44] then good Mrs. Blackwell.[45] Now Mr. Blackwell himself. Who can tell how soon we may follow them?

Mon. 29. I preached at West Street on the ministry of angels.[46] And many were greatly refreshed in considering the office of those spirits that continually attend on the heirs of salvation.

Friday, August 2, we observed as a day of fasting and prayer for a blessing on the ensuing Conference.[47] And I believe God

[42] Ebenezer Blackwell, banker (on whom see Feb. 10, 1751; 20:379, n. 54 in this edn.). His second wife, who survived him, was Mary Eden, niece of the wife of Bishop Lowth.

[43] On Mrs. Sparrow, see Sept. 29, 1747 (20:194-95, n. 33 in this edn.).

[44] Mrs. Hannah Dewal, who died in 1762 (see Nov. 6, 1762; 21:397, n. 21 in this edn.), was a member of the Blackwell family, constantly encountered at Lewisham in the *Journal* of CW.

[45] Elizabeth Blackwell died in 1772; see Feb. 26, 1772 (22:308, n. 46 in this edn.).

[46] Though JW believed that the Roman Catholic church inculcated the worship of angels and thereby erred grievously (*A Roman Catechism with a Reply* [vol. 13 in this edn.; Jackson, 10:103-4]; *Popery Calmly Considered*, 1779), he held that angels were among the orders of spirits to be discovered by faith, and that 'good angels are continually sent of God "to minister to the heirs of salvation" who will be "equals to angels" by and by, although they are now a little inferior to them'; Sermon 117, 'On the Discoveries of Faith', §6 (4:29-38 in this edn.); see also Sermon 71, 'Of Good Angels', on Heb. 1:14, published early in 1783 (3:3-15 in this edn.). This idea he employed in pastoral encouragement; Telford, 7:95-96.

[47] Having extended the Conference of 1780, and found the cost of the Conference of 1781 burdensome upon the hosts, JW this year cut the meetings short. The Conference business concerned two of JW's fears, the radicalism generated by the American War and the settlement of chapel trusts. It was resolved to exclude members of the Irish volunteers who exercised on the Lord's Day (though church parade and resistance to invasion were permitted). The other case was that of the Birstall preaching-house, built 1750-51 and much reshaped since. The Birstall trustees now required another deed and dunned JW, much against his will, to sign a deed which gave them the right to choose and dismiss preachers themselves; Telford, 7:124-25. Conference, however, resolved that if the Birstall trustees refused to settle the preaching-house 'on the Methodist plan', money should be raised nationally 'to build another preaching-house as near the present as may be'. A clash was avoided, and when the Birstall house case got into the vice-chancellor's court in 1853, it transpired that the trustees had never exercised the powers they claimed in the deed, and had always accepted the preachers sent by Conference; Simon, *The Last Phase*, pp. 194-95. This Conference, nevertheless, required 'a plain statement of the case to be drawn up' and this was published in 1783 as *The Case of the Birstall House* (9:505-9 in this edn.). Cf. Tyerman, *John Wesley*, 3:373-76.

clothed his word with power in an uncommon manner throughout the week. So that were it only on this account, the preachers who came from all parts found their labour was not in vain.

Tue. 13. Being obliged to leave London a little sooner than I intended, I concluded the Conference today and desired all of our brethren to observe it as a day of solemn thanksgiving. At three in the afternoon, I took coach. About one on Wednesday morning, we were informed that three highwaymen were on the road before us and had robbed all the coaches that had passed, some of them within an hour or two. I felt no uneasiness on the account, knowing that God would take care of us. And he did so, for before we came to the spot all the highwaymen were taken. So we went on unmolested and, early in the afternoon, came safe to Bristol.

Thur. 15. I set out for the west; preached at Taunton in the evening; Friday noon at Cullompton, and in the evening at Exeter. Here poor Hugh Saunderson[48] has pitched his standard and declared open war. Part of the society have joined him; the rest go on their way quietly, to make their calling and election sure.[49]

Sun. 18. I was much pleased with the decent behaviour of the whole congregation at the cathedral; as also with the solemn music at the post-communion, one of the finest compositions I ever heard.[50] The bishop[51] inviting me to dinner, I could not but observe, (1) the lovely situation of the palace,[52] covered with trees and as rural and retired as if it was quite in the country; (2) the plainness of the furniture, not costly or showy, but just fit for a

[48] On Hugh Saunderson, see June 4, 1774 (22:412, n. 19 in this edn.).

[49] See 2 Pet. 1:10.

[50] On a previous visit, JW had greatly admired the organ in Exeter Cathedral; see Aug. 29, 1762 (21:387 in this edn.). The organist from 1777 was the celebrated William Jackson (1730-1803), who composed songs, madrigals, and opera as well as liturgical music.

[51] The Bishop of Exeter from 1778 was John Ross (or Rosse) 1719-92, an attorney's son from Ross-on-Wye. He was educated at St. John's College, Cambridge, graduating B.A. 1741, M.A. 1744, B.D. 1751, and D.D. 1756. He was a fellow of the college, 1744-70. He rose rapidly, becoming preacher at the Rolls and royal chaplain in 1757, vicar of Frome in 1760, and canon of Durham in 1769. As bishop, he remained a considerable pluralist. In 1779, he advocated greater toleration for Dissenters and had a reputation for learning, modesty, and hospitality. The recollection of his clash, a generation before, with Bishop Lavington, Ross's immediate predecessor but one in that see, must have added spice to JW's dinner.

[52] The bishop's palace is situated to the south of the chancel and, along with the close, was in a very sheltered and secluded position until very recent years. The present palace contains medieval work, but dates mostly from 1848; the grounds were much restored by Butterfield.

Christian bishop; (3) the dinner sufficient, but not redundant; plain and good, but not delicate; (4) the propriety of the company, five clergymen and four of the aldermen; and (5) the genuine, unaffected courtesy of the bishop, who, I hope, will be a blessing to his whole diocese.

We set out early in the morning, Monday 19, and in the afternoon came to Plymouth. I preached in the evening, and at five and twelve on Tuesday, purposing to preach in the square at the dock in the evening. A little before I concluded, the commanding officer came into the square with his regiment, but he immediately stopped the drums and drew up all his men in order on the high side of the square. They were all still as night; nor did any of them stir till I had pronounced the blessing.

Thursday 22, I preached at St. Austell; Friday 23, at Truro and in the street at Helston. Saturday 24, I preached in Marazion at eleven, and in the evening at Penzance.

Sun. 25. We prayed that God would 'stay the bottles of heaven,'[53] and he heard our prayer. I preached at Mousehole about nine to a large congregation, to a larger at St. Buryan[54] about two. But that at St. Just in the evening exceeded both of them put together. After visiting the other societies, I came to Redruth on Saturday 31. I preached there in the evening and at noon, on Sunday, September 1; afterwards I expounded the parable of the sower at Gwennap[55] to how many thousands I know not—but all (I was informed) could hear distinctly. 'This is the Lord's doing.'[56]

Monday 2. I went on to Port Isaac. Tuesday 3, I preached in the street at Camelford. Being informed here that my old friend Mr. Thomson, rector of St. Gennys,[57] was near death and had expressed a particular desire to see me, I judged no time was to be lost. So borrowing the best horse I could find, I set out and rode as fast as I could. On the way I met with a white-headed old man who caught me by the hand and said, 'Sir, do you not know me?' I answered, 'No.' He said, 'My father, my father! I am poor John Trembath.'[58] I desired him to speak to me in the evening at Launceston, which he did. He was for some time reduced to

[53] Job 38:37.
[54] Orig., 'Beryam'.
[55] On Gwennap pit, see Sept. 5, 1762 (21:388, n. 75 in this edn.).
[56] Cf. Ps. 118:23.
[57] Orig., 'Ginny's'. On George Thomson, and the spelling of his name, see June 14, 1745 (20:69, n. 81 in this edn.).
[58] On John Trembath, see Oct. 22, 1745 (20:96, n. 68 in this edn.).

extreme poverty, so as to hedge and ditch for bread. But in his distress he cried to God, who sent him an answer of peace. He likewise enabled him to cure a gentleman that was desperately ill, and afterward several others, so that he grew into reputation and gained a competent livelihood. 'And now', said he, 'I want for nothing; I am happier than ever I was in my life.'

I found Mr. Thomson just alive, but quite sensible. It seemed to me as if none in the house but himself was very glad to see me. He had many doubts concerning his final state and rather feared than desired to die. So that my whole business was to comfort him and to increase and confirm his confidence in God. He desired me to administer the Lord's Supper, which I willingly did; and I left him much happier than I found him, calmly waiting till his change should come.

Newington, January 19, 1786.[59]

---

[59] The date JW finished preparing this Extract for publication; see *Diary*, Jan. 6–19, 1786.

A N

EXTRACT

OF THE

Rev. Mr. JOHN WESLEY's

JOURNAL,

FROM

Sept. 4, 1782, to *June* 28, 1786.

XX.

L O N D O N:

Printed for the Author; and fold at the New Chapel, City-
Road, and at the Rev. Mr. WESLEY's Preaching-Houfes
in Town and Country. 1789.

Journal

From September 4, 1782, to June 28, 1786[1]

Wednesday, Sept. 4, 1782, I preached in the market-house at Tiverton; Thursday 5, at Halberton, Taunton, and South Brent.[2] Friday 6 about ten, I preached at Shipham, a little town on the side of Mendip,[3] almost wholly inhabited by miners who dig up *Lapis Callaminoris*. I was surprised to see such a congregation at so short a warning, and their deep and serious attention seemed to be a presage that some of them will profit by what they hear. In the afternoon, we went on to Bristol.[4]

---

[1] The text for this Extract will follow the corrections incorporated into edn. B (1789).

[2] Halberton was a parish 3 1/2 miles east of Tiverton which attained some celebrity as the source of a durable stone which could easily be worked up into large blocks for use in canal-building. Lewis, *England*, 2:327-28. For South Brent see above, Sept. 3, 1779.

[3] Orig. 'Mendif'. Shipham was small parish 3 miles north-east of Axbridge. Lead and calamine (a zinc carbonate) long continued to be mined in the village, but despite JW's optimism, Methodism did not take root. Lewis, *England*, 4:73.

[4] It was on this occasion that the celebrated meeting took place between JW and Adam Clarke. Wesley had sent Clarke in great poverty to Kingswood school to train as a preacher, giving him a letter addressed to the headmaster, Thomas Simpson (on whom see above, Sept. 7, 1781; 22:19-20, n. 82 in this edn.). Simpson treated Clarke with the utmost callousness, and his wife thought it necessary, he being Irish, to coat him with 'infernal unguent', and an appeal was made to JW. The narrative in Clarke's own words probably puts greater claims into JW's mouth than he made for himself, but is an interesting commentary on his pastoral and preaching method:

At length Mr. Wesley returned to Bristol. The day he came, Mr. Simpson went in and had an interview with him; and I suppose told his own tale—that they had not room, that it was a pity I should not be out in the general work; and I was told that Mr. W. wished to see me.

I had this privilege for the first time on September 6th. I went into Bristol, saw Mr. Rankin [see Sept. 8, 1765], who carried me to Mr. Wesley's study, off the great lobby of the rooms over the chapel in Broadmead. He tapped the door, which was opened by this truly apostolic man. Mr. R. retired: Mr. W. took me kindly by the hand, and asked me, 'How long since I had left Ireland?' Our conversation was short. He said, 'Well, brother Clarke, so you wish to devote yourself entirely to the work of God?' I answered, 'Sir, I wish to *do* and *be* what God pleases!' He then said, 'We want a preacher for Bradford (Wilts.), hold yourself in readiness to go thither; I am going into the country, and will let you know when you shall go.' He then turned to me, laid his hands upon my head, and spent a few moments in praying to God to bless and preserve me, and to give success to the work to which I was called. I departed, having now received, in addition to my appointment from God to preach his gospel, the only authority I could have from man, in that line in which I was to exercise the Ministry of the Divine Word. That evening Mr. Wesley preached in the chapel from Zech. 4: 6,

Sun. 8. My brother read prayers and I preached to a very
uncommon congregation. But a far more numerous one met near
King Square in the evening, on whom I strongly enforced, 'Ye
cannot serve God and Mammon'.[5] Permit me to observe here
5 how you may distinguish a genuine small Field's Bible from a
spurious one.[6] The genuine reads here, 'Ye can serve God and
Mammon'. In the spurious the 'not' is supplied.

Mon. 9. About noon,[7] I preached at Paulton where the flame is

'Not by might, nor by power, but by my Spirit, saith the Lord of Hosts.' In this
sermon, which was little else than a simple narrative of facts, he gave a succinct
account of the rise and progress of what is called *Methodism:* its commencement
in Oxford, occasioned by himself and his brother Charles, and a few other young
men, setting apart a certain portion of time to read the Greek Testament, and
carefully to note the doctrines and precepts of the gospel, and to pray for outward holiness, &c. With and by these, God had condescended to work a work,
the greatest that had been wrought in any nation since the days of the Apostles.
That the instruments he employed were, humanly speaking, not at all calculated
to produce such a glorious effect; they had no *might* as to extraordinary learning,
philosophy or rhetorical abilities; they had no *power,* either ecclesiastical or civil;
could neither command attention, nor punish the breach of order; and yet by
these means was this extraordinary work wrought; and in such manner too as to
demonstrate, that as it was neither by *might nor power,* it *was by the Spirit of the
Lord of Hosts.* Had this relation been entirely *new* to me, I should have felt more
interest in the sermon. But I had already acquainted myself with the history of
Methodism [9:426-503 in this edn.], of which it was an abridgment. The sermon
had nothing great in it, but it was well suited to the purpose for which it was
preached; viz. to lead the people ever to consider the glorious revival of religion
which they witnessed, as the work of God alone; and to give him the glory; as to
Him alone this glory was due.

Clarke, *Life of Adam Clarke,* 1:165-66.
   [5] Matt. 6:24.
   [6] JW is here in error, and is too optimistic. John Field, printer to Parliament, produced a quarto English Bible in 1648, and then other editions in smaller formats, down
to one in 24ᵐᵒ, first printed in 1653, designed for the pocket. Of this edition it is said
almost 20,000 were circulated, despite numerous misprints. Kilburne notes: 'All the
dedications and titles of David's Psalms are wholly left out, being part of the original
text in Hebrew. . . . John 9:21, "Or who hath opened his eyes we know not". These
words are wholly omitted. Rom. 6:13, "Neither yield ye your members as instruments
of righteous men unto sin" for "unrighteousness". 1 Cor. 6:9, "Know ye not that the
unrighteous shall inherit the Kingdom of God?" for "shall not inherit".' Lea Wilson
mentions three other misprints: Matt. 6:24, 'Ye cannot serve and mammon' ('God'
omitted—here is JW's error); John 2:10, 'When they have' for 'when men have', and
3:21, 'might be manifest' for 'may be made manifest'. Many copies are thought to have
been corrected by cancel leaves, and later editions in this format were less inaccurate.
JW is said always to have used a small edition of Field's Bible when preaching out of
doors, and his copy is passed annually from President to President of Conference. A. S.
Herbert, *Historical Catalogue of Printed Editions of the English Bible, 1525-1961* (London, 1968), p. 200 (No. 635).
   [7] Edns. A and B (1789). Later editions read 'nine'.

abated but not quenched.[8] The same is the case at Shepton Mallet, where I preached in the evening. Tuesday 10, I went on to the simple-hearted colliers at Coleford,[9] abundance of whom met at six in the evening in a green meadow, which was delightfully gilded by the rays of the setting sun. Wednesday 11, I preached to a large and serious congregation at the end of the preaching-house at Frome.

After preaching at Rode,[10] Pensford, Trowbridge, and Freshford, on Friday 13, I preached at Bath. Sunday 15, I had a far greater number of communicants than usual. Both at this time and in the afternoon and the evening service, we had no common blessing.

On Monday and Tuesday, I preached at Chew Magna, at [Bishop] Sutton, [Chew] Stoke, and Clutton. In my way thither, I saw a famous monument of antiquity at Stanton Drew,[11] supposed to have remained there between two and three thousand years. It was undoubtedly a Druid's temple, consisting of a smaller and a larger circle of huge stones set on end, one would think, by some power more than human. Indeed such stones have been used for divine worship nearly, if not quite, from the time of the flood. On the following days, I preached at many other little places.

Sun. 22. After the service at Bristol, I hastened to Kingswood and preached a funeral sermon on Jenny Hall, a lovely young woman, who died in full triumph and desired a sermon might be preached on Rev. 7:13, and following verses.

On Monday, Tuesday, and Wednesday, I visited the classes and was concerned to find that for these two last years, the society has been continually decreasing. Thursday 26 and the following days, I visited the rest of the country societies.[12] For a day or two, I was

---

[8] The revival at Paulton is commented on above, Mar. 4, 1779, Sept. 8, 1779, Sept. 6 1780; and below, Apr. 12, 1785.

[9] Coleford, Somerset, on which see Jan. 31, 1745 (20:51 and n. 20, in this edn.).

[10] Orig., 'Road'.

[11] Stanton Drew was a small parish 1 1/2 miles west of Pensford. Lewis *(England,* 4:171) reports that 'the neighbourhood abounds with various objects of interest to the antiquary, the most prominent of which are, Maes Knoll Tump, a stupendous barrow, and an extensive Druidical temple of three circles of stones whose diameters are respectively 120, 43, and 32 yards, spreading itself over ten acres of ground: the stones which are of amazing dimensions, were apparently brought from the neighbouring quarries; many of them, however, now lie prostrate on the ground.' The modern literature, acknowledging that the three stone circles of Stanton Drew are the most important prehistoric monuments in Somerset, and a similar version of the great circles on Salisbury plain, is silent as to the Druids. Pevsner, *North Somerset and Bristol*, p. 263.

[12] Including Bath and Bradford-on-Avon. Clarke, *Life of Adam Clarke*, 1:169.

not well, but I went on with my work till Sunday, when I preached morning and evening at the New Room, and in the afternoon in Temple Church.[13]

Tuesday, October 1. I read among the letters, in the evening, the striking account of Robert Roe's death,[14] a burning and a shining light while alive, but early numbered with the dead. Saturday 5, I visited several that are yet in the body but longing to depart and to be with Christ. But many have this year stepped before them. For forty years I do not know that so many have, in the space of one year, been removed to Abraham's bosom.

Sun. 6. I preached in Temple Church, between our own morning and evening service. And I now found how to speak here so as to be heard by every one: direct your voice to the middle of the pillar fronting the pulpit.

Mon. 7. I left Bristol with much satisfaction, firmly believing that God will revive his work there. I preached at the Devizes about eleven, and in the evening at Salisbury; Tuesday 8, at Winchester, and at Portsmouth Common. Wednesday 9, we took a wherry for the Isle of Wight.[15] There was sea enough, which now and then washed over our boat. However, in about an hour we landed safe and walked on to Newport. This place seems now ripe

---

[13] On this church, see above, Sept. 24, 1780.

[14] Robert Roe (*c*. 1754-82) was the son of Charles Roe (on whom see July 19, 1764; 21:480, n. 88 in this edn.) of Macclesfield, who built Christ Church there and presented David Simpson to it. After the death of his first wife, Charles Roe's attachment to Methodism is said to have weakened, and Robert was sent to Brasnose College, Oxford, in 1774, with a view to ordination. Here he seems to have done well in college examinations, but was denied the grace to supplicate for his degree, and also permission to migrate, on a charge (which he denied) of attending illicit conventicles, which actually meant frequenting Methodist meetings. As he refused to give these up (despite Simpson's pleas to the contrary), he was denied the means of securing ordination. In chagrin his father banished him from the town, and the contretemps is believed to have hastened his death in 1782. When Charles Roe's estate was divided, Robert built a house in which his cousin, Hester Ann Rogers, and her mother, widow of James Roe, 'prime curate' of Macclesfield, lived till his death. Robert Roe's diary was serialized in the *Arminian Magazine* 6 (1783) and 7 (1784), the account of his examination before the college authorities being given in *Arminian Magazine* 7 (1784):134-37. See also Smith, *Macclesfield*, pp. 117, 130, 145-48, 187-91; Alfred Leedes Hunt, *David Simpson and the Evangelical Revival* (London, 1927), pp. 182-87; H. A. Rogers, *The Experience and Spiritual Letters of Mrs. Hester Ann Rogers* (London, 1840), pp. 37-38.

[15] The implication of Tyerman (*John Wesley*, 3:386) and the direct statement of Curnock (6:374) that on this occasion Robert Wallbridge (*c*. 1776-1837), whose younger sister Elizabeth was later immortalized by Legh Richmond as *The Dairyman's Daughter* (London, 1810), was converted under JW's preaching, are controverted by Wallbridge's obituary (*Wesleyan Methodist Magazine* 60 [1837]:318) which ascribes the episode to JW's visit in 1790 (see Sept. 30, 1790). See also Dyson, *Isle of Wight*, pp. 137-46.

for the gospel; opposition is at an end. Only let our preachers be men of faith and love, and they will see the fruit of their labours.

Fri 11. I returned to Portsmouth, took chaise at two the next morning, and in the afternoon came to London.

Mon. 14. I went to Wallingford. The house was filled in the evening with much affected hearers. Shall all our labour here be in vain? Lord, thou knowest!

Tue. 15. About noon I preached at Oxford. I have seen no such prospect here for many years. The congregation was large and still as night, although many gentlemen were among them. The next evening, the house would not contain the congregation. Yet all were quiet, even those that could not come in. And I believe God not only opened their understandings, but began a good work in some of their hearts.

Wed. 16. I preached at Witney, one of the liveliest places in the circuit, where I always find my own soul refreshed.

I saw such a garden at Oxford as, I verily believe, all England cannot parallel. It is triangular[16] and, I conjecture, contains about an acre of ground; it is filled with fruit trees of various sorts and all excellent in their kinds. But it is odd beyond all description, and superlatively whimsical. The owner has crowded together pictures, statues, urns, and antiques of various kinds; for all which why should not Mr. Babcock's name, as well as Mr. Robert's,[17] be consigned to posterity?

Thursday 17, I preached at Thame;[18] this evening and the next, at High Wycombe, and on Saturday returned to London.

Monday 21, I preached at Tunbridge Wells; Tuesday 22, at Sevenoaks. Wednesday 23, I visited the house of mourning at Shoreham and read the strange account at first hand. Not long after his former wife died, Mr. H. paid his addresses to Miss B.[19]

---

[16] Edn. A, 'three-square'.

[17] This is probably a printing error for Jacob Bobart the elder (1599–1680), or his son of the same name (1641–1719), who succeeded his father as superintendent of the Oxford Physic garden. The latter was also professor of botany in Oxford from 1684, and published the third part of Robert Morison's *Plantarum historiae universalis Oxoniensis*, 2 vols. (Oxford, 1680–99). The elder Bobart was born in Brunswick.

[18] Orig., 'Tame'.

[19] Elizabeth, Vincent Perronet's sole surviving daughter, in 1749 married William Briggs, of the Custom House, a leader at the Foundery, one of JW's secretaries, who in 1753 was appointed one of the two book stewards. He had been a preacher, or at least employed in visiting the societies, and was present at the Conference of 1748. *Arminian Magazine* 1 (1778):232–33; Tyerman, *John Wesley*, 2:176–80. The unfortunate lady here referred to must have been one of their daughters, though not Philothea Perronet

He had been intimately acquainted with her for some years. By immense assiduity and innumerable professions of the tenderest affection, he by slow degrees gained hers. The time of marriage was fixed. The ring was bought. The wedding clothes were sent
5   to her. He came on Thursday, a few days before the wedding-day, and showed the most eager affection. So he did on Saturday. He came again on the Wednesday following, sat down very carelessly on a chair, and told her with great composure that he did not love her at all and therefore could not think of marrying her. He talked
10 a full hour in the same strain, and then walked away!

Her brother sent a full account of this to Miss Perronet, who read it with perfect calmness, comforted her niece, and strongly exhorted her to continue steadfast in the faith. But the grief, which did not outwardly appear, preyed the more upon her spir-
15 its, till three or four days after, she felt a pain in her breast, lay down, and in four minutes died. One of the ventricles of her heart burst, so she literally died of a broken heart.

When old Mr. Perronet heard that his favourite child, the stay of his old age, was dead, he broke into praise and thanksgiving to
20 God, who had 'taken another of his children out of this evil world!'

But Mr. H. meantime has done nothing amiss. So both himself and his friends say!

Fri. 25. I returned to London and was glad to find Mr. Edward
25 Smyth[20] and his family just come from Dublin. Sunday 27 at ten, I took coach, reached Norwich on Monday noon, and preached at six in the evening. I stayed there on Tuesday; and Wednesday 30, went on to Yarmouth, where were the largest congregations I had seen for many years. Thursday 31, I went on to Lowestoft[21],
30 which is at present far the most comfortable place in the whole circuit. Friday, November 1, Mr. Smyth and his wife[22] gave us a strange account. A little before they were married, her brother

Briggs, who married Thomas Thompson, the Hull banker, in 1782. Five other children of this marriage actually outlived Vincent Perronet; *Methodist Magazine* 22 (1799):53. Sad though the story is, it is impossible not to note that the Perronet children inherited a predisposition to early death; Vincent had at least 12 children of whom only Elizabeth and Edward survived him. Of the two only Elizabeth had issue; her family on the whole did well, and their survival is rather more remarkable than the losses they incurred.

[20] On Edward Smyth, see June 2, 1777, and Nov. 22, 1779.

[21] Orig., 'Lostaffe'.

[22] Mrs. Edward Smyth (on whom see above, June 2, 1777) was born Agnes Higginson; her brother therefore was Samuel Higginson.

Samuel was about eight years old. One evening, as she was with Mr. Smyth, in one of the Rows at Yarmouth, both of them saw Samuel standing five or six yards off. She cried out, 'Sammy, come hither, I want you,' but instantly he was gone. Just then he fell into the river. A large water-dog which was on the bridge, directly leaped off, swam about, and sought him, but could not find him. He then came out and ran to his mother's house howling; nor would he leave her, till he was put out by force.

Sat. 2. About nine, I preached at Cove,[23] a village nine or ten miles from Lowestoft. The poor people presently filled the house and seemed to devour every word. About one, I preached at Loddon, and at Norwich in the evening.

Sun. 3. I administered the Lord's Supper to about an hundred and forty communicants. I preached at half past two and again in the evening, after which I requested them to go away in silence without anyone speaking to another. They took my advice. They went away in profound silence, so that no sound was heard but that of their feet.

Mon. 4. At five in the morning, the congregation was exceeding large. That in the evening seemed so deeply affected that I hope Norwich will again lift up its head. At nine, we took coach and, before eleven on Tuesday 4, reached Colchester. In order to strengthen this poor feeble society, I stayed with them till Friday, preaching morning and evening, and visiting in the day to as many as I could, sick or well. I divided the classes anew, which had been strangely and irregularly jumbled together, appointed stewards, regulated temporal as well as spiritual things, and left them in a better way than they had been for several years.

Monday 17 and the following days, I visited the societies in and about London.

Sun. 24. I preached at St. Clement's[24] in the Strand, the largest church I ever preached in at London, except (perhaps) St. Sepulchre's, to an immense congregation. I fully discharged my own

---

[23] Now North Cove, a small parish 3 miles east of Beccles.

[24] The rector of this church from 1756 was John Burrows LL.B. (*c.* 1733-86). He matriculated from Trinity College, Oxford, in 1750, and graduated in 1762. The last occasion on which JW records having preached in this church, which was one of the early centres of the religious societies, was Nov. 5, 1738. He then concluded: 'As this was the first time of my preaching here, I suppose it is to be the last' (see 19:20 and n. 86 in this edn.). St. Clement Dane goes back probably to Danish times. The medieval church was partly rebuilt in 1640, and rebuilt again by Wren, 1680-82. The church was burnt out in 1941, and restored, 1955-58, the interior now being entirely new.

soul, and afterwards took coach to Northamptonshire. On Monday 25, I preached at Towcester; on Tuesday, at Whittlebury, so called—but the true name of the town is Whittle;[25] on Wednesday, at Northampton; and on Thursday, I returned to London. Friday 29, I preached at Highgate in the Palace built in the last century by that wretched Duke of Lauderdale,[26] now one of the most elegant boarding-houses in England.[27] But alas! It is not Publow![28]

Monday, December 3, I preached at St. Neots[29] in Huntingdonshire. Tuesday 3, at Buckden about one, and in the evening at Huntingdon. Two clergymen were there, with one of whom I had much serious conversation.[30] Wednesday 4, I preached with great enlargement of spirit, to my old congregation at Bedford. Thursday 5, with some difficulty I crossed the country to Hinxworth[31] and preached to fifty or sixty plain people, who seemed very willing to learn. In the afternoon it, being impossible to drive a chaise strait round to Luton, I was obliged to go many miles about, and so did not reach it till after six o'clock. So I went directly to the preaching-house and began without delay enforcing those solemn words, 'Today, if ye will hear his voice, harden not your hearts.'[32]

Fri. 6. I could procure no other conveyance to St. Albans but in an open chaise. And hence (the frost being very sharp), I con-

[25] JW appears to have been misinformed. Whittlebury appears recognizably as Wytlbyr in a Northamptonshire survey as early as the twelfth century. *Victoria County History; Northamptonshire*, 1:373. Cf. George Baker, *History and Antiquities of the County of Northampton*, 2 vols. (London, 1822-30), 2:70.

[26] John Maitland, second Earl and first Duke of Lauderdale (1616-82), one of the leaders of the covenanting party in his youth, who later came round to the King's side, and, as secretary for Scottish affairs, 1660-82, aimed to make the Crown absolute in Scotland both in church and state. Doubtless regarded by JW as wretched because he was supposed to have advised the surrender of the King, Charles I, by the Scots to the English in January 1647, and because in 1679, Parliament approved an address to the King for his dismissal 'on account of his arbitrary and destructive counsels.'

[27] Miss Teulon's boarding school at Linden House, Highgate, visited again by JW on Dec. 13, 1787, and Dec. 15, 1788. Whether Miss Teulon was related to Melchior Teulon, one of the executors of JW's will, is not clear.

[28] On Miss Owen's school at Publow, see Sept. 6, 1772; 22:348, n. 41 in this edn.

[29] At this time Henry Venn and his newly ordained son, John, were supplying St. Neots Church, 'whence the curate had been suddenly called away.' *The Life and a Selection from the Letters of the late Rev. Henry Venn*, ed. Henry Venn (London, 1834), pp. 346, 350.

[30] These clergy may well have been members of the evangelical circle which associated with Henry Venn at Yelling, 6 miles from St. Neots.

[31] For the connection here, see above, July 17, 1782.

[32] Heb. 3:15; 4:7. In his Diary, however, JW cites Heb. 12:14, 'Follow peace with all men, and holiness, without which no man shall see the Lord'.

tracted a severe cold.[33] Monday 9, I had a better conveyance into Kent. In the evening, I preached at Canterbury; on Tuesday, at Dover; the next day, at Canterbury again. On Thursday 12 and on Friday morning, I preached at Chatham and, in the afternoon, returned to London.

Sat. 15. I found the cold which I had contracted in the way to St. Albans exceedingly increased, having a deep and violent cough, which continued at intervals, till spring.

Mon. 16. I retired to Hoxton[34] for a few days. Thursday 19 about eleven at night, a gun was fired at our chamber window, and at the same time, a large stone thrown through it, (probably in sport, by some that had been drinking). I presently went to sleep again.

Sat. 21. I visited Mr. Maxfield,[35] struck with a violent stroke of palsy. He was senseless and seemed near death. But we besought God for him, and his spirit revived, I cannot but think, in answer to prayer. Sunday 29, I buried the remains of Thomas Forfitt,[36] a rich, and yet a generous man. He was unwearied in well-doing, and in a good old age, without any pain or struggle, fell asleep. Tuesday 31, we concluded the year with a solemn watch-night.[37]

Wednesday, January 1, 1783. May I begin to live to-day! Sunday 5, we met to renew our covenant with God. We never meet on this occasion without a blessing. But I do not know that we had ever so large congregation before.[38]

Fri. 10. I paid one more visit to Mr. Perronet,[39] now in his 90th

---

[33] On the protracted bronchial trouble to which this led, see below, Dec. 15, 1782, Mar. 15-23, 1783.

[34] Here JW follows his usual custom of retiring to the house of a London lay friend, in this case his executor William Marriott (on whom see Jan. 15, 1771; 22:262, n.42 in this edn.), when there was writing to be done. As the Diary makes clear, the writing in this case was the laborious revision of the London class-papers conferring membership of the society. The Marriotts helped a good deal with this, and one member of the family became one of the earliest collectors of JW's letters and notebooks.

[35] On Thomas Maxfield, see May 20, 1739 (19:61, n. 5 in this edn.). He never fully recovered from this stroke, Atmore (*Memorial*, p. 269) noting that 'for some years before his death, he became very friendly with the Methodists; the preachers frequently supplied his chapel and preached to his congregation. He died very suddenly of a paralytic stroke, but undoubtedly he was prepared for the solemn change.' Cf. below, Feb. 2, 1783.

[36] Thomas Forfitt, of the parish of St. Luke, gentleman (1706-82), was connected with the Foundery society much of his life, and was a trustee of the City Road chapel for 3 years. Stevenson, *City Road*, pp. 181, 250, 557.

[37] For watch-night services, see Apr. 9, 1742 (19:258, n. 50 in this edn.).

[38] For covenant services, see Aug. 6, 1755 (21:23, n. 82 in this edn.).

[39] On Vincent Perronet, see Aug. 14, 1744 (20:35, n. 74 in this edn.).

year. I do not know so venerable a man. His understanding is little, if at all impaired, and his heart seems to be all love. A little longer, I hope, he will remain here to be a blessing to all that see and hear him.

5   Sun. 19. I preached at St. Thomas's Church[40] in the afternoon, and at St. Swithin's[41] in the evening. The tide is now turned, so that I have more invitations to preach in churches than I can accept of.

Saturday, February 1. I drank tea at Mr. A———'s in the Maze-
10 pond, Southwark. But both Mr. A——— and his wife informed me, they were determined to quit the house as soon as possible by reason of strange noises which they heard day and night, but in the night chiefly, as if all the tables and chairs had been thrown up and down in the rooms above and under them.

15 Sun. 2. Mr. Maxfield continuing ill, I preached this afternoon at his chapel. Prejudice seems now dying away. God grant it may never revive. Tuesday 11, I buried the remains of Sarah Clay,[42] many years a mother in Israel; the last of those holy women, who, being filled with love, forty years ago devoted themselves wholly
20 to God, to spend and be spent in his service. Her death was like her life, calm and easy. She was dressing herself when she dropped down and fell asleep.

Mon. 17. I had an opportunity of attending the lecture of that excellent man, Dr. Conyers.[43] He was quite an original: his 'mat-
25 ter' was very good, his 'manner' very bad. But it is enough that God owned him, both in the conviction and conversion of sinners.

Thur. 20. I went to Dorking and, in the afternoon, took a walk through the lovely gardens of Lord Grimston.[44] His father-in-law,

[40] St. Thomas's, Southwark, built 1702-3, then the chapel of the old St. Thomas's Hospital, now the Chapter House of Southwark Cathedral.

[41] On the church and rector of St. Swithin's, see above, Dec. 2, 1781.

[42] For Sarah Clay, see Jan. 28, 1774 (22:397, n. 31 in this edn.).

[43] For Richard Conyers, see Apr. 12, 1764 (21:452, n. 62, in this edn.).

[44] The estate at Bury Hill, about a mile south-west of Dorking (see map to W. Thorne, *The Garden of Surrey; or, A Sketch of Dorking* [Dorking, 1829]), here visited by JW, was created by Edward Walter M.P. of Stalbridge, Dorset, who 'accidentally seeing this country, was so pleased with it', that he bought properties till he was the principal landowner in the parish, and built a mansion at Bury Hill where he resided till his death in 1780. His daughter Harriet married James Bucknell Grimston, Viscount Grimston and Baron Duboyne in the Irish peerage (1747-1808), whose roots were in Hertfordshire. He was M.P. for St. Albans, 1783-84, and for Hertfordshire, 1784-90, when he was created Baron Verulam of Gorhambury, Herts. Harriet died in 1787, and on the

who laid them out, is some time since numbered with the dead. And his son-in-law, living elsewhere, has not so much as 'the beholding them with his eyes!'[45]

Fri. 21. At our yearly meeting for that purpose, we examined our yearly accounts and found the money received, (just answering the expense) was upwards of three thousand pounds a year. But that is nothing to *me*. What I receive of it yearly is neither more nor less than thirty pounds.

To-day Charles Greenwood[46] went to rest. He had been a melancholy man all his days, full of doubts and fears, and continually writing bitter things against himself. When he was first taken ill, he said he should die, and was miserable through fear of death. But two days before he died, the clouds dispersed, and he was unspeakably happy, telling his friends, 'God has revealed to me things which it is impossible for man to utter.' Just when he died, such glory filled the room that it seemed to be a little heaven —none could grieve or shed a tear, but all present appeared to be partakers of his joy.

Mon. 24. I buried the remains of Captain Cheesement,[47] one who, some years since, from a plentiful fortune, was by a train of losses utterly ruined. But two or three friends enabling him to

death of her husband in 1808, their son, the second Baron, sold the whole of the estates at Dorking. With the exception of an artificial lake 'judiciously managed' to look like a river, 'the general aspect of this estate [was] that of genuine and unadorned rusticity, without any of those costly elegancies and embellishments (so-called), which often tend to divest Nature of her sweetest charms.' J. Timbs, *A Picturesque Promenade round Dorking* (London, 1822), pp. 111-16.

[45] Cf. Eccles. 5:11.

[46] Charles Greenwood (1726-83) was the son of James Greenwood, and an early member of the select society at the Foundery (Stevenson, *City Road,* p. 33), and was himself one of the trustees of the City Road Chapel. He and his wife, Mary, have already appeared, nursing Fletcher of Madeley through a serious illness in their Stoke Newington home (see above, July 30, 1777), and they also provided a quiet retreat for JW's literary work. Greenwood was a successful upholsterer by trade, and a sidesman at St. Mary's, Stoke Newington. An account of his last hours was published in *Arminian Magazine* 6 (1783):306, 361, which was republished as a pamphlet including verses by CW. Stevenson, *City Road,* pp. 65, 81, 361-67, 448, 523; Luke Tyerman, *Wesley's Designated Successor; the Life, Letters, and Literary Labours of the Rev. John William Fletcher* (London, 1882), pp. 372-73, 382, 390, 392, 409, 432-33, 460, 516, 541. For Mary Greenwood, see Dec. 18, 1787.

[47] John Cheesement (1731-83) was born at Seaton, near Sunderland, and his money was made at sea. He was one of the first trustees of the City Road Chapel. The maritime style of this entry was sustained even more flamboyantly on his tombstone; Stevenson, *City Road,* pp. 81, 522-23. His widow married George Wolff (1736-1828), sometime Consul General to the court of Denmark, his native country, the last surviving executor of JW's will, and a liberal subscriber to Methodist causes. *Wesleyan Methodist Magazine* 51 (1828):286.

begin trade again, the tide turned; he prospered greatly, and riches flowed in on every side. A few years ago he married one equally agreeable in her person and temper. So what had he to do but enjoy himself? Accordingly he left off business, took a large,
5 handsome house, and furnished it in a most elegant manner. A little while after, showing his rooms to a friend, he said, 'All this will give small comfort in a dying hour.' A few days after, he was taken with a fever. I saw him twice. He was sensible, but could not speak. In spite of all means, he grew worse and worse, and in
10 about twelve days died. So within a few days we lost two of our richest[48] and two of our holiest members: Sarah Clay[49] and good old George Hufflet,[50] who had been for many years a burning and a shining light. He lay fourteen weeks praising God continually and had then a triumphant entrance into his kingdom.
15 Sunday, March 2. In the evening I took coach, and the next evening preached at Bath. Thursday 6, I went on to Bristol and found a family of love, so united as it had not been for some years. The next week I met the classes, and on Friday had a watch-night at Kingswood. But I was far from being well, the cold which I
20 caught in coming from Luton, rather increasing than decreasing. Saturday 15, I had a deep, tearing cough and was exceeding heavy and weak. However, I made shift to preach at Weavers' Hall and to meet the penitents. Sunday 15, I found myself considerably worse. However, I preached in the morning, but had such a fever
25 in the afternoon that I was obliged to take my bed.

I now knew not what to do, having fixed the next morning for beginning my journey into Ireland, and sent notice to Stroud, Gloucester, and various other places, of the days wherein I proposed to visit them! But Mr. Collins[51] kindly undertook to supply
30 my place at Stroud and the other places, as far as Worcester.

Lying down in bed I took part (being able to swallow no more) of a draught which was prepared for me.[52] It gave me four or five

---

[48] Charles Greenwood and John Cheesement.

[49] On whom see Jan. 28, 1774; 22:397, n. 31 in this edn.; and above, Feb. 11, 1783.

[50] George Hufflet (1726-83) of Grey Eagle Street, Spitalfields, had been JW's host at lunch as recently as Jan. 18 (see Diary; Stevenson, *City Road*, pp. 82, 523). JW had commended him in December 1780 as one who had 'far more *clear ideas of the life of faith* than' the 'honest George Clark' (Telford, 7:43). Hufflet's name suggests that he was descended from the old Huguenot community in Spitalfields.

[51] For Brian Bury Collins, see above, June 2, 1782.

[52] At the house of Ezekiel King, tallow chandler. *Methodist Recorder* (Aug. 20, 1903), p. 11.

and twenty stools and a moderate vomit, after which I fell fast asleep. Monday 17. Mr. Collins set out. About six in the morning, finding myself perfectly easy, I set out in the afternoon and over-took him at Stroud. But it was as much as I could do, for I was in a high fever, though without any pain. After giving a short exhorta-tion to the society, I was very glad to lie down. My fever was exactly of the same kind with that I had in the North of Ireland.[53] On Monday, Tuesday, Wednesday, and Thursday, I was just the same: the whole nervous system was violently agitated. Hence arose the cramp, with little intermission, from the time I lay down in bed till morning. Also a furious, tearing cough, usually recur-ring before each fit of the cramp. And yet I had no pain in my back or head or limbs, the cramp only excepted. But I had no strength at all, being scarce able to move, and much less to think. In this state I lay, till on Friday morning, when a violent fit of the cramp carried the fever quite away. Perceiving this, I took chaise without delay, and reached Worcester in the afternoon. Here I overtook Mr. Collins again, who had supplied all my appointments, and with a remarkable blessing to the people. But being much exhausted, I found rest was sweet. Saturday 22 in the morning, I gave a short exhortation, and then went on to Birmingham.

Sun. 23. Finding still some remains of the fever, with a load and tightness across my breast, and a continual tendency to the cramp, I procured a friend to electrify me thoroughly, both through the legs and the breast several times in the day. God so blessed this that I had no more fever or cramp, and no more load or tightness across my breast. In the evening, I ventured to preach three quarters of an hour and found no ill effect at all!

Tue. 25. In the afternoon I reached Hilton Park,[54] about six miles North of Wolverhampton. Here I found my old acquain-tance, Miss Freeman (whom I had known almost from a child),[55]

[53] Between June 13 and 28, 1775, when his life had been despaired of.

[54] Hilton Park was the estate of Sir Philip Gibbes. JW redeemed the hospitality some-what unflatteringly to write some 'Thoughts upon Dissipation' for the *Arminian Maga-zine* 8 (1785):643.

[55] JW had certainly sustained a correspondence of sorts with Miss Freeman for over a quarter of a century, complaining regularly that she did not answer his letters (Telford, 3:215; 4:159; 7:177, 275). CW also enthused at this time about 'our dear Miss Freeman'; *CWJ* 2:282. Just before his death in 1788, however, CW 'prayed, with many tears, for all his enemies, naming Miss Freeman. "I beseech thee, O Lord, by thine agony and bloody sweat . . . that she may never feel the pangs of eternal death" '; Jackson, *Charles Wesley*, 2:443. JW's correspondence contains a hint that the cause of the revulsion was

with Sir Philip Gibbes's lady and his two amiable daughters in a lovely recess. With these I spent this evening and the next day both profitably and agreeably.

Thur. 27. I crossed over the country to Hinckley and preached in the evening in the neat, elegant preaching-house. So I did morning and evening on the three following days to a serious, well-behaved people.

Here I met with Dr. Horne's Commentary on the *Psalms*,[56] I suppose the best that ever was wrote. Yet I could not comprehend his aggrandizing the *Psalms*, it seems, even above the New Testament. And some of them he hardly makes anything of, the eighty-seventh in particular.

Tuesday, April 1, etc., I went through several of the societies[57] till I reached Holyhead on Friday 11. We went on board without delay and, on Sunday morning the 13th, landed at Dunleary; whence (not being able to procure a carriage) I walked on to Dublin.

Here I spent two or three weeks with much satisfaction in my usual employments. Monday 21, I spent an hour with Mr. Skelton,[58]

that it was Miss Freeman who persuaded Charles's younger son, Samuel, to join the Roman Catholic Church, in which fold he remained for a number of years; Telford, 8:47: 7:230-31. But at the time of this entry, JW was able to give a favourable picture of the Hilton household and of Miss Freeman's role in it. 'Lady Gibbes put me in mind of one of Queen Elizabeth's dames of honour. Her daughters were exceedingly amiable, but sink under Miss Freeman's superior sense, and begin to feel that they are not Christians. She has been of great service to them, and hies at them day and night to show them what is real religion. On Wednesday night they were much struck; the younger sister could not contain herself, but burst out into a passion of tears. M. F. herself seems utterly disconcerted, seeking rest but finding none. If Sally [CW's daughter] is not hurt by her, she (Sally) will help her much.' Telford, 7:173.

[56] George Horne, *A Commentary on the Book of Psalms* (1776). JW's criticism seems harsh, though Horne started from the position that 'the Psalms are an epitome of the Bible adapted to the progress of devotion . . . [affording us] in perfection, though in miniature, everything that groweth elsewhere,' and set out to elucidate 'the *prophetical, evangelical, mystical* or *spiritual* sense' in which they testified to the Christ. Psalm 87 ('His foundation is in the holy mountains') is indeed treated somewhat flatly as an archetype of the church under the figure of Jerusalem, but concludes (as JW might have been expected to approve) with a paean upon the new birth as 'the only birth which we ought to value ourselves upon, because that alone gives us our title to "the inheritance of the saints in light".' *Commentary* (London, 1820), 1:v, vi, x; 2:70-73.

[57] These included Nottingham, where JW preached on April 6 (as his Diary shows) and, with the assistance of Coke, opened the new chapel at Hockley; cf. Harwood, *Nottingham*, p. 55; R. C. Swift, *Lively People—Methodism in Nottingham, 1740-1929* (Nottingham, 1982), p. 21. Cf. below, p. 308, n. 75.

[58] Orig., 'Shelton'. On Philip Skelton, see June, 14, 1771; 22:281, n. 12 in this edn. Samuel Bradburn in his note on the Journal says the name was Shetton. *WHS* 19 (1934):115.

I think full as extraordinary a man as Mr. Law:[59] of full as rapid a genius, so that I had little to do but *to hear*, his words flowing as a river.

Tue. 29. Our little Conference began and continued till Friday, May 2. All was peace and love, and I trust the same spirit will spread through the nation.[60]

Sat. 3. I made a little excursion to a nobleman's seat, a few miles from Dublin. It may doubtless vie in elegance, if not in costliness, with any seat in Great Britain. But the miserable master of the whole has little satisfaction therein. God hath said, 'Write this man childless.' For whom then does he heap up these things? He is himself growing old.[61]

> And must he leave this paradise? Then leave
> These happy shades, and mansions fit for gods?[62]

Sun. 4. There was an ordination at St. Patrick's. I admired the solemnity wherewith the Archbishop[63] went through the service. But the vacant faces of the ordained showed how little they were affected thereby. In the evening, multitudes met to renew their covenant with God. But here was no vacant face to be seen. For God was in the midst and manifested himself to many, particularly to a daughter of good William Penington.[64]

---

[59] William Law (1686-1761), the author of *A Serious Call to a Devout and Holy Life* (1729).

[60] In a letter to CW JW enlarged: 'We had an exceedingly *happy Conference*, which concluded this morning. I wish all our English preachers were of the same spirit as the Irish, among whom is no jarring string. I never saw such simplicity and teachableness run through a body of preachers before.' Telford, 7:177.

[61] Henry Loftus, Viscount Loftus of Ely and Baron Loftus of Loftus Hall in the Irish peerage (1709-83), created Earl of Ely in the Irish peerage in 1771. He died (in England) barely a fortnight after JW's visit to his estate, and all his honours became extinct.

[62] Altered from Milton's *Paradise Lost*, xi.269-71. Cf. above, p. 104, and Aug. 13, 1759 (21:225, n. 49 in this edn.).

[63] Robert Fowler (?1726-1801), Archbishop of Dublin from 1779. Fowler had been educated at Trinity College, Cambridge, graduating B.A. 1747, M.A. 1751, and D.D. 1764. He was chaplain to George II 1758, and prebendary of Westminster 1765. His first Irish preferment was to the see of Killaloe, 1771. His solemnity of manner was also noted by Philip Skelton; S. Burdy, *Life of Skelton* prefaced to *The Complete Works of the late Philip Skelton*, 6 vols. (London, 1824), 1:118. In 1782, Fowler with 12 other spiritual peers protested in the Irish House of Lords against a bill for the relief of Dissenters. *Gentleman's Magazine* 71 (1801):965, 1049.

[64] On William Penington, see above, Mar. 11, 1765 (21:500, n. 90 in this edn.). Miss Penington (b. *c.* 1767) had been converted, or brought to the brink of conversion, under the ministry of John Bredin at Athlone in 1781; Crookshank, *Ireland*, 1:354. She subsequently married a converted soldier, Joseph Burgess (1757-1839), who in 1790 became a Methodist itinerant of note; *Wesleyan Methodist Magazine* 62 (1839):420, 763; 63

Mon. 5. We prepared for going on board the packet.. But as it delayed sailing, on Tuesday 6, I waited on Lady Arabella Denny[65] at the Blackrock, four miles from Dublin. It is one of the pleasantest spots I ever saw. The garden is everything in miniature. On one side is a grove with serpentine walks, on the other is a little meadow and a green-house with a study (which she calls her chapel) hanging over the sea. Between these is a broad walk leading down almost to the edge of the water, along which run two narrow walks commanding the quay, one above the other. But it cannot be long before this excellent lady will remove to a nobler paradise.

The unusually large congregation in the evening was plentifully watered with the dew of heaven. I found a particular concern for the children, many of whom willingly attended.

Wed. 7. The packet still delaying, I exhorted a large congregation in the evening to take care how they 'built their house upon the sand',[66] and then cheerfully commended them to the grace of God!

Thur. 8. We rose at one, went down to the quay at two, and about four went on board the Hillsborough packet.[67] About five the wind turned fair, and between five and six in the evening brought us to Holyhead. About seven we took coach, and the next evening met our friends at Chester.[68]

(1840):537-56. Their son, William Penington Burgess (1780-1868), after teaching at Kingswood, became a Methodist minister and hymnologist; *Wesleyan Methodist Magazine* 91 (1868):947.

[65] Lady Arabella Fitzmaurice (1707-92), second daughter of Thomas Fitzmaurice, first Earl of Kerry (and hence, aunt of the Earl of Shelburne), married Arthur Denny of Tralee, M.P. for Co. Kerry, who died childless in 1742. Lady Denny subsequently devoted ample means to charitable causes, and in 1765 received the thanks of the Irish parliament, the freedom of the Guild of Merchants, and that of the City of Dublin for her charities to foundling children. In 1766, she founded the Magdalen Asylum in Dublin. On her death the Royal Irish Academy offered a prize medal worth 100 guineas for the best monody on the occasion, 'that esteemed lady's virtues and angelic life certainly afford[ing] an opportunity for touching the most delicate keys of the human heart'; *WHS* 5 (1905):73. Her estate, later known as Lisinaskea, was situated on the south side of Dublin bay between Blackrock and Williamstown, in an area of aristocratic houses and villas; many of the elms which bordered the broad-walk described by JW were destroyed in a great storm of Feb. 26, 1903. See also Edmund George Petty-Fitzmaurice, *Life of William, Earl of Shelburne*, 2 vols. (London, 1912), 1:5, 8-9.

[66] Cf. Matt. 7:26.

[67] Captain John Shaw.

[68] One of whom was George Walker, a Chester goldsmith (*The Chester Guide* [Chester, 1782], p.109), who had a handsome estate near Tarporley. He was a trustee of both the Octagon and John Street chapels. J. Janion, *Some Account of the Introduction of Methodism into the City and Some Part of the County of Chester* (Chester, 1833), pp. 30, 68.

Mon. 12. About eight, I preached at Preston on the Hill; about twelve, in Warrington; and in the evening, at Liverpool. Here the scandal of the cross seems to be ceased, and we are grown honourable men. Thursday 15, I preached about noon at Wigan, and in the evening at Bolton to a people much alive to God. Saturday 17, I went on to Manchester. Sunday 18, Mr. Bayley[69] came very opportunely to assist me in the morning service. Such a sight I believe was never seen at Manchester before. It was supposed there were thirteen or fourteen hundred communicants, among whom there was such a spirit as I have seldom found, and their whole behaviour was such as adorned the gospel.

Tue. 20. I met the select society,[70] consisting of between forty and fifty members. Several of these were lately made partakers of the great salvation, as several were above twenty years ago. I believe there is no place but London where we have so many souls so deeply devoted to God. And his hand is not shortened yet, but his work rapidly increases on every side.

About noon I preached at Stockport, and in the afternoon in the new church at Macclesfield.[71] This society seems as lively as even that at Manchester, and increases nearly as fast. Not a week passes wherein some are not justified and some renewed in love. Wednesday 21, I met a few of these and found them indeed

All praise, all meekness, and all love.[72]

[69] Orig., 'Bailey'. Cornelius Bayley (1751-1812), was a master at Kingswood School, 1773-83. While at Kingswood he published a Hebrew grammar entitled *An Entrance into the Sacred Language* (London, 1782), to which JW (for four copies) and numerous other Methodist preachers (including Adam Clarke) subscribed. After leaving Kingswood, Bayley obtained episcopal ordination, and built St. James's, Manchester, for himself in 1787. This church was much used by Manchester Methodists for sermon and sacrament, but at the turn of the eighteenth century Bayley was one of the Anglican clergy most active in breaking up the undenominational Sunday school in which Methodists were deeply involved, and establishing a system under exclusive church control; Ward, *Religion and Society*, pp. 40-41. He was admitted at Trinity College, Cambridge in 1789, and matriculated in 1792. He published a good deal and received the degrees of B.D. and D.D. from Cambridge in 1792 and 1800. It was Bayley's marriage at Buxton (see below, May 25, 1783) at which JW officiated the following week; *Wesleyan Methodist Magazine* 68 (1845):13n. His cooperation with JW at this stage is illustrated in *WHS* 9 (1914):193, but his later career reveals him as a leading member of a group of prickly evangelicals in the church of Wesleyan rather than Calvinist origin.
[70] Orig., 'Society Select'. For the select society, see Oct. 13, 1749 (20:307, n. 66 in this edn.).
[71] Christ Church, Macclesfield, built for David Simpson in 1775.
[72] CW, *Short Hymns on Scripture*, 2:49, line 8 of Charles's hymn no. 1391 on Ezekiel 36:26; *Poetical Works*, 10:57; see also *Collection of Hymns* (1780), no. 332, line 16 (7:489 in this edn.). See also above, June 9, 1777.

In the evening I exhorted them all to expect pardon or holiness *today*, not *tomorrow*. O let their love never grow cold!

Fri. 23. I set out for Derby, but the smith had so effectually lamed one of my horses that many told me he would never be able to travel more. I thought, 'Even this may be made matter of prayer,' and set out cheerfully. The horse, instead of growing worse and worse, went better and better and, in the afternoon (after I had preached at Leek by the way), brought me safe to Derby.

Sat. 24. Being desired to marry two of our friends at Buxton,[73] two and thirty miles from Derby, I took chaise at three and came thither about eight. I found notice had been given of my preaching in the church, and the minister[74] desired me to read prayers. By this means I could not leave Buxton till eleven, nor reach Nottingham till after seven, whereas I was to have preached at six. But Mr. Brackenbury[75] came to town just in time to supply my place.

Sun. 25. I had an easy day's work, as Mr. Bayley assisted me by reading prayers and delivering the wine at the Lord's Table.

Tue. 27. I preached at Loughborough in the morning, and at Mountsorrel[76] at one. While I was preaching, the rain which was so much wanted began and continued for eight and forty hours. In the evening, I preached at Leicester, where I always feel much liberty and yet see but little fruit. After preaching at Northampton, Bedford, and Hinxworth, on Saturday 31, I returned to London.

Sunday, June 1. I was refreshed by the very sight of the congregation at the New Chapel. Monday 2 and the following days, I employed in settling my business and preparing for my little excursion.[77] Wednesday 11, I took coach with Mr. Brackenbury,

---

[73] The wedding was that of Cornelius Bayley and Rachel Norton, who appears (from the Diary only) to have travelled up from Derby with JW in the chaise.

[74] The incumbent of St. Anne's, Buxton, was John Mellor. 'Prayers are read, during the season, in the assembly room, the chapel at Buxton being too small and in too ruinous a state for the company. The allowance for the minister is defrayed by subscription.' D. P. Davies, *A New and Historical View of Derbyshire* (Belper, 1811), pp. 623–24.

[75] On R. C. Brackenbury, see above, July 9, 1776.

[76] Mountsorrel was a decaying market town 7 1/2 miles north of Leicester, which produced stockings, lace and road-metal, and became a hotbed of dissent. Lewis, *England*, 3:310.

[77] JW had been invited to the Netherlands by William Ferguson (1735–1804) of Hoxton, a member and local preacher in the London society, who had handled his publications for circulation in the Netherlands since at least 1774. Facing bankruptcy in 1777, he went to Holland on the advice of his wife, Cecily Godbehave, apparently dealing in clocks and

Broadbent,[78] and Whitfield,[79] and in the evening we reached Harwich. I went immediately to Dr. Jones,[80] who received me in the most affectionate manner. About nine in the morning, we sailed and, at nine on Friday 13, landed at Hellevoetsluis. Here we[81] hired a coach for Brielle,[82] but were forced to hire a waggon also to   5 carry a box which one of us could have carried on his shoulders. At Brielle, we took a boat to Rotterdam. We had not been long there when Mr. Bennet,[83] a bookseller who had invited me to his house, called for me. But as Mr. Layal,[84] the Minister of the

watches, silver and gold, and created a successful business at The Hague. He quickly found spiritual fellowship and assistance with the language, and when he planned to return to England permanently he received so many invitations to come back that he felt obliged to do so in 1778. He was now introduced to the Prince of Orange, and became a citizen of The Hague. By 1780, he was deeply involved with Dutch groups sustaining a warm philadelphian piety, and had put them in touch with English Methodism. Among them were members of the social elite, and the groups JW met through his agency were one of the sources of the later revival movement in Holland. The Dutch lay preacher G. T. Beughel described how 'the Englishman Ferguson, who had a ship in Amsterdam, and a factory in London . . . was a preacher with the Methodists, and prevented from going to England by the war. He said he did not like to be silent, so he began work in Amsterdam, and announced that he did not mind what people said of him if he knew his end was proper, and he was right. This was a necessary lesson for every private Christian.' He belonged to the circle of the well-known Rotterdam preacher, J. L. Verster, a friend of the Moravians and a founder of the Dutch Missionary Society. Ferguson, who thus formed abiding connections in the Netherlands, was a native of Kelso, who had a devout and somewhat emotional upbringing. He subsequently fell out with the blasphemers and smugglers of Holy Island, was drawn into Newcastle Methodism, and deeply impressed by the preaching of JW himself. Receiving a vivid call to preach, he began to labour in the Alnwick area, but contrived to offend both the general public and his Methodist brethren. Another providential call brought him to London to work as a watchmaker. His son, Jonathan (1765–1845), acted as JW's interpreter. Jan van den Berg, 'John Wesley's Contacten met Nederland', *Nederlands Archief voor Kerkgeschiedenis*, N.S. 52 (1971):62–86; Moore, *Wesley*, 2:285–89; *WHS* 7 (1909):89; *Arminian Magazine* 5 (1782):292–97, 346–51; *Wesleyan Methodist Magazine* 68 (1845):292.

[78] On John Broadbent, see above, Aug. 17, 1779.

[79] On George Whitfield, JW's travelling companion, see above, Aug. 19, 1781.

[80] On John Jones, formerly a master at Kingswood and now vicar of Harwich, see Nov. 30, 1746 (20:150, n. 3 in this edn.).

[81] The party included, besides those already mentioned, JW's niece, Sarah Wesley. Telford, 7:181.

[82] Orig. 'Briel'. Brielle was an old fortified town about 10 kilometres north of Hellevoetsluis and across the river from Rotterdam. It was the first place to be captured by the 'sea-beggars' in 1572; Mary II is said to have seen her husband William off to England from Hellevoetsluis in 1688 from the top of Brielle church tower.

[83] Lambert Bennet, bookseller and politician of Orangist sympathies, had published a Dutch edition of the letter of James Hervey defending his *Theron and Aspasio* against JW. Van den Berg, 'Wesley's Contacten', p. 71; K. C. Hazewinkel, 'Rotterdamers Boekverkopers', in *Opstellen aangeboden an Dr. F. K. H. Kossman* (The Hague, 1958), pp. 35–58.

[84] Orig., 'Loyal'. Alexander Layal, a native of Melrose (*c.* 1739–96), was preacher at the Scots church in Rotterdam, 1770–96, having served the Scots church at Dordrecht,

Scotch congregation, had invited me, he gave up his claim and
went with us to Mr. Layal's. I found a friendly sensible, hospitable, and, I am persuaded, a pious man. We took a walk
together round the town, all as clean as a gentleman's parlour.
5 Many of the houses are as high as those in the main street at
Edinburgh, and the canals running through the chief streets make
them convenient as well as pleasant, bringing the merchants
goods up to their doors. Stately trees grow on all their banks. The
whole town is encompassed with a double row of elms, so that one
10 may walk all round it in the shade.

Sat. 14. I had much conversation with the two English ministers,[85] sensible, well-bred, serious men. These, as well as Mr.
Layal, were very willing I should preach in their churches, but
they thought it would be best for me to preach in the Episcopal
15 church.[86] By our conversing freely together, many prejudices were
removed, and all our hearts seemed to be united together.

In the evening, we again took a walk round the town, and I
observed: (1) Many of the houses are higher than most in Edinburgh. It is true, they have not so many stories, but each story is
20 far loftier. (2) The streets, the outside and inside of their houses
in every part, doors, windows, well-staircases, furniture, even
floors, are kept so nicely clean that you cannot find a speck of dirt.
(3) There is such a grandeur and elegance in the fronts of the
large houses as I never saw elsewhere, and such a profusion of
25 marble within, particularly in the lower floors and stair-cases, as I
wonder other nations do not imitate. (4) The women and children
(which I least of all expected) were in general the most beautiful I
ever saw. They were surprisingly fair and had an inexpressible air
of innocence in their countenance. (5) This was wonderfully set

1766–70. He was a Hebraist, and a student of prophecy who had published a pamphlet
on the downfall of the Turks. He was educated at Edinburgh, where he was a favourite
pupil of James Robinson. He was also celebrated for greatly developing the musical life
of the Scots Church in Rotterdam. W. Stevens, *The History of the Scottish Church, Rotterdam* (Edinburgh, 1832), pp. 203, 228; Scott, *Fasti*, 7:552; H. H. Barger, *J.Scharp. Een
predikent uit den patriottentijd* (Rotterdam, 1906), p. 54; Van den Berg, 'Wesley's Contacten', p. 72.

[85] I.e., the two ministers of the English Presbyterian church in Rotterdam, Thomas
Greaves, minister from 1755, and John Hall (1740–1829), minister from 1779 (Stevens,
Scottish Church, pp. 229, 335; Wilson, *Dissenting Churches*, 1:183). The 'prejudices'
doubtless arose from Calvinist mistrust of Arminians.

[86] JW had visited this church on Sept. 8, 1738 (19:12 in this edn.) and was to preach here
again on Aug. 13, 1786. The chaplain of this church, 1777–94, when he returned to England with ill-health, was William Williams, M.A. Stevens, *Scottish Church*, 329–30, 332.

off by their dress, which was *simplex munditis*, plain and neat in
the highest degree. (6) It has lately been observed that growing
vegetables greatly resist putridity. So there is an use in their
numerous rows of trees, which was not thought of at first. The
elms balance the canals, preventing the putrefaction which those   5
otherwise might produce.

One little circumstance I observed which I suppose is peculiar
to Holland. To most chamber-windows a looking-glass is placed
on the outside of the sash so as to show the whole street with all
the passengers; there is something very pleasing in these moving   10
pictures. Are they found in no other country?

Sun. 15. The Episcopal church is not quite so large as the
chapel in West Street. It is very elegant both without and within.
The service began at half past nine. Such a congregation had not
often been there before. I preached on 'God created man in his   15
own image.'[87] The people 'Seemed, all but their attention, dead.'[88]
In the afternoon the church was so filled, as (they informed me) it
had not been for these fifty years. I preached on, 'God hath given
us eternal life, and this life is in his Son.'[89] I believe God applied it
to many hearts. Were it only for this hour, I am glad I came to   20
Holland.

One thing which I peculiarly observed was this, and the same
in all the churches in Holland. At coming in, no one looks on the
right or the left hand or bows or curtsies to anyone, but all go
straight forward to their seats, as if no other person was in the   25
place. During the service, none turns his head on either side or
looks at anything but his book or the Minister. And in going out,
none takes notice of any one, but all go straight forward till they
are in the open air.

After church, an English gentleman invited me to his country-   30
house, not half a mile from the town. I scarce ever saw so pretty a
place. The garden before the house was in three partitions, each
quite different from the others. The house lay between this and
another garden, (nothing like any of the others) from which you
looked through a beautiful summer-house, washed by a small   35
stream, into rich pastures filled with cattle. We sat under an
arbour of stately trees between the front and back gardens. Here

[87] Gen. 1:27.
[88] Cf. William Congreve, *On Mrs. Arabella Hunt singing*, ver. 1, l. 12, in *Works*, 3:875.
See above, Oct. 16, 1778, and n.
[89] 1 John 5:11.

were four such children (I suppose seven, six, five, and three years old) as I never saw before in one family. Such inexpressible beauty and innocence shone together!

In the evening I attended the service of the great Dutch church,[90] as large as most of our cathedrals. The organ (like those in all the Dutch churches) was elegantly painted and gilded. And the tunes that were sung were very lively and yet solemn.

Mon. 16. We set out in a *trekschuit*[91] for the Hague. By the way we saw a curiosity: the gallows near the canal, surrounded with a knot of beautiful trees. So the dying man will have one pleasant prospect here, whatever befalls him hereafter! At eleven we came to Delft, a large, handsome town, where we spent an hour at a merchant's house, who, as well as his wife, a very agreeable woman, seemed both to fear and to love God. Afterwards we saw the great church,[92] I think nearly, if not quite, as long as York Minster. It is exceeding light and elegant within, and every part is kept exquisitely clean. The tomb of William the First is much admired, particularly his statue, which has more life than one would think could be expressed in brass.

When we came to the Hague, though we had heard much of it, we were not disappointed. It is indeed beautiful beyond expression. Many of the houses are exceeding grand and are finely intermixed with water and wood; yet not too close, but so as to be sufficiently ventilated by the air.

Being invited to tea by Madam de Wassenaar[93] (one of the first quality in The Hague), I waited upon her in the afternoon. She received us with that easy openness and affability, which is almost peculiar to Christians and persons of quality. Soon after, came ten or twelve ladies more, who seemed to be of her own rank (though dressed quite plain), and two most agreeable gentlemen, one of whom, I afterwards understood, was a colonel in the Prince's Guards. After tea, I expounded the three first verses of the thir-

---

[90] St. Laurenskerk.

[91] Orig. 'Track-skuit'. In Dutch 'trekschuit', or, in English, 'track-boat', a canal-barge towed from the tow-path.

[92] The Nieuwe Kerk. The building of this church commenced in 1381; it contains the family vault of the House of Orange.

[93] Orig. 'Vassenaar'. Anna, Baroness von Wassenaer (1716-1801), became the second wife of Wilhelm, Baron von Wassenaer (1712-83) in 1757. If Boswell was accurate with his titles, she could not have been the Mlle. Wassenaer with whom he danced 'one country-dance' in 1764. James Boswell, *Boswell in Holland, 1763-64*, ed. F. A. Pottle (London, 1952), p. 262.

teenth of the First Epistle to the Corinthians. Captain M——[94] interpreted, sentence by sentence. I then prayed, and Colonel V—— after me. I believe this hour was well employed.

Tue. 17. As we walked over the place, we saw the Swiss Guards at their exercise. They are a fine body of men, taller, I suppose, than any English regiment. And they all wear large whiskers, which they take care to keep as black as their boots. Afterwards, we saw the gardens at the old palace,[95] beautifully laid out, with a large piece of water in the middle and a canal at each end. The open walks in it are pleasant, but the shady, serpentine walks are far pleasanter.

We dined at Mrs. L——'s,[96] in such a family as I have seldom seen. Her mother, upwards of seventy, seemed to be continually rejoicing in God her Saviour. The daughter breathes the same spirit, and her grandchildren, three little girls and a boy, seem to be all love. I have not seen four such children together in all England. A gentleman coming in after dinner, I found a particular desire to pray for him. In a little while, he melted into tears, as indeed did most of the company. Wednesday 18 in the afternoon, Madam de Wassenaar invited us to a meeting at a neighbouring lady's house. I expounded Gal. 6:14, and Mr. M. interpreted as before.

Thur. 19. We took boat at seven. Mrs. L. and one of her relations, being unwilling to part so soon, bore us company to Leyden, a large and populous town, but not so pleasant as Rotterdam. In the afternoon we went on to Haarlem,[97] where a plain, good man and his wife received us in a most affectionate manner. At six we took boat again. As it was filled from end to end, I was afraid we should not have a very pleasant journey. After Mr. Ferguson had told the people who we were, we made a slight excuse and sung an hymn. They were all attention. We then talked a little, by means of our interpreter, and desired that any of them who pleased would sing. Four persons did so and sung well; after awhile, we sung again. So did one or two them, and all our hearts

[94] Kapitein Muyssen. Van den Berg, 'Wesley's Contacten', p. 76.
[95] Not the Binnenhof as noted by Curnock, but the Oude Hof, dating from 1565, and now with the Tourist Information Office annexed.
[96] Mrs. M. F. Loten was the mother of the young woman who became JW's most enthusiastic supporter in Holland, Johanna Carolina Arnodina Loten (on whom see below, June 26, 1783) and was the wife of Arnoud Loten, mayor of Utrecht.
[97] Orig., 'Haerlem'.

were strangely knit together, so that when we came to Amsterdam, they dismissed us with abundance of blessings.

Fri. 20. We breakfasted at Mr. Ferguson's, near the heart of the city. At eleven we drank coffee (the custom in Holland) at Mr. J——
—'s, a merchant,[98] whose dining-room is covered, both walls and ceiling, with the most beautiful paintings. He and his lady walked with us in the afternoon to the stadt-house, perhaps the grandest building of the kind in Europe. The great hall is a noble room indeed, near as large as that of Christ Church in Oxford.[99] But I have neither time nor inclination to describe particularly this amazing structure.

At five in the evening we drank tea at another merchant's, Mr. G——'s,[1] where I had a long conversation with Mr. de H——,[2] one of the most learned as well as popular ministers in the city, and (I believe what is far more important) he is truly alive to God. He spoke Latin well, and seemed to be one of a strong understanding, as well as of an excellent spirit. In returning to our inn, we called at a stationers,[3] and though we spent but a few minutes, it was enough to convince us of his strong affection, even to strangers. What a change does the grace of God make in the heart! Shyness and stiffness are now no more!

Sat. 21. We breakfasted with a very extraordinary woman,[4] who lamented that she could not talk to us but by an interpreter. However she made us understand that she had a little child some years since, three or four years old, that was praying continually; that

---

[98] This name appears in the Diary as 'Mr. Yoosden', perhaps Petrus Yoosten, who in 1794 bought a garden on town property in the new plantation in the middle road. JW also visited him in a house in the country 'in the Plantations' (see p. 288).

[99] For this comparison, see below, July 15, 1783.

[1] Probably Johann Ludwig Gregory, merchant and banker of Amsterdam (Van den Berg, 'Wesley's Contacten', p. 78, n. 1), father-in-law of the minister Allard Pierson from Alkmaar.

[2] Gerardus de Haas (1737-1817), minister in Amsterdam, 1781-1817, a man of Orangist sentiment. De Haas became a D. D. of Utrecht, and was a minister at Scharpenzeel, Amersfort, and Middelburg before serving in Amsterdam. He wrote poetry and Bible commentaries. P. C. Molhuysen, *Niew Nederlandsch Biografisch Woordenboek*, 11 vols. (Leiden, 1937), 3:519; Barend Glasius, *Godgeleerd Nederland; Biographisch Woordenboek van nederlandsche Godgeleerden*, 3 vols. (Hertogenbosch, 1851-56), 2:3.

[3] Petris Schouten, on whom see below, Aug. 19, 1786.

[4] The following story seems to be a bowdlerized and abbreviated version of 'A short account of two children at Amsterdam: in a letter from their mother', published in *Arminian Magazine* 7 (1784):591-92. The 'mother' of that paper (apparently the 'extraordinary woman' here) was born Hendrika Christina van Santbeek and married J. H. Rodenbeek in 1754.

one morning, having just dressed her, she said, 'Will you go kiss your sister!' She said, 'Yes, Mamma, and I will kiss *you* too,' and threw her arms about her mother's neck, who said, 'My dear, where will you go now?' She said, 'I will go to Jesus,' and died.

At eleven I spent an hour with a woman of large fortune,[5] who appeared to be as much devoted to God as her. We were immediately as well acquainted with each other as if we had known each other for many years. But indeed an easy good breeding (such as I never expected to see here) runs through all the genteeler people of Amsterdam. And there is such a childlike simplicity in all that love God as does honour to the religion they profess.

About two, we called upon Mr. V——n,[6] and immediately fell into close conversation. There seems to be in him a peculiar softness and sweetness of temper, and a peculiar liveliness in Mrs. V——n. Our loving dispute concerning deliverance from sin was concluded within an hour, and we parted, if that could be, better friends than we met. Afterwards we walked to Mr. J——'s house in the Plantations, a large tract of ground, laid out in shady walks. These lie within the city walls. But there are other walks, equally pleasant, without the gates. Indeed, nothing is wanting but the power of religion to make Amsterdam a paradise.

Sun. 22. I went to the New Church,[7] so called still, though four or five hundred years old. It is larger, higher, and better illuminated than most of our cathedrals. The screen that divides the church from the choir is of polished brass and shines like gold. I understood the psalms that were sung and the text well, and a little of the sermon, which Mr. de H—— delivered with great earnestness. At two, I began the service at the English church, an elegant building, about the size of West Street Chapel. Only it has no galleries; nor have any of the churches in Holland. I preached on Isaiah 55:6, 7, and I am persuaded many received the truth in the love thereof.

After service, I spent another hour at Mr. V——'s. Mrs. V——

[5] Cornelia Paulina van Valkenburg (1756–1822) who is introduced by name on JW's next visit, Aug. 18, 1786. She was the daughter of M. W. van Valkenburg, the mayor of Haarlem, and sister-in-law of Hieronymus van Alphen; she lived in a very large house on the Oude Gracht in Haarlem. JW seems to have been introduced to her by Miss Roucquet, who spoke English and French and seemed truly alive to God. She may have been the sister of the Haarlem doctor, Jacobus Rouquette, either Jeanne Marie (1738–1809) or Marie (1741–1809). Van den Berg, 'Wesley's Contacten', p. 87.

[6] This appears from the Diary to be 'Vanhousen', doubtless one of the two van Hoesens living in Amsterdam. Van den Berg, 'Wesley's Contacten', p. 78, n. 1.

[7] The building of this church began in 1408; it has been frequently damaged by fire, and since 1815 has been used for the coronation of Dutch monarchs.

— again asked me abundance of questions concerning deliverance from sin, and seemed a good deal better satisfied with regard to the great and precious promises. Thence we went to Mr. B.,[8] who had lately found peace with God. He was full of faith and love
5 and could hardly mention the goodness of God without tears. His wife appeared to be exactly of the same spirit, so that our hearts were soon knit together. From thence we went to another family, where a large company were assembled. But all seemed open to receive instructions and desirous to be altogether Christians.

10 After dinner, Mrs. J—— took me in a coach to the Mere, and thence round the country to Zeeburg. I never saw such a country before: I suppose there is no such summer country in Europe. From Amsterdam to Mere is all a train of the most delightful gardens. Turning upon the left, you then open upon the Texel,
15 which spreads into a sea. Zeeburg itself is a little house built on the edge of it, which commands both a land and sea prospect. What is wanting to make the inhabitants happy, but the knowledge and love of God?

Tue. 24. We took a view of the new workhouse, which stands
20 on one side of the Plantations. It much resembles Shoreditch Workhouse, only it is considerably larger. And the front of it is so richly ornamented that it looks like a royal palace. About four hundred are now in the house, which is to receive four hundred more, just half as many as are in the poorhouse at Dublin, which
25 now contains sixteen hundred. We saw many of the poor people, all at work, knitting, spinning, picking work, or weaving. And the women in one room were all sewing, either fine or plain work. Many of these had been women of the town, for this is a bridewell and workhouse in one. The head keeper was stalking to and fro
30 with a large silver-hilted sword by his side. The bedchambers were exceeding neat; the beds are better or worse, as are those that use them. We saw both the men in one long room, and the women in another at dinner. In both rooms, they sung a psalm and prayed before and after dinner. I cannot but think the man-
35 agers in Amsterdam wiser than those in Dublin. For certainly a little of the 'form of religion' is better than none at all!

Afterwards we spent an hour at Mrs. V——'s, a very extraordinary woman. Both from her past and present experience, I can have no doubt but she is 'perfected in love.' She said,

---

[8] Willem Box, the son of a schoolmaster. Van den Berg, 'Wesley's Contacten', p. 78, n. 1.

I was born at Surinam and came from thence when I was about ten years old. But when I came hither, my guardian would not let me have my fortune unless I would go back to Surinam. However, I got acquainted with some pious people, and made shift to live till I was about sixteen. I then embarked for Surinam, but a storm drove us to the coast of England, where the ship was stranded. I was in great distress, fearing I had done wrong in leaving the pious people. But just then God revealed himself to my soul. I was filled with joy unspeakable and boldly assured the people, who despaired of life, that God would preserve them all. And so he did; we got on shore at Devon. But we lost all that we had.

After a time, I returned to Amsterdam and lived four years in service. Then I married. Seven years after, it pleased God to work a deeper work in my heart. Since then I have given myself wholly to him. I desire nothing else. Jesus is my all. I am always pleased with his will. So I was, even when my husband died. I had not one discontented thought; I was still happy in God.

Wed. 25. We took boat for Haarlem. The great church[9] here is a noble structure equalled by few cathedrals in England, either in length, breadth, or height; the organ is the largest I ever saw, and is said to be the finest in Europe. Hence we went to Mr. Van Ka——'s,[10] whose wife was convinced of sin and justified by reading Mr. Whitefield's Sermons.

Here we were as at home. Before dinner we took a walk in Haarlem Wood. It adjoins to the town and is cut out in many shady walks, with lovely vistas shooting out every way. The walk from the Hague to Scheveling is pleasant; those near Amsterdam more so; but these exceed them all.

---

[9] The Groote Kerk of St. Bavo, completed in the sixteenth century, after more than a hundred years building. The organ was created by Christian Müller, 1735-38, and later played by Mozart. Frans Hals is buried here.

[10] JW was the guest of the van Kampen couple. It is not clear whether Willem van Kampen and his wife, or Willem's elder brother, Nicolaus van Kampen, and his wife, were the parents of the later Prof. N. G. van Kampen. The van Kampen family lived on a large nursery, the 'Cleraad van Flora', near the present Wilhelminapark, founded by the father of Nicolaus and Willem, who died in 1781, and founded an important bulb-exporting business which did active business in England. Old Mr. van Kampen was a Baptist who had formerly had strong Moravian sympathies; in the family circle there was a warm generous piety. In Willem's home they read Erasmus, Hugo de Groot, and Doddridge as well as the sermons of Whitefield here mentioned. Willem died at the end of October 1783 as the result of an accident; his widow then moved to town. So when JW stayed at the nursery again, Nicolaus was the host. It is clear that JW felt completely at home with the warm-hearted van Kampens. Van den Berg, 'Wesley's Contacten', p. 80.

We returned in the afternoon to Amsterdam, and in the evening took leave of as many of our friends as we could. How entirely were we mistaken in the Hollanders, supposing them to be of a cold, phlegmatic, unfriendly temper! I have not met with a more
5 warmly affectionate people in all Europe! No, not in Ireland!

Thur. 26. Our friends having largely provided us with wine and fruits for our little journey, we took boat in a lovely morning for Utretcht, with Mr. Van——'s sister, who in the way, gave us a striking account.

10   In that house, said she (pointing to it as we went by), my husband and I lived, and that church adjoining to it was his church. Five years ago, we were sitting together, being in perfect health, when he dropped down and, in a quarter of an hour, died. I lifted up my heart and said, 'Lord, thou art my husband now,' and
15 found no will but his.

This was a trial worthy of a Christian. And she has ever since made her word good. We were scarce got to our inn at Utrecht, when Miss L——[11] came. I found her just such as I expected. She came on purpose from her father's country-house, where all the family
20 were. I observe of all the pious people in Holland that, without any rule but the word of God, they dress as plain as Miss March[12]

[11] Johanna Carolina Arnodina Loten (1753-1823), daughter of Arnoud Loten, burgomaster of Utrecht. In 1788 she married Johannes van Doelen, later a burgomaster of Utrecht, whose library at the time of his death in 1828 included JW's *Earnest Appeal to Men of Reason and Religion* and part of the *Journal*. JW offered her to Elizabeth Ritchie as a pattern of Christian perfection (Telford, 7:184). Her son predeceased her, leaving a daughter who married J. A. Grothe of the Stichtse revival circle and an original member of the Utrecht missionary society. JW had been put in touch with Miss Loten by letter through Ferguson beforehand, and corresponded with her till his death, but the correspondence does not survive; Telford, 7:197; *Arminian Magazine* 15 (1792):50-51. The Lotens belonged to the Gereformeerde Kerk. Van den Berg, 'Wesley's Contacten', p. 81; Moore, *Wesley*, 2:291; Telford, 8:171.

[12] Miss J. C. March, who here makes her sole appearance in the *Journal*, was one of JW's most important correspondents, over 40 of the letters which he wrote surviving. Very little is known of her, except that she was the 'lady of fortune and piety' who engaged Miss Thornton, later Mrs. Greenwood, as a companion (*Methodist Magazine* 28 [1805]:37), 'a lady of good education [who] devoted her life and all she had in doing good. She sometimes made excursions to Bristol and other parts of the country where she met classes, etc.'; Jackson, *Early Methodist Preachers*, 6:25. She was at Bristol during the Conference of 1774 (see Aug. 9, 1774) and probably stayed with JW at Elizabeth Johnson's, a similarly pious lady with whom her name is here coupled. JW regarded each as 'a *rara avis in terris*'; Telford, 5:84. JW's correspondence with Miss March, which was predominantly upon spiritual matters, ceased on Dec. 10, 1777. She had had periods of ill-health for some time, and the implication of the past tense here is that she had died some years previously.

did formerly and Miss Johnson[13] does now! And considering the vast disadvantage they are under, having no connection with each other and being under no such discipline at all as we are, I wonder at the grace of God that is in them!

Fri. 27. I walked over to Mr. L——'s country-house about three miles from the city. It is a lovely place, surrounded with delightful gardens, laid out with wonderful variety. Mr. L—— is of an easy, genteel behaviour, speaks Latin correctly, and is no stranger to philosophy. Mrs. L—— is the picture of friendliness and hospitality, and young Mr. L—— seems to be cast in the same mould. We spent a few hours very agreeably. Then Mr. L—— *would* send me back in his coach.

Being sick of inns (our bill at Amsterdam alone amounting to near an hundred florins), I willingly accepted of an invitation to lodge with the sons-in-law of James Oddie.[14]

Sat. 28. We went over to Zeist, the settlement of the German brethren.[15] It is a small village, finely situated with woods on every side, and much resembles one of the large colleges in Oxford.

---

[13] The spiritual reputation of Elizabeth Johnson (1720-98), JW's 'lovely woman' (Telford, 5:313), 'an angel here below' (ibid., 6:129), who was converted in 1744, has been sufficiently illustrated; see previous note; also above, Sept. 29, 1778; Sept. 12, 1780. JW was glad to use her as an example and a counsellor, especially to women, and frequently to take advantage of her hospitality when he was in Bristol. Her father, a West India merchant, disinherited her because she was a Methodist, but her uncle bequeathed her £400 a year, and she lived with her sister to whom her father left £1000 a year. On her sister's death in 1783, Elizabeth received the legacy her father had denied her. For her contribution to early Africa evangelisation, see Tyerman, *John Wesley,* 3:272. After JW's death she was opposed to the separation of Methodism from the Church of England implied by the administration of the sacraments by the itinerant preachers; *Wesleyan Methodist Magazine* 124 (1901):128. A memoir and extracts from her diary were published in *An Account of Mrs. Elizabeth Johnson* (Bristol, 1799).
[14] On James Oddie, see Oct. 16, 1762 (21:391 and n. 90 in this edn.). According to Curnock the sons-in-law were the two Fergusons.
[15] I.e., the Moravian congregation at Zeist. Tyerman, *John Wesley,* 3:395, gives a rather free translation of the German entry in the diary of the congregation (which is partly printed by Van den Berg, 'Wesley's Contacten', p. 82): '1783. June 28. We kept the children's prayer day. The Rev. John Wesley, the well-known Methodist minister, arrived here in the afternoon, with several other ministers. After visiting his old friend, Brother Anton, he paid a rather hurried visit to the brethren's house, and the sisters' house; and then attended the children's love-feast, at three o'clock; on which occasion as it happened to be his eightieth birthday, the children sang a few benedictory verses for him; the congregation closing the service by singing "The grace of the Lord be with us all!". At 4.30 p.m. he and his companions returned to Utrecht, where he had preached the day before.' The official history of the Brethren recalls the visit as one of unbroken harmony, adding that JW still retained his understanding of German, though he could no longer speak it readily. J. C. Hegner, *Fortsetzung von David Cranzens Brüderhistorie,* 4 sections (Barby/Gnadau, 1791-1816), 3:7-8.

Here I met with my old friend Bishop Anton,[16] whom I had not seen for near fifty years. He did not ask me to eat or drink, for 'it is not their custom!' And there is an inn! But they were all very courteous. And we were welcome to *buy* anything that we pleased
5 at their shops! I cannot see how it is possible for this community to avoid growing immensely rich.[17]

I have this day lived fourscore years, and, by the mercy of God, my eyes are not waxed dim, and what little strength of body or mind I had thirty years since, just the same I have now. God grant
10 I may never live to be useless. Rather may I

> My body with my charge lay down,
> And cease at once to work and live.[18]

Sun. 29. At ten, I began the service in the English church in Utrecht.[19] I believe all the English in the city were present, and
15 forty or fifty Hollanders. I preached on the thirteenth of the First of Corinthians; I think as searchingly as ever in my life. Afterwards a merchant invited me to dinner. For six years he had been at death's door by an asthma, and was extremely ill last night. But this morning, without any visible cause he was well and walked
20 across the city to the church. He seemed to be deeply acquainted with religion, and made me promise, if I came to Utrecht again, to make his house my home.

In the evening a large company of us met at Miss L——'s, where I was desired to repeat the substance of my morning ser-
25 mon. I did so, Mr. Tydeman[20] (the Professor of Law in the Uni-

[16] Orig., 'Antone'. Anton Seiffert, 1712-85 (on whom see 18:151, 362; 20:477 in this edn.), was the ordinand whom JW still mistakenly imagined he had seen consecrated a bishop in Georgia in 1736. In fact, as the entry in the congregation diary (immediately above) shows, he had never been and was never to be made a bishop. When a system of government was set up for the Moravian Church in America, he assisted Peter Böhler as President of the Pennsylvania synod, and served in Ireland in the 1760s. J. Taylor Hamilton, *A History of the Church known as the Moravian Church or the Unitas Fratrum* (Bethlehem, Pa., 1900), pp. 79, 80, 110, 139, 241.

[17] This comment, together with the reference in the congregation diary to JW's haste, suggests a degree of irritation on both sides. JW clearly had no conception of the burden still borne by the Brethren in paying off Zinzendorf's debts.

[18] CW, *Short Hymns on Scripture*, No. 254, lines 7-8; see *Poetical Works*, 9:80.

[19] I.e., the English Presbyterian Church, which originated in the early seventeenth century in a chaplaincy to British troops, and met in the Mariakerk in Utrecht, now demolished. The minister from 1778 till he was driven out by the French in 1794 was William Laurence Brown (b. 1755).

[20] Orig., 'Toydemea'. Mainard Tydeman, a man of outspoken Orangist sympathies and pietist inclinations who ran two class-meetings. He was interested in Jung-Stilling. Van den Berg, 'Wesley's Contacten', p. 84, n. 2.

versity) interpreting it sentence by sentence. They then sung a Dutch hymn, and we an English one. Afterwards Mr. Regulet, a venerable old man, spent some time in prayer for the establishment of peace and love between the two nations.[21]

Utrecht has much the look of an English town. The streets are broad and have many noble houses. In quietness and stillness it much resembles Oxford. The country all round is like a garden. And the people I conversed with are not only civil and hospitable, but friendly and affectionate, even as those at Amsterdam.

Mon. 30. We hired a coach for Rotterdam at half a crown per head. We dined at Gouda at Mr. Van Flooten's,[22] minister of the town, who received us with all possible kindness. Before dinner we went into the church, famous for its painted windows. But we had not time to survey a tenth part of them. We could only observe, in general, that the colours were exceeding lively, and the figures exactly proportioned. In the evening, we reached once more the hospitable house of Mr. Layal[23] at Rotterdam.

Tuesday, July 1. I called on as many as I could of my friends, and we parted with much affection. We then hired a yacht,[24] which brought us to Hellevoetsluis about eleven the next day. At two, we went on board, but, the wind turning against us, we did not reach Harwich till about nine on Friday morning. After a little rest, we procured a carriage, and reached London about eleven at night.

I can by no means regret either the trouble or expense which

[21] From the beginning of the American War of Independence there was friction between Britain and the Netherlands over the maritime rights of neutrals, the huge arms traffic with the Americans through the Dutch West Indies, and the supply of naval stores to France and Spain by Dutch merchants. These irritations led to a British declaration of war on the Dutch at the end of 1780, and though the shape of the peace terms (based on the restoration of wartime conquests) was clear by the beginning of 1783, peace was not finally concluded till May 1784.

[22] Orig., 'Flooten's'. Wilhelmus Antonius van Vloten (1740-1809), minister at Waddingsveen, 1767-70, lived in retirement at Utrecht, Gouda, Leiden, and Amsterdam. He wrote extensively in the fields of practical and biblical theology; Molhuysen, *Biografisch Woordenboek*, 10: 1126; Glasius, *Godgeleerd Nederland*, 3:524-26. Van Vloten thought the modernized Augustinian theological system of the Gereformeerde Kerk more hazardous to virtue and holiness than Roman Catholicism; Van den Berg, 'Wesley's Contacten', pp. 84-85. The fifteenth century Sint Janskerk at Gouda, the largest church in the Netherlands, possesses 64 windows glazed with almost half an acre of stained glass, reputed to approach that of Chartres in delicacy of colour and boldness of design, and executed between 1555 and 1603.

[23] On whom see above, June 13, 1783.

[24] Orig., 'yatch'.

attended this little journey. It opened me a way into, as it were, a new world, where the land, the buildings, the people, the customs were all such as I had never seen before. But as those with whom I conversed were of the same spirit with my friends in England, I was as much at home in Utrecht and Amsterdam as in Bristol and London.

Sun. 6. We rejoiced to meet once more with our English friends in the New Chapel, who were refreshed with the account of the gracious work which God is working in Holland also.

Wed. 9. I spent a melancholy hour with Mr. M——[25] and several others, who charged him with speaking grievous things of me, which he then knew to be utterly false. If he acknowledges his fault, I believe he will recover; if not, his sickness is unto death!

These four days, Tuesday, Wednesday, Thursday, and Friday, were as hot as the midsummer days in Jamaica. The summer heat in Jamaica usually raises the thermometer to about eighty degrees.[26] The quicksilver in my thermometer now rose to eighty-two.

Mon. 14. I took a little journey into Oxfordshire and found the good effects of the late storms. The thunder had been uncommonly dreadful, and the lightning had tore up a field near High Wycombe and turned the potatoes into ashes. In the evening I preached in the new preaching-house at Oxford, a lightsome, cheerful place, and well filled with rich and poor scholars, as well as townsmen. Tuesday 15, walking through the city, I observed it swiftly improving in everything but religion. Observing narrowly the hall at Christ Church,[27] I was convinced it is both loftier and larger than that of the stadt-house in Amsterdam. I observed also, the gardens and walks in Holland, although extremely pleasant, were not to be compared with St. John's or Trinity gardens,[28] much less with the parks, Magdalen water-walks, etc., Christ Church Meadow, or the White-walk.

Wed. 16. I went on to Witney. There were uncommon thunder and lightning here last Thursday. But nothing to that which were

---

[25] For Thomas Maxfield, see May 20, 1739, and June 21, 1745 (19:61, n. 5; 20:71 in this edn.).

[26] A curious affirmation from one who had never been to Jamaica.

[27] The hall is 115 by 40 by 50 feet high, and is the largest pre-Victorian hall in Oxford or Cambridge.

[28] St. John's: 'The Garden is very extensive and tastefully laid out'; Trinity: 'The gardens are large and well laid out'. *The Strangers' Guide through the University and City of Oxford* (Oxford, 1838), pp. 70, 65.

there on Friday night. About ten, the storm was just over the town. And both the bursts of thunder and lightning, or rather sheets of flame, were without intermission. Those that were asleep in the town were waked, and many thought the day of judgment was come. Men, women, and children, flocked out of their houses and kneeled down together in the streets. With the flames, the grace of God came down also in a manner never known before. And as the impression was general, so it was lasting. It did not pass away with the storm, but the spirit of seriousness, with that of grace and supplication, continued. A prayer-meeting being appointed on Saturday evening, the people flocked together so that the preaching-house was more than filled, and many were constrained to stand without the door and windows. On Sunday morning before the usual time of service, the church was quite filled. Such a sight was never seen in that church before. The rector himself was greatly moved and delivered a pressing, close sermon with uncommon earnestness. When I came on Wednesday, the same seriousness remained on the generality of the people. I preached in the evening at Woodgreen,[29] where a multitude flocked together, on the 'Son of man coming in his glory.'[30] The word fell heavy upon them, and many of their hearts were as melting wax. Thursday 17 at five, they were still so eager to hear that the preaching-house would not near contain the congregation. After preaching, four and thirty persons desired admission into the society, every one of whom was (for the present at least) under very serious impressions. And most of them, there is reason to hope, will bring forth fruit with patience. In the evening, I preached to a lovely congregation at Stroud and, on Tuesday afternoon, came to Bristol.

Monday, Tuesday, and Wednesday I spent at Bath. Thursday 24, I went with a few friends to Blaise Castle.[31] The woods on

---

[29] Woodgreen is described above (Aug. 26, 1767) as 'near the town' of Witney. Thunderstorms in the South and South Midlands were the worst in the month for many years. At Witney, in quite separate incidents, a man and a woman were killed in the fields. *Gentleman's Magazine* 53 (1783):621.

[30] Cf. Matt. 25:31.

[31] Blaise Castle House was built for a Quaker banker only in 1796. Blaise Castle itself, built by a previous owner, the merchant Thomas Farr, in 1766, was an early example of a sham castle built to crown a hill in the grounds. Kings Weston was designed by Vanbrugh for Sir Edward Southwell *c.* 1710, the gardens featuring two loggias and other buildings; Pevsner, *North Somerset and Bristol*, pp. 470, 471. JW came this way again on July 24, 1788.

the side of the hill, cut through various directions, are the pleasantest I ever saw, little inferior to the Leasowes,[32], and by the
beautiful prospects far superior to Stowe gardens.[33] Afterwards
we took a view of Lord Clifford's woods at Kings Weston. They
5 are amazingly beautiful; I have seen nothing equal to them in
the West of England and very few in any other parts. In the
evening, I read to the congregation an account of our brethren
in Holland, and many thanksgivings were rendered to God on
their account.

10 Tue. 29. Our Conference began,[34] at which two important
points were considered, first, the case of Birstall House,[35] and secondly, the state of Kingswood School.[36] With regard to the former, our brethren earnestly desired, that I would go to Birstall
myself, believing this would be the most effectual way of bringing
15 the trustees to reason. With regard to the latter, we all agreed that
either the school should cease or the rules of it be particularly
observed; particularly, that the children should never play and
that a master should be always present with them.

Tuesday, August 5. Early in the morning I was seized with a

[32] For these gardens, see above, July 13, 1782.

[33] Stowe gardens are described above, Oct. 13, 1779.

[34] Apart from the topics here mentioned, Conference condemned the 'needless multi-
plying of preaching-houses', and forbade begging for chapel-building outside the
immediate circuit concerned; *Minutes*, 1:167. A letter presented to the Conference of
1785 (ibid., p. 181) also makes it clear that one vital matter was raised which was not
minuted: 'We whose names are underwritten, do declare that Mr. Wesley was desired at
the last Bristol Conference, without a dissentient voice, to draw up a deed which should
give a legal specification of the phrase, "The Conference of the People called
Methodists". . .'.

[35] The Birstall Chapel case had occupied the previous Conference (and is described
above, Aug. 2, 1782). After recovering from the illness which afflicted him at this Conference, JW went on to Birstall with results described below, Sept. 3-4, 1783. Birstall
was not mentioned in the minutes, but there was a resolution dispatching Dr. Coke
throughout the English societies to get all the preaching-houses settled on the Conference plan, and requiring assistants 'to give him all the support in their power.'

[36] The *Minutes* (1:166) make it clear that Conference recognized that the school was
suffering from general incompetence and disorganisation, not just children who played,
and that there was more to a master than the simple demand for perennial oversight, for
the children 'run up and down the wood, and mix, yea fight, with the colliers' children'.
Adam Clarke's ill reception had clearly shown that something was wrong (see above,
Sept. 6, 1782), and, brief as was his connection with the school, his denunciation of it
lacked nothing in circumstantial detail; Clarke, *Life of Adam Clarke*, 1:159-69. But what
to do with Thomas Simpson, the headmaster? Conference answered: 'He deserves to be
an itinerant preacher.' This embarrassment was, however, avoided by his setting up a
school of his own in Keynsham (on which JW commented favourably, below, Oct. 5,
1787), where his son later became vicar. A. G. Ives, *Kingswood School in Wesley's Day
and Since* (London, 1970), p. 97.

most impetuous flux.[37] In a few hours it was joined by a violent and almost continual cramp: first, in my feet, legs, thighs, then in my side and my throat. The case being judged extreme, a grain and a half of opium was given me in three doses. This speedily stopped the cramp, but at the same time, took away my speech, hearing, and power of motion, and locked me up from head to foot, so that I lay a mere log. I then sent for Dr. Drummond,[38] who from that time attended me twice a day. For some days, I was worse and worse, till on Friday, I was removed to Mr. Castleman's.[39] Still my head was not affected, and I had no pain, although in a continual fever. But I continued slowly to recover, so that I could read or write an hour or two at a time. On Wednesday 12, I took a vomit, which almost shook me to pieces but, however, did me good. Sunday 17 and all the following week, my fever gradually abated, but I had a continual thirst and little or no increase of strength. Nevertheless, being unwilling to be idle, on Saturday 23, I spent half an hour with the penitents; and finding myself no worse, on Sunday 24, I preached at the New Room, morning and afternoon. Finding my strength was now in some measure restored, I determined to delay no longer, but setting out on Monday the 25th, reached Gloucester in the afternoon. In the evening, I preached in the town-hall, I believe, not in vain. Tuesday 26, I went on to Worcester, where many young people are just setting out in the ways of God. I joined fifteen of them this afternoon to the society, all of them I believe athirst for salvation. Wednesday 27, I preached at Birmingham and had a comfortable season. Thursday 28, I paid another visit to the amiable family at Hilton Hall.[40] Friday 29 about ten, I preached for the first time at Stafford, to a large and deeply attentive congregation. It is now the day of small things here. But the grain of mustard seed may grow[41] into a great tree.

[37] John Pawson noted of this Conference that 'Mr. Wesley was dangerously ill, and we were obliged to do a considerable part of our business without him'; Jackson, *Early Methodist Preachers*, 4:50. This accounts sufficiently for the minutes being fuller than usual, and for the preachers' concern that the Conference itself should have a proper legal definition.

[38] Probably Dr. Archibald Drummond (d. 1801) who pulled down Highfield House; *Transactions of the Bristol and Gloucestershire Archaeological Society* 64 (1943):115. He had attended a friend of CW at Bristol. *CWJ*, 2:261.

[39] On John Castleman, surgeon, see above, Mar. 8, 1782.

[40] The Gibbes family, on whom see above, Mar. 25, 1783.

[41] Edn. A reads 'grow up'. JW's optimism here was ultimately justified, but, despite his visits in each of the next three years, regular preaching was not established till 1803; *Wes-*

Hence, I rode to Congleton. I had received abundance of complaints against the Assistant of this circuit, James Rogers.[42] Saturday 30, I heard all the parties face to face and encouraged them all to speak their whole mind. I was surprised: so much prejudice, anger, and bitterness on so slight occasions I never saw. However, after they had 'had it out', they were much softened, if not quite reconciled.[43] Sunday 31, I preached in the new church at Macclesfield,[44] both morning and afternoon. I believe we had seven hundred communicants.

Monday, September 1. We clambered over the mountains to Buxton. In the afternoon I preached in Fairfield[45] Church about

leyan Methodist Magazine 49 (1826):426. The society at Stafford was at this time in its infancy. Jeremiah Brettel, reappointed in 1779 to Macclesfield, relates how, 'in passing through Stafford, with Dr. Coke, while dining at an inn, the bellman was sent about to say, that the Rev. Dr. Coke, from Oxford, was going to preach at the market-place. The Doctor mounted a table, which I took from the inn for the purpose: the people came and looked at us from a distance: but shortly drew near, and heard with attention. Some came to the inn, and expressed a wish to be visited again. Their request was complied with, and afterwards a little society was formed.' *Wesleyan Methodist Magazine* 53 (1830):657.

[42] James Rogers (1749-1807) was born at Marsk in the North Riding of Yorkshire, and, after a childhood much marked by fear of judgment, and by the death of his father, was converted by the preaching of one of his childhood companions, and put in touch with a neighbouring society at Guisborough. He became a firm Methodist from the time he went to Whitby in 1768, and aspired to entire sanctification and to preach. In 1772 when one of the preachers appointed for York went to America, JW asked Rogers to take his place. The Conferences of 1782 and 1783 appointed him to Macclesfield where he endured a double crisis. 'As the circuit was large and unwieldy [he relates] four preachers were sent, with instructions to divide it. We did this in the best manner we could. . . . But this with some other amendments, such as furnishing the preachers' dwelling-house by subscription, changing the stewards &c. gave deep offence to a few individuals; but the hearts of the people were united to their preachers; and notwithstanding all the difficulties we met with, we were greatly comforted among them . . . and had the satisfaction of leaving them considerably increased in number'; Jackson, *Early Methodist Preachers*, 4:306. At the same time his wife died leaving him with two small boys. Rogers thereupon (in 1784) married one of her friends, Hester Ann, daughter of Rev. James Roe of Macclesfield. Subsequently Rogers gave distinguished service in Ireland, but was with JW in London when he died.

[43] JW is reported also to have preached at Congleton 'on the raising of the ruler's daughter, which he applied to the conversion of our relations', a sermon which gave especial heart to John Boothby, of Kettleshulme. He relates: 'For twenty years only six persons of our family were in connexion; however, I had confidence that the Lord would bring them all in; but "hope deferred maketh the heart sick". I began to be discouraged, and almost left off praying for them. [JW's encouragement kept him going with the result that] my wife and seven children, and sixteen other near relatives, are now in society; besides some who are gone to their everlasting rest', an interesting example of conversion by clan which required much perseverance by the paterfamilias. *WHS* 4 (1903):32; Dyson, *Congleton*, p. 89.

[44] Christ Church, built for David Simpson, on whom see Apr. 3, 1774.

[45] Fairfield was a small chapelry in the parish of Hope, a mile north-east of Buxton. The phrase 'clambered over the mountains' is a further illustration of the distress

half a mile from the town. It was thoroughly filled with serious
and attentive hearers. Tuesday 2, we went to Leeds, where I was
glad to find several preachers.

Wed. 3. I consulted the preachers, how it was best to proceed
with the trustees of Birstall House to prevail upon them to settle   5
it on the Methodist plan. They all advised me to begin by preaching there. Accordingly, I preached on Thursday evening and met
the society. I preached again in the morning. Friday 5 about nine,
I met the nineteen trustees. And after exhorting them to peace
and love, said, 'All that I desire is that this house may be settled on   10
the Methodist plan, and the same clause may be inserted in *your*
deed which is inserted in the deed of the New Chapel in London,
viz., "In case the doctrine or practice of any preacher should, in
the opinion of the major part of the trustees, be not conformable
to Mr. W[esley]'s Sermons and Notes on the New Testament; on   15
representing this to the nearest Assistants, after a proper hearing,
another preacher shall be sent within three months." 'Five of the
trustees were willing to accept of our first proposals, the rest were
not willing.[46]

Although I could not obtain the end proposed, and in that   20
respect had only my labour for my pains, yet I do not at all repent
of my journey. I have done *my* part; let others bear their own burden. Going back nearly the same way I came, on Saturday 13, I
reached Bristol. I had likewise good reward for my labour, in the
recovery of my health by a journey of five or six hundred miles.   25

On Wednesday 17 and the two following days, I visited several
of the country societies and found most of them not only increasing in number but in the knowledge and love of God.

Fri. 26. Observing the deep poverty[47] of many of our brethren, I

caused to JW's sensibilities by hill country. Buxton had grown up at a junction of
Roman roads, and its communications were relatively good.

[46] Edn. A omits 'to the nearest . . . hearing' from the quoted clause. On January 13,
the trustees agreed to accept financial assistance offered by JW, and also a new deed giving Conference authority to appoint the preachers. Many of the documents relative to
this case are to be found in Tyerman, *John Wesley*, 3:373-83. See also *The Case of
Birstall House* (9:505-9 in this edn.); Telford, 7:124-25. This episode, not to mention
the Dewsbury case which followed (see Aug. 1, 1789), sufficiently illuminates the
improvidence of the exchange in the Conference of 1779:

'Q. 22. Some Trustees may abuse their power after my death. What can be done to
prevent this?

A. It seems, we need take no thought for the morrow. God will provide when need
shall be'. *Minutes*, 1:136.

[47] Michaelmas corn prices in 1783 had not been exceeded since the famine year of
1709, and were not to be exceeded again till the near-famine year of 1795.

determined to do what I could for their relief. I spoke severally to some that were in good circumstances and received about forty pounds. Next I inquired who were in the most pressing want, and visited them at their own houses. I was surprised to find no mur-
5 muring spirits among them, but many that were truly happy in God. And all of them appeared to be exceeding thankful for the scanty relief which they received.

Sun. 28. It being a fair day, I snatched the opportunity of preaching abroad to twice or thrice as many as the room would
10 have contained. Wednesday, October 1. I preached at Bath to such a congregation as I have not seen there of a long season. All my leisure hours this week I employed in visiting the remaining poor and in begging for them. Having collected about fifty pounds more, I was enabled to relieve most of those that were in pressing
15 distress.

Mon. 6. Leaving the society in a more prosperous way than it had been for several years, I preached in the Devizes about noon, and at Salisbury in the evening. Captain Webb lately kindled a flame here, and it is not yet gone out.[48] Several persons were still
20 rejoicing in God, and the people in general were much quickened. Tuesday 7, I found his preaching in the street at Winchester had been blessed greatly. Many were more or less convinced of sin, and several had found peace with God. I never saw the preaching-house so crowded before with serious and attentive hearers.
25 So was that at Portsmouth also. Wednesday 8, we took a wherry for the Isle of Wight. Before we were half over, the sea rose and the water washed over us. However, we got safe to Wootton Bridge,[49] and then walked on to Newport. There is much life among the people here, and they walk worthy of their profession.
30 Thur. 9. I went to Newtown[50] (two miles from Newport), supposed to be the oldest town in the Isle—but its glory is past! The church lies in ruins, and the town has scarce six houses remaining. However, the preaching-house was thoroughly filled, and the

---

[48] This work is referred to above, Oct. 3, 1780. For Captain Webb, see Feb. 2, 1773; 22:359, n. 73 in this edn.

[49] Orig. 'Wotton-bridge'. On Wootton Bridge, see above, Oct. 6, 1758 (21:166, n. 57 in this edn.).

[50] Newtown, 5 miles west from Newport, and until 1832, a burgage borough represented in Parliament. Even in the nineteenth century when the harbour was used by the preventive service, Newtown had only a handful of inhabitants. But it had a charter dating from the thirteenth century, and a titular mayor (who was also returning officer) was chosen by the 33 burgage-holders.

people appeared to be all of one rank: none rich and none extremely poor, but all were extremely serious and attentive.

Fri. 10. I crossed over to Southampton and found two or three there also who feared and loved God. Then I went to Winchester and had the pleasure of dining with Mr. Lowth[51] and supping with Mrs. Blackwell. Her six lovely children are in admirable order; it is a pleasure to see them. A clergyman having offered me his church, I purposed beginning at five. But the key was not to be found. So I made a virtue of necessity and preached near the cross-street, probably to double the congregation which would have been in the church.

Many of the Dutch prisoners[52] remaining here, I paid them a short visit. When they were brought hither first, one of them prayed with as many as desired it and gave them a word of exhortation. Presently one found peace with God, and joined him in that labour of love. These increased, so that they have now five exhorters; many are justified, and many more convinced of sin. About two hundred of them were met together when I came. They first sung a hymn in their own language. I then gave them a short exhortation in English, for which they were extremely thankful.

Sat. 11. Just at twelve (the same hour as at Bristol), I was taken exceeding ill, and so continued till three. I then took chaise, as I had appointed, and was better and better every stage, and quite well when I came to London.

Mon. 13. I preached at Wallingford. Tuesday 14, I went on to Oxford and found both the congregation and society increased in zeal as well as in number. Wednesday 15, I came to Witney. The flame which was kindled here by that providential storm of thunder and lightning is not extinguished but has continued ever since with no discernible intermission. The preaching-house is still too small for the congregation. Thursday 16, I preached at High Wycombe and, on Friday, returned to London.

Sun. 19. I took the Diligence for Norwich and preached there the next evening to more than the house would contain. And both

---

[51] The second Mrs. Blackwell, Mary Eden, was a niece of the wife of Robert Lowth, Bishop of London, and it was through this connexion that JW had last met the bishop; see above, Nov. 24, 1777. This Mr. Lowth was probably the bishop's elder brother, William (*c.* 1707-95), who was a demy of Magdalen College, Oxford, 1724-32, graduating B.A. in 1728, and M.A. in 1730, and was a prebendary of Winchester from 1759.

[52] I.e., prisoners taken during the American War of Independence; peace with the Dutch was not yet concluded, see above, June, 29, 1783.

this night and following, we sensibly felt that God was in the midst of us. Wednesday 22, I went to Yarmouth. Often this poor society had been well-nigh shattered in pieces, first by Benjamin Worship,[53] then a furious Calvinist, tearing away near half of them; next by John Simpson, turning antinomian and scattering most that were left. It has pleased God, contrary to all human probability, to raise a new society out of the dust; nay, and to give them courage to build a new preaching-house which is well finished and contains about five hundred persons. I opened it this evening, and as many as could get in seemed to be deeply affected. Who knows, but God is about to repair the waste places and to gather a people that shall be scattered no more?

Thur. 23. We went to Lowestoft, where the people have stood firm from the beginning. Observing in the evening that forty or fifty people were talking together as soon as the service was over (a miserable custom that prevails in most places of public worship, throughout England and Ireland), I strongly warned the congregation against it, as I had done those at Norwich and Yarmouth. They received it in love, and the next evening, all went silently away. But this warning must be given again and again in every place, or it will not be effectual.

Sat. 25. I preached in Lowestoft at five; at eight to an earnest, lively people at [North] Cove; and at one to a more numerous, but not more lively, congregation at Loddon. The most numerous was that at Norwich in the evening, many of whom were truly alive to God.

Sun. 26. I gave the Sacrament at seven; at nine, I preached at Ber Street, where I am in hopes considerable good will be done. The most serious congregation in our house we had at two, but the most numerous at six, though not above half of those that came could get in. Those that could hear, did not lose their labour, for God 'satisfied the hungry with good things.'[54]

---

[53] On Benjamin Worship and John Simpson, see Jan. 20, 1761 (21:300, n. 54 in this edn.). For the history of Yarmouth Methodism, see above, Oct. 24, 1781.

[54] Cf. Luke 1:53. The text had an unusual resonance for JW on this occasion, for 'when leaving, [he] had a whole host of poverty-stricken people about his carriage. His purse was low, containing only what was necessary to take him back to London; and the clamour of the mendicant crowd, for once, disturbed his temper. Somewhat sharply he said: "I have nothing for you. Do you suppose I can support the poor in every place?" At the moment he was entering his carriage, his foot slipped; and he fell upon the ground. Feeling as though God himself had rebuked him for his hasty words, he turned to Joseph Bradford [on whom see June 17, 1775] and, with subdued emphasis, remarked: "It is all right, Joseph; it is all right; it is only what I deserved; for if I had no

Mon. 27. I talked at large with M—— F——. Such a case I have not known before. She has been in the society nearly from the beginning. She found peace with God five and twenty years ago and the pure love of God a few years after. Above thirty years she has been a class- and a band-leader and of very eminent use. Ten months since, she was accused of drunkenness and of revealing the secret of her friend. Being informed of this, I wrote to Norwich (as I then believed the charge) that she must be no longer a leader, either of a band or a class. The preacher told her, further, that in his judgment she was unfit to be a member of the society. Upon this she gave up her ticket, together with the band and her class-papers. Immediately all her friends (of whom she seemed to have a large number) forsook her at once. No one knew her or spoke to her. She was a dead thing out of mind!

On making a more particular inquiry I found that Mrs. N—— (formerly a common woman) had revealed her own secret to Dr. Hunt,[55] and twenty people besides. So the first accusation vanished into air. As to the second, I verily believe the drunkenness with which she was charged was in reality a falling down in a fit. So we have thrown away one of the most useful leaders we ever had for these wonderful reasons!

Wed. 29. I crossed over to [King's] Lynn and found things much better than I expected. The behaviour of Mr. G—— (which one would have imagined would have done much harm) had rather done good. People in general cried, 'Let that bad man go, they will do better without him.' And the house was sufficiently crowded with serious hearers. November 1, I returned to London.

In the two following weeks, I visited the classes both in London and the neighbouring societies. Sunday 16, being much importuned, I preached in the evening at Mr. Maxfield's chapel.[56] But I dare not do so again, as it can't contain one third of that congregation at the New Chapel.

Mon. 17. I preached at Sevenoaks and, on Tuesday 18, at

other good to give, I ought at least to have given them good words" '; Tyerman, *John Wesley*, 3;405, quoting James Everett, *Adam Clarke Portrayed*, 3 vols. (London, 1843–49), 1:94. JW's own straits are mentioned below, Jan. 12, 1784.

[55] Dr. Hunt was JW's host in Norwich. See Diary for Oct. 20, 25, 1783.

[56] On the improved relations between Maxfield and the Methodists, see above, Dec. 21, 1782; but also see below, Dec. 6, 1783. He died on March 18, 1784.

Mount Ephraim[57] near Tunbridge Wells. Wednesday 19, I came once more to the lovely family at Shoreham. A little longer that venerable old man[58] is permitted to remain here, that the flock may not be scattered.[59]

5   When I was at Sevenoaks, I made an odd remark. In the year 1769, I weighed a hundred and twenty-two pounds. In 1783, I weighed not a pound more or less. I doubt whether such another instance is to be found in Great Britain.[60]

Mon. 24. I preached at Canterbury, and again on Wednesday; on Tuesday 25, at Dover; Thursday 27, at Sheerness, where Mr. Fox read prayers[61] and I preached on those words in the Second Lesson, 'Today if ye will hear his voice, harden not your hearts.'[62]

Fri. 28. I returned to London. Tuesday, Dec. 2, I married Mr. Rutherford and Miss Lydia Duplex.[63] Wednesday 3, I took a little journey into Hertfordshire and, having preached at Hinxworth and Wrestlingworth, on Friday 5, I preached at Barnet and, on Saturday 6, returned to London.

I now inquired more carefully and particularly into the strange case of poor Mr. M——.[64] But the more I inquired, the worse the matter appeared to be. It was plain, by the evidence of many unexceptional witnesses, that he had told innumerable lies: affirming, denying, and affirming again! And this man, who has

---

[57] Mount Ephraim was one of the four districts which formed the hamlet of Tunbridge Wells (Hasted, *Kent*, 3:276). According to Curnock (6:461) the Countess of Huntingdon had a house here.

[58] Vincent Perronet, on whom see Aug. 14, 1744 (20:35, n. 74 in this edn.).

[59] Robert Miller (1763-1829), then a preacher on trial, preached at Shoreham in 1790 and was assailed by 'two men who were made drunk by persons who ought to have known better, purposely while I was preaching in the street,' but by skilful badinage transformed them into bodyguards for the day who 'kept others that would have disturbed me, in awe, by repeatedly declaring, that if any attempted to meddle with me, they would knock them down.' *Methodist Magazine* 24 (1801):193.

[60] Always astonishingly confident of the virtues of his regimen, JW here unwittingly reveals the venial pride of the elderly. Age was beginning to leave its mark on him.

[61] 'There is a chapel erected here at the expense of government, for the use of the garrison, &c., but all christenings, marriages, burials and other ecclesiastical rites, are performed at the mother church of Minster which has the entire ecclesiastical jurisdiction over this ville. The chaplain is appointed by government to the care of this chapel' (Hasted, *Kent*, 6:233). This was probably Mr. Fox.

[62] Heb. 3:7-8. In his Diary, JW cites Heb. 3:7 as his text.

[63] This couple are otherwise unknown. JW's Diary indicates an interview with John Duplex, presumably the bride's father, immediately before the wedding. He was one of the original trustees of City Road, and is described as 'of the parish of Christ Church, weaver'. Stevenson, *City Road*, p. 250.

[64] On the apparently better Methodist relations with Thomas Maxfield, see above, Nov. 16, 1783; Dec. 21, 1782.

lived above twenty years in a constant course of lying and slandering, tells you, 'He enjoys constant communion with God, and that nothing can make him happier but heaven!'

Thur. 18. I spent two hours with that great man, Dr. Johnson, who is sinking into the grave by a gentle decay.[65] Wednesday 24, while we were dining at Mr. Blunt's,[66] his servant-maid, ill of a sore throat died. Saturday 27, I dined at Mr. Awbrey's[67] with Mr. Wynantz,[68] son of the Dutch merchant at whose house I met with Peter Böhler[69] and his brethren forty-five years ago.

Wed. 31. We concluded the year at the New Chapel with the voice of praise and thanksgiving.

Thursday, Jan. 1, 1784. I retired for two or three days to Peckham.[70] Sunday 4, though it rained violently, we had, I believe, upwards of eighteen hundred people at the renewal of the covenant.[71] Many found an uncommon blessing therein. I am sure I did, for one.

Tue. 6. At noon, I preached at Barking and, in the evening, at Purfleet[72] to a people that were all alive. Wednesday 7, I went on to Colchester and, on Friday 9, returned to London.

[65] Coming so soon after JW's confident self-estimate (Nov. 17, 1783), this comment sounds less kindly than it really was. Johnson had suffered a stroke on June 17, 1783, and had been increasingly afflicted with bronchitis, dropsy, and rheumatoid arthritis. A few days before JW's visit, he had another attack of what seems to have been coronary thrombosis, and JW was one of a host of visitors who now called with good wishes and presents for convalescence. W. Jackson Bate, *Samuel Johnson* (London, 1978), pp. 575-78, 584.

[66] John Blunt was frequently JW's host at this time (see Diary July 9, 1783; Jan. 27, 1785), and raised a family which did well in church and state. But before the present journal was published he had annoyed his father-in-God both as a class-leader and as a contemptuous critic of the preachers, and had received a memorable rebuke: 'Of all the men I have conversed with in London or in England, you are above measure self-conceited and full of yourself. Whereas you are by no means equal even in sense to those whom you despise—Mr. Bradburn, Moore and John Edwards, for instance. Their natural understanding is stronger than yours, and is likewise far better improved.' Telford, 8:103.

[67] JW visited Awbrey again in 1785 (Diary, Jan. 13) and 1791 (Diary, Jan. 28).

[68] On Francis Wynantz the elder, a naturalized Danzig merchant, see Feb. 7, 1738 (18:223, n. 14 in this edn.).

[69] On Peter Böhler, see ibid., n. 15.

[70] During this retirement he wrote the preface to the *Arminian Magazine* for the year, defending its polemical title, and expressing satisfaction at the rising demand for it, 600 copies more being printed than for the year before.

[71] On this service see Aug. 6, 1755 (21:23, n. 82 in this edn.).

[72] Purfleet was a chapelry in the parish of West Thurrock, 16 1/2 miles east of London, where a small harbour had been made at the junction of a tiny tributary and the Thames. It has a curious indirect link with early Methodist history. The explosion at the Foundery, which led to the Board of Ordnance moving their cannon-founding

Mon. 12. Desiring to help some that were in pressing want, but not having any money left, I believed it was not improper in such a case to desire help from God. A few hours after, one from whom I expected nothing less, put ten pounds into my hands.

5   Wed. 21. Being vehemently accused by a well-meaning man of very many things, particularly of covetousness and uncourteousness, I referred the matter to three of our brethren. Truly, in these articles, 'I know nothing by myself. But he that judgeth me is the Lord.'[73]

10   Sat. 24. I began visiting the classes in the town and country. Sunday 25, I preached in the afternoon in St. George's Southwark,[74] a very large and commodious church. [Thursday, February 5, I went down to Nottingham and preached a charity sermon for the General Hospital.[75] The next day, I returned to London.]

15   In the following week, I visited the country societies. Saturday 14, I desired all our preachers to meet and consider thoroughly the proposal of sending missionaries to the East Indies. After the matter had been fully considered, we were unanimous in our judgment that we have no call thither yet, no invitation, no provi-

20   dential opening of any kind.[76]

Thur. 19. I spent an agreeable hour with the modern Hannibal, Pascal Paoli,[77] probably the most accomplished general that is now in the world. He is of a middle size, thin, well-shaped, genteel, and has something extremely striking in his countenance. How

25   much happier is he now, with his moderate pension, than he was in the midst of his victories!

On Saturday, having a leisure hour, I made an end of that

operations out to Woolwich on the south bank of the Thames, and so to the premises being available for Methodist use, led also to their moving gunpowder stores out to Purfleet on the north bank.

[73] Cf. 1 Cor. 4:4.

[74] St. George's, Southwark, was built, 1734–36, by John Price to replace a medieval church. Though badly built, it is now assessed as 'a sound sturdy church, uncommonly well sited'. Pevsner, *London*, 2:297.

[75] JW has misplaced this and the following sentence, as his Diary and letters confirm. He had, in fact, preached a charity sermon (on Isa. 55:6) for the General Hospital at Nottingham when he was there the previous year on April 6. He later preached charity sermons there for the hospital on Nov. 11, 1787, and July 11, 1788. There were also charity sermons for the Nottingham General Hospital by Methodist preachers stationed in the circuit in 1784 and 1786; Swift, *Nottingham*, p. 23. On the hospital itself, see below, Sept. 8, 1786.

[76] Conference had similarly declined to send missionaries to Africa in 1778.

[77] Orig., 'Paschal Paöli'. On Pascal Paoli, Corsican general, see Nov. 11, 1768. JW was again impressed by him on a later visit, see below, Nov. 6, 1784.

strange book *Orlando Furioso.*[78] Ariosto had doubtless an uncommon genius, and subsequent poets have been greatly indebted to him. Yet it is hard to say which was most out of his senses, the hero or the poet. He has not the least regard even to probability: his marvellous transcends all conception. Astolpho's shield and horn and voyage to the moon; the lance that unhorses everyone, the all-penetrating sword, and I know not how many impenetrable helmets and coats of mail; leaves transformed into ships, and into leaves again; stones turned into horses, and again into stones—are such monstrous fictions as never appeared in the world before, and one would hope, never will again. O who that is not himself out of his senses, can compare Ariosto with Tasso![79]

Monday, March 1. I went to Newbury and preached in the evening to a large and deeply affected congregation. Tuesday 2 and Wednesday 3, I preached at Bath and, on Thursday 4, went on to Bristol. Friday 5, I talked at large with our masters in Kingswood School, who are now just such as I wished for.[80] At length the rules of the house are punctually observed, and the children are all in good order.

Sat. 6. I spent a few melancholy minutes at Mr. Henderson's with the lost Louisa.[81] She is now in a far more deplorable case than ever. She used to be mild, though silly, but now she is quite furious. I doubt the poor machine cannot be repaired in this life.

The next week, I visited the classes at Bristol. Friday 12, being at Samuel Rayner's in Bradford[-on-Avon], I was convinced of

[78] Lodovico Ariosto, *Orlando Furioso*, first published at Ferrara, 1516. Thomas Macaulay was prepared to compare Ariosto with Tasso on more than one occasion; *Critical and Historical Essays*, ed. F. C. Montague, 3 vols. (London, 1903), 1:252-53; 2:490.

[79] On February 28, between this entry and the next, JW signed the Deed of Declaration requiring trustees to hold the chapel premises for such preachers as John and Charles Wesley should appoint, or, after their deaths, as Conference should appoint; the deed further named the Legal Hundred who were to constitute the Conference, who should fill up vacancies by co-optation. The document is printed in George Smith, *Wesleyan Methodism*, 1:705-9; Rupert Davies, A. Raymond George, and Gordon Rupp, eds., *A History of The Methodist Church in Great Britain*, 4 vols. (London: Epworth, 1965-88), 4:195-96.

[80] The only master remaining from the old staff was Vincent de Boudry, the Frenchman. The next headmaster was Thomas McGeary A.M. The assistant masters, who proved difficult to recruit, were Richard Dodd and William Winsbeare. A. H. Hastling, W. A. Willis, and W. P. Workman, *The History of Kingswood School* (London, 1898), p. 80.

[81] On Richard Henderson and his private asylum, see above, Sept. 29, 1781. On Louisa, 'the maid of the haystack', see above Mar. 15, 1782.

two vulgar errors: the one, that nightingales will not live in cages; the other, that they only sing a month or two in the year. He has now three nightingales in cages, and they sing almost all day long from November to August. Saturday 13 about nine, I preached at
5　Trowbridge, where a large congregation quickly[82] attended. Returning to Bristol, I lodged once more at E—— J——'s,[83] a genuine old Methodist. God has lately taken away her only brother, as well as her beloved sister. But she was still able to say, 'It is the Lord: let him do what seemeth him good.'[84]
10　　Mon. 15. Leaving Bristol after preaching at five, in the evening I preached at Stroud, where to my surprise, I found the morning preaching was given up, as also in the neighbouring places. If this be the case while I am alive, what must it be when I am gone? Give up this, and Methodism too will degenerate into a mere sect,
15　only distinguished by some opinions and modes of worship.[85]
　　Tue. 16. I preached in Painswick at noon, and at Gloucester in the evening. The room was full at five in the morning, and both the preachers and people promised to neglect the early preaching no more. Wednesday 17, we went to Cheltenham, which I had not
20　seen for many years.[86] I preached at noon to half a houseful of hearers, most of them cold and dead enough. I expected to find the same at Tewksbury but was agreeably disappointed. Not only the congregation was much larger, but I admired their teachableness. On my mentioning the impropriety of *standing* at prayer and
25　sitting while we were singing praise to God, they all took advice, kneeling while we prayed and stood up while we sung psalms.
　　Thur. 18. We crossed over to Bengeworth, where Mr. Cooper[87]

---

[82] Edn. A, 'quietly'.

[83] On Elizabeth Johnson, see above, June 26, 1783.

[84] 1 Sam. 3:18.

[85] The early preaching was not the only example of accumulated devotions in early Methodism which failed to take root, and died out within a few years of JW's death, a victim not merely of changed social circumstances, but of the increased activism required of Methodists in other ways, especially in administration and fund-raising. The archetype of the new activism, Jabez Bunting, signed the death warrant of the old, in his first appointment in London in 1803. 'September 8th. I was so weary and drowsy this morning, at five o'clock, that, though I heard Mr. Taylor going out to preach, I had neither curiosity enough, nor piety enough, to rise and hear him'; Bunting, *Life of Jabez Bunting*, 1:112. Cf. below, Apr. 5, 7, 1784.

[86] JW notes that he was in Cheltenham on Aug. 4, 1774; 22:423 in this edn. and was in the immediate district on Mar. 16-19, 1778.

[87] On Edward Cooper, perpetual curate of Bengeworth (b. 1739), see Apr. 19, 1764; 21:455, n. 69 in this edn. He was a negligent head of Prince Henry's Grammar School, Evesham, till 1807. *Victoria County History; Worcestershire*, 4:506.

read prayers and I preached. Friday 19, being informed that my chaise could pass part of the way to Broad Marston, I went boldly for awhile and then stuck fast. I borrowed a horse and went on. At five, I preached in Pebworth Church, and at five in the morning in our own chapel at Broad Marston. As we rode back to Bengeworth, the cold was so intense, that it had an effect I never felt before; it made me downright sick. However, I went on and preached in the church at eleven and, in the evening, at Worcester. Sunday 21, I preached to a crowded audience in St. Andrew's Church. The vicar read prayers[88] and afterwards told me, 'I should be welcome to the use of his church whenever I came to Worcester.'

Mon. 22. In the evening, I preached at Birmingham. Tuesday 23, I preached in the church at Quinton[89] to a congregation gathered from all parts. Not many appeared to be unaffected, for the power of God was eminently present.

After preaching at various other places,[90] on Saturday 27, I went to Madeley and, at Mr. Fletcher's desire, revised his letters to Dr. Priestley.[91] I think there is hardly another man in England

[88] William Warmington (*c.* 1745-1828) was incumbent of St. Andrew's, Worcester, from 1775; T. R. Nash, *Collections for the History of Worcestershire*, 2 vols. (London, 1882), vol. 2, App., p. 124. He matriculated from Brasenose College, Oxford, in 1761, and graduated B.A. in 1764. He was vicar of Norton with Lenchwick, Co. Worcester, 1785 till his death.

[89] On this Quinton in West Midlands, see above, Mar. 24, 1781. As there was no church there till 1840, the entry may refer to the parish church at Halesowen. Cf. *WHS* 5 (1905):92.

[90] Besides preaching JW also paid a visit to Hilton Park, the home of Sir Philip Gibbes (on whom see above, Mar. 25, 1783) from which on Mar. 26, 1784, he dated an account of the ghostly disturbances in his father's house, published in *Arminian Magazine* 7 (1784):548-50, 606-8, 654-57.

[91] Joseph Priestley (1733-1804), at this time minister of the New Meeting, Birmingham, was the most famous of the Presbyterians moving into unitarianism, and was as celebrated for his scientific inquiries as for his sceptical theological views, which had most recently been embodied in his *History of the Corruptions of Christianity* (Birmingham, 1782) which was burned by the common hangman at Dort in 1785. Fletcher of Madeley (on whom see Feb. 13, 1757; 21:88-89, n. 33 in this edn.) set out to defend the doctrines of the Trinity and Divinity of Christ against him, but, in 1785, died before the work was published. JW asked Joseph Benson to edit and publish what Madeley had written, and this he did (with much material of his own) under the titles: *A Rational Vindication of the Catholic Faith; being the First Part of a Vindication of Christ's Divinity; inscribed to the Reverend Dr. Priestley* (Hull, 1788; London, 1790), and *Socinianism Unscriptural; or, The Prophets and Apostles Vindicated from the Doctrine of Christ's mere Humanity; being the Second Part of a Vindication of His Divinity* (Birmingham, 1791). It is noteworthy that when in 1791 Priestley prefixed to his *Original Letters by the Rev. John Wesley and his Friends* an *Address to the Methodists*, Benson declined to reply. Priestley was at that time the worst-afflicted victim of the Church-and-King mobs, and Benson forbore to add to his troubles.

so fit to encounter him. Sunday 28, notwithstanding the severe weather, the church was more than filled. I preached on part of the Epistle (Heb. 9:13, etc.); in the afternoon on, 'The grace of God that bringeth salvation',[92] and, I believe, God applied it to
5 many hearts.

Mon. 29. I gave an exhortation at Sheriffhales[93] in my way to Stafford. When I came thither, I found no notice had been given, so I had only a small company in a deplorable hole, formerly a stable. Hence we went to Lane End,[94] a village two or three miles
10 from Newcastle-under-Lyme. It was still piercingly cold. But the preaching-house would not hold a fourth part of the people, so I preached in the open air, the moon giving us clear light, though not much heat. The house was filled at five in the morning. And God again applied his word.

15 Tue. 30. I preached in the new preaching-house at Hanley Green, but this was far too small to hold the congregation. Indeed this country is all on fire, and the flame is still spreading from village to village. The preaching-house at Newcastle just held the congregation, many being kept away by the election, especially
20 the gentry. But still the poor heard the gospel preached, and received it with all readiness of mind.

Tue. 31. I reached Burslem,[95] where we had the first society in the country, and it is still the largest and the most in earnest. I was obliged to preach abroad. The house would but just contain the
25 societies at the love-feast, at which many, both men and women, simply declared the wonderful works of God.

I did not find so lively a people at Congleton. Although the wounds made by prejudice were nearly healed, yet a faintness and deadness remained.[96] I found the same sad effects of prejudice at
30 Macclesfield. But there are so many here truly alive to God that his work goes on still, only not in so rapid a manner as it might otherwise have done.

---

[92] Titus 2:11; in his Diary, JW gives 2:13 as his text.

[93] On Sheriffhales, a place where the old dissent had established itself in the Restoration period, see above, Mar. 25 1782.

[94] Lane End was a market town with Longton, and a chapelry in the parish of Stoke-upon-Trent, 4 miles south-east from Newcastle-under-Lyme.

[95] It has been learnedly held that this was the occasion when JW sat for the modelling of one of the best known of his early busts by Enoch Wood; but it is noteworthy that no mention of this is made in his tightly-packed diary for the day. *WHS* 6 (1907):17-23.

[96] The *Journal* itself is sufficient testimony to the capacity of Congleton people, Anglican and Methodist, for sustaining mutual acrimony. See above, Mar. 31, 1776; Mar. 29, 1779; Mar. 28, 1782; Aug. 29, 1783.

Sunday [April] 4. I preached at the New Church, morning and evening to a London congregation. Monday 5 about noon, I preached at Alpraham to an unusually large congregation. I was surprised when I came to Chester to find that there also, morning preaching was quite left off, for this worthy reason, 'Because the people will not come, or at least, not in the winter.' If so, 'the Methodists are a fallen people.' Here is proof. They have 'lost their first love!'[97] And they never will or can recover it till they 'do the first works.'[98]

As soon as I set foot in Georgia, I began preaching at five in the morning. And *every communicant,* that is, every serious person in the town, *constantly* attended throughout the year; I mean, came every morning, winter and summer, unless in the case of sickness. They did so till I left the province. In the year 1738, when God began his great work in England, I began preaching at the same hour, winter and summer, and never wanted a congregation. If they will not attend now, they have lost their zeal; and then it cannot be denied, 'they are a fallen people.'

And in the mean time, we are labouring to secure the preaching-houses to the next generation.[99] In the name of God, let us if possible, secure the present generation from drawing back to perdition! Let all the preachers that are still alive to God join together as one man, fast and pray, lift up their voice as a trumpet, be instant, in season, out of season, to convince them they are fallen, and exhort them, instantly to 'repent, and do the first works.'[1] This in particular, rising in the morning, without which neither their souls nor bodies can long remain in health.

Wed. 7. I crossed over the water to Liverpool. Here I found a people much alive to God, one cause of which was, that they have preaching several mornings in a week and prayer-meetings on the rest, all of which they are careful to attend. On Good Friday, April 9, I went to Warrington. In the morning, I read prayers, preached, and administered the Lord's Supper to a serious congregation. I preached at five again, and believe few were present who did not feel that God was there of a truth.

Sat. 10. I preached to a huge congregation at Manchester, and to a far larger at ten in the morning, being Easter day. It was sup-

---

[97] Cf. Rev. 2:4.
[98] Rev. 2:5. Cf. above Mar. 15, 1784.
[99] On the Deed of Declaration, see above Feb. 28, 1784.
[1] Rev. 2:5.

posed, there were near a thousand communicants.[2] But hitherto the Lord has helped me in this respect also. I have found no congregation which my voice could not command.

Mon. 12. I found a lovely congregation at Stockport, much
5   alive to God. So was that at Oldham the next day, which was not perceptibly lessened, though it blew a storm and poured down with rain. Here a young woman of unblameable character (otherwise I should not have given her any credit) gave me a remarkable account.[3] She said, 'I had totally lost the sight of my right eye,
10   when I dreamed one night that our Saviour appeared to me, that I fell at his feet, and he laid his hand upon my right eye. Immediately I waked and, from that moment, have seen as well with that eye as with the other.'

I applied to a very large congregation the case of the Rechabites
15   (Jer. 35). I asked, (1) does it appear that these owed to Jehonadab more than the Methodists owe to me? (2) Are they as observant of *my* advices[4] (although both scriptural and rational, to instance only in dress and rising early) as the Rechabites were of *his* advices (of drinking no wine and living in tents, which had nei-
20   ther scripture nor reason to support them)?

I think every member of the society at Bolton does take my advice with respect to other things as well as with respect to dress and rising early, in consequence of which they are continually increasing in number as well as in grace.

25   Fri. 16. I preached, about ten, at Wingates,[5] a village five or six miles from Bolton. I was constrained by the multitude of people to preach abroad, though it was exceeding cold, on 'All things are ready; come unto the marriage.'[6] Truly the people were ready too. They drank in every word.

---

[2] Thomas Taylor (on whom see May 31, 1767:22:82, n. 89) in his MS diary put it at 1200. Tyerman, *John Wesley*, 3:411.

[3] The young woman was Ann Brooks (1763-91), who had vivid religious impressions at school, deepened by reading Edward Young's *Night Thoughts* and James Hervey's *Meditations*, which culminated in conversion under the preaching of Matthew Mayer (on whom see June 21, 1763; 21:419, n. 10 in this edn.) and Joseph Benson. Not long after her admission to the Methodist society in June 1781, her acute eye trouble (more fully described in *Arminian Magazine* 16 [1793]:146-47) began, which defied all the medical assistance available. On the Saturday before Christmas 1781, 'hearing a person read in the *Arminian Magazine*, of a woman being cured by the power of faith', she commended herself to God's mercy at night, and the remarkable dream leading to the cure followed.

[4] These themes are treated further in Sermon 39, 'Catholic Spirit' (2:81-95 in this edn.), and Sermon 97, 'On Obedience to Pastors' (3:374-83 in this edn.).

[5] Wingates was a village 4 miles west of Bolton.

[6] Matt. 22:4.

In the evening, we had a very uncommon congregation at Wigan. Only one gentlewoman behaved 'as she used to do at church' (so several afterwards informed me): talking all the time, though no one answered her! But the rest were deeply attentive and, I trust, will not be forgetful hearers. I had designed to go from hence to Blackburn, but hearing that one of our society near Preston was at the point of death, I turned a little out of my way to spend half an hour with her. I found Mrs. Nuttal,[7] a lovely, patient creature, praising God continually, though worn away with pining, sickness, and long-continued pain. Having paid the last office of friendship here, I went to Preston and preached to a serious congregation. In the evening, I preached at Blackburn, where also the society is lively and continually increasing.

Sun. 18. After preaching at five to a numerous congregation (but not one rich or well-dressed person among them either morning or evening! poor Blackburn!), I hastened on to Gisburn. The church was so full that a few were obliged to stand without the doors. The word was quick and powerful. So it was afterward at Settle. Sufficient for this day was the labour thereof.

Mon. 19. I went on to Ambleside, where, as I was sitting down to supper, I was informed, 'Notice had been given of my preaching, and that the congregation was waiting.' I would not disappoint them, but preached immediately on 'Salvation by faith.' Among them were a gentleman and his wife who gave me a very remarkable relation. She said,

She had often heard her mother relate, what an intimate acquaintance had told her, that her husband was concerned in the Rebellion of 1745. He was tried at Carlisle and found guilty. The evening before he was to die, sitting and musing in her chair, she fell fast asleep. She dreamed one came to her and said, 'Go to such a part of the wall, and among the loose stones you will find a key, which you must carry to your husband.' She waked but, thinking it a common dream, paid no attention to it. Presently she fell asleep again and dreamed the very same dream. She started up, put on her cloak and hat, and went to that part of the wall, and

---

[7] Mrs. Nuttal was a lady of independent means of Walton-le-Dale, and one of the earliest Methodists in the neighbourhood. JW had corresponded with her in 1782. Telford 7:122, 132; Richard Allen, *History of Methodism in Preston* (Preston, 1866), p. 35; W. Pilkington, *The Makers of Wesleyan Methodism in Preston* (London, 1890), p. 20.

among the loose stones found a key. Having with some difficulty procured admission into the jail, she gave this to her husband. It opened the door of his cell, as well as the lock of the prison door. So at midnight, he escaped for life.

Tue. 20. We went to Whitehaven, where there is a fairer prospect than has been for many years. The society is united in love, not conformed to the world, but labouring to experience the full image of God wherein they were created. The house was filled in the evening and much more the next, when we had all the church ministers and most of the gentry in the town; but they behaved with as much decency as if they had been colliers.

Thur. 22. I preached in the market-house at Cockermouth. In our way thence, we had some of the heaviest rain I have seen in Europe. The Sessions being at Carlisle, I could not have the court-house; but we had a good opportunity in our own house. Friday 23, we travelled through a lovely country to Longtown, the last town in England, and one of the best built in it, for all the houses are new from one end to the other.[8] The road from hence to Langholm is delightfully pleasant, running mostly by the side of a clear river. But it was past seven before we reached Selkirk.

Sat. 24. We had frost in the morning, snow before seven, piercing winds all day long, and in the afternoon vehement hail; so that I did not wonder we had a small congregation at Edinburgh in the evening.

Sun. 25. I attended the Tolbooth Kirk[9] at eleven. The sermon was very sensible but, having no application, was no way likely to

---

[8] Longtown was a market town in the parish of Arthuret, 8 miles north of Carlisle. It was 'eminently indebted to the liberality and public spirit of the late Dr. [Robert] Graham [D. D.] who was mainly instrumental in raising it from the state of a poor village to its present improved condition. . . . The situation is pleasant and healthy, the houses are neatly built, and the streets are spacious, but not regularly paved nor lighted: the inhabitants [who were weavers working for Carlisle manufacturers] are supplied with water from wells'; Lewis, *England*, 3:145. Graham (d. 1782) also built the family seat at Netherby, later occupied by his son, Sir James Graham. William Hutchinson, *History of Cumberland*, 2 vols. (Carlisle, 1794), 2:532-33.

[9] The Tolbooth parish was erected by the Edinburgh Town Council Dec. 24, 1641, and the west portion of St. Giles (formerly used as the Tolbooth, from which the name of the parish has arisen) was appropriated for its use. After a repair or alteration it was opened on Apr. 20, 1656. On the New Assembly Hall being built, this building was appropriated for the use of the Tolbooth parish, and opened Nov. 5, 1843. Who delivered the boring sermon is not clear, for Alexander Webster (1707-84), the minister of the parish from 1737, a distinguished statistician, royal chaplain, and apologist for the revival at Cambuslang, had died on January 25, and was not succeeded by another evangelical, Thomas Randall (1746-1827), until June 1785. Scott, *Fasti*, 1:49-52.

awaken drowsy hearers. About four, I preached at Lady Maxwell's,[10] two or three miles from Edinburgh, and at six in our own house. For once it was thoroughly filled. I preached on 'God is a spirit, and they that worship him, must worship him in spirit and truth.'[11] I am amazed at this people. Use the most cutting words and apply them in the most pointed manner; still they *hear*, but *feel* no more than the seats they sit upon!

Mon. 26. I went to Glasgow and preached in the evening to a very different congregation. Many attended in the morning, although the morning preaching had been long discontinued both here and at Edinburgh. In the evening, many were obliged to go away, the house not being able to contain them. Wednesday 28, we found the same inconvenience, but those who could get in found a remarkable blessing. Thursday 29, the house[12] was thoroughly filled at four, and hearts of the people were as melting wax. Afterwards, I returned to Edinburgh, and in the evening the house was well filled. So that we must not say, 'The people of Edinburgh love the word of God only on the Lord's Day.'

Fri. 30. We went to Perth, now but the shadow of what it was, though it begins to lift up its head. It is certainly the sweetest place in all north Britain, unless perhaps Dundee. I preached in the Tolbooth to a large and well-behaved congregation. Many of them were present again at five in the morning, May 1. I then went to Dundee, through the Carse of Gowrie, the fruitfullest valley in the kingdom. And I observe a spirit of improvement prevails in Dundee and all the country round about it. Handsome houses spring up on every side. Trees are planted in abundance. Wastes and commons are continually turned into meadows and fruitful fields. There wants only a proportionable improvement in religion, and this will be one of the happiest countries in Europe.

In the evening, I preached in our own ground to a numerous congregation, but the next afternoon to one far more numerous, on whom I earnestly enforced, 'How long halt ye between two

---

[10] In 1783 Lady Maxwell (on whom see above, May 31, 1782) had moved to Coates Hall, described by JW (below, May 27, 1786) as 'my lovely lodging at Coates'.

[11] John 4:24.

[12] The preaching-room in Glasgow, from 1765 till the first chapel was opened in John Street in 1787, was in the Barbers' Hall in Stockwell Street, described by John Pawson in 1785 as 'miserable . . . , ugly beyond description, up a nasty narrow passage, and not large enough to hold one half of the people that would come to it, bad as it is.' Swift, *Scotland*, pp. 49-50.

opinions?"[13] Many of them *seemed* almost persuaded to halt no longer, but God only knows the heart.

Mon. 3. I was agreeably surprised at the improvement of the land between Dundee and Arbroath. Our preaching-house at Arbroath[14] was completely filled. I spoke exceeding plain on the difference of 'building upon the sand'[15] and building 'upon the rock'.[16] Truly these 'approve the things that are excellent',[17] whether they practise them or no.

I found this to be a genuine Methodist society: they are all thoroughly united to each other. They love and keep our rules. They long and expect to be perfected in love. If they continue so to do, they will and must increase in number as well as in grace.

Tues. 4. I reached Aberdeen between four and five in the afternoon. Wednesday 5, I found the morning preaching had been long discontinued; yet the bands and the select society were kept up. But many were faint and weak for want of morning preaching and prayer-meetings, of which I found scarce any traces in Scotland.

In the evening, I talked largely with the preachers and showed them the hurt it did both to them and the people for any one preacher to stay six or eight weeks together in one place. Neither can he find matter for preaching every morning and evening, nor will the people come to hear him. Hence he grows cold by lying in bed, and so do the people. Whereas if he never stays more than a fortnight together in one place, he may find matter enough, and the people will gladly hear him. They immediately drew up such a plan for this circuit, which they determined to pursue.

Thur. 6. We had the largest congregation at five which I have seen since I came into the 'kingdom'. We set out immediately after preaching and reached Oldmeldrum about ten. A servant of Lady Banff's was waiting for us there, who desired I would take post-horses to Forglen.[18] In two hours, we reached an inn which, the servant told us, was four little miles from her house. So we

---

[13] 1 Kgs. 18:21.
[14] Built in 1772.
[15] Matt. 7:26.
[16] Matt. 7:24.
[17] Cf. Phil. 1:10.
[18] Forglen was the house of the Abercromby family (and also a parish a mile west of Turriff). Lady Banff (who d. in 1790) was the mother of Jean, wife of Sir George Abercromby of Birkenbog and Forglen, and the widow of Sir Alexander Ogilvie of Forglen, who succeeded as seventh Baron Banff in the Scottish peerage in 1746 and died at Forglen in 1771. JW visited her again on May 24, 1790.

made the best of our way and got thither in exactly three hours. All the family received us with the most cordial affection. At seven, I preached to a small congregation, all of whom were seriously attentive, and some, I believe, deeply affected.

Fri. 7. I took a walk round about the town. I know not when I have seen so pleasant a place. One part of the house is an ancient castle, situated on the top of a little hill. At a small distance runs a clear river, with a beautiful wood on its banks. Close to it is a shady walk to the right, and another on the left hand. On two sides up the house there is abundance of wood; on the other, a wide prospect over fields and meadows. About ten, I preached again with much liberty of spirit, on 'Love never faileth.'[19] About two, I left this charming place and made for Keith. But I know not how we could have got thither had not Lady Banff sent me forward through that miserable road with four stout horses.

I preached about seven to the poor of this world.[20] Not a silk coat was seen among them; and to the greatest part of them at five in the morning. And I did not at all regret my labour.

Sat. 8. We reached the banks of the Spey.[21] I suppose, there are few such rivers in Europe. The rapidity of it exceeds even that of the Rhine, and it was now much swelled with melting snow. However we made shift to get over before ten and, about twelve, reached Elgin. Here I was received by a daughter of good Mr. Plenderleath,[22] late of Edinburgh; with whom, having spent an agreeable hour, I hastened toward Forres. But we were soon at a full stop again, the river Findhorn[23] also was so swollen that we were afraid the ford was not passable. However, having a good guide, we passed it without much difficulty. I found Sir Lodowick Grant[24] almost worn out. Never was a visit more seasonable. By free and friendly conversation his spirits were so raised, that I am in hopes it will lengthen his life.

---

[19] Cf. 1 Cor. 13:8.

[20] On 'the town of beggars' at Newmill near Keith, see above, May 20, 1776.

[21] Orig., 'Spay'.

[22] Orig., 'Plenderlaith'. David Plenderleath, minister of Ormiston 1732-46, Dalkeith 1746-64, and of the second charge of the Tolbooth Church, Edinburgh, 1764, till his death in 1779. David Plenderleath, whose death was said to be 'deeply regretted by the pious', was the son of the famous Patrick Plenderleath of Saline, of whom a friend declared 'I never knew a man in whom more of the Lord's image shined'; D. Fraser, *Life and Diary of the Rev. Ralph Erskine* (Edinburgh, 1834), pp. 127-28. Lady Maxwell had enjoyed his preaching at Elgin. JW wrote to him in 1768. Telford 5:89-91.

[23] Orig., 'Findam'.

[24] On Sir Lodowick Grant, who died in 1790, see June 7, 1764 (21:469, n. 34 in this edn.).

Sun. 9. I preached to a small company at noon, on 'his commandments are not grievous'.[25] As I was concluding, Colonel Grant and his Lady came in, for whose sake I began again and 'lectured', as they call it, on the former part of the 15th chapter of St. Luke. We had a larger company in the afternoon, to whom I preached on 'judgment to come'.[26] And this subject seemed to affect them most.

Mon. 10. I set out for Inverness. I had sent Mr. M'Allum[27] before, on George Whitfield's[28] horse, to give notice of my coming. Hereby I was obliged to take both George and Mrs. M'Allum with me in my chaise. To ease the horses, we walked forward from Nairn, ordering Richard[29] to follow us as soon as they were fed. He did so, but there were two roads. So as we took one, and he the other, we walked about twelve miles and a half of the way through heavy rain. We then found Richard waiting for us at a little ale-house and drove on to Inverness. But, blessed be God, I was no more tired than when I set out from Nairn. I preached at seven to a far larger congregation than I had seen here since I preached in the kirk. And surely the labour was not in vain, for God sent a message to many hearts.

Tue. 11. Notwithstanding the long discontinuance of morning preaching, we had a large congregation at five. I breakfasted at the first house I was invited to at Inverness, where good Mr. M'Kenzie[30] then lived. His three daughters live in it now, one of whom inherits all the spirit of her father. In the afternoon, we took a walk over the bridge into one of the pleasantest countries I have seen. It runs along by the side of the clear river and is well cultivated and well wooded. And here first we heard abundance of

---

[25] 1 John 5:3.

[26] In the Diary, JW cites Rev. 20:12 as his text on this occasion.

[27] Duncan M'Allum (1755-1834), one of the stupendous autodidacts of Scottish Methodism. Of little formal education, he was early converted by Methodist agency and disclosed a consuming passion for knowledge which led him into 'Latin, Greek, Hebrew and Syriac, . . . civil and ecclesiastical history, and . . . most branches of mental and physical science'. JW appointed him to a circuit in 1775, and he served mostly in Scotland, preaching much in Gaelic. A legend in his lifetime, his obituary declared that 'perhaps no Wesleyan minister in Scotland was ever better known, more generally esteemed, or more useful; and among his sincerest admirers were many of the clergy of the Scottish Church, and professors of the Scottish universities.' *Wesleyan Methodist Magazine* 57 (1834):717. He himself wrote an obituary of his wife; *Methodist Magazine* 37 (1814):207–12.

[28] On George Whitfield, itinerant, see above, Aug. 19, 1781.

[29] JW's personal servant, on whom see below, Nov. 23, 1784.

[30] On Murdach Mackenzie, see Apr. 27, 1770 (22:226 in this edn.).

birds welcoming the return of spring. The congregation was larger this evening than the last, and great part of them attended in the morning. We had then a solemn parting, as we could hardly expect to meet again in the present world.

Wed. 12. I dined once more at Sir Lodowick Grant's, whom likewise I scarce expect to see any more. His Lady is lately gone to rest, and he seems to be swiftly following her. A church being offered me at Elgin[31] in the evening, I had a multitude of hearers, whom I strongly exhorted to 'seek the Lord while he may be found.'[32] Thursday 13, we took a view of the poor remains of the once magnificent cathedral.[33] By what ruins are left, the workmanship appears to have been exquisitely fine. What barbarians must they have been who hastened the destruction of this beautiful pile by taking the lead off the roof!

The church was again well filled in the evening by those who seemed to *feel* much more than the night before. In consequence, the morning congregation was more than doubled, and deep attention sat on every face. I do not despair of good being done even here—provided the preachers be sons of thunder.

Fri. 14. We saw at a distance the Duke of Gordon's new house, six hundred and fifty feet in front![34] Well might the Indian ask,

[31] There were two charges attached to the parish church in Elgin. The senior charge was filled in 1778, after much opposition, by the incumbent of the second charge (1774-78), presented by George III, William Peterkin A.M. (d. 1788), a graduate of Aberdeen, remembered as the first incumbent of the parish who had recourse to pulpit notes. The second charge was vacant at the moment. Scott, *Fasti*, 6:391, 394.

[32] Cf. Isa. 55:6.

[33] The 'poor remains' of Elgin Cathedral were indeed a sad mixture of squalour and splendour. Founded by the Bishop of Moray in 1224, the cathedral was burned by Alexander Stewart, the Wolf of Badenoch, subsequently restored, 'and continued in all its original magnificence till the year 1568, when the Regent Morton directed the lead to be stripped off its roof, in order to pay his troops. From its exposure to the weather, it now began to decay; the woodwork of the great tower in time perished, and the foundation sinking, it fell in 1711.' Originally the cathedral, 264 feet in length, had five towers, and on the same site were a chapter house, conventual buildings and a bishop's palace. Samuel Johnson found that the result produced in Scotland by barbarism, would in England be produced by neglect; Johnson, *Western Isles* (Yale edn., 1971), pp. 23-24. But 'by the laudable exertions of the barons of the exchequer of Scotland (*c.* 1820), and the commissioners of woods and forests of England, much of the accumulated rubbish' was eventually removed, and other interesting features brought to light. Lewis, *Scotland*, 1:399. Cf. John Shanks, *Elgin: and a Guide to Elgin Cathedral* (London, 1866), chs. 3 & 4.

[34] Gordon Castle, near Fochabers, was 'considered the most magnificent and princely mansion north of the Firth of Forth. The edifice was originally a gloomy tower, in the centre of a morass called the Bog of Gight, and accessible only by a narrow causeway, and a drawbridge. It [became] a vast structure, of which the exterior measures 570 feet

'Are you *white* men no bigger than we *red* men? Then why do you build such lofty houses?'[35] The country between this and Banff is well cultivated and extremely pleasant. About two, I read prayers and preached in the Episcopal Chapel at Banff, one of the neatest
5   towns[36] in the kingdom. About ten, I preached in Lady Banff's dining room at Forglen[37] to a very serious, though genteel, congregation, and afterwards spent a most agreeable evening with the lovely family.

Sat. 15. We set out early and dined at Aberdeen. On the road, I
10 read Ewen Cameron's translation of *Fingal*.[38] I think he has proved the authenticity of it beyond all reasonable contradiction. But what a poet was Ossian! Little inferior to either Homer or Virgil; in some respects superior to both. And what an hero was Fingal. Far more humane than Hector himself, whom we cannot
15 excuse for murdering one that lay upon the ground. And with whom Achilles, or even pious Aeneas, is not worthy to be named. But who is this excellent translator, Ewen Cameron? Is not his other name, Hugh Blair?

Sun. 16. I went to Newburgh, a small fishing town fifteen miles
20 north of Aberdeen. Here is at present, according to its bigness, the liveliest society in the kingdom.[39] I preached in a kind of

---

in length; and the building consists of four lofty stories, with spacious two-storied wings, and connecting galleries or arcades of similar height. From behind the centre rises a ponderous square tower of the eleventh century, nearly ninety feet high, overlooking the stately pile.' The bog was transformed into a magnificent park with trees and classical statuary. Lewis, *Scotland*, 1:434.

[35] Another version of this apothegm was reported by JW from Georgia, July 1, 1736 (18:163 in this edn.).

[36] JW made a similar observation above, May 20, 1776. Before the sixteenth century, Banff was an inconsiderable fishing village, and it suffered a good deal during the civil war of the seventeenth century. This, combined with the demolition of older property, meant that the town was in a great measure newly built, with regular and spacious streets. It was in keeping with this character that piped water was put in as early as 1810, and 'hot, cold and shower baths fitted up with every accommodation'. Lewis, *Scotland*, 1:102.

[37] Orig., 'Fortglen'. On Lady Banff and Forglen, see above, May 6, 1784.

[38] *Fingal, an Ancient Epic Poem in Six Books; together with several other poems composed by Ossian, and son of Fingal, translated from the Gaelic language* (London, 1762). These poems were in fact the work of James Macpherson (1736-96). Earlier poems of his, published as *Fragments of Ancient Poetry, Collected in the Highlands and Translated from the Gaelic or Erse Languages* (Edinburgh, 1760) had been shown to Hugh Blair (on whom see above, May 10, 1779) who was impressed by them, and who argued for the authenticity of the later poems in *A Critical Dissertation on the Poems of Ossian, the Son of Fingal* (1763). See also July 17, 1767 (22:91 in this edn.).

[39] Orig., 'Newborough'. Newburgh was one of the many places in Scotland where Methodism took root, but given the superior competitive power of the Kirk in which

square to a multitude of people. And the whole congregation appeared to be moved and ready prepared for the Lord.

At two in the afternoon, Mr. Blake[40] read prayers and I preached in Trinity Chapel. It was crowded with people of all denominations. I preached from 1 Cor. 13:1, 2, 3, in utter defiance of their common saying, 'He is a good man, though he has bad tempers.' Nay, if he has *bad tempers* he is no more a *good man* than the devil is a *good angel.* At five, I preached in our own chapel, exceedingly crowded, on 'The form and power of godliness.'[41] I am now clear of these people and can cheerfully commend them to God.

Mon. 17. I reached Arbroath and inquired into that odd event which occurred there in the latter end of the last war. The famous Captain Fall[42] came one afternoon to the side of the town and sent three men on shore, threatening to lay the town in ashes unless they sent him thirty thousand pounds. That not being done, he began firing on the town the next day and continued it till night. But perceiving the country was alarmed, he sailed away the next day, having left some hundred cannon balls behind him, but not

---

for another half-century the evangelical party gained in strength, and given also the lack of clarity in Methodist connexional policy in Scotland, never thrived and finally died out. A chapel was built at Newburgh *c.* 1795, and a new one (which was assisted by the Distressed Chapels Fund) in 1818. This was sold in 1827, repurchased in 1831, and finally closed soon afterwards. Swift, *Methodism in Scotland*, p. 91.

[40] Orig., 'Black'. In the 1690s, at Presbyterian instigation, the Privy Council deposed (among others) the Episcopal minister of the West Church of St. Nicholas, Aberdeen, and closed the church to the congregation. The latter, however, established themselves in the Hospital and Church of the Trinity Friars, and used this Trinity Chapel until they were again deprived of a pastor and premises after the rebellion of 1715, building Old St. Paul's in 1721. From at least 1753, however, they were using the chapel again, and in 1770, they called the Rev. William Blake, minister of Ellon, whom JW encountered, as a third minister to assist at both chapels, confining him to Trinity Chapel in 1776. Blake took his congregation to a new St. James's Chapel in Netherkirkgate in 1791, and died in 1804. The congregation was dissolved in 1806. *The Church of St. Paul's in Loch Street, Aberdeen* (Aberdeen, 1946), pp. 7-8, 10, 13 (I owe a loan of this work to the kindness of the Rev. D. Strachan).

[41] Cf. 2 Tim. 3:5.

[42] Orig., 'Fell'. Captain William Fall, commander of the *Fearnought* cutter of Dunkirk, operated as a privateer during the American War of Independence. On May 23, 1781, he sailed into Arbroath Bay and demanded submission to the French flag under penalty of bombardment. The Town Council played for time till evening, and then requested terms. Fall, late that night, demanded £30,000 and six chief men of the town as hostages. Resistance was now led by the minister of Arbroath, Alexander Mackie (1731-87), and Fall was dared to bombard the town, which he proceeded to do. The next morning, troops arrived from Montrose, and a defiant answer was sent to Captain Fall. After bombarding the town with red-hot balls and ransoming two small Arbroath vessels which he had captured, Fall sailed off before noon. *WHS* 4 (1904):200-201; Hay, *Arbroath*, pp. 346-52.

having hurt man, woman, or child, or any thing else, save one old barn door.

Tue. 18. I preached at Dundee. Wednesday 19, I crossed over the pleasant and fertile county of Fife to Melville House,[43] the grand
5 and beautiful seat of Lord Leven. He was not at home, being gone to Edinburgh as the King's Commissioner. But the Countess was with two of her daughters and both her sons-in-law. At their desire, I preached in the evening, on 'It is appointed unto man once to die.'[44] And I believe God made the application. Thursday 20, it
10 blew a storm. Nevertheless, with some difficulty, we crossed the Queensferry. Friday 21, I examined the society and found about sixty members left. Many of these were truly alive to God. So our labour here is not quite in vain. Saturday 22, I had some close conversation with L———— M————,[45] who appeared to be clearly
15 saved from sin, although exceedingly depressed by the tottering tenement of clay. About noon, I spent an hour with her poor scholars, forty of whom she has provided with a serious master, who takes pains to instruct them in the principles of religion as well as in reading and writing. A famous actress[46] just come down from Lon-
20 don (which [is], for the honour of Scotland, just during the sitting of the Assembly), stole away a great part of our congregation tonight. How much wiser are these Scots than their forefathers!

---

[43] Orig., 'Melval-house'. Melville House, erected in 1692 about a mile east of Collessie, was the seat in Co. Fife of David, sixth Earl of Leven (1722-1802), who was High Commissioner to the General Assembly of the Church of Scotland, 1783-1801. The countess, Wilhelmina (*c.* 1724-98), was a posthumous daughter of William Nisbet of Dirleton, Co. Haddington, the sister of Lady Banff (encountered by JW on May 6, 1784), and is said to have been converted at the age of 19 by George Whitefield. Her exemplary piety was praised by the Countess of Huntingdon. 'She was one of a band of excellent ladies in high rank, who united in establishing a meeting for reading the Scriptures, to be held alternately at each other's houses. It continued to be well attended and singularly useful for many years. It was strictly confined to a select circle of women in high life, many of whom were ornaments to the Christian church by a life of holiness. The Countess of Northesk and Hopetoun, daughter to Lord and Lady Leven, Lady Glenorchy, Wilhelmina, Countess of Leven, and her excellent sisters, Lady Ruthven and Lady Banff, etc., were valuable members of that select band.' Sir William Fraser, *The Melvilles, Earls of Melville, and the Leslies, Earls of Leven*, 3 vols. (Edinburgh, 1890), 1:350; Seymour, *Huntingdon*, 1:100-101.

[44] Cf. Heb. 9:27.

[45] On Lady Maxwell, see above, May 31, 1782. The reference to the 'tottering tenement of clay' is misleading; Lady Maxwell was in her early forties and survived till 1810. Her school is described above, June 1, 1782.

[46] Sarah Siddons (1755-1831) appeared for the first of nine performances in her famous role of Belisidora in Thomas Otway's tragedy in blank verse, *Venice Preserved*, at the Royalty Theatre on May 22, 1784. It is said that on one day, 2575 applications were made for 630 places.

Sun. 23. I went in the morning to the Tolbooth Kirk,[47] in the afternoon to the Old Episcopal Chapel. But they have lost their glorying: they *talked* the moment service was done, as if they had been in London. In the evening, the octagon was well filled, and I applied with all possible plainness, 'God is a Spirit; and they that worship him, must worship him in spirit and in truth.'[48]

Mon. 24. I preached at Dunbar. Tuesday 25, I spent an hour with Mr. and Mrs. F[all],[49] a woman every way accomplished. Neither of them had ever yet heard a sermon out of the kirk. But they ventured that evening, and I am in hope they did not hear in vain. Wednesday 26, we went on to Berwick-upon-Tweed. The congregation in the town-hall was very numerous. So it was likewise at five in the morning. Thursday 27, we travelled through a delightful country to Kelso. Here the two seceding ministers[50] have taken true pains to frighten the people from hearing us by retailing all the ribaldry of Mr. Cudworth,[51] Toplady,[52] and Rowland Hill.[53] But God has called one of them to his account already, and in a fearful manner. As no house could contain the congregation, I preached in the churchyard,[54] and a more decent behaviour I have scarce ever seen. Afterwards, we walked to the Duke of Roxburgh's[55] seat, about half a mile from the town, finely situated on a rising ground[56] near the ruins of Roxburghe Castle. It has a

---

[47] On the Tolbooth Kirk, see above, Apr. 25, 1784.

[48] John 4:24.

[49] JW had taken tea with this couple at Haddington and was to visit them again two years later. Diary, May 25, 1784; May 30, 1786.

[50] There were meeting-houses for Burghers and Antiburghers in Kelso. Haig, *Kelso*, pp. 122-23.

[51] On William Cudworth, see Mar. 25, 1759 (21:180, n. 12 in this edn.).

[52] On Augustus Montague Toplady, see Nov. 29, 1775 (22:474 in this edn.).

[53] On Rowland Hill, see above, June 26, 1777.

[54] It seems to have been on this occasion that Sir Walter Scott, then a boy of twelve, heard JW preach, 'standing on a chair in Kelso churchyard. . . . He told many excellent stories. One I remember which he said had happened to him at Edinburgh. "A drunken dragoon", said Wesley, "was commencing in military fashion, 'G-d eternally d—n me', just as I was passing. I touched the poor man on the shoulder, and when he turned round fiercely, said calmly, you mean '*God bless you*'." In the mode of telling the story he failed not to make us sensible how much his patriarchal appearance, and mild yet bold rebuke, overawed the soldier, who touched his hat, thanked him, and, I think, came to chapel that evening.' J. G. Lockhart, *Memoirs of the Life of Sir Walter Scott*, 10 vols. (2nd edn., Edinburgh, 1839), 6:46.

[55] John Ker, third Duke of Roxburgh (1740-1804), a celebrated book-collector and intimate of George III, at whose wedding his sisters were bridesmaids.

[56] The Ker family inherited the property of Kelso Abbey at the Dissolution, and in 1718 built Floors Castle, 'a stately edifice . . . after a design by Sir John Vanbrugh, and situated in an extensive park embellished with stately timber and rich plantations. In the

noble castle: the front and the offices round make it look like a little town. Most of the apartments within are finished in an elegant,
but not in a costly manner. I doubt whether two of Mr. Lascelle's
rooms at Harewood House[57] did not cost more in furnishing than
twenty of these. But the Duke's house is far larger, containing no
less than forty bedchambers. But it is not near finished yet, nor
probably will be till the owner is no more seen.

Fri. 28. I entered into England once more and, in the evening,
preached in the town hall at Alnwick. Saturday 29, I should have
preached in the town hall at Morpeth, but it was pre-engaged by a
company of strolling players. So we retired into our own preaching-house. In the afternoon, I went on to Newcastle.

May 30, Whitsunday, the rain obliged us to be in the orphan-
house both morning and evening. But in the afternoon, I was
forced to preach abroad at the Fell by the multitudes that flocked
together, partly moved by the death of William Bell and his wife,[58]
one so soon after the other.

Tuesday, June 1. About nine I preached to a large number of
the poor people at Howden Pans,[59] at noon in North Shields, and
in the evening at Newcastle, where I had now great satisfaction,
the congregation both morning and evening being larger than
they had been for many years, and the society being much alive
and in great peace and harmony.[60] Friday 4, I went over to Sunderland and found the work of God here also in a prosperous

park is a holly bush of venerable growth which marks out the spot where James II [of
Scotland] was killed by the bursting of a cannon, while employed in the siege of Roxburghe Castle, in 1460.' Lewis, *Scotland*, 2:8.

[57] Orig., 'Harwood-house'. On Edward Lascelles and Harewood House, see above,
Apr. 30, 1779.

[58] William Bell, who died on Jan. 1, 1784, aged 84, and his wife Jane who followed
him on Feb. 10, 1784, aged 71, were bakers in Gateshead, who, losing their only child
young, devoted their energies and resources to the Methodist cause. They erected the
first Methodist chapel in Co. Durham at Low Fell in 1754, and on their death left it to
the connexion. One of the earlier Methodist Sunday schools in the region was attached
to it in 1789. *WHS* 20 (1936):124-26; Thomas Wilson, *The Pitman's Pay, and other
Poems* (Gateshead, 1843), p. 97, n. 6.

[59] Howden Pans was a township in the parish of Wallsend, 2 miles south-west of
North Shields. Situated on the Tyne, the place obtained its name from the presence of
numerous saltpans, but this business was gradually displaced by the export of coal.
Lewis, *England*, 2:475.

[60] William Smith, JW's step-son-in-law, noted of this visit: 'We have been favoured
lately with Mr. Wesley's company. His visit was highly pleasing and I hope very profitable.
He preached admirably well [and] was attended with the largest congregations I ever
remember, and his whole behaviour and temper of mind was truly apostolical.' MS Corr.
of Wm. Smith and Joseph Benson, July 16, 1784, in Methodist Archives, Manchester.

state. Saturday 5, I saw as many of the people, sick or well, as I could and was much comforted among them. Sunday 6, I preached at eight in the Room; at eleven, in Monkwearmouth Church.[61] I purposed preaching abroad at Newcastle in the evening, but the weather would not permit. So I preached in the house, on 'This is the record, that God hath given unto us eternal life; and this life is in his Son.'[62]

Mon. 7. About noon I preached at Durham,[63] and in the evening in the town hall at Hartlepool, where I had not been for sixteen years.[64]

Tue. 8. I came to Stockton-on-Tees. Here I found an uncommon work of God among the children. Many of them from six to fourteen were under serious impressions and earnestly desirous to save their souls. There were upwards of sixty who constantly came to be examined and appeared to be greatly awakened. I preached at noon, on 'The kingdom of heaven is at hand,'[65] and the people seemed to feel every word. As soon as I came down from the desk, I was enclosed by a body of children, one of whom and another sunk down upon their knees, until they were all kneeling. So I kneeled down myself and began praying for them. Abundance of people ran back into the house. The fire kindled and ran from heart to heart, till few, if any, were unaffected. Is not this a new thing in the earth? God begins his work in children. Thus it has been also in Cornwall, Manchester, and Epworth. Thus the flame spreads to those of riper years, till at length they all know him and praise him, from the least unto the greatest.

Wed. 9. I went to Barnard Castle.[66] Here I was informed, that my

[61] On former Methodist relations with Monkwearmouth Church, see May 31, 1761 (21:326, n. 48 in this edn.). The perpetual curate from 1768 to his death in 1792 was Jonathan Ivison. He had been curate of Whitburn from 1751 till at least 1770, and was vicar of West Torrington, Lincs., from 1763 till his death; Lincs. Record Office, Lincs. Episc. Reg. 39, p. 15. In 1792 he said he resided on his living at Monkwearmouth (Auckland Castle, MS Monkwearmouth Visitation Return, 1792). *Ex inf.* Miss M. McCallum.

[62] 1 John 5:11.

[63] Orig., 'Anham'.

[64] The last visit recorded in the Journal was on July 7, 1766; 22:48 in this edn. Hartlepool was at this time a small seaside spa, boasting 'scenery . . . of a romantic character particularly along the seashore, where the shelving precipitous rocks, which the lashing of the waves has hollowed into caverns and recesses, present a wild and picturesque appearance.' The town was governed by a mayor, recorder, and twelve capital burgesses, who did their business in the town hall where JW preached; it was one of their recent improvements, being built about 1750. Lewis, *England*, 2:368.

[65] JW noted the text in his Diary as Mark 1:15, 'The kingdom of God is at hand.'

[66] Here his host was Anthony Steele, the father of the historian of Dales Methodism and one of the trustees of the Barnard Castle property. Steele, *Dales*, p. 155, 145.

old school-fellow, Mr. Fielding[67] and his wife, were gone to rest. His son, not choosing to live there, had let his lovely house to a stranger. So in a little time his very name and memory will be lost!

Sun. 10. After preaching at five, I took horse for the Dales and, about eight, preached at Cotherstone. Here I had the pleasure of seeing some of our brethren who had been long at variance, cordially reconciled. Hence, we rode through the rain and wind to Newbiggin in Teesdale. Being but a poor horseman and having a rough horse, I had just strength for my journey, and none to spare. But after resting awhile, I preached without any weariness.

Having then procured an easier horse, I rode over the great mountain into Weardale. But I found not my old host; good Stephen Watson[68] was removed to Abraham's bosom. So was that mother in Israel, Jane Nattrass[69] (before, Salkeld), the great instrument of that amazing work among the children. But God is with them still: most of the leaders and many of the people are much alive to God, as we found in the evening, when we had such a shower of grace as I have seldom known.

Fri. 11. About ten, riding through a village called Middleton,[70] I was desired to preach there. So I began in the street without delay. A large number of people came together and received the word with gladness. Afterwards we rode at leisure to Barnard Castle and, on Saturday 12, to Darlington.

Sun. 13. We had a sound, useful sermon at church.[71] At eight, I preached in our own Room, designing to preach abroad in the afternoon, but the rain prevented. Monday 14 about noon, I preached at Northallerton, and I believe God touched many hearts, as also at Thirsk, where I preached in the evening to an attentive congregation.

---

[67] On George Fielding, see May 9, 1764 (21:464, n. 7 in this edn.).

[68] Presumably the husband of Jane Watson. Steele, *Dales*. p. 107.

[69] Orig. "Nattres'. On Jane Nattrass, née Salkeld, see June 5, 1772 (22:334, n. 71 in this edn.) in a long passage giving JW's own account of the Weardale revival to which he here refers. Curnock notes that 43 children joined the Weardale society at this visit.

[70] This slightly derogatory reference obscures the fact that Middleton in Teesdale was a market town and parish, and, in consequence of the development of lead-mining, the major population centre in the west of the county.

[71] Who preached this valuable sermon is quite uncertain. Darlington was a perpetual curacy which passed from Henry Hemington (1772-84) to William Gordon (1784-1830) at precisely this time; and both were resident in Kent, the one at Westerham and the other at Hastings. There were also subcurates from time to time. Gordon died in 1830 at the age of 84, and was also rector of Speldhurst, Kent, 1816-30. W. H. D. Longstaffe, *The History and Antiquities of the Parish of Darlington* (Darlington, 1854), p. 227.

Tue. 15. I preached once more to my old friends at Osmotherley. About noon, I preached at Potto and, in the evening, at Hutton Rudby, where we had a glorious opportunity: some great persons who were present seemed to be struck and almost persuaded
to be Christians. Wednesday 16, I preached in Stokesley about
eight, in Guisborough at noon, and in the evening at Whitby.[72]

The morning congregation filled the house. Indeed, the society
here may be a pattern to all in England. They despise all ornaments but good works, together with a meek and quiet spirit. I
did not see a ruffle, no nor a fashionable cap among them, though
many of them are in easy circumstances. I preached at the market-
place in the evening, where were at least thrice as many as the
house could contain.

Sat. 19. I met such a select society as I have not seen since I left
London. They were about forty, of whom I did not find one who
had not a clear witness of being saved from inbred sin. Several of
them had lost it for a season, but could never rest till they had
recovered it. And every one of them seemed now to walk in the
full light of God's countenance.

About one, I preached to another congregation of plain people
at Robin Hood's [Bay]. Here was the first society in all these
parts, several years before there was any in Whitby. But their continual jars with each other prevented their increase either in grace
or number. At present they seem to be all at peace. So I hope we
shall now have joy over them.

In the evening, I preached to a large congregation at Scarborough. Sunday 20, the new vicar showed plainly why he refused
those who desired the liberty for me to preach in his church. A
keener sermon I never heard. So all I have done to persuade the
people to attend the church is overturned at once! And all who
preach thus, will drive the Methodists from the church, in spite
of all that I can do. I preached in the evening, on 1 Cor. 13:1, 2, 3.
And God mightily confirmed his word, applying it to the hearts
of many of the hearers.

---

[72] It was on this occasion that JW said to the wife of William Ripley, stone-mason,
builder, preacher of the gospel and leading light of the Whitby society, 'Sister Ripley,
if you want your husband to die, keep him at home, but if you want him to live, let
him go and travel with me a few weeks. I will take care of him.' After an emotional
family parting, Ripley travelled with JW till the following Conference at the beginning of August. On the advice of the physician, William Hey, he was then sent on a
sea voyage to London, but still died the following December. *WHS* 4 (1904):127–32;
6 (1907):37–42.

Mon. 21. The rain drove us into the house at Bridlington.[73]
Tuesday 22, we stopped at a little town[74] where Mr. Osbaldeston
lately lived, a gentleman of large fortune whose lady was as gay
and fashionable as any. But suddenly she ran from east to west.
5 She parted with all her clothes, dressed like a servant, and scarce
allowed herself the necessaries of life. But who can convince her
that she is going too far? I fear nothing less than Omnipotence.

About one, I preached to a large and remarkably serious congregation at Beverley; about six, at [Kingston upon] Hull. After-
10 wards, I met the society and strongly exhorted them 'to press on
to the prize of their high calling'.[75] Thursday 24, I preached about
one at Pocklington, and in the evening at York, where I enforced,
'Thou shalt worship the Lord thy God, and him only shalt thou
serve.'[76] Friday 25, many were in tears, and a fire seemed to run
15 through the whole congregation, while I opened that Scripture,
'They shall rest in their beds, each one walking in his uprightness.'[77] Such another opportunity we had in the evening, while I
was explaining the words of our Lord to the centurion, 'Go thy
way; and as thou hast believed, so be it done unto thee.'[78]

20 Sat. 26. About two, I preached at Thorne and inquired what
fruit remained of the great work of God there? Some, I found,
had drawn back to their sins, but many held fast what they
received. Hence I rode to Epworth, which I still love beyond most
places in the world. In the evening, I besought all them that had
25 been so highly favoured, 'Not to receive the grace of God in
vain'.[79]

Sun. 27. I preached at Misterton at eight, and at Upperthorpe[80]

---

[73] Orig. 'Burlington'.

[74] There is an editorial problem relating to the compilation of the Journal here. There
is no doubt that the 'little town' is the parish of Hunmanby 8 miles south-east of Scarborough. A society had been formed there which worshipped in a barn till 1816. The
manor house was occupied by Humphrey Brooke Osbaldeston (1745-1835) who had
come into the estate in 1778. He married Catherine, daughter of Sir Joseph Pennington,
Bart., who is the eccentric wife to whom JW refers; *WHS* 5 (1906):249. Why JW uses
the past tense ('lately lived') is not clear: this journal extract was published in 1789. The
schedule listed in the Diary suggests that JW could have stopped at Hunmanby
(halfway between Scarborough and Bridlington) on the morning of the 21st; backtrack-
ing there on the 22nd would not allow for an early arrival at Beverley, which is confirmed by both JW's Diary and that of William Ripley.

[75] Cf. Phil. 3:14.

[76] Matt. 4:10.

[77] Isa. 57:2.

[78] Matt. 8:13.

[79] Cf. 2 Cor. 6:1.   [80] Orig. 'Overthorp'.

about one. At four, I took my stand in Epworth market-place and preached on those words in the Gospel for the day, 'There is joy in heaven over one sinner that repenteth, more than over ninety and nine just persons that need no repentance.'[81] It seemed, as if very few, if any, of the sinners then present were unmoved. 5

Mon. 28. I inquired into the state of the work of God which was so remarkable two years ago.[82] It is not yet at an end, but there has been a grievous decay owing to several causes: (1) the preachers that followed Thomas Tattershall[83] were neither so zealous nor so diligent as he had been; (2) the two leaders to whom the young 10 men and lads were committed went up and down to preach and so left them in a great measure to themselves, or rather to the world and the devil; (3) the two women[84] who were the most useful of all others forsook them, the one leaving town and the other leaving God; (4) the factories which employed so many of the 15 children failed, so that all of them were scattered abroad; (5) the meetings of the children by the preachers were discontinued, so their love soon grew cold; and as they rose into men and women, foolish desires entered, and destroyed all the grace they had left. Nevertheless, great part of them stood firm, especially the young 20 maidens, and still adorn their profession. This day, I met the children myself and found some of them still alive to God. And I do not doubt but if the preachers are zealous and active, they will recover most of those that have been scattered.

Today I entered on my eighty-second year and found myself 25 just as strong to labour, and as fit for any exercise of body or mind, as I was forty years ago. I do not impute this to second causes, but to the sovereign Lord of all. It is he who bids the sun of life stand still, so long as it pleaseth him.

---

[81] Cf. Luke 15:7.

[82] On this revival see above, May 14, 1782.

[83] Thomas Tattershall (*c.* 1754-1822) was admitted to the itinerancy in 1782 with the reputation of an energetic and zealous man; *Wesleyan Methodist Magazine* 45 (1822):414, 615. He had been admitted on trial in 1781, and stationed at Epworth with James Barry and John Morris. The next two years saw five changes among the three circuit staff, only John Beanland serving for the whole period, and another complete revolution followed at the Conference of 1784. Tattershall's part in the Epworth revival of 1782 is mentioned frequently in *Arminian Magazine* 7 (1784):45-50, 103-7. William Ripley noted that 'Mr. Wesley severely condemned the preachers for three things, viz. neglecting the select society, the meeting of the children, and not going to the poor house. "It is time for me", said he, "to be taken away when I am entirely disregarded," a message which reads oddly beside his birthday celebration below. *WHS* 4 (1904):128.

[84] Ann Field and Ann Towris; which was which is not known.

I am as strong at eighty-one, as I was at twenty-one, but abundantly more healthy, being a stranger to the head-ache, tooth-ache, and other bodily disorders which attended me in my youth. We can only say, 'The Lord reigneth!'[85] While we live, let us live
5 to him!

In the afternoon, I went to Gainsborough and willingly accepted the offer of Mr. Dean's chapel.[86] The audience was large and seemed much affected; possibly some good may be done, even at Gainsborough! Tuesday 29, I preached in the street at
10 Scotter to a large and deeply attentive congregation. It was a solemn and comfortable season. In the evening, I read prayers and preached in Owston [Ferry] Church, and again in the morning. Wednesday 20 in the evening, I preached at Epworth. In the residue of the week, I preached morning and evening in several of
15 the neighbouring towns.

Sunday, July 4. I read prayers and preached in Owston [Ferry] Church, so filled as probably it never was before; and believe everyone, awakened or unawakened, felt that God was there. The congregation in the afternoon at Epworth market-place was
20 thought to be larger than ever it was before. And great was the Holy One of Israel in the midst of them.

Mon. 5. At twelve, I preached in the elegant house at Doncaster, for once pretty well filled, and spoke more strongly, indeed more roughly, than I am accustomed to do. It was sultry hot (as it
25 has been once or twice before) while we went to Rotherham, where I preached abroad to a larger congregation, both of rich and poor, than even at Epworth and earnestly enforced on those who are called believers, 'By their fruits ye shall know them.'[87]

Tue. 6. I joined again the select society, which was fallen in
30 pieces, and prayed them to be wiser for the time to come. I break-

[85] 1 Chron. 16:31; Ps. 93:1; 96:10; 97:1, 99:1.

[86] William Ripley places this service the following morning, saying, 'we had a good sermon at Gainsborough in a gentleman's meeting-house, and a parting blessing, when Mr. Wesley explained the rise and progress of Methodism. The preacher of the place desired licence to show his catholic love and exhort us to the same after Mr. Wesley had done'; *WHS* 4 (1904):128. The chapel was used by a congregation of Independents who had seceded from the Presbyterian congregation as it moved towards unitarianism. It had been opened by the Countess of Huntingdon's Anglican friend, Rev. Cradock Glascott, and was secured financially by John Dean, of Gainsborough, wharfinger, and subsequently by his son, Joseph, a cheesefactor, and first chairman of the Gainsborough Bridge Company.

[87] Matt 7:20. The Diary gives Matt 7:16, 'Ye shall know them by their fruits', as JW's text.

fasted at that amiable old man's, Mr. Sparrow,[88] elder brother to his twin-soul, whom I knew at Westminster. Thence I went on to Sheffield, where the society is increased to near some hundred members. How swiftly does the work of God spread among those who earn their bread 'by the sweat of their brow?'[89]

Wed. 7. It was supposed there were a thousand persons present at five in the morning. A young gentlewoman was with us at breakfast, who was mourning and refused to be comforted. We prayed for her in faith, and in a few hours she was enabled to rejoice in God her Saviour. In the afternoon, the heat was scarce supportable, and it seemed to increase every hour. But between two and three in the morning, Thursday 8, came a violent storm followed by uncommon thunder and a flood of rain which continued about three hours. This entirely cooled the air and, ceasing just as we set out, left us a pleasant journey to Wakefield.[90]

I recommended to the congregation here (and afterwards in many other places) the example of the people in Holland (at least wherever I have been) who never *talk* in a place of public worship, either before or after the service. They took my advice. None curtsied or bowed or spoke to anyone, but went out in as decent a manner and in as deep silence as any I saw at Rotterdam or Utrecht.[91]

Fri. 9. I preached at Huddersfield in the morning, at Longwood House[92] at noon, and in the evening at Halifax. Sunday 11, I

---

[88] JW's connection with Westminster was through his elder brother Samuel who was an usher there, 1712-32, and his younger brother Charles, who was a pupil, 1716-26. JW lodged in his brother Samuel's house in Dean's Yard during his vacations from Charterhouse. The twin-soul whom JW knew and with whom he corresponded was Samuel Sparrow, a London merchant, who wrote a few spiritual works. Two years before his death in 1776, Samuel Sparrow wrote to JW insisting that 'though we cannot quite agree on some few subjects, yet I hope that will not prevent such a friendship as will last for ever. . . . True religion lies more in the heart than in the head, more in practice than in speculation; in faith that works by love and manifests itself in fidelity to God and love to men.' His brother, with whom JW now breakfasted, was John Sparrow, formerly of London and now of Wincobank near Sheffield, where he was still alive in 1785 at the age of 82. Neither are known to have been connected with Mrs. Sparrow of Lewisham, on whom see Sept. 29, 1747 (20:194-95, n. 33 in this edn.).

[89] Cf. Gen. 3:19.

[90] William Ripley notes that 'we got safe to a little place nigh Daw Green to preach at eleven o'clock, in a new [preaching] house, where my good old father Wesley enforced the words of the Canaanitish woman, "Lord keep me," with all the power of speech he was master of. O, how did he labour to bring people to believe NOW'; *WHS* 4 (1904):129. John Valton had been collecting for this chapel all the year, and preached at its foundation on April 29; *WHS* 6 (1907):34-35.

[91] See above, June 15, 1783.

[92] On Longwood House, see above, July 27, 1781.

preached in the morning at Greenland House, at one and in the
evening at Halifax. The house would in no wise contain the people, yet the wind was so high that I could not preach abroad.[93]

Mon. 12. Mr. Sutcliffe[94] read prayers and I preached at Hep-
5 tonstall, where many poor souls were refreshed. Between one and
two I preached in Todmorden Church,[95] and at five in our own
preaching-house,[96] boldly situated on the steep ascent of a tall
mountain.

Tue. 13. I went to Burnley,[97] a place which had been tried for
10 many years, but without effect. It seems the time was now come.
High and low, rich and poor, now flocked together from all quarters. And all were eager to hear, except one man, who was the
town-crier. He began to bawl amain, till his wife ran to him and
literally stopped his noise. She seized him with one hand and
15 clapped the other upon his mouth, so that he could not get out
one word. God then began a work which I am persuaded will not
soon come to an end. Wednesday 14, I preached at Colne. Thursday 15, I retired to Otley and rested two days.[98] Sunday 18, I

[93] It is clear from the independent accounts of Joseph Benson (Curnock, 6:525n.) and
William Ripley (*WHS* 4 [1904]:130) that JW preached out of doors twice, once at noon
when he was unable to make himself properly heard, and, in the evening 'upon a table
before our garden', very successfully.

[94] On Tobit Sutcliffe, minister of the chapelry of Heptonstall, see Apr. 18, 1774
(22:404, n. 72 in this edn.).

[95] Orig. 'Tedmorden-Church'. On church and incumbent, see above, Apr. 27, 1780.
In 1815, it was reported that 'the present very worthy curate, and truly gospel preacher .
. . has been the "good parson" there above 40 years.' *Methodist Magazine* 38 (1815):445.

[96] This chapel had been built in 1783, and in the view of the congregation, its 'bold
situation rendered it very inconvenient'. It cost them, however, a generation's effort to
get another, which was opened by Jabez Bunting in 1828; *Wesleyan Methodist Magazine*
51 (1828):482. William Ripley mentions that JW opened this chapel, still 'not quite finished . . . and called Pool of Bethesda', and that his host, Mr. Crosby, was 'a good man
of great substance and of good nature'. *WHS* 4 (1904):131.

[97] Orig., 'Beverley'; the Diary clearly says 'Burnley'. JW here takes a short way with
the sinners of Burnley. A society had been formed there in 1763, but after Grimshaw's
death in that year, it apparently died out. However, Thomas Dixon, one of the preachers appointed to the Colne circuit at the next Conference, noted in his unpublished
diary that 'the work of God at Burnley at this period was very young, but many in 1784
were converted.' The property owners of the town served notice on the Methodist congregation to leave their chapel, and prepared to boycott any alternative. Peter Harg-
reaves, joiner, however, allowed Methodists to meet in his workshop from the end of
1784 until the Keighley Green Chapel was built. B. Moore, *History of Wesleyan
Methodism in Burnley and East Lancashire* (Burnley, 1899), pp. 55-56.

[98] This usually means that JW was writing diligently, and the Diary confirms that he
was working on an 'Answer to Appeal', i.e., an answer to the circular written by John
Hampson, Sen., a preacher enraged at being omitted from the Deed of Declaration, *An
Appeal to the Reverend John and Charles Wesley; to All the Preachers who act in Connexion*

preached morning and afternoon in Bingley Church,[99] but it would not near contain the congregation. Before service, I stepped into the Sunday-school,[1] which contains two hundred and forty children, taught every Sunday by several masters and superintended by the curate. So, many children in one parish are restrained from open sin and taught a little good manners, at least, as well as to read the Bible. I find these schools springing up wherever I go. Perhaps God may have a deeper end therein than men are aware of. Who knows but some of these schools may become nurseries for Christians?

Tue. 20. Though it rained all day, in the morning we had a good congregation at five. Wednesday 21, I met the society and found but one or two of the original members, most of them being gone to Abraham's bosom. I was a little surprised to find that only two or three of the rest had stood fast in the glorious liberty. But indeed, most of them recovered their loss four years ago.

Thur. 22. Although it rained, yet I met the congregation in the morning, and most of them were athirst for full salvation. Friday 23, abundance of people were present at five in the morning, and such a company of children as I have hardly seen in England.

Sat. 24. In the evening, I went to Hanging Heaton, a little village near Dewsbury.[2] Some months since, an uncommon work of

---

with Him, and to Every Member of their Respective Societies in England, Scotland, Ireland and America; Smith, *Wesleyan Methodism*, 1:492. One of the signs of JW's advancing years was that his literary fertility was now diminished, and no work corresponding to this short title seems ever to have been published. JW, however, published a brief apologia, clearly written after the event, in *Arminian Magazine* 8 (1785):267–69.

[99] The vicar of Bingley, 1741–89, was Richard Hartley.

[1] Bingley Sunday School was an undenominational school in which general cooperation lasted till 1810, when it broke up under pressure of disagreements about extempore prayer, and of the opportunity given the established clergy to go their own way by the building of a National School; John Ward, *Historical Sketches of the Rise and Progress of Methodism in Bingley* (Bingley, 1863), p. 55. JW's next comments accurately reflect not only the enormous impetus given to the Sunday school movement by the organisation of nondenominational schools in Manchester, but also how little the central organisation of Methodism had to do with it. The withdrawal of Anglicans from so much of the nondenominational enterprise in the twenty years after JW's death left many Sunday schools in Methodist hands; Ward, *Religion and Society*, pp. 40–44, 53; T. W. Laqueur, *Religion and Respectability* (New Haven, 1976), pp. 65–74. But JW, who had more sympathy for the schools than some of his preachers, printed a letter on the subject from Robert Raikes in *Arminian Magazine* 8 (1785):41–43.

[2] John Valton, with the assistance of Elizabeth Ritchie, had been looking after the classes here for some weeks. He records: '24 July . . . This evening, Mr. Wesley preached at Hanging Heaton to a very large concourse of people. As we walked up to the village many of the people met him very lovingly and welcomed him into the town. 25 July. Mr. Wesley having walked from Hanging Heaton to Daw Green, preached a

God broke out here: the whole town was in a flame. There are now about two hundred in the society, and very few that do not know God. I was obliged to preach abroad by the multitude that flocked together. And many of them found that God was there, to
5 their unspeakable comfort.

Sun. 25. I preached to several thousands at Birstall, and to at least as many at Leeds. Tuesday 27, our Conference began,[3] at which four of our brethren, after long debate (in which Mr. Fletcher took much pains), acknowledged their fault, and all that
10 was past was forgotten. Thursday 29, being the public Thanksgiving day,[4] as there was not room for us in the old church, I read prayers, as well as preached, at our Room. I admired the whole

profitable sermon. He then walked to Birstal, 3 1/2 miles, and preached at Brown Hill to a vast large congregation; the one half could not hear him. Afterwards he set out to Leeds to hold the Conference.' *WHS* 8 (1911):35.

[3] The minutes of this Conference are less informative than the average. The great debate was about the Deed of Declaration (on which, see above, Feb. 22, 1784), establishing the membership of the legal Conference after JW's death. Moved, he claimed, partly by considerations of expense (which had recently occasioned complaints), he named fewer than half the present preachers to form the Legal Hundred, and, prudently making a choice in every age-group, necessarily excluded some seasoned preachers who felt they had a good claim to inclusion. Tempers ran high on both sides, till John Fletcher intervened: 'Never', recounted Charles Atmore, 'never while memory holds her seat, shall I forget with what ardour and earnestness Mr. Fletcher expostulated, even on his knees, both with Mr. Wesley and the preachers. To the former he said, "My father! my father! they have offended, but they are your children." To the latter he exclaimed, "My Brethren! my brethren! he is your father!" and then, portraying the work in which they were unitedly engaged, fell again on his knees and with much fervour and devotion engaged in prayer. The Conference was bathed in tears; many sobbed aloud.' *Wesleyan Methodist Magazine* 68 (1845):14-15. Four preachers nevertheless retired from the work, the Hampsons, father and son (on whom see Apr. 14, 1753; 20:451-52, n. 7 in this edn.), Joseph Pilmore (see Aug. 3, 1769; 22:197, n. 37 in this edn.), and John Atlay (see June 29, 1766; 22:46-47, n. 4 in this edn.). JW went some way to meet fears that he was creating a hierarchy, by depositing a letter with his travelling companion to be read after his death, imploring them not 'to assume any superiority over' their brethren (*Minutes.* 1:233-34). But even so, James Oddie, a former preacher and now a draper at Keighley (see Oct. 16, 1762; 21:391, n. 90 in this edn.) and Robert Oastler, grocer of Thirsk, got up a petition to the Legal Hundred begging them to give written assurance to the preachers not named in the deed that they would be treated with complete equality when the deed came into operation on JW's death; Tyerman MSS, 2, fols. 29-30, in Methodist Archives, Manchester. Oddie seceded with John Atlay to Dewsbury, and Oastler later became a Kilhamite.

[4] This celebration was in connection with the final conclusion of peace with Britain's enemies in the American War of Independence, the main lines of which had been agreed in the autumn of 1782; *Gentleman's Magazine* 54 (1784):552. A great Yorkshire recorder of sermons noted: 'Thursday . . . at ten in the forenoon, being the General Thanksgiving, Rev. Dr. Coke and the Rev. Dr. [Cornelius] Bayley read prayers in the Methodist Chapel, Leeds: Mr. Wesley preached from 1 Cor. 13:1-14. Mr. Wesley preached again at six in the evening from Matt. 22:39.' *WHS* 9 (1914):193.

service for the day. The prayers, scriptures, and every part of it, pointed at one thing. 'Beloved, if God so loved us, we ought also to love one another.'[5] Having five clergymen[6] to assist me, we administered the Lord's Supper, as was supposed, to sixteen or seventeen hundred persons.

Sunday, August 1, we were fifteen clergymen at the old church.[7] Tuesday 3. Our Conference concluded, in much love, to the great disappointment of all. This evening, I went as far as Halifax and, the next day, to Manchester.[8] Thursday 5, we set out early but, being obliged to go round about, could not reach Shrewsbury till half past seven. I began preaching immediately in memory of good John Appleton,[9] lately called away, on 'Whatsoever thy hand findeth to do, do it with thy might, for there is no work, nor device, nor knowledge, nor wisdom in the grave whither thou goest.'[10] Friday 6, I preached at Birmingham and, on Saturday 7, at Worcester.

Sun. 8. I preached in the afternoon in St. Andrew's Church[11] and was agreeably surprised to observe the congregation deeply attentive while I applied the story of Dives and Lazarus.

Mon. 9. I rode over Malvern Hills, which affords one of the

---

[5] 1 John 4:11.

[6] Thomas Coke, John Fletcher, Cornelius Bayley (on whom, see above, May 18, 1783), David Simpson (see Apr. 3, 1774; 22:402, n. 59 in this edn.), and Richard Dillon, an Oxford graduate, who was stationed with other clergy in London.

[7] The vicar of Leeds was Samuel Kirshaw, who was admitted to St. Catherine's College, Cambridge in 1723, and graduated B.A. 1728, M.A. 1731, D.D. 1760. He was rector of Coningsby in 1732, vicar of Leeds from 1751 till his death in 1786, and rector of Ripley in 1759. Joseph Hunter, *Familiae Minorum Gentium*, 4 vols. (London, 1894-96), vols. 37-41 in Publications of the Harleian Society, n.s., 37:156.

[8] This curious route to Manchester was occasioned by JW's having seen two ladies from Halifax, Mrs. Swaine and her sister, Miss Haughton, at the Conference service and, on this evening, inviting himself as their overnight guest, driving them home in his chaise. Walker, *Halifax Methodism*, pp. 163-64.

[9] John Appleton, currier, a native of Shropshire, had been converted in Bristol under impressions created by the spectacle of a clergyman who attacked Methodism being 'suddenly seized with a rattling in his throat, attended with a hideous groaning, [who] fell backwards against the door of the pulpit, burst it open and fell down the stairs, dying the next day'. Returning to Shrewsbury, he fitted up a room in 1761 for preaching, where for many years he preached twice in the week and twice on Sundays to good congregations. Like the later Ranters, 'he had great power in prayer, and his petitions were so constantly granted, that he said he was almost afraid to ask for fear he should ask amiss.' He had built the new Shrewsbury Chapel at his own expense in 1781 (see above, Mar. 27, 1781). He died on May 1, 1784. *Arminian Magazine* 13 (1790):636-40; W. Phillips, *Early Methodism in Shropshire* (Shrewsbury, 1896), p. 9; Skinner, *Nonconformity in Shropshire*, pp. 61, 64, 65.

[10] Eccles. 9:10.

[11] On this church and rector, see above, Mar. 21, 1784.

finest prospects in the kingdom,[12] to Ledbury, then through miserable roads to Ross[-on-Wye]. I preached in the evening at Monmouth, to a very quiet and civil congregation. Tumults were now at an end, as I lodged at the house of a gentleman[13] whom none
5 cared to oppose. And even in the morning, we had a large congregation both of rich and poor.

Tue. 10. I took a walk to what is called the Bowling-green House,[14] not a mile from the town. I have hardly seen such a place before. A gravel walk leads through the most beautiful meadows,
10 surrounded on all sides by fruitful hills, to a gently rising ground on the top of which is a smooth green, on which the gentry of the town frequently spend the evening in dancing. From hence, spread various walks bordered with flowers, one of which leads down to the river, on the back of which runs another walk, whose
15 artless shades are not penetrated by the sun. These are full as beautiful in their kind as even the hanging-woods at Brecon.[15] Wednesday 11, it was with some difficulty that I broke from this affectionate people and went on through a most lovely country to Brecon.

20 Thur. 12. I found the little flock were in great peace and increasing in number as well as in strength. I preached in the town hall. I never saw such a congregation in Brecon before, no, not even when I preached abroad. And I scarce ever found the power of God so present. It seemed as if everyone *must* know the
25 Lord, 'from the least to the greatest'.[16]

Fri. 13. We went on to Carmarthen. After preaching, I advised

---

[12] Cf. above, Sept. 9, 1777.

[13] Probably William (Catchmayd) Gwinnett, with whom he had stayed on May 14, 1781 (see above), and who had kept down the mob on that occasion. But the Diary reference on August 10, 'at brother John's', opens the possibility that he stayed with Thomas Johnson (1731-1815), four times mayor of Monmouth, with whom he stayed on his next visit, Aug. 15, 1788, after (as he put it) Gwinnett had 'done with us'.

[14] On a previous visit to this region (see Aug. 25, 1769; 22:201, n. 65 in this edn.), JW had revelled in the beauties of Piercefield near Chepstow. On this occasion, the destination was probably Beaulieu Grove on the Kymin, the sedulously developed, picturesque charms of which are described by Charles Heath, *Descriptive Account of the Kymin Pavilion and Beaulieu Grove* (Monmouth, 1807); also to be found in C. Heath, *Historical and Descriptive Accounts . . . of the Town of Monmouth* (Monmouth, 1804); W. Coxe, *An Historical Tour in Monmouthshire* (London, 1801), pp. 300-301; Williams, *Wesley in Wales*, p. 112, n. 3.

[15] Hanging woods are situated on a steep slope, 'so as to hang over or appear to do so'; *OED*. The reference may be to Priory Groves, Brecon, or to Priory Wood, about 3 miles north-east of Hay-on-Wye. Williams, *Wesley in Wales*, p. 112, n. 3.

[16] Heb. 8:11.

all the audience to copy after the decent behaviour of the Hollanders in and after public worship.[17] They all took my advice: none opened their lips till they came into the open air.

Sat. 14. Was the hottest day we have had this summer. We reached Tenby soon after one. After dinner, we took a walk through the town. I think there is not such a town in England. It is the Kilmallock of Great Britain.[18] Two thirds of the ancient town are either in ruins or vanished away. In the evening, I preached in the street to a large congregation of rich and poor, all quiet and attentive. I cannot but think salvation is at length come to this town also. I preached again in the morning, Sunday 15, and the word seemed to sink into the hearts of the hearers. Thence we went by Pembroke to St. Daniel's. It was a comfortable season. We had such another at Pembroke in the evening. Many mourned after God, and many rejoiced with joy unspeakable.

Mon. 16. I preached at Haverfordwest. Tuesday 17, we rode over to Roch, eight miles from Haverfordwest. The new preaching-house[19] was pretty well filled, and I was glad to find that a little ride did me no harm. Wednesday 18, I went to Admiral Vaughan's at Trecwn,[20] one of the pleasantest seats in Great Britain. The house is embosomed in lofty woods and does not appear till you drop down upon it. The Admiral governs his family, as he did in his ship, with the utmost punctuality. The bell rings, and all attend without delay, whether at meals or at morning and evening prayer. I preached at seven on Phil. 3:8 and spent the evening in serious conversation.

[17] Cf. above, June 15, 1783.

[18] Tenby, in ancient times a fishing village, was the site of a plantation of Flemings under Henry I in the twelfth century, and became one of the fortified towns by which the Norman hold on South Wales was maintained. The fortifications were restored in the fifteenth century and again as a defence against the Armada in 1588, but suffered when the town repeatedly changed hands during the civil wars. The town itself decayed until a decade after JW's death, when it enjoyed a modish revival as a bathing resort. Kilmallock, a Norman town, 16 miles south from Limerick, had been described by JW on visits of 1749 and 1750 as a 'vast heap of ruins'; see May 29, 1749; May 18, 1750 (20:277, n. 88; 20:336 in this edn.). By west-of-Ireland standards, it was not a negligible town, but it was distinguished by 'the magnificence of its ruins' and especially the fortifications, the repair of which had been endowed by Edward III with tolls and customs; Lewis, *Ireland*, 2:135-36. A visual impression of the place may be derived from T. Crofton Croker, *Historical Illustrations of Kilmallock* (London, 1840).

[19] Apparently JW performed the official opening of the chapel for the society, which had long met in the house of Henry Child. *Wesleyan Methodist Magazine* 59 (1836):139; D. Young, *The Origin and History of Methodism in Wales and the Borders*, (London, 1893), p. 115, n. 1.

[20] Orig. 'Tracoon'. On Vaughan and Trecwn, see above, July 16, 1777.

Thur. 19. I went on to Mr. Bowen's[21] at Llwyn-gwair, another most agreeable place; the more so because of the company, Mr. and Mrs. Bowen, his brother, and six of their eleven children, two of whom are lately come from the university. Friday 20 about eight, I preached in the church at Newport[22] and spoke strong words, if haply some might awake out of sleep. Thence, we went to Haverfordwest, it being the day when the bishop held his visitation. As I was returning in the afternoon from visiting some of the poor people, a carriage in the street obliged me to walk very near a clergyman, who made me a low bow. I did the same to him, though I did not then know the bishop,[23] who has indeed won the hearts of the people in general by his courteous and obliging behaviour.

Sun. 22. I heard a good sermon in the church at Camarthen; being the Assize Sermon, on *There is no power but of God.*[24] In the evening, I preached in the market-place to, I think, the largest congregation I ever saw in Wales. Thursday 26, on the road I read over Voltaire's 'Memoirs of himself.'[25] Certainly never was a more consummate coxcomb! But even his character is less horrid than that of his royal hero![26] Surely so unnatural a brute never disgraced a throne before! *Cedite Romani Catamiti! Cedite Graii!*[27] A monster that made it a fixed rule to let no woman and no priest

[21] On George Bowen, see Aug. 20, 1772; 22:346, n. 32 in this edn. He and his wife Easter (or Hester) had six sons and six daughters, but one of the sons died in infancy. On the family, see W. Islwyn Morgan in *Bathafarn* 21 (1966):37-48; 23 (1968):14-24; Williams, *Wesley in Wales*, p. 115, n. 2.

[22] JW always used the church at Newport, where the rector was the friendly David Pugh (on whom see Aug. 20, 1772; 22:347, n. 33 in this edn.).

[23] Edward Smallwell (*c.* 1721-99), Bishop of St. David's, 1783-88. He matriculated from Christ Church in 1739, and graduated B.A. 1743, M.A. 1747, B.D. 1755, D.D. 1775. He was a canon of Christ Church from 1775, and rector of Batsford, Glos., from 1757, both till his death. He became a chaplain to the King in 1766 and was Bishop of Oxford, 1788-99.

[24] Rom. 13:1

[25] François Marie Arouet de Voltaire, *Memoires pour servir a la vie de M. de Voltaire, écrits par lui-même* (Londres, 1784).

[26] Frederick the Great. In Voltaire's picture of Frederick, 'neither women nor priests entered the palace,' and homosexual 'schoolboy sports' had ten minutes' precedence over affairs of state at the levee; *Memoirs of the Life of Voltaire* (Eng. trans., London, 1784), pp. 86, 91. Modern inquiry concludes that these allegations, made after Voltaire had quarrelled with Frederick, and simply parrotted by other writers, are in the last degree unlikely to be true. G. B. Volz, 'Friedrich der Grosse und seine sittlichen Anklager', *Forschungen zur Brandenburgischen und Preussischen Geschichte* 6 (1928):1-37.

[27] Adapted from Propertius, *Elegies*, II.34, 65, 66, which has *scriptories (writers)* rather than *catamite* (boys kept for homosexual practices). JW's Latin was rendered by Thomas Jackson with astounding verbosity: 'Ye Catamites among the Romans and Greeks, concede to this wretch the palm of criminality' (Jackson, 4:287).

enter his palace, that not only gloried in the constant practice of sodomy himself, but made it free for all his subjects! What a pity that his father had not beheaded him in his youth and saved him from all this sin and shame.

In the evening, I preached in the town hall at Cardiff and showed the scriptural meaning of that much mistaken term, 'a Christian'. Friday 27, I preached at Newport. I hardly know such another place. The people hear and hear, and are as much moved as the benches they sit upon. I spoke as strong as I possibly could on 'Awake thou that sleepest!'[28] And I judged from the number who attended at five in the morning that it was not all lost labour.

Sat. 28. Being informed the boat would pass at eight, we hastened to the New Passage. But we were time enough, for it did not set out till past six in the evening. However, we got into[29] the boat about seven and, before nine, reached Bristol.

Tue. 31. Dr. Coke, Mr. Whatcoat,[30] and Mr. Vasey[31] came down from London in order to embark for America.

Wednesday, September 1. Being now clear in my own mind, I

---

[28] Eph. 5:14.

[29] Samuel Bradburn altered this phrase in his copy of the journal to 'got out of'. *WHS* 19 (1934):115.

[30] Richard Whatcoat (1736-1806) was born at Quinton, Glos., and early orphaned. Apprenticed at Darlaston, Staffs., and then employed at Wednesbury, he first made contact with evangelical religion under Methodist preaching in the latter place, and became overwhelmingly convinced of living under judgment. In 1761, with the assistance of Alexander Mather, he came through this, 'stripped of all but love', and began to exhort. In 1769, he got John Pawson to propose him at Conference as an itinerant, and he subsequently served in England, Wales, and, for some tough years, in Ireland. This experience doubtless recommended him to JW for service in America, including ordination. JW's attempt in 1787 to impose him on the American Methodists as superintendent (or bishop) evoked strenuous resistance from them, in consequence of which JW's own name was left out of the American Minutes. But in 1800, Whatcoat was finally raised to the episcopate by his fellow itinerants in America. His distinguished service there was almost interrupted by discouragement and a return to England in the mid-1790s, but he became so important a prop to the authority of Francis Asbury that, upon Whatcoat's death, Asbury tried (in vain) to get a 'contingent General Conference' called to provide for the episcopal succession on his own demise. Whatcoat's MS journal is preserved at Garrett Theological Seminary. *Arminian Magazine* 4 (1781):190-95; *Methodist Magazine* 30 (1807):423-24; E. S. Bucke, ed., *History of American Methodism*, 3 vols. (Nashville, 1964), 1:229-31, 425-26, 451, 475.

[31] Thomas Vasey (1745-1826), early orphaned, was educated by an uncle 'zealously attached to the Church of England', who required him to choose as a young man between membership in the Methodist society and his expectations under his uncle's will. This was the first of a series of renunciations. Admitted to the itinerancy (under his initials) in 1775, Vasey was instructed by JW not to 'turn again into folly but watch and pray that you enter not into temptation' (Telford, 6:170). Having accepted ordination from JW, Vasey was much disturbed by 'the prevalence of republican opinions in

took a step which I had long weighed in my mind and appointed
Mr. Whatcoat and Mr. Vasey to go and serve the desolate sheep in
America.[32] Thursday 2, I added to them three more, which I verily believe will be much to the glory of God.[33] Friday 3, I preached
5 at Guinea Street, and the word of God was with power, in consequence of which there was a large congregation at five in the
morning, although they had not been accustomed before to any
service at that hour. Saturday 14 in the evening, I preached at
Bath. Sunday 5, I read prayers, preached, and administered the
10 Sacrament to a large congregation. But it was larger in the afternoon, and largest of all in the evening when I opened and applied,
'Thou shalt love thy neighbour as thyself.'[34] And many were laid
in the balance and found wanting, even of those who had often
appealed to this very rule.
15   Wed. 8. I preached at Kendleshire,[35] where I do not remember
to have been for near forty years. On the two following days, I
preached at Clutton[36] and Coleford. After preaching to an earnest

America' and, having accepted a second ordination from Bishop White of the Protestant
Episcopal Church, returned home after two years. JW allowed him to accept a curacy,
but in 1789, he returned to the itinerant work 'with much zeal and success'. From 1811
to 1826, he enjoyed a congenial appointment to conduct the liturgical services at City
Road, London, and then retired to Leeds on account of the strength of the select bands
in the town, spending nearly one third of his remaining days in prayer. He died suddenly of a fit. *Wesleyan Methodist Magazine* 50 (1827):142, 644.

[32] The use of the word 'appointed' here in the Journal, while in the private Diary
'ordained' is used for the same act, says much about JW's belief about ordination, as
well as the deviousness to which he was driven by the hostility of his brother. For a
good account of the whole transaction taking the usual view that 'ordination is separation', see Baker, *Wesley and Church*, pp. 256–82. For a different view, stressing the
interrelation between the necessities of the American Episcopalians in creating a
national episcopacy and the need of JW to create a constitutional structure for an international movement, see W. R. Ward, 'The Legacy of John Wesley: the Pastoral Office
in Britain and America' in *Statesmen, Scholars, and Merchants*, ed. A. Whiteman, J. S.
Bromley, and P. G. M. Dickson (Oxford, 1973), pp. 329–35.

[33] This sentence, which appeared in the first edition in 1789, was suppressed by JW in
a revised edition which appeared in the same year. The Diary makes it clear that Whatcoat and Vasey were ordained deacons on Wednesday, September 1, and elders (or
presbyters) on Thursday, when Coke was also ordained Superintendent. The journal
entry may have been suppressed because it could be understood to mean, not three more
ordinations, but three more persons. These transactions took place in the house of Dr.
John Castleman (on whom see above, Mar. 8, 1782), 6 Dighton Street, Bristol. JW was
assisted by Coke and James Creighton (on whom see May 23, 1773; 22:369, n. 19 in this
edn.), presbyters of the Church of England.

[34] Cf. Luke 10:27.

[35] Orig. 'Kendalshare'. Kendleshire was last mentioned in the Journal on Jan. 17, 1740
(19:135 in this edn.), and in the Diary on May 21 and 24, 1741 (19:462).

[36] Orig. 'Chelton'.

congregation at Coleford, I met the society. They contained themselves pretty well during the exhortation, but when I began to pray, the flame broke out. Many cried aloud, many sunk to the ground, many trembled exceedingly, but all seemed to be quite athirst for God and penetrated by the presence of his power. 5

Sun. 12. Dr. Coke read prayers and I preached in the New Room. Afterward, I hastened to Kingswood and preached under the shade of that double row of trees which I planted about forty years ago. How little did any one then think that they would answer such an intention! The sun shone as hot as it used to do 10 even in Georgia. But his rays could not pierce our canopy. And our Lord meantime shone upon many souls and refreshed them that were weary.

Mon. 13. I visited one[37] that was confined to her bed and in much pain, yet unspeakably happy, rejoicing evermore, praying 15 without ceasing, and in everything giving thanks; yea, and testifying that she had enjoyed the same happiness without any intermission for two and twenty years.

Tue. 14. I preached at Bath and Bradford[-on-Avon]; Wednesday 15, at Trowbridge[38] and Frome. Thursday 16, I went to 20 Ditcheat,[39] a village near Castle Cary, where I found a friendly, hospitable family. I preached in the evening to a numerous and earnest congregation. Friday 17, the house would not contain half the people. Hence we passed through a delightful country to the Nunnery,[40] a more elegant trifle, near King Alfred's Tower, a lofty, 25

[37] Perhaps Ann Noble, on whom see below, Mar. 20, 1785.

[38] For early evangelical and Methodist religion in Trowbridge, see Sept. 17, 1754 (20:492, n. 96 in this edn.), Sept. 12, 1780, Sept. 27, 1781, and Edward Dyer, *Wesleyan Methodism in Trowbridge* (Trowbridge, 1862). After a few years' trial, the original chapel in Trowbridge had been given up. But John Mason had founded a class in 1781, and on this or some other occasion soon afterwards, 'having put on his canonicals in Mr. Knapp's parlour, Wesley preached near the bridge to a large assembly,' with the result that in 1790, John Valton was able to open a new chapel there. *WHS* 8 (1912):117-18; Jackson, *Early Methodist Preachers*, 6:130-31.

[39] Ditcheat was a substantial parish 3 miles north-west of Castle Cary. The 'friendly hospitable family' was that of John Goodfellow and his wife, who had just been admitted to society membership. He describes the occasion in his diary: 'On Thursday the 16th of September, the Rev. Mr. Wesley came to my house and preached in the churchyard (Mr. L[ea]r[s] having refused to let him have his church to preach in) to about 900 people and again next morning to about 300.' *WHS* 20 (1935):76.

[40] The Nunnery (otherwise the Convent) is one of the buildings in Stourhead Gardens which (nude statues apart) had delighted JW on Sept. 12, 1776 (see above). It is 'a picturesquely irregular thatched stone cottage with three turrets'. The building contained 'painted panels with nuns in the clothes of various orders and stained glass from Glastonbury'. Pevsner, *Wiltshire*, p. 450. King Alfred's Tower had been built in 1772 in

triangular building standing [on] the highest part of the country, on the very spot (as is supposed) where he drew up his army against the Danes. About eleven, I preached at Castle Cary to a quiet and attentive multitude. In the evening, I preached at Shep-
5 ton Mallet, where the people at length know the day of their visitation. Saturday 18, I preached in the neat, cheerful church at Midsomer Norton.[41]

   Monday 20, Tuesday, and Wednesday, I met the classes, but found no increase in the society.[42] No wonder, for discipline had
10 been quite neglected, and without this, little good can be done among the Methodists. Thursday 23, I preached at Paulton about one, and at Pensford in the evening. The gentlemen at Chew Magna having sent me word 'I was welcome to preach in the church,' I went thither the next morning. But they now sent me
15 word 'they had changed their minds',[43] so I preached in our own preaching-house, on 'If we let him alone, all men will believe on him.'[44]

   Thur. 30. I had a long conversation with John McGeary,[45] one of our American preachers, just come to England. He gave a
20 pleasing account of the work of God there, continually increasing,

---

the south-west extremity of the parish of Kilmington by Henry Hoare, who had purchased the adjoining Stourhead estate. The tower featured an inscription commemorating Alfred as a forerunner of the Enlightenment: 'to him we owe the origin of juries and the creation of a naval force. Alfred, the light of a benighted age, was a philosopher and a Christian, the father of his people and the founder of the English monarchy and liberties.' Collinson, *Somerset*, 3:39; Pevsner, *Wiltshire*, p. 450. JW's Diary indicates that he actually visited the tower area en route from Frome to Ditcheat on Thursday, not on Friday as the Journal implies.

[41] The rector was Edward Ford, who matriculated from University College, Oxford, in 1757, aged 21, and graduated B.A. 1761, M.A. 1772, B.D. 1772.

[42] I.e., at Bristol. Compare JW's previous visitation, Sept. 17, 1783.

[43] The patron of Chew Magna was the Rev. Mr. Lindsey; I have not traced the incumbent.

[44] Cf. John 11:48.

[45] John McGeary was an Irishman who had worked with Asbury in America for two years and had now returned to England at the end of the war and to service in the Liverpool circuit (Telford, 7:266). At the following Conference, JW appointed him to Newfoundland, where the work had already been commenced by other Irishmen, Laurence Coughlan and John Stretton, a local preacher. McGeary, a man 'naturally of a bold, forward temper', did not get on with the Newfoundlanders, made an unfortunate marriage, and became 'utterly discouraged, not only through want of success, but through want of conveniences, yea, necessaries of life, and returned to England in 1788'. He served again in Newfoundland, 1790-92, when he took an English circuit. He ceased to travel in 1793. Telford, 7:260, 266, 371; 8:48, 119; George G. Findlay and William W. Holdsworth, *The History of the Wesleyan Methodist Missionary Society*, 5 vols. (London, 1921), 1:267-68.

and vehemently importuned me to pay one more visit to America before I die. Nay, I shall pay no more visits to new worlds till I go to the world of spirits.

Saturday, October 2, it pleased God once more to pour out his spirit on the family at Kingswood. Many of the children were much affected. I talked particularly with some who desired to partake of the Lord's Supper. They did so the next morning. Afterwards, I spent a little time with all the children and easily observed an uncommon awe resting upon them all. In the evening, we renewed our covenant with God in the New Room at Bristol. It was supposed, we had a thousand communicants, and I believe none went empty away.

Mon. 4. I set out for London. About eleven, I preached at the Devizes, and in the evening at Salisbury.[46] A grievous stumbling-block was lately thrown in the way of this poor people. A young gentlewoman, after being deeply convinced of sin, found peace with God in a glorious manner. She was unspeakably happy but, not long after, suddenly fell into black despair and, afterwards, into melancholy madness, wherein she continued about two years. Here was an occasion of offence for them that sought occasion, which they took care to improve.

Wed. 6. About eleven, I preached at Winchester and, in the evening, at Portsmouth Common. Those who could not get in, at first made a little noise, but in a short time, all was quiet. Thursday 7, I crossed over to the Isle of Wight. In the afternoon, I preached at Newtown, once the largest town in the Isle, but now not having six houses together. In the evening, all the ministers and most of the Gentry at Newport attended the preaching. Who hath warned them to flee from the wrath to come? O may many 'bring forth fruit with patience?'[47] Friday 8, we returned to Portsmouth Common and, Saturday 9, to London.[48]

Mon. 18. I set out for Oxfordshire and, in the evening,

---

[46] On Luke 12:7 and Phil. 4:7, respectively. George Story took shorthand notes on these two sermons, which are preserved in the Story Papers, Manuscript Department, Perkins Library, Duke University, Durham, NC. The MSS, as well as the Diary, indicate that the sermon at Salisbury was on Tuesday (not Monday) evening; see also 4:517 in this edn.

[47] Luke 8:15.

[48] The Diary entries suggest that this was the occasion of the anecdote related by Henry Moore: 'When Mr. Wesley was upwards of eighty, he said to me—after he had travelled from Portsmouth to Cobham, in Surrey, which he reached before 1 o'clock— "We should lose no time, we have not, like the Patriarchs, 700 or 800 years to play with." ' *Wesley*, 1:143n.

preached at Wallingford. Tuesday 19, I spent an hour at Lord
Harcourt's seat[49] near Nuneham [Courtenay], one of the pleasantest spots I have seen. It stands on a gently rising hill and commands a most delightful prospect. The rooms are not so grand as
5 some, but elegant in the highest degree. So is also the front of the
house and what is called the flower garden, a small enclosure surrounded by lofty trees and filled with all the beauties that nature
and art can give.

The house at Oxford was thoroughly filled, and students as
10 well as townsmen were deeply serious. Thursday 21, I preached at
Witney, on 'As thou hast believed, so be it done unto thee.'[50] We
had a large congregation at five in the morning; at twelve, I met
the children and was pleased to find that the impression which
was made on them by the storm last year is not yet worn out. And
15 the whole society, still double to what it was, appears to be much
in earnest.

After preaching in the evening, I met the select society and
found many of them who for several years have lost nothing of
what they had received, but do still love 'God with all their heart',[51]
20 and in consequence, 'rejoice evermore, pray without ceasing, and
in everything give thanks'.[52] Tuesday 22, I preached at High
Wycombe about noon and, in the afternoon, went on to London.

Sun. 24. I preached at Shadwell Church,[53] which was exceed-

---

[49] George Simon, second Earl and third Viscount Harcourt (1736-1809), had been a
page at the coronation in 1761. The church, manor house, and village of Nuneham
Courtenay were built by the first Earl, who in 1760 had swept away the old church and
village to make way for a classical landscape. The tenants' cottages were built out of the
sight of the house, and the church was erected as an ornamental temple in the park. The
site of the house was chosen with a view to its landscaping possibilities and its prospect
of the domes and spires of Oxford. But the house itself was an unsatisfactory compro-
mise between the compact Palladian villa originally designed as a leisure retreat and the
family seat into which it was subsequently turned by the addition of state rooms, servants' quarters, etc. In 1786, Fanny Burney described it as 'straggling, half new, half
old, half comfortable, half forlorn, begun in one generation and finished in another'.
Pevsner, *Oxfordshire*, pp. 725-27.
[50] Matt. 8:13.
[51] Cf. Matt. 22:37.
[52] 1 Thess. 5:16, 17, 18.
[53] The incumbent of St. Paul's, Shadwell, from 1741 till his death, was Joseph Butler
(*c.* 1716-98), who matriculated from Exeter College, Oxford, in 1732, graduated B.A.
1736, M.A. 1738. The church in which JW preached had been built in 1656 as a chapel
of ease to St. Dunstan's, Stepney, and was renowned as the church of the sea-captains,
the names of 175 commanders and their wives (including Captain Cook) appearing in
the registers, 1730-90; Blatch, *Guide*, p. 410. The present church was erected by the
Church Building Commissioners between 1817 and 1821.

ingly crowded with rich and poor, who all seemed to receive the truth in love. In the evening, I took coach and, the next evening, preached at Norwich. Afterwards, I advised the people to go away in silence.[54] And they did so: neither man nor woman spoke till they were out of the house. The following days, I visited the other societies in the circuit and, on Tuesday, November 1, returned to London.

Fri. 5. We had a solemn watch-night.[55] Saturday 6, I was an hour or two in conversation with that truly great man, Pascal Paoli,[56] who is a tall, well-made, graceful man, about sixty years of age—but he does not look to be above forty. He appears to have a real regard for the public good, and much of the fear of God. He has a strong understanding and seemed to be acquainted with every branch of polite literature. On my saying, 'He had met with much the same treatment with that of an ancient lover of his country, Hannibal,' he immediately answered, 'But I have never yet met with a King of Bithynia.'[57]

Mon. 8. This week, I visited the societies near London, a very heavy but necessary work. Thursday 18, I visited two persons in Newgate who were under sentence of death. They seemed to be in an excellent temper, calmly resigned to the will of God. But how much stress can be reasonably laid on such impressions it is hard to say. So often have I known them vanish away as soon as ever the expectation of death was removed.

[54] Here JW is again enforcing the reverence of behaviour he had admired in the Netherlands (see above, June 15, 1783). There were, however, special reasons for his counsel here. The Norwich circuit had been again badly divided on the Calvinist controversy, and immediately before JW's arrival, Charles Atmore, himself a Norfolk man, had left his Colne circuit to assist in allaying the 'spirit of unhallowed contention and strife'. His journal supplies some of what is missing from that of JW: 'Tuesday, Oct. 26th. I was once more honoured with the sight of that great and good man, Mr. Wesley, who was in perfect health. He preached an excellent sermon from Hosea 14:4 and, in the evening, explained the nature and property of love from 1 Cor. 13:1–3. Wednesday, Oct. 27th. He preached a very comfortable, although at the same time alarming sermon, at Mr. Cripps's, from "It is appointed unto men once to die, but after this the judgment." We were honoured with his company at Haddiscoe to dine. He afterwards preached a short but sweet sermon from Heb. 7:25. He then rode to Yarmouth, where he addressed a tolerable congregation, from John 4:26. Thursday, Oct. 28th. At five a.m., Mr. Wesley preached from Rom. 13:11–14, and then set off for Lowestoft.' *Wesleyan Methodist Magazine* 68 (1845):15–16.

[55] For watch-night services, see Apr. 9, 1742 (19:258, n. 50 in this edn.).

[56] On Pascal Paoli, see Nov. 11, 1768 (22:164, n. 10 in this edn.).

[57] Prusias, King of Bithynia, provided a refuge from the Romans for Hannibal in 190 B.C. The Romans, however, put him under severe diplomatic pressure to surrender Hannibal, who took poison, *c.* 183 B.C.

Sat. 20. At three in the morning, two or three men broke into our house[58] through the kitchen window. Thence they came up into the parlour and broke open Mr. Moore's bureau, where they found two or three pounds. The night before, I had prevented his leaving there seventy pounds which he had just received. They next broke open the cupboard and took away some silver spoons. Just at this time the alarm, which Mr. Moore by mistake had set for half past three (instead of four) went off, as it usually did, with a thundering noise. At this, the thieves ran away with all speed, though their work was not half done, and the whole damage which we sustained scarce amounted to six pounds.

Mon. 22, I preached at Northampton and, on Tuesday 23, at Whittlebury.[59] Here my servant[60] was seized with a fever, attended with eruptions all over, as big as peppercorns. I took knowledge of the 'prickly heat', as we called it in Georgia, termed by Dr. Heberden,[61] the 'nettle rash', and assured him he would be well in four and twenty hours. He was so, and drove us on to Banbury, where, on Wednesday 24, I met with a hearty welcome from Mr. George, formerly a member of the London society. The Presbyterian minister[62] offering me the use of his meeting, I willingly accepted his offer. It was, I believe, capable of containing near as

[58] This was the house in City Road. Henry Moore (1751-1844), born near Dublin, the son of a yeoman, was educated under a scholarly clergyman with a view to entering Trinity College, a prospect cut short by the death of his father. Apprenticed to a Dublin artist, he moved to London, 'where he devoted many of his leisure hours to what is usually called pleasure'. Converted after deep convictions of sin, he was admitted to the itinerancy on trial in 1779 and, at this moment, was stationed in London and sharing the house in City Road. He won a considerable reputation as a preacher and Bible scholar, and had an incisiveness of judgment, which in his later years made him difficult to deal with. JW's friend and often his travelling companion, he was appointed by will his literary executor along with Thomas Coke and John Whitehead, and published one of the more valuable biographies of his hero, 1824-25. *Wesleyan Methodist Magazine* 67 (1844):481-82, 770-71.

[59] JW had been invited to Whittlebury to minister to Mrs. Henson who was dying, and was already too weak to converse much with him when he arrived. She died shortly afterwards. *Arminian Magazine* 8 (1785):249.

[60] The Diary entry for Nov. 23 reveals that this was Richard, who appeared in the Journal above, May 10, 1784.

[61] On William Heberden the elder, physician, see Apr. 19, 1774; 22:405, n. 76 in this edn.

[62] Rev. George Hampton M.A. (1716-96), pastor of the Old Meeting, Banbury, from 1739 till his death. About 1742, the meeting-house replaced a barn in which the congregation had met since 1716, and lasted till the present Unitarian Church was built in 1850. *WHS* 13 (1921):82; A. D. Tyssen, 'The Old Meeting House Banbury, and its Successor, the Unitarian Church', *Transactions of the Unitarian Historical Society* 1 (1916/18):280-86.

many people as the chapel at West Street. But it would not near contain the congregation. And God uttered his voice, yea, and that a mighty voice; neither the sorrow nor the joy which was felt that night will quickly be forgotten.

Thur. 25. I desired the people would sit below in the morning, supposing not many would be present. But I was much mistaken. Notwithstanding the darkness and rain, the house was filled both above and below. And never did I see a people who appeared more ready prepared for the Lord. Returning through Brackley, I was informed that notice had been given of my preaching there at nine in the town hall.[63] So I began without delay. The congregation was large and attentive, but seemed to understand me no more than if I had been talking Greek. But the society seemed alive to God and striving to enter in at the strait gate.

In the evening, I preached at poor, dead Towcester. But is not God able to raise the dead? There was a considerable shaking among the dry bones. And who knows but these dry bones may live?

Fri. 26. I returned to London. Sunday 28, I preached a charity sermon at St. Paul's, Covent Garden.[64] It is the largest and the best constructed parish church that I have preached in for several years. Yet some hundreds were obliged to go away, not being able to get in. I strongly enforced the necessity of that humble, gentle, patient love, which is the very essence of true religion. Monday 29 in the evening, I preached at Hinxworth in Miss Harvey's new house.[65] Tuesday 30, I visited my old friends at Bedford, but found Mr. Hill[66] was gone to rest and Mr. Parker[67] was just quivering on the verge of life. However, I rejoiced to find him clearly possessed of that *perfect love* which he had so long opposed.

[63] Brackley town hall, 'a handsome building in the centre of the town, supported on arches, under which the market is held, was erected in 1706, by Scroop, Duke of Bridgwater, at an expense of £2000'. Lewis, *England*, 1:282.

[64] At this moment, the living of St. Paul's, Covent Garden, was vacant, Richard Bullock D.D., being presented by the Duke of Bedford the very next day, November 29. The church, more picturesquely known as 'the handsomest barn in England', is a perfectly plain parallelogram with no internal subdivision, and fronted to the east by a pillared portico and sham door. Designed by Inigo Jones and consecrated in 1638, it was intended to be the chief feature of the west side of Covent Garden Square, the south being taken up by Bedford House. Pevsner, *London*, 1:55, 283.

[65] On Miss Harvey's chapel-building in and about Hinxworth, see above, July, 17, 1782.

[66] This is thought to be John Hill, landlord of the Rose, High Street, Bedford. JW had visited him as recently as Dec. 4, 1782 (see Diary) and had written up part of his Journal in his house.

[67] On William Parker, see Oct. 8, 1753 (20:476, n. 23 in this edn.).

Wednesday, December 1, I preached at St. Neots to the largest congregation I ever saw here. And I know not that ever I knew them so affected. It seemed as if God touched all their hearts. Thursday 2, I preached about noon at Buckden and, in the evening, to a crowded congregation at Huntingdon.[68] I wondered that I saw nothing here of a young clergyman[69] who last year professed much love and esteem. But I soon heard, his eyes were opened to see *the Decrees*. So he knows *me* no more!

Fri. 3. Partly riding and partly walking through wind and rain and water and dirt, we got at last to Luton, where I found a large congregation, and we greatly rejoiced in God our Saviour. Saturday 4, I went on to London.

Mon. 6. I went to Tunbridge Wells, but not without difficulty, part of the road being made scarce passable through the abundance of rain. I preached in the large Presbyterian meeting-house,[70] but the violent rain thinned the congregation. Yet on Tuesday 7, we set out in a lovely morning. But in about an hour, just as a pack of hounds came on in full cry, a furious storm of hail met them in the teeth and utterly silenced them. It soon turned snow, which so covered the road that we could scarce get on, though we walked good part of the way. So that we could not get to Robertsbridge till after the time appointed. The snow likewise so retarded us in our journey to Rye that we were above an hour in the night. However, the house was well filled with serious hearers, so that I did not repent of my labour.

Wed. 8. With great difficulty with two pair of good horses, we got on fifteen miles in five hours. But we could not reach Sevenoaks till the congregation had been long waiting. Thursday 9, going on to Shoreham, we found that venerable man, Mr. Perronet,[71] ninety-one years of age, calmly waiting for the conclusion of good warfare. His bodily strength is gone, but his understanding is little impaired, and he appears to have more love than ever. After preaching to an earnest congregation in the evening and to great part of them in the morning, I returned to London.

Monday 13 and the two days following, I preached at Canterbury, Dover, and Sittingbourne. Thursday 16, I went to Sheerness, where Mr. Fox[72] read prayers and I preached on those words

---

[68] Orig. 'Binlington'. [69] On this episode, see above, Dec. 3. 1782.
[70] On this meeting-house, see above, Jan. 19, 1778.
[71] Vincent Perronet lived another five months; see below, May 7, 1785.
[72] On this clergyman, see above Nov. 25, 1783.

in the Second Lesson, 'If the righteous scarcely be saved, where shall the ungodly and the sinner appear?'[73] I hardly ever spoke stronger words. May God make the application! I never before found this society in such a state as they were now, being all in general athirst for God and increasing in number as well as in grace. Friday 17, I preached at Chatham, where likewise I found only peace and love; and, on Saturday 18, cheerfully returned to London.

Mon. 20. I went to Hinxworth, where I had the satisfaction of meeting Mr. Simeon,[74] Fellow of King's College in Cambridge. He has spent some time with Mr. Fletcher at Madeley—two kindred souls, much resembling each other both in fervour of spirit and in the earnestness of their address. He gave me the pleasing information that there are three parish churches in Cambridge wherein true scriptural religion is preached, and several young gentlemen who are happy partakers of it.

I preached in the evening on Gal. 6:14. Tuesday 21, I spent a little time with the children at Miss Harvey's school,[75] whom she likewise carefully instructs herself. After dinner, we set out for Wrestlingworth, and, having a skillful guide who rode before the chaise and picked out the best way, we drove four miles in only three hours. Wednesday 22, I returned to London and concluded my journeys for the present year.

Sat. 25. We met as usual, in the New Chapel at four; at ten and in the afternoon, I preached in West Street, and afterwards spent a comfortable hour in meeting the society.

---

[73] 1 Pet. 4:18.

[74] Charles Simeon (1759–1836) went up to King's College, Cambridge, from Eton on a scholarship in 1779 and soon acquired pronounced religious convictions. A fellowship at King's opened the way to ordination. His views were given a further slant by contact with John Venn and his father, Henry. He worked first in the parish of St. Edward's, Cambridge, and entered on the living of Holy Trinity, Cambridge, in 1783. Here he remained the rest of his life, combining a succession of college offices with laborious parish work and with the intellectual leadership of what became the evangelical party. He also overcame much local opposition. As the political storm brewed against itinerant preaching, 1799–1800, he was one of the many evangelicals who ceased to itinerate and who cooled in their relations with Methodists and others who continued to do so. These ill relations account for the fact that neither William Carus's *Memoirs of the Life of Charles Simeon* (London, 1847) nor Joseph Benson's *Fletcher*, which was ill received by the evangelical *Christian Observer*, mentions the warm relations between their heroes. They are discussed, however, in Tyerman's *Wesley's Designated Successor*, pp. 551–52. The three Cambridge churches were probably St. Edward's, Holy Trinity, and Great St. Mary's, evangelicalism being stronger in colleges than parishes.

[75] On Miss Harvey of Hinxworth, see above, July 17, 1782.

Sun. 26. I preached the condemned criminals' sermon in New-gate. Forty-seven were under sentence of death. While they were coming in, there was something very awful in the clink of their chains. But no sound was heard, either from them or the crowded audience, after the text was named: 'There is joy in heaven over one sinner that repententh, more than over ninety and nine just persons, that need not repentance.'[76] The power of the Lord was eminently present, and most of the prisoners were in tears. A few days after, twenty of them died at once, five of whom died in peace. I could not but greatly approve of the spirit and behaviour of Mr. Villette,[77] the Ordinary. And I rejoiced to hear that it was the same on all similar occasions.

Fri. 31. We had a solemn watch-night[78] and ushered in the new year with the voice of praise and thanksgiving.

Saturday, January 1, 1785. Whether this be the last or no, may it be the best year of my life! Sunday 2, a larger number of people were present this evening at the renewal of our covenant with God[79] than was ever seen before on the occasion.

Tue. 4. At this season, we usually distribute coals and bread among the poor of the society. But I now considered they wanted clothes as well as food. So on this and the four following days, I walked through the town and begged two hundred pounds in order to clothe them that wanted it most. But it was hard work, as most of the streets were filled with melting snow which often lay ankle deep, so that my feet were steeped in snow-water nearly from morning till evening. I held it out pretty well till Saturday evening I was laid up with a violent flux which increased every hour, till at six in the morning Dr. Whitehead[80] called upon me.

---

[76] Cf. Luke 15:7.

[77] John Villette (d. 1799) was highly spoken of by Johnson: 'Let me observe in justice to the Reverend Mr. Villette, who has been Ordinary of Newgate for no less than eighteen years [according to Venn, since 1774], in the course of which he has attended many hundreds of wretched criminals, that his earnest diligence is highly praiseworthy, and merits a distinguished reward'; Boswell, *Johnson*, 4:329. Villette, the son of a City clergyman, was admitted sizar at St. John's College, Cambridge, in 1765, and graduated B.A. and was priested in 1771. Despite the championship of Boswell and Johnson, no further preferment came his way.

[78] On watch-night services, see Apr. 9, 1742 (19:258, n. 50 in this edn.).

[79] On the origins of the Covenant Service, see Aug. 6, 1755 (21:23, n. 82 in this edn.).

[80] John Whitehead (1740-1804), born at Dukinfield, Cheshire, of parents converted to Moravianism. He was converted by the preaching of Matthew Mayer (Tyerman, *John Wesley*, 2:474) and was admitted to the itinerancy in 1765, after participating as a preacher on trial in a notable revival in Cornwall in 1764; *Methodist Magazine* 27 (1804):271-72. He then travelled for four years, finally studying at Kingswood and hoping to become a mas-

His first draught made me quite easy, and three or four more perfected the cure. If he lives some years, I expect he will be one of
the most eminent physicians in Europe.

I supposed my journeys this winter had been over, but I could
not decline one more. Monday 17, I set out for poor Colchester to   5
encourage the little flock. They had exceeding little of this
world's goods, but most of them had a better portion. Tuesday 18,
I went on to Mistley,[81] a village near Manningtree. Some time

ter there (Telford, 5:142, 178). 'He then married and settled in business at Bristol. From
thence he removed to Wandsworth . . . and opened a school. He there became acquainted
with Dr. Lettsom, two of whose sons were his pupils. Under the doctor's direction, he
studied physic, and by his recommendation he obtained from the late Mr. Barclay, an
eminent Quaker, the appointment of guardian to his son, who was pursuing his studies at
Leiden in Holland. Mr. Whitehead himself at the same time completed his own studies at
that University, and returned to England with the diploma of Doctor of Medicine. He
had, sometime before, joined the Society of Quakers; and, by their influence chiefly, he
obtained the situation of physician to the London Dispensary. After a few years he again
joined the Methodist society and was received by Mr. Wesley with his usual kindness';
Moore, *Wesley*, 1:v–vi. JW would not, however, have him back as a preacher, but he
served in London as a local preacher and rendered valuable medical services to JW and
other preachers. By his will of Feb. 20, 1789, JW left all his MSS to Thomas Coke, Dr.
Whitehead, and Henry Moore, 'to be burned or published as they see good'. When after
JW's death the preachers heard that John Hampson, Jun., no longer a Methodist, was to
publish a life of JW, they pressed Whitehead to write an 'authorized' *Life*, based on published Journals and MSS, for which he would receive an honorarium of 100 guineas in
compensation for loss of professional time. This whole project became involved in the
divisions which afflicted Methodism in the 1790s in ways that have never been fully
explained, although Whitehead published his side of the story in the introduction to the
biography, and Moore outlined (but never published) his view in 'A Plain Account of the
Conduct of Dr. Whitehead respecting Mr. Wesley's Manuscripts, etc., in reply to what
the Doctor has published on that subject' (in R. Heitzenrater, *Faithful unto Death: Last
Years and Legacy of John Wesley* [Dallas, 1991], pp. 83–125). The problems began when
Whitehead objected to the financial terms of the arrangement and, once given the MSS,
refused to let his fellow literary trustees examine them or critique his own writing. The
other trustees (Coke and Moore) quickly put together a *Life of the Rev. John Wesley* (London, 1792) which appeared in print more than a year before the first volume of Whitehead's two-volume work of the same title (1793–96). Legal disputes over the possession of
the papers followed which burdened the London society with over £2000 in costs. Whitehead returned the papers to the City Road house after his *Life* was finished in 1796.
Whitehead's championship of Charles Wesley greatly irked the preachers, and during the
disputes his membership of the society was terminated. It was, however, restored in 1797.
Whitehead wrote the inscription on JW's memorial tablet, and was buried in his grave.
And when in 1824–25, Moore wrote another *Life* of JW, this time in reply to Robert
Southey, he made extensive unacknowledged use of Whitehead's biography; Stevenson,
City Road, pp. 177–78. Extracts from a MS biography of Whitehead by John Pawson are
to be found in Tyerman MSS, 3, fols. 43–72, in Methodist Archives, Manchester.

[81] Orig. 'Mistleythorn'. Mistley was a small parish half a mile east of Manningtree,
situated on the navigable river Stour at a point that could be reached by vessels of 300
tons burden at the spring tides. It did a brisk business in corn, malt, and coal. Lewis,
England, 1:287. Methodist preaching had only reached Manningtree in 1782. *Wesleyan
Methodist Magazine* 56 (1833):307.

since, one of the shipwrights of Deptford Yard, being sent hither to superintend the building of some men-of-war, began to read sermons on a Sunday evening in his own house. Afterwards, he exhorted them a little and then formed a little society. Some time after, he begged one of our preachers to 'come over and help them'.[82] I now found a lively society and one of the most elegant congregations I had seen for many years. Yet they seemed as willing to be instructed as if they had lived in Kingswood. Wednesday 19, I returned to Colchester and, on Thursday 20, preached to a lovely congregation at Purfleet[83] and, the next morning, returned to London.

Sun. 23. I preached morning and afternoon at West Street and, in the evening, in the chapel at Knightsbridge. I think it will be the last time, for I know not that I have ever seen a worse behaved congregation.

Tue. 25. I spent two or three hours in the House of Lords.[84] I had frequently heard that this was the most venerable assembly in England. But how was I disappointed! What is a lord, but a sinner, born to die!

Sunday, January 30. From those words, 'Righteous art thou, O Lord, and true are thy judgments,'[85] I endeavoured to point out those sins which were the chief cause of that awful transaction we commemorate this day. I believe the chief sin which brought the king to the block was his persecuting the real Christians. Hereby he drove them into the hands of designing men, which issued in his own destruction.

Sunday, February 6. We had a love-feast. I could not but observe the manner wherein several of them spoke one after another; not only the matter, but the language—the accent, the tone of voice—wherewith illiterate persons, men and women,

[82] Cf. Acts 16:9.

[83] On this place and congregation, see above, Jan. 6, 1784.

[84] JW chose a bad day. The Lords and Commons met to hear and reply to the King's speech on the opening of Parliament. Much of the substance of that speech was provided by financial matters, the suppression of smuggling, and the prosecution of the work of the commissioners on the public accounts, which were in the first instance Commons matters and evoked livelier discussion there. W. Cobbett, *The Parliamentary History of England*, 36 vols. (London, 1806–20), 24:1332–1413.

[85] Ps. 119:137 (BCP). JW's sermon register indicates that he did preach regularly on Jan. 30, the celebration of King Charles the Martyr, but it is quite impossible to know the topics that he developed from his texts. His own succinct summary in this instance suggests an ingenious adjustment of the Jacobitism of his early milieu to the respect for Puritan vital religion which he had acquired.

young and old, spoke, were such as a scholar need not be ashamed of.[86] 'Who teacheth like him!'[87]

Sun. 13. I met the single women and exhorted them to consider, to prize, and to improve the advantages they enjoyed. On the following days, I visited many of our poor to see with my own eyes what their wants were and how they might be effectually relieved?

Sun. 20. I preached in Spitalfields Church in the morning and, in the afternoon, at St. Ethelburga's[88] and, in the evening, in the New Chapel. On Monday, Tuesday, and Wednesday, I visited the residue of the sick and poor. Friday 25, I received letters from the preachers, stewards, and leaders at Plymouth Dock informing me that William Moore[89] had renounced the Methodists, hired a place to preach in, and drawn away about forty of our members to form a society for himself. They therefore begged I would come down as soon as possible to quench the kindling fire. I saw no time was to be lost and therefore immediately took places in the Exeter Diligence.

Sun. 27. I preached in Stepney Church,[90] one of the largest parish churches in England. Monday 28, the Diligence reached Salisbury about eight in the evening. About nine, we left it. So keen a frost I hardly ever felt before. And our carriage let in the air on all sides, so that we could hardly preserve life. However, soon after five on Tuesday evening we got to Exeter. Wednesday, March 2, we went on to Plymouth Dock and found all that we

[86] Humanly speaking, one may suppose that the redemptive effect of many Methodist conversions consisted in their making people articulate in spiritual matters who had not previously been articulate about anything (cf. below, Aug. 27, 1785; June 11, 1786). The love-feast with its personal testimonies afforded every opportunity for both the use and the abuse of this gift. The popularity of London love-feasts in the 1760s is suggested by heavy expenditure on 'bunns' in the accounts of the London circuit; *WHS* 15 (1926):175. The complaint in 1789 that 'the whole lasted about 3/4 hour, so that there was scarce time for half a dozen people to speak.' suggests that eloquence was well bridled; *WHS* 23. (1942):103. Cf. below, Mar. 27, 1785; July 3, 1786; Nov. 16, 1786; Apr. 8, 1787.

[87] Job 36:22.

[88] The rector, 1775-1807, was William Gilbank (*c.* 1740-1807), formerly scholar of St. John's College, Cambridge, a Bible scholar and chaplain to the Duke of Gloucester from 1781. St. Ethelburga, Bishopsgate, an undistinguished church of late fourteenth-century origins, with a bell-tower said to date from the mid-eighteenth century, now houses the Church's Ministry of Healing. Pevsner, *London,* 1:64, 144-45.

[89] On Moore and this secession, see July 26, 1762 (21:377, n. 47 in this edn.).

[90] St. Dunstan's, Stepney, which began as a village church with a Saxon past, is mostly of fifteenth-century origins, but the outer walls of the chancel are thirteenth century. Pevsner comments, 'Nearly 150 feet long, that is large for a village church.' *London,* 2:410, 413. The rectory may have been vacant, for Giles Fairclough Haddon, D.D. (*c.* 1724-85), the incumbent, died about this time.

had heard confirmed. But I verily believe we are better without
William Moore than with him, as his heart is not right with God.

To quiet the minds of many well-meaning persons, I preached
on those comfortable words, 'Even the hairs of your head are all
numbered.'[91] And in the morning, on 'Despise not thou the chas-
tening of the Lord, nor faint when thou art rebuked of him.'[92]
Thursday 3 in the evening, I read to the whole congregation a
plain state of the case with regard to the Deed of Declaration,
which William Moore had so wonderfully misrepresented. And I
believe they were all fully satisfied.[93]

Fri. 4. I took a walk through the Royal Hospital for sick and
wounded sailors.[94] I never saw anything of the kind so complete:
every part is so convenient and so admirably neat. But there is
nothing superfluous and nothing purely ornamental, either
within or without. There seems to be nothing wanting but a man
full of faith and zeal to watch over the souls of the poor patients
and teach them to improve their affliction.

In the evening, I preached to a large congregation at Plymouth,
and it pleased God to give me uncommon liberty in describing
the power of faith. What a blessed proof of this has there been
here, since I was in the town before!

Preaching at the Dock in the evening, I besought all serious
people not to 'grieve the Holy Spirit of God',[95] but to 'put away all
bitterness and wrath, and anger, and clamour, and evil-speaking'.[96] I exhorted them in particular not to talk about Mr. Moore
at all, but to give him up to God.

[91] Cf. Luke 12:7, as noted in the Diary.

[92] Heb. 12:5; the Diary lists Heb. 12:7 as the text.

[93] This 'plain statement' was doubtless JW's *Thoughts upon some Late Occurrences*,
written on this day and published in the *Arminian Magazine* 8 (1785):267-69. In it JW
repeated the circumstances which necessitated an unambiguous definition of the Conference, and again based the restriction of the Legal Hundred to that number on the
need to save expense and provide pastoral oversight during Conference periods.

[94] The Royal Naval Hospital was established in 1762 and was a source of admiration
to visitors from at home (such as Howard, the philanthropist); Worth, *Devonport*, p. 17.
The hospital occupied a site of twenty-four acres, thirteen of which were lawn, a fair-
weather exercise-ground for convalescent patients. The hospital consisted of a quadrangle of ten buildings, each containing six wards capable of receiving sixteen patients each,
or more in a crisis. The buildings were isolated from each other to prevent the spread of
contagion, though they were linked by a piazza which permitted wet-weather exercise.
Separate pavilions were provided for stores, cookery, operations, and a 'pox ward'. A
further building contained a dispensary and a chapel, where a hospital chaplain officiated. Samuel Rowe, *The Panorama of Plymouth; or Tourist's Guide* (Plymouth, 1821),
pp. 82-86.

[95] Eph. 4:30.   [96] Cf. Eph. 4:31.

Sun. 6. I preached at the Dock at seven. Between one and two, I began at Plymouth, and as many as could get in seemed to be deeply affected with the application of those words, 'Go thy way, and as thou hast believed, so be it done unto thee.'[97]

In the afternoon, I accepted of an invitation from Dr. Gench, the Physician of the Hospital, and passed an agreeable hour with a man of sense and, it seems, of considerable learning. At five, I preached in the shell of the new house, on 'the form and power of godliness'.[98] In the evening, I met the society once more, confirmed in the truth more than ever and more determined to walk in the good old way wherein they had continued from the beginning.

Mon. 7. We had a pleasant journey to Exeter, and on Tuesday to Bath. But the coach did not come in soon enough for me to preach in the evening. Nevertheless, we had a large congregation in the morning. Wednesday 9, this society too is much improved since I was here last.[99] Many stumbling-blocks are removed out of the way, and brotherly love is increased.

Thur. 10. After spending a day or two at Bristol, on Saturday 12, I returned to Bath and preached to a numerous congregation. Great part of them were present again at six in the morning. Sunday 20, I went over to Kingswood and preached the funeral sermon of Ann Noble, an old member of the society who, having adorned the gospel above forty years, died in the full triumph of faith.

Mon. 21. I set out early and dined at Stroud. The death of Mr. Willis,[1] snatched away in the midst of his years but a few days before, brought abundance of people to the preaching-house. And most of them were deeply serious, so that we had a very solemn hour. Tuesday 22, I preached in Painswick at noon, and at six in the court-house at Gloucester.[2] A multitude of people flocked

---

[97] Matt. 8:13.

[98] Cf. 2 Tim. 3:5 (the Diary incorrectly cites 2 Tim. 2:5).

[99] This phrase is perhaps not intended quite literally; JW is reminded by the troubles occasioned by William Moore in Plymouth of the struggles he had at Bath in 1779 to contain the disputes concerning Alexander McNab (on whom see Nov. 22, 1779).

[1] This domestic tragedy was less recent than the Journal entry suggests. R. Willis, saddler and ironmonger of Stroud, lost his wife the previous November after a marriage of 64 years. At the funeral on November 4, he died also. *Gentleman's Magazine* 54 (1784):875.

[2] Gloucester was a centre for both Quarter Sessions and Assizes, which at this time met in the Boothhall in 'a large uncomfortable room supported by double rows of chestnut timber'; G. W. Counsel, *History of the City of Gloucester* (Gloucester, 1829). It was replaced by 'a magnificent shire-hall in the Grecian style', with semi-circular courtrooms, built for the purpose in 1814 to designs by Smirke. Lewis, *England*, 2:264.

together, many of whom were of the better sort. And most of
them appeared to be, for the present, almost persuaded to be
Christians. Wednesday 23 about eleven, I preached at Tewksbury
and, in the evening, at Worcester. Thursday 24, I breakfasted at
5 Mrs. Price's, a Quaker, who keeps a boarding-school.[3] I was much
pleased with her children, so elegantly plain in their behaviour as
well as apparel. I was led, I know not how, to speak to them
largely, then to pray. And we were all much comforted. The society is in great peace and striving together for the hope of the
10 gospel. I have not seen greater earnestness and simplicity in any
society since we left London.

I was now considering how strangely the grain of mustard seed,
planted about fifty years ago, has grown up. It has spread through
all Great Britain and Ireland, the Isle of Wight and the Isle of
15 Man, then to America, from the Leeward Islands through the
whole continent into Canada and Newfoundland. And the societies in all these parts walk by one rule, knowing religion is holy
tempers, and striving to worship God, not in form only, but likewise 'in spirit and in truth'.[4]

20 March 25, Good Friday, I hastened to reach Birmingham
before the church service began.[5] A sharper frost I never knew.
But indeed our house was hot enough in the evening, and I have
not seen a more earnest people. Such an advantage it is to be fully
employed! In every place we find labouring men most susceptible
25 of religion. Such a blessing results from that curse, 'In the sweat
of thy brow thou shalt eat bread.'[6]

Sat. 26. I had designed to rest, but notice had been given of my
preaching at Quinton[7] at noon. As the house would not hold the
people, I was constrained, cold as it was, to preach abroad. And
30 they all seemed to *feel* that solemn question, 'How shall we
escape, if we neglect so great salvation?'[8]

In the evening, my heart was enlarged in such a manner as I
have seldom known, so that I detained the congregation considerably longer than I am accustomed to do, and all the people seemed
35 determined to 'glorify God with their body and their spirit'.[9]

---

[3] JW's letter to Mrs. Howton at this school, Oct. 3, 1783, implies that he had placed a
child there. Telford, 7:190.
[4] Cf. John 4:23-24.
[5] For the Birmingham clergy, see below, Mar. 19. 1786.
[6] Cf. Gen. 3:19.
[7] On Quinton, see above, Mar. 21, 1784.
[8] Heb. 2:3.   [9] Cf. 1 Cor. 6:20.

March 27, Easter Day. I preached at seven on 'The Lord is risen indeed'[10] with an uncommon degree of freedom, and then met the local preachers, several of whom seemed to have caught the fashionable disease, desire of independency. They were at first very warm, but at length agreed to act by the rules laid down in the minutes of the Conference.

The weather now changed. Small rain fell some hours and then turned into snow; this made it very dirty. However, the poor people got through and filled Darlaston Church.[11] Hence I returned to Wednesbury but could not preach abroad, the ground being covered with snow. As many as could crowded into the house. A love-feast followed, at which many plain people spoke without reserve. The artless propriety with which they spoke must be truly astonishing to all who did not consider that promise, 'Ye shall be all taught of God.'[12]

Mon. 28. I preached a kind of funeral sermon on Sarah Wood,[13] one of the first members of the society. For above fifty years, she adorned the gospel, being a pattern of all holiness. She was confined to her bed for several months. Being asked, 'If time did not hang upon her hands?' she answered, 'No, the Bible is my delight.' 'How can that be', said her friend, 'when you cannot see?' 'Very well', said she, 'for the Lord brings it to my remembrance.' So without doubt or fear, she delivered up her soul to her merciful and faithful Creator.

About eleven, I preached at Wolverhampton and spent the afternoon with the amiable family at Hilton Park.[14] Tuesday 29 at noon, I preached in the room at Stafford[15] to a deeply affected congregation. This was the more strange, because there are few towns in England less infected with religion than Stafford. In the evening, I preached at Newcastle[-under-Lyme] to a very serious

---

[10] Luke 24:34.

[11] On the rector, Titus Neve, see above, July 11, 1782.

[12] Cf. 1 Thess. 4:9.

[13] Sarah Wood was a relative of John Wood, the Wolverhampton ironmonger and coal-owner, and her early adherence to Methodism was one of the things which led him to turn against the Methodists and take steps which led to the Wednesbury riots in 1743 and 1744. On these events, see Oct. 20, 1743 (19:344, n. 19 in this edn.); J. L. Waddy, *The Bitter Sacred Cup* (London, 1976), p.11.

[14] On the Gibbes family of Hilton Park, see above, Mar. 25, 1783.

[15] On JW's hopes for Stafford, see above, Aug. 29, 1783. The 'room' had been acquired earlier in the year to replace the stable where the congregation had previously met. Although Stafford became the head of a circuit in 1808, a chapel was not built till 1811. *Wesleyan Methodist Magazine* 49 (1826):428; *Methodist Recorder* (Apr. 30, 1908):9.

and much affected congregation. Wednesday 30, we found a difficulty at Lane End.[16] Even at noon, the house contained not a third of the congregation. The wind was piercing cold. Nevertheless, I preached abroad, and God warmed our hearts. In the evening, I
5 was greatly comforted among our brethren at Burselm, well established in grace. And such another congregation I met with, Thursday 31, at Congleton.

Friday, April 1. I came to Macclesfield, where Mr. Simpson[17] had given notice of my preaching in his church. Here I fully
10 delivered my own soul and, on Saturday 2, went on to Manchester. Sunday 3, our brethren flocking in from all parts, the house, large as it is, could not contain them. It was supposed we had twelve hundred communicants. Monday 4, I preached to our old, loving congregation at Bolton. Tuesday 5 at noon, I preached at
15 Wingates in the open air. The congregation were quite ripe for all the gospel blessings, devouring every word. In the evening, I preached at Wigan. I never before saw this preaching-house full. But it was more than full tonight, and with deeply attentive hearers. Wednesday 6, I preached at Liverpool, but I found no ship
20 there ready to sail. So Thursday 7 (after preaching at Warrington in the way), I hastened to Chester. Neither was there any ship at Parkgate ready to sail. So Friday 8, we took coach and reached Holyhead between four and five on Saturday in the afternoon. Between nine and ten, we went on board the Clermont packet.[18]
25 But it was a dead calm till past ten on Sunday 10, when the company desired me to give them a sermon. After sermon, I prayed that God would give us a full and speedy passage. While I was speaking, the wind sprung up and, in twelve hours, brought us to Dublin Bay. Does not our Lord still hear prayer? I found such a
30 resting place at our own house, as I never found in Ireland before, and two such preachers[19] with two such wives I know not where

---

[16] On Lane End and Longton, see above, Mar. 29, 1784.
[17] On David Simpson and Christ Church, Macclesfield, see Apr. 3, 1774; 22:402, n. 59 in this edn.
[18] Captain Richard Taylor, Dublin; see June 20, 1762 (21:370 in this edn.); *WHS* 5 (1905):78. JW was accompanied by George Whitfield (on whom see above, Aug. 19, 1781); *WHS* 2 (1900):137-38.
[19] James Rogers (see above, Aug. 29, 1783), who on Aug. 9, 1784, had married (secondly) Hester Anne Roe; and Andrew Blair (*c.* 1748-93). Blair, an Ulsterman with a natural propensity to study, was converted under Methodist preaching in 1771, and was received as a preacher upon trial at the Conference of 1778. He was 'regarded as an eminent messenger of the living God [with] . . . a more than ordinary knowledge of men and things . . . [and] mighty in prayer . . . in an uncommon degree.' Atmore, *Memorial*,

to find again. In the evening, and so every evening beside, we had Sunday evening congregations. And in the morning, they were larger by a third part than those I had when I was here last.

On Tuesday and the three following days, I examined the society. I never found it in such a state before: many of them rejoiced in God their Saviour and were as plain in their apparel, both men and women, as those in Bristol and London. Many, I verily believe, love God with all their hearts, and the number of these increase daily. The number of the whole society is seven hundred and forty-seven. Above three hundred of these have been added in a few months, a new and unexpected thing! In various places indeed we have frequently felt

> the overwhelming power of saving grace,[20]

which acted almost irresistibly. But such a shower of grace never continued long, and afterwards men might resist the Holy Ghost as before. When the general ferment subsides, every one that partook of it has his trial for life. And the higher the flood, the lower will be the ebb. Yea, the more swiftly it rose, the more swiftly it falls. So that if we see this here, we should not be discouraged. We should only use all diligence to encourage as many as possible to press forward in spite of all the refluent tide. Now especially we should warn one another not to grow weary or faint in our mind, if haply we may see such another prodigy as the late one at Paulton near Bath, where there was a very swift work of God, and yet, a year after, out of an hundred converted, there was *not one* backslider!

The number of children that are clearly converted to God is particularly remarkable. Thirteen or fourteen little maidens in one class are rejoicing in God their Saviour, and are as serious and stayed in their whole behaviour as if they were thirty or forty years old. I have much hopes, that half of them will be steadfast in the grace of God which they now enjoy.

Sun. 17. We had such a number of communicants at the cathe-

---

pp. 55-60. In 1792, he began to suffer 'evident symptoms of a dropsy', which even Bath waters and private nursing could not check, and he endured a painful but edifying death within a few months. Crookshank, *Ireland*, 1:251.

[20] CW, 'The Invitation', st. 10, in *Hymns on the Great Festivals* (1746), p. 46; reprinted in *Hymns and Sacred Poems* (1749), 1:260; *Poetical Works*, 5:64. Variations upon the same line appear in the Journal, June 20, 1769, June 7, 1788, and June 21, 1789. See also, Sermon 63, 'The General Spread of the Gospel', §12 (2:489, n. 27 in this edn.).

dral[21] as was scarce ever seen there before. In the evening many were cut to the heart; and I believe not a few comforted. A love-feast followed, at which many spoke what God had done for their souls with all plainness and simplicity.

5 Mon. 18. I went through a delightful country to Prosperous,[22] a little town begun five years ago by Captain Brooke,[23] just returned from the East Indies. Here he introduced every branch of the cotton manufactory on a most extensive plan. He built two rows of commodious houses with all convenient appurtenances. And he 10 now employs about two thousand men, women, and children on the spot, beside near the same number in other places.

They had a very large room, but not near large enough for the congregation. All that got in seemed much affected, as they did likewise at five in the morning. About fifty of them are already 15 joined in a society. Fair blossoms! But what will the fruit be?

A remarkable circumstance, we were informed, occurred near this place about three weeks before. A poor woman who owed her landlord fourteen pounds scraped seven together, which she brought him. But he absolutely refused to take less than the whole,

[21] St. Patrick's Cathedral, Dublin.

[22] Prosperous, at its peak a substantial township 11 miles from Leixlip, Co. Kildare, 'is situated near the Grand Canal, [and] owes its origin to Mr. Robert Brooke, who, toward the close of the last century, expended a large fortune in attempting to establish the cotton manufacture there. In less than three years, a town consisting of 200 houses was built: establishments were completed for all the various branches of that manufacture, including the printing of linen and cotton goods, and also for making the requisite machinery. In pursuing this object, that gentleman exceeded the limits of his own private fortune, and, upon application to Parliament, obtained a grant of £25,000. But in 1786, having again occasion to apply to Parliament for assistance, his petition was rejected, and the works consequently were discontinued. Upon this occasion 1400 looms were thrown out of employment, and every other branch of the manufacture ceased.' Weaving continued on a small scale till the place was burned down by rebels in 1798. JW encountered this experiment when it was at its most hopeful stage. See Crookshank, *Ireland*, 1:384.

[23] Robert Brooke (d. *c.* 1802) entered the service of the East India Company as an ensign in 1764, became a captain in 1767, and after distinguished service under Clive against Corsim Ali, Soojah Dowlah, and Hyder Ali, and having put down a revolt in the province of Corah, was rewarded with the lucrative collectorship of the province. His services against the Mahrattas and in the Rohilla War were warmly acknowledged by the directors of the company. It was the fortune he made in this service that he invested in the prematurely named Prosperous, a village to which he invited the Methodist preachers and provided them with every facility. The bulk of the workers were Catholic, who were provided with a room on condition that they did not interfere with the Methodists. The loss of his own fortune, that of his wife and elder brother Henry, in the enterprise, led to his appointment as governor of St. Helena *c.* 1787, where he capably trained East India Company troops and planned an invasion of the Cape of Good Hope, which was anticipated by an expedition from Britain. Crookshank, *Ireland*, 1:384; *DNB*.

yet detained her in talk till evening. She then set out on a car. When she was within a mile of home, she overtook a soldier, who said he was exceedingly tired and earnestly entreated her to let him ride with her on the car, to which she at length consented. When they came to her house, finding there was no town within two miles, he begged he might sit by the fireside till morning. She told him she durst not suffer it, as hers was a lone house, and there was none in it but herself and her girl. But at last, she agreed he should lie in the girl's bed, and she and the girl would lie together. At midnight, two men, who had blackened their faces, broke into the house and demanded her money. She said, 'Then let me go into the next room and fetch it.' Going in, she said to the soldier, 'You have requited me well for my kindness, by bringing your comrades to rob my house.' He asked, 'Where are they?' She said, 'In the next room.' He started up and ran thither. The men ran away with all speed. He fired after them and shot one dead, who being examined, appeared to be her landlord! So that a soldier was sent to protect an innocent woman and punish an hardened villain!

Tue. 19. I preached at ten to an uncommonly large and serious congregation at Edenderry. In the evening, I preached at Tyrrellspass, where a small, dead society is all that now remains. Such another I found at Coolalough[24] on Wednesday 20. Thursday 21, going to Athlone, I found the scene entirely changed: there has not been for many years so much life in the society. Many of the old dead members are quickened again. Many are added to them, and there is no jar of any kind among them: they provoke one another only to love and to good works.

Fri. 22. It is just seven years since I was here before, and I find little change in many, only that they are more dead to the world and consequently more alive to God. And for a few that have left them, God has given them double, that are either alive to God or athirst for him.

Sun. 24. In the afternoon, I preached at the east end of the market-house. I scarce ever saw so numerous a congregation at Athlone. And all were attentive: not a word was heard, and scarce any motion was to be seen. I trust the seed now sown will not wither away but grow up into everlasting life.

---

[24] Orig. 'Coolylough'. The decay of the societies at Tyrellspass and Coolalough shows how much both had depended on the personal influence of Samuel Handy (on whom see Apr. 5, 1748; 20:217, n. 16 in this edn.). He had moved from Tyrellspass to Brackagh Castle, Coolalough, and died there in 1779.

Mon. 25. Being desired to preach at Ballinsaloe[25] in my way to Aughrim, I stood about eleven in the shade of a large house and preached to a numerous congregation of Papists and Protestants, equally attentive, on 'The kingdom of God is at hand.'[26] As I
5 entered Aughrim, the rector,[27] who was waiting at his gate, welcomed me into the country and desired me to use his church, both now and whenever I pleased. I preached there at six. It was thoroughly filled with well-behaved hearers. But the society here, as well as that at Tyrrellspass, is wellnigh shrunk into nothing!
10 Such is the baleful influence of riches! The same effect we find in every place. The more men increase in goods (very few excepted), the more they decrease in grace.

Tue. 26. I went on to Eyrecourt.[28] Here also the minister gave me the use of his church, but the people seemed to understand
15 little of the matter. As I had not this privilege at Birr,[29] I went to the square, where the owner of a large house invited me to preach before it. The congregation was exceeding large, but many of them wild as colts untamed.[30] However, the far greater part of them were seriously attentive. I am in hopes the work of God will
20 revive here also, the rather because he has fully restored one of the most eminent backsliders in the kingdom.

When I came to Tullamore, the minister[31] was willing that I should preach in the church, where both the soldiers and all the officers attended.[32] And our great Captain was present also.

---

[25] Orig. 'Ballinasto'.

[26] Mark 1:15.

[27] Matthew Knaggs, vicar of Aughrim, 1767-1803.

[28] On Eyrecourt, see July 2, 1760 (21:266, n. 49 in this edn.) and Apr. 17, 1775 (22:447, n. 66 in this edn.).

[29] Birr (once known as Parsonstown) was a large market town 18 miles south-west of Tullamore and 60 miles west from Dublin, with, at this time, a brisk woollen trade employing several hundred weavers and combers. 'The principal streets, formed of modern houses and laid out in straight lines, terminate in Duke Square, in which is a statue of the Duke of Cumberland, on a Doric pillar 55 feet high, set up in 1747 in commemoration of his victory at Culloden.' Lewis, *Ireland*, 2:417. The house in this square before which JW preached was owned by a Mr. Marshall. Crookshank, *Ireland*, 1:397-98. The symbolism of this event was repeated when a Wesleyan chapel came to be built: it was situated in Cumberland street, just off the square, along with the court-house, jail, and excise office. C. Cooke, *The Picture of Parsonstown* (Dublin, 1826), pp. 210, 242-43.

[30] Cf. Daniel Defoe, *Col. Jack* (1722); see 21:188, n. 38 in this edn.

[31] James Maxwell was vicar of Tullamore (with Multifarnham), 1779-99. He entered Trinity College, Dublin, in 1763, graduated B.A. in 1768 and died in 1799.

[32] JW had been entertained to tea by the Quartermaster, Joseph Burgess, and his wife. In the evening they heard him preach on 'Fear God, Honour the King' (1 Pet. 2:17; although

Thur. 28. I supposed the house at Portarlington would have more than contained the congregation, but it would scarce contain a third part of them. So I removed to the market-house and preached on the general judgment. The word was quick and powerful, so that very few appeared to be unaffected.

In the evening, I preached in the church at Mountmellick. Perhaps such a congregation was never there before. But the greater part of them seemed to be of Gallio's mind, to 'care for none of these things'.[33]

Fri. 29. I preached in our own house at Kilkenny to just such another congregation. But those that attended in the morning were of a nobler spirit, and I found uncommon liberty among them.

Sat. 30. I preached at Waterford in the court-house,[34] one of the largest in the kingdom. A multitude of people quickly ran together, which occasioned some tumult at first; but it was quickly over, and all were deeply attentive. Surely God will have much people in this city.[35]

Sunday, May 1, at eight, I preached in the court-house to a larger congregation than before. At eleven, I went to the cathedral, one of the most elegant churches in Ireland. The whole service was performed with the utmost solemnity. After service, the senior prebend, Dr. Fell,[36] invited me to dinner and desired,

Wesley's Diary gives 2 Cor. 4:18 as his intentional text). *Wesleyan Methodist Magazine* 63 (1840):542. Burgess later became an itinerant preacher (see above, May 4, 1783).

[33] Cf. Acts 18:17.

[34] 'The court-house, and the city and county jail, occupy a considerable space of ground near the spot where St. Patrick's Gate stood, and are handsomely fronted with granite. The court-house, which is in the centre, was designed and executed by James Gandon, Esq. [in the previous year, 1784], on the recommendation of Howard, the philanthropist. The entrance leads into a hall, from which are seen the interiors of the city and county courts, which are well-arranged and lighted, but on a scale too confined to afford suitable accommodation to the public.' Lewis, *Ireland*, 2:643.

[35] JW's presence and personal counsel left an indelible impression upon at least two future preachers, William Gurley, who travelled in the Methodist Episcopal Church of America and who left a long account of the occasion (quoted in *WHS* 2 [1900]:138–39 from Leonard Burley, *Memoir of Rev. William Gurley* [Cincinnati, 1852], p. 34), and Samuel Wood who sought advice as to entering the ministry. JW replied, 'If the Lord has called you to wait on him, do not run before he sends you, and if he calls, do not fly from him as Jonah did. I will give you two words of advice, viz., read [Jonathan Edward's] *Brainerd's Life*, it will show you the true spirit of a gospel missionary; and read my *Notes on the New Testament*, they will teach you to think.' Curnock, 7:73n.

[36] Hans Thomas Fell (1724–98) was born in Waterford and educated at Trinity College, Dublin, graduating B.A. 1744, LL.B. 1748, LL.D. 1755. He was prebendary of Disert and Kilmoleran, 1749–79; precentor of Waterford, 1779–98; vicar-general of Waterford and Lismore and vicar of Rosbercon in 1769.

'when I came again, I would take a bed at his house.' I doubt that
will never be!

At four, I preached at the head of the Mall[37] to a Moorfields
congregation, all quiet and attentive. Monday 2, the congregation
at five in the morning was larger than that on Saturday evening,
and all of them appeared to have (for the present at least) a real
concern for their salvation. O that it may not pass away as the
morning dew!

I took a solemn farewell of this affectionate people, concluding
with those awful words,

> Now on the brink of death we stand;
>   And if I pass before
> You all may safe escape to land,
>   And hail me on the shore.[38]

Tue. 3. We set out for Dungarvan ferry.[39] But in spite of all the
speed we could make, the road was so horrible, that we could not
reach Youghal before six in the evening. At seven, the court-
house[40] was filled from end to end. And such was the attention of
all, high and low, that I hope many of them will bring forth fruit
to perfection.

Wed. 4. At five in the morning, the court-house was thoroughly
filled. So in the evening, I preached in the Mall, where the congregation was much the same as the last at Waterford. Only that
they were in general Protestants, as are most in the town, who are
also some of the most courteous and quiet people in the kingdom.

---

[37] 'At the east end of the city is the Mall, from which a spacious street has been
opened, forming the principal western entrance on the Cork road.' Lewis, *Ireland*,
2:638.

[38] JW here alters verse 5 of CW's funeral hymn 'How happy every child of grace';
Poetical Works, 6:217. The third line in the original reads 'They all shall soon escape to
land'. JW has typically personalized this reference to Acts 27:44.

[39] Dungarvan, Co. Waterford, on the road from Waterford to Cork, not Dungarvan,
Co. Kilkenny, on the road from Dublin to Waterford. The town was situated on a
peninsula formed by two arms of a spacious bay to which it gave its name; hence the
ferry.

[40] Youghal was commencing a period of steady growth and 'a valuable piece of slab [or
muddy ground] having been reclaimed by the corporation and their tenantry [in 1774],
Catherine Street, the Mall, and numerous extensive warehouses have been built on it. . . .
The Mall-house, in which the courts are held and the public business transacted, is a
handsome structure built by the corporation in 1779 on a site reclaimed from the slab. It
contains, besides the court-rooms, an assembly room, a reading room, and the magistrates' offices; adjoining it is an agreeable promenade.' Lewis, *Ireland*, 2:681. The Mall-
house also took in English and Irish newspapers, and maintained public backgammon-
tables. *The Ancient and Present State of Youghall* (Youghall, 1784), pp. 38-39.

Thur. 5. Before I came halfway to Cork, I was met by about thirty horsemen.[41] We dined at Midleton and then rode on through a pleasant, well cultivated country to Cork. In the evening, many in the crowded congregation were much comforted.

Fri. 6. I made an exact inquiry into the state of the society. I found the number was about four hundred, many of whom were greatly in earnest. Many children, chiefly girls, were indisputably justified; some of them were likewise sanctified and were patterns of all holiness.

But how shall we keep up the flame that is now kindled, not only in Cork, but in many parts of the nation? Not by sitting still, but by stirring up the gift of God that is in them, by uninterrupted watchfulness, by warning everyone and exhorting everyone, by besieging the throne with all the powers of prayer. And after all, some will, and some will not, improve the grace which they have received. Therefore, there must be a falling away. We are not to be discouraged at this, but to do all that in us lies[42] today, leaving the morrow to God.

Sat. 7. On this day that venerable saint, Mr. Perronet,[43] desired his granddaughter, Miss Briggs,[44] who attended him day and night, to go out into the garden and take a little air. He was reading and hearing her read the three last chapters of Isaiah. When she returned, he was in a kind of ecstasy, the tears running down his cheeks from a deep sense of the glorious things which were shortly to come to pass. He continued unspeakably happy that day, and on Sunday was, if possible, happier still. And indeed heaven seemed to be as it were opened, to all that were round about him. When he was in bed, she went into his room to see if anything was wanting, and as she stood at the feet of the bed, he smiled and broke out, 'God bless thee, my dear child, and all that belong to thee. Yea, he *will* bless thee!' which he earnestly

---

[41] This cortege was led by George Howes (1744-1831), who, converted as a child under Methodist preaching, became a pillar of Cork Methodism, a confidant of the preachers, a trustee of the Methodist chapel, and was appointed steward by JW on this visit. He was a notable visitor of prisoners and the sick. 'He possessed a more than ordinary degree of cheerfulness. His phraseology, which was peculiar, arrested attention; and even this he turned to good account.' Crookshank, *Ireland*, 1:399; *Wesleyan Methodist Magazine* 54 (1831):207.

[42] An obvious reiteration, late in life, of his longtime emphasis on *facere quod in se est* (see 1:72, n. 19 in this edn.).

[43] On Vincent Perronet, see Aug. 14, 1744 (20:35, n. 74 in this edn.).

[44] On whom, see above Oct. 23, 1782.

repeated many times, till she left the room. When she went in the
next morning, Monday 9, his spirit was returned to God!

So ended the holy and happy life of Mr. Vincent Perronet in
the ninety-second year of his age. I follow hard after him in years,
being now in the eighty-second year of my age. O that I may follow him in holiness! And that my last end may be like his!

Sun. 8. In the afternoon, I stood in the vacant space near the
preaching-house, capable of containing many thousands. An
immense number assembled. There was no disturbance; the days
of tumult here are over.[45] And God has now of a long season made
our enemies to be at peace with us.

Mon. 9. About noon, I preached at Kinsale in the old bowling-
green[46] which lies on the top of the hill and commands a large
prospect both by sea and land. All behaved well but a few officers,
who walked up and down, and talked together during the whole
service. The poor in Ireland in general are well-behaved; all the
ill-breeding is among well-dressed people. In the evening, I
preached in the main street at Bandon[47] to a very numerous congregation. But some of them were better clothed than taught, for
they laughed and talked great part of the time.

Such a transaction occurred here last week as has not occurred
this century. A soldier walking over the bridge met a countryman
and, taking a fancy to his stick, strove to wrench it from him. His
companion knocked the soldier down. News of this being carried
to the barracks, a whole troop of soldiers marched down and,
without any provocation, fell upon the countrymen coming into
the town, pursued them into the houses where they fled for shelter, and hacked and hewed them without mercy. Two and forty
were wounded, several maimed, and two killed upon the spot.

Wed. 11. I returned from Bandon to Cork, and, after endeav-

---

[45] On the Cork riots (1749), see July 20, 1749, Apr. 14, May 21-30, 1750 (20:285-90,
331-33, 338-43 in this edn.).

[46] Kinsale was rather shabbily built under Compass Hill and seems to have become
more fashionable the higher it rose. 'Towards the middle of the hill is a pleasant bowl-
ing green [where JW now preached], and, higher up, a road planted with trees, called
the Mall, where the ladies and gentlemen recreate themselves.' Charles Smith, *Ancient
and Present State of the County and City of Cork*, ed. R. Day and W. A. Copinger, 2 vols.
(Cork, 1893-94), 1:210 (view, 1:204a).

[47] Bandon, a Protestant town 15 1/2 miles south-west of Cork, at this time a thriving
centre of the woollen industry where Methodism took firm root, was situated on both
the north and the south banks of the river Bandon. On the south bank, settlements
extended for 1 1/2 miles under the names of Boyle Street, Shannon Street, and Main
Street. Lewis, *Ireland*, 1:170.

ouring to confirm those that were much alive to God, on Friday 13, with some difficulty, I broke loose from my affectionate friends and in two long stages reached Kilfinnane.[48] It being too stormy to preach abroad, I preached in the assembly-room. All the hearers were serious and well-behaved. I trust, some will bring forth fruit with patience.

Afterwards, I took a survey of the Danish mount near the town, the first I have seen surrounded with a triple ditch. But it is not either so high or so large as that near Dundee.[49] Is it not strange that the Irish, as well as the Scots, should so soon have driven out those merciless robbers who defied all the strength of England for so long a time? Saturday 14, I found a far greater curiosity, a large druidical temple. I judged by my eye, that it was not less than a hundred yards in diameter. And it was, if I remember right, full as entire as Stonehenge or that at Stanton Drew.[50] How our ancestors could bring or even heave these enormous stones, what modern can comprehend!

In the evening, we found many of our old friends at Limerick were removed to Abraham's bosom. May 15, Whitsunday, the service at the cathedral[51] began at eleven and lasted till three. It concluded a little sooner by *my* assisting at the Lord's Supper at the request of the clergymen. Between five and six, I took my

[48] Orig. 'Killfinnam'. Kilfinnane, a linen as well as a market town, had been settled as recently as 1740 by Palatines (on whom see May 12 1749; 20:272, n. 75), who successfully defended the place against Irish rebels in 1793. 'Outside the town [was] "the Danes' fort", a mound about 130 feet high, 50 feet in diameter at the base and 20 at the summit, encircled by seven earthen ramparts about 20 feet apart, gradually diminished in height, from the innermost to the outermost, which is about 10 feet high and 2000 feet in circuit; an extensive view is obtained from the summit.' Lewis, *Ireland*, 2:60.

[49] Which of the ancient relics (of which Co. Limerick was full) this was is uncertain. The bulk of them were military and included no less than one hundred castles of more recent times. JW seems not to have noticed the poignancy of the survival of these monuments to past failure to keep order in the midst of a new period of prolonged peasant warfare which had recommenced in 1762. He similarly persistently underestimated the Volunteers.

[50] 'The druidical temple at Stanton Drew, Somerset, consists of three circles of stones, many of them very large, of diameters 120, 43, and 32 yards, covering ten acres of ground.' Lewis, *England*, 4:171. The modern commentators regard the Stanton circles as the most important prehistoric monument in Somerset, a miniature version of the monuments on Salisbury Plain, but omit all mention of the Druids; Pevsner, *North Somerset and Bristol*, p. 263. Cf. above, Sept. 17, 1782.

[51] The cathedral at Limerick, served by a large chapter, was said to have been founded in the twelfth century, enlarged about 1200, adorned in the fourteenth century, partly rebuilt in the fifteenth century, much improved in the early seventeenth century, and restored at the end of the wars of that century. It was situated in the English town and surrounded with graduated battlements.

stand near the custom-house amidst an innumerable multitude of people. But they were

wild as the untaught Indian's brood.[52]

They made such a wonderful noise that I judged it best to give
5 them the ground, and retire to our own house. Monday 16, I
restored the select society, which had been quite neglected. In the
evening, I earnestly exhorted all our brethren to set out again in
the good old way and to run with patience the race that is set
before them.[53]

10 Tue. 17. In my way to Gort,[54] I was met by some of our brethren
of Kilcreest,[55] a village eight miles beyond it, giving me an invitation from Colonel Pearse[56] to lodge at his house. He sent me to
Kilchreest in one of his own carriages. There I found a large number of plain people, to whom I preached in the yard. Thence I
15 returned to the Colonel's, but the house being full of genteel company, I was as out of my element, there being no room to talk upon
the only subject which deserves the attention of a rational creature.

Wed. 18. Learning that a little girl[57] had sat up all night and then
walked two miles to see me, I took her into the chaise and was sur-
20 prised to find her continually rejoicing in God. The person with
whom the preachers lodge[58] informed me that she has been two
years possessed of his pure love. We breakfasted at Athenry,[59]

---

[52] From CW's *Hymns for those that seek . . . Redemption* (1747), No. 31, verse 3; *Poetical Works*, 4:251.

[53] See Heb. 12:1.

[54] Gort was a substantial market town 17 miles south-east of Galway.

[55] Orig. 'Killchrist'. Kilcreest was a parish 3 miles west of Loughrea on the road to Gort.

[56] According to Curnock, 7:79n, the name is given in George Taylor, *Taylor & Skinner's Maps of the Roads of Ireland* (2nd edn., London, 1783) as Persse, which may imply a connexion with Mrs. Persse of Castleboy 4 miles away; see May 18, 1787.

[57] Mary Brooke (1770-1845), who was converted at the age of about twelve, 'joined the Wesleyan Methodist society and for more than sixty years adorned the Gospel of Christ Jesus by the uniform tenor of her life', forty-seven of them as a servant in the household of the Irish itinerant, James Bell (1759-1844), whom she survived by a fortnight. *Wesleyan Methodist Magazine* 68 (1845):401, 189.

[58] The name 'Roxborough' in the Diary may be the clue to the identity.

[59] Athenry, a parish, market town, and (still) a borough, 11 miles east of Galway, had been the site of important monastic establishments in the Middle Ages, and was the chief burial place of the earls and principal families of the region. Twice sacked by Irish rebels in the reign of Elizabeth, it never recovered its importance. It lost its borough charter under the Municipal Reform Act. Despite all this, and the lugubrious description JW gave of it on his next visits (see May 19, 1787), it was still a modest town and a very populous parish.

once a populous city, but now *Seges est, ubi Troja fuit.*[60] In the afternoon we went on to Ballinrobe.

Having heard a remarkable account of the Charter School[61] here, I resolved to see it with my own eyes. I went thither about five in the afternoon, but found no master or mistress. Seven or eight boys and nine or ten girls (the rest being rambling abroad) dirty and ragged enough, were left to the care of a girl, half the head taller than the rest. She led us through the house. I observed first the schoolroom, not much bigger than a small closet. Twenty children could not be taught there at once with any convenience. When we came into the bedchamber, I inquired, 'How many children now lodge in the house?' and was answered, 'Fourteen or fifteen boys and nineteen girls.' For these boys there were three beds, and five for the nineteen girls. For food, I was informed, the master was allowed a penny farthing a day for each! Thus they were clothed, lodged, and fed! But what are they taught? As far as I could learn, just nothing! Of these things I informed the commissioners for these schools in Dublin. But I do not hear of any alteration. If this be a sample of the Irish Charter Schools, what good can we expect from them?

In my way from Limerick hither, I read and carefully considered Major Vallancey's Irish Grammar,[62] allowed to be the best extant. And supposing him to give a true account of the Irish language, it is not only beyond all comparison worse than any ancient language I know anything of, but below English, French, German, Italian, Spanish, or any other modern language. The difficulty of reading it is intolerable, occasioned chiefly by the insufferable number of mute letters, both of vowels and consonants, the like of which is not to be found in any language under heaven. The number of pronouns, and the irregular formation of the verbs, is equally insufferable. But nothing is so insufferable as their poetry, the whole construction of which is so trifling and childish, and yet requires more pains to write than either the

[60] Ovid, *Heroides*, I.53-54: 'Now are fields of corn where Troy once was' (Loeb).
[61] On the Irish Charter Schools, see May 15, 1773 (22:367, n. 12 in this edn.).
[62] Charles Vallancey, *A Grammar of the Iberno-Celtic, or Irish Language* (Dublin, 1773). Vallancey (1721-1812), the English-born son of a French Protestant, has more recently been described as 'the founder of a school of writers who theorize on Irish history, language, and literature, without having read the original chronicles, acquired the language, or studied the literature, and who have had some influence in retarding real studies, but have added nothing to knowledge.' *DNB*.

modern rhyme or the ancient attention to long and short syllables! Friday 20, I went on to Castlebar. Here I generally find a welcome reception. Almost all the inhabitants here love us well and believe the Methodists are good men.

5 Sat. 21. Mr. Brown of Rahins,[63] about three miles from Castlebar, invited us to his house. It is one of the pleasantest places I have seen in the kingdom. But it was not so pleasant as when I was there first, for his lovely wife and an amiable daughter are both gone into a better country.

10 May 22, Trinity Sunday, I preached in the morning, on 'There are three that bear record in heaven.'[64] The congregation at church was remarkably well-behaved, and the rector preached a sound, useful sermon. At five, I preached to an exceeding numerous congregation, and afterwards administered the Sacrament to 15 the society. Two clergymen were with us, the curate of Castlebar and the curate of a neighbouring parish, one of whom already enjoys the peace of God, and the other was earnestly seeking it.

Mon. 23. After a long day's journey, I preached in the new court-house[65] at Sligo to far the worst congregation that I have 20 seen since I came into the kingdom. Some (miscalled gentry) laughed and talked without fear or shame, till I openly reproved them. And the rabble were equally rude near the door. In the morning, I preached in our own preaching-house, chiefly for the sake of Mrs. Simpson, a mother in Israel, who has been long con-25 fined to her room. Walking about noon, I was catched in a heavy shower and contracted a severe cold. However, I preached in the evening to a far civiller congregation than the night before. So I think my labour here was not quite in vain.

Wed. 25. I preached about ten in the court-house[66] at 30 Manorhamilton, and then rode over the Black Mountain, now clothed with green, and through a delightful road to Florence

[63] Orig., 'Relins'. On Dodwell Browne, see June 1, 1771; 22:275, n. 92 in this edn.

[64] 1 John 5:7. Wesley had preached from this text ten years earlier at Cork; see Sermon 55, On the Trinity (2:374–86 in this edn.).

[65] Writing half a century later, Lewis (*Ireland*, 2:527) dismissed the court-house as 'too limited for the business of the town' and compared it unfavourably with the 'handsome and substantial' county jail.

[66] This was the sessions-house where petty sessions were held on alternate Wednesdays, and the full sessions quarterly. JW was the guest of Mr. Bradham, 'one of the first and most respectable Methodists in this country, who [in 1780] received the Wesleyan preachers into his house, and continued to entertain them and the venerable founder of Methodism during the remainder of his life.' *Wesleyan Methodist Magazine* 56 (1833):823.

Court. Here I observed the parti-coloured gates (as they were some years since) to be painted plain red. The wind was high and piercing cold. Yet the multitude of people obliged me to preach in the open air. Thursday 26, I preached in the assembly-room at Swanlinbar, but not without difficulty, my cold being so increased that I could not sing nor speak but just in one key.[67] However, I made shift to preach in the church at Ballyconnell[68] in the evening, though it was very full and, consequently, very hot. Friday 27, feeling myself much as I was eleven years ago and not knowing how short my time of working might be, I resolved to do a little while I could. So I began at five and, though I could scarce be heard at first, yet the more I spoke, the more my voice was strengthened. Before I had half done, everyone could hear. To God be all the glory!

About ten, I preached at Killashandra[69] to a multitude of people. But my voice was now so strengthened that everyone could hear. In the evening, there being no house at Kilmore[70] that could contain half the congregation, I was obliged again to preach abroad. There were several sharp showers, but none went away, for it pleased the Lord to send therewith gracious rain on the souls of them that feared him.

Sat. 28. At five, though I had not quite recovered my voice, I judged it best to speak as I could. So I preached in Mr. Creighton's barn, and at seven in the ball room at Cavan. I had designed to go straight from hence to Clones. But a friend sending me word that Mr. Sanderson was willing I should preach in his church at Ballyhaise,[71] I altered my purpose and went thither. Abundance of people were waiting for me. But Mr. Sanderson having changed his mind, I preached in the inn-yard to a very well-behaved congregation, of rich as well as poor. Hence I went on to Clones, where I found such a society as I had hardly seen in

[67] After the service 'a Mr. Pollock invited the venerable evangelist to his house, where he was the means of sowing the seed of eternal life in the family, and its fruits appear to the present day.' Crookshank, *Ireland*, 1:400.

[68] Ballyconnell was a small market town 12 1/2 miles north-west of Cavan.

[69] Killashandra was a market town and the centre of a populous parish 9 miles west of Cavan.

[70] Kilmore, Co. Cavan, was a parish and the seat of a diocese on the road from Killashandra to Cavan, and 3 miles south-west of the latter. Here JW was the guest of Robert Creighton, the brother of the Rev. James Creighton, on whom, see above, May 23, 1773; 22:369, n. 19 in this edn.

[71] Ballyhaise was a market town in the parish of Castleterra; the church stood just outside the town. Lewis, *Ireland*, 1:130, 296.

Ireland, making it a point of conscience to conform to all our
rules, great and small. The new preaching-house was exceeding
neat, but far too small to contain the congregation. The first time
I preached today, was with difficulty; the second and third with
less; the fourth with none at all.

Sun. 29. The morning service, so called, began between twelve
and one. At five, the storm was so high that I could not preach in
the market-place as I first designed. At length, we pitched upon a
sloping meadow near the town, where we were perfectly sheltered
by the hill. I supposed the congregation would have filled the
house at Dublin more than twice over. We had several showers,
but the people regarded them not, being wholly taken up with
better things.

Mon. 30. We went on to Caledon. A convenient preaching-
house is just built here, which (after the forms were removed) just
contained the congregation. The power of God was very unusually present among them. Many were cut to the heart and refused
to be comforted till God spoke[72] peace to their souls. And many
did already rejoice with joy unspeakable.

When we came to Armagh on Tuesday, the wind was extremely
high, and the air as cold as it used to be in December. However,
we had no place that could contain the congregation but Mr.
M'Geough's avenue.[73] And here the people, crowding close
together, did not seem to regard either cold or wind. Tuesday 31,
we took a walk to the primate's palace[74] and had a full view of the
house. It is elegant in the highest degree and yet not splendid,
and it is furnished throughout in a handsome though not in a
costly manner. Since I was here before, he has added an obelisk an
hundred feet high and a dairy-house, with many other conveniences, and a chapel, never yet used! But we were informed, 'He
designs to do many things more!' How well then may it be said
to *him*,

> *Tu secunda marmora*
> *Locas sub ipsum funus, et sepulchri*
> *Immemor, struis domos!*[75]

[72] Edn. A 'speak'.

[73] On this, see Apr. 17, 1769; 22:178-79, n. 58 in this edn.

[74] On Richard Robinson and his building at Armagh, see June 5, 1773; 22:374-75, n.
35 in this edn.

[75] Horace, *Odes*, ii.18, 17-19: 'Thou, on the grave's verge, dost contract for the cutting
of marble slabs, and forgetful of the tomb, dost rear a palace?' (Loeb).

At eleven, I preached in the avenue again. It rained all the time, yet the congregation was large and attentive. Afterwards, a decent woman, whom I never saw either before or since, desired to speak with me and said, 'I met you at Caledon. I had then a violent pain in my head for four weeks but was fully persuaded I should be well if you would lay your hand on my cheek, which I begged you to do. From that moment, I have been perfectly well.' If so, give God the glory. In the evening, the rain drove us into the market-house, where we were a little disturbed by two or three drunken men. But all the rest (a numerous congregation) behaved with deep seriousness.

Wednesday, June 1. I took my leave of my coeval, Mr. M'Geough, whom I scarce expect to see again in this world.[76] About ten, I preached at Blackwatertown in Mr. Roe's yard to a large and elegant congregation; and in the evening, to a larger still at the side of the fort at Charlemont. Mrs. T—— was an unspeakable blessing to this town, while Mr. T——[77] was stationed there. And the revival of religion which began then has been increasing ever since.

In the road to and from Charlemont, I had a good deal of conversation with that amiable women, Mrs. R——.[78] God has indeed dealt very mercifully with her, and her soul is at present much alive. I have great hopes that she and all her lovely family will be patterns to all that are round about them.

Thur. 2. I went to Mr. Caulfield's,[79] the rector of Killyman, three miles from Charlemont. His house is agreeably situated at the head of a beautiful avenue, in which I preached to a very numerous congregation, most of whom seemed to be deeply affected. I sent my horses on to Cookstown,[80] ten Irish miles, Mr. Caulfield sending *me* thither Friday 3, with a pair of his. At ten, I

---

[76] In fact the two met again twice; see June 18, 1787, June 16, 1789.

[77] Preachers had been stationed at Charlemont since 1780, but none with this initial. Perhaps Thomas Tattershall, honourably mentioned above (June 28, 1784), stationed in Londenderry, is meant.

[78] Perhaps Mrs. Roe.

[79] Charles Caulfield was the son of Rev. the Hon. Charles Caulfield, rector of Arboe and grandson of the second Viscount Charlemont. A scholar of Trinity College, Dublin, in 1757, he graduated B.A. in 1759, and M.A. in 1762. He was rector of Forkill, 1772-75, and of Killyman, 1775-1817. He was an active friend to the Methodist cause. J. B. Leslie, *Armagh Clergy and Parishes* (Dundalk, 1911), p. 338. The Caulfields were a clerical as well as an aristocratic family—Charles Caulfield's son was a clergyman, and his grandson, Charles, Bishop of Nassau.

[80] Orig. 'Mr. Cook's town'.

preached there and then hastened forward, but I could not reach Londonderry before seven. We then found (notwithstanding they had but short notice) a congregation gathered from all parts.

The society here has not been so well established for many years as it is now. What is principally wanting is zeal for God and entire self-devotion to him.

Sun. 5. At eight, I strongly applied the latter part of the thirteenth chapter to the Romans. We had a very decent congregation at church, but not so many communicants as I expected. At six, our room was thoroughly filled with as serious hearers as ever I saw. Monday 6, we had a numerous congregation in the morning, of rich as well as poor. But who is able effectually to warn these to flee from the wrath to come?

At eleven, I preached in an open place at Limavady[81] sixteen miles from Londonderry. In the evening, we had at Coleraine a larger congregation than at Clones itself. And they seemed a more intelligent people than most I have met with. Indeed the whole town is different from all that I have seen. There is no hurry or noise, but all quiet and still, both by day and by night,[82] so that no wonder so many here receive the gospel of peace and 'bring forth fruit unto perfection'.[83]

Tue. 7. I accepted the offer of the Presbyterian Meeting and preached there at noon and at six in the evening. Wednesday 8, after preaching in the morning, I left many of the loving people in tears and went on to Ballymoney, where I preached in the courthouse[84] to a very civil and a very dull congregation. From hence we went to Ballymena. In the afternoon, I walked over to Gracehill,[85] the Moravian settlement. Beside many little houses for them

[81] Orig. 'Newtown'. According to Lewis, *Ireland*, 2:401, the distance was 12 3/4 miles.

[82] JW arrived at Coleraine at the right time: the Saturday market in Coleraine was a very brisk affair for both linens and provisions. The next of the four fairs was not till July 5, and a thrice-weekly grain-market was not established till 1819. Lewis, *Ireland*, 1:372.

[83] Cf. Luke 8:14.

[84] Ballymoney court-house was in the centre of the town; the Antrim quarter sessions were held here and at Ballymena alternately.

[85] Moravian societies had been created in this district in 1746 by the preaching of John Cennick (on whom see Mar. 9, 1739; 19:36, n. *a* in this edn.) and Benjamin Latrobe (see Aug. 18, 1747; 20:190, n. 12 in this edn.). When in 1758, it was resolved to create a permanent settlement, three hundred sixty-one acres of the townland of Ballykennedy were obtained, 2 miles south-west of Ballymena, on a lease renewable forever. Each family had a plot to pasture a cow and produce potatoes and oats for home consumption. 'The village is chiefly formed by two parallel streets, terminated on the north by

that are married, they have three large buildings (on the same plan with that at Fulneck), having the chapel in the middle, the house for the single men on the left hand, that for the single women on the right. We spent one or two agreeable hours in seeing the several rooms. Nothing can exceed the neatness of the rooms or the courtesy of the inhabitants. But if they have most courtesy, we have more love. We do not suffer a stranger, especially a Christian brother, to visit us without asking him either 'to bite or sup'. 'But it is *their way*'. I am sorry to say, so it is. When I called on Bishop Anton[86] in Holland (an old acquaintance whom I had not seen for six and forty years, till both he and I were grown grey-headed), he did not ask me so much as to wet my lips! Is not this a shameful way! A way contrary not only to Christianity but to common humanity? Is it not a way that a Jew, a Mahometan, yea, an honest heathen would be ashamed of?

Having now finished an ingenious book, Le Vayer's *Animadversions on the Antient Historians*, I thought a few passages worth transcribing as containing some uncommon remarks. He says more for the veracity of Herodotus than ever I saw before, and convinces me that his authority is more to be relied on than that of Polybius, who,

> contrary to the truth of history, makes Scipio an example of *continence*, in giving up the fair captive to the Spanish prince; whereas in fact, he never would, nor did, restore her to her husband.
>
> There is not a more incredible relation in all the Roman history, than that Clelia and all the Roman virgins, who were hostages to the Etrurians,[87] swam over the river Tiber to Rome. Surely they

the road from Ballymena to Ahoghill, and leading to a square, of which their continuation composes two sides, and in which are situated the principal buildings of the Moravian establishment. These buildings include a chapel with dwellings for the minister and the warden; a house for unmarried brethren; the sisters' house; an academy for young gentlemen, and boarding school for young ladies; and an inn. On the fourth side of the square, which is unoccupied by buildings, are gardens and fields, sloping down to the river; and on the summit of a rising ground [just as in Herrnhut], at a short distance in the rear of the chapel, is the burial ground, which has an air of peculiar quiet and repose.' Lewis, *Ireland*, 1:134.

[86] On this episode and a further reference to Anton Seiffert, see above, June 28, 1783.

[87] Orig. 'Hetrurians'. 'When the Etruscan Lars Porsenna finally gave up his attempt to restore Tarquinius Superbus to the throne of Rome from which he had been expelled, he made a treaty with the Romans according to which they handed over hostages in exchange for the Janiculum Hill across the Tiber, which was to be returned by the Etruscans. One of the hostages was a girl called Cloelia, who, while in the Etruscans' camp, obtained permission to bathe in the Tiber. After sending her guards away while she undressed, she swam across the river to Rome, accompanied by other girl

would scarce have dared to look upon so rapid a river, much less to plunge into it! Especially when there was no necessity, for the peace was then almost concluded.

Some writers affirm, and it is earnestly believed, that Belisarius[88] was reduced to *beggary*. But it is a mere fable. On the contrary, the Emperor Justinian heaped titles and honours upon him to the last, although he recalled him out of Italy after he had been defeated there by the French. Procopius, who wrote largely concerning him, says not one word of his being reduced to poverty.[89]

Thur. 9. Between nine and ten, I preached in the court-house at Antrim[90] to a large staring congregation. Thence we went on to Belfast through miserable roads. O where is common sense? At six, I preached in the linen-hall[91] to a large congregation admirably well behaved. I often wonder that among so civil a people we can do but little good! Friday 10, we came to Downpatrick

hostages. The Etruscans shot at the swimming figures, but Cloelia was able to restore the whole band safe and sound to their families. Although Porsenna complained of the breach of treaty and demanded Cloelia's return, he was so impressed by her bravery that . . . [her] act opened up friendly relations between Porsenna and the new republic: and the Romans erected an equestrian statue of her on the Sacred Way.' M. Grant and J. Hazel, *Who's Who in Classical Mythology* (London, 1979), p. 92.

[88] Belisarius (*c.* 505-65), the greatest of Byzantine generals, was accused in 563 of conspiracy against the life of Justinian, his fortune was sequestered, and he soon died. A. P. Stanley noted in 1853 that 'it is remarkable that whilst his life is preserved to us with more than usual accuracy—by the fact of the historian Procopius having been his secretary . . . the circumstances of his disgrace and death are involved in great uncertainty. . . . This arises from the termination of the contemporary histories of Procopius and Agathias before the event in question.' Edward Gibbon followed certain sources to believe that he was merely imprisoned for a year in his own palace and restored to his honours eight months before his death, whilst Lord Mahon, on the authority of an anonymous writer of the eleventh century, sustained the story (which went into legend) that he had his eyes put out and passed the remainder of his life sitting in the streets of Constantinople begging. William Smith, *Dictionary of Greek and Roman Biography and Mythology*, 3 vols. (London, 1853-56), 1:478-80.

[89] François de La Mothe Le Vayer, *Notitia historicorum selectorum; or, Animadversions upon the Antient and Famous Greek and Latin Historians*, trans. from the French by William D'Avenant (Oxford, 1678), pp. 34-37, 5-7.

[90] 'The court-house is a large and handsome building nearly in the centre of the town; and under it is the bridewell.' Lewis, *Ireland*, 1:36.

[91] This was quite new, and arose from the determination of the powerful linen interest in and about Belfast to get the main market for their produce away from Dublin. 'In 1785 a spacious and handsome quadrangular building was erected in the centre of Donegal Square, by public subscription, and called the White Linen Hall. It affords great facility for making up assorted cargoes for foreign countries . . . and nearly all the London merchants are supplied by factors resident here. The Brown Linen Hall, created [in 1773], is in an inclosed space on the south side of Donegal Street . . . where the merchants attend every Friday for the purchase of brown webs from the weavers, who assemble here from the surrounding districts.' Lewis, *Ireland*, 1:185.

where, the preaching-house being too small, we repaired as usual to the Grove, a most lovely plain very near the venerable ruins of the cathedral. The congregation was as large as that at Belfast but abundantly more awakened. The people in general were remarkably affectionate. They filled the large preaching-house at five in the morning. And we seemed to be as closely united with them as with one of our old societies in England.

About eleven on Saturday, I preached in the linen-hall at Ballynahinch[92] to a numerous congregation. The country from hence to Lisburn is wonderfully pleasant and fruitful. At six, I preached in the Presbyterian Meeting,[93] a large and commodious building. And I was now with the most lively society that I have seen for many days, owing chiefly to the good providence of God bringing sister Johnson[94] hither. She came indeed in an acceptable time. For J—— W——[95] and his wife, who for many years had been pillars, had left the society. They had one child, a son about nineteen years old, of whom they were fond enough. By a fall from his horse, he was killed in a moment, leaving his parents inconsolable. Just then she came to Lisburn and visited them. God opened her mouth, both in exhortation and prayer. They saw and acknowledged his hand. She was enabled to give up her child to God; he cried out, 'Surely God has sent an angel from heaven to comfort us!' Both of them joined the society and are more in earnest for salvation than they have been for many years.

Sun. 12. We had a solemn opportunity in the morning. In the afternoon, as no building could contain the people, I stood abroad and proclaimed, 'There is joy in heaven over one sinner that repenteth, more than over ninety and nine just persons who need not repentance.'[96] The hearers (allowing five persons to a square yard) were seven or eight thousand.

At eleven, I preached in the churchyard at Lurgan. The sun shone extremely hot, but we were sheltered from it, partly by the church and partly by the spreading trees. In the afternoon, I went on to Tandragee, one of the pleasantest towns in Ireland, sur-

---

[92] Edn. A 'Ballinehunch'; edn. B, 'Ballinihanch' Ballynahinch was a market and post town in the parish of Magherdroll, half-way between Downpatrick and Lisburn.

[93] Described by Lewis, *Ireland*, 2:279, as first class.

[94] Formerly Dorothea King; see July 26, 1762 (21:376, n. 42 in this edn.). She became the second wife of the itinerant John Johnson (see May 5, 1757; 21:95, n. 70 in this edn.), with whom, when his itinerancy was ended by ill health, she settled at Lisburn.

[95] John Wilson. *WHS* 2 (1900):140.

[96] Cf. Luke 15:7.

rounded by woods and fruitful hills, with a clear river running between them. At six, I stood in the Grove, where the tall elms shaded both me and the numerous congregation. Several gentlemen and several clergymen were among them, and all behaved with serious attention.

I lodged at the Rev. Dr. L——'s,[97] where my time seemed exceeding short. Wednesday 15, the scene changed from a palace to a cottage at Derryanvil,[98] a small village surrounded by a bog but inhabited by lively Christians. About eleven, I preached in a shady orchard to an exceeding large congregation; in the evening, to a still larger at the Grange,[99] a small village on the top of a hill. Many showers went to the right and the left while I was preaching, but only a few drops fell upon us. Thursday 16 about eight, I preached at Richhill,[1] where there were many backsliders, on 'How shall I give thee up Ephraim?'[2] In the afternoon, I came to Newry, where I never before had any tolerable place to preach in. But the Presbyterians now offered me the use of their large and handsome meeting-house;[3] perhaps it never was filled before. I believe the occasion required me to speak very plain, which I did from Elijah's question, 'How long halt ye between two opinions?'[4] And I applied it to the conscience of each person, rich and poor, with all possible plainness.

Fri. 17. Many of our friends from Dublin gave us the meeting at Drogheda,[5] a large handsome town, which seemed to me to be little inferior to Waterford. After much opposition, a small society is formed here. I preached in the sessions-house,[6] a large commodious room, which was quickly filled with rich and poor. The

[97] On Henry Leslie, see June 13, 1773; 22:375-76, n. 39 in this edn.

[98] Where a chapel had been built the previous year. Crookshank, *Ireland*, 1:403.

[99] The Grange was a huge and populous parish comprising almost 6,800 acres, formed out of the parish of Armagh in 1777. Cf. May 6, 1765 (21:507 in this edn.).

[1] Richhill was a small parish 4 miles east of Armagh.

[2] Hos. 11:8.

[3] Described by Lewis, *Ireland*, 2:433, as 'large and elegant'. Later in the year a Methodist chapel was built on a site given by Mr. Boyd, one of the new members (Crookshank, *Ireland*, 1:403), and a high-pressure revival followed in 1790 and 1791. *Arminian Magazine* 14 (1791):413-16.

[4] 1 Kgs. 18:21.

[5] Drogheda was 23 miles north of Dublin.

[6] Crookshank (*Ireland*, 1:403) says, without quoting any source, that this meeting took place in the linen-hall (described by Lewis, *Ireland*, 1:484, as a spacious building of brick containing five halls), but there was a sessions-house at Drogheda, the Tolsel, 'a spacious and handsome building of hewn stone', well adapted for the purpose. Ibid., 1:485.

mayor himself and several of the aldermen took care that none should make any disturbance. God gave us an exceeding solemn season. After sermon, I gave a short account of the rise of Methodism. I believe all were so satisfied that there will scarce be any more persecution of the Methodists at Drogheda.

Sat. 18. Having visited all the places I proposed, I came back to Dublin just as well as I set out, my strength having been as my day.

Sun. 19. I exhorted a crowded audience 'to bring forth fruits meet for repentance'[7] and afterwards pressed the exhortation on our own society. Monday 20, I visited one ill of a violent fever and calmly triumphing over sickness and pain and death. In the evening, I received a letter from a physician, whom the next morning I carried to see her. He thoroughly understood her case. And from the day she followed his prescription, she began to recover. I feared very many of the society would be lost before my return. But I found only three, so that seven hundred and thirty-seven of them remained.

Tue. 28.[8] By the good providence of God, I finished the eighty-second year of my age. Is anything too hard for God! It is now eleven years since I have felt any such thing as weariness. Many times I speak till my voice fails, and I can speak no longer. Frequently, I walk till my strength fails, and I can walk no farther. Yet even then, I feel no sensation of weariness, but am perfectly easy from head to foot. I dare not impute this to natural causes. It is the will of God.

Wed. 29. I went with twelve or fourteen of our friends on the canal to Prosperous.[9] It is a most elegant way of travelling, little inferior to that of the *trekschuits*[10] in Holland. We had fifty or sixty persons in the boat, many of whom desired me to give them a sermon. I did so, and they were all attention. In the evening, I preached at Prosperous to a numerous congregation on the 'general judgment'.[11] After preaching at five in the morning, Thursday 30, I took boat with a larger company than before, who, about eleven, desired me to preach, for which they appeared to be exceeding thankful.

Friday, July 1. Most of our travelling preachers met to confer

---

[7] Luke 3:8, as noted in the Diary.

[8] In edn. A, this paragraph was misplaced after July 6 and the following paragraph misdated 'Wed. 22'; cf. Diary.

[9] For this township, see above Apr. 18, 1785.

[10] Orig. 'Track-skaits'; on this form of transport, the track-boat, see above, June, 16, 1783.

[11] JW's text was Rev. 20:12.

together on the things of God.[12] We began and ended in much peace and love, being all resolved not to 'do the work of the Lord so lightly'. Sunday 3, we had a larger congregation than ever at St. Patrick's, where many of our brethren found such a blessing that they will not easily be so prejudiced against the church as they were in time past.

Wed. 6. We concluded our Conference. I remember few such conferences, either in England or Ireland: so perfectly unanimous were all the preachers and so determined to give themselves up to God.

Sunday, July 10. I went on board the *Prince of Wales*,[13] one of the neatest ships I ever was in. We left the work of God increasing in every part of the kingdom, more than it has done for many years. About two in the morning, we sailed out of Dublin Bay and came into Holyhead Bay before one in the afternoon on Monday 11. That evening we went on to Gwyndy;[14] Tuesday 12, to Kinmel, one of the pleasantest inns in Wales,[15] surrounded with gardens and stately woods, which their late proprietor must see no more! Wednesday 13, we reached Chester. After preaching there between five and six in the evening, I stepped into the stage-coach, which was just setting out and, travelling day and night, was brought safe to London on Thursday 15 in the afternoon.[16]

[12] The Irish Conference reported a very substantial increase in membership, permitted the building of three new chapels, and gave its mind to the improvement of its financial administration; Crookshank, *Ireland*, 1:404. The mood of tranquil satisfaction, which is apparent in JW's birthday assessment of his health, is reflected also in his view of the state of the work and his own public position. To his brother he wrote: 'Here is a set of excellent young preachers. Nine in ten of them are much devoted to God. I think, number for number, they exceed their fellow-labourers in England. These in Dublin particularly [James Rogers and Andrew Blair] are burning and shining lights'; Telford, 7:274. And to Elizabeth Ritchie: 'Many years ago I was saying, "I cannot imagine how Mr. Whitefield can keep his soul alive, as he is not now going through honour and dishonour, evil report and good report, having nothing but honour and good report attending him wherever he goes." It is now my own case: I am just in the condition now that he was then in. I am become, I know not how, an honourable man. The scandal of the cross is ceased; and all the kingdom, rich and poor, Papists and Protestants, behave with courtesy—nay, and seeming goodwill! It seems as if I had wellnigh finished my course, and our Lord was giving me honourable discharge.' Telford, 7:277.

[13] The *Prince of Wales* was a Parkgate packet, Captain John Heird, Roger's Hotel, Rogerson's Quay, Dublin; *WHS* 5 (1905):78. See also below, July 11, 1787.

[14] Gwyndy was a chapelry 11 miles east of Holyhead, about half-way to the crossing from Anglesey to the mainland. JW had called there on Apr. 11, 1783 (see Diary). There was an inn on the post road.

[15] The Cross Foxes, Kinmel; Williams, *Wesley in Wales*, p. 119, n. 2. Kinmel is between Abergele and St. Asaph.

[16] On the 16th the preacher John Valton dined with JW and found him, so soon after his travels, as 'young and lusty as the eagle'. *WHS* 8 (1911):36.

Sun. 17. I preached both morning and evening on the education of children.[17] I now spoke chiefly to the parents, informing them that I designed to speak to the children at five the next morning. Monday 18 at five, not only the morning chapel[18] was well filled, but many stood in the large chapel. I trust they did not come in vain. The rest of the week, I was fully employed in writing for the magazine and preparing for the Conference. Sunday 24, I preached at West Street, morning and afternoon, when both the largeness and earnestness of the congregation gave me a comfortable hope of a blessing at the ensuing Conference. Tuesday 26, our Conference began, at which about seventy preachers were present whom I had invited by name.[19] One consequence of this was that we had no contention or altercation at all, but everything proposed was calmly considered and determined as we judged would be most for the glory of God.

Monday, August 1. Having, with a few select friends, weighed the matter thoroughly, I yielded to their judgment and set apart three of our well-tried preachers, John Pawson, Thomas Hanby, and Joseph Taylor, to minister in Scotland.[20] And I trust God will

[17] Cf. Sermon 95, 'On the Education of Children' (3:347-60 in this edn.).

[18] This was used mostly for the early preaching, which continued into the early nineteenth century; see above, Mar. 15, 1784.

[19] That is to say, JW invited fewer preachers than the hundred named in the Deed of Declaration, a number small enough to provoke the secession of eight preachers. The preachers who did attend were required to subscribe their support of that deed. In the Minutes for this Conference, JW did not publish the American membership figures, but included the letter he had given to Coke and Asbury appointing them Superintendents over the American flock and justifying his ordinations. The Conference also condemned selling books and the employment of hairdressers on the Lord's Day, as well as the sending of children to dancing schools on any day. *Minutes*, 1:179-82.

[20] The rationale of this act of ordination was like that of the American ordinations, viz., that JW felt entitled by virtue of his own ordination, to ordain, at any rate for areas outside the jurisdiction of the Church of England. He proved able to make two more visits to Scotland, but was already counting his days and wishing to provide a means by which the Scottish Methodists might enjoy the sacraments he was less and less able to bring to them. For John Pawson, see June, 21, 1767; 22:86, n. 4 in this edn.

Thomas Hanby (1733-96) was born at Carlisle, the son of a woollen manufacturer of Barnard Castle, who soon returned with him to that town. He was early converted through the agency of John Whitford (see above, Sept. 25, 1748; 20:249, n. 70 in this edn.), the first Methodist preacher to come to the town (who soon afterwards became a Calvinist and left the connexion). In 1755, he was admitted to the itinerancy, having been employed by Shent and other preachers to help out temporarily with their circuits, and acquired the reputation not only of a notable preacher but also of a man who combined a mild temper with rock-like convictions; Jackson, *Early Methodist Preachers*, 2:131-57. These swiftly proved very inconvenient to JW himself, for Hanby was unwilling to confine the administration of the sacraments to Scotland, claiming that he would not have accepted ordination if this limitation had been clear to him. His vigourous description of the result, written in 1789, speaks for itself:

bless their ministrations and show that he has sent them. Wednesday 3, our peaceful Conference ended, the God of power having presided over all our consultations.

Sun. 7. After preaching in the morning at West Street, and in
5 the afternoon at the New Chapel, I took a solemn leave of the society and, on Monday 8, went in the Diligence to Portsmouth Common. Here I found a lively and consequently an increasing society. Tuesday 9, I crossed over the Isle of Wight. Here also the work of God prospers. We had a comfortable time at Newport,
10 where is a very teachable though uncommonly elegant congregation. Wednesday 10, we took a walk to the poor remains of Carisbrooke Castle. It seems to have been once exceeding strong, standing on a steep ascent. But even what little of it is left is now swiftly running to ruin. The window indeed through which King
15 Charles attempted to make his escape is still in being and brought to my mind that whole train of occurrences wherein the hand of God was so eminently seen.[21]

> Mr. Mather sent me a threatening bull; Mr.Wesley a second; and, to complete the work, the clergy in London, Mr. Rankin, and Mr. Moore, joined their artillery. The last in command is my colleague, Joseph Taylor, who opposes me with the utmost warmth. . . . Mr. Wesley has for some years treated me contemptuously, putting me beneath the weakest and most suspicious characters (viz. Briscoe and Fenwick). . . . To be expelled the connexion, after thirty-five years of uninterrupted labour, is to me a very painful thought; but I see I must suffer it, and shall only take away with me this motto, "Driven from Methodism for defending the injured, and nearly abrogated and obsolete, ordinance of Christ."

Tyerman, *John Wesley,* 3:574–76. John Pawson caustically reported that 'the truth is, the good old man [JW] has been so pestered with his brother and the High Church bigots on all sides that I really believe he does not know what to do,' denying even any intention of secession from the Church of Scotland (*WHS* 12 [1920]:107-9). The confession helped to preserve Hanby's ground in the connexion. In 1791, within a month of JW's death, Hanby and Pawson were among those who advocated a Presbyterian system of connexional management, with an annually changing president, committees, and (if need be) local presidents to see to district affairs, and the filling up of the Legal Hundred by seniority (*WHS* 30 [1955]:165). He himself became the fourth President after JW's death, 1795-96.

Joseph Taylor (1752-1830) was born at Driffield near Derby and returned to Derby as a supernumerary for the last nine years of his long life. Early converted, he began early to preach, and he was taken into the itinerancy on trial in 1777. He so outlived his contemporaries that, at the time of his death, his colleagues did not know what to make of him, and he fell back on a theory that he had 'when young . . . unhappily injured his constitution, particularly when in Cornwall, during a great revival of religion [1782-84]. By over-exertion in this good work, he entailed upon himself infirmities which never left him, and which gave to his physical efforts in the pulpit an air of feebleness'; *Wesleyan Methodist Magazine* 53 (1830):642-43. His peers did not appoint him President till 1802, by which time Pawson had already been President twice.

[21] A comparison of this passage with that of July 10, 1753 (see 20:467 and note 82 in this edn.), shows how much JW's latent royalism had been sharpened by the American

Thur. 11. About noon, I preached in a little court in the town of Portsmouth.[22] The people were all attention. So there was a much larger congregation in the evening in St. George's Square. Surely after all the stumbling-blocks which have been thrown in the way, God will have many souls in this place.

Fri. 12. I preached at Winchester and, on Saturday 13, went on to Salisbury. As Captain Webb[23] had just been there, I endeavoured to avail myself of the fire which he seldom fails to kindle. The congregation in the evening was very large and seemed to be deeply affected. So they did again at eight on Sunday morning. But I believe the greatest blessing was in the evening, particularly during the prayer, wherein God was pleased to move many in an uncommon manner.

Mon. 15. I preached in Shaftesbury at nine to such a congregation as I had not seen there before. I was glad to see among them the gentleman who, thirty years ago, sent his officer to discharge me from preaching in his borough.[24] About two, I preached at Castle Cary to as many as could well hear. And I believe there were very few who did not feel that God was with us.

In the evening, I preached at Shepton Mallet, but the house would not near contain the congregation. For many years this society was remarkably dead, but it is now one of the liveliest in England.

Tue. 16. We went on to Taunton, where I expected little good. But I was agreeably disappointed. The house was thoroughly filled. A solemn awe sat upon the whole congregation, and God spoke to their hearts. The house was nearly filled at five in the morning, a sight never seen here before. Wednesday 17, Cullompton House[25] was more than filled, many being constrained to go away. And I found uncommon liberty of speech here, as well as at Exeter in the evening.

Thur. 18. I had a pleasant journey to Plymouth Dock, the rain having but just laid the dust. The late separation here seems to have done little hurt:[26] a few turbulent men have left us, but men

---

War; he is clearly not suggesting that the hand of God was seen in the way Charles I eventually paid with his life for a long career of duplicity.

[22] This obscure entry was thought by the historian of Portsmouth Methodism to show that there were now two Methodist preaching-houses, one in Old Portsmouth and one in Portsea. Henry Smith, *Wesleyan Methodism in Portsmouth* (London, 1895), p. 34.

[23] For Thomas Webb, see Feb. 2, 1773 (22:369, n. 73 in this edn.).

[24] For this episode, thirty-five years before, see Sept. 4, 1750 (20:360 in this edn.).

[25] I.e., preaching-house.

[26] See above, Feb. 25, 1785; and Sept. 28, 1757 (21:127 in this edn.).

of a more quiet spirit are continually added in their stead. So that on the whole we are gainers by our loss. Such is the wisdom of God!

Fri. 19. In the evening, I preached in the new house at Plymouth. This also was well filled. Sunday 21, I preached at the Dock at seven, and the house contained us pretty well. But in the evening, it was thought as many went away as got in. After preaching, I gave them a plain account of the beginning and progress of that great work of God, vulgarly called 'Methodism'.

Mon. 22. I took a cheerful leave of our brethren at the Dock, leaving them well united together, and on the following days preached at Liskeard, St. Austell, Sticker (a new place near it),[27] Helston, Marazion, and Penzance. Thursday 25 about nine, I preached at Mousehole, where there is now one of the liveliest societies in Cornwall. Hence we went to the Land's End, in order to which we clambered down the rocks to the very edge of the water. And I cannot think but the sea has gained some hundred yards since I was here forty years ago.[28] In the evening, I preached at St. Just, where are still many of our eldest brethren, although many are gone to Abraham's bosom.

Fri. 26. In the evening, I preached in the market-place at St. Ives to almost the whole town. This was the first place in Cornwall where we preached and where Satan fought fiercely for his kingdom. But now all is peace. I found old John Nance had rested from his labours. Some months since, sitting behind the preacher in the pulpit, he sunk down, was carried out, and fell asleep![29]

Sat. 27. About nine, I preached at the copper-works near the Hayle in the new preaching-house.[30] I suppose such another is not in England nor in Europe nor in the world. It is round, and all the

[27] Sticker was a village 3 miles south-west of St. Austell on the main road to Truro.

[28] JW's first visit here was on Sept. 11, 1743 (see 19:337 in this edn.). Why JW should have thought that this imperious cliff was crumbling at such a rate is hard to imagine.

[29] On John Nance, see Apr. 4, 1744 (20:20, n. 89 in this edn.).

[30] The industrial character of Hayle is borne out in the names of its two early Methodist preaching-houses, Foundery and Copperhouse (here referred to, and the name also of part of the town); Lewis, *England*, 2:390. The Copperhouse Chapel was circular with a conical roof, with windows at the top of the wall and a single door facing the road. It was constructed of a common building material in Hayle, blocks made from the molten dross remaining after the extraction of copper from the ore, which were brittle but very hard and durable; *WHS* 4 (1904):195. Smelting in Hayle did not long survive JW, the ore being shipped to South Wales where there was an abundant supply of coal; and the building which replaced this chapel in 1817 had a brick-tiled floor. T. Shaw, *History of Cornish Methodism* (Truro, 1967), p. 43.

walls are brass, that is, brazen slugs. It seems nothing can destroy this till heaven and earth pass away.

At two, the stewards of all the societies met at Redruth.[31] There is nothing but peace and love among them and among the societies from whence they came, and yet no great increase!

At our love-feast in the evening, several of our friends declared how God had saved them from inbred sin, with such exactness both of sentiment and language as clearly showed they were taught of God.[32]

Sun. 28. At half past eight, I preached at St. Agnes to the largest congregation I ever saw there. Between one and two, I preached in the street at Redruth to thousands upon thousands. And my strength was as my need. Yet I was afraid, lest I should not be able to make all those hear that assembled in the evening. But though it was supposed there were two or three thousand more than ever were there before, yet they heard (I was afterwards informed) to the very skirts of the congregation, while I applied those solemn words, 'One thing is needful.'[33]

Wed. 31. I preached at Launceston; September 1, in the market-place at Tiverton; and on Friday 2, opened the little preaching-house at Wellington. At noon, I preached in an ancient, venerable building once belonging to a Lord Chief Justice. It is oddly called Cathanger.[34] Having a stupid people to deal with, I spoke exceeding plain. And I think many of them, even Somersetshire farmers, felt as well as heard. Thence we went on to Ditcheat. The people here are all attention, so that I had nothing to do but apply the promises. The society is continually increasing, and more and more of the hearers are convinced and justified. What is the strangest thing is, there is no opposer in the town, but rich and poor all acknowledge the work of God. Saturday 2 in the afternoon, the good providence of God brought us once more well to Bristol.

---

[31] At this time, there were 45 societies in the Redruth circuit with a membership of 2517. The meeting was a business gathering as well as a spiritual occasion, and cast interesting light on the cost of itinerancy. The preachers were paid three guineas a quarter; house rent was £3. 2s. 3d. for *three* quarters; but horse-shoeing at Redruth alone came to £5. 16s. 0d., and 'horses and driver with Mr. Wesley £5. 0s. 6d.'. *WHS* 2 (1900):125-26.

[32] Compare the comment above, Feb. 6, 1785.

[33] Luke 10:42, probably JW's commentary on his sermon rather than his text, since the Diary cites John 4:24, 'God is a Spirit: and they that worship him must worship him in spirit and in truth.'

[34] On Cathanger, see above, Sept. 3, 1778.

Sun. 4. Finding a report had been spread abroad that I was just going to leave the church, to satisfy those that were grieved concerning it, I openly declared in the evening that I had now no more thought of separating from the church than I had forty years ago.

Tue. 6. I preached at Paulton and Coleford; Wednesday 7, in an open place near the road at Mells.[35] Just as I began, a wasp, though unprovoked, stung me upon the lip. I was afraid it would swell so as to hinder my speaking, but it did not. I spoke distinctly near two hours in all and was no worse for it. In the evening, I preached with much satisfaction at Frome to a mixed multitude of rich and poor, and afterwards strongly exhorted them that had believed to 'walk in love'[36] after the example of our great Master. On Thursday, I preached at Trowbridge, and on Friday at Bradford[-on-Avon], where the work of God has much increased lately. Indeed it has increased this year through the whole circuit as it has not done for twenty years before. On Saturday evening, I preached at Bath. Sunday 11, Mr. Bradburn[37] preached at seven, and Mr. Collins[38] about two in the afternoon. I began the service at eleven and preached on part of the Epistle, Ephesians 3:14, etc. Both then and in the evening the word 'distilled as the dew, and as the rain on the tender herb'.[39]

Tue. 13. I preached at [Chew] Stoke and, in the evening, at Pensford, where I fear, after all the pains we have taken, the generality of the people know just as much of religion as the Hottentots. Wednesday 14, I preached in the evening in Temple

---

[35] Mells was one of the Mendip coal parishes, 3 miles west of Frome.

[36] Eph. 5:2. Wesley had preached from 1 Pet. 1:18 (see Diary).

[37] Samuel Bradburn (1751-1816), admitted to the itinerancy on trial in 1774, and at this moment Superintendent of the Bristol circuit, was born in Gibraltar, the son of an army private. Returning to England at the age of twelve, he was apprenticed to a cobbler at Chester and, after youthful profligacy, became a Methodist at the age of eighteen. He speedily became one of the great Methodist orators of the day, his passionate eloquence finding a counterpart in his uninhibited devotion to his wives, and indeed his profligacy with money. In the early years after JW's death, he became a leading advocate of Methodist separate communion and the rights of congregations and preachers against the trustees, in the name of *vox populi* and the rights of man, but learning what these might imply in terms of government hostility and radical internal reform, changed front suddenly in 1795 (Ward, *Religion and Society*, pp. 29-39) and became President in 1799. It is plain, however, that many of the preachers never quite trusted Bradburn, and his official obituarist was not completely assured of his salvation. *Methodist Magazine* 39 (1816):707; Bradburn, *Memoirs*; Blanshard, *Life of Bradburn*.

[38] For Brian Bury Collins, see above, June 2, 1782.

[39] Cf. Deut. 32:2.

Church[40] on Psalms 74:12. In the old translation, it runs, 'The help that is done upon earth, God doth it himself' (a glorious and important truth!); in the new, 'Working salvation in the midst of the earth'. What a wonderful emendation! Many such emendations there are in this translation: one would think King James had made them himself.[41]

Thur. 15. I went over to Hanham once more and saw poor disconsolate Louisa,[42] still wrapping herself up naked in her blanket and not caring to speak to anyone. The late pretty tale of her being the emperor's daughter is doubtless a mere catch-penny, and her four and twenty examinations are as credible as Mahomet's journey through seventy thousand heavens.[43]

Sun. 18. I read prayers and preached at the New Room in the morning, at two under the sycamore in Kingswood, and at five near King Square in Bristol. In the following week, I visited the classes and was amazed to find there is no increase in the society, considering what able and diligent preachers they have had the last year![44]

Tue. 27. I visited the little flock at Almondsbury, humble, simple, and much devoted to God. Friday 30 about eleven, I preached in the church at Midsomer Norton to a numerous congregation. The curate (Mr. Sims) read prayers for me, and read them admirably well. About five, I began at Ditcheat, where it rained almost all the time I preached. But this did not much lessen the congregation. Indeed all of this town, hardly one excepted, seem to have a liking to the truth. Saturday, October 1,

---

[40] On this Bristol Church, see above, Sept. 24, 1780. JW lists his text incorrectly as Ps. 74:14.

[41] JW here again, with transparent sarcasm, shows his preference for the 'old' BCP (Coverdale) translation of Ps. 74:12 (numbered as verse 13 in the prayerbook) over that of the 'new' AV (1611 'King James' version).

[42] For Louisa, 'the maid of the haystacks', see above, Mar. 15, 1782.

[43] Wesley's source for this comment is probably Humphrey Prideaux, *The True Nature of Imposture Fully Displayed in the Life of Mahomet* (6th edn., London, 1716), which he had read in Georgia (see Jan. 22, 24, 1737; 18:465 in this edn.). However, JW misremembered the account of Mahomet's journey. There are seven heavens, not seventy thousand. When Mahomet had ascended to the seventh heaven, it was 'made up of divine light, and here he found Jesus Christ. . . . Here he saith he found a much greater number of angels than in all the other heavens besides, and among them an extraordinary angel having seventy thousand heads, and every head seventy thousand tongues, and every tongue uttering seventy thousand distinct voices at the same time, with which he continued day and night incessantly praising God' (p. 53).

[44] For the connexional year 1784–85, Samuel Bradburn, James Hall, and Thomas Lee (on whom see July 19, 1757; 21:115 and n. 47 in this edn.).

I preached at Shepton [Mallet][45] to a crowded audience. In the evening, I preached at Weavers' Hall to such a congregation as I had not seen there for many years. Sunday 2, after reading prayers and preaching, I administered the Sacrament to many hundred communicants. We then solemnly renewed our covenant with God.[46] And while we solemnly avouched him to be our God, I believe many felt with holy, humble joy, that he avouched us to be his people. At four, we went into the mail coach. At twelve, it being exceeding dark, the wheel of a wagon touched ours, and the coach was over in a moment, but just on the spot were some rails which stopped it so that it did not fall to the ground; so that it was easily set right again without any hurt to man or beast. About seven, we reached Hyde Park Corner, and the New Chapel at eight. Tuesday 4, I made a little excursion into Hertfordshire[47] and, on Friday 7, returned to London.

Mon. 10. Setting out for Oxfordshire, I preached at Wallingford in the evening and at five in the morning. I preached in Oxford at noon, and in the evening at Witney, where the power of God used to be eminently present. Thursday 13, returning to Oxford, I once more surveyed many of the gardens and delightful walks. What is wanting but the love of God to make this place an earthly paradise? I preached in the evening to a very serious audience, as also the next evening at High Wycombe. In all this circuit the work of God appears both to widen and to deepen.

Saturday 15, I returned to London. Sunday 16 at nine in the evening, I set out for Norwich. Tuesday 18 and the following days, I visited [Great] Yarmouth and the other parts of the circuit.

Sat. 22. I returned to Norwich and, in the evening, spoke home to an uncommonly large congregation, telling them, 'Of all the people I have seen in the kingdom for between forty and fifty years, you have been the most fickle and yet the most stubborn.'[48]

---

[45] Shepton Mallet was noted, not only for lead-mining, but also for the production of woollens, silks, lace, stockings, sail-cloth, and hair-seating.

[46] On the Covenant Service, see Aug. 6, 1755 (21:23, n. 82 in this edn.).

[47] As the Diary shows, to visit Miss Harvey of Hinxworth (on whom see above, July 17, 1782) and William Hicks, vicar of Wrestlingworth (on whom, see Nov. 6, 1758; 21:171, n. 79 in this edn.).

[48] The present trouble in Norwich was twofold. The congregations were loath to observe some Methodist customs such as five a.m. preaching, and were fond of innovations such as an increasing amount of music. What made all this worse was that the Superintendent, Thomas Wride (on whom see May 15, 1775; 22:450, n. 78 in this edn.), was one of the most contentious preachers and fought bitterly with his Norwich

However, our labour has not been lost, for many have died in peace. And God is able to say to the residue of these dry bones, 'Live!'[49]

Sun. 23. I administered the Lord's Supper to about a hundred and sixty communicants.

Tue. 25. I crossed over to [King's] Lynn, which has been of a long season a cold and comfortless place. But the scene is now entirely changed. Two young, zealous, active preachers,[50] strongly urging the people to expect a full and present salvation, have enlivened both the society and the congregation. But the difficulty was, how to get to London? No coach set out till Friday morning nor got in before Saturday night. So I took a post-chaise after preaching and reached Downham[51] between ten and eleven. But here we were informed that in so dark a night we could not travel over Ely roads, which run between two banks, across which are many bridges where the coachman must drive to an inch. But we knew in whom we trusted, and pushed forward, till about one on Thursday we reached London.

Mon. 31. I set out for Northamptonshire and, in the afternoon, came to Luton. For many years, I had lodged at Mr. Cole's in Luton,[52] but he was now gone to his long home. The room prepared for me now was very large and very cold and had no fireplace in it. After dinner, I called upon Mr. Hampson, the lawyer who had made Mr. Cole's will. He gave me with the utmost courtesy all the information I wanted, and afterwards invited me to lodge at his house, which I willingly did. In the evening, the preaching-house was thoroughly filled. And we had a blessed season, both now and in the morning.

Tuesday, November 1. When I came to Northampton, the new

colleagues, especially the probationer, John McKersey, as to what to do about it. If McKersey refused to preach at five on the grounds that he could not preach before breakfast, Wride told him to take his breakfast to bed. The extraordinary contraption invented by Wride to ensure his own early rising is described in 22:450, n. 78 in this edn. Early in 1786, JW bowed to the inevitable and moved Wride out of Norwich. McKersey had his probation extended till 1790 and, afflicted with ill health, had eventually to cease travelling. He died in 1800, favoured with only the briefest of notices in the Conference minutes. *Minutes*, 2:41.

[49] Cf. Ezek. 37:5-6.

[50] The preachers for 1784-85 had been John Barber and John McKersey; for the current year, 1785-86, William Palmer and Charles Bland. On the earlier history of Methodism at King's Lynn, see Nov. 6, 1771; 22:296, n. 89 in this edn.

[51] Downham was a substantial parish 3 miles north of Ely.

[52] On William Cole and his wife, see Apr. 30, 1754 (20:486, n. 64 in this edn.); also Davis, *History of Luton*, pp. 118-19.

Presbyterian meeting-house[53] was offered me, twice as large as
our own. The congregation was numerous and deeply attentive.
Many attended again in the morning; I trust, not without a blessing. Wednesday 2, I preached at Whittlebury. Thursday 3, I met
5　with Perry's *Treatise upon the Gravel and Stone.*[54] I had long supposed that there could not be in nature any such thing as a lithon-
triptic,[55] a medicine that could dissolve the stone without dissolv-
ing the bladder. But I am now convinced there is no arguing
against matter of fact. The facts here alleged are too recent to be
10　denied and too clear to be evaded. Therefore I cannot but
earnestly advise everyone that has this dreadful distemper to try
without delay, if he can afford it, this sovereign remedy.

　　Friday 4, I returned to London. Sunday 6, I preached a funeral
sermon for that great and good man, Mr. Fletcher,[56] and most of
15　the congregation felt that God was in the midst of them. In the
afternoon, I buried the remains of Judith Perry, a lovely young
woman, snatched away at eighteen. But she was ripe for the bridegroom and went to meet him in the full triumph of faith. Sunday
13, I preached at Shoreditch Church.[57] The congregation was
20　very numerous and the collection unusually large.

[53] This was a church in King's Head Lane built by the Rev. William Hextall for that
large part of the congregation of the Doddridge Church which had followed him when
he was dismissed as its pastor. Before it was built, Hextall had enjoyed the hospitality of
the Methodist chapel, a building originally erected by Strict Baptists. *WHS* 25
(1946):91.

[54] Charles Perry, *Disquisitions of the Stone and Gravel, and other Diseases of the Kidneys
and Bladder* (London, 1777). He also wrote *A Treatise of Diseases in General* (London,
1741).

[55] Orig. 'Lithorn–triple'. A word of Greek derivation, defined by *OED* as a medicine
'having the property of breaking up stone in the bladder'.

[56] See Sermon 114; 3:610-29 in this edn. JW's panegyric set Fletcher in a universal
context: 'For many years I despaired of finding any inhabitant of Great Britain that
could stand in any degree of comparison with Gregory Lopez or Monsieur de Renty.
But let any impartial person judge if Mr. Fletcher was at all inferior to them! . . . So
unblameable a character in every respect I have not found either in Europe or America.
Nor do I expect to find another such on this side of eternity' (ibid., pp. 627-28). Joseph
Benson, Fletcher's biographer, felt bound to question whether JW had not here been
blinded by personal affection and theological sympathy, yet reinforced his assessment
by that of Henry Venn: 'He was a luminary; a *luminary* did I say? he was a *sun.* I have
known all the great men for these fifty years: but I have known none like him.' This
striking testimony to Fletcher's winsomeness is also evidence that the bitter Calvinist
controversy of the 1770s was beginning to lose its compelling urgency in the evangelical
world. Benson, *Fletcher,* pp. 372-73.

[57] St. Leonard's, Shoreditch, dated from at least the twelfth century, and, being outside the City, survived the Great Fire, only to fall into ruin, part of the tower collapsing
in 1716. A new church designed by George Dance was erected, 1736-40, and it was in

Mon. 14. This week, I read over again and carefully considered Mr. Fry's Tract upon marriage.[58] I wonder it is not more known, as there is nothing on the head like it in the English tongue. I still think he has proved to a demonstration that no marriages are forbidden, either by the law of God or of England, but those of brothers and sisters, and those in the ascending and descending line. The contrary supposition seems to be built wholly in a misinterpretation of that expression in the eighteenth chapter of Leviticus, 'Thou shalt not *uncover her nakedness*.'[59] But this, he clearly shows, does not mean to *marry* a woman, but to *deflower* her.

Sun. 20. I preached in Bethnal Green Church[60] and spoke as plain as I possibly could on 'Having the form of godliness, but denying the power of it'.[61] And this I judged to be far more suitable to such a congregation than talking of 'justification by faith'.

Having promised our friends at Winchester to come and open their preaching-house when it was ready, I set out on Thursday 24, and preached there in the evening to a numerous congregation.[62] But I have not seen a people less affected: they seemed to be mere stocks and stones. However, I have 'cast my bread upon the water'. Possibly it may 'be found again after many days'.[63] On Friday evening, we went into the mail coach and reached London at eight in the morning.

Sun. 27. As soon as I had concluded my sermon at the New Chapel, I hastened away to preach at St. Luke's,[64] one of the largest parish churches in London. It was thoroughly filled, as it was seven years ago when I preached there before. God enabled me to speak strong words on the Epistle for the Day. And I believe some felt that it was now high 'time to awake out of sleep'.[65]

this that JW preached. This church suffered much remodelling and extensive damage from a bomb in 1944. The damage was made good, 1946–55. The vicar 1780–1801 was John Blake B.A.

[58] John Fry, *The Case of Marriages between near Kindred Particularly Considered* (London, 1756; 2nd edn., 1773). Cf. Sept. 11, 1756; 21:78, n. 97 in this edn.

[59] Lev. 18:7.

[60] St. Matthew's, Bethnal Green, built by George Dance the Elder, 1743–46, and rebuilt after a fire in 1859. The rector, 1766–1809, was William Loxham B.A.

[61] Cf. 2 Tim. 3:5.

[62] A weak Methodist cause in Winchester had lately been given new vigour by the labour of Captain Webb (on whom, see Feb. 2, 1773; 22:359, n. 73 in this edn.) and Thomas Coke (see Aug. 13, 1776), and they now built a chapel in Parchment Street. *Wesleyan Methodist Magazine* 57 (1834):727–28.

[63] Cf. Eccles. 11:1.

[64] On St. Luke's, Old Street, and its incumbent, see above, Nov. 29, 1778.

[65] Rom. 13:11.

Mon. 28. I went to Canterbury; the chapel was more than filled. On Tuesday, I found at Dover also a considerable increase of the work of God. Wednesday 30, I went on to Margate. Some years since, we had a small society here. But a local preacher took them to himself: only two or three remained, who from time to time pressed our preachers to come again. And to remove the objection that 'there was no place to preach in,' with the help of a few friends they built a convenient preaching-house.[66] Thursday, I opened it in the evening. The congregation was large and perfectly well behaved. And I cannot but hope that, after all the stumbling-blocks, there will be a people here who will uniformly adorn the gospel of Christ. On Friday, I returned to London.

Monday, December 5, and so the whole week, I spent every hour I could spare in the unpleasing but necessary work of going through the town and begging for the poor men who had been employed in finishing the New Chapel. It is true I am not obliged to do this. But if I do it not, nobody else will.

Sun. 11. I strongly enforced St. James' beautiful description of 'the wisdom from above'.[67] How hard is it to fix even on serious hearers a lasting sense of the nature of true religion! Let it be right opinions, right modes of worship, or anything, rather than right tempers!

Thur. 22. I preached at Highgate. Considering how magnificent a place this is, I do not wonder so little good has been done here. For what has religion to do with palaces?[68]

---

[66] Margate Methodism had begun in the mid-1760s (see Dec. 4, 1765; 22:27-28 and n. 6 in this edn.) when Thomas Coleman, who had been converted under JW's preaching in London, settled in the town as a schoolmaster. He fitted up his school in Love Lane as a preaching place and, preaching there and out of doors, gathered a good society. In 1778, he rented a chapel at Birchington and built another at St. Nicholas. He invited the preachers in the Canterbury circuit to join in the work, but cooperation was short-lived, as in 1779 JW wrote to the Margate society disclaiming all connection with him; Telford, 6:363. Coleman kept his own chapel at St. Nicholas and most of the congregation, and the preachers continued to labour at Birchington. 'Mr. William Brewer, who had been a great sinner, but was truly converted from the error of his ways, and one of Mr. Coleman's principal hearers at Margate, invited the preachers to Margate, where for a time they preached in a small room and had but few followers, but in 1785, with some difficulty, they built a small chapel which was opened by Mr. Wesley, and the cause prospered, and it is due to the memory of that excellent man, Mr. Brewer, to record his zeal and liberality in supporting the cause there for many years at no small sacrifice while in its infant state.' *WHS* 7 (1910):102-5; 17 (1929):72-75. Coleman is thought to have been the author of *A Letter to a Friend on Methodism* (Canterbury, 1782); Green, *Anti-Methodist Publications*, No. 528.

[67] Cf. Jas. 3:17.

[68] This reference is explained above, Nov. 29, 1782.

Sun. 25, being Christmas Day, I preached at the New Chapel early in the morning, and in the evening; about eleven, at West Street. Monday 26, I baptized a young woman brought up an Anabaptist. And God bore witness to his ordinance, filling her heart at the very time with peace and joy unspeakable. 5

This week I endeavoured to point out all the errata in the eight volumes of the *Arminian Magazine*. This must be done by *me*. Otherwise several passages therein will be unintelligible.[69]

Sunday, January 1, 1786. We began that solemn service, the renewing of our covenant with God,[70] not in the evening as 10 heretofore, but at three in the afternoon, as more convenient for the generality of the people. And God was with us of a truth.

Mon. 9. At leisure hours this week, I read the life of Sir William Penn, a wise and good man. But I was much surprised at what he relates concerning his first wife, who lived, I suppose, 15 fifty years and said a little before her death, 'I bless God I never did any thing wrong in my life!'[71] Was she then ever convinced of sin? And if not, could she be saved on any other footing than a *heathen*?

Tue. 24. I was desired to go and hear the King deliver his 20 speech in the House of Lords.[72] But how agreeably was I surprised? He pronounced every word with exact propriety. I much doubt whether there be any other king in Europe that is so just and natural a speaker.

Tue. 31. I had a more particular account of Joseph Lee[73] than 25

---

[69] The Diary shows that JW was kept occupied daily with the errata till January 5. He published six and a half pages of corrections in small print after the index to the *Arminian Magazine* 9 (1786), and in 1786 dropped Thomas Olivers, the itinerant whom he had so unsuccessfully employed as sub-editor. See Aug. 8, 1789.

[70] For the origins of the Covenant Service, see Aug, 6, 1755 (21:23, n. 82 in this edn.).

[71] See 'An Account of the Blessed End of my Dear Wife, Gulielma Maria Penn', in *A Collection of the Works of William Penn; to which is prefixed a journal of his life with many original letters and papers never before published*, 2 vols. (London, 1726), 1: 231: 'At another time as I was speaking to her of the Lord's love and witness of his Spirit that was with her, to give her the peace of well-doing, she returned to me, looking up, "For", said she, "I never did, to my knowledge, a wicked thing in all my life." '

[72] The King's speech was brief, referring to the improved prospects of maintaining peace in Europe and the better economic outlook at home. The resolutions upon free trade with Ireland had been communicated to the Irish Parliament, but no progress had been made. The Commons should maintain the navy and reduce the national debt. Cobbett, *Parliamentary History*, 25:985–86.

[73] John Nelson had written an 'Account of the Death of Joseph Lee' in 1768 as a warning to backsliders; *Arminian Magazine* 5 (1782):580–81. It did not contain the picturesque detail of JW's penultimate sentence, but added that 'he sometimes attended our preaching; but it was only to laugh at us.' To this account JW added a preface that 'Joseph Lee

ever I had before. When I went first to Newcastle upon Tyne, I chose him, being a man full of faith and love, to be one of the leaders, steward of the society, and caterer for our family. He discharged his trust with the utmost ability and integrity. He walked
5   humbly and closely with God and was a pattern to all the town as well as to all the society. But after some time, he was persuaded to quit Newcastle and settle at Nottingham. There he fell among antinomians and, trusting in his own strength, gradually sucked in their opinion, grew less and less strict, and lost first the power,
10 and then the very form, of religion. After he had lived some years openly and avowedly without God in the world, while he was one evening quite merry with his jovial companions, one of them said, 'Why, Mr. Lee, you was once very godly: you was one of those mad *Methodists!*' He answered not a word, but leaned his arm on
15 the table and died.

Sunday, February 5. In the morning, while I was applying at the New Chapel that solemn declaration, 'The Lord's hand is not shortened that he cannot save, nor is his ear waxed heavy, that he cannot hear,'[74] he did indeed speak aloud in his word, so that the
20 stout-hearted trembled. I broke out into prayer. The power of God came mightily upon us, and there was a general cry. But the voice of two persons prevailed over all the rest, one praying, and the other shrieking as in the agonies of death. God relieved the former in a few minutes; the other, not till evening.
25   This week in travelling, I read over Dr. Stuart's *History of Scotland*.[75] He is a writer indeed! As far above Dr. Robertson as Dr. Robertson is above Oldmixon.[76] He proved beyond all possibility of doubt that the charges against Queen Mary were totally

---

was one of our first society in Fetter Lane, and received remission of sins, one of the first in London. He worked in the same shop with Gascoign Graham and Matthew Errington, and was for several years a burning and shining light.' In 1745 he had been a member of Robert Hagley's band at the Foundery. Stevenson, *City Road*, p. 34.

[74] Cf. Isa. 59:1.
[75] Gilbert Stuart, *History of Scotland from the Establishment of the Reformation till the Death of Queen Mary* (London, 1782; enl. edn., 1784). Stuart (1742-86) was an able but spiteful journalist, not above boasting that he had written two articles on the same public figure, 'one a panegyric and the other a libel', for each of which he would receive a guinea. He believed that his failure to obtain a chair of public law in Edinburgh in 1779 had been due to the influence of William Robertson (on whom see Nov. 10, 1769), whom he pursued with deadly hatred and openly challenged to reply to his defence of Queen Mary. Robertson retorted with a charge of plagiarism. *DNB*.
[76] John Oldmixon (1673-1742), Whig historian and pamphleteer, had made it his business to attack the Tory historians of the seventeenth century, and produced his own *The History of England during the Reigns of the Royal House of Stuart* (London, 1730).

groundless: that she was betrayed basely by her own servants from the beginning to the end, and that she was not only one of the best princesses then in Europe, but one of the most blameless, yea, and the most pious women!

Monday 13, I went to Mitcham[77] and found a little company just started up, who were all on fire for God. The house being too small, I preached at the front of a house adjoining to the road, where the earnestness of the people made amends for the keenness of the north wind.

Sun. 19. I preached in Horsleydown Church,[78] where (to my no small surprise) no man, woman, or child seemed to know me, either by face or by name! But before I had done, many of the numerous congregation knew that God was there of a truth.

Mon. 20. I paid my last visit to that saint of God, Ann Sharland,[79] dying of a cancer in her breast, in continual pain, but triumphing over pain and death.

Sun. 26. I took a solemn leave of the congregation at the New Chapel, at West Street, and at Brentford. Monday 27, we went on to Newbury with little interruption from the snow, and I had a comfortable opportunity with a large and serious congregation. But I have not passed such a night for these forty years, my lodging room being just as cold as the outward air. I could not sleep at all till three in the morning. I rose at four and set out at five. But the snow which fell in the night lay so deep it was with much difficulty we reached Chippenham. Taking fresh horses there, we pushed on to Bath and found a larger congregation than could well be expected.

Wednesday, March 1. I had appointed to preach in Trowbridge[80] at noon. But we could not get thither till half an hour

[77] Mitcham was a parish 9 miles south from London, then separated from the parishes of Carshalton, Morden, Merton, and Wandsworth by a trout stream, and from Croydon by an extensive common. 'The greater portion of the land is laid out in vast plantations of chamomile, liquorice, peppermint, roses, lavender, and other aromatic plants.' Lewis, *England*, 3:287.

[78] St. John's, Horsleydown, a Southwark rectory in the gift of the crown, was one of the places of worship built under the 1711 Act for Fifty New Churches, but was not rebuilt after damage in the Second World War.

[79] Mrs. Anne Sharland (1736-86) was a Mayfair fruiterer who often entertained the Wesley brothers. JW spoke of her as 'that open, noble-spirited creature, Nancy Sharland, "In whom there is no guile"'; Telford, 7:39. Refusing to follow her predecessor's custom of Sunday trading, she lost only one customer, the rector of the parish. She was buried in City Road Chapel. John Telford, *Two West End Chapels* (London, 1886), pp. 62-63.

[80] Samuel Bradburn met JW here, and seems to have been with him for most of the following week. On the 7th, they met the Bristol classes together. Bradburn, *Memoirs*, p. 103.

after. I then preached without delay; and in the evening in Bristol, on 'O death, where is thy sting, O grave, where is thy victory!'[81] Afterwards, I visited one who could say with Mr. de Renty, 'I bear with me an experimental verity, and a plenitude of the presence of the ever-blessed Trinity.'[82] In the afternoon, I went over to Kingswood and found the school in excellent order.[83] Sunday 5, I read prayers and preached and administered the Sacrament to about five hundred communicants. At three, I preached in Temple Church; at five, in the New Room; on Friday, I baptized a young Negro, who appeared to be deeply serious and much affected, as indeed did the whole congregation. Saturday 11, I rode over to Churchill[84] about twelve miles from Bristol, where Dr. Barry read prayers, and I preached to a serious congregation.

Mon. 13. I left Bristol, taking Mr. Bradburn with me, as I judged a change of place and of objects would be a means of calming his mind, deeply affected with the loss of a beloved wife.[85] In the evening, I preached at Stroud; Tuesday 14 at noon, in Painswick with uncommon liberty; and in the evening, at Gloucester. I preached in the old church (now vanished away) belonging to St. Bartholomew's Hospital,[86] which I think was very considerably larger than the New Chapel in London.

Wed. 15. Much snow fell in the night and quite blocked up the road. Yet with some difficulty we got through to Tewksbury, where I preached at noon. Abundance of snow likewise fell in the

---

[81] 1 Cor. 15:55.

[82] Jean Baptiste de Saint-Jure, *The Holy Life of Monsr. de Renty* (London, 1658), p. 28. See also, Sermon 55, *On the Trinity*, §17 (2:385 and n. 36 in this edn.), where Wesley made the same reference to Monsr. de Renty.

[83] The Diary makes it clear that this Journal entry is an inaccurate conflation of the events of three days. The evening sermon on March 1 was at Bath, the sermon on 1 Cor. 15:55 was on March 2 at Bristol, and the visit to Kingswood School took place on March 3.

[84] Churchill was a modest parish with a handsome church, 4 miles north-east of Axbridge. The living was a perpetual curacy.

[85] The death of Mrs. Bradburn no doubt accounts for JW's choice of text in Bristol. Bradburn himself notes: 'My friends have forced me out in hopes of recovering my health.' Bradburn, *Memoirs*, p. 103.

[86] On June 26, 1343, Henry III annexed the Church of St. Nicholas to St. Bartholomew's Hospital. Both the church (in the remains of which JW here preached) and hospital were already in a poor state when taken over by the corporation in the reign of Elizabeth. 'The church is an ancient structure, in the early style of English architecture, with later additions and insertions; the tower, which is handsome, appears to have declined from the perpendicular by the sinking of the foundations; it is surmounted by a spire, the upper part of which has been removed for greater security.' Lewis, *England*, 2:265; Counsel, *Gloucester*, p. 148. The curate from 1735 was Samuel Gwinnet LL.B. Samuel Rudder, *A New History of Gloucestershire* (Cirencester, 1779), p. 201.

afternoon, but we pushed through it to Worcester. Thursday 16, it was not without some difficulty that we made our way through the snow to Bewdley. Prejudice is here now vanished away. The life of Mr. Clark turned the tide, and much more his glorious death.[87] I preached about noon, and at Worcester in the evening, where we had an uncommon blessing while I was enforcing, 'Thou shalt have no other gods before me.'[88]

Fri. 17. At eleven, I preached at Bengeworth, and again at six in the evening, I believe, not without effect. Saturday 18, I went on straight to Birmingham. Sunday 19, a large congregation attended in the morning. At ten, I went to St. Mary's,[89] where the curate preached an admirable sermon. At five, the preaching-house would not near contain the congregation. Afterwards, I administered the Lord's Supper to about five hundred communicants.

Mon. 20. I met the select society,[90] most of whom are clearly perfected in love. Tuesday 21 at three in the afternoon, I preached at Quinton[91] in the new preaching-house, and in the evening at Birmingham. Today, I read Dr. Withering's *Treatise on Foxglove*.[92] He says it frequently cures epilepsies, palsies, insanity, consumptions, and several other diseases. Sunday 26, the church[93] as usual was far too small to contain the congregation.

[87] See above, Mar. 18, 1779.

[88] JW quotes Exod. 20:3; but in the Diary gives Deut. 5:7, 'Thou shalt have none other gods before me.' as his text.

[89] The vicar of St. Mary's, 1774-90, was John Riland (on whom, see Apr. 19, 1764; 21:454, n. 69 in this edn.), and his curate and successor was Edward Burn (*c.* 1759-1837). He was an Irishman, educated at Trevecca, who itinerated for some years in the Countess of Huntingdon's connexion. Having obtained ordination from the Bishop of Coventry, he matriculated from St. Edmund Hall, Oxford, in 1784, graduating B.A. 1790, M.A. 1791. He became curate of St. Mary's Chapel, Birmingham, in 1785, retaining this post till his death. By this time he was also rector of Smethcott, Shrewsbury, and minister of St. James's Chapel, Ashted, Birmingham. He wrote against Priestley and, in his later years, was active in interdenominational enterprise in the Bible Society, and was first secretary of the Birmingham branch of the C.M.S. *DNB*; Seymour, *Huntingdon*, 1:394; 2:112, 187, 477; G. F. Nuttall, 'Students of Trevecca College, 1768-91', *Transactions of the Cymmrodorion Society* (1967, Part II):271.

[90] On this institution, see Oct. 13, 1749 (20:307, n. 66 in this edn.).

[91] On this place, see above, Mar. 24, 1781.

[92] William Withering, *An Account of the Foxglove, and Some of its Medicinal Uses; with Practical Remarks on Dropsy and Other Diseases* (Birmingham, 1785).

[93] At Madeley. JW had met Elizabeth Ritchie the week before at Birmingham and had had the inspiration of taking her on to Madeley to comfort her widowed friend Mary (Bosanquet) Fletcher. Miss Ritchie describes the effect of JW's sermon, in which he 'so delineated the character of the dear departed saint [John Fletcher], as greatly to affect me and many others, whose weeping eyes and sympathizing looks showed how greatly they revered and loved the memory of their dear departed pastor'. Bulmer, *Mrs. Mortimer*, p. 102.

I preached on Rev. 14:1-7, and exhorted the congregation to cherish that divine ambition of being found 'faultless before God'.[94] We had another large congregation in the afternoon, and all serious as death. I spent the evening at a neighbouring gentle-
5 man's house[95] in close conversation from the beginning to the end.

Tue. 28. After calling at Sheriffhales and giving them a short exhortation, I hastened to Stafford and found the congregation waiting. I strongly enforced upon them, 'The kingdom of God is
10 at hand,'[96] and then went on to Lane End.[97] It was past seven, and the wind was piercing cold. However, I was constrained to preach abroad, and none of us seemed to regard the weather, for God warmed our hearts.

I forgot to mention that the evening before, Madeley Church
15 was thoroughly filled, and God reserved the great blessing for the last. We had a glorious opportunity. He poured the dew of his blessing on many souls and caused many mourners to rejoice with joy unspeakable.

Wed. 29, We came to our old steady friends at Burselm. But he
20 with whom I used to lodge is no more seen.[98] He trusted the Americans with all his substance, and they cheated him out of all. So he came home and died, leaving an amiable widow and six or seven children.

Cold as it was, the multitude of people constrained me to
25 preach abroad. But I believe none went away. I preached on 'Truly our fellowship is with the Father, and with his Son, Jesus Christ.'[99] We have scarce seen such a time since we came from London. The place seemed to be filled with his glory.

After visiting Newcastle[-under-Lyme] and Congleton, on Sat-
30 urday, April 1, I came to Macclesfield. Here again, I had the satis-faction to find a people much alive to God. Sunday 2, we had a

---

[94] Cf. Rev. 14:5.

[95] Samuel Ferriday, at whose house JW had stayed at least once before, on Mar. 21, 1770 (*Methodist Recorder* [Apr. 3, 1902]:13-14), and was to stay at least once more, in 1789 (see Diary, Mar. 26, 1786, Mar. 23, 1789). Ferriday was Wilkinson's successor at the Bradley ironworks in 1808, and a coalmaster and banker. Having expanded too fast on credit, he went bankrupt in 1817. *Victoria County History: Staffordshire*, 2:124-25.

[96] Mark 1:15.

[97] At Longton; see above, Mar. 29, 1784.

[98] John Bourne of Burslem, master potter, who died in 1785. On a previous visit, JW had found Bourne's wife, Sarah, née Kent (1745-1835), very ill; he won lasting devotion by curing her with a special diet. *Wesleyan Methodist Magazine* 58 (1835): 631-32.

[99] 1 John 1:3.

large and serious congregation at the new church[1] both morning and afternoon. The organ is one of the finest toned I ever heard, and the congregation singing with it make a sweet harmony. Monday 3 about eleven, I preached to a crowded congregation in the new house near Chapel-en-le-Frith. Many of these lively people came from among the mountains and strongly reminded me of those fine verses wherein Dr. Burton paraphrases those plain words, 'The hills are a refuge for the wild goats, and so are the stony rocks for the conies.'

> *Te, domine, intonsi montes, te saxa loquentur*
> *Summa Deum, dum montis amat juga pendulus hircus,*
> *Saxorumque colit latebrosa cuniculus antra.*[2]

It is chiefly among these enormous mountains that so many have been awakened, justified, and soon after perfected in love. But even while they are full of love, Satan strives to push many of them to extravagance. This appears in several instances. (1) Frequently three or four, yea, ten or twelve, pray aloud all together. (2) Some of them, perhaps many, scream all together as loud as they possibly can. (3) Some of them use improper, yea, indecent expressions in prayer. (4) Several drop down as dead and are as stiff as a corpse, but in awhile they start up and cry, Glory! Glory! perhaps twenty times together. Just so did the French Prophets,[3] and very lately the Jumpers in Wales, bring the real work into contempt.[4] Yet whenever we reprove them, it should be in the most mild and gentle manner possible.

Tue. 4. In the evening, I preached to a lovely congregation at Stockport.[5] Friday 5, I went on as swiftly as I could through Man-

[1] Christ Church, Macclesfield, on the origins of which, see Apr. 3, 1774 (22:402, n. 59 in this edn.); and above, Oct. 1, 1782.

[2] On these lines and their author, John Burton, see Apr. 25, 1755 (21:8, n. 33 in this edn.).

[3] For the French Prophets, see above, Jan. 28, 1739 (19:32-33, n. 49 in this edn.).

[4] JW's distaste for hill-country, reinforced by the belief that mountains had their origin in the Flood and hence in human sin, here seems to heighten his dislike of Derbyshire enthusiasm, which he finds unusually unpalatable.

[5] Benson's diary fills out the itinerary: 'April 7. On Monday last, I met Mr. Wesley at Chapel-en-le-Frith and went along with him to Hayfield, New Mills, and Stockport, and preached in all these places. On Wednesday noon, he opened the new chapel at Bullock Smithy, Mr. [David] Simpson [on whom see Apr. 3, 1774; 22:402, n. 59 in this edn.] reading prayers. The congregation was very large. After dining at an inn with about forty persons, he set off for Manchester.' Curnock, 7:154, n. 1.

chester, Wigan, and Bolton. Sunday 16 (Easter Day), I crossed over to Warrington, whence, having read prayers, preached, and administered the Lord's Supper, I hastened back to Bolton. The house was crowded the more because of five hundred and fifty children who are taught in our Sunday schools. Such an army of them got about me when I came out of the chapel that I could scarce disengage myself from them.[6]

Mon. 17. I went on to Blackburn,[7] which was sufficiently crowded, it being the fair-day. No house would contain the people. So I stood abroad and expounded that awful Scripture, 'I saw the dead, small and great, stand before God.'[8] All were still as night, unless when they sung. Then their voices was as the sound of many waters.

Tue. 18. I preached at Padiham, Burnley,[9] Southfield,[10] and Colne. Thursday 20, I went to Otley and found God was there both in the evening and morning service. Friday 21, I preached at

---

[6] JW always had a special affection for the Sunday schools of Bolton. It may have been on this occasion that he preached to them a sermon on Ps. 34:11, using no word of more than two syllables, although the Diary does not confirm it. Tyerman, *John Wesley*, 3:472. Charles Atmore left an account of JW preaching from Ps. 34:11 to the children at Newcastle; see below, May 7, 1790.

[7] Here a new preaching-house had lately become necessary, and after much difficulty a site was found in what became a fashionable part of the town, the money being raised by George Walkden, yeoman, and William Banning, breadmaker. J. Ward, *Rise and Progress of Wesleyan Methodism in Blackburn* (Blackburn, 1871), pp. 23-24.

[8] Rev. 20:12.

[9] Methodist legend attributes the conversion of a pillar of the Burnley society, William Hopwood (1766-1828), to JW's sermon on this occasion; Moore, *Methodism in Burnley*, p. 57. Hopwood's obituary, in a different vein of romance, insists that 'through the instrumentality of an alarming dream, he was awakened to a sense of his danger as a sinner against God; and being invited to unite himself to the Methodist society, he gladly availed himself of the privilege and was shortly afterwards made happy in the enjoyment of the pardoning love of God.' *Wesleyan Methodist Magazine* 61 (1838):559.

[10] Southfield, about 2 miles east of Colne, was the residence of William Sagar (b. 1751), a cloth merchant, who contributed much to the ill-starred chapel at Colne; see above, June 11, 1777. JW usually stayed with him, as the preachers later stayed with his son Richard; *Wesleyan Methodist Magazine* 47 (1824):66-68. He now summoned Parson Greenwood, the Superintendent of Keighley circuit, to Southfield; Greenwood sent his assistant, John Barritt, an ex-farmer in his first year of travelling. He describes how he 'heard Mr. Wesley preach at Southfield in the afternoon, and at Colne in the evening; and had the unspeakable privilege of accompanying him to several places, where he addressed multitudes, and frequently with considerable power. I was led greatly to admire his manner and style of preaching; his capability of adapting himself to all classes of individuals, whether the rich or the poor, the learned or the illiterate. He gave me much advice respecting personal religion, and the ministerial work.' *Wesleyan Methodist Magazine* 66 (1843):180; Jessop, *Methodism in Rossendale*, pp. 114-15. Sagar did much to preserve the Southfield society from the influence of the Kilhamite agitation in the later 1790s. Laycock, *Haworth Round*, pp. 326-27; see also, Moore, *Methodism in Burnley*, pp. 31, 45.

Yeadon, where the work of God is rapidly going forward. Such a company of loving children I have nowhere seen but at Oldham near Manchester. Sunday 23, I preached in Haworth Church[11] in the morning, and Bingley Church in the afternoon. But as there were many hundreds that could not get in, Mr. Atmore[12] preached abroad at the same time. In the evening, I preached to an huge multitude at Bradford. Surely the people of this town are highly favoured, having both a vicar[13] and a curate that preach the truth.

Monday 24, I preached at Halifax; Tuesday 5 at ten, in Heptonstall Church[14] (the ugliest I know), and in the afternoon, at Todmorden Church. How changed are both the place and the people since I saw them first. 'Lo! the smiling fields are glad! And the human savages are tame!'

Thur. 27. I preached at Greetland at ten, and at Huddersfield in the evening. Friday 28, I preached at Longwood House,[15] the owners of which are a blessing to all the poor, both in spirituals and temporals. Saturday 29, the wind drove us in the evening into the cloth-hall in Gildersome,[16] where I expounded and applied, 'The things that are seen are temporal: but the things that are not seen are eternal!'[17]

[11] For the perpetual curate of Haworth, John Richardson, see Apr. 19, 1764 (21:454, n. 69 in this edn.).

[12] Charles Atmore (1759-1826), itinerant, at this time Superintendent of the Colne circuit. The son of a sea captain of King's Lynn, Atmore entered the itinerancy in 1781, and his preaching was popular as 'plain, sound, experimental, practical and often accompanied by much divine unction'. He was shortly preaching to hundreds more than the chapel would hold from the Sagar's garden wall (Tyerman MSS, 3, fol. 37, in Methodist Archives, Manchester). He regarded the revival he led in the area south of Pendle as the happiest and most useful episode of his life. At the Conference of 1786, Atmore was ordained by JW to administer the sacraments in Scotland, and was subsequently encouraged by Pawson to administer them privily in England (Tyerman MSS, 3, fol. 156). He was the chief influence in creating a Sunday school in Newcastle in 1790; *Wesleyan Methodist Magazine* 68 (1845):118-19; Tyerman MSS, 2, fol. 231. After JW's death, he began himself to ordain, but speedily regretted his action. Atmore became one of the leading historians and propagandists of the connexion, and, having had a prominent part in resisting Lord Sidmouth's bill to limit the Toleration Act, he was elected President of Conference in 1811; *Wesleyan Methodist Magazine* 49 (1826):644-45; J. S. Stamp, 'Memoir of the Rev. Charles Atmore', serialized in *Wesleyan Methodist Magazine* 68 (1845). Copies of 118 of John Pawson's letters to Atmore are preserved in Tyerman MSS, 3.

[13] John Crosse, on whom see June 28, 1770; 22:236, n. 2 in this edn.

[14] On Tobit Sutcliffe, the incumbent, see Apr. 18, 1774; 22:404, n. 72 in this edn.

[15] On Longwood House and its owner, Mr. Whitaker, see above, July 27, 1781.

[16] Gildersome, at this time a perpetual curacy in the parish of Batley, was situated 4 1/2 miles south-west of Leeds, and was a place engaged in the manufacture of both cotton and woollen textiles.

[17] Cf. 2 Cor. 4:18.

Sun. 30. I preached in the new house at Dewsbury[18] as I had intended. I could not preach abroad at Birstall at noon because of the boisterous wind. I got some shelter from it at Wakefield while I applied those words in one of the Psalms for the Day, 'He healeth them that are broken in heart, and giveth medicine to heal their sick-ness.'[19] On Monday, May 1, and Tuesday, I preached at Leeds; on Wednesday, at the church at Horsforth[20] with a remarkable blessing. Thursday 4, preaching at Tadcaster in the way, in the evening, I preached at York.[21] Sunday 7 in the morning, I preached in St. Sav-iour's Church,[22] thoroughly filled with serious hearers; and in the afternoon at St. Margaret's,[23] which was over-filled, many being con-strained to go away. We had a love-feast in the evening, at which many artlessly testified what God had done for their souls. I have not for many years known this society in so prosperous a condition. This is undoubtedly owing, first, to the exact discipline which has for some time been observed among them, and next, to the strongly and continually exhorting the believers to 'go on to perfection'.

Mon. 8. I preached about one, in the new house at Easingwold,[24] and in the evening, at Thirsk. Tuesday 9, I went on to Richmond. I alighted, according to his own desire, at Archdeacon Blackburne's house.[25] How lively and active was he some years ago! I find he is

[18] This chapel had been opened in 1784. John Valton preached at the laying of the foun-dation stone on Apr. 29, 1784, and he now records what was JW's other business here (see Diary for Apr. 28): 'Mr. Wesley met the Dawgreen trustees, who had determined on a most dangerous and treacherous settlement of the Dewsbury House. I confronted them with a clear state of the matter when the agreement was made. This I believe, brought them to terms of accommodation which soon took place.' *WHS* 8 (1911):35, 47.

[19] Ps. 147:3 (BCP).

[20] Horsforth, 4 miles north-west of Leeds, was a chapelry in the parish of Guiseley. The perpetual curate from 1783 till his death in 1823 was William Shepley M.A. Borth-wick Institute, York, MS A.B. 15, p. 325; 19, p. 88.

[21] According to the Diary, this sermon was given on Friday, May 5; JW did not arrive in York until 11:30 a.m. on the 5th.

[22] The rector of St. Saviour's, York, from 1754 till his death in 1796, was Richard Cordukes. He matriculated from Trinity College, Cambridge, 1734, aged 18, was scholar 1735, graduated B.A. 1737/8, M.A. 1741.

[23] The rector of St. Margaret's, York, from 1769 till his death in 1802 was John Bell.

[24] Easingwold was a modest market town and parish 12 miles north-west of York. JW's visit was to open the new chapel built by a class of seventeen members, the origins of which are described by Alexander Mather (on whom see Mar. 10, 1761; 21:309, n. 78 in this edn.): 'In many places where they have a preacher and would gladly support him, they cannot because of the inconveniences of the place preached in. Even in . . . Selby . . . it is so, and was so in . . . Easingwold *last year* till we struggled and got a little house which cost £140, of which £70 is still due.' Tyerman MSS, 2, fol. 246.

[25] The Diary indicates that JW had dinner and 'mostly religious talk' on this occasion with Francis Blackburne (1705-87). The former had earlier been made indignant by some

two years younger than me. But he is now a mere old man, being both blind and deaf and lame! Who maketh thee to differ? He durst not ask me to preach in his church, 'For fear somebody should be offended.' So I preached at the head of the street to a numerous congregation, all of whom stood as still (although it rained all the   5 time) and behaved as well as if we had been in the church.

Thur. 11. I rode through a lovely country to Barnard Castle and found much life in the congregation. Friday 12 about noon, we came to Appleby, the county town of Cumberland. A very large room being provided, I preached with much liberty, and   10 then cheerfully went on to Penrith.

In my way hither, I looked over Lord Bacon's Ten Centuries of Experiments.[26] Many of them are extremely curious, and many may be highly useful. Afterwards, I read Dr. Anderson's *Account of the Hebrides.*[27] How accurate and sensible a writer! But   15 how clearly does he show that through the ill-judged salt, the herring-fishery there, which might be of great advantage, is so effectually destroyed that the King's revenue therefrom is annihilated! Yea, that it generally, at least frequently, turns out some thousand pounds worse than nothing![28]   20

of the latter's literary effusions (see above, Dec. 20, 1768; 22:166, n 18 in this edn.). Blackburne, a native of Richmond, became rector of that parish in 1739 (it having been promised to him on the first vacancy) and resided there till his death. In 1750, he became archdeacon of Cleveland, and a prebendary of York. A liberal in opinions from his time at St. Catherine Hall, Cambridge (to which he was admitted in 1722), he became the spokesman of the extreme liberal party in the establishment and expounded his views in a series of works, of which the most famous was the *Confessional* (London, 1766), and led the Feathers Tavern movement against subscriptions in the early 1770s. Theophilus Lindsey, who married his step-daughter, and John Disney, who married his daughter, both left the Church to become Unitarians. Blackburne avoided any further subscription by declining later offers of preferment. About the time of JW's visit, Blackburne began to resign his public offices 'from a sense of increasing decay'. *Life,* prefixed to his *Works,* 7 vols. (Cambridge, 1804), 1:lxv; *DNB;* W. R. Ward, *Georgian Oxford* (Oxford, 1958), ch. 15.

[26] Francis Bacon, *Sylva sylvarum; or, A Naturall History, in Ten Centuries*, published after the author's death by Wm. Rawley, D.D. (London, 1627).

[27] James Anderson, *An Account of the Present State of the Hebrides and the West Coasts of Scotland* (Edinburgh, 1785).

[28] Anderson's argument that free importation of cheap English rock salt was needed to keep the Hebridean fisheries in operation was a one-sided support to a political agitation just commencing, and JW's summary of it is naive. The Scottish salt industry indeed declined throughout the eighteenth century, and, at the end, despite a pernicious system of indentured labour, suffered production costs about eight times (per unit of weight) those of Cheshire rock salt. But by the Act of Union, Scottish producers had been given perpetual exemption from two-thirds of the English salt tax and undercut the north of England industry by output which paid little duty, or (it was suspected) evaded duty altogether. A situation guaranteed to minimize the yield to the Exchequer was justified on the grounds of Scottish poverty. Even the new Salt Acts of 1780–82 were not allowed to upset

Friday 12, I preached at Carlisle; and Saturday 13, after a long day's journey, at Glasgow. After spending three days here fully employed, on Wednesday 17, we went on to Edinburgh. Here likewise I had much and pleasant work. On Friday 19, I went for-
5 ward to Dundee and, on Saturday 20, to Arbroath, where I spent the Lord's Day in the Lord's work.

Mon. 22. Having a long day's journey before us, we set out at half hour past three. So we came only to Aberdeen. Wednesday 24, we had an exceeding solemn parting, as I reminded them that
10 we could hardly expect to see each other's face any more till we met in Abraham's bosom.[29]

Thur. 25. We set out early. But when we came to Inverbervie,[30] the inn was full—there was no room for man or beast—so [we] were constrained to go a double stage to Montrose. But the storm was so
15 high we could not pass for several hours. However, we reached Arbroath soon after six. And a large congregation was deeply atten-tive while I applied, 'To him that hath shall be given: but from him that hath not shall be taken away, even what he assuredly hath.'[31]

[Fri. 26.] The storm was still so high that unless we set out at
20 night, we could not pass till nine in the morning. So we went on board at eleven. The wind was then so strong that the boat could scarce keep above water. However, our great Pilot brought us safe to land between one and two in the morning.[32] Saturday 27 about three [a.m.], we came to the New Inn[33] and rested till between six
25 and seven. Thence going gently on to Kinghorn,[34] we had a pleas-

---

the proportion between the Scottish and the English duties. What the Scots did not get was the extension of the bounty on foreign salt, permitted by the pre-Union fishing acts, to their own production, and what they could not now stop was the smuggling from Ire-land of cheap Cheshire salt, the legal entry of which they had sedulously refused. Free trade in native salt, which the Scots had all along opposed, was not introduced till 1825. E. Hughes, *Studies in Administration and Finance, 1558-1825* (Manchester, 1934), pp. 419-27.

[29] This sentiment is in common form with those JW had expressed in Ireland, but he was spared to visit Scotland (like Ireland) twice more in 1788 and 1790.

[30] Orig., 'Bervie'. Inverbervie was a small royal burgh in Kincardineshire, 14 miles south of Stonehaven. The Diary shows that JW had visited it before, on May 4 and 17, 1784.

[31] Cf. Luke 8:18.

[32] The Diary clarifies the fact that JW was in trouble with the weather on two ferry crossings on two successive days; the first on the afternoon of the 25th across the Mon-trose Basin, and the second over midnight on the 26th and 27th, when he crossed the Firth of Tay, 1 1/2 miles wide, from Dundee to Newport-on-Tay.

[33] According to Curnock (7:165), the New Inn is near Kingskettle, 19 miles south-west of Newport-on-Tay.

[34] Kinghorn, a royal burgh, in the county of Fife, is situated on the northern shore of the Firth of Forth directly across from Edinburgh, and on the great road from Dundee to Edinburgh. Lewis, *Scotland*, 2:75.

ant passage to Leith. After preaching, I walked to my lovely lodging at Coates[35] and found rest was sweet.

Sun. 28. I preached first at our own house and, at noon, on the
Castle Hill [Edinburgh]. I never saw such a congregation there
before. The chair was placed just opposite to the sun. But I soon 5
forgot it while I expounded those words, 'I saw the dead, small
and great stand before God.'[36] In the evening, the whole audience
seemed to feel, 'Without holiness no man shall see the Lord.'[37]

Tue. 30. I had the happiness of conversing with the Earl of
H[addington][38] and his Lady at Dunbar. I could not but observe both 10
the easiness of his behaviour (such as we find in all the Scottish nobil-
ity) and the fineness of his appearance, greatly set off by a milk-white
head of hair. Wednesday 31, I took a view of the stupendous bridge
about ten miles from Dunbar, which is thrown over the deep glen
that runs between the two mountains, commonly called The Pease.[39] 15
I doubt, whether Louis XIV[40] ever raised such a bridge as this.

In the evening, I preached at Berwick-upon-Tweed; Thursday,
June 1, at Alnwick. Friday 2, I was desired to lay the first stone of
the preaching-house there.[41] A very large congregation attending,

---

[35] Coates Hall, 3 miles from Edinburgh, the residence of Lady Maxwell, on whom see above, May 31, 1782.

[36] Rev. 20:12.   [37] Cf. Heb. 12:14.

[38] Charles Hamilton (1721-94), seventh Earl of Haddington, and his second wife Anne, daughter of Sir Charles Gascoigne, whom he married Mar. 8, 1786, 'much to the disgust of his family'; George Edward Cokayne, *The Complete Peerage of England, Scotland, Ireland, Great Britain, and the United Kingdom*, 13 vols. in 6 (Gloucester, 1910), s.v. Haddington's son, Charles, later the eighth Earl, married the daughter of the second Earl of Hopetoun (on whom see May 12, 1772; 22:323, n. 26 in this edn.).

[39] The Pease Bridge, 300 feet in length and 127 in height, was on the old road between Edinburgh and Berwick-upon-Tweed. The parish of Cockburnspath with Old Cambus, Berwickshire, is thus described: 'The scenery is in some parts, highly romantic; the glens are distinguished by a great variety of features, combining rocks and woods and streams which, frequently obstructed in their progress, form some beautiful cascades. On the precipitous ridge which incloses the Tower Glen, are the remains of the ancient castle; and over another called the Pease Den, which is remarkable for its depth, has been thrown a bridge of singular construction.' Lewis, *Scotland*, 1:206. When Thomas Lee (on whom see July, 19, 1757; 21:115, n. 47 in this edn.) went that way, probably in 1765 when he was in Edinburgh on chapel-building business (Hayes, *Edinburgh Methodism*, pp. 8, 11), it seems that the bridge was not built: 'The worst was when we came to the steep descent from the mountains called the Pease, where the hill had fallen into the deep road and made it utterly impassable. This obliged us to creep along a path like a sheep-track hanging over a deep vale. Meantime the snow and wind beat so furiously upon us, that we knew not if we should escape with life.' Jackson, *Early Methodist Preachers*, 4:163; cf. May 23, 1788.

[40] Orig. 'Lewis the XIVth'.

[41] The Alnwick society had first met in rooms and then in a chapel in the Green But, later demolished to make way for the new court-house. The new preaching-house for

we spent some time on the spot in solemn prayer and singing praise to God. About noon, I preached in the town-hall at Morpeth; in the evening, at Newcastle. How different is the spirit of this congregation to that of most of those I have seen lately!

Whitsunday, June 4. I preached at eight to an amazing congregation at the Ballast Hills.[42] But it was doubled by that at the Fell in the afternoon. But, it was supposed, that at the Garth Heads in the evening was as large as both together.

On Monday and Tuesday, the congregation was larger than I ever remember. Wednesday 7 at five, we had a solemn parting. About noon, I preached at North Shields in a tent erected near the town to a very numerous congregation.[43] In the evening, I preached at Sunderland; about eleven on Friday, I preached in the church at Monkwearmouth[44] on those words in the Second Lesson, 'If thou canst believe, all things are possible to him that believeth.'[45] Friday 9, I preached at Durham about eleven and, in the evening, at Hartlepool. I preached in the town-hall,[46] where

which JW now laid the foundation stone was opened in Dec. 1787. *WHS* 7 (1909):63-67, 93.

[42] For the Ballast Hills, see above, June 17, 1781.

[43] This bland entry conceals a lively contretemps. At the end of 1783, the lease of the old preaching-house at North Shields was about to expire, but the choice of a new site led to the formation of two parties led by Dr. Watson (and later John Reed) and by Edward Coates, a trustee of the old chapel. Each claimed JW's support; JW insisted that a local agreement be reached. When he arrived in North Shields, each party was building a preaching-house—hence JW's preaching in a tent. He is said, however, to have denounced the Reed party, and to have preached on the site of the Coates preaching-house in Millbourn Place, on the suggestive text, Mark 3:35. Coates and George Snowdon, the Newcastle Superintendent (on whom see May 3, 1775; 22:449, n. 75 in this edn.), pursued JW to Sunderland for further reassurance, and it transpired that each party wished only one North Shields preaching-house to be retained, the Newcastle preachers backing the Coates party with a view to incorporating their preaching-house into the Newcastle circuit, the Sunderland preachers backing their opponents with a view to incorporating their house into the Sunderland circuit. The issue went to and from Conference, and was still unresolved when JW returned to North Shields on May 30, 1788. By this time JW was convinced that the Coates party were proceeding on the contumacious principles of the Dewsbury trustees (see above, Apr. 30, 1786), and they were indeed in touch with John Atlay (see June 29, 1766; 22:46, n. 4 in this edn.), who had then left JW's connexion for Dewsbury. In 1789, the Millbourn Place trustees declined to settle their preaching-house on the Conference plan, and William Eels, Atlay's assistant, became their preacher. *WHS* 4 (1904):223-30; Tyerman, *John Wesley,* 3:573; [E. Coates], *A New Portrait of Methodism; Being a Circumstantial Account of the Dispute between the Rev. John Wesley and the Trustees of Millbourn Place Chapel* (Leeds, 1815); Tyerman MSS, 3, fols. 164, 182, 185, in Methodist Archives, Manchester.

[44] On Methodist relations with Monkwearmouth Church, see above, May 31, 1761 (21:326, n. 48 in this edn.). On Joseph Ivison, the present incumbent, see above, June 6, 1784.

[45] Mark 9:23.   [46] On which see above, June 7, 1784.

many appeared to be very deeply affected. Surely the seed will spring up at last, even here where we seemed so long to be ploughing on the sand.

Sat. 10. I went to Darlington. Since I was here last, Mr. ―― died and left many thousand pounds to an idle spend-thrift, but not one groat to the poor! O unwise steward of the mammon of unrighteousness! How much better for him had he died a beggar!

Sun. 11. I was obliged in the evening to preach abroad. Afterward we had a love-feast at which many plain people spoke the height and depth of Christian experience in the most plain and artless manner.

Mon. 12. We found still at Stockton much fruit of sister Brisco's[47] labours among the children. I preached here at noon, and at Yarm in the evening. Tuesday 13, the preaching-house at Hutton Rudby was well filled at nine. When I came to Guisborough, where I had no thought of preaching, I found the congregation waiting. So I began without delay, and it was a time of love. We had a warm ride in the afternoon to Whitby, where it has pleased God fully to make up the removal of William Ripley,[48] who was for many years a burning and shining light. In the evening, the house was well filled with people and with the power of God. And after preaching four times, I was no more tired than when I rose in the morning.

Thur. 15. I found the work of God at Scarborough more lively than it had been for many years. Friday 16 in the evening, I preached at Bridlington Quay to a numerous congregation. Saturday 17, I found Mr. Parker[49] at Beverley in a palace. The gentleman that owned it being gone abroad, it was let at a moderate rent. I preached here at twelve, about four at Newland,[50] and at

[47] The reference here is to JW's previous visit to Stockton (see above, June 8, 1784), when he stayed with Mrs. Brisco, the wife of the itinerant, Thomas Brisco (on whom see July 19, 1768; 22:149, n. 28 in this edn.), then Superintendent of the Yarm circuit. JW speaks elsewhere of her 'peculiar love for children, and . . . uncommon talent in building them up into Christians'. *WHS* 19 (1934):174.

[48] On William Ripley and his death in Dec. 1784, see above, June 16, 1784.

[49] On Thomas Parker, formerly of Shincliffe, see above, May 31, 1780.

[50] In Wesley's day, Newland was 'a pleasant village' 1 1/2 miles north-west from Kingston upon Hull, 'where several imposing mansions had been built by Hull merchants'. One of these was the home of Richard Terry (1734–1804), located at the corner of Beverley and Clough Roads, and variously called, 'Newland Hall', 'Newland Park', or 'Terry's House'. Originally a schoolmaster at Gilberdyke near Howden, he had now become 'one of the earliest and most successful Baltic merchants in Hull'. JW had been in touch with him here since at least 1774, when he discouraged him from setting up a free school in the Manor Alley Chapel, Hull. JW proposed to visit the Terrys in 1780

seven in [Kingston upon] Hull. Sunday 18, I was invited by the vicar[51] to preach in the High Church,[52] one of the largest parish churches in England. I preached on the Gospel for the Day, the story of Dives and Lazarus. Being invited to preach in the after-
5 noon, the church was, if possible, more crowded than before, and I pressed home the prophet's word, 'Seek ye the Lord while he may be found: call ye upon him while he is near.'[53] Who would have expected a few years since to see me preaching in the High Church at Hull? I had appointed to preach at Swinefleet, so I
10 went as far as Beverley this evening, and on Monday 19, set out early. But being vehemently importuned to go round by Malton, I did so and preached there at nine. Thence I hastened to Pockling-ton and, finding the people ready, stepped out of the chaise and preached without delay. We reached Swinefleet between six and
15 seven, having gone in all seventy-six miles. A numerous congre-gation was assembled under the shade of the tall trees. Sufficient for this day was the labour thereof.[54] But still, I was no more tired than when I rose in the morning. Tuesday 20, I preached in Crowle at noon and, in the evening, at Epworth.
20   Wed. 21. I preached at Scotter at nine and, at one, in Brigg in an open part of the town. All were still as night, the very boys and girls standing as quiet as their parents. Indeed, it seemed that the hearts of all were as melting wax before the Lord.[55] In the evening, the people flocking together on every side, I was con-
25 strained to preach in the market-place at Grimsby, where every-one behaved well except the Calvinist preacher! Thursday 22 in the evening, I preached at Louth. I never saw this people affected before. Friday 23 at nine, I preached at Tealby, where many of the people felt that God was with them in an uncommon manner.

(Telford, 7:16) and wrote to Richard after this present visit on the affairs of the Hull circuit; Telford, 7:337. Terry was thus now a pillar of the Methodist cause. In the 1790s he was reckoned a high-churchman and a munificent contributor to the churches of St. Mary, St. James, and St. John, and took a modest part in Hull public life. *WHS* 23 (1941):1-7.

    [51] Thomas Clark D.D., vicar of Holy Trinity, Hull, 1784-97.

    [52] Hull patriots in the nineteenth century claimed that Holy Trinity Church was 'the largest parish church (not being a cathedral) in the Empire', that it occupied an area of 2,230 square yards, and that 'the lightness and elegance of its workmanship are not to be surpassed by any similar structure.' *The Visitor's Guide to the Town of Hull* (Hull, 1852), p. 11.

    [53] Isa. 55:6.

    [54] See Matt. 6:34.

    [55] See Ps. 22:14, 97:5.

Having now given a second reading to *Fingal,* rendered into heroic verse, I was thoroughly convinced it is one of the finest epic poems in the English language.[56] Many of the lines are worthy of Mr. Pope:[57] many of the incidents are deeply pathetic, and the character of *Fingal* exceeds any in Homer, yea, and Virgil, too. No such speech comes out of his mouth, as

Sum pius Aeneas, fama super æthera notus:[58]

No such thing in his conduct as the whole affair of Dido is in the Trojan hero. Meantime, who is Ewen Cameron? Is it not Dr. Blair?[59] And is not one great part of this publication to aggrandize the character of the old Highlanders as brave, hospitable, generous men?

In the evening, I preached to a large congregation at Gainsborough in Sir Nevil Hickman's yard. But Sir Nevil is no more[60] and has left no son, so the very name of that ancient family is lost! And how changed is the house since I was young and good Sir Willoughby Hickman[61] lived here! One of the towers is said to have been built in the reign of King Stephen, above six hundred years ago. But it matters not: yet a little while, and the earth itself with all the works of it will be burned up.

---

[56] On Ossian and *Fingal,* see above, May 15, 1784.
[57] Alexander Pope (1688-1744), poet.
[58] Virgil, *Aeneid,* I.378-79. JW constructs one perfect hexameter out of two of Virgil's:

Sum pius Aeneas [raptas ex hoste penates
Classe veho mecum] fama super aethera notus.

Pious Aeneas am I, who am carrying with me in my fleet my household gods rescued from the foe, known by report high up in heaven.

WHS 5 (1905):90, quoted in Curnock, 7:172.

[59] On this mistaken identification, see above, May 15, 1784.
[60] On Sir Nevil Hickman (1727-81), see Aug. 3, 1759 (21:221, n. 39 in this edn.); also A. Stark, *History and Antiquities of Gainsborough* (London, 1843), p. 364.
[61] Sir Willoughby Hickman, a stout opponent of James II, died on Oct. 28, 1720; Stark, *Gainsborough,* pp. 461-62. Stephen had conveyed the castle (one tower of which still stood at the end of the house) with the manor in a charter granted to William, Earl of Lincoln, and the received opinion was that part of the old hall dated from Stephen's time; Allen, *History of Lincoln,* 2:23. In the early eighteenth century, the Hickmans moved to Thorock Hall nearby, and 'about 1760, Mr. Hornby obtained a lease of the Old Hall, for the purpose of establishing therein a coarse linen manufactory; but that not succeeding, the building was converted into separate dwelling-houses.' A few years later again, the large hall was turned into a theatre with considerable structural damage. Stark, *Gainsborough,* p. 419.

Sat. 24. I preached at Newton [on Trent];[62] afterwards at Newark[-on-Trent], one of the most elegant towns in England;[63] and in the evening, at Retford on 'I saw the dead, small and great, stand before God.'[64]

5 Sun. 25. I preached at Misterton. I was grieved to see so small a congregation at Haxey Church. It was not so when Mr. Hoole[65] lived here. O what a curse in this poor land are pluralities and non-residence![66] But there are evils that God alone can cure.

About one I preached at Upperthorpe, where the spreading 10 trees sheltered both me and the congregation. But we had a far larger at Epworth between four and five in the afternoon. Surely God will visit this place yet again and lift up them that are fallen.

Mon. 26. I read prayers and preached in Owston [Ferry] Church, thoroughly filled with attentive hearers; and again at nine 15 in the morning. Tuesday 27 at one in the afternoon, I preached at Belton. While I was preaching, three little children, the eldest six years old, the youngest two and a half, whom their mother had left at dinner, straggled out and got to the side of a well which was near the house. The youngest, leaning over, fell in; the others 20 striving to pull it out, the board gave way, in consequence of which they all fell in together. The young one fell under the bucket and stirred no more; the others held for a while by the side of the well and then sunk into the water, where, it was supposed, they lay half an hour. One coming to tell me, I advised immedi-25 ately to rub them with salt and to breathe strongly into their mouths. They did so, but the young one was past help. The others in two or three hours were as well as ever.

Wed. 28. I entered into the eighty-third year of my age. I am a

---

[62] Orig. 'New Inn'. The Diary reads 'Newton', but given Wesley's hand, the entry looks very similar to the 'New Inn' that he had written three pages earlier. Newton on Trent was a small parish 9 miles west of Lincoln.

[63] Despite this flattering description and being well supplied with public buildings, Newark was reckoned no more than 'neatly built', and its great age of improvement came only with an act of 1793. Its striking feature was the number of handsome bridges occasioned by its situation among the arms of the Trent and its tributaries, many of them recently built or rebuilt. The turnpike road from the north, built by Smeaton in 1770, had 14 bridges with 96 arches. Lewis, *England*, 3:326.

[64] Rev. 20:12.

[65] Orig. 'Harle', an error for Joseph Hoole, vicar of Haxey, 1712-36 (on whom see 18:129, n. 40 in this edn.).

[66] The reference probably included the extensive pluralism of Spencer Madan, vicar of Haxey, 1762-92 (on whom see July 17, 1774; 22:421, n. 54 in this edn.). He crowned a profitable career by elevation to the episcopate.

wonder to myself. It is now twelve years since I have any such sensation as weariness. I am never tired (such is the goodness of God!) either with writing, preaching, or travelling. One natural cause undoubtedly is my continual exercise and change of air. How the latter contributes to health I know not, but certainly it does.

This morning, Abigail Pilsworth, aged fourteen, was born into the world of spirits. I talked with her the evening before and found her ready for the bridegroom. A few hours after, she quietly fell asleep. When we went into the room where her remains lay, we were surprised. A more beautiful corpse I never saw. We all sung,

> Ah lovely appearance of death!
> What sight upon earth is so fair!
> Not all the gay pageants that breathe,
> Can with a dead body compare![67]

All the company were in tears. And in all (except her mother, who sorrowed, but not as one without hope) they were in tears of joy. O death, where is thy sting!

London, Jan. 20, 1789.[68]

FINIS

[67] This was one of CW's *Funeral Hymns* (1746); see *Poetical Works,* 6:193. JW included it as No. 47 in the *Collection of Hymns* (1780; 7:138 in this edn.), and it kept its place for almost a century. In its approach to grieving it is worth comparing and contrasting with a recent comment of Philippe Ariès: '[Embalming] has become a very widespread method of preparing the dead, a practice almost unknown in Europe and characteristic of the American way of death. The meaning could be that of a certain refusal to accept death. . . . In order to sell death it had to be made friendly. . . . [Funeral directors] presented themselves not as simple sellers of services, but as "doctors of grief" who have a mission, as do doctors and priests; and this mission, from the beginning of this century, consists in aiding mourning survivors to return to normalcy [in the shortest possible time]'. *Western Attitudes to Death* (Baltimore, 1974), pp. 98-99.

[68] The date JW finished preparing this Extract for publication; see Diary, Jan. 9-20, 1789.

A N

EXTRACT

OF THE

JOURNAL

OF THE

Rev. Mr. *JOHN WESLEY.*

From *June* 29, 1786, to *Oct.* 24, 1790.

XXI.

LONDON:

Printed by G. PARAMORE, North-Green, Worship-Street;
and sold by G. WHITFIELD, at the Chapel, City-Road; and
at the Methodist Preaching-Houses in Town and Country. 1794.

Journal[1]

June 29, 1786–October 24, 1790

Thursday, June 29, 1786. I took cheerful leave of my affectionate friends at Epworth, leaving them much more alive than I
found them. About one, I preached at Thorne, now one of the 5
liveliest places in the circuit, to a numerous congregation; and in
the evening, at Doncaster. I know not that ever I saw this preaching-house filled before. And many of them seemed to feel as well
as hear. It may be some will bring forth fruit with patience.

Fri. 30. I turned aside to Barnsley, formerly famous for all man- 10
ner of wickedness.[2] They were then ready to tear any Methodist
preacher in pieces. Now not a dog wagged his tongue. I preached

---

[1] It is appropriate to include Thomas Jackson's editorial note to this Journal extract,
which itself incorporates the note of the editors who, about June 1791, first published
this extract after JW's death:

> This part of Mr. Wesley's Journal was not transcribed and published by him-
> self, but by those persons who had access to his papers after his decease. They
> apologize for the imperfect form in which it appears by saying, at the conclusion,
> 'We are not sure that Mr. Wesley carried on his Journal any farther; but if any
> more of it should be found, it will be published in due time. There are unavoid-
> able chasms in this Journal, owing to some parts being mislaid, and it is probable
> that many of the proper names of persons and places are not properly spelled, as
> the whole of the manuscript was so ill written as to be scarcely legible.' It should
> also be stated that this portion of the Journal contains some passages which it is
> probable Mr. Wesley would never have committed to the press, and for the pub-
> lication of which he should not be made responsible.

Jackson, 4:339n.

[2] Barnsley had indeed a record of violence right down to this time. According to
James Everett's MS notes, in 1773 'Jerry Cocker [went] to Barnsley—the mob pulled
Cocker [on whom see above, July 17, 1776] down and dragged him down the street—
threw eggs, one with a gosling in it—unable to end the service—applied to the vicar of
Sheffield—the prosecutors bound over to Rotherham sessions—it was given in favour
of the rioters, because the preacher, though licensed, yet the *place* (market place) was
not licensed'; Tyerman MSS, 3, fol. 11, in Methodist Archives, Manchester. In 1783,
Henry Longden, like Cocker, an eminent Sheffield local preacher, was assaulted and
believed an attempt had been made on his life; Tyerman, *John Wesley*, 3:474. In 1785,
John Barber was stoned by the mob: 'He was hit by a stone and much hurt—a Quaker
took him into his house—he lives in "Barnsley Folly"—here Barber finished his sermon'; Tyerman MSS, 3, fol. 21. Raynor, the currier, whose house provided the society
with a meeting place until a room over a weaver's shop was found *c.* 1792, also suffered
abuse. Barnsley, a market town and chapelry in the parish of Silkstone, was a producer
of coal even at this date, but was noted principally for wire-drawing, and linen-weaving

403

near the market-place to a very large congregation, and, I believe, the word sunk into many hearts. They seemed to drink in every word. Surely God will have a people in this place.

Saturday, July 1. I went on to Bramley[3] about four miles from Sheffield, where a gentleman has built a neat preaching-house for the poor people at his own expense.[4] As the notice was short, I had no need to preach abroad. The congregation was deeply serious while I explained what it was to 'build upon a rock',[5] and what to 'build upon the sand'.[6] In the evening, I spoke very plain to a crowded audience at Sheffield on 'Now it is high time to awake out of sleep.'[7] One of the hearers wrote me a nameless letter upon it. But he could remember nothing of the sermon but only that 'The rising early was good for the nerves!'

Sun. 2. I read prayers, preached, and administered the Sacrament to six or seven hundred hearers. It was a solemn season. I preached soon after five in the evening on 'There is joy in heaven over one sinner that repenteth.'[8] Afterwards I gave an account of the rise of Methodism (that is, old scriptural Christianity) to the whole congregation, as truth will bear the light and loves to appear in the face of the sun.

Mon. 3. We had our Quarterly Meeting, followed by a love-feast, at which many spoke without reserve, and several of them admirably well, showing that with the fear of the Lord is understanding.[9]

was beginning a rapid development. All these trades produced strong men whose delight in vigourous horse-play was not always tempered by discretion. Rowland Jackson, *History of Barnsley* (2nd edn., London, 1858), pp. 163–69.

[3] Bramley was a small chapelry in the parish of Braithwell, 4 miles east of Rotherham and 10 miles from Sheffield.

[4] This chapel had been built opposite his own house by Matthew Waterhouse (*c.* 1741-1822) and opened on Dec. 11, 1785, by Joseph Benson. His sister-in-law, Mrs. A. Waterhouse, who lived at Beckingham, 18 miles from Bramley and 7 from Owston, informed him that JW was going to preach in Owston on June 26, staying with Gervase Woodhouse, and Waterhouse came over to invite JW to preach at Bramley. Samuel Russell, *Historical Notes of Wesleyan Methodism in the Rotherham Circuit* (Rotherham, 1910), pp. 32–34; *WHS* 28 (1951):45.

[5] Cf. Matt. 7:24.

[6] Cf. Matt. 7:26.

[7] Rom. 13:11.

[8] Cf. Luke 15:7.

[9] For a previous comment in this vein, see above, Feb. 6, 1785. On this occasion, JW baptized Joseph Benson's daughter; *Wesleyan Methodist Magazine* 59 (1836):166. James Everett commented upon JW's legendary visit in a note to Thomas Holy (1752-1831), a pillar of Sheffield Methodism: 'After preaching, the people, being much affected, followed him as usual in crowds to Mr. Holy's door. The streets were lined with people

Tue. 4. I met the select society, most of them walking in glorious liberty. Afterwards, I went to Wentworth House, the splendid seat of the late Marquis of Rockingham.[10] He lately had forty thousand a year in England and fifteen or twenty thousand in Ireland. And what has he now? Six foot of earth.   5

> A heap of dust is all remains of thee!
> 'Tis all thou art: and all the proud shall be.[11]

The situation of the house is very fine. It commands a large and beautiful prospect. Before the house is an open view, behind, a few acres of wood but not laid out with any taste. The green-   10 houses are large, but I did not observe anything curious in them. The front of the house is large and magnificent but not yet finished.[12] The entrance is noble, the saloon exceeding grand, and so are several of the apartments. Few of the pictures are striking: I think none of them to be compared with some in Fonmon Cas-   15 tle.[13] The most extraordinary thing I saw was the stables: a square

---

looking out at the windows as if the king were passing. Wesley passed on, noting the children that flocked round him and emptying his pockets to the poor. When he got before Mr. Holy's door, Mr. Holy went arm in arm with him on the green in the open air to pray with them and give them his blessing—they would not go—he prayed again. . . .' (Tyerman MSS, 3, fols. 28-29). This passage was embroidered by both Samuel Jackson, *Wesleyan Methodist Magazine* 55 (1832):10-11; and Tyerman, *John Wesley*, 3:475.

[10] Charles Watson-Wentworth, second Marquis of Rockingham (1730-82), the celebrated Yorkshire Whig magnate, and Prime Minister as recently as 1782. JW's politics had lately been anything but Rockinghamite, but he owed some familial gratitude to the family of Wentworth Woodhouse, who in 1729 had provided a fortnight's hospitality to him and his father to use the library for the latter's *Dissertations on the Book of Job*. Tenuous personal connections between the two visits are said to have led to JW's being asked to pray with the household on this occasion. See Curnock, 7:181, n. 2, for the tradition about JW's visit, the date corrected by his Diary, Oct. 26, 1729.

[11] Incorrectly quoted from Pope's *Elegy to the Memory of an Unfortunate Lady*, lines 73-74. See Dec. 5, 1750 (20:373 in this edn.); see also Sermon 126, 'On Worldly Folly', II.5 (4:136 in this edn.).

[12] One of the most remarkable erections of its kind, Wentworth Woodhouse (width 600 feet) has not only the largest frontage of any house in England, but consists of two eighteenth-century houses which cannot be seen together, one facing west, the other east, with a difference in height amounting almost to a story, though both were designed and built for Thomas Wentworth, first Marquis of Rockingham. He came into the estate in 1723 and died in 1750. Apart from a Van Dyck of Archbishop Laud and a Stubbs of Rockingham's favourite horse, the only pictures mentioned by Pevsner are 'a good set of paintings of Christ and the apostles, in Rubens's style'. Pevsner, *Yorkshire, West Riding*, pp. 539-45.

[13] The home, near Cardiff, of JW's old friend Robert Jones (on whom see Sept. 21, 1741; 19:227, n. 9 in this edn.). Old friendship and religious sympathy here clearly interfered with JW's ability to compare like with like.

fit for a royal palace, all built of fine stone and near as large as the old quadrangle at Christ Church in Oxford. But for what use were these built? To show that the owner had near threescore thousand pounds a year! O how much treasure might he have laid
5   up in heaven with all this mammon of unrighteousness! About one, I preached at Thorpe [Hesley] to three or four times as many as the preaching-house would have contained, and in the evening to the well-instructed and well-behaved congregation at Sheffield. O what has God wrought in this town! 'The leopard
10 now lies down with the kid.'[14]

Wed. 5. Notice was given, without my knowledge, of my preaching at Belper[15] seven miles short of Derby. I was nothing glad of this, as it obliged me to quit the turnpike road to hobble over a miserable common. The people, gathered from all parts,
15 were waiting. So I went immediately to the market-place and, standing under a large tree, testified, 'This is life eternal, to know thee, the only true God, and Jesus Christ whom thou hast sent.'[16] The house at Derby was thoroughly filled in the evening. As many of the better sort (so called) were there, I explained (what
20 seemed to be more adapted to their circumstances and experience), 'This only have I found, That God made man upright; but they found out for themselves many inventions.'[17]

Thur. 6. In going to Ilkeston,[18] we were again entangled in mis-

---

[14] Cf. Isa. 11:6. On the early violence in Sheffield, see July 1, 1748 (20:230, n. 77 in this edn.).

[15] Belper was a market town and chapelry in the parish of Duffield, 7 miles north of Derby, inhabited principally by nailers. A rapid growth and economic transformation of the town had begun in 1777 with the opening of Strutt's cotton mill. These changes were marked in Methodist history by the opening of a chapel in 1782 on a site given by Thomas Slater. But Thomas Slater's farmhouse, where the preaching began, continued to provide hospitality to preachers into the present century. G. A. Fletcher, *Records of Wesleyan Methodism in Belper* (Belper, 1903), pp. 26-28, 37, 65; *Methodist Recorder* (Apr. 2, 1903), p. 15. The first market was held in Belper in 1737, and JW's account of preaching under a tree suggests that the market-place retained something of its original character, 'mere waste ground, overgrown with grass and rubbish' on which stood several large trees. *WHS* 16 (1928):112.

[16] Cf. John 17:3.

[17] Cf. Eccles. 7:29.

[18] Ilkeston was a market town and parish 8 miles north-east of Derby, a centre for the mining of coal and ironstone, and the production of lace and stockings. The circumstances of the visit show how close Methodist history could be to legend. For many years there had been only one Methodist in Ilkeston. On her death, John Crook (on whom see above, June 6, 1781) preached an open-air sermon which deeply impressed the vicar, the Rev. George Allen, and led to an invitation to preach at the church door at the end of the next Sunday service. This sermon led in turn to the vicar's conversion,

erable roads. We got thither, however, about eleven. Though the church is large, it was sufficiently crowded. The vicar read prayers with great earnestness and propriety. I preached on 'Her ways are ways of pleasantness,'[19] and the people seemed all ear. Surely good will be done in this place, though it is strongly opposed both by the Calvinists and Socinians.

We went on in a lovely afternoon and through a lovely country to Nottingham. I preached to a numerous and well-behaved congregation. I love this people. There is something wonderfully pleasing both in their spirit and their behaviour.

Fri. 7. The congregation at five was very large, and convinced me of the earnestness of the people. They are greatly increased in wealth and grace, and continue increasing daily. Saturday 8, I walked through the General Hospital.[20] I never saw one so well ordered. Neatness, decency, and common sense shine through the whole. I do not wonder that many of the patients recover. I prayed with two of them. One of them, a notorious sinner, seemed to be cut to the heart. The case of the other was quite peculiar.[21] Both her breasts have been cut off, and many pins taken out of them, as well as out of her flesh in various parts. 'Twelve', the apothecary said, 'were taken out of her yesterday and five more today.' And the physicians potently believe she swallowed them all, though

and to his inviting JW on the present occasion. D. McAllum, *Memoirs of Rev. H. Taft, M.D.* (Newcastle, 1824), pp. 6-7. Calvinists and Socinians were present in force at Ilkeston, there being General and Particular Baptists, Independents, and Unitarians.

[19] Prov. 3:17.

[20] 'The General Hospital, a spacious and commodious building consisting of a centre and two projecting wings, was erected in 1781 [opening the following year] on the highest part of Standard Hill, on a site given by the corporation and the Duke of Newcastle. It is supported by funds arising from liberal donations and by annual subscription, and is . . . open to invalids from any part of the country'; Lewis, *England*, 3:404. JW's carefully phrased expectation that patients might sometimes recover was high praise; long afterwards Florence Nightingale introduced her *Notes on Hospitals* (London, 1859) with the observation (p. 2) that 'the function of a hospital [is not] to kill the sick,' and it was not till much later still that hospital patients could be reasonably certain of dying of the disease they went in with. JW had already preached on behalf of the hospital in 1784, and was to do so again in 1787 and 1788. *WHS* 5 (1906):163-64.

[21] This was the case of Kitty Hudson, who had been left in the care of her grandfather, the sexton of St. Mary's Church, and given the job of sweeping the church. When she found any pins or needles she kept them in her mouth to give to a woman who offered to reward her with toffee for collecting them. By the age of eighteen, she had swallowed so many that she had to enter the General Hospital, where pins were found all over her body. Kitty Hudson was not only one of the patients who recovered; she married a man named Goddard, bore 19 children, and for many years carried the mail twice a day from Arnold into Nottingham and back, becoming known as the 'Arnold Post'. Harwood, *Nottingham*, pp. 59-60; *WHS* 5 (1906):163-64; Swift, *Lively People*, p. 23.

nobody can tell when or how! Which is the great credulity? To believe this is purely *natural?* Or to ascribe it to preternatural agency?

In the evening many felt

Th' o'erwhelming power of saving grace.[22]

And many more on Sunday 9, when we had the largest number of communicants that ever were seen at this chapel, or perhaps at any church in Nottingham. I took a solemn leave of this affectionate congregation at five in the morning, Monday 10, not expecting to meet another such (unless at Birmingham) till I came to London.

About nine, I preached at Mountsorrel, and, though it was the fair-day, I saw not one drunken person in the congregation. It rained most of the way to Leicester, and some were afraid there would be no congregation. Vain fear! The house was extremely crowded with deeply attentive hearers while I applied our Lord's words to the centurion, in effect spoken to *us* also, 'As thou hast believed, so be it done unto thee.'[23] In the afternoon, we went on to Hinckley. It rained all the evening, yet we had more hearers than the house could contain, and hardly a trifler among them. A more serious, well-behaved people I have seldom seen.

This evening (I believe before I had done preaching), a remarkable instance of divine justice appeared. A man in the street was grievously cursing another and praying God 'to blast his eyes.' At that instant he was struck blind. So (I suppose) he continues ever since.[24]

Tue. 11. The poor, little flock at Coventry[25] have at length pro-

[22] CW, 'The Invitation', st. 10, in *Hymns on the Great Festivals* (1746), p. 46, repr. in *Hymns and Sacred Poems* (1749), 1:260; *Poetical Works*, 5:64; and as No. 9 in the 1780 *Collection* (7:92 of this edn.). See June 20, 1769 (22:189, and n. 11 in this edn.); above Apr. 12, 1785; June 7, 1788, and June 21, 1789; also Sermon 63, 'The General Spread of the Gospel', §12 (2:489, n. 27 in this edn.).

[23] Matt. 8:13.

[24] The unedifying end of this story (for which see Feb. 12, 1787) might have stood as a caution against early Methodist enthusiasm for special providences.

[25] 'The cause of Methodism in Coventry was for many years very low, in consequence of what Mr. Wesley calls in his journal the unjustifiable conduct of J. W., who was there at the beginning of it and fixed a stigma upon it which is scarcely wiped off to this day.' *Methodist Magazine* 40 (1817):326-27. Curnock conjectured that J. W. was James Wheatley, who was certainly a scoundrel (see Apr. 12, 1744; 20:23-24, n. 15 in this edn.), but is difficult to tie to the beginnings of Methodism at Coventry.

cured a neat, convenient room.[26] Only it is far too small. As many of the people as could get in were all attention. How is the scene changed here also! I know not, but *now* the corporation, if it had been proposed, would have given the use of the town-hall to *me* rather than to the dancing master![27] In the evening, I went on to   5
Birmingham and found the usual spirit in the congregation. They were much alive to God and consequently increasing in number as well as in grace.

Wed. 12. At noon, I preached in the new chapel at Deritend.[28] To build one here was an act of mercy indeed, as the church   10
would not contain a fifth, perhaps not a tenth, of the inhabitants. At six, I preached in our chapel at Birmingham[29] and, immediately after, took coach to London.

Thur. 13. We reached the town at two and settled all our business on this and the two following days. Sunday 16, my heart was   15
greatly enlarged in exhorting a very numerous congregation to 'worship God in spirit and in truth'.[30] And we had such a number of communicants as we have not had before, since the covenant night. I suppose fifty, perhaps a hundred, of them never communicated before. In the afternoon, I buried the remains of Thomas   20
Parkinson (who died suddenly two or three days before), one of our first members, a man of excellent spirit and unblamable conversation. Monday 17, after preaching at West Street, where many were impressed with a deep sense of the presence of God, I took coach for Bristol. We had a delightful journey. But having   25
the window at my side open while I slept, I lost my voice, so that I could scarce be heard across a room. But before Wednesday morning (by applying garlic as usual), it was instantly restored.

Thur. 20. I preached at the new room on, 'We have this trea-

---

[26] An auction room in the women's market. *WHS* 9 (1914):121, 167.

[27] See above, July 21, 1779.

[28] Orig. 'Derrington'. Deritend was a chapelry in the parish of Aston, north-east of Birmingham city centre. It was a hamlet that consisted 'principally of one spacious street from which several others diverge', at the point where the road from Coventry to Birmingham crossed the river Rea. It was already in a spate of industrial development, principally in the iron trades, which were shortly to make it an integral part of Birmingham. The church, St. James's, a square-towered brick building, regarded as 'a picturesque and interesting feature', was inadequate to the growth of the place. The living, a perpetual curacy, was in the gift of the inhabitants and householders of Deritend and Bordesley. Lewis, *England*, 2:39. The chapel was built in the main street. See Sheldon, *Birmingham*, p. 35.

[29] Cherry Street Chapel.

[30] Cf. John 4:24.

sure in earthen vessels.'[31] And the hearts of many, who had been
vexed with needless scruples, were mightily refreshed.

Fri. 21. I walked over to Kingswood School, now one of the
pleasantest spots in England. I found all things just according to
my desire, the rules being well observed and the whole behaviour
of the children showing that they were now managed with the
wisdom that cometh from above.

Sun. 23. I preached in the morning on those words in the Second Lesson, 'Lazarus, come forth,'[32] and I believe many that were
buried in sin heard the voice of the Son of God. In the evening, I
preached abroad on Matt. 5:20. In the middle of the sermon, it
began to rain, but not many went away. This put me in mind of
that remarkable circumstance respecting the late pope.[33] On that
solemn day when the pope rides on horseback to St. Peter's, a
violent storm scattered his whole retinue. When it abated, his
Holiness was missing; but they soon found him sitting quietly in
the church. Being asked how he could ride through such a storm,
he very calmly replied, 'I am ready to go not only through water,
but through fire also for my Lord's sake.' Strange! That such a
man should be suffered to sit two years[34] in the papal chair!

Tue. 25. Our Conference began.[35] About eighty preachers
attended. We met every day at six and nine in the morning, and at
two in the afternoon. On Tuesday and on Wednesday morning,
the characters of the preachers were considered, whether already
admitted or not. On Thursday in the afternoon, we permitted any
of the society to be present and weighed what was said about separating from the church. But we all determined to continue
therein, without one dissenting voice. And I doubt not but this
determination will stand, at least till I am removed into a better

[31] 2 Cor 4:7. See Sermon 129, 'Heavenly Treasure in Earthen Vessels' (4:161-67 in
this edn.).
[32] John 11:43. This service was in the New Room.
[33] Pope Clement XIV, 1769-74.
[34] Perhaps an error for the five years of Clement's rule. The only very short-lived
pope of the period was Innocent XIII, 1721-24.
[35] It is clear from this entry that the attendance was well short even of the Legal Hundred. The Diary shows that at least three ordinations took place, those of Joshua Keighley, appointed to Inverness (he died suddenly of fever in 1787; *Arminian Magazine* 10
[1787]:123-24; Atmore, *Memorial*, pp. 227-30), William Warrener, appointed to
Antigua, and William Hammet, appointed to Newfoundland. The Minutes (1:189-91)
include extensive papers by JW himself, justifying these ordinations and arguing that,
whatever might happen after his death, they did not imply present separation from the
Church of England.

world. On Friday and Saturday, most of our temporal business
was settled. Sunday 30, I preached in the room morning and
evening, and in the afternoon at Kingswood, where there is rather
an increase than a decrease in the work of God.

Mon. 31. The Conference met again, and concluded on Tuesday morning. Great had been the expectations of many that we
should have had warm debates.[36] But by the mercy of God, we
had none at all. Everything was transacted with great calmness,
and we parted as we met, in peace and love.

Tuesday, August 8. At seven, Mr. Brackenbury,[37] Broadbent,[38]
and I took coach for Harwich, which we reached about eight in the
evening. Wednesday 9, between two and three in the afternoon, we
went on board the *Besborough* packet, one of the cleanest ships I
ever saw, with one of the most obliging captains. We had many gentlemen on board, whom I was agreeably surprised to find equally
obliging. Thursday 10, the wind continuing small and the sea calm,
they desired me to give them a sermon. They were all attention.
Who knows but some among them may retain the impressions they
then received? Friday 11, for some time we had a dead calm. So
that we did not reach Hellevoetsluis till the afternoon, nor Rotterdam till between ten and eleven at night. We found Mr. Layal[39] was
not returned from a journey which he had begun a week or two
before. But Mrs. Layal gave us a hearty welcome.

Sat. 12. Mr. Williams,[40] minister of the Episcopal Church, and
Mr. Scott,[41] minister of the Scots Church, both welcomed me to
Holland. But the kindness involved me in an awkward difficulty:
Mr. Scott had asked the consent of his Consistory for me to
preach in his church on Sunday afternoon, but Mr. Williams had
given notice of my preaching in his church both morning and
afternoon; and neither of them [was] willing to give up his point.
I would fain have compromised the matter, but each seemed to
apprehend his honour concerned and would not in any wise give
up his point. I saw no possible way to satisfy both but by prolong-
ing my stay in Holland, in order to preach one Sunday, morning
and afternoon in the Episcopal, and another in the Scots Church.

---

[36] John Fletcher, peace-maker at the Conference of 1784, was now dead.
[37] For R. C. Brackenbury, see above, July 9, 1776.
[38] For John Broadbent, see above, Aug. 17, 1779.
[39] For Alexander Layal, see above, June 13, 1783.
[40] For William Williams, see above, June 14, 1783.
[41] Alexander Scott, a strict Calvinist, minister of the Scots Church, Rotterdam, 1780-95.

And possibly God may have more work for me to do in Holland than I am yet aware of.

Though Mr. Layal, with whom I lodged when I was in Rotterdam before, was not in town, being gone with a friend to Paris, yet I was quite as at home and went on in my work without any interruption. Sunday 13, the service began about ten. Mr. Williams read prayers exceeding well, and I preached on those words in the First Lesson, 'How long halt ye between two opinions?'[42] All the congregation gave a serious attention: but I fear they only *heard*, but did not *feel*. But many seemed to be much affected in the afternoon, while I opened and applied those words, 'There hath no temptation taken you, but what is common to men.'[43] In the evening, Mr. Scott called upon me and informed me that the elders of his church would not desire me to stay in Holland on purpose to preach, but would dismiss my promise. I then determined to follow my first plan and (God willing) to return to England in a fortnight.

Mon. 14. Taking boat at eight, we went at our ease through one of the pleasantest summer countries in Europe and reached the Hague between twelve and one. Being determined to lodge at no more inns,[44] I went with brother Ferguson[45] to his own lodging and passed a quiet and comfortable night. A few pious persons came to us in the evening, with whose spirits we quickly took acquaintance. I have not found any persons, since we crossed the sea, who seemed so much devoted to God.

Tue. 15. Making the experiment when we took boat, I found I could write as well in the boat as in my study. So from this hour, I continued writing whenever I was on board. What mode of traveling is to be compared with this? About noon we called on Professor Roers[46] at Leyden, a very sensible and conversable man. As he spoke Latin very fluently, I could willingly have spent some hours with him. But I had appointed to be at Amsterdam in the evening. We came thither between seven and eight and took up our abode with William Ferguson, who continued to lodge us all with tolerable convenience.

[42] 1 Kgs. 18:21.

[43] Cf. 1 Cor. 10:13.

[44] On his previous visit (see above, June 27, 1783), JW had become 'sick of inns' and the expense they occasioned.

[45] For William Ferguson, see above, June 2, 1783.

[46] Probably Carolus Boers, professor of theology, supporter of the Orange party, and friend of M. Tydeman, the great linguist. Molhuysen, *Biografisch Woordenbook*, 1:318; Glasius, *Biographisch Woordenboek*, 1:464.

Wed. 16. I spent the day very quietly in writing and visiting a few friends, who knew not how to be affectionate enough. In the evening, I spoke to a little company at my own lodgings on, 'It is appointed to men once to die.'[47]

Thur. 17. I breakfasted with a little company of truly pious people and afterwards went to see the manner wherein the deacons of Amsterdam relieve their poor weekly. I suppose there were two or three hundred poor, but the whole was transacted with the utmost stillness and decency.

Today, likewise, I visited more of my friends, who showed all possible affection. Friday 18, we went to Haarlem and spent an agreeable day with a few agreeable friends. We lodged at Mr. Van Kampen's,[48] a florist, and were perfectly at home. Both Mr. and Mrs. Van Kampen seemed deeply devoted to God, as much as any I have seen in Holland.

In the afternoon, we met a little company in the town who seemed to be truly alive to God, one Miss Rouquet[49] in particular, whose least recommendation was that she could speak both Dutch, French, and English. She spent the evening at Miss Valkenburg's,[50] the chief gentlewoman in the town. Here we supped. The manner was particular. No table-cloth was used, but plates with knives and forks and napkins to each person, and fifteen or sixteen small ones, on which were bread, butter, cheese, slices of hung beef, cakes, pancakes, and fruit of various kinds. To these were added music upon an excellent organ, one of the sweetest tones I ever heard.

Sat. 19. We took a walk in Haarlem wood. So delightful a place I scarce ever saw before. I judged it to be about a mile broad and two or three miles deep. This is divided into almost innumerable walks, some broad and some narrow, but diversified in a wonderful manner and skirted with elegant houses on both sides. In the afternoon, we returned to Amsterdam. In the evening, Mr. Schouten,[51] a bookseller (whose daughter had come with us in the boat to Amsterdam), an elder of the Holland's Church, invited us to supper and desired me to expound a portion of scripture,

---

[47] Cf. Heb. 9:27.
[48] On the Van Kampen family, see above, June 25, 1783.
[49] On the Rouquet sisters, see above, June 21, 1783.
[50] Orig. 'Falconberg'. On Cornelia Paulina van Valkenburg, see above, June 21, 1783.
[51] Orig. 'Shranten'. Petris Schouten, bookseller in the Kelverstraat, whom JW had visited on June 20, 1783.

which I did with liberty of spirit. Afterward, Mr. Brackenbury repeated to them in French the substance of what I had said.

Sun. 20. I expected to have preached in the English Church as I did before. But some of the elders were unwilling, so I attended
5 there as a hearer. And I heard as miserable a sermon as most I have heard in my life. It might have been preached either among Jews, Turks, or heathens without offending them at all. In the afternoon, I expounded to a company of serious Christians our Lord's account of 'building *our* house upon a rock'.[52] Jonathan
10 Ferguson[53] interpreted sentence by sentence. And God applied it to the hearts of the hearers.

Mon. 21. I spent an hour with great satisfaction at Mr. Nolthenius's[54] country house. Such a couple as him and his wife, I never saw since I left London. And both their children appeared to be
15 worthy of their parents, both as to persons, understanding, and temper.

Tue. 22. I spent great part of the day at Mr. Vankennel's[55] country house, having agreed with him to give me a private room to write in before and after dinner. At ten, a very sensible clergyman
20 came in, with whom I conversed very largely, as he talked elegant Latin and exceeding fluently, beyond any I have lately seen on the continent.

Having seen all the friends I proposed to see, on Thursday 24, I took my leave of this loving people and the pleasant city of Ams-
25 terdam, very probably for ever. And setting out at seven in the morning, between two and three in the afternoon came to Utrecht. Mr. Van Rocy,[56] the gentleman who had engaged me to lodge, sent a coach to wait for me at my landing, and received me with the courtesy and cordiality of an old Yorkshire Methodist.
30 Fri. 25. I kept close to my work all the day. I dined at Mr. Loten's,[57] where was such variety of food as I never saw at any nobleman's table either in England or Ireland! In the afternoon,

---

[52] Cf. Matt. 7:24.

[53] On Jonathan, son of William Ferguson, see above, June 2, 1783.

[54] Orig. 'Noltanu'. Probably Willem Hendrik Nolthenius (1726-96), who had two children and was a church worker. Van den Berg, 'Wesley's Contacten', p. 89, n. 2.

[55] The Diary suggests that this visit was on the 23rd. JW had been working daily on his life of John Fletcher for over two weeks.

[56] This is probably the person who invited JW on his last visit. The description suggests a member of the well-to-do bourgeoisie. The name could be in error; JW might be referring to Adrian van Romondt, a friend of Lotens and one of M. Tydeman's circle.

[57] On Arnoud Loten and his daughter, Johanna Carolina Arnodina, see above, June 17, 1783.

we took a view of a widow lady's gardens in the suburbs of Utrecht. I believe from the house to the end of the grand vista is about a mile. I think the gardens are not half as broad. But such exquisite beauty and symmetry I never saw before. In grandeur it is not to be named with a few places in England. But in elegance and variety, I verily believe it equals, if not exceeds, any place of the size in Europe.

In the evening, I expounded to a select company of very honourable ladies Matt. 7:24, Miss Loten interpreting for me sentence by sentence. And I know not but God might bless this poor way of preaching to the Dutch, as he did that to the Indians by David Brainerd.[58]

Sat. 26. I had a long conversation with a gentleman, whom almost all the religious world take for a madman. I do not know that I have found one of so deep experience since I left London. I have no doubt of his being perfected in love. He has a clear witness of it and has had many years without interruption. I had now an opportunity of being thoroughly informed concerning the University of Utrecht. As the young gentlemen are scattered over this town and live without the least control, they do anything they please. And as they have no tutors, they have none to check them. Most of them lounge from morning to night, doing nothing or doing worse. Well, bad as they are, Oxford and Cambridge are not Utrecht yet.

Sun. 27. I attended the service of the English Church, where about thirty persons were present. At five in the evening, I believe I had eighty or ninety hearers, and I had much liberty of speech among them. I cannot doubt but some of them found the word of God to be sharper than a two-edged sword.

After service, I went once more to Mr. Loten's. Both Mrs. Loten[59] and he came to town on purpose to see me. Otherwise he could find little comfort there during the present state of affairs. The burghers have all agreed to depose their burgo-masters[60] and elect new ones in their stead, who are tomorrow to take an oath on

---

[58] On David Brainerd, see Dec. 4, 1749 (20:315, n. 98 in this edn.).

[59] On Mrs. Loten, see above, June 17, 1783.

[60] Utrecht was a particularly vigorous centre of the Dutch Patriot movement, an agitation precipitated by the American War of Independence (known to the Dutch as the Fourth English War). Trouble had begun in 1775 when the Orange Stadtholder, William V, backed a request of the British government to withdraw the Scotch brigade from Dutch service for use in America, to find himself sharply opposed in some of the provincial estates. Van der Capellen, who led the resistance, was supported by many

a scaffold erected in the open market place, not to the Prince of
Orange but the city of Utrecht. To this end they had displaced all
the Prince's guards and placed burghers at all the gates. It is
thought the example will spread, and it will not be strange if all
5   Holland should soon be a field of blood.

Mon. 28. We took boat at seven, being informed that at eight,
all the city gates would be shut. In the evening, we reached Rotterdam and rejoiced to meet good Mr. Layal[61] once more. Here we
rested on Tuesday. Wednesday 30, we set out early and went
10   twelve miles in a coach, for which we had to pay six guilders and
no more. We then crossed the river, which cost four stivers, and
hired an open wagon for twenty-three stivers, which brought us
to the other river in half an hour. At the Brill, we hired another
coach, which cost us four guilders. I set down these little things
15   that others may not be cheated.

Wed. 30. We found company enough in our inn at Hellevoetsluis, genteel, good-natured, and sensible. But finding our conversation was not suited to their taste, we only dined with them on
this and the following days. Both on this Thursday and Friday,
20   the wind was quite contrary. But otherwise we could not have
sailed, for it blew a storm. So I took the opportunity of writing a
sermon for the Magazine.

Saturday, September 2. The storm abating, we set sail about

well-to-do merchants, bankers, and professors, who showed a common sympathy with
the American cause and a common sense of exclusion from public influence, either
because they did not belong to the families which controlled the town councils or
because they were dissenters from the Established Church. This 'democratic' wing of
the Patriot movement could expect some support from the oligarchic 'regents' who
filled the town councils and had their own feuds with the House of Orange, depending
heavily on court patronage and the Established Church. To the latter, the war seemed a
wanton indulgence of greed; to the former, it was a defence of national interests against
British depredations, and they organised uniformed Free Corps in various towns, open
to Protestant dissenters and Roman Catholics. In Utrecht, where the town council filled
its own vacancies and chose its burgomasters among men nominated by the
Stadtholder, an agitation against the oligarchy began in 1783 so vigorously that many
anti-Orange regents began to take alarm. Nevertheless, the movement increased in
strength, and in 1786 the Utrecht burghers finally ended their old council and chose
another by a general election—the event JW witnessed. His fears of civil war were
realised in 1787, when the King of Prussia, the brother of the Princess of Orange, sent
in his troops to restore order. With this intervention and heavy expenditure by the
British, the Orange regime was reconstituted and guaranteed by the two powers. Five to
six thousand of the Patriots, including many men of substance, went into exile. R. R.
Palmer, *The Age of the Democratic Revolution*, 2 vols. (Princeton, 1959-64), 1:324-40; E.
H. Kossmann, *The Low Countries, 1780-1940* (Oxford, 1978), pp.34-47.
    [61] For Alexander Layal, see above, June 13, 1783.

nine, though the wind was contrary. But in the afternoon it fell calm. The rolling of the ship made us sick. I myself was sick a few minutes; Mr. Broadbent (by times) for some hours; Mr. Brackenbury (who did not expect to be sick at all) almost from the beginning of the voyage to the end.[62]

Sun. 3. When we had been twenty-four hours on board, we were scarce come a third of our way. I judged we should not get on unless I preached, which I therefore did, between two and three in the afternoon, on 'It is appointed for men once to die,'[63] and I believe all were affected for the present. Afterwards, we had a fair wind for several hours, but it then fell dead calm again. This did not last long, for as soon as prayer was over, a fresh breeze sprung up and brought us into the bay. It being then dark, we cast anchor. And it was well, for at ten at night, we had a violent storm. I expected little rest. But I prayed, and God answered, so that I slept sound till my usual hour, four o'clock. The wind being again quite contrary, we were obliged to tack continually. But about nine, were brought safe to Harwich.[64] After resting about an hour, we took chaise and, about one, came to Colchester, where, Mr. Brackenbury being exceeding weak, we thought it best to stay till the morning.

In the evening, the house was thoroughly filled, and many received the truth in the love thereof, so that I did not at all regret my stopping here. Setting out early in the morning, Tuesday 5, I reached London before one o'clock and transacted most of my business in the afternoon. In the evening, I preached on Psalm 29:9, 10, and the voice of the Lord was indeed 'with power'.[65] Wednesday 6, I answered my letters and, on Thursday 7, set out for Bristol.

In the evening, I preached at Newbury. It rained and blew vehemently, yet the house was thoroughly filled, and I found uncommon liberty in pushing the inquiry, 'Who of you are building on sand; and who upon a rock?'[66] Friday 8 in the evening, I

[62] For JW's travelling companions, John Broadbent and R. C. Brackenbury, see above, Aug. 17, 1779, and July 9, 1776, respectively.

[63] Cf. Heb. 9:27.

[64] Sophie von La Roche, a German noblewoman, who was travelling to England from Rotterdam, left her own first-hand account of this voyage which included comments and vignettes of Wesley and his companions. *Sophie in London, 1786,* Eng. trans. by Clare Williams (London, 1933), pp. 66–81.

[65] See Ps. 29:4.

[66] See Matt. 7:24, 26.

preached at Bath to a more numerous congregation than I
expected; and more serious, for I do not find there were any careless or inattentive hearers. Saturday 9, we had a good congregation at five, although the weather continued stormy. Afterward, I
5 searched to the bottom a story I had heard in part, and found it
another 'tale of real woe'. Two of our society had lived together in
uncommon harmony, when one who met in band with E. F. (to
whom she had mentioned that she had '*found a temptation* toward
Dr. F.')[67] went and told her husband[68] 'she *was in love* with him,
10 and that she had it from her own mouth.' The spirit of jealousy
seized him in a moment and utterly took away his reason. And,
someone telling him 'his wife was at Dr. F's' (on whom she had
called that afternoon), he took a great stick and ran away and,
meeting her in the street, called out 'Strumpet; Strumpet!' and
15 struck her twice or thrice. He is now thoroughly convinced of her
innocence, but the water cannot be gathered up again! He sticks
there: 'I do thoroughly forgive you, but I can never love you
more.'

     Sun. 10. Our service began at ten. Mr. Creighton[69] (whose
20 health is a little recovered by rest and drinking the mineral
waters) read prayers and assisted at the Sacrament. I preached on
'The children are brought to the birth, and there is not strength
to bring forth.'[70] At half an hour past two, we had a far larger congregation and, I think, equally serious, on whom I enforced the
25 exhortation, 'Come unto me, all ye that are weary and heavy
laden.'[71] In the evening, I opened and largely applied those words
in the Gospel for the Day, 'Verily I say unto you, many prophets
and kings have desired to see the things which ye see, and have
not seen them, and to hear those things that ye hear, and have not
30 heard them.'[72]

---

[67] Thought to be William Falconer M.D. (1744–1824). Falconer received M.D.
degrees from both Edinburgh (1766) and Leiden (1767), and, after beginning a successful practice in his native town of Chester, was encouraged by Dr. John Fothergill, a
physician who was reckoned to have saved JW's life in 1753 (see Nov. 13, 1753; 20:481,
n. 38 in this edn.), to settle in Bath in 1770. In 1773 he became F.R.S. and was physician to Bath General Hospital, 1784–1819. He wrote very extensively on the Bath waters
and other medical topics, but also on spiritual and biblical themes, and was much prized
by men of letters, especially Samuel Parr. *DNB*.
[68] I.e., E. F.'s husband.
[69] On James Creighton, see May 23, 1773; 22:369, n. 19 in this edn.
[70] Cf. 2 Kgs. 19:3, the text given in the Diary; but see also Isa. 37:3; 66:9.
[71] Cf. Matt. 11:28.
[72] Cf. Luke 10:24. This was the Thirteenth Sunday after Trinity.

Mon. 11. Leaving the society here well united together, I went on and preached at Bristol in the evening and, on Tuesday 12, retired to a friend's house, where I went on in Mr. F[letcher]'s life[73] without interruption. But on Wednesday 13, I could not resist the desire of my friends to preach at Temple Church in the 5
evening. I never saw it so full in an evening before, nor felt so much of the power of God there.

Fri. 15. I had much satisfaction in the evening at the chapel in Guinea Street. It was thoroughly filled, and most of the people seemed much affected, while (from Heb. 12:1) I described what I 10
take to be the chief besetting sins of Bristol: love of money and love of ease. Indeed, God has already wrought a great deliverance for many of them, and we hope a far greater will ensue.

Sun. 17. I preached morning and evening at the room[74] and, in the afternoon, at Kingswood, where the work of God seems to stand 15
nearly at one stay, not sensibly increasing or decreasing. On Monday, Tuesday, and Wednesday, I met the classes at Bristol and, on the remaining days of the week, transcribed the society, considerably increased since last year, and I hope in grace as well as in number.[75]

Sat. 23. I read the general plan of Monsieur Gebelin's vast 20
work, designed to consist of twelve very large quarto volumes, eight of which are published, *The Primitive World Analysed and Compared with the Modern*.[76] He is a man of strong understanding, boundless imagination, and amazing industry. I think his first volume is a beautiful castle in the air. I admire it, but I do not believe 25
one word of it, because it is wholly built on the authority of Sanchoniatho,[77] whom no one could ever yet prove to have had a being. And I fear he was a deist, (1) because he nowhere lays the least stress upon the Bible; (2) because he supposes the original confusion of tongues to have been a merely natural event. Sunday 30
24, God was eminently present with us at the morning-service, as

---

[73] *A Short Account of the Life and Death of the Rev. John Fletcher*, which was to be published in Dec.-Jan. 1786-87; see vol. 14 in this edn.; Jackson, 11:273-365.
[74] I.e., the New Room.
[75] This membership roll is the last of three in JW's hand preserved at the New Room in Bristol. His writing was already shaky, and he did not attempt the task again. In 1789, he simply recorded the list of leaders. Bristol membership in the 1770s and early 1780s had remained steady at about 750. *WHS* 26 (1948):143-47.
[76] Antoine Court de Gebelin, *The Primitive World Analysed, and Compared with the Modern World; or, Enquiries into the Antiquities of the World* (Paris, 1773). The work extended to nine volumes.
[77] *Sanchoniatho's Phoenician History* [tr. from Eusebius *De praeparatione evangelica*]. With remarks by Richard Cumberland and Squier Payne (London, 1720).

well as at Temple Church in the afternoon, which I never saw so filled before; which is not at all strange, considering the spirit of the vicar[78] and the indefatigable pains which he takes with rich and poor. At five, I took the opportunity of a fair evening to
5 preach once more near King Square. And once more I declared to a huge multitude the whole counsel of God.

Mon. 25. We took coach in the afternoon and, on Tuesday morning, reached London. I now applied myself in earnest to the writing of Mr. Fletcher's life, having procured the best materials I
10 could. To this I dedicated all the time I could spare till November, from five in the morning till eight at night. These are my studying hours: I cannot write longer in a day without hurting my eyes.

Sat. 30. I went to bed at my usual time, half an hour past nine, and, to my own feeling, in perfect health. But just at twelve, I was
15 waked by an impetuous flux, which did not suffer me to rest many minutes together. Finding it rather increased than decreased, though (which I never knew before) without its old companion the cramp, I sent for Dr. Whitehead.[79] He came about four, and, by the blessing of God, in three hours I was as well as
20 ever. Nor did I find the least weakness or faintness, but preached morning and afternoon, and met the society in the evening, without any weariness. Of such a one I would boldly say with the son of Sirach, 'Honour the physician, for God hath appointed him.'[80]

Mon. 2. I went to Chatham and had much comfort with the
25 loving, serious congregation in the evening, as well as at five in the morning. Tuesday 3, we then ran down with a fair, pleasant wind to Sheerness. The preaching-house here is now finished, but by means never heard of. The building was undertaken a few months since by a little handful of men without any probable means of
30 finishing it. But God so moved the hearts of the people in the dock that even those who did not pretend to any religion—carpenters, shipwrights, labourers—ran up, at all their vacant hours, and worked with all their might without any pay! By this means, a large square house was soon elegantly finished both within and
35 without. And it is the neatest building, next to the New Chapel in London, of any in the south of England.[81]

---

[78] Joseph Easterbrook, for whom see above, Mar. 18, 1781.
[79] For John Whitehead, see above, Jan. 4, 1785.
[80] Cf. Ecclus. 38:1, which reads, 'Honour the physician . . . for the Lord created him.'
[81] The Sheerness preaching-house was erected opposite the pier, on a site next to the house of JW's host in the town, Edward Smith, rigger.

I preached in the evening on 'Stand ye in the old paths,'[82] to a lovely congregation, and then showed the society of how great importance it was that *their* light should 'shine before men'.[83] And indeed it does shine. They are of one heart and of one mind, striving for the hope of the gospel. I preached at Chatham on Thursday evening and, the next day Friday 6, returned to London.

Tue. 10. Having promised to preach in their new house at [King's] Lynn,[84] I thought it best to go while the good weather continued. I had ordered two places to be taken in the coach which would have reached [King's] Lynn on Tuesday noon. But my messenger, mending my orders, took them in the Diligence, which came in between nine and ten at night. By this means, I lost one of three evenings which I proposed to spend there.

I spent Wednesday and Thursday with much satisfaction with a very loving and lively people, increasing in grace as well as in number, and adorning the doctrine of God our Saviour. I had appointed to preach Mrs. Shewell's[85] funeral sermon at Barnet on Friday evening. And as we had only two light persons in the Diligence and no baggage, I hoped we should have come in time. But they were vain hopes. We did not reach Hoddesdon[86] till after sunset. I then took a post-chaise, for the Diligence went the other road. But as we had a rough by-road across the country without either moon or stars, we could not reach the chapel till half an hour after seven. About half the congregation were gone away, an officious man having informed them I would not come. With the other half, which pretty well filled the house, we had a solemn opportunity.

So I have lived to see the large family at Hadley, two brothers and three sisters, all removed. So does 'the earth drop its inhabitants, as the tree its leaves'.[87]

Mon. 16. I went to Hinxworth and preached in the evening to a more numerous congregation than I ever had seen there before. At length, Miss Harvey[88] sees some fruit of all the pains she has

---

[82] Cf. Jer. 6:16.   [83] Matt. 5:16.

[84] On the origins of Methodism at King's Lynn, see Nov. 6, 1771; 22:296–97, n. 89 in this edn.

[85] Elizabeth Shewell (for whom see Nov. 22, 1771; 22:298, n. 96 in this edn.), probably the widow of John Shewell whose funeral sermon JW had preached in 1771.

[86] Orig. 'Hodsdon'. Hoddesdon was a market town and chapelry extending into two parishes and situated 4 miles south-east from Hertford.

[87] Homer, *Iliad*, vi.146; see also above, July 10, 1779, and note.

[88] For Miss Harvey of Hinxworth, see above, July, 17, 1782.

taken. Tuesday 17, I met her poor children in the morning, twenty of whom she keeps at school in the village, as she is unwearied in doing good. In the evening, I preached in Mr. Hicks's church at Wrestlingworth.[89] I have not seen such a con-
5 gregation there for many years. Neither have I found so much of the power of God. Surely all our labour here will not be in vain. Thursday 19, I returned to London. In this journey I had a full sight of Lord Salisbury's[90] seat at Hatfield.[91] The park is delightful. Both the fronts of the house are very handsome, though
10 antique. The hall, the assembly-room, and the gallery are grand and beautiful. The chapel is extremely pretty. But the furniture in general (excepting the pictures, many of which are originals) is just such as I should expect in a gentleman's house of five hundred a year.

15 Sun. 22. I preached at West Street, morning and afternoon, and at All Hallows Church in the evening. It was much crowded, and gave us so remarkable a blessing as I scarce ever found at that church. Tuesday 24, I met the classes at Deptford and was vehemently importuned to order the Sunday service in our room[92] at
20 the same time with that of the church. It is easy to see, that this would be a formal separation from the church. We fixed both our morning and evening service all over England at such hours as not to interfere with the church, with this very design, that those of the church, if they chose it, might attend both the one and the
25 other. But to fix it at the same hour is obliging them to separate, either from the Church or us. And this I judge to be not only inexpedient, but totally unlawful for me to do.

Wed. 25. I went to Brentford, but had little comfort there. The society is almost dwindled to nothing. What have we gained by
30 separating from the Church here? Is not this a good lesson for others?

---

[89] Orig. 'Wastlingworth'. For William Hicks, see Nov. 9, 1758 (21:171, n. 79 in this edn.).
[90] James, seventh Earl and first Marquis of Salisbury (1748-1823). He was M.P. for Great Bedwin, 1774-80, and for Launceston, 1780. Created Marquis in 1789, he held minor household and political offices.
[91] Hatfield House was built by Robert Cecil, first Earl of Salisbury, 1608-12, and is reckoned by Pevsner to be 'the most important mansion in the county and one of the four or five most important Jacobean mansions in England.' The chief designer was Robert Lyinge, a carpenter. The features noted by JW still command admiration. Much redecoration was done in the nineteenth century. Pevsner, *Hertfordshire*, pp. 111-16.
[92] I.e., preaching-house.

Thur. 26. Mr. Holbrook[93] carried us to Hampton Court, far the finest palace which the King of England has. The buildings are a little town, and nothing can be pleasanter than the park. But above all, the three fronts of the house, the staircase, and the furniture and pictures in the apartments are worthy of a king and not equalled by any in the kingdom in some respects, not by Blenheim[94] itself; which exceeds it only in its front, in tapestry, and in shockingly immodest pictures.

In the evening, I preached to a large and serious congregation at Wandsworth. I think it was about two in the morning that a dog began howling under our window in a most uncommon manner. We could not stop him by any means. Just then William B[arke]r[95] died.

Fri. 27. I preached once more at Barnet, probably for the last time. Sunday 29, after preaching at West Street, I went directly to St. Giles's, where I preached before I went abroad two or three and fifty years ago.[96] And are they not passed as a watch in the night? My subject was, the 'joy in heaven over one sinner that repenteth'.[97] And truly God confirmed his word: many seemed to be partakers of that joy, and a solemn awe sat on the whole congregation.

Monday 30 and the ensuing days, I visited the classes. I was

---

[93] The Diary reveals that JW had frequently met the Brentford society or classes at Mr. Holbrook's house in recent years (Feb. 10, Nov. 11, 1784; Nov. 9, 1785; Feb. 26, 1786) and continued to do so (Feb. 7, Nov. 7, 1787; Feb. 17, 1791).

[94] Although there is no record in the Journal of JW's visiting the Duke of Marlborough's Oxfordshire palace at Blenheim, it was familiar to him from his Oxford days, and was often a standard of comparison with him. See Dec. 22, 1774 (22:440–41 in this edn.); Oct. 17, 1780.

[95] In recent years, JW had frequently enjoyed William Barker's hospitality at Lewisham (Diary, Feb. 14, 1783; Feb. 13, Nov. 12, 1784). The parish register records his burial on Oct. 31, 1786, at the age of fifty-six. J. T. Squire, ed., *The Registers of the Parish of Wandsworth, 1603–1787* (Lymington, 1889), p. 461.

[96] The Journal and published Diary record JW as having preached at St. Giles-in-the-Fields on Feb. 4, 1739 (19:34 in this edn.), but his reference here is so circumstantial as to favour the supposition that there was another occasion about 1734. St. Giles's began as the chapel of a leper hospital founded in 1101, and did not become a parish church until 1547, after the hospital had been dissolved by Henry VIII. In the seventeenth century, the building became ruinous and was replaced by a Gothic brick erection, 1623–30. This also became ruinous and was replaced, 1730–34, by a building in the tradition of Wren and Gibbs to a design by Flitcroft that was preferred to one by Hawksmoor. This building saw minor remodelling in the nineteenth century and superficial damage in the Second World War. Its present restored glory is overshadowed by Centre Point. Blatch, *Guide*, pp. 266–67. the rector, 1769–88, was John Smyth, A.M.

[97] Cf. Luke 15:7.

careful to take an exact account of the society. I was surprised to find only a hundred and fifty-nine.[98] I thought they had been double the number. I hope, by the assistance of God, within four months to see that none of these want either food or raiment.

Friday, November 3. Taking the advantage of a moonlight evening, I went down to the chapel in Rotherhithe.[99] I never saw it so well filled before, nor with such serious and attentive hearers. Is anything too hard for God? Shall *this* wilderness blossom and bud as the rose?

Sun. 5. I buried the remains of John Cowmeadow,[1] another martyr to loud and long preaching. To save his life, if possible, when he was half dead, I took him to travel with me. But it was too late. He revived a little, but soon relapsed, and after a few months, died in peace. He had the ornament of a meek and quiet spirit, and was of an exemplary behaviour.

Tue. 7. I visited the classes and found them much increased both in grace and number. The house was, as usual, well filled in the evening, and many were refreshed and comforted.

Thur. 9. In the evening, I preached at Stratford. And understanding I had 'many good sort of people' to deal with, I endeavoured to stir them up, by strongly showing what it is to 'build upon a rock',[2] after showing them the various ways whereby the generality of 'good men' (so called) usually 'build upon the sand'.[3]

Sun. 12. I preached morning and afternoon for the use of our little Charity School,[4] where forty boys and twenty girls are trained up both for this world and the world to come.

Mon. 13. I retired for a few days to Highbury Place,[5] that I

---

[98] The membership of the London societies was reported to the Conference of 1786 as 2,517, and was growing steadily. It is not quite clear why JW expected hard times, since at Michaelmas wheat prices had been at their lowest for a generation; but the Diary (Nov. 17, 24, 1786) shows that he appointed 'Fathers of the poor' to deal with the problem. See also Jan. 8, 1787.

[99] Orig. 'Redriff'.

[1] Atmore judges Cowmeadow somewhat less briskly than JW: 'He was a deeply pious young man, of an excellent spirit and unblameable in conversation. He was admitted on trial at the Conference in 1783, and as a preacher was acceptable and useful. He laboured in the vineyard, though with much weakness of body, till the year 1786, when the Lord removed him from his work and labour, and received him to his eternal reward.' *Memorial*, p. 89.

[2] Cf. Matt. 7:24.

[3] Cf. Matt. 7:26.

[4] This school had originally been run by Silas Told, the celebrated prison visitor, on whom see Nov. 13, 1748 (20:253, n. 89 in this edn.).

[5] The house of John Horton (for whom see above, Sept. 21, 1780), which, as the Diary shows, had very frequently provided a refuge for JW in recent years.

might go on in my work without interruption. I returned to town on Thursday 16 and, after preaching on 1 Tim. 6:20, had a comfortable meeting with the bands. Their shyness is vanished away, and we have only one inconvenience: we have not time to hear all those that are willing to speak.[6]

Sun. 26. After officiating at West Street morning and afternoon, I took coach at seven in the evening. We had a clear, pleasant night and reached Norwich about eleven on Monday the 27th. I found all things in peace through the zeal and prudence of Jasper Robinson[7] and his fellow labourers. The congregation in the evening was nearly as large as it usually is on Sunday, and more than twice as large at six in the morning as it is accustomed to be. Tuesday 28 about noon, I preached at Caistor[-on-Sea],[8] a little town twenty miles east of Norwich, to a little serious congregation; the greater part of them seemed to be ripe for a blessing. The house at [Great] Yarmouth was thoroughly filled in the evening, and many attended in the morning likewise. Once more the combatants here have laid down their arms[9] and solemnly promise to continue in peace and love.

Wednesday and Thursday I spent comfortably at Lowestoft among a quiet, loving people. Friday, December 1, I took a solemn leave of them at six. At nine, I preached at North Cove with much enlargement of spirit, and, about eleven, at Beccles to more than their preaching-house could contain. And all of them appeared as serious and attentive as the congregation at [Great] Yarmouth. In the evening, there seemed to be a considerable shaking even among the dry bones at Loddon,[10] and such a com-

[6] On the advantages and disadvantages of religious articulateness, see above, Feb. 6, 1785, and references there given.

[7] Jasper Robinson (1727-97), Superintendent of the Norwich circuit 1786-88. Born near High Wycombe, he became spiritually concerned in 1759 at Liverpool and, moving to Leeds in 1760, was converted and joined the Methodists. By 1763, he claimed full salvation and became very active as a class-leader, local preacher, and visitor of the sick and poor. In 1776, he became an itinerant, and, though it is said that 'his ministerial activities were not great.' he so attached himself by honest effort to his flock that an eyewitness of his funeral declared that he had not seen so many tears shed since the funeral of JW himself; Atmore, *Memorial*, pp. 375-76; *Methodist Magazine* 21 (1798):231-34. On the recent troubles at Norwich, which he helped to calm, see above, Oct. 22, 1785.

[8] Orig. 'Cayster'. Caistor-on-Sea was a modest union of two parishes east of Norwich. JW gives this topographical direction to distinguish it from Caistor St. Edmund, 3 miles south of Norwich.

[9] On the strife among Yarmouth Methodists, see Jan. 20, 1761 (21:300-301 in this edn.), Oct. 23, 1781, Oct. 22, 1783.

[10] Sufficient, indeed, at this time to bring about a change in the convictions of a convinced Calvinist, Mrs. Lydia Flagg (1753-1826). *Wesleyan Methodist Magazine* 49 (1826):861.

pany attended at Mr. Crisp's[11] in the morning as I never saw there before.

Sat. 2. I returned to Harwich and was much pleased in the evening with the largeness and seriousness of the congregation.
Sunday 3, I administered the Lord's Supper at eight, and afterwards attended our parish church. Besides the little company that went with me, and the clerk and minister, I think we had five men and six women. And this is a Christian country.

Our house could in no wise contain the congregation, either in the afternoon or in the evening. And at both times, great was the power of God in the midst of them. I have not seen for many years such a prospect of doing good in this city.

Mon. 4. I was strongly importuned by our friends at Long Stratton[12] to give them a sermon there. I heard of a young woman in that country who had uncommon fits, and of one that had lately preached, but I did not know that it was one and the same person. I found her in the very house to which I went, and went and talked with her at large. I was surprised: Sarah Mallet,[13] two or three and twenty years old, is of the same size that Jane Cooper[14] was and is, I think, full as much devoted to God and of as strong an understanding. But she is not likely to live, having a species of consumption which I believe is never cured. Of the following relation which she gave me, there are numberless witnesses.

Some years since, it was strongly impressed upon her, that she ought to call sinners to repentance. This impression she vehemently resisted, believing herself quite unqualified both by her sin and her ignorance, till it was suggested, 'If you do it not willingly, you shall do it whether you will or no.' She fell into a fit

[11] On occasion, the Loddon society dined with Mr. Crisp. *Arminian Magazine* 11 (1788):132.

[12] Long Stratton was a modest parish 10 miles south of Norwich and situated on the road from Norwich to London via Ipswich, which had been turnpiked in 1769. Albert, *Turnpike Road System*, p. 55.

[13] Sarah Mallet (b. 1768), one of the succession of early women preachers in the Norwich area, came to live with her uncle William Mallet at Long Stratton in 1780, and lived with him at intervals thereafter till she married a local preacher, William Boyce. Soon after her first arrival, she was converted and began to talk and preach in frequent fits. JW took to her and, understanding some of the difficulties she encountered as a self-supporting evangelist, wrote frequently with offers of spiritual counsel, money, and books. *Arminian Magazine* 11 (1788):91–93, 130–33, 185–88, 238–42; Telford, 8:15, 43, 77, 108, 118, 160, 190, 228, 250; *Methodist Recorder* (Winter No., 1895), p. 66.

[14] For Jane Cooper, a model of Christian perfection, see Nov. 19, 1762 (21:398, n. 23 in this edn.).

and, while utterly senseless, thought she was in the preaching house at Lowestoft, where she prayed and preached for near an hour to a numerous congregation. She then opened her eyes and recovered her senses. In a year or two, she had eighteen of these fits, in every one of which she imagined herself to be preaching in one or another congregation. She then cried out, 'Lord, I *will* obey thee, I *will* call sinners to repentance.' She has done so occasionally from that time. And her fits returned no more.

I preached, at one, to as many as the house could contain, of people that seemed ready prepared for the Lord. In the evening, the hearts of the whole congregation at Norwich seemed to be bowed as the heart of one man. I scarce ever saw them so moved. Surely God will revive his work in this place, and we shall not always find it so cold and comfortless as it has long been.

Tue. 5. In the afternoon, I took coach again, and returned to London at eight on Wednesday morning. All the time I could save to the end of the week, I spent in transcribing the society, a dull but necessary work which I have taken upon myself once a year for near these fifty years.

Wed. 13. I retired to Peckham where, the next evening, I preached to as many as the house would well contain and found much liberty of spirit in enforcing upon them the glorying only in the cross of Christ. Saturday 16, I returned to London.

Sun. 17. We had (as usual) a very solemn and comfortable season at Spitalfields. Wednesday 20, I retired to Highbury Place. But how changed! Where are the three amiable sisters? One is returned to her father, one deprived of her reason, and one in Abraham's bosom![15]

Sat. 23. By great importunity, I was induced (having little hope of doing good) to visit two of the felons in Newgate who lay under sentence of death. They appeared serious, but I can lay little stress on appearance of this kind. However, I wrote in their behalf to a great man. And perhaps it was in consequence of this that they had a reprieve.[16]

---

[15] The reference here is to the three Durbin sisters. Alice Durbin (1757-1834), Henry Durbin's youngest daughter, returned to her father in Bristol, where both later died; *WHS* 7 (1909):16. In 1790, John Valton prayed for the second 'Miss Durbin who has long been deranged in her faculties'; *WHS* 8 (1912):117. Mary Durbin, who married John Horton of Highbury Place, had died on May 16, 1786. John Horton also lost two new-born sons in 1782 and 1784. *WHS* 3 (1901):24.

[16] At this Old Bailey sessions, 23 received sentences of death and 52 of transportation. Of those sentenced to death at the previous sessions, 7 were granted a royal reprieve on condition of transportation. *Gentleman's Magazine* 56 (1786):1089.

Sun. 24. I was desired to preach at the Old Jewry.[17] But the church was cold, and so was the congregation. We had a congregation of another kind the next dayArt, Christmas Day, at four in the morning, as well as five in the evening, at the New Chapel, and at West Street Chapel about noon.

Sun. 31. From those words of Isaiah to Hezekiah, 'Set thy house in order,'[18] I strongly exhorted all who had not done it already to settle their temporal affairs without delay. 'Tis a strange madness which still possesses many that are in other respects men of understanding, who put this off from day to day, till death comes in an hour when they looked not for it.

---

[17] This was a Presbyterian meeting-house, built *c.* 1701 for a congregation originally gathered during the Restoration period by Edmund Calamy. Though now in decline, it was reckoned 'among the most respectable of the Presbyterian denomination'. The minister was Abraham Rees D.D. Wilson, *Dissenting Churches*, 2:304.

[18] Cf. Isa. 38:1 (Diary cites Isa. 38:5); see also 2 Kgs. 20:1.

APPENDIX

MANUSCRIPT DIARIES

EDITORIAL NOTE

These volumes are intended primarily to reproduce the public documents which Wesley himself prepared and published, such as his Journal. The private diary entries which lie behind the published material in this volume, however, are presented in this appendix.

A description of Wesley's diaries, a glossary of terms used therein, and the styling principles in this edition are found in the editorial introduction to the early diaries in volume 18 of this edition (pp. 302–310). As an example of the principles of transliteration followed by the editor, Wesley's use of 'p' in his MS has been rendered as 'prayed'; 'pr' as 'prayer'; 'pp' as 'read Prayers', each having a different sense (see Glossary, 18:308-9). One of JW's typical symbols, evident from his earliest diaries, is translated as 'sins'. His occasional use of a number in parenthesis after a sermon text reference may indicate that he was using more than one version of a sermon on that text.

The original holograph consists primarily of shorthand and abbreviated long-hand entries, which are here transliterated and/or expanded silently. Question-able or conjectural readings are placed within square brackets; unknown read-ings are indicated by a long dash. Modern spelling is used for place-names.

The diary material in the appendixes of this and the following volume comes from two documents:

(a) John Wesley Diary, Dec. 1, 1782–Jan. 31, 1790, in the Methodist Archives, The John Rylands University Library of Manchester (J.W.III.10); on 260 numbered pages, with a list of four resolutions on front flyleaf and financial accounts for Dec. 1782–Apr. 1790 (reading from the back) on pp. 268–337, end-ing with the note, 'N.B. For upwards of eighty-six years I have kept my accounts exactly. I will not attempt it any longer, being satisfied with the con-tinual conviction that I save all I can and give all I can, that is, all I have. John Wesley, July 16, 1790.'

(b) John Wesley Diary, Feb 1, 1790–Feb. 24, 1791, in the Morley Collection, Wesley College, Bristol; on 39 sometimes numbered pages, with four resolu-tions on front flyleaf dated Feb. 25, 1790 (same as those of 1783 in previous vol-ume), and note at end: 'Here ends the diary of this man of God! He continued it to Thursday the 24 of February, 1791, and died on Wednesday morning fol-lowing, viz., the 2nd of March, 1791. O, that I might so follow him as he fol-lowed Christ! Amen, Lord! Henry Moore.'

The resolutions that Wesley entered at the beginning of each volume read as follows:

I resolve Deo Juvante,

1. To touch no woman, look at, think of none, sole pleasure[?] .
2. To dedicate an hour, morning and evening; no excuse, reason, or pretence.
3. To converse κατα θεόν [according to God]; no anger, no εὐτραπελία [coarse jesting].
4. To pray every hour, seriously, deliberately, fervently.

Appreciation is extended to the Methodist Archives and Wesley College for permission to reproduce these documents in this edition. I would also thank Wanda Willard Smith for her long-time assistance in trying to make sense of these materials, especially for her work on Wesley's Sermon Register and her expertize in British geography and place-names.

R.P.H.

DIARY

December 1, 1782–December 31, 1786

SUNDAY, DECEMBER 1, 1782. 4 Prayed; letters. 8 The preachers; necessary business. 8.30 Read Prayers, 2 Timothy 3:5! Communion. 1 At sister Burgess's, dinner, religious talk; prayer; visited; slept; writ notes. 3 The leaders; tea; prayed. 5 Hebrews 7:25! Society; supper; prayer. 9.15 In the coach.

MONDAY, DECEMBER 2. 6 Religious talk! 7 Tea, religious talk. 8 Chaise. [1]0.15 St Neots; letters. 1.30 Dinner, religious talk; prayer. 3 Journal; prayed. 4 Visited; tea, religious talk; prayer; prayed. 6 Mark 9:23(2)! 7 Letters; supper, religious talk. 9 Prayer. 9.30.

TUESDAY, DECEMBER 3. 4 Prayed; letters. 6 Mark 9:23(2); journal. 8 Tea, religious talk; journal. 10 Coach. 11 Buckden; journal; dinner. 1 Ephesians 2:8; journal. 4 Prayed; tea, religious talk. 6 Chaise; Huntingdon; Hebrews 4:7! chaise; Godmanchester; supper! prayer. 9.45.

WEDNESDAY, DECEMBER 4. 4 Prayed; journal. 6 1 Corinthians 12:31; tea; prayer. 8 Chaise; Buckden; chaise; *Henry, Earl of Moreland.* 12.30 Bedford; at Mr Hill's, necessary talk (religious); journal. 1.30 Dinner, religious talk. 2.30 Journal. 4 Tea, religious talk; prayed. 6 Ephesians 3:14, etc! journal; supper; prayer. 9.30.

THURSDAY, DECEMBER 5. 4 Prayed; journal. 6 Matthew 5:6! tea, religious talk. 8 Chaise; Biggleswade; tea; chaise. 10.30 Hinxworth; religious talk; Hebrews 9:27; dinner. 1.30 Chaise. 6.15 Luton. 6.30 Hebrews 12:14! journal; supper, religious talk; prayer. 9.30.

FRIDAY, DECEMBER 6. 5 Prayed. 6 John 6:26; journal; tea, religious talk. 8 Chaise. 2.15 At home, dinner, letters; prayed. 5 Letters; the Committee. 8 Supper; prayer; necessary business. 9.30.

SATURDAY, DECEMBER 7. 4 Prayed; letters; tea; prayer; letters. 12.15 Dinner, religious talk; prayer; letters. 3 Prayed. 4 Visited; at brother Soper's, tea, religious talk; prayed. 6 Read Prayers, John 6:28, Communion; coach; supper; [Roger] Penry, necessary business. 9.30.

SUNDAY, DECEMBER 8. 4 Prayed; letters; walked. 8.15 Chapel, read Prayers, Romans 15:4, 5, Communion; coach. 1 At Mr Dixon's, dinner, religious talk. 3 St John's, read Prayers, James 1:27. 5 Tea. 5.45 Necessary business; prayed; Society; letters; supper; prayer. 9.30.

MONDAY, DECEMBER 9. 4 Prayed; tea. 5 Diligence with brother Atlay and sister Hall. 11 Rochester; tea. 11.45 Diligence. 4.30 Canterbury; dinner, religious talk; tea. 6 Colossians 1:10! at brother Thornton's, supper, religious talk; prayer. 9 At sister Biss[aker]'s; prayer. 9.30.

432

TUESDAY, DECEMBER 10. 4 Prayed; Magazine. 7 1 Timothy 6:20; tea, necessary talk (religious). 9.15 Chaise; necessary business. 1 Dinner; prayer. 3 Journal; prayed. 5 Tea, religious talk; prayer; necessary business. 6.30 Ephesians 3:14, etc! Communion; at sister Simmond's. 8 Supper, religious talk; prayer. 9.30.

WEDNESDAY, DECEMBER 11. 4 Prayed; Hebrews 6:1; Magazine; tea; prayer; necessary talk (religious). 9.30 Chaise. 12 Canterbury; necessary business. 1 Dinner. 2.30 Journal; prayed. 5 Tea, religious talk; prayer. 6.30 Ephesians 3:14, etc! Communion; supper; prayer. 9.30.

THURSDAY, DECEMBER 12. 4 Prayed; journal. 6 John 6:28; tea, religious talk; prayer. 8 Diligence. 12 Chatham; journal. 1 Dinner, religious talk; journal. 2.30 Walked. 3.30 Journal; prayed; tea; prayer. 6 2 Timothy 3:5! Communion. 8 Journal; supper, religious talk; prayer. 9.30.

FRIDAY, DECEMBER 13. 4 2 Timothy 3:4; tea, religious talk; prayer. 7 Diligence. 12.30 At home; letters. 2 Dinner; prayer. 3 Letters. 4 Visited; tea; prayed; letters. 8 Supper; prayer; necessary business. 9.30.

SATURDAY, DECEMBER 14. 4 Prayed; journal. 8 Tea, religious talk; prayer; necessary business. 12.30 Dinner, religious talk; prayer. 1.30 Magazine; visited. 4 Prayed; tea; prayed. 6 Read Prayers; 1 Peter 2:9! Communion; Penry. 9.30.

SUNDAY, DECEMBER 15. 4 Prayed; letters. 8 Spitalfields. 9.30 Prayed; 2 Timothy 3:4! Communion; at brother Dewey's. 1 Dinner, necessary talk (religious). 2 Slept; prayed; the leaders; prayed; tea; prayed. 5 Read Prayers, Isaiah 26 *ult.* 6.30 Society! supper; prayer; letters. 9.30.

MONDAY, DECEMBER 16. 4 Prayed; 1 Peter 3:8; Select Society; necessary business. 8 At W. Marriott's, tea; prayer; writ Society. 1 Dinner, religious talk. 1.30 Writ Society. 5 Tea, religious talk; prayed; writ Society. 8 Prayer; supper; prayed. 9.30.

TUESDAY, DECEMBER 17. 4 Prayed; writ Society. 8 Prayer; tea. 9 Married G[eorge] Shadford and E. Bai——. 11 Writ Society. 1 Dinner; Society. 5 Tea, religious talk; prayed; Society. 8 Prayer; supper, religious talk. 9.30.

WEDNESDAY, DECEMBER 18. 4 Prayed; Society. 8 Prayer; tea, religious talk; Society. 1 Dinner, religious talk. 1.30 Society. 5 Tea, religious talk; prayed. 6.30 Society. 8 Supper, religious talk; prayer. 9.30.

THURSDAY, DECEMBER 19. 4 Prayed; writ Society. 7 Writ letters. 8 Prayer; tea, religious talk; letters. 10 Visited. 11 Letters. 1 Dinner, religious talk. 1.45 Letters; Society; letters. 4 Prayed. 5 Tea, religious talk; writ Society. 8.30 Supper. 9 Prayer. 9.30.

FRIDAY, DECEMBER 20. 4 Prayed; Case of Birstall. 8 Prayer; tea, religious talk; Case. 11 At home; necessary business. 12 The female [bands]; letters. 1.30 Prayer. 2.15 Dinner, religious talk; prayer. 3.30 Letters; Magazine. 4.30 Tea, religious talk; prayed. 6 Read. 7 Magazine; supper, religious talk. 8.30 2 Thessalonians 2:7! 9.30 Coffee. 10 Prayer! 12.

SATURDAY, DECEMBER 21. 6.30 Prayed; Magazine. 8 Prayer; tea, religious talk. 9 Writ letters; necessary talk (religious) to many. 12 Necessary business. 1 Dinner, necessary talk (religious); prayer. 2 Letters; tea, necessary talk (religious); prayed. 4 At Mr Maxfield's. 5 Communion; prayer! coach. 5.45 Snowsfields; prayed. 6 Read prayers, 1 John 1:9, Communion; coach. 7.45 Supper; Penry, necessary business. 9.30 Laid down, could not sleep. 10 Ill.

SUNDAY, DECEMBER 22. 4 Prayed; slept; Magazine. 8 Chapel. 9.30 Read Prayers, 2 Thessalonians 2:7! Communion. 1 At brother Clulow's, dinner, religious talk; prayer; slept. 3 The leaders. 3.30 Read Prayers, Acts 22:16. 4 Tea; Society; coach; Society; supper, religious talk; letters; prayer. 9.30.

MONDAY, DECEMBER 23. 4 Prayed; 1 John 1:1-4; Select Society; letters. 8 Tea, religious talk; prayer; Magazine; visited. 12 Select Society. 1.15 At sister Key's, dinner, religious talk; prayer; necessary business; at children['s meeting?]. 3.30 Magazine. 4.30 Tea, religious talk; prayer. 5.30 Prayed. 6.15 Read Prayers; 1 John 3:1-3! supper; at bands; Magazine. 9.30.

[TUESDAY, DECEMBER 24. No entry.]

Christmas Day [WEDNESDAY, DECEMBER 25]. 3.30 Dressed. 4 Prayer; John 3:16! 6 Magazine; tea; coach; Chapel, read Prayers, John 3:16, Communion. 12 Coach; at brother Butcher's, dinner; prayer. 3 Slept; prayed; tea. 5 Prayed; Ephesians 1:9. 6 Society; single women. 7.30 Supper, religious talk; prayer; Magazine. 9.30.

THURSDAY, DECEMBER 26. 4 Prayed; sermon. 8 Tea, religious talk; prayer. 9 Sermon; sins! 1 At L. Halton's, dinner; prayer. 2 Visited. 2.30 Letters; tea; prayed. 6.15 Acts 7:55! the bands! supper, religious talk; prayer. 9 Kempis. 9.30.

FRIDAY, DECEMBER 27. 4 Prayed; letters; sermon; Magazine. 2.30 At Mr Pilgrim's, dinner, religious talk; prayer. 3.30 Visited; buried sister Gant; tea, religious talk; prayed. 6.30 Read Prayers, Revelation 22:17! 8 Supper; prayer. 9.30.

SATURDAY, DECEMBER 28. 4 Prayed; letters. 8 Tea, religious talk; prayer; letters; Magazine. 1 At Mr Ford's, dinner, religious talk. 3 Visited some. 5 At Mr Prelt's, tea, religious talk; prayer; prayed. 6 Read Prayers, 1 John 5:19! Communion; Penry, supper, necessary business. 9.30.

SUNDAY, DECEMBER 29. 4 Prayed; letters. 8 The preachers; prayed. 9.30 Read Prayers, Isaiah 37:3! Communion; Highbury. 1.30 Dinner, religious talk; coach. 3 The leaders; prayed; buried Thomas Forfit; tea; prayed. 5 Read Prayers, Philippians 1:21! Society; band; Love-feast. 8 Supper, necessary talk (religious); prayer. 9.30.

MONDAY, DECEMBER 30. 4 Prayed; 1 John 1:4, Communion; Select Society. 7 Writ the bands. 7.30 At sister Cockerot's. 8 Tea, religious talk; prayer; letter. 9 Writ the bands. 10 The preachers; accounts, ultimate. 11 Walked; Chapel; Select Society; visited; walked. 1.30 At Mr Atwood's, dinner. 3 Prayer. 4.30 Tea, religious talk; prayed. 6.30 Read Prayers, Psalms 147:3! supper; the bands. 9.30.

[TUESDAY, DECEMBER 31.] 4 Prayed; 1 John 1:1-4; writ bands. 8 Tea, religious talk. 9.15 At home; the bands. 11 The preachers; the bands. 1.30 At John Folgham's, dinner, religious talk; prayer; visited many; tea, religious talk; prayer. 6 Prayed; the bands; supper. 8.30 Psalms 106:24; prayer. 12.30.

[Texts noted at bottom of page:] Isaiah 37:3; 2 Thessalonians 2:7; Psalms 106:24.

WEDNESDAY, JANUARY 1, 1783. 7 Prayed. 8 Tea, religious talk; prayer; the preachers; letters. 1 At brother Ball's, dinner, religious talk; prayer. 2.30 Visited many. 5 At sister Halton's, tea, necessary talk (religious); prayed. 6 Read Prayers, Revelation 21:5! Communion; visited. 8.15 Supper; prayer. 9.30.

THURSDAY, JANUARY 2. 4 Prayed; letters. 8 Tea, religious talk; prayer; the preachers. 10 Journal. 1 Dinner, religious talk; prayer; visited many. 3.45 Prayed; tea, religious talk; letters. 8 Supper, religious talk; prayer. 9.30.

FRIDAY, JANUARY 3. 4 Prayed; 1 John 1:4-7, Communion; texts. 9 The preachers. 10 Texts. 1 Walked. 2 At Charles', Mr Galway! dinner, necessary talk (religious); walked. 5 At brother Ferguson's, tea, religious talk; prayer. 6 Prayed; audit; supper; prayer. 9.30.

SATURDAY, JANUARY 4. 4 Prayed; writ notes. 8 Prayer; tea, religious talk; the preachers. 9.30 Magazine. 12 Visited. 1 At Mr Thornton's, dinner, religious talk. 2.30 Magazine; prayed. 5 At sister Bicc——n's, tea, religious talk; prayer. 6 Read Prayers, Romans 3:22! Communion; supper; Penry, necessary business. 9.30.

SUNDAY, JANUARY 5. 4 Prayed; letters; the preachers. 9.30 Read Prayers, Deuteronomy 29:11! Communion. 1 At brother Duf——'s. 1 Dinner, religious talk; slept; the leaders. 4 Tea; prayed. 5 The covenant. 8 Supper, religious talk; prayer. 9.30.

MONDAY, JANUARY 6. 4 Prayed; Heb. 8:10, Select Society; necessary business; tea; prayer; the preachers. 9.30 Walked; Highbury Place. 10.30 Writ notes; texts. 3 Dinner, religious talk. 4 Texts; prayed. 6 Tea, religious talk; texts. 9 Supper, religious talk; prayer. 10.

TUESDAY, JANUARY 7. 4 Prayed; writ sermon. 8.30 Tea, religious talk; prayed. 9.30 Sermon. 2 Garden. 2.30 Dinner, religious talk. 4 Texts. 5 Prayed. 6 Tea, religious talk; texts. 8.45 Supper, religious talk; prayer. 9.45.

WEDNESDAY, JANUARY 8. 4 Prayed; texts. 8.30 Tea, religious talk; prayer. 9.30 Texts. 12 Magazine. 2 Dinner, religious talk. 3 Letters; prayed. 5 Prayed. 6 Tea, religious talk. 7 Letters. 8 Supper; prayer; religious talk. 9.45.

THURSDAY, JANUARY 9. 4 Prayed; letters. 8 Tea, religious talk; prayer. 9.15 Coach. 10.15 At home; sorted letters. 1 Dinner. 2 Visited some. 3.30 Religious talk to Charles; tea; prayed. 6.30 Read Prayers, Romans 8:3, 4. 8 The bands; supper, religious talk. 9.30.

FRIDAY, JANUARY 10. 4 Prayed; letters. 7 Chaise with Charles and Sally. 12.30 Shoreham; necessary talk (religious). 1 Dinner, religious talk. 2 Letters. 4 Tea; writ letters; prayed. 6 Luke 20:35, etc. 7 Society; letters; supper, religious talk; prayer. 9.30.

SATURDAY, JANUARY 11. 4 Prayed; letters. 7 Revelation 21:6; tea. 8 Chaise. 1 At home; letters. 2 Dinner, religious talk. 3 Letters; visited. 4.30 Tea, religious talk; prayer; prayed; letters; supper. 8.15 Penry, necessary business. 9.30.

[Texts noted at bottom of page:] Psalms 62:2; Romans 16:17.

SUNDAY, JANUARY 12. 4 Prayed; letters; Chapel, read Prayers, Psalms 62:2! Communion; Magazine. 1.30 Dinner. 2 Slept; prayed. 3 The leaders. 3.30 Read Prayers, Romans 10:4, etc; Society; coach; Society. 7.30 Supper, religious talk; prayer. 9.30.

MONDAY, JANUARY 13. 4 Prayed; 1 John 1:5-7; Select Society; letters. 7.30 Tea, religious talk; prayer; the preachers. 9 Letters; Magazine. 11.30 Magazine. 12 Select Society. 1.30 At sister Turner's, dinner, religious talk; prayer; visited many. 5 Tea, religious talk; prayed. 6.15 Read Prayers, Romans 11:26; supper; the bands; Magazine. 9.30.

TUESDAY, JANUARY 14. 4 Prayed; 1 John 1:6-7; Magazine. 7.30 Tea, religious talk; walked. 9 The preachers. 10 Magazine. 1.15 At sister Shakespeare's, dinner, religious talk; prayer; visited. 3 Prayed; Magazine; tea; prayed. 6.30 Read Prayers, Romans 12:2; the bands; supper; prayer. 9.30.

WEDNESDAY, JANUARY 15. 4 Prayed; letters; tea; prayer; the preachers. 10 Magazine; visited. 2.15 At brother Wright's. 3 Dinner, religious talk; prayed. 4.30 Prayer; at brother Thornton's, tea, religious talk; prayer. 6 Read Prayers, Romans 13:10. 7.30 Coach; supper; prayer. 9.30.

THURSDAY, JANUARY 16. 4 Prayed; letters. 7.30 Prayer; tea; the preachers. 9 Letters; Magazine. 1 At brother Ferguson's [?], dinner, religious talk; prayer; visited. 3 Prayed. 4 Magazine; tea, religious talk; prayer. 6.30 Read Prayers, Psalms 84:1. 7 The bands; supper, necessary talk (religious); prayer. 9.30.

FRIDAY, JANUARY 17. 4 Prayed; sermon. 1 Visited some; walked. 2.30 At brother Cheesement's, dinner, religious talk; prayer. 4 Walked; coach. 5 At brother Clulow's, tea, religious talk; prayer. 6.30 Slept; prayed; supper. 8.30 Psalms 106:24; coffee; prayer. 12.30.

SATURDAY, JANUARY 18. 7 Prayed; walked. 8 At brother Pocock's, tea, religious talk; prayer; walked. 9.30 Pupil; necessary business; Magazine. 12 Visited. 1 At brother Hufflet's, dinner, religious talk; Magazine; prayer. 4 Visited; tea; prayed. 6 Read Prayers, Romans 16:17, Communion; supper; Penry, necessary business. 9.30.

SUNDAY, JANUARY 19. 4 Prayed; sermon; Spitalfields. 9.30 Read Prayers, Matthew 17:20, Communion; at Mr Mark's; dinner, religious talk. 2.30 Prayed; slept; read Prayers, 1 Corinthians 1:30; coach; tea. 6 St Swithin's, read Prayers, 1 Corinthians 1:24. 7.30 Supper, religious talk; prayer. 9.30.

MONDAY, JANUARY 20. 4 Prayed; 1 John 1 *ad fin.*; Select Society; Magazine. 7.30 Prayer; tea; pupil. 9.30 Magazine. 12 Select Society. 1.30 At sister Well's, dinner, religious talk; prayer. 2.30 Magazine; the leaders. 4 Prayed. 4.30 Tea, religious talk; prayed. 6.15 Read Prayers, 1 Corinthians 2:2; supper; the bands; Magazine. 9.30.

TUESDAY, JANUARY 21. 4 Prayed; 1 Corinthians 2:6! Magazine. 8 At home; tea; pupil. 9 Letters. 1 At brother Cory's, dinner, religious talk; prayer. 2.30 Letters; prayed. 4.30 Tea, religious talk; prayer. 5.30 Prayed. 6.15 Read Prayers, 1 Corinthians 3:8. 7.30 The bands; supper; prayer. 9.30.

[Text noted at bottom of page:] Matthew 17:20.

WEDNESDAY, JANUARY 22. 4 Prayed; sermon. 7.30 Prayer; tea; sermon. 1 At brother Willan's, dinner, religious talk; writ Society; prayer. 4.30 Walked. 5 Tea, religious talk; prayer. 6 Read Prayers, 1 Corinthians 4:2, Communion. 8 Supper, religious talk; prayer. 9.30.

THURSDAY, JANUARY 23. 4 Prayed; letters; prayer; tea; pupil. 10 Letters. 1 At brother Marsden's, dinner, religious talk; prayer. 2.30 Necessary business; Magazine. 4.30 At T. Scolic's, tea, religious talk; prayer. 5.30 Prayed. 6 Read Prayers, 1 Corinthians 5:10! the bands; supper; prayer. 9.30.

FRIDAY, JANUARY 24. Prayed; sermon. 8.30 Pupil; accounts. 12 Magazine; prayer. 2.30 At brother Para[more's ?]. 3 Dinner, religious talk; prayer; visited; prayed. 4.30 Tea, religious talk; prayer; prayed. 6 The Committee. 7.30 Supper; read. 8 Prayer. 9.30.

SATURDAY, JANUARY 25. 4 Prayed; letters; tea; prayer; pupil; letters. 1 At brother Butcher's, dinner, religious talk; prayer; prayed. 4 Visited; at sister Clementson's, tea, religious talk; prayer. 6 Read Prayers, Acts 26:28, Communion; supper; Penry, necessary business. 9.30.

SUNDAY, JANUARY 26. 4 Prayed; letters; Chapel; read Prayers, Romans 12:21! Communion; dinner; slept; prayed. 3 The leaders. 3.30 Read Prayers, 1

Corinthians 7:29, etc! tea; Society; coach; Society; supper. 7.30 Necessary talk (religious); prayer. 9.30.

MONDAY, JANUARY 27. 4 Prayed; 1 John 2:1-4; Select Society. 7 Writ notes. 7.30 Prayer; tea; pupil. 9.30 Coach. 10.30 Peckham, necessary talk (religious); writ notes. 1 Dinner, religious talk. 2 Sermon. 5 Tea, religious talk; prayed. 6 Sermon. 8 Supper, religious talk; prayer. 9.30.

TUESDAY, JANUARY 28. 4 Prayed; sermon. 7.30 Prayer; tea, religious talk; sermon. 12 Garden; sermon. 2 Dinner; sermon. 5 Tea, religious talk; prayed; sermon. 6 At sister Fuller's; Galatians 6:14! sermon. 8 Supper, religious talk; prayer. 9.30.

WEDNESDAY, JANUARY 29. 4 Prayed; Magazine. 8 Prayer; tea, religious talk. 9 Magazine. 12 Garden; Horne; Magazine. 2 Dinner, religious talk; Mrs Fuller. 3 Magazine; prayed. 5 Tea, religious talk. 8 Supper; prayer. 9.45.

THURSDAY, JANUARY 30. 4 Prayed; letters. 8 Tea, religious talk; prayer; Magazine. 12.15 Garden. 1 Dinner, religious talk. 2.45 Coach. 4.30 At home; tea; prayer; letters; prayed. 6.30 Read Prayers, 2 Samuel 2:34; the bands; supper; prayer. 9.30.

FRIDAY, JANUARY 31. 4 Prayed; prayed; journal; necessary talk (religious) to some; journal. 2.30 Dinner; prayer; journal. 5 Tea; prayer; prayed; journal. 8 Supper; read; prayer. 9.30.

SATURDAY, FEBRUARY 1. 4 Prayed; letters. 8 Tea; prayer; letters; necessary talk (religious) to many. 1 Dinner; prayer; necessary business. 3 Letter; prayed. 4.30 Walked; at brother Adam's, tea, religious talk; prayer. 6 Read Prayers, 1 Corinthians 13:13! Communion; supper. 8.15 Penry, necessary business. 9.30.

SUNDAY, FEBRUARY 2. 4 Prayed; letters. 8 The preachers. 9.30 Read Prayers, Matthew 8:26! Communion; at sister Burgess's. 1 Dinner, religious talk; prayer. 2.15 Slept; prayed; at Mr Maxfield's, tea; prayed. 5 Read Prayers, 1 Corinthians 13:1, etc. 6.30 Society. 7.30 Supper, necessary talk (religious). 9.30.

MONDAY, FEBRUARY 3. 4 Prayed; 1 John 2:5-10; Select Society; class; tea. 8 Class. 1 Dinner; class. 4.30 At brother Graham's, tea, religious talk; class. 6 Read Prayers, 1 Corinthians 13:9; Society. 8.15 Supper, religious talk; prayer. 9.30.

TUESDAY, FEBRUARY 4. 4 Prayed; letters. 6 Class; tea. 8 Class. 1 At brother Rance's, dinner, religious talk. 2 Class. 5 At brother Tedford's, tea; prayer. 6 Prayed. 6.30 Read Prayers, 1 Corinthians 16:13. 7 The leaders; supper; prayer. 9.30.

WEDNESDAY, FEBRUARY 5. 4 Prayed; letters. 6 Class; tea. 8 Class. 1 At brother Kemp's, dinner, religious talk. 2 Class. 5 Tea, religious talk; prayed. 6 Letters. 8 Supper, necessary talk (religious); prayer! necessary business. 9.30.

THURSDAY, FEBRUARY 6. 4 Prayed; letters. 6 Class; tea; class. 1 At sister Westry's, dinner. 2 Class. 5 Tea. 5.15 Coach. 6.15 At Charles's concert! coach. 9.45.

FRIDAY, FEBRUARY 7. 4 Prayed; letters. 6 Class; tea; class. 11 At Mr Parkinson's; class. 1 Dinner, religious talk. 2 Class; necessary talk (religious); class. 5 Tea; prayed. 6 The committee. 8 Supper, necessary talk (religious); read; prayer. 9.30.

SATURDAY, FEBRUARY 8. 4 Prayed; letters. 6.30 Walked. 7 At brother Trig's; class; tea, religious talk. 8 At the Chapel; class. 12 At brother Collinson's; class; walked! 1 Dinner, religious talk. 2 Class. 4.45 Tea, religious talk; visited! 6 Read Prayers, 2 Corinthians 4:18! 7 Society. 8.15 Supper; necessary business. 9.30.

SUNDAY, FEBRUARY 9. 4 Prayed; letters; the Chapel. 9.30 Read Prayers, Colossians 3:12, etc! Communion. 1 At Mr Key's, dinner, religious talk. 2 Slept; prayed. 3 The Leaders. 3.30 Read Prayers. 4 2 Corinthians 5:16, etc, Society; coach; Society. 7.30 Supper; read. 9 Prayer. 9.15.

[Text noted at bottom of page:] 2 Corinthians 4:18.

MONDAY, FEBRUARY 10. 4 Prayed; 1 John 2:12, etc; Select Society. 7 At brother Raw's, tea; class. 11 Chapel; letters; Select Society. 1 At brother Dobson's, dinner; visited. 2 Class. 5.30 Prayed; necessary talk (religious). 6.30 Read Prayers, 2 Corinthians 6:2! supper; the bands! 9.30.

TUESDAY, FEBRUARY 11. 4 Prayed; 1 John 2:12; class; tea; class. 1 At brother Bower's, dinner, necessary talk (religious). 2 Walked; at home; necessary business; walked; buried Sarah Clay! coach; Westminster. 5.30 Class; prayed. 6.30 2 Corinthians 4:18! coach; Chapel; supper; prayer. 9.30.

WEDNESDAY, FEBRUARY 12. 4 Prayed; letters; class; tea. 7 Class. 12.30 Letters. 2 At brother Barr's, dinner. 3.30 Coach. 5 At brother Strong's, tea, religious talk; prayed. 6 Colossians 3:12, etc! 7 Class; prayed; supper! prayer. 9.30.

THURSDAY, FEBRUARY 13. 4 Prayed; Ephesians 4:30! Magazine; visited; at brother Blackall's, tea, necessary talk (religious). 7.30 Coach; walked. 10 Letters. 12.15 Coach; at brother Langford's, dinner; letters. 4 Coach. 5.15 Wandsworth; tea, necessary talk (religious); prayed. 6 Isaiah 37:3; class; supper, religious talk; prayer. 9.30.

FRIDAY, FEBRUARY 14. 4 Prayed; Psalms 106:24; at Mr Barker's, tea; the children. 7 Coach. 8.30 At home; letters; the bands; coach. 12 Stratford; Isaiah 55:7. 1 Class; dinner; chaise. 5 Hadley, tea, 2 Corinthians 6:2! class; supper; prayer. 9.30.

SATURDAY, FEBRUARY 15. 4 Prayed; Magazine; tea; chaise. 8.15 At home; necessary business; writ the bands. 1 Dinner. 2 Letters; necessary talk (religious) to many; necessary business; at Mr Maxfield's; Jasper Jane, etc! 4 Letters; tea, religious talk; prayed. 7 Religious talk, supper; Penry, necessary business. 9.30.

SUNDAY, FEBRUARY 16. 4 Prayed; letters; Spitalfields. 9.30 Read Prayers, Mark 16:16! Communion; visited. 1.15 Dinner; prayer. 2.30 Slept; letter; the leaders; tea; prayed. 5 2 Timothy 4:7! 7 Society! necessary talk (religious) to many. 8 Supper, religious talk; prayer. 9.30.

MONDAY, FEBRUARY 17. 4 Prayed; 1 John 2:15, etc; Select Society; letter. 8.15 Tea, religious talk; prayer; letter. 10 Walked; visited. 12 Poplar; 2 Corinthians 6:2; class; dinner; walked. 3.30 At Mr Dornford's. 4 Letters. 5 Prayed; tea, religious talk. 6.30 At Dr Conyers's! 8 Supper, religious talk. 9.45 Prayers. 10.15.

TUESDAY, FEBRUARY 18. 4 Prayed; Magazine; letters. 8 Prayer; tea, religious talk; letters. 12 Visited. 1 At brother Stan——'s, dinner, religious talk. 2 Letters; prayed. 4 Class. 5 At brother Ock's, tea, religious talk; class. 6.30 Mark 16:16! at sister Purnell's, supper, religious talk; prayer. 9.30.

WEDNESDAY, FEBRUARY 19. 4 Prayed; Magazine. 7 Tea, religious talk; prayer. 8 Walked. 9 At sister Wright's, tea, necessary talk (religious). 10 Visited; chaise. 11.30 Barking; necessary talk (religious). 12 2 Corinthians 8:9! class; dinner. 2 Chaise. 5 Lambeth; letters; tea. 6.30 Romans 14:17! class; supper; prayer. 9.30.

THURSDAY, FEBRUARY 20. 4 Prayed; Psalms 106:24; letters. 7 The leaders; letters. 8 Tea, religious talk. 9 Coach. 2 Dorking; dinner, religious talk. 3.15 Walked! 5 Tea, religious talk; prayed. 6.15 Ephesians 5:14! Communion; prayed; supper; necessary talk (religious); prayer. 9.30.

FRIDAY, FEBRUARY 21. 4 Prayed; journal. 6 Psalms 106:24; class. 8 Tea, religious talk; prayer. 9 Coach with sister Sparrow, etc, religious talk; Magazine. 2.30 At sister Rankin's, dinner, necessary talk (religious). 3.30 Prayer; necessary business. 4 Letters; tea; prayed. 6 Quarterly Meeting; committee. 8 Supper, necessary talk (religious); prayer. 9.30.

SATURDAY, FEBRUARY 22. 4 Prayed; letters. 8 Tea, religious talk; at Thomas Oliver's; Magazine. 1.30 Dinner; visited sister Greenwood! 5 At sister Day's, tea, religious talk; prayer. 6 Read Prayers, Galatians 5:5, Communion; supper; Penry, necessary business. 9.30.

SUNDAY, FEBRUARY 23. 4 Prayed; letters; Chapel. 9.30 Read Prayers, Psalms 41:1, Communion; at brother Folgham's. 1.30 Dinner. 3 The leaders. 4 Read Prayers, Galatians 5:15, Society; coach; Society; supper; prayer. 9.30.

MONDAY, FEBRUARY 24. 4 Prayed; 1 John 2 *ad fin.*; writ notes; tea; letters. 10 Coach; at brother Cheesement's. 11 Religious talk. 2.15 Buried him. 3 At brother Walter's, dinner; letters; tea; prayed. 6.30 Read Prayers, Ephesians 1:6. 7 Supper; the bands; journal. 9.30.

TUESDAY, FEBRUARY 25. 4 Prayed; Ephesians 1:13; journal; visited. 7.30 Tea, religious talk; walked; letters. 1.30 Dinner, religious talk; letters. 3.30 Tea, necessary talk (religious)! letter; at brother Float's, tea, religious talk; prayer; prayed; religious talk. 6.30 Read Prayers, Revelation 21:1-5! the leaders; supper; prayer. 9.30.

WEDNESDAY, FEBRUARY 26. 4 Prayed; letters; prayer. 8 Tea, religious talk; letters. 1 Walked; visited. 2.30 At brother Rankin's, dinner, religious talk; prayer; visited. 5 At W. Garret's, tea, religious talk. 6 Read Prayers, Ecclesiastes 9:10! Communion, coach. 8.30 Supper, religious talk; prayer. 9.30.

THURSDAY, FEBRUARY 27. 4 Prayed; letter; Magazine. 8 Tea, religious talk. 9 Magazine. 2 At Mr Judd's, dinner, religious talk. 3.30 Prayed. 4 Buried Charles Greenwood; tea; prayed. 6.30 Read Prayers, Ephesians 4:30! 7.30 The bands; supper, religious talk; prayer. 9.30.

FRIDAY, FEBRUARY 28. 4 Prayed; Magazine. 1.30 Coach. 2 At Mr Wolff's, dinner, religious talk; visited; tea; chaise. 5 Stratford; Hebrews 9:27! coach; Plaistow; opened letters. 8 Supper, religious talk; prayer. 9.30.

[Text noted at bottom of page:] Ephesians 6:11.

SATURDAY, MARCH 1. 4 Prayed; letters. 8 Tea, religious talk; prayer. 9 Coach. 10 At home; necessary talk (religious); writ letters. 1.30 Dinner; letters. 3.30 Prayed; visited; tea, religious talk; prayer. 6 Read Prayers, Ephesians 6:11! Communion, supper; Penry, necessary business. 9.30.

[SUNDAY, MARCH 2.] 4 Prayed; letters; the preachers; prayed. 9.30 Read Prayers, Job 3:17! Communion; walked; at Mr Horton's. 2 Dinner. 3.30 The leaders; tea; prayed. 5 Read Prayers, 1 Corinthians 13:8! Society! supper, necessary talk (religious); prayer. 8 Friday Street; coach; necessary talk (religious); slept. 10.

MONDAY, MARCH 3. 6 Necessary talk (religious). 7.30 Newbury; tea. 8.30 Coach; necessary talk (religious). 3.30 Chippenham, dinner. 4 Coach. 6 Bath; at brother Sinclair's, tea, necessary talk (religious). 6.30 1 Corinthians 13:8. 7.15 At brother Symes's, supper, religious talk; prayer. 9.30.

TUESDAY, MARCH 4. Prayed; 1 John 2:12, 13; class; visited. 8 Tea, religious talk; prayer. 9 Class. 11 Trustees. 1 At brother Sinclair's, dinner, religious talk; visited. 2.15 Letters. 4.30 Tea, religious talk; prayer. 5.45 Prayed. 6.30 Read Prayers, Philippians 3:8! class. 8.30 Supper, religious talk; prayer. 10.

WEDNESDAY, MARCH 5. 4 Prayed; Philippians 3:9; class; the stewards! 8 Tea, religious talk; prayer; visited. 10.15 Letters. 1 Dinner; prayer. 3 Accounts; necessary business. 4 Prayed. 5 Tea, religious talk; prayed. 6.30 Read Prayers, Philippians 3:15! Communion. 8.30 Supper, religious talk; prayer. 10.15.

THURSDAY, MARCH 6. 4 Prayed; 1 John 2:15! writ notes. 7.30 At Miss Cave's, tea, necessary talk (religious); visited. 9 Coach. 12 At home; necessary business. 2 At Mr Durbin's, dinner, religious talk; prayer. 3 Magazine. 4 Prayed; prayer;

at sister Lewis's, tea, religious talk; prayer; prayed. 6.30 Job 3:17! the bands; at sister Johnson's.

[FRIDAY, MARCH 7.] 4 Prayed; letters. 8 Tea; Magazine. 12 The females. 1 Prayer. 2.15 At brother Green's, dinner; prayer. 3.30 Magazine; prayed. 5 Tea, religious talk; prayer. 6.30 2 Thessalonians 2:7! at sister Castlemen's. 8 Supper, religious talk; prayer. 9.30.

SATURDAY, MARCH 8. 4 Prayed; letters; Magazine. 8 At Sa[lly] James's, tea, religious talk; prayer. 9 Magazine. 1 At R. Lewis's, dinner, religious talk; letters; prayed. 5 Visited; at brother Collins's, tea, religious talk. 6 Philippians 3:8; necessary business; Penry; at Miss Johnson's, supper; prayer; necessary business. 9.30.

SUNDAY, MARCH 9. 4 Prayed; Magazine. 8 Tea, religious talk; meditation. 9.30 Read Prayers, Genesis 19:17! Communion; at brother Ewer's, dinner; prayer. 2.30 Slept. 3 Read Prayers, 2 Corinthians 6:2; tea; prayed. 5 2 Corinthians 6:1. 6 Society; necessary business; supper, religious talk; prayer. 9.30.

MONDAY, MARCH 10. 4 Prayed; Philippians 3:14! class. 8 Tea, religious talk; prayer. 9 Class. 1 Dinner, religious talk. 2 Class. 4.45 Tea, religious talk; visited; prayed. 6.30 2 Thessalonians 2:7! at sister Castleman's, supper; read; prayer. 9.30.

TUESDAY, MARCH 11. 4 Prayed; class; tea; class. 1 Dinner, religious talk. 2 Class. 5 Tea; visited some. 6.30 Read. 7 The leaders; the leaders; at sister Johnson's, supper, religious talk; prayer. 9.30.

[Text noted at bottom of page:] Genesis 19:17.

WEDNESDAY, MARCH 12. 4 Prayed; classes; the preachers! 8 At brother Capel's, tea, religious talk; letters. 10 Class. 1 At brother Hopkin's, dinner, religious talk. 2 Class. 4 Visited many; tea, religious talk. 6.30 Guinea Street, Hebrews 8:10! 8 At sister Castlemen's, supper, necessary talk (religious); prayer. 9.30.

THURSDAY, MARCH 13. 4 Prayed; writ notes. 8 Tea; visited some; read Miss Boone. 1 Visited some. 1.30 At brother Stock's, dinner, religious talk; prayer. 4 Coach; visited. 5 Brislington; tea, religious talk; prayed. 6.30 Ecclesiastes 9:10! read; prayer. 8 Supper, religious talk; prayer. 9.30.

FRIDAY, MARCH 14. 4 Prayed; writ Magazine. 8 Tea, religious talk; prayer. 9 Chaise. 10 Read notes. 12 Females. 1 Prayer. 2 At Mr Castleman's, dinner, religious talk; prayer. 4 Chaise; tea, religious talk. 5 At the School; accounts. 6 Prayed; letter; supper; necessary talk (religious). 8.30 Ill; 2 Corinthians 4:18; necessary business. 10.

SATURDAY, MARCH 15. 5.30 Prayed; the children; chaise. 8 At brother Gee's, tea, religious talk; prayer; visited; slept. 10 Letters. 1 At brother Powell's, dinner, religious talk; prayer. 2.30 Letters. 4 Prayed; at sister Lydiard's [orig., Lyddiat's], tea, religious talk; prayer. 6 1 Corinthians 7:35! Penry; at sister Johnson's, supper, religious talk; prayer; necessary business. 9.15.

SUNDAY, MARCH 16. 4 Prayed; letters. 8 Tea, religious talk; necessary business; prayed. 9.30 Read Prayers, John 3:7! Communion; ill. 1 At brother Bullen's, dinner, religious talk; prayer. 2 Slept. 3.30 Necessary talk (religious). 4 Tea; writ; ill; chaise; at sister Johnson's; Mr Dyer. 6 No bands.

MONDAY, MARCH 17. 6 Prayed; tea. 9.30 Walked; home; tea; chaise. 2.45 Stroud; dinner, necessary talk (religious); ill. 4.30 Prayed; tea, religious talk; prayed; tea; prayer; necessary talk (religious); tea, religious talk. 8.15 Supper, necessary talk (religious); prayer. 9.30.

TUESDAY, MARCH 18. 6 Prayed; writ notes; [?]; tea, mostly religious talk; slept. 12.15 Chaise. 1.30 New house. 2 Dinner, religious talk; slept. 4.30 Tea, religious talk; chaise. 7.30 Society! total eclipse. 8 Religious talk; prayer. 9.45.

WEDNESDAY, MARCH 19. 6 Dressed; prayed; tea, necessary talk (religious); necessary business; read. 1 dinner, religious talk; prayer; read Cowper's *Poems.* 4 Chaise. 5 Tea, religious talk; Cowper; supper; prayer. 9.30.

THURSDAY, MARCH 20. 4 Very ill. 7 Tea, religious talk. 9 Diary; read notes. 1.30 Dinner; read Cowper. 4 Chaise. 5 At Mr Freeby's, tea, religious talk; prayer; necessary talk (religious); necessary business; supper. 9 Prayer. 9.30.

FRIDAY, MARCH 21. 5.30 Well! necessary business; tea, religious talk; prayer. 7.15 Chaise. 9.15 Gloucester; the people; tea; prayer. 11.30 Chaise. 1.30 Tewkesbury; dinner, religious talk. 2.45 Chaise. 5 Worcester; tea, religious talk; prayed. 6 Read letters. prayed. 8 Tea; prayer; necessary business. 9.30.

SATURDAY, MARCH 22. 5 Prayed; necessary business; tea. 7 Society; visited! 8 Chaise. 10.30 Inn. 11 Chaise. 1.30 At Mr Holden's, necessary talk (religious). 2 Dinner, necessary talk (religious); writ notes; prayed; tea; writ notes. 8.15 Supper; prayer. 9.30.

SUNDAY, MARCH 23. Ill. 6 Prayed; letters. 8.15 Tea, religious talk; writ journal; writ Magazine. 12 Electrified. 1 At Mr Pai[n]'s, dinner, religious talk; prayer. 2.30 Writ Magazine; prayed. 5 Tea, religious talk. 7 Society! 8 Supper, religious talk; prayer. 9.30.

MONDAY, MARCH 24. 4 Prayed; read Stonhouse. 8.15 At John Andr[ew's?], tea, religious talk; prayer. 9.30 Stonhouse; sins! 1 At brother Barnard's, dinner, religious talk; prayer; necessary business. 3 Magazine; prayed; tea, religious talk; prayer. 6 Ephesians 4:30! many such [?]. 8 Supper, religious talk; prayer. 9.30.

TUESDAY, MARCH 25. Prayed; necessary business; tea; prayer. 6.30 Chaise. 8 Wednesbury; religious talk, tea; visited. 9 John 6:69! necessary business. 11 Chaise. 1.30 Hilton Hall; religious talk. 4 Dinner, religious talk to Miss Freeman! prayed; tea, religious talk; supper, religious talk. 11.

WEDNESDAY, MARCH 26. 5 Prayed; letters. 9 Tea, religious talk. 10 Writ Magazine. 11 Garden with Miss Freeman, necessary talk (religious). 12.30 Magazine.

2.30 Dinner, religious talk. 4.30 Letter; prayed; journal. 7.30 Tea, necessary talk (religious). 9 Supper, religious talk; prayer! 10.

THURSDAY, MARCH 27. 5 Prayed; journal. 6.30 Miss Freeman, religious talk! 7 Tea, religious talk; prayer! 8.30 Chaise. 2.15 Paisly [i.e., Fazeley]. 3 Dinner, religious talk. 3.15 Chaise. 5.30 Hinckley, tea; 1 Corinthians 1:23! necessary talk (religious). 7 Writ notes. 8 Supper, religious talk; prayer. 9.30.

FRIDAY, MARCH 28. 4 Prayed; Romans 12:1! journal. 2:15 Dinner, religious talk; Horne; prayed. 5 Tea, religious talk; prayed. 6 Isaiah 55:6! Society! supper, religious talk; prayer. 9.30.

SATURDAY, MARCH 29. 4 Prayed; Hebrews 12:14! Horne; letters. 8 Tea, religious talk; prayer; letters. 12 Walked. 1 Dinner, religious talk; prayer. 2 Horne; prayed. 5 Tea, religious talk; prayer. 6 John 4:24! 7 Horne. 7.45 Supper, religious talk; prayer. 9.30.

SUNDAY, MARCH 30. 4 Prayed; ill; journal. 8 Tea, religious talk. 8.30 Romans 3:23! journal. 11 Read Prayers. 12 Dinner, religious talk. 1 Journal. 3.30 Prayed; read Prayers; journal; tea; John 17:3! Horne. 7.30 Supper, religious talk; prayer. 9.30.

MONDAY, MARCH 31. 4 Prayed; Psalms 147:3! Horne. 7 Tea, religious talk; prayer. 8 Chaise. 11.15 Ashby-de-la-Zouch. 12 Journal. 12.30 Dinner; journal. 3 Love-feast. 4.30 Prayer; tea. 6 Joshua 24:15. 7 Journal. 8 Supper, religious talk; prayer. 9.30.

TUESDAY, APRIL 1. 4 Prayed; journal; tea. 8 Chaise; visited. 10.30 Castle Donington; necessary business. 11 Matthew 7:24! 12 Dinner, religious talk. 1 Chaise. 3.30 Nottingham; leaders. 5 Tea; prayed. 6 Letters; 1 Samuel 20:3! supper, religious talk; prayer. 9.30.

WEDNESDAY, APRIL 2. 4 Prayed; 1 Peter 2:1, etc; journal. 7.15 Tea, religious talk; journal. 11.30 Walked. 12.30 Journal. 1 Dinner, religious talk. 2 Journal. 4.30 Tea, religious talk; prayed. 6 Matthew 11:28, etc! journal. 8 Supper, religious talk; prayer. 9.30.

THURSDAY, APRIL 3. 4 Prayed; journal. 7.30 Tea, religious talk; prayer; journal. 10 Letters; visited. 12.30 Dinner; journal. 3 Texts; Dr Coke, necessary talk (religious); prayed. 4.30 Tea, religious talk; prayer. 6 Acts 9:31. 7 Society; journal. 8 Supper, religious talk; prayer. 9.30.

FRIDAY, APRIL 4. 4 Prayed; letters. 6 Journal. 11.30 Visited. 12.30 Dinner, religious talk; journal. 4 Prayed; tea, religious talk; prayed. 6 1 Corinthians 1:24! Society! writ journal. 8 Supper, necessary talk (religious); prayer. 9.30.

SATURDAY, APRIL 5. 4 Prayed; journal; letters. 7.30 Tea, religious talk; prayer; letters. 12 Walked. 1 At brother Plat's, dinner, religious talk. 2 Letters; journal.

4 Prayed; tea, religious talk; prayed. 6 Zechariah 4:6; journal. 7.30 Journal; necessary business; supper, religious talk; prayer. 9.30.

SUNDAY, APRIL 6. 4 Prayed; letters. 8 Tea, religious talk; letters. 10 Read Prayers, Hebrews 9:13! Communion! 1 At brother Woodward's, dinner; prayer. 2 Journal; prayed; tea. 5 Isaiah 55:6! Society. 7.30 Prayed; supper, religious talk; prayer. 9.30.

MONDAY, APRIL 7. 4 Prayed; Mark 1:15; journal; tea, religious talk; prayer. 8 Chaise, Stapleford, tea. 10 Hebrews 8:10! chaise. 12.30 Derby; letter. 1.30 Dinner, religious talk; letters. 4 Prayed; tea, religious talk. 6 Isaiah 5:4! Society; supper, religious talk; prayer. 9.30.

TUESDAY, APRIL 8. 4 Prayed; Matthew 5:6! necessary business; tea. 7 Chaise. 10 Uttoxeter; tea, necessary talk (religious). 11 Chaise; sins! 1.30 Lane End [Longton]; religious talk, dinner; prayer; chaise. 4.30 Newcastle; tea, religious talk; writ notes; prayer. 7 Luke 10:42! supper; prayed. 9.30.

WEDNESDAY, APRIL 9. 4 Prayed; Philippians 3:13! tea. 6.45 Chaise. 9.45 Nantwich; tea, religious talk; prayer. 10.30 Chaise. 12 Alpraham; dinner, necessary talk (religious); prayer. 1.30 Chaise. 4 Chester. 5 Necessary business; tea; prayed. 7 Matthew 22:27! Society; at brother Sellers's, supper, religious talk; prayer. 10.30.

THURSDAY, APRIL 10. 4 Prayed; chocolate. 5 Chaise; Holywell. 12 St Asaph; dinner; chaise; Conway; writ notes; prayed. 8 Supper, religious talk; prayer. 9.45.

FRIDAY, APRIL 11. 4 Prayed. 5 Chaise. 8 Bangor Ferry; tea; chaise. 11.30 Gwyndy [orig., 'Gwindew']; dinner. 1 Chaise. 3 Holyhead; tea; writ notes. 5.30 On the *Bestboran.* 8 Lay down.

SATURDAY, APRIL 12. 4 Slept; necessary talk; walked. 8 Tea; prayed; dozed; prayed; tea. 9 Slept.

SUNDAY, APRIL 13. 4.30 Dressed; religious talk. 6 In the boat. 7 Dunleary. 7.30 Walked. 9.30 At Mr Smith's. 10 Tea; necessary business. 11.30 Read Prayers, Communion. 2 Dinner, religious talk. 4 Prayed. 5 Tea, religious talk. 6 Matthew 26:50, etc, Society; supper, religious talk; prayer. 9.30.

MONDAY, APRIL 14. 4 Prayed; 1 John 1:1-3! writ sermon. 8 At sister Keene's, tea, religious talk; prayer. 9.30 Sermon. 11 Sat for my picture. 12 Walked. 2 Dinner, religious talk. 3 Letters. 4 Prayed; tea, religious talk; prayer. 6.30 1 John 1:4! supper, religious talk; prayer. 9.30.

TUESDAY, APRIL 15. 4 Prayed; 1 John 1:5, 6! necessary talk (religious); sermon. 7.30 Tea, religious talk; prayer; sermon. 11 Sat; visited. 2 At Arthur Keene's, dinner, religious talk; prayed; visited; Communion. 5 Tea, religious talk; prayer; prayed. 6.30 Colossians 1:10! the bands. 8.15 Supper, necessary talk (religious); prayer. 9.30.

WEDNESDAY, APRIL 16. 4 Prayed; 1 John 1:7! necessary talk (religious); sermon. 7.30 Tea, religious talk; prayer; sermon. 1 Walked. 2 Dinner, necessary talk (religious). 3.30 Read notes. 4.45 Prayed; tea, religious talk. 6.30 1 Timothy 6:9! the leaders. 8 Supper, religious talk; prayer. 9.30.

THURSDAY, APRIL 17. 4 Prayed; 1 John 1 *ult.*; sermon; letters. 7.30 Tea, religious talk; prayer; sermon. 11 Letters. 1 Walked. 2 Dinner, religious talk; prayer. 3.30 Prayed; visited. 5 Tea, religious talk; prayer; prayed. 6.30 Ephesians 3:14, etc! the single men. 8 Supper, religious talk; prayer. 9.30.

Good FRIDAY [APRIL 18]. 4 Prayed; sermon. 8.30 Genesis 22:1! sermon. 11 Read Prayers! 2.30 Dinner, religious talk. 4 Prayed. 4.45 Tea, religious talk; prayer. 5.30 1 Peter 2:1, etc; the Love-feast. 8.15 Supper, religious talk; prayer. 9.30.

SATURDAY, APRIL 19. 4 Prayed; 1 John 2:1, 2; letters. 7.30 Tea, religious talk; prayer. 8.30 Letters. 12.30 Collin's. 2 Dinner, religious talk; prayer. 4 Sat; tea, religious talk. 6 Romans 8:3, 4; necessary business; supper; prayer. 9.45.

Easter Day [APRIL 20]. 4 Prayed; letters; tea, religious talk; prayer. 8.30 1 Peter 1:3; sermon. 11 St Patrick's, read Prayers, Communion. 2.30 Dinner, religious talk; prayer. 3.30 Sermon; prayed; tea. 5.30 Romans 6:23. 7 Society; supper, religious talk; prayers. 9.30.

MONDAY, APRIL 21. 4 Prayed; sermon. 8 Tea, religious talk; prayer. 9 Sermon. 1 At Mr Skelton's, religious talk! 2 At brother Tate's, dinner, religious talk; prayer. 4.45 Tea, religious talk; prayer. 5.30 Prayed. 6.30 Luke 24:25. 7.30 Select Society! supper, religious talk; prayer. 9.30.

TUESDAY, APRIL 22. 4 Prayed; sermon. 8 Tea, religious talk; prayer. 9 Writ notes. 12 Walked; writ notes. 2.15 Dinner, necessary talk (religious). 4 Prayer! 4.45 Visited. 5 At home; Mr Hales, etc! tea, necessary talk (religious). 6 Prayed. 6.30 Colossians 3:1, etc. 7.30 The bands! supper, religious talk; prayer. 9.30.

WEDNESDAY, APRIL 23. 4 Prayed; 1 John 2:3-12; writ notes. 8.30 At Mr Hales's, tea, necessary talk (religious). 10 Texts. 1 Walked. 2 At Mr Dolier's, dinner, religious talk. 4 Prayer! tea, religious talk; prayer. 6 Prayed. 6.30 1 John 5:20! the leaders; supper, religious talk; prayer. 9.30.

THURSDAY, APRIL 24. 4 Prayed; 1 John 2:13, etc; writ journal. 7.30 Tea, religious talk; prayer; journal. 12.30 Walked. 2.30 Dinner, religious talk. 3.45 Journal; prayed. 5.15 Tea; prayer. 6.30 2 John 8! letters. 8.15 Supper. 9 Prayer. 9.30.

FRIDAY, APRIL 25. 4 Prayed; letters. 10 Mr Skelton, necessary talk (religious). 11.15 Necessary talk (religious) to many. 12 Walked. 1 Prayer. 2 Dinner, religious talk. 4 Prayed; tea; at Mrs Glass's! 6 Prayed; Isaiah 59:1, 2; the singers. 8.30 Supper, religious talk; prayer. 9.30.

SATURDAY, APRIL 26. 4 Prayed; letters. 8 Tea, mostly religious talk; prayer. 9.15 Letters. 1.15 Walked. 2 At Mrs Car[r]'s, dinner, religious talk; prayer. 3.30 Visited; sat; at brother Cook's, tea, religious talk. 6.30 Daniel 9:24! prayed; necessary business. 8.15 Supper, religious talk; prayer. 9.45.

SUNDAY, APRIL 27. 4 Prayed; journal; tea; prayer. 8.30 1 Peter 2:9! journal. 11 Read Prayers, Communion. 2 Dinner, religious talk; prayer. 4 Prayed; tea. 6.30 1 John 5:11! Society; at Lady [Arabella] Denny's. 7.30 Tea, religious talk; at home; supper, religious talk; prayer. 9.45.

MONDAY, APRIL 28. 4 Prayed; 1 John 2 *ad fin.*; necessary talk! 8 Tea, religious talk; prayer. 9.30 Necessary talk (religious) to many. 10 Read notes. 11 Necessary talk (religious). 12 Visited! 2.30 At brother Hall's, dinner, religious talk; prayer; visited! tea, religious talk; prayer. 6.30 Zechariah 4:6! married persons; supper, religious talk; prayer. 9.30.

TUESDAY, APRIL 29. 4 Prayed; writ for Conference. 6 Conference. 8 Tea, religious talk. 9 Conference. 1.15 Necessary business. 2 At brother Keene's, dinner, religious talk. 3 Conference. 5 Tea, religious talk; prayer; prayed. 6.30 Jeremiah 6:16! the bands! 8 Supper, religious talk; prayer. 9.30.

WEDNESDAY, APRIL 30. 4 Prayed; writ Conference. 6 Conference. 8 Tea, religious talk; prayer. 9 Conference. 1 Necessary business; walked. 2 At sister Keene's, tea, religious talk; prayer. 3 Conference. 4.30 Tea, religious talk; prayer; visited. 6 Prayed. 6.30 Isaiah 5:4! the leaders. 8.15 Supper, religious talk; prayer. 9.30.

THURSDAY, MAY 1. 4 Prayed; writ for Conference. 6 Conference. 8 Tea, religious talk; necessary business. 9 Conference. 1 Necessary talk (religious); necessary business. 2.30 Dinner, religious talk. 3.30 Conference. 5 Tea; writ; prayed. 6.30 Hebrews 6:1; Select Society; supper; prayer. 9.30.

FRIDAY, MAY 2. 4 Prayed; John 6:28! Conference; Communion. 8 Letters. 1 Prayer. 2.15 At Mrs Pearse's. 3 Dinner, religious talk; prayer. 4 Prayed; tea, religious talk; prayer. 5.30 Tea, religious talk; prayer. 6.30 Deuteronomy 29:10. 8 The singers; supper, mostly religious talk; prayer. 9.30.

SATURDAY, MAY 3. 4 Prayed; letters; tea; prayer; letters. 10 Coach; Rathcormack! coach. 2.15 Dinner. 3.30 Visited! walked. 5.30 Tea, religious talk; prayer. 6.30 Proverbs 3:17; visited. 8.30 Supper, religious talk; prayer; necessary business. 10.

SUNDAY, MAY 4. 4.45 Prayed; journal; tea. 8.30 Matthew 7:16! journal. 11 St Patrick's [Dublin], read Prayers, ordination. 2.45 Dinner; visited; tea. 5.30 Numbers 23:10! the Covenant. 8.30 Supper, religious talk; prayer. 9.45.

MONDAY, MAY 5. 4 Prayed; Acts 22:16(2); necessary talk (religious); tunes. 8 Tea, religious talk; prayer; tunes. 1 Walked. 2.15 Dinner, religious talk; prayer. 4 Prayed; visited. 5 Prayed; tea, religious talk; prayer; prayed. 6.30 Ecclesiastes 7:29! tunes; supper, religious talk; prayer. 9.30.

TUESDAY, MAY 6. 4 Prayed; 1 Corinthians 13:8, etc; tunes. 7.45 Tea, religious talk; prayer; tunes. 10 Coach. 11.30 Blackrock; coach. 2 Tunes. 2.30 Dinner, religious talk. 4 Visited. 5 Tea, religious talk; prayer. 6.30 Colossians 3:11! the bands! supper, religious talk; prayer. 9.30.

WEDNESDAY, MAY 7. 4 Prayed. 1 Corinthians 15:58! letters. 8 Tea, religious talk; prayer. 9 Letters; necessary talk (religious) to some. 12.30 Coach. 1 Canal basin! 2 At sister Keene's, dinner, religious talk. 4 Visited; prayed; tea. 6.30 Matthew 7:26! the leaders. 8 Supper, religious talk; prayer. 9.30.

THURSDAY, MAY 8. 1 Tea; prayer; coach. 2.30 In the boat. 4 In the ship. 5 Sailed; Captain Cook. 6.30 Tea; Cook. 12 Dinner; Cook. 5.30 Holyhead; necessary business. 7 Coach. 9 Gwyndy; supper. 10.30.

FRIDAY, MAY 9. 3.30 Necessary business. 4 Coach; prayed; Survey of Ireland. 10 Conway; tea; boat. 11 Coach; Survey; necessary talk (religious). 9 Chester, at Miss Beddish's, supper, religious talk; prayer. 10.45.

SATURDAY, MAY 10. 5 Prayed; letters. 8 Tea, religious talk; prayer; letters. 1 Dinner, religious talk; prayer. 2 Letters; read notes. 3 Journal. 3.30 Walked. 4.30 Tea, religious talk; prayer; prayed. 6.45 Psalms 146:4! read; supper; prayer. 9.45.

SUNDAY, MAY 11. 4 Prayed; journal. 7 Philippians 3:13; tea, religious talk; prayer. 9.30 Writ sermon. 10.30 Read Prayers, necessary talk (religious). 1 At brother Walker's, dinner, religious talk; prayer. 2.30 Sermon; necessary talk (religious). 4 Prayed; visited; tea, religious talk. 5 Ezekiel 37:1, etc, Communion. 7.30 Prayed; supper, religious talk; prayer. 9.30.

MONDAY, MAY 12. 4 Prayed; Galatians 5:1! T. Be[ddis]h, etc, necessary talk; prayer. 6 Tea, religious talk; prayer; sermon. 12 Visited. 1 At Mr Gardiner's, dinner, religious talk; prayer. 2.30 Necessary talk (religious) to many; writ notes. 4.30 Prayed. 5 Tea, mostly religious talk. 6.30 Isaiah 59:1; Society; necessary business; supper, religious talk; prayer. 9.30.

TUESDAY, MAY 13. 4.15 Necessary business; prayed; tea. 5 Walked. 8 Pres-ton; Romans 3:23. 9.15 Chaise; Watson. 11 Warrington; read. 12 Jeremiah 8:20! 2 Chaise. 5 Liverpool; tea, religious talk; prayed. 6.30 Matthew 11:4; supper; prayer. 9.30.

WEDNESDAY, MAY 14. 4 Prayed; Acts 22:16(2); sermon. 8 Tea, religious talk; prayer; sermon; necessary talk (religious) to some. 12 Visited. 1 Dinner, religious talk. 2 Prayer. 2.30 Sermon; prayed. 4.15 Visited some. 5 Tea, religious talk; prayer; necessary talk (religious) to some. 6.30 Isaiah 38:5. 7.30 Society; supper; necessary talk (religious); prayer. 9.30.

THURSDAY, MAY 15. 4 Prayed; Isaiah 57:1, 2; necessary talk (religious) to many. 7 Tea. 7.30 Chaise; Arthur Young. 12 Wigan; Hebrews 9:27! at brother

Layland's, dinner, religious talk; prayer. 3 Chaise. 5 Bolton; tea, religious talk; prayed. 6 Daniel 9:24! Society; supper, religious talk; prayer. 9.15.

FRIDAY, MAY 16. 4 Prayed; Psalms 45:13; tunes. 8 Sermon. 11 Tunes; sins! walked. 1 At sister Thwaite's, dinner; the leaders; christened. 3 Tunes; tea; prayed. 6 Matthew 7:16; Society; tunes; supper, religious talk; prayer; necessary business. 9.30.

SATURDAY, MAY 17. 4 Prayed; Matthew 5:47! letters. 8 Tea, religious talk; prayer. 9.15 Chaise. 11.30 Manchester. 12 Sermon; letters. 1 Dinner, necessary talk (religious). 2 Letters; necessary talk (religious) to many. 4 Prayed; tea, religious talk; necessary talk (religious). 6.15 Luke 8:18; necessary business; supper; prayer. 9.30.

SUNDAY, MAY 18. 4 Prayed; sermon. 8 Tea, religious talk; prayer. 9.30 Read Prayers, Matthew 16:23! Communion. 1 Dinner. 2 Slept; sermon. 3 Prayed. 4 Tea, religious talk; prayed. 5.15 1 Corinthians 1:30! Society! necessary talk (religious) to many. 8 Supper, religious talk; prayer. 9.30.

MONDAY, MAY 19. 4 Prayed; Galatians 5:5; necessary talk (religious) to many; letters. 8 Tea, religious talk; prayer. 9 Letters. 12.30 Walked. 1 At brother Brierley's, dinner, religious talk; prayer. 2 Visited many. 5 Tea, religious talk; prayed. 6 Genesis 22:1, 2! Love-feast! necessary talk (religious); supper; prayer. 9.30.

TUESDAY, MAY 20. 4 Prayed; 2 John 8! Select Society! necessary talk (religious) to many. 8 Tea, religious talk; prayer; necessary business; prayer. 10 Chaise; Stockport; sermon. 12 Hebrews 2:3! walked. 1.30 At brother Moore's, dinner, religious talk. 3 Chaise. 5 Macclesfield; at sister Ryle's, tea, religious talk. 6 Read Prayers, 1 Corinthians 3:11, etc. 7.30 Society. 8 Supper, religious talk; prayer. 9.30.

WEDNESDAY, MAY 21. 4 Prayed; 1 Corinthians 3:8! necessary talk (religious). 7 Letters; read notes. 8 Tea, religious talk; prayer. 9 Journal. 12 Walked. 1 Dinner, religious talk. 2.30 Slept; read. 3 Prayed. 4 With E[lizabeth] R[itchie?], etc, religious talk; prayer. 5 Tea, religious talk; christened; prayer. 6 Mark 1:15(2)! Love-feast! sermon; supper, religious talk. 9 Prayer. 9.30.

THURSDAY, MAY 22. 4 Prayed; Romans 15:2! Select Society; sermon. 8 Tea, religious talk; prayer. 9 Sermon; necessary talk (religious) to many. 12 Visited some! 1 Dinner, religious talk; prayer; sermon. 4 Prayed. 5 Tea, religious talk; prayer. 6 Read Prayers, Ezekiel 37. 7.30 Society; supper, religious talk; prayer. 9.30.

FRIDAY, MAY 23. 4 Prayed; 1 Corinthians 15:58; tea. 6.30 Chaise. 9 Leek; tea, religious talk. 9.30 2 Corinthians 6:1. 10.30 Chaise. 1 Ashbourne; dinner. 2 Chaise. 4.15 Derby; necessary business. 5 Tea, religious talk; prayer. 6 Colossians 1:10! Society! supper, religious talk; prayer. 9.30.

SATURDAY, MAY 24. 2 Prayed; tea, religious talk. 3 Chaise; with Rachel Norton, religious talk. 8.15 Buxton; tea. 9 Married Mr Bailey and Rachel Norton; read Prayers, Isaiah 55:6! necessary business; necessary talk (religious). 11 Chaise; read Dillom. 3.30 Dinner; chaise. 7.30 Nottingham. 8 Necessary business; supper, religious talk; necessary business. 9.30.

SUNDAY, MAY 25. 4 Prayed; letters. 8.30 Tea, religious talk; meditation. 10 Read Prayers, John 16:31! Communion; visited. 1 Dinner, religious talk. 2 Slept; read sermon; prayed. 4 Tea, religious talk; journal. 5 James 1:27! Society. 7 Journal. 8 Supper, religious talk; prayer. 9.30.

MONDAY, MAY 26. 4 Prayed; Luke 8:18; letters. 8 Tea, religious talk; prayer. 9 Letters. 12 Dinner, religious talk. 1 Sermon. 3 Prayed; read. 4 Visited; Communion. 5 At brother Woodward's, tea, religious talk; prayer. 6.30 Mark 3:35; the leaders; visited; supper, religious talk; prayer. 9.30.

TUESDAY, MAY 27. 4 Prayed; Magazine; tea; prayer. 6.15 Chaise; with Mr Brackenbury; Loughborough. 9 Tea; Joshua 24:15! Chaise. 11 Mountsorrel; Magazine. 12 Luke 10:42! dinner; chaise; Leicester; necessary talk (religious); tea; prayed. 6.30 Ephesians 4:30! Society. 8 Supper; prayer. 9.30.

WEDNESDAY, MAY 28. 4 Prayed; 1 Corinthians 13:13; tea; chaise. 9 Welford; tea, religious talk. 10 Chaise. 1.30 Northampton; dinner, religious talk. 2.30 At sister Philips's, necessary talk (religious); tea, religious talk. 6.30 2 Corinthians 13:5, Society; supper, religious talk; prayer. 9.30.

THURSDAY, MAY 29. 3 Prayed; tea, religious talk. 4.15 Chaise; Dillom. 7 At brother Angrave, tea; prayer. 8 Chaise. 11 Bedford, necessary talk (religious). 12 2 Timothy 3:5! dinner, religious talk. 2.30 Miss Harvey. 3 Chaise. 5.15 Hinxworth; tea, religious talk; prayed; Proverbs 3:17; supper; prayer. 9.30.

FRIDAY, MAY 30. 3.30 Prayed; tea; read. 5 Chaise; Welwyn [orig., 'Welling']; tea, religious talk. 9 Chaise. 12 Barnet; Charles ate dinner. 2 Coach. 4.30 At home; tea; visited; necessary business; letters; supper; prayer. 9.30.

SATURDAY, MAY 31. 4 Prayed; letters. 8 At brother Rankin's, tea; prayer; letters. 1 Dinner, religious talk; letters; Magazine. 5 Tea, religious talk; letters; prayed. 7.45 Supper; Penry, necessary business. 9.30.

[Text noted at bottom of page:] 2 Corinthians 5:7.

SUNDAY, JUNE 1. 4 Prayed; letters. 7 Religious talk. 8 The preachers; prayed. 9.30 Read Prayers, 1 Peter 4:11! Communion; coach. 1.30 At brother Horton's, dinner. 3.15 The leaders; tea; prayed. 5 Read Prayers, 1 Corinthians 15:58! Society. 7 Read notes. 7.30 Supper, religious talk; prayer. 9.30.

MONDAY, JUNE 2. 4 Prayed; 1 Corinthians 15:41! Select Society; Magazine. 8 Tea; religious talk, prayer; Magazine. 10 Visited some! 12 Select Society; at brother Dobson's, dinner, religious talk. 2 Magazine; the children; prayed. 5

Tea, religious talk; prayer; prayed. 6.30 Read Prayers, 1 Corinthians 16:13! supper; the bands; Magazine. 9.30.

TUESDAY, JUNE 3. 4 Prayed; 1 Corinthians 15:41; Magazine; sins. 8 At brother Smyth's, tea, religious talk! visited. 10.30 Writ journal. 1 At sister Burgess's, dinner, religious talk; prayer. 2 Journal. 4 Prayed. 5 Tea, religious talk; prayer. 6 Prayer. 6.30 Read Prayers, 2 Corinthians 1:22; the leaders; supper, religious talk; prayer. 9.30.

WEDNESDAY, JUNE 4. 4 Prayed; 1 John 3:1-3! letters. 8 Tea, religious talk; prayer. 9.30 Journal; letters. 2 At Mr Wolff's, dinner, necessary talk (religious). 3 Journal. 4 Prayed; walked; tea, religious talk; prayer; coach. 6 Read Prayers, 2 Corinthians 3:18, Communion. 7 Coach. 8 Supper, religious talk; prayer. 9.30.

THURSDAY, JUNE 5. 4 Prayed; letters. 8 Tea, religious talk; prayer. 9 Journal. 12.30 Garden. 1 Charles ate dinner, religious talk. 2 Visited. 3.45 Prayed. 4.30 Visited; tea, religious talk. 6.30 2 Corinthians 4:5; the bands; visited; coach. 8.30 Highbury Place; necessary talk (religious). 9.15 Supper; religious talk; prayer. 10.15.

FRIDAY, JUNE 6. 4 Prayed. 5 Journal. 1 Garden. 2 Dinner, necessary talk (religious). 3 Journal. 5 Prayed. 6 Tea, religious talk. 7 Journal. 8 Garden; meditation; religious talk. 9 Supper, religious talk; prayer. 10.

SATURDAY, JUNE 7. 4 Prayed; letters; tea; prayer; walked. 8.30 At home; letters. 1 At brother Walter's, dinner, religious talk; prayer. 3.30 Magazine; prayed. 5 At James Smith's, tea, religious talk. 6 Read Prayers, 2 Corinthians 5:7! Communion. 7.45 Penry, necessary business. 9.30.

WHITSUNDAY, JUNE 8. 3.30 Prayer; Acts 2:1-4; slept; letters; walked. 8.15 Chapel. 9.30 Read Prayers, Psalms 68:18! Communion. 1 At brother Folgham's; religious talk, dinner. 3 The leaders. 3.30 Read Prayers, Acts 2:1-4! tea; Love-feast; coach; Society; supper. 7.30 Garden; religious talk; prayer. 9.30.
MONDAY, JUNE 9. 4 Prayed; John 7:37! Select Society; writ notes. 8 Tea, religious talk; prayer. 9 At sister Rankin's; Magazine. 1 Dinner, religious talk; Magazine; prayed. 3.15 Visited some. 5.30 At sister Loup——'s, tea, religious talk; prayer. 6.30 Read Prayers. 7 Acts 19:2; supper; the bands; coach; visited. 9.45.

TUESDAY, JUNE 10. 4 Prayed; letters. 8 At T. Oliver's, tea, religious talk; Magazine. 12.30 Walked. 1 At brother Holton's, dinner, religious talk; prayer. 2 Necessary business; visited; necessary talk (religious). 5 Tea; prayer; prayed. 6.30 1 John 4:1. 7.30 The leaders; supper, religious talk; prayer. 9.30.

WEDNESDAY, JUNE 11. 4 Prayer; tea, religious talk; prayer. 5 Coach. 8.15 Ingatestone [orig., 'Ingetston']; tea, religious talk. 9 Coach. 1 Coke. 2 Coach. 5.30 Harwich; at Dr Jones's, tea, necessary talk (religious). 8 Supper. 9 Prayer. 9.30.

THURSDAY, JUNE 12. 4 Prayed; Dr Horne. 8 Tea, religious talk; prayer. 8.30 On the *Besborough*; necessary business. 9 Set sail; read *Account of Holland*; religious talk. 12 Dinner, mostly religious talk. 1 *Account;* prayer. 5 Tea, religious talk; prayed; *Account*. 8 Supper, mostly religious talk. 9.30.

FRIDAY, JUNE 13. 4.30 Prayed; Account; necessary talk (religious), tea; prayer. 9 Hellevoetsluis [orig. 'Hoelvoets']; coffee; coach. 12 Delft; dinner, necessary talk (religious). 1 Boat; religious talk. 4 Rotterdam; at Mrs Young's. 5 Coffee; at Mr Loyal's, religious talk; walked. 8 Supper; prayer. 9.30.

SATURDAY, JUNE 14. 6 Prayed; Magazine. 8 Tea, religious talk; prayer. 9 Magazine. 12 Walked. 1 Dinner, religious talk. 2 Magazine. 4 Prayed. 5 At Mrs Monke's [Montie's?], tea, religious talk; prayer. 6.30 Walked! 8 Supper, religious talk; prayer. 9.45.

SUNDAY, JUNE 15. 4 Prayed; Magazine. 8 Tea, religious talk; prayer; Magazine. 9.30 Read Prayers, Genesis 1:27! visited. 12.30 At Mr Williams', dinner. 1.45 Slept; prayed. 2.30 Read Prayers, 1 John 5:11! 4.30 At Mr Smith's, tea; garden. 6.30 Read Prayers! 8 Supper, religious talk; prayer. 9.30.

MONDAY, JUNE 16. 4 Prayed; Magazine. 7.30 Tea, religious talk; prayer. 9 Boat; religious talk! 11 Delft; religious talk! 12 Walked! 1 Boat. 3 The Hague Inn; necessary business; dinner, religious talk; prayer. 6 At Madam van Wassenaar's, tea; 1 Corinthians 13:1–3! prayer! 7.30 Walked. 10.

[TUESDAY, JUNE 17.] 5 Prayed; journal. 7 Walked. 8 At Mrs Lieuliet's, tea, religious talk; prayer. 9.30 Magazine. 11 Walked. 12 At Mr Allen's, coffee; walked. 1 At Mrs Lieuliet's, dinner, religious talk; prayer! 3 Read. 4 Prayed. 5 At Mrs Wassenaar's, tea, religious talk; at [blank], Galatians 6:14; at sister Lieuliet's, supper, religious talk; prayer. 10.

WEDNESDAY, JUNE 18. 4.30 Prayed; journal. 8 Walked. 9 At Mrs Lieuliet's, tea, religious talk; prayer. 10 Magazine. 11.30 At Mr [blank], religious talk. 1 At Mr Allen's, dinner, religious talk; prayer; the Court! walked. 5 At Madam Wassenaar's, tea, religious talk; prayer. 7 2 Timothy 3:5! supper; prayer. 10.

THURSDAY [JUNE 19]. 4.15 Prayed; necessary talk; tea, religious talk. 7 Boat; mostly religious talk; sang. 11 Leyden; tea; walked! 1 Boat; writ. 5 Haarlem; tea, religious talk; prayer! 6 Boat; religious talk! 9 Amsterdam; the Swan; supper; prayer. 10.15.

FRIDAY, JUNE 20. 4.30 Prayed. 6 Magazine. 8 At brother Ferguson's, tea, religious talk; prayer; Magazine. 11 Visited! 12 Magazine. 1.30 Dinner; Magazine. 3 Stadthouse! 5 At Mr [blank]. 6 Tea, religious talk; prayer! 9 Supper; letter. 10.45.

SATURDAY, JUNE 21. 5.15 Prayed; letters; journal. 8 At sister Beam's, tea, religious talk; prayer; visited some; religious talk. 1.30 Dinner. 2 Visited Mr Vanhooven, religious talk! walked. 3.30 Mr Yooesden's. 4 Garden; tea, religious talk; walked! 8 At brother Ferguson's, supper, religious talk; necessary business. 10.

SUNDAY, JUNE 22. 4.30 Prayed; journal. 7.30 Tea, religious talk. 8.15 Read Prayers. 11 Magazine. 12.30 At Mr Pierson's. 1 Dinner, necessary talk (religious). 2 Isaiah 55:6! at Mr Vanhooven's, religious talk, tea; prayer; at Mr Box's! tea, religious talk; prayer. 7.30 At Mr [blank], religious talk; prayer! 9.30.

MONDAY, JUNE 23. 4 Prayed; journal; writ notes. 8 At brother Ferguson's, tea, religious talk; prayer. 9 Visited some; walked. 11 At sister Medcalf's, religious talk; prayer. 12 Magazine. 2 At Mr Pierson's, dinner, religious talk! 3.30 Coach; [the] Meer [orig. 'Mare']! tea, religious talk; coach. 8.45 At home; religious talk; prayer. 9.30.

TUESDAY, JUNE 24. 4 Prayed; journal; Magazine. 8 At Mrs [blank], tea, religious talk; prayer; visited some. 11 The Workhouse! 1 At sister Vanhousen's, religious talk. 2 At Mr Vanhingel's, dinner, religious talk; prayer; tea; visited. 7.30 At Mr Vanhousen's, religious talk; prayer; supper. 10.

[WEDNESDAY, JUNE 25.] 4.30 Prayed; journal. 7 In the boat; religious talk. 9.30 Haarlem; tea; in the church. 10 At Mr Van Campen's, religious talk; walked! garden; coffee, religious talk. 12 Haarlem; religious talk. 1 Dinner, religious talk; prayer. 3 Boat; religious talk. 6 At brother Box's, religious talk, supper; visited many; at home; necessary talk (religious); necessary business. 12.

THURSDAY, JUNE 26. 4 Prayed; writ notes. 6 Tea, religious talk; prayer. 7 Boat; sang; slept. 9 Coffee, religious talk; sang; read notes. 3 Utrecht; Miss Loten! 5.30 Walked; garden; religious talk. 7.15 Mr Loten. 7.30 Necessary talk (religious); prayer. 8 Supper, religious talk. 9.30.

FRIDAY, JUNE 27. 4 Prayed; journal. 8 Tea, religious talk; prayer; Temple of Sol; visited. 11 Walked. 12 At Mr Loten's, mostly religious talk. 1 Dinner, religious talk. 3.30 Coach; Utrecht; necessary business. 6 Visited many. 8 Supper, religious talk; prayer. 9.30.

SATURDAY, JUNE 28. 4 Prayed; journal. 8 At brother Thompson's, tea, religious talk; walked! 9 Necessary talk (religious); Ramsay. 12 Coach. 1.30 Zeist; with Antone! 3 Love-feast; dinner; coach. 6 Utrecht; at sister [blank], tea, religious talk; prayer. 8 At home; supper; read; prayer. 9.30.

SUNDAY, JUNE 29. 4 Prayed; journal; Ramsay; tea, religious talk. 9.15 Necessary business. 10 1 Corinthians 13:1-3! 12.15 At Mr Vanderloe's, dinner, religious talk. 2 Prayed; journal. 5 At Miss Loten's, tea; Gr——; sang an Exchange! 8.30 At home; supper; prayer. 9.30.

MONDAY, JUNE 30. 4 Prayed; tea, religious talk. 6 Coach. 11 Gouda; at Mr Van Vlooten's; in the kirk; dinner; read Prayers. 2 Chaise; religious talk; Ramsay. 5 Rotterdam; at Mr Loyal's, tea, religious talk; necessary business; prayed. 8 Supper, religious talk; prayer. 9.30.

TUESDAY, JULY 1. 4 Prayed; journal. 8 At Mr Williams', tea, religious talk. 9 Magazine. 10.30 Sister Lieuliet, etc, religious talk. 1 At Mrs Livingston's, dinner, religious talk. 2 Slept; prayed. 3 Magazine. 4.30 Visited! 7 Boat; necessary talk (religious), supper. 10.

WEDNESDAY, JULY 2. 4.30 Prayed; Magazine; tea; Magazine. 11 Hellevoetsluis; Magazine. 1 Dinner. 2 In the *Prince Henry*; Ramsay; prayed. 5 Tea, necessary talk (religious); prayed; Ramsay. 8 Supper, necessary talk (religious). 9.30 Laid down. 11 Slept.

THURSDAY, JULY 3. 4 Prayed; Ramsay. 7 Tea, necessary talk (religious); Ramsay. 2 Dinner; Ramsay; mostly religious talk. 8 Supper; Ramsay; mostly religious talk. 9.30.

FRIDAY, JULY 4. 4.30 Prayed; Ramsay; tea. 9 Harwich; tea; necessary business. 11 Coach; Manningtree. 1.30 Chaise; Colchester; dinner; chaise. 11 Lady Lane [London?], necessary business. 11.30.

SATURDAY, JULY 5. 4.45 Prayed; at home; letters. 7 Tea; prayer; letters. 12.45 Walked with Charles. 12.30 Dinner, religious talk; prayer. 1 Letters. 5 Tea; prayer; prayed. 6 Letters; supper; Penry; necessary business. 9.30.

SUNDAY, JULY 6. 4 Prayed; Magazine; sins. 8 The preachers. 9.30 Read Prayers, 1 Peter 5:10! Communion; at brother Horton's, dinner, religious talk. 3 The leaders; tea; prayed. 5 1 Peter 5:8; Society. 7 Writ notes. 7.15 Supper, religious talk; prayer. 9.30.

MONDAY, JULY 7. 4 Prayed; Matthew 19:6! Select Society; tea; prayer. 8.30 Magazine. 9 Chaise. 10 At sister Wright's. 10.30 Writ sermon. 1.45 Dinner, religious talk. 2.30 Sermon. 5 Prayed. 6 Tea, mostly religious talk. 7 Garden, necessary talk (religious); supper; prayer. 9.30.

TUESDAY, JULY 8. 4 Prayed; sermon. 8 Tea; prayer; sermon; letters. 1.30 Garden. 2.30 Dinner, mostly religious talk; sermon; chaise. 5 At home; tea, religious talk; prayer. 6.30 Read the letters; the leaders. 8 Chaise. 8.45 Walthamstow; supper; prayer. 10.

WEDNESDAY, JULY 9. 4.30 Prayed; sermon; sins! 8 Tea, religious talk; prayer; sermon. 11 Chaise; sermon. 2.15 At brother Blunt's, mostly religious talk, dinner. 4.15 At Mr Maxfield's, tea; chaise. 7 Leyton; Proverbs 3:17; chaise; supper; prayer. 9.45.

THURSDAY, JULY 10. 4 Prayed; sermon. 8 Tea, religious talk; prayer; letters. 11 Chaise; at home; necessary business. 1 At sister Burgess's, dinner, religious talk; prayer; Magazine; prayed; at sister Cheesement's, tea, religious talk; prayer. 6.30 Psalms 55:6; the bands; Highbury; supper; prayer. 10.30.

FRIDAY, JULY 11. 4.30 Prayed; sermon; tea; prayer; sermon. 2 Coach; at brother Gardiner's; christened; dinner. 7 Highbury; prayed; tea; sermon. 8.30 Supper, religious talk; prayer. 9.45.

SATURDAY, JULY 12. 4 Prayed; sermon. 7.30 Tea, religious talk; prayer; walked. 9.30 Sermon; letters. 1 At brother Da——'s, dinner, religious talk. 2.30 Sermon; prayed. 5 Tea, religious talk; prayed. 6 Read Prayers, 1 Thessalonians 4:7! supper; Penry, necessary business. 9.30.

SUNDAY, JULY 13. 4 Prayed; necessary business; letter; walked; Chapel; read Prayers, John 1:29! Communion; at Mrs Key's. 1.30 Dinner. 2.30 Slept; the leaders. 3.30 Read Prayers, 1 Thessalonians 5:19! Society. 6 Walked; Society; supper; necessary business; religious talk; prayer. 9.30.

MONDAY, JULY 14. 4 Prayed; tea. 5 Chaise with Mr Brackenbury, religious talk; Uxbridge; tea. 10.30 [High] Wycombe; necessary business. 11 Acts 9:31; dinner; visited. 1 Chaise; Tetsworth; chaise. 6 Oxford; tea; Romans 1:16! walked; supper; prayer. 9.30.

TUESDAY, JULY 15. 4 Prayed; Matthew 19:6! necessary business; letters. 7.30 Tea, religious talk, necessary talk (religious); visited. 10 Walked. 11.30 Visited; writ notes. 1 Dinner, necessary talk (religious). 3.30 Prayed. 4.30 Walked. 5.30 Tea, religious talk. 6.30 1 Corinthians 13:1-3! walked to supper, religious talk; prayer. 9.30.

WEDNESDAY, JULY 16. 4 Prayed. 1 Corinthians 13:13; necessary talk, tea; prayer. 7 Chaise. 9 Witney; necessary talk (religious); writ Dutch Grammar. 1.30 Dinner, religious talk. 3 Read notes. 4 Garden; prayed. 5 Prayed; tea. 6.30 +Matthew 25:31! Society; supper, religious talk; prayer. 10.

THURSDAY, JULY 17. 4 Prayed; Mark 4:3, etc; Society! tea. 7 Chaise with A. B., religious talk; Bibury. 10 Tea. 11 Chaise. 3 Stroud; dinner; writ notes; prayed. 5.30 Tea, religious talk, necessary talk (religious). 7 John 5:8! at brother Freeb——'s, supper, religious talk; prayer. 9.30.

FRIDAY, JULY 18. 4 Prayed; 2 John 8! tea, religious talk; prayer. 7 Chaise. 9.15 Newport; tea. 10.15 Chaise. 1.30 Bristol; prayer. 2.30 Dinner, religious talk; prayer. 3.15 Letters. 5 Prayer; tea; Conference. 7.45 Supper, necessary talk (religious). 8.30 Prayer; Matthew 19:6! prayer; necessary talk! 12.

SATURDAY, JULY 19. 4.45 Prayed; letters. 7 In the water. 8 Tea, necessary talk (religious); prayer. 10 Letters. 12.30 Visited. 1 At brother Pine's, dinner, religious talk; prayer. 2.30 Letters. 4.45 Prayer; tea, religious talk; prayed. 6.30 Writ notes. 7.30 Penry; at Mr Castleman's, supper, religious talk; prayer. 9.45.

SUNDAY, JULY 20. 4 Prayed; letters. 8 Tea, religious talk; prayed. 9.30 Read Prayers, John 8:12! Communion. 12.45 Dinner, religious talk; chaise. 2 At the School; +Mark 4:3, etc! chaise. 3.30 Prayed; tea. 5 Psalms 103:13; Society; letter. 8 Supper, necessary talk (religious); prayer. 9.30.

MONDAY, JULY 21. 4 Prayed; Ephesians 6:11; letter. 7 In the water. 8 Tea, religious talk; prayer. 9 Writ for Conference. 12 Select Society. 1 At R. Lewis's, dinner, religious talk; prayer. 2.30 Chaise. 4.30 At brother Timbrel's. 5 Prayed; tea. 6.30 Job 3:17; Society; religious talk, supper; prayer. 9.30.

[Texts noted at bottom of page:] Matthew 19:6; Psalms 55:6.

TUESDAY, JULY 22. 4 Prayed. Psalms 106:24! the leaders. 7 Conference. 8 Tea, religious talk; prayer. 9.30 Conference. 12 Visited! 1 Dinner, religious talk. 2.30 Conference. 4.15 Prayed; visited; tea, religious talk; prayer. 6.30 2 Corinthians 4:18! Society; supper, religious talk; prayer. 9.45.

WEDNESDAY, JULY 23. 4.15 Prayed; 1 Corinthians 7:35! chaise. 8.15 At Mr Thomas's, tea, religious talk; prayer; coach. 10 Writ for Conference. 1 At brother Stock's, dinner, religious talk, necessary talk (religious). 4 Prayed. 5.15 At brother Fr——'s, tea, religious talk; visited! 6.30 John 5:8! visited. 8 At Miss J[ohnson]'s, supper; prayer. 9.30.

THURSDAY, JULY 24. 4 Prayed; letter. 6 Coach; Blaise Castle; walked! tea; coach; Kings Weston. 10 Walked. 11 Coach. 12 Necessary business; visited some. 2.15 At Mr Durbin's, dinner, religious talk; prayer. 4 Necessary business. 5 Prayer; tea, religious talk. 5.30 Necessary business; prayed. 6.30 Read Account; Clifton; supper; prayer. 9.45.

FRIDAY [JULY 25]. 4 Prayed; writ Conference. 8 Tea, religious talk; Conference; letters. 3 Dinner, Dr Coke, etc. 4 Necessary talk (religious). 5 Tea; garden. 9 Supper, religious talk; prayer. 9.45.

SATURDAY, JULY 26. 4 Prayed; Dr Coke, necessary talk for Conference. 8 Tea, religious talk; prayer; writ Conference. 11 Visited many. 1 At John Ellison's, dinner, religious talk. 3 Necessary business; prayer. 5 Tea, religious talk; letters; necessary talk (religious). 8 At Mr Castleman's, supper, religious talk; prayer. 9.30.

SUNDAY, JULY 27. 4 Prayed; necessary business. 6 Chaise; Brislington; tea; coach. 9 Bath; Conference; read Prayers, Matthew 5:20! Communion. 1.30 At brother Sims's, dinner; slept; prayed. 2.30 Titus 2:12; tea, necessary talk (religious); chaise; visited. 7.45 Supper, religious talk; prayer. 9.30. Hot.

[MONDAY, JULY 28.] 4 Prayed; Zechariah 6:8! writ Conference; in the water. 8 Tea; Conference; letters. 1 At brother Colmer's, dinner, religious talk; prayer. 2 Read letters. 5 Prayer; tea; prayed. 6.30 Jeremiah 6:16! at sister Johnson's, religious talk; prayer. 9.30.

TUESDAY, JULY 29. 4 Prayed; 1 Corinthians 7:35! Conference. 8 Tea, religious talk. 9 Conference. 12 In the water. 1 Dinner. 2 Conference. 4.30 Tea, religious talk. 5.30 Prayed. 6.30 Acts 2:4; the leaders. 8 At sister Johnson's, supper, religious talk; prayer. 9.30.

WEDNESDAY, JULY 30. 4 Prayed; Acts 2:4; Conference. 8 Tea, religious talk; prayer. 9 Conference. 12 Necessary business. 1 At brother Green's, dinner, religious talk; letters. 5 Tea, religious talk; prayer. 6.30 Isaiah 5:4! necessary business. 8 At sister Johnson's, supper, religious talk; prayer. 9.30.

THURSDAY, JULY 31. 4 Prayed; writ notes. 6 Conference; tea; Conference. 12 Letters. 1 Dinner, religious talk. 2 Conference. 4.30 Necessary talk (religious) to many. 5 Tea; prayed; writ notes. 6.30 Mark 3:35; the bands. 8.30 At sister Johnson's, supper, mostly religious talk. 9.30.

FRIDAY, AUGUST 1. 4 Prayed; writ Conference. 6 Conference. 8 Writ notes. 9 Conference. 12.30 Writ Conference. 1 Prayer. 2 Dinner, mostly religious talk. 3 Conference. 4.15 Writ Conference. 5 Tea, religious talk; prayed; writ notes. 6.30 2 Timothy 3:5! necessary talk (religious) to many; at sister Johnson's, supper; prayer. 9.30.

SATURDAY, AUGUST 2. 4 Prayed; letter. 6 Conference. 8 Tea, religious talk. 9 Conference. 12 Writ notes. 1 Dinner; writ letters. 4.15 Visited some. 6 At Miss Johnson's; writ letters. 8 Supper, religious talk; prayer; necessary business. 9.30.

SUNDAY, AUGUST 3. 4 Ill; prayed; letters. 8 Tea, religious talk; necessary business. 9.30 Read Prayers, Acts 1:5! Communion. 1 At brother Ewer's, dinner, religious talk. 2.30 Slept; prayed; tea. 5 +Hebrews 6:1! Society; at Mr Castleman's, supper, religious talk; prayer. 9.30 Lay down. 1 Ill.

[MONDAY, AUGUST 4. No entry]

TUESDAY, AUGUST [5]. 4 Ill. 5 Colossians 1:26! ill; Mr Dyer; lay down; many visited. 11 Class; took jalap; Dr Drummond, necessary talk (religious); Mr Gold. 6 Tea, necessary talk (religious); lay down.

WEDNESDAY, AUGUST [6]. 6 Many called; tea, necessary talk (religious); Dr Drummond; Mr Gold; stupid [i.e., in a state of stupor]! 2 Lay down. 4 Tea, necessary talk (religious); Dr Drummond; Gold. 8.30 Prayer; lay down.

THURSDAY, AUGUST [7]. 7 Tea, necessary talk (religious); necessary business; Dr Drummond; Mr Goole; broth; necessary talk (religious); several called; read Mrs Smyth's letters! 4.30 Tea, religious talk; broth. 9.

FRIDAY, AUGUST [8]. 7 Prayed; tea, religious talk; writ to A—— B——. 8 Writ diary. 11.30 Chaise. 1 Dinner; read [?]; sister Smith's. 5 Tea, necessary talk (religious); supper. 8.30 Prayer; lay down.

SATURDAY, AUGUST [9]. 7 Tea, necessary talk (religious). 11.30 Chaise, with sister Boone. 12.30 Necessary talk (religious). 1 Dinner; writ letters. 5 Tea, religious talk! prayer! 8 Supper, religious talk. 9.30.

SUNDAY, AUGUST [10]. 6 Prayed; slept; tea; writ letter; slept. 11.30 Chaise; with Mrs Brackenbury. 1 Dinner; slept. 4 Religious talk! 5 Tea, religious talk; prayed! 6.30 Slept. 8.30 Supper. 9.

MONDAY, AUGUST [11]. 5 Prayed. 6 Slept. 8.30 Tea, necessary talk (religious); slept. 12.15 Chaise; with Mr Brackenbury. 1.45 Dinner. 3 Read. 3.30 Slept. 4.30 Prayed; tea, religious talk; read. 8.30 Supper, religious talk; prayer. 10.

TUESDAY, AUGUST [12]. 5 Prayed. 6 Slept. 7.30 Necessary talk (religious), tea, religious talk; read. 10 Lay down. 12 Chaise. 2 Dinner, religious talk; slept. 5 Prayed; tea, religious talk; prayed; read. 8 Supper, religious talk. 9.45.

WEDNESDAY, AUGUST [13]. 5 Prayed. 6 Slept; walked. 8 Religious talk, tea; read. 11 Walked; coach; slept. 2 Dinner, necessary talk (religious). 3.30 Slept. 4.15 Vomit! 5.30 Slept; ill. 8.30 Supper. 9.

THURSDAY, AUGUST [14]. 5 Prayed. 6 Slept. 7 Read; walked. 8 Tea, religious talk; prayer. 9 Read. 10 Slept. 11 Read; necessary talk (religious) to many. 12 Chaise; Hotwells; chaise. 2 Dinner, necessary talk (religious). 3 Slept. 4 Read; walked. 5 Tea, religious talk; prayer; read. 8 Supper, religious talk; prayer. 9 Could not sleep. 12.

FRIDAY, AUGUST [15]. 6 Prayed; walked. 8 Tea, religious talk; slept. 9 Read. 10.30 Visited! 11.45 Chaise. 2 Dinner. 3.30 Slept. 4 Prayed; walked. 5.15 Tea, necessary talk (religious); read. 8.15 Supper, necessary talk (religious); prayer. 9.30.

SATURDAY, AUGUST [16]. 5 Prayed; letters. 8 Tea; chaise. 9.30 Letters; necessary talk (religious) to many. 2 Dinner, necessary talk (religious). 3 Letters; prayed; walked. 5 At brother Hick's, Mr Sulger, etc, tea, religious talk! 6.30 Letters. 8 Supper, religious talk; prayer. 9.30.

SUNDAY, AUGUST [17]. 5.15 Prayed; letter. 8 Tea, religious talk; chaise. 10.30 Letters; read. 1.30 Dinner; letter. 3.30 Prayed. 4 Tea, religious talk; Magazine. 6.30 Walked. 7.30 Supper, necessary talk (religious) to many. 9 Prayed. 9.30.

MONDAY, AUGUST 18. 4.30 Ill; slept. 6 Magazine. 8 At brother White's, tea, religious talk; prayer; chaise, with sister Castleman. 10.45 Magazine. 1 At sister Johnson's, dinner, religious talk; prayer; letters. 4 Prayed; at sister Chapman's. 5 Tea, religious talk; prayer. 6.30 Read; supper, religious talk; prayer. 9.30.

TUESDAY, AUGUST 19. 4.15 Prayed; writ journal. 8 Tea, religious talk; prayer; chaise; visited. 11 Letters; sermon. 1 At brother Powel's, dinner, religious talk; prayer. 2.30 Prayed; letter. 4.30 Chaise; Bedminster; tea, necessary talk (religious); walked. 7.30 Prayed; supper; prayer. 9.30.

WEDNESDAY, AUGUST 20. 4 Prayed; slept; sermon. 7.30 Chaise. 8.30 At Mr Ireland's, tea, religious talk; garden. 10 Prayer. 10.15 Chaise! 11.30 At home; writ sermon; letter. 2 Dinner, religious talk; sermon; prayed. 4.30 Walked; at brother Lewis's, tea, religious talk; prayer; read; meditation. 8 Supper, necessary talk (religious); prayer. 9.30.

THURSDAY, AUGUST 21. 4 Slept; prayed. 6 Sermon. 8 Tea. 8.30 Chaise; Hotwells. 10 Sermon. 11 Letter; sermon. 1 At sister Dyer's, dinner, religious talk; prayer. 2.30 Slept. 3.15 Prayed. 4 Chaise, with sister Roberts. 5 The Cupolas; garden. 5.30 Tea, religious talk; prayer. 6.30 Chaise. 7.30 At Mr Castleman's; prayed; supper, religious talk; Dr Coke; prayer. 9.30.

FRIDAY, AUGUST 22. 4 Prayed; slept. 6 Sermon; letters. 8 Tea, religious talk; sermon; necessary talk (religious) to many. 2 Chaise; Bedminster. 2.30 Dinner, religious talk; garden; tea; chaise. 6.30 Prayed. 8 Supper; prayer.

SATURDAY, AUGUST 23. 4 Prayed; slept. 6 Sermon; letter. 8 At brother Gee's, tea, religious talk; prayer; visited. 9.30 Sermon; slept. 12 Read. 1 At John Ellison's, dinner, religious talk; prayer; visited. 3 Letters; prayed. 5 Tea, religious talk. 6 Read notes. 7.30 Penry! supper, religious talk; prayer; necessary business. 10.

SUNDAY, AUGUST 24. 4 Dressed; slept. 5.30 Prayed; letters. 8 Tea, religious talk; necessary business. 9.30 Read Prayers; Acts 22:16! Communion. 1 At Mr Castleman's, dinner; slept. 2 Prayed; letters. 4 Tea, religious talk. 5 Psalms 116:12! Society. 7 At sister Castleman's; prayed. 8 Supper, religious talk; prayer. 9.30.

MONDAY, AUGUST 25. 4 Prayed. 5 Chaise. 6.30 Almondsbury [orig., 'Amesbury']; tea, religious talk; prayer. 7 Chaise; Newport; coffee. 9.45 Chaise. 1 Gloucester; at sister Conybeare's; read notes. 2 Dinner, religious talk. 3 Read notes; prayed. 5 At brother Davi[es?]'s, tea, religious talk. 6 Isaiah 55:6! supper, prayer. 9.30.

TUESDAY, AUGUST 26. 4 Prayed; 2 Corinthians 2:2! tea; prayer. 7 Chaise; Tewkesbury; tea, religious talk; prayer; chaise. 1.30 Worcester; dinner; letters; prayed; tea, religious talk. 6 Ephesians 3:14! Society. 8 Supper, religious talk; prayer. 9.30.

WEDNESDAY, AUGUST 27. 4 Prayed; Judges 1:27! letter; tea; prayer. 7.15 Chaise. 9.45 Tea, religious talk. 10.45 Chaise. 1.30 Birmingham; at Mr Holden's, dinner, necessary talk (religious). 3 Necessary talk (religious); prayed. 5 At sister Jones's, tea, religious talk. 6 2 Timothy 3:5! Society! supper, religious talk; prayer. 9.30.

THURSDAY, AUGUST 28. 4 Prayed; Psalms 106:24! letter; tea. 7.15 The Chaise. 8.45 Wednesbury. 9 Tea, religious talk; prayer. 10 Chaise. 12.15 Hilton Hall, necessary talk (religious). 4 Dinner, religious talk. 5 Prayed; mostly religious talk. 7 Tea, mostly religious talk. 10 Supper; prayer. 11.

FRIDAY, AUGUST 29. 5 Prayed; tea, Miss G——, religious talk! 6.30 Chaise. 9.30 Stafford; tea; 2 Corinthians 8:9! 11 Chaise. 2.45 Newcastle[-under-Lyme]; dinner. 3.15 Walked; chaise. 5.30 Congleton; tea, religious talk; prayed. 6 Ephesians 4:1, etc! Society! supper, religious talk. 9.30.

SATURDAY, AUGUST 30. 4 Prayed; 1 Corinthians 7:35! letters. 8 Tea, necessary talk! 10 Chaise. 12.30 Macclesfield; writ notes. 1.30 Dinner, religious talk. 4.30

Prayed; visited; tea. 6.15 Isaiah 38:5! necessary talk (religious). 8 Supper, religious talk; prayer. 10.

SUNDAY, AUGUST 31. 4.15 Prayed; writ notes. 6 Necessary talk! 9 Tea. 10 Read Prayers, 1 Kings 5:11! Communion. 2 Dinner, religious talk. 3 Read Prayers, Romans 1:16. 4.30 Tea, necessary talk! 6.45 Society; supper, necessary talk (religious); prayer. 9.30.

MONDAY, SEPTEMBER 1. 4 Prayed; Mark 4:27; writ notes. 9 At brother Johnson's, tea, religious talk; prayer. 9.30 Visited some. 10.30 Chaise. 1 Buxton; necessary business; dinner, religious talk. 3 Prayed. 4 Read Prayers, Hebrews 9:27! tea, religious talk. 6 Walked; supper; prayer. 9.30.

TUESDAY, SEPTEMBER 2. 3 Prayed; tea. 4.15 Chaise. 6.30 [Stoney] Middleton. 7.30 Chaise. 10 Sheffield. 10 Tea, religious talk. 11 Chaise. 1 Barnsley; dinner. 2 Walked; chaise; Burnet. 5.15 Leeds; tea, necessary talk (religious); prayed. 6.30 Psalms 116:12; the preachers! 8.30 At Mr Hey's, supper, necessary talk (religious); prayer. 9.45.

WEDNESDAY, SEPTEMBER 3. 4.15 Prayed; letters. 8 Tea, religious talk; prayer. 9.30 The preachers! 11.30 Writ notes; at brother Floyd's. 1 Dinner, religious talk. 3 Prayed. 4 Elizabeth Ritchie! 4.45 Tea, religious talk; prayer. 5.45 Prayed. 6.30 Matthew 22:37. 7.30 Society; supper, religious talk; prayer. 10.

THURSDAY, SEPTEMBER 4. 4 Prayed. 1 Corinthians 7:35; the leaders; letters. 8.30 Tea; prayer; letters. 11 Chaise. 1 At John Taylor's, dinner, necessary talk (religious). 3 Letters; prayed; tea; chaise. 6 Psalms 116:12! 7 Chaise; Gomersal; supper, religious talk; prayer. 9.30.

FRIDAY, SEPTEMBER 5. 4 Prayed; Ephesians 4:1, etc! letters. 7.30 Tea, religious talk. 9 The Trustees! 1 Dinner, religious talk. 2 The Trustees! necessary talk (religious) to many. 5 Tea; prayed. 6 Matthew 7:16! 7.30 Prayed; supper, necessary talk (religious); prayer. 9.30.

SATURDAY, SEPTEMBER 6. 4 Prayed; Ephesians 4:30; writ journal. 7 Tea, necessary talk (religious); chaise. 9 Leeds; letters. 1 At sister Clapham's, dinner, religious talk; prayer; chaise. 4 Leeds; prayed; tea, religious talk; prayed. 6.30 Acts 2:5! Select Society; supper, religious talk; prayer. 10.

SUNDAY, SEPTEMBER 7. 4 Prayed; letter. 7 Philippians 1:21! necessary business; tea, religious talk; prayer. 9.30 Chaise. 11 Birstall; writ notes. 12 Dinner, religious talk. 1 Matthew 8:2! chaise. 4.30 Halifax; tea. 5 Romans 8:33! Society! prayed; supper, religious talk; prayer. 9.45.

MONDAY, SEPTEMBER 8. 4 Prayed; tea; prayer. 5 Chaise. 9 Rochdale; tea, religious talk. 10.30 Chaise. 12.45 Manchester; letters. 2 Dinner, religious talk. 3 Writ notes. 4 Prayed. 5 Tea, religious talk. 6 2 Timothy 3:5! Society, necessary talk (religious)! supper; prayer. 9.30.

Tuesday, September 9. 4 Prayed; 2 Timothy 3:4! necessary business; tea, religious talk; prayer. 7.30 Chaise. 9 At brother Mart[in's?], tea, religious talk; prayer. 10 Chaise. 12.15 Macclesfield; dinner, religious talk. 2 Chaise. 4.15 Congleton; tea. 5 Chaise. 6.30 Newcastle[-under-Lyme]; tea; Hebrews 9:27; supper; prayer. 9.30.

Wednesday, September 10. 4 Prayed; tea. 5 Chaise; Stafford; chaise. 1.15 Wednesbury; dinner; Acts 1:5. 3 Chaise. 4.30 Burslem; tea, religious talk; prayed; letters; tea; prayed. 7 Matthew 7:16! 8 Supper, religious talk; prayer. 9.30.

[Texts noted at bottom of page:] Luke 10:37; Job 7:18(2)

Thursday, September 11. 4 Prayed; letter. 5 2 Timothy 3:4! letters; tea. 7.30 Chaise; Bromsgrove. 10 Tea, religious talk; chaise. 2 Worcester; dinner, religious talk. 3 Necessary business; necessary talk (religious); prayed. 5 Tea, religious talk; prayed. 6 Acts 1:5! Society! supper, religious talk; prayer. 9.30.

Friday, September 12. 4 Prayed; tea. 5.15 Chaise. 8.45 Tewkesbury; tea. 9 1 Peter 4:18. 10 Chaise. 1 Gloucester; dinner, religious talk; prayer. 2.30 Chaise. 4.45 Letter; prayed. 6.30 1 Corinthians 1:23! Society; supper, religious talk; prayer. 9.30.

Saturday, September 13. 4 Prayed. 1 Corinthians 13:8! chaise; Ryeford [orig., 'Dryford']; tea, religious talk; prayer. 8 Chaise; Newport. 10 Tea. 11 Chaise. 1 Almondsbury; dinner, religious talk; prayer; chaise. 4 At home; necessary business; prayed. 5 Prayer; at Miss Johnson's, tea, religious talk. 6 Prayed; letters; supper; prayer; necessary business. 9.30.

Sunday, September 14. 4 Prayed; letters; journal; tea. 9.30 Read Prayers, Luke 10:24! Communion. 1 At sister Johnson's, dinner, religious talk. 2 Journal; slept; prayed. 5 Tea, religious talk; prayed. 5 Luke 10:37; Society; writ notes; supper, religious talk; prayer. 9.30.

Monday, September 15. 4 Prayed; Edwards; writ notes. 8 Tea, religious talk; prayer. 9 Magazine. 12 Select Society. 1 Mr Pine's, dinner, religious talk; prayer. 2.30 Slept; journal. 3.30 Prayed. 4.30 Tea, religious talk; prayer; Job 7:18! at Mr Castleman's, supper, religious talk; prayer. 9.30.

Tuesday, September 16. 1 At brother Story's, dinner, religious talk; prayer; Magazine; visited. 5 At sister Callow's, religious talk, prayer. 6 Necessary talk (religious); prayed. 6.30 1 John 2:15; leaders; supper; prayer; mend. 9.30.

Wednesday, September 17. 4 Prayed; letters. 8 At brother Rob——'s, tea, religious talk; prayer. 9.30 Chaise. 12 Bath; dinner, religious talk. 1 Ephesians 2:12! chaise. 4 Bradford[-on-Avon]; necessary talk (religious); tea; prayed. 6 Matthew 7:16! Society! at Mr Ball's, supper, religious talk; prayer. 9.30.

Thursday, September 18. 4 Prayed; 1 John 2:15! necessary talk (religious), tea, religious talk; chaise. 8 Trowbridge; tea, religious talk. 9 +Luke 10:42!

Society; chaise. 4 Hannam; dinner, religious talk; prayer! chaise. 4.30 Necessary business. 5 Prayer; tea; prayed. 7 Luke 18:25! the bands! at brother Castleman's, supper; prayer. 9.30.

FRIDAY, SEPTEMBER 19. 4 Prayed; letters; tea; letters. 12 The females. 1 Prayer; at Mr Durbin's, dinner, religious talk; prayer. 4 Chaise. 5 At the School; necessary talk (religious); tea; prayed. 8 Supper. 8.30 Acts 1:5! coffee; prayer. 10.

SATURDAY, SEPTEMBER 20. 6 Prayed; the leaders; children. 7 The accounts. 8.30 Chaise. 9.30 At home; letters; walked. 1 At sister Morgan's, dinner, religious talk; prayer. 2.30 Visited some; prayed. 5 At sister Marston's, tea, religious talk; prayer. 6 2 Corinthians 4:7! Penry; at sister Johnson's, supper, religious talk; necessary business; prayer. 9.30.

[Texts noted at bottom of page:] Acts 1:5; Luke 18:25; Matthew 11:10 [?]; Matthew 6:22; Luke 10:37.

SUNDAY, SEPTEMBER 21. 4.30 Prayed; letters. 8 Tea, religious talk; prayed; sins. 9.30 Read Prayers, 2 Corinthians 4:2! Communion. 1 At sister Ewer's, dinner, religious talk; prayer. 2.30 Slept; prayed; tea, religious talk. 5 2 Corinthians 4:5! Society; Taylor; supper, religious talk; prayer. 9.30.

MONDAY, SEPTEMBER 22. 4 Prayed; Edwards. 6 Class. 8 Tea, religious talk. 9 Class. 1 Dinner, religious talk; prayer. 2 Class. 5 Tea, religious talk; prayer; writ notes; prayed. 7 James 2:5! 8.30 At Mr Castleman's, supper, religious talk; prayer. 9.45.

[Pointing hand] TUESDAY, SEPTEMBER 23. 4 Prayed; writ notes. 6 Class. 8 Tea, religious talk; prayer. 9 Class. 1 Dinner, religious talk; prayer. 2 Class. 4.30 Necessary business. 5 Tea, religious talk; prayer; prayed. 6.30 Read the letters; the leaders; at sister Johnson's. 9 Supper, religious talk; prayer. 9.45.

WEDNESDAY, SEPTEMBER 24. 4 Prayed; letters. 8 At brother Cap[el]'s, tea; letters. 11 Class. 1 Dinner. 2 Class; tea. 5 Jacob's Wells; +Matthew 8:2! class; chaise; prayer. 8 At brother Castleman's, supper, religious talk. 9 Prayer. 9.30.

THURSDAY, SEPTEMBER 25. 4 Prayed; writ Society. 8 Tea, religious talk; writ Society. 10 Sat [saw?] the dwarf [?]; chaise. 12 Almondsbury; Acts 22:16! dinner, religious talk; prayer. 3 Chaise. 4.30 Tea, religious talk; prayer; at Cols[ton] School. 6.15 Prayed. 7 Micah 2:10; the bands; at sister Johnson's, supper; prayer. 9.45.

FRIDAY, SEPTEMBER 26. 4 Prayed; writ Society. 12 The females; writ Society. 1 Prayer; visited; at brother Sanders'. 3 Dinner; visited some. 4.30 Tea, religious talk; chaise. 6.15 At the School; necessary talk; prayer; writ Society. 8 Supper, religious talk; prayer. 9.30.

SATURDAY, SEPTEMBER 27. 4 Prayed; writ Society. 6 The children; writ Society; tea. 8 Chaise; writ the bands; letters. 1 At brother Green's, dinner; prayer.

2 Visited many. 5 At sister Lydiard's, tea, religious talk; prayer. 6 Matthew 6:22! Penry; at sister Castleman's, supper; prayer; necessary business. 9.30.

SUNDAY, SEPTEMBER 28. 4 Prayed; writ notes; letters; tea; necessary business; prayed. 9.30 Read Prayers, Mark 1:15(2)! Communion. 1 Dinner. 2 Slept; writ notes; prayed. 4 Tea; prayed. 5 Galatians 6:15! Society; read. 8 Supper, religious talk; prayer. 9.30.

MONDAY, SEPTEMBER 29. 4 Prayed; Jeremiah 35; letters; tea; letters. 11.30 Read; Select Society. 1 At brother Burgess's, dinner, religious talk; visited many. 5 Tea, religious talk; prayer. 6 Prayed. 7 Matthew 6:33! singers. 8.30 At sister Johnson's, supper, religious talk; prayer. 9.45.

TUESDAY, SEPTEMBER 30. 4 Prayed; letters. 8 Tea, religious talk; prayer. 9 Letters. 12 Necessary business. 1 At sister Lewis's, dinner, necessary talk (religious). 2.30 Visited many. 5 At sister Ran[kin]'s, tea, religious talk; prayer. 5.30 Prayed. 6.30 Matthew 6:22! the leaders. 8.15 At sister Castleman's, supper; prayer. 9.30.

[Texts noted at bottom of page:] Matthew 6:33, v. 34; James 2:5.

WEDNESDAY, OCTOBER 1. 4 Prayed; letters. 8 Tea, religious talk; prayer; letters; necessary business. 12 Chaise; Hannam; dinner, religious talk; prayer. 3.30 Chaise. 5 At brother Timbrel's; prayed; at brother Rogers's; christened; tea, religious talk; prayed. 6.15 Micah 2:10! 8 At brother Syme's, supper, religious talk; prayer. 9.30.

THURSDAY, OCTOBER 2. 4 Prayed; Matthew 6:22! read Bishop Wilson. 8 Tea, religious talk; prayer; read. 10 Chaise; Keynsham. 11.30 At Miss Bishop's, religious talk. 12 1 Peter 4:18! religious talk. 2 Dinner; the children; prayer. 3 Chaise; at Mr J——'s; visited. 4 Tea; chaise. 5 Visited; prayed. 7 Matthew 6:34; the bands; at sister Johnson's, supper; prayer. 9.45.

FRIDAY [OCTOBER 3]. 4 Prayed; letters. 8 Tea, religious talk; visited; letters. 12 The females; sins. 1 Prayer; necessary talk (religious) to many. 2.30 Dinner, religious talk; prayer. 3.30 Visited; chaise; at the School; necessary talk (religious); chaise. 6 At sister Hodges's, tea, religious talk. 6.30 1 Corinthians 13:13! 8 At Mr Castleman's, supper; prayer. 9.30.

SATURDAY, OCTOBER 4. 4 Prayed; letters; necessary business. 8 Tea, religious talk; visited. 9.30 Writ journal. 12.30 Visited. 1 At sister Lank's, dinner, religious talk; prayer; visited. 2.30 Necessary business; prayed. 4 Visited many. 6 Jeremiah 35 *ult.*! Penry. 8 At sister Johnson's, supper, religious talk; necessary business; prayer. 9.30.

SUNDAY, OCTOBER 5. 4 Prayed; letters; at brother Chapman's, religious talk, tea; prayer; necessary business; prayed. 9.30 Read Prayers, Ephesians 3:14, etc. 11 Communion. 1 At brother Cross's, dinner, religious talk; slept; letter; prayed. 4 Tea; prayed. 5 Malachi 4:2. 6 Society; the singers. 8 Supper, religious talk; prayer. 9.30.

MONDAY, OCTOBER 6. 3.15 Prayed; coffee. 4 Chaise. 6 Bath; tea. 6.45 Chaise. 10 Devizes; necessary talk (religious). 11 1 Samuel 21:8! at Mr Bailey's, dinner. 1 Chaise. 4.30 Salisbury [orig., 'Sarum']. 5 Tea; prayed. 6.30 Micah 2:10! Society! supper, religious talk; prayer. 9.45.

TUESDAY, OCTOBER 7. 4 Prayed. 5 [blank]; tea. 6.30 Chaise. 10 Winchester; necessary business; letters. 11 Matthew 7:24! dinner; prayer. 1.30 Chaise. 5.45 Portsmouth; at brother Singer's, tea, religious talk. 6.30 Matthew 6:22! Society! supper; prayer. 9.30.

WEDNESDAY, OCTOBER 8. 4 Prayed; Job 7:18(2); necessary business; at sister Paulby's, tea, religious talk. 8.30 Boat. 11 Wootton Bridge [orig., 'Woodden bri']; walked. 12.30 At Mr Clark's, religious talk. 2 Dinner. 3 Prayed; letters. 5 Tea, religious talk; prayed. 6.30 Matthew 11:28; Society; supper; prayer. 9.30.

THURSDAY [OCTOBER 9]. 4 Prayed; Matthew 12:43! letters. 7.30 Tea, religious talk; prayer; letters. 12.45 Dinner; chaise. 3 Newtown; ruin! Isaiah 55:6! chaise. 6 At Mr W. Clark's, tea, religious talk. 6.30 Matthew 7:14! Society! supper; prayer. 9.30.

FRIDAY, OCTOBER 10. 4 Prayed; Hebrews 8:10; tea; coach; Cowes. 7.30 Boat. 10.30 Southampton. 11 Chaise. 12 Winchester [orig., 'Winton']; letters. 2 At Mr Lowth's, dinner, religious talk; visited. 5 +2 Corinthians 8:9. 6 At Mrs Blackwell's, tea, necessary talk (religious). 8 Supper. 8.30 At brother W——'s. 9 Prayer. 9.30.

SATURDAY, OCTOBER 11. 2.30 Prayer. 3 Chaise; ill; Farnham; tea; chaise. 11 Staines; Charles [Hayes?], necessary talk (religious). 12.45 Dinner. 2 Coach. 5.30 At home; tea; letters. 7.45 Supper, necessary talk (religious); prayer; necessary business. 9.30.

SUNDAY, OCTOBER 12. 4 Prayed; letter; necessary business. 7.30 Walked; Chapel. 9.30 Read Prayers, Ephesians 4:3, etc! Communion. 1.30 At brother Horton's, dinner, religious talk; coach; the leaders; tea; prayed. 4 Read Prayers, Ezekiel 18:32. 6 Society; writ notes; supper, religious talk; prayer. 9.30.

MONDAY, OCTOBER 13. 4 Letter; tea. 6 Coach; Colnbrook [orig., 'Colebrook']; tea, religious talk; coach; Shakespeare. 2.30 Wallingford; dinner, necessary talk (religious). 3.30 Letters. 5 Tea; prayed. 6.30 Galatians 6:14! 8 Supper; prayer. 9.30.

TUESDAY, OCTOBER 14. 4 Prayed; Matthew 12:43! letters. 8 Tea; letters. 12 Dinner, religious talk. 1.15 Chaise. 3 Oxford [orig., 'Oxon']; necessary business; walked. 5 Tea, religious talk; prayed. 6.30 Philippians 3:8. 8 Supper, religious talk; prayer. 9.30.

WEDNESDAY, OCTOBER 15. 4 Prayed; 1 Corinthians 12:31; letter. 7 Walked. 8 Tea, religious talk; walked. 11 Chaise. 12.45 Witney. 1 Necessary talk (religious) to A. B.; letter. 2 Dinner, religious talk; letters. 4 Prayed; garden. 5 Tea, religious talk; prayer; prayed. 6.30 Philippians 1:21; Society! at sister — —'s, supper, religious talk; prayer. 9.30.

THURSDAY, OCTOBER 16. 4 Prayed; Job 7:18(2); chaise; Oxford; tea; chaise. 12 Wycombe; letters. 2 Dinner; letters. 4 Prayed; tea; prayer. 6.30 Micah 2:10! Society; supper; prayer. 9.30.

[FRIDAY, OCTOBER 17.] 4 Prayed; Psalms 106:24! tea, religious talk; prayer. 7 Chaise. 11.30 At home; letters. 3 Dinner. 3.30 Letters. 5 Tea; prayed; letters. 8 Supper; prayer. 9.30.

SATURDAY, OCTOBER 18. 4 Prayed; letters. 8 Tea, religious talk; prayer. 9 Letters. 12 Religious talk to Charles; walked. 1 Dinner; Charles [senior], Charles [junior], and Samuel, mostly religious talk. 3 Letters. 4.30 Tea; prayed; Magazine. 8 Supper; Magazine; necessary business. 9.30.

SUNDAY, OCTOBER 19. 4 Prayed; necessary business; letters; Spitalfields. 9.30 Read Prayers, Matthew 22:39, Communion; at brother Duplex's. 1 Dinner, religious talk; slept; letter; prayed; the leaders. 4 Tea; prayed. 5 Galatians 5:5; Society. 7 Necessary business; at brother Walter's, supper, religious talk. 9.15 Diligence [i.e., coach].

MONDAY, OCTOBER 20. 5.30 Prayed; read notes. 7 Newmarket; tea; Diligence; Shakespeare. 3.15 At Dr Hunt's, dinner, religious talk; Magazine. 5 Tea, religious talk; prayed. 6 Psalms 116:12! 8 At Dr Hunt's, supper, religious talk; prayer. 9.30.

TUESDAY, OCTOBER 21. 4 Prayed; Magazine. 8 Tea, religious talk; prayer. 9 Sermon. 12 Walked. 1 Dinner. 2.15 Sermon; prayed. 5 Tea; prayed. 6.30 Matthew 19:6; the leaders. 8.30 Supper, religious talk; prayer. 9.30.

[Text noted at bottom of page:] Luke 12:7!

WEDNESDAY, OCTOBER 22. 4.30 Psalms 106:24! sermon; tea. 8 Coach. 12 [Great] Yarmouth; walked. 1 At brother Hindmarsh's! dinner, religious talk. 2 Sermon; prayed. 4.45 At brother Warren's. 5 Tea, religious talk; prayer. 6 1 Corinthians 1:24! Society; supper, religious talk; prayer. 9.30.

THURSDAY, OCTOBER 23. 4 Hebrews 7:25; sermon. 8 Tea, religious talk; prayer. 9 Sermon. 10 Chaise. 11.30 Lowestoft [orig., 'Löstoffe']; read; necessary business. 12 Walked. 1 Dinner, religious talk. 2 Sermon; sins! 3.30 Read notes; prayed; visited; tea, religious talk; prayer. 6 Prayed. 6.30 2 Corinthians 4:18! Society. 8 Supper, mostly religious talk; prayer. 9.30.

FRIDAY, OCTOBER 24. 4 Prayed; journal. 6 Ephesians 6:11; journal. 10 Accounts; Magazine. 12 Walked. 1 At brother Mallet's, dinner, religious talk. 2.30 Magazine. 4 Prayed. 5 Tea, religious talk. 6 Prayed; Matthew 5:20! Society; supper, religious talk; prayer. 9.30.

SATURDAY, OCTOBER 25. 4 Prayed; Acts 1:5; tea. 6.45 Chaise. 8 [North] Cove; tea; Mark 1:15(2). 9 Chaise. 11.30 At brother Cross's, religious talk, dinner. 1 Hosea 14:4; chaise. 4.30 At Dr Hunt's, tea; prayed. 6.30 Mark 3:35; Society; supper, religious talk; prayer. 10.

SUNDAY, [OCTOBER 26]. 4 Prayed; letters. 7 Communion, 161; tea. 9 Romans 8:34! letters. 12.30 At Mr Thurston's. 1 Dinner, religious talk. 1.45 Meditation. 2 Luke 12:20; letters; prayed; tea. 6 Luke 12:7! 7 Magazine. 8 Supper, religious talk; prayer. 9.30.

MONDAY, OCTOBER 27. 4 Prayed; 1 Corinthians 7:35; sermon. 8 Tea, religious talk; prayer. 9 Sermon; letters. 11.30 Visited. 1 At Mr Ashley's, dinner, religious talk. 2.15 Magazine; prayed. 5 Tea, religious talk; prayed. 6.30 Luke 2:4; Magazine. 8 Supper, religious talk; prayer. 9.30.TUESDAY, OCTOBER 28. 4 Prayed; 1 Peter 3:8! sermon. 8 Tea, religious talk; prayer. 9 Sermon. 12.15 Walked; at Dr Hunt's. 1.30 Dinner, religious talk. 2.30 Sermon. 3 Prayed; tea. 6 Prayed; Matthew 22:39! 7.30 The leaders; supper; necessary business. 9.30.

WEDNESDAY, OCTOBER 29. 4 Prayed; 1 Corinthians 13:13; sermon; tea. 8 Diligence; Shakespeare. 4 [King's] Lynn; dinner. 4.30 Prayed. 5 Tea, religious talk. 6 Matthew 7:24! Society! 8 Supper, religious talk; prayer. 9.30.

THURSDAY, OCTOBER 30. 4 Prayed; Hebrews 6:1; sermon. 8 Tea, religious talk; prayer. 9 Sermon. 12 Walked. 1 At sister Register's, dinner, religious talk. 2.30 Sermon. 4 Prayed; tea, religious talk; prayed. 6.30 2 Timothy 3:5. 7 Society. 8 Supper, religious talk; prayer. 9.30.

FRIDAY, OCTOBER 31. 4 Prayed; Zechariah 4:7; sermon. 9 Read Clarkson, etc. 12 Walked. 1 Dinner, religious talk; prayer. 2.15 Writ notes. 5 Tea, religious talk; prayer; prayed. 6.30 Matthew 7:16! 7.30 Communion; supper, religious talk; prayer. 10 In the coach.

SATURDAY, NOVEMBER 1. 6 Necessary talk (religious); read Thomas Baker *On Learning*. 7 Newmarket; tea; coach. 2.30 Epping; dinner. 3.15 Coach; Baker, mostly religious talk. 6 At home; letters. 8 Supper, necessary talk! necessary business. 9.30.

SUNDAY, NOVEMBER 2. 5 Prayed; letters; the preachers. 9.30 Read Prayers, Matthew 22:4(2)! Communion. 1.15 At brother Deavy's, dinner, religious talk. 3 Slept; the leaders; tea; prayed. 5 Read Prayers, Ephesians 5:15. 6 Society; letters; supper, religious talk; prayer. 9.30.

MONDAY, NOVEMBER 3. 4 Prayed; Jeremiah 35:19! Select Society. 7 Class; tea; class. 12 At brother Wi——'s; class. 1 Dinner. 2 Class; tea. 6 Read Prayers, Colossians 3:11! class. 8.30 Supper; prayers. 9.30.

TUESDAY, NOVEMBER 4. 4 Prayed; letters. 6 Class; tea; class. 11 At brother Rance's, dinner. 1 Class. 4.30 Christened James Dornford; tea; prayer; necessary business; prayed. 6.30 Read Prayers, Luke 12:7! the leaders! supper; prayer. 9.30.

WEDNESDAY, NOVEMBER 5. 4 Prayed; letters. 6 Class; tea; class. 1 Dinner; class. 3 Coach. 5.15 Brentford. 5.30 Tea, religious talk. 6 Ephesians 4:1, etc! 8 At brother Blake's, supper, religious talk; prayer. 9.30.

THURSDAY, NOVEMBER 6. 4 Prayed; tea. 4.45 Chaise. 6.30 At home; letters. 7 Class; tea; class. 1 At sister Westry's, dinner. 2 Class. 4 Coach; Wandsworth; tea, religious talk; prayed. 6 Matthew 22:4. 7 Society! supper, religious talk; prayer. 9.30.

FRIDAY, NOVEMBER 7. 4 Prayed. 5 Chaise. 6.30 At home; writ notes. 7 Class; tea; class. 1 At brother Park's, dinner; class. 3 Chaise. 4.45 Hadley; tea; prayed. 6 Luke 12:7! 7 Society; read notes; supper. 9.45.

SATURDAY, NOVEMBER 8. 4 Prayed; tea. 5 Chaise. 6.30 Letters. 7 Class. 11 Letters. 12 Walked; dinner; prayer. 1.30 Letters; sins. 4 Prayed; walked; at Mr Collinson's, tea, religious talk. 6 Read Prayers, 1 Thessalonians 4:1, Communion; supper; Penry, necessary business. 9.30.

SUNDAY, NOVEMBER 9. 4 Prayed; letters. 8 Chapel. 9.30 Read Prayers, Ephesians 6:10, etc, Communion. 1.30 At Highbury; christened; dinner. 3.30 Read Prayers, 1 Thessalonians 5:19. 6 Society; coach; Society; supper, religious talk; prayer. 9.30.

MONDAY, NOVEMBER 10. 4 Prayed; Ephesians 2:8(3); Select Society; class; tea; class. 12 Select Society. 1 Dinner. 2 Class. 5 Tea, necessary talk (religious); prayed. 6.30 Read Prayers, Luke 12:7! supper; the bands; prayer. 9.30 Lay down.

[Texts noted at bottom of page:] Matthew 22:4(2); Ephesians 2:8(3); Jeremiah 23:27

TUESDAY, NOVEMBER 11. 4 Prayed; letter; Jeremiah 35; class; tea; class. 1 At brother Bower's, dinner. 2 Class. 4.30 At sister Hales's, tea, religious talk; class; prayed. 6.30 Hebrews 7:25! coach. 8 Chapel; supper; prayer. 9.30.

WEDNESDAY, NOVEMBER 12. 4 Prayed; letters; class; tea; class. 1.30 At Mr Brock's, dinner; christened. 3.30 Chaise. 4.30 Brentford; at brother Blake's, tea, religious talk; prayed. 6 Micah 2:10! class; supper, religious talk; prayer. 9.30.

THURSDAY, NOVEMBER 13. 4 Prayed; Mark 3:35; read notes; tea; prayer. 8 Coach. 10.30 At home; letters. 12.30 Coach. 1 Lambeth; writ Society. 2 Dinner; writ Society. 5 Prayed; tea; Society. 6.30 Micah 2:10; class; supper; prayer. 9.30.

FRIDAY, NOVEMBER 14. 4 Prayed; Ephesians 2:8(3); writ Society; tea; the children; Society. 11.30 Coach. 1 At brother Staniforth's, dinner; writ Society. 4 Class; tea. 6.30 Luke 12:7; Society. 8 At P. Lievre's, supper, religious talk; prayer. 9.30.

SATURDAY, NOVEMBER 15. 4 Prayed; at sister Purnell's, tea, religious talk; prayer. 6 Chaise. 7 Snowsfields; class; tea; class. 1 Dinner, religious talk; class. 4.30 Tea, religious talk; prayer. 6 Read Prayers, 1 Timothy 4:8! Society; coach. 8.15 Supper; necessary business. 9.30.

SUNDAY, NOVEMBER 16. 4 Prayed; Magazine. 8 Spitalfields. 9.30 Read Prayers, John 8:12! Communion; at Mr Maxfield's. 1.30 Dinner, religious talk; prayer; the leaders. 4 Tea, religious talk; at Mr Maxfield's, religious talk. 5.30 Read Prayers, Psalms 84:1; Society; Love-feast; supper; prayer. 9.30.

MONDAY, NOVEMBER 17. 4 Prayed; Matthew 6:34! Select Society. 7 Chaise; Farnborough; tea. 10.30 Chaise. 12.30 Sevenoaks; writ Society. 1.30 Dinner. 2.30 Writ Society. 4 Prayed. 5 Tea, religious talk. 6 Matthew 22:4(2)! Society; writ notes; supper; prayer. 9.30.

TUESDAY, NOVEMBER 18. 4 Prayed; writ Society. 6 Ephesians 2:8(3); Society. 8 Tea, religious talk; Society. 11 Chaise. 1.30 At Miss Boone's, necessary talk (religious). 2 Dinner, mostly religious talk. 3 Society. 4.30 Tea; prayed; Society. 6.30 Jeremiah 23:27! Society; supper; prayer. 9.45.

WEDNESDAY, NOVEMBER 19. 4 Prayed; Society. 7 1 Corinthians 13:8, etc; tea, religious talk; prayer. 9.15 Chaise; Sevenoaks. 12.15 Chaise. 1.15 Shoreham; dinner. 2 Society. 4 Tea, religious talk; prayed; Society. 6 1 Peter 1:13, etc! Society. 7.30 Supper, religious talk; prayer. 9.30.

THURSDAY, NOVEMBER 20. 4 Prayed; writ Society; necessary talk (religious). 7 Revelation 21:6; tea, religious talk; prayer. 9 Chaise. 10.30 Bromley. 11 Chaise. 1.30 Highbury; writ Society. 2.30 Dinner. 3.30 Writ Society. 5.30 Tea; prayed; Society; supper; prayer. 10.

FRIDAY, NOVEMBER 21. 4 Prayed; letters. 8 Tea; prayer; letters. 3 Dinner, necessary talk (religious). 4 Letters; prayed; tea; letters. 8.30 Supper, religious talk; prayer. 10.

[Pointing hand] SATURDAY, NOVEMBER 22. 4 Prayed; letters. 8 Tea; prayer; letters. 12.15 At Charles's, necessary talk (religious). 1.30 Dinner, religious talk. 3 Music. 3.45 Walked. 5 At brother Soper's, tea, necessary talk (religious); prayed. 6 Read the letters. 8.30 Supper; necessary business. 9.30.

SUNDAY, NOVEMBER 23. 4 Prayed; letters; chaise; the Chapel. 9.30 Read Prayers, Jeremiah 23:7! Communion; at Mr Brackenbury's. 1 Dinner, religious talk; visited. 3 The leaders; Titus 2:11; tea; Society. 6 Coach; Society; necessary business; supper, necessary talk (religious); prayer. 9.30.

MONDAY, NOVEMBER 24. 4 Prayed; tea. 5.15 Chaise; Dartford; tea; chaise. 12 Chatham; tea. 1 Chaise. 5.30 Canterbury; at brother Blackly's, dinner, tea, religious talk; prayer. 6 Luke 12:7! Society! at sister Bissaker's [?], supper, religious talk; prayer. 9.30.

Tuesday, November 25. 4 Prayed; Psalms 106:24! writ Society; tea, religious talk; prayer; Society. 10 Chaise. 1 Dover; dinner, religious talk; Society. 4 Walked; prayed; tea. 6 Matthew 22:4! supper. 8 Religious talk; prayer. 9.30.

Wednesday, November 26. 4 Prayed; letters. 6 Ephesians 4:1, etc! tea, religious talk; prayer. 8 Chaise. 11.30 Canterbury. 12 Society. 1 Dinner, religious talk. 2.30 Society; prayed. 5 Tea, religious talk; prayer; prayed. 6 [blank]. 7 Communion; at Mrs Simmond's, supper, religious talk; prayer. 9.30.

Thursday, November 27. 4 Prayed; tea. 5.15 Chaise; tea. 9 Kingsferry; chaise. 11 Sheerness; sins; Society. 1.30 Dinner; Society; prayed. 5 Tea, religious talk; prayer. 6 Read Prayers, Hebrews 3:7. 8 Supper, religious talk; prayer. 9.45.

Friday, November 28. 4 Prayed; letter. 5.30 1 Corinthians 15:58, Communion; tea; prayer. 8 Chaise. 11.30 Chatham. 12 Tea, religious talk; prayer; writ Society. 1 Dinner; Society. 4 Prayed; tea, religious talk. 6 2 Timothy 3:5. 7.30 Communion; supper, religious talk; prayer. 9.30.

Saturday, November 29. 4 Prayed. 5 Matthew 22:37; tea. 6 Chaise. 9.30 Welling; tea, necessary talk (religious); prayer. 10.30 Chaise. 12.30 At home; letters. 1 Dinner, necessary talk (religious); prayer. 2 Letters; tea; prayed; letters. 8.45 Necessary business. 9.30.

Sunday, November 30. 4 Prayed; letters; the preachers. 9.30 Read Prayers, Romans 13:11, etc! Communion! 1 Dinner, religious talk. 2 Slept; prayed; the leaders; tea; prayed. 5 Read Prayers, Hebrews 6:1, 2! Society. 7 Supper, necessary talk (religious); prayer. 9.30.

[Texts noted at bottom of page:] Romans 13:11, etc; 1 Peter 1:3, etc.

Monday, December 1. 4 Prayed; 1 Peter 3:8; Select Society; tea; letters. 11 Chaise; writ Society; Select Society. 1.30 At brother Clulow's, dinner, religious talk; prayer. 3 Writ Society. 4 Visited; tea, religious talk, necessary talk (religious). 6.30 Prayed; Hebrews 7:25! supper; the bands. 9.30.

Tuesday, December 2. 4 Prayed; 1 Peter 3:8; writ Society; visited; necessary business. 9 With John Duplex, tea, necessary talk (religious). 10 Married Lydia Duplex [to Mr Rutherford]; coach. 1 Richmond; walked; dinner, religious talk. 3 Coach; writ notes. 6.30 Read Prayers, Hebrews 8:10; the leaders; supper; necessary business; prayer. 9.30.

[Wednesday, December 3.] 4 Prayed; tea. 5 Chaise, with Mr Brackenbury, religious talk. 8 Tea, religious talk. 9 Chaise. 12.30 Baldock; Miss Harvey. 1 Chaise. 2 Hinxworth; writ Society. 2.30 Dinner, religious talk. 3.30 Writ Society; prayed; tea. 6 Ephesians 2:8; supper, religious talk; prayer. 9.30.

[Thursday, December 4.] 4 Prayed; writ Society. 8 Tea, religious talk; prayer; Society. 10.30 Visited; walked. 1 Dinner; letters. 3 Chaise. 4.30 At Mr Hick's, religious talk, tea; prayed. 6 Read Prayers, 2 Corinthians 8:9! 8 Supper, religious talk; prayer. 9.30.

FRIDAY, DECEMBER 5. 4 Prayed; read. 6.45 Tea, religious talk. 8 Chaise. 9.30 Hinxworth; tea, religious talk; prayer; chaise. 3 Old Bell; dinner; chaise. 4.45 Hadley; tea; prayed. 6 Matthew 22:4! Communion. 8 Supper, religious talk; prayer. 9.30.

SATURDAY, DECEMBER 6. 4 Prayed; writ Preface; tea. 6.15 Chaise. 8.15 At home; letters; Preface. 12.30 Dinner; prayer. 1 Preface. 4 Prayed; walked. 5 Tea, religious talk. 6 Read Prayers, Hebrews 12:28! Communion; supper; Penry, necessary business. 9.30.

SUNDAY, DECEMBER 7. 4 Prayed; Preface. 8 The preachers; prayed. 9.30 Read Prayers, Romans 15:4, 5. 12 Communion. 1 Dinner, religious talk. 3 The leaders; tea; prayed. 5 Read Prayers, Hebrews 13:22! 6 Society; necessary talk (religious) to many; supper, religious talk; prayer. 9.30.

MONDAY, DECEMBER 8. 4 Prayed; 1 Corinthians 13:9; Select Society; letter. 8 Tea, religious talk; prayer; visited; letters. 12 Select Society. 1.30 At brother Braun's, dinner, religious talk; visited. 3:30 Writ notes; tea, religious talk; prayed. 6.15 Read Prayers. 7 James 1:27! supper; the bands. 9.30.

TUESDAY, DECEMBER 9. 4 Prayed; 1 Corinthians 13:9! letters. 8 Tea, religious talk; prayer. 9.30 At home; letters. 1 At brother Sause's, dinner, religious talk. 2.30 Letters; prayed. 6.30 Read Prayers, James 2:5! the leaders. 8.30 Supper, religious talk; prayer. 9.30.

WEDNESDAY, DECEMBER 10. 4.15 Prayed; letters. 8 Tea, religious talk; letters; accounts; Magazine. 1 Dinner, religious talk. 2.30 Magazine. 5 Tea, necessary talk (religious); *The Adelphi* [by Terence]. 9.30 Chaise; supper; prayer; sins. 11.

THURSDAY, DECEMBER 11. 5 Prayed; journal. 8 Tea, religious talk; prayer. 9 Letter to T. Maxfield. 2 At brother Folgham's. 3 Dinner; christened! religious talk; chaise. 4.15 Tea, religious talk; prayer. 5.30 Prayed; Luke 18:25. 7.30 The bands; supper; prayer. 9.30.

FRIDAY, DECEMBER 12. 4 Prayed; letter; Magazine. 12.45 Visited. 1.30 Prayer. 3 At brother Wright's, dinner, religious talk. 5 At home; tea; prayed. 6 The Committee! read Barrington! 8 Supper, necessary talk (religious); prayer. 9.30.

SATURDAY, DECEMBER 13. 4 Prayed; Barrington. 8 Tea, necessary talk (religious); prayer; Barrington. 1 At brother Thornton's, dinner, religious talk. 2.30 Letters; prayer. 4.30 Tea, religious talk; prayer; prayed. 6 Read Prayers. 7 1 Peter 1:3, Communion; supper; Penry, necessary business. 9.30.

SUNDAY, DECEMBER 14. 4 Prayed; writ notes; Chapel; read Prayers, 1 Corinthians 4:2! Communion. 1 Dinner, religious talk. 2 Slept; prayed. 3 The leaders. 3.30 Read Prayers, James 2:5; Society; St Swithin's, read Prayers, 1 Peter 2:2. 7.30 Supper; prayer, read. 9.30.

MONDAY, DECEMBER 15. 4 Prayed; 1 Corinthians 8:1; Select Society; letters. 8 Tea, religious talk; prayer; Barrington. 11 Chaise; visited. 12 Select Society; at brother Wilson's, dinner; prayer. 2.30 Barrington; prayed. 4.45 Tea, religious talk; prayer. 6 A. B——n. 6.30 Read Prayers, Luke 18:25! supper; the bands. 9.30.

TUESDAY, DECEMBER 16. 4 Prayed; 1 Corinthians 8:1; letters. 8 Tea, religious talk; prayer; walked. 9.30 At home; letters; Barrington. 12.30 Visited. 1 At T. Rankin's, dinner, religious talk; prayer. 2.30 Barrington; prayed. 4 Tea, religious talk; prayer. 5.30 Prayed. 6.30 Read Prayers, Acts 16:31! the leaders; Society! supper; prayer. 9.30.

WEDNESDAY, DECEMBER 17. 4 Prayed; Barrington. 8 Tea, religious talk; prayer; Barrington. 1 Writ the bands. 2.30 At Mr Wolff's, dinner, religious talk; at Mr Rutherford's, tea, religious talk; prayer. 6 Read Prayers, 1 Peter 5:6! Communion; coach; supper, necessary talk (religious); prayer. 9.30.

THURSDAY, DECEMBER 18. 4 Prayed; letters. 8.15 Tea, religious talk; prayer; corrected Magazine. 2 At Dr Johnson's, dinner, mostly religious talk. 4 Buried; christened; tea, religious talk; prayer. 5.30 Prayed. 6.30 Read Prayers, 1 John 1:3! the bands; supper, necessary talk (religious); prayer. 9.30.

FRIDAY, DECEMBER 19. 4 Prayed; letters. 8 Magazine. 12 The females. 1.30 Prayer; at brother Owen's, dinner, religious talk; prayer; Magazine. 4.30 Tea, religious talk; prayer. 5.30 Prayed; Magazine. 8 Supper, necessary talk (religious); prayer. 9.30.

SATURDAY, DECEMBER 20. 4 Prayed; letters; Magazine. 8 At G. Clark's, tea, necessary talk (religious)! prayer; Magazine. 1 At sister Shakespeare's, dinner; letters; prayer; visited; tea, religious talk. 6 Read Prayers, 1 John 2:12! Communion; supper; Penry, necessary business. 9.30.

SUNDAY, DECEMBER 21. 4 Prayed; letters; Spitalfields; read Prayers, Matthew 24:27! Communion; at brother Teulon's. 1 Dinner, religious talk; prayer; visited. 3 The leaders; buried; prayed; necessary talk (religious); tea, religious talk. 6 St Swithin's, read Prayers, 1 John 1:3! 8 Supper; prayer! 9.30.

MONDAY, DECEMBER 22. 4 Prayed; Matthew 24:27; Select Society; tea; chaise. 9 Camberwell; texts. 3 Dinner, religious talk; Magazine, prayed. 6 Tea, religious talk; Magazine. 8.15 Supper, religious talk; prayer. 9.45.

TUESDAY, DECEMBER 23. 4 Prayed; Magazine. 8 Tea, religious talk; prayer; Magazine. 12 Walked. 1 Dinner, religious talk; Magazine. 4.45 At brother Smith's, tea, religious talk; prayer. 7 Prayed; Magazine. 8 Supper, religious talk; prayer. 9.45.

WEDNESDAY, DECEMBER 24. 4 Prayed; Magazine; tea; prayer. 7 Chaise. 8 At home; read notes; letters; Magazine; visited. 3 At brother Blunt's, dinner, religious talk; prayer. 4 Read Prayers. 5 At brother Garr——'s, tea, religious talk;

prayer. 6 Read Prayers, 1 John 4:15! Communion; supper, religious talk; prayer. 9.30.

CHRISTMAS DAY [THURSDAY, DECEMBER 25]. 3.30 Prayed; prayer; Genesis 3:15! 6 Slept; Magazine; tea; chaise. 9.30 Read Prayers, Genesis 3:15! Communion. 1.30 At brother Bat——'s, dinner, religious talk; prayer. 2.45 Magazine; prayed; tea, mostly religious talk. 5 Titus 3:4, etc; Society; Magazine; supper; prayer; read. 9.30.

FRIDAY, DECEMBER 26. 4 Prayed; letters. 10 Snowsfields; read Prayers, Acts 7:55! Communion; at brother Collinson's, dinner, religious talk; prayer. 3.30 Prayed; at brother Rankin's, tea, religious talk; prayer. 6 Read Prayers, John 4:24! supper, religious talk; prayer. 9.30.

SATURDAY [DECEMBER 27]. 4 Prayed; letters. 8 Tea, necessary talk (religious); letters; Magazine. 1 At brother Awbrey's, dinner, religious talk; prayer. 3 Prayed. 4 Chaise; at sister Bowman's, tea, religious talk; prayer. 6 Read Prayers, Revelation 22:20, Communion. 7.45 Supper, religious talk; necessary business. 9.30.

SUNDAY, DECEMBER 28. 4 Prayed; Magazine; Chapel. 9.30 Read Prayers, Revelation 14:1, etc, Communion; dinner, religious talk; prayer. 2.15 Slept; prayed; the leaders. 3.30 Read Prayers, 1 John 5:11! Society; chaise; Society; supper, religious talk. 8.30 Magazine. 9.30.

MONDAY, DECEMBER 29. 4 Prayed; Jeremiah 3:12; Select Society; necessary talk (religious). 8 Tea, necessary talk (religious); prayer. 10 Pupil. 12 Select Society. 1.30 At sister Sharland's, dinner, religious talk; prayer; visited! at sister Jacob's, tea, religious talk; prayer; prayed. 6.30 Read Prayers, John 4:24(2); supper; the bands. 9.30.

TUESDAY, DECEMBER 30. 4 Prayed; Matthew 24:27, Communion; Magazine; visited. 8 Tea, necessary talk (religious); prayer. 9.30 Necessary business. 10 Pupil; letter; Magazine. 1 Dinner, religious talk; prayer; visited; Workhouse! tea, religious talk; prayer. 5 Necessary business; prayed. 6.30 Read Prayers, 1 John 4:19! the leaders; supper, religious talk; prayer. 9.30.

WEDNESDAY, DECEMBER 31. 4 Prayed; Magazine. 8 Tea, religious talk; prayer; Magazine. 1 Dinner; visited; letters; tea; prayer; prayed; Magazine. 8 Tea. 8.30 Jeremiah 3:12! prayer. 9.15. 12.30.

[Texts noted at bottom of page:] Genesis 3:15; Acts 7:55; John 4:24(2); Jeremiah 3:12; 1 John 4:19.

THURSDAY, JANUARY 1, 1784. 6.30 Prayed; tea, religious talk; prayer. 10 Read Prayers, 2 Corinthians 5:15! Communion. 1 At brother Ball's, dinner, religious talk. 3 Peckham; Magazine. 5 Prayed; tea. 6.30 Magazine. 8.30 Supper. 9 Religious talk; prayer. 10.

FRIDAY, JANUARY 2. 4.30 Prayed; Magazine; texts. 8.30 Tea, religious talk; prayer; texts. 2.30 Dinner. 3 Religious talk; prayer. 4 Magazine; prayed. 5 Tea, religious talk; prayed. 6 1 John 4:19! Magazine. 8.30 Supper, religious talk; prayer. 10.30.

SATURDAY, JANUARY 3. 5 Prayed; texts. 8.30 Tea, religious talk; prayer; Magazine; chaise. 1 At brother Da——'s, dinner; letters; prayer. 4.30 Tea, religious talk; prayer. 6 Read Prayers, Romans 2:29, Communion. 8 Supper; Penry, necessary business. 9.30.

SUNDAY, JANUARY 4. 4 Prayed; letters; the preachers; prayed. 9.30 Read Prayers, 2 Kings 23:3, Communion; at sister Box's. 1 Dinner, religious talk; prayer. 2 Necessary talk (religious); slept. 3 Prayed; tea; prayed. 5 The Covenant! supper; prayer. 9.30.

MONDAY, JANUARY 5. 4 Prayed; Matthew 6:22! Select Society; letters. 8 Tea; letters. 12 Select Society. 1.30 Dinner; visited. 3.30 Letters; tea, religious talk; prayer; Magazine. 6.30 Read Prayers, Romans 4:9; supper. 8 The bands; Magazine. 9.30.

Tuesday, JANUARY 6. 4 Prayed; Matthew 6:22! letter; walked. 7.30 At home; tea; letters. 10 Chaise; Barking. 12 1 John 4:19! visited; dinner. 2 Chaise. 4 Rainham; tea. 5 Chaise; Purfleet; Matthew 8:2! Rainham; supper; prayer. 9.30.

[WEDNESDAY] JANUARY [7]. 4 Prayed; tea; prayer. 5 Chaise; Ingatestone; tea; chaise; Ariosto [*Orlando Furioso*]. 11.30 Witham. 1.30 Chaise. 3 Colchester; dinner; Magazine; tea; prayer. 7 Jeremiah 3:12! Magazine; supper, religious talk; prayer. 10.

THURSDAY, JANUARY 8. 4.15 Prayed; Magazine. 6 Luke 12:7! the leaders; writ Society. 8 Tea, religious talk; prayer. 9 Magazine. 1.30 Dinner; Magazine. 3 Visited; tea; prayer. 5 Magazine. 6.30 Matthew 24:4! Communion; supper; prayer. 9.30.

FRIDAY, JANUARY 9. 4 Tea; prayer. 5 Chaise. 8.30 Chelmsford; tea; walked; chaise. 1 Romford; chaise. 3 At home; dinner; letters; tea; prayer; letters; supper, religious talk; prayer. 9.30.

SATURDAY, JANUARY 10. 4 Prayed; letters. 8 Tea, religious talk; prayer; letters. 1 At brother Marsden's, dinner, religious talk; prayer. 2.30 Sorted letters; prayed; ——[?]; tea. 6 Read Prayers, Romans 8:3, 4, Communion; supper; Penry; necessary business. 9.30.

SUNDAY, JANUARY 11. 4 Prayed; letters; Chapel, read Prayers, Romans 12:1! Communion; at Mr Brackenbury's. 1.30 Dinner; slept; the leaders. 3.30 Read Prayers, Romans 12:2! Society; chaise; Society. 7 Prayed; supper, religious talk; prayer. 9.30.

MONDAY, JANUARY 12. 4 Prayed; Luke 2:51; Select Society; writ notes. 8 Tea, religious talk; prayer. 9 Letter. 10 Pupils. 12 Select Society; at Mr Brooks's, dinner, religious talk; prayer. 3 Letters; tea; prayed. 6.30 Read Prayers, Romans 10:4; supper; the bands; Magazine. 9.30.

TUESDAY, JANUARY 13. 4 Prayed; Luke 2:52; Magazine. 8 Tea, religious talk; prayer; walked. 9 Letters. 1.30 At brother Bird's. 2 Dinner, religious talk; prayer; visited. 3.30 Letters; tea. 5 Prayed; letters. 6.30 Read Prayers, Romans 11:33. 7 The leaders; supper, religious talk; prayer. 9.30.

WEDNESDAY, JANUARY 14. 4 Prayed; letters. 8 Tea, religious talk; prayer; letters. 1 At brother Love's, dinner, religious talk; prayer; at home. 3 Prayed; letters. 5 At brother L. Able's, tea, religious talk; prayer. 6 Read Prayers, Romans 12:1, Communion; supper; prayer. 9.30.

THURSDAY, JANUARY 15. 4 Prayed; letters. 8 Tea, religious talk; prayer; letters. 10 Pupils; Magazine. 1 At Thomas Olivers's, dinner. 2 Prayer. 2.30 Magazine; necessary business. 5 Mrs Tighe's, tea, religious talk; prayed. 6.30 Read Prayers. 7 Romans 13:10! the bands; supper, religious talk; prayer. 9.30.

FRIDAY, JANUARY 16. 4 Prayed; letters; Magazine; letters. 10 Pupils; letters. 12 The females; letters. 1.30 Prayer. 2.30 At brother Sause's. 3.30 Letter. 4.30 Tea, religious talk; prayed; letters. 8 Supper, religious talk; prayer. 9.30.

SATURDAY, JANUARY 17. 4 Prayed; accounts. 8 Tea, religious talk; Mr Collins, prayer, religious talk! necessary business. 10 Pupils; necessary business. 11.30 Magazine. 1 At brother Hussey's, dinner; prayer. 2 Magazine; prayed. 4.30 Tea; visited. 6 Read Prayers, Romans 15:2! Society; Communion; supper; Penry, necessary business. 9.30.

SUNDAY, JANUARY 18. 4 Prayed; letters; Spitalfields. 9.30 Read Prayers, Matthew 16:23! Communion; dinner, religious talk; prayed. 2.30 Slept; prayed. 3 The leaders; tea; prayed. 5 Read Prayers, Isaiah 53:4, 5! Society! 7 The Lovefeast; supper, religious talk; prayer. 9.30.

MONDAY, JANUARY 19. 4 Prayed; Romans 15:2; Select Society; necessary talk (religious); necessary business; tea; prayer. 9 Letters; pupils; necessary talk (religious). 12 Select Society; at Mr Atwood's, dinner, religious talk; prayer. 3.30 Chapel; prayed. 4.30 Tea, religious talk; prayer; prayed. 6.30 Read Prayers, Psalms 90:12! prayer; bands. 9.30.

[TUESDAY] JANUARY [20]. 4.45 Romans 15:2! Magazine; chaise. 8 At sister Cheesement's, tea, religious talk; prayer; chaise. 10 Newington; letters. 1.30 Dinner, necessary talk (religious). 2.30 Letters; prayed; tea; writ notes. 7 Daniel 2; supper, religious talk; prayer. 9.30.

WEDNESDAY, JANUARY 21. 4 Prayed; letters; Magazine. 8 Tea, religious talk; prayer; Magazine. 12 Walked with Thomas Rankin; visited. 1 At sister Cheesement's, dinner, religious talk; prayer. 3.30 At home; prayed; tea. 6 Mr Smyth. 7 Hammet, Crawford, Riley, supper, religious talk; prayer. 10.15.

[Texts noted at bottom of page:] Romans 11:33, Romans 15:2, Psalms 90:12.

THURSDAY, JANUARY 22. 4 Prayed; letters. 8 Tea, religious talk; letters. 10 Pupils. 11 Magazine; chaise. 1 Highgate; religious talk. 2 Dinner, religious talk. 3 Read notes; prayed. 5 Tea, religious talk; prayed. 6.30 Revelation 20:12! 7 Read! 9 Supper, religious talk; prayer. 10.30.

FRIDAY, JANUARY 23. 5 Prayer; Magazine. 7 1 Peter 1:24; tea; prayer. 9 Chaise. 10 Pupils; letters. 12 The females; letters. 1.30 Prayer; at brother Willan's, dinner, religious talk; prayer; visited. 4 Prayed; letters; tea. 6 Mr Smith, etc! 9 Supper, religious talk; prayer. 10.

SATURDAY, JANUARY 24. 4 Prayed; letters. 7 Class; tea; class. 12 At brother Collinson's; class. 1 Dinner. 2 Class. 4 Prayed; at brother Trigg's, tea, religious talk; prayer; prayed. 6 Read Prayers, 1 Corinthians 6:20! Society; communion; coach. 8.15 Supper; necessary business. 9.30.

SUNDAY, JANUARY 25. 4 Prayed; read notes. 6.30 Necessary talk (religious), with Charles; Chapel. 9.30 Read Prayers, Acts 22:16! 11 Communion; visited; at brother Dobson's, dinner, religious talk; prayer. 2.15 Slept; prayed; the leaders. 3.30 Read Prayers, Acts 26:18! Society; chaise; Society; supper, religious talk; prayer. 9.30.

MONDAY, JANUARY 26. 4 Prayed; Matthew 6:34; Select Society; class. 1 Dinner, religious talk. 2 Class; tea; class. 6 Read Prayers, 1 Corinthians 8:1; class, necessary talk! 8 Coach; supper, necessary talk (religious); prayer. 9.30.

[Pointing hand] TUESDAY, JANUARY 27. 4 Prayed; writ notes. 6 Class; tea; class. 1 At brother Hudson's, dinner, religious talk; prayer. 2 Class. 5 At home; prayed; necessary business. 6.30 Read the letters; the leaders; supper. 9 Prayer. 9.30.

WEDNESDAY, JANUARY 28. 4 Prayed; letter. 6 Class; tea; class. 12 Letters. 1 At brother Kemp's, dinner. 2 Class. 3.30 Letters; tea; Magazine; prayed; Magazine. 8 Supper, religious talk; prayer. 9.30.

THURSDAY, JANUARY 29. 4 Prayed; letters; class; tea; class. 1 At sister Westry's, dinner. 2 Class. 5 Tea, necessary talk (religious). 5.30 Chaise. 6.30 At Charles's, necessary talk (religious) to General Oglethorpe, etc; concert. 10.30 Supper. 11.

FRIDAY, JANUARY 30. 5 Prayed. 6 Class. 8 The leaders; class. 1 Dinner; at brother Parker's. 2 Class. 5 Tea, religious talk; prayer. 6 At brother Dewey's, etc! prayed. 8 Supper, religious talk. 9.30.

SATURDAY, JANUARY 31. 4 Prayed; letters. 7 Class; tea; class. 1 Dinner, religious talk. 2 Class; letters; walked. 5 Visited; tea. 6 Prayers. 1 Corinthians 12:31, Communion; supper; Penry, necessary business. 9.30.

[Texts noted at bottom of page:] Matthew 8:13; Acts 26:28.

SUNDAY, FEBRUARY 1. 4.15 Prayed; letters. 8 The preachers. 9.30 Read Prayers, Matthew 8:13! Communion; dinner, religious talk. 2.30 Slept; prayed; the leaders; buried. 4 Tea; prayed. 5 1 Corinthians 13:1, etc; Society. 7 [Met] the married [Society]! 8 Supper, necessary talk (religious); prayer. 9.30.

MONDAY, FEBRUARY 2. 4 Prayed; 1 Corinthians 13:8, etc! Select Society. 7 Class; tea; class. 12 Select Society; at brother Nelson's, dinner, religious talk. 2 Class; tea; class; read Prayers, 1 Thessalonians 4:7; the bands; supper, religious talk; prayer. 9.30.

TUESDAY, FEBRUARY 3. 3 Prayed; slept. 5 Letters. 7 Class; tea; class. 1 At brother Kemp's, dinner. 2 Class. 5 Westminster; tea; class. 6.30 Hebrews 12:14! Chapel. 8.15 Supper; prayer. 9.30.

WEDNESDAY, FEBRUARY 4. 4 Prayed; read notes. 7 Class; tea; class. 1 At brother Treble's, dinner, religious talk. 2 Class. 4.30 Chaise; Brentford; at brother Blake's, tea; prayed. 6.30 Acts 26:18! class; supper, religious talk; prayer. 9.30.

THURSDAY, FEBRUARY 5. 4 Prayed; 1 Corinthians 13:8, etc! prayed; tea. 7 Chaise. 9 At home; letters. 1 At Mr Judd's, dinner, religious talk; prayer; visited; prayed. 4 Chaise; Highgate; letters; tea, religious talk. 6 Letter. 6.30 1 Thessalonians 4:7! letters. 9 Supper, religious talk. 10.30.

FRIDAY, FEBRUARY 6. 4.45 Prayed; letters. 8 Micah 2:10! tea, religious talk; letters. 1 Dinner, religious talk; the children. 3 Chaise. 4.30 Hadley; prayed; read *Orlando [Furioso];* tea. 6 Hebrews 6:1. 7 Class; *Orlando [Furioso];* supper, religious talk; prayer. 10.15.

SATURDAY, FEBRUARY 7. 4.45 Prayed; letters; tea. 7 Chaise. 9 At home; letters. 1 At John Paramore's, dinner, religious talk. 2 Necessary business. 3 Necessary talk (religious); *Orlando [Furioso];* letters. 5 Tea; prayed; *Orlando [Furioso].* 8 Supper; read notes; necessary business. 9.30.

SUNDAY, FEBRUARY 8. 4 Prayed; sermon. 8 Chapel. 9.30 Read Prayers, Matthew 20:16! Communion; coach. 1 At Mr Pigeon's, necessary talk (religious), dinner. 3 St George's; read Prayers, 1 Corinthians 13:1, etc. 4 Tea, religious talk. 6 St Swithin's; read Prayers, 2 Corinthians 4:5; at home. 8 Supper, necessary talk (religious); prayer. 9.30.

MONDAY, FEBRUARY 9. 4 Prayed; 1 Corinthians 13, *ad fin;* Select Society; necessary business; tea. 8 Chaise; with brother Sause. 9 Shakespeare. 1 Dorking; writ notes. 2 Dinner; writ notes. 5 Prayed; tea. 6 Colossians 1:10! Communion; supper, religious talk; prayer. 9.30.

TUESDAY, FEBRUARY 10. 4 Prayed; writ notes. 6 Galatians 5:5; class; tea; prayer. 9 Chaise. 1.15 At Mr Dornford's. 2 Dinner, religious talk; prayer. 4 Class; tea; class. 6.30 Ephesians 3:14, etc! Society; at Mr Holbrook's, supper, religious talk; prayer. 9.30.

WEDNESDAY, FEBRUARY 11. 5 Prayed; sermon. 7 Tea, religious talk; prayer. 8 Chaise. 9.30 At home; writ sermon. 12 Chaise. 1 Lambeth; dinner; letters. 5 Prayed; tea; letters. 6.30 Luke 10:42. 7.30 Class; supper, religious talk; prayer. 10.

THURSDAY, FEBRUARY 12. 5 Prayed; letter. 7 Children; tea, religious talk. 8 Chaise; Shakespeare. 9 Letters. 10 Chaise; Bow; class. 12 1 John 4:19! chaise. 2 At brother Senol's, dinner, religious talk. 3 Visited; chaise. 4.30 Wandsworth; tea; prayed. 6.30 1 Thessalonians [4:]7! class. 8.30 Supper, religious talk; prayer. 10.

FRIDAY, FEBRUARY 13. 4.30 Prayed; writ sermon. 6 1 Corinthians 13:13; at brother Barker's, tea, necessary talk (religious); prayer. 8 Chaise. 9 Letters; chaise. 12 Poplar; Acts 26:18; class; dinner, religious talk. 2 Chaise. 3 At home; letters. 5 Tea; prayed. 6 The Committee. 8 Supper, religious talk; prayer. 9.30.

SATURDAY, FEBRUARY 14. 4 Prayed; letters; Magazine. 8 Tea, religious talk; prayer. 9 E[lizabeth] Ellison and sister Hall! read notes. 11 Dr Coke, etc! 1 At Samuel Bailey's, dinner, religious talk; prayer. 2 Magazine; prayed. 4.30 Tea, religious talk. 6 Read Prayers, Psalms 74:13, Communion; supper; Penry, necessary business. 9.30.

SUNDAY, FEBRUARY 15. 4 Prayed; read notes. 8 Spitalfields. 9.30 Read Prayers, John 15:7, etc, Communion; visited; at Mr Wil[la]n's. 2 Dinner, religious talk. 2.45 Read Prayers, Revelation 20:12! 5 Read Prayers, Genesis 6:5; Society; single women. 8 Supper, religious talk; prayer. 9.30.

MONDAY, FEBRUARY 16. 4 Prayed; Psalms 74:13! Select Society; read notes. 8 Tea, religious talk; prayer. 9 Letters. 12 Select Society; Communion. 1.15 At Mr Clulow's, dinner, necessary talk. 3 *Orlando [Furioso];* Magazine; prayed; at brother Davison's. 5 Tea, religious talk; prayer. 6.30 Read Prayers, 2 Corinthians 12:7; supper, religious talk; the bands. 9.30.

TUESDAY, FEBRUARY 17. 4 Prayed; Psalms 74:13; *Orlando [Furioso];* Magazine. 7.30 Tea, religious talk; chaise. 8.30 At home; Magazine. 11 Writ notes. 1 At brother Collinson's, dinner, religious talk; prayer. 2.30 Letters. 5 Tea, religious talk; prayer. 6 Prayed; read Prayers, 2 Corinthians 13:11; the leaders; supper; prayer; *Orlando [Furioso].* 9.30.

WEDNESDAY, FEBRUARY 18. 4 Prayed; journal. 8 At Mr Creighton's, tea, religious talk; prayer. 9 Letters; Magazine. 2 At Mr Wolff's, dinner, religious talk. 4.15 At R. Whitfield's, tea, religious talk; prayer. 6 Read Prayers, 2 Corinthians 5! Communion; supper; prayer; Ariosto [*Orlando Furioso*]. 9.30.

THURSDAY, FEBRUARY 19. 4 Prayed; writ letters. 8 Tea, religious talk; prayer; Ariosto [*Orlando Furioso];* letters. 1 At sister Mullis's, dinner, religious talk. 2 Prayer. 2.30 Magazine; prayed. 4.30 Chaise; at Charles's, tea, religious talk; prayed; Ariosto [*Orlando Furioso*]. 7 Concert; Pascal Paoli! 11.

[Texts noted at bottom of page:] Matthew 4:10; John 15:7, etc; Psalms 74:13; Acts 11:26; Psalms 90:12.

FRIDAY, FEBRUARY 20. 5.30 Prayed; writ my will. 10 Magazine. 12 The Temple; necessary talk (religious). 1.30 Prayer. 2.30 At George Clark's, dinner, religious talk; prayer. 4 Prayed; *Orlando [Furioso];* at sister Butcher's, tea, religious talk. 5 Prayer; prayed. 6 Quarterly Meeting! 8 Supper; prayer. 9.30.

SATURDAY, FEBRUARY 21. 4 Prayed; letters. 8 Tea, religious talk; prayer. 9 Letters; Magazine. 1 At brother Thurgood's, dinner, religious talk. 2.30 Prayer; Magazine. 3.30 Prayed; at Mr Waldron's, tea, religious talk; prayer. 6 Read Prayers, Acts 11:26(2), Communion; supper; Penry, necessary business. 9.30.

SUNDAY, FEBRUARY 22. 5 Prayed; Magazine. 8 The Chapel. 9.30 Read Prayers, Acts 11:26, Communion. 1 At sister Okerblum's, dinner, religious talk; prayer. 2 Slept; prayed. 3 The leaders. 3.30 Read Prayers, Ephesians 6:3! 5 Tea; Society; chaise; Society! the single men. 8 Supper, religious talk; prayer. 9.30.

MONDAY, FEBRUARY 23. 4 Prayed; Psalms 90:12; Select Society; Magazine. 8 Tea, religious talk; prayer; Magazine. 11.30 Read notes. 12 Select Society. 1.45 At Mr Griffith's, dinner, religious talk; prayer. 4 Prayed; read notes; at sister Hayne's. 5 Tea, religious talk; prayed. 6.30 Read Prayers, Galatians 6:15! necessary talk! supper; the bands. 9.30.

TUESDAY, FEBRUARY 24. 4 Prayed; Psalms 90:12; Magazine. 8 Tea, religious talk; prayer; visited some. 10 Ariosto [*Orlando Furioso*]. 11 Knightsbridge; read Prayers, Matthew 11:28! at sister Bar[nes]'s, dinner, religious talk; prayer. 4 Prayed. 5 Tea; prayer; necessary talk. 6.30 Read Prayers, Ephesians 1:13! the leaders. 8 Supper, religious talk; prayer. 9.30.

ASH WEDNESDAY, FEBRUARY 25. 4 Prayed; sermon. 10 Read Prayers, Matthew 6:17, Communion, sermon. 1 At Thomas Rankin's, dinner, necessary talk (religious); prayer. 2.30 Sermon. 4 Prayed. 5 At brother Wright's, tea, necessary talk (religious); prayer. 6 Read Prayers, Philippians 2:12! Communion; supper, religious talk; prayer. 9.30.

THURSDAY, FEBRUARY 26. 4 Prayed; sermon. 8 Tea, religious talk; prayer; sermon. 11 Visited; walked; Mr Best; visited. 1 At Mr Goslin's, dinner, religious talk; prayer. 3.30 At Mr Beardmore's; writ sermon. 5 Prayed. 5.30 Tea, necessary talk (religious); sermon. 8 Supper, religious talk; prayer. 10.

FRIDAY, FEBRUARY 27. 4.30 Prayed; sermon. 8 Tea; prayer; sermon. 2 Dinner, religious talk. 3 Sermon; prayed. 5.30 Tea, religious talk. 6.15 Sermon. 8.15 Prayed; supper, necessary talk (religious); prayer. 10 Thomas Tennant ill.

SATURDAY, FEBRUARY 28. 4.45 Prayed; sermon. 8 Tea; prayer; sermon. 11 At Mr Clulow's; necessary business; coach; Hampstead. 1 Visited. 2.30 At brother Wilson's, dinner; prayer; prayed. 5 Tea, religious talk; prayer. 6 Read Prayers, Ephesians 5:1, 2! Communion. 7 Penry, necessary business. 9.45.

SUNDAY, FEBRUARY 29. 4 Prayed; sermon; the preachers; read Prayers, Matthew 4:10! Communion; at brother Clulow's, dinner, religious talk; prayer. 2.30 Slept; the leaders; read Prayers, Genesis 22:1, 2; chaise. 6 Brentford; tea. 6.15 Acts 11:26! Communion; supper, religious talk; prayer. 9.30.

MONDAY, MARCH 1. 4 Prayed; tea; prayer. 5 Chaise; with G. Whitfield, Shakespeare. 8.15 The Crown [Inn]; tea, religious talk. 9 Walked; chaise. 12 Reading; Matthew 7:24; dinner. 2 Chaise. 5 Newbury; tea, religious talk; prayed; writ notes. 7.15 2 Corinthians 4:5! supper; prayer. 9.30.

[TUESDAY] MARCH [2]. 4 Prayed; the people. 5 Chaise. 9 Marlborough; tea. 10 Chaise. 1.30 Chippenham. 2 Dinner. 2.15 Chaise. 4.15 Bath; at brother Symes's, necessary talk (religious), tea; prayed; necessary talk (religious). 6.30 Acts 11:26(2)! writ notes; supper, necessary talk (religious); prayer. 9.30.

WEDNESDAY, MARCH 3. 4 Prayed; letters. 6 Matthew 6:34; letters. 8 Tea, religious talk; prayer; letters. 12 The leaders; tea, necessary talk. 1 At brother Timbrel's, dinner, religious talk. 2.15 Letters. 4.45 At brother Fowler's, tea, religious talk; prayer. 6.30 Matthew 4:10! Society; Magazine; supper; prayer. 9.30.

THURSDAY, MARCH 4. 4 Prayed; letter. 6 Hebrews 2:14; Magazine. 8 Tea, religious talk; visited. 9.30 Chaise. 11.30 Bristol. 12 Necessary business; letters. 2 At Mr Durbin's, dinner, religious talk; prayer. 3.30 Letters. 5 Prayer; tea, religious talk; prayer. 5.30 Prayed. 6.30 Psalms 90:12! the bands; at Mr Castleman's, supper, necessary talk (religious); prayer. 9.30.

[FRIDAY] MARCH 5. 4 Prayed; letters; tea; prayer; letters; accounts. 12 The females; prayed. 1 Prayer. 2 At sister Ewer's. 2 Dinner, religious talk; prayer. 3.30 Prayed. 4 Chaise; at the School, necessary talk (religious)! 5.30 Tea, religious talk; prayed; Magazine. 8 Supper, religious talk; prayer. 9.30.

SATURDAY, MARCH 6. 4 Prayed; Magazine; the children. 6.30 Necessary talk (religious) to the mothers; chaise. 8.30 Hannam; tea, necessary talk (religious); Louisa! chaise. 10 Necessary business; letters. 1 At brother Green's, dinner, religious talk; prayer. 2.30 Magazine; prayed. 4 Visited; tea. 6 John 15:7, etc; Penry; supper; prayer; necessary business. 9.30.

[SUNDAY] MARCH [7]. 4 Prayed; letter; journal. 8 Tea, religious talk; prayed. 9.30 Read Prayers, 1 Thessalonians 4:7! Communion; dinner, religious talk. 3 Temple Church; read Prayers, Matthew 4:10; tea; prayed. 5 1 Thessalonians 4:8! Society. 7 The singers; supper, religious talk; prayer. 9.30.

MONDAY, MARCH 8. 4 Prayed; Romans 13:11, etc! writ notes. 7 Class; tea; class. 1 At brother Robert's, dinner, religious talk. 2 Class; prayer. 5 Tea, religious talk; prayer; prayed. 7 Matthew 8:13! at Mr Castleman's, supper, necessary talk (religious). 9.45.

TUESDAY, MARCH 9. 4 Prayed; letters. 6 Class; tea, necessary talk (religious)! 9 Class. 1 At sister Stafford's, necessary talk (religious). 2 Class; visited! 5 Tea, necessary talk (religious); prayed. 6.30 Psalms 74:13; the leaders; Johnson; supper, religious talk; prayer. 9.30.

[WEDNESDAY] MARCH [10]. 4 Prayed; letters. 8 Tea; letters. 10 Prayer; class; visited some. 1 Dinner. 2 Class; visited some. 5 Tea; visited. 6.30 Matthew 22:4! at sister Thompson's; supper, necessary talk (religious); prayer. 10.

THURSDAY, MARCH 11. 4.15 Prayed; letters; Magazine. 8 At brother White's, tea, religious talk; prayer; visited. 9.30 Letters. 1 At brother Pine's, dinner, religious talk; prayer; letter. 3 Brother Simpson, etc, necessary talk! letter. 5 At brother Gee's, tea, religious talk; prayer. 6 Prayed.

FRIDAY, MARCH 12. 4 Prayed; letters. 7 Chaise; with E. Morgan. 8 Keynsham; tea, religious talk; Matthew 8:2. 10 Chaise; Cullen. 1.15 Bradford[-on-Avon]; at brother Rainer's, dinner! 2.30 Read notes. 4 Prayed; tea, religious talk. 6 Matthew 4:10! Society! at Mr Ball's, supper; prayer. 10.

SATURDAY, MARCH 13. 4 Prayed; Romans 13:11, etc! at Mr Shrabri——'s, tea; chaise; Trowbridge. 8 Tea; Job 22:21! chaise. 1.30 At John Ellison's, dinner; letters. 5 Tea; visited some. 6 Romans 11:33! Penry; at Miss Johnson's, supper, religious talk; prayer; necessary business. 9.30.

SUNDAY, MARCH 14. 4 Prayed; letters. 8 Tea, religious talk; prayer; necessary business. 9.30 Read Prayers, Luke 11:14, etc! Communion; christened. 1.30 At brother Cross's, dinner, religious talk. 2.30 Necessary business. 3.30 Slept; prayed. 4 Tea; prayed. 5 Matthew 4:10! 6 Society! the singers. 8 Supper, religious talk; prayer. 9.30.

MONDAY, MARCH 15. 4 Prayed. 5 John 4:24! chaise. 9.30 Newport; tea; necessary talk (religious). 10.30 Chaise; Atterbury. 1 Stroud; writ plan. 2 Dinner. 3 Plan. 5 Tea, religious talk. 6 Prayed. 6.30 Luke 12:7! Society! at brother Freeby's, supper, religious talk; prayer. 9.30.

TUESDAY, MARCH 16. 4 Prayed; Romans 13:11; plan. 8 Tea, religious talk; prayer; texts; chaise. 12 Painswick; Luke 11:14, etc; dinner. 2 Chaise. 3.30 Gloucester. 4 Necessary business; tea; prayed. 6 Acts 11:26! Society! supper, religious talk; prayer. 9.45.

WEDNESDAY, MARCH 17. 4 Prayed; Hebrews 12:14! letters. 8 Tea, religious talk; prayer. 9 Chaise; Atterbury. 12 Cheltenham. 12.30 Necessary business. 1 Dinner, religious talk. 2 No leader; chaise. 3.30 Tewkesbury; prayed; tea, religious talk. 6 Matthew 7:24! Society! supper, religious talk; prayer. 9.30.

THURSDAY, MARCH 18. 4 Prayed; Hebrews 3:7! letters. 8 Tea, religious talk; prayer. 9 Chaise. 12.30 Bengeworth; necessary business. 1 Dinner. 2 Magazine. 4 Prayed; visited; tea, religious talk; prayer; at Mr Beale's, religious talk. 6 Read Prayers, 1 Timothy 1:5! supper, religious talk; prayer. 9.30.

FRIDAY, MARCH 19. 4 Prayed; Magazine. 6 2 John 8! Magazine; tea, religious talk; at Mr Beale's, religious talk. 10 Chaise. 11 Visited! read. 12 [Broad]

Marston; Magazine. 1 Dinner. 2 Magazine; prayed; tea; walked. 5 Read Prayers, 1 Samuel 21:8; walked; supper, religious talk; prayer. 9.45.

SATURDAY, MARCH 20. 4 Prayed; Micah 2:10; Magazine; tea, religious talk; prayed. 8.15 Rode! 10 Bengeworth; at Mr Beale's, religious talk. 11 Read Prayers, John 7:37; necessary talk (religious); dinner. 1.30 Chaise. 4 Worcester; letters; tea; visited. 6.30 Matthew 4:10! letter; supper; prayer. 10.

SUNDAY, MARCH 21. 4 Prayer; letters. 7 Psalms 74:12! at brother King's, tea, religious talk; prayer; visited. 9 Writ notes. 11 Read Prayers; writ notes. 1 Dinner, religious talk; slept; prayed. 3 Read Prayers, 1 Corinthians 13:1, etc; tea, religious talk; prayed. 6 2 Corinthians 4:5! Society; visited. 8 Supper, religious talk; prayer. 9.30.

MONDAY, MARCH 22. 4 Prayed; Psalms 106:24; Select Society; tea, religious talk; prayer. 7.15 Chaise; Crab Inn. 9.30 Tea, religious talk. 10.30 Chaise. 1 Birmingham; at brother Jones's, dinner, religious talk. 2 Letters. 5 Prayed; tea. 6.30 Matthew 22:4! Society; supper. 9.30.

[TUESDAY] MARCH [23]. 4 Prayed; Matthew 6:34! letters. 8 Tea, religious talk; prayer; letters. 10.30 Coach. 11.30 Quinton. 12 John 4:24! dinner, religious talk; walked; garden. 2.45 Coach. 3.30 Read; sins. 4 Prayed; tea, religious talk. 6.30 Acts 17:30, Communion. 9 Supper, religious talk; prayer. 10.

WEDNESDAY, MARCH 2[4]. 4 Prayed; Psalms 50:23; journal. 8 Tea, religious talk; prayer. 9 Journal. 1 At brother Andr[ew's]. 1.30 Dinner, religious talk; prayer. 3 Chaise. 4.30 Tea, religious talk; letter; prayed. 6.30 John 4:14; Society. 8 Supper, religious talk; prayer. 9.30.

THURSDAY, MARCH 25. 5 Prayed; Romans 13:11, etc; Magazine. 8 Tea, religious talk; Magazine. 10 Chaise; Darlaston. 10.30 Visited! read Prayers, Romans 3:22! chaise. 1 Wednesbury; dinner, religious talk. 3 Chaise; Dudley; prayed; tea; Magazine; Matthew 8:13; Society; supper; prayer. 9.30.

[FRIDAY] MARCH [26]. 4.15 Prayed; Psalms 106:24; Magazine. 7.30 Tea; prayer; Magazine. 10.30 Chaise; Wolverhampton; Daniel 9:24! chaise. 1.30 Hilton Park. 2 Necessary talk (religious). 3 Dinner. 4 Magazine; prayed; tea, mostly religious talk. 10.30 Supper; prayer. 11.

SATURDAY, MARCH 27. 5.30 Prayed; read; tea, religious talk; prayer. 7.45 Chaise. 8.30 Wolverhampton; tea. 9 Matthew 7:24; chaise; Upton; chaise. 1.15 Madeley; dinner, religious talk, Mr Fletcher. 2 Prayed. 6 Tea, religious talk. 7.30 James 3:17; prayer; supper. 9.30.

[SUNDAY] MARCH 28. 4 Prayed; Magazine. 8 1 Corinthians 13:8, etc; tea, religious talk. 9 Magazine. 10 Read Prayers, Hebrews 9:13! 12.15 Dinner, religious talk; letters. 2.30 Read Prayers, Titus 2:13! 4 Tea, religious talk; Magazine. 8 Supper, religious talk; prayer. 10.

MONDAY, MARCH 29. 4 Prayed; letters. 6 Religious talk; prayer. 7 Chaise. 8 Sheriffhales; tea, religious talk; prayer. 9 Chaise. 12 Stafford; Proverbs 3:17! dinner. 2 Chaise. 5 Lane End [Longton]; tea, religious talk; prayed. 6 Ephesians 2:8! 7.30 Necessary talk (religious), supper, religious talk; prayer. 9.45.

TUESDAY, MARCH 30. 4 Prayed; Isaiah 66. 7 Letters. 8 Tea, religious talk; prayer; letters. 12 Dinner; chaise. 1 Hanley Green; Hebrews 8:11; chaise. 3 Newcastle[-under-Lyme]; Magazine. 5 Tea, religious talk. 7 Prayed; Mark 9:23; supper; prayer. 9.30.

[WEDNESDAY] MARCH [31]. 4 Prayed; Mark 9:29! letters; chaise. 8 Burslem; tea. 9 Visited. 10 Magazine; texts. 1 Dinner; prayer. 2 Writ journal. 4 Prayed; tea, religious talk. 5.30 Isaiah 59:1, 2! Love-feast! supper; prayer. 9.45.

THURSDAY, APRIL 1. 4 Prayed; Acts 22:16; letter. 8 Tea, religious talk; prayer. 9 Chaise. 11 Congleton; Magazine; E. Ro——'s! 1 Dinner. 2 Magazine; prayed; tea, religious talk. 6.30 Luke 12:7. 8 Society. 8.15 Supper, religious talk; prayer. 9.30.

FRIDAY, APRIL 2. 4 Prayed; Philippians 3:13! Magazine. 8 Tea, religious talk; prayer. 8.45 Chaise. 11 Macclesfield; necessary talk (religious); Magazine. 1.30 Dinner. 2.30 Magazine. 5 Tea; prayed; Magazine. 6.30 1 Peter 1:24! Society; supper, religious talk; prayer. 9.30.

SATURDAY; APRIL 3. 4 Prayed; Isaiah 57:1, 2; necessary talk (religious); Magazine. 8 Tea, religious talk; Magazine. 12 Visited. 1 Dinner, religious talk; Magazine; prayed. 5 Tea, religious talk; visited some. 6.30 Psalms 146:4, 5. 7 Select Society; supper, necessary talk (religious). 9.30.

SUNDAY, APRIL 4. 4 Prayed; letters; tea; letters. 10.15 Read Prayers, Titus 2:11, etc. 1 Dinner, religious talk; slept. 3 Read Prayers, Matthew 4:10; tea, religious talk; letter; walked. 7 The Love-feast! supper, religious talk; prayer. 10.

MONDAY, APRIL 5. 4 Prayed; tea, necessary talk (religious). 5 Chaise. 8.15 Middlewich; tea. 9.15 Chaise. 12 Alpraham; dinner. 1 Hebrews 6:1! 2 Chaise. 4.30 Chester. 5 Necessary talk (religious); tea; prayed. 6.30 Hebrews 9:13! the leaders; supper; prayer. 10.

TUESDAY, APRIL 6. 4 Prayed; writ journal. 8 Tea, religious talk; prayer; letters; walked. 1 Dinner; prayer. 2 Writ Lives of Preachers. 4.30 Walked; tea, religious talk; prayed. 6.15 John 4:24! 7 Love-feast; supper, religious talk; prayer. 9.30.

WEDNESDAY, APRIL 7. 4 Prayed; Matthew 12:43! letter. 8 Tea, religious talk; prayer; letter; necessary talk (religious); prayer. 10 Chaise; Eastham; dinner. 1.30 Boat. 3 Liverpool; read notes; prayed; tea, religious talk; prayed. 6 Daniel 9:24! Society; supper, religious talk; prayer. 9.30.

THURSDAY, APRIL 8. 4 Prayed; Romans 13:16; Magazine. 8 Tea, religious talk; prayer; Magazine. 12 Walked; visited. 1 Dinner, religious talk; prayer. 2.30

Magazine. 3.45 Prayed; tea, religious talk. 6 Matthew 4:10! the bands! supper; prayer. 9.30.

GOOD FRIDAY, APRIL [9]. 4 Prayed; Psalms 74:13; necessary talk (religious); chaise. 9.30 Warrington; necessary business; read Prayers. 11 Genesis 22:1, 2, Communion; dinner. 2 Christened; prayed. 4 Tea, religious talk. 5 Hebrews 4:13! Society! Magazine; supper, religious talk; prayer. 9.30.

SATURDAY, APRIL 10. 4 Prayed; Psalms 106:24; Magazine; tea. 9 Chaise. 12 Manchester; letters. 2 Dinner, religious talk. 2.15 Letters. 4.30 Tea, religious talk; prayer. 6 Romans 8:13! supper; prayer; Communion; necessary business. 9.45.

EASTER DAY [SUNDAY] APRIL [11]. 4 Prayed; letters. 8 Christened; tea; prayed. 10 Read Prayers, Luke 24:34, Communion. 1.30 Dinner, religious talk. 2.30 Slept; read sermon. 4 Tea, religious talk. 5.15 Colossians 3:1, etc; Society; supper, religious talk; prayer. 9.30.

MONDAY, APRIL 12. 4 Prayed; writ sermon. 8 Tea, religious talk; prayer; visited; sermon. 2 At brother Philips's, dinner; visited some; chaise. 4.30 Stockport; sermon; tea. 6 Romans 8:33; Society; walked; at brother Moore's, supper, religious talk; prayer. 9.45.

TUESDAY, APRIL 13. 4 Prayed; sermon. 8 Tea; visited! 9 Chaise. 11.15 Oldham; sermon, John 5:8. 1.15 Dinner. 3 Chaise. 4.30 Manchester; the preachers! tea, religious talk. 6 Acts 11:26! Society; supper, religious talk; prayer. 10.

WEDNESDAY, APRIL 14. 4 Prayed; Jeremiah 35 *ult.*; sermon. 8 Tea, religious talk; prayer. 9 Chaise. 11 Bolton; sermon. 1 Dinner, necessary talk (religious); sermon. 4 Prayed; tea, religious talk; prayer. 6 Matthew 8:13! 7 Society. 8 Supper, religious talk; prayer. 9.30.

THURSDAY, APRIL 15. 4 Prayed; sermon. 8 Tea, religious talk; prayer. 9 Sermon. 1 Dinner, religious talk; prayer. 2 Sermon; prayed. 4.15 Christened ten; tea, religious talk; prayed. 6 2 John 8! the bands; supper; prayer. 9.30.

FRIDAY, APRIL 16. 4 Prayed; John 4:24; letters. 8 Tea, religious talk; prayer; writ notes. 9.15 Chaise. 10.30 Wingates; +Matthew 22:4! chaise. 1.15 At brother Laland's. 1.30 Dinner; sermon; prayed; tea. 6 1 Corinthians 13:1, etc! supper; prayer. 9.30.

SATURDAY, APRIL 17. 4 Prayed; sermon. 6 Romans 12:1; tea, religious talk; prayer. 8 Chaise. 11 At sister Nuttal's, necessary talk (religious); chaise. 12 Preston; Hebrews 9:27; dinner, religious talk. 3 Chaise. 5 Blackburn; tea, religious talk. 6 John 17:3; Society; supper, religious talk; prayer. 9.30.

[SUNDAY] APRIL [18]. 4 Prayed; Hebrews 6:1; tea. 7 Chaise. 10.15 Gisburn; read Prayers, Isaiah 55:6, 7. 12.30 Dinner, religious talk. 1.30 Chaise. 4 Settle; necessary business; tea; letters. 5.15 1 John 5:11! 6.30 Society! sermon; supper; prayer. 9.30.

MONDAY, APRIL 19. 4 Prayed; 1 Samuel 21:8! tea. 6.30 Chaise. 9.30 Kirkby Lonsdale. 10 Tea; sermon. 10.45 Chaise. 1 Kendal; dinner. 2.30 Chaise. 6.15 Ambleside; sermon. 8 Ephesians 2:8. 8.45 Supper, religious talk. 9.30.

TUESDAY, APRIL 20. 4 Prayed. 4.45 Chaise. 8 Keswick; tea. 9 Chaise. 12 Cockermouth; dinner. 1 Chaise. 3.30 Whitehaven; at T. Hodge's; letters; prayed; tea; Psalms 146:4! Society; supper, religious talk; prayer. 9.30.

WEDNESDAY, APRIL 21. 4 Prayed; 1 John 2:12; journal; tea. 7.30 Sermon. 12 Walked; dinner. 1.30 Visited many. 3 Read; letters; prayed. 4.45 Tea, religious talk; prayer. 6 Revelation 14:1, etc! the bands; supper; prayer. 9.30.

THURSDAY, APRIL 22. 4 Prayed; Matthew 5:47! chaise. 8.30 Cockermouth; tea. 9 Luke 10:42! 10.15 Chaise. 12.45 Red Dial; dinner, religious talk; chaise. 4 Carlisle; necessary business; tea, religious talk. 6.30 Romans 3:23! supper, religious talk; prayer. 9.30.

FRIDAY, APRIL 23. 4 Tea; prayer. 5 Chaise; Langholm; tea; chaise. 11 Mosspaul Inn. 12 Chaise; Hawick; dinner; chaise. 7 Selkirk; supper; prayer. 9.30.

SATURDAY, APRIL [24]. 4 Prayed. 5 Chaise. 7.15 Stage Inn [?Stagehall]; tea; chaise. 11 Middleton. 12 Chaise. 2.15 Edinburgh; inn; dinner. 3 Letters. 5 Tea, religious talk; letters; prayed. 7 Luke 12:7! sister Thompson's, supper, religious talk; prayer. 10.

SUNDAY, APRIL 25. 4 Prayed; letters. 7 1 John 5:19! tea, religious talk; letters. 10.30 Read Prayers. 1 At Lady Maxwell's, dinner, religious talk; prayer. 2.15 Letters. 3.30 Prayed; tea; Revelation 20:12; walked; prayed. 6 John 4:24; Society. 8 At Mrs Caithness's, supper, mostly religious talk. 9.30.

MONDAY, APRIL 26. 4 Prayed Romans 13:11! letters; tea, religious talk. 8 Coach. 12 Dinner, necessary talk (religious). 1 Coach. 5.15 Glasgow; tea, religious talk. 6 Luke 16:31! Society! 8 At Mr Gillie's, supper, religious talk; prayer. 9.45.

TUESDAY, APRIL 27. 4 Prayed; Luke 1:72! letters. 8 Tea, religious talk; prayer; letters. 1 Dinner, religious talk; prayer. 3.30 Letter. 4.30 Tea, religious talk; prayer; prayed. 6 Ecclesiastes 7:29; Society! 8 At brother McKie's, supper, religious talk; prayer. 9.30.

WEDNESDAY, APRIL 28. 4 Prayed; Luke 12:7! letters. 8 Tea, religious talk; prayer. 9 Writ journal. 12 Walked. 1 At brother Richard's, dinner, religious talk; prayer; visited. 2.30 Writ logic. 4 Prayed; at Mr [blank]. 5 Tea, religious talk; prayer. 6 Luke 13:23, 24! Society; at brother Tassie's. 8 Supper, religious talk; prayer. 9.30.

THURSDAY, APRIL 29. 4 Prayed; 1 John 4:19; letter. 7 Tea, religious talk; prayer. 8 Walked; Diligence [coach]. 9 Read [Joseph] Spence's sermon. 1 At Mrs Henderson's, dinner. 1.45 Diligence. 5 Stream[?]. 5.30 Edinburgh; at brother Ross's, tea, religious talk; prayer. 6 Necessary business; prayed. 7 1 John 4:19; at Mrs Thompson's, supper religious talk; prayer. 10.

FRIDAY, APRIL 30. 4 Prayed; writ notes. 4.45 Chaise. 6.30 Queensferry; tea, necessary talk (religious); in the boat. 7.30 Chaise; Caesar; Greek Testament; sins! 10.30 Kinross. 11.45 Chaise; Greek Testament; Caesar. 2.15 Perth; dinner; writ notes; prayed. 5 Tea, necessary talk (religious). 6 Tolbooth; 1 Corinthians 13:1, etc! Society; supper, religious talk; prayer. 9.15.

SATURDAY, MAY 1. 4 Prayed; read notes. 6 1 Corinthians 13:13! tea, religious talk; prayer. 7.45 Chaise; Rait. 10 Chaise. 12.30 Dundee; writ notes. 1.30 Dinner, religious talk. 2.30 Texts. 4 Letters. 5 Tea, religious talk; prayer. 6 Hebrews 4:13; Society; supper, religious talk; prayer. 9.30.

SUNDAY, MAY 2. 4 Prayed; writ letter; tea. 7 Hebrews 8:10; letter. 9.30 Garden. 10.15 Read Prayers. 1 Dinner, religious talk; prayer. 2 Slept; prayed. 3 Read Prayers. 4.15 At sister Kay's, tea, religious talk. 5.30 1 Kings 18:21; Society; read. 8 Supper, religious talk; prayer. 9.30.

MONDAY, MAY 3. 4 Prayed; Matthew 12:43, etc; letter. 8 Tea, religious talk; prayer; visited. 9.15 Chaise. 12.15 Arbroath; Logic. 1.30 Dinner, religious talk. 2 Logic. 3.15 Prayed; walked. 6 Matthew 7:24! Society; necessary talk (religious)! supper; prayer. 9.30.

TUESDAY, MAY 4. 3 Necessary business. 4 Chaise. 6 Ferryden; tea. 7.45 Chaise. 10.15 Inverbervie [orig., 'Bervie']. 11.15 Chaise. 12 History of Perth. 1 Stonehaven [orig., 'Stonehith'; hithe = haven]; dinner. 2 Chaise. 4.45 Aberdeen. 5 Tea, religious talk; prayer. 6.30 Matthew 22:37; Society; supper; prayer. 9.30.

WEDNESDAY, MAY 5. 4 Prayed; Romans 13:11! letters. 8 Tea, religious talk; prayer; letters. 11 Read. 12 Walked. 1 Dinner. 2 Read. 4.15 Prayed. 5 Tea, religious talk; prayer. 6 Prayed. 6.30 Matthew 22:39! Society; the preachers! 8.30 Supper; prayer. 9.45.

THURSDAY, MAY 6. 4 Prayed; Genesis 49:4; tea. 6.15 Chaise. 10 Oldmeldrum; tea. 11 Chaise. 3 Forglen; religious talk; necessary business. 4 Dinner, religious talk. 5.30 Prayed; tea, religious talk; Proverbs 3:17. 8 Read letters. 9 Supper, religious talk; prayer. 10.30.

FRIDAY, MAY 7. 4.45 Prayed; letters. 9 Tea; writ letters. 12 1 Corinthians 13:8, etc! 1 Dinner, religious talk. 2 Chaise. 6.15 Keith; at Dr Ha——'s, tea; Hebrews 9:27! Society. 8.15 Supper, religious talk; prayer. 9.45.

SATURDAY, MAY 8. 4 Prayed. 5 Acts 16:31; tea; prayer. 6.30 Chaise. 8 [The River] Spey; tea. 10.15 Walked; chaise. 12 Elgin; letters; dinner. 2 Chaise. 5 Dalvey; necessary talk (religious); tea. 6.30 Necessary business; prayed; journal; Revelation 14:1, etc; supper, religious talk; prayer. 10.30.

SUNDAY, MAY 9. 4.30 Prayed; writ upon *Nervous Disorders*. 9 Prayer; tea, religious talk; writ *Thoughts*. 12.30 Read Prayers, 1 John 5:3, Luke 15:7. 2

Thoughts. 3 Dinner. 4.30 Revelation 20:12. 5.30 Prayed; tea; *Thoughts.* 7.30 Religious talk, supper; prayer. 10.15.

MONDAY, MAY [10]. 4.45 Prayed; *Thoughts;* garden. 8 Tea; prayer. 9 Chaise. 10.30 Nairn; walked. 3.30 Petty [Church]. 4.15 Chaise. 5.15 Inverness; at sister Livingston's. 5.15 Dinner, religious talk, tea. 6.45 Psalms 33:1! Society! supper, religious talk; prayer. 9.30.

TUESDAY, MAY 11. 4 Prayed; Luke 20:35; letters. 8 Tea, religious talk; prayer! 9 Letter; journal; sins! 12.30 Walked. 1.45 Dinner, religious talk. 3.15 Letters. 4 Prayed; tea, religious talk. 6.30 1 Samuel 20:3. 8 Read; supper, religious talk; prayer. 10.

WEDNESDAY, MAY 12. 4.30 Revelation 14:1, etc! letter; tea. 7.45 Chaise. 10.30 At Mr Dunbar's. 11 Chaise. 1.30 Dalvey; necessary talk (religious); dinner, religious talk. 2.15 Chaise. 4.45 Elgin; tea, religious talk. 6 Prayed. 6.30 Isaiah 55:6! prayed; supper, religious talk; prayer. 9.30.

THURSDAY, MAY 13. 4 Prayed; Mark 1:15; *Thoughts.* 8 Tea, religious talk; read notes. 12 Walked. 1 *Thoughts.* 2 Dinner, religious talk. 3 Letters. 5 Prayed; tea. 6.30 Matthew 16:26! Society; supper; prayer. 9.30.

[FRIDAY] MAY [14]. 4 Prayed; Ephesians 2:8! tea. 6.15 Chaise; *Fingal;* Cullen; tea; chaise. 1.15 Banff; necessary business; dinner. 2 Read Prayers, Romans 13:10. 3.30 Chaise. 5.30 Forglen; tea, mostly religious talk. 7 Job 22:21! supper, religious talk. 10.

SATURDAY, MAY 15. 4.15 Prayed; read; garden. 6 Tea, religious talk. 6.45 Chaise. 2 Aberdeen; letter; dinner; letter. 5 Tea, religious talk; prayed; letter. 7 Joshua 24:15; Society; supper, religious talk; prayer. 9.45.

SUNDAY, MAY 16. 4 Prayed; tea. 6.15 Coach. 9 Newburgh; tea; +Matthew 22:4! chaise. 1.15 Aberdeen; dinner, religious talk. 2.15 Read Prayers, 1 Corinthians 13:1, etc; tea, religious talk. 5 2 Timothy 2:5. 6 Society; letters; supper; prayer. 9.15.

MONDAY, MAY 17. 3.30 Prayed; tea. 4.30 Chaise. 9.30 Inverbervie; tea. 10.30 Chaise. 1 Montrose. 2 Dinner. 2.30 Chaise. 4.30 Arbroath; at Mr Watson's, mostly religious talk, tea. 6 1 Corinthians 1:24! Society; visited. 8.30 Supper; prayer. 9.30.

TUESDAY, MAY 18. 4 Prayed; Matthew 8:2! writ notes; visited. 8 Tea, religious talk; prayer. 9 Chaise. 12 Dundee; letter. 1 Dinner, religious talk. 2 Letters. 4 Prayed. 5 Tea, religious talk. 6 +John 5:8! 8 Society; supper; prayer. 9.30.

WEDNESDAY, MAY 19. 4 Prayed; Matthew 5:6! writ notes. 8 Tea, religious talk; prayer; writ notes. 11 Boat. 1 Walked. 1.30 Chaise. 4 Melville House; dinner. 5 Walked; religious talk. 7 Prayed; tea; Hebrews 9:27! 8.45 Supper, necessary talk (religious). 10.30.

THURSDAY, MAY 20. 4 Prayed; writ notes. 5.45 Chaise; Kinross; tea; chaise. 11.30 Queensferry. 12.45 Walked; chaise. 2.30 Edinburgh; at Lady Maxwell's, religious talk. 4 Dinner; letters; prayed; tea. 7 2 Timothy 2:5! chaise; supper; prayer. 10.

FRIDAY, MAY 21. 4 Prayed; 2 Timothy 2:4; letters. 8 Tea, religious talk; prayer. 9 Class. 2 At Mrs Cairn's, dinner, mostly religious talk. 3.30 Letters. 5 Leith; tea, religious talk; prayer; coach; prayed. 6.30 Psalms 74:12! Society. 8.15 Supper, religious talk; prayer. 9.45.

SATURDAY, MAY 22. 4.45 Prayed; letters; religious talk! walked. 8.15 Tea, religious talk; prayer; visited! 10.15 Letters. 12 At the School! 2 Dinner, religious talk; prayer. 3.30 Letter; prayed. 5 At brother Ross's, tea, religious talk. 6.30 Isaiah 57:1, 2; chaise; supper, religious talk; prayer. 9.45.

SUNDAY, MAY 23. 4 Prayed; read; tea; chaise. 7 Malachi 3:1! tea, religious talk; prayer; letters. 10.30 Read Prayers. 1 At Mr Ball's, dinner, religious talk; prayer. 2.30 Read Prayers! tea, religious talk; prayer. 4.15 Prayed; read! John 4:24! chaise. 8 Supper, religious talk; prayer. 9.30.

MONDAY, MAY 24. 4 Prayed; walked; Jeremiah 8:20! tea, religious talk; prayer. 7 Chaise. 10 Haddington; tea. 11.30 Chaise. 1 Dunbar; read. 2 Dinner, religious talk; letters. 5 Tea, religious talk; prayed; journal. 7 Daniel 9:24! supper, religious talk; prayer. 9.30.

TUESDAY, MAY 25. 4 Prayed; Hebrews 6:1; journal. 7.30 Tea, religious talk; journal. 9 Chaise; at Lady Haddington's [at Dunbar]. 10 Walked. 11.30 Chaise. 12.30 Chester Hall; dinner, religious talk; prayer; chaise. 3 At home; prayed; at Mr Fall's [at Dunbar], tea, mostly religious talk. 7 Mark 4:18! supper, religious talk; prayer. 10.

[WEDNESDAY] MAY [26]. 4 Prayed; Revelation 14:1, etc; tea; prayer. 6.30 Chaise; the Press [i.e., The Pease]; tea, religious talk; prayer. 10.45 Chaise. 1 Berwick[-upon-Tweed]; at Mr Tanner's; Magazine. 2 Dinner; Magazine. 4.30 Prayed; visited; tea, religious talk. 6 Hebrews 12:14! Society; supper; prayer. 9.30.

THURSDAY, MAY 27. 4 Prayed; 1 Thessalonians 5:19; tea; prayer. 6.30 Chaise. 9.30 Tea. 10.45 Chaise. 12.45 Kelso; necessary talk (religious); Magazine. 3 Dinner, necessary talk (religious). 4 Magazine. 5 Prayed; tea, religious talk. 6 Prayed. 7 +Romans 3:22; walked; Floors Castle [orig. 'the Fleur']! supper; religious talk; prayer. 11.

FRIDAY, MAY [28]. 4 Prayed; 2 Corinthians 6:1! tea, religious talk; prayer. 6.15 Chaise. 10.15 Water rose ahead. 10.30 Tea; walked; coach. 2.30 Alnwick; at brother Annet's, dinner; Magazine; tea, religious talk. 6 Prayed. 6.30 Colossians 1:10! Society; supper, religious talk; prayer. 9.30.

SATURDAY, MAY 29. 4 Prayed; Luke 9:62! tea, religious talk; prayer. 7 Chaise. 11 Morpeth; necessary talk (religious). 12 Isaiah 66:8, 9! dinner. 2 Chaise. 4.30

Newcastle [upon Tyne]; tea; necessary business; letter; prayed. 7 2 Corinthians 4:18! supper, religious talk; prayer; necessary business. 10.

WHITSUNDAY, MAY [30]. 4 Prayed; letters; tea. 8.30 Acts 2:4! letters. 12.30 Dinner. 1 Coach. 2 +John 14:21! coach. 4 Tea; prayed. 5 1 Thessalonians 4:8! Love-feast. 8 Supper, religious talk; prayer. 9.30.

MONDAY, MAY 31. 4 Prayed; John 16:8; the singers. 7 Letters. 8 Tea, religious talk; prayer; letters. 12 Visited. 1 At brother Batson's, dinner, religious talk; prayer. 2.30 Letters. 4 Prayed; tea, religious talk; letter. 6.30 John 16:8! necessary talk (religious); supper, religious talk; prayer. 9.30.

TUESDAY, JUNE 1. 4 Prayed; letters. 7 Tea, necessary talk (religious). 7.30 Chaise; Howdon Pans; Acts 19:2! 11 Chaise; North Shields; necessary talk (religious); John 7:37! dinner, religious talk; prayer; chaise. 5 At home; tea. 6 Prayed. 6.30 Luke 12:7; the leaders; supper, mostly religious talk; prayer. 9.30.

WEDNESDAY, JUNE 2. 4 Prayed; John 16:8! necessary talk (religious); texts. 8 Tea, religious talk; prayer; texts; letters. 12 Visited. 1 At brother Green's, dinner, religious talk; prayer; visited. 3 Letters; prayed. 5 Tea, religious talk; prayed. 6.30 John 16:8! Select Society; supper; prayer. 9.30.

THURSDAY, JUNE 3. 4 Prayed; John 16:8; necessary talk (religious); accounts; tea, religious talk; prayer. 8.30 Sermon. 11.30 Chaise. 12.30 At W. Smith's. 1 Garden; religious talk. 1.30 Dinner, religious talk; prayer. 3 Chaise. 4 Prayed; tea, religious talk; prayer. 6 Prayed; Romans 13:11! 7.30 The bands; supper, religious talk; prayer. 9.45.

FRIDAY, JUNE 4. 4 Prayed; Hebrews 13:1; sermon; prayer. 10 Chaise. 12.30 Sunderland; sermon. 1.30 Dinner, religious talk. 2.30 Letters. 4 Picture! 5 Tea, religious talk; prayer. 6 Prayed. 6.30 Acts 11:26! Society! supper. 8 Religious talk; prayer. 9.30.

SATURDAY, JUNE 5. 4 Prayed; Acts 20:23; sermon. 8 Tea, religious talk; prayer. 9 Sermon. 12 Walked. 1 Dinner, religious talk; prayer. 2 Visited some. 3 Necessary business; picture! 5 Tea, religious talk; prayer. 6.30 Matthew 7:14! 8 Supper, religious talk; prayer. 9.30.

SUNDAY, JUNE 6. 4 Prayed; Communion. 6 Sermon; tea, religious talk. 8 Genesis 1:27! the leaders. 10 Wearmouth; read Prayers, 1 John 5:7! 12.30 Dinner, religious talk; prayer. 2 Chaise. 4.15 Tea; prayed. 5 1 John 5:11! 6.30 Society; necessary business; at brother Batson's, supper, religious talk; prayer. 9.30.

MONDAY, JUNE 7. 4 Prayed; Matthew 12:43! letters; necessary business; tea; prayer. 9 Chaise. 12.30 Durham; Matthew 4:10! dinner, religious talk. 2 Chaise. 6 Hartlepool; tea; boat. 6.30 Matthew 7:24! boat; supper; prayer. 10.

TUESDAY, JUNE 8. 4 Prayed; Hebrews 6:1! boat; sermon; tea; prayer. 8 Chaise. 10.30 Stockton[-on-Tees]. 11 At sister Briscoe's; sermon. 12 Mark 1:15(2)! the children! 1.30 Dinner; prayer. 3 Chaise; Yarm; letter; tea; letter; prayed. 6.30 Acts 17:30! 7.30 Society. 8 Supper, religious talk; prayer. 9.30.

WEDNESDAY, JUNE 9. 4 Prayed; John 15:1, etc; tea; prayer; chaise; Darlington; tea. 10 Chaise; sins! 12.45 Barnard Castle; letter. 1.30 Dinner, religious talk; prayer; necessary talk (religious) to many. [4?] Tea, religious talk; prayer; prayed. 7 Revelation 3:20! Society! supper, religious talk; prayer. 9.30.

THURSDAY, JUNE 10. 4 Prayed; Revelation 2:4; necessary business; rode [horseback]; Cotherstone; John 5:8; tea, necessary talk (religious); prayer. 10 Rode; Newbiggin; dinner; Luke 9:62. 2 Rode. 4 Weardale; sermon; tea; prayed. 6.30 Mark 1:15(2)! Society! supper, religious talk; prayer. 9.30.

FRIDAY, JUNE 11. 4 Prayed; Matthew 22:4; rode. 8 Newbiggin; tea; sermon; prayer; rode. 10 Middleton; +2 Corinthians 8:9; rode. 12.30 Sandford [Startforth?]; sermon; dinner; prayer; rode. 3.30 Barnard Castle; visited; tea; prayed. 6.30 2 Corinthians 6:2; Society; supper; prayer. 9.30.

[SATURDAY] JUNE [12]. 4 Prayed; Job 7:18; Communion; necessary business. 7.30 Tea, religious talk; prayer. 9 Chaise. 10 Darlington. 12 Necessary business. 1 Dinner, religious talk; prayer. 3 Necessary business; letters. 5 Tea; prayed; letters. 6.30 1 Corinthians 3:11, etc; letters; supper, religious talk; prayer; necessary business. 9.45.

SUNDAY, JUNE 13. 4 Prayed; letters; tea. 8 Matthew 18:7! letters. 10 Read Prayers. 12 Dinner, religious talk; prayer. 1.15 Letters. 2.15 Read Prayers. 4 Prayed; tea, religious talk. 5 Luke 16, *ult!* Love-feast! necessary talk (religious). 8.15 Supper, religious talk; prayer. 9.30.

MONDAY, JUNE 14. 4 Prayed; Hebrews 2:14; necessary business. 6.30 Chaise. 9 Northallerton; tea; Isaiah 66:8! Society; letters; sermon. 12.30 Dinner; sermon. 2.30 Chaise. 4.15 Thirsk; sermon; prayed. 6.30 1 John 2:12; Society; supper; prayer. 9.30.

TUESDAY, JUNE 15. 4 Prayed; Communion; chaise. 8.30 Osmotherley; tea. 9 Luke 20:34; chaise. 12 Potto; dinner; 1 John 2:12, etc; sermon. 4 Tea, religious talk; chaise; Hutton Rudby; sermon. 6.30 Hebrews 9:27! at brother Suggel's, supper, religious talk; prayer. 9.30.

WEDNESDAY, JUNE 16. 4 Prayed; sermon; tea. 6.15 Chaise; Stokesley; Psalms 146:4! prayer! chaise. 11 Guisborough; +Galatians 3:22; dinner. 1 Chaise; Scaling; chaise. 5.30 Whitby.

THURSDAY, JUNE 17. 4 Prayed; Ecclesiastes 2:2; writ journal. 8 Tea, religious talk; prayer; visited. 9 Journal. 1.30 Dinner. 2 Prayer; religious talk. 2.30 Journal. 4.30 Visited; tea, religious talk; prayer; prayed. 6 Prayed. 6.30 +John 4:24. 7.30 Society! supper, religious talk; prayer. 9.30.

FRIDAY, JUNE 18. 4 Prayed; Galatians 5:1; letters; necessary talk (religious) to some. 11 Read Prayers; visited. 12 Read Prayers. 1 Dinner, religious talk. 2.30

Letter. 3.30 Prayed; visited; tea, religious talk; prayer. 5.30 Prayed. 6.30 Revelation 20:12! 8 The bands; supper; prayer. 9.30.

SATURDAY, JUNE 19. 4 Prayed; 1 Timothy 6:20; sermon. 8 Tea, religious talk; prayer; sermon; prayer. 10 Chaise; Robin Hood's Bay [orig., 'the Bay']. 11.30 Sermon. 12 Hebrews 2:3; chaise. 5 Scarborough; tea, religious talk; prayed. 6 Psalms 144:15! Society; supper, religious talk; prayer; necessary business. 9.45.

SUNDAY, JUNE 20. 5 Prayed; letters; tea. 8 Matthew 8:13! letters. 10 Read Prayers. 12.30 Dinner, religious talk; prayer. 1 Letters. 2.30 M. Fenwick, etc! 4 Visited; tea. 5 1 Corinthians 13:1, etc! the Love-feast! supper, religious talk; prayer. 9.30.

MONDAY, JUNE 21. 4 Prayed; 1 John 5:19! necessary business; Select Society. 7 Tea, religious talk. 8 Chaise. 12 Bridlington Quay [orig., 'Burlington Key']. 12.30 Dinner; letters; sermon. 4.45 Chaise; Bridlington; tea; prayed. 6 Psalms 90:12! 7 Society; chaise; the Quay; supper, religious talk; prayer. 9.30.

TUESDAY, JUNE 22. 4 Prayed; Zechariah 4:7! sermon; tea. 7.30 Chaise; inn. 12 Chaise. 12.30 Beverley. 1 Dinner, religious talk; 1 Corinthians 13:1, etc! chaise. 4 Newtown; tea, religious talk; christened; prayer. 5 Chaise; Hull; necessary talk (religious). 6 1 Kings 19:13! Society! visited; supper; prayer. 9.30.

WEDNESDAY, JUNE 23. 4 Prayed; Romans 13:11, etc! letters. 8 Tea, religious talk; prayer. 9 Sermon; letters. 1 Dinner, religious talk; prayer. 2.30 Sermon. 3 Prayed; sermon. 5 Tea, religious talk; prayer; necessary business. 6.30 2 Timothy 3:5! Society! supper; prayer. 9.30.

THURSDAY, JUNE [24]. 4 Prayed; Psalms 50:23! chaise. 9.15 Market Weighton [orig., 'Weeton']; tea; chaise. 11 Pocklington; necessary business; letters. 12 Dinner; Isaiah 59:1, 2; chaise. 4 York; letters. 5 Tea, religious talk; prayed. 6 Matthew 4:10! Society; supper, religious talk; prayer. 9.30.

FRIDAY, JUNE 25. 4 Prayed; letters. 6 Writ Conference. 10 Isaiah 57:1, 2! letters. 1 Dinner; letters. 2 Love-feast; letters; prayed. 5 Tea, religious talk; prayer; necessary business. 6.30 Matthew 8:13! the bands. 8 Supper, religious talk; prayer. 9.30.

SATURDAY, JUNE 26. 4 Prayed; 2 Corinthians 5:1, etc! tea; chaise. 8.30 At brother Dash's, tea, religious talk; chaise; Selby; religious talk; prayer. 10 Chaise. 1.45 Thorne; dinner; Revelation 2:5; visited. 2.30 Chaise. 4.30 Epworth; necessary business; tea, religious talk; prayer; necessary business; prayed. 6.30 2 Corinthians 6:1; supper; prayer. 9.45.

SUNDAY, JUNE 27. 4 Prayed; texts. 6 Chaise; Misterton; tea. 8 John 4:14! 9.30 Chaise. 10.30 Read Prayers; walked. 1 Dinner. 1.30 Luke 10:42! chaise. 3.30 Epworth; tea; prayed; +Luke 15:7! Society. 6 Necessary talk (religious); letter. 7 Supper, religious talk; prayer. 9.30.

MONDAY, JUNE 28. 4 Prayed; 1 Peter 5:10; letters. 8 Tea, religious talk; prayer; visited; letters. 11.30 Garden. 12 The children. 1 Dinner, religious talk. 2 Chaise. 4.45 Gainsborough; necessary business; tea, religious talk. 5.30 Prayed. 6.30 2 Corinthians 8:9! 8.15 Supper; walked; prayer. 9.30.

TUESDAY, JUNE 29. 4 Prayed; Mark 1:15(1); the preachers. 8 Tea, religious talk; prayer. 9 Chaise. 11 Scotter; Mark 1:15(2)! dinner. 12.45 Chaise. 2 Owston [Ferry]; letters. 4.30 Tea, religious talk. 5.30 Prayed; walked. 6.30 Read Prayers, Acts 4:31! necessary business. 8 Supper, mostly religious talk; prayer. 9.30.

WEDNESDAY, JUNE 30. 4 Prayed; letters. 7.30 Tea, religious talk; prayer; letters. 10.30 Walked. 11 Read Prayers, Psalms 146:4, 5; letter. 1 Dinner, religious talk. 2 Chaise. 3 Epworth; writ for Conference; tea. 5.30 Prayed. 6.30 Luke 12:7; Select Society! 8 Supper, necessary talk (religious). 9.30.

THURSDAY, JULY 1. 4 Prayed; Luke 2:52; writ journal; visited. 8 Tea, religious talk; prayer. 9 Letter; journal. 11 Chaise. 12 Crowle; Romans 1:16; dinner; prayer. 2 Chaise. 4 Swinefleet; necessary business; tea; accounts. 5 Prayed. 6 +Hebrews 2:3! Society; supper, necessary talk (religious). 9.30.

FRIDAY, JULY 2. 4 Prayed; Deuteronomy 33:26! sermon; tea; prayer. 8 Chaise. 11.15 Belton; sermon. 12 Dinner, religious talk. 1 +Titus 2:14! chaise. 2.30 Writ Conference. 5 Tea, religious talk; prayer. 6 Prayed; 2 Timothy 3:5! supper, religious talk; prayer. 9.30.

SATURDAY, JULY 3. 4 Prayed; Mark 4:26; letters. 8 Tea, religious talk; prayer. 9 Letters; writ notes. 12.30 Garden. 1 Dinner, religious talk; prayer; visited many. 4.30 Walked; tea, religious talk; prayer. 6.30 Zechariah 4:6! 7.30 Society; at Mr Ward's, supper, religious talk; prayer. 9.30.

SUNDAY, JULY 4. 4 Prayed; sermon. 7 Chaise; East Lound; tea, religious talk; prayer; chaise; Owston [Ferry]; read Prayers. 11 Luke 16:31! dinner, religious talk; prayer. 2.15 Chaise; slept; tea; prayed. 4 +Philippians 4:4. 5.15 The Love-feast. 7 Writ notes. 8 Supper, religious talk; prayer. 9.30.

MONDAY, JULY 5. 4 Prayed; Romans 13:11! letter. 7 Tea, religious talk; prayer. 8 Chaise. 11 Doncaster; Magazine. 12 Acts 11:26! dinner! 2 Chaise. 4.15 Rotherham; necessary business. 5 Tea, religious talk; prayed. 6.30 +Matthew 7:16! Society; supper, religious talk. 9.30.

TUESDAY, JULY [6]. 4 Prayed; Ephesians 4:1-4! Select Society; letters; tea. 9.30 Writ Conference. 1 Dinner. 2 Conference. 4.30 Tea, religious talk; prayed. 5.30 John 4:24! the Love-feast. 8.30 At Mr Holy's [at Sheffield], supper, necessary talk (religious). 9.45.

WEDNESDAY, JULY 7. 4 Prayed; Acts 22:16(2)! writ Conference. 8 Tea, religious talk; prayer; visited. 9.30 At brother Holy's, religious talk; letters; Conference. 12 Garden. 1 Dinner, mostly religious talk. 2 Magazine. 4.30 Prayed; tea, religious talk. 6.30 Colossians 1:10! Select Society; supper, religious talk; prayer. 9.45.

THURSDAY, JULY 8. 4 Prayed; Psalms 29:10! walked; tea; prayer. 7 Chaise; Barnsley; tea; chaise. 1 Wakefield; writ notes. 1.30 Dinner, religious talk. 2 Writ journal; prayed. 5 Tea, religious talk; prayer; prayed. 6.15 John 4:24; Society! 8 Supper, mostly religious talk; prayer. 9.30.

FRIDAY, JULY 9. 4 Prayed; Isaiah 57:1, 2; letters; tea, religious talk; prayer. 8.30 Chaise. 10.30 Mirfield. 11 Matthew 15:28; chaise. 1 Longwood House; necessary business. 2 Dinner, religious talk. 3 Letter. 4 Prayed; tea, religious talk; chaise. 6 Hebrews 13:22! Society; chaise; supper; prayer. 9.45.

[SATURDAY] JULY [10]. 4 Prayed; texts. 6 Hebrews 6:1; tea, religious talk! prayer! 9 Texts; Conference. 12 Walked. 1.30 Dinner, religious talk! prayer! 3 Chaise. 4.30 Halifax; tea, religious talk; prayed. 6 Psalms 116:12, 13! visited. 8 Supper, religious talk; prayer. 9.45.

SUNDAY, JULY 11. 4 Prayed; sermon; tea; prayer. 8 Chaise; Greetland; Matthew 7:16! chaise. 11.30 Halifax; letters; dinner. 1.30 +Matthew 22:4; Society; prayed; tea, religious talk. 5 +2 Timothy 3:5! letters. 7.30 Supper, religious talk; prayer. 9.30.

MONDAY, JULY 12. 4 Prayed; letters; tea. 7 Chaise; Heptonstall; tea. 9 Read Prayers, Psalms 62:1! chaise. 11 At brother Sutcliffe's; writ notes; dinner. 1 Read Prayers, 1 Thessalonians 4:7! at brother Crosby's, tea. 5 Letters; prayed; John 5:8! sermon. 8 Supper, religious talk; prayer. 9.30.

TUESDAY, JULY 13. 4 Prayed; sermon. 6 1 Corinthians 6:19 [JW left this space blank, but see William Ripley's diary for note on this sermon, *WHS* 4 (1904):131]; tea, religious talk. 8.30 Chaise. 11 Padiham; necessary talk (religious); dinner, religious talk. 1 Hebrews 4:14! chaise; Burnley; sermon; tea; prayed. 5 +Isaiah 55:7! 6.15 Chaise. 7.45 Southfield; supper, religious talk; prayer. 9.30.

WEDNESDAY, JULY 14. 4 Prayed; sermon. 7.30 Tea, religious talk; sermon. 12 Garden. 1 Dinner. 2 Sermon. 4 Chaise. 5 Colne; tea, religious talk; prayer. 6 Matthew 7:16. 7 Chaise. 8 Southfield; supper, religious talk; prayer. 9.30.

[THURSDAY] JULY [15]. 4 Prayed; sermon. 6 1 John 2:12; tea, religious talk; prayer. 7.45 Chaise. 9.45 Tea, religious talk. 10.45 Chaise! 2 Otley; dinner, religious talk; sermon. 5.30 Tea; prayed; sermon. 7.30 Prayed. 8 Supper, religious talk; prayer. 9.30.

FRIDAY, JULY 16. 4 Prayed; writ Answer to the Appeal. 7.30 Tea, religious talk; prayer; Answer. 12 Walked; Answer. 1.30 Dinner, religious talk; prayer; Answer. 5 Tea, religious talk; prayer; Answer. 6.30 Prayed. 7 Writ. 8 Supper, religious talk; prayer. 9.30.

SATURDAY, JULY 17. 4 Prayed; Appeal. 8 Tea, religious talk; prayer; sermon. 11 Letters. 12.30 Dinner, religious talk; prayer. 1.30 Chaise. 4 Keighley; visited; tea, religious talk. 6 Matthew 8:13; Society; supper; prayer. 9.15.

SUNDAY, JULY 18. 4 Prayed; letters. 8 Tea, religious talk; prayer; chaise; Bingley. 10.15 Read Prayers, Matthew 5:20! 1 At Mr Hartley's, dinner, religious talk. 2.30 Read Prayers, Psalms 90:12; chaise; Keighley; tea. 5.30 2 John 8! Society; necessary talk (religious); supper, religious talk; prayer. 9.15.

MONDAY, JULY 19. 4 Prayed; Judges 1:27; letters. 7.30 Tea, religious talk; prayed; letter. 10 Chaise; with Elizabeth Ritchie. 12 Baildon; dinner. 1 Matthew 15:28; chaise. 4 Otley; letters. 5 Tea; prayed. 6 Matthew 4:10! Society; supper, religious talk; prayer. 9.30.

TUESDAY, JULY 20. 4 Prayed. 2 Corinthians 5:1-4; letters. 8 Tea, religious talk; prayer. 9 Letters. 12.45 Dinner, religious talk. 2 Writ Magazine. 4 Prayed. 5 At Mr Hartley's, tea, religious talk; prayer. 6.30 Colossians 1:10! 7 The bands; supper; prayer; necessary business. 9.15.

WEDNESDAY, JULY 21. 4 Prayed; 1 Peter 1:9; Select Society; Magazine. 8 Tea, religious talk; prayer. 9 Magazine. 10.30 Chaise. 11.30 Park Gate; Dr Coke, etc. 1.30 Dinner. 2.30 Conference. 4 Prayed; tea, religious talk. 5.30 Chaise. 6 Mark 1:15(2)! Society; chaise; supper, religious talk. 9.30.

THURSDAY, JULY 22. 4 Prayed; 2 Corinthians 4:18! Conference. 8 Tea, religious talk; prayer. 9 Writ Answer to Appeal. 1 Dinner; writ Answer. 4 Garden; tea, religious talk; prayed; chaise. 6 Isaiah 59:1, 2! 7.30 Conference. 8 Supper, religious talk; prayer. 9.30.

FRIDAY, JULY 23. 4 Prayed; chaise; Mark 9:23(2)! letters. 7 Tea, religious talk; prayer; letters. 10 Religious talk. 10.30 Chaise. 12 Eccleshill; dinner; T[homas] R[ankin], etc, necessary talk. 1 Acts 11:26! chaise. 2.30 Bradford. 3 Conference. 4.30 Tea, religious talk; prayed. 6 +Matthew 22:37 [Acts 22:16 deleted]; Society! supper; prayer; necessary business. 9.30.

SATURDAY, JULY 24. 4 Prayed; Matthew 22:29! Select Society; Conference. 8 Tea, religious talk; prayer; Conference. 10.30 Chaise. 1 Dawgreen; dinner; Conference; prayed. 4.15 Walked. 5 Hanging Heaton; tea; prayed. 6.30 +Acts 22:16! Society! supper, religious talk; prayer; necessary business. 9.30.

SUNDAY, JULY 25. 4 Prayed; Conference. 6.30 Walked. 7 Dawgreen; tea, religious talk. 8 Matthew 8:2! 9.30 Walked. 11 Birstall; Conference; dinner; +Acts 9:31! 2.15 Chaise. 3.30 Leeds; at Mr Hey's, necessary business; +Revelation 20:12! Society! necessary business; supper, religious talk; prayer. 9.30.

MONDAY, JULY 26. 4 Prayed; Conference. 7.30 James 3:17; tea, religious talk; writ letters. 1.45 Dinner, religious talk; letters. 5 At brother Bradburn's, tea, religious talk; prayer. 6 Psalms 62:1; necessary talk (religious) to many. 8 Supper, religious talk; prayer. 9.30.

TUESDAY, JULY 27. 4 Prayed; letters. 6 Conference. 8 Tea, religious talk; letter. 9 Conference. 12 Letters. 1 Dinner, religious talk. 2 Conference; writ letters. 5 Tea, religious talk; prayed. 6 Luke 12:7! necessary talk (religious) to many. 8.15 Supper, religious talk; prayer. 9.30.

WEDNESDAY, JULY 28. 4 Prayed; writ Conference. 8 Tea, religious talk. 9 Conference. 12 Writ notes. 1 Dinner, religious talk; prayer. 2 Conference. 4.30 Writ notes; tea, religious talk; prayer. 6 Matthew 22:37! necessary business; supper; prayer. 9.30.

[THURSDAY] JULY [29]. 5 Prayed; writ notes; Conference; writ notes. 8 Tea; writ notes. 9 Conference. 10 Read Prayers, 1 Corinthians 13, Communion. 1.30 Dinner. 2.45 Conference. 5 Tea, religious talk; letter; prayed. 6 Matthew 22:39. 8 Writ notes; supper, religious talk; prayer. 9.30.

FRIDAY, JULY 30. 4 Prayed; letters. 6 Conference. 8 Tea; letters. 9 Conference. 12 Letters. 1 At Mr Appleby's, dinner, religious talk. 2 Conference. 5 Tea, religious talk; necessary business. 6 Letters. 8 Supper, religious talk; prayer. 9.30.

SATURDAY, JULY 31. 4 Prayed; letters. 6 Conference. 8 Tea, religious talk. 9 Conference. 12 Necessary talk (religious) to many. 1 At Mr Hey's, dinner, religious talk. 2 Conference; writ letters. 5 Tea, religious talk. 6 Prayed. 7 Letters. 8 Supper, necessary talk (religious); prayer; necessary business. 9.45.

SUNDAY, AUGUST 1. 4 Prayed; letters; tea. 10 Read Prayers, Communion. 1 At Dr Kershaw's, dinner. 2 Letters. 4 Tea; prayed. 6 +Matthew 7:16; Society. 7 Necessary talk; supper, religious talk; prayer. 9.30.

MONDAY, AUGUST 2. 4 Prayed; writ notes; Conference. 8 Tea, religious talk. 9 Conference. 12.15 Necessary talk (religious). 1 Conference. 4 Necessary talk (religious). 5 Tea, religious talk; prayer; prayed. 6 John 4:24! necessary talk (religious) with Dr Coke, etc. 8 Supper, religious talk; prayer. 9.30.

TUESDAY, AUGUST 3. 4 Prayed; Jeremiah 35; Conference; tea, religious talk. 9 Writ notes. 12 Necessary talk! 1 Dinner; Conference; tea; necessary business. 5 2 Timothy 3:5! 6 Chaise. 10 At sister Haugh[ton]'s, supper, religious talk; prayer. 11.45.

WEDNESDAY, AUGUST 4. 4.30 Prayed; tea; religious talk. 6 Chaise; with brother and sister Bayley. 9.30 Rochdale; tea, religious talk. 10.15 Chaise; Manchester; necessary business; dinner, necessary talk (religious); writ notes! 5 Prayed; tea. 6 Psalms 90:12; Society; visited. 8 Supper, necessary talk (religious); prayer. 10.

THURSDAY, AUGUST 5. 3 Prayed; tea. 4 Chaise. 8 Congleton; tea, religious talk; prayer. 9 Chaise. 11.30 Newcastle[-under-Lyme]. 12 Dinner. 1 Chaise. 4 Ternhill; tea. 4.30 Chaise. 7.30 Shrewsbury [orig., 'Salop']; Ecclesiastes 9:10! supper, religious talk; prayer. 10.

FRIDAY, AUGUST 6. 4 Prayed; Luke 12:7! tea, necessary talk (religious). 7 Chaise. 9 The Cock. 9.30 Chaise. 12.30 Wolverhampton. 1 Dinner. 2.30 Chaise. 4.45 Birmingham; tea, religious talk; prayed. 6.30 Matthew 7:16; Society; supper, mostly religious talk; prayer. 9.30.

SATURDAY, AUGUST 7. 4 Prayed; Psalms 74:13! necessary talk, tea; prayer. 7.15 Chaise; Crab Mill Inn. 9.30 Tea. 10.30 Chaise. 1 Worcester; necessary business. 1.30 Dinner, religious talk; prayer. 2.30 Spetchley [orig., 'Sketchly']. 4 Prayed. 5 Tea, religious talk; prayer; necessary business. 6.30 Ecclesiastes 7:29; writ notes; supper; necessary business. 9.45.

SUNDAY, AUGUST 8. 4 Prayed; Magazine. 7 Tea; prayer. 8 1 Peter 2:9! hymns. 11 Read Prayers; hymns. 1 Dinner. 2 Hymns; prayed. 3 Read Prayers, Luke 16:31! tea, necessary talk (religious); prayed. 6 1 Kings 19:13! 7 Society; writ notes; supper, religious talk; prayer. 9.30.

MONDAY, AUGUST 9. 4 Prayed; Psalms 62:1; Select Society; necessary talk, tea. 7 Chaise. 10 Ledbury; tea; visited. 11 Chaise. 1.30 Ross[-on-Wye]; dinner. 2.30 Chaise. 4.30 Monmouth; tea, religious talk; prayed. 6 John 17:3! Magazine; supper, mostly religious talk; prayer. 9.30.

TUESDAY, AUGUST 10. 4 Prayed; 1 Peter 2:1, etc; Magazine. 8 Tea, religious talk; journal. 12 Walked. 1.15 Dinner, necessary talk (religious). 2.30 Prayed. 3 Luke 7:36; at brother Johnson's, tea, religious talk; prayer. 6 1 Corinthians 13:1; walked; mostly religious talk. 8 Supper, religious talk; prayer. 9.45.

WEDNESDAY, AUGUST 11. 4 Prayed; writ notes. 6 Hebrews 6:1! tea, religious talk; prayer! 8 Chaise. 11 Abergavenny. 11 Tea. 12 Chaise. 3.30 Brecon; at brother Churchey's; necessary business; dinner; letters. 5.30 Prayed. 6.30 Isaiah 59:1, 2! Society; writ notes; supper; prayer. 9.30.

THURSDAY, AUGUST 12. 4 Prayed; Romans 13:11, etc; letters. 8 Tea, religious talk; accounts; letters. 12 Walked. 1.30 Dinner, religious talk. 2.30 Letters. 4.30 Prayed; tea, religious talk. 6.30 Proverbs 3:17! visited! 8 Supper, necessary talk (religious)! prayer. 9.30.

FRIDAY, AUGUST 13. 3.30 Necessary business. 4 Chaise; Penpont; tea; prayer; chaise. 9.15 Llandovery; tea. 10 Chaise. 12 Llandeilo. 1 Dinner, religious talk. 2 Chaise. 4.30 Carmarthen; at sister Lewis's, tea, religious talk; prayed. 6 Isaiah 66:8; supper; prayer. 9.30.

[SATURDAY] AUGUST [14]. 4 Prayed; Philippians 2:12! tea. 6.30 Chaise. 10 Tavernspite; tea. 10.45 Chaise. 1.15 Tenby; at Captain Farr's; Magazine; dinner. 3 Magazine. 4 Prayed; walked! 5 Tea, religious talk. 6 +2 Corinthians 8:9; religious talk; supper; prayer; necessary business. 9.45.

SUNDAY, AUGUST 15. 4 Prayed; Magazine. 6 Romans 12:1! 7.30 Chaise. 9.30 Pembroke; tea, religious talk; read. 10.30 St Daniel's, read Prayers, Acts 13:26,

Communion. 1 Hymns. 2 Dinner, religious talk; hymns; prayed; tea. 6 Luke 19:42! supper; prayer. 9.45.

[MONDAY] AUGUST [16]. 4 Prayed; letters. 7.15 Tea, religious talk; prayer. 8 Matthew 12:41; letter. 9.30 Rode chaise. 12.30 Haverfordwest; at Mr Davis's; hymns. 2 Dinner, religious talk. 3.30 Letters; prayed. 5.30 Tea, religious talk. 6.30 Matthew 7:24! Society; supper, religious talk; prayer. 9.45.

TUESDAY, AUGUST 17. 4 Prayed; 1 Corinthians 12:31! letters; texts. 8 Tea, religious talk; prayer. 9.15 Rode. 11 Roch; Ephesians 4:1, etc. 11.45 Rode. 1.15 At sister Warren's. 2 Visited; dinner, religious talk; prayer. 3.30 Necessary business; prayed; tea, religious talk. 6.30 Romans 8:4; Society; supper; prayer. 9.30.

[WEDNESDAY] AUGUST [18]. 4 Prayed; Judges 1:27; walked; letter. 8 Tea, religious talk; prayer; visited. 10.15 Chaise. 12.45 Trecwn; necessary talk (religious). 2 Dinner, mostly religious talk. 3.15 Writ notes. 5 Tea, religious talk; prayed; writ notes. 7 Philippians 3:8; supper, necessary talk (religious); prayer. 9.45.

THURSDAY, AUGUST 19. 4 Prayed; letters. 8 Prayer; tea, religious talk. 9.15 Chaise; visited. 12.30 Llwyn-gwair. 1 Mostly religious talk. 2.30 Dinner, religious talk. 4 Prayed; tea; Matthew 7:16! supper, mostly religious talk; prayer; hymns.

FRIDAY, AUGUST 20. 4 Prayed; letter. 7 Romans 8:3, 4; tea, religious talk; chaise; Newport; read Prayers. 9 1 Samuel 21:8! 9.30 Chaise. 11.30 New Inn [Ordnance Survey SN 0630]. 12 Chaise. 2 Haverfordwest; necessary talk (religious); dinner; visited many; tea; prayed. 6.30 John 4:24; supper; prayer. 10.

[SATURDAY] AUGUST [21]. 4 Prayed; Revelation 14:1, etc; tea; prayer. 6.30 Chaise; Narberth; Hebrews 9:27. 9.30 Chaise. 1.45 Carmarthen. 2.15 Dinner; letters; prayed. 5 Tea, religious talk; letters. 7 Matthew 11:30! supper, mostly religious talk; prayer; necessary business. 9.30.

SUNDAY, AUGUST 22. 4 Prayed; letters; tea. 8 Colossians 3:11; letters. 11 Read Prayers! 1 Dinner, religious talk. 2 Writ notes. 3 Prayed; tea, religious talk. 5 +Luke 18:10; Society; visited; supper, religious talk; prayer. 9.30.

MONDAY, AUGUST 23. 4 Prayed; Hebrews 2:3! letter; tea. 7.30 Chaise. 11 Llanelli; Hebrews 12:14. 12.30 Dinner. 1.45 Chaise; sins! 4.30 Swansea; tea, religious talk; necessary business. 6 +Psalms 24:3, 4! writ notes; supper, religious talk; prayer. 9.45.

TUESDAY, AUGUST 24. 4 Prayed; tea. 4.45 Chaise; Neath; tea, religious talk. 8 Psalms 144:15! chaise. 4 Cowbridge; at Mr Thomas's; necessary business; tea, religious talk; writ notes. 6.30 Micah 2:10; Society; necessary talk (religious); supper; prayer. 9.45.

WEDNESDAY, AUGUST 25. 4 Prayed; Magazine. 8 Tea, religious talk; prayer; letters; Magazine. 11 Read Prayers, Revelation 20:12. 1 Chaise. 2.30 Fonmon;

Magazine. 3 Dinner, good talk. 4 Magazine; prayed; tea. 6 Job 22:21! Magazine; supper, religious talk; prayer. 10 Ill.

THURSDAY, AUGUST 26. 5.15 Prayed. 6 Magazine. 8 Luke 12:7! tea, religious talk; Magazine; prayer. 11 Chaise. 1.30 Llandaff; read Voltaire. 2.30 Dinner, necessary talk (religious). 4 Voltaire; chaise. 5 Cardiff; tea; read; prayed. 6 Acts 11:26; Society; supper, religious talk; prayer. 9.30.

FRIDAY, AUGUST 27. 4 Prayed; Magazine. 8 Tea; letter. 9 Matthew 22:4. 10.15 Chaise. 12.15 Parsley Works [Cardiff]; walked. 2 Dinner, religious talk; prayer; chaise. 4 Newport; prayed; Magazine; tea. 6 Luke 13:23; Magazine; supper; prayer. 9.30.

SATURDAY, AUGUST [28]. 4 Prayed; Ephesians 5:14! tea. 6.30 Chaise. 9.15 [New] Passage; tea; Magazine. 1 Dinner; Magazine; prayed. 6 Boat. 6.30 Inn. 7 Chaise. 8.30 At sister Johnson's. 9 Supper; prayer; necessary business. 10 Ill.

SUNDAY, AUGUST 29. 4 Prayed; letters; tea; necessary business. 9.30 Read Prayers, Mark 7:37! Communion. 1 At brother Ewer's, dinner, religious talk. 2 Slept; necessary business; prayed; tea, religious talk.+ 5 Acts 28:32! Society! 7 The singers. 8 Supper, necessary talk (religious); prayer. 9.30.

MONDAY, AUGUST 30. 4 Prayed; Hebrews 6:1(2); writ plan. 8 Tea, religious talk; prayer; accounts; journal. 12 Select Society. 1 At brother Pine's, dinner, religious talk; prayer. 2.30 Letters; necessary talk (religious) to some; prayer. 5 At P. Gad's, tea, religious talk. 6 Prayed. 6.30 Luke 12:15; necessary talk (religious); supper, religious talk; prayer. 9.30.

TUESDAY, AUGUST 31. 4 Prayed; letters. 1 Tea, religious talk; prayer; letters. 12 Necessary business; Dr Coke, necessary talk (religious). 1 At John Ellison's with Charles, dinner, religious talk. 2.30 Writ notes; prayed; prayer. 5 Tea, religious talk. 6 Prayed. 6.30 Read the letters; the leaders; at sister Johnson's, supper, religious talk; prayer. 9.45.

[Texts noted at bottom of page:] Mark 7:38; Luke 12:15; 1 Corinthians 11:14.

WEDNESDAY, SEPTEMBER 1. 4 Prayed; ordained Richard Whatcoat and Thomas Vasey; letters. 8 Tea, religious talk. 9 Letters; writ notes. 2 Dinner, religious talk; prayer; visited some. 5 Tea, religious talk; prayer; visited. 6.30 Read Prayers, Romans 2:28! 8 At sister Johnson's, supper, religious talk; prayer. 9.30.

THURSDAY, SEPTEMBER 2. 4 Prayed; ordained Dr Coke! Magazine. 8 Tea; read Magazine. 12 Visited; at Mr Green's, dinner, religious talk; prayer; chaise; visited. 4 Keynsham; necessary talk (religious); read. 5 Tea, religious talk; prayed. 7 Ecclesiastes 9:10; prayer; supper, religious talk. 9.30.

FRIDAY, SEPTEMBER 3. 4 Prayed; writ notes. 6 Matthew 8:13! at Miss Bishop's; prayer; chaise. 8 At Mr Ireland's, tea, religious talk; prayer; chaise. 10 At home;

letters. 11 Prayer. 12 The females. 1 Prayer; at Mr Castleman's, dinner, religious talk. 3 Necessary business; prayed; tea. 6.30 Matthew 25:31! supper; prayer. 9.30.

[SATURDAY] SEPTEMBER [4]. 4 Prayed. 5 Guinea Street; 1 Peter 1:1, 2; read; tea, religious talk. 7 Necessary business. 8 Visited. 9 Letters. 12 Walked. 1 At sister Roach's, dinner, religious talk; prayer. 2.45 Chaise. 4.45 Bath; tea, religious talk; prayer. 6 Necessary business. 6.30 Luke 12:7! supper, religious talk; prayer. 9.30.

SUNDAY, SEPTEMBER 5. 4 Prayer; Magazine. 7.15 Tea, religious talk. 8 Class. 9.30 Magazine. 10.30 Read Prayers, 1 Kings 19:13! Communion. 1.15 Dinner, religious talk; slept. 2.30 Luke 10:23! class; tea, religious talk; prayed. 6 Luke 10:27; Society; supper; prayer. 9.30.

MONDAY, SEPTEMBER 6. 4 Prayed; Ephesians 4:1-6; class. 7.15 Visited. 8 Tea, religious talk; prayer. 9 Writ to Mr Pitt. 1 Dinner, religious talk; prayer. 2 Letter. 3.30 Read; prayed. 5 Tea, religious talk; walked; prayed. 6.30 Luke 10:27! the bands! supper, religious talk; prayer. 9.30.

TUESDAY, SEPTEMBER 7. 4 Prayed; Hebrews 6:1(2); the leaders; Magazine. 8 Tea, religious talk; walked. 9.30 Magazine. 10.45 Chaise. 12 Keynsham; Mark 9:23(2); dinner; chaise. 3.30 At home; writ notes; tea; prayed. 6.30 1 Peter 1:1, 2; the leaders; supper; prayer. 9.30.

WEDNESDAY, SEPTEMBER 8. 4 Prayed; letters. 8 Tea, religious talk; letters; sins! 1.15 Water. 2.15 Dinner, religious talk; necessary business. 4 Chaise. 5.15 Kendalshire; tea; John 5:8; chaise; the School; supper. 9 Prayer. 9.30.

THURSDAY, SEPTEMBER 9. 4 Prayed; the children; chaise. 7 At home; tea; letters. 10 Chaise. 12 Clutton; dinner; Isaiah 66:7; chaise. 5 Coleford; tea; prayed. 6 +Matthew 8:13! Society! supper, religious talk; prayer. 9.30.

FRIDAY, SEPTEMBER 10. 4 Prayer; Communion; visited; chaise. 7.45 [Midsomer] Norton; tea, religious talk; prayer. 9 Chaise. 12 At home; necessary business. 1 Prayer. 2 At brother Stock's, dinner, religious talk; prayer; necessary business. 4.30 Chaise. 5.30 At the School; tea; prayed; writ notes. 8 Supper, religious talk; prayer. 9.30.

SATURDAY, SEPTEMBER 11. 4 Prayed; writ notes; the children; letter. 7 Tea, religious talk. 8 Chaise. 9 Letters. 12.30 Walked. 1 At brother Emblem's, dinner, religious talk; prayer; visited. 2.45 Prayed; letter; prayer. 5 At sister Corsley's, tea, religious talk; prayer. 6 Isaiah 1:3(2)! Penry. 8 At brother Castleman's, supper, religious talk; prayer. 9.30.

SUNDAY, SEPTEMBER 12. 4 Prayed; letters. 8 Tea; necessary business. 9.30 Prayers, Galatians 5:22, Communion; chaise. 1 At the School; dinner. 2 +Psalms 146:4! chaise; tea; prayed.+ 5 Matthew 13:3, etc; Society; singers. 8 Supper, religious talk; prayer. 9.30.

MONDAY, SEPTEMBER 13. 4 Prayed; 1 Peter 1:3-6; letters. 8 Tea, religious talk; letters; visited. 12 Select Society! 1 At brother Hunt's, dinner, religious talk. 2.30 Writ notes. 3 Prayed. 4 Visited! 5 Tea, religious talk; prayer. 6 Letter. 6.45 1 Peter 1:7; at Mr Castleman's, supper, religious talk; prayer. 9.30.

TUESDAY, SEPTEMBER 14. 4 Prayed; sermon. 8 Tea; necessary business. 9.30 Chaise. 12 Bath; dinner. 1 Romans 12:2! 2.15 Chaise. 4.15 Bradford[-on-Avon]; tea, religious talk; prayed. 6 Matthew 4:10; Society! necessary business. 8 Supper, religious talk; prayer. 9.30.

WEDNESDAY, SEPTEMBER 15. 4 Prayed; Romans 13:11, etc! sermon; chaise. 8 Trowbridge; tea, necessary talk (religious). 9 +Matthew 8:2! chaise. 11.30 Frome; at Mr Blunt's; sermon. 1.30 Dinner, necessary talk (religious). 2.30 Sermon; prayed; tea, religious talk. 6 +2 John 8! Society; supper; prayer. 9.30.

THURSDAY, SEPTEMBER 16. 4 Prayed; Hebrews 2:3! sermon; tea. 7 Chaise. 10 Garden [of Stourhead House]. 11 Chaise; the Tower [King Alfred's Tower]; chaise. 2.30 Ditcheat; dinner, religious talk. 4 Prayed; tea. 5 +2 Corinthians 8:9! Society! 7 Sermon; prayed. 8 Supper, religious talk; prayer. 9.30.

FRIDAY, SEPTEMBER 17. 4 Prayed; +Acts 22:16! sermon. 7.30 Tea, religious talk; sermon. 10 Chaise; sermon. 11 +Isaiah 55:6, 7! sermon. 1.15 Dinner, religious talk; prayer. 3 Chaise; Shepton [Mallet]; necessary talk (religious); tea. 5 Prayed; tea, religious talk. 6 Matthew 8:13; Society; sermon; supper, religious talk; prayer. 9.30.

SATURDAY, SEPTEMBER 18. 4 Prayed; 1 Corinthians 10:13; sermon; tea, religious talk. 8.30 Chaise. 10.15 [Midsomer] Norton; sermon; read Prayers, Matthew 19:20! sermon. 1 Dinner, religious talk. 2 Chaise. 4.30 Necessary business; tea. 6 Isaiah 1:3(2); Penry; at Mr Castleman's, supper, religious talk; prayer. 9.30.

SUNDAY, SEPTEMBER 19. 4 Prayed; letters. 6.15 Chaise. 7 Class; tea; class. 9 John 4:24! Communion; class. 12.30 Dinner. 1.30 Slept. 1.45 +Galatians 6:14; Society; chaise; prayed; tea. 5 +Philippians 4:7! Society. 7 The singers; supper, religious talk; prayer. 9.30.

MONDAY, SEPTEMBER 20. 4 Prayed; 1 Peter 1:7-16; letter. 7 Class; tea; class. 1 Dinner. 2 Class. 5 Tea, necessary talk (religious); prayed. 6.45 1 Peter 1:16! at Mr Castleman's, supper, religious talk; prayer. 9.30.

[Text noted at bottom of page:] 1 Peter 1:16.

TUESDAY, SEPTEMBER 21. 4 Prayed; letters. 6 Class; tea; letters; class. 1 Dinner, religious talk. 2 Class; letters; prayer. 5 Tea, religious talk. 6.15 Prayed; read the letters; the leaders. 8.30 At Mr Castleman's, necessary talk (religious); prayer. 9.45.

WEDNESDAY, SEPTEMBER 22. 4 Prayed; letter. 6 Class; writ Society. 8 At brother Copel's, tea; writ Society. 10 Class. 1 Dinner, religious talk. 2 Class. 4

Tea, religious talk. 5 Romans 13:10; class. 7 Walked; at Mr Bowther's; writ Society; prayed; supper; prayer. 9.30.

THURSDAY, SEPTEMBER 23. 4 Prayed; writ Society; tea, religious talk; prayer; walked. 8.15 Necessary business; chaise; at Mr Punter's, coffee; prayer. 10.30 Chaise. 12 Paulton; dinner, religious talk. 1 +1 Samuel 20:3! writ Society; prayer. 4 Chaise; Pensford; tea, religious talk; Acts 16:31; chaise; at brother Wa——'s, supper, religious talk; prayer. 9.30.

FRIDAY, SEPTEMBER [24]. 4 Prayed; Society. 8 Tea; Society; letters. 11 Chaise. 11.45 Chew [Magna]; John 11:48; dinner. 2 Chaise. 2.30 [Chew] Stoke; read notes; prayed; tea; Psalms 144:15 [orig., 16]; read. 8 Supper, necessary talk (religious); prayer. 9.30.

SATURDAY, SEPTEMBER 25. 4 Prayed; Galatians 5:5; necessary business; tea. 7 Chaise. 8.30 At home; writ class. 2 At Mr J——'s, dinner, religious talk; prayer. 4 Chaise; visited some; tea, religious talk. 6 Isaiah 1:3! Penry. 8 At Mr Castleman's, supper, religious talk; prayer. 9.45.

SUNDAY, SEPTEMBER [2]6. 4 Prayed; letters; tea; necessary business. 9.30 Read Prayers, Deuteronomy 29:10! Communion. 1 Dinner, religious talk; letter. 3 Read Prayers, Ephesians 3:14, etc; tea; prayed. 5 Hebrews 8:10, etc; Society; the singers. 8 Supper; prayer. 9.30.

MONDAY, SEPTEMBER 27. 4 Prayed; 1 Peter 1:17-20; writ class; tea. 8 Chaise. 10 At Dr Camplin's, tea, religious talk; chaise. 12 John 4:24! dinner, religious talk; chaise. 4.30 Visited; tea, religious talk; prayed. 6.45 1 Peter 1:24! at Mr Castleman's, supper; prayer. 9.30.

TUESDAY, SEPTEMBER [28]. 4 Prayed; letter; writ class. 8 Tea, religious talk; prayer; writ class. 1 At brother Flar——'s, dinner, religious talk. 2.30 Letters; prayed. 5 Prayer; tea, religious talk; prayed. 6.30 2 Corinthians 11:14! the leaders. 8.30 At Mr Castleman's, supper, religious talk; prayer. 9.30.

WEDNESDAY, SEPTEMBER 29. 4 Prayed; letters. 6 Writ the bands. 1 Dinner, religious talk; visited many. 5.15 Tea, religious talk; visited. 6.30 Hebrews 7:25; Society; at Mr Thomas's, supper, religious talk; prayer. 9.30.

THURSDAY, SEPTEMBER 30. 4 Prayed; Zechariah 4:7; writ sermon. 7.30 Tea; John McGeary! sermon. 9.30 Sermon. 11 Newgate; read Prayers, Psalms 146:4; walked. 2 Hanham. 3 Dinner, religious talk. 3.30 Walked; at the School; walked. 5.15 Tea; prayed; 1 Peter 2:1; the bands; supper; prayer. 9.30.

FRIDAY, OCTOBER 1. 4 Prayed; journal; letters. 8.30 Necessary business; religious talk. 9 Prayer. 10.30 Visited some. 1 Prayer; communion. 3 Dinner, religious talk; visited some. 5.15 Tea; prayed; sermon; supper. 8.30 Matthew 13:31, 32. 10 Coffee; sermon; prayer. 12.30.

SATURDAY, OCTOBER 2. 6 Prayed; letters. 8 Tea, religious talk; letters. 11 Visited some. 1 Dinner, religious talk; prayer. 2.30 Sins; writ notes; prayed. 3.30

Visited many; tea, religious talk. 6 1 Corinthians 13:8, etc! Penry; at Mr Castleman's, supper, religious talk. 9 Prayed; necessary business. 9.30 Dream!

SUNDAY, OCTOBER 3. 4 Prayed; letters. 7.30 Chaise; at the School! tea, religious talk. 9 Deuteronomy 29:10! Communion! 11 The servants; the children! chaise; at home; necessary business. 1 Dinner, religious talk; slept. 3 Prayed. 4 Tea, religious talk. 4.30 Ephesians 4:1-3! the Covenant! 9 Necessary business; supper; prayer. 10.

MONDAY, OCTOBER 4. 3 Necessary business; prayed; tea. 4 Chaise. 6.30 Bath; tea. 7 Chaise; sins. 10.30 Devizes; necessary talk (religious). 11 Luke 15:7! at Mr Bailey's, dinner, religious talk. 1 Chaise. 5.30 At Mr Gifford's [at Salisbury], tea, religious talk; prayed. 6.30 2 Corinthians 6:1! Society; supper; prayer. 9.30.

TUESDAY, OCTOBER 5. 4 Prayed. 5 Hebrews 13:22! sermon. 8 Tea, religious talk; prayer. 9 Sermon. 12.30 Garden. 1 Dinner, religious talk. 2 Sermon. 3 Visited some. 4.30 Prayed; tea. 6.30 Luke 12:7! [George Story took down this sermon in shorthand] Society. 8.30 Supper. 9 Prayer. 9.30.

WEDNESDAY, OCTOBER 6. 2 Prayed. 5 Philippians 4:7! chaise; Stockbridge; tea; chaise. 11 Winchester [orig., 'Winton']; John 4:24! dinner. 12.45 Chaise. 5.15 Portsmouth Common; tea, religious talk. 6 Prayed. 6.30 Matthew 5:47! Society! supper, necessary talk (religious); prayer. 9.30.

THURSDAY, OCTOBER 7. 4 Prayed; Galatians 5:1! necessary business; tea, religious talk. 7.30 Boat. 9 Wootton Bridge. 9 Walked. 9.30 Chaise. 10 Newport; visited. 11 At Mr Clark's; sermon. 12 Dinner. 12.30 Chaise; Newtown; Matthew 11:28; chaise; tea; prayed. 6.30 Acts 21:26! supper, religious talk; prayer. 9.30.

FRIDAY, OCTOBER 8. 4 Prayed; Revelation 14:1, etc! sermon; tea. 7.30 Chaise; Ryde [orig., 'Wride']. 9.30 Boat. 11.30 At Point; walked; read notes. 1 Point; dinner. 2 Matthew 22:4! walked. 3.30 Necessary business. 4 Prayed; tea, necessary talk (religious). 6.30 2 Corinthians 11:14; supper; prayer. 9.30.

SATURDAY; OCTOBER 9. 1.30 Tea. 2 Chaise. 8.45 Godalming; tea, religious talk. 9.30 Chaise; [read] Walsh. 11.45 Cobham; brother Duplex, etc, dinner; coach. 5 At home; necessary business; tea; prayed; supper; letters; prayer. 9.30.

[SUNDAY] OCTOBER [10]. 4 Prayed; hymns; walked; Chapel; the preachers. 9.30 Read Prayers, Psalms 50:12, Communion. 1 Dinner, religious talk; Charles. 2.30 Slept; the leaders; hymns; tea, religious talk; prayer. 5 Read Prayers, Psalms 50:23; Society; hymns; supper; prayer. 9.30.

MONDAY, OCTOBER 11. 4 Prayed; 1 Peter 1:1-9! Select Society. 7 Hymns. 8 At Thomas Rankin's, tea, religious talk; prayer. 9 Hymns. 12 Necessary business; garden. 1.30 At brother Todd's, dinner, necessary talk (religious); prayer; hymns. 4 Visited; tea, religious talk; prayed; hymns. 8 Supper, religious talk; prayer. 9.30 Sins.

TUESDAY, OCTOBER 12. 4 Prayed; hymns. 8 At Thomas Rankin's, tea; prayer; hymns. 12 Necessary business; necessary talk (religious). 1 Dinner; hymns. 4 Prayed; tea, religious talk. 5.30 Necessary business; prayed. 6.30 Read Prayers, 1 Peter 1:9! the leaders. 8.30 Supper, religious talk; prayer. 9.30.

WEDNESDAY, OCTOBER 13. 4 Prayed; 1 Peter 1:10–15; tunes; tea; prayer; letters. 10 Tunes. 1.15 Dinner, religious talk; prayer; letters. 4.30 Visited. 5 Tea; prayer; prayed. 6 Letters. 8 Supper, necessary talk (religious); prayer. 9.30.

THURSDAY, OCTOBER 14. 4 Prayed; letters. 7 Necessary business; prayer; tea, religious talk; writ notes. 1 Dinner, religious talk; sermon; hymns. 4 Writ notes. 4.30 Visited; tea, necessary talk (religious)! prayer. 6 Prayed; read Prayers, 1 Peter 1:16; the bands; supper; prayer. 9.30.

[FRIDAY] OCTOBER [15]. 4 Prayed; sermon; letters. 12 The females; letters. 1.30 Prayer. 2.30 Dinner, religious talk. 3 Letters. 5 Visited; tea; prayer. 6 Prayed; letter. 7.45 Supper, religious talk; prayer. 9.30.

SATURDAY, OCTOBER 16. 4.15 Prayed; hymns. 8 Tea; prayer. 9 Hymns. 12 Walked with Charles. 1 Dinner; prayer. 1.30 Necessary business. 3 Read; prayed. 4.30 Visited some; tea, religious talk. 6.15 Letters; supper; Penry, necessary business. 9.30.

SUNDAY, OCTOBER 17. 4.15 Prayed; read notes. 8 Spitalfields. 9.30 Read Prayers; Daniel 3; Communion. 1 At brother Kemp's, dinner, necessary talk (religious). 2 Slept; letter; prayed; tea. 5 Read Prayers, Galatians 6:10; Society; read notes. 8 Supper, religious talk; prayer. 9.30.

MONDAY, OCTOBER 18. 3.30 Necessary business. 4 Chaise; Brentford; tea. 6.15 Chaise. 9.30 Maidenhead; tea. 10 Walked; chaise; read Walsh. 2 Wallingford; dinner. 3 Walsh; prayed. 5 Tea, religious talk. 6 Genesis 22:1, 2! Society. 8 At Mr Ludg——'s, supper; prayer. 9.30.

TUESDAY, OCTOBER 19. 4.30 Ill; prayed. 6 Luke 12:7; tea, religious talk. 7.30 Chaise. 9 Nuneham; walked; chaise. 12 Oxford; at brother Wickins'; writ shorth[and]s. 1 Dinner; shorthand. 3 Sins! prayed. 4 Walked! tea, religious talk. 6 Acts 11:26! Love-feast; supper; prayer. 9.30.

WEDNESDAY, OCTOBER 20. 4 Prayed; Magazine. 6 Romans 13:11, etc! Magazine. 8 Tea, religious talk; prayer; walked. 10 Chaise. 12 Witney; Magazine. 2 Dinner; Magazine. 4 Walked; Magazine; prayed. 5 Tea, religious talk. 6 Matthew 8:13! Society! supper; prayer. 9.30.

THURSDAY, OCTOBER 21. 4 Prayed; Isaiah 59:1, 2! journal. 8 Tea, religious talk; journal; Magazine. 12 The children. 1 Magazine. 2 Dinner; Magazine. 4 Prayed; walked. 5 Tea, religious talk; prayed. 6.30 1 Corinthians 13:1, etc. 7.30 Select Society; supper; religious talk; prayer. 9.30.

FRIDAY, OCTOBER 22. 4 Prayed. 5 1 Corinthians 13:8, etc! chaise; Oxford; tea. 8 Chaise. 10 Tetsworth. 11 Tea, religious talk. 11.45 Chaise. 12.30 [High]

Wycombe; Magazine. 1.30 Dinner, religious talk. 2.30 Journal. 3.30 Magazine; prayed; tea, religious talk. 6 John 4:24! Society; supper, religious talk; prayer. 9.45.

SATURDAY, OCTOBER 23. 4 Prayed. 5 Philippians 4:7! tea. 6.30 Chaise. 11.30 At home; letters. 1.30 Dinner, religious talk; letters. 3 Hymns. 5 Tea; writ class. 7 Prayed; supper; Penry; necessary business. 9.30.

SUNDAY, OCTOBER 24. 4 Prayed; hymns; walked. 8 Chapel. 9.30 Read Prayers, Matthew 22:13, etc! Communion. 1 Dinner, religious talk; visited. 2.30 Coach. 3 Shadwell; read Prayers, Luke 10:42! tea, religious talk. 6 Writ notes; Society. 7.30 Necessary business; supper; prayer. 9 Coach. 10 Slept.

MONDAY, OCTOBER 25. 6 Newmarket; tea; coach; read *Corsica;* mostly religious talk. 1.45 Norwich. 2 Walked. 2.15 Coach; dinner; prayer; walked. 4.30 Prayed; tea, religious talk. 6 Genesis 22:1, 2! 7.30 Writ notes. 8.15 Supper, religious talk; prayer. 9.30.

TUESDAY, OCTOBER 26. 4.30 Prayed; Luke 12:7! letters. 8 Tea, necessary talk (religious); prayer. 9 Letters. 10 Walked; chaise. 12.30 Loddon. 1 Dinner, religious talk; chaise; Hosea 14:4; chaise; letters. 4 Prayed; chaise; tea. 5 Religious talk, prayer! 6 1 Corinthians 13:1! chaise; supper, religious talk; prayer. 9.30.

WEDNESDAY, OCTOBER 27. 4 Prayed; Hebrews 9:27! letters. 8 Tea, religious talk; prayer. 9 Chaise. 12 Haddiscoe; dinner; Hebrews 7:25; chaise; [Great] Yarmouth; tea; prayed. 6 John 4:24! supper; prayer. 9.30.

[THURSDAY] OCTOBER [28]. 4 Prayed; Romans 13:11; journal; read notes. 8 Tea, religious talk; prayer. 9 Walked; chaise. 11.15 Lowestoft; read Reynolds. 1 Dinner, religious talk. 2.30 Sermon. 4 Prayed; tea, religious talk. 6 Matthew 8:13! Society! supper, religious talk; prayer. 9.30.

FRIDAY, OCTOBER 29. 4 Prayed; sermon. 6 Psalms 74:12; sermon. 8 Tea, religious talk; prayer. 9 Sermon. 12 Walked; visited. 1 Dinner, religious talk; prayer. 2 Sermon. 3 Letters; tea; prayed. 6 1 John 4:19. 7 Communion; supper, religious talk; prayer. 9.30.

SATURDAY, OCTOBER 30. 4.15 Isaiah 59:1, 2; tea, religious talk; prayer; necessary business. 7 Chaise; [North] Cove; tea, 1 Corinthians 1:30. 10 Chaise. 12 Loddon; dinner, religious talk; prayer. 1.15 Chaise. 3.45 At home; necessary business; tea, religious talk. 6 Prayed. 6.30 Matthew 4:10; Society; supper; prayer. 10.30.

SUNDAY, OCTOBER 31. 4.15 Prayed; letters. 7 Communion. 8 Tea, religious talk; prayer; letters. 12.30 Dinner, religious talk; Ephesians 6:11, etc. 3 Slept. 3.15 1 Corinthians 13:1, etc! letters. 4.30 Tea, religious talk; prayed. 6 Colossians 1:9, 10. 7.45 Supper, religious talk; prayer. 9.30.

MONDAY, NOVEMBER 1. 4 Prayed; Psalms 74:12; sermon. 8 Tea, religious talk; prayer. 9 Mr Kay! sermon. 9.30 Sermon. 12.15 Walked. 1 At Dr Hunt's, dinner, necessary talk (religious). 2.30 Letters; sermon; prayed. 4.30 Tea, religious talk. 5 Ephesians 2:8; Ch[arles]. 6 Acts 11:26; the leaders; supper. 10 Diligence.

TUESDAY, NOVEMBER 2. 6 Necessary talk (religious); *Corsica.* 7 Tea; Diligence. 2.30 At home; dinner; necessary business; chaise. 4 Deptford; class; tea; class. 6.30 Matthew 8:13; Society. 8 At sister Pur——'s, supper, religious talk; prayer. 9.30.

WEDNESDAY, NOVEMBER 3. 5 Prayed; letters. 8 Tea, religious talk; prayer; letters. 1.30 At Mr Dornford's, dinner, religious talk; prayer. 3 Letters. 5 Tea, religious talk; prayer; prayed; letters. 8 Supper, mostly religious talk; prayer. 9.30.

THURSDAY, NOVEMBER 4. 4 Prayed. 5 Sermon. 8 Tea, religious talk; prayer. 9 Letters; sermon. 1 Dinner, necessary talk (religious); prayer. 2.30 Chaise. 3 Visited. 3.30 At Thomas Rankin's; sermon; prayed. 5 Tea, religious talk; prayer. 6 Sermon. 8 At home; supper, religious talk; prayer. 9.30.

FRIDAY, NOVEMBER 5. 4 Prayed; writ notes. 8 Sermon; letters. 12 The females. 1 Necessary talk (religious) to John Atlay. 1.30 Prayer; dinner; prayer. 3 Writ sermon; visited. 5 Tea, religious talk. 6 Prayed; letters; sermon; supper. 8.30 2 Corinthians 11:14; coffee; prayer. 12.30.

SATURDAY, NOVEMBER 6. 7 Prayed. 8 Tea; letters; necessary talk (religious). 11 Chaise; at Charles's, Pascal Paoli! 2 Dinner, religious talk; prayer. 3.30 Chaise. 4 Letters; sister P——! 5 Tea, religious talk; prayer; prayed; letters. 8 Supper; Penry; necessary business; sins! 9.30.

SUNDAY, NOVEMBER 7. 4 Prayed; letters. 8 The preachers. 9.30 Read Prayers, Hebrews 13:17! Communion; at James Ham[mond]'s. 2 Dinner, religious talk. 2.30 Slept; prayed; tea. 5 Read Prayers, Proverbs 3:17! Society; supper, religious talk. 9 Prayer. 9.15.

MONDAY, NOVEMBER 8. 4 Prayed; 1 Peter 1:1-4; Select Society. 7 At brother Raw's, tea; class. 10.30 Necessary business. 11 Class. 12 Select Society. 1.30 Dinner; class. 5.30 Tea, religious talk; prayer. 6.30 Read Prayers, 1 Thessalonians 4:7! supper; the bands! 9.30.

TUESDAY, NOVEMBER 9. 4 Prayed; 1 Peter 1:1-5; class. 7 Tea; class. 1 At brother Bowers's, dinner, religious talk. 2 Class; visited; class; tea. 6.15 Matthew 8:13! 8.30 Supper; prayer. 9.30.

WEDNESDAY, NOVEMBER 10. 4 Prayed; letters. 6 Class; tea; class. 12 Letters; walked. 1 Dinner, religious talk; letters. 3 Mr Osbaldiston, religious talk! 4 Chaise. 5.15 Brentford; tea, religious talk. 6 Matthew 8:13! class! at Mr Holbrook's, supper, religious talk; prayer. 10.15.

THURSDAY, NOVEMBER 11. 4 Prayed. 5 1 Corinthians 10:13! writ Society. 8 Tea, religious talk; prayer; necessary business. 10. Chaise. 11.45 Lambeth; 1

Peter 1:24; class. 2 Dinner, religious talk; writ notes. 4.15 Chaise. 5.15 Wandsworth; tea, necessary talk (religious). 6 Psalms 146:4, 5; class; supper; prayer. 9.30.

FRIDAY, NOVEMBER [12]. 4 Prayed; writ notes. 6 At Mr Barker's, tea, religious talk; prayer. 7 Chaise. 8.15 At home; letters. 11 Chaise. 11.45 Bow; writ notes; Galatians 3:22; class; dinner. 2 Chaise. 4.45 Hadley. 5 Tea, religious talk; prayer. 6 John 4:24! class. 8 Supper, religious talk; prayer. 9.30.

SATURDAY, NOVEMBER 13. 4 Prayed; Magazine; tea; prayer; necessary talk! chaise. 9.30 Letters. 12.15 Dinner; prayer. 1 Visited; necessary business. 2.30 Letters; prayed. 4.30 Walked; at brother Trigg's; tea, religious talk. 6 Read Prayers, 1 Timothy 1:5! 7 Communion; supper; Penry, necessary business. 9.30.

SUNDAY, NOVEMBER 14. 4 Prayed; letters; chaise; the preachers; prayed. 9.30 Read Prayers. 2 Corinthians 11:14! Communion. 1 Dinner, religious talk. 2 Slept; prayed; the leaders. 3.30 Read Prayers, John 6:28; tea; Society; coach. 6.30 Society; Love-feast. 8 Supper, religious talk; prayer. 9.30.

MONDAY, NOVEMBER 15. 4 Prayed; 1 Peter 1:14-19; Select Society. 7 Chaise; tea; class. 1 Dinner. 2 Visited; class. 5 Tea, religious talk; class. 6 Read Prayers, 1 Timothy 4:8! Society. 8 Coach; supper, religious talk; prayer; necessary business. 9.30.

TUESDAY, NOVEMBER 16. 4 Prayed; necessary business. 6 Class; tea; class. 1 Dinner, religious talk. 2 Class. 4 Tea; necessary business. 5 Writ notes; prayed. 6.30 Read Prayers, 1 Peter 1:18-20! the leaders; supper. 9 Prayer. 9.30.

WEDNESDAY, NOVEMBER 17. 4 Prayed; necessary business. 6 Class; tea; class. 1 At brother Kemp's, dinner. 2 Class. 5 At sister Mackril's, tea, necessary talk (religious). 5.30 Letters; prayed. 8 Supper, religious talk; prayer. 9.30.

THURSDAY, NOVEMBER 18. 4 Prayed; letters. 6 Class; tea; class. 12 Newgate! 1.30 Dinner. 2.30 Slept; letter; prayed. 4 Chaise; Highgate; tea, religious talk; prayer. 6.30 Acts 11:26; class; Magazine; supper; prayer. 10.

FRIDAY, NOVEMBER 19. 3.30 Dressed; necessary business. 4.30 Chaise; at home; necessary business. 6 Class. 1 Dinner, at brother Parker's. 2 Class; tea. 4.45 Walked. 5.45 Highbury Place; tea, religious talk; visited! 7 Prayed; Magazine. 8.30 Supper, religious talk; prayer. 10.

SATURDAY, NOVEMBER 20. 4 Prayed. 5 Walked. 6 At home; class! walked. 7 Class; tea; class. 1 Dinner. 2 Class. 4.30 Tea, religious talk. 6 Read Prayers, 1 Peter 1:17; Society; the leaders; Charles. 8.30 Supper, necessary talk. 9.30.

[Texts noted at bottom of page:] 1 Timothy 1:5, 4:8; 1 Peter 1:18.

SUNDAY, NOVEMBER 21. 4 Prayed; necessary business; letters. 8 Spitalfields. 9.30 Read Prayers, 1 Peter 1:18! Communion; at brother Duplex's. 2 Dinner, religious talk; slept. 3 The leaders. 4 Tea, necessary talk (religious). 5 Read Prayers, Revelation 3:5! Society. 7.30 Supper; necessary business; prayer; notes read; sins! 9.30.

MONDAY, NOVEMBER 22. 3 Necessary business; tea. 4 Chaise; Barnet; tea; chaise; Hockliffe [orig., 'Hockley']; chaise. 1.45 Newport [Pagnell]; dinner. 3.15 Chaise. 6 Northampton; tea, religious talk. 7 John 4:24! supper, religious talk; prayer. 9.30.

TUESDAY, NOVEMBER 23. 4 Prayed; Magazine. 6 1 Corinthians 10:13! religious talk; Magazine; tea, religious talk; prayer. 9 Chaise. 12.30 Whittlebury; sermon. 1.30 Dinner, religious talk; sermon. 4.30 Tea, religious talk; prayer. 5.30 Prayed. 6.30 Matthew 8:13! supper, religious talk; prayer; Richard! 9.30.

WEDNESDAY, NOVEMBER 24. 4 Prayed; sermon. 6 Luke 20:34! sermon; tea; prayer. 8 Chaise. 10.15 Brackley. 11 Tea; Society. 11 Chaise. 1.45 Banbury; necessary talk (religious). 2 Dinner; sermon. 4.30 Tea, religious talk; prayer. 5.30 Prayed. 6.30 Isaiah 55:7! 8 Supper, religious talk; prayer. 9.30.

THURSDAY, NOVEMBER 25. 4 Prayed; sermon. 6 Romans 12:1! chaise. 9.15 Brackley; tea, religious talk. 9.30 2 Corinthians 8:9! chaise. 1 Towcester; dinner; sermon. 4 Prayed; tea, religious talk. 6 1 Peter 4:18! sermon; supper; prayer. 9.30.

FRIDAY, NOVEMBER 26. 2.45 Necessary business; tea. 4 Chaise; Brickhill; tea, religious talk; chaise; Redburn [near St Albans]. 12 Dinner. 12.30 Chaise. 5 At home; tea; prayed; letters. 8.30 Supper; prayer. 9.30.

SATURDAY, NOVEMBER 27. 4 Prayed; letters; tea; letters. 12 Garden. 1 At G. Clark's, dinner; prayer. 2 Letters. 4.15 Prayed; walked; at brother Freeman's, tea, religious talk; prayer; prayed. 6 Read Prayers, Hebrews 3:15, Communion. 8 Supper, religious talk; necessary business. 9.30.

SUNDAY, NOVEMBER 28. 4 Prayed; letters; walked; Chapel. 9.30 Read Prayers, 1 Peter 1:18! Communion; dinner, religious talk; prayer. 2 Slept; prayed. 3.30 Covent Garden; read Prayers, 1 Corinthians 13:1, etc; coach; Society. 7 Letters. 8 Supper; prayer; necessary business. 9.30.

MONDAY, NOVEMBER 29. 3.30 Prayed. 4 Chaise. 7.15 Tea; chaise. 1 Hinxworth; necessary talk (religious); writ Society. 2 Dinner, necessary talk (religious). 3 Writ Society. 5 Tea; prayed; Society. 6.30 Jeremiah 8:22. 8 Supper, religious talk; prayer. 9.30.

TUESDAY, NOVEMBER 30. 4 Prayed; writ to John Ha[mpso]n. 8 The children! tea, religious talk. 9 Writ Society. 1 Dinner, religious talk. 2 Chaise. 5 Bedford; at brother Eagle's, tea, religious talk. 6 John 4:24! Society; supper, religious talk. 9 Prayer. 9.30.

[Texts noted at bottom of page:] Revelation 3:5; Hebrews 13:17.

WEDNESDAY, DECEMBER 1. 4 Prayed; journal. 6 1 Corinthians 15:58! journal. 8 Tea, religious talk; prayer; religious talk; prayed. 9.15 Chaise. 12.15 St Neots; necessary talk (religious); Magazine. 1.30 Dinner. 2.30 Writ Society. 4 Prayed; tea, religious talk; prayer; prayed. 6 Proverbs 3:17! journal. 9 Supper, religious talk; prayer. 10.30.

THURSDAY, DECEMBER 2. 4.30 Prayed; sermon. 6 Romans 13:11! writ notes. 8 Tea, religious talk; prayer; sermon. 10 Chaise; Buckden. 11.30 2 Corinthians 6:2! chaise. 1 Godmanchester; sermon. 3 Dinner, religious talk; prayed. 5 Tea. 6 Huntingdon; 1 Corinthians 13:1, etc; writ notes. 8 Supper, religious talk; prayer. 9.30.

FRIDAY, DECEMBER 3. 4 Prayed; chaise. 7.30 St Neots; tea, religious talk; chaise. 2 Walked! 3 Luton; dinner; Magazine; prayed. 5 Tea, religious talk. 6 Matthew 8:13! Magazine; supper, religious talk; prayer. 9.30.

SATURDAY, DECEMBER 4. 4 Prayed; tea. 4.30 Chaise. 9 Barnet; tea, necessary talk. 9.30 Chaise. 11.30 At home; letters. 1 Dinner; prayer; letters. 4.30 Coach; at John Hallam's; tea, necessary talk (religious). 6 Read Prayers, Hebrews 10:36, Communion; supper; Penry, necessary business. 9.30.

SUNDAY, DECEMBER 5. 4 Prayed; letters; the preachers. 9.30 Read Prayers, Psalms 24:3, 4, Communion. 1 Dinner; visited. 3 The leaders; tea; prayed. 5 Hebrews 11:1! Society; letter; necessary business; supper, religious talk; prayer. 9.30.

MONDAY, DECEMBER 6. 4 Prayed; tea. 4.30 Chaise; tea; chaise. 2 Mount Ephraim [near Tunbridge Wells]; dinner; writ sermon; tea, religious talk. 6 Prayed. 6.30 Hebrews 4:14; writ notes. 8 Supper, religious talk; prayer. 9.30.

TUESDAY, DECEMBER 7. 4 Prayed; sermon. 6 Hebrews 10:19; tea; prayer. 7.45 Chaise! 1 Robertsbridge; dinner, religious talk; prayer. 2 Chaise. 5 Rye; tea, necessary talk (religious). 6 Luke 15:7! Society! 7.30 At sister Barnes's, supper, religious talk; prayer. 9.30.

WEDNESDAY, DECEMBER 8. 4 Prayed; tea; prayer. 5.30 Chaise! 10 Robertsbridge; tea, religious talk; prayer. 11 Chaise. 4 Woodgate [coaching stop near Tunbridge Wells]; dinner; chaise. 6.30 Sevenoaks. 7 1 Peter 1:18; Magazine. 8 Supper, religious talk; prayer. 9.45.

THURSDAY, DECEMBER 9. 4.30 Prayed; Magazine. 6 Matthew 8:13! Magazine. 8 Tea, religious talk; prayer; Magazine. 10.30 Prayer; chaise. 12.30 Shoreham; religious talk! 1 Dinner; Magazine. 4 Tea, religious talk. 5 Prayed. 6 Luke 12:7! Magazine; supper, religious talk; prayer. 9.30.

FRIDAY, DECEMBER 10. 4 Prayed; Magazine. 7 Matthew 8:13; tea; prayer. 8 Chaise! 3 At sister Cheesement's, dinner, religious talk; prayer; walked. 4.30 At home; tea; prayer; letters; prayed. 8 Supper; prayer. 9.30.

SATURDAY, DECEMBER 11. 4.15 Prayed; letters. 8 Tea, religious talk; prayer; letters. 1 Dinner, religious talk; prayer; read notes; letters. 3 Accounts. 4 Prayed; walked. 5 Tea, religious talk. 6 Read Prayers, James 4:4, Communion; supper; Penry. 9 Necessary business. 9.30.

[Texts noted at bottom of page:] James 4:4; 1 Peter 1:18.

SUNDAY, DECEMBER 12. 4 Prayed; letters; Chapel. 9.30 Read Prayers, Revelation 2:5! Communion; dinner, religious talk. 2.30 Slept; prayed; the leaders. 3.30 Read Prayers, Leviticus 19:17; Society; chaise; Society; prayed. 7.30 Writ notes; supper; prayer. 9.30.

MONDAY, DECEMBER 13. 4 Prayed; tea. 6 Diligence. 11.30 Chatham; tea; prayer. 12 Diligence. 4.30 Canterbury; at brother Hagel's, dinner, religious talk, tea. 6.30 Acts 11:26! 7 Society; supper, religious talk; prayer. 10.

TUESDAY, DECEMBER 14. 4 Prayed; writ Society! 6 Romans 13:11; Society. 8 Tea, religious talk; prayer. 9 Chaise. 12 Dover; Society. 1.30 Dinner; Society. 4 Visited; tea, religious talk; prayed. 6 Matthew 22:37! Society; supper, mostly religious talk! prayer. 9.30.

WEDNESDAY, DECEMBER 15. 4 Prayed; writ notes. 7 Matthew 22:39. 8 Tea, religious talk; prayer; chaise. 1 At brother Collier's, dinner, religious talk; prayer; writ notes; prayed. 4.30 Tea, religious talk; prayer. 6.15 John 4:24! Communion. 8 Supper; prayer. 9.45.

THURSDAY, DECEMBER 16. 4 Prayed; writ Society; 1 Peter 5:10! at brother Saddleton's. 7 Tea, religious talk; prayer. 7.30 Chaise. 9.45 Sittingbourne; tea; 1 Corinthians 15:58. 11 Chaise; walked. 2 Sheerness; dinner; writ notes; tea! read Prayers, 1 Peter 4:18! Society; supper; prayer. 9.30.

[FRIDAY] DECEMBER [17]. 4 Prayed. 5.15 Psalms 64:1, Communion; tea; necessary business; prayer. 9.30 In the boat. 2.30 Chatham; dinner, necessary talk (religious)! prayed; tea; prayer. 6 Revelation 2:5! Communion; supper, religious talk; prayer. 9.30.

SATURDAY, DECEMBER 18. 4 Prayed; 1 Peter 1:18! chaise. 12 At home; writ letters. 1.30 Dinner; prayer. 2 Writ letters. 4 Magazine; prayed; coach. 5 Tea, religious talk; prayer. 6 Read Prayers. 2 Peter 1:5, etc, Communion; supper; Penry; A. Mo——! sins. 10.

SUNDAY, DECEMBER 19. 4 Prayed; letters; the preachers. 9.30 Read Prayers, Acts 19:2! Communion. 1 Dinner. 2.30 Slept; prayed; tea. 5 Read Prayers, 1 Peter 4:9 [orig., '2 Pet. 4:9']; Society; Magazine; supper; prayer. 9.30.

[MONDAY] DECEMBER [20]. 4 Prayed; Leviticus 19:17; Select Society; tea. 7 Chaise. 10.30 Hatfield; Miss Harvey; chaise. 2.30 Hinxworth. 3 Dinner, Mr Simeon! writ Society. 5 Tea, religious talk. 6.30 Galatians 6:14. 8.30 Supper, religious talk; prayer. 9.45.

Tuesday, December 21. 4 Prayed; Society. 7.30 Matthew 13:3, etc; Society. 9 Tea, religious talk; Society. 2.30 Chaise! 5.30 Wrestlingworth; tea, religious talk; Revelation 20:12; supper; prayer. 9.15 At Mr Sales's. 9.45.

Wednesday, December 22. 4 Prayed; necessary business; tea. 5.45 Chaise with Miss Harvey. 12 Hatfield; dinner. 12.30 Chaise. 4 At home; writ notes; tea; prayed; writ Society. 8 Supper, religious talk; prayer. 9.30.

Thursday, December 23. 4 Prayed; Society. 8 At Thomas Rankin's, tea, religious talk; prayer; Society. 12.30 Visited. 1 Dinner, Dr Whitehead, necessary talk (religious). 2 Society. 4 Tea, necessary talk (religious). 5.30 At home; 1 John 3:1, etc! the bands; supper; prayer. 9.30.

Friday, December 24. 4 Prayed; letters. 12 The females. 1 Prayer. 2 Dinner; prayer. 3 Writ lettters. 5 Tea; prayer. 6 Letters; supper, religious talk; prayer. 9.30.

Christmas Day, Saturday, December 25. 3.30 Prayed. 4 Prayer; Matthew 1:21; writ letters; tea; chaise. 9 Chapel. 9.30 Read Prayers, Luke 2:14, Communion. 1 Dinner, religious talk; coach. 2.30 Slept; prayed. 3 Read Prayers, Isaiah 11:10, Society! tea, religious talk; writ letters; supper; prayer; necessary business. 9.30.

Sunday, December 26. 4 Prayed; Magazine; tea; letters. 10.15 Newgate; read Prayers. 11 Luke 15:7! 1 At sister Box's, dinner, religious talk; prayer. 2.15 Slept; prayed. 3 The leaders. 4 Tea; prayed. 5 Acts 7:55; Society; supper, religious talk. 9.30.

Monday, December 27. 4 Prayed; 1 Peter 1:5, etc; Select Society; letters. 8 Tea, religious talk; writ notes; Chapel. 9.30 Read Prayers, 1 John 3:1, etc! Communion; at sister Keysall's, dinner, religious talk; prayer; Chapel. 3 Writ notes; tea, religious talk. 6.30 Read Prayers, Revelation 22:20! supper; the bands! 9.30.

[Tuesday] December [28]. 4 Prayed; 1 Peter 4:11! Communion; writ notes. 7 Tea, religious talk; prayer. 8.30 At home; letters. 10 Read Prayers. 11 Revelation 14:1, etc, Communion; writ notes. 1 At Dr Whitehead's, dinner, necessary talk (religious); prayer. 3 Writ notes. 4.30 Tea, religious talk; prayer; prayed; read Prayers, 1 John 5:3! the leaders; supper; prayer. 9.30.

[Wednesday] December 29. 4 Prayed; 1 Peter 4:11; Communion; writ notes. 7.30 Prayer; tea; writ Society. 1.30 Visited. 3 At brother Wright's, dinner, religious talk. 5 At Mr Rutherford's, tea, religious talk; prayer. 6 Read Prayers, 2 John 8, Communion. 8 Supper, religious talk; prayer. 9.30.

Thursday, December 30. 4 Prayed; writ journal. 8 Prayer; tea, religious talk; journal. 1 At sister Shakespeare's, dinner, religious talk; prayer. 2.30 Letters. 4.30 Tea, religious talk; prayer; prayed. 6.30 Read Prayers, Psalms 147:3; the bands! 8 Supper, religious talk; prayer; necessary business. 9.30.

FRIDAY, DECEMBER 31. 4 Prayed; letters. 12 The females; sorted letters. 2 Dinner, religious talk; prayer. 3.30 Slept; prayed. 4.30 Tea, religious talk; prayer. 5.30 Prayed; writ notes; Committee; supper; 1 Peter 4:7! prayer. 12.30.

[Texts noted at bottom of page:] Isaiah 11:10; Leviticus 19:17; 1 Peter 4:

SATURDAY, JANUARY 1, 1785. 6.45 Prayed. 8 Tea, religious talk; prayer; writ notes. 10 Read Prayers, 2 Corinthians 5:17, Communion; writ notes. 1 At brother Ball's, dinner, religious talk; prayer; visited. 3.30 Prayed; chaise; tea, religious talk; prayer. 6 Read Prayers, 2 Corinthians 6:17, Communion; supper; Penry, necessary business. 9.30.

SUNDAY, JANUARY 2. 4 Prayed; letters. 8 The preachers. 9.30 Read Prayers, Joshua 24:15! Communion; at brother Bumsted's. 2 Visited; slept. 3 The leaders; tea; prayed. 5 The Covenant. 8 Supper, religious talk; prayer. 9.30.

[MONDAY, JANUARY 3.] 4 Prayed; Psalms 76:11; Select Society; writ notes. 7 Tea; walked. 8 Tea; necessary business; went begging [for] the poor. 1 At Thomas Olivers's, dinner, religious talk. 3 Went [begging]! visited; christened Josiah Dornford; prayer. 7 Necessary business; prayed; supper; Mr Collins; prayer. 9.30.

[TUESDAY, JANUARY 4.] 4 Prayed; letters; tea; prayer. 8 Went begging; visited. 3 Dinner, religious talk. 4 Went [begging]; tea, religious talk; prayer. 6 Read Prayers, Romans 4:9! Communion; low. 8 Supper, religious talk; prayer. 9.30.

[WEDNESDAY, JANUARY 5. No entry.]

THURSDAY, JANUARY 6. 4 Prayed; letters; tea; prayer. 8 Went [begging]; visited. 1 At brother Marsden's, dinner; prayer. 2.30 Went [begging]. 4 Prayed; tea, religious talk; prayer. 5.30 Prayed; letters. 7.30 The bands; supper, religious talk; prayer; ill. 9.30.

FRIDAY, JANUARY 7. 4.30 Prayed; letters; slept. 8 Tea; letters. 10 Went [begging]. 1 Writ notes. 2 At brother Dewey's, dinner, religious talk. 3 Chaise. 5 Hadley; tea, religious talk. 6 Luke 20:34! Communion; supper, religious talk; prayer. 9.30. Ill.

SATURDAY, JANUARY 8. 4.30 Prayed; Magazine; tea. 6 Chaise. 8 At home; necessary business. 8.30 Went [begging]. 1 At brother Thornton's, dinner, religious talk; prayer. 2.30 Went [begging]. 3.30 Prayed. 4.15 Tea, religious talk; prayer. 6 Read Prayers, Romans 6:23! 7 Communion, coach. 8 Ill; supper; necessary business. 9.30.

SUNDAY, JANUARY 9. 4 Very ill. 8 Rose; prayed; tea; read Magazine; Dr Whitehead; Magazine. 1 Dinner, religious talk; Magazine. 4 Tea; Magazine; prayed; letter. 8 Supper, religious talk; prayer. 9.30.

MONDAY, JANUARY 10. 5 Prayed. 6 Letters; writ notes. 8 Tea, religious talk; prayer; writ notes. 12 Chaise; went [begging]. 1 At sister Well's, dinner, religious talk; prayer; coach. 3 Magazine. 5 Tea; prayer; Magazine. 8 Supper; prayer. 9.30.

TUESDAY, JANUARY 11. 4 Prayed; Magazine. 8 Tea, religious talk; prayer; went [begging]. 1 At brother Gouthit's, dinner, religious talk; prayer. 2 Went [begging]. 4.30 At home; tea, religious talk; prayer. 5.30 Prayed. 6.30 Read Prayers, Romans 9:16; the leaders! 8.30 Supper, necessary talk (religious); prayer. 9.30.

WEDNESDAY, JANUARY 12. 4 Prayed; letters; tea, religious talk. 9 Went [begging]. 10.15 Letters. 1 At brother Love's, dinner, necessary talk (religious); prayer; went [begging]; visited. 4 Tea, religious talk; prayer. 6 Read Prayers, Romans 10:4! Communion; supper; prayer. 9.30.

THURSDAY, JANUARY 13. 4 Prayed; letters. 8 Tea, religious talk, prayer; went [begging]. 10.30 Letters; writ notes. 1.15 At Mr Awbrey's. 2.30 Dinner, religious talk; prayer. 4 Prayed; tea, religious talk; prayer; prayed. 6.15 Read Prayers, Romans 11:32; the bands. 8.15 Supper, religious talk; prayer. 9.30.

FRIDAY, JANUARY 14. 4 Prayed; letters. 11.30 The females. 12 Chaise; went [begging]. 2.30 At Mr Judd's, dinner, religious talk; prayer. 4 Prayed; tea, religious talk. 6.15 The Committee. 7.30 Magazine. 8 Supper, religious talk; prayer. 9.30.

SATURDAY, JANUARY 15. 4 Prayed; letters. 7.30 Tea, religious talk; prayer; letters. 10 Went begging. 1.15 At brother Day's. 2 Dinner; read notes; prayer; visited. 5 At Ka—— Harding's, tea, religious talk; prayer. 6 Read Prayers, Romans 13:10, Communion; supper; Penry, necessary business. 9.30.

SUNDAY, JANUARY 16. 4 Prayed; letters. 8 Spitalfields. 9.30 Read Prayers, Matthew 14:31! Communion. 1 Dinner, religious talk; prayer. 2 Slept; prayed; the leaders. 4 Tea, religious talk; prayed. 5 Read Prayers, Romans 14:17! Society; the married persons. 8 Supper, religious talk; prayer. 9.30.

MONDAY, JANUARY 17. 4 Tea. 5 Chaise; Magazine; Romford; tea; chaise; Magazine; Ingatestone. 11 Chaise. 4.45 Colchester; dinner, religious talk, tea. 6 Prayed; Matthew 7:16! 8 Supper; prayer. 9.30.

TUESDAY, JANUARY 18. 4 Prayed; Magazine. 6 Revelation 2:5! the leaders. 8 Tea, religious talk; prayer; visited some. 10 Read notes. 10.30 Chaise. 12 Mistley [orig., 'Mistly Thorn']; at Mrs Parmenter's; Magazine. 2 Dinner, religious talk. 3.30 Prayed; read the *Shipwreck!* 5 Tea, religious talk; prayer. 6 Isaiah 55:6! 7.30 At home; supper, religious talk; prayer. 9.45.

WEDNESDAY, JANUARY 19. 4 Prayed; read Walsh. 6 Mark 1:15! *Shipwreck.* 8 Tea, religious talk; prayer; *Shipwreck;* prayer. 10 Chaise. 11.30 Colchester. 1 At sister Woodcock's, dinner, necessary talk (religious); prayer. 2 Visited some; *Shipwreck.* 4 Prayed; tea, religious talk. 6 John 4:24! Communion; at [blank]. 8.30 Supper, religious talk; prayer. 9.45.

THURSDAY, JANUARY 20. 4 Tea; prayer. 5 Chaise; Witham; tea; chaise; Ingatestone; chaise. 2 Magazine. 3.30 Rainham; dinner, religious talk; prayer; tea; chaise. 6 Purfleet; Hebrews 7:25! chaise; Rainham; supper; prayer, 9.30.

FRIDAY, JANUARY 21. 4 Prayed; tea; prayer. 6 Chaise. 9.15 At home; letters. 12 The females. 12.45 Coach; Mr Best! 2 At Mr Goslin's, religious talk, dinner; prayer. 4 Coach; at home; letters; prayed; tea. 6 The Committee. 7 Letters; prayed. 8 Supper, religious talk; prayer. 9.30.

SATURDAY, JANUARY 22. 4 Prayed; letters. 8 Tea; prayer; letters. 1 At Mr Bicc——n's, dinner, religious talk; prayer. 3.30 Visited; tea, religious talk; prayer. 6 Read Prayers, 1 Corinthians 4:5, Communion. 8.30 Supper. 9 Necessary business; sins! 9.30.

SUNDAY, JANUARY 23. 4 Prayed; letters; sins! Chapel. 9.30 Read Prayers, Matthew 20:15! Communion. 1 Dinner. 2 Slept; prayed; the leaders. 3.30 Read Prayers; [1 Cor. 6:5 deleted] Matthew 21:21! Society; Knightsbridge; tea. 6 Read Prayers, John 4:24! chaise; supper; prayer. 9.30.

MONDAY, JANUARY 24. 4 Prayed; 1 Peter 1:12, etc; Select Society; tea; letters. 12 Select Society; writ notes. 2 At Mr Griffith's, dinner, religious talk; prayer. 3.30 Prayed; tea. 6.30 Read Prayers, 1 Corinthians 6:20(2)! supper; the bands. 9.30.

[Pointing hand] TUESDAY, JANUARY 25. 4 Prayed; 1 Peter 1:12, etc; necessary talk (religious); letter. 7.30 Tea, religious talk; letters. 12 Dinner; necessary business. 1 House of Lords; walked. 4.30 Tea, religious talk; prayed. 6.30 Read the letters; the leaders. 8.30 Supper, religious talk; prayer. 9.30.

WEDNESDAY, JANUARY 26. 4 Prayed; 1 Peter 1:16, etc; letters; tea; letters. 12 Visited. 12.45 At sister Cheesement's. 1 Dinner; prayer. 2.30 Chaise. 4.45 Brentford; tea; prayed. 6.30 Matthew 21:21! Society; supper, religious talk; prayer. 9.30.

THURSDAY, JANUARY 27. 4 Prayed; Romans 13:11, etc; Magazine; tea. 7 Chaise; visited. 10 Writ notes. 1 At brother Blunt's, dinner, necessary talk (religious); Magazine; prayer. 4.45 Tea, religious talk; prayer; prayed. 6.30 Read Prayers, 1 Corinthians 8:2; the bands; supper, religious talk; prayer. 9.30.

FRIDAY, JANUARY 28. 4 Prayed; letters. 9 Prayer; letters. 1 Prayer; Communion. 3 Dinner, religious talk; prayer. 4 Tea; visited. 5.30 Slept; prayed; writ notes; supper. 8.30 Prayer; Hebrews 12:1, 2. 10.

SATURDAY, JANUARY 29. 4.15 Prayed; letters. 7 Class; tea; class. 1 Dinner. 2 Class. 4.30 Visited some. 5.15 Tea, religious talk; prayer. 6 Read Prayers, 1 Corinthians 10:12! Class. 8 Supper; Penry; necessary business. 9.45.

SUNDAY, JANUARY 30. 4 Prayed; letters; the preachers. 9.30 Read Prayers, Psalms 119:137, Communion; dinner; letters. 2 Slept; the leaders; tea; prayed. 5

Read Prayers, Hebrews 12:7! St Antholin's; read Prayers, 1 Corinthians 13:1, etc; supper, religious talk; prayer. 9.30.

MONDAY, JANUARY 31. 4 1 Peter 1 *ad fin;* Select Society; class; tea; class. 1 Dinner; class; tea; read Prayers, 1 Corinthians 13:8, etc; class; supper; religious talk; prayer. 9.30.

[Texts noted at bottom of page:] Psalms 68:12; 1 Corinthians 8:2, etc; 10:12; Hebrews 12:7; 2 Corinthians 1:22; 2:11; 15:19.

TUESDAY, FEBRUARY 1. 4 Prayed; 1 Peter 1 *ad fin;* letter; class; Spitalfields; class; tea; class. 1 At brother Hudson's, dinner; class. 5 Tea, religious talk; prayer; prayed. 6.30 1 Corinthians 15:42; class; the leaders. 8 Supper, religious talk; N. Norton; prayer. 9.30 Sins!

WEDNESDAY, FEBRUARY 2. 4 Prayed; letters; class; tea; class. 1 Dinner, religious talk. 2 Class. 5 Tea, religious talk; prayer; prayed. 6.30 Writ letters. 8 Supper, religious talk; prayer. 9.30.

THURSDAY, FEBRUARY 3. 4 Prayed; letters. 6 Class; tea; class. 1 At sister Westry's, dinner, religious talk; prayer. 2 Class. 5 Tea, religious talk; prayer. 6.30 1 Corinthians 16:13; class; the bands. 8 Supper, religious talk; prayer. 9.30.

FRIDAY, FEBRUARY 4. 4 Prayed; writ notes. 6 Class; tea; class. 10 Writ notes. 10.30 Class. 1 Dinner, religious talk; class. 5 At sister Box's, tea, religious talk; prayer. 6 Prayed; letters. 8 Supper, religious talk; prayer. 9.30.

SATURDAY, FEBRUARY 5. 4 Prayed; writ class. 8 Tea; class. 12 Necessary talk (religious) to many. 1 Dinner, religious talk; prayer. 2 Class. 4.30 Chaise. 5 Tea, religious talk; prayer. 6 Read Prayers, 2 Corinthians 1:22! Communion. 7.30 Class; supper; Penry, necessary business. 9.30.

SUNDAY, FEBRUARY 6. 5 Prayed; letters. 8 The preachers. 9.30 Read Prayers, 1 Corinthians 13:13! Communion. 1 At brother W. Leet's. 2 Dinner, religious talk; prayer. 2 Writ class; the leaders. 4 Tea; prayed. 5 2 Corinthians 2:11; Society. 7 Love-feast! supper. 9.30.

MONDAY, FEBRUARY 7. 4 Prayed; Psalms 68:12! Select Society. 7 Class. 12 Select Society. 1 At G. Whitfield's, dinner, religious talk. 2 Class. 5 Tea, religious talk; prayer; prayed. 6.30 Read Prayers, 2 Corinthians 3:17; class; supper; the bands. 9.30.

TUESDAY, FEBRUARY 8. 4 Prayed; writ notes. 1 Peter 1 *ad fin;* class; tea; class. 1 At brother Bower's, dinner. 2 Class. 5 Tea, religious talk; prayer; class. 6.30 Hebrews 12:7, etc! coach. 8 Supper. 9 Prayer. 9.30.

WEDNESDAY, FEBRUARY 9. 4 Prayed; writ class; tea. 7 Class. 1 Necessary business. 2 At brother Bar——'s, dinner, necessary talk. 4 Chaise. 5 Brentford; tea, religious talk; prayed; writ class. 6.30 2 Corinthians 2:11; class; supper. 9 Prayer. 9.30.

THURSDAY, FEBRUARY 10. 4 Prayed; Luke 16:31! tea, religious talk; writ class. 7.30 Chaise. 9 Lambeth; writ class. 1 Dinner, religious talk. 2 Class. 4.30 At brother Gibson's, tea, religious talk; prayer. 6.30 Revelation 20:12! class; supper, religious talk; prayer. 10.

FRIDAY, FEBRUARY 11. 4 Prayed; class. 6 Isaiah 57:1, 2! tea, religious talk; in the School. 8.30 Class. 10.30 Chaise. 11.30 Stratford [London]; necessary talk. 12.15 Hebrews 9:27! 2 Class; dinner. 2.30 Chaise. 5.30 Hadley; tea, religious talk. 7 1 Corinthians 16:13! 7 Class; supper, religious talk; prayer. 9.30.

SATURDAY, FEBRUARY 12. 4 Prayed; journal. 7 Chaise. 9 At home; letters. 1 At brother Paramore's, dinner, religious talk. 2 Letters. 4 Necessary talk (religious) to many; chaise. 5 Visited; tea, religious talk; prayer. 6 Read Prayers. 7 Hebrews 12:7, Communion; supper; Penry, necessary business. 9.30.

SUNDAY, FEBRUARY 13. 4.30 Prayed; ill; letters; the Chapel; the preachers, necessary talk. 9.30 Read Prayers, 2 Corinthians 6:2. 11.30 Communion. 1 At brother Dobson's, dinner, religious talk; prayer; slept; prayed; the leaders. 3.30 Read Prayers, 1 Corinthians 16:13; tea, Society; coach; Society; the single women; supper, religious talk; prayer. 9.30.

MONDAY, FEBRUARY 14. 4 Prayed; 1 Peter 2:1, etc; Select Society; writ notes. 8 Tea, religious talk; prayer. 9 Necessary talk (religious) to many; writ letters. 2 At Dr Whitehead's, dinner, religious talk; prayer. 3.30 Visited; chaise. 5.30 Wandsworth. 6 Tea. 6.30 Hebrews 12:7! Society! at brother Crowther's, supper; prayer. 9.30.

TUESDAY, FEBRUARY 15. 5 Prayed; read letters. 6 Luke 9:62; tea; chaise. 9 At home; letters; chaise. 1 Deptford; at P. Hore's, dinner, religious talk; letters. 4 Class; tea; class. 6.30 Matthew 21:21! Society. 8 Supper, religious talk; prayer. 10.

WEDNESDAY, FEBRUARY 16. 4.45 Prayed; letters. 8 Tea, religious talk; prayer; letters; writ Society. 11.30 Visited. 1 At sister Pearson's, dinner, religious talk; prayer; chaise. 4 At home; visited; chaise. 5.30 Highgate; tea, religious talk. 9 Ecclesiastes 9:10! prayed. 8 Supper; prayer. 10.

THURSDAY, FEBRUARY 17. 4 Prayed; letters; tea. 8 1 Corinthians 15:19! necessary talk (religious); chaise. 11 Letters. 2 Dinner, religious talk; prayer. 3.30 Necessary business; letters. 4.30 Tea, religious talk; prayer; letter. 6.45 At [his nephew] Charles's concert. 10 At home; supper; prayer. 10.30.

FRIDAY, FEBRUARY 18. 5 Prayed; letters; tea. 8 Chaise. 10 Ewell. 11 Chaise. 1 Dorking; Magazine. 2 Dinner. 3 Letters. 4 Prayed; tea. 6 2 Timothy 2:3! Communion. 7 Class; supper; prayer. 9.45.

SATURDAY, FEBRUARY 19. 4 Prayed; writ notes. 6 Revelation 2:5! writ Society. 8 Chaise. 12.30 At brother Ormes's; writ Society. 1 Dinner, religious talk. 2 Visited many; tea; prayed. 6 Read Prayers, Psalms 101:2, Communion; supper; Penry, necessary business. 9.45.

SUNDAY, FEBRUARY 20. 4.45 Prayed; letters; Spitalfields. 9.30 Read Prayers, 1 Thessalonians 4:3, Communion; read letters. 1 Dinner. 2.15 Necessary talk. 3 St Ethelburga's; read Prayers, Galatians 3:22! tea; prayed. 5 Read Prayers, Psalms 101:2; Society; class; prayed. 8 Supper, religious talk; prayer. 9.30.

MONDAY, FEBRUARY 21. 4 Prayed; 1 Peter 2:6-8; writ notes; visited many. 12 Select Society. 1.15 Dinner, religious talk; prayer. 2 Visited many. 5 Tea, religious talk; prayed. 6.30 Psalms 101:2! supper; the bands. 9.30.

TUESDAY, FEBRUARY 22. 4 Prayed; 1 Peter 2:6-8; letters; tea; writ Society. 2 At Mr Atwood's, dinner, religious talk; prayer. 3.30 Walked. 4.30 Tea, religious talk; John Duplex, necessary talk; prayed. 6.30 Read Prayers, Galatians 5:22! 7.30 The leaders. 8.30 Supper, religious talk; prayer. 9.30.

WEDNESDAY, FEBRUARYY 23. 4 Prayed; letters. 8 Tea, religious talk; letters. 10 Visited many. 2 At Mr Dethi——'s, dinner, religious talk. 3 Visited many. 5 Tea, religious talk; prayer. 6 Read Prayers, Galatians 6:15, Communion; coach. 8 Supper; prayer; A. M.! 9.30 Sins.

THURSDAY, FEBRUARY 24. 4 Prayed; letters. 8 Tea, necessary talk (religious); letters. 11.30 Visited. 12.15 Letters. 1 Charles, etc; dinner, necessary talk (religious); prayer; letters. 4.30 Tea, religious talk; prayer. 5.30 Prayed. 6.30 Read Prayers, Ephesians 1:13! the bands! supper. 9 Prayer. 9.30.

FRIDAY, FEBRUARY 25. 4 Prayed; writ letters. 11 Accounts. 12 The females; visited many. 2.30 Dinner, religious talk; prayer. 3.30 Magazine. 4.30 Tea, religious talk; prayer. 5.30 Prayed; letters. 8 Supper. 8.30 1 Peter 2:9-11! 10.30.

SATURDAY, FEBRUARY 26. 5.15 Prayed; letters. 8 Tea, religious talk; prayer; letters; necessary business. 1 At brother Hamilton's, dinner, religious talk; prayer. 2 Necessary business. 3.30 Prayed. 5 Tea, religious talk. 6 Read Prayers, Ephesians 3:14, etc, Communion; supper; Penry, necessary business. 9.30.

SUNDAY, FEBRUARY 27. 4 Prayed; letters; Chapel; read Prayers, Ephesians 5:1, 2! Communion; class. 1 At sister Keysall's; Communion; dinner, religious talk; prayer; coach. 3 Stepney; read Prayers, 1 Corinthians 13:1, etc; at brother Bar——'s; New Chapel; Ephesians 4:30; General Love-feast. 8 Supper, religious talk; necessary business; prayer. 9.30.

MONDAY, FEBRUARY 28. 4 Prayed; necessary business; tea. 6 Diligence. 10 Tea; Diligence. 3 Overton; dinner; Diligence. 8 Salisbury; at Mr Gifford's, supper, religious talk. 8 Diligence very cold! 12.

[Texts noted at bottom of line:] 1 Thessalonians 4:3; Psalms 101:2; Galatians 4:3, etc; Psalms 101:2.

TUESDAY, MARCH 1. 5 Slept. 6 Magazine. 9 Bridport; tea; Diligence. 2 Honiton; dinner; Diligence. 5.30 Exeter [orig., 'Exon']; at brother Eastlake's, tea; prayed; writ notes. 7 Job 22:21! supper, religious talk; prayer. 9.30. Ill.

WEDNESDAY, MARCH 2. 5 Prayed; tea. 6.30 Diligence; Ashburton; tea; Diligence. 3.30 The Dock; dinner, necessary talk (religious). 5 Tea; prayed. 6.30 Luke 12:7; at brother Walter's, supper, religious talk; prayer. 9.30.

THURSDAY, MARCH 3. 4 Prayed; Hebrews 12:7; writ journal. 8 Tea, religious talk; prayer; writ *Thoughts on the Deed* [of Declaration]. 12 Walked. 1 Dinner, religious talk; journal. 2 In the Dock. 3 Journal. 4 Prayed; tea, religious talk; prayer. 6.30 John 4:24! supper, religious talk; prayer. 9.30.

FRIDAY, MARCH 4. 4 Prayed; Ephesians 4:1-6! sermon. 8 Tea, religious talk; prayer; sermon. 12 Trustees. 1.30 At sister Mitchell's, dinner, religious talk; prayer. 2.15 Journal. 3 Prayed; walked; Royal Hospital; tea, religious talk; prayer. 5.30 Plymouth; supper. 6.30 Matthew 21:21! Love-feast; supper; prayer. 9.30.

SATURDAY, MARCH 5. 4 Prayed; Isaiah 59:1, 2; sermon; tea, religious talk; prayer. 7.30 Walked. 8.30 Dock; sermon. 1 At brother Hoare's, dinner, religious talk; prayer. 3 Necessary business. 4 Prayed; tea, religious talk; prayer; prayed. 6.30 Ephesians 4:30! 7.30 Society; supper, religious talk; prayer. 10.

SUNDAY, MARCH 6. 4 Prayed; sermon. 7 Matthew 22:37! visited; tea, religious talk; walked; Plymouth. 10.30 Read Prayers. 12 Dinner; sermon. 1.30 Matthew 8:13! sermon. 3.30 At Dr Gench's, religious talk! walked; tea. 5 2 Timothy 2:5, Communion; supper, religious talk; prayer. 9.45.

MONDAY, MARCH 7. 4 Prayed; tea; prayer. 6 Diligence. 10.30 Ashburton; tea; Diligence. 3 Exeter; dinner, necessary talk (religious). 4.30 Prayed; tea, religious talk; prayer; prayed. 6.30 John 4:24! supper; prayed. 9.30.

TUESDAY, MARCH [8]. 4 Prayed; tea. 5 Coach; Mr Cummin's! Collins; tea; coach. 1.30 Pips Inn. 2 Dinner. 2.45 Coach; mostly religious talk. 7.30 Bath; at brother Fowler's, necessary business, supper; prayer. 9.30.

WEDNESDAY, MARCH 9. 4 Prayed; 1 Corinthians 16:13, necessary talk (religious). 6.30 Writ sermon. 8 Tea, religious talk; prayer. 9.30 Sermon; visited some! 1.30 At brother Webb's, dinner, religious talk; prayer; necessary talk to Mr Collins! sermon; prayed. 5 Tea, religious talk; prayer. 6.30 1 Thessalonians 4:3! Society! supper, religious talk; prayer. 9.30.

THURSDAY, MARCH 10. 4 Prayed; John 1:47! sermon. 8 Tea, religious talk; prayer; visited; chaise. 11.30 At the Room, necessary business. 1 At sister Johnson's, dinner, religious talk; prayer; letters. 5 Tea; prayer; prayed. 6.30 Galatians 4:3, etc! the bands. 8.30 Supper, religious talk; prayer; necessary business. 9.45.

FRIDAY, MARCH 11. 4 Prayed; letters; tea; prayer; letters. 12 Females. 1 Prayer. 2 At Mr Castleman's, dinner, religious talk; prayer. 3.30 Letters; prayed. 5 Tea, religious talk; prayer; prayed; necessary business. 7 1 Timothy 1:5; at sister Johnson's, supper; prayer. 9.30.

[Texts noted at bottom of page:] John 1:47; Galatians 4:3, etc; Psalms 103:14.

SATURDAY, MARCH 12. 4 Prayed; letters; tea; prayer; letters; sermon. 1 At John Ellison's, dinner, mostly religious talk. 2.30 Necessary business. 3 Chaise. 5 Bath; tea, religious talk; prayer. 7 Matthew 21:21; supper; prayer. 9.30.

SUNDAY, MARCH 13. 4 Prayed; tea. 6 Hebrews 12:5! chaise; tea. 9.30 Read Prayers, Psalms 68:1, 2. 11.30 Communion. 1 Dinner, religious talk; prayer. 2.30 Slept; letters; tea; prayed. 5 1 Thessalonians 4:11, etc. 7 Society; the singers. 8 At Mr Castleman's, supper; prayer. 9.30.

MONDAY, MARCH 14. 4 Prayed; John 1:47; letter. 7 Class; tea; class. 1 Dinner, necessary talk (religious); prayer. 2 Class. 4.30 Writ notes. 7 John 1:47! class; at Mr Johnson's, supper, necessary talk (religious); prayer. 10.

TUESDAY, MARCH 15. 4 Prayed; letter. 6 Class. 8 Tea, religious talk. 9 Class. 1 Dinner, religious talk; prayer. 2 Class. 4 Visited many. 5 At sister Callow's, tea, religious talk; prayer. 6 Prayed. 6.30 1 Thessalonians 4:3! the leaders; at Mr Castleman's, supper, religious talk; prayer. 9.30.

WEDNESDAY, MARCH 16. 4 Prayed; letter. 6 Class. 7 Letter. 8 Tea, religious talk; class. 1 At brother Hopkins's, dinner; class. 4 At sister Knight's, tea, religious talk; prayer. 5 Micah 2:10; chaise; at home. 8 At sister Johnson's, supper, religious talk; prayer. 9.30.

[Pointing hand] THURSDAY, MARCH 17. 4 Prayed; journal. 8.15 Tea, religious talk; prayer. 9 Visited many. 1 At sister Ewer's, dinner, religious talk; prayer. 2 Visited many. 4.30 Tea, religious talk; prayer; prayed. 6.30 Read the letters; class. 8.30 At sister Johnson's. 9 Supper, religious talk; prayer. 9.30.

FRIDAY, MARCH 18. 4 Prayed; accounts; prayer; sermon. 12 The females. 1 Prayer. 2.30 At brother Roberts's. 3 Dinner. 3.45 Chaise; at the School; necessary talk (religious)! prayer; tea. 6 Prayed; letters; supper, religious talk; prayer. 9.30.

SATURDAY, MARCH 19. 4 Prayed; the leaders; letter; chaise. 8 At brother Robin's, tea, religious talk; prayer; christened. 9 Necessary business. 10 Letters; necessary business; visited. 1 At brother Stocks's, dinner, religious talk; prayer; visited many. 5 Tea, religious talk! sermon. 6 1 Peter 1:18; Penry; at Mr Castleman's, supper, religious talk; prayer. 9.45.

SUNDAY, MARCH 20. 4 Prayed; ill! slept; prayed; tea; prayer. 9.30 Read Prayers, Psalms 103:14, Communion; chaise. 1.30 At the School; dinner. 2 Psalms 90:12; Society; chaise. 4 Tea; prayed. 5 1 Timothy 4:8! Society! 7 Religious talk. 8 Supper, religious talk; prayer. 9.45.

MONDAY, MARCH 21. 4 Prayed; tea. 5 Chaise. 8 Newport; tea, religious talk. 9 Chaise; read [John] Mills on [the Management of] Bees. 11 Stroud; writ texts. 2 Dinner, religious talk; prayer. 3 Texts; prayed. 5 Tea, religious talk; prayer; prayed. 6.30 Luke 20:3; Society; supper; prayer. 9.30.

TUESDAY, MARCH 22. 5 Hebrews 12:5; writ texts. 8 At sister Willis's, tea, religious talk; prayer; texts. 10.15 Chaise. 11.30 Painswick; religious talk. 12 John 6:28; dinner. 2.15 Chaise. 3.30 Gloucester [orig., 'Gloster']; prayed, tea; religious talk. 6 John 17:3! Society! supper; prayer. 9.45.

WEDNESDAY, MARCH 23. 4 Prayed; writ notes. 6 Job 22:21! tea, necessary talk (religious); prayer. 8.45 Chaise. 10.30 Tewkesbury. 11 Matthew 4:10! necessary talk (religious), dinner. 1.45 Chaise. 4 Worcester; prayed; tea, necessary talk (religious). 6.30 Proverbs 3:17! Society; supper, mostly religious talk; prayer. 9.30.

THURSDAY, MARCH 24. 4 Prayed; Matthew 5:6; writ texts. 8 At sister Howton's, tea, religious talk; prayer. 9 Texts. 1.30 Dinner, religious talk; texts. 4.15 Prayed; tea, religious talk; prayer. 6.30 John 5:8! the bands. 8 Supper, religious talk; prayer. 9.45.

GOOD FRIDAY, MARCH 25. 4 Prayed; tea; prayer. 5 Chaise; tea; chaise. 10.30 Birmingham; writ letters. 2 Dinner; letters; prayed. 5 At sister Kempson's, tea, religious talk; prayer. 6 Hebrews 9:13! Society; supper, religious talk; prayer. 9.30.

SATURDAY, MARCH 26. 4 Prayed; Revelation 2:5; texts. 8 Tea, religious talk; prayer; journal. 10.30 Coach; Quinton; necessary talk (religious). 12 +Hebrews 2:3! dinner, religious talk; coach. 3.30 At home; read notes! 5 Tea, religious talk; prayer. 6 1 Corinthians 6:19! 8 Supper, religious talk; prayer. 10.30.

EASTER DAY, MARCH 27. 4.30 Prayed; texts; tea. 8 Luke 24:34! the preachers; chaise. 11.30 Wednesbury; letters; dinner; chaise. 2 Darlaston; read Prayers, Romans 8:33. 3.30 Chaise; Wednesbury; tea, religious talk. 5 Luke 24:26, Lovefeast! supper; prayer. 9.30.

[MONDAY, MARCH 28.] 4 Prayed; letter; tea. 7 Revelation 14:1, etc; chaise; Wolverhampton; tea, religious talk; prayer. 11 Luke 12:7; chaise. 1.15 Hilton [Park]; mostly religious talk. 3 Dinner, mostly religious talk. 5 Prayed; read. 6.15 Tea, necessary talk (religious). 9 Supper, mostly religious talk. 10.30 Prayer. 11.

TUESDAY, MARCH 29. 6 Prayed; journal. 8.15 Tea, mostly religious talk. 9 Chaise; with Miss Gibbes, religious talk. 10 Read. 11.15 Stafford, necessary talk (religious). 12 1 Corinthians 1:23; dinner. 2 Chaise. 4.30 Newcastle[-under-Lyme]. 5 Tea; prayed. 6 [Blank, no text;] Society; supper; prayer. 9.30.

WEDNESDAY, MARCH 30. 4 Prayed; Colossians 3:1-4; sermon. 8 Tea, religious talk; prayer; sermon; sins! 10 Chaise. 11.15 Lane End [Longton]; read notes. 12 +Matthew 22:4! dinner, religious talk; prayer. 3 Chaise. 4.30 Burslem; tea, religious talk; prayer; prayed. 6 Galatians 4:3, etc. 6 Society! supper, religious talk; prayer. 9.30.

THURSDAY, MARCH 31. 4 Prayed; Romans 13:11; Magazine. 8 Tea, religious talk; prayer; necessary business. 9.30 Chaise. 11.30 Congleton; writ sermon. 1

Dinner, necessary talk. 2 Sermon. 4.30 Prayed; tea, religious talk. 6 1 Peter 1:9. 7 Society; supper, religious talk; prayer. 9.45.

FRIDAY, APRIL 1. 4 Prayed; 1 Peter 1:9; sermon. 8 Tea, religious talk; prayer; sermon. 10 Chaise. 12.30 Macclesfield; necessary talk (religious). 1 Dinner, religious talk; prayer; sermon; prayed. 5 Tea, religious talk. 6 Read Prayers, Hebrews 3:7; Love-feast. 8.30 Supper, religious talk; prayer. 9.15.

SATURDAY, APRIL 2. 4 Prayed; Isaiah 59:1, 2; sermon. 7 Tea, religious talk; prayer. 7.30 Chaise. 9 At brother Mayer's [orig., 'Mare's'], tea, religious talk; prayer. 10.30 Chaise. 11.30 Manchester; necessary talk (religious); writ notes. 1 Dinner, religious talk. 2.30 Letters. 4 Prayed; tea. 6 1 Thessalonians 4:3! necessary talk (religious)! supper, religious talk; prayer. 9.45.

SUNDAY, APRIL 3. 4 Prayed; letters; tea. 9 Necessary business; prayed. 10 Read Prayers, John 21:22! Communion. 1.30 Dinner, religious talk; prayer; slept. 3 Letter; tea; prayed. 5 1 John 5:11, Society. 7.30 Prayed. 8 Supper, necessary talk (religious); prayer. 9.30.

MONDAY, APRIL 4. 4 Prayed; Luke 12:7! Dr Bailey, etc, necessary talk! 8 Tea, religious talk; sermon. 12.15 Walked. 1 At brother Brierly's, dinner, religious talk. 2.30 Chaise. 4.30 Bolton; necessary business; tea; prayed. 6 Matthew 21:21, Society! sermon; supper, religious talk; prayer. 9.30.

TUESDAY, APRIL 5. 4 Prayed; Hebrews 12:5; sermon. 8 Tea, religious talk; sermon. 10 Chaise. 11 Wingates; +Mark 1:15(2)! 12 Chaise. 1.15 Wigan; dinner, religious talk. 2.15 Sermon; walked. 4 Prayed; walked; tea, religious talk. 6 Matthew 8:2, Society; walked; supper; prayer. 9.30.

WEDNESDAY, APRIL 6. 4 Prayed; sermon. 6 Psalms 90:12; tea. 7.30 Chaise; Prescot; chaise. 12 Liverpool; necessary talk (religious); sermon. 1.15 Dinner, religious talk; prayer; sermon; letters. 4 Prayed. 4.30 Tea, religious talk; prayer; prayed. 6.30 Romans 11:13! Society; supper; prayer. 9.45.

THURSDAY, APRIL 7. 4 Prayed; Revelation 2:5; necessary business; tea; prayer. 7.15 Chaise. 10.15 Warrington; Luke 20:34! sermon; dinner. 1.30 Chaise. 4.30 Chester; at John Seller's, tea, religious talk; prayer. 5 Writ notes. 6 Ecclesiastes 9:10! Society; supper; prayer. 9.30.

FRIDAY, APRIL 8. 4 Prayed; Hebrews 3:15! tea, religious talk; prayer. 7 Coach. 10.45 Holywell; tea. 11.30 Coach; read Boyle. 2.15 Dinner. 3.30 Coach. 7 Conway; prayed; letter. 8 Supper, necessary talk (religious); prayer. 9.30.

SATURDAY, APRIL 9. 4 Prayed; letters. 6.15 Coach. 11 Bangor Ferry; tea. 11.30 Walked. 12.30 Coach; prayed. 4.30 Tea; letters; prayed; read; supper. 9.30 On the *Clermont*. 10.

SUNDAY, APRIL 10. 5 Prayed; read. 8 Tea; read. 10.30 Hebrews 9:27; prayer! read. 1 Dinner, religious talk; read; prayed. 6 Tea, religious talk; read. 9.30.

MONDAY, APRIL 11. 2 Landed [Dublin Bay]. 3 Slept. 6.30 Walked; necessary talk (religious); writ notes. 8 At sister Blackp——'s, tea, religious talk; prayer! 9 Writ felon's letters; walked. 2 Dinner, religious talk; prayer. 3 Letters. 4.30 Prayed; tea, religious talk; prayer; prayed. 7 Matthew 8:13! supper, religious talk; prayer. 9.30.

TUESDAY, APRIL 12. 4 Prayed; Romans 13:11! class. 8 Tea, religious talk; prayer; journal. 10 Class. 12 Journal. 1 Prayer. 2 Dinner, religious talk; prayer. 4 Class. 5 Tea, religious talk; prayer; prayed. 6.30 Matthew 9:5! 8 Supper, religious talk; prayer. 9.30.

WEDNESDAY, APRIL 13. 4 Prayed; Matthew 22:37; class. 8 Tea, religious talk; prayer; visited. 10 Class; letter; walked. 2 Dinner, religious talk; prayer. 4 Class. 5 Tea, religious talk; prayer; prayed. 6.30 Matthew 22:39! the leaders. 8 Supper, religious talk; prayer. 9.30.

[Pointing hand] THURSDAY, APRIL 14. 4 Prayed; Psalms 106:24; class. 8 Tea, religious talk; prayer; class. 12 Letter; necessary talk (religious). 2 At brother Brooke's, dinner, religious talk; visited. 4 Class; tea, religious talk; prayer. 6.30 The leaders; Select Society. 8.15 Supper, religious talk; prayer. 9.30.

FRIDAY, APRIL 15. 4 Prayed; Luke 12:7! class. 7.30 Journal. 10 Class. 11.30 Writ notes. 12 Read Prayers; class. 2 Walked; Mount Pleasant [Dublin]; dinner, religious talk; prayer; coach. 3.30 Visited many. 5 Tea, religious talk. 6 Prayer. 6.15 Prayed. 6.30 Hebrews 12:5! prayed; supper, necessary talk (religious); prayer. 9.30.

SATURDAY, APRIL 16. 4 Prayed; texts. 8 Tea, religious talk; prayer; visited many. 2 Dinner, religious talk; prayer; visited some. 5 Tea, religious talk; prayer; prayed. 6 Psalms 62:1! visited! at sister Fetherston's. 8 Prayer; supper. 9.30.

SUNDAY, APRIL 17. 4 Prayed; journal. 7 Ephesians 3:14, etc! necessary talk (religious) to some; tea, religious talk! prayer; prayed. 10.45 Read Prayers, Communion. 2 At Mr Smith's, dinner, religious talk; prayer. 3.30 Conference; prayed; tea, religious talk; prayer. 5.30 1 Peter 2:11, the Love-feast. 8.30 Supper, religious talk; prayer. 9.30.

MONDAY, APRIL 18. 4 Prayed; Philippians 2:12! tea, religious talk. 8.15 Chaise. 10 Sedgel [i.e., Celbridge?]; walked. 11.15 Chaise. 1 Prosperous; walked! 2 Dinner, religious talk; prayer; letters. 5 Tea, religious talk; prayed. 6 Isaiah 55:6! Society; at T. Brooke's, supper, necessary talk (religious); prayer. 9.30.

TUESDAY, APRIL 19. 4 Prayed; Hebrews 9:27! tea. 6.30 Chaise! 9 Edenderry; tea, religious talk. 10 2 Corinthians 8:9! chaise; sins! 2 Tyrrellspass; dinner, religious talk. 3 Journal; tea, religious talk. 6 Micah 2:10! religious talk, supper; prayer. 9.30.

WEDNESDAY, APRIL 20. Prayed; texts. 7 Mark 4:3, etc; tea, religious talk; prayer; visited. 9.30 Chaise. 11.15 Coolalough; texts. 2 Dinner, religious talk. 3

Texts. 4.30 Prayed; tea, religious talk. 6 Psalms 146:4, 5; prayed. 7.45 Chaise; sick; supper, mostly religious talk; prayer. 9.30.

THURSDAY, APRIL 21. 4 Prayed; texts. 7 2 John 8; tea, necessary talk (religious); prayer. 9.30 Chaise. 12.30 Athlone. 1 Collected John Walsh. 3 At brother Dean's, dinner, necessary talk (religious). 4.30 Prayed; tea, religious talk. 6 Proverbs 3:17! prayed. 8 Supper, religious talk; prayer. 9.45.

FRIDAY, APRIL 22. 4 Prayed; Colossians 1:10! Walsh. 8 Tea; Walsh. 12 Visited; Communion; visited some. 2 Dinner, religious talk. 3.30 Walsh. 4 Prayed. 5 Tea, religious talk; prayer. 6 Hebrews 7:25! 7 Society; supper, religious talk; prayer. 9.30.

SATURDAY, APRIL 23. 4 Prayed; Galatians 5:1; Walsh. 8 Tea, religious talk; prayer. 9 Walsh. 1 Walked. 2 At brother Rutli[dge]'s, dinner, religious talk; read notes. 4 Letters. 5 Tea, necessary talk (religious); prayer. 6.30 John 4:24! the bands! supper, religious talk; prayer. 9.30.

SUNDAY, APRIL 24. 4 Prayed; Walsh; tea. 8 Ephesians 3:14! Walsh. 11.30 Read Prayers; Walsh. 2.30 Dinner; letter; prayed. 5 Tea, religious talk. 5.30 +Luke 19:42! Communion! supper; prayer. 9.30.

MONDAY, APRIL 25. 4 Prayed; 1 Corinthians 13:8, etc! letter; tea, religious talk; prayer. 8 Chaise. 10.30 Ballinasloe. 11 +Mark 1:15(2)! chaise. 1.15 Aughrim; Walsh. 2 Dinner. 3 Walsh; prayed; tea. 6 Isaiah 55:6; visited some; supper, religious talk; prayer. 9.30.

TUESDAY, APRIL 26. 4 Prayed; Isaiah 57:1, 2; necessary talk (religious), tea. 7.15 Chaise. 9.15 Eyrecourt; Acts 16:30. 11 Chaise. 1.30 Birr; Walsh. 2.30 Dinner, religious talk. 3.30 Walsh; prayed. 5 Tea, necessary talk (religious). 6 Job 22:21; Society, necessary talk (religious)! supper, religious talk; prayer. 9.30.

WEDNESDAY, APRIL 27. 4 Prayed; Isaiah 59:1, 2; letter; tea, religious talk. 7.15 Chaise. 8 At Mr Barry's, tea, mostly religious talk. 9.30 Chaise. 12.30 Tullamore; Walsh. 2 Dinner; Walsh. 4 Prayed. 5 Tea, religious talk; prayed; Walsh. 6.30 2 Corinthians 4:18! Society; supper; prayer. 9.30.

THURSDAY, APRIL 28. 4 Prayed; 2 Timothy 3:5! 6 Magazine. 8 Tea, religious talk; prayer. 9 Chaise; Portarlington. 12.30 Revelation 20:12; dinner, religious talk; prayer; chaise. 4 Mountmellick; prayed; tea, religious talk; prayer. 6 In the church, Hebrews 9:27, Society; visited! supper; prayer. 9.30.

FRIDAY, APRIL 29. 4 Prayed; chaise. 8 Tea, religious talk; prayer; chaise. 11.30 Ballyragget [orig., 'Ballinagget']. 1 Chaise. 1.45 Kilkenny; necessary business; dinner; walked. 5 Prayed; tea. 6.30 1 Peter 1:24! writ notes; supper, religious talk; prayer. 9.30.

SATURDAY, APRIL 30. 4.30 1 Peter 4:18! tea, necessary talk (religious). 7 Chaise. 9 Knocktopher; tea, religious talk. 10 Chaise. 1 Ferry [at Waterford]. 2 At

James Deaves's, dinner; letters; necessary talk (religious). 5 Tea, religious talk. 6 Prayer; prayed. 6.30 Matthew 22:4! necessary talk (religious); supper, religious talk; prayer. 9.30 Necessary business. 9.45.

SUNDAY, MAY 1. 4 Prayed; letters; journal; tea. 8 Daniel 9:24; journal. 11 Read Prayers, Communion. 2 Dinner, religious talk. 3 At Dr Fall's, mostly religious talk. 4 Tea, religious talk. 5 +1 Corinthians 13:1, etc! 6.30 Love-feast. 8 Supper, religious talk; prayer. 9.30.

MONDAY, MAY 2. 4 Prayed; journal. 6 2 John 8; necessary business. 8 Tea, religious talk; prayer; visited many. 10 Letters. 1 The children; dinner, religious talk. 3 Letter; prayed; tea, religious talk; prayed. 6.30 +Revelation 14:1, etc! supper. 9 Prayer. 9.30.

TUESDAY, MAY 3. 3.30 Prayed; tea; prayer. 4.30 Chaise. 7.30 Kilmacthomas; tea, religious talk. 8.30 Chaise. 11.15 Dungarvan; dinner. 1.15 Chaise; walked; chaise. 6 Youghal; necessary business; tea. 7 Matthew 22:4! 8 Supper; prayer. 9.30.

WEDNESDAY, MAY 4. 4 Prayed; journal. 6 Matthew 8:2! journal. 8 Tea, necessary talk (religious)! prayer. 10 Journal. 12 Walked. 1 Dinner, religious talk. 2 Letter. 3 Read notes; prayed. 5 Tea, religious talk; prayer. 6 Read. 6.30 The Mall, +John 5:8! 7.30 Society. 8.30 Supper, religious talk; prayer. 10.

THURSDAY, MAY 5. 4 Prayed; read. 6 Ephesians 4:1, etc! necessary business. 8 Tea, religious talk; prayer. 9 Chaise. 11.30 Midleton; many! necessary talk (religious), dinner. 1.30 Chaise. 4 Cork; at brother Laffan's; necessary business. 5.15 Tea, religious talk; prayed. 6 Letters. 7 Isaiah 66:8! supper, religious talk; prayer. 9.30.

FRIDAY, MAY 6. 4 Prayed; Ecclesiastes 2:2! letters. 8 Tea, religious talk; prayer; letters. 12 Walked. 12.30 Prayer. 2 Dinner, religious talk; prayer. 4 Prayed. 5 Tea, religious talk; prayer. 6.30 Matthew 22:37! Select Society; supper; prayer. 9.30.

SATURDAY, MAY 7. 4 Prayed; Matthew 22:39; letter; writ journal. 8 Tea, religious talk; prayer; journal. 12 Necessary talk (religious). 1 Walked. 2 Dinner, religious talk; prayer. 4 Prayed; tea, religious talk; prayer. 6.30 Isaiah 59:1, 2. 8 Supper, mostly religious talk; prayer; necessary business. 9.45.

SUNDAY, MAY 8. 4 Prayed; journal; texts; tea. 8 Ephesians 3:14, etc! letters. 11 Read Prayers, Communion. 2 Dinner, religious talk; prayer. 3.30 Slept; prayed; tea, religious talk. 5 +1 Peter 4:7, Love-feast. 8.30 Supper, religious talk; prayer. 9.30.

MONDAY, MAY 9. 4 Prayed; Matthew 12:43! letters. 8 Tea, religious talk; prayer. 8.45 Chaise. 11.30 Kinsale. 12 +1 Kings 19:13; dinner, religious talk. 2.30 Chaise. 4.30 Bandon; necessary business; tea; prayed. 6.30 +Ecclesiastes 7:29! Society; at Mrs Barr's, supper, religious talk: prayer. 9.30.

TUESDAY, MAY 10. 4 Prayed; Matthew 22:21! letters. 8 Tea, religious talk; prayer; letter. 12 Visited many. 2 Dinner, religious talk. 4 Slept; prayed. 5.30 Tea, religious talk. 6.30 +John 4:24! visited. 8.30 Supper, necessary talk (religious); prayer. 10.

WEDNESDAY, MAY 11. 4 Prayed; Romans 13:11, etc; journal; tea, religious talk; prayer. 8 Visited; chaise. 11.30 Cork; letter. 2 Dinner, religious talk. 4 Prayed; tea. 6.30 Colossians 1:10; the leaders. 8.30 Supper, religious talk; prayer. 10.

THURSDAY, MAY 12. 4 Prayed; Luke 12:7; Magazine; sins! 8 Tea, religious talk; prayer; Magazine. 12 Walked! 2 Dinner, religious talk; prayer. 4 Prayed; tea, religious talk. 6.30 Job 22:21! Communion. 9 Visited. 9.30 Supper, religious talk; prayer. 10.30.

FRIDAY, MAY 13. 4 Prayed; Luke 20:34! tea, religious talk; prayer. 7 Chaise. 10.45 Mallow; tea. 11.45 Chaise. 3.45 Kilfinnane; at brother Upton's, dinner, religious talk; prayed. 5 Tea. 6 Luke 10:42! walked! 8 Supper, religious talk; prayer. 9.30.

SATURDAY, MAY 14. 4 Prayed; Hebrews 2:3! tea; chaise. 8.30 Bruff; C. Har——, etc, tea, religious talk. 9.30 Chaise. 12.15 Limerick; necessary business; letters. 2 Dinner, religious talk; prayer; necessary talk (religious). 4 Prayed; tea, religious talk. 6 Matthew 8:13! walked; supper, mostly religious talk. 9.30.

WHITSUNDAY, MAY [15]. 4 Prayed; sermon. 7 Tea, religious talk; prayer. 8 Acts 2:4! sermon. 11 Read Prayers, Communion. 3 Dinner, religious talk; slept; prayed. 5 Tea. 5.30 +John 7:37! 7 The Love-feast. 8.30 At Mr Bean's, supper, religious talk; prayer. 9.30.

MONDAY, MAY 16. 4 Prayed; sermon. 7 Tea, religious talk; prayer. 8 Galatians 5:22! Select Society. 10 Sermon; visited. 2.15 Dinner, mostly religious talk. 3.15 Prayed; visited; tea. 6 Hebrews [6]:1! Society; supper, religious talk; prayer. 9.30.

TUESDAY, MAY 17. 4 Prayed; Isaiah 57:1, 2! tea; prayer. 6.30 Chaise. 10 At Mr Blood's, tea, religious talk; prayer. 11 Chaise. 1 Crusheen; dinner. 2 Chaise. 4 Gort; tea. 4.45 Chaise. 6.45 Roxborough. 8 Necessary talk (religious); chaise; Kilchreest; +Proverbs 3:17; Roxborough; necessary talk; supper. 10.30.

WEDNESDAY, MAY 18. 4.30 Necessary business; chaise; Kilchreest; tea, religious talk; prayer. 6 Chaise; Athenry; tea. 9 Chaise. 12 Claremorris; dinner. 1 Chaise; prayed. 4 Ballinrobe; religious talk; sermon; tea. 6.30 Isaiah 1:3! sermon. 8.30 Supper, religious talk; prayer. 9.45.

THURSDAY, MAY 19. 4 Prayed; sermon; tea. 8 Matthew 7:24! sermon; journal. 1 Walked. 2.45 Dinner, religious talk; journal. 5.30 Tea; visited. 6.15 Matthew 25:31! prayed; supper, religious talk; prayer. 9.45.

FRIDAY, MAY 20. 4 Prayed; letters; tea. 8 1 Samuel 21:8; chaise. 12.15 Castlebar. 1 Writ texts. 2 Dinner, necessary talk (religious). 3.30 Prayed; walked. 5

Tea, religious talk. 6 Matthew 7:16. 7 At John Carr's, necessary talk. 8 At John Langst——'s, supper, religious talk; prayed. 9.30.

SATURDAY, MAY 21. 4 Prayed; 1 Peter 3:8; texts. 8 Tea, religious talk; prayer; laid the stone! 10 Texts. 1.30 Chaise; Rahans [orig. 'Rehins']; necessary talk (religious), dinner, religious talk. 4.30 Chaise; tea, religious talk; prayed. 6.30 2 Corinthians 4:18! Society! supper, religious talk; prayer. 9.30.

[Text noted at bottom of page:] 1 Pet. 3:8.

SUNDAY, MAY 22. 4 Prayed; texts. 7 Tea, religious talk. 8 1 John 5:7; journal; sins. 11.30 Read Prayers; visited. 2 Dinner, necessary talk (religious); prayer. 3 Prayed. 4 Tea, religious talk. 5 Genesis 1:27! Society, Communion. 8 Supper, religious talk; prayer. 9.15.

MONDAY, MAY 23. 4 Prayed; 2 Corinthians 5:1, etc! tea; prayer. 6.15 Chaise. 9 Swinford; tea. 10 Chaise. 12.30 Tobercurry [orig., 'Tubbe']; dinner. 1.30 Chaise. 5 Sligo; prayed; tea; necessary business. 7 Acts 11:26! supper, mostly religious talk; prayer. 9.30 Lay down. 11.

TUESDAY, MAY 24. 4 Prayed; Isaiah 38:5; sermon. 7.30 Tea, religious talk; prayer; sermon. 1 Dinner, religious talk; sermon. 4 Walked; tea, religious talk. 6 1 Corinthians 13:1, etc; Society, Communion. 8.30 Supper, religious talk; prayer. 9.45.

WEDNESDAY, MAY 25. 4 Prayed; 1 Corinthians 15:58; tea; prayer. 7 Chaise. 9.30 Manorhamilton; tea. 10 2 Corinthians 5:17, etc! chaise. 3.45 Mount Florence; dinner, religious talk; necessary business. 5 Tea; prayed. 6 +Hebrews 4:13! sermon. 7.30 Religious talk; supper; prayer. 9.30.

THURSDAY, MAY 26. 4 Prayed; Matthew 5:6; journal. 7 Tea, religious talk; prayer. 8 Chaise; Swanlinbar [orig., 'Swadlebar']. 9.30 Matthew 4:10! chaise. 12.30 Ballyconnell; journal; necessary talk (religious) to many. 2 Dinner; journal; walked; tea. 6 Jeremiah 6:16! Society; prayed; supper; prayer. 9.45.

FRIDAY, MAY 27. 4 Prayed; Hebrews 12:6! tea, necessary talk (religious); prayer. 7 Chaise. 8.15 Killashandra; tea, religious talk. 9.30 +Matthew 8:2! necessary talk (religious) to many. 12.30 Chaise. 1.45 Kilmore; dinner, mostly religious talk. 4 Walked; prayed; tea. 6 +Mark 16:16! Society; supper; prayer. 9.30.

SATURDAY, MAY 28. 4 Prayed; Galatians 5:5; chaise. 7 Cavan; Micah 2:10; chaise. 8.30 Ballyhaise [orig., 'Ballinhay']; tea; John 17:3! chaise. 1 Clones; writ notes. 2 Dinner, religious talk. 3 Journal; prayed; tea. 5 Prayed; prayed. 6 Isaiah 37:3! necessary talk; supper; prayer. 9.45.

SUNDAY, MAY 29. 4 Prayed; journal. 7 Tea, religious talk. 8 1 John 4:19! writ conference. 12 Read Prayers. 2 Dinner, necessary talk. 3.45 Slept; read Prayers; Luke 16:2; Communion. 8 Supper, religious talk; prayer. 9.45.

MONDAY, MAY 30. 4 Tea; prayer. 4.45 Chaise. 8.30 Caledon; tea, religious talk; letters. 11 Hebrews 8:11! 12 Society! 1 Dinner. 2.15 Chaise. 3.45 Armagh; walked; tea, religious talk. 5.30 Religious talk. 6 +Matthew 7:16! visited. 8 Supper, religious talk; prayer. 9.30.

TUESDAY, MAY 31. 4 Prayed; texts. 8 Tea, religious talk; prayer; walked; ill. 10 Read notes. 11 +Isaiah 59! 12 Read notes. 2 Dinner, religious talk; prayer. 4 Tea, religious talk; prayer; prayed. 6 +Acts 16:31; Society. 8 Necessary talk (religious), supper; prayer. 9.30.

WEDNESDAY, JUNE 1. 4 Prayed; letters. 7 +Acts 16:31. 8 At Dr Gruber's, tea, religious talk; visited. 9.30 Chaise; Blackwatertown. 11 +1 Peter 1:24; letter; writ notes. 2 Dinner, religious talk. 3 Writ conference. 4 Prayed; tea; chaise. 6 +Malachi 3:1; Society; chaise; supper; prayer. 10.15.

THURSDAY, JUNE 2. 4.15 Writ Conference. 8.15 Tea, religious talk; necessary business; chaise. 10 Charlemont; +Acts 9:31; Communion. 1 Chaise; Killyman; necessary talk (religious); dinner, religious talk. 3.30 Letter; prayed; tea, religious talk. 6 +Hebrews 9:27! prayed; garden, religious talk. 8 Supper, religious talk; prayer. 9.30.

FRIDAY, JUNE 3. 4 Prayed. 4.30 Chaise. 7 Cookstown; tea; Jeremiah 8:22! Society. 9 Chaise. 12.30 Gortin. 1.30 Chaise. 3.45 Strabane. 4.15 Chaise. 6.45 Londonderry. 7 Tea, religious talk; Colossians 1:10! supper, necessary talk (religious). 10.15.

SATURDAY, JUNE 4. 4 Prayed; letters. 8 Tea, religious talk; prayer; letters. 12 1 John 5:19; walked! 2.30 Dinner, religious talk. 4.45 Prayed. 5.30 Tea, religious talk. 6.30 Micah 2:10; Society; supper, mostly religious talk; prayer; necessary business. 10.15.

SUNDAY, JUNE 5. 4 Prayed; slept; letters; tea. 8 Romans 13:11, etc! letters; read notes. 11.30 Read Prayers, Communion. 2.30 Dinner, religious talk; letters; prayed. 5.15 Tea, religious talk. 6 Luke 14:17! Society, necessary talk (religious). 8.30 Supper, religious talk; prayer. 9.45.

MONDAY, JUNE 6. 4 Prayed; journal. 6 Isaiah 57:1, 2; tea, religious talk; prayer; writ. 8.15 Chaise. 10.45 Limavady [orig., 'Newtown']; +2 Cor 6:1. 12 Chaise. 2.15 Coleraine; journal. 3 Dinner, religious talk. 4 Prayed; walked. 5 Tea, religious talk; prayed. 6.30 +1 Kings 18:21! supper; prayer. 9.30.

TUESDAY, JUNE 7. 4 Prayed; read Horneck. 8 Tea, religious talk; prayer; letters. 12 Mark 4:3, etc. 1.15 Journal. 2 At Mr Davey's, dinner, religious talk. 4 Prayed; tea, religious talk. 6 1 Corinthians 13:13! 7 Love-feast; supper, religious talk; prayer. 9.30.

WEDNESDAY, JUNE 8. 4 Prayed; letter. 5 Revelation 14:1, etc; tea. 6.30 Chaise. 8.30 Ballymoney. 9 Romans 3:27! chaise. 11 Tea, religious talk. 12 Chaise; Ballymena; necessary talk (religious). 2.30 Dinner. 3.15 Walked! [to Gracehill] 5 Read; chaise; tea. 6 +Hebrews 4:14! Love-feast! supper, religious talk. 10.

THURSDAY, JUNE 9. 4 Prayed; Isaiah 30:18! tea. 6.30 Chaise. 9 Antrim; tea; Revelation 20:12! 11 Chaise. 2 Belfast; necessary business. 3 Dinner, necessary talk (religious); prayed; tea. 6 +Job 22:21! 7 Love-feast; necessary talk (religious); supper; prayer. 9.45.

FRIDAY, JUNE 10. 4 Prayed; letters. 6 +Luke 20:34! tea, religious talk; prayer. 7.45 Chaise; Saintfield [orig., 'Send——']; tea. 11 Chaise to Downpatrick; letters. 3 Dinner, religious talk. 4 Prayed; walked. 5 Tea; prayed. 6 +1 Corinthians 1:30; Communion. 8.15 Supper, necessary talk (religious). 9.30.

SATURDAY, JUNE 11. 4 Prayed; journal. 6 1 John 2:12! journal; tea, religious talk; prayer. 8.30 Chaise. 10.30 Ballynahinch. 11 +Matthew 7:24! journal; dinner. 1.30 Chaise. 3.30 Lisburn; necessary talk (religious); letters; tea. 6 Psalms 62:1! Society; supper, religious talk; prayer. 9.30.

[SUNDAY] JUNE [12]. 4 Prayed; [writ] *Thought upon Marriage*; tea, religious talk. 8 Ephesians 3:14, etc; *Thought*. 11 Read Prayers. 1.30 At John Johnson's, dinner, religious talk; prayed; slept. 4.15 Tea, religious talk. 5 +Luke 15:7! Communion. 7.45 Prayed. 8 Supper; prayer. 9.30.

MONDAY, JUNE 13. 4 Prayed; journal. 6 1 Samuel 20:3; necessary talk (religious) to many; tea; prayer. 8.15 Chaise. 10.30 Lurgan; necessary business. 11 +Romans 1:16! visited. 1.15 Dinner, religious talk. 2 Chaise. 5.45 Tandragee, necessary talk (religious); tea; prayed. 6 +Ezekiel 18:31! Society; to Dr Leslie's; supper. 10.15.

[TUESDAY, JUNE 14.] 4.15 Prayed; read; +Luke 12:7; writ notes; tea; writ notes. 1 Visited. 2 At Dr Leslie's, dinner, religious talk. 4 Necessary talk (religious) to many; prayed. 5 Tea, religious talk. 6 Proverbs 3:17! walked to Dr Leslie's, supper, religious talk. 9.45.

WEDNESDAY, JUNE 15. 4 Prayed; writ notes. 6 +1 Peter 4:7; necessary talk to many; tea; prayer. 8 Chaise. 9.45 Derryanvil. 10 Writ notes. 10.45 +Acts 2:4! Communion. 1 Dinner, religious talk. 2 Chaise. 3.30 The Grange. 4 Writ journal; prayed; tea. 6 +Matthew 5:47! supper, religious talk; prayer. 9.30.

THURSDAY, JUNE 16. 4 Prayed; journal. 6 Matthew 12:43; chaise. 8 Richhill; tea; Hosea 11:8 [orig., '8:11'; cf. journal]. 9.45 Chaise. 12.45 Newry; necessary business. 1.30 Dinner, religious talk; visited! 5 Tea, religious talk; prayed. 6 1 Kings 18:21! Love-feast! supper, religious talk; prayer. 9.30.

FRIDAY, JUNE 17. 4 Letter; prayed; Revelation 21:6! letter; tea. 7.30 Chaise. 10.30 Dundalk; tea. 11.45 Chaise. 2 Drogheda; letters. 3 Dinner, necessary talk (religious). 4 Letters; prayed. 5 Tea, religious talk; prayed. 7 Isaiah 55:6! supper, religious talk; prayer. 9.30.

SATURDAY, JUNE 18. 4 Prayed; Mark 1:15! tea. 6.30 Chaise. 8.45 Man-of-War; tea, necessary talk (religious). 9.30 Chaise. 10.30 Swords; necessary talk. 11 Coach; sister Keene, etc, religious talk; visited some. 2 At brother Keene's, dinner; letters; prayed; tea. 6 Acts 9:31! letters; supper; prayer. 9.30.

SUNDAY, JUNE 19. 4 Prayed; letters; tea. 8 1 Peter 4:18! Magazine. 11 Read Prayers, Communion. 2 At Mr Smith's, dinner, religious talk; prayer. 3.30 Prayed; slept; letter. 4.30 Tea, religious talk. 5.30 Luke 3:8! Society! visited. 8.30 Brother Keene's, supper, religious talk; prayer. 9.30.

MONDAY, JUNE 20. 4 Prayed; 1 John 1:1; class. 8 Tea, religious talk; prayer. 9 Class. 1 Visited. 2 At Mr Boswell's, dinner, religious talk; prayer. 3 Class; letters. 5 Tea, religious talk; prayer; prayed. 6.30 1 John 1:1, 2; necessary talk (religious) to some. 8 Cha[rles?]; supper, religious talk; prayer. 9.30.

[Pointing hand] TUESDAY, JUNE 21. 4 Prayed; 1 John 1:1-3; class. 7.30 Letter. 8 Tea, religious talk; prayer. 9 Letters. 10 Class. 12.30 Letters; visited. 2 Dinner, religious talk; prayer; letter. 4 Class. 5 Tea, religious talk; prayer; prayed. 6.15 Read the letters. 8.30 Supper, religious talk; prayer. 9.45.

WEDNESDAY, JUNE 22. 4 Prayed; 1 John 1:2-4; class; letters. 8 Tea, religious talk. 10 Class; letters; visited; coach. 1.45 Sandymount. 2 Dinner, religious talk. 3 Letters. 4.30 Tea, religious talk; walked; coach. 6.30 Luke 22:19; the leaders; coach; supper, religious talk; prayer. 9.45.

THURSDAY, JUNE 23. 4 Prayed; 1 John 1:5-7! class. 8 Tea, religious talk; prayer; letter; writ conference. 10 Class. 12 Class. 1 Visited. 2.15 Dinner, religious talk; prayer; visited some. 5 Tea, religious talk; prayer; visited! 6.30 1 John [1]:8-10. 7.30 Select Society; coach; supper, religious talk; prayer. 9.45.

FRIDAY, JUNE 24. 4 Prayed; letters. 6 Class; letters. 10 Class. 12 Visited; at Dr Fisher's! 2.15 Dinner; prayer. 4.30 Tea, religious talk; prayer. 5.30 Prayed. 6.30 Matthew 21:21! the singers! coach. 8.30 Supper, religious talk; prayer. 9.45.

SATURDAY, JUNE 25. 4 Prayed; letters. 8.30 Tea, religious talk; Hospital, Ranelagh! 12 Visited; letter. 2 At Mr. Smith's, dinner, religious talk; prayer. 4 Prayed. 5 Tea, religious talk; prayer. 6 Acts 11:26! garden. 8 Supper, religious talk; prayer; necessary business. 9.45.

SUNDAY, JUNE 26. 4 Prayed; letters. 7 Tea, religious talk; prayer. 8 Psalms 106:24; letter; visited. 11 Read Prayers, Communion. 2.30 Dinner, religious talk; prayer. 4 Prayed. 4.30 Tea, religious talk; prayer. 5.30 Luke 9:62! Society! 8 Supper, religious talk. 9 Prayer. 9.30.

MONDAY, JUNE 27. 4 Prayed; 1 John 2:1-10; letters. 8 Tea, religious talk; prayer; letter. 10 Trustees; letter. 1 Visited; necessary business. 2 Dinner, religious talk; prayer. 4 At brother Ashton's, tea, religious talk. 5 At sister [blank]. 5 Tea, religious talk; prayer. 6.30 1 John 2:11, 12! necessary talk (religious); supper; prayer. 9.30.

TUESDAY, JUNE 28. 4 Prayed; Psalms 116:12; writ Society. 8 Tea, religious talk; prayer; Society. 2 At A. Keene's, dinner, religious talk. 3.30 Society; prayed. 5.15 At sister Blashford's, tea, religious talk; prayer. 6.30 1 Corinthians 6:20! 7.30 The bands; supper, religious talk; prayer. 9.45.

WEDNESDAY, JUNE 29. 4 Prayed; letters. 6 Walked. 7 The boat; religious talk. 9 Tea, necessary talk (religious). 10.30 Proverbs 3:17! 11 Walked. 12 Boat; chaise. 2.15 Prosperous; read. 3 Dinner. 4 Writ Society. 5 Prayed; tea, religious talk. 6.30 +Revelation 20:12; Society; supper; prayer. 9.30.

THURSDAY, JUNE 30. 4 Prayed; letter; Ecclesiastes 9:10! tea. 6.30 Chaise. 8 The boat; writ Society. 9.30 Tea; read. 11 1 Corinthians 13:1-3. 3 At Mr. D'Olier's, dinner. 4.15 Prayed. 5 At Miss Moore's, religious talk; prayer. 6 Prayed. 6.30 1 John 2:15, etc! visited; necessary talk (religious); prayer. 9.30.

FRIDAY, JULY 1. 4 Prayed; Matthew 13:27; Conference. 8 Writ notes. 9 Conference. 1 Visited; writ notes. 2 Dinner, religious talk; prayer. 5 Tea, religious talk; prayer; visited. 6.30 1 Timothy 6:20! the singers. 8.30 Supper; prayer. 9.30.

SATURDAY, JULY 2. 4 Prayed; writ notes. 6 Conference. 8 Tea, religious talk; Conference. 12.30 Letters; visited. 2 At home; dinner; letters. 5 Tea, religious talk; prayer. 6.15 Writ Society. 8 Supper, religious talk; prayer; coach. 10.

SUNDAY, JULY 3. 4 Prayed; Magazine; letters; tea. 8 2 Timothy 3:5! letters; visited! letters. 11 Read Prayers. 2.15 At G[eorge] Grant's, dinner, religious talk; slept. 4 Prayed; tea. 5.30 Matthew 13:32. 6.30 Love-feast; coach; supper, religious talk. 9.45.

MONDAY, JULY 4. 4 Prayed; letters; Conference. 8 Tea, religious talk. 9 Conference. 1 Visited. 2 Dinner, religious talk; prayer. 3.15 Conference. 5 Tea, religious talk; prayer; prayed. 6.30 2 Corinthians 4:7! coach; supper; prayer. 9.45.

TUESDAY, JULY 5. 4 Prayed; letters; Conference; tea; Conference. 12.30 Visited; writ notes. 2 Dinner, religious talk; prayer. 3.15 Conference. 5 Tea, religious talk; prayer. 6.30 Matthew 8:2! the bands; supper, religious talk; prayer. 9.45.

WEDNESDAY, JULY 6. 4 Prayed; letters; Conference; Communion; tea, religious talk; visited. 9.30 Letters. 10.30 Letters. 12 Visited; chaise! visited! 2 Dinner, religious talk; prayer. 3.30 Prayed; tea, religious talk; prayer; writ notes. 6.30 Micah 2:10! the leaders; coach. 8 Supper, religious talk; prayer. 9.45.

THURSDAY, JULY 7. 4 Prayed; letters. 8 Tea, religious talk; prayer; read; class. 12 Necessary business; chaise. 2 Dinner, necessary talk (religious); prayer. 4 Prayed. 5 Tea, religious talk; prayed. 6.30 1 Corinthians 12:31! the leaders; coach; supper, religious talk; prayer. 9.30.

FRIDAY, JULY 8. 4 Prayed; letters. 9 Writ Society. 1 Chaise. 2 Dinner, religious talk; prayer. 3.30 College. 5 Prayed; tea, religious talk. 6.30 2 Corinthians 4:18! the singers; coach; supper, religious talk; prayer. 9.45.

SATURDAY, JULY 9. 4 Prayed; letters. 6.30 Writ class. 8 Tea, religious talk; prayer; writ class. 12.30 Chaise. 2 Dinner, religious talk; prayer; writ class; visited; tea, religious talk; prayer; visited. 7 Necessary business. 8 Supper, religious talk; prayer; necessary business. 10.

SUNDAY, JULY 10. 4 Prayed; letters. 7 Tea, religious talk; prayer. 8 John 4:24; chaise! prayer. 10 Necessary business; letter; read Prayers; Communion. 2 Dinner, religious talk; prayer; slept; letters; prayed; tea. 6.30 Psalms 50:21. 7 Society; supper. 9 Chaise; in the boat. 11 *Prince of Wales.* 12.

[MONDAY] JULY [11.] 6 Prayed; [William] Coxe's *Travels [in Poland, Russia, Sweden, and Denmark*]. 9 Tea; Coxe; Holyhead; letter; tea, necessary talk (religious). 5 Walked. 7.15 Chaise. 8 Gwyndy; supper, religious talk; prayer. 10.

[Text noted at bottom of page:] Matthew 13:32.

TUESDAY, JULY 12. 4.30 Prayed; necessary business. 6 Chaise; prayed; Coxe. 8.30 Bangor Ferry; tea, necessary talk (religious). 10 Chaise; Coxe; walked. 1.30 Conway; walked; boat; dinner. 4.45 Chaise. 6 Walked; chaise. 8 Kinmel [Bay]; supper; prayer; sins. 10.

WEDNESDAY, JULY 13. 4.30 Prayed. 5.30 Chaise; Holywell; tea; chaise. 1 Chester; dinner. 2 Necessary talk (religious); religious talk; necessary business. 3 Slept; prayed; writ notes; prayed; tea. 5.30 Matthew 13:32! 7 Coach. 10.30 Slept.

THURSDAY, JULY 14. 4 Prayed; read Coxe's *Travels.* 7 Eccleshall; tea. 7.30 Coach; Coxe; necessary talk (religious). 2 Atherstone [orig., 'Attershall']; dinner. 3 Coach; Hinckley; tea, religious talk. 6 Coach. 8.30 Lutterworth. 9 Necessary talk (religious). 10 Slept.

FRIDAY, JULY [15]. Prayed; Coxe; mostly religious talk. 5 Stony Stratford; tea; coach; Coxe; religious talk. 3 London; coach; at home; necessary business; prayed. 8.30 Supper, religious talk; prayer. 10.15.

SATURDAY, JULY [16]. 4.45 Prayed; letters. 7.30 Tea, necessary talk (religious) with Charles; letters. 12.30 Walked. 1 Dinner, religious talk; prayer. 2 Letters. 5 Tea, religious talk; prayer; prayed; necessary talk (religious). 7 Letters. 8 Supper, religious talk; necessary business. 9.30.

SUNDAY, JULY 17. 4 Prayed, letters. 8 The preachers. 9.30 Read Prayers; Proverbs 22:6! Communion; at brother Beardmore's, dinner; christened; slept. 3 The leaders; prayed. 5 Read Prayers, Proverbs 22:6; Society; necessary talk (religious) to many; supper, religious talk; prayer. 9.30.

MONDAY, JULY 18. 4 Prayed; Colossians 3:10! Select Society; letters. 8 At Thomas Rankin's, tea, necessary talk (religious); prayer; Magazine; sins. 1 Dinner, religious talk. 2 Magazine. 5.30 Tea, religious talk; prayed; Magazine. 8.15 Supper, religious talk; prayer. 9.30.

TUESDAY, JULY 19. 4 Prayed; Magazine. 6 Dr Coke, etc, necessary talk (religious). 8 Tea, religious talk; prayer; walked; visited. 11 At sister Greenwood's; Magazine. 1.30 Dinner, religious talk. 2.30 Magazine. 5 Tea, religious talk; prayer. 6 Prayed. 7 Magazine; supper; prayer. 9.30.

WEDNESDAY, JULY 20. 4 Prayed; sermon. 8 Tea, religious talk; prayer; sermon. 1.30 Dinner, religious talk. 2.30 Sermon. 5 Tea; prayed; sermon. 6.30 Micah 2:10! sermon; letters; garden. 8.30 Supper, religious talk; prayer. 9.30.

THURSDAY, JULY 21. 4 Prayed; letter; walked. 6.30 At home; necessary business; tea. 7.45 Walked. 8.45 Peckham. 9 Tea; prayer; letter; journal. 3 Dinner, religious talk; prayed; writ journal. 6 Tea, religious talk. 7 Micah 2:10; garden; religious talk. 9.15 Supper, religious talk; prayer. 10.

FRIDAY, JULY 22. 4 Prayed; sermon. 8 Tea, religious talk; prayer; sermon. 12.30 Letters. 3 Dinner, necessary talk (religious); garden. 5.30 Prayed. 6 Letters. 7 Tea, mostly religious talk. 8 Dr Coke, necessary talk (religious). 9 Supper, religious talk; prayer. 10.30.

SATURDAY, JULY 23. 4 Prayed; letters. 8 At sister Thornton's, tea, religious talk; prayer. 9 Walked. 10.15 At home; letters. 1.15 Dinner. 2 Letters. 5 Tea; letters; necessary talk (religious) to many. 8 Supper, religious talk; necessary business. 9.45.

SUNDAY, JULY 24. 4 Prayed; letters. 6 Religious talk; coach. 8 The preachers. 9.30 Read Prayers, Proverbs 22:6! Communion. 1.15 Dinner, religious talk; prayer; coach; slept. 3 The leaders. 3.30 Read Prayers, 1 Kings 19:9! tea; Society; coach; Society. 6 Prayed; supper, religious talk; prayer. 9.45.

MONDAY, JULY 25. 4 Prayed; Ephesians 2:8; letters. 8 Tea, religious talk; letters. 1 At Dr Whitehead's, dinner, religious talk. 2 Writ Conference. 5 Tea; the Trustees; prayed. 6.30 1 Peter 1:3-5; Cabinet; supper; prayer. 9.45.

TUESDAY, JULY 26. 4 Prayed; letters. 6 Conference. 8 Tea, religious talk. 9 Conference. 12 Cabinet. 1 Dinner. 2 Conference; tea. 5 Read letters; necessary business; prayed. 6.30 1 Peter 4:11! necessary talk (religious) to many. 8 Supper, religious talk; prayer. 9.30.

WEDNESDAY, JULY 27. 4 Prayed; writ notes. 6 Conference. 8 Tea, religious talk. 9 Conference. 12 Cabinet; dinner, religious talk. 2 Conference. 2.30 Writ notes. 4 Cabinet! 5 Tea, necessary talk (religious); Cabinet. 6.15 Prayed. 6.30 2 Corinthians 4:5! Cabinet; supper, religious talk; prayer. 9.30.

THURSDAY, JULY 28. 4 Prayed; Cabinet. 6 Conference. 8 Tea, religious talk. 9 Conference. 12 Cabinet. 1 Dinner, religious talk. 2 Conference. 4 Cabinet. 5 Tea, religious talk; prayed; letter. 6.30 Romans 15:2; writ Conference. 8 Supper, religious talk; prayer. 9.30.

FRIDAY, JULY 29. 4 Prayed; Conference. 8 Tea; writ notes. 9 Conference. 12.30

Writ notes. 2 Dinner, religious talk. 3 Conference. 4.30 Necessary talk. 5 Tea, necessary talk! 5.30 Prayed; letters. 8 Supper, religious talk; prayer. 9.30.

SATURDAY, JULY 30. 4 Prayed; writ notes. 6 Conference. 8 Tea, religious talk; prayer. 9 Conference. 12 Letters; necessary talk (religious). 2 Dinner, religious talk. 3 Letters. 5 Tea; prayed; letters; walked; supper; necessary business. 9.30.

SUNDAY, JULY 31. 4 Prayed; letters; tea. 8.15 Married sister Sparrow. 9.30 Read Prayers, Hebrews 12:1, 2, Communion. 1 Dinner, religious talk; prayer; slept; prayed; the leaders; tea; prayed. 5 Read Prayers, Hebrews 3:15. 6 Letter. 6.30 Love-feast. 8 Supper, religious talk; prayer. 9.30.

MONDAY, AUGUST 1. 4 Prayed; ordained three. 6 Conference. 8 Tea; writ Conference. 9 Conference; letters. 1 Dinner. 2 Conference. 4 Letters. 5 Tea; prayed. 6.30 Mr Collins! necessary talk (religious); supper, religious talk; prayer. 9.30.

TUESDAY, AUGUST 2. 4 Prayed; ordained. 6 Conference. 8 Tea; Conference. 12 Writ notes. 1 Dinner, religious talk. 2 Conference; necessary talk (religious). 5 Tea, religious talk; prayed. 6.30 Ephesians 3:14, etc; the leaders; supper, religious talk; prayer. 9.30.

WEDNESDAY, AUGUST 3. 4 Prayed; religious talk. 6 Conference. 8 Tea, religious talk. 9 Communion [blotted out?]; letters. 12 Highbury Place. 2 Dinner, necessary talk (religious). 3 Magazine. 5 Prayed; tea; Magazine. 8 Walked. 8.30 Supper, religious talk; prayer. 10.

THURSDAY, AUGUST 4. 4.30 Prayed; Magazine. 8 Tea, religious talk; prayer; accounts. 10 Walked. 10.45 At home; necessary business. 12.30 Coach. 2 Balham; garden. 3 Dinner, religious talk. 4 Magazine; prayed. 6 Tea, religious talk; Magazine; garden; religious talk. 8.15 Supper, religious talk; prayer. 10.

FRIDAY, AUGUST 5. 4 Prayed; Magazine. 8 Prayer; tea; religious talk; Magazine. 10 Coach. 11.30 Writ notes. 1 Prayer; dinner, religious talk. 3 Visited; letter; prayed. 5 Tea; prayer; prayed. 6 Committee. 8 Supper; prayer. 9.30.

SATURDAY, AUGUST 6. 4 Prayed; Magazine. 8 Tea, religious talk; prayer; corrected Magazine; letters. 1.15 Dinner, religious talk; prayer. 2.30 Necessary business; prayed; coach. 5 At Mr Collins's, tea, religious talk; prayed. 6 Read Prayers, Hebrews 9:14! Communion. 8 Supper, religious talk; Penry, necessary business. 9.30.

SUNDAY, AUGUST 7. 4 Prayed; Magazine; letter; coach; Chapel. 9.30 Read Prayers, Luke 18:10! Communion. 1 Dinner, religious talk; prayer. 2.30 Slept; letter. 5 Read Prayers, Hebrews 10:19; Society; necessary business; supper; prayer. 9.30.

[MONDAY] AUGUST [8.] 4 Prayed; tea. 5 Walked. 5.30 Diligence; Kingston; tea; Diligence; read; mostly religious talk. 1.45 Liphook; dinner. 2.30 Diligence;

read; sang; mostly religious talk. 6.15 The Common. 6.30 Tea; 1 Peter 1:24; supper, religious talk; prayer. 9.30.

TUESDAY, AUGUST 9. 4 Prayed; Romans 13:11; writ notes. 7 Tea, religious talk. 8 Boat. 10.30 Wootton Bridge; chaise. 11.30 Necessary talk (religious). 12 Read Walsh. 1.30 Dinner, religious talk. 2.30 Read Fisher. 4 Prayed; tea, religious talk. 6.30 Matthew 8:13! Society; supper; prayer. 9.30.

WEDNESDAY, AUGUST 10. 4 Prayed; 1 Corinthians 10:12! walked; the Castle [Carisbrooke]. 8 Tea, religious talk; prayer. 9 Sermon; sins. 12 Garden. 1 Dinner, religious talk; prayer. 2.30 Necessary talk (religious); coach; garden. 5 Read notes; prayed. 5.15 Tea, religious talk; prayed. 6.15 Matthew 9:5; Society; supper, religious talk; prayer. 9.30.

THURSDAY, AUGUST 11. 4 Prayed; Luke 20:34; necessary business; tea; prayer. 7.15 Chaise. 9 Boat. 11 At home [Portsmouth]; necessary business. 12 +2 Corinthians 6:2! at brother Webb's; garden; dinner, religious talk; prayer. 3.30 Read; prayed. 5 Tea; prayed. 6.30 +Revelation 20:12! Society; supper, religious talk; prayer. 9.30.

FRIDAY, AUGUST [12]. 4 Prayed; Isaiah 57:1, 2; letter; tea. 7 Chaise. 9 Wickham; tea. 9.15 Chaise. 12 Winchester [orig., 'Winton']; writ notes. 1.15 Dinner, religious talk. 2.15 Letter; read John Walsh; prayed. 4 Walked; visited; tea. 6.30 Matthew 22:27; Society; supper; prayer. 9.45.

[SATURDAY] AUGUST [13.] 4 Prayed; Matthew 22:35; letter; tea; prayer. 6.45 Chaise; tea; chaise. 12.30 Salisbury [orig., 'Sarum']. 1 Writ notes. 2 Dinner; letter; prayed; tea, necessary talk (religious); prayed; Walsh. 7 John 5:8; supper; prayer; prayer; necessary business. 10.

SUNDAY, AUGUST 14. 4 Prayed; letters; tea. 8 Hebrews 2:3! Walsh. 10.30 Read Prayers, Communion. 1 Dinner, Walsh. 4 Walsh, prayed, tea. 5.30 Revelation 20:1, etc! Society; Walsh. 8.30 Supper; religious talk; prayer. 9.30.

MONDAY, AUGUST 15. 4 Prayed; tea. 4.45 Chaise; with Mr Green. 8 Shaftesbury [orig., 'Shaston']; tea, necessary talk (religious). 8.45 Micah 2:10! 10 Chaise. 12.45 Castle Cary; writ notes. 1 +Psalms 147:3; dinner, religious talk. 2.45 Chaise; Shepton [Mallet]; visited! tea; prayed; Luke 12:7! supper; prayer. 9.15.

[TUESDAY] AUGUST [16.] 4 Prayed; Psalms 106:24! tea. 7 Chaise. 10.30 Tea. 11.30 Chaise. 1.30 Taunton; dinner, religious talk; texts. 4 Prayed; tea; Walsh. 6.15 Hebrews 7:25! 8 Supper, religious talk; prayer. 9.30.

WEDNESDAY, AUGUST 17. 4 Prayed; Ephesians 4:1-5; Walsh; tea; prayer. 7 Chaise. 11 Cullompton; Walsh. 12 Colossians 1:10! dinner. 2 Chaise. 4 Exeter [orig., 'Exon']; prayed; tea. 6.30 1 Corinthians 13:1, etc! at Mr Moxy's, supper, religious talk; prayer. 9.30.

THURSDAY, AUGUST 18. 4 Prayed; tea. 4.30 Chaise; Ashburton; tea, religious talk; prayer; chaise. 12 Ivybridge; necessary talk (religious), dinner. 1.30 Chaise. 4 The Dock; letter; prayed; tea. 6.30 Isaiah 59:1, 2! necessary talk (religious), supper; prayer. 9.30.

FRIDAY, AUGUST 19. 4 Prayed; Isaiah 57:1, 2; letters. 10 Journal. 12 Prayers; journal. 1.30 Dinner, religious talk. 2 Prayers; letters; prayed. 4 Walked; Plymouth; tea; read; prayed. 6.30 Ephesians 5:14! 8 Supper, religious talk; prayed. 9.30.

SATURDAY, AUGUST 20. 4 Prayed; Ephesians 3:14! Walsh. 7 Tea, religious talk; prayer; visited; walked. 10.30 Dock; Walsh. 1.15 Dinner, religious talk; prayer. 3 Walsh. 5 Tea, religious talk; prayed. 6.30 1 Corinthians 13:8, writ notes; supper, religious talk; prayer; necessary business. 10.

SUNDAY, AUGUST 21. 4 Prayed; letter. 7 2 Corinthians 3:18! tea, religious talk; chaise. 9.15 Plymouth; Walsh. 10.30 Read Prayers. 1 Dinner. 1.30 Galatians 3:22! visited. 4 Slept; prayed. 5 Tea, religious talk; Luke 10:34. 7.30 Society; necessary talk (religious); supper, religious talk; prayer. 9.30.

MONDAY, AUGUST 22. 3 Necessary business; prayed; tea. 4.15 Chaise. 9 Liskeard; tea; Acts 16:31; chaise. 2 St Austell; dinner, religious talk; Walsh; letter; prayed. 6 +Galatians 6:15. 7 Society! necessary talk (religious), supper; prayer. 9.30.

TUESDAY, AUGUST 23. 4 Prayed; Magazine; tea; prayer; chaise. 9 Sticker; Mark 1:15(2)! chaise. 12 Truro; 1 Peter 4:18! dinner, necessary talk (religious). 2.30 Chaise. 4.30 Penryn. 5 Tea, religious talk; prayed. 6 +Job 22:21! Society; supper, religious talk; prayer. 9.30.

WEDNESDAY, AUGUST 24. 4 Prayed; Job 7:18! letter. 8 Tea, religious talk; prayer. 8.45 Chaise. 10.45 Helston; necessary talk (religious). 12 2 Timothy 3:5! dinner, religious talk; prayer. 2.30 Chaise. 4 Marazion; Job 28:28. 5 Chaise; Penzance; tea. 6 +Daniel 9:24! Society; supper, religious talk; prayer. 9.30.

THURSDAY, AUGUST 25. 4 Prayed; 2 John 8; letter; tea; chaise. 8.30 Mousehole; tea; Hebrews 6:1! 10.30 Chaise; Land's End! 2.15 St Just; dinner; letter; necessary talk (religious), tea. 5 Tea; prayed. 6 John 5:8; Society; supper, religious talk; prayer. 9.30.

FRIDAY, AUGUST 26. 4 Prayed; Malachi 3:1; tea; prayer. 6.45 Chaise; visited. 8.30 Tea, religious talk; prayer. 9.15 Chaise. 10.30 St Ives; Walsh. 11 Read Prayers. 12 Walsh. 1 Dinner, religious talk; prayer. 2 Visited. 3 Walsh. 4 Prayed; tea. 6 +Isaiah 66:8; Society; supper, religious talk; prayer. 9.30.

SATURDAY, AUGUST 27. 4 Prayed; Ephesians 4:1-7; walked; chaise. 7 Copper Works; tea; 1 John 5:19; chaise. 12 Redruth; letters. 1 Dinner; the Stewards. 4 Necessary talk. 4.30 Prayed; tea. 6 1 Peter 4:7! Love-feast! supper, religious talk; prayer. 10.

SUNDAY, AUGUST 28. 4 Prayed; slept; letters; tea; chaise. 8 St Agnes; tea. 8.30 +Matthew 8:13! chaise. 10.30 Letters. 12.30 Dinner. 1.30 +Matthew 22:21! letters; prayed; tea. 4.15 Chaise. 5 +John 4:24! Society; visited. 8 Supper; prayer. 9.30.

MONDAY, AUGUST 29. 4 Prayed; chaise. 5 Kerley [Downs]; tea; 2 Corinthians 5:1, etc; chaise. 9 *Indian Queen*; 1 Corinthians 1:30; chaise. 2 Port Isaac; dinner; letters; prayed. 6 +Hebrews 2:3; Society; supper; necessary business; prayer. 9.15.

TUESDAY, AUGUST 30. 4 Prayed; Luke 20:34; letters. 7.30 Tea, religious talk; letter; Magazine. 11 Chaise. 1 Visited! dinner; Communion! 2.45 Chaise. 4 Camelford; writ notes; tea. 5 Prayed. 6 1 Corinthians 13:1-3; Society; supper, religious talk; prayer. 9.30.

WEDNESDAY, AUGUST 31. 4 Prayed; letter. 8 Tea, religious talk; accounts. 11 Matthew 12:43! dinner; prayer. 1.15 Chaise. 4 Launceston; prayed; tea. 6 1 Kings 19:9! necessary talk (religious) to many; supper, religious talk; prayer. 9.30.

THURSDAY, SEPTEMBER 1. 3.30 Prayed; tea. 4.15 Chaise. 7.30 Okehampton; tea. 8.15 Walked; coach. 12 Crediton; dinner. 12.30 Chaise. 3 Tiverton; letters; tea, religious talk; sermon; prayed. 6 +Isaiah 1:3. 7 Society; supper; prayer. 9.30.

FRIDAY, SEPTEMBER 2. 3.30 Tea. 4.15 Chaise; Cicero. 7 Wellington; tea, religious talk; Hebrews 9:27! chaise. 10 Taunton; necessary talk (religious); prayer. 10.30 Chaise. 11.30 Cathanger; Luke 9:62! dinner; chaise; Ditcheat; tea; Matthew 8:2; supper; prayer. 9.30.

SATURDAY, SEPTEMBER 3. 4 Prayed. Matthew 8:13! writ notes; tea. 7.30 Chaise; Shepton [Mallet]. 9 Matthew 7:24; chaise. 2 At Mr Durbin's, necessary talk (religious), dinner; read notes; prayer. 4 Necessary business; letters. 5 Prayer; tea, religious talk; letters. 7.30 At Miss Chapman's, supper, religious talk; prayer; necessary business. 9.30.

SUNDAY, SEPTEMBER 4. 4 Prayed; letters. 8 Tea, religious talk; necessary business. 9.30 Read Prayers; Matthew 5:48! Communion. 1 At brother Ewer's. 2 Religious talk; prayer. 2.30 Slept; letters. 4 Tea; prayed. 5 Matthew 6:24; Society; singers. 8 Supper, religious talk; prayer. 9.30.

MONDAY, SEPTEMBER 5. 4 Prayed; Matthew 20:6; letters. 8 Tea, religious talk; prayer; letters. 10.30 Buried brother King. 12 Select Society. 1 At Miss Johnson's, dinner, religious talk. 2 Writ texts. 4 Sins! prayed; tea, religious talk; prayed. 6.30 Luke 12:7! at sister Chapman's, supper, religious talk; prayer. 9.30.

TUESDAY, SEPTEMBER 6. 4 Prayed; letter. 8 Tea, religious talk; prayer. 9.15 Necessary business. 9.45 Chaise; [read] Buchan. 12 Paulton; dinner; Matthew

5:47! 2 Chaise. 4 Coleford; writ notes; prayed; tea. 5.30 Prayed; 2 Corinthians 1:22; Communion; supper, religious talk; prayer. 9.30.

WEDNESDAY, SEPTEMBER 7. 4 Prayed; letters; tea; prayer. 8.15 Chaise; Mells; +Isaiah 55:7! chaise. 11.15 Frome; letters. 1 Dinner, religious talk. 2 Letters; journal. 5 Tea, religious talk; prayed. 6 1 Peter 1:18! Society! supper, necessary talk (religious); prayer. 9.30.

THURSDAY, SEPTEMBER 8. 4 Prayed; Magazine. 7.30 Tea, religious talk; prayer. 8.30 Writ notes. 10.30 Chaise; Rode [Som.]. 12 Dinner; +1 Samuel 20:3; chaise. 3.30 Trowbridge; necessary talk (religious); letter; prayed. 6 +John 17:3; christened two; Society; read notes; supper, religious talk; prayer. 9.30.

FRIDAY, SEPTEMBER 9. 4 Prayed; letters. 7.30 Tea, religious talk; prayer. 8 Letters. 11 Religious talk; walked. 12.30 Letter. 1 Dinner, religious talk; prayer. 2 Chaise; religious talk; Bradford[-on-Avon]; letters; tea. 5 Prayed. 6 Matthew 8:13; Society; supper, religious talk; prayer. 9.30.

SATURDAY, SEPTEMBER 10. 4 Prayed; 1 Peter 1:18; read letter. 8 Tea, religious talk. 8.45 Chaise. 10.15 Bath; at brother Giles's. 11 Read letter. 1 Dinner, religious talk; letters. 4 Walked; tea, religious talk; prayed. 6 Micah 2:10! 7.30 Prayed; supper, religious talk; prayer. 9.30.

[Text noted at bottom of page:] 1 Peter 2.

SUNDAY, SEPTEMBER 11. 4 Prayed; sermon. 8 Tea, religious talk; prayer. 9 Writ notes. 10 Read Prayers, Ephesians 3:14! Communion; visited. 1 Dinner, religious talk; slept. 2.45 Mr Collins; prayed. 4.30 Tea, necessary talk (religious); prayer; visited. 5.30 Romans 12:1! 7 Society; supper, mostly religious talk; prayer. 9.30.

MONDAY, SEPTEMBER 12. 4 Prayed; sermon. 6 Romans 12:2! necessary business; tea; prayer; visited. 9 Chaise. 11.30 Kendleshire. 12 +Isaiah 57:1, 2! chaise. 1.30 Dinner. 2 Chaise. 3 At home; necessary business. 4 Letters. 5 Prayer; tea; prayed. 6.30 1 Peter 2:1-5; at sister Chapman's, supper, religious talk; prayer. 9.30.

TUESDAY, SEPTEMBER 13. 4 Prayed; letters. 8 Tea, religious talk; prayer; letters. 10 Chaise. 12 [Chew] Stoke; John 9:4! dinner, necessary talk (religious). 2 Prayer. 2.15 Chaise. 3.15 Belluton [orig., 'Belton']; letter; prayed; tea; walked. 6 Pensford; 2 Timothy 3:5! walked; Belluton; supper, religious talk; prayer. 9.30.

WEDNESDAY, SEPTEMBER 14. 4 Prayed; sermon. 7 Tea, religious talk; prayer; chaise. 9 At home; letter; sermon. 12.30 Visited some. 1.15 At Mr. Stock's, dinner, religious talk; prayer; visited; Communion. 3.30 Letters; prayed; tea, religious talk. 6.30 Temple [Church]. 7 Read Prayers, Psalms 74:12! [orig., 74:14; cf. Journal]; supper, religious talk; prayer. 9.30.

THURSDAY, SEPTEMBER 15. 4 Prayed; sermon. 8 Tea, religious talk; prayer; letters; sermon. 12.15 Chaise. 1 Hanham; garden! necessary talk (religious). 2

Dinner, religious talk; prayer; chaise. 4 Prayed. 5 Tea, religious talk; prayer; prayed. 6.30 1 Peter 2:5-9! 8 Supper, religious talk; prayer. 9.30.

FRIDAY, SEPTEMBER 16. 4 Prayed; sermon. 11 Necessary talk (religious) to some; sins! 12 The females; sermon. 1 Prayer. 2 At Mr Castleman's, dinner, religious talk; prayer. 3.30 Prayed. 4.15 Chaise; at the School; prayer; necessary talk (religious); tea. 6 Sermon; garden; supper. 8.30 1 Peter 4:18! coffee; prayer. 12.

SATURDAY, SEPTEMBER 17. 6 Prayed; sermon; the children. 8 Tea, necessary talk; letters; garden. 1 At brother de Boudry's, dinner, religious talk; prayer; chaise. 3.30 Necessary talk! visited; tea, religious talk; prayer. 6 1 Peter 2:9! Penry. 8 At sister Chapman's, supper, religious talk; prayer. 9.30.

SUNDAY, SEPTEMBER 18. 4 Prayed; letters. 8 Tea, religious talk; prayer; necessary business. 9.30 Read Prayers, Matthew 19:29! Communion; chaise. 1 At the School; dinner, necessary talk (religious). 2 +Matthew 19:31 [i.e., 19:30?]; Society; chaise; slept. 4 Tea; prayed. 5 +Matthew 19:20, 21; Society! necessary talk (religious); the singers; supper, religious talk; prayer. 9.30.

MONDAY, SEPTEMBER 19. 4 Prayed; 1 Peter 2:11-15! writ notes. 7 Class; tea, necessary talk (religious). 9 Class. 12 Necessary business; class. 1 Dinner, religious talk. 2 Class. 4 Sermon; prayed; tea, religious talk. 5 Tea, religious talk; prayer. 6 Prayed. 6.30 1 Peter 2:11! 8 At sister Chapman's, supper, religious talk; prayer. 9.30.

TUESDAY, SEPTEMBER 20. 4 Prayed; ill; letter. 6 Class. 8 Tea, religious talk; prayer. 9 Class. 1 Dinner, religious talk; prayer. 2 Class. 4 Prayed; necessary talk (religious). 5 Tea, religious talk; prayer; prayed. 6.30 1 Peter 2:17! the leaders! supper, religious talk; prayer. 9.30 Ill.

   [Texts noted at bottom of page:] Hebrews 8:10; Matthew 19:29; 1 Peter 2:11, 16, 17 (twice).

WEDNESDAY, SEPTEMBER 21. 4.30 Prayed. 6 Class. 8 Tea, religious talk. 9 Class. 1 At brother Hopkins's, dinner, religious talk. 2 Class. 4 Jacob's Wells; tea, religious talk; prayer. 5 Psalms 90:12! class; walked; at Mr Bowsher's; writ Society; supper, religious talk; prayer. 9.30.

THURSDAY, SEPTEMBER 22. 4.15 Prayed; writ Society. 7.30 Tea, religious talk; prayer; walked. 9 Writ Society; good talk!. 1 At John Ellison's. 2 Mostly religious talk. 3 Society. 4 Prayed; tea, religious talk. 6.30 1 Peter 2:17! the bands. 8.15 At sister Chapman's, supper, religious talk; prayer. 9.30.

FRIDAY, SEPTEMBER 23. 4 Prayed; letters. 10 Writ Society. 12 The females; necessary talk (religious) to some. 1 Prayer. 2.15 Dinner, religious talk. 4 Visited some; tea, religious talk. 6 Guinea Street; Romans 1:16! Society. 7.30 At brother Stock's, supper, religious talk; prayer. 9.30.

SATURDAY, SEPTEMBER 24. 4 Prayed; letters; tea; chaise. 8 At Mr Ireland's, tea, religious talk; prayer; chaise. 10.30 At home. 11 Writ Society. 2.30 At Mr. Durbin's, dinner, religious talk; prayer; visited some; tea, religious talk. 6 Matthew 6:33; Penry; at sister Johnson's, supper, religious talk; prayer; necessary business. 9.30.

SUNDAY, SEPTEMBER [25]. 4 Prayed; journal; letters; tea, religious talk; prayer. 8.30 Necessary business; prayed. 9.30 Read Prayers, Matthew 25:12, Communion. 1 At brother Wait's, dinner, religious talk; slept; Temple [Church]. 3 Read Prayers, 1 Corinthians 10:13! tea; prayed. 5 Hebrews 8:10! Society; supper, religious talk; prayer. 9.15.

[MONDAY] SEPTEMBER [26]. 4 Prayed; Psalms 139 *ult;* letters. 8 Tea, religious talk; prayer. 9 Letters. 12 Select Society. 1 At brother Cross's, dinner, religious talk; prayer. 2.30 Visited many. 4.30 Prayed. 5 Tea; prayed. 6 Committee! 7 1 Peter 2:17(2); supper, religious talk; prayer. 9.30.

[Pointing hand] TUESDAY, SEPTEMBER 27. 4 Prayed; letters; sermon. 8 Tea, religious talk; prayer. 9 Writ notes. 10.30 Chaise; Almondsbury [orig., 'Amesbury']. 12 Hebrews 2:14; dinner, religious talk; prayer. 2.30 Chaise. 4 Writ notes; prayed; visited. 5 Tea, necessary talk (religious). 6 Prayed. 6.30 Read the letters; the leaders. 8.30 Supper; prayer. 9.30.

WEDNESDAY, SEPTEMBER 28. 4 Prayed; letters. 8 Tea, religious talk; prayer; writ notes. 9.30 Brother Lock, etc, necessary talk. 12 Visited some. 1 At brother Lane's, dinner, religious talk; prayer. 2.30 Necessary business; prayed; tea, religious talk. 6.30 Read Prayers, 1 Corinthians 13:13! at sister Johnson's, supper, religious talk; prayer. 9.30.

THURSDAY, SEPTEMBER 29. 4 Prayed; letters. 8 Tea, religious talk; prayer; letters. 1 Dinner, religious talk; prayer. 2.30 Visited some. 4.30 At sister Philips's, tea, religious talk. 6 Committee. 6.30 1 Peter 2:22. 7.30 The bands; supper, religious talk; prayer. 9.30.

FRIDAY, SEPTEMBER 30. 4 Prayed; letters. 6.15 Chaise. 9 Midsomer Norton; tea, religious talk. 11 Read Prayers, Mark 3:32! dinner; prayer. 1.30 Chaise. 4.15 Ditcheat; tea, religious talk. 5 +Matthew 15:28! Society; necessary talk (religious); supper; visited; prayer. 9.30.

[Text noted at bottom of page:] Mark 12:44.

SATURDAY, OCTOBER 1. 4 Prayed. 5 Hebrews 6:1; tea, religious talk. 7 Chaise. 8 Shepton [Mallet]; 1 Peter 2:16. 9 Chaise. 1.15 At home; necessary business. 2 Dinner; visited many. 5 Tea, religious talk; prayer. 6 Hebrews 2:15; Penry; at sister Johnson's, supper, religious talk; prayer. 9.30.

SUNDAY, OCTOBER 2. 4 Prayed; letters; tea. 8 Necessary business; prayed. 9.30 Read Prayers, Ephesians 4:17, Covenant! 1.30 Dinner; visited; prayed. 4 Mail coach; slept. 12.

MONDAY, OCTOBER 3. 7 London; chaise; necessary talk (religious); tea; prayed; prayer; letters. 1 Dinner, religious talk; prayer; letters. 4 Garden. 5 Tea, religious talk; prayed; letters; necessary talk (religious) to many. 8 Supper, necessary talk (religious); prayer. 9.30.

TUESDAY, OCTOBER 4. 4 Prayed; writ letters. 8 Tea, religious talk; prayer; writ accounts; sorted my books. 12 Garden. 1 Dinner, religious talk; prayer; necessary business. 4.15 Visited; tea, religious talk. 5.30 Prayed. 6.30 Read Prayers, 1 Peter 2:13-16; the leaders; supper, religious talk; prayer. 9.30.

WEDNESDAY, OCTOBER 5. 4 Prayed; letters; tea. 6.15 Chaise; Hatfield; tea. 10.15 Miss Harvey; chaise. 2.30 Hinxworth; dinner, religious talk. 3.30 Read notes; Magazine. 5 Prayed; tea; Magazine. 6.30 Romans 3:22; Magazine; supper, religious talk; prayer. 9.30.

THURSDAY, OCTOBER [6]. 4 Prayed; Magazine. 7 The children; tea, religious talk. 9 Magazine. 12 Walked. 1 Dinner, religious talk; necessary business. 3 Chaise. 4.30 Wrestlingworth; tea, necessary talk (religious); prayed. 6 Read Prayers, 2 Corinthians 5:17, etc! 8 Supper, religious talk; prayer. 9.30.

FRIDAY, OCTOBER 7. 4 Prayed; Magazine. 6.15 Cart. 7.45 Hinxworth; tea, religious talk; prayer. 9 Chaise. 12.45 Hatfield; dinner, religious talk. 2.30 Chaise. 4 At home; letters; tea; prayer; writ notes. 6 The audit; supper, necessary talk (religious); prayer. 9.30.

SATURDAY, OCTOBER 8. 4.30 Prayed; letters. 8 Tea, religious talk; prayer; letters. 11 Errata. 12.30 Walked. 1 Dinner, religious talk; prayer. 2 Errata; letters. 5 Tea; prayed; letters; supper. 8.15 Penry, necessary business. 9.30.

SUNDAY, OCTOBER 9. 4 Prayed; letters. 8 The preachers. 9.30 Read Prayers; Mark 12:44! Communion. 1 At brother Hammond's, religious talk, dinner. 2.30 Slept; prayed; read Prayers, 1 Peter 1:24; Society; Love-feast! 8 Supper, religious talk; prayer. 9.30.

MONDAY, OCTOBER 10. 4 Prayed; necessary business. 4.30 Chaise; Brentford; tea; chaise; Salt Hill; tea; chaise. 12.30 Henley[-on-Thames]; chaise. 2.30 Wallingford; at Mr Lindgr——'s, dinner; Magazine. 5 Prayed; tea. 6 John 5:8! Magazine; supper, religious talk; prayer. 9.30.

TUESDAY, OCTOBER 11. 4 Prayed; Isaiah 57:1, 2! walked; chaise; Nuneham! walked; tea; christened. 10 Chaise. 11 Oxford; Magazine. 12 Hebrews 2:15! 1 Dinner, religious talk. 2.30 Chaise. 4.30 Witney; necessary business; tea; Magazine. 6.30 1 Thessalonians 4:3! Society; supper, necessary talk (religious); prayer. 9.30.

WEDNESDAY, OCTOBER 12. 4 Prayed; Mark 1:15(2); sermon. 8 Tea, religious talk; prayer; visited! sermon. 2 Dinner, mostly religious talk. 3 Sermon; prayed. 5 Tea, religious talk; prayer; sermon. 6.30 Mark 12:34! 8 Necessary talk (religious) to A[nn] B[olton]. 8.30 Supper; prayer. 9.30.

THURSDAY, OCTOBER 13. 4 Prayed; 1 Peter 4:7! tea, religious talk; prayer. 7 Chaise. 9 Oxford; tea; prayer; walked. 11.30 Necessary business. 12 Sermon. 1 Dinner, religious talk; walked. 3.45 Sermon; prayed. 5 Tea, religious talk; prayer; visited. 6 John 4:24! 7.30 Sermon; supper, religious talk; prayer. 9.30.

FRIDAY, OCTOBER 14. 4 Prayed; Psalms 84:1! tea; prayer. 6.45 Chaise. 9 Tetsworth. 10 Chaise. 12 [High] Wycombe; letters. 2 Dinner, religious talk. 3 Letters. 4 Prayed. 5 Tea, religious talk. 6.30 Ecclesiastes 7:29; Society. 8 Supper, religious talk; prayer. 9.30.

SATURDAY, OCTOBER 15. 4 Prayed; Isaiah 59:1, 2; tea. 6.30 Chaise. 9 Uxbridge; tea. 9.30 Chaise. 12.30 At home; letters. 1 Dinner, religious talk; prayer; Mr. Bethell, etc!. 2.30 Letters. 5 Tea; prayer; letters; supper; Penry, necessary business. 9.30.

SUNDAY, OCTOBER 16. 4 Prayed; letters; walked; Chapel; read Prayers, Ephesians 6:11, Communion; dinner, religious talk; prayer. 3 The leaders. 3.30 Read Prayers, Psalms 84:1; Society; chaise; Society; necessary business. 8 Supper; prayer. 9 [Mail] coach. 12.

MONDAY, OCTOBER 17. 6 Religious talk. 7 Newmarket; tea, religious talk. 7.30 Coach; religious talk; Magazine. 2.30 Norwich; at home; dinner; prayer; letters. 5 Tea, religious talk; prayed. 6.30 Mark 3:35! Magazine; supper, necessary talk (religious); prayer. 9.30.

TUESDAY, OCTOBER 18. 4 Prayed; Isaiah 57:1, 2; letters; tea. 8 Coach. 12 [Great] Yarmouth; letters. 1.30 Dinner, religious talk; prayer. 3 Sermon; prayed. 4 Walked; prayed. 5.15 Tea, religious talk; prayer. 6.30 Luke 12:7. 8 Supper, religious talk; prayer. 9.30.

WEDNESDAY, OCTOBER 19. 4 Prayed; Hebrews 6:1; prayer; sermon. 8 Tea, religious talk; prayer. 9.30 Sermon; necessary talk (religious)! 12 Walked. 1 Sermon. 1.30 Dinner, religious talk; sermon. 4 Prayed. 5 Tea, religious talk; prayed. 6.30 John 5:8; supper; prayer. 9.30.

THURSDAY, OCTOBER 20. 4 Prayed; Ephesians 4:30, etc; sermon. 8 Tea, religious talk; prayer; sermon. 10.30 Chaise. 12 Lowestoft. 12.15 Walked. 1 Dinner, religious talk. 2 Sermon. 4 Prayed; walked; tea; prayer. 6.30 Mark 1:15(2). 7.30 Society; supper; prayer. 9.30.

FRIDAY, OCTOBER 21. 4 Prayed. 6 1 Corinthians 12:31; tea, religious talk; prayer. 8 Chaise; [North] Cove; tea; Mark 9:23. 10.30 Chaise. 1 Loddon; read. 1.45 Dinner, religious talk. 2.45 Journal; prayed. 5 Prayed; religious talk; prayer. 6.30 Ecclesiastes 7:29! Society; walked; supper; prayer. 9.30.

SATURDAY, OCTOBER 22. 4 Prayed; Matthew 5:6; tea, religious talk; prayer. 7 Whisk [i.e., whist]. 9 Norwich; letters. 11 Sermon. 2 At Dr Hunt's, mostly religious talk. 3.30 Sermon. 4.45 Tea; prayed. 6.30 1 Peter 1:18! Society! 8.30 Religious talk, supper, religious talk; prayer. 9.30.

SUNDAY, OCTOBER 23. 4 Prayed; Magazine. 7 Communion; tea. 8.45 Sermon. 10 Read Prayers, Communion. 1 Dinner, religious talk; sermon. 2.30 Luke 9:62; sermon. 4.30 Tea; prayed. 5.30 Luke 9:55; Society; sermon. 8 Supper, religious talk. 9 Prayer. 9.30.

MONDAY, OCTOBER 24. 4 Prayed; 1 Corinthians 10:12! sermon. 8 Tea, religious talk; prayer; sermon. 12 Visited some. 1.15 Dinner. 3 Sermon. 5 Tea, religious talk; prayer. 6.30 Matthew 5:20! the leaders; supper; prayer; necessary business. 9.30.

TUESDAY, OCTOBER 25. 4 Prayed; 1 Peter 4:7! letter; tea; prayer. 8 Machine. 10 Tea; machine. 12.30 Dinner, necessary talk (religious). 2 Machine. 4.30 [King's] Lynn; tea, religious talk; prayer; prayed. 6.30 Micah 2:10. 7 Society; supper, necessary talk (religious); prayer. 9.45.

WEDNESDAY, OCTOBER 26. 4 Prayed; Isaiah 59:1, 2; necessary talk; letters. 8 Tea, religious talk; prayer; necessary business. 9 Sermon. 12.30 Dinner, religious talk. 2 Visited some. 3.15 Letters; tea; prayed. 6 John 4:24! Communion. 8 Supper, religious talk; prayer. 9 Chaise. 12.

THURSDAY, OCTOBER 27. 4 Chaise. 7.30 Royston; tea. 8 Chaise. 1 New Chapel [City Road]; necessary business; dinner, necessary talk (religious). 3 Chaise. 4.30 Deptford; letters. 5 Tea, religious talk; letters; prayed. 8 Supper, religious talk. 9 Prayer. 9.30.

FRIDAY, OCTOBER 28. 6 Prayed; letters. 8 Tea, religious talk; prayer; letters. 1 Dinner, religious talk; prayer. 2 Letters. 5 Tea; prayed; tunes. 8.15 Supper, religious talk; prayer. 9.30.

SATURDAY, OCTOBER 29. 4.15 Prayed; tunes. 8 Tea, religious talk; tunes. 10 Prayer; visited; chaise. 11 London; necessary business; tunes. 1 Dinner, religious talk; tunes; necessary business. 2 Letters. 4.30 Tea, religious talk; prayer. 6 Prayed. 7 Letters; supper; Penry, necessary business. 9.30.

SUNDAY, OCTOBER 30. 4 Prayed; letters; Spitalfields; read Prayers; Luke 16:31, Communion; visited; dinner; the leaders; tea; prayed. 5 Read Prayers, Philippians 4:7! Society; supper, religious talk; prayer; necessary business. 9.30.

MONDAY, OCTOBER 31. 4 Prayed; Mark 4:19; tea. 6.15 Chaise. 8.30 Barnet; tea, religious talk; chaise. 11 St Albans; within; chaise. 2 Luton; dinner, necessary talk! Magazine; necessary business. 5 At Mr. Hampson's, tea, necessary talk (religious). 6.30 Philippians 4:7! Society! 8 Supper; prayer. 9 At Mr Hampson's, mostly religious talk. 9.30.

TUESDAY, NOVEMBER 1. 4 Prayed; 1 Corinthians 15:58! Society! tea. 6.45 Chaise; Woburn; tea; chaise. 12 Newport [Pagnell]; within; chaise. 3 Northampton; Magazine. 4.30 Tea, religious talk. 6 Prayed. 6.30 Mark 3:35! Magazine; supper, religious talk; prayer. 9.30.

WEDNESDAY, NOVEMBER 2. 4 Prayed; Hebrews 12:5! necessary talk (religious), tea; prayer. 8.15 Chaise. 10.30 Necessary business. 11 Errata. 12.30 Dinner, religious talk; visited! journal; prayed. 5 Tea, religious talk, necessary talk (religious) to many; prayer. 6.30 1 Peter 1:18. 7.30 Society; supper, religious talk; prayer. 9.30.

THURSDAY, NOVEMBER 3. 4 Prayed; journal. 6 1 Peter 5:10! journal. 8 Tea, religious talk; journal. 9.15 Chaise. 10.15 Necessary talk (religious); journal. 1 Dinner, religious talk; read Perry! 5 Tea, religious talk; prayed. 6.30 1 Peter 4:7. 8 Supper, religious talk; prayer. 9.30.

FRIDAY, NOVEMBER 4. 3 Tea, religious talk; prayer. 4 Chaise; Fenny Stratford; tea; chaise. 9.45 Dunstable. 10.30 Chaise. 12.15 St Albans; chaise. 2.45 Barnet; dinner, religious talk. 4 Coach. 6.15 At home; letters; prayed. 8 Supper, religious talk; prayer. 9.30.

SATURDAY, NOVEMBER 5. 4 Prayed; letters. 8 Tea, religious talk; prayer; letters. 1 Dinner, religious talk; prayer; visited some; letter. 3.15 Prayed. 4 Walked; visited; tea, religious talk. 6 Read Prayers, Luke 9:55, Communion; supper, religious talk; Penry, necessary business. 9.30.

SUNDAY, NOVEMBER 6. 4 Prayed; letters. 7 Read notes. 8 The preachers. 9.15 Read Prayers, Psalms 37:37! Communion. 1 At sister Box's, dinner, religious talk; slept; the leaders; tea; buried Judith Perry; prayed, 1 Corinthians 15:55! Society; supper, necessary talk (religious); prayer. 9.30.

MONDAY, NOVEMBER 7. 4 Prayed; 1 Peter 2:11, 12! Select Society; letters. 8 Tea, religious talk; prayer; letters; necessary talk (religious). 1 Dinner, religious talk; prayer. 2 Letter; prayed. 3 Chaise. 4 Wandsworth; religious talk, tea; prayed. 6 John 4:24! class! 8 At brother Crowther's, supper, religious talk; prayer. 9.30.

TUESDAY, NOVEMBER 8. 4 Prayed; read notes. 6 1 Peter 4:7! tea, necessary talk; prayer. 7.30 Chaise. 8.30 At home; letters. 12 Chaise. 1.15 At P. Lievre's, necessary talk. 2 Dinner, necessary talk. 3 Magazine. 4 Class. 5 Tea; class. 6.30 1 Peter 1:18; class; supper; prayer. 9.30.

WEDNESDAY, NOVEMBER 9. 4 Prayed; journal; tea, mostly religious talk. 7.30 Chaise. 8.45 At home; letters. 1.15 At Miss Well's, dinner, religious talk. 3.30 Chaise; visited. 4.30 Brentford; tea; Magazine. 6.30 Mark 3:35! class. 8 At Mr Holbrook's, supper, religious talk; prayer. 9.30.

THURSDAY, NOVEMBER 10. 4 Prayed; Magazine. 6 Mark 4:25; at Mr. Holbrook's, necessary talk, tea; prayer; chaise. 10.30 Lambeth; Magazine. 1 Dinner; Magazine; prayed. 5 Tea, religious talk. 6 Magazine. 6.30 1 Corinthians 15:55! class; supper, religious talk; prayer. 9.30.

[Text noted at bottom of page:] 1 Corinthians 15:55.

FRIDAY, NOVEMBER 11. 4 Prayed; Magazine. 6 1 Peter 5:10; the children! tea, religious talk; chaise. 9 At home; letters. 11 Chaise. 12 Stratford [London]; 1 Corinthians 13:13! class. 2 Dinner; chaise. 5.45 Hadley; tea; Hebrews 12:14! class; supper; prayer. 9.30.

SATURDAY, NOVEMBER [12]. 4 Prayed; writ notes; tea, religious talk. 7 Chaise. 9 At home; letters; necessary talk (religious) to some. 1 Dinner; read notes. 3 Magazine; prayed; tea; visited. 6 Read Prayers, 2 Thessalonians 3:15! Communion; Society. 8.15 Supper; necessary business. 9.30.

SUNDAY, NOVEMBER 13. 4 Prayed; letters. 8 The preachers; Magazine. 10.30 Shoreditch; read Prayers. 12 1 Corinthians 13:1, etc. 1 Dinner; walked. 3 Chapel; the leaders; read Prayers. 4 Psalms 37:37! Society; coach; supper; prayer. 9.30.

MONDAY, NOVEMBER 14. 4 Prayed; 1 Peter 2:13-15; Select Society; class; tea; class; dinner. 2.30 Wapping; class; tea; class. 6.15 Read Prayers, Revelation 14:1, etc; coach. 8.15 Supper, necessary talk; prayer. 9.45.

TUESDAY, NOVEMBER 15. 4 Prayed; letters. 6 Class; tea; class. 1 At brother Hudson's, dinner, religious talk. 2 Class. 4.45 Tea; prayed. 6.30 1 Peter 2:16; the leaders; supper. 8 Necessary talk (religious); prayer. 9.30.

WEDNESDAY, NOVEMBER 16. 4 Prayed; letters. 6 Class; tea; class. 1 At brother Kemp's, dinner, religious talk. 1 Class. 4.45 Tea, necessary talk; prayed; letters; read; sins! 8.15 Supper, necessary talk (religious). 9 Prayer. 9.30.

THURSDAY, NOVEMBER 17. 4 Prayed; letters. 6 Class; tea; class. 1 Dinner, religious talk. 2 Class. 5 Tea; prayed. 6.30 Read Prayers, 1 Peter 2:17; the bands; supper, religious talk; prayer. 9.30.

FRIDAY, NOVEMBER 18. 4 Prayed; letters. 6 Class; tea; class. 1 At brother Park's, dinner, religious talk. 2 Class. 4.30 Tea; necessary business; slept. 6 The Committee. 7.30 Prayed; religious talk. 8 Supper. 8.30 1 Peter 2:17(2)! 9.45.

SATURDAY, NOVEMBER 19. 4 Prayed; letters. 7 Class; tea; class. 1 Dinner, at brother Collinson's, necessary talk (religious). 2 Class; prayed. 4.30 Tea, religious talk; prayed. 6 Read Prayers, 2 Timothy 2:19! class; Society. 8 Supper, necessary talk (religious); necessary business. 9.30.

SUNDAY, NOVEMBER 20. 4 Prayed; letters. 8 Spitalfields. 9.30 Read Prayers, Jeremiah 23:6, Communion; dinner, religious talk. 2.30 Bethnal Green; read Prayers, 2 Timothy 3:5! tea; prayed. 5 Read Prayers, 2 Timothy 3:4; Society; necessary business. 8 Supper, religious talk; prayer. 9.30.

MONDAY, NOVEMBER 21. 4 Prayed; 1 Peter 2:17(2); Select Society. 7 Class; tea; class. 12 Select Society. 1 Dinner, religious talk. 2 Class. 5 Tea, religious talk; prayed. 6.30 Read Prayers, 2 Timothy 3:4! supper. 8.15 The bands. 9.30.

TUESDAY, NOVEMBER 22. 4 Prayed; 1 Peter 2:17(2); class; tea; class. 1 Dinner, religious talk. 2 Class. 4.30 Visited; class; tea. 6.30 2 Peter 2:9! supper; prayer. 9.30.

WEDNESDAY, NOVEMBER 23. 4 Prayed; letters; class; tea; class. 1 Dinner, religious talk; class; coach. 4.30 Necessary business. 5 Tea; prayed. 6 The committee! letter; supper; necessary business; prayer. 9.30.

THURSDAY, NOVEMBER 24. 3 Necessary business. 4 Coach. 6 Necessary talk (religious). 7.15 Tea; coach; necessary talk (religious)! 3.15 Winchester; dinner. 4 Necesssary business; prayed; tea. 6 1 Corinthians 1:24; Society; writ notes; supper; prayer. 9.30.

FRIDAY, NOVEMBER 25. 4 Prayed; letters. 8 Tea; letters. 12 Hebrews 4:14; letters. 2 At Mr Blackwell's. 2 Dinner, necessary talk (religious). 3 Letters; brother Winscom, etc, necessary talk! tea. 6 Isaiah 55:6, 7! writ notes. 8 Supper, religious talk; prayer; necessary talk (religious). 10.30 Coach.

SATURDAY, NOVEMBER 26. 4 Slept. 9 At home, tea, religious talk, letters. 1.15 Dinner; prayer. 2 Slept; letters. 5 Tea, religious talk; prayed. 6.30 Letters; supper; Penry, necessary talk (religious), necessary business. 9.30.

SUNDAY, NOVEMBER 27. 4 Prayed; letters; the preachers; read Prayers, Romans 13:12, 13; St Luke's, Romans 13:11, etc! at brother Sturly's; dinner, religious talk. 2 Slept; letter; the leaders. 4 Tea; prayed. 5 Read Prayers, Hebrews 3:7; Society; necessary business; supper; prayer. 9.30.

MONDAY, NOVEMBER 28. 4 Prayed; tea, necessary talk (religious). 5.30 Diligence; necessary talk (religious); Magazine. 10.45 Rochester; tea, religious talk; prayer. 11.45 Diligence; Magazine. 4.15 Canterbury; at brother Hagel's, dinner, religious talk. 5 Necessary business; prayed; tea; prayer. 6.30 Revelation 7:9, etc! Society! supper; prayer. 9.30.

TUESDAY, NOVEMBER 29. 4 Prayed; letters. 7 Hebrews 12:5. 8 Tea, religious talk; prayer. 9.30 Chaise. 12.30 Dover; read notes. 1 Dinner, religious talk. 2 Magazine. 4 Prayed. 5 Tea, religious talk. 6 John 4:24! 7 Society! supper, religious talk; prayer. 9.30.

WEDNESDAY, NOVEMBER 30. 4 Prayed; Magazine. 6 Galatians 5:5! tea, religious talk; prayer. 8 Chaise. 10.45 Sandwich. 11 Chaise. 1 Margate; dinner; Magazine. 4.30 Tea; prayed. 6.30 Mark 3:35! 7.30 Magazine; supper, religious talk; prayer. 9.30.

[Texts noted at bottom of page:] Revelation 7:3–5; Psalms 126:6; 1 Peter 2:21.

THURSDAY, DECEMBER 1. 4 Prayed; Magazine. 8 Tea, religious talk. 8.30 Revelation 20:12! chaise. 1.30 Canterbury; at brother Callard's, dinner, religious talk; prayer. 3 Magazine; prayed; tea, religious talk; prayer. 6 Ephesians 5:14(2)! 7 Communion; supper; religious talk; prayer. 10.

FRIDAY, DECEMBER 2. 4 Prayed; tea. 5 Coach; Rochester; tea; coach. 4 At home; dinner; prayed; tea; letters. 8 Supper. 9 Religious talk; prayer. 9.30.

SATURDAY, DECEMBER 3. 4 Prayed; letters. 8 Tea; prayer; necessary business; letters. 1.15 Dinner, religious talk; prayer; necessary business. 2.30 Visited many; tea; prayed. 6 Read Prayers, Hebrews 9:7! Communion; supper; Penry, necessary business. 9.30.

SUNDAY, DECEMBER 4. 4 Prayed; letter. 8 The preachers. 9.30 Read Prayers, Romans 15:6, Communion; at brother Teulon's. 1 Dinner, necessary talk (religious). 2.15 Slept; prayed; the leaders; tea; prayed. 5 Read Prayers, Hebrews 10:36! 6 Society; Love-feast; supper, religious talk; prayer. 9.30.

MONDAY, DECEMBER 5. 4 Prayed; 1 Peter 2:17(4); Select Society; tea; writ notes; visited many. 12 Select Society. 1 At brother Snall's, dinner, religious talk; prayer; visited many. 5 Tea, religious talk. 6.30 Read Prayers, Hebrews 11:1! supper; the bands; prayer. 9.30.

TUESDAY, DECEMBER 6. 4 Prayed; 1 Peter 2:17(4); letters. 8 Tea, religious talk; prayer; visited many. 11 Letters. 1.30 Visited. 2 Dinner, religious talk; prayer; visited. 4.30 Letters; necessary talk (religious), tea; prayer; prayed; writ notes. 6.30 Read Prayers, Hebrews 12:28; the leaders; supper, necessary talk (religious); prayer. 9.30.

WEDNESDAY, DECEMBER 7. 4 Prayed; letters; tea; prayer. 8.15 Visited many. 11.30 Letters. 12 Visited many. 2.30 At W. Wright's, dinner, religious talk; prayed. 5 Tea, religious talk. 6 Read Prayers, Hebrews 13:22! 7 Communion; chaise. 8 Supper, necessary talk (religious); prayer. 9.30.

THURSDAY, DECEMBER 8. 4 Prayed; letters. 7.30 Walked; at sister Cheesement's, tea, religious talk; prayer; walked. 9.30 [Stoke] Newington. 10 Letters; Magazine. 1.30 Dinner, religious talk; Magazine; prayed. 5.30 Tea, religious talk; prayed; Magazine. 8.30 Supper; prayer. 9.30.

FRIDAY, DECEMBER 9. 4 Prayed; journal. 9.30 Accounts. 11 Read notes. 2 Dinner, religious talk; prayer. 4.30 Prayed; tea, necessary talk (religious). 7 1 Peter 1:18; supper, necessary talk (religious); prayer. 9.30.

SATURDAY, DECEMBER 10. 4 Prayed; letters; read notes. 8 Tea, religious talk; prayer; walked; visited. 10.30 Letters; necessary business. 1 At brother Thornton's, dinner; letters. 4.15 Prayed; tea; visited. 6.30 Read Prayers, Philippians 2:13! Communion; supper; Penry, necessary business. 9.30.

SUNDAY, DECEMBER 11. 4 Prayed; letters; Chapel. 9.30 Read Prayers, Psalms 126:6! Communion; dinner; slept; prayed; the leaders; read Prayers; James 3:17! tea. 5 Society; coach; Society; writ notes; supper, religious talk; prayer. 9.30.

[Texts noted at bottom of page of page:] Hebrews 9:8; Psalms 126:6.

MONDAY, DECEMBER 12. 4 Prayed; 1 Peter 2:21! Select Society; necessary talk (religious); tea; prayer. 8.30 Begged. 12 Select Society; dinner; walked. 3 Visited; tea. 5.30 Prayed. 6.30 Read Prayers, James 5:10, etc; supper; the bands. 9.30.

TUESDAY, DECEMBER 13. 4 Prayed; 1 Peter 2:21; tea; walked; letters. 1.15 Dinner, religious talk; prayer; visited some. 4 Letter; prayed. 5 Tea, religious talk. 6 Read notes. 6.30 Read Prayers, 1 Peter 2:21; the leaders; supper, religious talk; prayer. 9.30.

WEDNESDAY, DECEMBER 14. 4 Prayed; letters. 8 Tea, religious talk; prayer; begged. 11 At home; letters; visited. 2.30 At Mr. Wo[lff]'s, dinner, religious talk. 4 Prayed. 5 Tea, religious talk. 6 Read Prayers, 1 Peter 2:24, etc! Communion. 8 Supper, religious talk. 9 Prayer. 9.30.

THURSDAY, DECEMBER 15. 4 Prayed; letters; tea; prayer. 9 Begged. 11.30 Letters. 1 Chaise; Shacklewell; Magazine. 2 Dinner, religious talk. 4 Prayed. 5 Tea, religious talk. 6.30 Hebrews 9:27! Magazine. 8 Supper, religious talk. 9.30 Prayer. 10.

FRIDAY, DECEMBER 16. 4.30 Prayed; Magazine. 7 Tea, religious talk; prayer. 8 Coach. 9 Prayer. 11 Letters. 1 Prayer; Communion; dinner. 3 Letters. 4 Visited; tea; Chapel; letters; supper; 1 Peter 2:25! coffee; prayer. 12.30.

SATURDAY, DECEMBER 17. 6 Prayed; tea; walked. 8 Necessary business; letters. 1 At sister Shakespeare's, dinner, religious talk; Magazine. 3.30 Prayed. 4 Tea, religious talk; walked; tea, religious talk; prayer. 6 Read Prayers, 2 Corinthians 6:2! Communion; supper. 8.15 Penry, necessary business. 9.30.

SUNDAY, DECEMBER 18. 4 Prayed; errata; Spitalfields. 9.30 Isaiah 30:18! Communion; visited. 1 Dinner, religious talk; prayer. 2 Slept; prayed. 3 St Swithin's, read Prayers, Matthew 7:24; tea. 5 Read Prayers, 2 Peter 1:5, etc; Society; Magazine; supper; prayer. 9.30.

MONDAY, DECEMBER [19]. 4 Prayed; 1 Peter 3:1-8; Select Society; tea; errata. 10 Visited. 12 Select Society; coach. 1 At brother Caddic's, dinner, religious talk; prayer. 3.30 Chapel; errata; tea, religious talk; prayer; errata. 6 Prayed; read Prayers, 2 Peter 2:9! supper; the bands; errata. 9.30.

TUESDAY, DECEMBER 20. 4 Prayed; 1 Peter 3:7, 8; errata; walked. 8 Visited; errata; dinner, religious talk; prayer. 4 Prayed. 4.30 Tea, religious talk; prayed. 6.30 Read Prayers, 2 Peter 3:6, etc! the leaders. 8 Supper, religious talk; prayer. 9.30.

WEDNESDAY, DECEMBER 21. 4 Dressed; slept; errata. 7.30 Walked; Highbury Place; tea, religious talk; letters; errata. 2 Dinner, religious talk; errata. 5 Prayed; errata. 8.15 Supper, religious talk; prayer. 9.45.

[Texts noted at bottom of page:] Deuteronomy 5:7; 1 John 4:19! 1 Corinthians 1:18; Luke 2:14.

THURSDAY, DECEMBER 22. 4 Prayed; errata. 8 Tea, religious talk; prayer; walked; errata. 12 Coach; Highgate. 1 Dinner, religious talk; errata. 4.30 Prayed; tea, religious talk. 6 2 Corinthians 6:1. 7.30 Errata; supper, religious talk; prayer. 10.

FRIDAY, DECEMBER 23. 4.45 Prayed; errata. 7 Tea, religious talk. 8 Deuteronomy 5:7! prayer; religious talk. 10 Coach. 11 Letters; errata. 2 Coach; at sister Cheesement's, religious talk, dinner; prayer. 4 Walked; at home. 5 Tea, religious talk; prayed; errata. 8 Supper, religious talk; prayer. 9.30.

SATURDAY, DECEMBER 24. 4 Prayed; letters. 8 Tea; letters. 1.15 Dinner, religious talk; prayer; visited some. 4.30 Tea, religious talk; prayer. 6 Read Prayers, 1 John 4:19! supper; religious talk; Penry! Mrs Wraxal! necessary business. 9.30.

CHRISTMAS DAY [SUNDAY, DECEMBER 25]. 3.30 Dressed; prayer, 1 Corinthians 1:18; tea; writ notes. 8 Chapel. 9.30 Read Prayers; Luke 2:14; Communion. 1 At sister Keysall's, dinner, religious talk; prayer. 3 Slept; the leaders; tea; prayed; Luke 2:14! the Love-feast; supper, religious talk; prayer. 9.30.

MONDAY, DECEMBER 26. 4 Prayed; 1 Peter 3:8, etc; Select Society; errata. 8 Tea; visited some. 10 Chapel; read Prayers, Acts 7:55, etc! Communion. 1 Dinner, religious talk; prayer; errata. 4 Prayed; at sister Blu——d's. 5 Tea, religious talk; prayer. 6.30 Read Prayers, Daniel 5:7! supper; christened! the bands! 9.30.

TUESDAY, DECEMBER 27. 4 Prayed; 1 Peter 3:6, etc; errata; walked; errata. 10 Read Prayers, John 21:22, Communion. 1 At brother Barr's, dinner, religious talk; prayer. 3.30 Errata; prayed. 4.30 At Thomas Rankin's. 5 Tea, religious talk; prayer. 6 Read Prayers, Ecclesiastes 6:12; the leaders. 8 Supper, religious talk; prayer. 9.30.

WEDNESDAY, DECEMBER 28. 4 Prayed; errata. 8 Tea, necessary talk (religious); prayer; read notes. 1.30 At Mrs Tighe's. 2 Dinner, religious talk. 3.30 Prayed; tea. 5 Coach. 6 Read Prayers, 1 John 5:3, Communion; supper, religious talk; prayer. 9.30.

THURSDAY, DECEMBER 29. 4 Prayed; 1 Peter 3:14, etc, Communion; letters. 8 Tea, religious talk; prayer; errata. 1.15 At Thomas Olivers's, necessary talk (religious). 3 Errata; prayed. 4.30 At Thomas Rankin's, tea, religious talk; prayer; prayed. 6.30 Read Prayers, Hebrews 8:10! 7.30 The bands; supper, necessary talk (religious); prayer. 9.30.

FRIDAY, DECEMBER 30. 4 Prayed; letters; errata. 12 The females. 1 Prayer. 2 Visited some. 2.30 Dinner. 3 Religious talk, prayer; visited. 4 Prayed; tea, religious talk; prayer. 6 Prayed. 7 Errata; supper; prayer. 9.30.

SATURDAY, DECEMBER 31. 4 Prayed; letters; tea; prayer. 8.15 Magazine. 1 Dinner, religious talk; visited. 2.30 Errata; prayed. 4 Walked; tea, religious talk.

5.30 Prayed. 6 Read Prayers, Jude 21, Communion; supper; Penry, necessary business. 9.30.

[Texts noted at bottom of page:] 1 Corinthians 1:18; Jude 21.

SUNDAY, JANUARY 1, 1786. 4 Prayed; errata. 8 The preachers. 9.30 Read Prayers, Deuteronomy 5:7! Communion. 1 At brother Hammond's, dinner, religious talk. 2.15 Slept; prayed. 3 The Covenant. 6 Prayed; errata. 8 Supper, religious talk; prayer. 9.30.

MONDAY, JANUARY 2. 4 Prayed; 1 Peter 2:21! Select Society; tea; errata. 11 Walked; errata. 12 Select Society. 1.30 At sister Dixon's, dinner, religious talk; prayer; errata; visited! 5.45 Prayed. 6.30 Read Prayers, Romans 1:16; supper; the bands. 9.30.

TUESDAY, JANUARY 3. 4 Prayed; 1 Peter 2:21; errata. 8 Tea, religious talk; prayer; errata. 1.30 Dinner. 3 Visited; walked. 4 Hackney; religious talk; prayer! coach. 5 Tea, religious talk; prayer. 6 Prayed. 6.30 Read Prayers, Romans 2:29; the leaders; supper, religious talk; prayer. 9.30.

WEDNESDAY, JANUARY 4. 4 Prayed; letters; tea; prayer. 8 Errata. 12 Visited. 1 Dinner, religious talk; prayer. 3 Errata; prayed; tea, religious talk; prayer. 5 Errata. 6 Mr Wolff, etc! 8 Supper, religious talk; prayer. 9.30.

THURSDAY, JANUARY 5. 4 Prayed; letters; errata. 7.30 Tea; prayer; errata. 10 Necessary business. 12.30 Visited. 1.30 Dinner, religious talk. 2 Prayer. 2.30 Visited. 3 Errata; tea; prayed. 6.30 Read Prayers, Romans 4:9! the bands. 8 Supper; prayer. 9.30.

FRIDAY, JANUARY 6. 4 Prayed; writ journal. 2.45 Dinner, religious talk; prayer. 4 Prayed; tea; writ notes. 6.30 Audit. 8 Supper, necessary talk (religious); prayer. 9.30.

SATURDAY, JANUARY 7. 4 Prayed; letters; tea; prayer. 8 Letters; journal. 1.30 At brother Da——'s, dinner, religious talk; journal; prayed. 5 At brother Thomas's, tea, religious talk; prayer; prayed. 6 Read Prayers, Romans 6:23! Communion. 7.30 Visited; supper; Penry, necessary business. 9.30.

SUNDAY, JANUARY 8. 4 Prayed; journal; Chapel; prayed. 9.30 Read Prayers, Romans 12:2, Communion. 1 Dinner. 2.15 Slept; prayed. 3 The leaders; read Prayers, Romans 12:21; Society; coach; Society. 7 Married persons. 8.15 Supper, religious talk; prayer. 9.30.

MONDAY, JANUARY 9. 4 Prayed; 1 Peter 3 *ad fin;* Select Society; tea; prayer; journal. 11 Coach; Stratford [London]; read journal. 2 Dinner. 3 Journal; prayed. 5 Tea, religious talk; prayed; journal. 8 Supper, religious talk; prayer. 9.30.

TUESDAY, JANUARY 10. 4 Prayed; journal. 8 Prayer; tea, religious talk; journal. 2 Dinner, religious talk; journal. 4 Prayed. 5 Tea, religious talk. 6 Journal. 8.15 Supper, religious talk; prayer. 9.30.

WEDNESDAY, JANUARY 11. 4 Prayed; journal. 8 Prayer; tea, religious talk; journal. 2 Dinner, religious talk; journal; prayed. 5.30 Tea, religious talk. 6.30 John 17:3! journal. 8.30 Supper, religious talk; prayer. 9.45.

THURSDAY, JANUARY 12. 4 Prayed; journal. 8.30 Prayer; tea, religious talk; journal. 1.15 Mostly religious talk. 2 Dinner, religious talk. 3 Journal; prayed. 4.45 Tea, religious talk; prayer; journal. 8.30 Supper, religious talk; prayer. 9.30.

FRIDAY, JANUARY 13. 4 Prayed; journal. 8 Prayer; tea, religious talk; journal. 12.30 Coach. 1.30 Visited; necessary business. 2.30 Dinner, religious talk; prayer. 5 Prayed; the preachers; tea, religious talk; writ notes. 8 Supper. 8.30 Prayer; Mark 9:23! coffee; prayer. 12.30.

SATURDAY, JANUARY 14. 6.30 Prayed; letters. 8 Tea, religious talk; prayer; letters. 1 Dinner, religious talk. 2.30 Letters. 1.30 Dinner, religious talk; prayer. 3 Letters. 5 Tea, religious talk; prayer; prayed; letters. 7.45 Supper; Penry, necessary business. 9.30.

SUNDAY, JANUARY 15. 4 Prayed; letters; Spitalfields. 9.30 Read Prayers, Matthew 13:3, etc! Communion; at Mr [blank], dinner; meditation. 3 St George's, read Prayers, Romans 13:10! tea. 5.30 At home; prayed; letters. 6.30 Society; supper, religious talk; prayer. 9.30.

MONDAY, JANUARY 16. 4 Prayed; 1 Peter 4:1-6; Select Society; tea; prayer; letters. 11 Walked; Select Society; dinner, religious talk. 2 Visited many. 5 Tea, religious talk; prayer. 6.30 Read Prayers, Romans 14:17! supper; the bands. 9.30.

TUESDAY, JANUARY 17. 4 Prayed; 1 Peter 4:1, 2! writ journal. 8 Tea, religious talk; prayer; walked. 9.30 Letters; journal. 1 Dinner, religious talk. 2.30 Journal; prayed. 4.30 Tea, religious talk; prayer. 6.30 James 2:22! the leaders. 8 Supper, religious talk; prayer. 9.30.

WEDNESDAY, JANUARY 18. 4 Prayed; journal. 7.30 Tea, religious talk; prayer; letters; journal. 1 Dinner, religious talk; prayer. 2.30 Walked. 3.30 [Stoke] Newington. 4 Journal. 5 Tea, religious talk; prayed; journal. 8 Supper, religious talk; prayer. 9.30.

THURSDAY, JANUARY 19. 4 Prayed; journal. 8 Tea, religious talk; prayer. 9 Journal. 1.30 Dinner, necessary talk (religious). 2.30 Journal; prayed. 5 Tea, religious talk; prayed. 6 Journal. 8 Supper, religious talk; prayer. 9.30.

FRIDAY, JANUARY 20. 4 Prayed; journal. 8 Tea, religious talk; prayer. 9 Journal. 1.30 Mr Rutt——, dinner, religious talk. 2.30 Writ notes. 4 Prayed. 5 Tea, religious talk; writ notes. 7 Hebrews 11:1(1)! writ notes. 8 Supper, religious talk; prayer. 9.30.

SATURDAY, JANUARY 21. 4 Prayed; read journal. 7.30 Tea, religious talk; prayer. 8.15 Coach. 9 At home; necessary business; writ letters. 1 At Thomas

Rankin's, dinner, religious talk; prayer. 2 Letters. 3 Prayed. 4.30 Walked; tea. 6 Read Prayers, 1 Corinthians 3:9. 7 Supper, religious talk; Penry, necessary business. 9.30.

[Text noted at bottom of page:] 1 Corinthians 10:31.

SUNDAY, JANUARY 22. 4 Prayed; letters; Chapel. 9.30 Read Prayers, Isaiah 55:6! Communion; dinner, religious talk; prayer; slept. 3 The leaders; read Prayers, 1 Corinthians 4:2! Society; coach; Society; writ notes; supper, religious talk; prayer. 9.30.

MONDAY, JANUARY 23. 4 Prayed; 1 Peter 4:8; Select Society; tea; writ sermon. 12 Select Society; at sister Dixon's, dinner, religious talk; prayer. 2.30 Sermon; prayed; tea, religious talk; prayer. 6.30 Read Prayers, 1 Corinthians 5:9; supper; the bands. 9.30.

TUESDAY, JANUARY 24. 4 Prayed; 1 Peter 4:8! sermon; tea; sermon. 12.30 House of Lords. 3.30 At Mr. Griffith's, dinner, religious talk; coach. 6 Tea; prayed. 6.30 Read Prayers, 1 Corinthians 6:20(2)! the leaders. 8 Supper, religious talk; prayer. 9.30.

WEDNESDAY, JANUARY 25. 4 Prayed; sermon. 7.30 Tea, religious talk; prayer; sermon. 2.15 At brother Wright's, dinner, religious talk; read notes. 5 At brother Garrett's, tea, religious talk; prayer. 6 Read Prayers, Acts 26:28! Society, Communion. 8 Supper, religious talk; prayer. 9.45.

THURSDAY, JANUARY 26. 4 Prayed; letters; tea, religious talk; prayer; letters; necessary business. 11 Coach. 12.30 Peckham; journal. 2 Dinner. 3 Journal; prayed. 5 Tea, religious talk; journal. 7 Deuteronomy 5:7! journal. 8.45 Supper. 9 Writ; prayer. 10.15.

FRIDAY, JANUARY 27. 4.30 Prayed; journal. 8 Tea, religious talk; prayer; journal; accounts. 1.30 Dinner, religious talk. 3 Writ notes. 5 Prayed; tea, religious talk. 6 Read notes. 8.30 Supper, necessary talk (religious); prayer. 10.30.

SATURDAY, JANUARY 28. 4.45 Prayed; read notes. 8 Tea, religious talk; prayer. 9 Read notes; letters. 12 Accounts. 2 Dinner, religious talk. 3 Writ notes; religious talk. 4.30 Coach; at sister Asker's, tea, religious talk. 6 Read Prayers, 1 Corinthians 9:16, etc, Communion; coach; supper, necessary talk (religious); Penry, necessary business; religious talk. 10.

SUNDAY, JANUARY 29. 4 Prayed; letters; writ notes. 8 The preachers. 9.30 Read Prayers, Isaiah 57:16, etc, Communion; at brother Dewey's, dinner, religious talk. 2 Slept; prayed; tea, religious talk. 5 Read Prayers, 1 Corinthians 10:31! Society; Love-feast! supper, necessary talk (religious). 9.30.

MONDAY, JANUARY 30. 4 Prayed; 1 Peter 4:12; Select Society; class; tea; class. 1 Dinner. 2 Class; tea; class. 6 Read Prayers, Mark 4:26; class. 8 Necessary talk (religious); supper; prayer. 9.45.

TUESDAY, JANUARY 31. 4 Prayed; letter; class. 8 Tea, necessary talk; class. 1 Dinner, religious talk; prayer. 2 Class. 3 Death of Joseph Lee. 4.30 Tea, religious talk; prayer; necessary business; prayed. 6.30 Read Prayers, 1 Peter 4:7! the leaders; supper; prayer. 9.30.

WEDNESDAY, FEBRUARY 1. 4 Prayed; letters. 6 Class; tea. 8 Class. 1 At brother Kemp's, dinner, religious talk. 2 Class; tea, necessary talk (religious). 5.30 Necessary business; prayed. 6 My committee, necessary talk. 8.30 Supper. 9 Prayer. 9.30.

THURSDAY, FEBRUARY 2. 4 Prayed; letter. 6 Class; tea; class. 1 At sister Westry's, dinner, religious talk. 2 Class; prayed; tea. 6 Prayed. 6.30 1 Peter 4:11! the bands; supper, religious talk; prayer. 9.30.

FRIDAY, FEBRUARY 3. 4 Prayed; class; tea; class. 11.30 Visited; class. 1 Dinner, religious talk. 2 Class. 4.30 Tea, religious talk. 5.30 Prayed. 6 Yearly Meeting. 8 Supper. 8.30 Necessary talk (religious); prayer. 9.30.

SATURDAY, FEBRUARY 4. 4 Prayed; writ notes. 7 Class. 8 Tea; class; writ notes. 11 Class; writ letters. 1 Dinner; writ. 2 Class; writ notes; visited. 5 Tea, religious talk; prayed. 6 Read Prayers, 1 Corinthians 16:13. 7 Society; class. 8.15 Supper, religious talk; necessary business. 9.30.

SUNDAY, FEBRUARY 5. 4 Prayed; writ notes. 8 The preachers. 9.30 Read Prayers, Isaiah 59:1, 2! Communion. 1 Dinner. 2 Visited; slept; prayed; tea, religious talk. 5 Read Prayers, Isaiah 64:1, 2, Society; single women; supper; lay down; sins! 9.45.

MONDAY, FEBRUARY 6. 4 Prayed; 1 Peter 4:17; Select Society. 7 Class. 8 Tea, religious talk; class. 12 Select Society; dinner. 2.30 Class. 5 Tea, religious talk; prayer; necessary talk (religious); prayed. 6.30 Read Prayers, Isaiah 59:1, 2; supper; the bands; the leaders! 10.

TUESDAY, FEBRUARY 7. 4 Prayed; 1 Peter 4:18; class; tea. 8 Class. 1 At brother Bower's, dinner. 2 Class. 5 Tea, religious talk; class. 6.30 1 Corinthians 10:13! class. 8 Chapel; supper; prayer. 9.15.

WEDNESDAY, FEBRUARY 8. 4 Prayed; letters; class; tea; class. 1 Dinner, religious talk; visited. 3.30 Chaise; read Dr Stuart. 5 Tea; prayed. 6.30 Matthew 7:26! Class. 8 Supper, religious talk; prayer. 9.30.

THURSDAY, FEBRUARY 9. 4 Prayed; letters. 6 1 Peter 4:18! tea; letters. 8.15 Coach. 10 Lambeth; letters. 1.30 Dinner, religious talk; letters. 5 Tea; prayed. 6.30 1 Peter 4:18; class. 8 Supper, religious talk; prayer. 9.30.

FRIDAY, FEBRUARY 10. 4 Prayed; writ Society. 6 ['1 Peter' deleted]; the children. 8 At Mr [blank]; walked; tea. 9.30 Sat; coach. 11 Necessary business; walked; coach. 12 Bow; Acts 16:31! 2 Class; dinner; coach; necessary business. 3 Coach. 6 Barnet; tea; 2 Corinthians 5:18. 7 Class; read Hall. 8 Supper, religious talk; prayer. 9.30.

SATURDAY, FEBRUARY 11. 4 Prayed; Hall! 6 Tea, necessary talk (religious). 6.45 Chaise. 8.30 At home; writ Society. 1 Dinner, religious talk. 2 Writ Society. 4 Christened R. Cheesement; Society; tea; prayed. 6 Society; supper, religious talk; Penry, necessary business. 9.30.

SUNDAY, FEBRUARY 12. 4 Prayed; letters. 8 The Chapel. 9.30 Read Prayers, Proverbs 22:6, Communion. 1 Dinner, religious talk. 2.15 Slept; prayed; the leaders. 3.30 Read Prayers, Proverbs 22:6! Society. 6 Chaise; Society; writ letter; supper, mostly religious talk; prayer. 9.30.

MONDAY, FEBRUARY 13. 4 Prayed; 1 Peter 4 *ult;* Select Society; tea; visited; writ Society. 10.30 Chaise. 11 With sister Wright. 12 Mitcham; +Isaiah 66:8; class! 2 Dinner; walked; Wandsworth; Society; tea; Revelation 20:12; chaise; at home; supper; prayer. 9.45.

TUESDAY, FEBRUARY 14. 4 Prayed; writ Society. 8 Tea; prayer; Society. 11 Walked; coach. 12.30 At sister Philip's; read Society. 2 Dinner, religious talk; Society; prayed; class; tea; class. 6.30 1 Corinthians 10:31! supper, religious talk; prayer. 9.30.

WEDNESDAY, FEBRUARY 15. 4 Prayed; writ Society. 8 Tea; prayer; Society. 1 Dinner, necessary talk (religious). 2 Writ Society. 4 Necessary talk (religious), tea. 6 Prayed; Society. 8 Supper, religious talk; prayer. 9.30.

THURSDAY, FEBRUARY 16. 4 Prayed; Society. 6 Tea; prayer. 6.30 Walked. 8 Tea, religious talk; coach! 1 Dorking; dinner, religious talk. 2 Writ Society. 5 Prayed; tea, religious talk. 6 Romans 1:16, Communion; class. 8 Supper, religious talk; prayer. 9.30.

FRIDAY, FEBRUARY 17. 4 Prayed; Society. 6 1 Corinthians 6:20; Society; tea, religious talk; prayer. 8 Coach. 1.30 At home; Society; walked. 3 At Sir Philip Gibbes's, mostly religious talk. 4 Dinner. 5.30 Walked; my Committee; letters; prayed; supper, religious talk; prayer. 9.30.

SATURDAY, FEBRUARY 18. 4 Prayed; writ Society. 8 Tea, religious talk; prayer; Society. 1.30 At Dr Whitehead's, dinner, religious talk. 3 Visited E. Brig, necessary talk (religious). 4 Prayed; walked; tea. 6 Read Prayers, Matthew 18:7, Communion; John Okey, etc! supper; Penry, necessary business. 9.30.

SUNDAY, FEBRUARY 19. 4 Prayed; letters; Spitalfields. 9.30 Read Prayers, Luke 8:18! Communion; at Edward Collinson's, dinner, religious talk. 3 St John's, Horsleydown; read Prayers, Revelation 20:12! 5 Coach; tea; read Prayers, Galatians 3:20; Society. 7 The single men; supper; prayer. 9.30.

[Text noted at bottom of page:] Luke 8:18.

MONDAY, FEBRUARY 20. 4 Prayed; Matthew 18:7; Select Society; letters; tea; letters. 12 Select Society. 1.30 Dinner, religious talk; prayer. 3 Letter. 3.30 Visited some! tea, religious talk; prayer. 6.30 Read Prayers, Galatians 3:22; supper; the bands. 9 Necessary business. 9.30.

TUESDAY, FEBRUARY 21. 4 Prayed; Matthew 18:7; necessary talk (religious); letters. 8 Tea, religious talk; prayer. 9.30 Writ letters. 2 Dinner, religious talk; prayer; chaise. 4 Letters; tea, religious talk; prayed. 6.30 Read Prayers, Isaiah 58:13, 14; the leaders; letters; supper; prayer. 9.30.

WEDNESDAY, FEBRUARY 22. 4 Prayed; letters; tea; letters. 11.30 Chaise. 12.30 Hornsey [London]; necessary talk (religious). 1.30 Dinner, religious talk. 2.30 Prayer; chaise. 4.30 At John Fenwick's, tea, religious talk. 6 Read Prayers, Galatians 5:5, Communion. 8 Supper; prayer. 9.30.

THURSDAY, FEBRUARY 23. 4 Prayed; letters; tea. 8.30 Coach. 3.30 Chatham; dinner, necessary business, necessary talk (religious). 5 Tea, religious talk; prayed. 6.30 Deuteronomy 5:7! Communion. 8 Supper, religious talk; prayer. 9.30.

FRIDAY, FEBRUARY 24. 4 Prayed; Luke 8:18! tea, religious talk. 6.30 Coach; Shakespeare! 12 At home; letters. 3 Dinner; visited. 5 Letter; tea; prayed; necessary talk (religious)! 8 Supper, religious talk; prayer. 9.30.

SATURDAY, FEBRUARY 25. 4 Prayed; letters. 8 Tea, religious talk; prayer; letters. 1 Charles, etc, dinner, religious talk; writ letters. 4.30 Visited! 5 Tea, religious talk; prayer. 6 Read Prayers, Ephesians 2:8! Communion; supper; Penry, necessary business. 9.30.

SUNDAY, FEBRUARY 26. 4 Prayed; letters; the preachers. 9.30 Read Prayers, 1 Corinthians 13:13! Communion. 1 Dinner, religious talk; prayer. 2.45 Chapel; read Prayers, Ephesians 2:8! 4 Chaise. 5.15 Brentford; tea; prayed. 6 Deuteronomy 5:7! Society; at Mr Holbrook's, supper, religious talk; prayer. 9.30.

MONDAY, FEBRUARY 27. 4 Prayed; choc[olate]. 5 Chaise. 7.30 The Windmill [inn in Salt Hill]; tea, necessary talk (religious). 8.30 Chaise. 9 Read Guthrie. 11.30 Reading, the Crown; dinner, necessary talk (religious). 12.30 Chaise; Guthrie. 3.30 Newbury; at brother Collin's. 4 Prayed; tea, religious talk. 6.30 Romans 1:16! Society; supper; prayer. 9.30. Could not sleep.

TUESDAY, FEBRUARY 28. 4 Prayed; tea, religious talk. 5 Chaise. 7 Hungerford; tea, religious talk. 7.45 Chaise; read Mr Buchan. 11.30 Dinner; walked; chaise. 5 Bath; at brother Webster's, tea, necessary talk (religious); prayed. 6.30 Deuteronomy 5:7! supper, necessary talk (religious); prayer. 9.30.

WEDNESDAY, MARCH 1. 4 Prayed; writ sermon. 8 Tea, religious talk; prayer; sermon; chaise. 12.30 Trowbridge; Hebrews 7:25! 1.30 Dinner, religious talk; prayer. 2.45 Chaise. 5 Bath; tea, religious talk; prayed; sermon. 6.30 Luke 8:18; Society; supper, religious talk; prayer. 9.45.

THURSDAY, MARCH 2. 4 Prayed; sermon. 6 1 John 3:8; sermon. 8 Visited; tea, religious talk; prayer. 9 Chaise; visited! 11.30 Bristol; necessary business. 1 At Miss Johnson's, dinner, religious talk. 2.30 Sermon. 5 Tea, religious talk; prayed. 6.30 1 Corinthians 15:55; the bands; at sister Johnson's, supper; prayer. 9.30.

FRIDAY, MARCH 3. 4 Prayed; sermon; tea; letters. 11 The females; visited! 2 Dinner, religious talk; prayer. 3.30 Writ notes; prayed; tea, religious talk; prayed. 5.30 Chaise; at the School; necessary talk (religious). 6.30 Letters. 8 Supper, religious talk; prayer. 9.30.

SATURDAY, MARCH 4. 4 Prayed; read. 6 The children, necessary talk (religious); chaise. 8 At Miss Morgan's, tea, religious talk; prayer. 9 Letters. 2 At Mr Durbin's, dinner, religious talk; prayer. 4 Prayed; tea, religious talk. 6 Guinea Street, Job 22:21! Penry; at Mr Castleman's, supper, religious talk; prayer. 9.30.

SUNDAY, MARCH 5. 4 Prayed; journal; tea; prayed. 9.30 Read Prayers, 2 Corinthians 6:2(4)! Communion. 1 Dinner, religious talk; prayed. 3 Read Prayers. 3.30 Philippians 4:9! tea; prayed. 5 Genesis 22:1, 2; Society; the singers. 8 Supper, religious talk; prayer. 9.30.

MONDAY, MARCH 6. 4 Prayed; 1 Peter 2:20, etc; letter. 7 Class; tea; class. 1 At sister Stafford's, dinner, religious talk. 2 Class. 4.30 Prayed; tea, religious talk; prayer; writ notes; prayed. 7 1 Peter 2:25, 26 [sic]; at Miss Johnson's. 8 Supper, religious talk; prayer. 9.30.

[Pointing hand] TUESDAY, MARCH 7. 4 Prayed; writ notes. 6 Class. 8 Tea, religious talk; letters. 9 Class. 1 Dinner, religious talk. 2 Class; read notes. 5 Tea, religious talk; prayed. 6.30 Read the letters; the leaders. 8 At sister Johnson's. 9 Supper, religious talk; prayer. 9.30.

WEDNESDAY, MARCH 8. 4 Prayed; writ journal. 8 Tea, religious talk; prayer; walked. 10 At home; letters; sins! 1 At brother Hopkins's, dinner, religious talk; prayer. 2 Class; chaise; Jacob's Wells, tea. 5 [Blank]; class; Clifton; writ notes; supper, religious talk; prayer. 9.30.

THURSDAY, MARCH 9. 4 Prayed; letters. 8 Tea, religious talk; prayer. 9 At home; letters. 1 Dinner, religious talk; prayer. 2.30 Letters. 5 Tea, religious talk; prayer. 6 Prayed. 6.30 Deuteronomy 5:7! the bands; at sister Johnson's, supper, religious talk; prayer. 9.30.

FRIDAY, MARCH 10. 4 Prayed; texts. 11 Necessary talk (religious) to many. 12 The females. 1 Prayer; christened! 2 Dinner, religious talk! 3 Visited many. 5 Tea, religious talk; prayer. 6 Guinea Street, Luke 18:8! visited; at sister Johnson's. 8 Supper, religious talk; prayer. 9.30.

SATURDAY, MARCH 11. 4 Prayed; texts. 8 Tea, religious talk; prayer. 9 Chaise. 11.15 Churchill; read Prayers, Isaiah 55:6; chaise; Wrington; dinner, religious talk; prayer; chaise. 5.30 At home; tea; prayed; necessary business. 7.30 Penry; at Mr Castleman's, supper, religious talk; prayer. 9.30.

SUNDAY, MARCH 12. 4 Prayed; letters; tea; prayed. 9.30 Read Prayers, 1 Thessalonians 4:5! Communion; chaise; at the School; dinner, religious talk; prayer. 2 Matthew 15:28! chaise; visited; tea; prayed. 5 1 Thessalonians 4:8! Society; letters. 8 Supper; prayer. 9.30.

MONDAY, MARCH 13. 4 Prayed; tea. 5 Chaise. 8.15 Newport; tea, religious talk. 9.45 Chaise. 12.30 Stroud. 1 Letters. 2 Dinner, religious talk. 3 Letters; prayed. 5 Tea, religious talk; prayer. 6 Titus 2:11, etc; Society; supper, religious talk; prayer. 9.30.

TUESDAY, MARCH 14. 4 Prayed; letters. 8 Tea, religious talk; prayer; letters. 11 Chaise. 12 Painswick; Isaiah 57:1, 2! dinner, religious talk. 2 Chaise. 4 Gloucester; writ notes; prayed; tea, religious talk. 6 Read Prayers, Isaiah 55:6, 7! Society! supper, religious talk; prayer. 9.30.

WEDNESDAY, MARCH 15. 4 Prayed; letter. 8 Tea, religious talk; prayer. 9 Necessary talk (religious). 9.30 Chaise. 11.15 Tewksbury; religious talk. 12 Mark 3:35! dinner, religious talk. 2 Chaise. 4.30 Worcester; letter. 5 Tea, religious talk. 6 John 4:24! Society! visited; supper, religious talk; prayer. 9.30.

THURSDAY, MARCH 16. 4 Prayed; writ notes. 6 John 6:28; writ notes. 8 Tea, religious talk; prayer. 9 Chaise. 11.30 Bewdley; religious talk. 12 Titus 2:11; dinner, religious talk; prayer. 2 Chaise. 5.30 Tea, religious talk. 6 Deuteronomy 5:7! the bands; supper, religious talk; prayer. 9.30 Sins!

FRIDAY, MARCH 17. 4 Prayed; writ notes. 6 1 Peter 4:7! tea, religious talk. 8 Chaise. 10.30 Bengeworth; visited; read Prayers, John 4:24! 1 Dinner, religious talk; letter; prayer; writ notes; prayed; at Mr Beale's! 5.30 Read Prayers, Job 22:21! texts; supper, religious talk; prayer. 9.30.

SATURDAY, MARCH 18. 4 Prayed; A. Bla[ir?]; tea; prayer. 6.30 Chaise. 8.45 Studley; tea. 9.45 Chaise. 12.45 Birmingham; Elizabeth Ritchie! 1.30 Dinner, religious talk. 3 Necessary business. 4 Prayed; tea, religious talk; writ notes. 7 Mark 3:35; writ notes; supper, religious talk; prayer. 9.30.

SUNDAY, MARCH 19. 4 Prayed; journal. 7 Tea, religious talk. 8 Isaiah 40:1! journal. 10 Read Prayers! 12.15 Writ notes. 12.45 Dinner, religious talk; prayer. 2 Letter; prayed. 4 Tea, religious talk; prayer. 5 Isaiah 55:1! Communion. 8.30 Supper, religious talk; prayer. 9.30.

MONDAY, MARCH 20. 4 Prayed; Matthew 12:43! letters. 8 Tea, religious talk; prayer; letters. 11 Select Society! visited! 1 Dinner; prayer; letters; prayed. 5 Tea, religious talk; prayer. 6.30 Matthew 9:5! supper, religious talk! prayer. 9.45.

TUESDAY, MARCH [21]. 4 Prayed; letters; journal. 8 Tea, religious talk; prayer; texts; letters. 1 Dinner; coach. 3 Quinton; Isaiah 1:3(2); coach. 5.15 Birmingham; tea, religious talk; prayer; read. 6.30 Ephesians 3:14, etc! 7.30 The bands; supper, religious talk; prayer. 9.30.

WEDNESDAY, MARCH 22. 4 Prayed; 1 Peter 4:7; writ letters. 8 Tea, religious talk; prayer. 9 Letter; necessary talk (religious) to some. 10 Necessary business; prayer. 11 Chaise; with Elizabeth Ritchie. 12.30 Wednesbury; writ notes. 1 Dinner, religious talk; prayer. 2.30 Journal. 4 Prayed; tea. 6 Acts 17:30! Society! supper; prayer. 9.30.

THURSDAY, MARCH 23. 4 Prayed; texts; sermon. 7.30 Tea, religious talk; prayer. 8.30 Sermon. 11 Chaise. 11.30 Darlaston; sermon. 12 Dinner; sermon. 1.30 Read Prayers; 2 Timothy 1:7; chaise; sermon; prayed. 6 Matthew 7:16! the bands! supper, religious talk; prayer. 9.30.

FRIDAY, MARCH 24. 4 Prayed; Matthew 5:6! sermon. 7.30 Tea; prayer; sermon. 11 Chaise. 12.15 Dudley. 12.30 Texts. 1.30 Dinner; texts; prayed; visited; tea, religious talk; prayed. 6 John 4:24! 7 Society! supper, religious talk; prayer. 9.30.

SATURDAY, MARCH 25. 4 Prayed; 1 Thessalonians 5:19! tea; chaise. 8 Wolverhampton; tea, religious talk; prayer. 9 Isaiah 55:1! 10.15 Chaise. 1.30 Madeley; dinner, religious talk; corrected. 5 Tea, religious talk; read papers; prayed; prayer. 8 Supper, religious talk; prayer; necessary business. 9.30.

SUNDAY, MARCH 26. 4 Prayed; papers. 7.30 James 3:17; tea, religious talk; texts. 10 Read Prayers, Revelation 14:1, etc. 12 Texts. 1 Dinner, religious talk; slept; texts. 2 Read Prayers, Mark 16:16. 4 Texts; prayed; tea, religious talk. 5 Prayed; journal. 8 At Mr Ferriday's, religious talk, supper; prayer. 9.30.

MONDAY, MARCH 27. 4 Prayed; letters. 7 Prayer; tea, religious talk; chaise. 7 Coalbrookdale; Isaiah 66:8! chaise. 9.30 Letters. 12 Writ texts. 12.30 Dinner, religious talk. 2 Read to Mrs Fletcher, to Elizabeth Ritchie. 4 Prayed; tea, religious talk. 6.30 Read Prayers, John 14:22! 8 Supper, religious talk; prayer. 9.30.

TUESDAY, MARCH 28. 4 Prayed; Isaiah 30:18; prayed. 7 Chaise. 8.30 Sheriffhales; tea; [1] Peter 1:24! 9.45 Chaise. 1 Stafford; Mark 1:15(2); dinner. 2.30 Chaise; Lane End [Longton]. 5 Tea, necessary talk (religious). 6 +Romans 8:33; prayed. 8 Supper, religious talk; prayer. 9.30.

WEDNESDAY, MARCH 29. 4 Prayed; Hebrews 6:1; sermon. 7.30 Tea; prayer; sermon. 10 Necessary talk (religious). 11.15 Chaise. 12.30 At Mr [Enoch] Wood's, dinner, religious talk. 2.30 Chaise; at brother Robinson's; sermon; prayed. 5 Tea, religious talk; prayer. 6 1 John 1:3! Society! supper, religious talk; prayer. 9.30.

THURSDAY, MARCH 30. 4 Prayed; 1 Corinthians 12:31; sermon. 8 Visited; tea; prayer; chaise. 9.30 Newcastle[-under-Lyme]. 10 Sermon. 1 Dinner; sermon; letters. 5 Prayed; tea. 6 John 5:19! Society. 8 Supper, religious talk; prayer. 9.30.

FRIDAY, MARCH 31. 4 Prayed; Psalms 50:23; letters. 8 Tea; letters. 10 Chaise. 12 Congleton; Magazine. 1 Dinner, religious talk. 2 Magazine. 4 Prayed; tea. 6 Matthew 4:10. 7 Society; supper; prayer. 9.30.

SATURDAY, APRIL 1. 4 Prayed; Romans 1:16; accounts; read. 8 Tea, religious talk; prayer. 9 Chaise. 11 Macclesfield; letters. 1 Dinner, religious talk; letters. 3.30 Prayed; necessary business; tea, religious talk. 5.30 Prayed. 6 Revelation 3:20. 7 Read. 8 Supper, religious talk; prayer; necessary business. 9.45.

SUNDAY, APRIL 2. 4 Prayed; journal. 7 Tea, religious talk; journal. 10 Read Prayers, Hebrews 4:7; writ notes; dinner, religious talk; slept. 2 Read Prayers, Hebrews 4:14, etc; prayed; letters; tea, religious talk; prayed. 5 Proverbs 22:6; Love-feast! 8.15 Supper, religious talk; prayer. 9.30.

MONDAY, APRIL 3. 4 Prayed; Hebrews 4:9; letters. 7 Tea, religious talk; prayer. 8.15 Chaise; sins! 11 Chapel[-en-le-Frith]; Acts 18:19! dinner, religious talk. 1 Chaise; visited; chaise; sins! 1.30 Hayfield. 4 Prayed; tea. 4.30 1 Corinthians 6:19! 7 New Mills; prayed; supper; prayer. 9.30.

TUESDAY, APRIL [4]. 4 Prayed; journal. 8 Tea, religious talk; [read] *Siege!* [probably John Hughes, *The Siege of Damascus*] 10 Malachi 3:1! Society! *Siege.* 1 Dinner, religious talk. 2 Chaise. 4 Stockport; prayed; tea; walked. 6 Matthew 22:37; Society. 7 Read *Siege!* 8 Supper, religious talk; prayer. 9.30.

WEDNESDAY, APRIL 5. 4 Prayed; read *Siege.* 8 Tea, religious talk; *Siege.* 10 Chaise; Bullocksmithy [now Hazel Grove]. 11 Read Prayers, Acts 2:4! dinner, religious talk. 2 Chaise. 3.30 Manchester; prayed; tea, necessary talk (religious). 6 Deuteronomy 5:7! necessary talk (religious). 8 Supper, religious talk; prayer. 9.30.

THURSDAY, APRIL 6. 4 Prayed; letters. 7 Tea, religious talk. 8 Chaise. 9.15 Ashton[-under-Lyne]; John 17:3! chaise. 11.30 New Hall. 12 John 4:24! chaise. 3 Slept; sermon; prayed. 5 Tea, religious talk; prayer. 6 Luke 8:18! sermon; supper, religious talk; prayer. 9.30.

FRIDAY, APRIL 7. 4 Prayed; sermon. 8 Tea; prayer; sermon. 9 Chaise. 10 Failsworth; Hebrews 9:27. 12 Chaise. 1 Oldham; dinner; +1 John 5:19; chaise. 4 Manchester; ill; writ notes. 5 Tea, religious talk; prayed. 6.30 1 Corinthians 10:12! supper, religious talk; prayer; necessary business. 9.45.

SATURDAY, APRIL 8. 5 Ill; prayed; letters. 8 Tea, religious talk; prayer; slept; the painter. 12 Slept. 1 Dinner, religious talk; prayer. 2.30 Slept; necessary business. 4 The painter. 5 Tea, religious talk; prayed. 6.30 Mark 3:34! 8 Read; supper, religious talk; prayer. 9.45.

SUNDAY, APRIL 9. 4.30 Prayed; letters. 8.15 Tea, religious talk; letters. 10 Read Prayers, Philippians 4:5! Communion. 1.30 Dinner, religious talk; slept. 4 Prayed; tea. 5.15 Hebrews 5:7! Society! necessary business. 8 Supper, religious talk; prayer. 9.30.

MONDAY, APRIL 10. 4 Prayed; 1 Peter 4:7; tea. 6.30 Chaise. 8.30 Bucklow Hill; tea; chaise. 11 Northwich; letters. 12 Ecclesiastes 7:29! dinner. 2 Chaise. 5.15 Chester; tea. 6 Deuteronomy 5:7! Society. 8 Supper; prayer; at John Sellers's. 9.30.

TUESDAY, APRIL 11. 4 Prayed; Revelation 2:5! Gouge. 8 Tea, religious talk; prayer; Gouge. 12.30 Walked. 1 Dinner, religious talk; prayer. 2.30 Gouge! prayed. 5 Tea, religious talk; prayer. 6 John 14:22! 8 The Society; supper! prayer. 9.30.

WEDNESDAY, APRIL 12. 4 Prayed; Revelation 2:5; necessary business. 6.30 Tea; prayer. 7 Chaise. 10 Tea; Rock [Ferry]; boat. 11.30 Liverpool; at Mr Wagner's; letters. 1 Dinner, religious talk; prayer; necessary business; prayed. 6.30 Deuteronomy 5:7! Society; supper, religious talk; prayer. 9.30.

THURSDAY, APRIL 13. 4 Prayed; 1 Corinthians 10:12! Select Society! letters. 8 Tea, religious talk; prayer. 9 Letters. 1 Dinner, religious talk. 2.30 Letters; prayed; tea. 6 Luke 12:20! Communion. 9 Supper, religious talk; prayer. 10.

GOOD FRIDAY, APRIL [14]. 4 Prayed; 1 Corinthians 6:20! coffee. 6 Chaise; Prescot; tea; chaise. 10.30 Wigan. 11 Read Prayers. 12 Dinner. 1 2 Corinthians 8:9! chaise. 5 Bolton; tea; prayed. 6 Hebrews 9:13; Society; supper, religious talk; prayer. 9.30.

SATURDAY, APRIL 15. 4 Prayed; Romans 8:4; letters; tea, religious talk. 8.30 Chaise. 11 Rochdale. 12 Isaiah 66:8! dinner. 2.30 Chaise. 4 Bury; tea; prayed. 5 Galatians 6:14! chaise. 8 Bolton; supper, religious talk; necessary business. 9.30.

EASTER DAY [April 16]. 4 Prayed; tea. 5 Chaise. 7.30 Warrington; tea, religious talk; Magazine. 10 Read Prayers, Luke 24:25, Communion. 12.15 Dinner. 1 Chaise; Bolton; tea; prayed. 5 1 Peter 1:3; Society! supper; prayer; religious talk. 9.30.

MONDAY, APRIL 17. 4 Prayed; Colossians 3:1-4; letters; chaise. 8 Tea, religious talk; prayer; chaise. 11.30 Blackburn. 12 Letters. 1.30 Dinner, religious talk; texts. 4 Prayed; tea. 6 +Revelation 20:12! 7 Society! supper, religious talk; prayer. 9.30.

TUESDAY, APRIL 18. 4 Prayed; journal; tea, religious talk. 8 Chaise. 9.30 Padiham. 10 Romans 8:33! Communion. 12.30 Necessary talk (religious). 1 Dinner, religious talk. 1.45 Chaise. 2.30 Burnley; +Mark 1:15! 4 Tea; chaise. 7.30 Southfield; letter; prayed; supper; prayer. 9.30.

WEDNESDAY, APRIL 19. 4 Prayed; sermon. 8 Tea, religious talk; sermon. 12 Dinner. 1 Matthew 25:1, etc! sermon. 3 Chaise. 4 Colne; tea, religious talk; prayed. 5 1 John 5:19! Communion. 7 Chaise. 8 Southfield; supper, religious talk. 9 Prayed. 9.30.

THURSDAY, APRIL 20. 4 Prayed; sermon. 6 Acts 22:16(2); tea, religious talk; prayer. 7.45 Chaise. 10.30 Inn [near Keighley?]. 11.30 Chaise. 1.45 Otley; sermon; dinner; sermon. 4 Prayed; tea, religious talk. 6 Galatians 5:1! 7 Society! supper, necessary talk (religious); prayer. 9.30.

FRIDAY, APRIL 21. 4 Prayed; Job 7:17! sermon. 8 Tea, religious talk; sermon. 11 Prayer; chaise. 12 Park Gate; sermon. 2 Dinner, religious talk. 3 Sermon; prayed. 6.30 Yeadon; Isaiah 66:9! 8 Chaise; supper, religious talk; prayer. 9.45.

SATURDAY, APRIL 22. 4 Prayed; sermon. 8 Tea, religious talk; prayer. 9 Chaise; Baildon; Mark 3:35! chaise. 12.30 Keighley; letters. 1.30 Dinner; letters;

prayed. 5 Visited; tea, religious talk. 6 Isaiah 57:1, 2. 7 Society; letters; supper, religious talk; prayer; necessary business. 9.45.

SUNDAY, APRIL 23. 4 Prayed; letters. 8 Tea, religious talk; chaise. 10 Haworth; read Prayers, 1 John 5:11! dinner. 1 Chaise. 2.30 Bingley; read Prayers, Luke 8:18; chaise. 5 Bradford; at Mr Cross's, tea, religious talk. 6 Prayed; +Mark 3:35; Society; supper; prayer. 9.45.

MONDAY, APRIL 24. 4 Prayed; Psalms 106:24; letters. 7 Tea, religious talk; prayer; letters. 10.30 Chaise. 12.30 Halifax. 1.30 Dinner, religious talk; letters. 4.15 Prayed; tea, religious talk. 6.30 2 Corinthians 5:1, etc; Society; supper; prayer. 9.45.

TUESDAY, APRIL 25. 4 Prayed; sermon. 6 Luke 20:34, etc; letters; tea. 8 Chaise. 10 Heptonstall; read Prayers, Acts 22:16; Society; Communion. 1 Dinner, necessary talk (religious); prayer. 2 Chaise. 3 At Mr Sutcliffe's [at Hoo Hole]; sermon; tea; prayed. 5 [At Todmorden Church] Read Prayers, Matthew 15:28! sermon; supper, religious talk; prayer. 9.30.

WEDNESDAY, APRIL 26. 4 Prayed; sermon. 6 Matthew 8:2! at Mr Sutcliffe's, tea, prayer. 8.15 Chaise. 10.30 Halifax; letters; sermon. 12.30 Walked. 1 Dinner, religious talk; prayer. 2.30 Sermon; letter; prayed; tea, religious talk. 6.30 2 Timothy 3:5! Society. 8 Supper, religious talk; prayer. 9.30.

THURSDAY, APRIL 27. 4 Prayed; letters. 8 Tea, religious talk; prayer. 9 Chaise; Greetland; Matthew 7:16. 11 Chaise. 12 Longwood House; sermon. 1.30 Dinner, religious talk. 2.30 Sermon. 5 Tea, religious talk; chaise [to Huddersfield]. 6 Isaiah 59:1, 2! chaise. 9 Supper; prayer. 10.

FRIDAY, APRIL 28. 4.45 Prayed. 6 Ephesians 4:30, etc! writ Conference. 7 Tea, religious talk; prayer; writ Conference. 11 Chaise. 12.30 Dewsbury; Conference. 1 Dinner; Conference. 3 Trustees. 5 Tea; prayed. 6.30 Matthew 22:37! Society; supper, religious talk; prayer. 9.30.

SATURDAY, APRIL 29. 4 Prayed; writ texts. 6 1 Corinthians 13:13! letters. 8 Tea, religious talk; prayer; writ Conference. 11 Chaise. 12 Gildersome; writ for Conference. 1 Dinner, religious talk; letters. 4 Prayed. 5 Tea, religious talk. 6 Cloth Hall; 2 Corinthians 4:18! read; prayed. 8 Supper, religious talk; prayer. 9.30.

SUNDAY, APRIL 30. 4 Prayed; letters. 6.30 Tea, religious talk; chaise. 8 Dewsbury; Matthew 22:39! chaise. 10.30 Birstall; letters. 12 Dinner; Psalms 144:15; letter. 2.30 Chaise. 4.15 Wakefield; tea. 5 +Psalms 147:3! letter; prayed. 7.30 Supper, religious talk; prayer. 9.30.

MONDAY, MAY 1. 4 Prayed; letters. 8 Tea, religious talk; prayer; sermon. 11 Chaise. 12.30 Leeds; necessary business. 1.30 Dinner, religious talk. 3 Read notes; prayed. 5 Tea, religious talk; prayer; read. 6.15 Ephesians 2:12; the leaders. 8.30 At Mr Hey's, supper, religious talk; prayer. 10.

TUESDAY, MAY 2. 4 Prayed; 1 Peter 5:10; the leaders, necessary talk (religious); prayer. 8 Tea, religious talk; prayer; visited. 9 Letters. 11 Journal; necessary talk (religious) to many. 1 At brother Floyd's, dinner, religious talk. 2.30 Writ notes; prayed. 5 Tea, religious talk. 6 Jeremiah 6:16! Society! supper, religious talk; prayer. 9.45.

WEDNESDAY, MAY 3. 4 Prayed; 1 Peter 2:8! letters. 8 Tea, religious talk; prayer. 9.15 Chaise. 10.30 Horsforth; read Prayers, Mark 1:15! at Mr Shapley's, necessary talk (religious), dinner; prayer; chaise. 3.30 At home; writ notes; prayed. 5 Tea, religious talk; prayer. 6.30 Luke 8:18; the bands; supper; prayer. 9.45.

THURSDAY, MAY 4. 4.15 Prayed; 1 Peter 4:7! necessary talk (religious); letter. 8 Tea, religious talk; prayer. 9.30 Chaise. 12 Tadcaster; necessary talk (religious). 1 Dinner; writ notes. 4 Prayed. 5 Tea, religious talk; prayed. 6 Mark 1:15! Society; supper; prayer. 9.30.

FRIDAY, MAY 5. 4 Prayed; Heb 6:1; letters; sermon. 8 Tea, religious talk; prayer; letter. 10 Chaise. 11.30 York; at brother Felt——'s; read notes. 1 Dinner, religious talk; letters; necessary talk (religious); prayed; tea, religious talk. 6 1 Thess 4:3! Select Society. 8 Supper, religious talk; prayer. 9.30.

SATURDAY, MAY 6. 4 Prayed; letters; sermon. 8 Tea, religious talk; prayer; sermon. 12 Walked. 1.15 Dinner, religious talk; letters. 4 Prayed. 5 Tea, religious talk; prayer. 6 Mark 9:23! Society. 8 At brother Spense's, supper, religious talk; prayer. 9.30.

SUNDAY, MAY 7. 4 Prayed; letters. 7 Tea, religious talk; sermon. 10.15 St Saviour's, read Prayers, Matthew 5:3, etc, Communion; dinner, religious talk. 2.30 St Margaret's, read Prayers, Romans 6:23; ill; tea; prayed. 5 Matthew 5:49. 6.30 Love-feast. 8 Supper, religious talk; prayer. 9.45.

MONDAY, MAY 8. 4 Prayed; 1 Peter 2:11; sermon. 8 Tea, religious talk; prayer. 9.30 Chaise. 11.30 Easingwold. 12 Dinner, religious talk; Galatians 3:23! 2 Chaise. 3.30 Thirsk; writ notes; prayed. 5 Tea. 6 Psalms 146:4! Communion; supper, religious talk; prayer. 9.30.

TUESDAY, MAY 9. 4 Prayed; 1 Corinthians 15:58! letter; tea. 7 Chaise. 9.30 Tea; chaise. 12 Richmond; at the Archdeacon's, religious talk. 2 Dinner, mostly religious talk; walked. 4.45 Marske [orig., 'Usk']; tea, religious talk; walked. 6 +Isaiah 55:6! Society! supper, religious talk; prayer. 9.30.

WEDNESDAY, MAY 10. 4 Prayed; Hebrews 7:25! letters; tea; necessary business. 7.30 Chaise. 10.30 Barnard Castle; read notes; necessary talk (religious) to many. 12.30 Dinner, religious talk; writ notes. 4 Prayed. 5 Tea; visited. 6 Matthew 20:16! Society! supper, religious talk; prayer. 9.30.

THURSDAY, MAY 11. 4 Prayed; Matthew 5:6! letter; tea. 7 Walked; chaise. 10 Brough; tea; prayer. 11 Chaise. 12.15 Appleby; dinner; John 17:3! visited. 2.30 Chaise. 4.30 Penrith; tea; prayed. 6 Rev. 20:12! supper; prayer. 9.30.

FRIDAY, MAY 12. 3.15 Prayer. 4 Chaise; read Dr Anderson. 7.30 Carlisle; necessary talk (religious), tea; prayer. 9 Chaise; Anderson. 12 Steetinghill [near Ecclefechan, the coach stop]; dinner. 1 Chaise; read. 4 Dinwoodie Green [orig., 'Wood Green']; tea; chaise. 7 Moffat; supper; prayer. 9.30.

SATURDAY, MAY 13. 3.30 Prayer. 4 Chaise. 6.30 Elvanfoot; tea. 7.30 Chaise; read; Douglas. 11 Douglas Mills. 12.15 Chaise; Machan. 4 Hamilton; dinner. 4.45 Chaise. 6.15 Glasgow; at brother Richard's, tea, necessary talk (religious). 7 Mark 3:35; necessary talk (religious), supper; prayer. 9.30.

[SUNDAY, MAY 14.] 4 Prayed; letters; tea; texts. 10.30 Read Prayers, Matthew 13:31. 1 At brother McKay's! dinner; prayer; slept. 2 Matthew 5:20! prayed. 4.30 Tea, religious talk. 5 Prayed; writ notes. 6 +2 Corinthians 8:9; Society; supper, religious talk; prayer. 9.30.

MONDAY, MAY 15. 4 Prayed; Hebrews 6:1; writ Magazine. 8 Tea, religious talk; prayer. 9 Read notes. 10.30 Walked; necessary talk. 11.30 Read. 1 Dinner, religious talk; prayer. 2 Letters; read. 4 Tea, religious talk; prayer. 5 Prayed. 6 Matthew 7:24. 7 The bands. 8 At Mr Rent's, supper, necessary talk (religious); prayer. 9.30.

TUESDAY, MAY 16. 4 Prayed; Matthew 8:2! writ notes; journal. 1 Walked. 2 At Dr Gillies's, dinner, religious talk; prayer. 3 Walked. 4 Read Prayers; tea. 6 2 Timothy 3:5! Society; supper; prayer. 9.30.

[WEDNESDAY, MAY 17.] 4 Prayed; Communion. [?].15 Chaise; tea; chaise. 10 Within. 11 Chaise. 2 Coates [Hall]; religious talk. 3 Dinner, religious talk. 4 Writ notes; prayed. 5 Tea, religious talk; coach. 6 Acts 11:26! coach. 8 Supper, religious talk; prayer. 9.30.

THURSDAY, MAY 18. 4 Prayed; Psalms 106:24! letters. 8 Tea, religious talk; prayer; letters. 12.30 Coates [Hall]. 1 Class! 3 Dinner, religious talk; prayer! 4 Prayed; slept; tea; prayed. 6.30 Matthew 15:28. 8 Supper, religious talk; prayer. 9.30.

FRIDAY, MAY 19. 3.15 Prayed; chaise; Leith; tea. 5.45 Boat. 7.30 Walked; chaise. 10.30 Inn; tea. 11.30 Chaise. 3.15 Boat. 4 Dundee; Thomas Hanby, necessary talk (religious), tea; prayed. 7 Mark 3:35; read; supper, necessary talk (religious); prayer. 9.45.

SATURDAY, MAY 20. 4 Prayed; Matthew 5:48; sermon. 8 Tea, religious talk; sermon. 11.30 Visited. 12.30 Dinner. 1.30 Chaise. 5 Arbroath; brother McAllum, tea, religious talk; prayer; prayed. 7 Hebrews 12:14. 8 Read; supper; prayer; necessary business. 9.45.

SUNDAY, MAY 21. 4 Prayed; sermon. 8 Tea, religious talk; sermon. 10.30 Read Prayers! 2 Kings 5:12; sermon; christened. 1 Dinner; slept. 2.30 Matthew 5:24; sermon; prayed; tea. 6 Luke 16:31! sermon; supper. 9 Prayer. 9.30.

MONDAY, MAY 22. 3.30 Tea. 4 Chaise. 6 Montrose; tea. 7 Chaise. 9.30 Inverbervie [orig., 'Bervie']. 10.15 Chaise. 12 Stonehaven; dinner. 1.15 Chaise. 4 Aberdeen. 5 Sermon; tea; prayed. 7 Matthew 4:10; supper, religious talk; prayer. 9.30.

TUESDAY, MAY 23. 4 Prayed; Hebrews 6:1; necessary talk (religious); sermon. 8 Tea, religious talk; prayer; sermon. 12 Necessary talk (religious); walked. 1 Dinner, religious talk. 2 Sermon. 4 Necessary business; tea, religious talk; prayer. 6.30 1 Peter 1:18! Society. 8 Supper, religious talk; prayer. 9.30.

WEDNESDAY, MAY 24. 4 Prayed; Matthew 13:3, etc; Select Society; journal. 8 Tea, religious talk; prayer. 9 Journal; necessary talk (religious); at Mrs B——'s; prayer. 10 Sins! letters. 12 Walked. 1.15 Dinner; Magazine. 3 Read notes; R. W.; letter; prayed; 2 Corinthians 5:1, etc! supper, religious talk; prayer. 9.30.

THURSDAY, MAY [25]. 3 Prayed; tea. 3.30 Chaise. 6 Stonehaven; tea. 7 Walked; chaise. 11.30 Montrose. 12 Dinner; high wind. 4 Walked; chaise. 6 Arbroath; necessary business; tea. 7 Luke 8:18. 8.30 Supper, religious talk; prayer. 9.30.

FRIDAY, MAY 26. 4 Prayed; 1 Corinthians 10:13; Magazine. 8 Tea, religious talk; prayer. 9.30 Chaise. 1 Dundee. 1.45 Dinner, religious talk. 3 Magazine. 4 Prayed; tea. 6 Deuteronomy 5:7! Magazine; supper, religious talk. 9.30 Slept. 11 In the boat! 12.45 Chaise.

SATURDAY, MAY 27. 4.30 New Inn; slept. 6.30 Tea. 7.15 Chaise. 9.30 Kinghorn; read. 11.30 Boat. 12.45 Leith; Magazine. 2.45 Dinner, religious talk. 3.30 Letter; prayed; tea. 6 Galatians 6:14. 7 Walked; Coates [Hall]; supper, religious talk; prayer. 9.30.

SUNDAY, MAY 28. 4.30 Prayed; letters; tea; prayer; chaise. 7.30 Psalms 50:23; letters. 10.30 Read Prayers, +Revelation 20:12; dinner; letters; read Prayers! 3.45 Letters; prayed. 5.30 Tea. 6 Isaiah 55:6, 7! chaise. 8.30 Supper, religious talk; prayer. 9.30.

MONDAY, MAY 29. 4 Prayed. 5 1 Corinthians 10:12; letters. 8 Tea, religious talk; walked. 10 Letters. 2 Dinner, religious talk; prayer; visited some. 5 Tea, religious talk; prayer; letters; prayed. 6.30 1 Peter 4:11; Society; chaise; supper. 9 Religious talk; prayer. 9.30.

TUESDAY, MAY 30. 4 Prayed; 1 Corinthians 15:55; tea, religious talk; prayer. 7 Chaise; Haddington; tea. 10 Chaise. 12 At Dr Hamilton's; christened; necessary talk (religious); chaise. 2.30 At Mr Fall's, dinner; letter; prayed. 5 Tea. 6 Prov 3:17! religious talk! chaise; supper, religious talk; prayer. 9.30.

WEDNESDAY, MAY 31. 4 Prayed; walked. 5 1 Peter 1:24! tea. 7 Chaise; the Arch [i.e., Pease Bridge]! 9.30 Tea. 10.30 Chaise. 12 Berwick[-upon-Tweed]; letters. 1.30 Dinner, religious talk; letters. 4 Prayed. 5 Tea, religious talk. 6 2 Timothy 3:5. 7 Society; walked; supper; prayer. 9.30.

THURSDAY, JUNE 1. 4 Prayed; 1 Peter 1:18! tea; prayer. 7 Chaise. 9.30 Belford; tea. 10.30 Chaise. 1 Alnwick; necessary business. 2 Dinner; necessary business; letters. 4 Prayed; tea; letters. 6 1 Thessalonians 4:3. 7 Society; letter; supper, religious talk; prayer. 9.30.

FRIDAY, JUNE 2. 4 Prayed; Matthew 13:31! laid the foundation! [of the preaching-house at Alnwick] 7 Chaise; with Jenny Smith [step-granddaughter]. 9.30 Tea; chaise. 11.30 Morpeth; Matthew 25:31. 1 Dinner; chaise. 4 At W. Smith's, tea, necessary talk (religious). 6 Psalms 74:14! Select Society; supper; prayer. 9.30.

SATURDAY, JUNE 3. 4 Prayed; Matthew 5:6! necessary talk (religious) to many; letters. 8 Tea, religious talk; prayer; letters; writ notes. 12.45 At W. Smith's; writ notes; dinner, religious talk. 2 Writ Conference. 4.15 Prayed. 5 Tea, religious talk; prayer. 6 Prayed; necessary business. 7 Mark 7:37! Leezes, supper; prayer. 9.30.

WHITSUNDAY, JUNE 4. 4 Prayed; letters. 8 Ballast Hills; tea, religious talk; +Matthew 8:2! letters. 12 Dinner; coach. 2.30 John 14:21! coach; tea, religious talk. 5 Garth Heads; Acts 2:4! 6.30 Love-feast! supper, religious talk; prayer. 9.30.

MONDAY, JUNE 5. 4 Prayed; Mark 9:23(2)! letters. 8 Tea, religious talk; prayer; letters; necessary talk (religious) to many. 1 Dinner, necessary talk (religious). 2.30 Letters; prayed. 4.45 Tea, religious talk; prayer. 6 Acts 19:2! Leezes. 7.30 Walked; supper, religious talk; prayer. 9.30.

TUESDAY, JUNE 6. 4 Prayed; Ephesians 2:8; letters. 8 Tea, religious talk; prayer; visited some. 10 Letters. 1 At brother Green's, dinner, religious talk; visited some. 3.30 Prayed; tea, religious talk; prayer. 6 Galatians 5:22! the leaders. 8 Supper, religious talk; prayer. 9.30.

WEDNESDAY, JUNE 7. 4 Prayed; 1 Peter 5:10! necessary business; tea, religious talk; prayer. 7.30 Chaise. 10.30 Shields. 11 Walked; necessary business. 12 +Mark 3:35! dinner. 1.30 South Shields; Society. 3 Chaise. 4.30 Sunderland; necessary business; tea. 6 John 7:37! Society; supper; prayer. 9.30.

THURSDAY, JUNE 8. 4 Prayed; Psalms 106:24! letters. 8 Tea, religious talk; prayer; letters; accounts. 10.30 Read Prayers, Mark 9:23! writ notes. 1.15 Dinner, religious talk. 2.15 Journal; prayed; tea, religious talk; prayer. 6 Matthew 21:21! Communion; supper, religious talk; prayer. 10.

FRIDAY, JUNE 9. 4 Prayed; Isaiah 57:1, 2; necessary talk (religious) to many; tea; prayer. 8.30 Chaise. 10.30 Durham. 1 Read notes. 12 Luke 8:18! dinner; prayer. 2 Chaise. 5 Hartlepool; tea; Romans 3:22. 7.45 Prayed; supper, religious talk; prayer. 9.30.

SATURDAY, JUNE 10. 4 Prayed; Hebrews 13:22! journal; necessary talk (religious), tea; visited; prayer. 8.15 Chaise. 10.15 At brother Walk[er's]. 11 Chaise.

1 Darlington; dinner; letters. 4.30 Prayed; tea. 6 Psalms 50:23! 7 Letters; supper, necessary talk (religious); prayer. 9.45.

SUNDAY, JUNE 11. 4 Prayed; letters. 7 Tea, religious talk. 8 1 Samuel 21:8; letter. 10 Read Prayers, Communion. 1 Dinner, religious talk; prayer. 2 Slept; journal; prayed; tea. 5 +1 John 5:7! Love-feast! 8 Supper, religious talk; prayer. 9.30.

MONDAY, JUNE 12. 4 Prayed; 1 Corinthians 10:12; letters. 7 Tea, religious talk; prayer. 8.30 Chaise. 11 Stockton[-on-Tees]; letter. 12 1 Timothy 4:8. 1 Dinner, necessary talk! prayer; visited! chaise. 4 Yarm; prayed; tea, religious talk. 6 Matthew 22:39, Communion; supper; prayer. 9.30.

TUESDAY, JUNE 13. 4 Prayed; Hebrews 6:1; chaise. 7.15 Potto; tea, religious talk; prayer; chaise. 9 Hutton [Rudby]; 2 Timothy 2:5; chaise. 11.30 Guisborough; +Ezekiel 18:31; dinner. 1.15 Chaise. 5.15 Whitby; tea; prayed. 6.30 2 Corinthians 3:18! Society; supper; prayer. 10.

WEDNESDAY, JUNE [14]. 4 Prayed; Isaiah 57:1, 2! letters. 8 Tea, religious talk; prayer; visited some. 10 Letters; walked. 1 Dinner; prayer. 2 Letters. 4 Prayed; tea, religious talk; prayer. 6 Romans 8:3, 4! Love-feast. 8 Supper, religious talk; prayer. 9.30.

THURSDAY, JUNE 15. 4 Prayed; 2 Corinthians 5:1, etc; Select Society; tea, religious talk. 8 Chaise. 11.30 Scarborough; read notes. 1.30 Dinner, religious talk. 2.45 Writ notes. 4 Prayed. 5 Tea, religious talk; prayed. 6 Matthew 25:31! Society; supper, necessary talk (religious); prayer. 9.30.

FRIDAY, JUNE 16. 4 Prayed; writ sermon. 8 Tea, religious talk; prayer; sermon. 10 Writ notes. 11 Hebrews 2:3! dinner, religious talk; slept. 1.30 Walked; chaise. 4.30 Bridlington Quay; necessary business; tea, religious talk. 5.30 Prayed. 6 +Matthew 9:5! 8 Supper, religious talk; prayer. 9.30.

SATURDAY, JUNE 17. 4 Prayed; Zechariah 4:4!; tea. 7.45 Chaise; *Fingal.* 9.15 Inn. 10 Chaise. 11 Beverley; at Mr Parker's; sermon. 12 Dinner. 1 Matthew 4:10; christened. 1.30 Chaise; Newland; Ephesians 2:8; tea; chaise. 6 Galatians 4:3; sermon; supper; prayer. 10.15.

SUNDAY, JUNE 18. 4 Prayed; sermon; letters. 8 Tea, religious talk; letters. 10.15 Read Prayers; Luke 16:31! letter; dinner, religious talk. 2 Slept; prayed. 3 Read Prayers, Isaiah 55:6! Love-feast; chaise. 8.30 Beverley. 9 Supper; prayer. 10.

MONDAY, JUNE 19. 3.30 Tea, religious talk. 4 Chaise. 8.30 Malton; tea; John 4:24! chaise. 1 Pocklington; dinner. 2 Chaise. 5 Boat. 5.30 Chaise. 6.30 Swinefleet; tea. 8 Supper, religious talk; prayer. 9.30.

TUESDAY, JUNE 20. 4 Prayed; [blank]; letter. 8 Tea, religious talk; prayer. 9 Chaise. 10.45 Crowle; letters. 12 Dinner; Matthew 22:39; Society! 3 Chaise. 4.30 Epworth; tea, religious talk; letter. 7 Mark 3:35. 8 Supper, religious talk; prayer. 9.

WEDNESDAY, JUNE 21. 3.30 Prayed; tea. 4.15 Chaise. 7 Scotter; letters; tea. 8.30 1 Corinthians 10:12! necessary talk (religious)! 9.30 Chaise. 12 Brigg; dinner. 1 +Isaiah 59:1! 2.15 Chaise. 5.15 Grimsby; tea. 6 +1 Peter 2:24! Society; supper; prayer. 9.30.

THURSDAY, JUNE 22. 4 Prayed; read journal. 8 Tea, religious talk; prayer; journal; letter. 11 2 Timothy 3:5! dinner; visited some 2.15 Chaise; Ludborough! tea, religious talk; prayer; chaise. 5 Louth; tea; prayed; sermon. 6.30 Acts 17:30! Society! supper, religious talk; prayer. 9.30.

FRIDAY, JUNE 23. 4 Prayed; Acts 22:16(2)! chaise. 8.15 Tealby! at James Kershaw's, tea, necessary talk (religious). 9 Luke 12:15! 10.15 Chaise. 12 Dinner; sermon. 2 Chaise. 3.45 Gainsborough.

SATURDAY, JUNE 24. 4 Sermon; prayed. 5.30 Chaise. 8 Newton [on Trent]; tea; +Psalms 90,12 chaise; Newark[-on-Trent]; necessary talk (religious); dinner. 1 Ecclesiastes 9:10! 2.45 Chaise; Tuxford. 4 Tea. 4.30 Chaise. 6.15 Retford; sermon; prayed; Revelation 20:12! supper; prayer. 9.30.

SUNDAY, JUNE 25. 4 Prayed; sermon. 5.30 Chaise; Misterton; tea. 8 +2 Corinthians 5:19! chaise; sermon. 10.30 Read Prayers; coach. 1 Dinner, religious talk; +Luke 8:3, etc; chaise; Epworth; tea; prayed. 3.30 +Matthew 22:4! Love-feast! supper, religious talk; prayer. 9.30.

MONDAY, JUNE 26. 4 Prayed; Luke 9:62; sermon. 8 Tea, religious talk; prayer; sermon. 12 Chaise; Owston [Ferry]; prayer. 1 Dinner, religious talk. 2 Sermon. 3 Walked; religious talk! tea, religious talk; prayed. 5.50 Read Prayers, Proverbs 3:17! 7.30 Supper, religious talk; prayer. 9.30.

TUESDAY, JUNE 27. 4 Prayed; letters. 7 Tea, religious talk; prayer; read notes. 9 Read Prayers, 1 Samuel 21:8; prayer; chaise. 12 Belton; dinner. 1 +Romans 8:3, 4; letters. 4.30 Tea, religious talk; prayer; chaise; walked. 6.15 Prayed. 7 Micah 2:10; visited; supper, religious talk; prayer. 9.30.

WEDNESDAY, JUNE 28. 4 Prayed; 1 Thessalonians 5:19! sermon. 7.30 Tea, religious talk; prayer; visited. 9 Sermon. 12.30 Garden. 1 Dinner, religious talk; sermon. 3.30 Prayed. 4 Visited some; tea, religious talk. 6 Prayed. 6.30 1 Corinthians 6:20! religious talk. 8.15 Supper; prayer. 9.30.

THURSDAY, JUNE 29. 4 Prayed; 1 Corinthians 15:58; letters. 7.30 Tea, religious talk; prayer; necessary business. 9 Chaise; visited! 10.45 Thorne; letter; dinner, religious talk. 1 Colossians 1:10! chaise. 4.15 Doncaster. 5 Necessary talk (religious); tea, religious talk. 6 Prayer. 6.30 John 4:24! supper, religious talk; prayer. 9.30.

FRIDAY, JUNE 30. 4 Prayed; journal. 7 Tea, religious talk. 8 Isaiah 59:1, 2! chaise. 12 Barnsley; dinner. 1.30 +Hebrews 9:27! 2.45 Chaise. 5 Rotherham; tea, religious talk. 6 +Matthew 8:13! Society; supper, religious talk; prayer. 9.30.

SATURDAY, JULY 1. 4 Prayed; Matthew 5:6; Select Society; letters. 8 Tea, religious talk; prayer; letters; visited. 10.30 Chaise. 12 Bramley; Matthew 7:24! at Mrs Spencer's, dinner, mostly religious talk. 3 Chaise. 5 Sheffield; tea. 6 Romans 13:11! necessary business; supper; prayer. 9.30.

SUNDAY, JULY 2. 4 Prayed; letters. 8 Tea, religious talk; letter. 9.30 Read Prayers, Luke 14:17, Communion. 2 Dinner; slept; letter. 3.45 Prayed. 4.30 Tea, good talk. 5 Luke 15:7; Society! letter. 8 Supper, mostly religious talk; prayer. 9.30.

MONDAY, JULY 3. 4 Prayed; Psalms 50:23! letters. 8 Tea, religious talk; prayer; sermon. 12.45 Quarterly Meeting; dinner. 1.30 Magazine. 3 Love-feast. 4.30 Tea, religious talk; visited; Communion. 6.30 2 Timothy 3:5! 8 Prayed; supper, religious talk; prayer. 9.30.

TUESDAY, JULY 4. 4 Prayed; 1 John 2:15! Select Society; necessary business; tea. 8 Chaise. 10 Wentworth; walked in the house [Wentworth Woodhouse]; choc[olate]; walked. 12.45 Thorpe [Hesley]; +Mark 3:35; chaise. 2.15 At Mr Sparrow's. 2.30 Dinner, religious talk; prayer. 4 Chaise; necessary business; tea; prayed. 6.30 Mark 9:23; Society; supper; prayer. 9.30.

WEDNESDAY, JULY 5. 4 Prayed; 1 Corinthians 15:58; tea. 6.45 Chaise. 9.15 Chesterfield; tea. 10 Chaise; visited. 1 Belper; +John 17:3; dinner, religious talk; prayer. 3.15 Chaise. 4.30 Derby; necessary talk (religious), tea. 5.30 Prayed. 6.30 Ecclesiastes 7:29! Society; supper; prayer. 9.30.

THURSDAY, JULY 6. 4 Prayed; Revelation 2:5; Society; necessary talk (religious); letter; tea; prayer. 8.30 Chaise; visited. 11.30 Ilkeston; prayers, Proverbs 3:17; necessary talk (religious), dinner. 3 Chaise. 4.30 Nottingham; tea. 5 Prayed. 6 Letter. 7 Daniel 9:24; the bands. 8 Supper, religious talk; prayer. 9.30.

FRIDAY, JULY 7. 4 Prayed; Matthew 20:15; letters. 11 Necessary business. 12.30 Dinner, religious talk; prayer. 3 Necessary business; religious talk; prayer. 4.30 Prayed; tea, religious talk; prayer. 6.30 Matthew 20:16; the leaders. 8 Supper, religious talk; prayer. 9.30.

SATURDAY, JULY 8. 4 Prayed; 1 Corinthians 11:28; letters; accounts. 8 Tea, religious talk; prayer; writ journal; necessary business. 12 Chaise. 1 At brother Hall's, religious talk, dinner; prayer. 2.30 Chaise. 3 Nottingham; necessary business; prayed. 4 Infirmary! 5.30 Tea, religious talk; prayer; religious talk! 7 1 Peter 1:18! religious talk to many; supper; prayer; sins! 10.

SUNDAY, JULY 9. 4 Prayed; letters; Magazine. 8.30 Tea, religious talk; prayer. 9.30 Read Prayers, Luke 8:18, Communion. 1.30 Dinner, religious talk. 2.30 Magazine. 4 Prayed. 5 Tea, religious talk. 5.30 Luke 8:18! Society. 8 Supper, religious talk; prayer. 9.30.

MONDAY, JULY 10. 4 Prayed; 1 Thessalonians 5:23; tea. 6 Chaise. 9 Mountsorrel; Romans 1:16; chaise. 11.30 Leicester; dinner. 1 Matthew 8:13! chaise. 4.30 Hinckley! tea; prayed. 6.30 Matthew 7:24. 8 Supper; prayer. 9.30.

TUESDAY, JULY 11. 4 Prayed. 5 Judges 1:27; Magazine; tea. 9 Chaise. 11 Coventry; necessary business. 12 Matthew 22:4! dinner. 2 Chaise. 4 Birmingham; tea, religious talk. 5 Necessary business; prayed. 6.30 John 4:24; the bands; supper, religious talk; prayer. 9.30.

[Text noted at bottom of page:] 2 Corinthians 4:7.

WEDNESDAY, JULY 12. 4 Prayed; 2 Corinthians 4:7! letters. 8 Tea, religious talk; prayer; letters. 11 Read notes. 12 Deritend [Birmingham]; 2 Corinthians 4:18. 2 Dinner, religious talk; prayer; at sister Philips's; prayed; tea. 6 1 Corinthians 13:8, etc; post coach.

THURSDAY, JULY 13. 4 Read; good talk; Oxford; tea. 5 Coach. 2 London; dinner; necessary business; prayer. 5 Tea; prayed; necessary business. 6.30 1 Thessalonians 5:23; the bands; supper, religious talk; prayer. 9.30.

FRIDAY, JULY 14. 4 Prayed; 2 Corinthians 4:7! brother Moore, etc. 8 Tea, religious talk; prayer. 9 Brother Moore, etc. 12.30 Walked. 1 Dinner, religious talk; letters. 5 Tea, religious talk; prayer. 6 Letters; prayed. 8 Supper, religious talk; prayer. 9.30.

SATURDAY, JULY 15. 4 Prayed; writ notes. 6 Brother Moore, etc. 8 Tea, religious talk; prayer. 9 Letters. 11 Necessary business. 12 Journal; garden. 1 Dinner, religious talk; prayer. 2 Letters. 3.30 Prayed; walked; tea, religious talk. 6 Read Prayers, 2 Thessalonians 2:13, Communion; Magazine; supper; Penry, necessary business. 9.30.

SUNDAY, JULY 16. 4 Prayed; Magazine. 8 The preachers; prayed. 9.30 Read Prayers, John 4:24! Communion! 1.30 Dinner, religious talk; prayer; slept. 3 The leaders; buried Thomas Parkinson! tea; prayed. 5 Read Prayers, 1 Samuel 17! Society; Love-feast. 8 Supper, religious talk; prayer. 9.30.

MONDAY, JULY 17. 4 Prayed; Psalms 84:1! Select Society; writ notes. 8 Tea, religious talk; prayer; walked. 10 Chapel; read notes. 12 Select Society; necessary talk (religious)! dinner, religious talk; visited some. 5 Tea, religious talk; prayer; visited. 6.15 Read Prayers, 1 Timothy 1:5! supper. 8.30 Mail coach; necessary business. 10.

TUESDAY, JULY 18. 4 Read; religious talk. 9.30 Bath; tea; coach. 12 Necessary business. 1 Dinner, religious talk; writ letters. 5 Tea, religious talk; hoarse! prayed; letters. 8 Supper, religious talk; prayer; applied garlic. 9.30.

WEDNESDAY, JULY 19. 4.30 Prayed; Conference; religious talk. 8 Tea, religious talk; prayer; writ for Conference; necessary talk (religious) to many; necessary business. 2.15 At Mr Durbin's, dinner, necessary talk (religious); prayer. 3.30 Conference; prayed. 5.30 Tea, religious talk; prayer. 6.30 Writ Conference. 8 Supper, religious talk; prayer. 9.30.

THURSDAY, JULY 20. 4 Prayed; Conference; in the water; Conference. 8 Tea, religious talk; prayer; Conference. 2 Dinner, religious talk; prayer. 4 Prayed. 5

Tea, religious talk; necessary business. 6.30 2 Corinthians 4:7! the bands; necessary talk (religious) to some. 8 Supper, religious talk; prayer. 9.30.

FRIDAY, JULY 21. 4 Prayed; read letters. 6 In the water. 7 Read letters; writ Conference. 10 Writ letters. 2.30 Dinner; walked. 5 At the School; necessary talk (religious); tea; walked; prayed. 7 Letters; supper, religious talk; prayer. 9.30.

SATURDAY, JULY 22. 4 Prayed; letters; the children; letters; walked. 8 At brother Rhodes's, tea, religious talk; prayer. 9 Letters. 12 Dr Coke, etc, necessary talk (religious)! 1.30 Cotham; mostly religious talk. 2 Dinner, necessary talk (religious); walked! 4.30 Letters. 5 Tea, religious talk. 6 Letters. 8 Supper; religious talk, prayer. 9.30.

[Text noted at bottom of page:] Jeremiah 48:10.

SUNDAY, JULY 23. 4 Prayed; letters. 8 Tea, religious talk; necessary business. 9.30 Charles read Prayers, John 11:43, Communion. 1 At brother Ewer's, dinner, necessary talk (religious); prayer. 2.45 Slept; prayed. 4 At sister Stafford's, tea, religious talk; prayed. 5 +Matthew 5:20! Society; read letters. 8 Supper, religious talk; prayer. 9.30.

MONDAY, JULY 24. 4 Prayed; Mr Pawson, etc. 6 Writ letters. 8 Tea, religious talk; prayer. 9 Writ letters. 11 Necessary talk (religious) to many; letters. 1 At brother Cross's, dinner, religious talk; prayer. 2 Letters; necessary talk (religious) to many. 4 Letter; prayed. 5 Tea, religious talk; prayed. 6.30 1 Corinthians 10:32! necessary talk (religious) to many. 8 Supper, necessary talk (religious); prayer. 9.30.

TUESDAY, JULY 25. 4 Prayed; brother Pawson, etc. 6 Conference. 8 Tea, religious talk; prayer. 9 Conference. 12 Writ narrative. 1 Dinner, religious talk; prayer. 2 Conference. 4 Brother Pawson, etc. 5 Tea, religious talk. 6 Prayed. 6.30 Jeremiah 48:10! writ notes; supper, religious talk; prayer. 9.30.

WEDNESDAY, JULY 26. 4 Prayed; brother Pawson, etc. 6 Conference. 8 Tea, religious talk; prayer. 9 Conference. 12 Writ notes. 1 Dinner. 2 Conference. 4 Brother Pawson, etc. 5 Tea, religious talk; prayer. 6 Writ notes; letters. 8 Supper, necessary talk (religious); prayer. 9.30.

THURSDAY, JULY 27. 4 Prayed; Committee. 6 Conference. 8 Tea, religious talk; prayer. 9 Conference. 12 Writ notes. 1 Dinner. 2 Conference! 4 Committee. 5 Tea, religious talk; visited. 6 Prayed, Ephesians 5:25! the bands! 8.15 Supper, mostly religious talk; prayer. 9.30.

FRIDAY, JULY 28. 4 Prayed; ordained Joshua Keighley, William Warrener, and William Hammet. 6 Conference. 9 Prayer. 10 Conference. 12.30 Writ notes. 2 Dinner, religious talk; prayer. 3.30 Letters; prayed. 5 Tea, religious talk; prayed. 6 Prayed; letters; supper. 8.30 Ephesians 4:11, etc! prayer. 10.

SATURDAY, JULY 29. 4 Prayed; ordained! Conference. 8 Tea, religious talk; prayer. 9 Conference. 12.30 Necessary business. 1 Dinner, religious talk. 2 Conference. 3 Letters. 5 Tea, necessary talk (religious). 6 Necessary business; necessary talk (religious). 7.30 Prayed; supper, religious talk; prayer; necessary business. 9.30.

SUNDAY, JULY 30. 4 Prayed; letters. 8 Tea; necessary business. 9.30 Read Prayers, Romans 6:23, Communion; coach. 1.30 At the School. 2 Dinner. 2.15 Psalms 146:4; coach; prayed; tea. 5 Hebrews 2:3; Society. 8 Supper, religious talk; prayer. 9.30.

MONDAY, JULY 31. 4 Prayed; letters. 6 Conference. 8 Tea, necessary talk (religious); Conference. 12 Writ Conference. 1 Dinner, religious talk; prayer. 2 Conference. 4 Letter; visited some; tea. 6 Prayed; Hebrews 11; in the water; supper, religious talk; prayer. 9.30.

[Texts noted at bottom of page:] Ephesians 4:11, etc; 5:25; 1 Corinthians 10:32; Hebrews 11:40.

TUESDAY, AUGUST 1. 4 Prayed; Acts 22:16(2)! Conference. 8 Tea; letters. 11.30 Necessary business. 1 Dinner, religious talk; prayer. 2 Letter; tea. 4 Coach. 9.30 Supper; slept.

WEDNESDAY, AUGUST 2. 4.30 Read; sang. 8.15 North Green; tea; prayer; letters. 12 At home; necessary business; mostly religious talk. 1 North Green; dinner; letters. 5 Tea, religious talk; prayer; prayed. 6.30 Letters. 8 Supper; prayer. 9.30.

THURSDAY, AUGUST 3. 4.15 Prayed; accounts. 8 Tea, religious talk; prayer; writ journal. 11 At home; necessary business. 12 Walked; visited. 1.15 Dinner, religious talk; prayer. 3.30 Read letters; Magazine. 4.15 Prayed; tea, religious talk; prayer. 6 Necessary business. 6.30 Hebrews 6:1! necessary talk (religious) to many; supper. 9.30.

FRIDAY, AUGUST 4. 4 Prayed; Acts 22:16; tunes. 8 Read notes; tunes. 12 Necessary talk (religious). 12.30 Letters. 2.30 Dinner, religious talk; writ 'Thoughts upon Methodism'. 5 Tea, religious talk; garden. 6.30 Prayed; writ notes. 8 Supper, religious talk; prayer. 9.30.

SATURDAY, AUGUST 5. 4 Prayed; writ Mr Fletcher's *Life*. 8 Tea, religious talk; prayer; writ *Life*. 12.30 Necessary business. 1 Dinner; prayer. 2.30 *Life*. 5 Tea, religious talk. 6 Prayed; *Life*. 7.30 Supper, religious talk; Penry, necessary business. 9.30.

SUNDAY, AUGUST 6. 4 Prayed; *Life*. 8 The preachers; letter. 9.30 Read Prayers, Matthew 7:16! Communion; dinner. 2 Slept; prayed. 3 Leaders. 4 Tea, religious talk; prayer. 5 Read Prayers, 2 Timothy 4:7, 8! buried. 6.30 Society; necessary talk (religious) to some. 8 At Thomas Rankin's, supper, religious talk; prayer. 9.30.

MONDAY, AUGUST 7. 4 Prayed; Acts 22:16(2)! Select Society; letters; tea, religious talk; letters. 12.30 Necessary business. 1 Dinner, religious talk; prayer. 2 Necessary business; letter. 5 Westminster; tea; *Life*. 6.15 Read Prayers, Hebrews 10:36; the bands; Charles; prayer. 9.30.

TUESDAY, AUGUST 8. 4 Prayed; *Life*. 6 Tea, religious talk. 7 Coach. 10 Ingatestone; tea, necessary talk (religious). 10.30 Coach. 2.30 Colchester; dinner; the Castle; walked. 4.30 Coach. 8 Harwich; supper, necessary talk (religious). 9.30.

WEDNESDAY, AUGUST 9. 4 Prayed; *Life;* letters. 8 Tea; letters; *Life*. 12.30 Visited. 1.30 Dinner. 2.30 Ship, the *Besborough;* necessary talk; read Told. 5 Prayed; tea; Told; mostly religious talk; supper. 9 Mostly religious talk. 9.30.

THURSDAY, AUGUST 10. 4 Prayed; Told. 8 Tea; Smollett; Proverbs 3:17; religious talk; Smollet. 2 Dinner, religious talk; Smollet; tea; prayed; Smollet; supper, mostly religious talk. 9.30.

FRIDAY, AUGUST 11. 4.30 Prayed; Smollet. 8 Tea, necessary talk (religious); Smollet. 2 Dinner. 4 Hellevoetsluis; necessary business. 4.45 Coach. 10 Rotterdam; necessary business; at Mrs Loyal's, supper. 11.

[SATURDAY] AUGUST 12. 5.30 Prayed; letter; *Life*. 8 Tea, religious talk; *Life*. 12.30 Visited; *Life*. 2 Dinner, religious talk. 3.30 *Life*. 5 At Mr Hall's, tea, religious talk. 6 Prayed; *Life*. 8.30 Supper, religious talk; prayer. 10.

SUNDAY, AUGUST 13. 4.30 Prayed; *Life*. 8 Tea, religious talk; *Life*. 10 Episcopal Church, read Prayers, 1 Kings 18:21. 12 *Life;* at Mr Williams's, dinner; *Life*. 2.30 Read Prayers, 1 Corinthians 10:13! visited; tea, religious talk. 6 *Life;* prayed; walked. 8.30 Supper, religious talk; prayer. 10.

MONDAY, AUGUST 14. 4.30 Prayed; *Life*. 7.30 Tea. 8 Boat; read History. 10.30 Delft; religious talk. 11.30 Boat. 12.30 Hague; at Mr Allen's; *Life*. 3 Dinner; *Life*. 5 Tea. 6 *Life*. 7.30 Walked; religious talk! supper; prayer. 10.

TUESDAY, AUGUST 15. 4.30 Prayed; *Life;* tea. 7 Boat; *Life*. 11 Leyden [orig., 'Luden']; visited some. 12.30 Boat. 5 Haarlem. 5.30 Boat. 7.30 Amsterdam; walked. 8 At brother Ferguson's, supper, necessary talk (religious); prayer. 10.

WEDNESDAY, AUGUST 16. 4.30 Prayed; *Life*. 7.30 Tea, religious talk; prayer; *Life*. 12.30 Walked; *Life*. 2 Dinner; *Life*. 4 At Mrs Yeaston's, tea, religious talk; prayer. 7.30 Hebrews 9:27; supper, necessary talk (religious); prayer. 9.30.

THURSDAY, AUGUST 17. 4 Prayed; *Life*. 8 At brother Dykeman's, tea, religious talk; prayer; visited. 10 Deacons. 11 *Life*. 1 Walked; at Mr Vanhingel's, dinner, religious talk; prayer. 4.15 Walked. 5 At Mrs Melv——'s! tea, necessary talk (religious). 6 *Life;* prayed. 7.30 Supper, religious talk; prayer. 9.30.

FRIDAY, AUGUST 18. 4 Prayed. 6 Boat; religious talk. 9.30 Haarlem; tea; read Prayers; visited; walked. 1 At Mr Van Kampen's [orig., 'Van Campen's'], garden, religious talk; prayer. 2.30 *Life.* 5 Visited; tea, religious talk. 7 At Miss Valkenburg [orig., 'Falconberg'], music, religious talk. 9 Supper, mostly religious talk. 10 Coach. 10.30.

SATURDAY, AUGUST 19. 5 Prayed; *Life.* 8 Tea, religious talk; *Life.* 11 Walked. 1 Dinner, religious talk. 3 Boat; *Life.* 6 At home; tea; prayed. 6.30 At Mr Schouten's, music; Ephesians 2:8! supper, religious talk; prayer. 9.30.

SUNDAY, AUGUST 20. 4 Prayed; *Life.* 7 Tea, religious talk; *Life.* 9.30 English Church, read Prayers! *Life.* 12.30 Dinner, religious talk; *Life.* 1.30 Read Prayers. 3 *Life.* 4 At brother Dykeman's, tea; Matthew 7:24! 6.30 At Mr Vankennel's [orig., 'Vanhingel's'], religious talk, supper. 8.30 At home; prayer. 9.15.

MONDAY, AUGUST 21. 4.30 Prayed; *Life.* 7 Tea, religious talk; prayer; *Life.* 12 Visited. 1 Dinner, religious talk; *Life.* 3.30 Walked. 4 At Mrs Yeaston's, religious talk; prayer; walked; at Mr Nolthenius's [orig., 'Noltani's'], tea, religious talk, garden! 7 Coach; walked. 8 Supper, religious talk; prayer. 9.30.

TUESDAY, AUGUST 22. 4 Prayed; *Life;* blin[d]! 8.30 At Mr Dykeman's, tea, religious talk; prayer! visited. 10.30 At home; *Life.* 1.30 Dinner, religious talk; *Life.* 4 Prayed. 5 At Mr Genan's, tea, religious talk. 7.30 *Life.* 8.30 Supper, religious talk; prayer. 9.30.

WEDNESDAY, AUGUST 23. 4 Prayed; *Life.* 7.30 Tea, religious talk; *Life.* 10.30 Necessary talk (religious); walked. 12 At Mr Vankennel's; *Life.* 3 Dinner, religious talk; *Life.* 4.45 Garden; tea, religious talk; walked. 7.30 *Life.* 8 Supper, religious talk; prayer. 9.30.

THURSDAY, AUGUST 24. 4.30 Prayed; tea. 7 Boat; writ journal. 2.30 Utrecht; at Mr Van Rocy's. 3 Dinner, necessary talk (religious); diary; prayed. 5 Tea, religious talk; visited some. 7 *Life.* 8.30 Supper, religious talk. 9 Prayer. 10.

FRIDAY, AUGUST 25. 4 Prayed; *Life.* 8 At Mr Russel's, tea, mostly religious talk. 9 *Life;* at Miss Loten's, dinner, religious talk; prayer. 4 Garden! 5.15 At Mr Thompson's, tea, religious talk; visited. 6 *Life.* 7 At Miss Loten's; Matthew 7:24; religious talk. 9.30 Supper, religious talk. 10.30 At home.

SATURDAY, AUGUST 26. 5 Prayed; *Life.* 7 Ill, lay down, slept. 10 Visited some. 1 At home; dinner, religious talk. 3 *Life;* prayed. 5 At Mr [blank], tea, religious talk; prayer; visited, religious talk!. 8 Supper, religious talk; prayer; necessary business. 9.30.

SUNDAY, AUGUST 27. 4 Prayed; *Life.* 7.30 Tea; *Life.* 9.30 At the English Church. 10 Read Prayers, sermon! 11.30 *Life.* 1 At Mr Russel's, dinner, necessary talk (religious). 3 *Life.* 4 Prayed; tea. 5 Read Prayers, Isaiah 55:6! visited; at Mr Loten's, religious talk; prayer! visited. 9 Supper. 9.45.

MONDAY, AUGUST 28. 4.15 Prayed; *Life;* tea, religious talk. 7 Boat; *Life.* 1.30 Gouda; at Mr [blank]. 2 Dinner, religious talk. 3.15 Coach. 5.30 Rotterdam; tea, necessary talk (religious). 6.30 Tea; supper; prayer. 9.30.

TUESDAY, AUGUST [29]. 4.15 Prayed; writ diary; tea; read notes. 2.30 Dinner. 4 Read notes; tea; prayed; supper; prayer. 9.45.

WEDNESDAY, AUGUST [30]. 4 Prayed; tea. 6 Coach. 12.30 Hellevoetsluis; read. 1.45 Dinner. 3 Writ notes; tea; supper; prayer. 9.30.

[THURSDAY, AUGUST 31.] 4 Prayed; read notes. 8 Tea; read notes; letters; walked. 2.30 Dinner. 4 Prayed; walked; tea. 7 Read notes. 8 Supper, necessary talk (religious); prayer. 9.30.

FRIDAY, SEPTEMBER 1. 4.30 Prayed; sermon. 8 Tea; sermon; walked. 2.30 Dinner; sermon. 4.30 Walked. 5 Sermon; tea; prayed; sermon. 8 Supper, religious talk; prayer. 9.30 Lay down. 11 Slept.

SATURDAY, SEPTEMBER 2. 4.15 Prayed; sermon; tea. 9 On board; read. 1 Dinner; read *Excerpta*. 5.30 Tea; prayed. 6 Read *Excerpta;* necessary talk (religious); supper; *Excerpta*. 9.30.

SUNDAY, SEPTEMBER 3. 4.30 Prayed; read *Excerpta*. 8 Tea; *Excerpta;* necessary talk (religious). 1 Dinner. 2 Prayed; Hebrews 9:27! *Excerpta;* religious talk; tea; prayed; supper. 9.30.

MONDAY, SEPTEMBER 4. 4 Prayed; *Excerpta;* mostly religious talk. 9 Harwich; tea, religious talk. 10 Chaise. 1 Colchester; at Inn, dinner, religious talk. 2 Diary; writ diary; prayed; tea; writ letters. 6.30 Prayed. 7 Luke 8:18! supper; prayer. 9.30.

TUESDAY, SEPTEMBER 5. 4 Prayed; tea. 5.15 chaise; Ingatestone; tea; chaise. 1 At home; dinner; prayed. 2 Necessary business; at Thomas Rankin's, necessary business; writ notes. 5 Tea, religious talk. 6.30 Psalms 29 *ult!;* at Thomas Rankin's, supper, religious talk; prayer. 9.30.

WEDNESDAY, SEPTEMBER 6. 4 Prayed; letters. 6 Dr Coke, etc, necessary talk (religious). 7 Letters. 8 Tea, religious talk; prayer. 9 Letters; sins! letters. 1.30 Dinner, religious talk; letters. 5 Tea, religious talk; visited; necessary business. 8 Supper, religious talk; prayer. 9.30.

THURSDAY, SEPTEMBER 7. 3.30 Prayed; tea. 4.30 Chaise; Colnbrook; tea; chaise. 12 Reading; chaise. 2.30 Newbury; dinner, religious talk; *Life.* 5 Tea, religious talk; prayed. 6.30 Matthew 7:24! supper, religious talk; prayer. 9.30.

FRIDAY, SEPTEMBER 8. 3.30 Tea. 4.15 Chaise; Smollett; Hungerford; tea, religious talk; chaise. 10 Beckhampton [orig., 'Beckington']; chaise; Melksham; dinner. 2.30 Chaise. 4 Bath; writ notes; prayed; tea, religious talk. 6.30 1 Thessalonians 4:8! supper; prayer. 9.30.

SATURDAY, SEPTEMBER 9. 4 Prayed; 2 Corinthians 4:7! letters. 8 Tea, necessary talk! prayer. 10 Letter; read. 1 Dinner, religious talk. 2 Necessary business; letter; prayed. 5 Tea, religious talk; Magazine. 7 1 Thessalonians 4:3! 8 Supper, religious talk; prayer. 9.30.

SUNDAY, SEPTEMBER 10. 4 Prayed; Magazine. 8 Tea; Magazine. 10 Read Prayers, 2 Kings 19:3, Communion. 1 Dinner. 2 Necessary business; slept. 2.30 Matthew 11:28; prayed; tea; visited; Magazine. 5.30 Luke 10:23! Society! Magazine; supper; prayer. 9.30.

[Text noted at bottom of page:] Matthew 18:3.

MONDAY, SEPTEMBER 11. 4 Prayed. 6 Psalms 50:23; necessary talk (religious), tea. 8 Chaise. 10 Hanham; Charles, religious talk. 11 Magazine. 2 Dinner, religious talk; chaise. 4 At home; necessary business; prayed; tea, religious talk. 6 Prayed; Magazine; 1 Peter 3:7; Magazine; supper; Magazine; prayer. 9.30.

TUESDAY, SEPTEMBER 12. 4 Prayed; letter; Magazine. 7.30 At Mr Stock's, tea; Magazine. 1 At brother Cross's. 2 Dinner. 2.30 Magazine; prayed. 5 At Mr King's, tea, religious talk. 6 Prayed. 6.30 1 Peter 3:10, etc. 7.30 The leaders; at brother Stock's, supper, religious talk; prayer. 9.30.

WEDNESDAY, SEPTEMBER 13. 4 Prayed; *Life.* 8 Tea, religious talk; prayer; *Life;* sins! 2 At Mr Durbin's, tea. 2.30 Dinner; prayer. 3.30 *Life;* prayed; at brother Collins's, tea, religious talk. 6.30 Temple Church. 7 Read Prayers, Romans 14:17! 8 Supper, religious talk; prayer. 9.30.

THURSDAY, SEPTEMBER 14. 4 Prayed; *Life.* 8 Tea, religious talk; prayer. 9 *Life.* 1 At brother Green's, dinner, religious talk. 2 Prayer. 2.30 *Life.* 5 Tea, religious talk; prayed. 6 *Life.* 8 Supper, religious talk; prayer. 9.30.

FRIDAY, SEPTEMBER 15. 4 Prayed; *Life.* 12 Magazine; read notes. 2 At brother Roberts's, dinner, religious talk. 3 Prayer. 3.30 Visited some. 5 Tea, religious talk. 6.30 Guinea Street; Hebrews 12:1(2). 8 Supper; prayer. 9.30.

SATURDAY, SEPTEMBER 16. 4 Prayed; letters. 8 Tea, religious talk; prayer. 9.30 At home; necessary business; read notes. 1 At brother Pine's, dinner; prayer. 3 *Life;* necessary business; prayed. 5 At brother Gifford's, tea, religious talk; *Life.* 7 Penry. 8 At Mr Pownal's, supper, religious talk; prayer. 9.30.

SUNDAY, SEPTEMBER 17. 4 Prayed; letters; *Life.* 8 Tea, religious talk; prayer. 9.30 Coach; read Prayers, Matthew 18:3, Communion; chaise. 1.30 At the School. 2 Dinner; Matthew 18:14, etc; Society; writ notes; supper, religious talk; prayer. 9.30.

MONDAY, SEPTEMBER 18. 4 Prayed; Matthew 18:3; *Life.* 7 Class; tea. 9 Class. 1 Dinner, religious talk. 2 Class. 4 Writ notes. 5 Tea, religious talk; prayer. 6.15 Prayed. 7 1 Peter 3:10, etc! 8 At Mr Castleman's, supper, necessary talk (religious); prayer. 9.30.

TUESDAY, SEPTEMBER 19. 4 Prayed; writ Society. 6 Class. 7 Tea, religious talk; prayer. 9 Class. 1 Dinner, religious talk; prayer. 2 Class. 3 Writ Society; prayer. 5 Tea, religious talk; prayer. 6 Prayed; 1 Peter 3 *ad fin;* the leaders. 8 At Mr Castleman's, supper, religious talk; prayer. 9.30.

WEDNESDAY, SEPTEMBER 20. 4 Prayed; writ Society; read! 8 Tea; class. 1.30 Dinner. 2 Class. 4.15 Tea, religious talk. 5 Isaiah 37:3; class. 7 Clifton; writ Society. 8 Supper, religious talk; prayer. 9.30.

[Text noted at bottom of page:] Hebrews 12:1(2).

THURSDAY, SEPTEMBER 21. 4 Prayed; Society. 8 Tea, religious talk; prayer; writ Society. 1.30 At Mr Gifford's, dinner, mostly religious talk; writ letters. 4.15 Prayed. 5 Tea, religious talk; prayed. 6.30 1 Peter 4:1-6; the bands. 8 At Mr Gifford's, supper, religious talk; prayer. 9.30.

FRIDAY, SEPTEMBER 22. 4.15 Prayed; sermon. 8 Tea; prayer; sermon. 10 Writ notes; read Gebalin. 12 The females. 12.30 Visited. 1 Prayer. 2.15 Dinner, religious talk; prayer. 4 Prayed; tea, religious talk. 5.30 Prayed. 6 Writ sermon. 8 Supper, religious talk; prayer. 9.30.

SATURDAY, SEPTEMBER 23. 4 Prayed; sermon. 8 Tea, religious talk; prayer; read Gebalin. 12 Visited some. 2 At Mr Durbin's, dinner, religious talk; prayer. 4 Slept; visited. 5 Tea, religious talk; prayer. 6 Prayed. 7 Penry; at brother Pownal's, supper, religious talk; prayer. 9.30.

SUNDAY, SEPTEMBER 24. 4 Prayed; letters. 8 Tea, religious talk; necessary business. 9.30 Charles read Prayers, 1 Corinthians 12:31! Communion; dinner, religious talk; meditation. 3 Temple [Church]; read Prayers, Galatians 6:16! tea, religious talk; prayed. 5 +Galatians 6:17! Society; the singers; supper, religious talk; prayer. 9.30.

MONDAY, SEPTEMBER 25. 4 Prayed; 1 Peter 4:7, 8! letters; necessary business. 8 Tea, religious talk; letters. 12 Select Society. 1 Dinner. 2 Letters. 4 Coach; with Miss Ki—— and brother Broadbent; religious talk, sang, supper. 12.

TUESDAY, SEPTEMBER 26. 6 Read. 9 At home; tea, necessary business; letters. 1 Dinner; prayer; letters. 5 At Thomas Rankin's, tea, religious talk. 6 Prayed; *Life.* 8 Supper, religious talk; prayer. 9.30.

WEDNESDAY, SEPTEMBER 27. 4 Prayed; *Life.* 8 Tea, religious talk; *Life;* walked. 11 [Stoke] Newington; *Life.* 1.30 Dinner, religious talk. 2.30 *Life.* 5 Tea, religious talk; prayer. 6.30 *Life.* 8 Supper, religious talk; prayer. 9.30.

THURSDAY, SEPTEMBER 28. 4 Prayed. 5 *Life.* 8 Tea, religious talk; prayer; *Life.* 10.30 Walked; at sister Cheesement's. 11 Religious talk; prayer! walked. 12.30 Necessary business. 1 At brother Willan's, dinner, religious talk; prayer. 3 Visited; *Life;* tea, religious talk. 6 Necessary business. 6.30 Read Prayers, 1 Chronicles 4:10! the bands; supper; prayer. 9.30.

[FRIDAY, SEPTEMBER 29.] 4 Prayed; *Life.* 11.45 Necessary business. 12 The females; prayer. 2 Dinner. 3 *Life;* visited many. 5 Tea; prayed; *Life.* 8 Tea, religious talk; prayer, *Life.* 11.30.

[SATURDAY, SEPTEMBER 30.] 11.30 Visited! 1 At home; dinner. 2 Prepared hymn-book. 5 Tea, religious talk; prayer; hymn-book. 8 Supper; Penry, necessary business. 9.30. 12 Ill.

[Text noted at bottom of page:] 1 Chronicles 4:10.

SUNDAY, OCTOBER 1. 7 Prayed; necessary business. 8 The preachers. 9.30 Read Prayers, 1 Corinthians 12:31! Communion. 1 Dinner, religious talk; prayer; slept. 3 The leaders. 4 Tea; prayed. 5 Read Prayers, Ephesians 3:14; Society; religious talk, supper; prayer. 9.30.

MONDAY, OCTOBER 2. 4 Necessary business; tea. 5 Coach; History; religious talk. 11.15 Chatham; letters. 1.15 Dinner. 2 Letters. 5 Tea, religious talk; prayed. 6.30 1 Chronicles 4:10! supper; prayer. 9.30.

TUESDAY, OCTOBER 3. 4 Prayed; Matt 12:43! sermon; tea, religious talk; prayer. 8.30 In the boat; read; prayer. 10.30 Sheerness; sermon. 12.30 Walked. 1 At Mr Greathead's, dinner, religious talk; prayer. 2.30 Sermon. 4 Prayed. 5 Tea, religious talk; prayed. 6.30 Jeremiah 6:16! Society! supper; prayer. 9.30.

WEDNESDAY, OCTOBER 4. 4 Prayed; Mark 4:26; sermon. 8 Tea, religious talk; visited some. 10 Walked; Queenborough. 11 Revelation 20:12! visited; walked. 1 Dinner; sermon. 4 Prayed. 5 Love-feast! Ecclesiastes 9:10, Communion. 8.30 Supper, religious talk; prayer. 9.30.

THURSDAY, OCTOBER 5. 4 Prayed; Mark 9:23; tea, religious talk; prayer. 7.30 In the boat; read; sang; prayer. 10.30 Chatham; sermon. 12 Dinner; sermon. 2 Visited. 4 Sermon; tea, religious talk; prayer; prayed. 6.30 Luke 10:34! Communion; supper, religious talk; prayer. 9.30.

FRIDAY, OCTOBER 6. 4 Prayed; Mark 9:23(2); tea. 6.30 Coach; Smollett; tea, religious talk. 11.30 At home. 12 The females; letters. 2 Dinner; prayer; letters. 5 Tea, necessary talk (religious). 5.30 Prayed; letters; audit. 8 Supper, religious talk; prayer. 9.30.

SATURDAY, OCTOBER 7. 4 Prayed; sermon; read; sins! 8 Tea, religious talk; necessary business. 10 Writ notes. 11 Chaise. 12 Garden with Charles. 1 Dinner, religious talk. 2 Writ notes; prayed. 4 Visited! tea, religious talk. 6 Read prayers, 2 Corinthians 6:16. 7 Communion; supper; Penry, necessary business. 9.30.

SUNDAY, OCTOBER 8. 4 Prayed; letters; chaise; the preachers; prayed. 9.30 Read Prayers, 1 Corinthians 12:31! Communion. 1 Dinner, religious talk; prayer; slept; prayed. 3 The leaders; read Prayers, 2 Corinthians 7:1; Society; tea; Society. 7 Necessary business; supper; prayer. 9.30.

MONDAY, OCTOBER 9. 4 Prayed; 1 Peter 5:1-4; Select Society; necessary business. 8 Tea, religious talk; prayer; chaise; visited! 10 Letters. 11 Visited; necessary business. 1 Dinner, religious talk; prayer; letters. 5 Tea, religious talk; prayed; letters. 8 Supper, religious talk. 9 Prayer. 9.30.

TUESDAY, OCTOBER 10. 4 Prayed; tea. 5 Diligence; Ware; tea; Diligence. 1 Cambridge; dinner. 2 Diligence. 9 [King's] Lynn; supper; prayer. 10.30.

WEDNESDAY, OCTOBER 11. 4 Prayed; Luke 10:34; *Life.* 8 Tea, religious talk; prayer; *Life.* 1 Dinner, religious talk; prayed; *Life.* 4 Prayed. 5 Tea, religious talk; prayer. 6.30 1 Corinthians 12:31! Society! 8.30 Supper, religious talk. 9 Prayer. 9.30.

[Text noted at bottom of page:] 2 Corinthians 6:16.

THURSDAY, OCTOBER 12. 4 Prayed; Mark 9:23(2); *Life.* 8 Tea, religious talk; prayer. 9 *Life;* read notes. 1 Dinner, religious talk; prayer. 2 Necessary talk; letters. 4.30 Prayed; tea, religious talk; prayer. 6.30 2 Corinthians 4:18. 7.30 Communion; supper, religious talk; prayer. 9.30.

FRIDAY, OCTOBER 13. 4 Prayed; tea. 5 Diligence; read Whiston; Ely; tea; Diligence; Royston. 1 Dinner; Diligence. 5.30 Hoddesdon; chaise. 7.30 Barnet; Ecclesiastes 9:10; Hadley; supper; prayer. 10.

SATURDAY, OCTOBER 14. 4 Prayed; *Life.* 7 Tea, necessary talk (religious); prayer. 8 Chaise. 9.45 At home; letters. 1 Dinner, religious talk; prayer. 2 Letters; *Life;* prayed. 5 Tea, religious talk. 6 Read Prayers, 2 Corinthians 13:10! Communion. 8 Supper; Penry, necessary business. 9.30.

SUNDAY, OCTOBER 15. 4.45 Prayed; letters. 8.15 Spitalfields. 9.30 Read Prayers, Luke 1:72! Communion. 1.30 Dinner, religious talk. 3.30 The leaders. 4 Tea; prayed. 5 Deuteronomy 5:6; Society. 7 Letter. 8 Supper, religious talk; prayer. 9.30.

MONDAY, OCTOBER 16. 4 Prayed; coffee. 5 Chaise. 7 Barnet; tea, religious talk. 8 Chaise. 9.30 Hatfield. 10 The House. 11 Miss Harvey. 11.30 Chaise. 3 Hinxworth; dinner, necessary talk (religious); prayed. 6.15 2 Corinthians 4:18! supper, religious talk; prayer. 9.30.

TUESDAY, OCTOBER 17. 4 Prayed; *Life.* 6.30 Matthew 25:1, etc. 7.30 Tea, religious talk; *Life.* 10.30 Garden. 11.30 *Life.* 12.30 Dinner, religious talk; *Life.* 3 Chaise. 5 Wrestlingworth; tea, religious talk. 6 Read Prayers, Galatians 3:22! mostly religious talk, supper; prayer. 9.30.

WEDNESDAY, OCTOBER 18. 4 Prayed; *Life.* 7.30 Tea; prayer. 9 Chaise. 11.30 Hinksworth; *Life.* 1.30 Dinner. 2.30 Letters. 4 Walked. 4.45 Prayed. 5 Tea, religious talk; prayed. 6.30 *Life;* supper, religious talk; prayer. 9.30.

THURSDAY, OCTOBER 19. 4 Prayed; *Life;* Matthew 25:1, etc. 7 Tea, religious talk; prayer; *Life.* 1.30 Dinner, religious talk; *Life.* 5 Tea; prayed; *Life.* 6.30 Revelation 7:8, etc! *Life;* supper, religious talk; prayer. 9.30.

FRIDAY, OCTOBER 20. 4 Prayed; *Life.* 7 2 Corinthians 6:2; tea; prayer; *Life.* 12 Walked! 2 Dinner, religious talk; prayer. 4 Chaise; at home; necessary business; tea. 6 The Trustees! 8 Supper; prayer. 9.30.

SATURDAY, OCTOBER 21. 4 Prayed; letters. 8 Tea, religious talk; prayer; letters. 12 Garden. 1 Dinner, religious talk; prayer; visited. 5 Tea, religious talk. 6 Necessary talk (religious); letters. 7.45 Supper; Penry, necessary business. 9.30.

[Texts noted at bottom of page:] Revelation 7:8, etc; 2 Corinthians 13:10; Deuteronomy 5:6.

SUNDAY, OCTOBER 22. 4 Prayed; letters. 8 Chapel. 9.30 Read Prayers, Ephesians 4:30! Communion; dinner, religious talk; slept. 3 The leaders. 3.30 Read Prayers, Ephesians 2:12; Society; coach; tea. 6.30 Allhallows. 7 Ephesians 2:8! supper, religious talk; prayer. 9.30.

MONDAY, OCTOBER 23. 4 Prayed; 1 Peter 5:1-5; Select Society; tea; *Life*. 12 Select Society. 1.30 Dinner, religious talk. 2.30 *Life*. 3 The children; *Life;* prayed. 5 Tea, religious talk; prayer; prayed. 6.15 Read Prayers, Daniel 6:18! supper. 8 The bands; *Life*. 9.30.

TUESDAY, OCTOBER 24. 4 Prayed; James 2:22; letter; *Life*. 7 Tea, religious talk; prayer; walked. 8 At home; letters; *Life*. 12 Chaise; at brother Dornford's, dinner; *Life*. 4 Class; tea; class. 6.30 Ephesians 2:8. 7.30 The leaders! at sister Philips's, supper, religious talk; prayer. 9.30.

WEDNESDAY, OCTOBER 25. 4 Prayed; *Life*. 8 Tea, religious talk; prayer. 9 *Life*. 12 Walked. 12.30 Dinner; prayer; chaise. 2.30 At home. 3 Necessary business. 3.30 Chaise. 5 Brentford; tea, necessary talk (religious); prayed. 6 Daniel 6:20. 7 Class; prayed. 8 Supper, necessary talk (religious); prayer. 9.30.

THURSDAY, OCTOBER 26. 4 Prayed; letters. 6 [Blank]. 7 Tea, necessary talk (religious); letters. 10 Chaise! 2 At Mr Holbrook's. 2.30 Dinner, religious talk; prayer. 3.45 Chaise. 4.45 Wandsworth; tea; prayed. 6 Hosea 14:4. 7 Society; supper, religious talk; prayer. 9.30.

FRIDAY, OCTOBER 27. 4 Prayed; read. 6 Hebrews 12:13; at Mr Barker's! tea; prayer; chaise. 9 Letters. 12 The females. 12.30 Letters. 2 Dinner, religious talk; prayer. 3 Chaise. 5 Barnet; tea, necessary talk (religious). 6 Ecclesiastes 6:12! class; at brother For[d's], supper; at brother Pa[wson's]. 9 Prayer. 9.30.

SATURDAY, OCTOBER [28]. 4 Prayed; chaise. 6.45 At brother Briggs's; class. 8 Tea; class; *Life*. 11 Class. 12 Letters. 1 Dinner. 2 Class. 4 Visited; tea, religious talk; prayed. 6 Read Prayers, Philippians 2:5, etc, Communion; Society. 8 Supper; necessary business. 9.30.

SUNDAY, OCTOBER 29. 4 Prayed; letters. 8 Tea, religious talk; chaise. 9.30 Read Prayers, Ephesians 5:15! St Giles. 12 Luke 15:7! coach; at sister Box's, dinner, religious talk; prayer; the leaders; tea; prayed. 5 Philippians 3:13; Society; Love-feast! supper, religious talk; prayer. 9.30.

MONDAY, OCTOBER 30. 4 Prayed; James 2:22; Select Society. 7 Class; tea; class. 1 Dinner; class. 5 Tea; class; read Prayers, Philippians 4:4, etc; Society; class; supper; prayer. 9.30.

TUESDAY, OCTOBER [31]. 4 Prayed; letters. 6 Class; tea; class. 1 Dinner; class. 4.30 Tea; prayer; necessary business; prayed. 6.30 Read the letters; the leaders; supper, necessary talk (religious); prayer. 9.30.

WEDNESDAY, NOVEMBER 1. 4 Prayed; letter. 6 Class; tea; class. 1 Dinner, religious talk. 2 Class. 5 Tea, necessary talk (religious); prayer. 6 Prayed; *Life.* 8 Supper, religious talk; prayer. 9.30.

THURSDAY, NOVEMBER 2. 4 Prayed; class; tea. 8 Class. 1 At sister Westry's, necessary talk (religious); prayer. 2 Class. 4.30 *Life.* 5 Tea, religious talk; prayer; prayed. 6.30 Read Prayers, Colossians 2:6! the bands. 8 Supper, religious talk; prayer. 9.30.

FRIDAY, NOVEMBER 3. 4 Prayed; *Life;* class. 1 Dinner, religious talk. 4 Tea; chaise. 6 Rotherhithe; Hebrews 12:5! class. 8 At brother Crookenden's [orig., 'Cookendale'], supper, religious talk; prayer. 9.30.

SATURDAY, NOVEMBER 4. 4 Prayed; *Life;* christened Caleb C[rookenden]; tea. 7 Chaise. 8 Letters; dinner, religious talk; prayer; letters; *Life.* 4 Prayed; walked. 5 Tea, religious talk. 6 Read the letters. 7 Communion; supper; Penry, necessary business. 9.30.

SUNDAY, NOVEMBER 5. 4 Prayed; letters. 8 The preachers. 9.30 Read Prayers, 1 Peter 3:4, 5! Communion. 1 Dinner, religious talk; prayer. 2.15 Slept; prayed; buried John Cowmeadow! leaders; tea; prayed. 5 Philippians 3:13; Society; necessary talk (religious), supper; prayer. 9.30.

MONDAY, NOVEMBER 6. 4 Prayed; 1 Peter 5:4, etc; Select Society. 7 Class; tea; class. 12 Select Society; dinner. 2 Class. 5 Tea, religious talk; prayed. 6.15 Read Prayers, Mon——, Matthew 6:19; supper. 7.30 The bands. 9.30.

TUESDAY, NOVEMBER 7. 4 Prayed; 1 Peter 5:4, etc; class; tea; class. 1 Dinner, necessary talk (religious). 2 Class. 4.30 At brother Hales's, religious talk. 5 Class. 6.30 Philippians 3:14! 8 At the Chapel; supper; prayer. 9.30.

WEDNESDAY, NOVEMBER 8. 4 Prayed; *Life.* 6 Class; tea; class; chaise. 1 At home; necessary business; chaise. 2 Highbury Place; dinner, religious talk; *Life.* 5 Tea, religious talk; prayed; *Life.* 8 Supper, religious talk; prayer. 9.30.

THURSDAY, NOVEMBER 9. 4 Prayed; *Life.* 8 Tea, religious talk; prayer; *Life.* 12.30 At home; necessary business. 1.45 Stratford [London]; dinner; *Life;* tea. 5 Class. 6 Matthew 7:24; supper; prayer. 9.45.

FRIDAY, NOVEMBER 10. 4 Prayed; *Life.* 8 Tea; prayer; *Life.* 1 Dinner, religious talk; *Life.* 5 Tea, religious talk. 6 Prayed; read notes. 8 Supper, religious talk; prayer. 9.30.

[Texts noted at bottom of page:] 2 Timothy 1:7; 2 Thessalonians 2:16.

[SATURDAY, NOVEMBER 11.] 4 Prayed; letters. 8 Tea, religious talk; prayer; letters. 12 Chaise; at home. 1 Dinner, religious talk; prayer. 2 Letters. 4 Prayed; at Adam Clarke's; tea, religious talk. 6 Read Prayers, 2 Thessalonians 2:16, Communion. 8 Supper, religious talk; Penry, necessary business. 9.30.

SUNDAY, NOVEMBER 12. 4 Prayed; letters; chaise; Chapel; prayed. 9.30 Read Prayers, Matthew 18:3! Communion. 1 Dinner; slept; prayed; the leaders. 3.30 Read Prayers, 2 Thessalonians 3:13! Society. 6 Chaise; Society; prayed; religious talk, supper; prayer. 9.30.

MONDAY, NOVEMBER 13. 4 Prayed; 1 Peter 5:10! Select Society; necessary talk (religious). 8 Tea, necessary talk (religious); prayer; letters; writ Society. 1 At brother Gouthit's, dinner, religious talk; prayer. 2 Chaise; Highbury Place; writ Society; tea. 5 Prayed. 6.15 Read Prayers, Matthew [text deleted]; supper; prayed. 9.30.

TUESDAY, NOVEMBER 14. 4 Prayed; hymns. 8 Tea, religious talk; prayer. 9 Hymns. 1 Dinner; writ for the pocket hymn-book. 5 Tea, religious talk; prayed; writ hymns. 8 Supper, religious talk; prayer. 9.30.

WEDNESDAY, NOVEMBER 15. 4 Prayed; hymns. 7.30 Tea, necessary talk (religious); prayer; hymns. 2 Mr Dodwell; John Atlay; dinner, religious talk. 3.30 Hymns; prayed. 5 M Owen; Morgan; Colston. 5 Tea, religious talk. 7.30 Prayed. 8 Supper, religious talk; prayed. 9.45.

THURSDAY, NOVEMBER 16. 4 Prayed; hymns. 7.30 Tea, religious talk; prayer; writ for the poor. 10 Letters; chaise. 12 At home; letter. 1 At brother Urling's, dinner, religious talk; prayer. 2.30 At home; letters. 5 Tea, religious talk; necessary talk (religious) to some! 6.30 Read Prayers, 1 Timothy 6:20. 7.30 The bands; supper, religious talk; prayer. 9.30.

FRIDAY, NOVEMBER 17. 4 Prayed; letters; necessary talk (religious) to some. 12 The females. 1 Prayer. 2 Dinner; Magazine. 4 The Fathers of the Poor! 5.15 At Mrs Rankin's, Miss Morgan. 6 Tea, religious talk; prayer. 8 Supper, religious talk; prayer. 9.30.

SATURDAY, NOVEMBER 18. 4 Prayed; writ journal. 8 Tea, religious talk; prayer. 9 Writ Society. 11 Writ journal. 1 Dinner; prayer. 2 Read; prayed. 3 Visited many. 5 Tea, religious talk. 6 Read Prayers, 2 Timothy 1:7! Communion; the leaders; supper, religious talk; necessary business. 9.30.

SUNDAY, NOVEMBER 19. 4.45 Letters. 7.45 Spitalfields. 9.30 Read Prayers, John 11:43, 44! Communion. 1 At brother Fellows's, dinner, religious talk; coach. 2.45 Shadwell. 3 2 Timothy 2:19; tea, religious talk; coach. 5.45 Letter; prayed; Society; Love-feast! supper, religious talk. 9 Prayer. 9.30.

[Text noted at bottom of page:] 2 Timothy 2:9.

MONDAY, NOVEMBER 20. 4 Prayed; 2 Peter 1:4; Select Society; writ Society. 8 Tea, religious talk; prayer; visited some. 12 Select Society. 1.30 At brother

Barr's, necessary talk! 2.30 Dinner; prayer; visited; tea; prayed. 6.30 Read Prayers, 1 Timothy 3:5! supper; the bands. 9.30.

TUESDAY, NOVEMBER [21]. 4 Prayed; 1 Peter 5:10! writ Society; tea. 8 Walked; Lambeth. 9 Writ Society. 1 Dinner, religious talk. 2 Society. 5 Tea, religious talk; prayed. 6.30 1 Peter 3:4. 7.30 Class; supper, religious talk; prayer. 9.30.

WEDNESDAY, NOVEMBER [22]. 4 Prayed; Society. 6 2 Timothy 1:7! Society; tea, religious talk. 8 Visited many. 10.30 Chaise; necessary business. 11.30 Visited many! 2 At Mr Wo——'s, dinner; prayer; visited many. 5 Tea, religious talk; prayer. 6 Read Prayers, Titus 1:9, Communion; chaise; supper; prayer. 9.30.

THURSDAY, NOVEMBER [23]. 4 Prayed; letters. 8 Tea; prayer; *Life.* 1 Dinner, necessary talk (religious); prayer; A Jacobs; *Life.* 4.30 Sins! tea, necessary talk (religious). 5.30 Prayed. 6.30 Titus 2:11, 12; the bands! supper, religious talk; prayer. 9.30.

FRIDAY, NOVEMBER [24]. 4 Prayed; *Life.* 12 The females. 1 Prayer. 2 Dinner, religious talk; prayer. 3 Society. 4 The Fathers [of the Poor]; necessary talk (religious); prayer. 5 Tea, necessary talk (religious); prayed. 6.30 Read Magazine. 8 Supper, religious talk! prayer. 9.30.

SATURDAY, NOVEMBER 25. 4 Prayed; letters. 8 Tea, religious talk; prayer; letters. 11 Necessary business; Magazine. 1.30 Dinner; prayer. 2 Necessary business; prayed. 3 Visited many; tea; prayed; religious talk. 6 Read Prayers, Hebrews 1:14! Society, Communion. 8 Supper; Penry, necessary business. 9.30.

SUNDAY, NOVEMBER 26. 4 Prayed; letters; Chapel; read Prayers, Colossians 1:10! dinner; christened; prayed; the leaders. 3.30 Read Prayers, Hebrews 2:3; tea; Society; supper. 7 Coach; mostly religious talk. 11.30.

[MONDAY, NOVEMBER 27.] 6 Religious talk, tea; coach. 11 Norwich; at Mr Hunt's; letters. 1 Dinner. 2 Read notes. 3 Read; prayed; tea; coach. 5.30 Prayed. 6 2 Timothy 1:7! Supper; prayer. 9.30.

TUESDAY, NOVEMBER 28 [Entry misdated for Wednesday; cf. Journal text.]

[WEDNESDAY, NOVEMBER 29]. 4 Prayed; Magazine. 6 Luke 9:62! the preachers, etc, necessary talk; necessary talk! prayer; tea, religious talk; prayer; visited; read. 10 Chaise. 12 Lowestoft; Magazine. 1.30 Dinner. 2.30 Magazine; prayed; tea, religious talk. 6.30 1 Corinthians 12:31; Society; supper; prayer. 9.30.

[THURSDAY, NOVEMBER 30.] 4 Prayed; Magazine. 6 Hebrews 12:1; Magazine. 8 Tea, religious talk; prayer; letters. 12.30 Visited. 1 At brother McAllum's, dinner; Magazine; prayed; tea. 6.30 Deuteronomy 5:7! Society; supper, religious talk; prayer. 9.30.

FRIDAY, DECEMBER 1. 4 Prayed; Magazine. 6 Luke 1:72! tea. 7.30 Chaise; North Cove; 1 John 1:3! 10 Chaise. 11 Beccles; Matt 22:4! chaise. 1.30 Loddon.

2 Dinner, religious talk. 3 Magazine; prayed. 4.15 Tea; prayed. 6 1 Peter 4:18! supper, religious talk; prayer. 9.30.

[SATURDAY, DECEMBER 2.] 4 Prayed; Magazine. 6 1 Samuel 21:8! Magazine; tea, religious talk. 9 Coach. 11 Norwich; necessary business; Magazine. 1 At Dr Hunt's, dinner, religious talk; slept; prayed. 2.30 John 4:24; letters; tea. 5.30 Necessary business; prayed; 1 Corinthians 15:55! supper; prayer. 9.45.

SUNDAY, DECEMBER 3. 4 Prayed; letters; tea. 8 Communion. 9 Letters. 11 Read Prayers. 1 Dinner, religious talk. 2.15 Slept. 2.30 Romans 13:10! prayed; tea, religious talk. 5 Prayed. 5.30 Romans 13:11, etc! Society; Magazine. 8 Supper, religious talk; prayer. 9.30.

MONDAY, DECEMBER 4. 4 Prayed; Magazine. 6 Ephesians 6:11; Magazine. 7.30 Tea, religious talk; prayer; Magazine. 10.30 Chaise. 12 [Long] Stratton; Sarah Mallet, religious talk; prayed! 1 Dinner, religious talk. 2 1 Corinthians 1:23; chaise; tea; prayed. 6 Luke 8:18! the leaders; supper; prayer. 9.30.

TUESDAY, DECEMBER 5. 4 Prayed; Magazine. 6 1 Corinthians 10:31! necessary talk (religious). 7.30 Tea, religious talk; prayer; visited many! 11 Magazine. 2 At Mr Thurgar's, necessary talk (religious), dinner. 3 Magazine; prayed. 4 Tea, religious talk. 4.30 Mail coach. 8 Supper, necessary talk (religious); slept.

WEDNESDAY, DECEMBER 6. 6 Mostly religious talk. 8 At brother Bumstead's, tea, religious talk; letters. 2.30 At brother Wright's. 3 Dinner; visited many. 5 At brother Wright's, tea, religious talk. 6 Read Prayers, Hebrews 12:14! 7 Communion; coach; supper, religious talk; prayer. 9.30.

THURSDAY, DECEMBER 7. 4 Prayed; Magazine; letters. 8 Tea; prayer; necessary business. 9.30 Coach; Highbury Place; writ Society. 1.30 Garden; dinner, religious talk. 3 Society. 5.30 Tea; Society; prayed; Society. 8 Supper, religious talk; prayer. 9.30.

FRIDAY, DECEMBER 8. 4 Prayed; writ Society. 8 Tea, religious talk; prayer; Society. 12 Necessary business. 1 Society. 2 Dinner. 3 Writ Society. 6 Tea; prayed; Society; supper; prayer. 9.30.

SATURDAY, DECEMBER 9. 4 Prayed; letters; tea; prayer; coach. 9 At home; letters. 1.30 At brother Butcher's, dinner, religious talk. 2 Letters; prayed. 4.30 Tea, religious talk. 6 Read Prayers, James 2:22! Society; Communion; supper. 8.15 Penry, necessary business. 9.30.

SUNDAY, DECEMBER 10. 4 Prayed; letters; Chapel. 9.30 Read Prayers, Acts 10:34! Communion; dinner. 2.30 Slept; prayed; the leaders. 3.30 Read Prayers, James 3:17! Society; coach; Society; the bands. 9.30.

MONDAY, DECEMBER [11]. 4 Prayed; 2 Peter 1:5-9; letters. 8 Tea, religious talk; prayer; letters. 10.30 Chapel; Captain Smith! Select Society. 1.15 Dinner, religious talk; prayer; letters. 4 Visited some. 6.30 James 4:14. 8 Supper, religious talk; prayer. 9.45.

TUESDAY, DECEMBER 12. 4 Prayed; 2 Peter 1:5-9; A Ja[cobs]! sins; writ notes. 7 Tea, religious talk; prayer; walked. 9 At home; letters. 1 Dinner, religious talk. 2 Letters. 4.30 Sister Westry's! tea. 6 Prayed. 6.30 Read Prayers, James 4:13; the leaders; supper, necessary talk (religious); prayer. 9.30.

WEDNESDAY, DECEMBER 13. 4 Prayed; letters. 8 Tea, religious talk; prayer; letters. 10 Visited; coach. 12.30 Peckham; writ Society. 2 Dinner, religious talk. 3 Society; prayed. 5.30 Tea, religious talk; Society; prayed. 8.30 Supper, religious talk; prayer. 10.

THURSDAY, DECEMBER 14. 4 Prayed; writ Society. 8 Tea, religious talk; prayer; Society. 1 At Mr Godden's, dinner, religious talk; prayer. 3 Letters; prayed. 5 Tea, religious talk! 6 Letters. 7 Galatians 6:14! letters. 8.30 Supper, religious talk. 9 Prayer. 9.45.

FRIDAY, DECEMBER 15. 4 Prayed; letters. 8 Tea, religious talk; prayer. 9 Letters. 1 Walked. 1.30 Dinner, religious talk. 2 Letter. 4 Prayed; at sister Thornton's! tea, religious talk; prayer. 7 Prayed; writ notes; supper; prayer. 9.45.

SATURDAY, DECEMBER 16. The frost began! 4 Prayed; Will; letters. 8 Tea, religious talk; prayer; writ Society. 11.30 Coach. 12 At brother Thornton's; letters. 1 Dinner, religious talk. 2 Writ Society; letter; prayed. 5 Tea, religious talk. 6 Read Prayers, 1 Peter 4:7! Communion; supper; Penry, necessary business. 9.30.

SUNDAY, DECEMBER 17. 4 Prayed; letters. 8 Spitalfields. 9.30 Read Prayers, Acts 17:30! Communion. 1 At brother Duplex's, dinner, religious talk; prayer; slept. 3 The leaders. 4 Tea, religious talk; prayed. 5 Prayers, 1 Peter 5:10! 6 Society. 7 Necessary talk (religious). 8 Supper, religious talk; prayer. 9.30.

MONDAY, DECEMBER 18. 4 Prayed; 2 Peter 1:11, etc; necessary talk (religious) to some. 8 Visited; tea, religious talk; prayer. 9 Necessary talk; letter. 12 Select Society. 1.30 Dinner, religious talk; prayer. 3 Read notes; prayed; visited; tea, religious talk; prayer! 6.15 Read Prayers, 2 Peter 1:5, etc; supper; the bands; read notes. 9.30.

TUESDAY, DECEMBER 19. 4 Prayed; 2 Peter 1:9, etc; read notes. 7 Tea, religious talk; prayer; walked. 9 Letters. 1 Dinner. 2 Letters. 4.30 Tea, religious talk; prayer; prayed. 6.30 Read Prayers, 2 Peter 2:9! the leaders; supper; prayer. 9.30.

WEDNESDAY, DECEMBER 20. 4 Prayed; letters. 8 Tea; prayer; necessary business. 10 Highbury Place; writ sermon. 2 Dinner. 3.30 Writ notes; prayed. 5 Tea, religious talk; prayed; sermon. 8 Supper, religious talk; prayer. 10.

THURSDAY, DECEMBER 21. 4 Prayed; sermon. 8 Tea; prayer; sermon. 2 Dinner; sermon. 5 Tea, religious talk; prayed; sermon. 8 Supper, religious talk. 9 Prayer. 9.30.

FRIDAY; DECEMBER 22. 4 Prayed; sermon. 8 Tea, religious talk; prayer; writ notes. 2 Dinner, religious talk; prayer; coach. 4 At home; letters. 5 Tea; prayed; Magazine. 8 Supper, religious talk; prayer. 9.30.

SATURDAY, DECEMBER 23. 4 Prayed; letters. 8 Tea, religious talk; writ notes. 12 Newgate! 1.15 At sister Sha[dfor]d's, dinner, religious talk; letter; prayed. 5 Tea, necessary talk (religious). 6 Read Prayers, 1 John 4:19! Communion. 8 Supper; Penry. 8.30 Necessary business. 9.30.

SUNDAY, DECEMBER 24. 4 Prayed; Bible; walked. 8 Chapel. 9.30 Read Prayers, Acts 24:16. 11.45 Old Jewry; read Prayers, Acts 24:25! at brother Cary's, dinner. 2.30 Slept; tea; prayed. 5 Read Prayers, 1 John 4:19! Society; necessary talk (religious); supper; prayer. 9.30.

MONDAY, DECEMBER 25. 3.30 Read Prayers; John 3:17; Select Society; necessary talk (religious); tea; married C Wheeler; tea; walked. 9.45 Chapel. 10 Read Prayers, Psalms 45:13! at sister Braun's, dinner, religious talk; prayer. 3 Read; prayed; tea, religious talk. 5 Read Prayers, John 1:18! the married men; prayed; supper; prayer. 9.30.

TUESDAY, DECEMBER 26. 4 Prayed; letters. 8 Tea, religious talk; prayer; letters. 10 Read Prayers, Persecution, Communion; visited! 1.30 Dinner, religious talk; prayer. 3 Writ notes; necessary talk (religious); tea; prayed. 6 Read Prayers, Psalms 119 *ult;* the leaders; supper, religious talk; prayer. 9.30.

WEDNESDAY, DECEMBER 27. 4 Prayed; letters. 8 Tea; letters; walked. 10 Chapel, read Prayers, John 21:21! Communion. 1 At brother Jacob's, dinner, religious talk; prayer; visited some; walked. 4 North Green; writ. 4.30 Tea, religious talk; prayed; writ notes. 8 Supper, religious talk; prayer. 10.

THURSDAY, DECEMBER 28. 4 Prayed; writ notes; letter. 8 Tea, religious talk; prayer; letter. 1 At Mr Ford's, dinner. 2 Religious talk; prayer. 4 Prayed; tea, religious talk. 6 Magazine. 8 Supper, religious talk; prayer. 9.45.

FRIDAY, DECEMBER 29. 4 Prayed; sermon. 9 E. B.! sins! sermon. 12 The females; sermon. 1 Prayer; at Thomas Olivers's. 2.30 Dinner, necessary talk (religious); prayer; visited; tea, religious talk; prayed; sermon. 8 Supper, religious talk; prayer; necessary business. 10.

SATURDAY, DECEMBER 30. 4 Prayed; sermon. 8 Tea, religious talk; prayer. 9 Sermon. 12.30 Walked. 1 Dinner, religious talk; sermon. 3.30 Prayed. 4.30 At sister Freeman's, tea, religious talk; prayer. 6 Read Prayers, John 21:21, Communion; supper; Penry, necessary business. 9.30.

SUNDAY, DECEMBER 31. 4 Prayed; sermon. 8 Tea, religious talk; prayer. 9.30 Read Prayers, Isaiah 37:3, Communion. 1 Dinner, religious talk. 2.15 Slept; prayed. 3 The leaders. 4 Tea; prayed. 5 Read Prayers, Isaiah 38:5! Society; the married women; supper; necessary business; supper, religious talk. 9.15.